Houghton Mifflin Harcourt

Texas History

HISTORY

Experience it @

hmhsocialstudies.com

BULLOCK TEXAS STATE HISTORY MUSEUM

Cover: Architectural details on the Texas State Capitol celebrate the state's long and diverse history. Photo copyright ©David Gilder/Fotolia

Printed in the U.S.A.

ISBN 978-0-544-32030-7

4 5 6 7 8 9 10 0918 22 21 20 19 18 17 16 15

4500535398 B C D E F G

CONTENTS

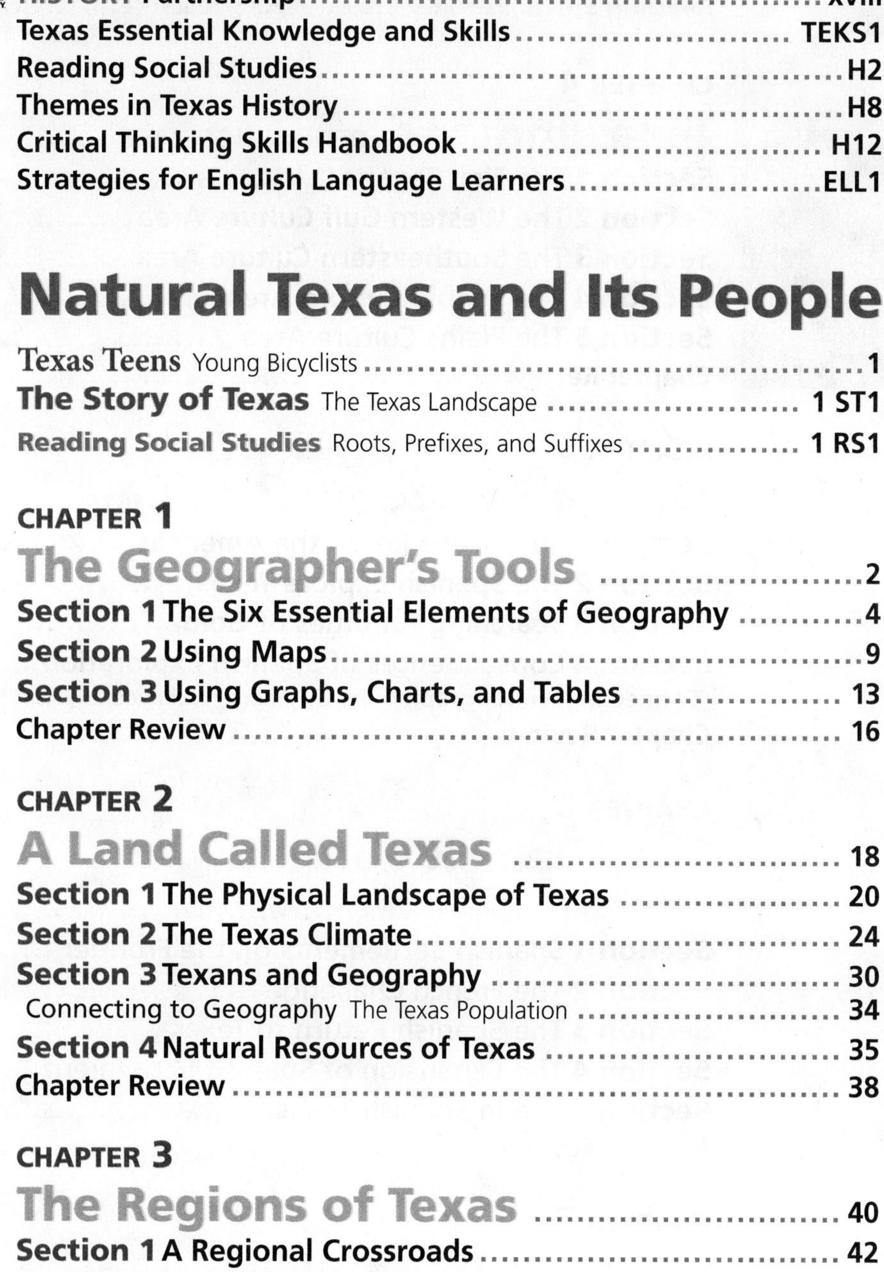

UNIT 1

Natural Texas and Its People

UNIT 2 The Spanish in Texas, BEGINNINGS–1821

Senior Texas Reviewer

Dr. Jesús F. de la Teja is Jerome H. and Catherine E. Supple Professor of Southwestern Studies and Regents' Professor of history and serves as director of the Center for the Study of the Southwest at Texas State University in San Marcos, Texas. He holds a Ph.D. in Latin American History from The University of Texas at Austin, and before coming to the university in 1991 he worked in the Archives and Records Division of the Texas General Land Office. His research interests focus on the northeastern frontier of Spanish colonial Mexico and Texas through the Republic era. He is the author of *San Antonio de Béxar: A Community on New Spain's Northern Frontier* (1995); co-author of *Texas: Crossroads of North America* (2004), a college-level survey of the state's history; and editor of *Tejano Leadership in Mexican and Revolutionary Texas* (2010). In addition to his research activities he serves as a consultant for the Bullock Texas State History Museum in Austin and as book review editor of the *Southwestern Historical Quarterly.* In 2005 Dr. de la Teja became the first-ever state historian of Texas and has also served as a Social Studies Expert Reviewer for the Texas Education Agency.

Texas Review Panel

Valerie Garnier
Social Studies Consultant
Coppell, Texas

Kerry Green
Sunnyvale High School
Sunnyvale, Texas

Kristin Harman
Bailey Junior High
Arlington, Texas

Aderienne Shaw-Kelly
E. B. Comstock Middle School
Dallas, Texas

The Mexican National Period, 1820–1835

UNIT 4

Revolution and Republic, 1835–1845

Early Statehood, 1845–1861 310

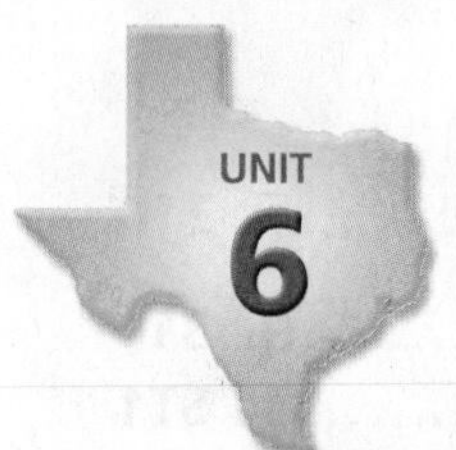
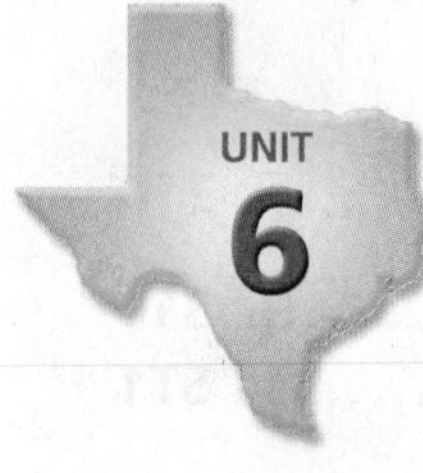

UNIT 6

Texas in the Civil War and Reconstruction, 1861–1880

Image Credit: ©Bob Thomas/Getty Images

Cotton, Cattle, and Railroads, 1860–1920

UNIT 8

Prosperity and the Great Depression, 1870–1939 494

The Modern Era, 1939–PRESENT

UNIT 10

Handbook of Texas, 1845–PRESENT

Image Credit: ©Neal and Molly Jansen/Alamy

REFERENCE SECTION

The BULLOCK MUSEUM

Want to know the story of Texas? Visit the Bullock Texas State History Museum and discover extraordinary exhibits and films. Located in Austin just blocks from the Texas Capitol, there's always something new to see at the museum.

WHAT CAN YOU DO AT THE BULLOCK MUSEUM?

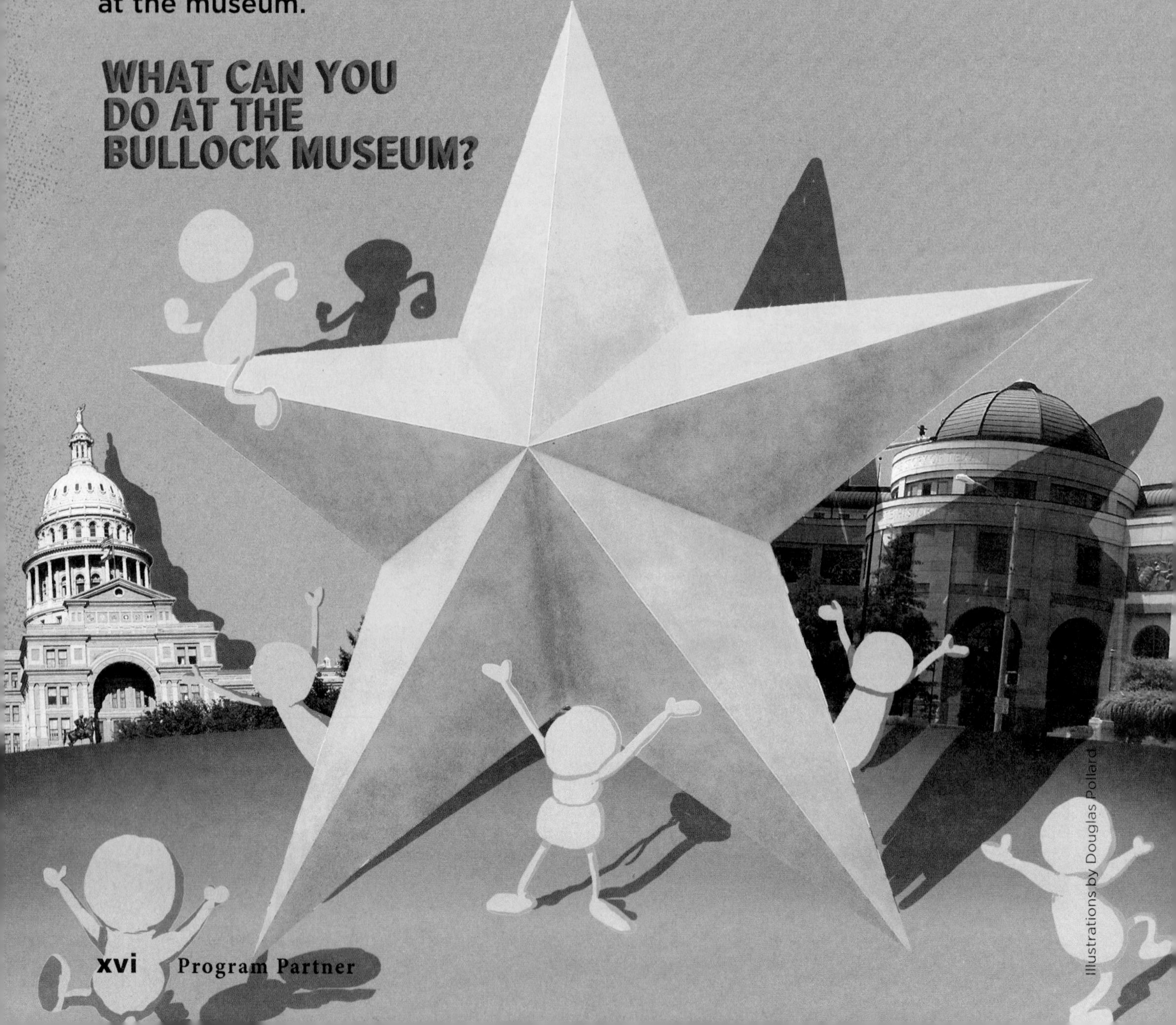

Illustrations by Douglas Pollard

Survive
A TORNADO AND A HURRICANE IN THE SAME BUILDING!

Meet
THE UGLIEST WOMAN IN TEXAS

Take
A PHOTO WITH BOB; YES, HE FOUNDED THE MUSEUM

Tour
EXHIBITS SO BIG THEY CAN FIT AN ENTIRE WWII AIRPLANE INSIDE

HISTORY® is the leading destination for revealing, award-winning, original non-fiction series and event-driven specials that connect history with viewers in an informative, immersive and entertaining manner across multiple platforms. HISTORY is part of A&E Television Networks (AETN), a joint venture of Hearst Corporation, Disney/ABC Television Group and NBC Universal, an award-winning, international media company that also includes, among others, A&E Network™, BIO™, and History International™.

HISTORY programming greatly appeals to educators and young people who are drawn into the visual stories our documentaries tell. Our Education Department has a long-standing record in providing teachers and students with curriculum resources that bring the past to life in the classroom. Our content covers a diverse variety of subjects, including American and world history, government, economics, the natural and applied sciences, arts, literature and the humanities, health and guidance, and even pop culture.

The HISTORY website, located at **www.history.com**, is the definitive historical online source that delivers entertaining and informative content featuring broadband video, interactive timelines, maps, games, podcasts and more.

"We strive to engage, inspire and encourage the love of learning..."

Since its founding in 1995, HISTORY has demonstrated a commitment to providing the highest quality resources for educators. We develop multimedia resources for K–12 schools, two- and four-year colleges, government agencies, and other organizations by drawing on the award-winning documentary programming of A&E Television Networks. We strive to engage, inspire and encourage the love of learning by connecting with students in an informative and compelling manner. To help achieve this goal, we have formed a partnership with Houghton Mifflin Harcourt.

In addition to premium video-based resources, **HISTORY** has extensive offerings for teachers, parents, and students to use in the classroom and in their in-home educational activities, including:

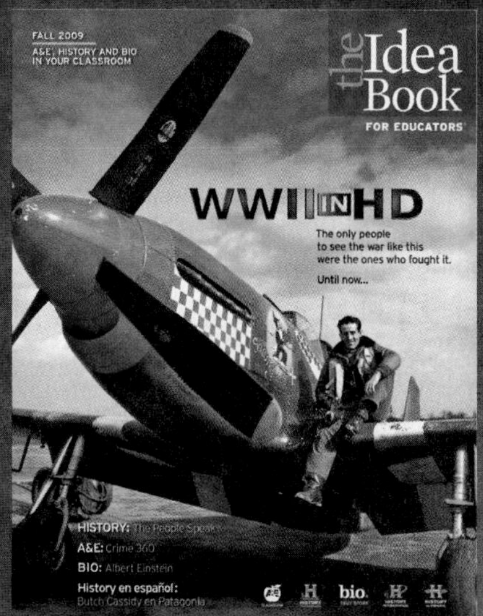

The Idea Book for Educators

- ***The Idea Book for Educators*** is a biannual teacher's magazine, featuring guides and info on the latest happenings in history education to help keep teachers on the cutting edge.

Classroom resources that bring the past to life

- **HISTORY Classroom (www.history.com/classroom)** is an interactive website that serves as a portal for history educators nationwide. Streaming videos on topics ranging from the Roman aqueducts to the civil rights movement connect with classroom curricula.

- **HISTORY email newsletters** feature updates and supplements to our award-winning programming relevant to the classroom with links to teaching guides and video clips on a variety of topics, special offers, and more.

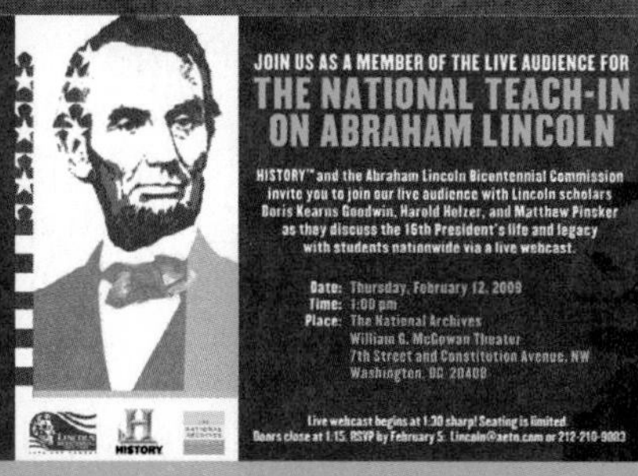

Live webcasts

- **Live webcasts** are featured each year as schools tune in via streaming video.

- **HISTORY Take a Veteran to School Day** connects veterans with young people in our schools and communities nationwide.

HISTORY Take a Veteran to School Day

In addition to **HOUGHTON MIFFLIN HARCOURT**, our partners include the *Library of Congress*, the *Smithsonian Institution, National History Day, The Gilder Lehrman Institute of American History*, the *Organization of American Historians,* and many more. HISTORY video is also featured in museums throughout America and in over 70 other historic sites worldwide.

 Texas Essential Knowledge and Skills

In this course you will learn about the history of Texas from early times to the present. This course is based on the Texas Essential Knowledge and Skills (TEKS) for Social Studies, Grade 7. The TEKS identify the student expectations for this course—the things that you should be able to identify, explain, and accomplish by the end of the year. Read through these expectations now for a preview of the content you will study this year. Later, as you read through this book, you will see TEKS codes listed on the opening pages of chapters and sections. The TEKS codes indicate which TEKS are being covered. Refer back to these pages if you want to see the full text of each TEKS code.

History

TEKS 1 The student understands traditional historical points of reference in Texas history. The student is expected to:

1A identify the major eras in Texas history, describe their defining characteristics, and explain why historians divide the past into eras, including Natural Texas and its People; Age of Contact; Spanish Colonial; Mexican National; Revolution and Republic; Early Statehood; Texas in the Civil War and Reconstruction; Cotton, Cattle, and Railroads; Age of Oil; Texas in the Great Depression and World War II; Civil Rights and Conservatism; and Contemporary Texas;

1B apply absolute and relative chronology through the sequencing of significant individuals, events, and time periods; and

1C explain the significance of the following dates: 1519, mapping of the Texas coast and first mainland Spanish settlement; 1718, founding of San Antonio; 1821, independence from Spain; 1836, Texas independence; 1845, annexation; 1861, Civil War begins; 1876, adoption of current state constitution; and 1901, discovery of oil at Spindletop.

TO LEARN MORE: For eras and dates, see content throughout the book, including Units 1 through 9. For chronology and sequence, see the Unit 2 Reading Social Studies lesson.

TEKS 2 The student understands how individuals, events, and issues through the Mexican National Era shaped the history of Texas. The student is expected to:

2A compare the cultures of American Indians in Texas prior to European colonization such as Gulf, Plains, Puebloan, and Southeastern;

2B identify important individuals, events, and issues related to European exploration of Texas such as Alonso Álvarez de Pineda, Álvar Núñez Cabeza de Vaca and his writings, the search for gold, and the conflicting territorial claims between France and Spain;

2C identify important events and issues related to European colonization of Texas, including the establishment of Catholic missions, towns, and ranches, and individuals such as Fray Damián Massanet, José de Escandón, Antonio Margil de Jesús, and Francisco Hidalgo;

2D identify the individuals, issues, and events related to Mexico becoming an independent nation and its impact on Texas, including Texas involvement in the fight for independence, José Gutiérrez de Lara, the Battle of Medina, the Mexican federal Constitution of 1824, the merger of Texas and Coahuila as a state, the State Colonization Law of 1825, and slavery;

2E identify the contributions of significant individuals, including Moses Austin, Stephen F. Austin, Erasmo Seguín, Martín De León, and Green DeWitt, during the Mexican settlement of Texas; and

2F contrast Spanish, Mexican, and Anglo purposes for and methods of settlement in Texas.

TO LEARN MORE: See Units 2 and 3.

TEKS 3 **The student understands how individuals, events, and issues related to the Texas Revolution shaped the history of Texas. The student is expected to:**

- **3A** trace the development of events that led to the Texas Revolution, including the Fredonian Rebellion, the Mier y Terán Report, the Law of April 6, 1830, the Turtle Bayou Resolutions, and the arrest of Stephen F. Austin;
- **3B** explain the roles played by significant individuals during the Texas Revolution, including George Childress, Lorenzo de Zavala, James Fannin, Sam Houston, Antonio López de Santa Anna, Juan N. Seguín, and William B. Travis;
- **3C** explain the issues surrounding significant events of the Texas Revolution, including the Battle of Gonzales, William B. Travis's letter "To the People of Texas and All Americans in the World," the siege of the Alamo and all the heroic defenders who gave their lives there, the Constitutional Convention of 1836, Fannin's surrender at Goliad, and the Battle of San Jacinto; and
- **3D** explain how the establishment of the Republic of Texas brought civil, political, and religious freedom to Texas.

TO LEARN MORE: See Chapter 11.

TEKS 4 **The student understands how individuals, events, and issues shaped the history of the Republic of Texas and early Texas statehood. The student is expected to:**

- **4A** identify individuals, events, and issues during the administrations of Republic of Texas Presidents Houston, Lamar, and Jones, including the Texas Navy, the Texas Rangers, Edwin W. Moore, Jack Coffee Hays, Chief Bowles, William Goyens, Mary Maverick, José Antonio Navarro, the Córdova Rebellion, the Council House Fight, the Santa Fe Expedition, public debt, and the roles of racial and ethnic groups;
- **4B** analyze the causes of and events leading to Texas annexation; and
- **4C** identify individuals, events, and issues during early Texas statehood, including the U.S.-Mexican War, the Treaty of Guadalupe-Hidalgo, population growth, and the Compromise of 1850.

TO LEARN MORE: See Chapters 12 through 17.

TEKS 5 **The student understands how events and issues shaped the history of Texas during the Civil War and Reconstruction. The student is expected to:**

- **5A** explain reasons for the involvement of Texas in the Civil War such as states' rights, slavery, sectionalism, and tariffs;
- **5B** analyze the political, economic, and social effects of the Civil War and Reconstruction in Texas; and
- **5C** identify significant individuals and events concerning Texas and the Civil War such as John Bell Hood, John Reagan, Francis Lubbock, Thomas Green, John Magruder and the Battle of Galveston, the Battle of Sabine Pass, and the Battle of Palmito Ranch.

TO LEARN MORE: See Chapters 18 and 19.

TEKS 6 The student understands how individuals, events, and issues shaped the history of Texas from Reconstruction through the beginning of the 20th century. The student is expected to:

- **6A** identify significant individuals, events, and issues from Reconstruction through the beginning of the 20th century, including the factors leading to the expansion of the Texas frontier, the effects of westward expansion on American Indians, the buffalo soldiers, and Quanah Parker;
- **6B** identify significant individuals, events, and issues from Reconstruction through the beginning of the 20th century, including the development of the cattle industry from its Spanish beginnings and the myths and realities of the cowboy way of life;
- **6C** identify significant individuals, events, and issues from Reconstruction through the beginning of the 20th century, including the effects of the growth of railroads and the contributions of James Hogg; and
- **6D** explain the political, economic, and social impact of the agricultural industry and the development of West Texas resulting from the close of the frontier.

TO LEARN MORE: See Chapters 20, 21, 22, and 24.

TEKS 7 The student understands how individuals, events, and issues shaped the history of Texas during the 20th and early 21st centuries. The student is expected to:

- **7A** explain the political, economic, and social impact of the oil industry on the industrialization of Texas;
- **7B** define and trace the impact of "boom-and-bust" cycles of leading Texas industries throughout the 20th and early 21st centuries such as farming, oil and gas production, cotton, ranching, real estate, banking, and computer technology;
- **7C** describe and compare the impact of the Progressive and other reform movements in Texas in the 19th and 20th centuries such as the Populists, women's suffrage, agrarian groups, labor unions, and the evangelical movement of the late 20th century;
- **7D** describe and compare the civil rights and equal rights movements of various groups in Texas in the 20th century and identify key leaders in these movements, including James L. Farmer Jr., Hector P. Garcia, Oveta Culp Hobby, Lyndon B. Johnson, the League of United Latin American Citizens (LULAC), Jane McCallum, and Lulu Belle Madison White;
- **7E** analyze the political, economic, and social impact of major events, including World War I, the Great Depression, and World War II, on the history of Texas; and
- **7F** analyze the political, economic, and social impact of major events in the latter half of the 20th and early 21st centuries such as major conflicts, the emergence of a two-party system, political and economic controversies, immigration, and migration.

TO LEARN MORE: See Units 7, 8, and 9.

Geography

TEKS 8 The student uses geographic tools to collect, analyze, and interpret data. The student is expected to:

- **8A** create and interpret thematic maps, graphs, charts, models, and databases representing various aspects of Texas during the 19th, 20th, and 21st centuries; and
- **8B** analyze and interpret geographic distributions and patterns in Texas during the 19th, 20th, and 21st centuries.

TO LEARN MORE: See content, maps, charts, and graphs throughout the book, including Chapter 1.

TEKS 9 The student understands the location and characteristics of places and regions of Texas. The student is expected to:

- **9A** locate the Mountains and Basins, Great Plains, North Central Plains, and Coastal Plains regions and places of importance in Texas during the 19th, 20th, and 21st centuries such as major cities, rivers, natural and historic landmarks, political and cultural regions, and local points of interest;
- **9B** compare places and regions of Texas in terms of physical and human characteristics; and
- **9C** analyze the effects of physical and human factors such as climate, weather, landforms, irrigation, transportation, and communication on major events in Texas.

TO LEARN MORE: See Chapters 2 and 3.

TEKS 10 **The student understands the effects of the interaction between humans and the environment in Texas during the 19th, 20th, and 21st centuries. The student is expected to:**

- **10A** identify ways in which Texans have adapted to and modified the environment and analyze the positive and negative consequences of the modifications; and
- **10B** explain ways in which geographic factors such as the Galveston Hurricane of 1900, the Dust Bowl, limited water resources, and alternative energy sources have affected the political, economic, and social development of Texas.

TO LEARN MORE: See content throughout the book, including Chapters 24, 28, and 29.

TEKS 11 **The student understands the characteristics, distribution, and migration of population in Texas in the 19th, 20th, and 21st centuries. The student is expected to:**

- **11A** analyze why immigrant groups came to Texas and where they settled;
- **11B** analyze how immigration and migration to Texas in the 19th, 20th, and 21st centuries have influenced Texas;
- **11C** analyze the effects of the changing population distribution and growth in Texas during the 20th and 21st centuries and the additional need for education, health care, and transportation; and
- **11D** describe the structure of the population of Texas using demographic concepts such as growth rate and age distribution.

TO LEARN MORE: See content throughout the book, including Chapters 2, 13, and 29.

Economics

TEKS 12 **The student understands the factors that caused Texas to change from an agrarian to an urban society. The student is expected to**

- **12A** explain economic factors that led to the urbanization of Texas;
- **12B** trace the development of major industries that contributed to the urbanization of Texas such as transportation, oil and gas, and manufacturing; and
- **12C** explain the changes in the types of jobs and occupations that have resulted from the urbanization of Texas.

TO LEARN MORE: See content throughout the book, including Chapters 27, 28, and 29.

TEKS 13 **The student understands the interdependence of the Texas economy with the United States and the world. The student is expected to:**

- **13A** analyze the impact of national and international markets and events on the production of goods and services in Texas such as agriculture, oil and gas, and computer technology;
- **13B** analyze the impact of economic concepts within the free enterprise system such as supply and demand, profit, government regulation, and world competition on the economy of Texas; and
- **13C** analyze the impact of significant industries in Texas such as oil and gas, aerospace, medical, and computer technologies on local, national, and international markets.

TO LEARN MORE: See Chapter 32.

Government

TEKS 14 **The student understands the basic principles reflected in the Texas Constitution. The student is expected to:**

- **14A** identify how the Texas Constitution reflects the principles of limited government, republicanism, checks and balances, federalism, separation of powers, popular sovereignty, and individual rights; and
- **14B** compare the principles and concepts of the Texas Constitution to the U.S. Constitution, including the Texas and U.S. Bill of Rights.

TO LEARN MORE: See Chapter 30.

TEKS 15 **The student understands the structure and functions of government created by the Texas Constitution. The student is expected to:**

- **15A** describe the structure and functions of government at municipal, county, and state levels;
- **15B** identify major sources of revenue for state and local governments such as property tax, sales tax, and fees; and
- **15C** describe the structure, funding, and governance of Texas public education, including local property taxes, bond issues, and state and federal funding supported by state and federal taxpayers.

TO LEARN MORE: See Chapters 30 and 31.

Citizenship

TEKS 16 **The student understands the rights and responsibilities of Texas citizens in a democratic society. The student is expected to:**

- **16A** identify rights of Texas citizens; and
- **16B** explain and analyze civic responsibilities of Texas citizens and the importance of civic participation.

TO LEARN MORE: See Chapter 31.

TEKS 17 **The student understands the importance of the expression of different points of view in a democratic society. The student is expected to:**

- **17A** identify different points of view of political parties and interest groups on important Texas issues, past and present;
- **17B** describe the importance of free speech and press in a democratic society; and
- **17C** express and defend a point of view on an issue of historical or contemporary interest in Texas.

TO LEARN MORE: See Chapter 31.

TEKS 18 **The student understands the importance of effective leadership in a democratic society. The student is expected to:**

- **18A** identify the leadership qualities of elected and appointed leaders of Texas, past and present, including Texans who have been president of the United States; and
- **18B** identify the contributions of Texas leaders, including Lawrence Sullivan "Sul" Ross, John Nance Garner ("Cactus Jack"), James A. Baker III, Henry B. González, Kay Bailey Hutchison, Barbara Jordan, Raymond L. Telles, Sam Rayburn, and Raul A. Gonzalez Jr.

TO LEARN MORE: See content throughout the book, including Chapters 24 through 29.

Culture

TEKS 19 **The student understands the concept of diversity within unity in Texas. The student is expected to:**

- **19A** explain how the diversity of Texas is reflected in a variety of cultural activities, celebrations, and performances;
- **19B** describe how people from various racial, ethnic, and religious groups attempt to maintain their cultural heritage while adapting to the larger Texas culture;
- **19C** identify examples of Spanish influence and the influence of other cultures on Texas such as place names, vocabulary, religion, architecture, food, and the arts; and
- **19D** identify contributions to the arts by Texans such as Roy Bedichek, Diane Gonzales Bertrand, J. Frank Dobie, Scott Joplin, Elisabet Ney, Amado Peña Jr., Walter Prescott Webb, and Horton Foote.

TO LEARN MORE: See content throughout the book, including Chapters 2, 6, and 29.

Source: The provisions of this §113.19 adopted to be effective August 23, 2010, 35 TexReg 7232.

Science, Technology, and Society

TEKS 20 **The student understands the impact of scientific discoveries and technological innovations on the political, economic, and social development of Texas. The student is expected to:**

- **20A** compare types and uses of technology, past and present;
- **20B** identify Texas leaders in science and technology such as Walter Cunningham, Michael DeBakey, Denton Cooley, Benjy Brooks, Michael Dell, and Howard Hughes Sr.;
- **20C** analyze the effects of various scientific discoveries and technological innovations on the development of Texas such as advancements in the agricultural, energy, medical, computer, and aerospace industries;
- **20D** evaluate the effects of scientific discoveries and technological innovations on the use of resources such as fossil fuels, water, and land; and
- **20E** analyze how scientific discoveries and technological innovations have resulted in an interdependence among Texas, the United States, and the world.

TO LEARN MORE: See content throughout the book, including Chapters 21 through 23.

Social Studies Skills

TEKS 21 **The student applies critical-thinking skills to organize and use information acquired through established research methodologies from a variety of valid sources, including electronic technology. The student is expected to:**

- **21A** differentiate between, locate, and use valid primary and secondary sources such as computer software, databases, media and news services, biographies, interviews, and artifacts to acquire information about Texas;
- **21B** analyze information by sequencing, categorizing, identifying cause-and-effect relationships, comparing, contrasting, finding the main idea, summarizing, making generalizations and predictions, and drawing inferences and conclusions;
- **21C** organize and interpret information from outlines, reports, databases, and visuals, including graphs, charts, timelines, and maps;
- **21D** identify points of view from the historical context surrounding an event and the frame of reference that influenced the participants;
- **21E** support a point of view on a social studies issue or event;
- **21F** identify bias in written, oral, and visual material;
- **21G** evaluate the validity of a source based on language, corroboration with other sources, and information about the author; and
- **21H** use appropriate mathematical skills to interpret social studies information such as maps and graphs.

TO LEARN MORE: See Social Studies Skills and Reading Social Studies lessons throughout the book.

TEKS 22 **The student communicates in written, oral, and visual forms. The student is expected to:**

- **22A** use social studies terminology correctly;
- **22B** use standard grammar, spelling, sentence structure, punctuation, and proper citation of sources;
- **22C** transfer information from one medium to another, including written to visual and statistical to written or visual, using computer software as appropriate; and
- **22D** create written, oral, and visual presentations of social studies information.

TO LEARN MORE: See content throughout the book, including the Social Studies Skills lesson in Unit 10.

TEKS 23 **The student uses problem-solving and decision-making skills, working independently and with others, in a variety of settings. The student is expected to:**

- **23A** use a problem-solving process to identify a problem, gather information, list and consider options, consider advantages and disadvantages, choose and implement a solution, and evaluate the effectiveness of the solution; and
- **23B** use a decision-making process to identify a situation that requires a decision, gather information, identify options, predict consequences, and take action to implement a decision.

TO LEARN MORE: See the Social Studies Skills lessons in Units 2 and 3.

Become an Active Reader

Did you ever think you would begin reading your social studies book by reading about reading? Actually, it makes better sense than you might think. You would probably make sure you learned some soccer skills and strategies before playing in a game. Similarly, you need to learn some reading skills and strategies before reading your social studies book. In other words, you need to make sure you know whatever you need to know in order to read this book successfully.

Tip #1
Use the Reading Social Studies Pages

Take advantage of the two pages on reading at the beginning of every unit. Those pages explain a reading skill or strategy and identify key terms.

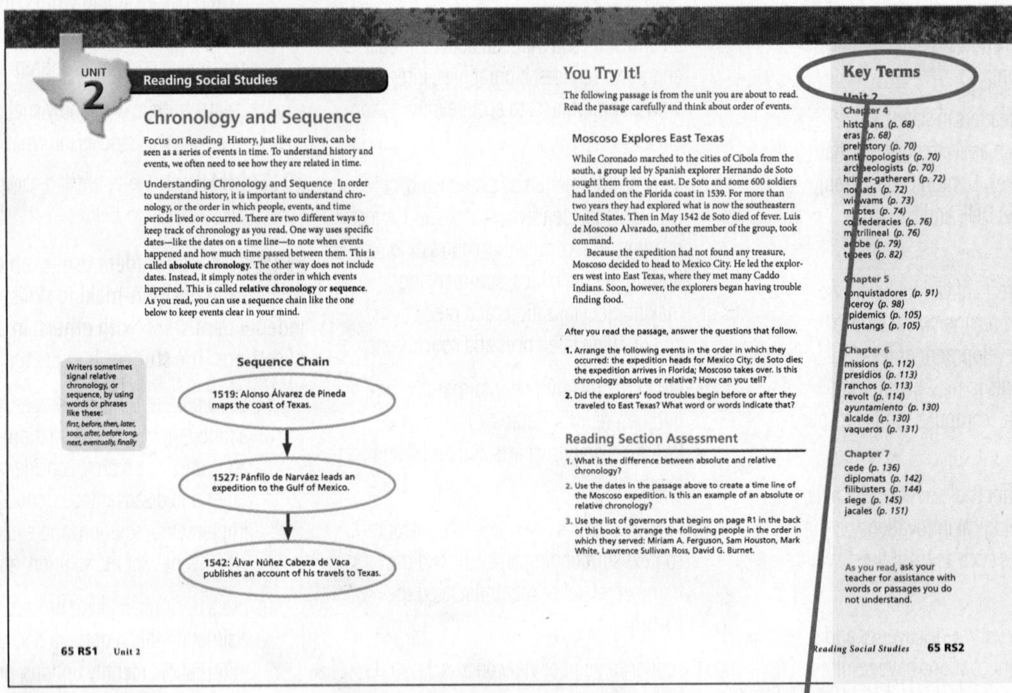

UNIT 2

Reading Social Studies

Chronology and Sequence

Focus on Reading History, just like our lives, can be seen as a series of events in time. To understand history and events, we often need to see how they are related in time.

Understanding Chronology and Sequence In order to understand history, it is important to understand chronology, or the order in which people, events, and time periods lived or occurred. There are two different ways to keep track of chronology as you read. One way uses specific dates—like the dates on a time line—to note when events happened and how much time passed between them. This is called **absolute chronology**. The other way does not include dates. Instead, it simply notes the order in which events happened. This is called **relative chronology** or **sequence**. As you read, you can use a sequence chain like the one below to keep events clear in your mind.

Writers sometimes signal relative chronology, or sequence, by using words or phrases like these: *first, before, then, later, soon, after, before long, next, eventually, finally*

Sequence Chain

1519: Alonso Álvarez de Pineda maps the coast of Texas.

1527: Pánfilo de Narváez leads an expedition to the Gulf of Mexico.

1542: Álvar Núñez Cabeza de Vaca publishes an account of his travels to Texas.

65 RS1 Unit 2

You Try It!

The following passage is from the unit you are about to read. Read the passage carefully and think about order of events.

Moscoso Explores East Texas

While Coronado marched to the cities of Cíbola from the south, a group led by Spanish explorer Hernando de Soto sought them from the east. De Soto and some 600 soldiers had landed on the Florida coast in 1539. For more than two years they had explored what is now the southeastern United States. Then in May 1542 de Soto died of fever. Luis de Moscoso Alvarado, another member of the group, took command.

Because the expedition had not found any treasure, Moscoso decided to head to Mexico City. He led the explorers west into East Texas, where they met many Caddo Indians. Soon, however, the explorers began having trouble finding food.

After you read the passage, answer the questions that follow.

1. Arrange the following events in the order in which they occurred: the expedition heads for Mexico City; de Soto dies; the expedition arrives in Florida; Moscoso takes over. Is this chronology absolute or relative? How can you tell?
2. Did the explorers' food troubles begin before or after they traveled to East Texas? What word or words indicate that?

Reading Section Assessment

1. What is the difference between absolute and relative chronology?
2. Use the dates in the passage above to create a time line of the Moscoso expedition. Is this an example of an absolute or relative chronology?
3. Use the list of governors that begins on page R1 in the back of this book to arrange the following people in the order in which they served: Miriam A. Ferguson, Sam Houston, Mark White, Lawrence Sullivan Ross, David G. Burnet.

Key Terms

Unit 2

Chapter 4
historians *(p. 68)*
eras *(p. 68)*
prehistory *(p. 70)*
anthropologists *(p. 70)*
archaeologists *(p. 70)*
hunter-gatherers *(p. 72)*
nomads *(p. 72)*
wigwams *(p. 73)*
mitotes *(p. 74)*
confederacies *(p. 76)*
matrilineal *(p. 76)*
adobe *(p. 79)*
tepees *(p. 82)*

Chapter 5
conquistadores *(p. 91)*
viceroy *(p. 98)*
epidemics *(p. 105)*
mustangs *(p. 105)*

Chapter 6
missions *(p. 112)*
presidios *(p. 113)*
ranchos *(p. 113)*
revolt *(p. 114)*
ayuntamiento *(p. 130)*
alcalde *(p. 130)*
vaqueros *(p. 131)*

Chapter 7
cede *(p. 136)*
diplomats *(p. 142)*
filibusters *(p. 144)*
siege *(p. 145)*
jacales *(p. 151)*

As you read, ask your teacher for assistance with words or passages you do not understand.

Reading Social Studies 65 RS2

Reading Skill or Strategy

Good readers use a number of skills and strategies to make sure they understand what they are reading. These lessons will give you the tools you need to read and understand social studies.

Reading Practice

After you learn a reading skill or strategy, it is important to practice using it to improve your ability to learn. You wouldn't play in a band concert, dance in a recital, or pitch in a baseball game without practicing, would you? Just like music, dance, or sports, reading is a skill that you have to practice to improve.

Key Terms

Before you read the unit, review these words and think about them. Have you heard the word before? Then watch for these words and their meanings as you read the chapter.

Tip #2

Read like a Skilled Reader You will never get better at reading your social studies book—or any book for that matter—unless you spend some time thinking about how to be a better reader.

Skilled readers do the following:

- They preview what they are supposed to read before they actually begin reading. They look for vocabulary words, titles of sections, information in the margin, or maps or charts they should study.
- They divide their notebook paper into two columns. They title one column "Notes from the Chapter" and the other column "Questions or Comments I Have."
- They take notes in both columns as they read.
- They read like active readers. The Active Reading list below shows you what that means.
- They use clues in the text to help them figure out where the text is going. The best clues are called signal words.

Chronological Order Signal Words: first, second, third, before, after, later, next, following that, earlier, finally

Cause and Effect Signal Words: because of, due to, as a result of, the reason for, therefore, consequently

Comparison/Contrast Signal Words: likewise, also, as well as, similarly, on the other hand

Active Reading

Successful readers are **active readers**. These readers know that it is up to them to figure out what the text means. Here are some steps you can take to become an active, and successful, reader.

Predict what will happen next based on what has already happened. When your predictions don't match what happens in the text, re-read the confusing parts.

Question what is happening as you read. Constantly ask yourself why things have happened, what things mean, and what caused certain events.

Summarize what you are reading frequently. Do not try to summarize the entire chapter! Read a bit and then summarize it. Then read on.

Connect what is happening in the part you're reading to what you have already read.

Clarify your understanding. Stop occasionally to ask yourself whether you are confused by anything. You may need to re-read to clarify, or you may need to read further and collect more information before you can understand.

Visualize what is happening in the text. Try to see the events or places in your mind by drawing maps, making charts, or jotting down notes about what you are reading.

Tip #3
Pay Attention to Vocabulary

It is no fun to read something when you don't know what the words mean, but you can't learn new words if you only use or read the words you already know. In this book, we know we have probably used some words you don't know. But, we have followed a pattern as we have used more difficult words.

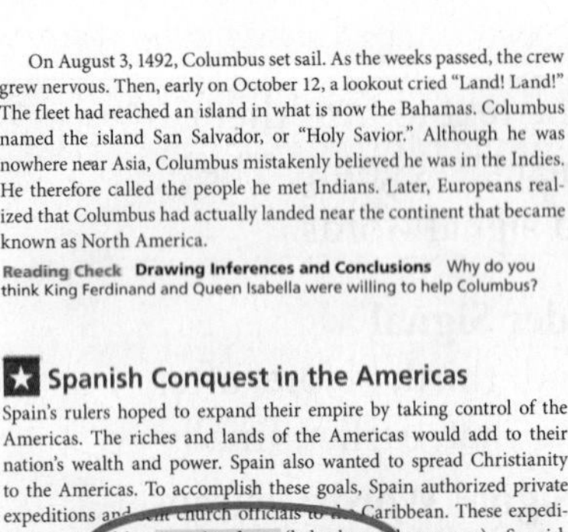

On August 3, 1492, Columbus set sail. As the weeks passed, the crew grew nervous. Then, early on October 12, a lookout cried "Land! Land!" The fleet had reached an island in what is now the Bahamas. Columbus named the island San Salvador, or "Holy Savior." Although he was nowhere near Asia, Columbus mistakenly believed he was in the Indies. He therefore called the people he met Indians. Later, Europeans realized that Columbus had actually landed near the continent that became known as North America.

Reading Check **Drawing Inferences and Conclusions** Why do you think King Ferdinand and Queen Isabella were willing to help Columbus?

That's Interesting!

Pigs on the Loose
Christopher Columbus and other early explorers carried livestock with them on their trips. This is how the first pigs came to the Americas. Many Spanish explorers let the pigs they brought roam free to live off grasses, nuts, and roots. These pigs turned wild, and their population in the Americas grew quickly. These abandoned pigs provided a source of food for later explorers.

★ Spanish Conquest in the Americas

Spain's rulers hoped to expand their empire by taking control of the Americas. The riches and lands of the Americas would add to their nation's wealth and power. Spain also wanted to spread Christianity to the Americas. To accomplish these goals, Spain authorized private expeditions and sent church officials to the Caribbean. These expeditions were led by **conquistadores** (kahn-kees-tuh-DAWR-ez)—Spanish soldier-adventurers in search of glory, gold, and land.

Conquistadores wore suits of armor and steel helmets in battle. They carried muskets and finely crafted swords. A few rode mighty horses. To Caribbean Indians, who had never seen horses or steel weapons, the conquistadores were a frightening sight. With this advantage and their superior military technology, the Spanish soon conquered many of the Caribbean Islands. They then turned to the American mainland.

Reading Check **Summarizing** What advantages helped the conquistadores conquer the Caribbean?

Interpreting Visuals

Contact. Columbus claimed the land he had found for Spain. *According to this painting, how did American Indians react to Columbus's arrival?*

Image Credit: (bl) ©Wikimedia Commons

The Age of Contact 91

While exploring the coast, the Spaniards saw some American Indians wearing gold jewelry. They excitedly asked where they could find more of the metal. The American Indians described Apalachee, a northern region that they said was rich in gold. Eager to find treasure, Narváez divided his force. He sent the ships in search of a harbor, while he and 300 soldiers set off for Apalachee.

Struggling through the Florida swamps, the Spaniards soon became lost. They ran out of food and grew weak. Many were wounded or killed in American Indian attacks. When the explorers at last found Apalachee, there was no gold. The discouraged Spaniards slowly began making their way back to the coast.

When the explorers neared shore, they searched for their ships without success. Unknown to the group, the ships had returned home. The stranded and starving explorers had to eat their horses to survive. Explorer **Álvar Núñez Cabeza de Vaca** (kah-BEH-sah deh BAH-kah) described their desperation. "It became clear that we could leave this terrible land only by dying."

As a last resort, the Spaniards used what materials they could find to build several small, flimsy boats. About a month after they set sail, a huge storm arose. Three of the boats, including Narváez's, washed up on the Texas coast, probably in or near Matagorda Bay. Narváez, however, disappeared when his poorly anchored boat washed out to sea. The other two boats shipwrecked on a Texas island—perhaps Galveston or San Luis. Only about 80 explorers had survived to reach the island.

Stranded once again, the explorers had lost most of their supplies. Many had even lost their clothes at sea and had nothing to wear. With winter approaching, the situation was grim. Just as they were losing all hope, a group of Karankawa Indians appeared. This meeting in 1528 marked the beginning of the Age of Contact in Texas.

Shocked by the strangers' condition, the Karankawas took the men in and shared their supplies with them. Food and clothing were scarce, however, and most of the Spaniards died during that winter. The few who lived were held captive and forced to work very hard. For the next few years Cabeza de Vaca worked as a servant, a trader, and a healer. He traveled along the Texas coast gathering sea shells and mesquite beans to trade for animal skins. He later wrote about his experiences in Texas.

TEXAS VOICES

"Throughout all this country we went naked, and . . . twice a year we cast our skins like serpents. The sun and air produced great sores on our [chests] and shoulders. . . . The country is so broken and thicket, that often after getting our wood in the forests, the blood flowed from us in many places."

—Álvar Núñez Cabeza de Vaca, *The Narrative of Álvar Núñez Cabeza de Vaca*

Reading Check **Summarizing** What tragedy struck the Narváez expedition when the explorers tried to sail to Mexico?

LINKING Past to Present

Cartography
In 1519 Alonso Álvarez de Pineda created the first map of the northern Gulf of Mexico. To create the map, he used his observations and simple tools such as a compass. Today mapmakers create extremely accurate maps using computers and satellites. The *Landsat 7* and *GOES* satellites provide detailed images of Earth that are used to make maps. *How have mapmaking techniques improved?*

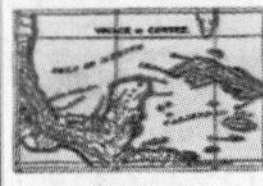

A map of the Gulf of Mexico made in the 1500s

Image Credit: ©North Wind/North Wind Picture Archives

The Age of Contact 95

Key Terms

At the beginning of each section you will find a list of key terms that you will need to know. Be on the lookout for those words as you read through the section.

Key People

Also included in the list at the beginning of each section are key people, the important figures who helped shape history. Keeping an eye out for their names will help you make sense of what you read.

Words to Know

As you read this social studies textbook, you will be more successful if you know or learn the meanings of the words on this page. There are two types of words listed here. The first list contains academic words. These words are important in all classes, not just social studies. The second list contains words that are special to this particular topic of social studies, Texas history. Knowing both types of words will help you succeed in this course.

Academic Words	
acquire	to get
affect	to change or influence
agreement	a decision reached by two or more people
aspect	part
conflict	an open conflict between two groups
consequences	effects of a particular event or events
contemporary	modern
defend	to protect from danger
distribute	to divide among a group of people
efficient	productive and not wasteful
establish	to set up or create
features	characteristics
function	work or perform
influence	change, or have an effect on
method	way of doing something
motive	reason for doing something
policy	rule, course of action
primary	main, most important
principles	basic beliefs or rules
process	a series of steps by which a task is accomplished
purpose	the reason something is done
role	a part or function; assigned behavior
vary	to be different

Social Studies Words	
administration	term a public official spends in office
agriculture	farming and ranching
border	a line separating one political unit, like a country, from another
boundary	the edge of a region where it meets another region
century	a period of 100 years
culture	the knowledge, beliefs, customs, and values of a group of people
decade	a period of 10 years
democracy	governmental rule by the people, usually on a majority rule principle
economy	the system in which people make and exchange goods and services
expansion	growth of territory
geography	the study of the earth's physical and cultural features
independence	freedom from forceful rule
politics	activities related to the shaping of government policies and programs
rebellion	an organized resistance to the established government
republic	a government in which people elect their leaders
revolution	the attempt to change one form of government for another
society	a group of people who share common traditions
South	the region of the United States sometimes defined by the states that seceded from the Union to form the Confederate States of America
West	the part of the United States west of the Mississippi River that was settled by Americans after 1800

Make This Book Work for You

Studying Texas history will be easy for you using this textbook. Take a few minutes to become familiar with the easy-to-use structure and special features of this history book. See how this Texas history textbook will make history come alive for you!

Unit

Each unit opener provides a visual that gives you an overview of the exciting topics celebrating Texas and connecting Texas Teens with the topics being studied.

Reading Social Studies provides lessons to teach reading skills with opportunities for practice.

Social Studies Skills provides opportunites to practice the skills presented in the unit.

History in Action provides opportunities for you to propose solutions to problems through simulations based on the topics within the unit.

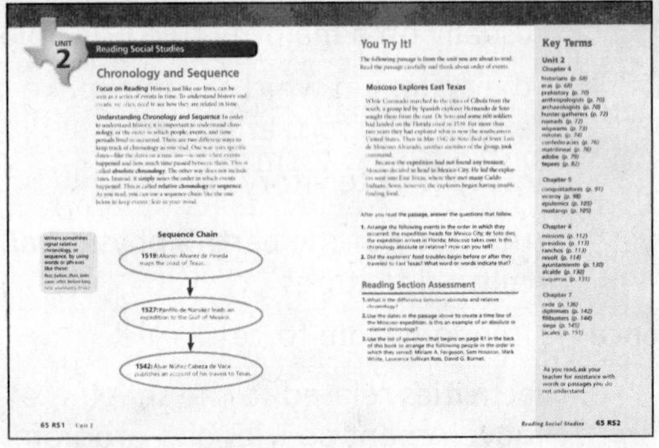

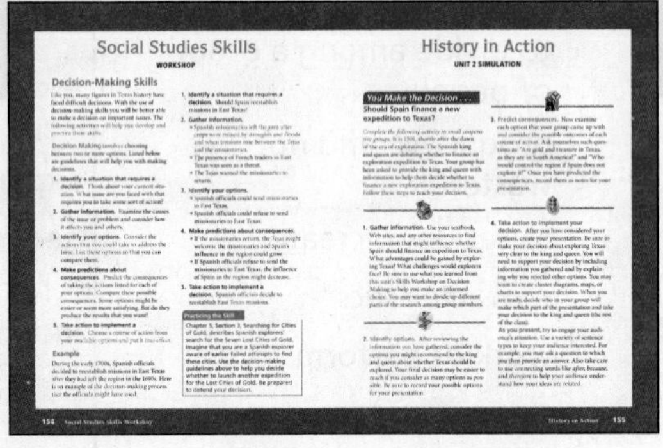

Chapter

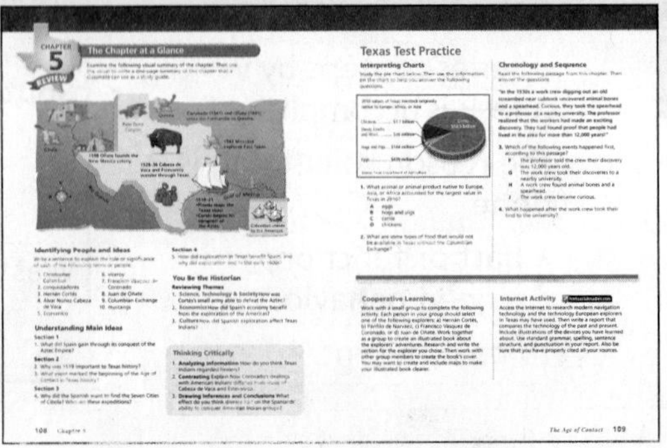

Each chapter begins with an introduction that lists the important ideas covered focusing on a particular time period. Each chapter ends with a **Chapter Review.**

Section

The Section opener pages include Main Idea statements and lists of Key Terms and People. In addition, each section includes the following special features.

Why It Matters Today
helps you make connections between what you are reading in your history book and the world around you.

The Story Continues
features an interesting episode from Texas history that shows you that history is not just a collection of facts but a blend of many individual stories and adventures.

myNotebook
allows you to write down the most important information from the section in a usable format.

Short sections of content
organize the information in each section into small chunks of text that you should not find too overwhelming.

Reading Check
questions end each section of content so that you can test whether or not you understand what you have just studied.

Section Assessment
boxes provide an opportunity for you to make sure that you understand the main ideas of the section. We also provide assessment practice online!

Europeans Reach the Americas

Main Ideas
1. Explorer Christopher Columbus reached the Americas from Europe in 1492.
2. The Spanish wanted to control the Americas to obtain gold, spread Christianity, and gain glory.
3. In 1519 Hernán Cortés conquered the Aztec Empire.

Key Terms and People
- Christopher Columbus
- conquistadores
- Hernán Cortés
- Moctezuma II

Why It Matters Today
Early explorers sailed uncharted waters and visited new lands. Use current events sources to find information about exploration today, such as space or deep-sea exploration.

TEKS: 1B, 1C, 2B, 20A, 21B, 21C, 21H, 21I

myNotebook
Use the annotation tools in your eBook to take notes on the arrival of Europeans in the Americas.

The Story Continues
A cookbook from the 1500s advised cooks to carefully "grind spices . . . [so] you do not lose any speck." Seasonings were far too valuable to waste. Cooks for wealthy Europeans used salt to help keep meat from spoiling and spices to make rotting foods taste better. Spices and salt were carried to Europe from Asia and Africa across dangerous routes. Merchants in the spice trade risked death in harsh deserts and murder by bandits. Such risks and long journeys made spices very expensive. One pound of salt could cost as much as two pounds of gold!

Columbus Sails to the Americas
The spices so valued by Europeans came from Asia, as did other valuable products such as Chinese silk. The dangers of overland trade routes made such goods costly. As a result, in the late 1400s nations in western Europe raced to find an all-water route to Asia. An Italian sailor named **Christopher Columbus** believed he could reach Asia by sailing west across the Atlantic Ocean. The idea was daring because no one knew just how big the Atlantic was or what lay beyond it. King Ferdinand and Queen Isabella of Spain eventually gave Columbus three ships—the *Niña*, the *Pinta*, and the *Santa María*.

90 Chapter 5

Cortés Conquers the Aztecs
The Aztecs had large amounts of gold, precious gems, and silver. Moctezuma gave Cortés peace offerings from this treasure, but the gifts were not enough. Cortés took Moctezuma captive and considered how to conquer the Aztecs. But before he could act, fighting broke out between the Aztecs and the Spaniards. On the night of June 30, 1520, the Spaniards fled the city. Cortés then planned a new assault. He convinced more Mexican Indians to join him and had his men build boats armed with cannons. In May 1521 the Spaniards and their allies attacked Tenochtitlán. After a long and brutal fight, they defeated the Aztecs in August. Many of the Aztecs were killed or enslaved. Tenochtitlán lay in ruins.

Spain had captured the great wealth and land of the Aztec Empire. The Spanish sent much of the Aztec gold and silver, including treasures, to Spain. On top of the ruins of Tenochtitlán, Cortés built Mexico City. It became the capital of New Spain, which eventually extended from California to Florida to Mexico. Along with the Caribbean Islands, Mexico became a common starting point for Spanish exploration in the Americas. Such exploration increased the size of Spain's empire, which by 1600 included much of North and South America.

Reading Check **Comparing** How were the Aztec Empire and Spanish America similar?

CONNECTING TO
ECONOMICS AND MATH

Gold and the Spanish Empire
Spanish explorers sent the gold and silver they found in the Americas back to Spain. As the amount of gold in Spain rose, prices of goods also rose. Spain produced few goods itself, so much of its wealth left the country to pay for goods made elsewhere.

The chart below lists the value of gold and silver sent to Spain from the Americas between 1516 and 1660. Use the information to create a bar graph.

YEAR	VALUE OF GOLD AND SILVER
1516–1520	993,000 pesos
1536–1540	3,938,000 pesos
1556–1560	7,999,000 pesos
1576–1580	17,252,000 pesos
1596–1600	34,429,000 pesos
1616–1620	30,112,000 pesos
1636–1640	16,315,000 pesos
1656–1660	3,361,000 pesos

Interpreting Data
1. During what years did the value of gold and silver sent to Spain peak?
2. By what percentage did the value of gold and silver increase between 1536 and 1560?

Section 1 Review

hmhsocialstudies.com
ONLINE QUIZ

1. **Define and explain:**
   - conquistadores
2. **Identify and explain** the significance of each of the following:
   - Christopher Columbus
   - King Ferdinand and Queen Isabella
   - Hernán Cortés
   - Moctezuma II
3. **Summarizing** Copy the web diagram below. Use it to show why Spain wanted to gain an empire in the Americas.

   Spanish Conquest of the Americas

4. **Finding the Main Idea**
   a. What did Christopher Columbus accomplish in 1492?
   b. Why was the building of Mexico City in 1519 significant?
5. **Writing and Critical Thinking** WriteSmart
   Sequencing Imagine that you are a member of Cortés's army in 1519. Write journal entries describing your experiences in Mexico. Describe events in their proper order.
   Consider the following:
   - the march to Tenochtitlán
   - the conquest of the Aztec Empire

The Age of Contact 93

Themes in Texas History

Each chapter in this book with a set of theme statements under the heading You Be the Historian. These statements are drawn from several broad themes central to nearly any study of history: Geography; Economics; Government; Citizenship; Culture; Science, Technology & Society; Constitutional Heritage; and Global Relations. As you begin each chapter, you will be asked to respond to the theme statements in a general way, based on your previous knowledge. At the end of the chapter, you will be asked to respond to more specific questions about the themes, based on the chapter content.

Geography

Geography is the study of the world, including its landforms, water features, climates, and resources. It is also the study of how people interact with and alter the world around them. The vast and diverse geography of Texas has played an important role in the state's history. As you will learn in this course, the landforms and climates of Texas have influenced where in the state people live. The distribution and development of the state's resources has helped shape its economy, society, and politics. Even as the land has shaped people's lives, though, people have reshaped the land. From digging canals and building dams to create waterways and lakes to clearing forests to make rooms for cities, Texans have had a tremendous impact on the Texas landscape.

Economics

Economics is the study of how people make a living, from the earliest farmers in the state to modern software engineers. As you study, you will explore the relationship between history and economics in Texas. You will learn about the growth of new industries and the ever changing relationship between government, business owners, and labor in Texas. You will also learn about the American free-enterprise economic system and how it has influenced American politics, as well as the lives of individual Texans and Texas society as a whole.

Government

Government is the structure that people set up to provide order and security in their lives. Every group in Texas history has had some form of government. Those governments have taken various forms, from independent bands of American Indians to a colonial government ruled by Spain to an independent Republic to a modern democratic state. In studying Texas history, you will explore the workings of each of these systems of government. In addition, you will learn about the functions and roles of county and municipal governments, including how they receive and spend money.

Stagecoach lines were big business in the early days of Texas statehood. Coaches carried passengers, cargo, and mail over long distances.

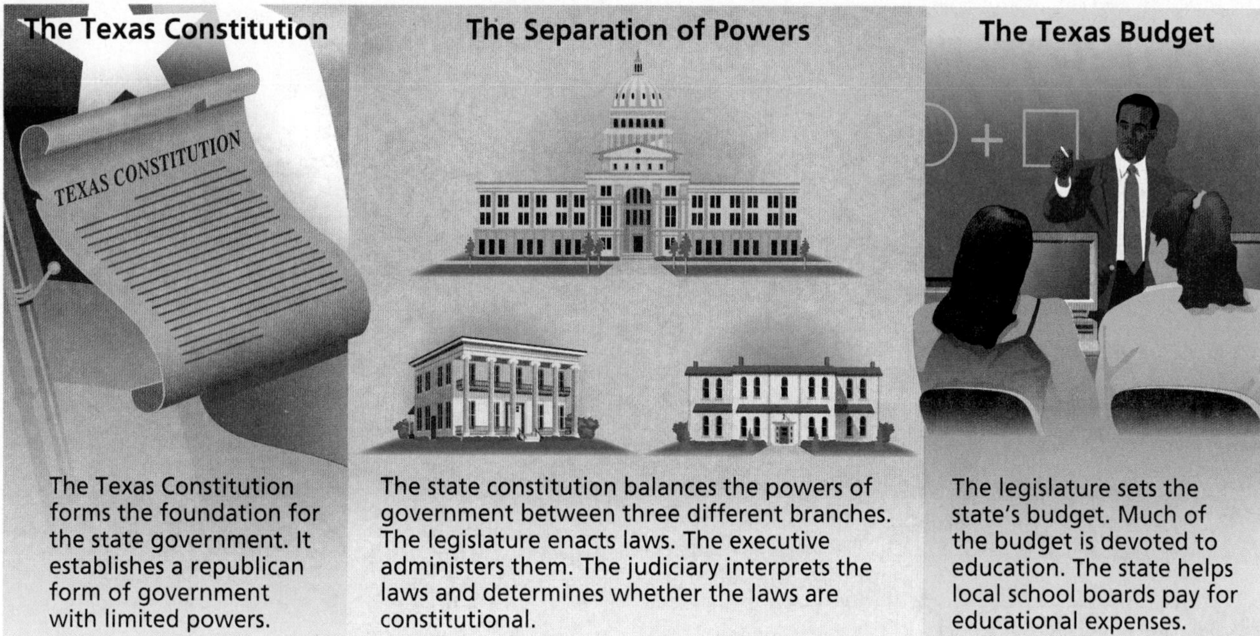

The Texas Constitution forms the foundation for the state government. It establishes a republican form of government with limited powers.

The state constitution balances the powers of government between three different branches. The legislature enacts laws. The executive administers them. The judiciary interprets the laws and determines whether the laws are constitutional.

The legislature sets the state's budget. Much of the budget is devoted to education. The state helps local school boards pay for educational expenses.

Citizenship

Citizenship means belonging to a particular country or society. Being a citizen means having certain rights and responsibilities. As Texas and U.S. citizens, we enjoy a number of basic rights, from freedom of speech and religion to the right to vote. Throughout history, however, Texans have had to struggle to define exactly what their rights were and to protect them. At times, certain members of society found their rights limited or denied, and they had to struggle to find full equality under the law. Texans have also worked to uphold the responsibilities of citizenship—such as voting and taking part in government—that accompany membership in our democracy.

Culture

Culture is defined as the set of knowledge, beliefs, and customs that a group of people share. It includes such elements as language, religion, celebrations, art, and cuisine. Texas has a rich and diverse culture influenced by the many ethnic, racial, and religious groups who have settled in the state. As you study Texas history, you will learn about the ways in which these groups maintained distinct cultures—such as maintaining traditional holidays and festivals—while adding to the greater Texas culture. For example, Tex-Mex cooking, influenced by cooking styles brought to the state by Mexican settlers, is popular throughout Texas. In addition, many cities and physical features in the state bear Spanish place-names.

Texans celebrate their culture with dances, music, food, and many other festivities and ceremonies.

NASA astronauts first landed on the Moon in 1969 and made several return trips in the following years.

Science, Technology & Society

From the development of barbed wire and the windmill to the growth of aerospace, medical, and computer research and technology in Texas, science and technology have influenced every aspect of our culture and society. As you read, you will learn about the many scientific and technological advances that Texans have made through our state's history. You will also learn about how these developments influenced the Texas economy and the lives of people across the state, the country, and the world.

World War I veterans

Constitutional Heritage

No study of Texas history would be complete without examining the Texas Constitution, the document that provides the legal framework for our state's democratic government. As you progress through this course, you will learn about the Constitution's origins and how it was influenced by both the U.S. Constitution and older Mexican and Spanish laws. You will understand why the writers of the Constitution included such elements as a separation of powers and an amendment process. You will also see how the Texas Constitution helps preserve the basic rights of all Texans.

Global Relations

Since Spanish explorers first arrived in Texas, the state has been involved in global events. In the years that followed the first contact between Spaniards and American Indians, Texans have served as world leaders, fought in several foreign wars, and formed trade relationships with countries around the world. As you read, you will be able to trace ways in which the state's political, social, and economic development has affected—and been affected by—other countries and their people.

Essential Elements of

Geography

History and geography are closely related. The events you study in history are strongly influenced by the landscapes of the places in which they occur. Similarly, the places you study in geography are shaped by the events that took place there. To describe a series of events without placing them in their physical settings is to tell only part of the story. The essential elements listed below are the basic ideas around which the study of geography is organized.

1. **The World in Spatial Terms** The first essential element refers to the way geographers view the world. They look at where things are located and how they are arranged on Earth's surface. Central to this way of looking at the world is the use of maps and models. Maps allow geographers to organize information in a visual form, one that allows them to see patterns that might otherwise be difficult to determine.

2. **Places and Regions** This essential element deals with the physical and human characteristics that make particular parts of Earth special. Every place on Earth has characteristics that define it, from what the land looks like to how often it rains to how the people who live their act. A region is an area with common characteristics that make it different from surrounding areas. People create regions as a convenient way to study the world. Regions can be large, like North America, or small, like a neighborhood.

3. **Physical Systems** This element deals with the world's physical features: mountains, plains, oceans, rivers, and so on. Geographers want to know not only where these features are located but also how they came to be there. As a result, they study the physical processes that shape and change Earth's physical features and environments.

4. **Human Systems** The element of human systems is concerned with the world's population. Geographers want to know where people live and why. They examine how populations grow, change, and move. They also investigate elements of the world's cultures to better understand how people in various parts of the world live.

5. **Environment and Society** One of the most important topics in geography is how people interact with the environment. The landforms and climate of a region shape various elements of people's lives, from what sort of clothing they wear to how they make their living. At the same time, however, people's actions can change their environments. These changes can be positive, such as bringing water to previously dry areas, or negative, such as causing pollution.

6. **The Uses of Geography** The study of geography has many uses. Historians use geography to understand the past. But understanding geography is important to the present as well. People use geography every day to explore such topics as where to build roads, what kinds of crops to grow in an area, and how to use Earth's limited resources more effectively to ensure the success of future generations.

Critical Thinking

Throughout this book, you will be asked to think critically about the events and issues that have shaped Texas history. Critical thinking is the reasoned judgment of information and ideas. The development of critical thinking skills is essential to effective citizenship. Such skills empower you to exercise your civic rights and responsibilities. The following critical thinking skills appear in the section reviews and chapter reviews of the book.

1. **Analyzing Information** is the process of breaking complex information down into its parts and examining the relationships between those parts. By looking at small bits of information, you can begin to better understand the whole. For example, if you are asked to analyze the effects of railroads on the development of Texas, you might begin by analyzing its effects on various elements of Texas culture, such as farming, the settlement of the frontier, or the growth of cities. Understanding the effects of railroads on these individual areas will help you more clearly express their effects on the state as a whole.

Early Texas farm

2. **Sequencing** means listing events in chronological order, or the order in which they occurred. Knowing the order in which events took place can help you understand the relationships among them. There are two basic types of sequencing you will use in this course: absolute and relative chronology. Absolute chronology involves arranging events by the specific date on which they occurred. Placing events on a time line is one example of absolute chronology. Relative chronology is less exact. It involves listing events in the order they happened without the need for dates. You only need to know what happened first, second, third, and so on.

3. **Categorizing** involves sorting items, people, or events into lists that share common characteristics. For example, if you were given a list of important figures in Texas history you could categorize them as political leaders, military leaders, and cultural leaders. If asked to discuss the effects of the discovery of oil in Texas, you could categorize them into economic effects, social effects, and political effects. Sorting people, items, or events into categories makes you consider their individual traits and what various people, items, or events have in common. It also makes it easier to see differences among them.

The issue of slavery was one cause of the Civil War.

4. **Identifying Cause and Effect** is an important part of interpreting the relationships between historical events. A cause is an action that leads to a particular event. An effect is what happens as a result of that event. As you read, you will learn that historical events often have many causes and lead to many effects. For example, Mexican president Santa Anna's abandonment of the Constitution of 1824, Stephen F. Austin's arrest, and the arrival of Mexican troops in Texas were all causes that led to the Texas Revolution. The revolution had many effects, including the formation of the Republic of Texas. Remember, however, that sequence and causation are not the same. The fact that one event took place before another does not necessarily mean that it caused the second event to take place. Similarly, not everything that happens after a particular event is an effect of that event.

5. **Comparing and Contrasting** means examining events, situations, or points of view to uncover their similarities and differences. Comparing two items or events means looking to see what they have in common. Contrasting items or events means looking to see how they are different. For example, a comparison of the Coastal Plains and Great Plains regions of Texas would reveal, among other similarities, that the two regions have similar physical features. Contrasting the two would show that the Coastal Plains receive much more rain each year than do the Great Plains and that different types of plants grow in each region as a result.

6. **Finding the Main Idea** involves sifting through a passage of text to determine the point that its writer was trying to make. Most historical writing consists of a series of main ideas supported by examples and details. It is important to be able to identify the main idea to be sure you understand what you are reading. In some cases, the main idea will be stated clearly in a sentence within a paragraph or section of text. In other cases, the main idea may be implied without being directly stated. In either case, it can be helpful to ask yourself, "What is the writer trying to say here?" each time you finish reading a paragraph or passage.

Texans celebrated the 100th anniversary of Texas independence in 1936.

7. **Summarizing** is the process of taking a large amount of information and boiling it down into a short, clear statement. Summarizing can be particularly useful in helping you review a long story or event. For example, the story of how cattle ranching developed in the Texas Panhandle is a detailed one, spanning more than 200 years and involving thousands of people. However, you won't need to remember every detail of that long saga to understand the state's history. It may be easier for you to remember with a short summary like this one: "Cattle ranching began during the Spanish period on isolated ranches. With the removal of the Plains Indians from West Texas in the 1880s, the region was opened to ranching. The grassland and aquifers in the region provided plenty of food and water for cattle, and ranching became a major industry in Texas."

8. **Making Generalizations and Predictions** asks you to interpret information to make general statements about what has taken place and to use that information to make educated guesses about what will happen next. A generalization is a broad statement about events or issues. It may not be true in every possible scenario, but it covers most situations. Making generalizations can help you see the big picture of historical events, keeping you from being bogged down in details. You must be careful, however, to avoid stereotypes, or overgeneralizations about groups of people. A prediction is an educated guess about the possible outcome of a series of events. When you read history, you should ask yourself questions like, "What will happen next? If this person does this, what will that mean for other people?", and so on.

9. **Drawing Inferences and Conclusions** means taking what you know about an event, a situation, or a problem and extracting new information from it. An inference is an assumption about a situation based on general information, including what you already know. For example, if you read that African Americans in the 1890s had few rights, you might draw on your knowledge that people without rights are often unhappy to infer that many African Americans were unhappy with their situation. A conclusion is a prediction about the outcome of a situation based on specific information. For example, consider the facts that many African Americans and Mexican Americans fought for their country in World War II and that several movements for equal rights began shortly after the war. From these, you might conclude that the experiences of African American and Mexican American soldiers led them to call for equality.

10. **Identifying Points of View** is the process of determining how an individual or group felt about an issue or event. A person's point of view is shaped by his or her frame of reference: his or her beliefs and attitudes as well as factors such as age, gender, religion, race, and economic status. The ability to identify points of view helps you understand why people see things as they do and reinforces the knowledge that people's views may change over time or with a change in circumstances.

11. **Supporting a Point of View** involves taking a stand about an event or issue and arguing persuasively for that position. When supporting a point of view, you should set up a clear, well-organized argument based on specific evidence that supports your point of view. For example, consider the points of view involved in the Populists' effort to regulate Texas railroads during the late 1800s. Whether you choose a position in favor of the farmers or in favor of the railroads, you should state your opinion clearly and give reasons that defend it. From time to time you may be called upon to support a point of view on a controversial or emotional issue.

12. **Identifying Bias** means identifying how the opinions and personal feelings of a writer, artist, politician, or other figure colors his or her work. Bias is an opinion based on prejudice or emotions rather than on fact. A biased writer presents a slanted view of issues or events, rather than reporting only what happened. A historian who is biased against American Indians, for example, might downplay the accomplishments of these groups. When looking at historical sources, it is always important to identify any biases the author may hold. You must keep those biases in mind while reading such sources.

13. **Evaluating** means judging the merits or significance of something. For example you might be asked to determine whether a reform movement was successful, whether the actions of a president were justified, or whether an event was good or bad for Texas. Any evaluation of this type should be carefully considered. Don't just toss out a simple answer, but really think about the event and its effects for everyone involved. Carefully consider both the positives and the negatives, and then make your final evaluation.

14. **Problem Solving** is the process of posing workable solutions to difficult situations. When presented with a historical problem, first gather information about it, including factors that helped bring the problem about and the challenges it brings to various people. List and consider possible options for solving the problem. For each possible solution, weigh its advantages and disadvantages before choosing what you think is the best solution.

15. **Decision Making** involves reviewing a situation and then making decisions or recommendations for the best possible course of action for the people involved. Before making any decision, gather information relevant to the issue at hand. You may need to do some background research to study the history of the situation and consider the points of view of the individuals involved. For each potential course of action, consider consequences that might result if it were followed. Then make a recommendation and follow through on any tasks that it requires.

Strategies for English Language Learners

Are you learning English? You can learn social studies and English at the same time. You already know a lot about social studies from knowing what's going on in the world. You can also learn English while learning social studies. Your teacher and other students will be happy to help you. Some of the ideas below will help you get ready to learn English. Some ideas will help you learn better in class and while you read. Other ideas will help you remember and use what you learn.

Get Ready to Learn

You can do these things before you go to social studies class.

Visit Your Classroom and Teacher

Go to your classroom with other students if you can. Look carefully around the room.

- Ask your teacher to tell you the names of things you do not know. You can ask, "What is this?" or "Will we use this in class?" or "What does it do?"
- Learn how to say and read the names of things you will use in class.
- Are there signs on the wall? What do they say? If you do not know, ask your teacher or other students, "What does this say? What does it mean?"
- Remember the words on signs. You may see these same words in other places.

Learn Some Social Studies Words

You will learn a lot of new words in your social studies class. Some of these new words will be social studies words. Other new words may not be social studies words but will still be important to learn.

- Ask your teacher to say and write some words you need to know.
- Ask what the words mean.
- Learn how to say and read the words.

Ask Your Teacher for Help with Reading

Your teacher can help you read your social studies book. He or she can help you learn new words that you need to know before you read.

- Your teacher might give you a list of the important words or ideas you will read or a list of questions to answer as you read.
- Your teacher might give you a graphic organizer to help you understand what you read. A graphic organizer is a drawing that shows how ideas are connected.

Look at Pictures Before You Read

Before you read your social studies book, look at the pictures. It will be easier to read the pages if you already know a little bit from looking at the pictures.

- As you look at the pictures, think about what you already know.
- If there are words with the pictures, read the words. Try to figure out the meaning of the words by what the pictures show.

Read Before Class

Your teacher may tell you what he or she will talk about tomorrow. If you read that part of the book today, you will already know some of what the teacher will say. Then it will be easier for you to understand when the teacher talks.

Before reading a section, look at the information in the Section Opener. This information introduces you to some of the words and ideas you will learn in the section.

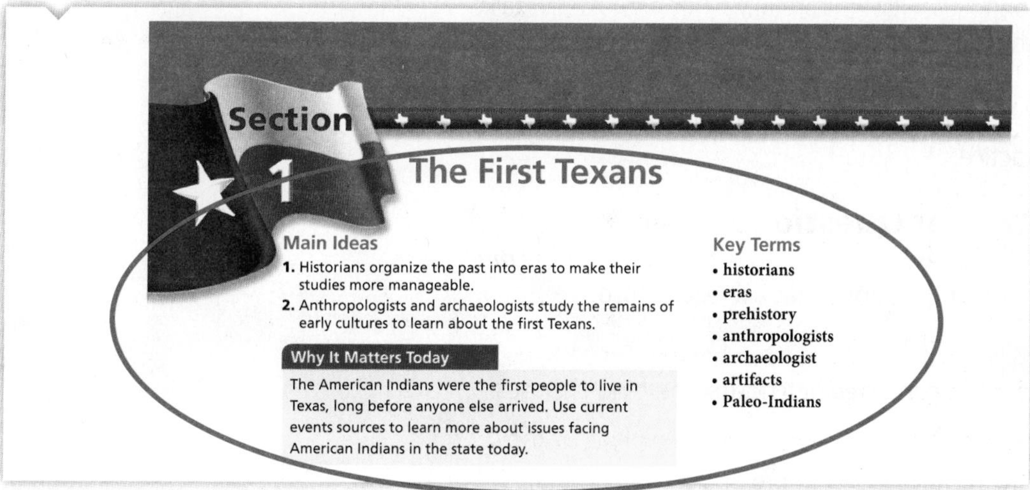
Section 1

The First Texans

Main Ideas

1. Historians organize the past into eras to make their studies more manageable.
2. Anthropologists and archaeologists study the remains of early cultures to learn about the first Texans.

Why It Matters Today

The American Indians were the first people to live in Texas, long before anyone else arrived. Use current events sources to learn more about issues facing American Indians in the state today.

Key Terms

- historians
- eras
- prehistory
- anthropologists
- archaeologist
- artifacts
- Paleo-Indians

Start Taking Notes Before Class

Taking notes means writing something to help you remember what you read or hear. Do not write all the words you read or hear. Write just the most important words, or make drawings.

- It can be hard to take notes when you listen. It is easier if you start your notes before class, when you read your book.
- Write down important words that you read, or draw something to help you remember important ideas. Leave lots of space on your paper.

- Then, take your notes to class. Use the same paper to take notes when you listen in class. Write more notes in the space you left.

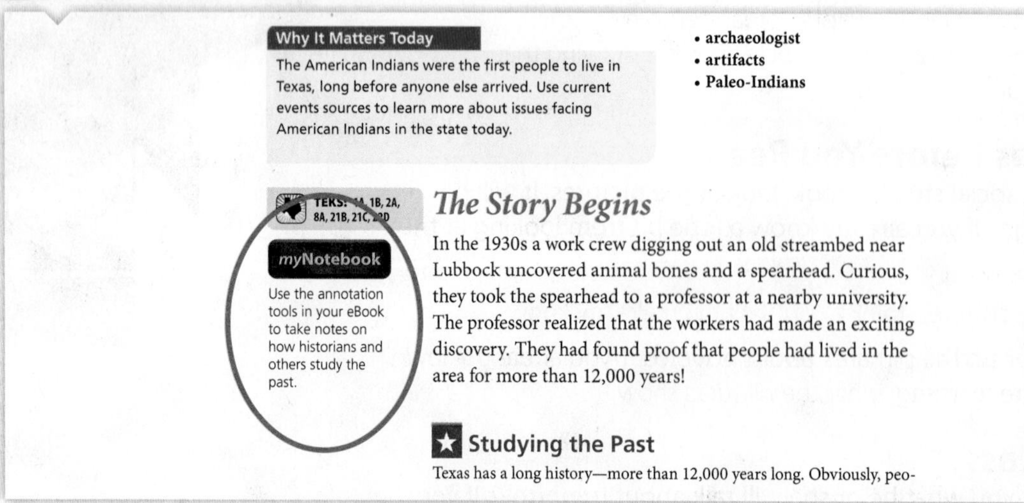

Why It Matters Today

The American Indians were the first people to live in Texas, long before anyone else arrived. Use current events sources to learn more about issues facing American Indians in the state today.

- archaeologist
- artifacts
- Paleo-Indians

TEKS: 1A, 1B, 2A, 8A, 21B, 21C, 22D

myNotebook

Use the annotation tools in your eBook to take notes on how historians and others study the past.

The Story Begins

In the 1930s a work crew digging out an old streambed near Lubbock uncovered animal bones and a spearhead. Curious, they took the spearhead to a professor at a nearby university. The professor realized that the workers had made an exciting discovery. They had found proof that people had lived in the area for more than 12,000 years!

Studying the Past

Texas has a long history—more than 12,000 years long. Obviously, peo-

Get Ready to Ask Questions

You might have questions about what you read before class.

- First, write down your question or words that you do not understand.
- Practice your question.
- Bring your question to class. Listen carefully when the teacher talks about the same thing as your question. Your teacher may answer the question.
- If you still do not have an answer, raise your hand. Ask the question you wrote and practiced.

Get Ready to Answer Questions

Learn these question words: ***what, where, when, who, why, how much, is it, will it***. Learn how to answer questions that use each word.

- *What*: Tell the name of a thing.
- *What will happen, what happened*: Tell how something changes.
- *Where*: Tell a place.
- *When*: Tell a time (you can also say before or after something).
- *Who*: Tell a person. Your teacher might ask, "Who can tell me . . .?" That means, "Do you know the answer?" If you do, raise your hand.
- *How much*: Tell an amount.
- *Why*: Tell what made something happen, or explain a reason.
- *Is it* or *Will it*: Answer yes or no. You can also give a reason for your answer.

If you do not know the exact words to answer a question, try using words you know to describe your ideas.

While You Learn

You can do these things in your social studies class.

Use What You Know

When you hear or read about something new, think about what you already know.

If a new word sounds like a word you already know, maybe the two words mean almost the same thing. Maybe you already know something about a new idea. Use what you know to help you understand new words and ideas.

Talk to your teacher and classmates about how what you already know relates to what you are learning.

Take Notes During Class

As you learn new words and ideas in class, listen carefully to your teacher and take notes. The type of notes you take will depend on the topic you are learning about. Here are some suggestions:

Write down the main ideas that your teacher explains.

- Write down important words and their meanings.
- Make lists of characteristics, causes, effects, and examples.
- Number the steps in a process.
- Draw pictures.

Put a question mark next to any notes that you do not understand.

Understand Instructions

Instructions tell you how to do something. They are sometimes called directions. You need to follow instructions many times in social studies class. Sometimes your teacher says the instructions. Sometimes you need to read the instructions.

Some instructions have some parts, called steps. Sometimes the teacher or book will use numbers (1, 2, 3 . . .) to tell you the order of steps.

Other times, instructions use words. Learn the words that tell you when to do things: first, then, next, before, after, while, last. Listen and look for these words in instructions. Use them to help you know when to do things.

You can also use these words to give other people instructions. You can use them to write or tell about something you did.

Learn Some Signal Words

Signal words are words that show how ideas are connected. Learn the words below, look for them as you read, and listen for them when people are speaking.

- These signal words show how things are the same or almost the same: *and, also, another, like.*
- These signal words show how things are different: *but, however, although, instead.*
- These signal words show how one thing causes another: *so, because, as a result.*

Look for Different Kinds of Sentences

There are four main kinds of sentences. They are listed below. Look for these kinds of sentences when you are reading. Listen for them when someone else is speaking. Practice using all types of sentences when you are speaking.

Sentence type	Example
Statements end with a period and tell you something.	Texas won its independence from Mexico in 1836.
Commands tell you to do something. You will see these sentences when there is something for you to do in the book or when you are doing a project.	Write down the year in which Texas won its independence.
Questions end with a question mark. When you are listening, listen for the speaker to pause after they ask a question. The pause gives you time to think about the question or to give an answer to the question.	When did Texas win independence from Mexico?
Exclamations show excitement or surprise and end with an exclamation point.	Texas was independent!

Get Help If You Do Not Understand

If you don't understand something that you hear or read, get help.

- Ask your teacher or another student. Raise your hand and ask in class, or wait until the teacher is finished talking.
- If you do not understand a word, try to say the word. Then ask, "What does that word mean?"
- If you do not know how to do something, ask, "How do I do this?"
- If you do not understand an idea or picture, tell what you do know. Then ask about the part you do not understand.

Answer Questions

When your teacher asks you a question, you need to answer. Here are some things that can help you:

- Listen carefully to the question. If you do not understand the words, you can ask, "Could you repeat the question?" or "Can you say that more slowly?"
- Listen for the question word. It tells you what kind of answer to give.
- If the teacher is pointing at something, the question is probably about that thing. You can talk about that thing in your answer.
- Remember what the teacher said before the question. The question might be about what the teacher said. Maybe you can use some of the teacher's words in your answer.
- If you do not know an answer, tell the teacher. You can say, "I don't know" or "I did not understand that very well" or "I don't remember that."

Talk in Groups

In social studies class, you often work with other students. You need to understand what your group should do.

- Read instructions if you have them. You can ask, "Can I have some more time to read?"
- If you do not understand the instructions, you can ask, "Can you help me understand this?"
- Talk about the instructions after you read. Tell what you can do. Ask the other students what they will do.
- As you work, you can ask your partner for help. You can say, "What do we do next?"
- Be sure to help your partner. You can ask, "What can I do to help?"
- If you have an idea, you can say, "I think we should do it this way" or "I have an idea."

Remember and Use What You Learn

You can do these things to help you learn important social studies words and ideas. Do them before class, in class, or after class.

Say It Again (and Again and Again)

One way to learn new words is to repeat them, or say them many times.

- First, make sure that you can say the word correctly.
- Be sure you know what the word means, too. Ask a friend or your teacher if you need to say the word differently or if you do not have the right meaning.

- When you can say the word correctly and know what it means, say the word several times. With a partner, take turns saying the word and telling each other the meaning.
- You will remember better if you say the meaning in your own words. You will remember even better if you say your own sentence that uses the word. Try to say a different sentence each time you repeat.

Use Flash Cards

Flash cards help you learn new words.

- To make flash cards, use some pieces of paper that are all the same size. What words do you need to learn?
- Write one word on a piece of paper. Turn the paper over. Write the meaning of the word. Use your own words or draw pictures to help you remember.
- Write the other words and their meanings on other pieces of paper.

To use flash cards, look at a word. Say what you think it means. Check the back of the paper for the word's meaning. Do this with all your words.

- If you get the meaning right, you may not need to look at that card again.
- If you get some wrong, look at them again and again.

You can use flash cards alone or with a partner.

Tell Somebody

Ask a friend or a person in your family to help you learn. Have the person ask you a question. If you need to learn some social studies words, have him or her ask you what the words mean.

If you need to remember what something in social studies means, have the person ask you. Then use your own words to tell what you know from your book or class. Tell the person what the words mean.

Answer all the person's questions. Helping that person understand helps you understand and remember too.

Make a Picture

Sometimes a picture can help you remember better than words can. You can draw pictures when you take notes. Draw your own picture, or use a graphic organizer.

There are many different graphic organizers. Here are some examples of graphic organizers used in this book.

A **Venn diagram** (Figure 1.A.) shows how things are the same and how they are different.

- Write how they are different in the circles.
- Write how they are the same where the circles come together.

You might be asked to complete a Venn diagram in this book.

A **concept map** (Figure 1.B.) shows how information is connected. Write an important word or idea in the big circle. Draw lines to smaller circles. In the smaller circles, write words that tell more about the idea in the big circle.

Figure 1.A. **Venn Diagram**

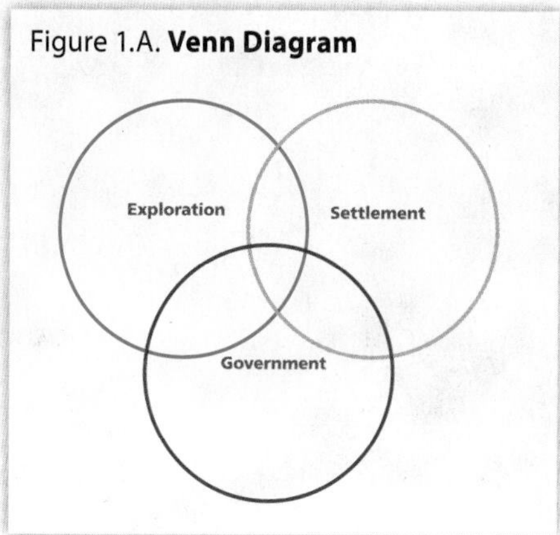

Figure 1.B. **Concept Map**

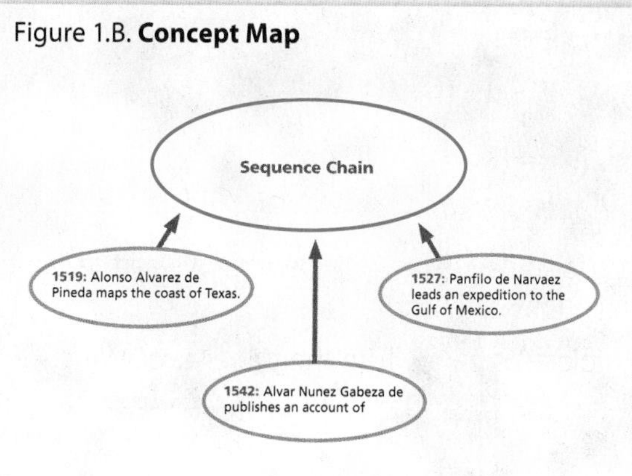

Summarize

Summarizing can help you remember what you read or hear. A summary includes only the most important ideas.

- You can summarize what you read.
- You can summarize what your teacher says in class.

When you summarize, write or say the most important ideas using your own words. You will remember better if you use your own words.

This book has a Visual Summary at the end of every chapter. The Visual Summary has important pictures and ideas from the chapter. Reading the Visual Summary will help you remember better.

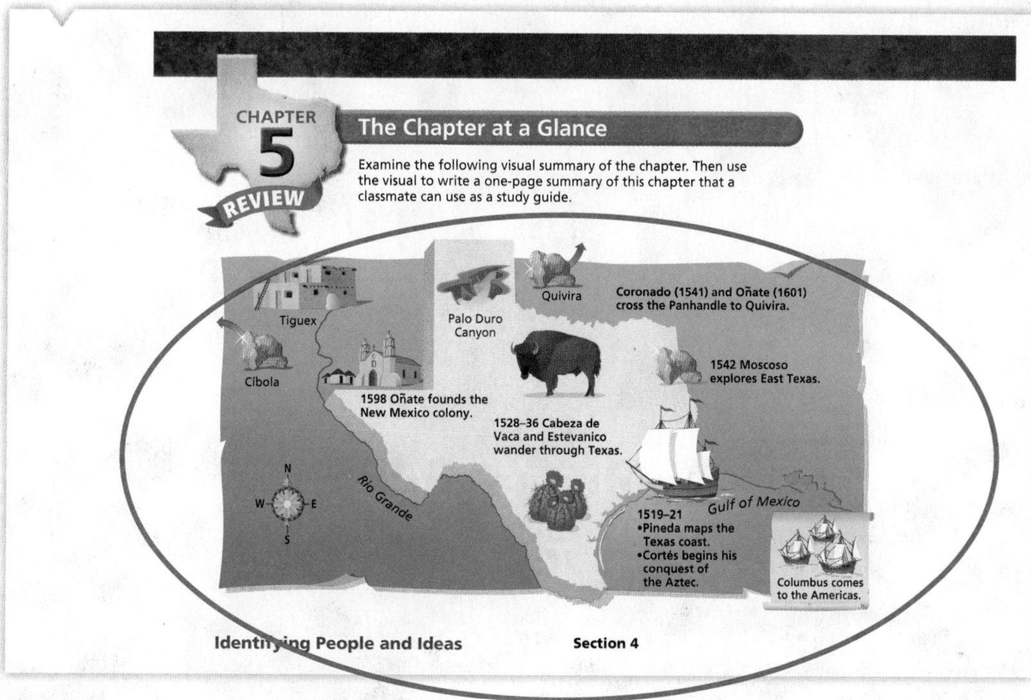

UNIT 1

Natural Texas and Its People

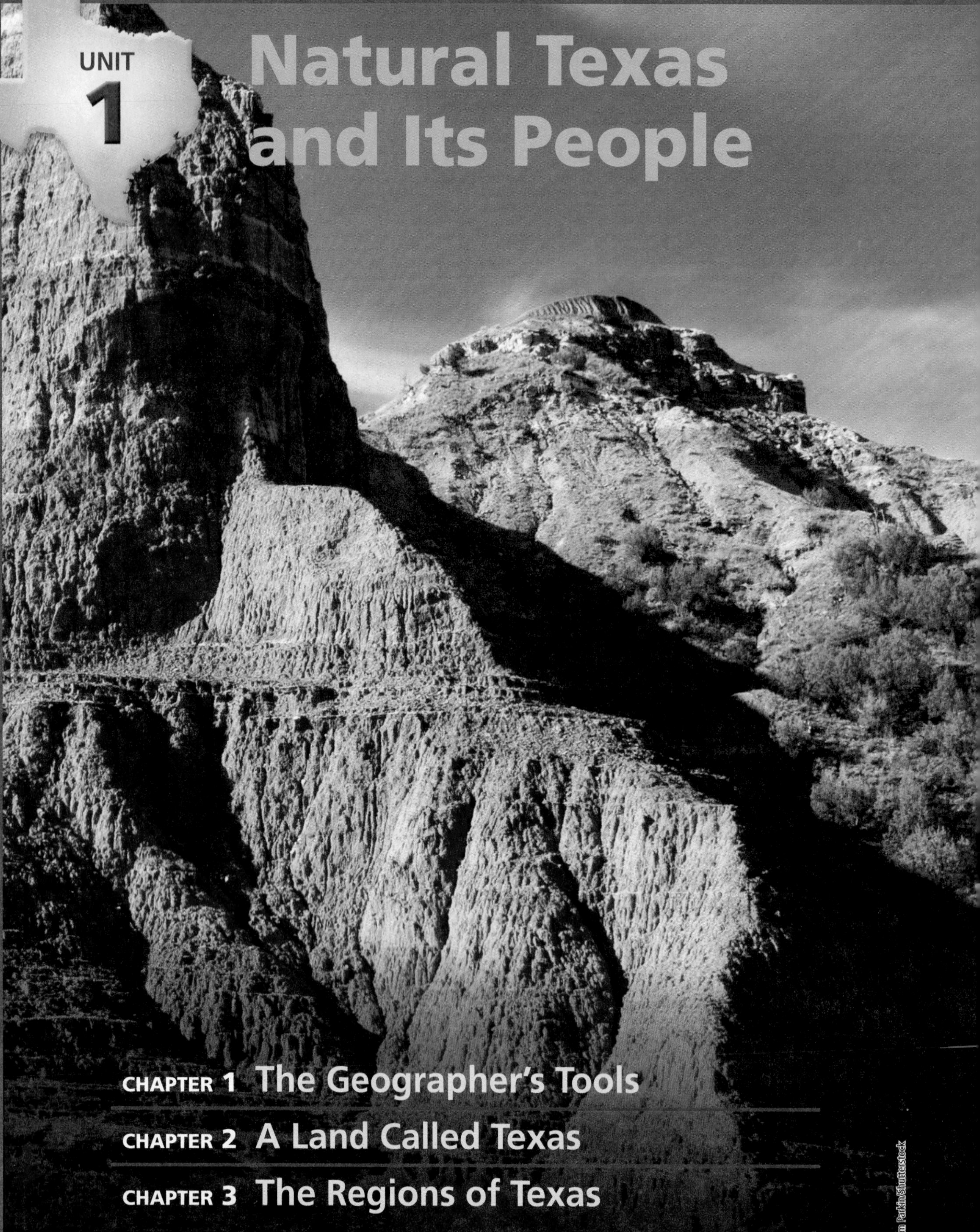

The Texas landscape at Palo Duro State Park is characterized by rugged red cliffs and yucca plants.

Image Credit: ©Jim Parkin/Shutterstock

Texas Teens

Young Bicyclists

Texas is known for its breathtaking natural scenery and its wide variety of landscapes. The chance to explore the beautiful vistas of the state inspires thousands of young Texans to take to their bicycles each year.

The Texas Parks and Wildlife Department maintains more than 1,000 miles of biking trails within the state's parks. These trails wind through every part of the state and through every kind of landscape. From the Piney Woods of northeast Texas to the Davis Mountains of the far west, from the ocean views of Galveston Island to the wide-open prairies, teenagers can find trails that appeal to nearly any taste.

Bicyclists who enjoy rugged terrain are drawn to places like Palo Duro Canyon. Biking trails twist through the canyon's rough terrain and steep, rocky walls rise high to either side. Wildlife ranging from deer to bobcats to rattlesnakes adds to the area's atmosphere. Active mountain bikers share the trails with hikers, horseback riders, and others enjoying nature.

Teens who prefer smoother rides might prefer the paved roads that run through the Hill Country west of Austin and San Antonio. Vast fields of wildflowers add color as the trails wind their way over the area's rolling hills. It is not uncommon to see long trains of cyclists making their way together through the region's broad expanses.

Wherever they ride, careful teens remember to practice bicycling safety. They wear helmets and reflective clothing so that other people can see them. They also bring plenty of water with them to prevent dehydration. And they bring repair equipment in case of emergency. Most of all, though, they remember to have fun. **In what ways do young Texas bicyclists take advantage of the state's great outdoors?**

In this unit you will learn more about the geography, climates, landforms, and regions of Texas. You will also learn about the people and culture of Texas.

The Texas Landscape

Texas is a large state, with many different kinds of landforms and environments. The Texas landscape includes dry, rugged deserts in the west; flat, treeless plains in the north; thick, piney forests in the east; and marshes and prairies along the Gulf Coast. From the Panhandle to the Rio Grande and from West Texas to the Hill Country and Gulf of Mexico, the Texas landscape provides a rich land and home for millions of people.

Texas is very rich in natural resources, which have contributed to the state's growth and economic development. Its climates, soils, and water resources have long made Texas a leading farming and ranching state. Many different crops are grown, including citrus fruits, corn, cotton, nuts, rice, sorghum, and wheat. The main livestock include cattle, horses, sheep, goats, and pigs. With its large size and diverse landscapes, Texas is the second-leading agricultural state in the nation.

Underneath Texas lie valuable natural resources—oil and natural gas. These energy sources have shaped Texas history since 1901, when a huge oil field was discovered at Spindletop, launching the Texas Oil Boom. Since then, the Texas oil industry has grown to lead the nation.

A rich land, so rich in resources, Texas also has a rich history, which you will learn about as you explore the story of Texas. From the earliest American Indians to the Tejanos, settlers, immigrants, and cowboys who have called Texas home, the people of Texas have all shaped the Lone Star State.

Exploring Museum Resources

The Bullock Texas State History Museum has more information about Texas geography, natural environments, and resources. Visitors can identify the natural resources found throughout Texas, evaluate how water is used around the state, and investigate some of the tools used to harvest crops and produce goods. Explore some of these resources online. You can find museum resources at hmhsocialstudies.com

Map Analyze a map to learn more about the geography and landscapes of Texas. What are some of the major features and landforms found in the state?

Photograph Learn more about how Texas resources have shaped the state's history and economy.

Artifact Early Texans used surveying equipment like this Gurley transit to map the seemingly endless Texas frontier. Learn more about this artifact online.

UNIT 1

Reading Social Studies

Roots, Prefixes, and Suffixes

Focus on Reading Figuring out the meaning of words and knowing how they connect with each other to make meaning is the key to understanding what you read. Learning to recognize and understand frequently used word parts is a valuable skill that will help you in all your studies.

Understanding Word Parts Many English words are made up of several word parts: roots, prefixes, and suffixes. **Roots** are the fundamental parts of a word. For example, *-loc-* is a Latin root for "place." The English word *locate* is based on the Latin root *-loc-*. **Prefixes** are word parts that are added to the front of a word, and **suffixes** are word parts that are added to the back of a word. Both prefixes (*dis*locate) and suffixes (loc*ation*) alter the meaning of a word. The following charts list roots, prefixes, and suffixes commonly found in many English words. As you read the charts, think about other words you know that contain these parts.

Common Roots

Root	Meaning	Sample Words
-dem-	people	democracy
-geo-	earth	geology
-graph-	write, writing	photograph
-loc-	place	location
-pop-	people; nation	population

Common Prefixes

Prefix	Meaning	Sample Words
de-	away from; off; down	decode
im-	into; within	import
inter-	between; among	interpersonal
non-	not	nonsense
re-	again	return

Common Suffixes

Suffix	Meaning	Sample Words
-able	able; likely	comfortable
-al	relating to	personal
-er	one who	teacher
-ion, -tion	act or condition of	election
-ment	result; act of	enjoyment

You Try It!

The passage below is from the unit you are about to read. With a partner, take turns reading sentences out loud to each other. As your partner reads, listen to how the words and word parts in each sentence help you figure out the meaning of what is being said.

Environment and Society

One of the most important topics in geography is how people interact with the environment. Human activities can have positive effects on the environment. For example, people help restore the environment by planting trees in areas that have been deforested. However, human activities can also affect the environment negatively. Some Texans have tried to limit the harm humans do to the natural environment.

Reread the underlined words in the passage above. For each of the underlined words, do the following: First, separate any prefixes and suffixes, and then identify the root of each word. Refer to the charts to help you define the root, prefix, or suffix. Then write a definition of each word.

Reading Section Assessment

Refer to the charts and answer the questions below.

1. How many root words does the term *demography* contain? What are they? Write a definition of *demography*.
2. What's the prefix in the word *renewable*? The suffix? Write a definition of *renewable*. Based on your definition, what does *nonrenewable* mean? How do you know?
3. How many more words can you think of that use a root, prefix, or suffix from the charts on the previous page? Make a list and share it with your classmates.

Key Terms

Unit 1

Chapter 1

culture *(p. 4)*
ecosystem *(p. 7)*
migration *(p. 7)*
urbanization *(p. 7)*
relative location *(p. 9)*
absolute location *(p. 9)*
latitude *(p. 10)*
longitude *(p. 10)*
map projections *(p. 12)*
statistics *(p. 13)*

Chapter 2

plateaus *(p. 21)*
tributaries *(p. 22)*
reservoirs *(p. 23)*
aquifers *(p. 23)*
humidity *(p. 25)*
erosion *(p. 29)*
habitat *(p. 29)*
immigration *(p. 31)*
birthrate *(p. 32)*
death rate *(p. 32)*

Chapter 3

natural regions *(p. 44)*
subregions *(p. 45)*
bayous *(p. 47)*
petrochemicals *(p. 47)*
lignite *(p. 49)*
escarpments *(p. 54)*
fault *(p. 55)*
basins *(p. 57)*
tourism *(p. 58)*

Before you read, look at the pictures and illustrations in a chapter. In many cases, this will help you know what you will read about and will make understanding the content easier.

CHAPTER 1

The Geographer's Tools

Texas Essential Knowledge and Skills (TEKS) 8A, 8B, 9A, 9B, 10A, 10B, 11A, 11D, 19D, 20A, 20D, 21A, 21B, 21C, 21H, 22A, 22C, 22D

This Texas snowman was made in Dallas.

Guadalupe Peak is in West Texas.

TEXAS

Coldest Spot
The lowest recorded temperature in Texas was a chilly –23°F, occurring in 1899 at Tulia and in 1933 at Seminole.

Hottest Spot
The highest recorded temperature in Texas was a blistering 120°F, occurring in 1936 at Seymour and in 1994 at Monahans.

Longest River
The Rio Grande, which begins in Colorado and flows along the Texas-Mexico border, runs 1,896 miles.

U.S. and WORLD

Coldest Spot
Vostok, Antarctica, had a record low of –129°F in 1983.

Hottest Spot
El Azizia, Libya, had a record high of 136°F in 1922.

Longest River
The Nile River flows some 4,160 miles through northeast Africa.

If you were a geographer . . .
How would you describe Texas?

Build on What You Know

Have you heard that everything is bigger in Texas? The state is second in the nation in size—behind Alaska. This large area offers a variety of terrain and natural scenery. To understand this large state, geographers use a variety of tools, including maps and charts.

The Rio Grande winds through the Big Bend region.

Horned lizards enjoy the dry climate of West Texas.

Driest Place
Wink received just 1.76 inches of rain in 1956.

Wettest Place
In 1873 Clarksville received 109.4 inches of rain.

Highest Point
Guadalupe Peak is the highest point in the state, at 8,749 feet above sea level.

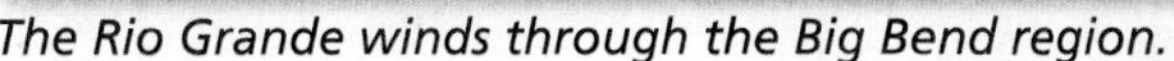

Driest Place
Arica, Chile, receives an average of just 0.03 inches of rain per year.

Wettest Place
Lloro, Colombia, receives an average of 523.6 inches of rain per year.

Highest Point
Mount Everest is the highest point in the world, at 29,035 feet above sea level.

You Be the Geographer

myNotebook

What's Your Opinion? Do you agree or disagree with the following statements? Support your point of view in your notebook.

- **Geography** Larger states have more geographic variety than smaller ones.
- **Culture** Geographers are not interested in human activity or cultures.
- **Economics** The economy of a region is directly dependent on its geography.

Section 1

The Six Essential Elements of Geography

Main Ideas

1. Geographers study physical and human systems.
2. The six essential elements of geography are a way for geographers to organize their studies.

Why It Matters Today

People have lived in Texas and influenced its environment for thousands of years. Use current events sources to find information about how people affect the Texas landscape today.

Key Terms and People

- **geography**
- **environment**
- **culture**
- **geographic information systems**
- **ecosystem**
- **migration**
- **urbanization**
- **Roy Bedichek**

TEKS: 8A, 8B, 9B, 10A, 10B, 19D, 20A, 20D, 21A, 21B, 21C, 22A

***my*Notebook**

Use the annotation tools in your eBook to take notes on the physical and human systems that geographers study.

The Geographer's World

Educator Roy Bedichek moved to a ranch near Austin in 1946. Writing to a friend, he described the natural beauty of the Hill Country. "A gentle rain started on the corrugated [grooved] iron roof a moment ago and I pulled the curtain of the southwest window to take a peep. . . . Suddenly as a flash on a motion-picture screen an *upright* rainbow in full and vivid colors appeared. . . . [I] stood there transfixed, a witness to a miracle."

The World in Spatial Terms

In order to understand the history of Texas, you must first learn about its geography. **Geography** is the study of the world, its people, and the interaction between them. Geographers study many aspects of the world, like how people adapt to their **environment**, or physical surroundings. They also study **culture**, or shared beliefs, traits, and values.

Texas is big—it covers about 267,000 square miles and has a population of more than 25 million. It is the second largest state in both size and population. Most Texans live in cities rather than in rural, or agricultural, areas. Yet Texas has close to 250,000 farms and some 130 million acres of farm and ranch land—more than any other state.

Geographers look at where things are on Earth's surface. For example, geographers studying Texas cities might find that they are typically located near sources of water, transportation centers, or other important cities. Changes in settlement patterns over time are also important.

Geographers use many tools in their studies, including maps, charts, and graphs. They also use field notes, interviews, photographs, reference books, and videos. High-tech tools such as satellites provide detailed images of Earth. Computer databases, like **geographic information systems** (GIS), store huge amounts of data, or information. Geography helps in planning for the future, including where new dams or roads should be built in Texas.

Reading Check **Finding the Main Idea** Explain the importance of geographic knowledge.

CONNECTING TO
SCIENCE AND TECHNOLOGY

GEOGRAPHIC TOOLS

Geographic information systems (GIS) are among the many tools used by geographers. Geographers also use technology such as computers, digital imagery, remote sensing, and satellites such as LANDSAT and GOES (Geostationary Operational Environment Satellite) to get satellite imagery of Earth. **How do you think these tools help students?**

★ Places and Regions

People's culture and experiences affect their ideas of places and regions. A place has physical and human characteristics that make it special. Physical characteristics include animal and plant life, sources of water, climate and weather, landforms, and soils. Landforms are the natural shapes on Earth's surface, such as mountains, hills, and valleys. Human characteristics include ethnicity, language, political and economic systems, population distribution, religion, and standards of living.

A region is an area with common characteristics that make it different from surrounding areas. People define regions to organize the world. Regions can be as large as Texas, or as small as a neighborhood. A *formal* region has one or more shared characteristics. A formal region might be based on physical features such as the plant life that grows there. Formal regions could also be cultural, economic, or political. Countries, states, and cities are examples of formal political regions.

Interpreting Visuals

Landscapes. *The Texas landscape is diverse with deserts, forests, plains, mountains, and swamps.* ***What does this image of Guadalupe Mountains National Park tell you about some of the landscape?***

A *functional* region is made up of different places that function together as a unit. A newspaper's subscription area and a metropolitan area such as Dallas–Fort Worth are examples of functional regions. A *perceptual* region is defined by people's shared attitudes, culture, and feelings about an area. Perceptual regions, such as Central Texas or the Panhandle, often have vague borders. Geographers try to learn what defines a place or region and what makes it special.

Reading Check **Categorizing** Choose a place or region and list three of its physical features and three of its human features.

★ Physical Systems and Human Systems

Geographers study the physical processes and interactions among four physical systems—Earth's atmosphere, land, water, and life. Physical processes shape and change Earth's physical features and environments. For example, Padre Island's coastline changes as tides from the Gulf of Mexico move beach sand. Climate and weather affect humans. For example, people might choose to live in an area that has a mild climate.

Texas Landforms

The Texas landscape is diverse. Traveling across the state, you could find plains, rivers, hills, deserts, and even mountains. Each of the landforms and waterways in this diagram can be found in Texas.

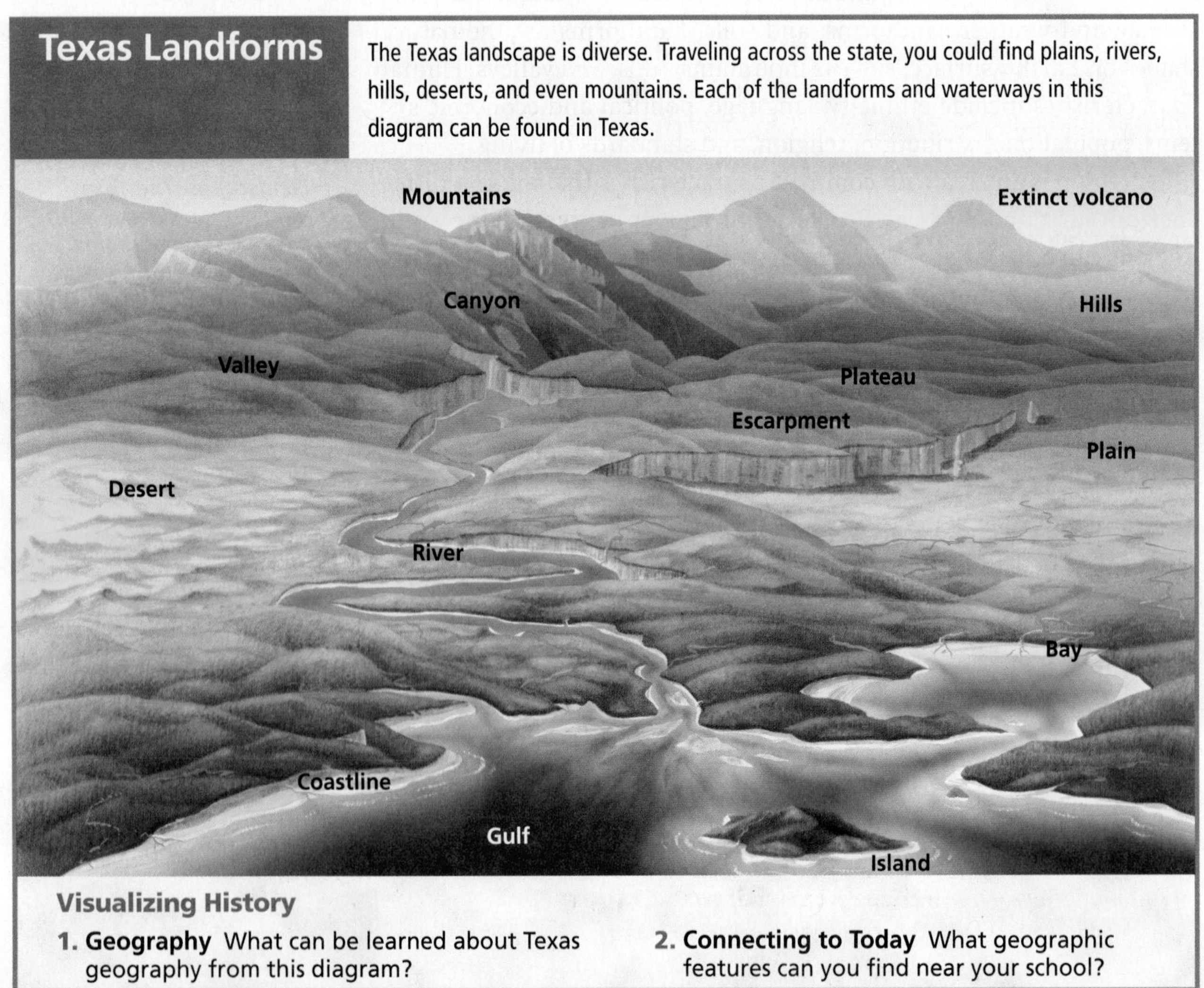

Visualizing History

1. **Geography** What can be learned about Texas geography from this diagram?
2. **Connecting to Today** What geographic features can you find near your school?

In some Central and North Texas areas the clay soil shrinks or swells depending on the weather. This affects how people build houses.

An **ecosystem** is all of an area's plants and animals together with the nonliving parts of their environment. A beach, an island, and a pond are ecosystems. Earth is the largest ecosystem. Natural events and human activity can change ecosystems. For example, in the 1930s drought and overgrazing led to the loss of topsoil and plant life in parts of North and West Texas. This hurt farming and ranching in the area. Studying physical processes and ecosystems is important because the environment is the setting for all life on Earth.

Studying human systems such as population distribution, growth, and movement helps in understanding human events and geography. Population growth is affected by a population's age, birthrate, death rate, and life expectancy. Changes in human activity such as advances in medical care and food production have led to population growth. Geographers also look at where people live and how crowded a region or place is when they study population density. They also study **migration**, or the movement of people. One specific type of migration is known as **urbanization**, which is an increase in people living or working in cities. Texas, like many places, is part of this trend.

Many geographers study the features of cultural groups. People often create groups that separate, organize, or unify areas. Geographers also consider human systems of communication, trade, and transportation in the global economy. Such human activities help explain how humans interact with one another and with the environment.

Reading Check **Identifying Cause and Effect** How did the weather change in the 1930s? How did this change affect the Texas economy?

BIOGRAPHY

Roy Bedichek (1878–1959) Roy Bedichek was an educator, folklorist, and journalist who moved to Texas from Illinois when he was about six years old. He attended the University of Texas, earning a bachelor of science and a master of arts. After college, he taught high school. Bedichek was a strong promoter of higher education. For many years he served as director of the University Interscholastic League (UIL). Bedichek was a gifted storyteller and wrote several books, including *Adventures with a Texas Naturalist*, *Karánkaway Country*, and a history of the UIL. **In what ways was Bedichek a leader in natural sciences and education?**

Environment and Society

One of the most important topics in geography is how people interact with the environment. Human activities can have positive effects on the environment. For example, people help restore the environment by planting trees in areas that have been deforested. However, human activities can also affect the environment negatively. As Houston's industry and population have grown, air pollution there has greatly increased. Some Texans have tried to limit the harm humans do to the environment. More than 60 years ago, Texas naturalist **Roy Bedichek** warned of the dangers of changing the environment.

TEXAS VOICES

"The gentle gardener poisons his soil to kill pillbugs and in so doing annihilates [wipes out] great numbers of beneficial creatures, including the lowly and lovely earthworm."

—Roy Bedichek, quoted in *Three Men in Texas*, by Ronnie Dugger.

Analyzing Primary Sources
Identifying Cause and Effect
According to Bedichek, why do some gardeners change the environment? to what effect?

That's Interesting!

Miles and Miles of Texas

Getting around Texas can take a while. Distances within the state are huge. Texas spans more than 800 miles from its northwest corner to its southern tip. El Paso, in far West Texas, is closer to Los Angeles, California, than to Orange in East Texas.

The environment affects humans as well. Physical features such as landforms and rivers can influence where people live, and people depend on the environment for survival. Human life requires three basic resources—air, water, and land. Other natural materials, such as wood and coal, are also important resources. As the world population grows, demands on resources increase. Geographers study the location, quality, and quantity of Earth's resources and the effect of human activity on these resources. Historians use geography to understand history. They look not only at when things happened but also at where and why they happened. For example, suppose you need to know when, where, and why the first settlement in San Antonio was built. You would need to know that water sources such as the San Antonio River influenced the settlement's location.

Geography helps people understand the present as well as the past. For example, the growing population of Texas has placed greater demands on the environment. In response, many communities in Texas have created water-conservation programs to help preserve this important natural resource. These programs are one way that Texans are using their knowledge of geography to plan for the future. Many geographers use the six essential elements to organize their studies and to help them understand the geography of Texas.

1. The World in Spatial Terms
2. Places and Regions
3. Physical Systems
4. Human Systems
5. Environment and Society
6. The Uses of Geography

Reading Check **Analyzing Information** Explain how human actions could cause water pollution. What are the possible results for the natural resources of Texas?

Section 1 Review

hmhsocialstudies.com
ONLINE QUIZ

1. Define and explain:
- geography
- environment
- culture
- geographic information systems
- ecosystem
- migration
- urbanization

2. Identify and explain the significance of:
- Roy Bedichek

3. Categorizing
Copy the table below. List the six essential elements of geography. Then describe each element.

Essential Element	Purpose

4. Finding the Main Idea

a. Describe the types of information geographers study.

b. How do humans adapt to and modify the physical environment?

5. Writing and Critical Thinking myWriteSmart

Analyzing Information Imagine that you are a geographer scheduled to speak to a classroom. Write a speech describing geography and what you do. Consider the following:
- the definition of geography
- the importance of geography

Section 2

Using Maps

Main Ideas

1. Maps are useful tools for finding the locations of places.
2. The main parts of a map include a title, scale, legend, and compass rose.
3. Geographers create maps for many different purposes.

Why It Matters Today

Maps are essential tools for geographers and many other professionals, but they can also be useful in your daily life. Use current events sources to find a recent news article that uses a map to explain a subject.

Key Terms

- **relative location**
- **absolute location**
- **latitude**
- **longitude**
- **equator**
- **prime meridian**
- **compass rose**
- **scale**
- **legend**
- **reference maps**
- **thematic maps**
- **map projections**

TEKS: 8A, 9A, 9B, 21B, 21C, 22A

myNotebook

Use the annotation tools in your eBook to take notes on how to use maps to learn about the characteristics of places and regions.

The Geographer's World

In 1724, engineer and mapmaker Francisco Álvarez Barreiro set off on a journey through Spanish lands in North America. In about four years, he traveled nearly 7,000 miles. As he traveled, he took careful notes and made sketches. From these, Barreiro created six maps, including one of Texas. He was the first professional mapmaker ever to see Texas for himself, and his map was prized for its accuracy.

Maps and Models

Have you ever used a map to find your way to a location or through a park? If so, you understand how useful maps can be. Maps are important tools for geographers and historians. By representing a place in graphic form, maps can show information about its physical and human features. With maps, many types of information can be organized visually.

Maps can also be used to locate places. Geographers describe location in two ways. **Relative location** describes where a place is in relation to other places. The relative location of a place is noted by its distance and direction from another place. For example, Dallas is 225 miles northwest of Houston or 33 miles east of Fort Worth. **Absolute location** is the exact position of a place on Earth. The absolute location of the Texas Governor's Mansion can be expressed as 1010 Colorado Street in Austin or as 36°16′N latitude and 97°44′W longitude.

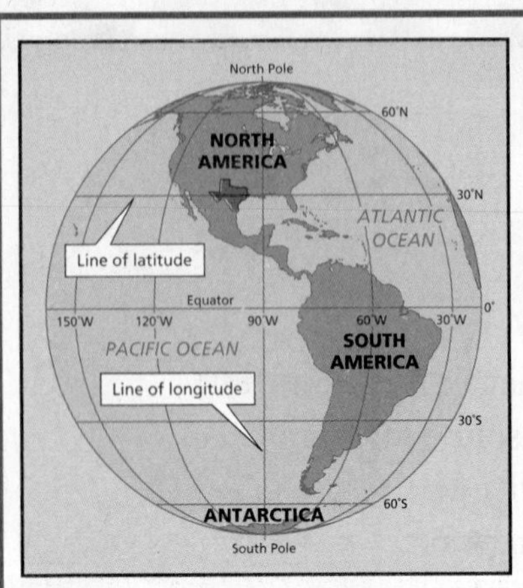

Latitude and Longitude

Interpreting Maps Lines of latitude run east and west, while lines of longitude run north and south. *Locate* What major line of latitude runs through Texas?

A model is similar to a map in that it shows the physical and human characteristics of a place. But where maps are flat and show locations in two dimensions, models show them in three dimensions. For example, look at the model of a Spanish mission on page 113 of this book. On a map the mission's walls would appear only as lines. Using the model, you can get a better sense of what the mission actually looked like.

Reading Check **Finding the Main Idea** Why do people use maps?

★ Latitude and Longitude

To locate an exact spot on Earth, people use a more complex grid system. This system uses **latitude** and **longitude**, which are imaginary lines circling the globe. While latitude lines run east-west, longitude lines run north-south.

Lines of latitude and longitude measure distance in degrees—360 of which circle Earth. Each degree is divided into 60 minutes, and each minute is divided into 60 seconds. The symbol for degree is °. Minutes are marked ′ and seconds, ″. Latitude lines measure distance north and south of the **equator**. The equator is an imaginary line circling the globe exactly halfway between the North and South Poles. Latitudes north of the equator are labeled *N* on maps. Those south of the equator are labeled *S*. Lines of latitude range from 0° at the equator to 90°N at the North Pole and 90°S at the South Pole.

Longitude lines measure distance east and west of the **prime meridian**. The prime meridian is an imaginary line that runs around the globe from the North Pole, through Greenwich, England, to the South Pole. Longitude lines range from 0° at the prime meridian to 180° at a line exactly halfway around the globe from the prime meridian. On maps, lines of longitude west of the prime meridian to 180° are labeled *W*. Those east of the prime meridian to 180° are labeled *E*.

The absolute location of any place on Earth can be given as a combination of latitude and longitude. For example, the latitude of San Antonio, Texas, is 29°25′N. The city's longitude is 98°30′W. Because Texas is a large state, it covers several degrees of latitude and longitude. North to south, Texas stretches from latitude 36°30′N to 25°50′N. East to west, the state extends from longitude 93°31′W to 106°36′W.

Reading Check **Comparing and Contrasting** Identify how latitude and longitude are different and the same.

★ The Parts of a Map

In some ways, maps are like coded messages. Mapmakers provide elements that make maps easier to read, such as a map's title. The title for the map on the next page tells you that the map shows the state's environmental regions. A map's directional indicator shows which directions are north, south, east, and west. North is usually at the top of a map. To show direction, some maps have a **compass rose** that points to all four cardinal points—north, south, east, and west.

A map's **scale** is the relationship between a measurement on the map and the actual distance on Earth's surface. Perhaps the most useful part of a map is the **legend**, or key. The legend explains the meaning of all the symbols on a map. This information typically appears in a box near the edge of the map. Map symbols may include colors, numbers, patterns, or small drawings.

Some maps include additional inset maps or locator maps, which are smaller maps set inside or next to the main map. Inset maps show more detail than the main map. For example, a map of Houston might have an inset map showing downtown Houston. Locator maps place the area in a map in its larger geographic surroundings.

Reading Check **Summarizing** List the parts of a map and what they do.

★ Types of Maps

Mapmakers have developed many types of maps, including **reference maps** and **thematic maps**. Reference maps are used to find locations. Two common types of reference maps are political and physical. Political maps show information such as boundaries, capitals, and cities. Physical maps show natural features such as landforms, rivers, and other bodies of water. Some maps include both political and physical information.

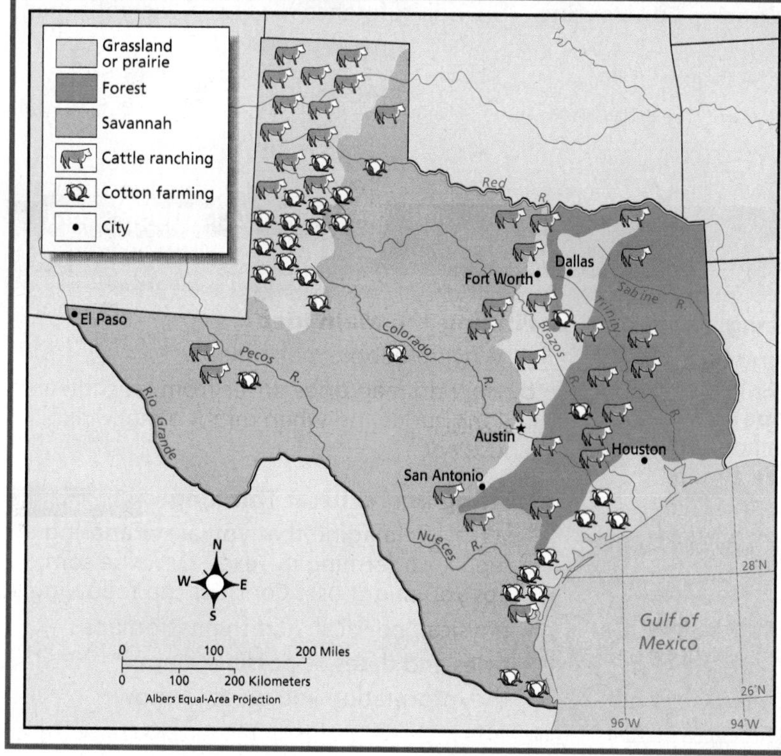

The Environment of Texas

Interpreting Maps Texas has a variety of vegetation, and Texas farmers have been able to use the land in many different ways.

1. Locate Where is cotton grown?

2. Comparing and Contrasting How is plant life in East Texas similar to and different from plant life in West Texas?

Interpreting Visuals

Cartography. *Imagine you were peeling Earth like an orange. If you were to flatten Earth on a table, it would split and create gaps.* ***How does the shape of Earth affect mapmaking?***

Thematic maps show a specific topic, theme, or spatial distribution of an activity. Subjects might include cattle ranching, climates, population density, rainfall, soil types, or world religions.

With the exception of globes, maps are usually flat, but Earth is round. This difference makes it difficult to create accurate maps. To address this problem, mapmakers have developed **map projections**. Mapmakers use map projections to create a flat representation of Earth's surface. To create a Mercator projection, mapmakers first transfer an image of Earth's features onto a cylinder-shaped surface. This map projection is useful because it shows true direction and shape. However, landmasses near the North and South Poles appear larger than they really are. For example, the sizes of northern areas like Greenland, Canada, and Europe are enlarged while the sizes of tropical areas are diminished. Other types of projections show the sizes of landmasses more accurately but distort their shapes. The many types of map projections each have specific advantages and disadvantages.

Reading Check **Contrasting** How do reference maps and thematic maps differ?

Section 2 Review

hmhsocialstudies.com
ONLINE QUIZ

1. Define and explain:
- relative location
- absolute location
- latitude
- longitude
- equator
- prime meridian
- compass rose
- scale
- legend
- reference maps
- thematic maps
- map projections

2. Summarizing Copy the graphic organizer below. Use it to describe how different map parts help decode a map.

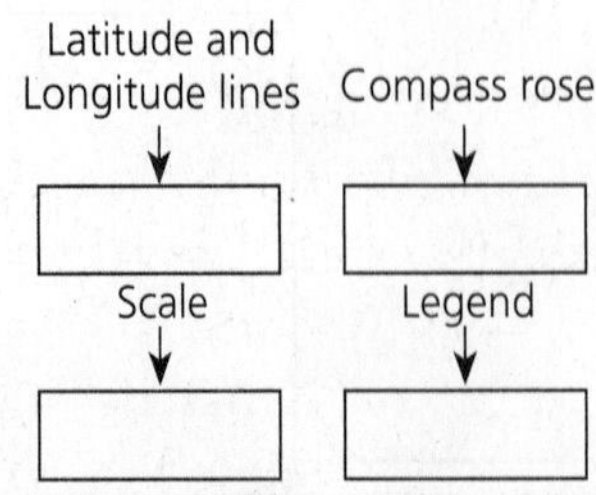

3. Finding the Main Idea

a. Why do people make maps?

b. How do map grids differ from latitude and longitude, and when might a mapmaker use each?

4. Writing and Critical Thinking myWriteSmart

Evaluating Imagine that you are preparing a report on farming in Texas. Describe some maps you might use. Consider the following:
- physical, political, and thematic maps
- titles and dates of possible maps
- the information you want to show

Section 3

Using Graphs, Charts, and Tables

Main Ideas

1. Bar graphs, line graphs, pie charts, and tables are useful for making comparisons and showing relationships.
2. Time lines, flowcharts, and causation charts are often used by geographers and historians.

Key Terms

- **statistics**
- **bar graph**
- **line graph**
- **pie chart**
- **time line**
- **flowchart**
- **causation chart**

Why It Matters Today

Lists of names, facts, statistics, and similar types of information are often clearest when presented visually. Use current events sources to find a news article that includes a chart or graph to present information. What is the visual's purpose?

TEKS: 8A, 10B, 11D, 21B, 21C, 21H, 22A

myNotebook

Use the annotation tools in your eBook to take notes on the different ways you can visually present statistical information.

The Geographer's World

In the spring of 2010, the U.S. government began taking a census, or count, of the population. To ensure that everyone was counted, the government hired census takers, like Texan Patrick Huck. In their work, Huck and other census takers collected a huge amount of data. The government then organized all this information for research and public use.

★ Using Graphs

Sometimes the best way to convey an idea or information is graphically, or with pictures. Geographers and historians have many tools, such as graphs, for presenting information visually. Graphs make it easier to compare facts and see the relationships between them. They are also useful for showing **statistics**—information in the form of numbers.

A **bar graph** is useful in comparing information about different places or time periods. Bar graphs use bars of different lengths to represent numbers and percentages. The bars may extend sideways or stand on end. Each graph has a horizontal axis and a vertical axis. The horizontal axis is the line across the bottom of the graph. The vertical axis is the line along the side. One axis has a number scale giving the value shown by the bars. The other axis may represent another variable, such as a time period. Colors sometimes define the bars instead of labels. A legend explains what each color means. The bar graph in the chapter review makes it easy to see which Texas city has the largest population.

Texas Population Growth, 2000–2010

Texas Counties	Population Growth
Harris	20.3%
Bexar	23.1%
Tarrant	25.1%
Travis	26.1%
Collin	59.1%

Interpreting Tables During the 2000s, many Texas counties experienced large population growth. What was the difference in population growth between Collin and Harris Counties?

A **line graph** indicates a trend, or pattern. It may show if something is increasing, decreasing, or staying about the same over time. Like bar graphs, line graphs have a horizontal and a vertical axis. The line graph below provides a simple visual record of population changes in Texas.

Reading Check **Finding the Main Idea** How are graphs useful to geographers and historians?

★ Using Charts, Tables, and Databases

A **pie chart**—or circle graph—shows how the parts of a whole are divided. The pie—or circle—represents the whole item or total amount. The pie pieces—or segments of the pie—represent a percentage of the whole. To make pie charts easier to read, segments are often colored. A legend may be used to define each color. The pie chart on the next page shows the origins of immigrants to Texas in 2011. The circle represents the total number of immigrants. Each segment represents the percentage of immigrants from one part of the world. A pie chart clearly summarizes a large amount of information.

Tables and databases help organize and categorize information. They are particularly useful when information is both descriptive and statistical. The table on this page lists names and statistical information. The database of Texas counties in the back of this book lists data about all of the counties in Texas. Both tables and databases use grids with columns and rows of boxes. Each box is called a cell. Labels often appear at the top of each column and at the left of each row.

Texas Population, 1900–2010

Interpreting Graphs The population of Texas has grown every 10 years since 1900. How have Texas population patterns changed since 1960?

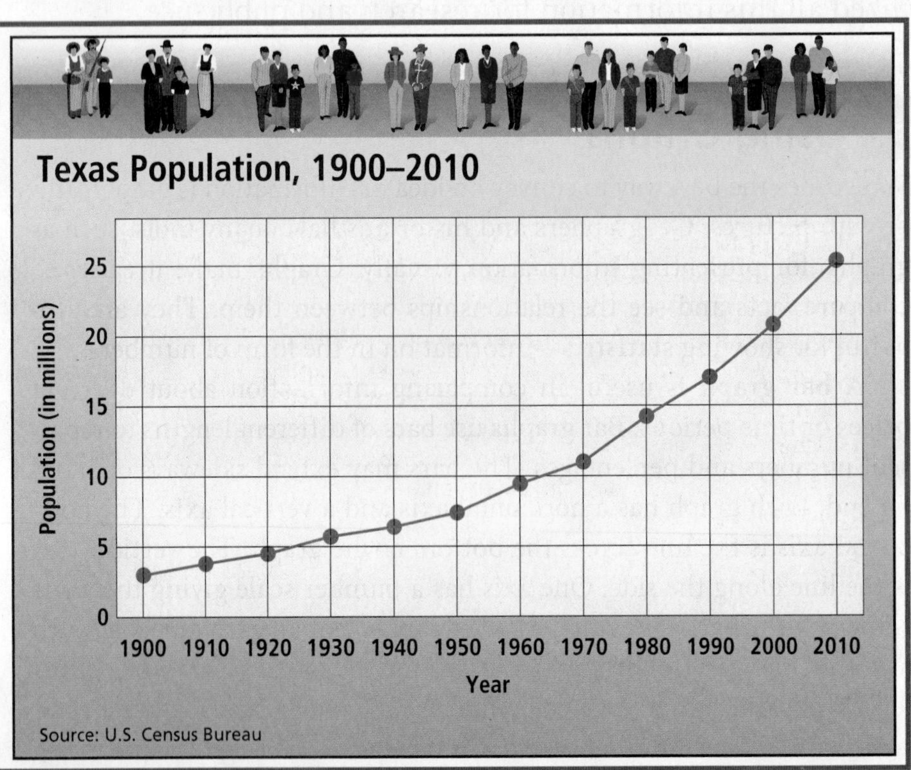

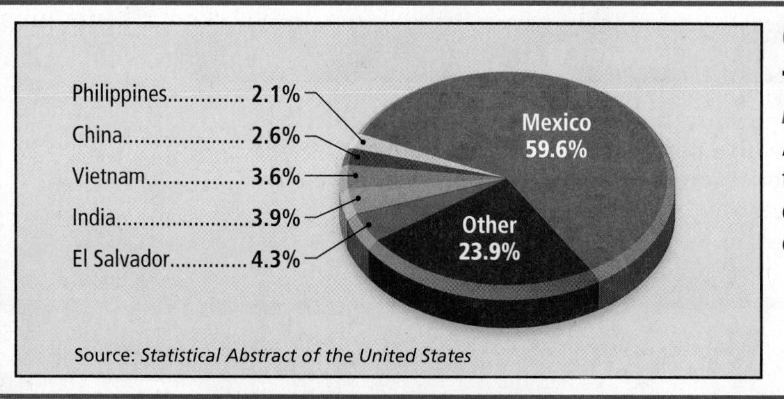

Origin of Immigrants to Texas, 2011

Interpreting Charts New immigrants from Asian and Latin American countries have added to the diversity of Texas. What percentage of immigrants to Texas came from Asian countries?

Charts show the relationship between different subjects. A **time line** shows the sequence of events. Time lines are useful for studying how one event may have led to or caused later events. A **flowchart** uses boxes, arrows, and sometimes images to show a series of activities or steps. For example, a flowchart could describe the steps it takes to turn trees into paper. Although it is similar to a flowchart, a **causation chart** focuses on cause and effect. These charts can take several forms. They may use pictures or diagrams to show the causes and effects of events. Some causation charts have boxes and arrows pointing out the effects of an event or idea. Others show events as steps or as a ladder. When an event has many causes or effects, a web diagram is useful. In a web, an event appears in the center. Its causes or effects surround it. In general, most charts contain information that is difficult to show in graphs or tables or to describe in text.

Reading Check **Analyzing Information** When might a geographer or historian choose to use a pie chart or a table instead of a line or bar graph?

Section 3 Review

hmhsocialstudies.com
ONLINE QUIZ

1. Define and explain:
- statistics
- bar graph
- line graph
- pie chart
- time line
- flowchart
- causation chart

2. Categorizing
Copy the web diagram below. Use it to explain how different charts, graphs, and tables help geographers and historians.

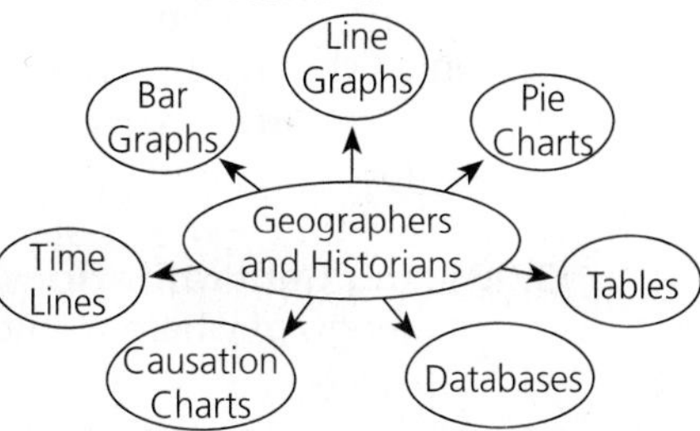

3. Finding the Main Idea
a. Why do people use graphs?
b. Describe three types of charts and explain their primary uses.

4. Writing and Critical Thinking myWriteSmart
Drawing Inferences and Conclusions Imagine that you are writing a newspaper article about a drought. Create a thematic chart, table, or database for your article. Consider the following:
- the causes, events, and results
- the farmers, crops, and geography

CHAPTER 1 REVIEW

The Chapter at a Glance

Examine the following visual summary of the chapter. Discuss the visual summary with a partner to be sure you both understand the material you read in this chapter. If you have any questions, ask your teacher or classmates for assistance.

Students of Texas history often use maps, charts, and other geographic tools to learn more about the state.

Identifying People and Ideas

Review the meanings of the following terms.

1. geography
2. Roy Bedichek
3. longitude
4. equator
5. compass rose
6. legend
7. thematic maps
8. time line
9. pie chart
10. causation chart

Understanding Main Ideas

Section 1

1. What are the six essential elements of geography?
2. In what ways do humans modify the environment, and what are some results of those modifications?

Section 2

3. What kinds of information can geographers organize and interpret from maps and models?
4. What are the parts of a map?

Section 3

5. Why are databases useful?
6. Why might a geographer choose to use a chart rather than a graph?

You Be the Geographer

Reviewing Themes

1. **Geography** How is the size of Texas related to its geographic diversity?
2. **Culture** How do geographers learn about human activities and cultures?
3. **Economics** How might geography affect the types of businesses and industries that develop in an area?

Thinking Critically

1. **Summarizing** Describe an idea for a Texas map showing regions based on one physical and one human characteristic.
2. **Drawing Inferences and Conclusions** Why are flowcharts and time lines often used by historians?
3. **Making Generalizations and Predictions** How will geography help in understanding Texas history?

Texas Test Practice

Interpreting Graphs

Study the graph below. Then use the information in the graph to help you answer the questions that follow.

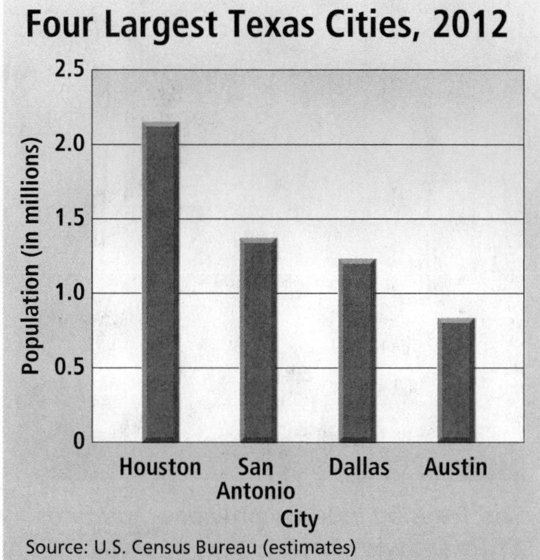

1. Approximately how much larger is Houston's population than that of the next largest city?
   - **A** 1,500,000 people
   - **B** 1,000,000 people
   - **C** 100,000 people
   - **D** 50,000 people

2. What advantages does a bar graph have in presenting the information on population distribution?

Analyzing Primary Sources

Read the following quote from early Texas settler Noah Smithwick. Then answer the questions.

"[Growing corn] was no very difficult matter near the coast, where there were vast canebrakes [thickets] all along the rivers. The soil was rich and loose from the . . . crops of [wild] cane that had decayed on it. In the fall, when the cane died down, it was burned off clean. The ground was then ready for planting, which was done in a very primitive manner, a sharpened stick being all the implement [tool] necessary. With this they made holes in the moist loam [soil] and dropped in grains of corn. . . . The only water obtainable was that of the sluggish river, which crept along between low banks thickly set with tall trees, from branches of which . . . [hung] long streamers of Spanish moss swarming with mosquitoes and malaria."

3. Which of the following statements would be least important to a geographer?
   - **F** The quote describes the arrangement of things in the landscape of an area.
   - **G** The quote describes a relationship between environment and society.
   - **H** The quote offers clues to the physical and human systems operating in Texas.
   - **J** The quote is of historical value.

4. Based on this quote, what conclusions could be drawn about where pioneers settled and why?

Linking to Community

Think about some of the physical and human characteristics that help define an area in your community. Physical characteristics might include the plant life, landforms, or climate of your community. The human characteristics might include the types of industry, location of roads, or location of people's homes. Create a map of the area and label some of the characteristics you have included.

Internet Activity 

Use the Internet to research how maps and models are made, what they can illustrate, and how they are formatted. Then apply what you have learned by creating a map or model that illustrates the relative and absolute location of your school. Make sure you include a directional indicator, a legend, and a scale.

CHAPTER 2

A Land Called Texas

Texas Essential Knowledge and Skills (TEKS) 8A, 8B, 9A, 9B, 9C, 10A, 10B, 11A, 11B, 11C, 11D, 16B, 18B, 19A, 19B, 19C, 19D, 20D, 21A, 21B, 21C, 21H, 22A, 22D

The Texas oil industry provides thousands of Texans with jobs.

TEXAS	In 2012 Texas produced about 730 million barrels of crude oil worth some $55 billion.	Texas has an estimated 23 billion tons of lignite, a type of coal.	More than 6 million acres of Texas land are irrigated.	The Ogallala Aquifer is the largest underground water source in Texas.
U.S. and WORLD	In 2012 the United States produced more than 2.3 billion barrels of oil.	The United States produced more than 80.9 million tons of lignite in 2012.	The United States used about 46 trillion gallons of water for irrigation in 2005.	The Ogallala Aquifer is also the largest aquifer in North America.

If you were a geographer . . .

What would you find most interesting about Texas geography?

Build on What You Know

Texas is a large and diverse state. The tools of geography will help you learn about the climate, landforms, people, and resources of Texas. The state's diverse population and wide variety of physical features help make Texas unique.

Image Credit: ©Jaochainoi/Shutterstock

Caddo Lake is a popular recreation area in East Texas.

Texas parks and natural areas provide a winter home for the endangered whooping crane.

Texas	World/U.S.
In 2012 there were more than 244,700 farms in Texas.	In 2012 there were 2.2 million farms in the United States.
Agriculture added some $36 billion to the Texas economy in 2012.	Agriculture added more than $297 billion to the U.S. economy in 2012.
Toledo Bend Reservoir on the Sabine River holds more than 5.5 billion cubic meters of water.	The largest reservoir in the world is Lake Kariba in Zambia-Zimbabwe.
Caddo Lake is the largest natural lake in Texas, covering more than 39 square miles (half of which are in Louisiana).	The largest natural lake in the world is the Caspian Sea, which covers more than 143,000 square miles.

You Be the Geographer myNotebook

What's Your Opinion? Do you **agree** or **disagree** with the following statements? Support your point of view in your notebook.

- **Geography** A region's physical features, such as land and water, are always modified by humans.
- **Culture** Immigrants moving into an area add to its cultural traditions.
- **Economics** A region's resources always influence its economy.

Section 1

The Physical Landscape of Texas

Main Ideas

1. Hills, mountains, plains, and plateaus are some of the landforms found in Texas.
2. Texas water resources include rivers, lakes, and aquifers.

Why It Matters Today

Texans have long relied upon the state's sources of water. Texas has many different water resources, including aquifers and reservoirs. However, increased usage has led to water shortages. Use current events sources to learn about water resources.

Key Terms

- **plains**
- **plateaus**
- **ranges**
- **tributaries**
- **reservoirs**
- **irrigation**
- **aquifers**
- **Ogallala Aquifer**
- **Edwards Aquifer**

TEKS: 8A, 8B, 9A, 9B, 10A, 10B, 21A, 21B, 21C, 22A, 22D

myNotebook

Use the annotation tools in your eBook to take notes on the landforms and water features in Texas.

The Geographer's World

In the summer of 1956, Jack Burch and James Papadakis discovered a small opening in a West Texas limestone cliff. They decided to squeeze through the 18-inch hole. Once inside, the two adventurers found a large cave with beautiful rare stalactites—rock formations that hang like icicles. The men had discovered one of the hidden natural treasures of Texas. The cavern was opened for public tours four years later. The Caverns of Sonora are among the most beautiful caves in the world.

★ Landforms of Texas

The Caverns of Sonora are just one of many natural treasures in Texas. To locate Texas on a globe, find the Northern Hemisphere. This northern half of the planet lies between the North Pole and the equator. Texas is also in the Western Hemisphere—the half of the planet west of the prime meridian. Located in the southern half of the North American continent, Texas borders a large body of water called the Gulf of Mexico. The state is located in the central and southern region of the United States. Texas is just north of Mexico, west of Louisiana, south of Oklahoma, and east of New Mexico. Arkansas borders the northeastern corner of Texas.

The varied landscape of Texas includes canyons, islands, valleys, and even extinct volcanoes. The four major landforms in Texas are hills, mountains, plains, and plateaus. **Plains** are areas of flat or gently rolling land without a sharp rise or fall in elevation. **Plateaus** are areas of flat elevated land that drop sharply on one or more sides.

Plains cover much of the Gulf Coast, the Panhandle, North Texas, South Texas, and West Texas. These flatlands help to define the Texas landscape. One visitor noted that the Gulf Coast plains were "so perfectly flat that the eye embraced an extent [distance] of many miles." Many of the Texas plains are interrupted by hills. The easternmost part of Texas is covered by forests. To the west lie gently rolling prairies, or treeless grasslands. Central Texas has rugged hills, including those in the Hill Country. West of the Hill Country lies the Edwards Plateau, which rises in elevation from east to west.

West of the plateau, the landscape becomes rocky. Several **ranges**, or groups of mountains, rise west of the Pecos River. The state's highest point, Guadalupe Peak, is in the Guadalupe Mountains. Although West Texas has some mountains, most of the state is covered by plains.

Reading Check **Summarizing** How does the Texas landscape and elevation change from east to west?

The Texas River System

Texas has several water features, including lakes, rivers, and streams. The largest body of water is the Gulf of Mexico, which is an important resource for Texas. It provides a source for fishing and shrimping. More important, the Gulf of Mexico serves as a major route for international trade. Because of its location on the Gulf, Texas is one of the country's leaders in shipping goods to other countries.

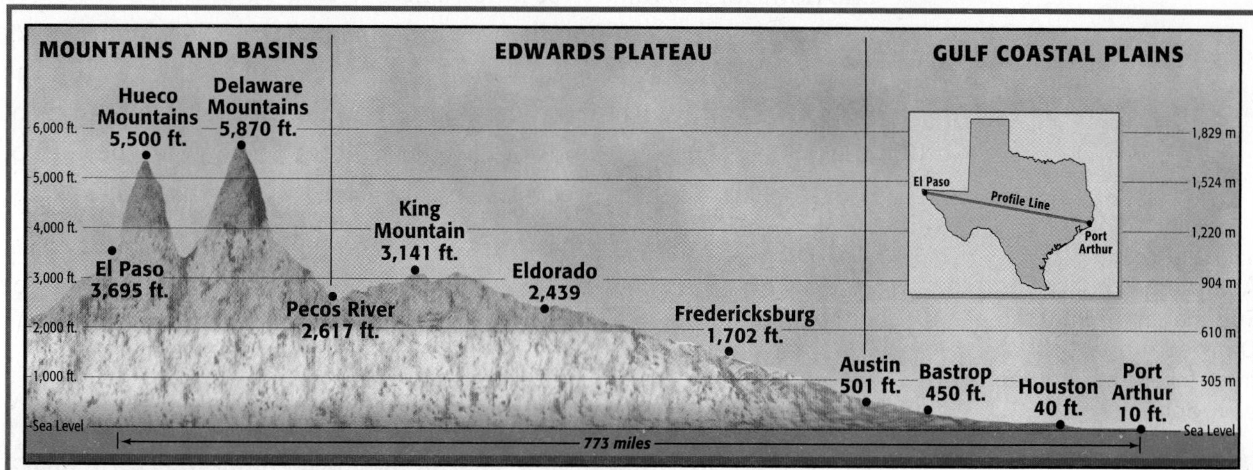

Interpreting Charts Moving from east to west, the elevation of Texas rises and the landscape becomes more rugged. How much higher are the Delaware Mountains than Port Arthur?

Interpreting Visuals

The majority of Texas rivers run through the central and eastern part of the state. ***How does the availability of water affect plant life?***

Texas has more than a dozen major rivers and some 11,000 streams. The Texas river system can be divided into several groups. A number of rivers and smaller streams in the northern part of the state flow into the Mississippi River. These include the Red River and Canadian River. A second group of rivers begins in Texas and neighboring states. These rivers flow parallel with one another directly into the Gulf of Mexico. They include the Brazos, Colorado, Neches, Nueces, Sabine, and Trinity. The third group consists of the Rio Grande and its **tributaries**. A tributary is any smaller stream or river that flows into a larger stream or river. The Pecos River is an important tributary to the Rio Grande.

Every one of these Texas rivers has its own special character. The Rio Grande is by far the longest. It begins as a snow-fed mountain stream in Colorado. From there, it flows 1,896 miles through New Mexico down desert canyons and coastal lowlands to the Gulf of Mexico. For 1,254 miles the Rio Grande forms the international boundary between the United States and Mexico.

The Comal—one of the shortest rivers in Texas—rises from a spring and flows for less than three miles. The Colorado River travels some 600 miles across Texas. Along the way it drains nearly 40,000 square miles of Texas landscape. It is the largest river contained entirely within the state. The Trinity River travels some 550 miles through the prairies of North Texas and the woods of East Texas. It then flows into the Gulf of Mexico. Park designer Frederick Law Olmsted traveled through Texas in the 1850s and commented on the river.

Analyzing Primary Sources
Summarizing What did Olmsted suggest about how Texans modify the environment?

TEXAS VOICES

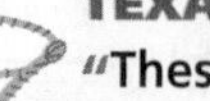

"These bottom lands bordering the Trinity [River] are among the richest of Texas. . . . High up, in the region of the Forks of the Trinity [River], are lands equally suitable to cotton, wheat, and corn."

—Frederick Law Olmsted, *Journey through Texas*

Reading Check **Contrasting** How do Texas rivers differ from each other?

★ Texas Lakes and Aquifers

Texas has few natural lakes. Caddo Lake, in Northeast Texas, is the largest. However, the state has hundreds of lakes built by people. Texans built dams along rivers to help control floods and to produce electricity.

Many dams also create **reservoirs**. These artificial lakes store water that is often used as drinking water for towns and cities. Reservoirs also serve as places for recreation. Some reservoirs are important sources for **irrigation**, or watering of crops.

Water is also found in the state's **aquifers**. Aquifers are formations of natural gravel, rock, and sand that trap and hold rainwater underground. Refilling, or recharging, them with water is typically a slow process.

In Texas several major aquifers provide water for farms, homes, and industry. The **Ogallala Aquifer** is the largest underground water source in the state. It is also the largest in North America, stretching below portions of eight states and covering about 174,000 square miles. Almost 96 percent of the water pumped out of the Ogallala Aquifer is used for irrigation.

Just to the south, the **Edwards Aquifer** provides water for San Antonio, Austin, and the rest of Central Texas. The largest springs in Texas come from the Edwards Aquifer. A spring is a natural outpouring of water from underground. These springs provide a place of recreation as well as a source of water.

Reading Check **Analyzing Information** How have Texans used the state's natural water resources?

CONNECTING TO Literature

Goodbye to a River
John Graves

John Graves grew up near Fort Worth and visited the Brazos River as a child. As an adult, Graves traveled by boat down the Brazos. The following excerpt is from an account of his journey, published in 1961.

For scores of years no [population] boom has brought people to its banks; booms elsewhere have sucked them thence. Old respect for the river's occasional violence makes farmers and ranchers build on high ground away from the stream itself, which runs primitive and neglected. When you paddle and pole along it, the things you see are much the same things the Comanches and the Kiowas used to see, riding lean ponies down it a hundred years ago to raid the new settlements in its valley. **According to Graves, why do farmers and ranchers build on high ground away from the river?**

★ Section 1 Review

hmhsocialstudies.com ONLINE QUIZ

1. Define and explain:
- plains
- plateaus
- ranges
- tributaries
- reservoirs
- irrigation
- aquifers

2. Identify and explain the significance of:
- Ogallala Aquifer
- Edwards Aquifer

3. Evaluating
Copy the graphic organizer below. Use it to explain how each feature of Texas geography affects life in the state.

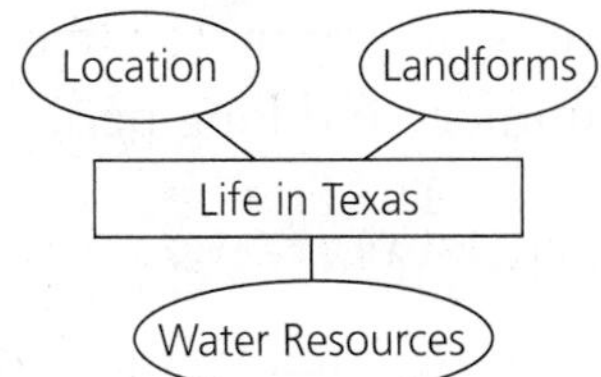

4. Finding the Main Idea
a. Describe the location of Texas.
b. What landforms and water resources exist in Texas?

5. Writing and Critical Thinking myWriteSmart
Drawing Inferences and Conclusions Write an interview with a geographer about the different geographical features of Texas. Be sure to include questions and potential answers.
Consider the following:
- landforms and water resources
- how Texans use these resources

Section 2 The Texas Climate

Main Ideas

1. The climate and weather of Texas affects life in the state, as well as its economy.
2. Texas plants and animals are affected by the state's changing landscape and climate.

Key Terms and People

- **humidity**
- **drought**
- **Lady Bird Johnson**
- **erosion**
- **habitat**
- **extinct**

Why It Matters Today

Texas experiences many types of severe weather. Use current events sources to learn about recent occurrences of severe weather.

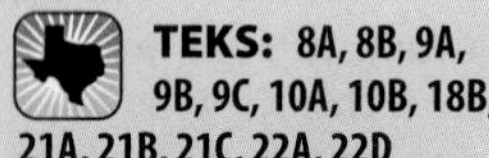
TEKS: 8A, 8B, 9A, 9B, 9C, 10A, 10B, 18B, 21A, 21B, 21C, 22A, 22D

myNotebook

Use the annotation tools in your eBook to take notes on how weather and climate affects life in Texas.

The Geographer's World

In 1947, residents of Lipscomb County heard a loud, train-like noise. One resident stepped out of his front door and saw an approaching tornado. The tornado picked the man up hundreds of feet into the air. Another person went to the door after the man disappeared and was also swept up. After a few scary moments, both men were set down uninjured. However, nothing was left of the house but the foundation and a couch. Sitting on the couch was the first man's family, who were all unhurt—but understandably frightened.

★ Weather and Climate

What is the weather like where you live? It it hot all summer? Does it rain often? Are you likely to see snow in the winter? All of these factors—temperature, rain, snow—are part of your area's climate. Climate is an area's pattern of weather over a long period of time. Although Texas weather can change quickly and dramatically, its climate is more stable.

The state's climate, particularly its temperature, is affected by its location. Texas is much closer to the equator than to the North Pole. The equator receives sunlight most directly. As a result, most of Texas experiences hot summers and long periods of sunshine. On some days temperatures rise above 110°F.

Wind patterns also affect the climate of Texas regions. The highest temperatures occur most often in the Rio Grande Valley and areas of north-central Texas. These areas are hotter because of winds that blow in from the west. These western winds cross deserts and carry warmer, drier air into the state.

The temperature of water rises and falls more slowly than that of land. Thus, the Gulf of Mexico acts as an air conditioner for the Texas coast. In the summer, sea breezes keep nearby land areas cooler than areas farther inland. In the winter, the Gulf keeps coastal lands warmer. However, Texans who live along the Gulf Coast experience higher **humidity**—the amount of moisture in the air. The high humidity often makes the warm temperatures along the Gulf Coast feel even hotter.

The Panhandle is also affected by winds. Winds that blow in from the north usually bring cooler temperatures to the Panhandle during winter months. The area often experiences cold fronts, or air masses, called northers. Temperatures can drop in a matter of minutes when a norther hits. A norther's effects are sometimes felt as far south as Central Texas and along the coast of the Gulf of Mexico. In winter, a northern air mass can blow in with freezing winds, ice, and snow. One Texan in the 1840s described a norther.

GLOBAL CONNECTIONS

El Niño

Sometimes global trends in weather affect Texas. Every few years, the ocean temperature rises along the west coast of South America. This trend, called El Niño, brings more winter rain than average to Texas. Most of this rain soaks the normally dry regions of West Texas and the Panhandle. **How does El Niño affect the Texas climate?**

TEXAS VOICES

"These winds commonly burst forth so suddenly that the first notice of their advent [arrival] is a violent gust that almost checks respiration [takes your breath away]. . . . The temperature frequently falls fifteen to twenty degrees in as many minutes."

Francis Moore Jr., quoted in *Texas: A Geography,* by Terry G. Jordan et al.

Analyzing Primary Sources
Finding the Main Idea
According to Moore, how does one know a norther has arrived?

Elevation can also affect temperature. The temperature can be cooler in higher elevations because the air is not as dense. Air that is less dense does not absorb heat as well. Therefore, the higher elevations of West Texas generally have a cooler climate than the rest of the state.

Reading Check **Summarizing** How do weather patterns differ across Texas?

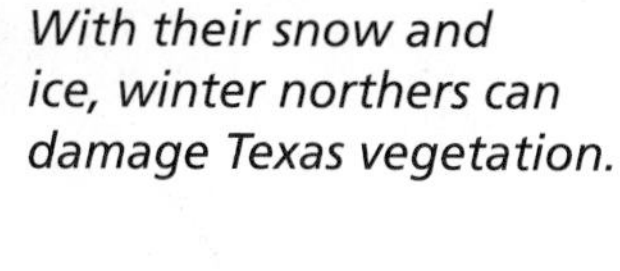

With their snow and ice, winter northers can damage Texas vegetation.

Zones of Annual Average Precipitation

Interpreting Maps As you move from east to west, Texas receives less and less rainfall.

1. ***Places and Regions*** Which region of Texas receives the most precipitation?
2. ***Analyzing Information*** How much rain does the westernmost region receive?

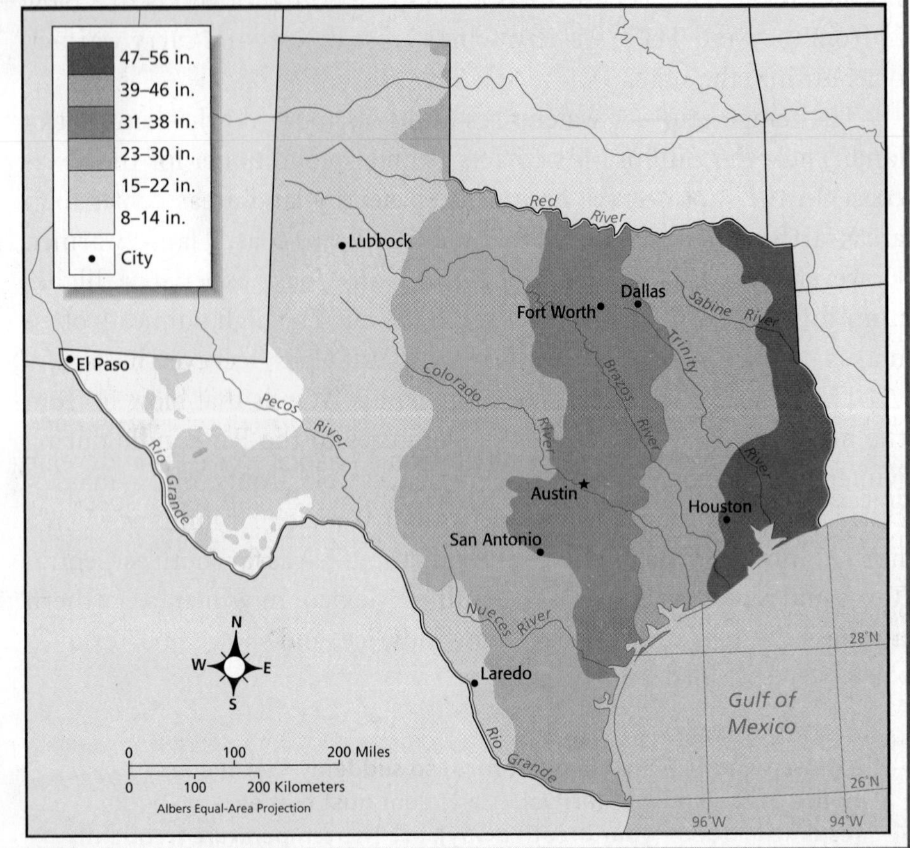

★ Rainfall in Texas

An area's climate is also determined by precipitation, or moisture falling as rain, snow, sleet, hail, or mist. In Texas the amount of precipitation increases across the state from west to east. While the average rainfall total in West Texas is 8–14 inches per year, East Texas receives 39–56 inches of rain annually. One reason the eastern half of Texas receives more rain is that it is closer to the Gulf of Mexico. The northern area of Texas receives part of its moisture from snow. The Panhandle usually gets several heavy snows each winter. The largest snowfall on record in Texas occurred in 1956, when the Amarillo area was blanketed by more than 30 inches of snow.

When rainfall is much less than the average, Texans experience a **drought**. These long periods without much rain cause damage to crops and livestock. Historically, Texas has experienced serious droughts every few decades. In the early 2000s, many areas of Texas suffered moderate to severe droughts. In 2011, for example, the state's average rainfall was just 14.8 inches.

The growth of industry, irrigation, and population have placed greater demands on water resources such as aquifers. As a result, water supplies in some Texas towns have fallen to very low levels during dry summer months. Droughts are particularly damaging to the Texas farming and ranching industries.

Floods are another threat to Texans and their property. Within minutes, calm streams can become raging rivers. Rivers can overflow their banks and cover neighboring lands. Dams have helped control flooding in many areas of Texas. But other places, like the Hill Country, still have floods following heavy downpours.

Reading Check Evaluating How can changes in rainfall affect the economy of Texas?

VIDEO
Tornado Alley
Twister
hmhsocialstudies.com

 Severe Weather

Texas gets its share of severe weather—including tornadoes, hurricanes, and blizzards. Tornadoes are violent funnel-shaped storms that develop inside severe thunderstorms. Their swirling winds can reach speeds of more than 300 miles per hour. Texas is in the southern edge of "Tornado Alley," a region of the midwestern United States. In Texas, tornadoes usually appear in the Panhandle or the north-central part of the state. One account of a tornado in May 1868 described its effects. "[It] blew cattle into the air, lodging them in trees, sucked all water from the Brazos River for a short distance and dumped a fifty-pound fish on dry land."

In 2009 approximately 129 tornadoes struck Texas. Tornadoes have claimed hundreds of lives and caused millions of dollars in damage. Tornado season is usually from spring until the beginning of summer.

Toward midsummer, the season for hurricanes starts. The season lasts through early fall. These huge storms develop over the waters of the Atlantic Ocean and Gulf of Mexico. They come ashore with high winds, heavy rains, and enormous tidal surges from the Gulf. In 1900 some 6,000 to 8,000 people were killed when a hurricane hit Galveston.

Interpreting Visuals

Hurricanes. *In 2008 floods caused by Hurricane Ike left highways in Galveston underwater.* ***How do you think storms like Hurricane Ike could affect the Texas economy?***

BIOGRAPHY

Lady Bird Johnson

(1912–2007) Claudia Alta "Lady Bird" Taylor grew up near the East Texas town of Marshall. Claudia was nicknamed Lady Bird as a child. After earning a master's degree at the University of Texas, Lady Bird married schoolteacher Lyndon B. Johnson in 1934. Lady Bird helped her husband's political career as he rose to become a U.S. president during the 1960s.

Later in her life, Lady Bird Johnson became concerned about the decline of wild plant life. Lady Bird explained why she founded a center to study wildflowers in Austin. "The founding of the National Wildflower Research Center was my way of repaying some of the debt for the delight . . . Nature has given me all my life."

Why did Lady Bird Johnson establish the wildflower center?

An even larger storm, Hurricane Ike, swept over Galveston and Houston in 2008. Winds rose to 110 miles per hour, and storm tides reached 22 feet above normal. Despite early warnings, 37 people died and nearly 3,000 had to be rescued. Thousands were displaced from their homes. In addition, Ike caused billions of dollars worth of damage to property.

Texas also gets hit by blizzards, or large snow storms. Those storms bring high winds, ice, and snow. They usually strike the Texas Panhandle or the north-central area of Texas. Blizzards are particularly dangerous to cattle and other livestock. The Great Blizzard of 1886–87 nearly destroyed the Texas cattle industry for almost a decade.

With new research and technology, scientists are better able to predict when and where severe weather will strike. These developments have saved hundreds of lives.

Reading Check **Categorizing** When and where do Texans experience tornadoes, hurricanes, and blizzards?

★ Texas Vegetation

The diversity of the Texas climate has provided a hospitable place for native plants. All kinds of brush, bushes, native grasses, trees, and wildflowers are native to Texas. Climate, landforms, and soil all help to determine where a plant will grow. For example, only native plants that can survive long periods without water can grow in the dry lands of far West Texas. Short grasses grow in clumps there, as do cacti and plants such as yucca. Groups of coniferous, or cone-bearing, trees are found in the mountains. These trees include junipers, piñon pines, and ponderosa pines. In contrast, the prairies of the central and eastern regions of Texas have rich native grasslands.

The plains of South Texas are also hot and dry. However, they get a bit more rain than West Texas does. South Texas is often called "brush country" because it is covered by shrubs and small trees. Mesquite trees are scattered throughout this part of Texas. Oaks are also found in places with more rain. Palm trees grow along the warm Gulf Coast of South Texas. Cacti and various grasses add to the variety of the landscape. In the Panhandle, the plains stretch for miles without trees. However, the soil conditions and annual rainfall support many different kinds of grasses. Unlike in far West Texas, grasses cover most of the land in the Panhandle.

In contrast to dry western Texas, the eastern third of the state receives plenty of rain. The soil is also very fertile. As a result, bushes, forests, and tall grasses can easily grow there. Forests cover the Piney Woods in East Texas. Gideon Lincecum visited the region in the 1830s. He wrote that it was "the thickest woods I ever saw." The Piney Woods is full of loblolly, longleaf, and shortleaf pine trees. Elm, hickory, and oak trees are also common in East Texas.

Lady Bird Johnson, the wife of U.S. president Lyndon B. Johnson, worked to keep Texas highways beautiful by leading the effort to plant bluebonnets and other wildflowers along the state's roads. She also helped establish the National Wildflower Research Center in Austin. The center provides information on native plants. These plants help to prevent **erosion**, or soil loss, by holding soil in place with their roots. Many wild plants also contribute beauty to the Texas landscape.

Reading Check **Contrasting** How do the climate and geography of West Texas differ from those of East Texas? How do these factors affect plant life in Texas?

Texas Wildlife

The vegetation of Texas provides a **habitat**, or environmental home, to a wide variety of animals. The forests and prairies of Texas are home to many wild animals. These include armadillos, bears, deer, javelinas, prairie hens, raccoons, skunks, wildcats, wild turkeys, and wolves. Texas waters are also full of wildlife. These animals include alligators, catfish, oysters, redfish, shrimp, and hundreds of other types of water animals.

As the state's environment has changed, the habitats of some animals have been destroyed. Because of this destruction, several species have become **extinct** in Texas. To be extinct means to die out completely or disappear. Several other species are endangered, or at risk of becoming extinct. Among them are the whooping crane and the Attwater Prairie Chicken. The populations of some animals that were once threatened with extinction have grown in recent years. For example, the buffalo population has grown dramatically.

Reading Check **Summarizing** What consequences have come from the modification of animal habitats in Texas?

Section 2 Review

hmhsocialstudies.com ONLINE QUIZ

1. Define and explain:
- humidity
- drought
- erosion
- habitat
- extinct

2. Identify and explain the significance of:
- Lady Bird Johnson

3. Analyzing Information Copy the graphic organizer below. Use it to explain how each type of weather affects Texas.

	Where they occur	Effects on life and economy
Droughts		
Floods		
Tornadoes		
Hurricanes		
Blizzards		

4. Finding the Main Idea

a. How does the climate of East Texas differ from that of West Texas?

b. What weather and geographic features affect plant and animal life?

5. Writing and Critical Thinking myWriteSmart

Summarizing In a letter to a friend, describe how the weather differs between East and West Texas.

Consider the following:
- weather trends in different regions
- the time of year

Section 3

Texans and Geography

Main Ideas

1. Texans come from many different countries and have diverse backgrounds.
2. Immigration, a rising birthrate, and a falling death rate have led to the growth of the Texas population.

Key Terms

- **immigration**
- **demography**
- **growth rate**
- **birthrate**
- **death rate**
- **age distribution**

Why It Matters Today

Texas has a rapidly growing population. Use current events sources to learn about population changes in Texas today.

TEKS: 8A, 8B, 10B, 11A, 11B, 11C, 11D, 19A, 19B, 19C, 19D, 21B, 21C, 21H, 22A, 22D

myNotebook

Use the annotation tools in your eBook to take notes on the characteristics of Texas's diverse population.

The Geographer's World

Texas is home to people from many different countries. These newcomers have brought cultural traditions with them. According to one Texan of Czech heritage, some Czech settlers practiced a special ritual. On Easter morning, a young Czech man would wash the face of the woman he liked. If the woman liked the young man as well, she would wash his face the day after Easter. This ritual marked the beginning of a relationship. While this old Czech tradition has faded from use, many other cultural traditions are preserved by Texans.

Who Texans Are

Texas is mostly populated by people who moved from other lands. As a result, Texans have many backgrounds, ethnicities, and races. Newcomers have brought unique cultural traditions and beliefs from their homelands. These differences contribute to the state's cultural diversity.

The first people to live in Texas were American Indians who moved to the area thousands of years ago. After Europeans arrived, the population of American Indians began dropping rapidly, mostly because of warfare and diseases that the Europeans carried. Over the centuries since then, American Indian groups have moved into and out of Texas, often driven by other people. In 2010 about 171,000 American Indians lived in Texas. Many hold religious ceremonies and practice traditional ways of life. For example, the Alabama-Coushatta Indians hold traditional dances on their reservation near Lake Livingston.

Many Texans trace their ancestry to people who came from Mexico in the 1700s and 1800s. At the time Mexico was a Spanish colony that included modern Texas. These early migrants brought with them the Spanish language and the Catholic faith. In recent times immigration to Texas from Mexico and other parts of Latin American has continued. **Immigration** is the movement of people from one country to another. In 2010 more than 9.4 million Hispanics lived in Texas. This number is more than 37 percent of the Texas population.

In 2010 the number of Texans who considered themselves white and not Hispanic was about 11.4 million—about 45 percent of the state's population. Some of these people's families first came to Texas in the early 1800s when settlers from the United States began coming to Texas. They helped shape the economy, education system, and laws of Texas.

European immigration also influenced Texas culture. Significant numbers of German, Czech, French, Irish, and other Europeans came to Texas during the 1800s and 1900s. Their presence is seen in place-names, foods, and other cultural traditions of Texas. For example, German polka music and food, such as sauerkraut, are common in some Texas Hill Country towns.

African Americans also have a long history in Texas. Many people of African origin were brought to Texas as slaves by Spanish and American settlers during the 1700s and 1800s. The African American population in Texas grew during the 1900s. In 2010 the state's African American population numbered more than 2.9 million, or about 12 percent of the Texas population that year. African Americans have influenced music, religious practices, and many other cultural traditions of Texas. For example, Scott Joplin and other African Americans in Texas helped develop ragtime, blues, and jazz.

In recent years more Asian Americans have made Texas their home. As of 2010 more than 960,000 Asian Americans lived in the state. An estimated 16.4 percent of immigrants to Texas in 2011 were Asian Americans. These immigrants have brought many foods and traditions. Asian Americans have brought religions such as Buddhism, Hinduism, and Islam to Texas, adding to the state's diversity.

Reading Check **Summarizing** What cultural activities have different racial and ethnic groups contributed to Texas?

Religious Diversity in Texas

During its history, Texas has attracted many different groups of people. As new groups came, they brought their religious beliefs with them. Early Spanish settlers in Texas established Catholic churches. Later, American and European settlers built Methodist, Baptist, Lutheran, and other Protestant churches in their communities. Jewish settlers built synagogues. Today new groups continue to arrive in Texas. Buddhists from Vietnam and other Asian countries have built temples in several large Texas cities. Middle Eastern and Indian newcomers have established Islamic mosques and Hindu and Sikh temples. **How does the growing population of Texas affect the state's religious diversity?**

★ Where Texans Have Settled

Some regions of Texas have been settled by people with a similar ethnic background. These groups have influenced the areas they settled. For example, people from Mexico have been migrating to the Rio Grande Valley for many years. As a result, Mexican influences are strong in South Texas. For example, many businesses and cultural institutions in this region have Spanish names.

Interpreting Visuals

Cultural celebrations. *These children are participating in a Hindu festival outside of Austin. Asian immigrants have brought new cultural traditions to Texas.* ***How do you think cultural celebrations like this one help Asian immigrants maintain their cultural heritage?***

Most early settlers from the southern United States made their home in East Texas. Many did so because the climate and soil are similar to those of the American South. Large groups of German and Czech immigrants settled in Central Texas. These European immigrants have left their mark on the area. This can be seen in the place-names, foods, and cultural activities in the region. For example, German immigrants established the towns of Fredericksburg and New Braunfels. In these towns people still hold German music festivals called Sängerfests.

Historically, most Texans lived in rural areas. As Texas industries grew, people began to move to cities. By 1950, more Texans lived in urban areas than on farms and ranches. As of 2010, about 87 percent of Texans lived in cities. Houston, Dallas, and San Antonio are three of the largest cities in the United States. Because most larger cities are in the central and eastern areas of Texas, the majority of Texans live in these regions. This growing population of city-dwellers marks a big change from the early days of rural settlement in Texas.

Reading Check **Finding the Main Idea** What settlement patterns have appeared in Texas?

★ The Growing Population of Texas

Texas is becoming more diverse as its population increases. In 2010 Texas had a population of more than 25 million. To understand why the Texas population continues to grow, you must learn about **demography**. Demography is a branch of geography that studies human populations.

When studying population **growth rate**—the speed of growth—demographers look at several factors. One factor is the **birthrate**, the number of births per 1,000 people each year. Another factor is the **death rate**, the number of deaths per 1,000 people each year. In 2010 the birthrate in Texas was 15.3, and the death rate was 6.6.

Better health care is allowing more Texans, like other Americans, to live longer. As a result, the death rate has dropped. More Texans are being born than are dying. These two factors are contributing to the growing population of Texas.

Immigration and migration are also factors in the growth of the Texas population. In 2011 more than 117,000 people came to Texas from foreign countries. Many of these newcomers have arrived from such different countries as Mexico, India, and Vietnam.

The growing population has brought many changes to Texas, including the age of the Texas population as a whole. As Texans live longer and more are born, the **age distribution** of the state changes. The age distribution is the portion of the population at each age. Some populations are, on the average, younger than others. This means they have a greater percentage of young people than other regions. With a higher percentage of young people, Texas is a younger state than most.

Gender distribution also affects population. As in other parts of the United States, women make up a higher percentage of the population in Texas. One reason for this is the fact that women tend to live longer than men. In 2010 there were 98.4 men for every 100 women. This has not always been the case, however.

At the beginning of the 1900s, there were approximately 110 men for every 100 women. Because Texas has a growing population, the age distribution and diversity of the state will continue to change. In addition, the population growth rate of the state will most likely increase over time.

Reading Check **Summarizing** What factors have contributed to the growth rate of the Texas population?

Section 3 Review

hmhsocialstudies.com
ONLINE QUIZ

1. Define and explain:
- immigration
- demography
- growth rate
- birthrate
- death rate
- age distribution

2. Evaluating
Copy the graphic organizer below. Use it to explain why the population of Texas continues to grow.

IMMIGRATION
\+ BIRTHS
− DEATHS
= GROWTH

3. Finding the Main Idea
a. What groups of people came to Texas, and where did they settle in the state?
b. How have the changes in the age distribution and growth rate affected the population?
c. How have Texans from various backgrounds maintained their cultural heritage while adapting to the larger culture?

4. Writing and Critical Thinking myWriteSmart
Analyzing Information Write an entry to a guidebook on Texas culture. Explain how these cultures benefit Texas. Consider the following:
- where people have settled
- how immigration and migration have influenced Texas since the 1800s

Connecting To

Geography

The Texas Population

The population of Texas is expected to keep growing. Projections, or estimates, of future populations help the government and businesses plan to meet the future needs of populations. Geographers can use pie graphs and charts to show changes in the racial and ethnic makeup of Texas.

Geography **Skills**

Interpreting Data and Charts

1. What percentage of Texans have Hispanic and Asian American heritage?
2. In which age groups do women outnumber men in Texas?
3. How much is the total population of Texas expected to grow between 2010 and 2025?
4. Which group's population is expected to grow fastest between 2010 and 2025?
5. What effects do you think the changes in population will have on Texas?

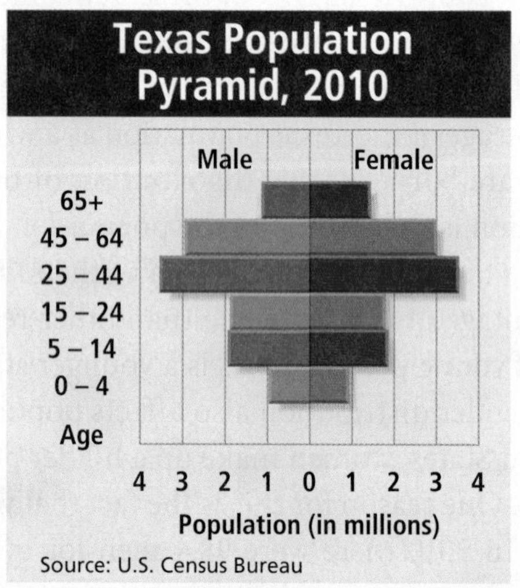

Racial and Ethnic Heritage of Texas, 2010

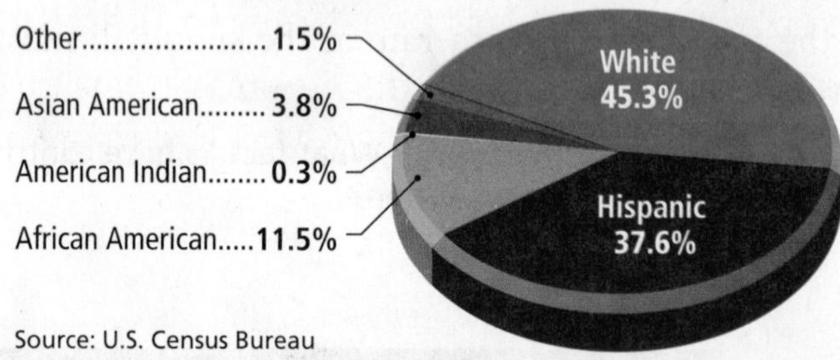

Source: U.S. Census Bureau

Texas Population

	2010	2025*
TOTAL POPULATION	25,145,561	27,183,000
WHITE	11,397,345	12,501,000
HISPANIC	9,460,921	10,230,000
AFRICAN AMERICAN	2,979,598	3,871,000
ASIAN AMERICAN	964,596	1,065,000
AMERICAN INDIAN	170,972	159,000

Source: U.S. Census Bureau *Figures for 2025 are estimates.

Section 4

Natural Resources of Texas

Main Ideas

1. Texas has many valuable agricultural and energy resources.
2. Texans use natural resources to build and support a strong economy.

Key Terms

- **agriculture**
- **nonrenewable resources**
- **renewable resources**

Why It Matters Today

Texans raise a wide variety of crops and animals on farms and ranches throughout the state. Use current events sources to learn more about crops and livestock in Texas today.

TEKS: 9B, 10A, 10B, 16B, 20D, 21B, 22A, 22D

myNotebook

Use the annotation tools in your eBook to take notes on the important natural resources found in Texas.

The Geographer's World

In June 1919, farmer Ruth Jones was planning to marry. Ruth and her sisters worked on their family's East Texas farm right up to the day before the wedding. Saturday afternoon, they leaned their hoes against a dead tree in the field and went home to prepare for the wedding on Sunday. On Monday morning, they were back working in the fields. Farmers like Jones rarely took a break from their fields.

Agricultural Resources

Texas has a wealth of natural resources that have contributed to the state's growth. Climate, soil, and water resources are all important to the Texas economy. Some Texans make their living from **agriculture**, or growing crops and raising animals. East Texas receives a lot of rainfall and has rich soil. Farmers in this region grow a wide range of crops, including fruits, nuts, and vegetables. Corn, tomatoes, and watermelon are some of the area's important crops. The greater amount of rainfall in East Texas also supports the growth of forests, which in turn supports a large timber industry. Along the southeastern Gulf Coast, farmers grow rice and vegetables. These crops do well in the region's warm wet climate.

Farmers in drier regions of Texas often use aquifers and rivers to irrigate their crops. The use of irrigation helps Texans overcome the climate limitations of many drier regions. In South Texas, farmers grow crops such as alfalfa, citrus fruits, cotton, melons, and vegetables. The warm winters in the region allow farmers to grow crops year-round.

Daily Life

Future Farmers of America

Learning to take care of livestock is an important undertaking for many Texas students. Many young Texans belong to organizations such as the Future Farmers of America (FFA). The FFA helps students learn and demonstrate the skill of raising livestock. The organization has about 7,500 chapters and more than 555,000 members. It helps students learn about the business of agriculture and livestock. The organization also helps to teach skills in leadership and teamwork.

Why do some young Texans join the Future Farmers of America?

Southern farmers can often grow two sets of crops per year. Farmers in the Panhandle can grow huge crops of wheat and cotton by drilling and pumping water from the Ogallala Aquifer to irrigate their fields.

The livestock industry is also an important part of the Texas economy. The main types of livestock in Texas include cattle, chickens, horses, pigs, sheep, and turkeys. The native grasses and generally warm climate of Texas provide a natural place to raise livestock. Many animals range the prairie regions of Central Texas, the Gulf Coast, and the Panhandle. In the dry Panhandle, ranchers pump water from aquifers and rivers for their livestock. Cattle ranching is a big business in Texas. In 2011, Texas ranchers had some 13.3 million head of cattle worth over $6 billion. In the rockier regions of Texas, ranchers raise goats for their mohair, which is used in clothing. Texas produces more mohair than any other state in the nation.

Reading Check **Evaluating** How do climate and other geographic features affect what crops and animals are raised in different regions of Texas?

★ Energy Resources

Some of the state's most valuable natural resources are energy resources such as coal, natural gas, and oil. Energy resources are important because they supply fuel to run automobiles, heat homes, and power industry. The production of oil and natural gas in Texas is worth over $67 billion per year. Texans have drilled oil wells in almost every region of the state and built refineries to process these resources. Thousands of Texans depend on jobs in the oil industry.

Coal, natural gas, and oil are **nonrenewable resources**. They cannot be replaced by Earth's natural processes. As a result, there is a limited supply of nonrenewable resources. Some Texans have turned to **renewable resources**—ones that are easily replaced by Earth's natural processes. Examples of renewable energy resources include sunshine, trees, and wind. Texas is the country's leading producer of wind energy.

Texas has a number of other resources that are important to its economy. For example, the construction industry uses sand and gravel to make concrete and other building products. Texans also mine minerals such as copper, salt, and sulfur. These natural resources provide important products for the daily lives of Texans. The production of these materials also provides many jobs to Texans.

Reading Check **Analyzing Information** How have Texans developed technology to use the state's natural resources?

Using Resources Wisely

Texas has a wide variety of abundant natural resources. Many Texans have used these rich natural resources to build successful businesses. For example, the state's climate, soil, and water have enabled Texas farmers to raise crops, creating a multibillion-dollar agricultural industry in the state. Many other Texas industries, from oil production to construction, have grown by using fossil fuels and other natural resources of the state. A large part of the Texas economy relies upon these resources.

Texans work to balance the state's economic growth and the needs of the future. For example, an abundant supply of water in Texas aquifers is important to farmers and ranchers in drier regions of Texas. Every year billions of tons of water are pumped out of Texas aquifers for farming and human consumption. In some years enough water is pumped out of Texas aquifers to cover roughly 11 million acres of land to a depth of one foot. However, in many years only some 5 million acre-feet worth of water is refilled. The slow process of refilling aquifers has led some Texans to organize water conservation districts to manage water resources. These districts were created to help to ensure the long-term use of aquifers for irrigation and allow for a productive agricultural economy in the state. In 2013, Texans approved the creation of a $2 billion fund to help pay for and manage state water projects.

Scientific and technological innovations have always helped Texans use natural resources. Advances in drilling technology have made removing oil, natural gas, and water from underground more efficient and profitable. New advances in science and technology will bring further changes to the use of the state's natural resources.

Reading Check **Making Generalizations and Predictions** How do you think future scientific discoveries and technological innovations will affect the use of natural resources?

Recycling

Some Texas businesses have turned to recycling as a way to reduce costs and manage their use of resources. Recycling is the reuse of materials. Recycling can save energy, money, and natural resources. Texans have formed groups like the Recycling Coalition of Texas and the Texas Corporate Recycling Council. Organizations such as these have established conferences, education programs, and partnerships with Texas industries. **What have some organizations done to promote recycling?**

Section 4 Review

hmhsocialstudies.com
ONLINE QUIZ

1. **Define and explain:**
   - agriculture
   - nonrenewable resources
   - renewable resources

2. **Comparing and Contrasting**
   Copy the graphic organizer below. Use it to explain the benefits of and problems with the use of natural resources.

   Natural Resources
   - Benefits Provided
   - Problems from Use

3. **Finding the Main Idea**
   a. How have geography and climate affected where Texans grow crops and raise livestock?
   b. How do Texans make use of renewable and nonrenewable energy sources?

4. **Writing and Critical Thinking** myWriteSmart
   Evaluating Imagine that you are writing a friend from out of state. Explain how Texans have adapted to and changed their environment to make use of its resources. Consider the following:
   - Texans using aquifers to irrigate in dry regions
   - Texans drilling for oil and natural gas
   - Texans using grasslands for livestock

CHAPTER 2 REVIEW

The Chapter at a Glance

Examine the following visual summary of the chapter. Then use the visual to create a model of life in Texas.

Landforms, Water, and Weather

The landforms and weather of Texas vary greatly. However, Texans have learned to adapt and use these geographic features.

People of Texas

People have come to Texas from many different places. More Texans today live in cities than in rural areas.

Natural Resources

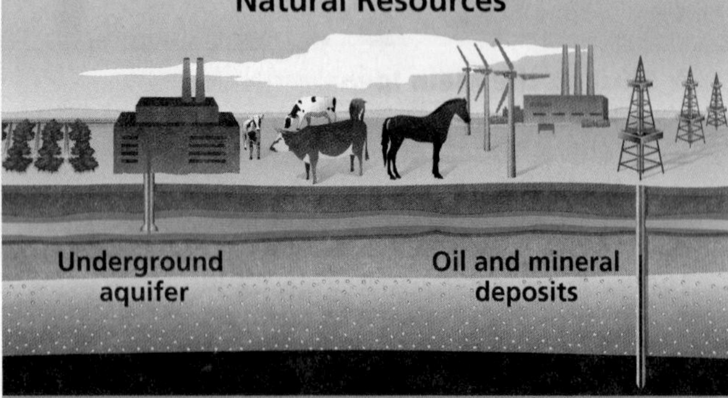

The state's natural resources have led to the growth of farming, ranching, energy production, and many other industries.

Identifying People and Ideas

Review the meanings of the following terms.

1. plains
2. irrigation
3. aquifers
4. humidity
5. drought
6. Lady Bird Johnson
7. growth rate
8. birthrate
9. death rate
10. age distribution

Understanding Main Ideas

Section 1

1. What types of landforms can be found in Texas?
2. How do some Texans use water resources?

Section 2

3. What types of severe weather threaten Texas?
4. How are Texas plants and animals affected by climate?

Section 3

5. What factors have contributed to a rising population growth rate in Texas?
6. How has the age distribution of Texas changed?

Section 4

7. What types of crops and livestock are raised in Texas?
8. What natural resources can be found in Texas?

You Be the Geographer

Reviewing Themes

1. **Geography** How have Texas farmers and ranchers changed the landscape of Texas?
2. **Culture** How have people of different racial and ethnic backgrounds added to the diversity of Texas culture?
3. **Economics** In what ways have the natural resources and weather of Texas affected the economy of the state?

Thinking Critically

1. **Analyzing Information** How have Texans adapted to and modified the natural environment? What are some of the positive and negative effects of these efforts?
2. **Evaluating** How does Texas benefit from the state's diversity of physical and human characteristics?
3. **Drawing Inferences and Conclusions** Make several predictions about how Texas and its natural resources will be affected by future scientific discoveries and technological innovations.

Texas Test Practice

Interpreting Maps

Study the map below. Then use the information on the map to answer the questions that follow.

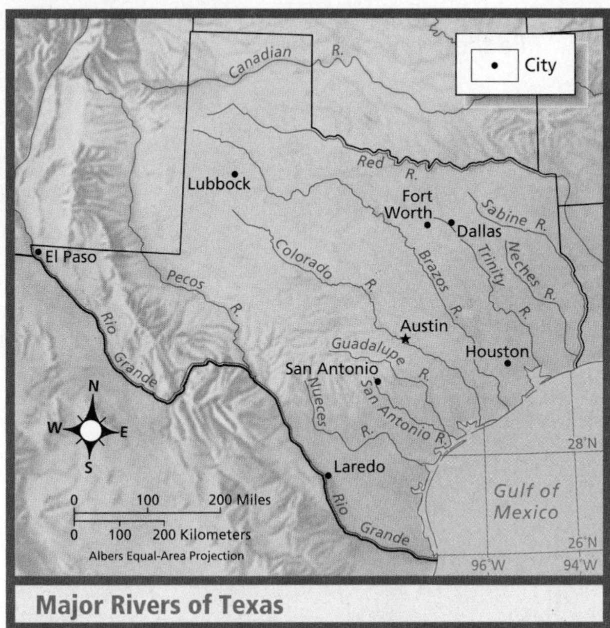

Major Rivers of Texas

1. Which region of Texas has the fewest rivers?

- **A** East Texas
- **B** the Gulf Coast
- **C** South Texas
- **D** West Texas

2. How do you think these sources of water have affected where Texans have settled?

Interpreting Outlines

Study the outline below. Then answer the questions that follow.

Natural Resources

I. Agricultural Resources
 A. Crops
 B. Livestock
  1. Cattle
  2. Horses
 C. Timber
II. Energy Resources
 A. Nonrenewable
  1. Coal
  2. Gas
  3. Oil
 B. Renewable
  1. Sunshine
  2. Trees
  3. Wind

3. Oil is which type of natural resource?

- **F** renewable energy
- **G** nonrenewable energy
- **H** renewable agricultural
- **J** none of the above

4. Reorganize the information in this outline into a visual format, such as a graph, chart, table, or graphic organizer.

Linking to Community

One challenge that some new arrivals in Texas face is learning a new language. Prepare a "Welcome to the Classroom" kit for new students who might speak little English. Look around the room and listen to what people say to make a list of common words and phrases that a student might need to know. Examples include words that appear in your classroom, like on signs or posters, and academic and vocabulary words that your teacher and classmates use regularly. For each word or phrase, write a meaning that could help a new student learn what he or she needs to know to do well in class. In your kit, remind students to practice using these words while speaking and that they can always ask the teacher or classmates for help.

Internet Activity 

Conduct Internet research to learn more about the characteristics of Texans today. Identify examples of cultural influences on Texas place names, vocabulary, religion, architecture, food, and the arts. Be sure to include information on various cultural activities, celebrations, and performances. Then write an informative essay to report what you have found. Make sure you use standard grammar, spelling, sentence structure, and punctuation.

CHAPTER 3

The Regions of Texas

Texas Essential Knowledge and Skills (TEKS) 8A, 8B, 9A, 9B, 10A, 10B, 12A, 12B, 13A, 13C, 19D, 20C, 21A, 21B, 21C, 22A, 22C, 22D

Texas cotton is made into textiles like these bolts of fabric.

TEXAS	The Texas timber industry earned more than $1.9 billion in 2007.	Texas contains more than 60 million acres of forests and woodlands.	In 2011 the value of Texas cotton production reached over $1.5 billion.
U.S. and WORLD	The American timber industry earned more than $20 billion in logging and sawmill production in 2009.	In 2007 the United States contained more than 751 million acres of forests and woodlands.	American farmers harvested more than $6.5 billion worth of cotton in 2011.

If you were a geographer . . .
How would you describe your region?

Build on What You Know

Texas has a wide variety of landforms, water resources, climates, and plant and animal life. In many cases, geographers use these physical features to describe the different regions of the state. From the Piney Woods of East Texas to the dry deserts in the west, Texas is a land of many contrasts.

Big Bend National Park attracts tourists with its views and dramatic landscape.

Texans develop and produce new electronic technology.

With 800,000 acres of land, Big Bend National Park is the largest national park in Texas.

The largest national park in the United States is the Wrangell–St. Elias Park, which covers more than 8 million acres of Alaska.

Sales of Texas livestock totaled more than $10.8 billion in 2007.

In 2009, sales from the meat and poultry industry were nearly $155 billion.

Texas exports of computers and electronics were worth more than $45 billion in 2012.

In 2012, United States exports of computer and electronic products were worth more than $123 billion.

You Be the Geographer *my*Notebook

What's Your Opinion? Do you **agree** or **disagree** with the following statements? Support your point of view in your notebook.

- **Geography** Agriculture can be an important part of an area's economy only if the region has fertile soil and a warm climate.
- **Economics** Geographic factors affect all industries.
- **Science, Technology & Society** People have to adapt to their environment.

Section 1 A Regional Crossroads

Main Ideas

1. Texas is considered the crossroads of natural regions.
2. There are four main natural regions found in Texas.

Why It Matters Today

Texas has several regions, each with its own distinct landforms and climates. Use current events sources to find information about how natural landforms affect people's lives.

Key Terms

- **Sunbelt**
- **natural regions**

TEKS: 8A, 9A, 9B, 21B, 21C, 22A, 22C, 22D

myNotebook

Use the annotation tools in your eBook to take notes on the natural regions found in Texas.

The Geographer's World

In the 1880s, two ranch workers were exploring a canyon in far West Texas. Looking over the canyon ledge, they saw almost 20 horses, but no people. They climbed down the steep canyon walls but could not find a way to get the horses out. Nor could they figure out how the horses had gotten into the canyon. There was little they could do for the horses. With only a few plants to eat, the animals soon starved. The workers named the spot Dead Horse Canyon.

★ Common Regional Names

Many places have unusual names that describe some geographic characteristic or feature. For example, the southern region of the United States is often called the **Sunbelt**. This name emphasizes the warm climate that has attracted many new residents to the region. Texas is part of the Sunbelt. Northwestern Texas is often called the Panhandle because the region's shape looks much like the handle of a pan. Other regions of Texas are named for their geographic features. The Redlands is an old name for an area of northeastern Texas that has reddish soil. The Coastal Bend, centered around Corpus Christi, gets its name from an area where the Gulf Coast "bends."

Texas is often divided into regions named for their general locations—East Texas, West Texas, South Texas, or North Texas. These regions have vague boundaries because they are based on perceptions, or points of view. For instance, people might have differing opinions about the boundaries of West Texas. Some say Fort Worth is in West Texas because the city has close economic and historical ties to the region's cattle industry. Fort Worth, though, is actually located in the eastern half of North Texas.

Other types of perceptual regions are cultural or political regions. These are based on human characteristics. For example, the German Hill Country is a cultural region named for its early German settlers, whose cultural legacy is still seen in the area. Another example of a cultural region is the Metroplex, the area around Dallas and Fort Worth. The region's culture is shaped by its nearness to two large cities.

Political regions are based on the political boundaries into which Texas has been divided, such as cities or counties. Tom Green County is an example of a political region, as is the city of El Paso. The legislative districts into which Texas is divided are also political regions.

Reading Check **Summarizing** What characteristics of a region help to determine its name?

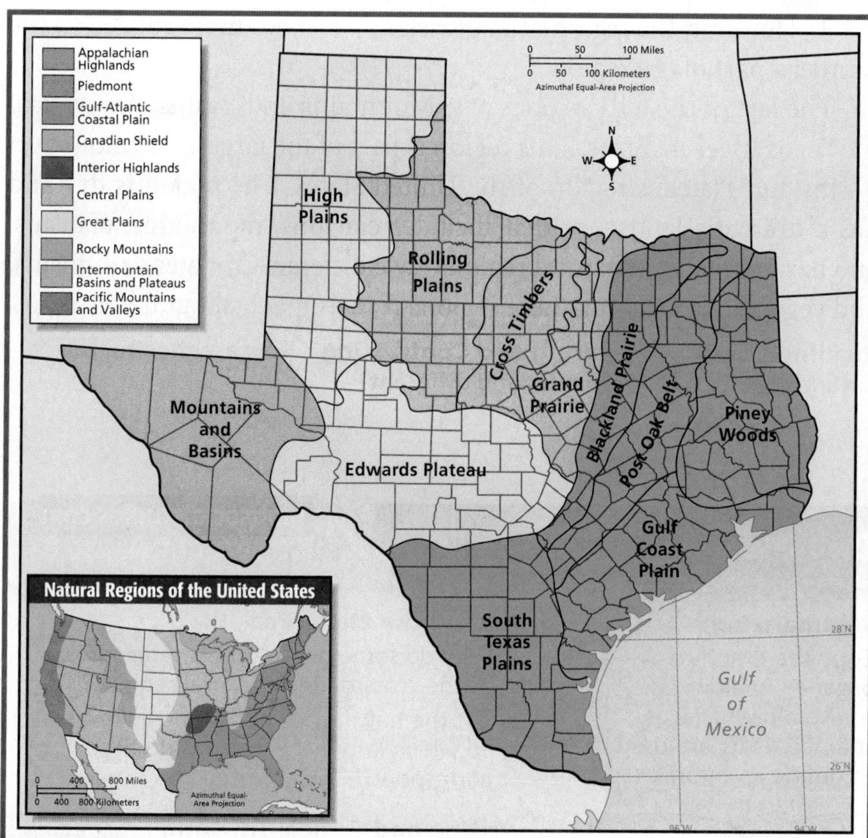

Natural Regions of Texas

Interpreting Maps Many geographers classify 10 natural regions in the United States. The four natural regions found in Texas have their own unique features; however, they maintain the characteristics of the larger natural regions of the United States.

Locate What four natural regions are found in Texas?

★ Natural Regions of Texas

Geographers study **natural regions** to compare and contrast different areas. A natural region is an area with a common physical environment. Natural regions are defined by physical features. These features include types of climate, landforms, plant life, and soil. For travelers, physical features are clues that they are leaving one region and entering another.

Some geographers divide the continental United States into 10 major natural regions. Parts of four natural regions are found in Texas, which is more than in any other state. For this reason, Texas is called the crossroads of natural regions.

The Coastal Plains is one of the largest natural regions in Texas. As part of the larger Gulf-Atlantic Coastal Plain, the region covers the entire coast of Texas and extends a few hundred miles inland. The land along the coast is usually marshy, while the land inland has both dense forests and grassy prairies. The North Central Plains region is part of the larger U.S. region known as the Central Plains. This region is characterized by gently rolling prairies that offer abundant resources for ranching and farming. The Great Plains region is known as one of the flattest areas on Earth. However, the region's flat grassland becomes more rugged in the southern part of the region.

The last of the four regions, the Mountains and Basins, lies west of the Pecos River in Texas. This region is part of the larger Intermountain Basins and Plateaus region of the United States. The region is dry and has a dramatic landscape that includes canyons, mountains, plateaus, and basins. The four natural regions have different climates, landforms, and vegetation. Studying these regions reveals much about life in Texas.

Reading Check **Comparing and Contrasting** How are the four major natural regions of Texas similar and different?

★ Section 1 Review

hmhsocialstudies.com
ONLINE QUIZ

1. Define and explain:
- natural regions

2. Locate on a map:
- Sunbelt
- Coastal Plains
- North Central Plains
- Great Plains
- Mountains and Basins

3. Summarizing
Copy the graphic organizer below. Use it to explain what types of characteristics are used to define a region.

4. Finding the Main Idea

a. Why do some geographers refer to Texas as the crossroads of natural regions?

b. List the natural regions found in Texas. To which larger U.S. regions do they correspond?

5. Writing and Critical Thinking myWriteSmart

Contrasting Write a letter to someone in another region. Tell that person about some of the interesting physical and human characteristics of your region. Consider the following:
- the name of your region
- characteristics that make your region similar to and different from other regions

Section 2 The Coastal Plains

Main Ideas
1. The five subregions of the Coastal Plains have varied landscapes and economies.
2. Texans in the Coastal Plains have both changed and adapted to their environment.

Key Terms
- **subregions**
- **bayous**
- **petrochemicals**
- **Rio Grande Valley**
- **lignite**
- **Metroplex**

Why It Matters Today
The Coastal Plains receive more rainfall than any other region in Texas. Use current events sources to find information about the problems too much rainfall can cause.

TEKS: 8A, 9A, 9B, 10A, 10B, 12A, 12B, 13A, 13C, 21A, 21B, 21C, 22A

myNotebook

Use the annotation tool found in your eBook to take notes on the physical and human features found in the subregions of the Coastal Plains.

The Geographer's World

As a boy, Texas naturalist Lance Rosier loved to explore the woods of East Texas. He knew the woods like the back of his hand. One overcast day, Rosier guided a friend into the woods to photograph a rare flower. He marched straight through the woods for two miles. Without searching, he stopped at a spot that had no landmarks. Astonishing his friend, Rosier said, "I saw it two years ago. Oh, here it is!"

★ The Piney Woods

The Coastal Plains can be divided into five **subregions**, or smaller regions. The easternmost subregion of the Coastal Plains is called the Piney Woods. It is part of a pine forest that covers the entire southern United States from the Atlantic Ocean to Texas. Most of the land in the Piney Woods is rolling hills. The Piney Woods also has one of the wettest climates of any Texas subregion. Rainfall helps support a large timber industry in the heavily forested areas of the Piney Woods. Gum, hickory, oak, and pine trees are an important source of timber and wood products for the subregion. Farming is also an important part of the subregion's economy. The rich soils and wet climate are ideal for producing many fruits and vegetables. In areas where farmers have cut down forests, tall grasses have grown. Farmers raise cattle in these open grassy areas.

Oil is another valuable natural resource in this subregion. Large amounts of oil were discovered here in the 1930s. The oil industry contributes to the economy of many regional cities such as Henderson and Kilgore. The subregion's creeks, lakes, and rivers also provide it with significant water sources. The area includes the Neches, Sabine, and Trinity Rivers as well as the Toledo Bend and Sam Rayburn Reservoirs. These rivers and reservoirs provide many Texans with drinking water and places of recreation.

Many people in the Piney Woods live in rural areas or small towns. These towns serve as local markets for farmers and the lumber industry. The subregion's largest cities are Longview and Texarkana. These cities have prospered as the agricultural, oil, and lumber industries have grown.

Texans have taken action to preserve some of the area's natural resources. The Big Thicket National Preserve was established to protect about 85,000 acres of trees and wildlife in the Piney Woods. This subregion also has four national forests: the Angelina National Forest, Davy Crockett National Forest, Sabine National Forest, and Sam Houston National Forest. The state conserves the natural resources of these forests. When trees are cut down, new trees are planted in their place.

Reading Check Analyzing Information How have the natural resources of the Piney Woods affected its economy?

Subregions of the Coastal Plains

Interpreting Maps With Houston and Dallas located in the region, the Coastal Plains region is the most populated in Texas.

1. ***Locate*** What rivers form the boundaries of the Coastal Plains region in Texas?
2. ***Contrasting*** How do the physical characteristics differ in the five subregions?

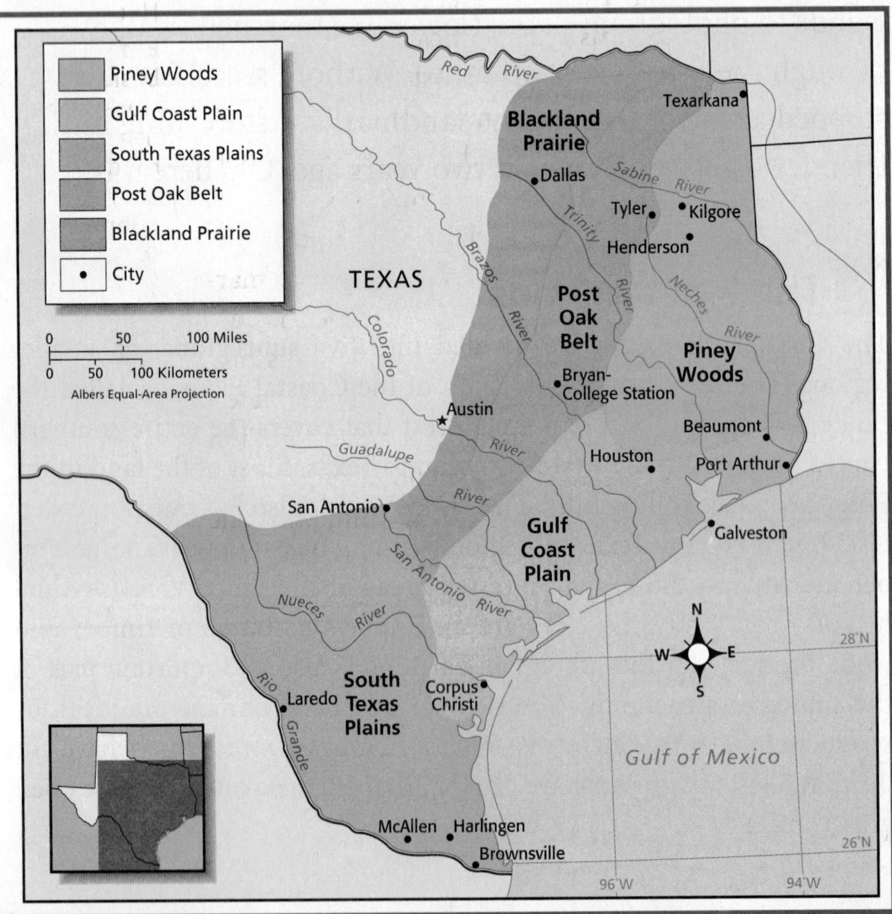

The Gulf Coast Plain

South and west of the Piney Woods lies the Gulf Coast Plain. This subregion extends south along the Gulf Coast from the Sabine River to Corpus Christi Bay. A chain of barrier islands runs nearly the entire length of the Texas coast. These islands are covered by brush, grasses, and sand. Shallow bays separate the islands from the mainland. On the mainland near the coast, the land is marshy and full of **bayous**. A bayou is a slow-moving, swampy section of a river or a lake. Inland, scattered groves of trees dot the plain's lush grasslands .

The soil and climate of the Gulf Coast Plain have made it a rich agricultural area. Farmers grow rice in the eastern areas near the coast. Farther south, in the Coastal Bend area, farmers produce cotton and grains. The coastal grasslands also support one of the largest livestock industries in Texas. The Gulf waters are another valuable resource. Fishing and shrimping are major sources of income for many Texans.

Oil is another resource, with offshore oil rigs providing many jobs for Texans. The center of the Texas and U.S. oil-refining industry lies between Beaumont and Houston. The area also has a large **petrochemicals** industry. Petrochemicals are chemicals made from oil and natural gas. They are used in most industries. Ports provide another boost to the economy of the Gulf Coast Plain. Some of the largest cities in this subregion are port cities: Houston, Corpus Christi, Beaumont, Galveston, and Port Arthur. Products are shipped in and out of these ports to destinations worldwide. As global markets have expanded, these ports have become increasingly busy. Houston is the largest city in Texas and has the fourth-largest population in the United States. Houston–The Woodlands–Sugarland is a metropolitan area that stretches for more than 10,000 square miles and, with a population of more than 6 million, is the fifth-largest metropolitan area in the nation. Although Houston lies about 50 miles inland, a huge channel connects the city with the Gulf of Mexico. Houston is one of the largest seaports in the nation and a major center for international shipping. The natural resources of the Gulf Coast Plain boost its industry and attract many people to this subregion.

Reading Check **Evaluating** How have national and international markets affected the Gulf Coast Plain?

★ Texas Cities ★

Houston

History: Houston was founded in August 1836 by Augustus and John Allen. The Allen brothers chose a site along the Buffalo Bayou, hoping the town would become an important port. Houston was the capital for a short period during the days of the Republic. However, the town did not begin to boom until the 1900s when the oil industry grew.

Population in 2012: 2,160,821 (estimate)

Relative location: Houston is located in the southeast corner of Texas.

Region: Gulf Coastal Plain

County: County seat of Harris County

Special feature: Largest city in Texas

Origin of name: Houston was named by the Allen brothers in honor of Sam Houston.

Economy: Houston has one of the busiest ports in the nation, making the city a global trade center. Houston also has many oil drilling, refining, and other production facilities. Oil-related industries, such as plastics and petrochemicals, have boomed in this region. Houston is also home to the Lyndon B. Johnson Space Center.

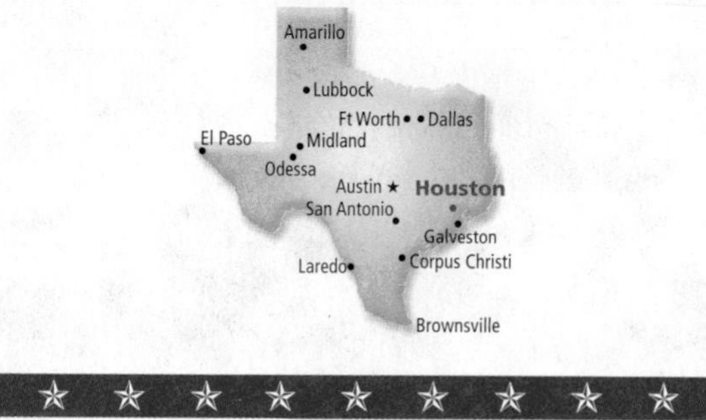

Analyzing Primary Sources
Identifying Bias Do you think DeWees liked the South Texas landscape?

The South Texas Plains

The South Texas Plains subregion lies to the west of the Gulf Coast Plain. The South Texas Plains extends south to the Gulf of Mexico, where the land is low and flat. In the northern and western areas of the subregion, the land rises gradually and becomes more hilly. The climate in this subregion is drier than in the Gulf Coast Plain. Grasslands cover the coastal section, but dense brushlands characterize the subregion farther inland. One early traveler in South Texas noted the interesting plant life of the region.

TEXAS VOICES

"The road is oftimes [often] completely hedged in [lined] for miles by long rows of prickly pear. . . . All the shrubbery throughout this country is covered with thorns."

—William B. DeWees, quoted in *Texas: A Geography*, by Terry Jordan, et al.

Padre Island

One of the most unusual features of the Coastal Plains region is Padre Island. This 133-mile-long island has the longest sand beach in the United States. The island is covered in sand dunes and is home to more than 600 different types of plants. The Padre Island National Seashore helps protect the island's natural beauty. Thousands of visitors come to relax and take in the scenery. **What is the most notable feature of Padre Island?**

The South Texas Plains subregion has many natural resources. One of the richest farming areas in the nation—the **Rio Grande valley**—lies in this subregion. Temperatures there are warm for most of the year, and freezes are rare. The Valley has fertile soils from sediment washed down the Rio Grande. Farmers grow citrus fruits, such as grapefruits and oranges, in large quantities. Vegetable crops, sugarcane, and specialty crops such as aloe vera add to the area's wealth. Many people in the Valley work in farming-related businesses.

Ranches are also common throughout the South Texas Plains. King Ranch is the largest of these ranches, stretching for more than 1 million acres, or 1,562 square miles. Oil and natural gas wells dot the landscape, but farming and ranching are the main sectors of this subregion's economy.

Although the South Texas Plains subregion is largely rural, it does include several cities. The subregion's largest city is San Antonio. Founded in 1718 by Spaniards, the city is home to many historic buildings and is

one of the state's most popular tourist attractions. San Antonio is also home to several large military bases. These bases play an important role in the local economy. San Antonio is a retail trade center for the South Texas region and a major center for international trade with Mexico.

Although San Antonio is the largest city in this subregion, Laredo is the fastest growing. Other border towns such as Brownsville, Harlingen, and McAllen are also expanding rapidly. While tourism and international trade are important to these cities, farming is still the area's most important economic activity.

Reading Check **Summarizing** What are the natural resources of the South Texas Plains, and how do Texans use them to develop the subregion's economy?

★ The Post Oak Belt

The Post Oak Belt subregion begins just outside of San Antonio and stretches north to the Red River, covering a considerable area in east-central Texas. The Post Oak Belt lies west of both the Piney Woods and the Gulf Coast Plain. The belt has a similar climate to the Piney Woods but receives a little less rainfall. The area's soil is sandier, and its land is mostly flat. In addition, grassland prairies cover parts of the Post Oak Belt.

A few parts of the Post Oak Belt are covered in trees such as post oak, blackjack oak, elm, hickory, pecan, and walnut. Mesquite trees have become increasingly common in the Post Oak Belt. Early settlers cleared many of the subregion's native trees for farming. Cotton is a major crop in this area.

Other important crops are corn and sorghum—a grain grown to feed livestock. Livestock is a major industry in the Post Oak Belt, with many farmers raising cattle and hogs. The regional economy also depends on natural energy resources found underground, such as oil and natural gas. In addition, deposits of **lignite**, a type of soft coal, are mined there.

As in the Piney Woods, most residents of the Post Oak Belt live in rural areas. However, a number of towns and small cities are scattered throughout the area. The largest cities are Bryan–College Station and Tyler. Manufacturing industries such as food processing, furniture construction, and metalworking have developed in these cities. Texas A&M University, one of the state's top educational institutions, is located in this subregion.

Reading Check **Drawing Inferences and Conclusions** How have Texans changed and adapted to the environment of the Post Oak Belt?

Interpreting Visuals

Downtown Dallas.** Many corporations have located their headquarters in downtown Dallas.* ***How do you think these businesses have affected the growth of the city?

★ The Blackland Prairie

The Blackland Prairie subregion stretches west alongside the Post Oak Belt. The climate here is similar to the Post Oak Belt climate; it is wet and mild. Rolling prairies cover the landscape. The area's rich black soils make it ideal for farming. Farmers here grow cotton, grains, and vegetables. Farmers also raise cattle, chickens, and hogs.

The Blackland Prairie is one of the most heavily populated subregions in Texas. Its many cities include Dallas, Garland, Grand Prairie, Mesquite, Plano, Richardson, Sherman, Temple, and Waco. Dallas, which is located in the northern area of the Blackland Prairie, is the third-largest city in Texas. This city has many industries. Home to a Federal Reserve Bank, Dallas is the center of the banking industry in both Texas and most of the Southwest. Many national insurance and oil companies have their corporate headquarters there. Dallas is also a major center for the international cotton market. The computer age began there at Texas Instruments. The Dallas economy is based in part on the manufacture of items ranging from computer electronics to missile parts and high-fashion clothing.

Dallas lies 33 miles east of Fort Worth, a city in a neighboring subregion. The economies of the two cities—and the cities that surround them—are so interlinked that people refer to them as the **Metroplex**. The two cities are a major transportation hub. The Dallas–Fort Worth International Airport is located between them. Interstate 35 is an important trade route that runs through both Dallas and Fort Worth. The highway starts at the Mexican border and runs through the United States almost to Canada. The many roads and railroads around the Metroplex help to promote the area's growth.

Reading Check Evaluating How has transportation affected the Blackland Prairie region?

★ Section 2 Review

hmhsocialstudies.com
ONLINE QUIZ

1. Define and explain:
- subregions
- bayous
- petrochemicals
- lignite

2. Locate on a map:
- Rio Grande valley
- Piney Woods
- Gulf Coast Plain
- South Texas Plains
- Post Oak Belt
- Blackland Prairie

3. Categorizing
Copy the table below, adding a column for each subregion. Identify the subregions, their location, and their special physical and human features.

Subregion	
Location	
Special Physical and Human Features	

4. Finding the Main Idea

a. What industries have encouraged the growth of cities in the Coastal Plains region?

b. How are the South Texas Plains and the Blackland Prairie similar and different?

5. Writing and Critical Thinking myWriteSmart

Summarizing Compare the subregions of the Coastal Plains and describe how Texans have adapted to and modified their environments. Consider the following:
- climate, landscape, minerals, and soils
- human economic activity in each subregion

Section 3 The North Central Plains

Main Ideas

1. The Grand Prairie, Cross Timbers, and the Rolling Plains are the subregions found in the North Central Plains.
2. The physical features of the North Central Plains affect industry in the region.

Key Term

- **transportation center**

Why It Matters Today

Ranching is big business in the North Central Plains. Use current events sources to find information about ranching today.

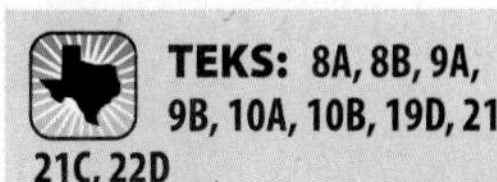
TEKS: 8A, 8B, 9A, 9B, 10A, 10B, 19D, 21B, 21C, 22D

myNotebook

Use the annotation tools in your eBook to take notes on the North Central Plains region.

The Geographer's World

In May 1849 U.S. Army major Ripley Arnold and a group of soldiers entered the Central Plains. Their orders were to build a fort on the Texas frontier. They traveled up the Trinity River, passing through a wild and beautiful prairie. Arnold decided to build the fort there. The outpost was named Fort Worth. Early visitors to the fort praised Arnold for choosing such a rich land for the settlement.

★ The Grand Prairie

The North Central Plains contains three main subregions: the Grand Prairie, the Cross Timbers, and the Rolling Plains. The Grand Prairie's climate is very similar to that of the Blackland Prairie to the east. However, the soil is thinner than that of the blacklands. The Grand Prairie is covered by grasses, shrubs, and small trees. These grasslands are particularly well suited for raising cattle. Other important livestock in this subregion include goats, hogs, poultry, and sheep. Although the area has an agricultural economy, the thin soil of the subregion limits crop production. Corn, oats, sorghum, and hay are grown primarily as animal feed. Farmers also grow cotton in some areas of this subregion.

Fort Worth is by far the largest city in the Grand Prairie and is also the largest city in the Texas Central Plains. The city plays a vital role in the subregion's economy. With some of the busiest rail yards in the nation, Fort Worth is a **transportation center**, or place where goods arrive to be shipped to many destinations. The city is also a major

Subregions of the North Central Plains

Interpreting Maps The Cross Timbers subregion forms two belts of forest land that divide the prairies of the Central Plains.

1. Locate What two major rivers create natural boundaries to the north and south of the North Central Plains region?

2. Drawing Inferences and Conclusions What do you think the number of cities in Eastern Cross Timbers says about the region's settlement patterns?

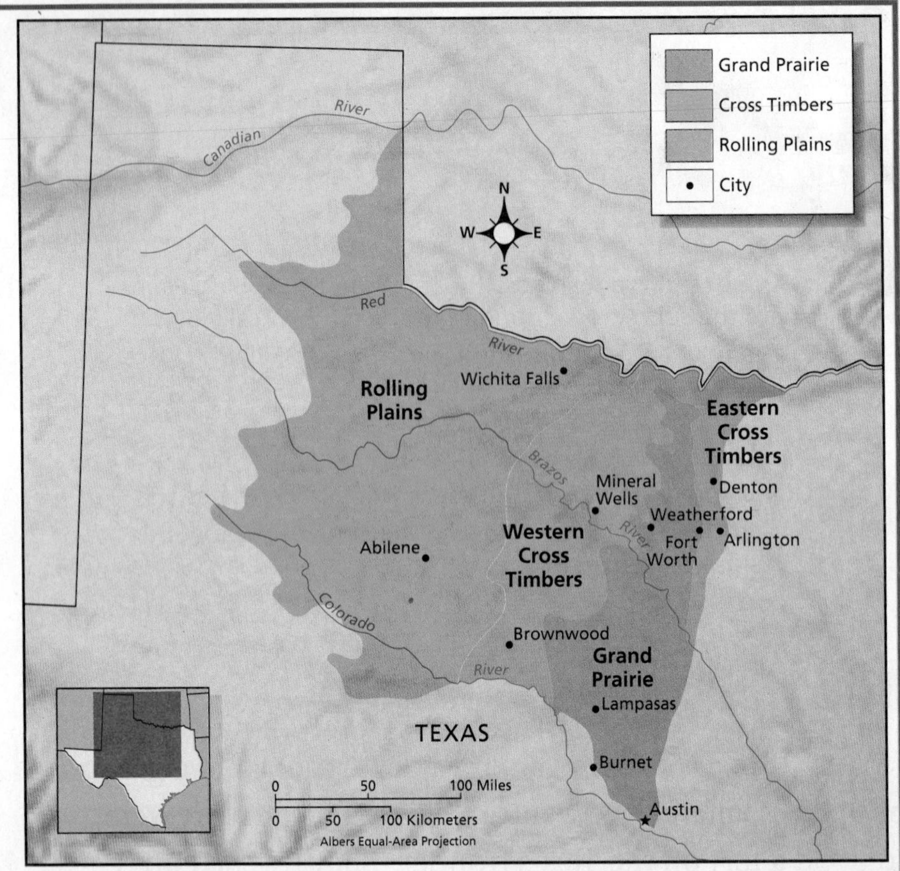

processing and transportation center for livestock and farm products. Most important, however, are Fort Worth's manufacturing industries. The city specializes in the manufacture of airplanes, electronics equipment, and helicopters.

Reading Check **Evaluating** How do the natural resources of the Grand Prairie affect its economy?

★ The Cross Timbers

Early visitors and settlers noted how the Cross Timbers forestland divided the surrounding prairie land. Two belts of forestland made up the Cross Timbers: the Western Cross Timbers and the Eastern Cross Timbers. The Western Cross Timbers lies west of the Grand Prairie. The Eastern Cross Timbers is located between the Grand Prairie and Blackland Prairie. The Eastern Cross Timbers is narrower than the Western Cross Timbers, averaging about 15 miles across.

When farmers moved into the region, they cut down many trees. Some of the native forest vegetation can still be found, however. The Eastern Cross Timbers contains some elms, hickories, and post oaks. Blackjack oak, cedar, hickory, mesquite, pecan, and post oak trees all grow in the drier Western Cross Timbers. The sandy soil of the Cross Timbers absorbs water well, making it a particularly good place for farming. Farmers grow crops ranging from peanuts to corn, cotton, and hay. Ranchers raise cattle, horses, and sheep there. Since 1917 the subregion has also provided Texas with energy resources such as oil and natural gas.

The Eastern Cross Timbers cuts the Metroplex in half, running between Dallas and Fort Worth. Cities such as Denton have manufacturing plants. While the Western Cross Timbers has no large cities, its towns include Brownwood and Mineral Wells.

Reading Check **Analyzing Information** How have farmers modified the landscape of the Cross Timbers subregion?

BIOGRAPHY

Walter Prescott Webb (1888–1963)
When Walter Prescott Webb was a child, his family moved from East Texas to the drier Central Plains. The differences between the two regions later influenced his work. After studying history at the University of Texas, Webb wrote and edited more than 20 books. His subjects varied from the Texas Rangers to the frontier to conservation of natural resources. **What was an early influence on Webb's research?**

★ The Rolling Plains

The Rolling Plains are located in the westernmost part of the Central Plains. Prairie grasses cover most of its hilly terrain. The thin soil of the subregion also supports some brush, hardwood trees, and mesquite trees. The Rolling Plains subregion is particularly well suited for cattle ranching. Steep valleys provide shelter for cattle, while the grasslands and rivers provide them with food and water. In areas with poorer vegetation, ranchers raise goats and sheep.

Where there is good farmland, farmers grow cotton, sorghum, and wheat. The Rolling Plains are also a source of oil and natural gas. The population of the Rolling Plains is much smaller than that of subregions in eastern Texas. Abilene and Wichita Falls are its largest cities. Both cities have meat and dairy processing facilities and serve as distribution centers for this subregion. Small market towns are also scattered throughout the area.

Reading Check **Comparing and Contrasting** How is the Rolling Plains subregion similar to and different from the Cross Timbers?

Section 3 Review

hmhsocialstudies.com
ONLINE QUIZ

1. Define and explain:
- transportation center

2. Locate on a map:
- Grand Prairie
- Cross Timbers
- Rolling Plains

3. Comparing and Contrasting
Copy the graphic organizer below. Use it to compare and contrast the physical and human features of the North Central Plains.

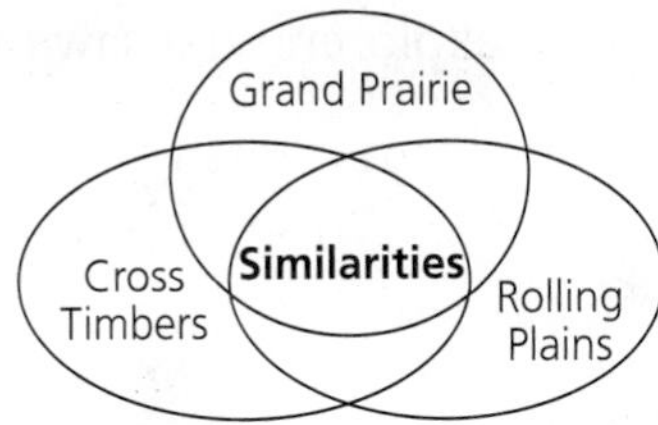

4. Finding the Main Idea

a. Compare the population distribution of the subregions found in the North Central Plains.

b. How have the region's geographic features affected its economy?

5. Writing and Critical Thinking myWriteSmart

Drawing Inferences and Conclusions Create a journal of a trip across the North Central Plains, explaining how life and the landscape differ between the subregions. Consider the following:
- the physical features of the region
- industries in each subregion

Section 4

The Great Plains

Main Ideas

1. The Great Plains region is divided into the High Plains and the Edwards Plateau subregions.
2. Texans have modified the region's environment to build and support its ranching and oil industries.

Key Terms and Places

- **Caprock**
- **escarpments**
- **fault**

Why It Matters Today

Erosion has affected the landscape of the Great Plains. Use current events sources to find information about erosion or other problems that farmers in Texas face today.

TEKS: 8A, 9A, 9B, 10A, 10B, 13C, 21B, 21C, 22A, 22D

myNotebook

Use the annotation tools in your eBook to take notes on the subregions of the Great Plains.

The Geographer's World

Gilbert Jordan grew up in a ranching community in the Hill Country. Ranch life was full of challenges. Weeds called cockleburs grew in nearby pastures and were a particular burden to ranchers. These burs get caught in the wool of the sheep and irritate cattle and horses. Ranchers had to pull cockleburs out of the pastures by hand. As Jordan remembers, "Pulling up cockleburs was a hot, mean job"—and every year the cockleburs would reappear in the pastures.

The High Plains

The Texas Great Plains includes two subregions: the High Plains and the Edwards Plateau. The High Plains subregion covers most of the Texas Panhandle. The land of the High Plains is higher than the Central Plains region. A hard bed of rock below the soil known as the **Caprock** is another noticeable physical feature in the area. Erosion of the rock has created cliffs—called **escarpments**—along its eastern and western sides. Over millions of years the Red River has cut a deep canyon into the Caprock. Palo Duro Canyon is at least 800 feet deep and more than 60 miles long. However, the High Plains subregion is mostly flat open prairie. When Spanish explorers first saw the High Plains they named it Llano Estacado.

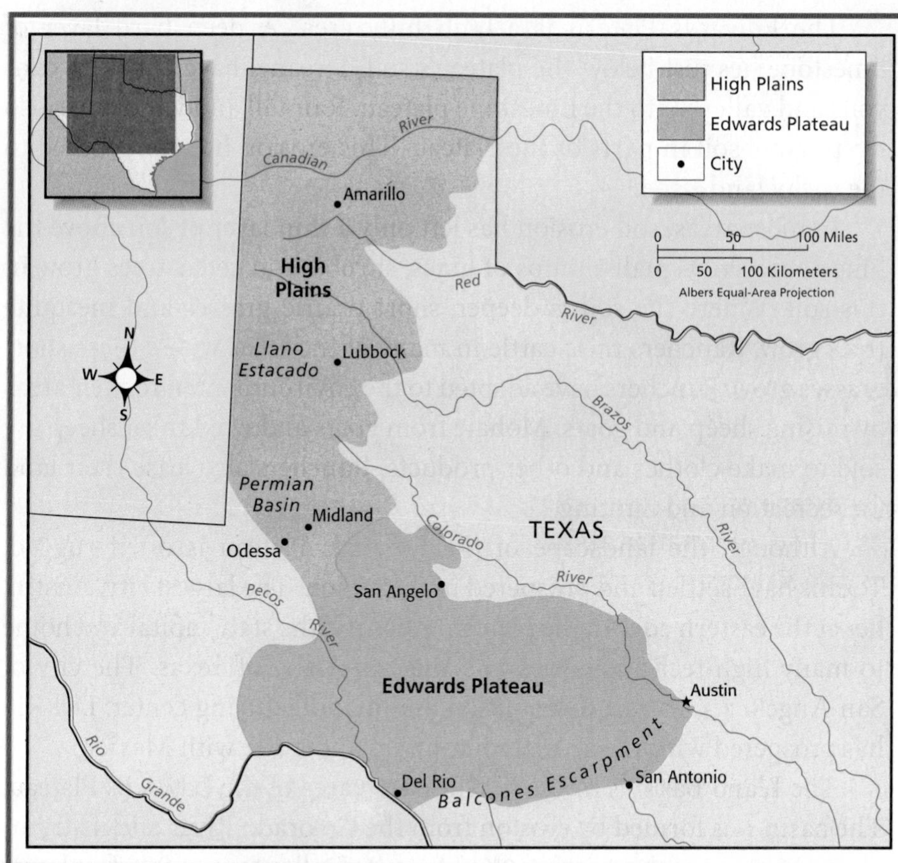

Subregions of the Great Plains

Interpreting Maps The Edwards Plateau has a more rugged landscape than the High Plains.

1. Locate What major landforms make up the Great Plains region?

2. Contrasting How do you think the landscape has affected the growth of cities in the Edwards Plateau subregion?

The High Plains receives little regular rainfall. Early settlers were certain that the land could not be farmed. However, the rich grassland did attract cattle ranchers. Today, feedlots—where cattle are raised on feed rather than grass—are scattered throughout the High Plains. In recent decades much of the grassland has been turned into farmland. Farmers pump water out of the Ogallala Aquifer to irrigate their fields of wheat and cotton.

Texans have discovered large deposits of oil and natural gas in the High Plains area. Oil wells dot the subregion. The few cities in the subregion provide services for the ranching, farming, and oil industries. For example, Lubbock and Amarillo serve as meat processing and distribution centers, while Midland and Odessa have several oil companies.

Reading Check **Finding the Main Idea** How have Texans adapted to and modified the environment of the High Plains?

Llano Estacado

Some historians once thought that *Llano Estacado* meant "Staked Plain." They believed that Spaniards used stakes to mark their path across the flat, treeless grassland. Other historians disagree. They doubt the Spanish could have found stakes on the treeless plains. Instead, they believe that *Llano Estacado* means "Stockaded Plain" and refers to the Caprock Escarpment, which looks like the wall of a fortress rising from the ground.

★ The Edwards Plateau

The Edwards Plateau subregion lies just south of the High Plains. The Edwards Plateau is separated from the Gulf Coastal Plain by the Balcones Escarpment. This limestone ridge lies on a **fault**, or break in Earth's crust. This fault extends up from the southwestern part of Texas through San Antonio and Austin.

CONNECTING TO

Literature

The Wind

Dorothy Scarborough

Folklorist and novelist Dorothy Scarborough wrote The Wind *in 1927. This excerpt describes the struggle of a pioneer woman in the Great Plains town of Sweetwater, where Scarborough grew up.*

For endless miles there seemed nothing but wind and sand and empty, far off sky. . . . But perhaps you do not understand the winds of West Texas. . . . Civilization has changed them. . . . Man, by building houses here and there upon the plains, by stretching fences, by planting trees, has broken the sweep of the wind. **What do you think life was like for Scarborough in Texas?**

The Edwards Plateau is a high hilly area. A deep hard layer of limestone lies just below the plateau's soil. Streams have cut deep canyons and valleys into the limestone plateau. Rainfall and wind have also swept away soil in parts of the plateau. This erosion has contributed to the rocky landscape.

In most areas, soil erosion has left only a thin layer of soil above the limestone. Only small clumps of grass, shrubs, and cedar trees grow in this soil. Where the soil is deeper, short prairie grasses and mesquite trees grow. Ranchers raise cattle in many of the areas where these short grasses grow. Ranchers have adapted to the environment in rockier areas by raising sheep and goats. Mohair from goats and wool from sheep are sold to make clothes and other products. Ranchers also lease their land for recreation and hunting.

Although the landscape of the Edwards Plateau is often rugged, Texans have settled and prospered in the region. The largest city, Austin, lies at the eastern edge of the plateau. Austin is the state capital and home to many high-tech industries and the University of Texas. The city of San Angelo serves as a distribution and manufacturing center. Del Rio has prospered with the growth of tourism and trade with Mexico.

The Llano Basin is in the northeastern area of the Edwards Plateau. The basin was formed by erosion from the Colorado River and its tributaries. Because of this erosion, the Llano Basin lies some 1,000 feet lower than the Edwards Plateau. There are few towns in the basin. Most residents are farmers or ranchers. Hunting and tourism also contribute to the basin's economy.

Reading Check **Analyzing Information** How has erosion affected the landscape of the subregion?

Section 4 Review

hmhsocialstudies.com
ONLINE QUIZ

1. Define and explain:
- Caprock
- escarpments
- fault

2. Locate on a map:
- High Plains
- Edwards Plateau

3. Categorizing Copy the graphic organizer below. Use it to identify, categorize, and compare the physical and human characteristics of the subregions of the Great Plains.

Subregion	Physical Characteristics	Human Characteristics

4. Finding the Main Idea

a. What are some common physical characteristics of the High Plains?

b. How does the physical geography of the High Plains affect the region's economy?

5. Writing and Critical Thinking my WriteSmart

Making Generalizations and Predictions Write a short editorial about the Great Plains, focusing on changes to the environment and potential consequences. Consider the following:
- how Texans modify the environment
- how erosion has affected the landscape of the Great Plains

Section 5

The Mountains and Basins

Main Ideas

1. The Mountains and Basins region is characterized by its dramatic landscape and dry desert climate.
2. The natural features of this region affect human activity there.

Key Terms and Places

- **basins**
- **Guadalupe Peak**
- **tourism**
- **Big Bend National Park**

Why It Matters Today

Big Bend National Park is one of the most popular tourist destinations in the region and the state. Use current events sources to find information about national parks.

TEKS: 8A, 9A, 9B, 10A, 10B, 13C, 21A, 21B, 21C, 22A, 22D

myNotebook

Use the annotation tools in your eBook to take notes on the features of the Mountains and Basins region.

The Geographer's World

The high mountains, deep canyons, and desert views of West Texas have excited the imaginations of Texans for years. According to one old story, a West Texas cowboy gave some strange directions to eastern visitors. "Go south from Fort Davis until you come to the place where rainbows wait for rain, and the big river is kept in a stone box, and water runs uphill." Despite the cowboy's directions, the confused visitors probably found their way and discovered the magical landscape of West Texas.

★ Mountains and Basins

The Mountains and Basins region dominates the landscape of far West Texas. Mountains, plateaus, **basins**, and canyons form the landscape of the subregion. A basin is a lowland surrounded by higher land. With its high mountains and low basins, the area's elevation varies greatly. The lowest point is in a canyon cut by the Rio Grande. The bottom of this canyon sits 1,700 feet above sea level. The highest point in this subregion and in Texas is **Guadalupe Peak**, which reaches 8,749 feet above sea level. The peak is part of the Guadalupe Mountains near the New Mexico border. The Davis Mountains rise in the central area of the region. Several peaks in the Davis Mountains reach more than 7,000 feet. The Chisos Mountains are near the Rio Grande.

The Mountains and Basins Region

Interpreting Maps This region is characterized by little rainfall and a dramatic desert landscape.

1. ***Locate*** Where is this Texas subregion located?
2. ***Drawing Inferences and Conclusions*** How do you think the environment has affected city growth in this subregion?

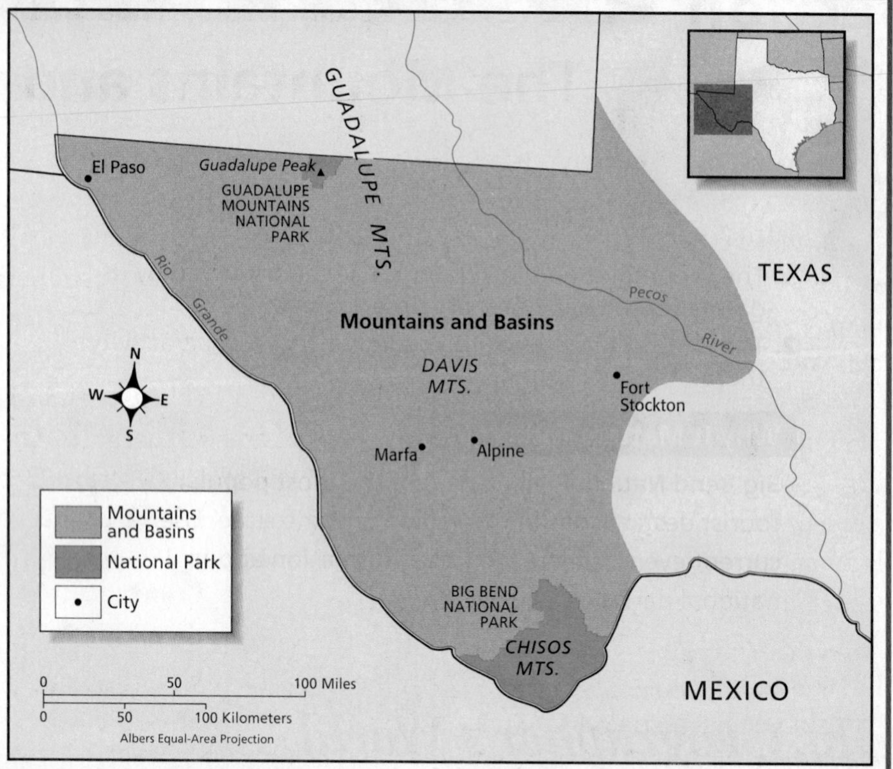

That's Interesting!

Vast Western Spaces

The Mountains and Basins region extends from the Rio Grande east to the Pecos River. Because most of the region lies west of the Pecos River, it is sometimes called the Trans-Pecos area. *Trans* means "across" or "beyond."

The climate of the region is also extreme. Summers are very hot, and winters can be cold. Whatever the temperature, this region is almost always dry. In the western areas of the region the average rainfall is less than 9 inches a year. The desert climate and landscape have limited the plant life in the area. Desert grasses, shrubs, mesquite trees, and cacti grow in the dry rocky soil.

The desert climate has also limited farming and ranching. Local ranches must be large because the desert grasses and plants offer a limited food source for cattle, sheep, and goats. Some Texans have managed to farm in the region by using irrigation. These farmers grow alfalfa, cotton, pecans, and vegetables. The region's economy has also been boosted by discoveries of oil, sulfur, and silver. The dramatic landscape has made **tourism** a large part of the economy. Tourism is the business of attracting visitors to a region or place.

The region has a small population and only a few small towns. The exception is El Paso, one of the largest cities in Texas. It sits along the Rio Grande in the westernmost corner of the state. Military bases and trade with Mexico have boosted the city's economy. In addition, Interstate 10—one of the most important U.S. highways—runs through El Paso. This major east–west shipping route has increased trade in the region.

Reading Check Evaluating How have Texans adapted to the geography and climate in the subregion?

Texas National Parks

Many businesses in El Paso have prospered by offering services to tourists. The beauty of the landscape also provides towns such as Alpine and Marfa with a major source of income. These towns serve as entrance points to one of the most popular tourist areas in Texas—**Big Bend National Park**. The park, which was named after its location in the bend of the Rio Grande, covers some 800,000 acres. Big Bend protects a wide variety of plants and animals, including the endangered peregrine falcon and the Mexican long-nosed bat.

Guadalupe Mountains National Park and Big Bend National Park offer many recreational activities, including bird-watching, camping, hiking, and river rafting. The National Park Service describes Big Bend as "the [most] outstanding scenic area of Texas." It has a dramatic landscape of towering peaks and deep river canyons. In 1899 geologist Robert T. Hill described one canyon there.

Interpreting Visuals

Big Bend National Park. *A variety of plant life exists within the park.* ***What types of vegetation can you identify?***

TEXAS VOICES

"The scene within this canyon is of unusual beauty. . . . The austerity [severeness] of the cliffs is softened by colors which camera or pen cannot reproduce. These rich tints are like the yellow marble of Portugal and Algiers, warmed by reddening tones which become golden in the sunlight."

—Robert T. Hill, quoted in *The Story of Big Bend National Park,* by John Jameson

Analyzing Primary Sources
Finding the Main Idea According to Hill, what attractions does Big Bend offer?

Reading Check **Summarizing** How have the landforms of the Mountains and Basins subregion affected the area's economy?

Section 5 Review

hmhsocialstudies.com
ONLINE QUIZ

1. **Define and explain:**
   - basins
   - tourism
2. **Locate on a map:**
   - Mountains and Basins region
   - Guadalupe Peak
   - El Paso
   - Big Bend National Park
3. **Identifying Cause and Effect**
   Copy the graphic organizer below. Use it to identify how the physical features of the subregion limit some economic activities and support others.

   Physical Characteristics
   Economic Limits | Economic Benefits

4. **Finding the Main Idea**
   a. What are the physical features of the region?
   b. Why are tourism and national parks important to the Mountains and Basins subregion?
5. **Writing and Critical Thinking** myWriteSmart
   Drawing Inferences and Conclusions Imagine that you are writing a story about the history of El Paso. Write a short paragraph describing why the population is limited in the region and why El Paso has grown. Consider the following:
   - how geography limited the region's population
   - the industries and other economic factors that have led to El Paso's growth

CHAPTER 3 REVIEW

The Chapter at a Glance

Examine the following visual summary of the chapter. Then discuss the main ideas of the chapter with a partner. If you cannot remember a particular word during your discussion, try to find another word that has the same meaning.

Natural Regions of Texas

Great Plains

North Central Plains

Mountains and Basins

Coastal Plains

Identifying Ideas

Review the meanings of the following terms.

1. natural regions
2. subregions
3. petrochemicals
4. Metroplex
5. Caprock
6. escarpments
7. Guadalupe Peak
8. tourism

Understanding Main Ideas

Section 1

1. Identify and describe the location of the four natural regions found in Texas.

Section 2

2. How have geographic factors led to urban growth in the Coastal Plains?

Section 3

3. What features of the North Central Plains affect its economy?

Section 4

4. How have the physical features of the Edwards Plateau limited human activities in the region?

Section 5

5. How does the landscape of the Mountains and Basins region affect the economy there?

You Be the Geographer

Reviewing Themes

1. **Geography** Identify some of the positive and negative consequences of Texans' modifications of the environment.
2. **Economics** Explain ways in which geographic factors have affected the economic development of Texas.
3. **Science, Technology & Society** In what ways have Texans adapted to the environment?

Thinking Critically

1. **Comparing and Contrasting** How are the physical and human characteristics of the Mountains and Basins region similar to and different from those of the Great Plains region?
2. **Analyzing Information** Driving from the Coastal Plains into the North Central Plains, how would the landscape change during your trip?
3. **Categorizing** What economic and geographic factors have contributed to the growth of cities in the Coastal Plains region?

Texas Test Practice

Interpreting Maps

Study the map below. Then use the information on the map to help answer the questions that follow.

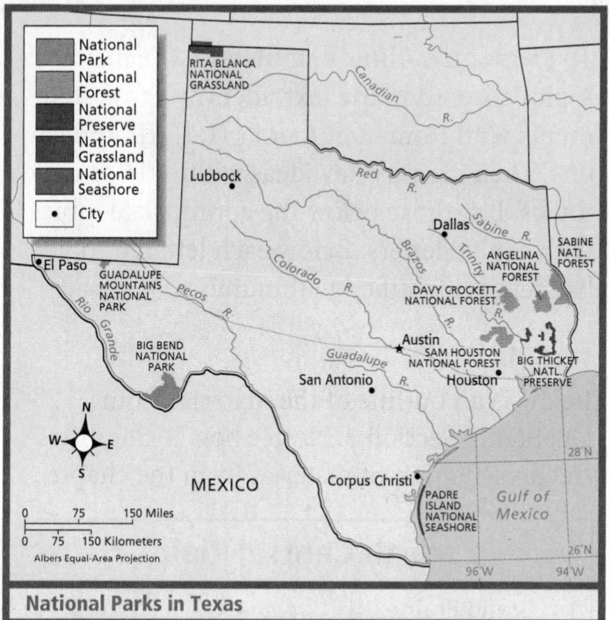

National Parks in Texas

1. Which region has the most national forests?
   - **A** Great Plains
   - **B** Mountains and Basins
   - **C** Coastal Plains
   - **D** North Central Plains

2. How does the physical geography of the state change from west to east?

Analyzing Primary Sources

Read the following quote by Walter Prescott Webb and answer the following questions.

"A plains environment is . . . sub-humid [dry] . . . The Great Plains offered such a contrast to the [eastern] regions . . . as to bring about a marked change in the ways of pioneering and living. For two centuries American pioneers had been working out a technique for the utilization [use] of the humid regions east of the Mississippi River. . . . Then . . . they . . . came out on the Great Plains, an environment with which they had had no experience. . . . The ways of travel, the weapons, the method of tilling the soil, the plows and other agricultural implements, and even the laws themselves were modified."

3. In what ways did settlers have to adapt to deal with the physical features of the Great Plains?
   - **F** They had to develop new methods of farming in dry regions.
   - **G** They changed the farming practices they used in the East only slightly.
   - **H** The settlers were unable to farm.
   - **J** They had to develop new methods for farming in wet regions.

4. How do you think these early pioneers modified the environment of the Great Plains?

Cooperative Learning

Work with a small group to complete the following activity. Each person in your group should select one of the following regions of Texas: a) Coastal Plains b) North Central Plains c) Great Plains d) Mountains and Basins. Each member should complete a model that shows the region's features, including natural resources, economic activities, educational institutions, and recreational opportunities in the area. Then work together as a group to create a brochure that compares the regions for tourists.

Internet Activity 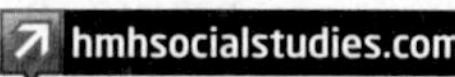

Use the Internet to research the location, wildlife, land features, and main cities of a region in Texas. Then create a radio script in which you tell an audience about your region. You might want to record your radio script. Make sure you cover each of the topics written above and use standard spelling, sentence structure, grammar, and punctuation.

Social Studies Skills

WORKSHOP

Using Reports and Outlines

During your study of Texas history, you will encounter a great deal of information. Some of that information will be presented in a clear and straightforward manner. Some of it, though, may take a little more effort to fully understand.

Reports are simple presentations of information. A report generally lists only facts without interpretation or opinions. Many government agencies produce reports to share information about the state of affairs within an area. Listed below are guidelines that will help you interpret any reports you may encounter this year.

1. **Determine who created the report.** Knowing who is presenting information can help you understand its significance.
2. **Understand the topic.** Read the title and opening of the report carefully. You can usually determine the main idea of the report from these pieces.
3. **Examine how the information is organized.** Does the report list events in the order they occurred? Does it list points in order of importance?
4. **Reorganize the information.** If you are unclear about the meaning of the report, try reorganizing the information it contains in a different form. That may help clarify what you have read.

Outlines can help you make sense of more complicated text. An outline is a visual representation of the main ideas and details found in a written text. If you find yourself confused by the material you are reading, it many help to stop and create an outline of the text. Seeing the information in outline form many help you interpret what the author is trying to say.

To create an outline, first identify the major topics covered in the text. Identify those statements with Roman numerals (I, II, III and so on). Then identify key ideas within those major topics. List those below the appropriate topics with capital letters. Below each lettered topic, list details identified with numbers.

Example

Below is an outline of the material from Chapter 3, Section 3. Notice how it simplifies the presentation of material from the chapter.

North Central Plains

I. Grand Prairie
   A. Wet, mild climate
   B. Covered in grasslands
      1. Good for raising cattle
      2. Limited crop production
   C. Fort Worth is largest city
II. Cross Timbers
   A. Forestland
   B. Good agricultural area
   C. Two divisions
      1. Eastern Cross Timbers
      2. Western Cross Timbers
III. Rolling Plains
   A. Covered in prairie grasses
   B. Well suited for cattle ranching
   C. Some farming

Practicing the Skill

Chapter 2, Section 3 describes where Texans live. Find a report online about settlement patterns in Texas. Write a statement about the author's main point. Then prepare an outline of the information in the report. Trade outlines with a classmate. From the outline you have received, can you interpret what your partner's report was about?

History in Action

UNIT 1 SIMULATION

You Solve the Problem . . .

How can you help the state's parks?

Complete the following activity in small cooperative groups. You and several other members of your community want to ensure that Texas state parks are well maintained. Your group would like to encourage other Texans to help in the effort. Follow these steps to solve your problem.

1. Gather information. Use your textbook, Web sites, government reports, and other resources to find information that might influence your plan of action for preserving the state's parks. Create an outline to organize the information you have found. Be sure to use what you learned from this unit's Skills Workshop on Using Reports and Outlines to help you interpret information a find an effective solution to this problem. You may want to divide up different parts of the research among group members.

2. List and consider options. Review the information you have gathered, and then list and consider the options you might recommend for successfully convincing Texans to take action to maintain their state parks. Your solution to the problem may be easier to reach if you consider as many options as possible. Record possible options that you could present on a poster.

3. Consider the advantages and disadvantages. Now consider the advantages and disadvantages of taking each option. Ask yourselves questions such as, "How will working together help the state's parks?" Once you have considered the advantages and disadvantages, record them as notes for use in preparing your poster.

4. Choose, implement, and evaluate a solution. After considering the advantages and disadvantages, prepare your poster. Clearly state your reasons for urging Texans to help maintain their state parks. You will need to support your reasons with information you gathered and explanations of why you rejected other options. Your poster needs to be visually appealing to attract the attention of other Texans. When you are ready, decide which group members will present the poster, and then take your solution to the community (the rest of the class).

As an audience member, listen carefully as other groups present their posters. Take notes about what each group is saying in its presentation. If you are unclear about what a group has said or if you want more details about its proposal, ask the group members for more information. After the class has asked its questions, vote on whether you would accept the group's proposal.

UNIT 2

The Spanish in Texas

(BEGINNINGS–1821)

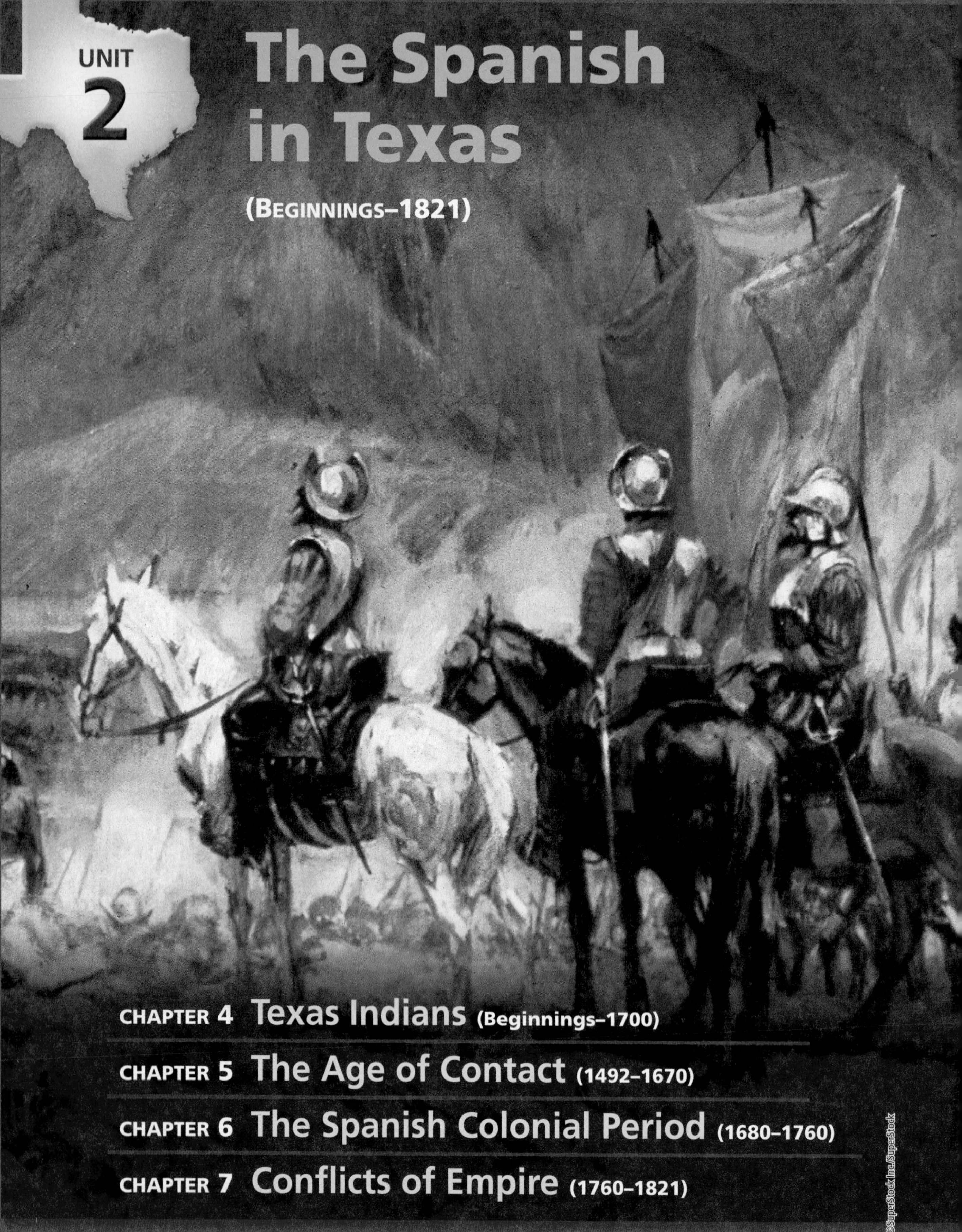

Francisco Vásquez de Coronado and more than 300 Spanish soldiers set out across Texas in search of gold and American Indian settlements.

Texas Teens

Young American Indians

Old Spanish accounts tell of a helpful young American Indian woman known only as Angelina. This was not her birth name. She was given the name Angelina, which means "little angel," for her eagerness to help the Europeans and to learn their language.

Angelina belonged to an American Indian group called the Hasinai, part of a larger body known as the Caddo Confederacy. Like many American Indians, her family traveled widely. At various times in her life she is believed to have lived in areas as far apart as Coahuila, Mexico, and East Texas.

It was in East Texas that she encountered Spanish explorers Alonso de León and Father Massanet around 1690. The men had traveled to the region to introduce Christianity and Spanish customs to the American Indians there. They built a mission called San Francisco de los Tejas as a base for their efforts. To their joy, Angelina was willing to become a Christian. She also learned both Spanish and French and was able to serve as a interpreter for other explorers through the area.

Angelina continued to help explorers, both Spanish and French, for many years. Various Europeans who traveled through Texas during this period reported encountering a helpful Caddo woman named Angelina. Their reports praise her for her intelligence and her wisdom. At times she may have lived and traveled with these explorers and missionaries.

Angelina made such an impression on the priests that they named a river after her, the Angelina. She is one of only a few American Indians honored by the Spanish in this way. The county of Angelina and the Angelina State Forest also bear her name today. A bronze statue honoring her can be found in Lufkin, across from the Museum of East Texas. **What role did Angelina play in Texas history?**

In this unit you will learn more about American Indians and Spanish settlement in Texas. You will also learn about the interactions between American Indians and the first European explorers and settlers.

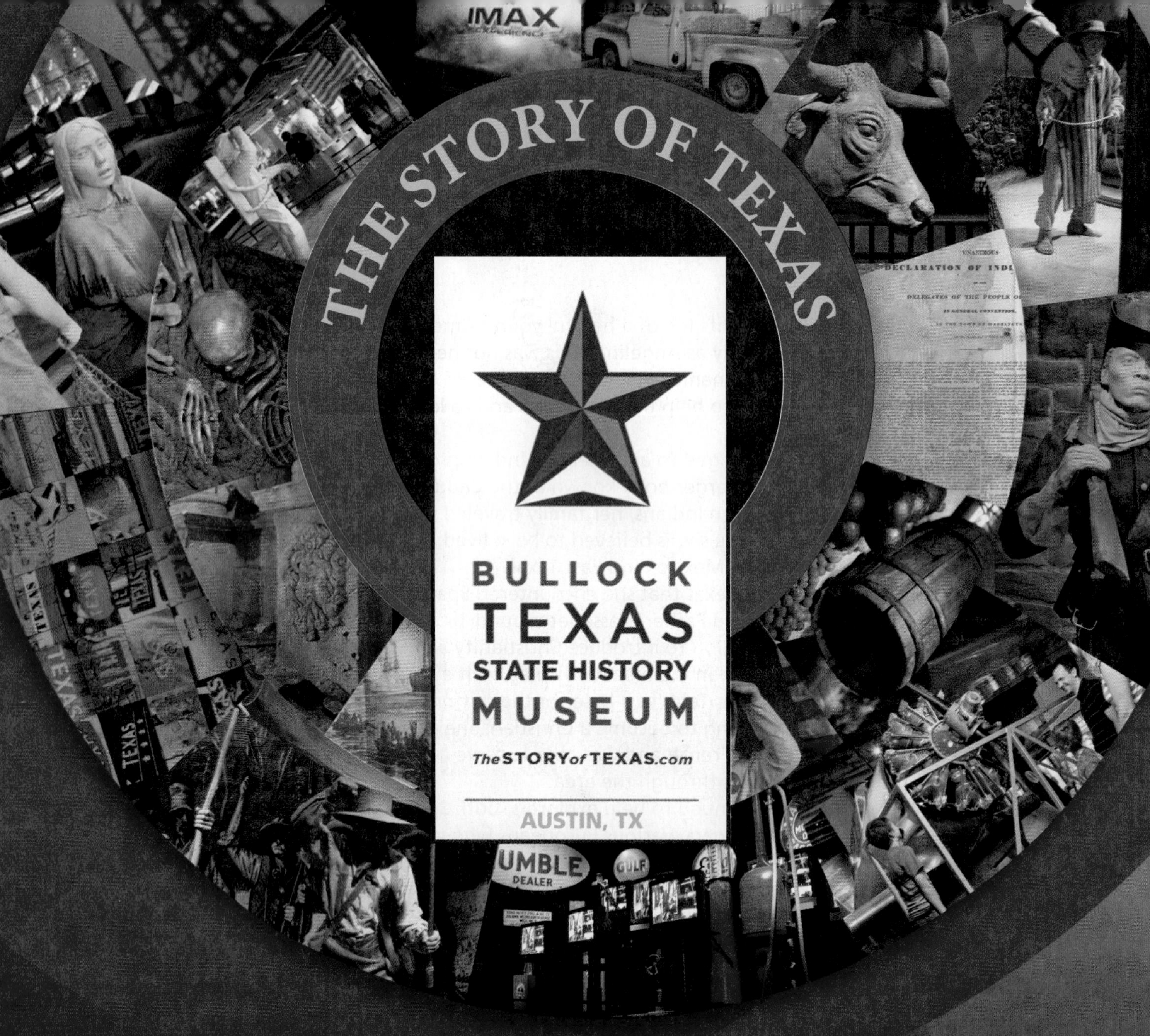

La Belle: Doomed from the Start

On a stormy day in 1686 a French ship named *La Belle* sank in Matagorda Bay, Texas. It was part of an expedition led by explorer René-Robert Cavelier, Sieur de la Salle. *La Belle* had sailed from France with three other ships and about 300 people to establish a French colony at the mouth of the Mississippi River. Because of poor planning, inaccurate maps, and bad luck, the expedition actually ended up in Texas, some 400 miles away from its intended target. Along with its passengers, *La Belle* carried a wide range of supplies to start a new colony. These supplies included woodworking tools, gunpowder, cannon balls, bottles, cups, plates, and more.

La Salle's expedition seemed destined for disaster. On the way, one ship was captured by pirates in the Caribbean. Then another ship ran aground and was lost, and a third returned to France. Only the supply ship *La Belle* was left. Despite losing all their ships, the colonists tried to set up a new colony, Fort St. Louis. La Salle and some of his crew left the struggling colony in search of the Mississippi. However, in 1687, La Salle was murdered by one of his own men.

Those left behind at the colony did not do well. They had little food, and many colonists were sick. Some were killed by local Indians. When *La Belle* ran aground and sank, they lost many of their remaining supplies and any chance of returning to France. By 1687, only 20 colonists remained alive at Fort St. Louis. In the end, the French attempt to build a colony failed.

Exploring Museum Resources

After it sank, *La Belle* and its cargo lay in the murky waters of Matagorda Bay for more than 300 years. Then, in 1995, a team of archaeologists found the lost ship and began the long, slow process of excavating one of the most important shipwrecks ever discovered in North American waters. Explore some of the artifacts from *La Belle* online. You can find museum resources at **hmhsocialstudies.com**

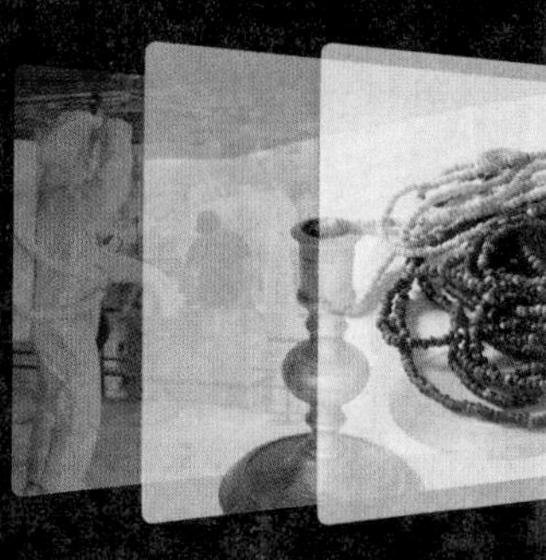

Artifact What did this cannon reveal about the *La Belle* shipwreck? Go online to find the answer and see more artifacts.

Artifact Why did French colonists bring thousands of glass beads like these with them on their journey to the New World?

Artifact Go online to see what these candlesticks reveal about La Salle's failed expedition.

Chronology and Sequence

Focus on Reading History, just like our lives, can be seen as a series of events in time. To understand history and events, we often need to see how they are related in time.

Understanding Chronology and Sequence In order to understand history, it is important to understand chronology, or the order in which people, events, and time periods lived or occurred. There are two different ways to keep track of chronology as you read. One way uses specific dates—like the dates on a time line—to note when events happened and how much time passed between them. This is called **absolute chronology**. The other way does not include dates. Instead, it simply notes the order in which events happened. This is called **relative chronology** or **sequence**. As you read, you can use a sequence chain like the one below to keep events clear in your mind.

Writers sometimes signal relative chronology, or sequence, by using words or phrases like these:
first, before, then, later, soon, after, before long, next, eventually, finally

Sequence Chain

1519: Alonso Álvarez de Pineda maps the coast of Texas.

↓

1527: Pánfilo de Narváez leads an expedition to the Gulf of Mexico.

↓

1542: Álvar Núñez Cabeza de Vaca publishes an account of his travels to Texas.

You Try It!

The following passage is from the unit you are about to read. Read the passage carefully and think about order of events.

Moscoso Explores East Texas

While Coronado marched to the cities of Cíbola from the south, a group led by Spanish explorer Hernando de Soto sought them from the east. De Soto and some 600 soldiers had landed on the Florida coast in 1539. For more than two years they had explored what is now the southeastern United States. Then in May 1542 de Soto died of fever. Luis de Moscoso Alvarado, another member of the group, took command.

Because the expedition had not found any treasure, Moscoso decided to head to Mexico City. He led the explorers west into East Texas, where they met many Caddo Indians. Soon, however, the explorers began having trouble finding food.

After you read the passage, answer the questions that follow.

1. Arrange the following events in the order in which they occurred: the expedition heads for Mexico City; de Soto dies; the expedition arrives in Florida; Moscoso takes over. Is this chronology absolute or relative? How can you tell?
2. Did the explorers' food troubles begin before or after they traveled to East Texas? What word or words indicate that?

Reading Section Assessment

1. What is the difference between absolute and relative chronology?
2. Use the dates in the passage above to create a time line of the Moscoso expedition. Is this an example of an absolute or relative chronology?
3. Use the list of governors that begins on page R1 in the back of this book to arrange the following people in the order in which they served: Miriam A. Ferguson, Sam Houston, Mark White, Lawrence Sullivan Ross, David G. Burnet.

Key Terms

Unit 2

Chapter 4

historians *(p. 68)*
eras *(p. 68)*
prehistory *(p. 70)*
anthropologists *(p. 70)*
archaeologists *(p. 70)*
hunter-gatherers *(p. 72)*
nomads *(p. 72)*
wigwams *(p. 73)*
mitotes *(p. 74)*
confederacies *(p. 76)*
matrilineal *(p. 76)*
adobe *(p. 79)*
tepees *(p. 82)*

Chapter 5

conquistadores *(p. 91)*
viceroy *(p. 98)*
epidemics *(p. 105)*
mustangs *(p. 105)*

Chapter 6

missions *(p. 112)*
presidios *(p. 113)*
ranchos *(p. 113)*
revolt *(p. 114)*
ayuntamiento (p. 130)
alcalde *(p. 130)*
vaqueros *(p. 131)*

Chapter 7

cede *(p. 136)*
diplomats *(p. 142)*
filibusters *(p. 144)*
siege *(p. 145)*
jacales *(p. 151)*

As you read, ask your teacher for assistance with words or passages you do not understand.

CHAPTER 4

Texas Indians

(Beginnings–1700)

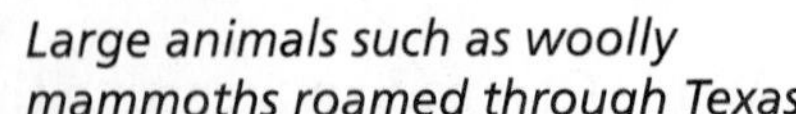

Large animals such as woolly mammoths roamed through Texas.

Texas Essential Knowledge and Skills (TEKS) 1A, 1B, 2A, 8A, 9B, 10A, 19C, 20A, 21B, 21C, 22A, 22B, 22D

TEXAS

c. 10,000 B.C. Proto-Indians live at the Gault site.

c. 1500 B.C. Coastal American Indians make knives and scrapers from stone.

c. A.D. 100 American Indians living near Galveston Bay begin making pottery.

10,000 B.C. | **1500 B.C.** | **500 B.C.** | **A.D. 500**

U.S. and WORLD

c. 1000 B.C. A clay tablet made in Babylon is an early attempt to create a map of the world.

c. A.D. 1 American Indians now known as the Hohokam create farming communities in present-day Arizona.

If you were there . . .

How would you survive in early Texas?

Build on What You Know

Environments in Texas vary widely between regions. Some regions are good for farming, while others are too dry. American Indians adapted to these regions in many ways. The food they ate, the homes they lived in, and the tools they used reflected their environments.

Early Texans used flint to make weapons and tools like this arrowhead.

Caddo Indians had a complex society based on farming.

c. A.D. 1000
The Caddos grow many kinds of crops in East Texas.

A.D. 1528
Europeans arrive in Texas and encounter the Karankawas.

A.D. 1000 — **A.D. 1200** — **A.D. 1400** — **A.D. 1600**

c. A.D. 900
The Anasazis start building large houses in Chaco Canyon in present-day New Mexico.

A.D. 1492
Explorer Christopher Columbus reaches islands off the southeastern coast of present-day Florida.

You Be the Historian

myNotebook

What's Your Opinion? Do you **agree** or **disagree** with the following statements? Support your point of view in your notebook.

- **Geography** People doing the same work in different regions lead similar lives.
- **Culture** People who rely on the same resources for survival are always the same culturally.
- **Science, Technology & Society** Changes in technology affect a group's culture.

Section 1

The First Texans

Main Ideas

1. Historians organize the past into eras to make their studies more manageable.
2. Anthropologists and archaeologists study the remains of early cultures to learn about the first Texans.

Why It Matters Today

The American Indians were the first people to live in Texas, long before anyone else arrived. Use current events sources to learn more about issues facing American Indians in the state today.

Key Terms

- **historians**
- **eras**
- **prehistory**
- **anthropologists**
- **archaeologist**
- **artifacts**
- **Paleo-Indians**

TEKS: 1A, 1B, 2A, 8A, 21B, 21C, 22D

myNotebook

Use the annotation tools in your eBook to take notes on how historians and others study the past.

The Story Begins

In the 1930s a work crew digging out an old streambed near Lubbock uncovered animal bones and a spearhead. Curious, they took the spearhead to a professor at a nearby university. The professor realized that the workers had made an exciting discovery. They had found proof that people had lived in the area for more than 12,000 years!

Studying the Past

Texas has a long history—more than 12,000 years long. Obviously, people living that long ago did not live like we do today. They had no electronics and no money. The earliest people did not even have farms to grow food. Such advances came with the passing of centuries.

Historians—people who study the past—examine how people and societies change over time. They study how people lived, worked, and thought. But 12,000 years is a long span of time to study. To make their work manageable, historians divide the past into shorter periods called **eras**. If you think of history as a long book, each era is like a chapter. Eras can be of any length. One might be only a few years long. Another might span hundreds of years. The chart on the next page lists major eras in Texas history. How do historians decide what makes an era? They look for a block of time that has some defining characteristic. It might be a political distinction, such as the time Texas belonged to Spain. It might be cultural or economic, like when oil dominated the Texas economy.

Some eras are defined by specific events. For example, the Mexican National Period began when Mexico won its independence from Spain. It ended when Texas formed its own country. Other eras have less defined time spans. The era of Cotton, Cattle, and Railroads refers to a time when farming and ranching were central to the Texas economy. No particular events mark its beginning or end. Because some eras have no clear start or end dates, they can overlap, as you can see on the chart.

Every historian views the past differently. As a result, two historians might divide their studies differently. The chart below shows one way to organize Texas history, but it is not the only way. There is no single way to organize the study of the past.

Reading Check **Finding the Main Idea** What are eras, and how are they useful to historians?

ERAS IN TEXAS HISTORY

ERA	DATES	DEFINING CHARACTERISTICS
Natural Texas and Its People	Before 1528	Before Europeans arrived in Texas, American Indians lived in the region. They built complex societies in many parts of the state.
Age of Contact	1528–1690	When Spanish explorers arrived in Texas in 1528, they met American Indians for the first time. The contact between the Spanish and American Indians during this period set the stage for future relations between the groups.
Spanish Colonial Period	1690–1821	During this era, the Spanish worked to establish control of Texas. They built missions, forts, and other settlements. Their efforts sometimes resulted in conflict with American Indians, the French, and others.
Mexican National Period	1821–1836	This era began when Mexico won its independence from Spain. The Mexican government worked during this time to encourage settlement in Texas and to maintain control of the area.
Revolution and Republic	1835–1845	During this era, Texans rebelled against the Mexican government and won their independence. The new Republic of Texas then had to figure out how to deal with the challenges confronting a young country.
Early Statehood	1845–1861	The Early Statehood era began when Texas joined the United States in 1845. The state faced several challenges during this period, including war, boundary disputes, and population increases.
Texas in the Civil War and Reconstruction	1861–1874	In 1861 Texas withdrew from the United States. It fought on the side of the South during the Civil War. The period of Reconstruction that followed caused great changes in the state's economy, society, and government.
Cotton, Cattle, and Railroads	1865–1900	During this era, the Texas economy recovered from the Civil War. Cotton farming and cattle ranching were major industries. The expansion of railroads helped both industries to grow.
Age of Oil	1894–1935	The discovery of vast oil fields in Texas led to major changes in the state's economy. The wealth that oil brought to Texas increased the state's influence in the country and the world.
Texas in the Great Depression and World War II	1929–1945	During this era, Texans suffered severe economic hardship brought on by the Great Depression. World War II brought economic revival and led to cultural changes in the state.
Civil Rights and Conservatism	1945–1980	Following World War II, various groups within Texas called for equality and social change. State politics changed as Texans increasingly began to side with the conservative Republican Party.
Contemporary Texas	Since 1980	The period since 1980 has seen significant economic and political growth in Texas. New issues and conflicts challenge Texans as they move toward the future.

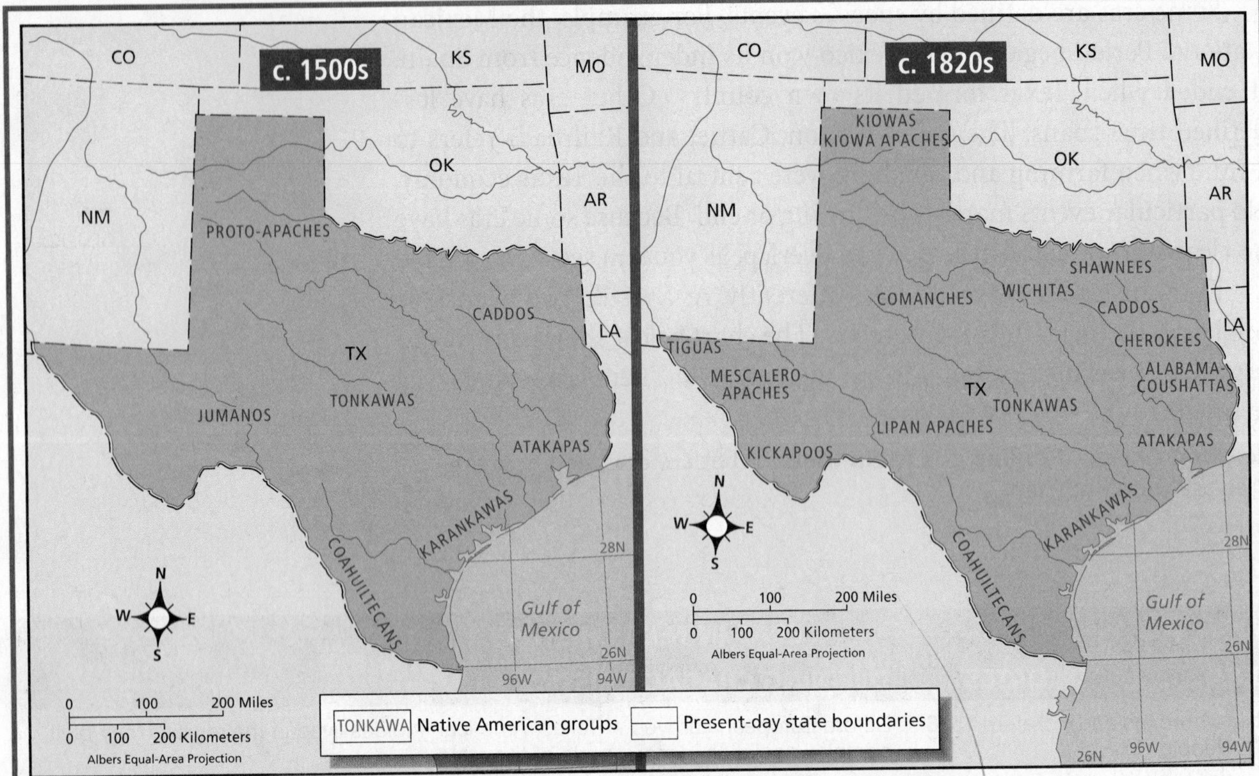

American Indians in Texas, c. 1500s and c. 1820s

Interpreting Maps The westward migration of settlers in North America forced new American Indian groups to move to parts of Texas in which other groups had not yet settled.

Human Systems How did the distribution of American Indian groups in the 1820s compare to their distribution in the 1500s? What factors might account for the changes?

★ The First Texans

As you have read, people have lived in Texas for more than 12,000 years. The earliest Texans lived long before the invention of writing. They left no written records behind to explain how they lived. We refer to this period before written records as **prehistory**.

Rock art from Seminole Canyon State Park

Even without records, we have learned a great deal about how early Texans lived. Most of what we know comes from the work of scholars called **anthropologists**. They want to understand how people live and relate to each other, whether today or in the past. One type of anthropologist, the **archaeologist**, studies the objects that people in the past left behind. Archaeologists sift through layers of earth and explore the oceans looking for **artifacts**—tools, weapons, and other objects made by people. Artifacts give clues about how people lived in the distant past.

Some artifacts had clear uses. Arrowheads, for example, were used for hunting and fighting. Axes and choppers were handy tools. Other artifacts are not so easy to understand. In parts of Texas, including the Pecos River valley, Seminole Canyon, and Big Bend, scholars have found images painted onto or carved into stone. These images often show important events, such as hunts or wars. Some use vividly colored paints made from local rocks. Archaeologists are not sure what the meaning of this rock art is. Some think the art was used to teach lessons. Others think it may have been part of religious rituals.

A few sites in Texas have proved to be particularly valuable to our study of the **Paleo-Indians**, another name for the first Americans. (*Paleo* means "old" or "ancient.") One such site is Lubbock Lake in the High Plains region. Hundreds of fossils found in that region have helped scholars learn about the types of animals early people hunted. Another valuable site is called the Gault site. Just west of Georgetown, it is filled with artifacts of the Clovis culture. The Clovis culture appeared in North America between 11,000 and 12,000 years ago. Not far away from Gault in Salado, diggers at the Buttermilk Creek site have found even older artifacts. These could be as old as 15,500 years, created long before the Clovis culture developed.

Over the centuries, Paleo-Indian culture changed. Many animals that early people hunted, including mammoths and giant bison, became extinct. As a result, people had to adapt to new ways of life. In the process, they developed distinct cultures with their own languages and belief systems.

Groups moved into and out of Texas. Some moved in search of new lands, while others were forced to leave their old lands. The maps on the previous page show the movement of some American Indian groups in Texas. Because many groups lived in the same area, they tended to develop some similar culture traits. Bands that lived in the same area and shared customs are called culture groups. You will learn more about some of the culture groups that lived in Texas in the following sections.

Reading Check **Analyzing Information** How do anthropologists and archaeologists learn about the distant past?

Alibates Flint Quarries

The Alibates flint quarries are located in the central Panhandle of Texas. The flint beds cover about 10 square miles. American Indians used Alibates flint to make tools and weapons. Spearheads made from Alibates flint have been found as far away as Colorado. In 1965 the flint quarries were declared a national monument. Today visitors can see waste flint, broken tools, and stones that American Indians used as hammers. Why has Alibates flint been found far away from the quarries?

Section 1 Review

hmhsocialstudies.com
ONLINE QUIZ

1. Define and explain:
- historians
- eras
- prehistory
- anthropologists
- archaeologist
- artifacts

2. Identify and explain the significance of the following in Texas history:
- Paleo-Indians

3. Sequencing
Copy the graphic organizer below. Use it to identify, in sequence, the major eras in Texas history. For each era, list its defining characteristics.

Era	Defining Characteristics

4. Finding the Main Idea
a. Why do historians divide the past into eras?
b. What have archaeologists discovered about Paleo-Indians in Texas?

5. Writing and Critical Thinking myWriteSmart
Analyzing Information Identify one particular era of Texas history that you would like to study. Write a paragraph describing why you find that era interesting.
Consider the following:
- the eras into which Texas history is divided
- the events and ideas that define each era of Texas history

Section 2

The Western Gulf Culture Area

Main Ideas

1. The Karankawas, who lived along the Gulf Coast, hunted and gathered plants to survive.
2. The Coahuiltecans lived in dry southern Texas.

Key Terms and People

- **hunter-gatherers**
- **nomads**
- **wigwams**
- **mitotes**

Why It Matters Today

American Indians near the Texas coast knew that the Gulf of Mexico could be a major food source. Use current events sources to learn about commercial fishing in the Gulf today.

TEKS: 2A, 9B, 10A, 21B, 22D

***my*Notebook**

Use the annotation tools in your eBook to take notes on the cultures that lived near the Gulf Coast.

The Story Continues

A mystery had arisen. Archaeologists working near Corpus Christi had found several human skeletons. Who were these people? The archaeologists identified them as the remains of Karankawa Indians. But another puzzle remained. One skeleton came from a person who was six feet tall, taller than the average early American Indian. The others were also unusually large for people of their time. Scientists struggled to explain why the Karankawa were larger.

★ The Karankawas

Known for their height, the Karankawas were hunter-gatherers who lived from the area near present-day Galveston south to Corpus Christi Bay. **Hunter-gatherers** are people who hunt wild animals and gather plants for food. The Karankawas fished, hunted sea turtles, and collected shellfish. They also gathered eggs and hunted deer and small animals.

The Karankawas were **nomads**, or people who moved from place to place. Within the Karankawa home range were a variety of ecosystems. Different parts of this territory were better suited to life at different times of the year. Each season, the Karankawas relocated to a region that could provide everything they needed to live at that time of the year. They had designated camp sites to which they returned every year as the seasons changed. During the fall and winter months when fish were plentiful, they lived along the Gulf Coast. They used dugout canoes to paddle through the bays and inlets. During the spring and summer, when herds of bison and deer were more common, they moved inland. Because of this migration, the Karankawas enjoyed a rich and varied diet, which may help explain their large stature. A French explorer described a summer among the Karankawas.

TEXAS VOICES

"I passed the entire summer in this country with them in going everywhere in search of food because they possess no cabins or fields. That is why they travel in this manner the entire summer. The men kill a few deer and a few buffaloes and the women search for wild potatoes."

—Simars de Bellisle, quoted in *The Karankawa Indians of Texas,* by Robert A. Ricklis

Analyzing Primary Sources
Analyzing Information What part of Bellisle's description suggests that the Karankawas moved from place to place?

Karankawa men hunted with large wooden bows and arrows. To fish, they used bows and arrows or fish traps. Women collected plants, cooked food, and took care of camps. They built portable huts called **wigwams** from bent poles covered with animal skins and reed mats. Each wigwam could house seven or eight people.

Reading Check **Finding the Main Idea** Why did the Karankawas move to different regions at different times of the year?

★ Daily Life of the Karankawas

Because the Gulf Coast has hot summers and mild winters, the Karankawas did not need much clothing. Some men did not wear anything. Others wore deerskin breechcloths, short cloths worn around the waist. Women wore skirts of deerskin or grass. In addition, both men and women painted themselves with bright colors. To keep insects away, the Karankawas rubbed alligator fat and dirt on their skin.

Europeans who arrived in Texas in the 1500s noted that the Karankawas treated their children with kindness. Each Karankawa child was given two names, one of which was known only to close family members. The Karankawas believed that the secret name carried magic that protected children from danger.

Nothing could protect them from European diseases, however. The Karankawas, like other Texas Indian groups, had never been exposed to European diseases. The Karankawas fell ill and died at an alarming rate. In addition, they fought with other American Indians, the French, the Spanish, and later, Americans. By the mid-1800s there were no Karankawas left.

Reading Check **Evaluating** Analyze the impact of European contact on the Karankawas.

Interpreting Visuals

Karankawas. *The Karankawa Indians lived along the Texas Gulf Coast.* ***What tools are these Karankawas using?***

★ The Coahuiltecans

The Coahuiltecans and other Texas Indians hunted deer.

Southwest of the Karankawas lived a people that historians call the Coahuiltecans. They lived in far southern Texas and northern Mexico, where the dry climate would not support much farming. The Coahuiltecans were not a single, unified group. Rather they included many independent groups who happened to live near each other. Spanish writers describing their ways of life lumped all of these groups together. Like other coastal groups, the Coahuiltecans moved with the seasons.

Many archaeologists believe that the Coahuiltecans made few tools. But they did have stone hammers and knives, and they used bows and arrows to hunt. They hollowed out gourds, such as melons and squashes, and wove baskets to store food. Because they were nomads, the Coahuiltecans did not build permanent houses. Instead, they placed animal skins over bent branches for shelter. Inside these huts were grass or deerskin beds and fire for cooking and heating. The men wore little clothing, and the women wore grass or deerskin skirts. Both men and women wore their hair long, hanging down to the waist.

The Coahuiltecans worked hard to survive, but they also made time for fun. At times groups would gather for feasting and dancing. They held all-night celebrations that the Spanish later called **mitotes**. These gatherings celebrated major events, such as religious ceremonies, victory in battle, or the gathering of a plentiful food supply.

The arrival of Europeans changed the lives of the Coahuiltecans. Many died from European diseases. Those remaining faced attacks from Apache Indians, who had been driven into Coahuiltecan territory. Many Coahuiltecans began to live among the Spanish and abandon their traditional ways of life. By 1800 few Coahuiltecan groups remained. The few who were left joined other Indian groups.

Reading Check **Analyzing Information** How did the Coahuiltecan use wildlife and plants to survive?

★ Section 2 Review

hmhsocialstudies.com ONLINE QUIZ

1. Define and explain:
- nomads
- wigwams
- mitotes

2. Comparing and Contrasting
Copy the graphic organizer below. Use it to show what the Karankawas and Coahuiltecans had in common and how life was different for the two groups.

3. Finding the Main Idea
a. How did seasonal migration help the Karankawas adapt to their environment?
b. Who were the Coahuiltecans?

4. Writing and Critical Thinking myWriteSmart
Summarizing Write a one-page short story about the Karankawas.
Consider the following:
- their seasonal movement
- their food, clothing, tools, and shelter

Image Credit: (tl) ©TxDOT Photo

Section 3

The Southeastern Culture Area

Main Ideas

1. The Caddos of East Texas were advanced farmers.
2. The Wichitas hunted and farmed to survive.
3. Atapaka settlements developed differently based on their locations.

Why It Matters Today

Important archaeological sites need to be preserved for future study. Use current events sources to learn more about working at an archaeological site.

Key Terms

- **crop rotation**
- **confederacies**
- **allies**
- **matrilineal**

TEKS: 2A, 10A, 19C, 20A, 21B, 22D

The Story Continues

The Caddo Indians told many stories to their children. The following story taught the importance of farming. "As Snake-Woman gave each person the seeds, she told him that he must plant them, and must care for the plants that grew from them, but must allow no one, especially children, to touch them. . . . She said that until the seeds were ripe they belonged to her, and if anyone gathered them too soon she would send a poisonous snake to bite him."

myNotebook

Use the annotation tools in your eBook to take notes on the lives and cultures of the peoples of the southeastern culture area.

The Caddos and Farming

The Caddo emphasis on farming grew out of the area in which they lived. They emerged in eastern Texas, Arkansas, Louisiana, and Oklahoma more than 1,000 years ago. The rich soil and abundant rain of eastern Texas allowed Caddo farmers to grow many crops.

Unlike the nomads of the Gulf Coast, the Caddos built permanent settlements. Over the years, they became expert farmers, developing agricultural techniques still used today. For example, the Caddos practiced **crop rotation**, planting different crops on a plot of land each year. This rotation prevents the soil from wearing out. The Caddos also set aside extra seeds each year for the next year's crop. In addition, the Caddos burned forests to provide lands for growing crops. On this land, the Caddos grew beans, corn, squash, sunflower seeds, and tobacco.

In many other Texas Indian groups, women did all the farming while men hunted. The Caddos, however, valued farming so highly that men shared the responsibility for growing crops. The men cleared the fields and made farm tools. Women did the rest of the farm work. In addition to their work in the fields, Caddo women gathered wild plants, cooked, and cleaned the houses.

Reading Check **Summarizing** What types of farming methods did the Caddos use that are still practiced today?

★ Caddo Society

With a plentiful supply of food available, the Caddo population grew quite large. With their efficient farming system, some people were able to take on special jobs not related to farming. Some became skilled at working with pottery or making tools. Others took on political or religious roles. Over time, the Caddos developed one of the more complex societies in Texas.

By the time European explorers arrived in the region, the Caddos were politically organized into three **confederacies**, or loose associations who worked together. The confederacies were called the Hasinais, the Kadohadachos, and the Natchitoches Caddos. The three groups shared a common language and were **allies**, or friends who supported one another. Although conflicts sometimes arose between them, the groups were usually on good terms. Each confederacy built temples and mounds for religious events. The mounds were also used as burial sites.

The Caddos were a **matrilineal** society. This means families were traced through the mother's side. Family names came from the mother, not the father. In addition, when couples married, they lived with the wife's family. Women cared for the household and made the important decisions concerning the family. In each house, an older woman directed the activities of the 10 to 20 people who lived there.

In addition to their farming duties, men fished and hunted. Hunters used bows and arrows to kill buffalo, deer, and small animals. Their skill with bows also made Caddo men respected warriors. During the cold winter months, men and women wore clothing made from animal skins. In summer, men wore deerskin breechcloths, while women wore clothes made from grass and straw. Both men and women tattooed and painted their bodies. Caddo homes were built from wooden poles covered with grass. Some homes were also plastered with mud.

When European explorers came to Texas, the Caddos were one of the first groups they met. The Europeans came to know the Caddos as *Tejas,* the origin of the name *Texas*. Despite the changes and difficulties the Europeans brought to their society, the Caddos would continue to play a role in the state's history for years to come.

Reading Check **Analyzing Information** What aspects of Caddo culture suggest that their society was successful?

LINKING
Past to Present

Studying the Caddo Mounds

Three huge mounds at the Caddo Mounds State Historic Site near Alto have drawn attention from archaeologists for decades. Built by the Hasinai Caddos, who lived at the site from about A.D. 780 to 1260, two of the mounds were used for public ceremonies. The third served as a burial site. Artifacts found at the site have taught us a great deal about Caddo life. They have also revealed that earlier Indians and Paleo-Indians lived on the site long before the Caddos. The state of Texas opened the site to the public in 1982. **What have scholars learned about the three American Indian mounds?**

The Wichitas

To the west of the Caddos along the Red River lived the Wichita Indians. The Wichita confederacy included four groups—the Wacos, the Taovayas, the Tawakonis, and the Wichitas. Originally from Kansas and Oklahoma, the Wichitas moved into north-central Texas in the 1700s. Some Wichitas lived as far south as present-day Waco.

The Wichitas lived mainly along creeks and rivers, where they grew beans, corn, melons, and squash. They used horses to hunt buffalo and deer. Like the Caddos, the Wichitas lived in permanent villages. One Spanish explorer in Kansas described a Wichita house.

TEXAS VOICES

"[The houses are] all round, built of forked poles . . . and on the outside covered to the ground with dry grass. Within, on the sides, they had frameworks or platforms which served them as beds on which they slept. Most of them were large enough to hold eight or ten persons."

—Don Juan de Oñate, quoted in *Spanish Exploration in the Southwest, 1542–1706,* by Herbert E. Bolton

Like the Caddos, the Wichitas tattooed their bodies. However, most Wichitas had more tattoos than the Caddos did. Women drew circles around their eyes and lines from their lips to their chins. Men tattooed their eyelids and drew short lines at the corner of each eye. Because these tattoos made them look like raccoons, the Wichitas called themselves *Kitikiti'sh,* or "raccoon eyes."

Reading Check **Finding the Main Idea** Where did most Wichitas live, and why?

Interpreting Visuals

Horses. *The Wichitas and other groups first got horses from Spanish settlers. Hunters would later capture wild horses to tame.* ***How did horses help Texas Indians?***

Our Caddo Name

In eastern Texas, the Spanish encountered a group of Caddos known as the Hasinais. The Spanish called the Hasinais by the group's word for friend—*Tejas* (TEH-hahs). The state of Texas takes its name from this word.

CONNECTING TO Literature

American Indian Stories

Most cultures have stories and tales to explain the origin of people and animals. These tales are called origin or creation stories. The Wichitas told how people got what they needed to survive. According to the story, people had many things but did not know how to use them. Then a man called Having-Power-to-Carry-Light and a woman called Bright-Shining-Woman appeared. Having-Power-to-Carry-Light showed the men how to make a bow and arrow and how to hunt. Bright-Shining-Woman brought corn and told the women to plant it. Having-Power-to-Carry-Light then became the first star seen in the morning, and Bright-Shining-Woman became the moon. **What does this story suggest about the role of hunting and farming in Wichita society?**

★ The Atakapas

Between the Caddos and the Gulf of Mexico lived a people called the Atakapas. Their territory ran from Galveston Island to the Sabine River and into parts of present-day Louisiana. Atakapa communities developed very different ways of life based on where in this territory they lived.

Atakapas who lived in inland areas far from the Gulf of Mexico had good land for farming. They grew many vegetables, but corn was their most important crop. Some scholars think that these Atakapas learned about farming from the Caddos who lived nearby. In addition to farming, the Atakapas used bows and arrows to hunt wild game. Buffalo and alligators formed part of their diet.

Other Atakapas lived closer to the coast, where the land was marshy. Saltwater sometimes flooded the land, so farming was impossible in this area. The ocean, however, provided an abundant supply of food. The Atakapas used wooden traps to catch fish and canoes to gather shellfish, which they raked from the sea bottom. The coastal Atakapas also gathered berries, birds' eggs, and nuts.

Regardless of where they lived, all Atakapas had some traits in common. They probably lived in huts made from brush, though historians are uncertain. They also made pottery and wove baskets. Atakapa clothing was simple, consisting of breechcloths for men and skirts for women. Some groups tattooed their faces and bodies.

Little remains of the Atakapa culture. European diseases had a terrible effect on the Atakapas, and by the early 1900s there were very few left.

Reading Check **Comparing and Contrasting** In what types of environments did Atakapa groups live, and how did these environments affect their way of life?

★ Section 3 Review

hmhsocialstudies.com
ONLINE QUIZ

1. Define and explain:
- crop rotation
- confederacies
- allies
- matrilineal

2. Analyzing Information
Copy the graphic organizer below. Use it to describe four aspects of Caddo culture.

Caddos

3. Finding the Main Idea

a. How did the Caddo culture adapt to and modify the environment?

b. Where did the name *Texas* come from?

c. Where did the Atakapas live, and how did they adapt to their environment?

4. Writing and Critical Thinking myWriteSmart
Comparing Write a short report comparing the Caddos, Wichitas, and Atakapas.
Consider the following:
- how they obtained food
- how they made houses and clothing

Section 4

The Pueblo Culture Area

Main Ideas

1. Some Jumanos were farmers who lived in villages, while others roamed the plains hunting buffalo.
2. Disease, drought, and attacks ended Jumano culture.

Key Terms

- **adobe**
- **hides**

Why It Matters Today

Drought affected the lives of hunter-gatherers and farmers in early Texas. It continues to affect Texans today. Use current events sources to learn more about drought problems today.

TEKS: 2A, 9B, 10A, 20A, 21B, 22D

myNotebook

Use the annotation tools in your eBook to take notes on Jumano culture in West Texas.

The Story Continues

The old buildings of sun-baked earth had withstood years of heat, rain, and wind. They had long outlasted the people who built them. The empty village now stood on the Texas plain, silent proof of a once-thriving society. The homes were built close to one another, as if huddled against the harsh elements. What happened to the people who lived there? Scholars had much to learn before they would know the secrets of the village.

The Jumanos

Buildings like the ones described above were built in Texas by a group of American Indians called the Jumano (zhoo-muh-NOH) people. Descendants of the earlier Anasazi culture, the Jumanos built permanent houses out of **adobe** bricks, which they made by drying clay mud in the sun. The early Jumanos lived in villages along the Rio Grande. Although the region was dry and rugged, they grew corn and other crops by placing fields near the river. When the Rio Grande overflowed, the fields filled with water.

VIDEO
Adobe
hmhsocialstudies.com

The Jumanos also gathered wild plants for food and hunted buffalo. Some became nomads and moved onto the plains of western and central Texas. They supplied the Jumanos near the Rio Grande with meat and **hides**, or animal skins. The Jumanos also traded goods with other American Indian groups to the east and the west.

Interpreting Visuals

Jumanos. *Like other Indians of the Southwest, the Jumanos lived in adobe homes and made pottery from clay.* ***How did the Jumanos adapt to their natural environment?***

The Jumanos who remained near the Rio Grande lived in large villages. All together, some 10,000 people lived in the five Jumano villages near La Junta de los Ríos, north of Big Bend. In some villages, the Jumanos built their houses around a central plaza. About 30 to 40 people lived in each house, usually made of adobe and wood. The roofs were flat and probably made from tree branches. Inside the house, the Jumanos often painted black, red, white, and yellow stripes on the walls.

Those Jumanos who did not live in villages probably lived in separate adobe houses or in grass huts. Those who hunted buffalo on the plains lived in temporary shelters made from animal hides or grass.

The Jumanos used bows and arrows to hunt buffalo. They used the hides of the buffalo they killed to make many objects. For example, Jumano warriors used shields of buffalo hide along with heavy clubs. Nearly everyone wore clothing and shoes made from hides as well.

In addition to their hide clothing, many Jumanos wore jewelry. This jewelry was made from copper, coral, and turquoise. They also tattooed or painted their faces with striped lines. Jumano hairstyles could be quite ornate, as one Spanish explorer described.

Analyzing Primary Sources
Comparing and Contrasting How did the hairstyles of Jumano women differ from those of the men?

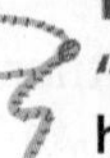

TEXAS VOICES

"The women . . . wear their hair long and tied to the head. The men have their hair cut very short, up to the middle of their heads, and from there up they leave it two fingers long and curl it with . . . paint in such a way that it resembles a small cap. They leave on the crown a large lock of hair to which they fasten feathers of white and black."

—Diego Pérez de Luxán, quoted in *The Indians of Texas,* by W. W. Newcomb Jr.

Reading Check **Analyzing Information** What innovation helped the Jumanos acquire food?

★ Troubled Times for the Jumanos

When the Spanish first arrived in Texas, they traded goods with the Jumanos. The Jumanos were particularly interested in the horses the Spanish had brought to the Americas. Horses made travel and buffalo hunting much easier. However, the Spanish arrival also marked the beginning of a difficult time for the Jumanos. The Spaniards brought diseases that killed many Jumanos.

The Jumanos faced other problems as well. Drought had always made life in western and central Texas difficult. In the early 1500s some Jumanos told a Spanish explorer that it had not rained for two years in a row. When periods of drought became longer during the 1600s and 1700s, many rivers in Texas dried up. Farming became very difficult, and many crops failed. Much of the grass on the plains also died, prompting the buffalo herds in western and central Texas to move away. The Jumanos, who had depended on the buffalo for meat and hides, lost an important resource.

The Jumanos also suffered from attacks by the Apaches, who lived in the plains to the north. The Apaches wanted control of Jumano hunting territories and trade. In the early 1680s a group of Jumanos, led by a chief named Juan Sabeata, asked the Spanish for protection against the Apaches. Sabeata had dealt extensively with the Spanish. He knew their customs and language, and he also knew the people of northern Mexico. Even so, the Spanish did little to help the Jumanos.

By the mid-1700s the Jumanos had lost control of much of their land to the Apaches. Historians think some Jumanos probably survived in small groups that eventually joined other American Indian groups. Some probably even joined the Apaches.

Reading Check **Summarizing** What three major events caused problems for the Jumanos?

LINKING Past to Present

Pueblo Culture

The Jumanos were a part of the larger Pueblo culture of the southwestern United States. The Pueblos lived in huge adobe buildings. They farmed, growing several varieties of corn and other crops. Skilled pottery makers, they used decorated jars for food storage. The Pueblos also held elaborate dances and ceremonies, many of which reflected the importance of agriculture to their society. Although historians believe that the Jumanos joined other American Indian groups, the Pueblo culture survived and flourishes today in the American Southwest. **How did Pueblo culture reflect the environment in which it developed?**

Section 4 Review

hmhsocialstudies.com ONLINE QUIZ

1. Define and explain:
- adobe
- hides

2. Locate on a map:
- Rio Grande

3. Summarizing Copy the graphic organizer below. Use it to show what the Jumanos did to survive in the dry climate of western Texas.

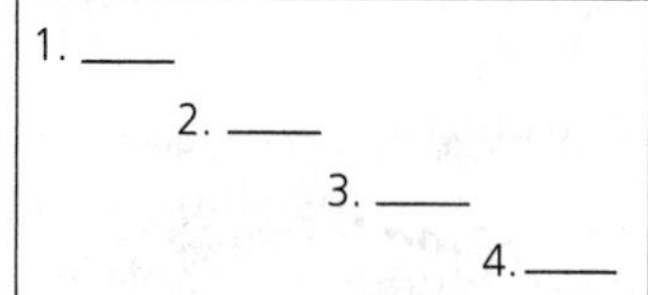

4. Finding the Main Idea

a. Why did the Jumanos migrate to the Rio Grande region?

b. What problems caused the decline of the Jumano culture?

5. Writing and Critical Thinking myWriteSmart

Comparing and Contrasting Imagine you are an anthropologist. Write a paragraph describing similarities and differences in the lives of the Jumanos and the Caddos.

Consider the following:
- farming techniques
- housing and clothing

Section 5

The Plains Culture Area

Main Ideas

1. Plains Indians, including the Tonkawas, hunted buffalo.
2. The Apaches, Comanches, and Kiowas were fierce warrior groups in Texas.

Key Terms

- **tepees**
- **bands**
- **Comanchería**

Why It Matters Today

The Plains Indian groups depended on the buffalo, which was later driven nearly to extinction. Use current events sources to learn more about the buffalo or an animal that is in danger of disappearing.

TEKS: 2A, 8A, 10A, 20A, 21B, 22D

myNotebook

Use the annotation tools in your eBook to take notes on the American Indians of the Great Plains.

The Story Continues

The hunters had finally killed their prey. The buffalo would provide food for everyone, but the hunters had to quickly prepare the buffalo and move on. If they lost track of the herds, the people might starve. A European explorer described how they removed the buffalo hide. "They cut the hide open at the back and pull it off . . . using a flint as large as a finger, tied in a little stick. . . . The quickness with which they do this is something worth seeing."

★ The Indians of the Plains

The Great Plains on which the buffalo roamed for centuries stretch from Canada into southern Texas. Before the arrival of Europeans, American Indian groups farmed on the edges of the plains. From time to time, they entered the plains to hunt the buffalo. These animals were enormous—some weighed 1,600 pounds and were 6 feet tall at the shoulder and 10 feet long. Men and women together hunted the buffalo on foot, sometimes chasing them over cliffs to kill many at once.

Buffalo hunting changed dramatically when the Spanish introduced horses to the region. By 1700 most southern Plains Indians owned horses. Once mounted, they moved out onto the plains to follow the buffalo herds. Their hunting grounds had become much larger.

Most Plains Indian groups shared some common cultural characteristics. Most lived in **tepees**, movable homes made from animal hides stretched over long poles. They made food, clothing, tools, and weapons from various parts of the buffalo. For example, women made a food called pemmican from dried buffalo meat. They pounded the meat into a powder to which they added nuts and berries. In summer Plains Indian **bands**, usually a few families, gathered for celebrations.

Reading Check **Drawing Inferences and Conclusions** Why did the Plains Indians move after they got horses?

VIDEO
Great Plains Indians
hmhsocialstudies.com

The Tonkawas

One group of Plains Indians, the Tonkawas, lived on the north-central plains of Texas and on the Edwards Plateau. Like most Plains groups, the Tonkawas depended on the buffalo for food, clothing, and shelter. Because they lived south of the largest buffalo herds, though, the Tonkawas also had to rely on other food sources. They hunted small animals, such as rabbits, rattlesnakes, and skunks, and gathered berries, fruits, and nuts. Like other Plains Indians, the Tonkawas wore clothing made from buffalo skins. The men wore their hair long and parted in the middle, while women wore their hair either long or short. Both men and women painted their bodies.

In the 1700s the Tonkawas were driven from their hunting grounds by the Apaches. The Tonkawas tried to adjust to the loss of their major source of food and hides—the buffalo—but had little success at farming. Surviving Tonkawas often joined other American Indian groups, and by the 1900s the Tonkawas no longer existed as a separate group.

Reading Check **Analyzing Information** Why did the Tonkawa lifestyle change after they were driven from their hunting grounds?

Interpreting Visuals

Buffalo. *Texas Indians used a variety of techniques to hunt buffalo.* ***What hunting method is illustrated in this painting?***

Image Credit: (bl) ©George Catlin/Smithsonian Art Museum, Washington, D.C. USA/Art Resource, NY

That's Interesting!

Naming the Apaches

Although we call them the Apaches, the group did not refer to itself by that name. They called themselves either the Inde or Diné, both of which mean "people." The term *Apache* probably comes from one of two sources. It could derive from the Ute name *Awa'tehe*, or it could come from the Zuni word *apachu*, which means "enemy."

★ The Apaches

The Apaches were another American Indian group that lived on the Texas plain. Scholars believe that the Apaches migrated to the American Southwest between A.D. 1000 and 1400. Their original homeland was far to the north in Canada. Two Apache groups, the Lipan Apaches and the Mescalero Apaches, settled in Texas. The Lipans lived between the Texas Hill Country and the Rio Grande. The Mescaleros, who lived in western Texas, eventually were forced to move to present-day New Mexico.

The Apaches were organized into bands that traveled, hunted, and fought together. The bands were made up of extended families, led by the most prominent family member. Groups of bands often lived close together for defensive purposes or for ceremonies. Like other groups, the Apaches adapted quickly to the introduction of the horse to the Americas, and horseback riding changed their way of life. Apache hunters were skilled riders, and riders often worked as a team when hunting buffalo. They surrounded buffalo herds and used bows and arrows to kill the animals.

Because buffalo were so large, hunters could not easily transport the bodies of animals they killed. Instead, they collected everything they could use off the body out on the plains. They preserved buffalo meat and used hides for many purposes. For example, if they needed to cross a river, they stretched hides over branches to make tub-shaped boats. Like other Plains groups, the Apaches also used buffalo hides for making clothing and shelter.

Some Lipan Apaches farmed, which was unusual for Plains Indians. Their crops included beans, corn, pumpkins, and watermelons. When the buffalo moved, however, the Lipan Apaches followed. Some Apaches who did not farm traveled to New Mexico to trade for food with other American Indian groups there.

Most Lipan Apache men cut their hair very short on the left side but allowed the hair on the right side to grow long. The men tied feathers and other decorations to their hair. They also plucked out all their beard and eyebrow hair. Both men and women wore earrings. Women also wore copper bracelets.

The Apaches often raided their neighbors for goods. Because mounted Apaches could easily attack Pueblo villages and Spanish towns, they became feared throughout Texas. However, the arrival of the more powerful Comanches, along with pressure from the Spanish, led to the decline of the Apaches. In addition, many Apaches died from European diseases. By the early 1800s, many Apaches had been driven out of Texas.

Reading Check **Summarizing** How did the presence of horses shape Apache culture?

★ The Comanches and Kiowas

The Comanches originally lived in what is now the western United States. After they acquired horses, though, the Comanches moved onto the Great Plains. In the early 1700s, they moved into Texas. Like the Apaches, the Comanches lived in bands. Each band was headed by a peace chief and a war chief. The peace chief was usually an older man, while the war chief was the band's best rider and fighter. These leaders, with assistance from other respected men, made important decisions for the band.

Their skill as buffalo hunters quickly made the Comanches a wealthy group. They traded goods made from the buffalo with other American Indians. The Comanches were also skilled fighters. They controlled much of the plains, including northern and western Texas, which the Spanish called the **Comanchería**.

The Kiowas were the last Plains group to arrive in Texas. They moved from the northern plains sometime in the early 1800s to escape from enemies. The Kiowas hunted buffalo and gathered berries, fruits, and nuts. Although they did not farm, the Kiowas did trade with neighboring groups. Kiowa men did the hunting and fighting. They wore their hair long, but over their right ear the hair was cut short. Kiowa women prepared buffalo hides, sewed clothing, and made pemmican. Skilled fighters, the Kiowas became allies of the Comanches. Both groups fiercely resisted being forced from their Texas hunting grounds and abandoning their way of life.

Reading Check **Comparing** How were the Comanches and Kiowas similar?

Comanche Migration to Texas 1700–1800

Interpreting Maps During the 1700s the Comanches migrated into the Great Plains region of Texas, which had been Apache territory.

Human Systems How did the migration of one American Indian group affect the lives of other American Indians?

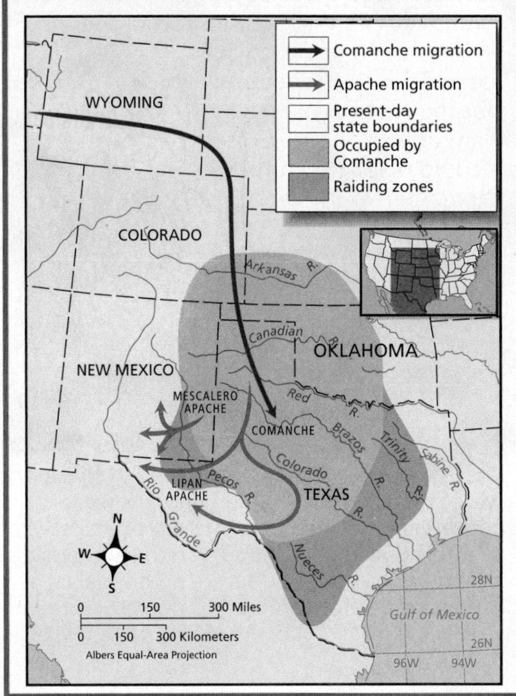

★ Section 5 Review

hmhsocialstudies.com ONLINE QUIZ

1. **Define and explain:**
   - hunting grounds
   - tepees
   - bands

2. **Identify and explain** the significance of each of the following in Texas history:
   - Comanchería

3. **Evaluating** Copy the graphic organizer below. Use it to explain why the buffalo was important to Plains Indians.

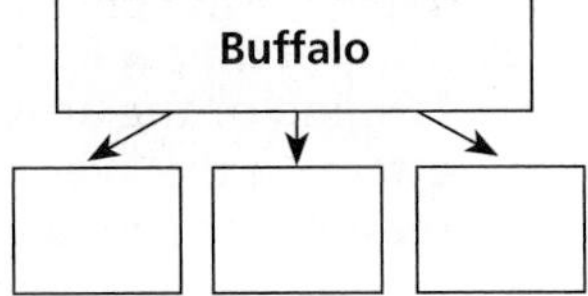

4. **Finding the Main Idea**
   a. Describe Plains Indian culture.
   b. Compare the Apaches, Comanches, Kiowas, and Tonkawas.

5. **Writing and Critical Thinking** *my*WriteSmart
   Analyzing Information Imagine that you are a Plains Indian. Write a short song explaining how the arrival of Europeans affected you.
   Consider the following:
   - how horses affected hunting
   - the movement of groups into Texas

CHAPTER 4 REVIEW

The Chapter at a Glance

Examine the following visual summary of the chapter. Working with a partner, take turns asking and answering questions about the material you read in this chapter.

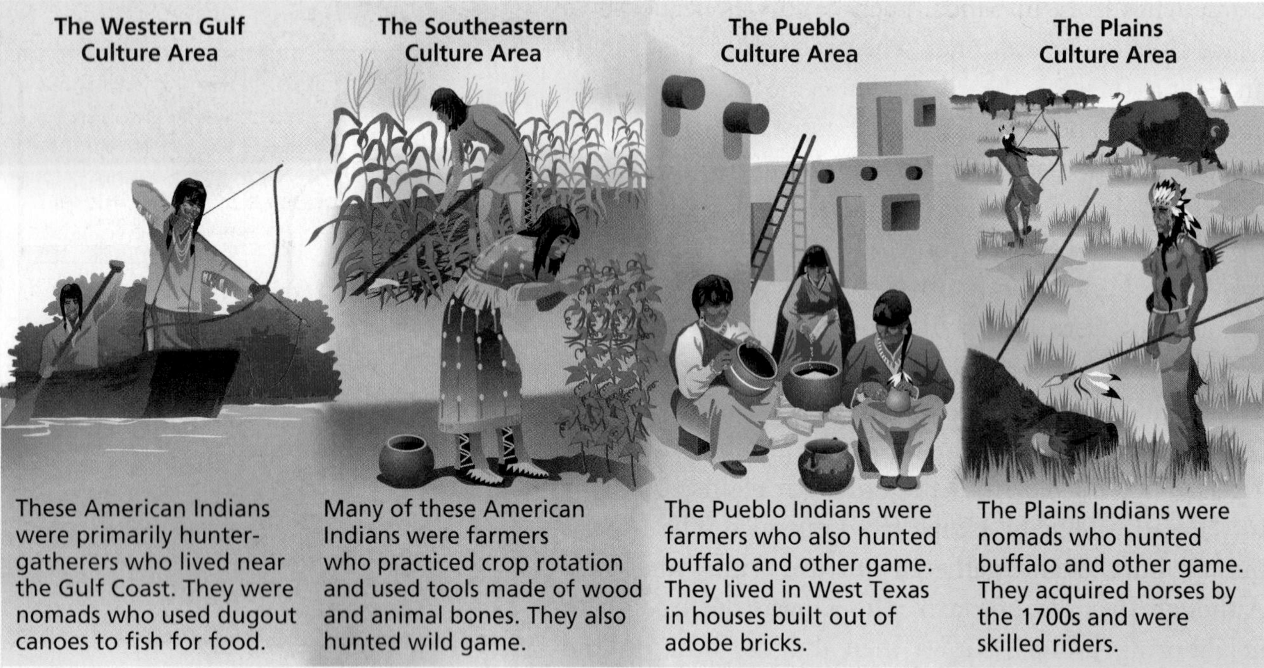

These American Indians were primarily hunter-gatherers who lived near the Gulf Coast. They were nomads who used dugout canoes to fish for food.

Many of these American Indians were farmers who practiced crop rotation and used tools made of wood and animal bones. They also hunted wild game.

The Pueblo Indians were farmers who also hunted buffalo and other game. They lived in West Texas in houses built out of adobe bricks.

The Plains Indians were nomads who hunted buffalo and other game. They acquired horses by the 1700s and were skilled riders.

Identifying People and Ideas

Write a sentence to explain the role or significance of each of the following terms or people.

1. artifacts
2. era
3. nomads
4. crop rotation
5. confederacies
6. matrilineal
7. adobe
8. allies
9. tepees
10. bands

Understanding Main Ideas

Section 1

1. What era in Texas history took place between 1835 and 1845?

Section 2

2. Why were the Karankawas nomads?
3. How did the Coahuiltecans survive in the dry southern Texas environment?

Section 3

4. How were the Caddo farming methods similar to those used today?

Section 4

5. What farming method did the Jumanos use to adapt to their environment?

Section 5

6. How did the horse aid the Plains Indians?

You Be the Historian

Reviewing Themes

1. **Geography** Why were the lives of the Caddos similar to and different from those of the Jumanos?
2. **Culture** In what ways were Texas Plains Indian groups similar to one another?
3. **Science, Technology & Society** How did new tools and technologies affect American Indians?

Thinking Critically

1. **Contrasting** How did the lives of hunter-gatherers in Texas differ from those of farmers?
2. **Drawing Inferences and Conclusions** How did the environment influence the way Texas Indians obtained food in the four cultural regions?
3. **Supporting a Point of View** Do you think farming or the arrival of the horse had a greater effect on the lives of Texas Indians? Provide reasons for your answer.

Texas Test Practice

Interpreting Maps

Study the map below. Then use the information on the map to answer the questions that follow.

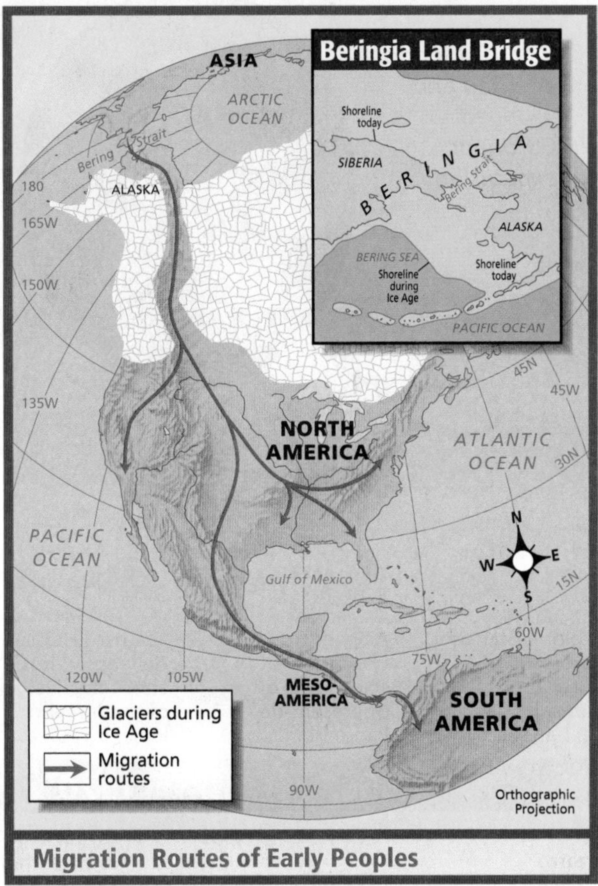

Migration Routes of Early Peoples

1. What geographic feature enabled people to travel to the Americas?

- **A** Mesoamerica
- **B** the Gulf of Mexico
- **C** the Beringia Land Bridge
- **D** the Arctic Ocean

2. How did this geographic feature affect the development of Texas?

Analyzing Primary Sources

Read the following quote by a Spanish explorer about the Karankawas. Then answer the questions.

"The Indians . . . left the island and passed over in canoes to the main [land], into some bays where [there] are many oysters. . . . There is [a] great want of wood; mosquitos are in great plenty. The houses are of mats, set up on masses of oyster shells, which they sleep upon."

3. Which of the following statements best describes the author's point of view?

- **F** The Indians are not using all the resources available to them.
- **G** The Indians were starving.
- **H** The Indians did not trust the explorer.
- **J** The Indians relied on food sources and materials that they could find.

4. What shows that the explorer observed the Indians adapting to their environment?

Interdisciplinary Connection to Geography

Work with a small group to complete the following activity. Each person should select a Texas Indian group discussed in the chapter. Use the library to find information to create a section for a guide to Texas Indian life. Let each group share its findings with the class. Once all groups have shared, create an illustrated map showing how Indian groups obtained food in the four cultural regions. Be sure to use standard grammar, spelling, sentence structure, and punctuation and to cite your sources.

Internet Activity

Access the Internet to research the lifestyles of two American Indian groups mentioned in the chapter and the environments in which they lived. Create an illustrated booklet that compares and contrasts how the groups adapted to their environment. Write at least one paragraph for each group, describing its food sources and its environments.

CHAPTER 5

The Age of Contact

(1492–1670)

Texas Essential Knowledge and Skills (TEKS) 1A, 1B, 1C, 2B, 8A, 9C, 20A, 21A, 21B, 21C, 21D, 21H, 22A, 22B, 22C, 22D

Viceroy Mendoza planned and supplied Coronado's expedition.

TEXAS

1519 Alonso Álvarez de Pineda maps the Texas coast.

1541 Explorer Francisco Vásquez de Coronado crosses the Texas Panhandle.

1554 A Spanish treasure fleet shipwrecks off of present-day Padre Island.

1581 Spaniard Hernán Gallegos writes about the lives of the Jumano Indians in Texas.

1490 — 1510 — 1530 — 1550 — 1570

U.S. and WORLD

1492 Christopher Columbus first reaches the Bahamas.

1519 Hernán Cortés begins his conquest of the Aztec Empire.

1532 Francisco Pizarro begins his defeat of the Inca Empire in South America.

1565 Pedro Menéndez de Avilés founds St. Augustine, Florida, the first European settlement in the present-day United States.

1574 An estimated 152,500 Spanish settlers live in the Americas.

If you were there . . .

Would you become an explorer?

Build on What You Know

Europeans arrived in Texas in the early 1500s. At the time, many different American Indian groups already lived in the area. Their lives would be permanently changed as European explorers and others began to enter and settle on their land.

Spanish conquistadores brought the first horses to Texas.

Spanish soldiers and conquistadores often wore large helmets.

Spanish conquistadores brought the first horses to Texas.

1601
Juan de Oñate crosses the Texas Panhandle on his way to Quivira.

1609
English captain Henry Hudson explores the eastern coast of North America and sails up the river that now bears his name.

1621
Potatoes native to the Americas are planted in Germany for the first time.

1657
The English navy destroys the Spanish West Indian fleet during a war between England and Spain.

1659
Spaniards first record seeing Apache Indians riding horses

1590 | 1610 | 1630 | 1650 | 1670

You Be the Historian

myNotebook

What's Your Opinion? Do you agree or disagree with the following statements? Support your point of view in your notebook.

- **Science, Technology & Society** A small army with superior weapons can defeat a great empire.
- **Economics** A nation can gain power and wealth by exploring and settling other lands.
- **Culture** People always benefit culturally from exploration.

Section 1

Europeans Reach the Americas

Main Ideas

1. Explorer Christopher Columbus reached the Americas from Europe in 1492.
2. The Spanish wanted to control the Americas to obtain gold, spread Christianity, and gain glory.
3. In 1519 Hernán Cortés conquered the Aztec Empire.

Key Terms and People

- **Christopher Columbus**
- **conquistadores**
- **Hernán Cortés**
- **Moctezuma II**

Why It Matters Today

Early explorers sailed uncharted waters and visited new lands. Use current events sources to find information about exploration today, such as space or deep-sea exploration.

TEKS: 1B, 1C, 2B, 20A, 21B, 21C, 21H, 22D

myNotebook

Use the annotation tools in your eBook to take notes on the arrival of Europeans in the Americas.

The Story Continues

A cookbook from the 1300s advised cooks to carefully "grind spices . . . [so] you do not lose any speck." Seasonings were far too valuable to waste. Cooks for wealthy Europeans used salt to help keep meat from spoiling and spices to make rotting foods taste better. Spices and salt were carried to Europe from Asia and Africa across dangerous routes. Merchants in the spice trade risked death in harsh deserts and murder by bandits. Such risks and long journeys made spices very expensive. One pound of salt could cost as much as two pounds of gold!

★ Columbus Sails to the Americas

The spices so valued by Europeans came from Asia, as did other valuable products such as Chinese silk. The dangers of overland trade routes made such goods costly. As a result, in the late 1400s nations in western Europe raced to find an all-water route to Asia. An Italian sailor named **Christopher Columbus** believed he could reach Asia by sailing west across the Atlantic Ocean. The idea was daring because no one knew just how big the Atlantic was or what lay beyond it. King Ferdinand and Queen Isabella of Spain eventually gave Columbus three ships—the *Niña*, the *Pinta*, and the *Santa María*.

On August 3, 1492, Columbus set sail. As the weeks passed, the crew grew nervous. Then, early on October 12, a lookout cried "Land! Land!" The fleet had reached an island in what is now the Bahamas. Columbus named the island San Salvador, or "Holy Savior." Although he was nowhere near Asia, Columbus mistakenly believed he was in the Indies. He therefore called the people he met Indians. Later, Europeans realized that Columbus had actually landed near the continent that became known as North America.

Reading Check **Drawing Inferences and Conclusions** Why do you think King Ferdinand and Queen Isabella were willing to help Columbus?

Spanish Conquest in the Americas

Spain's rulers hoped to expand their empire by taking control of the Americas. The riches and lands of the Americas would add to their nation's wealth and power. Spain also wanted to spread Christianity to the Americas. To accomplish these goals, Spain authorized private expeditions and sent church officials to the Caribbean. These expeditions were led by **conquistadores** (kahn-kees-tuh-DAWR-ez)—Spanish soldier-adventurers in search of glory, gold, and land.

Conquistadores wore suits of armor and steel helmets in battle. They carried muskets and finely crafted swords. A few rode mighty horses. To Caribbean Indians, who had never seen horses or steel weapons, the conquistadores were a frightening sight. With this advantage and their superior military technology, the Spanish soon conquered many of the Caribbean Islands. They then turned to the American mainland.

Reading Check **Summarizing** What advantages helped the conquistadores conquer the Caribbean?

That's Interesting!

Pigs on the Loose

Christopher Columbus and other early explorers carried livestock with them on their trips. This is how the first pigs came to the Americas. Many Spanish explorers let the pigs they brought roam free to live off grasses, nuts, and roots. These pigs turned wild, and their population in the Americas grew quickly. These abandoned pigs provided a source of food for later explorers.

Interpreting Visuals

Contact. *Columbus claimed the land he had found for Spain.* ***According to this painting, how did American Indians react to Columbus's arrival?***

Interpreting Visuals

Cortés. *Cortés led a fleet with 11 ships and about 600 soldiers to Mexico.* ***What technological advantages do you think the Spaniards had over the Aztecs?***

KEY DATE 1519
Hernán Cortés establishes the first Spanish settlement on the American mainland.

VIDEO
The Arrival of the Spanish
hmhsocialstudies.com

★ Cortés Marches through Mexico

In 1519 conquistador **Hernán Cortés** sailed from Spanish Cuba to the eastern coast of Mexico. There he founded La Villa Rica de Vera Cruz, the first Spanish settlement on the American mainland. The settlement still exists as the city of Veracruz. After landing, the Spaniards learned of the powerful and wealthy Aztec Empire, led by **Moctezuma II** (MAWK-teh-soo-mah). Cortés decided to find Moctezuma "wherever he might be. . . . [And] take him alive in chains or make him subject to [Spain]."

To make certain his soldiers would not retreat, Cortés sank his ships. He meant to have victory at any cost. However, he faced overwhelming odds. The Aztecs had conquered a vast area and ruled several million people. An Indian woman named Malintzin (mah-LINT-suhn)—also called Malinche (mah-LEEN-cheh)—helped Cortés overcome these odds. With her help, he gained allies among the conquered peoples. Thousands joined Cortés as he marched toward the Aztec capital, Tenochtitlán.

After arriving at Tenochtitlán, Cortés and his soldiers marveled at its great size and beauty. One soldier described the city, which was situated in the middle of a huge lake.

TEXAS VOICES

"When we saw all those cities . . . built in the water, and other great towns on dry land, . . . we were astounded. These great towns and temples and buildings rising from the water, all made of stone, seemed like an enchanted vision."

—Bernal Díaz del Castillo, quoted in *Cortés and the Downfall of the Aztec Empire*, by Jon Manchip White

Reading Check **Analyzing Information** What weakness in the Aztec Empire did Cortés use to increase the size of his army?

★ Cortés Conquers the Aztecs

The Aztecs had large amounts of gold, precious gems, and silver. Moctezuma gave Cortés peace offerings from this treasure, but the gifts were not enough. Cortés took Moctezuma captive and considered how to conquer the Aztecs. But before he could act, fighting broke out between the Aztecs and the Spaniards. On the night of June 30, 1520, the Spaniards fled the city. Cortés then planned a new assault. He convinced more Mexican Indians to join him and had his men build boats armed with cannons. In May 1521 the Spaniards and their allies attacked Tenochtitlán. After a long and brutal fight, they defeated the Aztecs in August. Many of the Aztecs were killed or enslaved. Tenochtitlán lay in ruins.

Spain had captured the great wealth and land of the Aztec Empire. The Spanish sent much of the Aztec gold and silver, including treasures, to Spain. On top of the ruins of Tenochtitlán, Cortés built Mexico City. It became the capital of New Spain, which eventually extended from California to Florida to Mexico. Along with the Caribbean Islands, Mexico became a common starting point for Spanish exploration in the Americas. Such exploration increased the size of Spain's empire, which by 1600 included much of North and South America.

Reading Check **Comparing** How were the Aztec Empire and Spanish America similar?

CONNECTING TO ECONOMICS AND MATH

Gold and the Spanish Empire

Spanish explorers sent the gold and silver they found in the Americas back to Spain. As the amount of gold in Spain rose, prices of goods also rose. Spain produced few goods itself, so much of its wealth left the country to pay for goods made elsewhere.

The chart below lists the value of gold and silver sent to Spain from the Americas between 1516 and 1660. Use the information to create a bar graph.

YEAR	VALUE OF GOLD AND SILVER
1516–1520	993,000 pesos
1536–1540	3,938,000 pesos
1556–1560	7,999,000 pesos
1576–1580	17,252,000 pesos
1596–1600	34,429,000 pesos
1616–1620	30,112,000 pesos
1636–1640	16,315,000 pesos
1656–1660	3,361,000 pesos

Interpreting Data

1. During what years did the value of gold and silver sent to Spain peak?
2. By what percentage did the value of gold and silver increase between 1536 and 1560?

★ Section 1 Review

hmhsocialstudies.com ONLINE QUIZ

1. **Define and explain:**
   - conquistadores
2. **Identify and explain** the significance of each of the following:
   - Christopher Columbus
   - King Ferdinand and Queen Isabella
   - Hernán Cortés
   - Moctezuma II
3. **Summarizing** Copy the web diagram below. Use it to show why Spain wanted to gain an empire in the Americas.

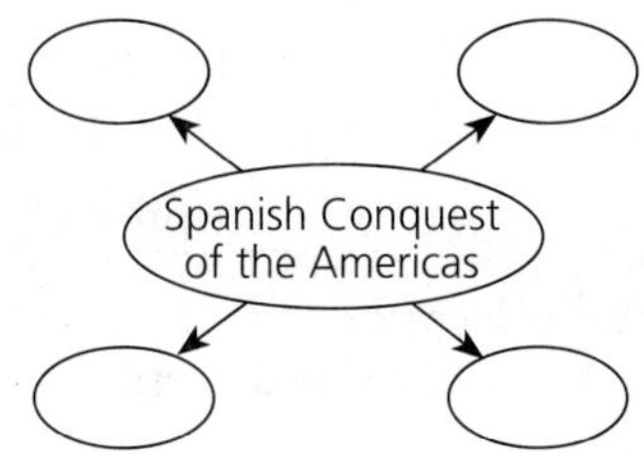

4. **Finding the Main Idea**
   a. What did Christopher Columbus accomplish in 1492?
   b. Why was the building of a settlement in Mexico in 1519 significant?
5. **Writing and Critical Thinking** myWriteSmart
   Sequencing Imagine that you are a member of Cortés's army in 1519. Write journal entries describing your experiences in Mexico. Describe events in their proper order.
   Consider the following:
   - the march to Tenochtitlán
   - the conquest of the Aztec Empire

Section 2

The Spanish Explore Texas

Main Ideas

1. Pineda mapped the Texas coast in 1519.
2. The Narváez expedition was shipwrecked on the coast of Texas, but few of its members survived.
3. Cabeza de Vaca and Estevanico traveled widely through Texas in search of a way back to Spanish lands.

Key People

- **Alonso Álvarez de Pineda**
- **Pánfilo de Narváez**
- **Álvar Núñez Cabeza de Vaca**
- **Estevanico**

Why It Matters Today

Early Spanish explorers visited the Gulf Coast of Texas. Today the Gulf Coast contains several of our state's cities. Use current events sources to find information about regional growth along the Gulf or in other parts of Texas.

TEKS: 1A, 1C, 2B, 8A, 9C, 20A, 21A, 21B, 21C, 22D

myNotebook

Use the annotation tools in your eBook to take notes on early Spanish exploration in Texas.

The Story Continues

In 1519 Spanish explorer Alonso Álvarez de Pineda sailed with a fleet from Jamaica into the Gulf of Mexico. He had been sent to explore the land between Florida and Mexico, both of which the Spanish already controlled. Sailing west from Florida, Pineda reached a large river—the Pánuco—along which were several American Indian villages. Pineda and some of his soldiers decided to establish a colony there, and he sent his ships back to Jamaica. When the ships returned with supplies, though, they found the settlers had been killed in Indian attacks.

The Narváez Expedition

Alonso Álvarez de Pineda and his crew were the first Europeans to see the Texas coast. In addition, Pineda was the first to map the northern Gulf of Mexico. Although no evidence exists that he and his crew entered Texas, their voyage increased Spanish interest in the region.

In 1527 **Pánfilo de Narváez** (PAHN-fee-loh deh nahr-BAH-ehs) led another voyage to the Gulf of Mexico. Like other Spanish explorers in the Americas, he dreamed of finding riches. The Narváez expedition included five ships with some 600 soldiers, plus horses. The explorers reached Florida in April 1528 and went ashore near Tampa Bay.

KEY DATE 1519
Alonso Álvarez de Pineda is the first European to map the Texas Gulf Coast.

While exploring the coast, the Spaniards saw some American Indians wearing gold jewelry. They excitedly asked where they could find more of the metal. The American Indians described Apalachee, a northern region that they said was rich in gold. Eager to find treasure, Narváez divided his force. He sent the ships in search of a harbor, while he and 300 soldiers set off for Apalachee.

Struggling through the Florida swamps, the Spaniards soon became lost. They ran out of food and grew weak. Many were wounded or killed in American Indian attacks. When the explorers at last found Apalachee, there was no gold. The discouraged Spaniards slowly began making their way back to the coast.

When the explorers neared shore, they searched for their ships without success. Unknown to the group, the ships had returned home. The stranded and starving explorers had to eat their horses to survive. Explorer **Álvar Núñez Cabeza de Vaca** (kah-BEH-sah deh BAH-kah) described their desperation. "It became clear that we could leave this terrible land only by dying."

As a last resort, the Spaniards used what materials they could find to build several small, flimsy boats. About a month after they set sail, a huge storm arose. Three of the boats, including Narváez's, washed up on the Texas coast, probably in or near Matagorda Bay. Narváez, however, disappeared when his poorly anchored boat washed out to sea. The other two boats shipwrecked on a Texas island—perhaps Galveston or San Luis. Only about 80 explorers had survived to reach the island.

Stranded once again, the explorers had lost most of their supplies. Many had even lost their clothes at sea and had nothing to wear. With winter approaching, the situation was grim. Just as they were losing all hope, a group of Karankawa Indians appeared. This meeting in 1528 marked the beginning of the Age of Contact in Texas.

Shocked by the strangers' condition, the Karankawas took the men in and shared their supplies with them. Food and clothing were scarce, however, and most of the Spaniards died during that winter. The few who lived were held captive and forced to work very hard. For the next few years Cabeza de Vaca worked as a servant, a trader, and a healer. He traveled along the Texas coast gathering sea shells and mesquite beans to trade for animal skins. He later wrote about his experiences in Texas.

TEXAS VOICES

"Throughout all this country we went naked, and . . . twice a year we cast our skins like serpents. The sun and air produced great sores on our [chests] and shoulders. . . . The country is so broken and thickset, that often after getting our wood in the forests, the blood flowed from us in many places."

—Álvar Núñez Cabeza de Vaca, *The Narrative of Álvar Núñez Cabeza de Vaca*

Reading Check **Summarizing** What tragedy struck the Narváez expedition when the explorers tried to sail to Mexico?

LINKING Past to Present

Cartography

In 1519 Alonso Álvarez de Pineda created the first map of the northern Gulf of Mexico. To create the map, he used his observations and simple tools such as a compass. Today mapmakers create extremely accurate maps using computers and satellites. The *Landsat 7* and *GOES* satellites provide detailed images of Earth that are used to make maps. How have mapmaking techniques improved?

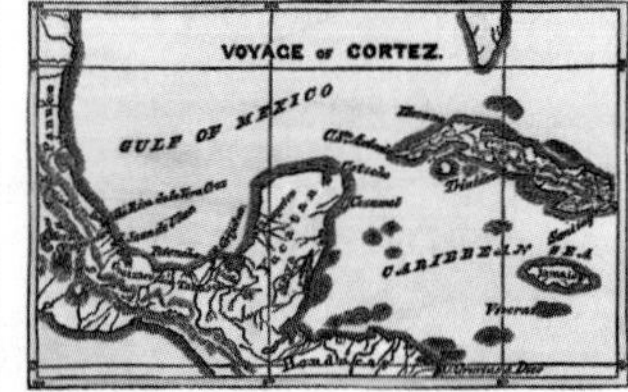

A map of the Gulf of Mexico made in the 1500s

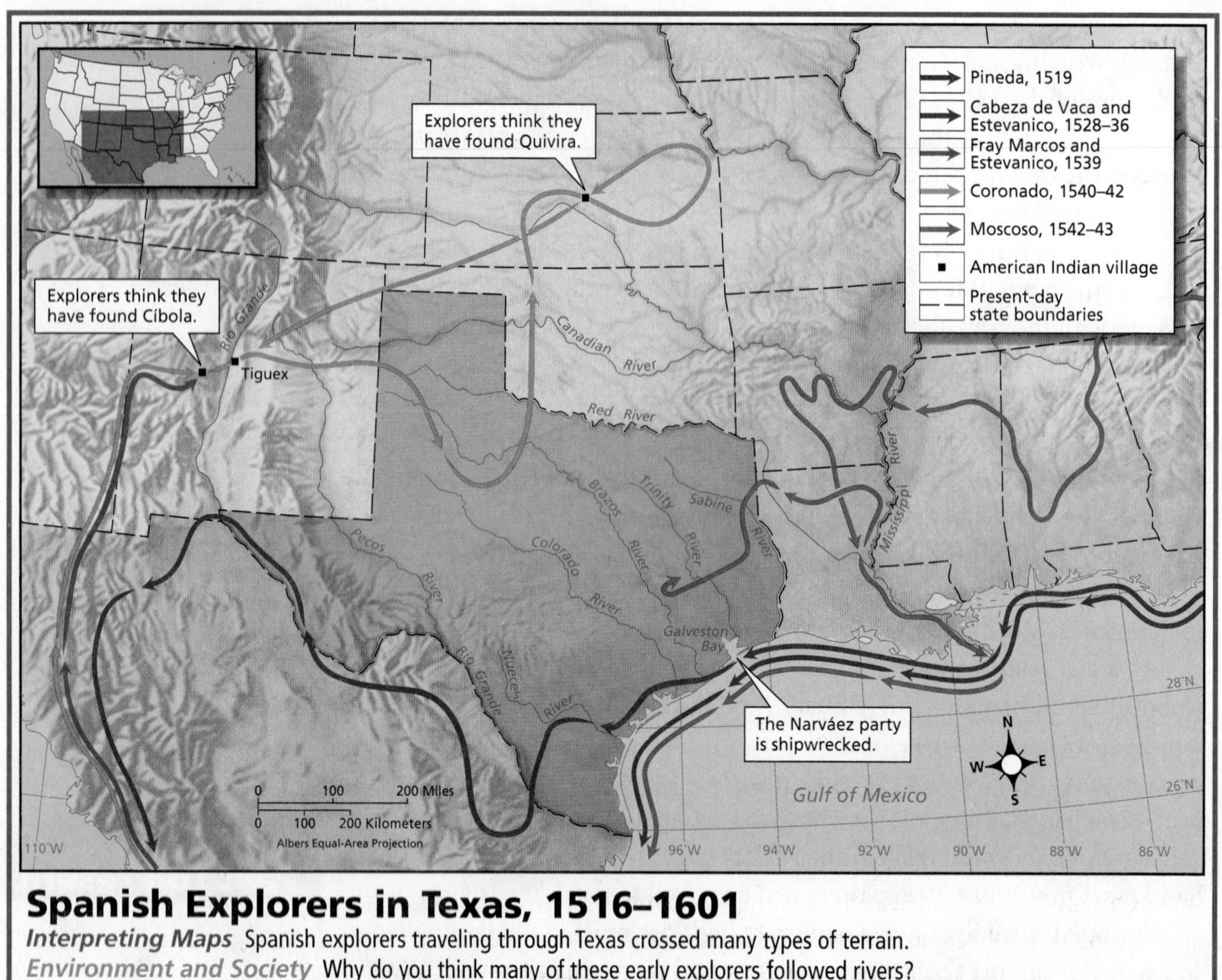

Spanish Explorers in Texas, 1516–1601

Interpreting Maps Spanish explorers traveling through Texas crossed many types of terrain.
Environment and Society Why do you think many of these early explorers followed rivers?

★ The Spaniards' Adventures in Texas

Eventually Cabeza de Vaca was captured by Coahuiltecan Indians. While in captivity, he met three other survivors of the Narváez expedition who had become slaves of the Coahuiltecans. Two of them—Alonzo del Castillo and Andrés Dorantes—had served as captains under Narváez. The third was a North African slave named **Estevanico** (eh-steh-bah-NEE-koh).

After two years of planning, the four men escaped and set off along the coast in search of Mexico. During their travels, they encountered the Atakapas and Karankawas in addition to the Coahuiltecans. The Spaniards traveled from one American Indian village to another. At one village, Cabeza de Vaca removed an arrowhead from a man's chest and then stitched up the wound. The operation amazed the American Indians who watched. As a result, the Spaniards became celebrated as healers among some Indian tribes. Cabeza de Vaca later described how the explorers' growing fame as healers helped them survive.

TEXAS VOICES

"This cure gave us control throughout the country. . . . We drew so many followers that we had no use for their services. . . . Frequently we were accompanied by three or four thousand persons, and . . . had to breathe upon and sanctify [bless] the food and drink for each."

—Álvar Núñez Cabeza de Vaca, *The Narrative of Álvar Núñez Cabeza de Vaca*

Estevanico's skill at communicating with different American Indian groups also helped the explorers survive. Cabeza de Vaca wrote that Estevanico "talked with [the Indians] constantly, found out about the ways we wanted to go . . . and the things we wished to know." By the end of their journey, the men were escorted from village to village by huge crowds of American Indian men, women, and children.

In 1536, almost eight years after their shipwreck, Cabeza de Vaca and his companions came across a group of Spanish soldiers. The explorers explained who they were, and the astonished soldiers took them to Mexico City. There they met with the viceroy, whom they told of their travels. Cabeza de Vaca later returned to Spain.

In 1542 he published the story of his travels as *The Narrative of Álvar Núñez Cabeza de Vaca*. It was the first European description of the land and people of North America. In it, Cabeza de Vaca described the lives and cultures of the American Indian groups he and his companions had met. Among other topics, he discussed what types of food people ate and how they treated their children. He also described the landscapes through which they had traveled. His book contains the first European description of a buffalo and descriptions of many Texan plants.

Reading Check **Identifying Points of View** Why did many American Indians in Texas follow the four Spanish explorers?

BIOGRAPHY

Álvar Núñez Cabeza de Vaca

(c. 1490–c. 1560) From an early age, Álvar Núñez Cabeza de Vaca heard tales of exploration and conquest. His grandfather had conquered the Canary Islands. As a teenager, Cabeza de Vaca joined the Spanish army, serving in Spain and Italy. After the disastrous Narváez expedition, Cabeza de Vaca became governor of a colony in Paraguay. When the settlers rebelled, he returned to Spain in disgrace. **How did Cabeza de Vaca's early experiences help him on his travels through Texas?**

Section 2 Review

1. **Identify and explain** the significance of each of the following in Texas history:
   - Alonso Álvarez de Pineda
   - Pánfilo de Narváez
   - Álvar Núñez Cabeza de Vaca
   - Estevanico

2. **Summarizing** Copy the chart below. Use it to describe the actions and results of each expedition.

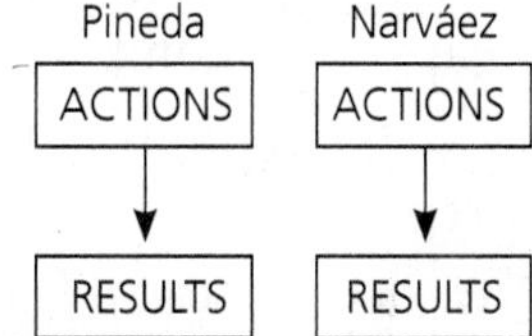

3. **Finding the Main Idea**
   a. Based on the map, which explorers passed through each region of Texas?
   b. What adventures did Cabeza de Vaca and Estevanico have during their time in Texas?

4. **Writing and Critical Thinking** myWriteSmart
   Supporting a Point of View Imagine that you are second-in-command of the Narváez expedition. Write a memo to Narváez giving your opinion about the division of his forces. Provide reasons to support your position.
   Consider the following:
   - the swamps the Spaniards would have to cross
   - other actions Narváez might have taken

Section 3

Searching for Cities of Gold

Main Ideas

1. Fray Marcos and Estevanico believed that they had found the fabled cities of gold called Cíbola.
2. Coronado traveled through Texas and surrounding areas in search of gold and silver.
3. The Moscoso expedition traveled through Texas on its way to Mexico but failed to find riches.

Key Terms and People

- **viceroy**
- **Francisco Vásquez de Coronado**
- **Moscoso expedition**

Why It Matters Today

Conquistadores explored the Americas in search of gold, silver, and other valuable metals. Use current events sources to learn more about the economic importance of minerals and other natural resources today.

TEKS: 1B, 2B, 20A, 21A, 21B, 21C, 21D, 22D

myNotebook

Use the annotation tools in your eBook to take notes about the Spanish search for gold in Texas.

The Story Continues

A Spanish legend described the Seven Cities of Gold. According to the story, seven bishops fled Portugal when the country was invaded in the A.D. 700s. After crossing the Atlantic Ocean, they came to a land filled with gold and jewels. There, the bishops built seven fabulously wealthy cities. Although no one knew the cities' location, many Spaniards thought they might be in the Americas. After all, some wealthy empires had already been found there. Surely others lay hidden away.

The Search for Lost Cities of Gold

Before returning to Spain, Cabeza de Vaca reported his adventures to officials in Mexico. He told of hearing of "mountains to the north, where there were towns of great population and great houses." He also said that he had seen signs of gold in the mountains.

Cabeza de Vaca's report excited the **viceroy**, or royal governor, of New Spain. In 1539 the viceroy sent a Catholic friar named Marcos de Niza north to find these cities. Fray Marcos was an experienced and skilled explorer. Because Estevanico knew the land, the viceroy sent him to serve as Fray Marcos's guide. Some 300 Mexican Indians also went along to provide protection for the explorers.

Fray Marcos and his company crossed what is now Arizona into New Mexico. Estevanico and several others went ahead of the main group to scout the way. This advance group eventually sent word back to Fray Marcos that they had seen a large city. As the friar continued on, he met some of the advance group fleeing his way. They reported that they had reached one of the seven cities and seen people wearing gold jewelry and drinking from golden cups. However, Estevanico had angered the villagers. They had attacked, killing him and many of the others.

To avoid a similar fate, Fray Marcos moved to high ground to view the city from afar. There, he saw it shining in the distance, with buildings that sparkled like gold in the desert sun. Satisfied that he had found great treasure, Fray Marcos returned home to Mexico City. He excitedly reported finding seven wealthy cities, which the Spanish called Cíbola. As wild rumors of Cíbola's wealth quickly spread, officials planned an expedition to claim its treasure.

Reading Check **Analyzing Information** Why might officials in Mexico City have questioned Fray Marcos's description of the cities of Cíbola?

BIOGRAPHY

Estevanico (c. 1501–1539) Estevanico was born around 1501 in Morocco. During his late teens, he was a slave for Spaniard Andrés Dorantes. In 1527 Dorantes joined the Narváez expedition and took Estevanico along. Estevanico thus became the first African to explore Texas. Later, in 1539, he guided a small group searching for gold. He was the first in the party to reach a Zuni village. Although Estevanico had gotten along well with many other American Indians, some of his actions angered the Zuni. Outside the village, they killed him. **In what two expeditions did Estevanico participate?**

★ Coronado's Search for Cíbola

To conquer Cíbola, the Spanish organized the largest force they had ever sent into North America. Some 300 soldiers, several religious officials, and more than 1,000 Mexican Indians led herds of cattle, horses, and sheep. **Francisco Vásquez de Coronado**, a 30-year-old conquistador, commanded this force. Riding a stallion, Coronado made an impressive sight in gold-plated armor and a steel helmet with bright feathers. With Fray Marcos serving as guide, the force set off in April 1540.

Interpreting Visuals

Searching for gold. *This early map of the Americas shows what Europeans knew of the region.* ***Based on this map, why do you think Spanish explorers believed they might find the Seven Cities of Cíbola?***

Interpreting Visuals

Coronado. *Coronado led his large expedition across the dry regions of what is now the southwestern United States.* ***How do you think they may have adapted to the environment of the region during their trip?***

When Coronado reached the city that Fray Marcos had seen, he found a force of Zuni Indians waiting. A short but hard-fought battle followed. The Spaniards, with their muskets and swords, soon defeated the Zuni. The conquerors' joy of victory did not last long, however. As they searched the cities, they did not find any gold or silver. The cities of Cíbola were not the legendary lost cities of gold but rather Zuni Pueblo villages. The Zuni had houses made of adobe brick, not gold. It had only looked like gold to Fray Marcos as it sparkled in the sunlight. Coronado was furious and sent the friar back to Mexico City in disgrace.

Reading Check **Drawing Inferences and Conclusions** How did physical and human features lead the Spanish to think Cíbola was made of gold?

★ Coronado Hears of Quivira

Although disappointed not to find Cíbola, Coronado nonetheless sent groups out to explore the land and search for treasure. The members of one group, led by García López de Cárdenas, became the first known Europeans to see the Grand Canyon. Another group traveled east to Tiguex (tee-GWAYSH), an area near the Rio Grande in what is now New Mexico. This area was home to the Tigua Indians, who proved friendly to the Spanish. Coronado soon moved his main force to the area.

While at Tiguex, the Spaniards met an American Indian from farther east whom they called the Turk. He told tales of Quivira, a nearby region where the cities were said to be full of gold. After the experience at Cíbola, many Spaniards doubted the Turk's story. Yet Coronado thought

Image Credit: ©Private Collection/The Bridgeman Art Library

finding Quivira was worth the risk and planned an expedition for the coming spring. That winter, the Spaniards' supplies ran out and they began forcing the Tigua Indians to give them food and clothing. The Tigua grew angry, and fighting soon broke out between them and the Spaniards. The Spaniards killed many Tigua before establishing control.

Reading Check **Finding the Main Idea** Who was the Turk, and why did the story he told interest Coronado?

★ Coronado Travels through Texas

Guided by the Turk, Coronado set out in search of Quivira in the spring of 1541. The explorers traveled onto the flatlands of the Texas Panhandle. One soldier described the area's high plains.

TEXAS VOICES

"The country . . . was so level and smooth that . . . if a man lay down on his back he lost sight of the ground. . . . Several lakes were found at intervals; they were round as plates. . . . The grass grows tall near these lakes; away from them it is very short. . . . In traveling over those plains, [we left] no more trace . . . than if nothing had been there."

—Pedro de Castañeda, quoted in *Spanish Explorers in the Southern United States, 1528–1543*

The expedition continued across the Llano Estacado. There the explorers also saw what they thought were strange humpbacked "cows," which were actually American buffalo. As the explorers traveled, they met many American Indians. Coronado and his army noted how skilled these Plains Indians were at hunting the buffalo. Moving east, the expedition crossed onto the Caprock Escarpment. This area of cliffs and canyons divides the Texas High Plains from the lower interior plains. There the explorers came upon another unusual sight—a deep gorge cut into the land. This gorge was likely Palo Duro Canyon.

The explorers camped in this canyon, and then the expedition headed north. Near what is now Wichita, Kansas, they reached Quivira and once again met with disappointment. Instead of treasure, they found only grass huts and corn. Coronado became angry and asked the Turk why he had deceived them. The Turk explained that the Tigua had made him tell the story so that the explorers would leave their village. Coronado had the Turk killed for his actions.

Coronado returned to Mexico City in 1542. In his report of the journey, he described the Llano Estacado as a fine land similar to parts of Spain. He noted that the huge buffalo herds might provide a source of wealth. Because he had not found any gold or other treasure, Spanish officials considered the expedition a failure, however.

Reading Check **Categorizing** What animals and geographic features did Coronado see while crossing the Texas Panhandle?

Interpreting Visuals

Armor. Conquistadores wore armor to protect themselves in battle. ***How might this armor have been a disadvantage during an expedition in Texas?***

Daily Life

What's for Dinner?

Before a voyage, explorers loaded their ships with barrels of flour, cattle, and other foods and livestock. These supplies often ran out before the ships landed. In such cases, some explorers ate wormy biscuits or rats to stay alive. When traveling overland in the Americas, hungry explorers copied the diets of local American Indians. Depending on where they were, explorers ate corn, fish, prickly pear fruit, and roots. In desperate times, some explorers even ate tree bark or their horses to survive. **How did explorers in the Americas learn which local plants or animals were suitable to eat?**

★ Moscoso Explores East Texas

While Coronado marched to the cities of Cíbola from the south, another group led by Spanish explorer Hernando de Soto sought them from the east. De Soto and some 600 soldiers had landed on the Florida coast in 1539. For more than two years they had explored what is now the southeastern United States. Then, in May 1542, De Soto died of fever. Luis de Moscoso Alvarado, another member of the group, took command. As a result, the later portion of the journey has become known as the **Moscoso expedition.**

Because the expedition had not found any treasure, Moscoso decided to head to Mexico City. He led the explorers west into East Texas, where they met many Caddo Indians. Soon, however, the explorers began having trouble finding food, and the Caddo had none to spare. Realizing they had little chance of making it to Mexico City on foot, Moscoso returned to the Mississippi River. Like Narváez, the explorers built small boats to sail to Mexico. Their attempt was successful, and in 1543 some 300 members of the original force of 600 reached Mexico.

In Mexico City, Moscoso made a report of his expedition. Parts of his report sounded much like Coronado's. Moscoso described Texas as a geographically varied land. He also mentioned seeing a thick, black goo seeping from the ground. Although he did not know it, Moscoso had seen petroleum, or oil. This would one day become the "black gold" of Texas and a source of great wealth for many Texans. However, the Spanish were interested only in gold and silver, and neither Coronado nor Moscoso had found any. The expeditions to Texas had failed to produce the riches the Spanish desired.

Reading Check **Making Generalizations and Predictions** After Moscoso's report, do you think Spanish officials were eager to send other expeditions to Texas? Why or why not?

★ Section 3 Review

hmhsocialstudies.com
ONLINE QUIZ

1. Define and explain:
- viceroy

2. Identify and explain the significance of each of the following in Texas history:
- Francisco Vásquez de Coronado
- Moscoso expedition

3. Sequencing Copy the graphic organizer below. Use it to identify in order the stories and events that led to Coronado's exploration of the American Southwest.

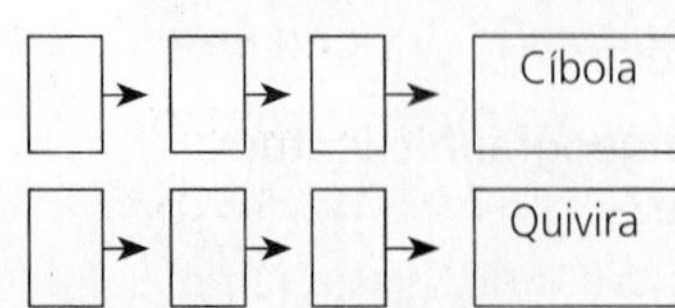

4. Finding the Main Idea

a. What happened on the Fray Marcos expedition to Cíbola?

b. Compare and contrast the Coronado and De Soto–Moscoso expeditions.

5. Writing and Critical Thinking myWriteSmart

Identifying Points of View Imagine that you are a Zuni Indian living in the American Southwest. Describe your opinion of the Spaniards looking for Cíbola. Consider the following:
- Spanish actions toward the Zuni
- Zuni actions toward the Spanish

Section 4

Consequences of Spanish Exploration

Main Ideas

1. Juan de Oñate founded the colony of New Mexico.
2. Interaction between Europeans and American Indians changed both societies.
3. The Columbian Exchange brought both devastating disease and useful horses to North America.

Key Terms and People

- **Juan de Oñate**
- **epidemics**
- **Columbian Exchange**
- **mustangs**

Why It Matters Today

The transfer of plants and animals between the Americas and other parts of the world greatly changed people's lives. Use current events sources to find information about the worldwide exchange of goods or ideas today.

The Story Continues

TEKS: 2B, 8A, 9C, 21B, 21C, 22D

myNotebook

Use the annotation tools in your eBook to take notes on the effects of Spanish exploration on both Europeans and American Indians.

In January 1598 Juan Pérez de Bustillo left Mexico with his wife and children. With more than 500 other settlers, they headed north into the Chihuahuan Desert. The settlers brought supplies for a colony as well as thousands of animals. Water was often scarce. During one long dry stretch, the thirsty colonists prayed for a miracle. Suddenly, a rainstorm arose, forming pools of water. The grateful colonists named the spot Socorro del Cielo, or "Aid from Heaven."

Oñate Founds New Mexico

After the Coronado and de Soto–Moscoso expeditions, Spanish officials lost interest in northern New Spain. The region had not produced any gold or other valuable metals. Yet rumors of marvelous golden cities to the north did not go away. In the late 1500s these tales again drew Spanish explorers to the Pueblo region in New Mexico. A few of these travelers also entered Texas. Some of the explorers who made the trips greatly exaggerated the region's potential wealth.

Between 1550 and the 1590s, settlement in New Spain had been slowly spreading northward. King Philip II of Spain wanted to control this expanding settlement. He decided to colonize the land of the Pueblo Indians. By doing so, he also hoped to increase Spain's wealth and spread Christianity to the Pueblo.

Juan de Oñate traveled across the rugged and dry terrain of the Texas Panhandle during his expedition.

To accomplish this mission, King Philip granted **Juan de Oñate** (ohn-YAH-teh) the right to settle and govern the colony. Oñate was from a wealthy Spanish family that had profited from silver mining in Mexico. The colony he was sent to establish was to be named New Mexico.

In early 1598 Oñate led more than 500 colonists north across the Chihuahuan Desert. The settlers struggled through the hot, dry land. When they reached the Rio Grande after three months in the desert, it seemed like an oasis with its shady willow trees and cool water. The thankful settlers held a feast to celebrate their survival. The area where they celebrated was located in a narrow pass between two mountain ranges. It therefore became known as El Paso del Norte, or the Pass of the North. Near what is now San Elizario, Texas, Oñate claimed the entire area drained by the Rio Grande for Spain.

The colonists continued upriver until they reached several Pueblo villages north of where Santa Fe, New Mexico, lies today. There they built the first Spanish settlement in New Mexico. Life in the colony was hard. The settlers had few comforts and found no gold. Oñate decided to explore northeast toward Quivira, in hopes of finding treasure where Coronado had failed. In 1601 Oñate set out with a small group across the Texas Panhandle. Like Coronado, he failed to find any gold.

The lack of treasure in Texas and the surrounding areas caused the Spanish to lose interest in the region. Few explorers entered the area for the next 80 years. The New Mexico colony continued to thrive, though. Travelers moved regularly between New Mexico and Mexico, passing through El Paso del Norte. Eventually, in 1689, a group of friars decided to establish a settlement along the route. This was the first settlement in the Trans-Pecos, which became part of Texas more than 100 years later.

Reading Check **Finding the Main Idea** What did Juan de Oñate accomplish in 1598?

GLOBAL CONNECTIONS

The Reformation

While the Spanish were spreading the Catholic faith in the Americas, Catholicism was under attack in Europe. In 1517 a Catholic priest named Martin Luther listed the problems he found with the Church. Luther posted his list on the door of a church in Wittenberg, Germany. The event led to a religious reform movement called the Protestant Reformation. In time, this movement resulted in the development of Protestant churches. What event sparked the Reformation?

★ The Effects of Spanish Exploration

Although the Spanish failed to find gold, their exploration of Texas was important. It gave Spain a strong claim to the area. The Spanish also gained valuable knowledge about the land and people of Texas. In addition, Texas served as a buffer between Spanish settlements to the south and American Indians and other, later European colonies.

At the same time, Spanish exploration greatly changed the lives of American Indians in Texas. During their travels, European explorers unknowingly spread diseases such as measles and smallpox. Although most Europeans recovered from such illnesses, American Indians often died because they had never been exposed to these diseases. **Epidemics**, or widespread outbreaks of disease, killed thousands of American Indians. In time, many Indians in Texas died from European diseases and from conflicts with Europeans.

The spread of diseases from Europe to the Americas was part of the **Columbian Exchange**. This term refers to the transfer of plants, animals, and diseases between the Americas and other continents. The Columbian Exchange is so named because it began with Christopher Columbus's arrival in the Americas in 1492. The Spanish brought to the Americas new plants and animals, such as bananas, cattle, and horses. When they returned to Europe, explorers took back American plants and animals, such as corn, peanuts, and turkeys.

Reading Check **Summarizing** What is the Columbian Exchange, and how did it affect Texas Indians?

The Rise of a Plains Horse Culture

The wild offspring of the horses the Spanish brought to the Americas became known as *mesteños,* or **mustangs**. In the 1600s American Indians in Texas began obtaining mustangs through trade and raids. As you read in the previous chapter, horses greatly changed Indian life, particularly on the plains. Using horses, Indians could move their belongings more easily. Some Indians became more nomadic, or mobile, as they used horses to follow the buffalo herds. On horseback, Indians became more effective hunters and fighters. They could ride deep into enemy territory, strike quickly, and then vanish into the plains.

Spaniards in New Mexico first recorded seeing Apache Indians riding horses in 1659. The sight horrified the Spanish—they had lost an important military advantage. They were no longer the only ones in the area with horses. The rise of a plains horse culture marked the start of a new phase in Spanish-Indian relations and warfare.

Reading Check **Identifying Cause and Effect** What led to the development of a Plains Indian horse culture, and how did this development affect the Spanish?

Texas Mustangs

The small horses brought by the Spanish to the Americas were tough and able to live off the land. In time, some escaped, and their wild offspring were called mustangs. By the mid-1800s more than 2 million mustangs roamed the North American grasslands. Hunting later decreased this number to as low as 20,000. A 1971 federal law protecting wild horses on public lands has helped restore the mustang herds. **How do mustangs represent the Spanish heritage of Texas?**

★ The Apaches Dominate the Plains

The Apaches in Texas and New Mexico had initially been friendly to the Spanish. While traveling through the Texas Panhandle, the explorers Coronado and Oñate both had met groups of Apaches. A member of Coronado's force described them.

TEXAS VOICES

"These folks live in tents made of the tanned skins of the cows [buffalo]. They travel around near the [buffalo], killing them for food. . . . They have better figures [than other Indians], are better warriors, and are more feared. They travel like the Arabs [nomads], with their tents and troops of dogs loaded with poles. . . . These people eat [the buffalo's] raw flesh and drink [its] blood. . . . They are a kind people and not cruel."

—Pedro de Castañeda, quoted in *Spanish Explorers in the Southern United States, 1528–1543*

After the Spanish began settling among the Pueblos, their relationship with the Apaches changed. The Apaches, who had raided the Pueblos for years, began to view the Spanish as enemies. Bands of Apaches raided the New Mexico settlements, taking horses and supplies. They proved unstoppable on horseback, despite the Spaniards' superior weapons. The Apaches soon ruled the Texas Plains, which the Spanish called Apachería, meaning "Apache land."

The conflict between the Spanish and the Apaches was one of many between Europeans and American Indians. The Spanish and other Europeans saw American lands as theirs to claim. American Indians—who had lived on this land for generations—saw it as their home. In Texas, clashes between these two points of view would continue for over a hundred years.

Reading Check Contrasting How did relations between the Apaches and the Spanish change?

★ Section 4 Review

1. Define and explain:
- epidemics
- Columbian exchange
- mustangs

2. Identify and explain the significance of the following in Texas history:
- Juan de Oñate

3. Locate on a map:
- Panhandle

4. Summarizing
- Copy the diagram below. Use it to list the effects of Spanish exploration in Texas.

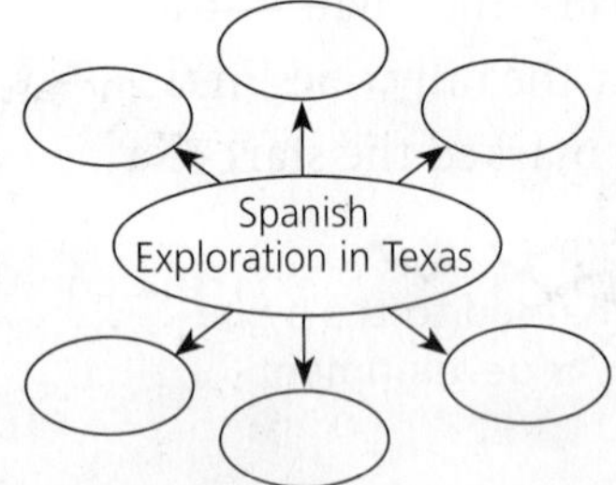

5. Finding the Main Idea

a. What did Juan de Oñate achieve, and how did his travels affect Texas?

b. How did the Spanish benefit from their exploration of Texas?

6. Writing and Critical Thinking *my*WriteSmart

Analyzing Information Write one paragraph explaining positive and one paragraph explaining negative effects of the Columbian Exchange in Texas.

Consider the following:
- the transfer of new animals and plants
- the spread of European diseases

Connecting To
Geography

The Columbian Exchange

The Columbian Exchange began when Columbus first arrived in the Americas. This process involved the transfer of plants, animals, and diseases between the Americas and Europe, Africa, and Asia. Explorers brought European plants and animals with them to the Americas. When explorers went home, they brought American plants and animals back with them. These plants and animals gradually spread from Europe to Africa and Asia.

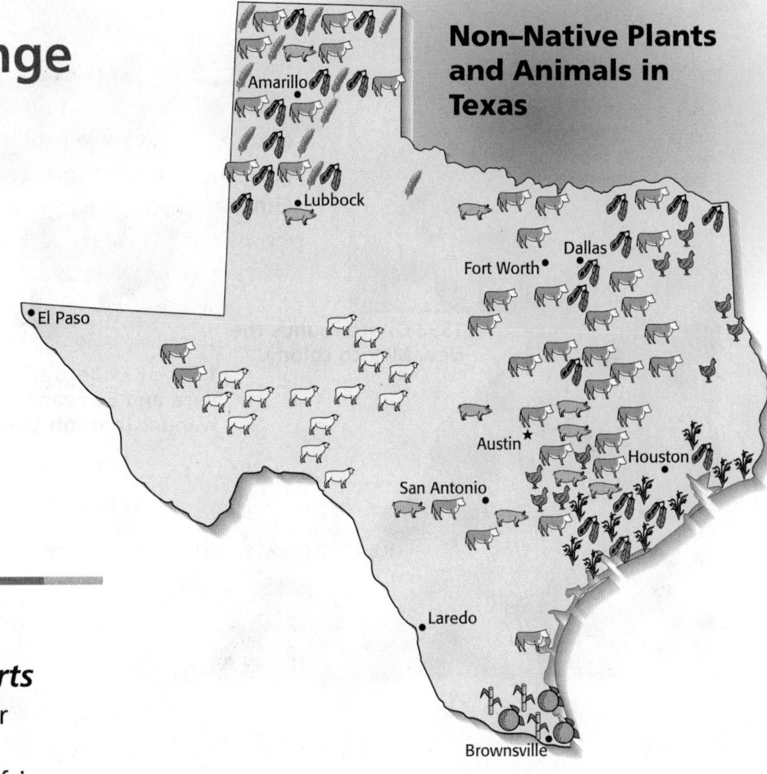

Geography **Skills**

Interpreting Thematic Maps and Charts

1. What food crops native to Europe, Asia, or Africa now grow in the Texas Panhandle?
2. What animals native to Europe, Asia, or Africa are now raised in South Texas?
3. What animals native to Europe, Asia, or Africa are most commonly found in Texas today?

Origins of Plants and Animals

	THE AMERICAS	EUROPE, ASIA, OR AFRICA
FOOD PLANTS	avocados, beans, cashews, cassava roots, cocoa beans, corn, papayas, peanuts, pecans, peppers, pineapples, potatoes, squash, tomatoes, vanilla beans, wild rice	barley, oats, rice, wheat, bananas, chickpeas, coffee, grapes, lemons, lettuce, okra, olives, onions, oranges, peaches, pears, radishes, soybeans, sugarcane, watermelons
OTHER PLANTS	cotton, marigolds, rubber, tobacco	bluegrass, couchgrass, crabgrass, daisies, dandelions, roses
ANIMALS AND INSECTS	gray squirrels, guinea pigs, hummingbirds, muskrats, potato beetles, rattlesnakes, turkeys	chickens, cows, domestic cats, goats, hogs, honey bees, horses, Japanese beetles, mice, rabbits, rats, sheep, sparrows, starlings

CHAPTER 5 REVIEW

The Chapter at a Glance

Examine the following visual summary of the chapter. Then use the visual to write a one-page summary of this chapter that a classmate can use as a study guide.

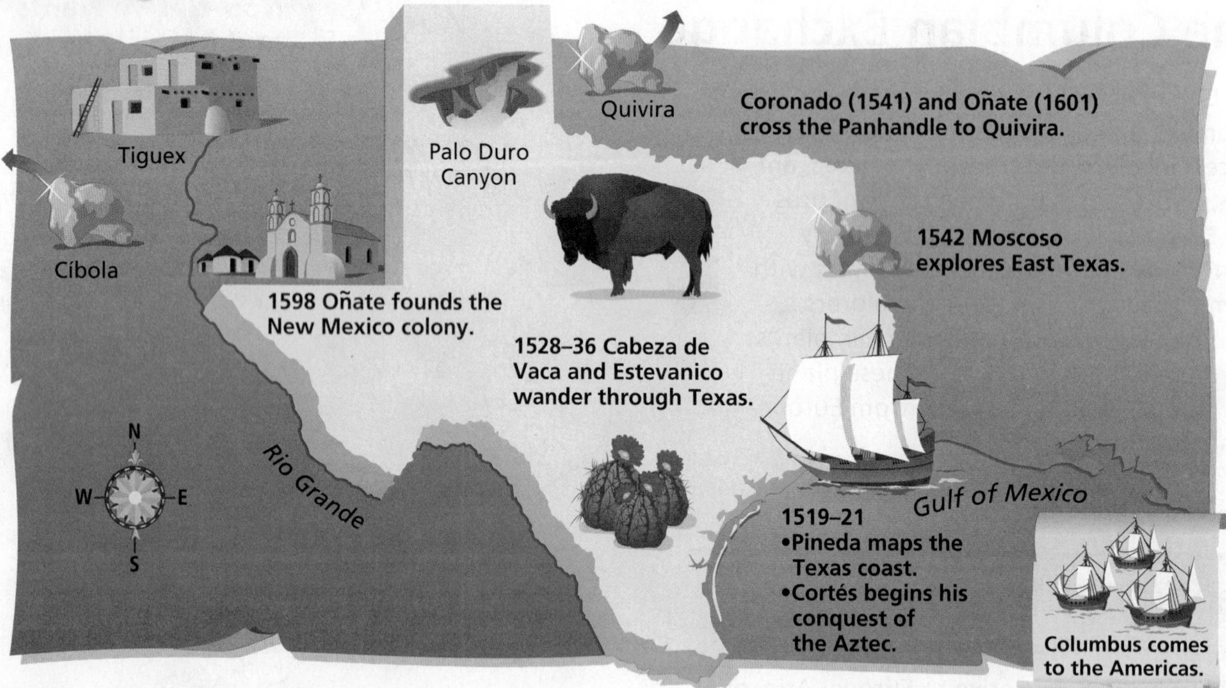

Identifying People and Ideas

Write a sentence to explain the role or significance of each of the following terms or people.

1. Christopher Columbus
2. conquistadores
3. Hernán Cortés
4. Álvar Núñez Cabeza de Vaca
5. Estevanico
6. viceroy
7. Francisco Vásquez de Coronado
8. Juan de Oñate
9. Columbian Exchange
10. mustangs

Understanding Main Ideas

Section 1

1. What did Spain gain through its conquest of the Aztec Empire?

Section 2

2. Why was 1519 important to Texas history?
3. What event marked the beginning of the Age of Contact in Texas history?

Section 3

4. Why did the Spanish want to find the Seven Cities of Cíbola? Who led these expeditions?

Section 4

5. How did exploration in Texas benefit Spain, and why did exploration end in the early 1600s?

You Be the Historian

Reviewing Themes

1. **Science, Technology & Society** How was Cortés's small army able to defeat the Aztec?
2. **Economics** How did Spain's economy benefit from the exploration of the Americas?
3. **Culture** How did Spanish exploration affect Texas Indians?

Thinking Critically

1. **Analyzing Information** How do you think Texas Indians regarded healers?
2. **Contrasting** Explain how Coronado's dealings with American Indians differed from those of Cabeza de Vaca and Estevanico.
3. **Drawing Inferences and Conclusions** What effect do you think disease had on the Spaniards' ability to conquer American Indian groups?

Texas Test Practice

Interpreting Charts

Study the pie chart below. Then use the information on the chart to help you answer the following questions.

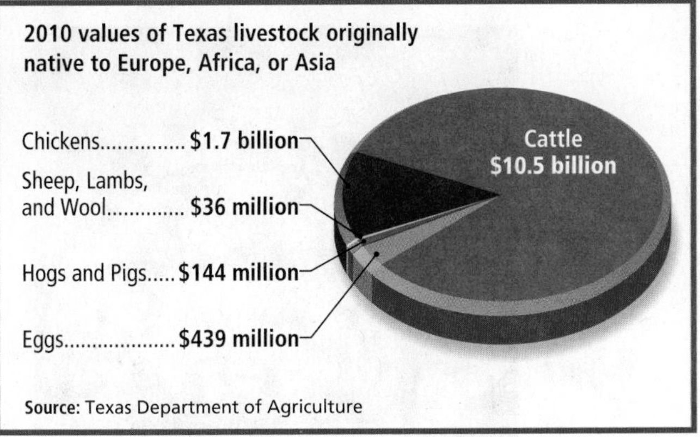

1. What animal or animal product native to Europe, Asia, or Africa accounted for the largest value in Texas in 2010?

- **A** eggs
- **B** hogs and pigs
- **C** cattle
- **D** chickens

2. What are some types of food that would not be available in Texas without the Columbian Exchange?

Chronology and Sequence

Read the following passage. Then answer the questions.

"In the 1930s a work crew digging out an old streambed near Lubbock uncovered animal bones and a spearhead. Curious, they took the spearhead to a professor at a nearby unversity. The professor realized that the workers had made an exciting discovery. They had found proof that people had lived in the area for more than 12,000 years!"

3. Which of the following events happened first, according to this passage?

- **F** The professor told the crew their discovery was 12,000 years old.
- **G** The work crew took their discoveries to a nearby university.
- **H** A work crew found animal bones and a spearhead.
- **J** The work crew became curious.

4. What happened after the work crew took their find to the university?

Cooperative Learning

Work with a small group to complete the following activity. Each person in your group should select one of the following explorers: a) Hernán Cortés, b) Pánfilo de Narváez, c) Francisco Vásquez de Coronado, or d) Juan de Oñate. Work together as a group to create an illustrated book about the explorers' adventures. Research and write the section for the explorer you chose. Then work with other group members to create the book's cover. You may want to create and include maps to make your illustrated book clearer.

Internet Activity 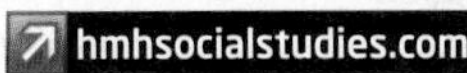

Access the Internet to research modern navigation technology and the technology European explorers in Texas may have used. Then write a report that compares the technology of the past and present. Include illustrations of the devices you have learned about. Use standard grammar, spelling, sentence structure, and punctuation in your report. Also be sure that you have properly cited all your sources.

CHAPTER 6

The Spanish Colonial Period

(1680–1760)

Texas Essential Knowledge and Skills (TEKS) 1A, 1B, 2C, 2F, 8A, 9A, 10A, 19A, 19C, 19D, 21A, 21B, 21C, 21D, 22A, 22B, 22C, 22D

Mission San Juan was one of the early Spanish missions established near what is now San Antonio.

TEXAS

1685 A group of colonists led by French explorer René-Robert Cavelier, Sieur de La Salle lands in Matagorda Bay in Texas.

1690 The Spanish build a mission named San Francisco de los Tejas.

1680 — 1690 — 1700 — 1710

U.S. and WORLD

1688 The Glorious Revolution in England led to the removal of the Catholic ruler James II and the appointment of William and Mary to the English throne.

1694 The French begin trading with American Indians along the Mississippi River for beaver pelts that are made into fur hats.

1700 More than 250,000 people live in the English colonies of North America.

If you were there . . .

Would you have settled in Texas?

Build on What You Know

Many Spaniards came to the Americas seeking gold and glory. Their search for gold brought several explorers trekking through Texas, where they reported on the land and its people. In the 1680s the Spanish began building churches and forts in Texas to extend their influence into the area.

The interiors of some missions were painted with bright, vibrant colors.

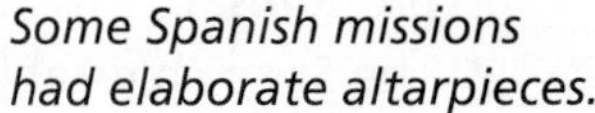

Some Spanish missions had elaborate altarpieces.

1718
Martín de Alarcón establishes the San Antonio de Valero mission.

1731
Settlers from the Canary Islands arrive in San Antonio.

1755
Rancher Tomás Sánchez establishes the town of Laredo.

1720 — **1730** — **1740** — **1750** — **1760**

1718
The French found New Orleans.

1732
Benjamin Franklin begins to publish *Poor Richard's Almanack.*

1759
Charles III takes the throne of Spain. He would later become known as one of the nation's best kings.

You Be the Historian

*my*Notebook

What's Your Opinion? Do you **agree** or **disagree** with the following statements? Support your point of view in your notebook.

- **Culture** When people move to a new region, they adapt to the culture that is already there.
- **Geography** A settlement's chances of success are not affected by its location.
- **Global Relations** Conflicts between countries always affect their overseas territories.

Section 1

Spanish Settlements on the Frontier

Main Ideas

1. Spanish officials promoted the building of missions, presidios, towns, and ranches in the borderlands.
2. The Spanish established missions along the western Rio Grande during the 1680s.

Key Terms

- **missions**
- **presidios**
- **ranchos**
- **revolt**

Why It Matters Today

The crops that Spaniards and American Indians grew were important sources of food for the missions. Use current events sources to learn more about farming in Texas today.

TEKS: 1A, 2C, 2F, 8A, 10A, 19C, 21B, 21C, 22D

myNotebook

Use the annotation tools in your eBook to take notes on the types of settlements the Spanish built in Texas.

The Story Continues

Francis di Bernardone, an Italian knight from Assisi, fought his first battle when he was 20. Soon after, he became ill. As he lay sick in bed, he thought about the meaning of his life. When he recovered, he was a changed man. He gave up soldiering and devoted his life to religion. In 1209 he founded a religious group. Many of its members, called Franciscans, became missionaries. Some 400 years later, Franciscans came to Texas to convert American Indians to Catholicism.

The Mission-Presidio System

At first, the Spanish were the only Europeans settling in North America. But by the early 1600s other nations had founded settlements too. Royal officials wanted to protect New Spain's northern frontiers. Because few Spaniards lived in these borderlands, the Spanish sent missionaries there to establish **missions**, or religious communities. Alongside the missionaries, the Spanish sent soldiers and civilian settlers. The soldiers were to provide protection for their fellow Spaniards. The arrival of the first Spanish in Texas ushered in the Spanish colonial period.

Missions had two purposes. Primarily, they were intended to convert American Indians to Catholicism and teach them about the Spanish way of life. At the same time, missions helped create a Spanish presence in a territory. Some missions developed into larger settlements, increasing the Spanish occupation of the borderlands.

The Spanish built missions near rivers to ensure a good water supply. Each mission usually included a church, dormitories, workrooms, barns, fields, and gardens. The Spanish wanted local American Indians to live within the mission walls. With the support of Spanish civilians, missionaries could teach the Indians about Catholicism and farming. In time, many thought, the Indians would become Spanish citizens.

Many American Indians helped build and maintain the missions. But many other Indians did not want missions on their lands and opposed Spanish attempts to change their ways of life. To protect the missions from attack, the Spanish built **presidios**, or military bases, near the missions. Soldiers in these forts were generally responsible for protecting several missions. Many soldiers brought their families with them to presidios, which later became centers of settlement in Texas.

When civilians came to the borderlands, they built settlements near missions and presidios. Some of these settlements became small towns. Farmers and merchants in these towns provided products and services for the missions and presidios. Other Spaniards lived on **ranchos**, or ranches. Some ranchos belonged to missions, while others were privately owned. Over time, some of these ranches grew into small settlements, increasing the Spanish presence in the borderlands.

Reading Check **Analyzing Information** How did the Spanish try to establish control of Texas?

Life in a Spanish Mission

Spanish officials established missions to spread Catholicism and encourage settlement. Missionaries and American Indians built churches, grew crops, and created irrigation systems. This model shows a well-established mission after several years of settlement.

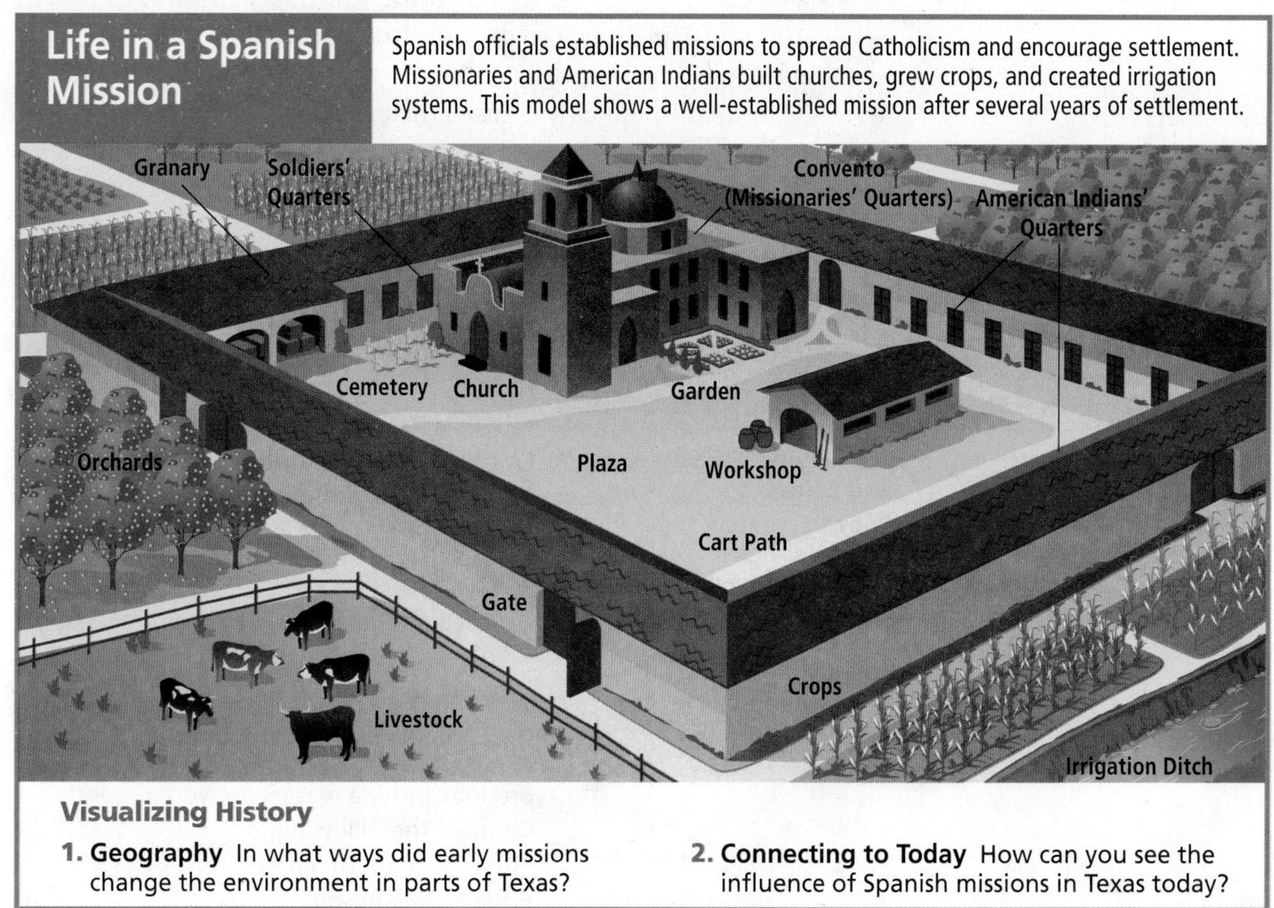

Visualizing History

1. **Geography** In what ways did early missions change the environment in parts of Texas?
2. **Connecting to Today** How can you see the influence of Spanish missions in Texas today?

Our Cultural Heritage

Spanish Place Names

The evidence of early Spanish exploration and settlement in Texas can be seen today. Many names of Texas cities and rivers, such as Amarillo and the Rio Grande, are Spanish. In the 1600s various teams of Spanish explorers named the rivers they crossed as they headed to East Texas. Among them were the San Antonio and Guadalupe rivers, both named for religious figures. **How did many cities, rivers, and places acquire Spanish names?**

★ New Settlements along the Rio Grande

In the 1600s the Spanish settled along the upper Rio Grande in New Mexico. They built missions among the Pueblo Indians as well as ranches and towns, including Santa Fe, founded in 1610. Tensions arose when the Spanish tried to make the Pueblos grow food for them. In addition, missionaries attempted to stop the Pueblo from practicing their traditional religious beliefs. In 1680 a Pueblo spiritual leader named Popé (poh-PEH) led a **revolt**, or revolution, against the Spanish. This Pueblo Revolt forced the Spanish settlers out of northern New Mexico.

The Spanish survivors of the Pueblo Revolt fled south along the Rio Grande. Some 2,000 refugees settled at El Paso del Norte, which had been made a part of New Mexico. Included among these refugees were about 300 Pueblos who had sided with the Spanish. The governor of New Mexico decided to establish settlements for these new arrivals.

By 1684 five settlements had been established along the south bank of the Rio Grande. Among these settlements was Ysleta (ees-LEH-tah), established as a home for Tigua Indians. The settlement included a mission church and homes for both Spanish and Indian families. Ysleta was founded on the south bank of the Rio Grande, but flooding altered the river's course in the 1800s. This left Ysleta on the north bank, in what is now Texas. As a result, it is considered the oldest Hispanic settlement in the state.

In the midst of this activity, however, the Spanish received some shocking news. The French had entered the Gulf of Mexico—Spanish waters. The Spanish quickly focused their attentions on protecting their territory along the Gulf Coast.

Reading Check **Finding the Main Idea** Why did the Spanish build settlements along the Rio Grande?

★ Section 1 Review

1. **Define and explain:**
   - missions
   - presidios
   - ranchos
   - revolt
2. **Locate on a Texas map:**
   - Ysleta
3. **Identifying Cause and Effect**
   Copy the graphic organizer below. Use it to describe Spain's goals for the borderlands and how Spain tried to accomplish those goals.

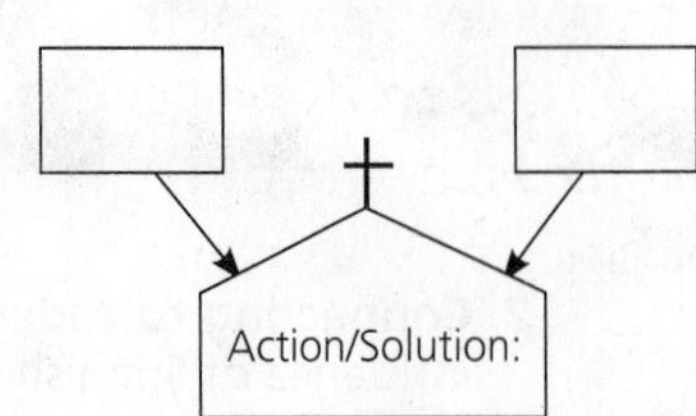

4. **Finding the Main Idea**
   a. What types of settlements were in the borderlands? Why was each built?
   b. How is early Spanish influence still seen in West Texas?
   c. Based on the model, what were the parts of a mission?
5. **Writing and Critical Thinking** myWriteSmart
   Supporting a Point of View Write a letter to an official in Mexico City requesting a new presidio. Include reasons for your request. Consider the following:
   - the functions of a presidio
   - the Pueblo Revolt

Section 2

The French Challenge

Main Ideas

1. The French under La Salle established a settlement on the Texas coast, but it failed.
2. The French presence in Texas led the Spanish to create new missions in the region.
3. The first Spanish missions in East Texas failed.

Key Terms and People

- **La Salle expedition**
- **Fort St. Louis**
- **Alonso de León**
- **Damián Massanet**
- **San Francisco de los Tejas**

Why It Matters Today

In the 1600s people from France, Spain, and other European nations settled in the Americas. Use current events sources to learn more about immigration to Texas and the United States today.

TEKS: 2C, 21B, 21C, 21D, 22D

myNotebook

Use the annotation tools in your eBook to take notes on the arrival of French settlers in Texas and the Spanish reaction to them.

The Story Continues

Diego de Peñalosa was bitter. The former Spanish governor of New Mexico had been found guilty of several crimes and exiled from all of New Spain in the 1660s. He went to England and then to France, seeking to undermine Spain's power in the Americas. To the French king Peñalosa proposed that France build a colony on the Rio Grande and slowly move into Texas. The king liked the idea. Peñalosa's hopes of leading the expedition soon died, however. The king picked another river and another explorer for the colony.

★ La Salle's Expedition

By the 1600s Spain was no longer the only European power in North America. England was beginning to establish colonies along the East Coast. France also posed a threat to Spain's control of the borderlands. To the north France had claimed Canada. French fur trappers were exploring the Great Lakes and the Ohio, Missouri, and Mississippi Rivers. In 1682 French explorer René-Robert Cavelier, Sieur de La Salle expanded France's empire. He canoed down the Mississippi River to its mouth at the Gulf of Mexico. There he planted the French flag and claimed all of the land drained by the Mississippi for France. This land extended from the Great Lakes to the Gulf of Mexico.

CONNECTING TO
SCIENCE AND TECHNOLOGY

La Belle

In 1686 La Salle's ship *La Belle* wrecked in Matagorda Bay. Divers found *La Belle* in 1995. Archaeologists wanted to examine the ship, so engineers designed an enormous steel structure to hold back the bay's water. Scholars spent months examining *La Belle.* The ship and its artifacts were then taken to a laboratory at Texas A&M University for further study. Some discoveries from the shipwreck are displayed at the Bullock Texas State History Museum in Austin. **How did scholars arrange to study *La Belle*?**

La Salle named the region Louisiana for his king, Louis XIV. After exploring the area, he returned to France and asked the king for permission to establish a settlement near the river's mouth. La Salle pointed out that the settlement would strengthen France's claim to Louisiana. The colony would serve as a military base from which to conquer the Spanish silver mines of New Spain. It would discourage other Europeans from moving into the area. The French also would gain a port for the valuable fur trade and perhaps even trade with the Spanish colonies.

King Louis agreed to La Salle's proposal. Because they knew a colony so close to Texas would anger the Spanish, the French kept their plan a closely guarded secret. They hoped to sneak up the Mississippi River and establish the colony before the Spanish found out.

The **La Salle expedition** left France in the summer of 1684. It had four ships and about 300 soldiers and settlers. The expedition ran into trouble when Spanish pirates captured one ship. Then some of the sailors deserted. They later told the Spanish of La Salle's plans. Despite these problems, La Salle sailed on. He became lost, however, and the ships missed the mouth of the Mississippi. The group finally came ashore in February 1685 at Matagorda Bay on the Texas coast. While entering the bay, one ship ran aground with valuable supplies aboard. Then another ship returned to France. The colonists were left with very little food and few other supplies. They were ill prepared for life in the wilderness.

Reading Check **Finding the Main Idea** What was the purpose of the La Salle expedition?

Fort St. Louis

La Salle and the others quickly realized they could not live on the coast's marshy lowlands. They moved inland several miles and built a settlement called **Fort St. Louis** near Garcitas Creek. The settlement consisted of several simple houses and a five-room fort made of timbers from the wrecked ship. One of the rooms in the fort served as a chapel. For protection, the settlers put eight cannons on the fort's walls.

As the settlement was being built, La Salle led a small group west toward the Rio Grande. They may have been searching for Spanish mines or food supplies. La Salle was away from the fort from October 1685 to March 1686. He probably reached the Rio Grande before he realized that Fort St. Louis was west of the Mississippi.

Meanwhile, life was not going well at the settlement. Hunger and disease killed many settlers. In addition, the colonists had to defend themselves against attack by the Karankawa Indians, whom La Salle and his men had angered. By the end of July 1685, more than half the settlers were dead. The situation became worse as the colony's leaders quarreled. La Salle returned in March 1686 to a colony in crisis. The colonists' condition grew more desperate when the last remaining ship, *La Belle*, wrecked during a storm and stranded the settlers.

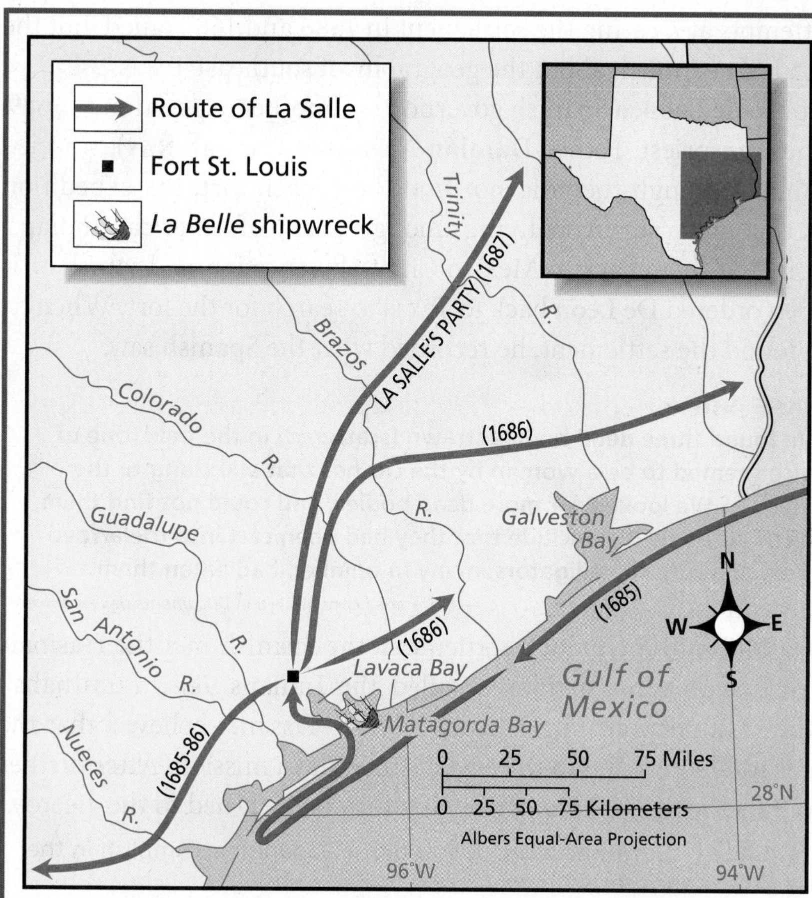

La Salle and the French in Texas

Interpreting Maps French explorer La Salle led several expeditions in Texas, although historians are not sure exactly where he and the colonists traveled.

Human Systems Why do you think La Salle's actions in Texas alarmed Spanish officials?

The first mission in East Texas, San Francisco de los Tejas, was a simple building like this reconstruction.

La Salle decided to go to Canada for help. However, the eastward journey through the wilderness to the Mississippi was difficult, and the expedition ended in failure. In early 1687 La Salle and 17 men went east again. While they marched through southeast Texas, tensions mounted. The men argued about how poorly things had turned out. Violence resulted, and La Salle was murdered by one of his own soldiers. Only six members of La Salle's party made it back to Canada.

Back at the settlement, fewer than 30 people were left, mostly women and children. Karankawa Indians attacked and overran the fort in late 1688 or 1689. They killed all of the adult settlers and destroyed the fort. Five children were taken captive by the Karankawas. The children were kept by the Karankawas until they were rescued later.

The La Salle expedition had ended in disaster. Despite its failure, the expedition gave France a claim to Texas. It also challenged Spain's empire north of the Rio Grande.

Reading Check **Analyzing Information** Why did Fort St. Louis fail?

★ The Spanish Search for La Salle

Soon after the founding of Fort St. Louis, the Spanish tried to drive the French from Texas. Officials sent six expeditions by land and five by sea. Attempts at locating the settlement in 1686 and 1687 failed, but the Spanish learned much about the geography of southeast Texas.

Alonso de León, a Spanish governor, led another expedition in 1689. A Franciscan priest, Father **Damián Massanet** (mas-ah-NAY), traveled with him. Although they did not find the French fort, the expedition found two French survivors living among a group of American Indians. De León took them back to Mexico City to be questioned. Spanish officials then ordered De León back to Texas to search for the fort. When he finally found the settlement, he recorded what the Spanish saw.

Analyzing Primary Sources
Drawing Inferences and Conclusions What did the Spaniards find that suggested that the French wanted to establish a permanent colony?

TEXAS VOICES

"We found three dead bodies strewn [scattered] in the field, one of which seemed to be a woman by the clothes that still clung to the bones. . . . We looked for more dead bodies, and could not find them, which caused us to conclude that they had been cast into the arroyo [creek] and that the alligators, many in number, had eaten them."

—Alonso de León, quoted in *Documents of Texas History*

In addition to the French settlement, the Spanish met the Hasinais on their travels. The Spaniards called the Indians *Tejas* (TEH-hahs), after the Hasinai word for "friend." Father Massanet believed that the Hasinais were interested in the establishment of a mission. After further exploration, the Spanish reported what they had learned to the viceroy.

Reading Check **Summarizing** What did the Spanish accomplish in the search for the French settlement?

Spanish Missions in East Texas

Alonso de León and Father Massanet had been impressed by the land and the Tejas. Upon their return to Mexico City, each advised the viceroy on how to set up missions in the region. De León wanted to built presidios alongside the missions to provide a strong military presence. Massanet argued that soldiers would only interfere with the work of the missionaries. Spanish officials soon approved Massanet's plan.

In early 1690 De León and Massanet returned to Texas with several missionaries and about 100 soldiers. Arriving in the land of the Tejas, the Spanish claimed the region for their king. They then picked a site west of the Neches River. The Spanish set to work building a mission. After only a few days, they finished building **San Francisco de los Tejas**. De León and Father Massanet soon returned to Mexico, leaving three missionaries and three soldiers at the mission. Both the Tejas and the missionaries were hopeful about the mission's future.

In 1691 Father Massanet returned to the mission with Domingo Terán de los Ríos, the first governor of Spanish Texas. Disputes arose between the two men, however, creating tension between missionaries and the government. The tension grew worse as droughts and floods ruined the mission's crops. Supplies were scarce, and the Spanish had to live on corn cakes. The Tejas at the mission ate cow skins to survive.

The Spanish became even more discouraged after discovering that the Tejas did not want religious instruction. After an outbreak of disease, the Tejas turned on the Spanish, blaming them for bringing the deadly disease. The Spaniards realized that they had to leave. On the night of October 25, 1693, the Spanish burned the mission to the ground. They buried the mission bells and fled to Mexico.

Reading Check **Finding the Main Idea** Why did the Spaniards leave East Texas?

That's Interesting!

Mud Volcanoes

Many Spaniards traveled along the San Marcos River to reach the East Texas missions. Some travelers saw an odd sight along the way—mud volcanoes. One priest noted, "These move when we ride near them on horseback and even discharge some water." These "volcanoes" were actually marshy patches that "erupted" under pressure. They are known as quaking bogs. Today visitors to Palmetto State Park can still see mud volcanoes.

Section 2 Review

hmhsocialstudies.com
ONLINE QUIZ

1. **Identify and explain** the significance of each of the following in Texas history:
   - La Salle expedition
   - Fort St. Louis
   - Alonso de León
   - Damián de Massanet
   - San Francisco de los Tejas
2. **Analyzing Information** Copy the graphic organizer below. Use it to show why the Spanish decided to build a mission in East Texas.

Reasons for a mission
1. ________
2. ________

3. **Finding the Main Idea**
   a. Why did La Salle establish Fort St. Louis, and what happened to it?
   b. What steps did Spanish officials take to stop French settlement in Texas?
4. **Writing and Critical Thinking** my WriteSmart
   Identifying Cause and Effect Write a short article about the founding and failure of the East Texas mission.
   Consider the following:
   - why it was established
   - the challenges it faced

Section 3

The Spanish Return to Texas

Main Ideas

1. In response to a perceived threat from the French, the Spanish resettled in East Texas in the early 1700s.
2. The Spanish built several missions, a presidio, and the region's first civil settlement near what is now San Antonio.

Key Terms and People

- **Francisco Hidalgo**
- **Louis Juchereau de St. Denis**
- **Domingo Ramón**
- **Antonio Margil de Jesús**
- **Martín de Alarcón**
- **El Camino Real**

Why It Matters Today

The Spanish tried to protect their hold on Texas by barring foreign trade in the region. Use current events sources to learn more about free trade issues or a trade dispute between nations today.

TEKS: 1B, 2C, 9A, 21A, 21B, 21C, 22D

myNotebook

Use the annotation tools in your eBook to take notes on the return of Spanish missionaries and settlers to Texas.

The Story Continues

Father Francisco Hidalgo was a patient but persistent man. Since becoming a Franciscan at the age of 15, he had longed to become a missionary, travel, and spread the Catholic faith. After arriving in New Spain, the young priest heard many stories about Texas. He became determined to go there to teach Texas Indians about Catholicism. Delay after delay prevented Father Hidalgo from reaching them. But he knew that his chance would come.

Back to East Texas

After the failure of San Francisco de los Tejas, the Spanish largely ignored East Texas for more than 20 years. Several missionaries were not happy with that policy. Among them was the Franciscan Father **Francisco Hidalgo** (ee-DAHL-goh). Years before, he had served at San Francisco de los Tejas. After it was abandoned, Father Hidalgo helped found the San Juan Bautista mission along the Rio Grande, but he was not content there. He wanted to return to East Texas and work with local American Indians. He repeatedly asked Spanish officials to reestablish the Tejas mission, but they refused.

Unwilling to give up, Father Hidalgo eventually looked elsewhere for help. He wrote a letter asking the French governor of Louisiana to help build missions in East Texas. Sending that letter was a daring move because, as you have seen, France and Spain were longtime enemies.

The French in Louisiana had been looking for an opportunity to trade with Spanish colonists in Mexico. However, Spain would not allow it. When the governor of Louisiana received Hidalgo's letter, he saw a chance. In 1713 he sent explorer **Louis Juchereau de St. Denis** (luh-wee zhew-shuh-roh duh-sand-uh-nee) to Texas. St. Denis's stated mission was to find Father Hidalgo. At the same time, the governor wanted him to make contact with the Spanish in hopes of later trade.

St. Denis headed north first. In 1713 he built a trading post near the Red River that grew into the town of Natchitoches, Louisiana. He then traveled southwest into Texas. Eventually he reached the presidio near the San Juan Bautista mission where Father Hidalgo lived.

As a French citizen in Spanish territory, St. Denis was arrested. However, the presidio commander, Diego Ramón, treated him well. The Frenchman enjoyed his stay at the mission, even courting Ramón's granddaughter. Eventually, though, Ramón sent St. Denis to Mexico City to meet the viceroy.

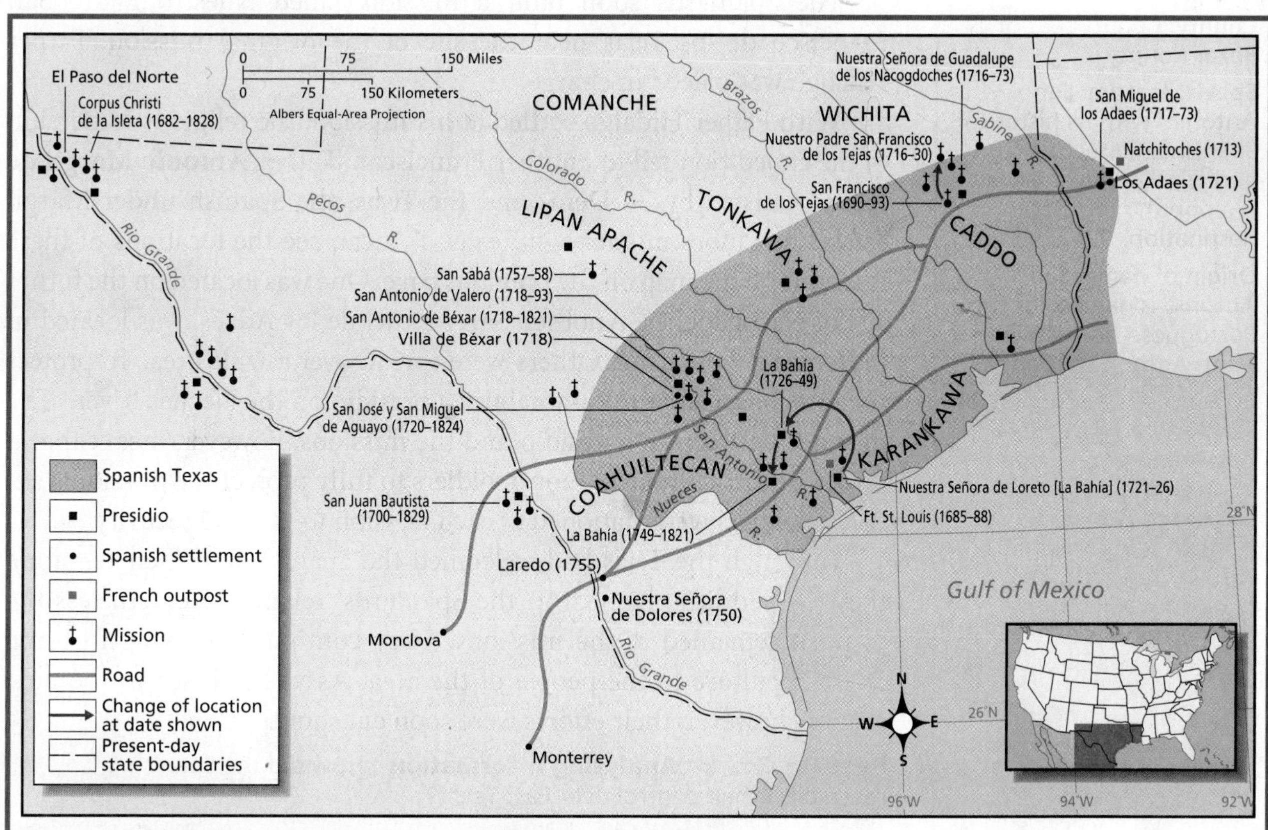

Texas Under Spanish Rule, c. 1750

Interpreting Maps During the 1600s and 1700s Spain established missions, presidios, and other settlements in Texas.

Places and Regions In what areas of present-day Texas were most of the Spanish settlements located?

★Texas Cities★

San Antonio

History: Martín de Alarcón, a Spanish official, founded a mission and presidio on the site of the city in 1718. The mission later became known as the Alamo. It became the site of an important battle in the Texas Revolution.

Population in 2012: 1,382,951 (estimate)

Relative Location: South-central Texas on the San Antonio River

Region: South Texas Plains

County: County seat of Bexar County

Special feature: San Antonio, with its historical Spanish architecture and winding River Walk, is a popular tourist destination.

Origin of name: San Antonio is named for the Portuguese-born Italian saint, Anthony of Padua.

Economy: The economy of San Antonio depends on public and private operations. Military establishments such as Fort Sam Houston, tourism, and medical research play important roles in the city's economy.

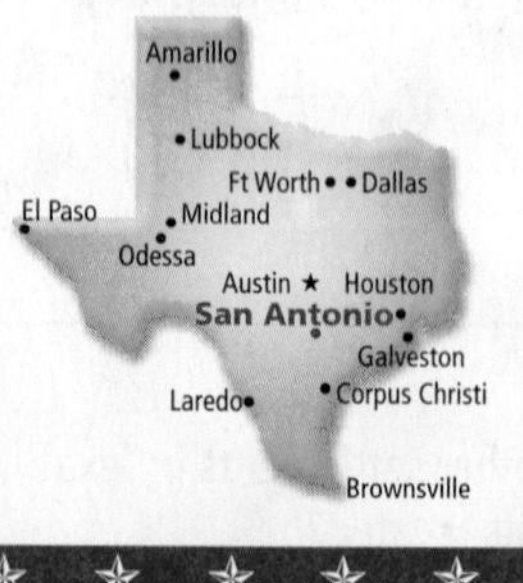

★ ★ ★ ★ ★

The information St. Denis gave to the viceroy convinced the Spanish that the French wanted to move into Texas. To protect their claim to the region, the Spanish decided to build new missions in East Texas. These missions were to be located near French territory. This would allow soldiers stationed at the missions to monitor French activity. Father Hidalgo was one of the priests chosen to set up the missions.

The expedition to establish the new missions was led by **Domingo Ramón**, son of the commander at San Juan Bautista. Although he was a Frenchman, St. Denis was hired as the expedition's guide. In addition, the expedition included Spanish priests, soldiers, and civilians. Some of the soldiers also brought their wives. These women were probably the first female Spanish settlers in Texas. Besides necessary supplies, the Spanish also brought gifts for the Tejas who lived in the region.

In late June 1716 the settlers arrived in East Texas, where the Tejas warmly received them. A priest described their first meeting.

TEXAS VOICES

"About eight o'clock in the morning thirty-four Indians arrived. . . . We went to greet and embrace them, our hearts overflowing with joy. . . . [We] served chocolate to them. . . . This day was most pleasing to us, holding out, as it did, such great prospects of attaining our end and achieving the purpose so much desired."

— Isidro Félix de Espinosa, quoted in *Documents of Texas History*

The Spaniards soon built a mission called Nuestro Padre San Francisco de los Tejas near the site of the original mission. Father Hidalgo was placed in charge.

With Father Hidalgo settled at his mission, the religious leadership of the expedition fell to another Franciscan, Father **Antonio Margil de Jesús**. Assisted by St. Denis and the Tejas, the Spanish under Margil established more missions in Texas. You can see the locations of these missions on the map on the previous page. One was located on the future site of Nacogdoches. Another, San Miguel de los Adaes, was located in present-day Louisiana. Others were spread over a wide area. To protect the missions, Captain Ramón built a presidio on the Neches River. The distance between the presidio and the missions, however, meant that it would be difficult for Ramón's soldiers to fully protect the missionaries. A few soldiers were stationed at each mission to provide security.

Although the Tejas had welcomed the Spanish into their territory, they showed little interest in the Spaniards' religion. Nevertheless the Spanish remained at the missions. They continued working to bring Spanish culture to the people of the area. As you will see in the next section, however, their efforts were soon cut short.

Reading Check **Analyzing Information** How did the Spanish reestablish their control over East Texas?

Image Credit: ©Jeremy Woodhouse/Photodisc/Getty Images (tl)

★ The San Antonio Settlements

The Spanish were determined to firmly establish settlements in East Texas. Officials knew that the first mission failed partly because of its distant location. It was more than 500 miles from the nearest Spanish settlements. Getting supplies to the mission had been difficult. The journey was long and dangerous, with the threat of raids by Texas Indians. Desperate Spanish settlers sometimes even turned to nearby French settlements for supplies. Because of these problems and the experiences of earlier Texas missions, the Spanish decided to set up an outpost between the East Texas missions and the Rio Grande.

KEY DATE 1718
Martín de Alarcón establishes a mission and a presidio at the site of present-day San Antonio.

Spanish officials wanted to make communication and travel between East Texas and Mexico easier. To accomplish that goal, they decided to build a mission-presidio outpost along the San Antonio River. In 1718 **Martín de Alarcón**, the governor of Texas, led a group of colonists to the area. Near the river, they built a mission called San Antonio de Valero. It was a simple structure made of branches, mud, and straw. The group then moved about a mile away and built a presidio named San Antonio de Béxar (BEH-har).

The San Antonio River area was a good location for a settlement. Winters were usually mild. Summers were hot but not very humid—unlike those in East Texas. Cottonwood trees dotted the landscape. One Spaniard called it "the most beautiful part of New Spain."

Over the next few years, the Spaniards built several more missions along the San Antonio River. In 1720 Antonio Margil de Jesús, who had supervised earlier missions in Texas, established San José y San Miguel de Aguayo. By 1721, more than 200 Indians lived in the mission. Over time, it would become the finest mission in Texas. A two-story stone building became the priests' residence. In the 1780s, an elaborately decorated church was built as well. As the years passed, the mission added a sugar mill, where workers made delicious brown sugar cones.

Interpreting Visuals

San Antonio. *The San Antonio has long been important to life in the city of San Antonio, as this image from the 1800s shows.* ***Based on the art, how do people in San Antonio use the river?***

BIOGRAPHY

Martín de Alarcón
(in office 1705–1708 and 1716–1719) Martín de Alarcón arrived in the Americas sometime before 1691. He later became the governor of Spanish Texas. After founding San Antonio, Alarcón set out on a dangerous trip to supply the missions in East Texas. He distributed supplies and talked with the French. Shortly after his journey to East Texas, Alarcón returned to Mexico. **How did Alarcón contribute to Spanish settlement in Texas?**

Many Indian groups, including the Coahuiltecans, lived and worked at the San Antonio missions. The missions soon became ranching centers, with many cattle roaming the area's pastures. They came to be the most successful missions in Texas.

Spanish officials did not want to have only soldiers and priests living in San Antonio. They wanted to establish a civil presence in the area. Alarcón had tried to establish a town in 1718, but he could not convince settlers to move there. In 1731, however, the Spanish developed a new plan. They recruited 15 families of Canary Islanders to move into a town near the San Antonio presidio. The town, San Fernando de Béxar, had the first organized civil government in Texas. Together, the missions, presidio, and town along the San Antonio River officially came to be known as San Antonio de Béxar. It was more commonly called Béxar or San Antonio.

In time, San Antonio became an important stop on the Texas part of **El Camino Real** (kah-MEE-noh reh-AHL), or royal road. This long road led from the East Texas missions south to Mexico City. It was the major route for travel into Texas. Some segments of the road had begun as trails linking American Indian settlements. Others were built or improved by the Spanish.

Despite its importance, El Camino Real was a rough road. Its path crossed several rivers that could cause problems for careless travelers. Nevertheless, the road was important. It linked Texas to Mexico and helped increase Spanish settlement in Texas, particularly in San Antonio.

Reading Check **Identifying Cause and Effect** Why were the San Antonio settlements established?

Section 3 Review

1. Identify and explain the significance of each of the following in Texas history:
- Francisco Hidalgo
- Louis Juchereau de St. Denis
- Domingo Ramón
- Antonio Margil de Jesús
- Martín de Alarcón
- El Camino Real

2. Locate on a Texas map:
- San Antonio

3. Categorizing Copy the graphic organizer below. Use it to identify the steps the Spanish took to settle San Antonio.

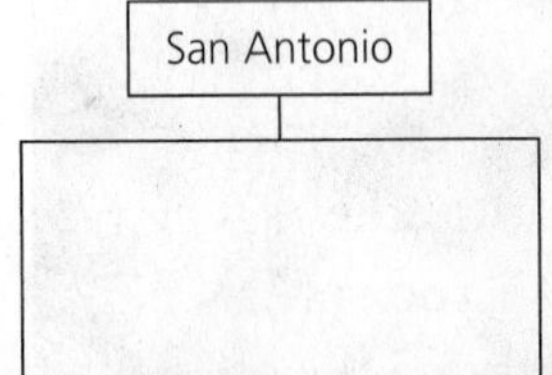

4. Finding the Main Idea

a. Why did St. Denis go to Texas, and how did the Spanish respond?

b. What did the Spanish hope to achieve in East Texas?

c. Look at the map. Where were presidios located in relation to missions?

5. Writing and Critical Thinking myWriteSmart

Identifying Cause and Effect Write a short story about why and how the Spanish founded the first mission and presidio in San Antonio in 1718.

Consider the following:
- the location of San Antonio
- the events surrounding the founding

Section 4

The Expansion of Spanish Settlement

Main Ideas

1. The Aguayo expedition reopened missions in East Texas.
2. José de Escandón helped settle the Rio Grande valley.
3. Missions in Central Texas were attacked by the Apaches.

Key Terms and People

- **Aguayo expedition**
- **Los Adaes**
- **La Bahía**
- **José de Escandón**

Why It Matters Today

In the 1600s several European nations had many colonies in the Americas. Use current events sources to learn more about these nations and their territories today.

myNotebook

Use the annotation tools in your eBook to take notes on the expansion of Spanish settlement in the early to mid-1700s.

The Story Continues

In June 1719 a band of French soldiers surprised the two Spaniards at a mission near what is now Robeline, Louisiana. The French took supplies, including several chickens from the mission's henhouse. Pleased with the raid, the French lieutenant tied several chickens to his saddle. But the chickens scared his horse and it threw the lieutenant to the ground. In the confusion, one of the Spaniards ran off. He raced to a nearby mission and told the people there of the incident, which has become known as the Chicken War.

★ The Aguayo Expedition

The Chicken War was an extension of a conflict between France and Spain in Europe. Although it was a minor incident, it had significant effects in Texas history. Fearing that the raid on the mission indicated the possibility of a large-scale French attack, the Spanish in the area decided to flee. Because of a small band of soldiers, the Spanish pulled out of East Texas entirely.

The Spanish did not stay gone for long, though. On orders from Spain, the viceroy of Mexico set out to retake and fortify the region. He sent the Marqués de San Miguel de Aguayo, the governor of Coahuila and Texas, to drive the French from the region and rebuild the missions. The **Aguayo expedition** set out in 1720.

BIOGRAPHY

José de Escandón

(1700–1770) José de Escandón was born in Spain but moved to Mexico at age 15. He joined the army and rose through the ranks to become a respected commander, known for his victories over hostile Indians. In 1747 he was sent to inspect the region around the mouth of the Rio Grande, an area later named Nuevo Santander. The next year he was named governor of Nuevo Santander and began to recruit colonists to move to the area. For his efforts in settling this area, Escandón has been called the father of the lower Rio Grande valley. **Why is José de Escandón called the father of the lower Rio Grande valley?**

By the time the expedition arrived in East Texas in 1721, the war between France and Spain had already ended. The few French troops remaining in Texas quickly agreed to withdraw to Louisiana. The well-equipped Spaniards quickly reoccupied the missions that had been abandoned. Aguayo also built a number of new missions nearby and new presidios to guard them.

Before the Aguayo expedition, East Texas had only two active missions and one presidio. By the time he left, it had 10 missions and four presidios. Among the presidios he founded were two that later played important roles in Texas. One was Nuestra Señora del Pilar de los Adaes. **Los Adaes** later served as the capital of Spanish Texas. The other was Nuestra Señora de Loreto de la Bahía del Espiritu Santo, or **La Bahía.** La Bahía, later known as Goliad, became one of the largest settlements in Texas.

The Aguayo expedition strengthened Spanish control of East Texas. As a result, the French never again threatened to take over the region.

Reading Check **Evaluating** Was the Aguayo expedition successful? Why or why not?

New Settlements on the Rio Grande

The Aguayo expedition had secured East Texas for Spain. However, a long stretch of the Gulf Coast south of Texas remained inhabited only by American Indians. Spanish officials were concerned that an enemy—such as the French or English—could sail in and claim that territory. They needed a way to secure their hold on the land.

In 1746, the Spanish turned to a military officer named **José de Escandón** to solve their problem. Escandón thought that the best way to secure Spain's claim was to establish a colony in the region. His first action was to move La Bahía, which Aguayo had founded some 20 years earlier, to a new location. Now located on the San Antonio River, La Bahía thrived in its new setting. The population grew, and a ranching industry developed. The missionaries at La Bahía also improved Spain's relationship with the Karankawa Indians, who lived nearby.

Escandón also established a series of settlements along the Rio Grande. To lure colonists from other parts of Mexico to the region, he offered them free land. The first settlements, built in 1749, were successful, and more colonists moved to the area. As the population grew Escandón built more settlements farther south, away from the river. In all, he founded 24 settlements in just six years. Among them was Laredo, settled in 1755. He also built 15 missions and two mining camps. More than 6,000 people lived in Escandón's colonies. In comparison, the settlements of Texas all together had only 1,800 Spanish settlers.

Reading Check **Summarizing** How did José de Escandón contribute to the Spanish presence in Texas?

★ Clashes on the Frontier

Interpreting Visuals

Presidios. *This presidio near modern Goliad protected the mission La Bahía.* ***What features might have helped this presidio protect the Spanish mission?***

Well north of Escandón's settlements, other Spaniards dreamed of establishing more missions. Eager missionaries hoped to convert the American Indians of the region to Catholicism. In addition, some Indian groups had asked to be taught Spanish culture. In the eyes of the missionaries, both sides would benefit from increased missionary work.

An early attempt to build a mission along the San Gabriel River failed due to squabbling and disease. However, the missionaries did not give up. When some Apache chiefs asked to be taught about Spanish life, a group of Franciscans seized the opportunity. In 1757, they built a mission called San Sabá. A presidio was built several miles away.

The Spanish had little success converting the Apaches, however. Many Apaches came to the mission, but they did not stay. They left to hunt and to raid their enemies. Then in March of 1758, some of those enemies decided to retaliate. They decided to attack the Apaches and their allies at San Sabá. About 2,000 enemies of the Apaches, including Comanches, Caddos, Tonkawas, and other groups, attacked. Many were armed with weapons they had gotten from the French. The attackers burned the mission, killing a number of people, including two of the three missionaries. A few weeks earlier, they had stolen many of the presidio's horses, leaving the soldiers there unable to ride to the mission's assistance. The Spanish later sent a counterattack against the Indians, but it failed to drive the Indians away.

The attack at San Sabá spelled the end of Spanish attempts to spread into Central Texas. Their missions and presidios were not sufficient to protect settlers from American Indians in the region. Even as areas to the south were flourishing under Spanish control, Texas remained largely empty of Spanish settlements.

Reading Check **Analyzing Information** What problems did the Central Texas missions face?

★ Section 4 Review

hmhsocialstudies.com
ONLINE QUIZ

1. Identify and explain the significance of each of the following in Texas history:
- Aguayo expedition
- Los Adaes
- La Bahía
- José de Escandón

2. Locate on a Texas map:
- Goliad (La Bahía)

3. Summarizing Copy the graphic organizer below. Use it to identify reasons that Spanish settlements had limited success in Texas.

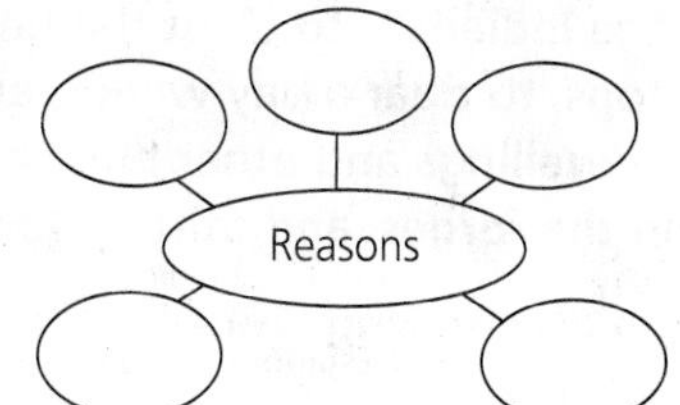

4. Finding the Main Idea

a. How did the conflict between France and Spain affect Texas, and what role did the Aguayo expedition play?

b. How successful were the missions in converting the Apaches and Comanches?

5. Writing and Critical Thinking myWriteSmart

Analyzing Information Write two paragraphs identifying and describing some of the Texas missions and settlements founded after 1740. Consider the following:
- the missions along the San Gabriel River
- the settlements on the southern Rio Grande

Section 5

Life in Spanish Texas

Main Ideas

1. Mission life was structured around prayer and work.
2. The life of a presidio soldier could be harsh.
3. Life in Spanish settlements reflected the influence of Spanish culture, which is still felt in Texas today.

Key Terms

- *ayuntamiento*
- alcalde
- vaqueros

Why It Matters Today

Many states in the American Southwest still show signs of a strong Spanish influence. Use current events sources to identify one way this influence is felt in your area of Texas today.

TEKS: 2C, 2F, 10A, 19C, 19D, 21B, 21C, 22D

myNotebook

Use the annotation tools in your eBook to take notes on life in Spanish Texas.

The Story Continues

The mission bells rang as daylight began to brighten the dark Texas sky. Rising from buffalo-skin mattresses, American Indians walked to the chapel. The priests counted the churchgoers as they entered. Then the congregation chanted and prayed. Later, the Spaniards and the Indians rose to sing a song called *El Alabado.* It told the churchgoers to lift their hearts and praise God. It was the start of another day at a Spanish mission in Texas.

Life in the Missions

The Spanish wanted Texas Indians to live in the missions and learn the Spanish way of life. In the missions, life followed a regular pattern of worship and work. The day started at dawn with religious services. For at least an hour, priests taught mission Indians about the Catholic faith. Then the Indians' workday began under the direction of the priests, soldiers, and civilians, including women. One priest described the work.

TEXAS VOICES

"The labor of the Indians is to plant the fields, look after the cattle, to water the crops, to clear away weeds, and to gather their grain, to [build] their dwellings and other buildings. . . . Some work at weaving and in the forges, and others work as carpenters and bricklayers."

—Isidro Félix de Espinosa, quoted in *Spanish Expeditions into Texas, 1689–1768,* by Nancy Haston Foster

American Indian men tended crops of beans, corn, and cotton. The women made pottery, cared for livestock, wove cloth, and ran the mission kitchen. The day ended with prayers and dinner—usually thin cereal. When they were not in church or working, mission Indians also learned Spanish songs and dances. The Spanish hoped these lessons would encourage Indians to abandon their traditional celebrations. This strategy rarely worked, as one missionary complained. "When the ministers are not watching them they go off to the woods, and there hold their dances." Some Indians also left the missions during hunting or fishing seasons. Most Texas Indians attempted to keep their own culture and traditions despite pressure from the missionaries.

Mission life was often harsh for the Indians who lived there. The missionaries forced them to work growing food both for themselves and for the Spaniards. Indians often were forced to stay in small, closed quarters so they could not leave the missions. In addition, the foods available at missions was less varied than what Indians had in their own settlements. As one missionary noted, "The meals consisted of nothing more than a little purslane [a wild herb] seasoned with salt and pepper." Cramped conditions and a restricted diet led to illness for many Indians.

Nevertheless, some missions, particularly those at San Antonio, became substantial communities. By the 1720s, Indians were irrigating the missions' crops. By 1750, one mission had 2,000 cattle and 1,000 sheep. Mission Indians harvested 2,400 bushels of corn that year. Missions near El Paso and San Antonio thrived because Indians there adopted Spanish cultures. Other missions, such as those in East Texas and La Bahía, helped the Spanish gain a presence in the borderlands.

Reading Check **Evaluating** How did some Texas Indians adapt to Spanish culture while maintaining their Indian traditions?

★ Life in the Presidios

A mission was more likely to succeed if it had a presidio nearby. These military outposts were built of adobe, stone, and timber. Each presidio had a chapel, barracks for soldiers, storage rooms, and a headquarters building. Sometimes a stockade, or wall, surrounded these buildings.

Soldiers in the presidios had several duties. They guarded the missions and protected the Spaniards' herds of horses. They helped supervise the American Indians who lived there. They also provided escorts for travelers, delivered mail, and performed construction work. At times, missionaries and soldiers argued about who had the higher authority in the borderlands. This tension added to the hardship of living in the small, isolated presidios. Although their work was risky, the soldiers received low wages. Many soldiers fell into debt because their pay was late in coming. In addition, the soldiers had poor equipment. Their uniforms were often worn and ragged.

CONNECTING TO

The Arts

Mission Architecture

Many of the early mission chapels in Texas were simple, rough structures made of wood. As the Spanish continued to settle in Texas, they began using stone to build mission villages. The buildings had baroque, or fancy, details. Carvings and sculptures decorated arched windows and doorways. Soaring bell towers stood high against the Texas sky. Mission San José in San Antonio is often called the Queen of Texas Missions. It includes a domed chapel and bright wall paintings. It also has a sculpted window known as the Rose Window. **Why might Spanish missionaries have wanted to create beautiful and fancy chapels?**

CONNECTING TO
Music

Romances Corridos
Romances corridos, or folk songs, were very popular in Spanish settlements in the 1700s and 1800s. These songs, sometimes accompanied by guitar, dealt with many different subjects—love, heartbreak, and bravery. *Romances corridos* continue to appeal to many Texans. The tunes have new words. Even so, they can be traced to the songs that Spanish settlers sang to entertain themselves on the frontier. **How are *romances corridos* from frontier times similar to popular songs of today?**

Despite the harsh conditions, some soldiers brought their families with them. Eventually, a few of these families moved from the presidios and helped start Spanish settlements.

Reading Check Comparing How was life in the presidios similar to life in the missions?

★ Life in the Settlements

Texas settlements had a diverse population of Spaniards, American Indians, and people of African descent. Most of the Spanish had moved north from Mexico in search of good land for farming or ranching. Some settlers were former soldiers who had married Texas Indians. Others were free African Americans, many of whom were of mixed descent.

A few permanent Texas towns grew from the mission-presidio system. As they grew, these Spanish settlements shared some similarities with modern towns. Many had well-defined streets leading past houses and government buildings. There were many different stores, including bakeries and candle shops. In San Antonio, by far the largest settlement, dams were built to create an irrigation system of canals.

San Antonio was the first town in Texas that allowed people to participate in their government. When the Canary Islanders first came, they were given lands and a charter for their settlement, San Fernando de Béxar. They elected an ***ayuntamiento*** (ah-yoon-tah-MYEN-toh), or governing council, to enforce royal and local laws. One member, the **alcalde** (ahl-KAHL-deh), held both judicial and law enforcement powers. However, the viceroy in Mexico City still had authority over all settlements in New Spain, including Texas. The viceroy appointed a governor to act as his representative in Texas and the neighboring state of Coahuila.

The economy of the settlements was mostly based on farming and ranching. Both men and women helped with the planting and harvesting of crops. The cattle business helped San Antonio and other towns grow. **Vaqueros** (vah-KEHR-ohz), or cowboys, worked on ranches near the settlements. Vaqueros were well known for their skilled horse riding and cattle handling. The Spanish also used their skills at horse riding to provide entertainment. Horse racing was a popular event.

Most social activities centered around the family and the church. Religious holidays offered opportunities for worship and socializing. On other special occasions, residents gathered at fandangos, or dances. As the Spanish settlements grew, they developed more cultural activities.

Spanish influences on the culture and history of Texas can still be seen today. Some Spanish missions are still active churches. The restored La Bahía presidio can be seen near present-day Goliad. The Spanish also laid out the first Texas roads, such as El Camino Real. Many of the place names of cities and natural features, such as rivers, are Spanish.

Many Texas traditions also reflect Spanish influence. For example, the Spanish had introduced horses and cattle ranching to the Americas. They settled in Mexico and then moved north, bringing cattle with them. Cowboys later used the equipment developed by the vaqueros. Spanish law also helped shape life in Texas. For example, early Spanish laws protected the property rights of women. Women continued to benefit from these laws when Texas became part of the United States. Spanish architecture, art, food, language, and music are alive in Texas today.

Reading Check **Drawing Inferences and Conclusions** What influence did the Spanish have on Texas place names and the cattle industry?

Section 5 Review

hmhsocialstudies.com
ONLINE QUIZ

1. Define and explain:
- *ayuntamiento*
- alcalde
- vaqueros

2. Comparing and Contrasting
Copy the graphic organizer below. Use it to compare and contrast the defining characteristics of life in Spanish Texas with present-day Texas.

Spanish Texas | Similarities | Modern Texas

3. Finding the Main Idea

a. What were some elements of life in the missions and presidios?

b. What was life in the Spanish settlements like?

4. Writing and Critical Thinking *my*WriteSmart

Evaluating Write a short speech describing examples of Spanish influence on place names or towns in Texas.

Consider the following:
- architecture, food, and music
- languages spoken there

CHAPTER 6 REVIEW

The Chapter at a Glance

Examine the following visual summary of the chapter. Then use it to create an oral presentation describing life in Spanish Texas.

Spanish Missions in Texas

Missions were built to spread the Catholic faith to American Indians and to gain control of the frontier.

Presidios in Texas

Presidios were built to protect the missions and guard against French forces and American Indians on the frontier.

Spanish Settlements in Texas

Spanish settlements grew near missions and presidios, providing valuable supplies. These settlements reinforced the Spanish presence in Texas.

Identifying People and Ideas

Write a sentence to explain the significance of each of the following terms or people.

1. missions
2. José de Escandón
3. La Salle expedition
4. San Francisco de los Tejas
5. Francisco Hidalgo
6. Domingo Ramón
7. Martín de Alancón
8. El Camino Real
9. Aguayo expedition
10. *ayuntamiento*

Understanding Main Ideas

Section 1

1. How did the Spanish try to control the borderlands?

Section 2

2. How did La Salle change Spanish policy in Texas?

Section 3

3. Why is 1718 an important year in Texas history?

Section 4

4. How did the Chicken War lead to the Aguayo expedition, and what were the effects of this expedition?

Section 5

5. What was life like for the Spanish and the American Indians in the missions?
6. Identify some examples of Spanish influence on modern-day Texas.

You Be the Historian

Reviewing Themes

1. **Culture** How did the Spanish attempt to change American Indian culture?
2. **Geography** How did San Antonio's climate and location help the settlement become successful?
3. **Global Relations** How did the war between France and Spain affect Texas?

Thinking Critically

1. **Comparing** Compare how the French and Spanish interacted with Texas Indians.
2. **Sequencing** Identify the order in which the Spanish built missions in the different regions of Texas, and what prompted them to build in those regions.
3. **Identifying Points of View** How did the missionaries' beliefs affect Spanish settlement in Texas?

Texas Test Practice

Interpreting Maps

Study the map below. Then use the information on the map to answer the questions that follow.

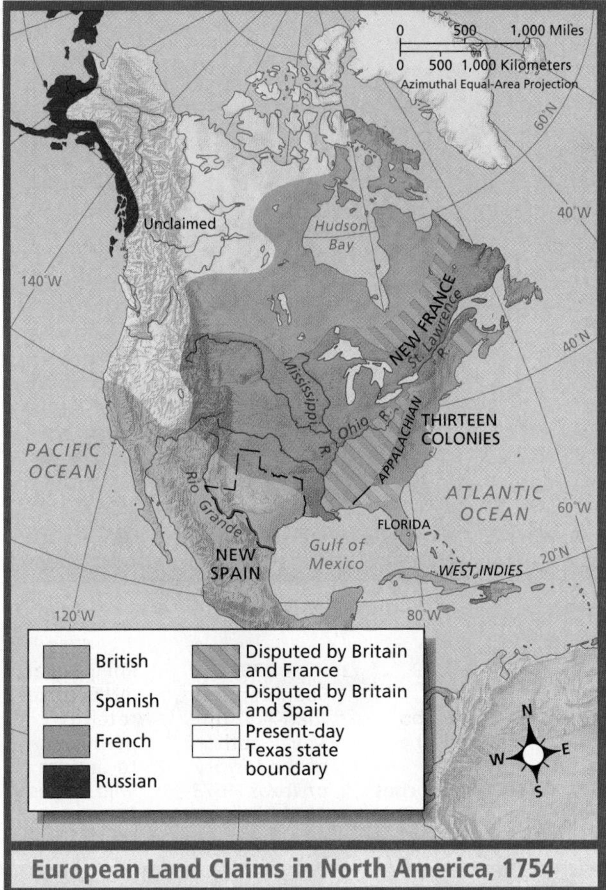

European Land Claims in North America, 1754

1. Which of the following statements is correct?
   - **A** France and Spain claimed the same area.
   - **B** England and Russia claimed the same area.
   - **C** Spain and France shared a border.
   - **D** Spain had no territory in present-day Texas.

2. Which countries claimed parts of present-day Texas?

Analyzing Primary Sources

Read the following quote about the presidio at San Sabá. Then answer the questions.

"The ease with which the enemy has been seen to maintain himself in its vicinity [area] . . . will someday suggest to them the ease with which this presidio can be surrounded. . . . Their numbers will not be small; the captain states that at times as many as three thousand [American Indians] have come to attack the presidio."

3. Which of the following statements best describes the author's point of view?
   - **F** The American Indians might soon realize how easy it would be to capture the presidio.
   - **G** The Spanish should not abandon the presidio because it is easy to defend.
   - **H** The Spanish outnumber the Indians.
   - **J** The Indians will never attack the presidio.

4. Based on the chapter, do you think the author's concerns were reasonable?

Linking to Community

Create a list of all the things in your community that have Spanish place names. Pick four of those names. Then do some research about the origins and meanings of these names. Finally, create a visual display about the place names you have found. If the place name is named for someone, be sure to include information about that person. Include any interesting facts related to the place names. Present what you have learned to your class.

Internet Activity

Access the Internet to find secondary sources describing how people from different racial, ethnic, and religious groups maintain their cultural heritage while adapting to the larger Texas culture. Create a written presentation in which you explain your findings. Be sure to use standard grammar, spelling, sentence structure, and punctuation and to properly cite your sources.

CHAPTER 7

Conflicts of Empire

(1760–1821)

Texas Essential Knowledge and Skills (TEKS) 1B, 2C, 2D, 2F, 8A, 9C, 17C, 19A, 19B, 21A, 21B, 21C, 21D, 21E, 21G, 22A, 22B, 22C, 22D

American Indians battled Spanish forces in Texas.

TEXAS

1766 The Marqués de Rubí expedition begins.

1779 Antonio Gil Ybarbo founds the town of Nacogdoches in East Texas.

1783 Spanish priest Juan Agustín Morfi, author of the *History of Texas, 1673–1779,* dies.

1791 Philip Nolan, a U.S. citizen, receives permission to capture wild horses in Texas.

1760 | 1770 | 1780 | 1790

U.S. and WORLD

1763 France, Great Britain, and Spain sign the Treaty of Paris, officially ending the Seven Years' War.

1775 The American Revolution begins.

1789 The French Revolution begins.

If you were there . . .
Would you join the movement for independence from Spain?

Build on What You Know

The Spanish tried to control Texas by building missions, presidios, and small towns. When the French were no longer a threat, Spanish officials lost interest in Texas. However, Spain soon faced new threats to its control of Texas and the rest of Mexico.

Image Credit: (tr) ©Album/Superstock

Mexican priest Miguel Hidalgo y Costilla called for freedom from Spanish rule.

Mexico won its independence in 1821.

1800

1803
France sells Louisiana to the United States. The purchase doubles the nation's size.

1810

1810
Father Miguel Hidalgo y Costilla's Grito de Dolores, or "Cry of Dolores," sparks Mexico's War of Independence.

1819
U.S. citizen James Long and a small force invade Texas, only to be defeated by Spanish forces.

1820

1821
Mexico, which includes Texas, wins its independence from Spain.

1821
Venezuela joins other Latin American nations in winning independence from Spain.

You Be the Historian

myNotebook

What's Your Opinion? Do you **agree** or **disagree** with the following statements? Support your point of view in your notebook.

- **Economics** Economic ties promote goodwill between nations.
- **Geography** Changing borders do not affect national policy.
- **Global Relations** National leaders and other individuals can dramatically influence politics in other countries.

Section 1

Changes in Spanish Texas

Main Ideas

1. In the 1760s the Spanish abandoned much of Texas.
2. New settlements and new policies improved relations with American Indians in the 1770s.

Why It Matters Today

Settlers in East Texas migrated to new homes in the 1770s. Use current events sources to find information about migration between regions today.

Key Terms and People

- **cede**
- **Marqués de Rubí**
- **Tejanos**
- **Antonio Gil Ybarbo**

TEKS: 2C, 2F, 8A, 9C, 21A, 21B, 22D

myNotebook

Use the annotations tools in your eBook to take notes on changes in Texas in the 1760s and 1770s.

The Story Continues

At the San Sabá presidio, Colonel Diego Ortiz Parrilla was worried. War had broken out between British and French colonists northeast of Texas. Parrilla told Spanish officials that he had heard rumors about the fighting. Both the British and the French were giving guns to the Wichita in hopes of winning them as allies. However, American Indians with guns could pose a serious threat to Spain's hold on Texas. Already, armed Indians had attacked his fort. Parrilla urged officials to strengthen the weak Texas defenses.

★ The Marqués de Rubí Report

The war between France and Great Britain about which Parrilla was worried had begun in 1754. The war, fought for control of the Ohio River valley, was called the French and Indian War. In 1762 Spain joined the war as well, as allies of the French. Only one year later, though, the British forced the French to sign a peace treaty. The effects of this treaty greatly changed the map of North America.

The 1763 Treaty of Paris required France and Spain to **cede**, or officially give, territory to Britain. France gave up Canada and all its claims east of the Mississippi River. Spain ceded Florida. Under a separate treaty, Spain gained New Orleans and Louisiana, which included all French territory west of the Mississippi River. With the loss of this huge region, France no longer posed a threat to Texas. The French had no land left on the mainland of North America.

Although it had been on the losing side of the war, Spain's holdings in North America had grown. Curious about the state of his overseas territory, the king of Spain sent trusted officials to report on conditions in Spanish America. In 1766 the **Marqués de Rubí** began a tour of the presidios of New Spain.

As he traveled through Texas the next year, Rubí grew concerned about conditions there. Most of the presidios needed repairs and were staffed by soldiers who lived in poverty, often without decent uniforms or equipment. One soldier reported, "This company lacks arms, horses, coats, and in a word everything necessary to carry out its obligations [duties]." Of all the presidios in Texas, only La Bahía and San Antonio de Béxar were in decent shape. Rubí also noted that Spanish attempts to befriend and convert the Apaches had failed. Even worse, enemies of the Apaches, such as the Comanches, now saw the Spanish as enemies.

In all, Rubí spent some two years and traveled more than 7,000 miles touring northern New Spain. He understood—as did many Spanish officers stationed on the frontier—that Spain did not have the power, wealth, or people necessary to hold such a huge, remote region. In 1768 Rubí issued a report of his findings. He urged Spain to pull back to the "real" frontier, the borderlands just north of Mexico. To protect this frontier, he proposed a string of 15 forts, each about 100 miles apart, from lower California to southern Texas. Only San Antonio and Santa Fe would remain north of this line of forts. Rubí did not think that a Spanish presence in East Texas was needed because the area no longer bordered French land. He recommended the following policy changes for Texas.

1. Spain should abandon all missions and presidios except those at La Bahía and San Antonio.
2. San Antonio should replace Los Adaes as the capital of Texas.
3. The Spanish population in East Texas should be moved to San Antonio to strengthen its defenses.
4. The Spanish should befriend the Comanches and seek their help in fighting the Apaches.

Reading Check Summarizing Why did Marqués de Rubí recommend withdrawing from much of Texas?

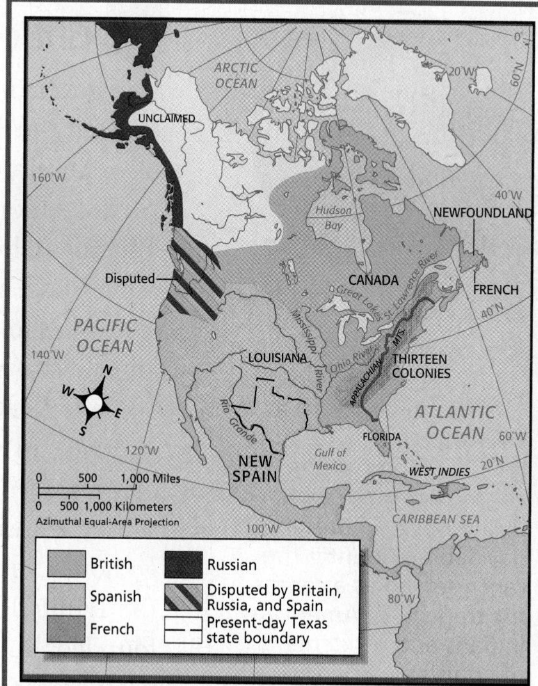

European Land Claims in North America, 1763

Interpreting Maps During the 1700s several European powers claimed land in North America.

Locate Which country controlled the area of present-day Texas?

BIOGRAPHY

Antonio Gil Ybarbo

(1729–1809) Antonio Gil Ybarbo was born at Los Adaes. As an adult, he established a large and prosperous ranch, El Lobanillo, in present-day Sabine County. The ranch served as a center for trade with American Indians and residents of Louisiana. Ybarbo became an important leader. In recognition, Spanish officials made him lieutenant governor, chief justice, and captain of the militia at Nacogdoches. **What role did Ybarbo play in Spain's colonization of Texas?**

★ Changes in Texas Policies

The government approved Rubí's recommendations. In 1773 officials ordered the Spanish withdrawal from East Texas. This was not an easy task. Several hundred people lived in the region in and around Los Adaes. Among the American Indians and French residents were many **Tejanos** (teh-HAH-nohs)—Texas settlers of Spanish descent. They had established homes, farms, and ranches in the area and did not want to leave. However, the Spanish were insistent. One man recalled how an official "went from house to house, driving the people from them." Some settlers died during the hard, three-month trek to San Antonio.

Once in San Antonio—now the capital of Texas—many of the newcomers were unhappy. They found that the best farmland around the settlement was already taken. Many grew homesick and began asking to go home. In 1774 they were given permission to return east, but only to the Trinity River. Led by **Antonio Gil Ybarbo** (ee-BAHR-boh), the group founded Bucareli in present-day Madison County. At first, Bucareli prospered. Comanche raids, disease, and flooding soon became serious problems, however, as Ybarbo described in a letter.

TEXAS VOICES

"On the night of February 14, the river went out of its banks and inundated [flooded] everything on both sides. . . . [The women and children] were got out on boards and doors and taken to the highest point in the vicinity, where a few days later Comanches fell upon us."

—Antonio Gil Ybarbo, quoted in *Documents of Texas History*

In 1779 Ybarbo and the others decided to move farther east. They founded the town of Nacogdoches on the site of an old mission and an even older Caddo settlement. The town prospered. Deep in the Piney Woods, it was not as exposed to attack from hostile Indians as other towns. In addition, the Tejanos who lived in the area were friendly to the Spanish. Nacogdoches developed a brisk trade with Louisiana and nearby Indians. Although Spain officially prohibited such trade, Nacogdoches was far from officials in San Antonio. The town soon became the main gateway for people and goods entering Texas from Louisiana.

Relations between the people of Nacogdoches and the Tejanos reflect a new Spanish attitude toward Texas Indians. Although some Coahuiltecans and other Indians had adapted to life at La Bahía and San Antonio, few other missions had achieved their goal of making Indians into Spanish citizens. Officials therefore decided to adopt a new policy of befriending American Indians whenever possible by trading with them and giving them gifts. The French had successfully used such an approach in their colonies for years.

A former French commander named Athanase de Mézières (mayz-yehr) was chosen to direct the new Texas Indian policy. Mézières was a good choice. He had several years of experience dealing with Indians and spoke several Indian languages. He lost no time in contacting Texas

In 1785 the Spanish signed a peace treaty with the Comanches.

Indians. During the 1770s he established peace with several northern Indian groups.

Overall, Spain's new policy seemed successful. In 1785 the Spanish signed a peace treaty with the Comanches. The Comanches agreed to stop raiding Spanish settlements in return for yearly gifts, including such items as beads, clothes, mirrors, and shoes. After a while, the Spanish even gave the Comanches guns. The treaty maintained a degree of peace with the Comanches for some 30 years.

Apache attacks in Texas continued, however. In 1790 a large Spanish army joined with Comanches, Wichitas, and others. At Soledad Creek west of San Antonio, this force won a major victory over the Apaches. This loss weakened Apache strength in Texas for many years.

Reading Check **Sequencing** List in order what happened to the East Texas settlers from 1773 to 1779.

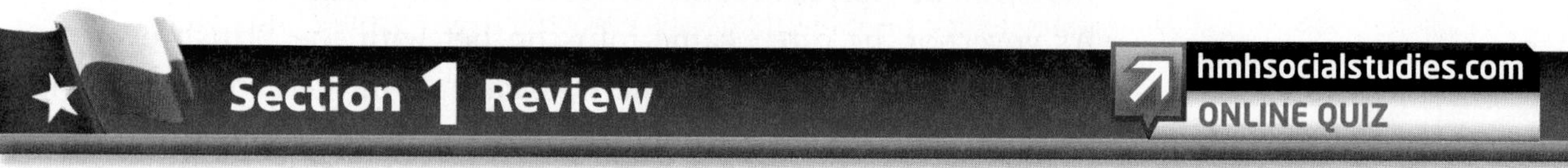

Section 1 Review

1. Define and explain:
- cede
- Tejanos

2. Identify and explain the significance of each of the following:
- Marqués de Rubí
- Antonio Gil Ybarbo

3. Locate on a map:
- Nacogdoches

4. Identifying Cause and Effect
Copy the graphic organizer below. Use it to identify the problems Rubí found in Texas and the actions Spanish officials took to address them.

Problems	Rubí's Report	Actions

5. Finding the Main Idea
a. What led to the Rubí inspection tour?
b. How did Spanish relations with Texas Indians change in the late 1700s?

6. Writing and Critical Thinking myWriteSmart
Sequencing Write a paragraph describing in order the movement of Spanish settlers from and back to East Texas.
Consider the following:
- why the East Texans had to move
- the events of the move

Section 2

Disputes with the United States

Main Ideas

1. Some Spanish officials saw the growth of the United States as a threat to their land in North America.
2. Disputes arose over the border between Texas and Louisiana.

Key Terms and People

- **Louisiana Purchase**
- **Neutral Ground**
- **diplomats**
- **Adams-Onís Treaty**

Why It Matters Today

Spain and the United States could not agree about the border between their territories. Use current events sources to learn about border disputes in the world today.

TEKS: 1B, 2C, 8A, 9C, 21B, 21C, 21E, 22D

***my*Notebook**

Use the annotation tools in your eBook to take notes on disputes between Spain and the United States.

The Story Continues

Bernardo de Gálvez eyed the British fort in Pensacola, Florida, determined to take it. If he did, Spain would regain control of Florida. Gálvez directed the 7,000 soldiers and 35 ships at his command to attack. Inside the fort, though, the 1,600 British troops were not easily defeated. They held out for two months. Then on May 9, 1781, a huge explosion ripped through the fort—a Spanish shell had hit the main gunpowder site. Florida was Spanish once more.

The Growing U.S. Threat

Bernardo de Gálvez became the governor of Spanish Louisiana in 1777. As governor, he often came into conflict with the British over trade issues. Several years after American Patriots in the 13 British colonies declared independence from Great Britain, Spain declared war on the British. Gálvez led Spanish forces in retaking Florida, winning victories against the British in the Bahamas and Louisiana. While fighting in Louisiana, Gálvez ordered officials in Texas to send him cattle to feed his troops. Between 1779 and 1782, Tejanos drove some 10,000 cattle into Louisiana. These were some of the earliest Texas cattle drives.

In 1783 the United States officially won its independence. Though Spain had helped win that independence, the new nation grew so quickly that some Spanish officials began to see it as a threat.

U.S. settlers pushed west as far as the Mississippi River. Without seeking permission, some continued into Spanish Louisiana to the Red River. Although this region belonged to Spain, few Spanish settlers lived there. Nor did many Spaniards live in East Texas, as one Spaniard noted.

TEXAS VOICES

"All the souls, which on our part, populate such a rich and vast province, are to be found in one villa, two presidios, . . . six ranches, seven missions and . . . Bucareli. . . . If one thinks about the millions of souls who could maintain themselves there, . . . the fertility of the land . . . one would not see this abandon without indifference."

—Father Juan Agustín Morfi, quoted in *Spanish Texas, 1519–1810,* by David M. Vigness

Despite some misgivings, Spanish leaders in Louisiana decided to allow U.S. immigration to boost the population. But officials in Texas put troops at Nacogdoches to keep unwanted foreigners out. As the U.S. population grew, Texans watched anxiously. Their anxiety increased in 1800 when Spain returned Louisiana to France. Just three years later, France sold the territory to the United States for $15 million. The deal, known as the **Louisiana Purchase**, doubled the size of the young nation.

Reading Check **Finding the Main Idea** Why did some Spanish officials see the United States as a threat to Spain's colonies?

That's Interesting!

Bernardo de Gálvez

Bernardo de Gálvez's contributions during the Revolutionary War did not end with the fighting. Gálvez represented Spain in negotiating the peace treaty. The U.S. Congress later honored him for his help in gaining U.S. independence. In addition, the region's largest bay was named Galveston in his honor.

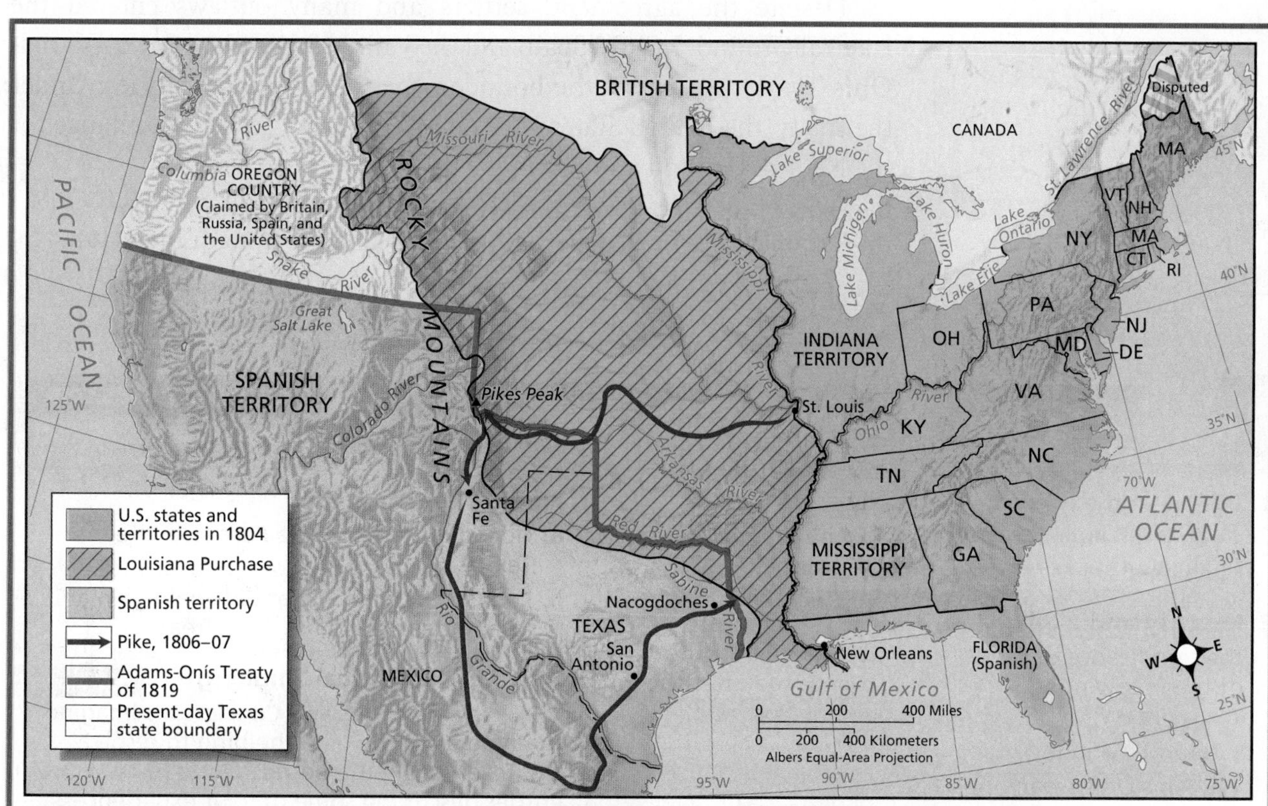

The Louisiana Purchase and the Adams-Onís Treaty

Interpreting Maps The Adams-Onís Treaty defined the border of the Spanish territory.

Places and Regions What rivers helped define the boundaries set by the Adams-Onís Treaty?

★ Border Disputes in Texas

Many Spanish were alarmed that New Spain now shared a border with the rapidly growing United States. To make matters worse, that border was not clearly defined. According to U.S. officials, the Louisiana territory extended as far west as the Rio Grande. Spanish officials disagreed. They claimed that Louisiana ended at the Arroyo Hondo, known today as the Calcasieu River. Fearing that the disagreement could lead to violence, the Spanish brought troops to East Texas.

Meanwhile even more Americans moved west. In 1806 a U.S. army captain named Zebulon Pike set out to explore the Louisiana territory for the government. Spanish soldiers captured him in New Mexico and accused him of spying. In time, the Spanish commander agreed to release Pike. He went home by way of northern Mexico and Texas, which he later described in a book as full of game, herds of mustangs, and wild cattle. His book added to U.S. interest in the region.

In late 1806 Spanish and U.S. military leaders met to discuss the disputed boundary. To prevent violence, they declared the area between the Sabine and the Arroyo Hondo neutral, meaning it did not belong to either side. This territory became known as the **Neutral Ground**. Both countries would remain out of the area until **diplomats** set the official border. Diplomats are officials who represent countries in foreign affairs.

Despite the agreement, settlers and many outlaws entered the Neutral Ground. In 1819 Spain and the United States signed the **Adams-Onís Treaty**, which set the boundary between their territories. Under the treaty, the United States gave up all claims to Texas in exchange for the Neutral Ground and Florida.

Reading Check **Making Generalizations and Predictions** Do you think conflict continued between New Spain and the United States? Why?

★ Section 2 Review

hmhsocialstudies.com
ONLINE QUIZ

1. **Define and explain:**
   - Louisiana Purchase
   - diplomats
2. **Identify and explain** the significance of each of the following in Texas history:
   - Neutral Ground
   - Adams-Onís Treaty
3. **Sequencing** Copy the graphic organizer below. Use it to describe in order the series of events in the border dispute that occurred after the Louisiana Purchase.

   Dispute → Temporary Solution → Permanent Solution

4. **Finding the Main Idea**
   a. How did the Louisiana Purchase affect Texas?
   b. Look at the map. What did Spain gain and lose under the Adams-Onís Treaty?
5. **Writing and Critical Thinking** *my* WriteSmart
   Drawing Inferences and Conclusions Imagine that you are a diplomat helping to resolve the Texas–Louisiana border. Write journal entries describing some of your experiences. Consider the following:
   - issues involved in the border dispute
   - your personal point of view about where the border should be located

Section 3

Unrest and Revolution

Main Ideas

1. The Spanish feared U.S. agents were active in Texas.
2. Mexico began a fight for independence in 1810.
3. Filibusters and rebels tried to take control of Texas.

Why It Matters Today

In the late 1700s some U.S. citizens fought to free Texas and Mexico from Spain. Use current events sources to find information about U.S. involvement in foreign conflicts today.

Key Terms and People

- **Philip Nolan**
- **filibusters**
- **Miguel Hidalgo y Costilla**
- **José Gutiérrez de Lara**
- **Republican Army of the North**
- **siege**
- **Battle of Medina**
- **James Long**

TEKS: 2D, 17C, 19A, 19B, 21B, 21D, 21E, 22D

myNotebook

Use the annotation tools in your eBook to take notes on the struggle for Mexican independence and its effects in Texas.

The Story Continues

To Philip Nolan, the mustangs roaming the Texas plains gleamed like gold. Horses were valuable items, and in Texas, they ran free. All you had to do was catch them. Nolan became a mustanger, capturing wild horses in Texas and driving them to Louisiana. There he sold them at a hefty profit. Then Spanish officials heard rumors of a U.S. plot to invade northern New Spain. Was Nolan a U.S. spy?

The Philip Nolan Expeditions

When they first heard of his actions, Spanish officials thought that **Philip Nolan** was searching for wealth. Nolan, a U.S. citizen, had first come to Texas in 1791 as a mustang trader. Three times Nolan entered Texas with the government's permission, but some Spanish leaders grew suspicious. They had heard rumors that Nolan was acting as a spy for General James Wilkinson, the U.S. commander in Louisiana and Nolan's former boss.

In late 1800 Nolan and some 20 men returned to Texas, this time without permission. Spanish soldiers sent to arrest Nolan found his camp about 40 miles northwest of Waco. Nolan, however, resisted arrest and was killed. Most of his men were captured, tried, and imprisoned. Whatever Nolan's motives may have been, his actions increased Spanish fears of U.S. expansion.

Father Miguel Hidalgo was a leader in the fight for Mexican independence.

The Spanish reaction to the presence of U.S. citizens in Texas was not unreasonable. For years to come, Texas would suffer raids by **filibusters**, military adventurers who tried to stir up rebellion in other countries. Some of these filibusters wanted to free Texas from Spanish rule, either to become an independent country or to join the United States. Others just hoped to profit by causing chaos in Texas. Some Spanish officials also believed that agents of the U.S. government were being sent specifically to cause trouble in Texas, as one Texas governor wrote.

TEXAS VOICES

"The king [of Spain] has been informed . . . that the United States has ordered emissaries to move here and work to subvert the population. . . . Avoid the entry of any foreigner or any suspected person."

—Pedro de Nava, quoted in *Spanish Texas, 1519–1821*, by Donald E. Chipman

Reading Check **Identifying Points of View** Why did Spanish officials grow suspicious of Philip Nolan?

The Call for Mexican Independence

In 1808, Napoleon, the emperor of France, invaded Spain and removed the Spanish king from power. This conquest would have profound effects in Mexico. Nearly all Mexicans supported their deposed king. However, a struggle for power broke out between creoles—people of Spanish descent who had been born in Mexico—and *peninsulares*, who had been born in Spain. In 1808 the *peninsulares* overthrew the viceroy and took control of the country. In response, creole groups across Mexico began to talk of taking up arms against the government.

On September 16, 1810, Father **Miguel Hidalgo y Costilla** (ee-DAHL-goh ee kohs-TEE-yah), a creole priest in Dolores, Mexico, rang a church bell and called for an end to rule by the *peninsulares*. "Will you not defend your religion and rights as true patriots? Long live our Lady of Guadalupe! Death to bad government! " This passionate cry, called the Grito de Dolores or "Cry of Dolores," sparked a war. What began as a revolt against the governing *peninsulares* became a war against Spain for Mexican independence.

VIDEO
Miguel Hidalgo's Call to Arms.

hmhsocialstudies.com

Supporters flocked to Father Hidalgo's cause. He soon led an army of more than 50,000. Support continued to grow as this army marched across Mexico. However, in 1811, Spanish soldiers captured and executed Father Hidalgo.

Still, the revolution did not end with Father Hidalgo's death. Among those who rose up were many Texans. In January 1811 a group of Hidalgo supporters in San Antonio led by Juan Bautista de las Casas drove the Spanish governor of Texas from office. Their revolt did not last long, though. Rebels quarreled among themselves, and Spanish loyalists quickly took the city back.

Reading Check **Analyzing Information** How did the call for Mexican independence affect life in Texas?

★ The Green Flag over Texas

As Mexico was struggling to become independent, some people decided that Texas should be independent too. One of those was **José Gutiérrez de Lara**. When Hidalgo's revolution began, Gutiérrez de Lara, a native of Revilla on the Rio Grande, went to the United States to win support for the rebels. After Hidalgo's death, Gutiérrez decided to use Texas as a base from which to continue the fight.

With secret support from the United States, Gutiérrez raised an army in Louisiana. One of his recruits was a U.S. Army officer, Augustus William Magee, who became co-commander of the force. Gutiérrez and Magee named their army, which included both Mexicans and U.S. citizens, the **Republican Army of the North**.

Flying a solid green flag, the Gutiérrez-Magee expedition invaded Texas in August 1812. The army quickly took Nacogdoches. At La Bahía, though, the expedition had more difficulty. The rebels took control of the presidio, but Spanish soldiers laid **siege** to it. A siege is a military blockade of a city or fort.

Despite a four-month siege, the Spanish army failed to take the fort. In March 1813 the Spanish army, led by the governor, left La Bahía to return to San Antonio. Gutiérrez and his army followed and defeated the Spanish force just outside of San Antonio. Gutiérrez took the governor prisoner. On April 6, 1813, the rebels declared Texas independent.

The Republican Army's military success was soon overshadowed by problems, though. After the rebels' *peninsular* prisoners, including the governor, were brutally executed, many soldiers became upset and left the army. Many who remained were unhappy with Gutiérrez's leadership. They forced him from power and replaced him. .

Meanwhile, a royalist army under General Joaquín de Arredondo moved into Texas from the south. On August 18, 1813, his army met the smaller Republican Army of the North, now composed mostly of Mexican rebels, in the **Battle of Medina**. Arredondo won a decisive victory. More than 1,000 rebels lay dead. He then led a campaign of revenge across Texas, executing or arresting hundreds of Tejanos.

Reading Check **Identifying Cause and Effect** What problems arose for the Republican Army of the North, and how was the army affected by them?

Diez y Seis de Septiembre

On September 16, 1810, Father Hidalgo delivered his historic Grito de Dolores. Today many Texans celebrate Diez y Seis de Septiembre, or the "Sixteenth of September." Festivities include speeches, parades, and traditional Mexican foods, music, and dancing. Some Texas towns also hold *charreadas*, Mexican-style rodeos exhibiting skilled horse riding. These celebrations honor an important day in Mexican and Texas history. **What event does Diez y Seis de Septiembre honor?**

Interpreting Visuals

Galveston. *Based on this image, why do you think Galveston was a popular base for pirates and rebels?*

★ Pirates and Rebels on the Coast

Despite General Arredondo's punishing actions, filibuster and revolutionary activity continued in Texas. Henry Perry, a veteran of the Gutiérrez-Magee expedition, gathered a force of about 300 soldiers on Galveston Island. Before long another filibuster force under Spaniard Francisco Xavier Mina also came to Galveston. They were joined there by Louis Michel Aury, a French pirate-adventurer. Aury was working with Mexican rebels and raiding Spanish ships in the Gulf of Mexico. He hoped to use the Mexican struggle for independence as a way to make a profit for himself.

Perry, Mina, and Aury planned to work together to invade Mexico. In April 1817, though, Perry broke away from the others and took a small force into Texas. They attacked La Bahía, where Perry demanded the surrender of the Spanish garrison. When the Spanish refused and prepared to attack, Perry and his men fled. Spanish forces soon surrounded the group, killing or wounding most of them. Perry later died after being wounded in the fighting. The planned invasion of Mexico never happened.

Aury was not the only pirate to operate from Galveston at this time. French pirate Jean Lafitte also had a base there. Lafitte had been a pirate and smuggler in Louisiana for many years. He had also fought for the United States at New Orleans in the War of 1812. To thank him, the U.S. president had given Lafitte a pardon for his crimes. Like Aury, Lafitte raided Spanish ships in the Gulf. Although he too claimed to be fighting for Mexican independence, he most likely was interested only in Spanish treasure. After Lafitte began to attack American ships, though, the U.S. Navy forced him to leave Galveston Island in 1820.

Reading Check **Finding the Main Idea** Where was filibuster activity based after the Gutiérrez-Magee expedition?

The Long Expeditions

Perhaps the best known of all filibusters in Texas was **James Long** from Natchez, Mississippi. Long was not happy with the way the United States had settled the boundaries of Louisiana. He thought that Texas was part of the Louisiana Purchase and should have become U.S. territory. Determined to do something about the situation, Long organized an army to invade Texas.

In 1819 Long and his army invaded Texas and captured Nacogdoches. He declared Texas independent, stating that the people of Texas had wanted to join the United States. Long won the support of a few Tejanos, but it was not enough to preserve his claim. Long and his army were soon driven out of Texas by Spanish forces.

Refusing to give up, Long planned a second invasion. In 1820 his new army sailed for Texas, landing at Point Bolivar. In late 1821 he captured La Bahía, but Spanish forces quickly took it back and forced Long to surrender. While awaiting trial, Long was shot and killed by a Spanish soldier. Officials claimed the death was accidental, but Long's friends called it murder. His death ended the early filibuster period in Texas.

Long's wife Jane had accompanied him to Texas and awaited his return at Point Bolivar. With her were two young girls—her daughter, Ann, and a slave named Kian. When the army failed to return, the Longs struggled through a difficult winter. At one point, several Karankawa Indians appeared, but Long fired a cannon and scared them away. Eventually, Jane Long learned of her husband's death. She traveled back to the United States, hoping one day to return to Texas.

Reading Check **Identifying Points of View** Why did James Long decide to invade Texas?

GLOBAL CONNECTIONS

Revolutions in Latin America

The Mexican rebellion was part of a revolutionary wave that swept Latin America in the early 1800s. These revolts led to the creation of several nations, including Argentina, Brazil, Peru, and Venezuela. Simon Bolívar, nicknamed the Liberator, led many of these struggles for independence. The nation Bolivia is named in his honor. By 1830 Spain had lost all of its American empire except the islands of Cuba and Puerto Rico.

Who was "the Liberator"?

Section 3 Review

hmhsocialstudies.com ONLINE QUIZ

1. Define and explain:
- filibusters
- siege

2. Identify and explain:
- Philip Nolan
- Miguel Hidalgo y Costilla
- José Gutiérrez de Lara
- Republican Army of the North
- Battle of Medina
- James Long

3. Categorizing Copy the graphic organizer below. Use it to identify the filibusters and to describe their actions and goals.

Filibuster Expedition	Actions	Goals

4. Finding the Main Idea

a. What goal did José Gutiérrez de Lara hope to achieve in Texas?

b. What was the outcome of the Battle of Medina?

5. Writing and Critical Thinking myWriteSmart

Supporting a Point of View Imagine that you live in San Antonio de Béxar. Write an article either supporting or opposing the Republican Army of the North's activity.

Consider the following:
- the reasons the army was fighting
- the events that occurred during and after the army's expedition in Texas

Section 4

Spanish Rule Ends in Mexico

Main Ideas

1. Mexico won its independence from Spain in 1821.
2. The Mexican War for Independence was very costly for Texas and its people.

Key Terms and People

- **Agustín de Iturbide**
- **jacales**

Why It Matters Today

The end of Spanish rule in Mexico led to great changes in the country. Use current events sources to find information about issues facing the government and people of Mexico today.

TEKS: 1B, 2D, 21B, 21C, 22D

myNotebook

Use the annotation tools in your eBook to take notes on the end of Spanish rule in Mexico and its effects on Texas.

The Story Continues

Early on July 19, 1821, the people of San Antonio de Béxar gathered in the town's plaza. They had only recently learned the news—the war was over, and Mexico had won its independence from Spain. Texas governor Antonio María Martínez stood solemnly with the others. Slowly, the Spanish flag in the plaza was lowered, and another flag was raised in its place. Standing before a crucifix, the group began reciting an oath of loyalty to Mexico.

Mexico Wins Independence

While some people were trying to free Texas, others had continued to fight for Mexico's independence. After the Spanish captured and executed Father Hidalgo, a priest named José María Morelos y Pavón took control of the revolution. Morelos wanted to break away from the Spanish monarchy and establish a republic in Mexico. A strong military leader, he won numerous battles. Morelos and his troops gained control of much of Mexico. In 1815, however, the Spanish captured Morelos and executed him.

The death of Morelos was a blow to the revolution. Although a few bands of rebels led by Vicente Guerrero, Guadalupe Victoria, and others continued to harass the Spanish army, few people held out much hope. The struggle for Mexican independence seemed at its end.

Then in 1820 surprising events in Europe breathed new life into the uprising. A new group rose to power in Spain. This group held views with which many Spanish loyalists in Mexico did not agree. As a result, many of those loyalists changed sides. No longer supporters of the Spanish king, they joined the movement for independence instead.

Among those former loyalists who switched sides was **Agustín de Iturbide** (ee-toor-BEE-deh). Iturbide had been a leader of the Spanish forces trying to put down the revolution. In fact, he had led the forces that defeated and captured Morelos. Fearing that the new government in Spain would take away some of his power, Iturbide joined forces with Guerrero's rebels. He declared his three goals: Mexico would be free from Spain. All people in Mexico would be equal. And the Roman Catholic Church would be Mexico's official religion.

Together the armies of Iturbide and Guerrero defeated the Spanish in 1821. Mexico had won its independence. Now free from Spanish rule, Mexico needed a new government. Although they had planned to share power, Iturbide forced Guerrero aside and took power for himself. In 1822 he declared himself Emperor Agustín I. His reign would not last long, and the Mexican people soon turned against him. However, his position in Mexican history was secured.

KEY DATE 1821
Mexico, including Texas, wins independence from Spain.

Reading Check **Sequencing** Describe in order the final events leading to Mexican independence.

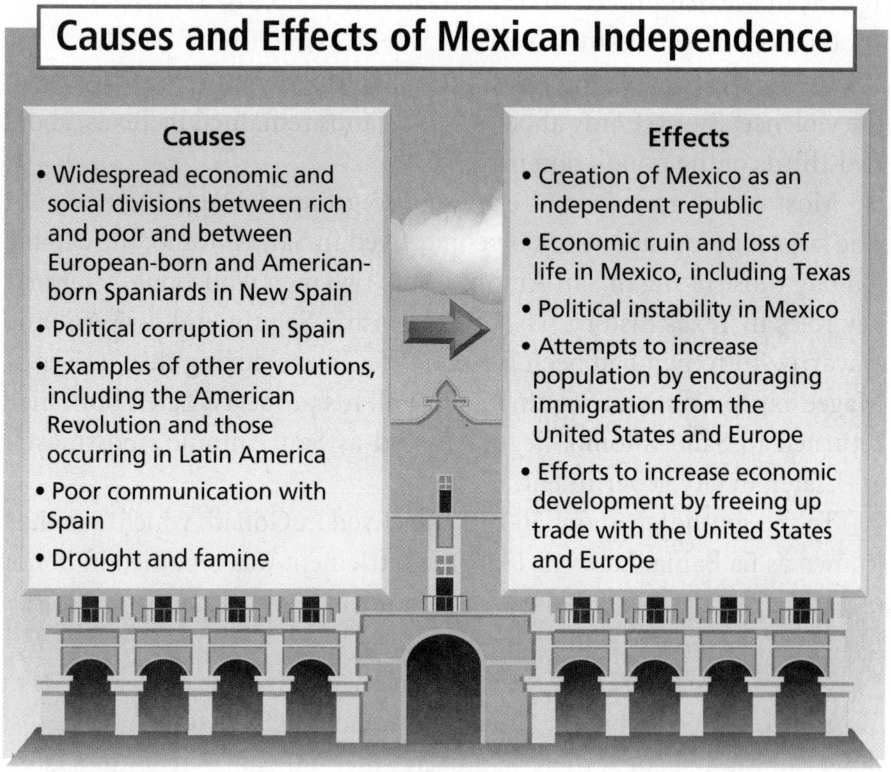

Causes and Effects of Mexican Independence

Causes	Effects
• Widespread economic and social divisions between rich and poor and between European-born and American-born Spaniards in New Spain • Political corruption in Spain • Examples of other revolutions, including the American Revolution and those occurring in Latin America • Poor communication with Spain • Drought and famine	• Creation of Mexico as an independent republic • Economic ruin and loss of life in Mexico, including Texas • Political instability in Mexico • Attempts to increase population by encouraging immigration from the United States and Europe • Efforts to increase economic development by freeing up trade with the United States and Europe

Interpreting Visuals

Ranchos. *Ranching in early Texas was often hot, dusty work.* ***What does this painting suggest about ranchers of this period?***

★ The War's Impact on Texas

Although many Texans had supported Mexican independence, few were prepared for the costs of the fight. Years of fighting in Texas and by Texans in Mexico proved to be costly for the people of Texas.

One of the greatest costs of the war was the loss of people. Many Tejanos had been killed in the fighting, and many more had fled from the violence. By 1821 only about 3,000 Tejanos remained in Texas, about two-thirds of the population in 1810.

Most of the remaining Tejanos were grouped in two settlements. The largest group, about 1,500 people, lived in San Antonio, the capital. Among those living in San Antonio were two men who would later play key roles in Texas history. They were Erasmo Seguín and José Antonio Navarro. Both men had been forced to flee Texas during the Gutiérrez-Magee expedition, and Seguín had lost all his property. Later, both men returned to San Antonio. Seguín served as San Antonio's postmaster and, later, in city government.

To the southeast, about 500 Tejanos lived in Goliad, which was then known as La Bahía. Later, in 1829, the settlement was renamed in honor of Father Hidalgo. The name *Goliad* came from rearranging the letters in the name *Hidalgo*, minus the silent *H*.

Nacogdoches in East Texas had been one of the largest settlements in Texas before the revolution. After the war, however, the town was almost deserted. Many people there had been killed during Arredondo's campaign of revenge, and many more had fled to Louisiana.

To the south and west—an area that is part of Texas today but was not at the time—several thousand people lived along the Rio Grande. They were grouped mostly around El Paso del Norte and Laredo. Unlike the people in East Texas, however, they lived in small settlements. Many lived on isolated ranches. The scrub and semi-arid grasslands along the lower Rio Grande helped the region develop into a major ranching area. Livestock included cattle, horses, mules, sheep, and goats.

Ranching was not easy after the war. The fighting had left the Texas economy in ruins, with livestock lost and crops destroyed. Governor Antonio María Martínez expressed his sorrow.

TEXAS VOICES

"[The armies] have drained the resources of the country, and laid their hand on everything that could sustain [support] human life. [Texas] has advanced at an amazing rate toward ruin and destruction.

—Antonio María Martínez, quoted in *The Mexican Frontier, 1821–1846*, by David Weber

The ranching industry recovered quickly, however. A steady horse trade developed between Texas and markets in the United States.

The Tejanos were not the only residents in Texas after the War of Independence. About 30,000 American Indians also lived in the region. However, events during the war had caused strain between Tejanos and Indians. As a result, the years following the fighting saw an increase in American Indian attacks on Texas settlements.

To guard against such attacks, wealthy ranchers built stone houses that resembled small forts. They put bars and shutters over their windows, and some built watchtowers. Others built homes of adobe. Less fortunate Tejanos lived in **jacales** (hah-KAH-lehs), one-room huts made of sticks and mud. These structures provided little safety from attacks.

Reading Check **Analyzing Information** How did Tejanos adapt to their environment?

Section 4 Review

1. Define and explain:
- jacales

2. Identify and explain the significance of the following in Texas history:
- Agustín de Iturbide

3. Locate on a map:
- San Antonio
- Goliad
- Nacogdoches

4. Summarizing
Copy the graphic organizer below. Use it to summarize how the Mexican War of Independence affected Texas.

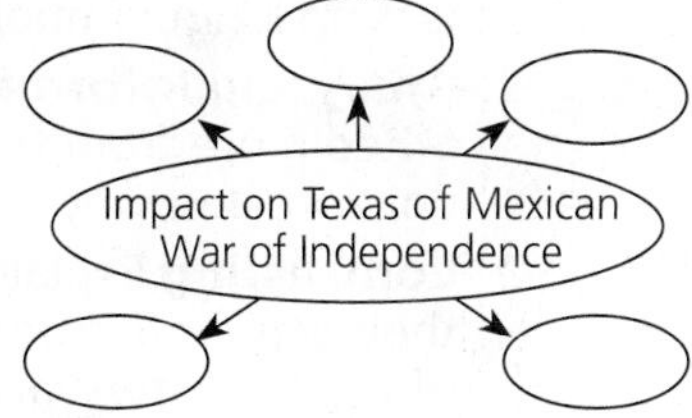

5. Finding the Main Idea

a. What was ranch life like in Texas?

b. What was the impact of Mexico's War of Independence on Texas?

c. What is the significance of the year 1821 in Texas?

6. Writing and Critical Thinking myWriteSmart

Sequencing Write a paragraph describing in order the final events of the Mexican War of Independence.

Consider the following:
- the rise of new leaders
- the effects of the war on Texas

The Chapter at a Glance

Examine the following visual summary of the chapter. Then use the visual to organize the information into an outline that a classmate can use as a study guide for the chapter.

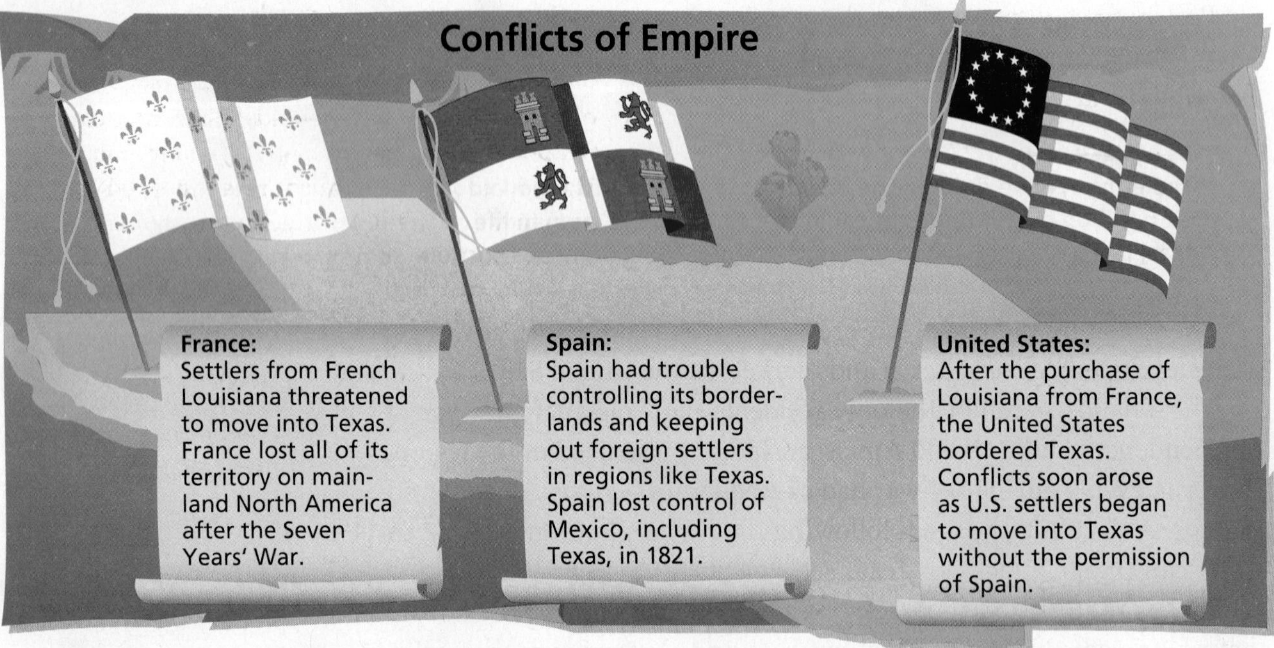

Identifying People and Ideas

Write a sentence to explain the role or significance of each of the following terms or people.

1. Tejanos
2. Antonio Gil Ybarbo
3. Louisiana Purchase
4. Adams-Onís Treaty
5. José Gutiérrez de Lara
6. filibusters
7. Miguel Hidalgo y Costilla
8. Marqués de Rubí
9. James Long
10. Philip Nolan

Understanding Main Ideas

Section 1

1. What actions did the Marqués de Rubí report lead to in Texas?

Section 2

2. What was the significance of the Louisiana Purchase for Texas?
3. What issue created territorial conflicts between Louisiana and New Spain, and how was it resolved?

Section 3

4. What did the filibusters hope to accomplish with their activities?
5. What problems weakened the Republican Army of the North?

Section 4

6. What roles did Texans play in the struggle for Mexican independence?

You Be the Historian

1. **Economics** What economic approach did the Spanish use to improve their relations with Texas Indians?
2. **Geography** How did the Louisiana Purchase affect Spanish policy in Texas?
3. **Global Relations** How did U.S. citizens try to influence events in Mexico and Texas?

Thinking Critically

1. **Supporting a Point of View** Do you agree with the Marqués de Rubí that defending East Texas was no longer important? Support your answer.
2. **Analyzing Information** Which country benefited more from the Adams-Onís Treaty, in your opinion, and why?
3. **Contrasting** Explain how the filibusters' views of their actions differed from Spanish officials' views of the filibusters' actions.

Texas Test Practice

Interpreting Maps

Study the map below. Then use the information on the map to help you answer the questions that follow.

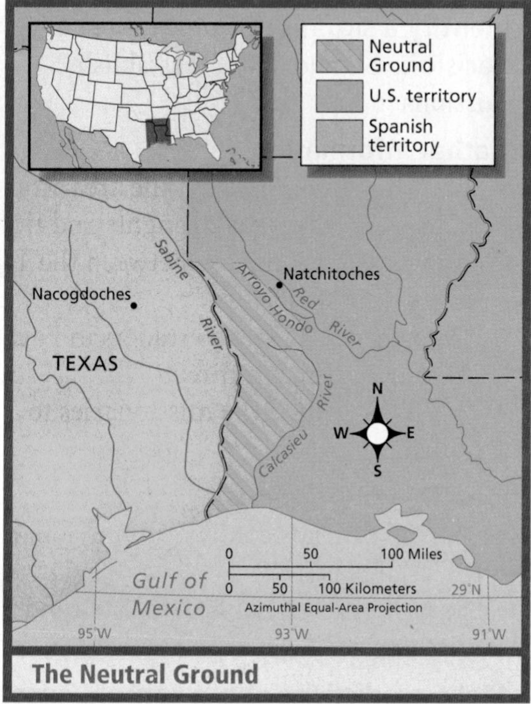

The Neutral Ground

1. Which streams and rivers helped define the boundaries of the Neutral Ground?
   - **A** the Sabine, the Arroyo Hondo, and the Red
   - **B** the Sabine and the Red
   - **C** the Calcasieu, the Sabine, and the Arroyo Hondo
   - **D** the Red and the Calcasieu

2. Why was the location of the Neutral Ground important?

Analyzing Primary Sources

Read the following quote by historian Anna Pennybacker, from her book *A History of Texas for Schools* (1895). Then answer the questions.

"In San Antonio lived many descendants of aristocratic Spanish families; the army officers were generally men of polished manners, as they often came from the Vice-Regal Court of Mexico; the priests were men of learning and refinement. The governor gave frequent receptions, while each night on the public square the people met to dance, converse, to promenade [walk], and to visit."

3. According to the author, what were some of the qualities of the leaders in early San Antonio?
   - **F** generous, talkative, liked to dance
   - **G** rugged, moderately wealthy, happy
   - **H** aristocratic, polished, educated, refined
   - **J** educated, ill-mannered, religious

4. Based on the above quote, what were some respected occupations in early San Antonio?

Linking to Community

Work with your classmates to create a multimedia display illustrating Spanish heritage in Texas and in your community. You may need to do additional research about Spaniards and Tejanos who lived and worked in the area in the 1700s and 1800s. Prepare material showing what affect they had on the region where you live. Be sure to include brief biographical material on the people you are researching. Then hold a Spanish heritage day at your school for students, parents, and teachers.

Internet Activity 

Access the Internet to locate and read primary and secondary sources on filibusters and revolutionaries in Spanish Texas. As you read, try to evaluate the validity of each source based on its language and what you know about the author. You may wish to corroborate what you read with other sources as well. Share your findings with the class.

Social Studies Skills

WORKSHOP

Decision-Making Skills

Like you, many figures in Texas history have faced difficult decisions. With the use of decision-making skills you will be better able to make a decision on important issues. The following activities will help you develop and practice these skills.

Decision Making involves choosing between two or more options. Listed below are guidelines that will help you with making decisions.

1. **Identify a situation that requires a decision.** Think about your current situation. What issue are you faced with that requires you to take some sort of action?
2. **Gather information.** Examine the causes of the issue or problem and consider how it affects you and others.
3. **Identify your options.** Consider the actions that you could take to address the issue. List these options so that you can compare them.
4. **Make predictions about consequences.** Predict the consequences of taking the actions listed for each of your options. Compare these possible consequences. Some options might be easier or seem more satisfying. But do they produce the results that you want?
5. **Take action to implement a decision.** Choose a course of action from your available options and put it into effect.

Example

During the early 1700s, Spanish officials decided to reestablish missions in East Texas after they had left the region in the 1690s. Here is an example of the decision-making process that the officials might have used.

1. **Identify a situation that requires a decision.** Should Spain reestablish missions in East Texas?
2. **Gather Information.**
   - Spanish missionaries left the area after crops were ruined by droughts and floods and when tensions rose between the Tejas and the missionaries.
   - The presence of French traders in East Texas was seen as a threat.
   - The Tejas wanted the missionaries to return.
3. **Identify your options.**
   - Spanish officials could send missionaries to East Texas.
   - Spanish officials could refuse to send missionaries to East Texas.
4. **Make predictions about consequences.**
   - If the missionaries return, the Tejas might welcome the missionaries and Spain's influence in the region could grow.
   - If Spanish officials refuse to send the missionaries to East Texas, the influence of Spain in the region might decrease.
5. **Take action to implement a decision.** Spanish officials decide to reestablish East Texas missions.

Practicing the Skill

Chapter 5, Section 3, Searching for Cities of Gold, describes Spanish explorers' search for the Seven Lost Cities of Gold. Imagine that you are a Spanish explorer aware of earlier failed attempts to find these cities. Use the decision-making guidelines above to help you decide whether to launch another expedition for the Lost Cities of Gold. Be prepared to defend your decision.

History in Action

UNIT 2 SIMULATION

You Make the Decision . . .

Should Spain finance a new expedition to Texas?

Complete the following activity in small cooperative groups. It is 1501, shortly after the dawn of the era of exploration. The Spanish king and queen are debating whether to finance an exploration expedition to Texas. Your group has been asked to provide the king and queen with information to help them decide whether to finance a new exploration expedition to Texas. Follow these steps to reach your decision.

1. **Gather information.** Use your textbook, Web sites, and any other resources to find information that might influence whether Spain should finance an expedition to Texas. What advantages could be gained by exploring Texas? What challenges would explorers face? Be sure to use what you learned from this unit's Skills Workshop on Decision Making to help you make an informed choice. You may want to divide up different parts of the research among group members.

2. **Identify options.** After reviewing the information you have gathered, consider the options you might recommend to the king and queen about whether Texas should be explored. Your final decision may be easier to reach if you consider as many options as possible. Be sure to record your possible options for your presentation.

3. **Predict consequences.** Now examine each option that your group came up with and consider the possible outcomes of each course of action. Ask yourselves such questions as: "Are gold and treasure in Texas, as they are in South America?" and "Who would control the region if Spain does not explore it?" Once you have predicted the consequences, record them as notes for your presentation.

4. **Take action to implement your decision.** After you have considered your options, create your presentation. Be sure to make your decision about exploring Texas very clear to the king and queen. You will need to support your decision by including information you gathered and by explaining why you rejected other options. You may want to create cluster diagrams, maps, or charts to support your decision. When you are ready, decide who in your group will make which part of the presentation and take your decision to the king and queen (the rest of the class).

   As you present, try to engage your audience's attention. Use a variety of sentence types to keep your audience interested. For example, you may ask a question to which you then provide an answer. Also take care to use connecting words like *after, because,* and *therefore* to help your audience understand how your ideas are related.

UNIT 3

The Mexican National Period

(1820–1835)

During the Mexican period, many Texans—both Tejanos and new immigrants—worked in ranching.

Texas Teens

Young Ranchers

When Mexico won its independence from Spain, Texas became part of the new Mexican republic. There were not many permanent settlements in what is today Texas. The huge amount of available space made Texas an ideal place for ranching. Spanish settlers brought huge herds of cattle and other animals to Texas. After Mexico became independent, the children and grandchildren of those early settlers continued to tend their herds.

When new settlers arrived in Texas in the 1820s, they admired the skill with which young Tejano ranchers rode horses. These young men spent most of their days in the saddle. One observer noted that ranchers seldom walked, preferring to ride even over short distances. Ranchers were attached to their horses, treating them almost like companions. People generally did not refer to their mounts just as horses. They used more descriptive terms, such as "the lively gray mare."

Besides their horsemanship, many Tejanos were known for their ability to use a lariat. A skilled rancher could easily stop a charging steer with a rope around its neck or legs. In addition to being an essential ranching tool, the lariat was also a useful method of self-defense. A well-thrown lariat could ensnare an attacker, allowing the rancher to make a quick getaway.

The life of a young rancher was not all work, though. Young men in Tejano communities liked to gather together for contests that tested their skills. These competitions were called *días de toros*, or days of the bulls. Various contests gave participants the opportunity to display their skills at riding and roping.

In addition to races and roping challenges, competitors took part in more unusual events. In one event, for example, riders on horseback took off at full speed, leaning down from their saddles to try to grab objects half buried in the sand. **What was life like for young Tejano ranchers in Mexican Texas?**

In this unit you will learn more about the period during which Texas was part of Mexico. You will also learn about the arrival of new settlers in Texas and the issues that arose between them and the Mexican government.

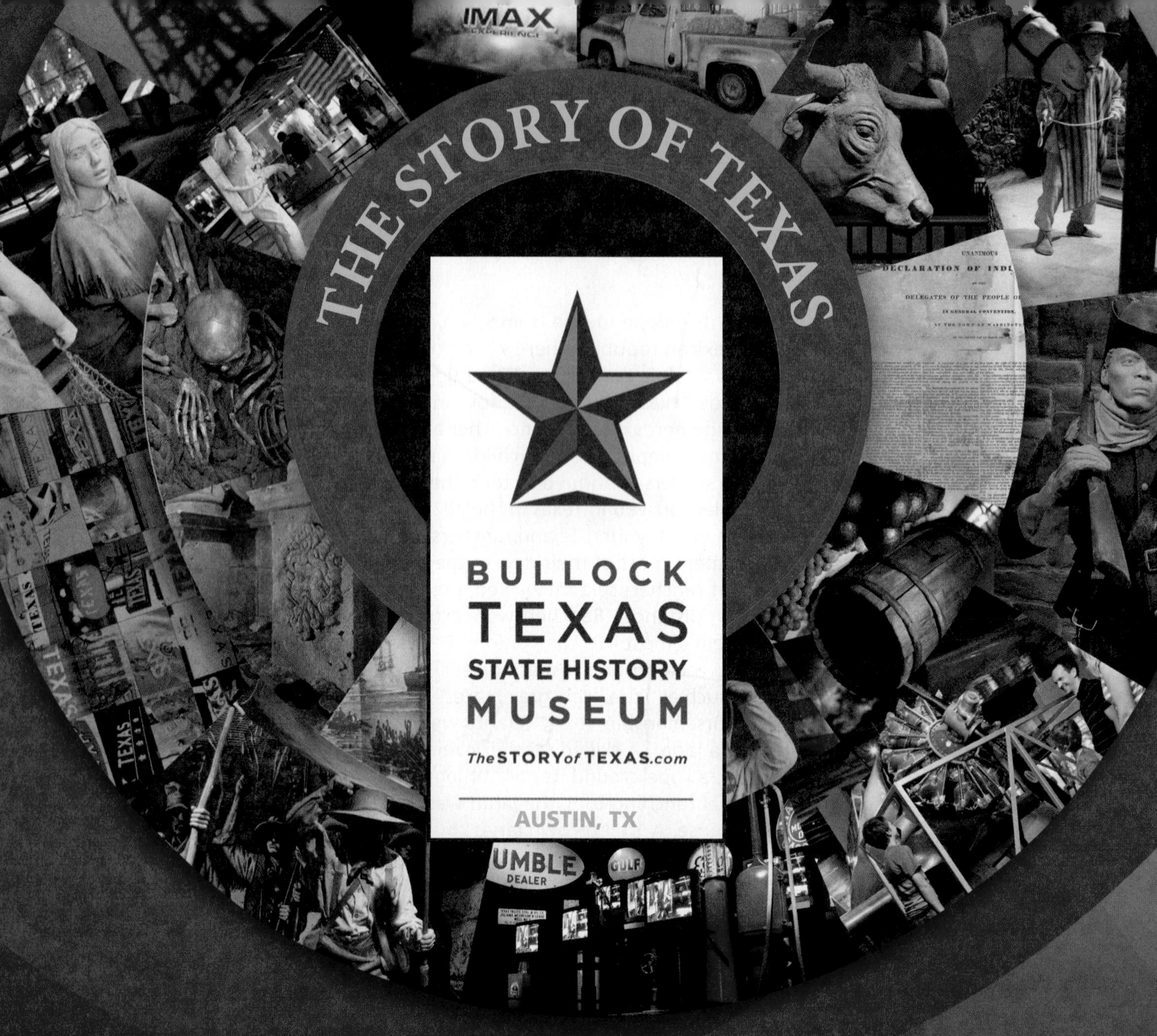

A Growing Sense of Separateness

In 1821 Mexico won independence from Spain. However, parts of the vast country, including Texas, had few Mexican residents and were vulnerable to attack by neighbors and American Indian tribes. As a result, the Mexican government encouraged immigration from the United States to Texas. It was hoped that Anglo immigrants would provide some protection from attack and strengthen the economy by farming, ranching, and paying taxes.

The government hired land agents called *empresarios* to bring settlers to Texas. Among them was Stephen F. Austin. He persuaded hundreds of American settlers to move to Texas in exchange for land.

By the late 1820s, however, Mexican leaders had begun to rethink this immigration policy. Some Anglo settlers were ignoring Mexican laws. Others were arriving illegally and occupying land that they had no legal claim to. In addition, Mexican leaders feared that the United States might try to annex Texas—and that Anglo settlers might support such a move. As a result, they passed the Law of April 6, 1830, banning American immigration to Texas.

Angered by the new law, some Anglo settlers called for its repeal. Stephen F. Austin traveled to Mexico City to speak on their behalf. While he was there, Austin wrote to some citizens of Texas suggesting that they organize a state government. He was arrested for encouraging rebellion. Austin remained in prison in Mexico for months, where he began to support the idea of Texas independence.

Exploring Museum Resources

How did Stephen F. Austin spend his time imprisoned in Mexico City? What was his jail cell like? Find the answers to these questions and explore some of the artifacts from this period of Texas history online. You can find museum resources at

hmhsocialstudies.com

PRIMERA SECRETARIA
DE ESTADO.
DEPARTAMENTO DEL INTERIOR.
Seccion 1.ª

El Escmo Sr. Vice-Presidente de los Estados-Unidos Mexicanos, en ejercicio del supremo poder ejecutivo, se ha servido dirigirme el decreto que sigue.

"El Vice-Presidente los Estados-Unidos Mexicanos á los habitantes de la República sabed: Que el congreso general ha decretado lo siguiente.

Art. 1.º "Se permite la entrada en los puertos de la República de los géneros de algodon prohibidos en la ley de 22 de mayo del año anterior, hasta el dia 1.º de enero del de 1831, y por los puertos del mar del Sur hasta fin de junio del mismo año.

Historic Document Analyze what the Law of April 6, 1830 says about immigration to Texas to see how it affected Texas history.

Artifact Examine the desk of Stephen F. Austin and find out how it was saved from destruction.

Diary Entries Read and listen to entries from the diary that Austin kept while he was in prison. What do they reveal about his hopes for Texas's future?

UNIT 3

Reading Social Studies

Main Ideas and Their Support

Focus on Reading A main idea may be a kind of summary statement, or it may be a statement of the author's opinion. Either way, a good reader looks to see what support—facts and various kinds of details—the writer provides. If the writer does not provide good support, the ideas may not be trustworthy.

Understanding Ideas and Their Support A writer can support main ideas with several kinds of details. These details might be facts, statistics, eyewitness accounts, examples, definitions, comments from experts on the subject, or brief stories known as anecdotes. Notice how the passage below uses facts and details to support the main idea.

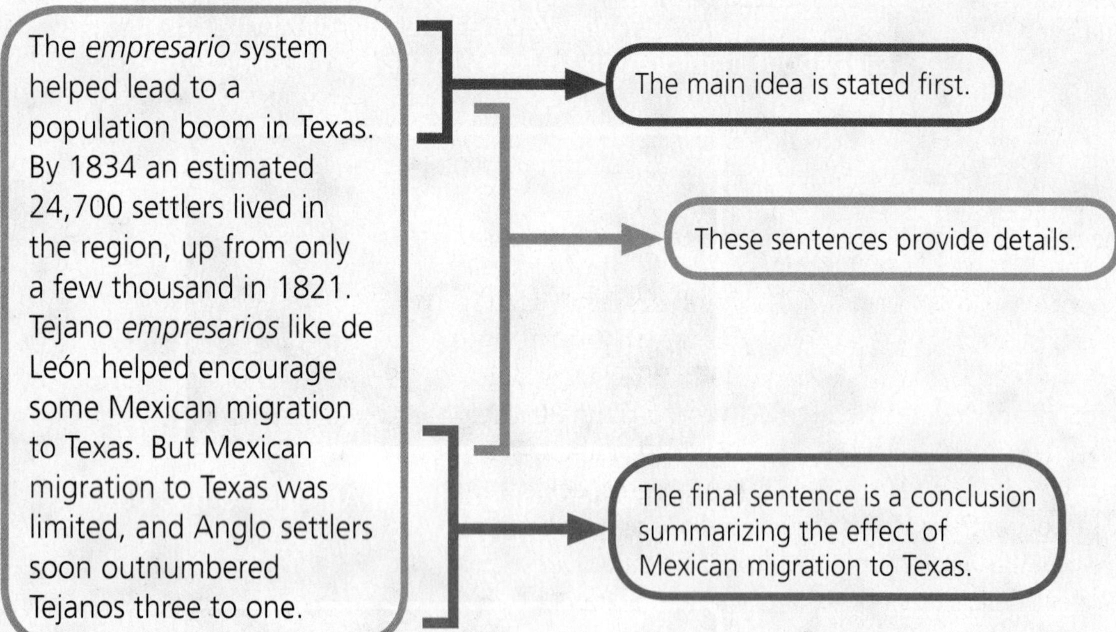

You Try It!

Read the following passage from the unit you are about to read. As you read, look for the writer's main idea and supporting details. Then answer the questions.

Mexico's New Colonization Laws

One concern of the new Mexican government was immigration. The National Colonization Law of 1824 allowed each Mexican state to set its own colonization policies. The law did create some new limits on immigrants, though. Unlike Stephen F. Austin, new U.S. immigrants could not establish colonies near the nation's borders or along the coast. Mexico hoped this restriction would help protect its northern territory.

1. Which sentence best states the writer's main idea?

2. Which method of support is not used to support the main idea?

Reading Section Assessment

Read the passage below and answer the questions that follow.

Austin's plan also detailed how he would distribute land to his colonists. Each household would receive 640 acres of land. A married man could claim another 320 acres, plus 160 acres for each child. Slaveholders could claim 80 acres per slave. In addition, settlers who provided valuable services or who brought items such as cotton gins, devices that separate cotton fibers from seeds, might receive extra land. Where possible, each land grant would lie on a river to provide water for farming and transportation. Settlers would pay Austin a fee of 12.5 cents per acre for his services. This fee covered the costs of surveying the land and recording land titles, the legal documents proving ownership.

1. Which sentence best states the main idea of the passage?
2. Which sentence in this passage provides an example?
3. Which methods used to support a main idea are not used in this passage?

Key Terms

Unit 3

Chapter 8

frontier *(p. 160)*
buffer *(p. 160)*
Anglos *(p. 161)*
secularize *(p. 162)*
militia *(p. 167)*
republic *(p. 172)*
empresarios (p. 174)

Chapter 9

squatters *(p. 184)*
flatboats *(p. 185)*
dogtrot cabin *(p. 187)*
quilting bees *(p. 187)*
buckskin *(p. 187)*
venison *(p. 188)*
barter *(p. 193)*
sawmills *(p. 193)*
exports *(p. 193)*
imports *(p. 193)*
plantations *(p. 195)*

Chapter 10

customs duties *(p. 205)*
resolutions *(p. 209)*
reforms *(p. 212)*
delegates *(p. 212)*
faction *(p. 217)*

Before you read, discuss with your teacher and classmates what you already know about the topics in each chapter, based on the headings and pictures within the chapter. Strong background knowledge can help you better understand what you read.

CHAPTER 8

Texas on the Mexican Frontier

(1820–1835)

Texas Essential Knowledge and Skills (TEKS) 1A, 1B, 2D, 2E, 2F, 8A, 8B, 9A, 9C, 10B, 11A, 11B, 17C, 18A, 19A, 19B, 21A, 21B, 21C, 21D, 21E, 21F, 21H, 22A, 22B, 22C, 22D

Stephen F. Austin fulfilled his father's plan to establish a colony in Texas.

TEXAS

1821 The Spanish government grants Moses Austin permission to found a colony in Texas.

1823 About 3,000 Anglo settlers live in Texas without the permission of the Mexican government.

1824 *Empresario* Martín de León settles families on the lower Guadalupe River.

1826 An American Indian attack on the Green DeWitt colony forces settlers to flee Gonzales.

1820 — 1822 — 1824 — 1826

U.S. and WORLD

1824 Charles Grandison Finney receives a license as a Presbyterian minister and begins preaching throughout the United States.

1826 Fur trapper and explorer Jedediah Smith blazes an overland route to California.

If you were there . . .

How would you encourage more families to settle in Texas?

Build on What You Know

In the early 1800s the people of Mexico fought for independence from Spanish rule. In 1821 Mexico became an independent country. Many Tejanos were glad to be part of Mexico. However, the war had left Texas unprotected. Mexico needed a larger population if it was to maintain control of the region.

U.S. immigrants settling in Texas brought candleholders like this one to light their new homes.

Settlers coming to Texas received land grants from empresarios *like Stephen F. Austin.*

1828 — **1830** — **1832** — **1834**

1828
Andrew Jackson is elected president of the United States.

1829
The *Texas Gazette* newspaper begins publication in Austin's colony.

1830
A cholera epidemic spreads west from Asia across Europe.

1832
George Catlin paints portraits of American Indians as he travels across the American West.

1835
Texas settlers hold about 3,500 land grants.

1835
Samuel Colt obtains a British patent for his single-barreled revolver. He obtains a U.S. patent the next year.

You Be the Historian

myNotebook

What's Your Opinion? Do you **agree** or **disagree** with the following statements? Support your point of view in your notebook.

- **Citizenship** Patience and persistence are important leadership qualities.
- **Economics** People who move to another country usually do so for financial reasons.
- **Geography** Many people choose where to live on the basis of climate and other geographic factors.

Image Credit: (tl) ©Dallas Historical Society; (tr) ©Bettmann/Corbis

Section 1

New Policies Toward Texas

Main Ideas

1. To protect the rest of the country, Mexico encouraged people to move to Texas and other frontier regions.
2. The Spanish, Mexicans, and Anglos who settled in Texas had different purposes and methods in doing so.

Key Terms

- **frontier**
- **buffer**
- **Anglos**
- **secularize**

Why It Matters Today

The Mexican government wanted to attract people to Texas to protect the rest of the country. Use current events sources to find information about why governments encourage immigration today.

TEKS: 1A, 2D, 2F, 11A, 21B, 21D, 21F, 22D

myNotebook

Use the annotation tools in your eBook to take notes on Mexico's policies regarding Texas.

The Story Continues

Miguel Ramos Arizpe wanted people to move to Texas. A high-ranking official in the state of Coahuila, he argued that Texas was important to the country's security. However, there were very few people living there. Somehow, the government needed to convince more people to move to Texas.

The Search for More Texans

The creation of independent Mexico in 1821 marked the beginning of the Mexican National period in Texas. During this period, which lasted until 1836, the Mexican government established new policies to deal with affairs in Texas. One of its major goals was attracting new settlers into the region, as Miguel Ramos Arizpe had recommended.

Like Ramos Arizpe, many Mexican officials viewed Texas and other northern frontier territories as vital in protecting the rest of the country. A **frontier** is a region marking the farthest edge of settlement by a country or group of people. Besides Texas, territories on the Mexican frontier included New Mexico, Arizona, and California.

The value of Texas and the other frontier territories was not in their resources or their people. Instead, it was based on their location. These frontier territories could serve as a **buffer**, or zone of protection, between Mexico and its northern neighbors. Officials in Mexico City were deeply concerned about attacks on their country. They feared that the United

States or American Indians could invade at any time. Before any attack could get to the heart of Mexico, though, it would have to pass through these frontier zones. This would give the Mexican army time to respond to the threat.

VIDEO
Mexico: From Independence to the Alamo
hmhsocialstudies.com

As you read in the previous chapter, the Texas population was greatly reduced by the Mexican War of Independence. As a result, there were not enough people living in Texas to make it an effective buffer. Invaders or attackers could pass through the territory with no resistance. The Mexican government therefore looked for ways to bring new settlers to the area. First, officials encouraged people from other parts of Mexico to move into Texas. However, few people were willing to make this move. Most Mexicans viewed the frontier as a harsh, distant land. They feared living too close to hostile Indian groups.

Mexico next turned to a new source of settlers—the United States. Many American farmers were eager to move into the rich prairies of Texas. The Mexican government agreed to give land to some of these farmers if they would bring settlers into Texas. To distinguish them from the Tejanos who already lived in Texas, historians refer to these new, mostly white, settlers from the United States as **Anglos**. Over the next several years, the Mexican government passed several sets of laws allowing and regulating Anglo settlement.

Reading Check **Finding the Main Idea** Why did the Mexican government want to encourage settlement in Texas?

★ Different Views of Settlement

By the 1830s, three distinct groups had been involved in the settling of Texas: Spaniards, Mexicans, and Anglos. Each group had its own purposes for and methods of settling the region.

HISTORIC DOCUMENT

Colonization Law of 1824

In 1824 the Mexican Congress passed a law allowing Anglo settlers to move to Texas. The law set guidelines for new settlers.

"ART. 1.—The Mexican Nation offers to those foreigners who may be desirous of settling in her territory security for their persons and property, provided they obey the laws of the country.

ART. 2.—This law relates to those lands, national property, which, as belonging to no individual, corporation or town, may be occupied by settlers. . . .

ART. 4.—No lands lying within 20 leagues of the boundaries with any foreign nation, nor within 10 leagues of the coast, can be occupied by settlers . . ."

Analyzing Primary Sources

1. **Finding the Main Idea** What restrictions did this law place on potential settlers?
2. **Drawing Conclusions** Why do you think settlers were not allowed to live near national boundaries or the coast?

As you recall, when the Spanish arrived in Texas they built presidios, missions, ranches and towns throughout Texas. Each type of settlement had a unique purpose. The presidios were created to defend the northern borders of New Spain from attacks. The missions were intended to teach Christianity to the American Indians. The Spanish hoped that Indians would live in the missions and adopt the Spanish way of life. Then they could become Spanish subjects.

By the time Mexico won its independence, the presidios and missions of Texas were in decline. Many presidios had only a few soldiers, and some were falling apart. The missions, too, were in bad shape. Few Indians lived there. Not wanting to pay for failing missions, the government chose to **secularize** them, or move them from religious to civil control. By 1831, all Texas missions had been secularized.

Like the Spanish, the Mexicans sought to increase settlement in Texas for defense. Rather than building presidios, though, the Mexican government largely counted on settlers to defend themselves. Some soldiers were sent to Texas for defense against Indian attacks, but there were not enough to completely secure the land. The government hoped that free or cheap land would draw people willing to risk some danger.

Among those who accepted this risk were many Anglos. Unlike the Spanish and Mexican governments, Anglo settlers of Texas were mostly drawn there for economic reasons. As you will read in the next chapter, Anglo businessmen created settlements throughout Texas. They established farms and ranches and, along the coast, built ports to ship goods back to the United States. Unlike the Spanish, most Anglo settlers had little interest in sharing their culture with the Indians. Indeed, many sought to drive the Indians away from their settlements completely.

Reading Check **Contrasting** How were Anglo settlements in Texas different from earlier settlements?

Section 1 Review

1. Define and explain:
- frontier
- buffer
- Anglos
- secularize

2. Analyzing Information
Copy the graphic organizer below. Use it to compare each group's purposes for and methods of settlement in Texas.

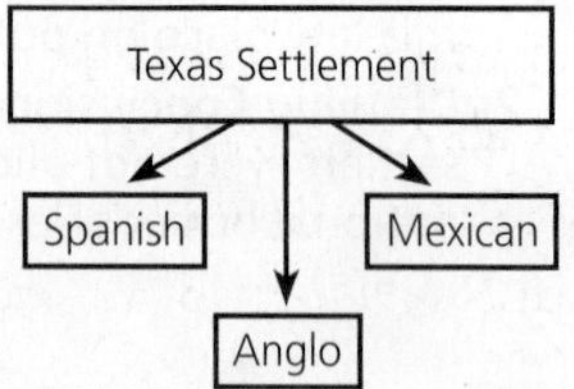

3. Finding the Main Idea
- **a.** What event marked the beginning of the Mexican National period in Texas?
- **b.** Where did the Mexican government find settlers for Texas?

4. Writing and Critical Thinking myWriteSmart
Evaluating Write a short entry on Mexican settlement in Texas for a Texas history book. Consider the following:
- the government's view of life on the northern frontier
- comparisons between Mexican and other patterns of settlement in Texas

Section 2

The Austins Come to Texas

Main Ideas

1. Moses Austin made plans to establish a colony in Texas but died before he could accomplish them.
2. Stephen F. Austin continued his father's plan and brought the first Anglo settlers to Texas.
3. Austin's colony faced many challenges in the first few years of its existence.

Why It Matters Today

During the 1820s Anglo settlers came to Texas hoping to improve their lives. Use current events sources to find information about reasons for immigration to Texas today.

Key Terms and People

- **Moses Austin**
- **Stephen F. Austin**
- **Baron de Bastrop**
- **Erasmo Seguín**
- **cotton gins**
- **militia**

TEKS: 1B, 2D, 2E, 2F, 8A, 8B, 9A, 11A, 18A, 21A, 21B, 21C, 22D

myNotebook

Use the annotation tools in your eBook to take notes on the lives and achievements of Moses and Stephen F. Austin.

The Story Continues

Moses Austin was ruined. He had moved to Spanish Missouri after his lead mines in Virginia failed. He had found success in Missouri, befriending many Spanish officials. When Missouri became part of the United States, Austin's success had continued. He had even become a part owner of the Bank of St. Louis. But in 1819, his luck changed. An economic crisis created a depression. Many banks failed, including the Bank of St. Louis. Austin lost his entire fortune. What was he to do?

★ Moses Austin's Texas Dream

Though he was broke, **Moses Austin** was not defeated. He had profited once by moving to a Spanish land—Missouri—and perhaps such a move could work again. Austin soon developed a plan to establish a colony of American families in Texas. By charging them fees, he could regain his wealth. Hopeful again, Austin set out for Texas.

On his way to Texas, Austin visited his son **Stephen F. Austin** in Arkansas Territory. The younger Austin had doubts about his father's plans, but Moses remained determined. He set out for Texas with a slave named Richmond. The two crossed into East Texas in November 1820.

BIOGRAPHY

Moses Austin

(1761–1821) Moses Austin was born in Connecticut. In his twenties he entered the lead-mining business in Virginia. After a few years of success, Austin's business ventures failed. In 1798, Austin moved his family to Missouri, which was then a part of Spanish Louisiana. There he created the area's first lead industry. His business expanded, amassing him a fortune of $190,000. When he went to Texas in 1820, however, most of this fortune was gone. Austin was the first person to get permission to bring Anglo settlers into Texas.

How did Moses Austin shape Texas history?

Reaching San Antonio in December, Austin met with Spanish governor Antonio María Martínez. The governor, however, did not trust U.S. citizens. He ordered Austin out of the city. However, a chance encounter changed the situation. In the city, Austin met the **Baron de Bastrop**, a Dutch businessman. Although he called himself a baron, Bastrop had not been born noble. Born Philip Hendrik Nering Bögel, he had fled the Netherlands in 1793 after being accused of theft. While on the run, he adopted his fake title and settled in San Antonio. There he became a successful businessman and a respected statesman.

Austin told Bastrop about his colonization plan, and Bastrop decided to help him. Together, the two men met with Martínez. They pointed out that Austin's colony would improve the Texas economy. His presence would also help protect the area from attacks by American Indians or U.S. soldiers. They also noted that Austin had become a Spanish citizen in Missouri and would be loyal to New Spain. Convinced, Martínez agreed to propose the plan to his superiors.

Satisfied, Austin returned to Missouri to await news. In the spring of 1821, he learned that Spanish officials had agreed to his plan. Austin had their permission to settle 300 Catholic families from Louisiana in Texas. Before he could act on his plans, however, Moses Austin became ill and died. The fate of his colony now lay in the hands of his son.

Reading Check **Summarizing** Why did Moses Austin want to create a colony in Texas, and why was that colony never established?

★ Stephen F. Austin Takes Over

Stephen F. Austin was 27 years old when he learned of his father's death. Austin became determined to carry out his father's plan to bring U.S. settlers to Texas. He traveled to San Antonio de Béxar in August 1821. **Erasmo Seguín**, a rancher and the alcalde of the town, led Austin to Governor Martínez. The Baron de Bastrop was on hand to translate. Martínez offered to support Austin's efforts to fulfill his father's plans. But in the time since Moses Austin had received his contract, Mexico had won independence from Spanish rule. Consequently, Austin needed a new contract from the Mexican government. Martínez agreed to help him get approval for that contract from officials in Mexico City.

Austin spent the next few months exploring the land east of San Antonio. He was seeking a good location for his colony. In the end, he picked the rich farmland in the area of the Brazos and Colorado River valleys—some 11 million acres on the Gulf Coast Plain. A colony there would have a mild climate, fertile soil, water, and plenty of timber for building. Wild game was also plentiful. In addition, the site was near the coast, where settlers and supplies could arrive by ship. In his journal, Austin described his chosen location.

TEXAS VOICES

"The Prairie comes to the river . . . and affords a most beautiful situation for a Town or settlement. The bluff is about 60 feet high—The country back of this place and below for about 15 miles (as far as we went) is as good in every respect as man could wish for, Land all first rate, plenty of timber, fine water—beautifully rolling."

—Stephen F. Austin, quoted in *Stephen F. Austin: Empresario of Texas*, by Gregg Cantrell

With a location chosen, Austin returned to the United States to prepare. From Louisiana he sent a report to Governor Martínez. It specified the colony's proposed location, which include land along the Gulf for a port.

Austin's plan detailed how he initially intended to distribute land to his colonists, although these terms later changed. Each household would receive 640 acres of land. Those who provided valuable services or items, such as **cotton gins**—devices that separate cotton fibers from seeds—would receive extra land. Where possible, each land grant would lie on a river to provide water for farming and transportation. Settlers would pay Austin a fee of 12.5 cents per acre for his services.

Austin's proposed terms were very attractive to people in the United States, where land cost at least $1.25 an acre. In addition, U.S. law required settlers to buy at least 80 acres and to pay the full price in cash. Few people had the $100 in cash needed to buy this much land. Austin, however, would accept goods as payment or allow settlers to pay the fees over time. Austin advertised for settlers in New Orleans, and applications poured in from eager men and women.

BIOGRAPHY

Stephen F. Austin

(1793–1836) Stephen F. Austin was studying law in New Orleans when he decided to help with his father's Texas colony. The younger Austin was an energetic, intelligent, patient man. Soft-spoken, cultured, and soon fluent in Spanish, he was equally at ease with frontier settlers and Mexican officials. He was devoted to his colonists and served as their adviser, banker, diplomat, and judge. His efforts brought prosperity to many and earned him the title the Father of Texas. **What qualities and experiences helped Austin become an important Texas leader?**

Austin's Colony

Interpreting Maps Stephen F. Austin established his colony on the Gulf Coast Plain.

1. Physical System What physical factors might have influenced Austin's choice for the location of his colony?

2. Evaluating What advantages do you think rivers provided to early settlements?

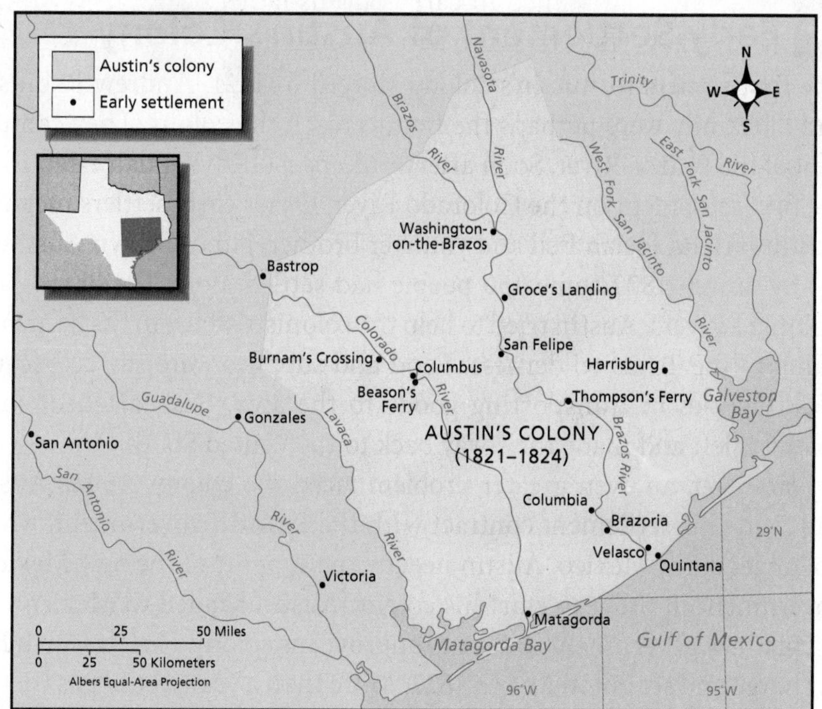

Interpreting Visuals

Colonial life. *Settlers in Austin's colonies built log cabins and planted crops.* ***What kinds of physical features might affect where and how people in the colonies lived?***

Austin was careful in selecting settlers. He believed his colony's success depended upon having hardworking, law-abiding people. All settlers also had to become Mexican citizens and convert to Catholicism.

With plans in place, Austin went to New Orleans to arrange for the colony's finances. While there, he formed a partnership with Joseph H. Hawkins, a friend and lawyer. Hawkins provided Austin with financial support and a ship. His backing secured, Austin set out for his colony.

Reading Check **Analyzing Information** How did Stephen F. Austin attract potential settlers for his Texas colony?

★ Early Settlement of Austin's Colony

The first settlers to Austin's colony arrived in 1821. Andrew Robinson and his family were perhaps the first to reach the colony. They camped west of the Brazos River. Soon afterward, Joseph Kuykendall established the first settlement on the Colorado River. Other early settlers included Austin's friend Josiah Bell and younger brother, James Brown Austin.

By March 1822 some 150 people had settled along the Brazos and Colorado Rivers. Austin tried to help the colonists adjust to the hardships of life in the Texas wilderness. Food and supplies were scarce because of difficulties in transporting goods to the area. Disheartened, some colonists left and made their way back to the United States.

However, an even greater problem faced the colony. Moses Austin had made his settlement contract with the Spanish government, which no longer ruled Mexico. Austin needed the support of the new Mexican government in order to start his colony. Austin headed to Mexico City to convince government leaders to approve his colony. He left Josiah Bell in charge and set out in March 1822. More than a year would pass before

he saw Texas again. The journey was more than 1,000 miles through rugged and dangerous land. At one point some 50 Comanches captured Austin's group, but the party was released unharmed. At another point, Austin dressed as a beggar to fool robbers.

Once in Mexico City, Austin found officials struggling to organize a new government. As a result, they had little time to deal with Texas matters. Austin, however, was determined to wait as long as it took. Between meetings with officials, he studied Spanish to become fluent.

Stephen F. Austin created this map of his colony in 1833.

Austin's patience eventually paid off. In January 1823 the Mexican government passed the Imperial Colonization Law. Under this law, Austin's land grant was secure and he could continue to bring in settlers from the United States. Families of farmers in the colony would receive 177 acres, and ranching families would receive 4,428 acres. Single men would receive one-third of these amounts. To get the greatest possible amount of land, most settlers in Austin's colony claimed to be both farmers and ranchers. In addition, settlers were exempt, or free, from paying taxes for six years. Austin himself would receive about 100,000 acres once he had settled 300 families in the colony.

As the colony's leader, Austin was charged with forming a local government and acting as judge. He was also empowered to form a **militia**, or army made up of citizens who serve when necessary.

Austin's determination and willingness to work with Mexican officials won him success. In the end, his colony was the only one ever to operate under the Imperial Colonization Law. The ruler who had issued it, Agustín de Iturbide, gave up power, and the new government had its own plans for colonization. However, they allowed Austin to maintain his colony under the old law. In April 1823 Austin headed back to Texas.

Reading Check **Identifying Cause and Effect** Why did Stephen F. Austin travel to Mexico, and what was the outcome of his trip?

Section 2 Review

hmhsocialstudies.com ONLINE QUIZ

1. Define and explain:
- cotton gins
- militia

2. Identify and explain the significance of each of the following in Texas history:
- Moses Austin
- Stephen F. Austin
- Erasmo Seguín

3. Summarizing Copy the graphic organizer below. Use it to describe Stephen F. Austin's colony.

Austin's Colony	
Location	
Size	
Final Land Terms	
Date of Start of Settlement	
Date of Final Approval	

4. Finding the Main Idea

a. Why did Moses Austin want to establish a colony in Texas, and why did his plans fail?

b. What personality traits helped Stephen F. Austin win approval for his colony?

5. Writing and Critical Thinking myWriteSmart

Sequencing Write a paragraph describing in order the steps Stephen F. Austin took to carry out his father's colonization contract. Consider the following:
- Austin's travels in Texas
- Austin's trip to Mexico City

Section 3

The Austin Colonies

Main Ideas

1. In its first years, Austin's colony faced problems that threatened to drive everyone away.
2. The Old Three Hundred helped make Austin's colony, centered on San Felipe de Austin, a success.
3. After the success of his first colony, Austin established four more colonies in Texas.

Key Terms and People

- **Old Three Hundred**
- **Jane Long**
- **San Felipe de Austin**
- **Little Colony**

Why It Matters Today

Austin's colony experienced many problems during its early years. Use current events sources to find out about problems communities today face and the solutions they use to fix those problems.

TEKS: 2E, 2F, 9A, 9C, 10B, 11A, 11B, 21A, 21B, 22D

myNotebook

Use the annotation tools in your eBook to take notes on life in Stephen F. Austin's colonies.

The Story Continues

Life in the Texas colonies was hard. Early settlers lived in crude log cabins without any floors or windows. Frightened families huddled together in small villages in hopes of fending off American Indian attacks. Swarms of mosquitoes pestered people along the hot and humid Gulf Coast, spreading deadly diseases. Alligators prowled at night, eating dogs and—on rare occasions—even people. Despite the discomfort caused by such harsh conditions, many settlers stayed, and even more kept coming.

★ Early Problems in Austin's Colony

Stephen F. Austin returned to his colony in August 1823. With him was the Baron de Bastrop, who had been appointed to issue the land titles. When they reached the colony, though, they found that many of the settlers were discouraged. Several had left to return to the United States, and several more were threatening to leave. A number of problems had arisen during Austin's absence. A bad drought had ruined the colony's first crop. Low on food, the settlers had eaten wild game to survive. In addition, the Karankawas, Tonkawas, and other local American Indians did not like the colonists living on their land and had raided the colony.

Austin tried to reassure the settlers, telling them that Mexico had approved the contract for the colony. To help bring order to the colony, he established a headquarters near present-day La Grange. There he set up a system of government and created rules to guide the colony. These rules blended Mexican and U.S. laws. Austin tried, with limited success, to form peaceful relations with nearby Texas Indians. At the same time, though, he also formed a militia for protection from raids. As he dealt with these problems, Austin began to look upon the settlers "as one great family who are under my care." With Austin working to restore good spirits to the colonists, people stopped leaving. Gradually the population of the colony increased.

Reading Check **Summarizing** What early problems affected settlers in Austin's colony, and how did Austin try to solve them?

★ The Old Three Hundred

By the fall of 1824, Austin had nearly fulfilled his contract with the Mexican government. In all, 297 families and single men had received land in his colony. Together these settlers became known as the **Old Three Hundred.** Most of them had come from the southern United States, particularly Louisiana. They were mostly farmers, and some were also slaveholders. Of the 1,790 colonists living in Austin's colony in 1825, about 440 were enslaved African Americans. Jared Groce, the wealthiest colonist, had brought some 90 slaves to the colony.

The settlers were fairly well educated. Only four of the white colonists could not read, a low figure for the time. Settlers also tended to be law-abiding, largely because of Austin's strict regulations.

Well-known members of the Old Three Hundred included Samuel May Williams and John P. Coles. Williams served as Austin's colonial secretary, and Coles built a sawmill that supplied lumber to the colony. Because many colonists brought their families with them to Texas, the colony was home to many women and children.

Daily Life

Hospitality in Austin's Colonies

While waiting to receive a land grant, Texas settlers occasionally stayed in hotels. One traveler in 1831 shared his Texas hotel room with 30 other men. Each man paid $1 for a place to put his bedroll on the floor. "In order to place thirty men in a horizontal position, on a space about twenty feet square . . . required no small care," he wrote. Many Texas families were also willing to put up strangers. The settlers, many of whom lived in isolated areas, gathered eagerly to hear the latest news. **How did travelers in Texas help settlers deal with the isolation of frontier life?**

BIOGRAPHY

Jane Long
(1798–1880) Jane Long was one of the Old Three Hundred. With her daughter Ann she obtained land in present-day Fort Bend and Waller Counties. On her land, Long ran boardinghouses, started a farm, raised cattle, and even tried raising sheep. Like many colonists, Long used slave labor in these efforts. In 1850 Long's plantation was worth more than $10,000. She never remarried, but tradition holds that some of the leading men of Texas courted her. **How did Jane Long contribute to the colonization of Texas?**

In addition, a few women held land grants on their own. **Jane Long,** the widow of filibuster James Long, received land in Austin's colony in 1824. She became one of the most famous of the Old Three Hundred. Another widow, Rebekah Cumings, came to the colony in 1822 with her children. She claimed land in present-day Brazoria and Waller Counties.

Reading Check **Analyzing Information** Explain the significance of the term Old Three Hundred.

★ San Felipe de Austin

By 1824, Austin felt that his colony needed a capital. In that year he founded **San Felipe de Austin,** better known as San Felipe. The town was located in present-day Austin County along the Brazos River. This site had several advantages. It was in the center of the colony, halfway between the coast and El Camino Real. Because travelers between Mexico, San Antonio, and East Texas traveled along the road, many people passed through San Felipe. The town sat on a high bluff, which aided in its defense. Below the bluff, the river provided a source of water. In addition, a ferry was located at the site.

San Felipe soon became the heart of Austin's colony. The town's population grew quickly as settlers moved to the capital. Austin placed his land office there and built a cabin on the edge of town. Other well-known residents included Gail Borden Jr. and Robert Williamson. Borden, with his brother Thomas and Joseph Baker, published the *Telegraph and Texas Register* newspaper. He also worked as a surveyor and inventor. Williamson was a judge who wore a wooden peg to support the knee of a weak leg. Known as Three-Legged Willie, Williamson would later help form the Texas court system. By 1827 San Felipe had between 100 and 200 residents. One settler described the town as it looked at the time.

Analyzing Primary Sources
Drawing Inferences and Conclusions Considering the colonists' building materials, how do you think they adapted to the environment of the region?

TEXAS VOICES

> **"Twenty-five or perhaps thirty log cabins strung along the west bank of the Brazos River was all there was of it. . . . The buildings all being of unhewn [rough] logs with clapboard roofs, presented few distinguishing features. . . . Every fellow built to suit himself . . . so that the town was strung along either side of the road something like half a mile . . . 'Pretty good as to length, but rather thin.'"**
>
> —Noah Smithwick, *The Evolution of a State, or Recollections of Old Texas Days*

By the early 1830s San Felipe was the second largest business center in Texas, after San Antonio. Homes and stores lined Atascosito Road, the town's main street. A lumber mill, newspaper office, and post office provided needed services. The town even had a hotel for weary travelers. Austin's colony was a success.

Reading Check **Evaluating** What geographic factors helped San Felipe de Austin thrive?

Austin's Other Colonies

Several Tejano leaders helped Austin succeed in his colonization efforts. José Miguel de Arciniega, Gaspar Flores de Abrego, José Antonio Saucedo, and Erasmo Seguín all gave valuable assistance. With their help, Austin was able to acquire contracts for four more colonies between 1825 and 1831. Each of them overlapped his first colony except for one. This one isolated colony became known as Austin's **Little Colony**.

Austin's contract for the Little Colony provided for settlement of 100 families north of the Old San Antonio Road and east of the Colorado River. This was an isolated location on the western edge of Texas settlement. The colony's main town of Bastrop was near Comanche hunting grounds and, as a result, suffered attacks.

Because of its isolation, the Little Colony grew slowly. Austin tried to help the colony thrive by organizing a militia and recruiting some Tonkawas as allies. Although these efforts helped, the colony remained small. In 1830 just one bachelor and two families lived in Bastrop.

Despite the slow growth of the Little Colony, Austin's other colonization efforts were a success. Austin described his feelings about his achievements in 1829.

Robert Williamson was one of the most famous residents of San Felipe.

TEXAS VOICES

"My ambition has been to succeed in redeeming [freeing] Texas from its wilderness state by means of the plough alone. . . . In doing this I hoped to make the fortune of thousands and my own amongst the rest. . . . I think that I derived more satisfaction from the view of flourishing farms springing up in this wilderness than military or political chieftains do from . . . their victorious campaigns."

—Stephen F. Austin, quoted in *Stephen F. Austin: Empresario of Texas,* by Gregg Cantrell

Analyzing Primary Sources
Analyzing Information What did Austin say was his goal in settling Texas?

Reading Check **Finding the Main Idea** In total, how many colonies did Stephen F. Austin establish in Texas?

Section 3 Review

hmhsocialstudies.com
ONLINE QUIZ

1. Identify and explain the significance of each of the following in Texas history:
- Old Three Hundred
- Jane Long
- San Felipe de Austin
- Little Colony

2. Locate on a Texas map:
- San Felipe

3. Categorizing Copy the graphic organizer below. Use it to identify three characteristics of the Old Three Hundred.

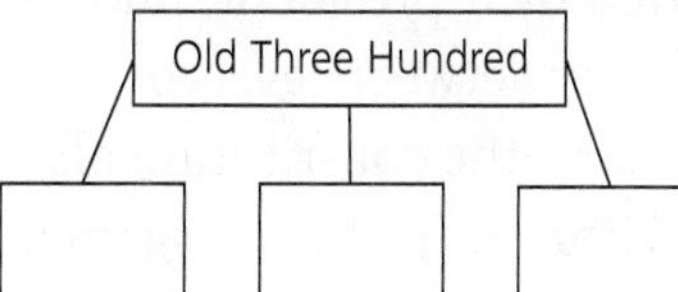

4. Finding the Main Idea

a. Why did some settlers threaten to leave Austin's colony, and how did Austin react?

b. What geographic factors caused Bastrop to grow more slowly than San Felipe?

5. Writing and Critical Thinking myWriteSmart

Summarizing Imagine that you live in San Felipe de Austin. Write a letter home describing life in the settlement.

Consider the following:
- its location
- the town's residents and buildings

Section 4

Empresarios and Tejanos

Main Ideas

1. Under Mexico's Federal Constitution of 1824, Texas was united with the state of Coahuila.
2. New colonization laws in Mexico allowed *empresarios* to receive contracts to bring settlers to Texas.
3. Many Tejanos supported immigration to Texas from the United States, though relations later became strained.

Why It Matters Today

Texas experienced a population boom in the 1820s and 1830s. Use current events sources to find information about areas experiencing population booms around the world today.

Key Terms and People

- **Federal Constitution of 1824**
- **republic**
- **Coahuila y Texas**
- **State Colonization Law of 1825**
- ***empresarios***
- **Green DeWitt**
- **Martín de León**

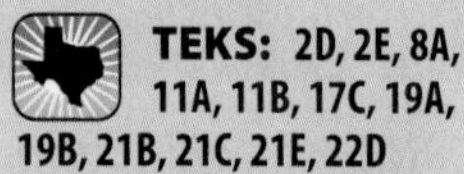

TEKS: 2D, 2E, 8A, 11A, 11B, 17C, 19A, 19B, 21B, 21C, 21E, 22D

myNotebook

Use the annotation tools in your eBook to take notes on the role of *empresarios* in Texas and the reactions of Tejanos to them.

The Story Continues

The news spread through Texas that the Mexican Congress had approved a new constitution. Stephen F. Austin had advised the officials who had written the document, and Erasmo Seguín had represented Texas at the constitutional assembly. Texas farmers had donated corn to cover Seguín's expenses. The people of Texas had done their part. They now waited to learn how the constitution would affect them.

★ A New Constitution for Mexico

After Mexican leader Agustín de Iturbide lost power, the Mexican people wanted a change of government. They called a constitutional assembly to draft a new constitution. Representing Texas was Erasmo Seguín of San Antonio. On October 24, 1824, the assembly officially adopted the **Federal Constitution of 1824**.

Under the new constitution, Mexico became a **republic**, a government in which people elect their leaders. Power was divided between the national government, headed by a president, and individual state governments. This division of power between levels of government is called federalism. As part of the division, the constitution also reorganized Mexico into 19 states and five territories. In this reorganization, Texas was united with the province of Coahuila into the new state of **Coahuila y Texas**.

Many Texans were not happy with this union. Seguín had argued fiercely against it in the assembly. He feared that Coahuila, which had a much larger population than Texas did, would dominate state politics. At the same time, Texas was not ready to be a state on its own. Instead, he believed, Texas should become a territory. When Seguín and Texas leaders learned that as a territory Texas would not control its own affairs, they agreed to a merger with Coahuila.

In the end, Seguín's fears proved somewhat justified. When the state's legislature met at the capital, Saltillo, 10 of the 12 members were from Coahuila. Only two were from Texas.

Reading Check **Identifying Cause and Effect** Why were some Texans opposed to unification with Coahuila?

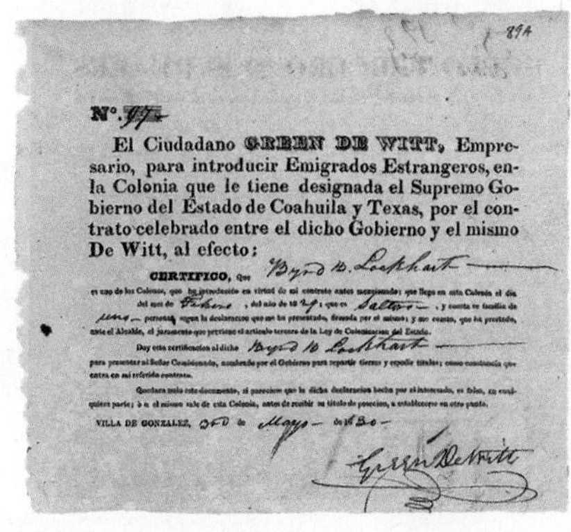

N°.

El Ciudadano GREEN DE WITT, Empresario, para introducir Emigrados Estrangeros, en la Colonia que le tiene designada el Supremo Gobierno del Estado de Coahuila y Texas, por el contrato celebrado entre el dicho Gobierno y el mismo De Witt, al efecto:

CERTIFICO, que

VILLA DE GONZALEZ,

Empresarios *received contracts from the Mexican government to bring settlers to Texas.*

Mexico's New Colonization Laws

One concern of the new Mexican government was immigration. The National Colonization Law of 1824 allowed each Mexican state to set its own colonization policies. The law did create some new limits on immigrants, though. Unlike Stephen F. Austin, new U.S. immigrants could not establish colonies near the nation's borders or along the coast. Mexico hoped this restriction would help protect its northern territory.

Coahuila y Texas in 1825

Interpreting Maps In 1824 the separate Mexican province of Texas was joined with the state of Coahuila. As the population grew, Texas was divided into political departments. By 1834 it had been divided into three departments: Béxar, Nacogdoches, and Brazos.

1. ***Locate*** San Antonio was the capital of which department?
2. ***Drawing Inferences and conclusions*** How did geographic features such as rivers affect the political boundaries of Texas?

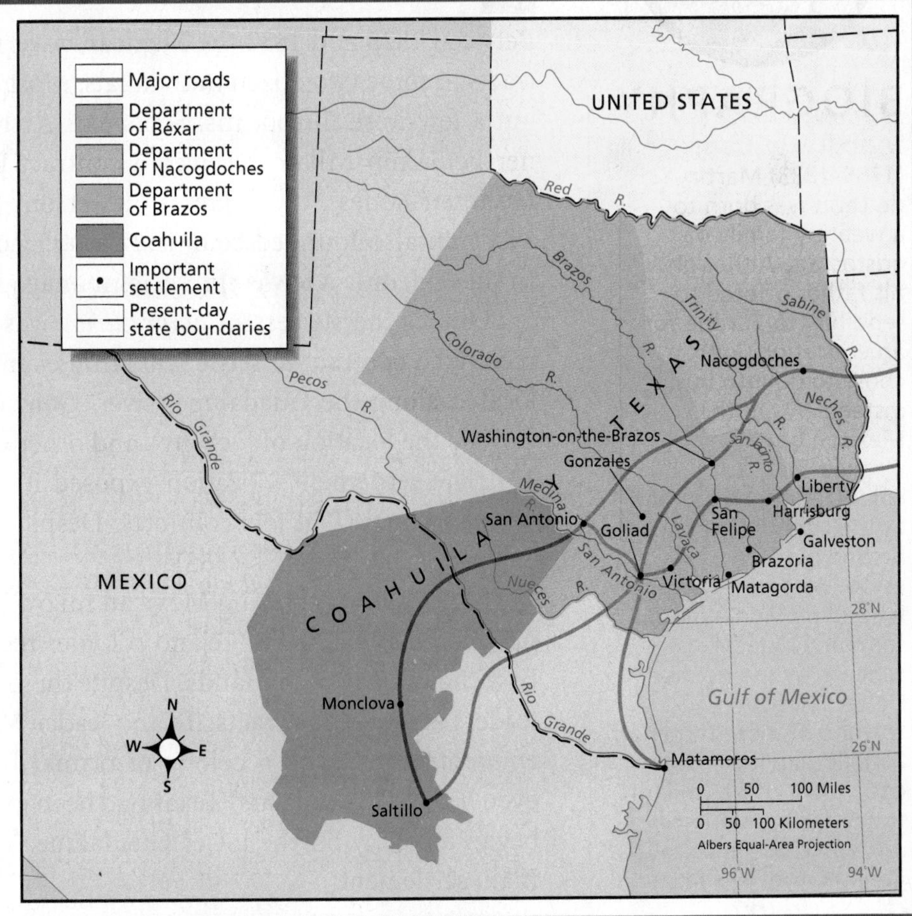

As a state, Coahuila y Texas had its own immigration policy. The Baron de Bastrop and other well-to-do Tejanos wanted to see Texas grow. They hoped U.S. settlers and other immigrants would provide protection against American Indians. They also believed that new settlement would raise land values in the region and provide new markets for Tejano merchants. These beliefs led the Mexican Congress to pass the **State Colonization Law of 1825**. This law further opened Texas to settlement and immigration.

Under the new colonization law, many people followed in the footsteps of Stephen F. Austin and became ***empresarios***. These businesspeople promoted settlement in Texas. Each *empresario* received 67,000 acres of land for every 200 families he brought to Texas. The head of a household could receive 4,428 acres of land for just pennies an acre. New settlers would not have to pay taxes for 10 years. The law's only requirements were that settlers become Catholics and Mexican citizens of good character. The *empresarios* introduced a huge wave of U.S. immigration to Texas.

Reading Check **Finding the Main Idea** Who were *empresarios*, and what role did they play in settling Texas?

BIOGRAPHY

Martín de León

(1765–1833) Martín de León was born to a wealthy family of aristocrats. Although his father offered to send him to Europe for an education, Martín chose to go into business instead. When the Mexican government opened Texas to colonization, he jumped at the chance. The ranch he and his wife Patricia established near Victoria helped provide a model for many later Texas ranches. When he died, De León left behind a fortune of more than half a million dollars—the equivalent of $13 million today. **How did Martín de León contribute to the beginning of the Texas cattle industry?**

The *Empresario* Colonies

Between 1825 and 1832 the Mexican government gave *empresario* contracts to some two dozen individuals. Most *empresarios* were American, but a few were Europeans. Scotsman Arthur G. Wavell and his partner Benjamin Milam received a contract to settle in northeast Texas. Irishmen James Power, James Hewetson, John McMullen, and James McGloin also founded colonies, though none were terribly successful. In the end, only a few *empresarios* managed to create lasting colonies.

One of the successful *empresarios* was **Green DeWitt**. In 1825 he received a contract to settle 400 families in Texas. DeWitt's colony was located along the Guadalupe River. Gonzales was its main town. You can see the location of DeWitt's and other colonies on the map on page 177. The settlement's location exposed it to American Indian attacks, and the people had few comforts. Despite these hardships, more than 525 people lived there by 1831.

In hopes of increasing Mexican migration to Texas, officials sought out Tejano *empresarios*. Tejano colonies received privileges, such as the first choice of available lands. Despite these privileges, only a few Tejano leaders accepted contracts. Tejano leader **Martín de León** was the only *empresario* to found a colony of primarily Mexican settlers. In 1824, even before Coahuila and Texas had been joined, he and his wife Patricia began a colony on the lower Guadalupe. The town of Victoria was its main settlement.

By 1834 some 300 people—mainly Mexicans but also a few Irish, Tejano, and U.S. settlers—lived in De León's colony. Despite some hardships, including attacks by American Indians, the colony thrived. It soon developed into a major ranching center. The colony also served as an important trade center. Much of this trade was conducted through the town of Linnville. Founded in 1831, it became an important Texas port.

As the De León colony prospered, Patricia de León worked to improve social and cultural life there. She established a school and brought traditional Spanish and Mexican culture into Victoria. After her husband died, she continued to live in the De León colony for a few years.

Another Tejano who took advantage of the government's offer was Lorenzo de Zavala. A wealthy citizen of Mexico City, he got permission in 1829 to build a settlement on the Sabine River south of Nacogdoches. Before long, though, he sold his contract and abandoned the idea.

Reading Check **Evaluating** After Stephen F. Austin, which *empresarios* were the most successful in establishing colonies in Texas?

Our Cultural Heritage

Tejano Culture

Tejano communities enjoyed many social activities, as shown in this painting of women gathered together to make tortillas. In Tejano communities today, people have carried on many traditions while adapting to the larger culture. Neighbors and relatives still gather for dances, fiestas, and holidays. They eat Spanish-Indian foods such as corn tortillas and frijoles, or beans. Many Tejanos also preserve their Spanish Catholic heritage. Tejano traditions remain a vibrant part of the state's diverse culture. **How have Tejanos maintained their culture?**

★ Tejano Leadership

The *empresario* system helped lead to a population boom in Texas. By 1834 an estimated 24,700 settlers lived in the region, up from only a few thousand in 1821. Tejano *empresarios* like De León helped encourage some Mexican migration to Texas. But Mexican migration to Texas was limited, and Anglo settlers soon outnumbered Tejanos three to one.

Image Credit: (b) ©North Wind Picture Archives

In the beginning, most Tejanos were eager to increase immigration to Texas. They believed that American settlers would help improve the economy of Texas. Many Tejanos, including Erasmo Seguín, wanted to develop a cotton industry in Texas. For such an industry to succeed, they thought they would need experts and workers from the United States.

The question of cotton led to a division among Tejanos. In the United States, most labor on cotton plantations was provided by slaves. To develop an American-style cotton industry in Texas, therefore, would mean introducing slavery to Texas. Some Tejano leaders viewed slavery as necessary for the economic success of Texas. Both Seguín and José Antonio Navarro, for example, supported the idea of cotton planters bringing slaves to Texas. Others were opposed to slavery in any form.

As time passed and new settlers arrived, some Tejanos developed less favorable views of their new neighbors. Conflicts sometimes arose. These conflicts often dealt with land or property. For example, a dispute arose in 1826 between Tejano residents of De León's colony and American settlers in DeWitt's colony. Livestock that had gone missing from De León's colony was found on DeWitt's land. The dispute almost resulted in violence, but war was prevented by the intervention of two men. One was Stephen F. Austin. The other was Rafael Antonio Manchola, a son-in-law of Martín de León. Manchola was a leader of the local militia.

Although the Tejano population of Texas was outnumbered, individuals like Seguín, Navarro, and Manchola remained important figures in state affairs. Their actions helped ensure that the Tejano point of view was represented in decision making, even as more American colonists became active in Texas politics.

Reading Check **Analyzing Information** How did Tejano views of Anglo settlers changed over time?

Section 4 Review

hmhsocialstudies.com
ONLINE QUIZ

1. **Define and explain:**
   - republic
   - *empresarios*
2. **Identify and explain** the significance of each of the following:
   - Federal Constitution of 1824
   - Coahuila y Texas
   - State Colonization Law of 1825
   - Green DeWitt
   - Martín de León
3. **Comparing**
   Copy the graphic organizer below. Use it to explain the creation of the *empresario* system and the feelings of Tejano leaders.

State Colonization Law
Empresario contracts
Tejano leadership

4. **Finding the Main Idea**
   a. How did the Mexican colonization laws affect immigration to Texas?
   b. What regions of Texas did *empresarios* help settle during the 1820s, and what geographic factors drew immigrants to those regions?
5. **Writing and Critical Thinking** *my*WriteSmart
   Supporting a Point of View Write a paragraph from the point of view of a Tejano supporting or opposing Anglo settlement in Texas.
   Consider the following:
   - the goals of Anglo colonies
   - the relationships between other Tejanos and settlers they have encountered

Connecting To Geography

Land in Mexican Texas

Many settlers came to Texas in search of land in the 1820s. *Empresarios* offered cheap land to immigrants. In return, the *empresarios* received contracts for land of their own.

Land Grants

The following table lists early settlers and the size of each of their land contracts. A *sitio* of land equals about 4,428 acres, and a *labor* of land equals about 177 acres. Convert the *sitios* and *labores* to acres and create a bar graph of this information.

NAME	CONTRACT
Elijah Alcorn	1.5 *sitios;* 1 *labor*
Stephen F. Austin	22.7 *sitios;* 3 *labores*
Josiah H. Bell	1.5 *sitios*
James Cummins	6 *sitios;* 1 *labor*
Antonio Flores	13 *labores*
John Foster	2.5 *sitios;* 3 *labores*
Jared E. Groce	10 *sitios*
Jane Long	1 *sitio;* 1 *labor*

Mexican Land Grants, 1821–1836

- Austin's colonies (1825–1828)
- Austin and William's (1831) (Robertson's contract, 1825)
- Burnet's grant (1826)
- Cameron's grant (1827 and 1828)
- De León's colony (1824)
- DeWitt's colony (1825)
- Filisola's grant (1831)
- McMullen and McGloin's colony (1828)
- Milam's contract (1826)
- Power and Hewetson's colony (1826)
- Wavell's contract (1826)
- Woodbury's grant (1826–1834)
- Vehlein's grant (1828)
- Zavala's grant (1828)
- Grant and Beales (1832)
- Padilla and Chambers (1830)
- Col. Juan Domínguez (1829)
- Exeter and Wilson (1826 and 1828)
- • Important settlement
- — — Present-day state boundaries

Geography **Skills**

Interpreting Thematic Maps and Data

1. Which person in the table owned the largest amount of land?
2. In what part of Texas were the first land contracts issued?
3. What geographic patterns can you see in the distribution of land contracts? Why do you think that pattern existed?

CHAPTER 8 REVIEW

The Chapter at a Glance

Examine the following visual summary of the chapter. Then use the visual to create a table that lists the benefits of the *empresario* system for the Mexican government, *empresarios*, and settlers.

Identifying People and Ideas

Write a sentence to explain the role or significance of each of the following terms or people.

1. Moses Austin
2. Erasmo Seguín
3. Baron de Bastrop
4. Stephen F. Austin
5. frontier
6. Coahuila y Texas
7. Old Three Hundred
8. *empresarios*
9. Green DeWitt
10. Martín de León

Understanding Main Ideas

Section 1

1. For what purpose did the Mexican government want to bring settlers to Texas?

Section 2

2. What difficulties did Stephen F. Austin face in getting a contract for his colony?
3. Why did many Anglo settlers immigrate to Austin's colony?

Section 3

4. Where did most of the Old Three Hundred come from in the United States, and what did they have in common?
5. What was the capital of Austin's first colony, and how did Austin expand his colonization efforts in Texas?

Section 4

6. Who were some successful *empresarios*?
7. How did Austin and the other *empresarios* affect settlement in Texas?

You Be the Historian

Reviewing Themes

1. **Government** How did Mexico's Federal Constitution of 1824 bring changes to Texas?
2. **Economics** Why did so many Anglo settlers come to Texas during the 1820s?
3. **Geography** What factors did Texas settlers consider when deciding where they should live?

Thinking Critically

1. **Comparing and Contrasting** How were the mission system and *empresario* system similar? How were they different?
2. **Summarizing** What were Tejanos' reactions to the idea of bringing Anglo settlers to Texas?
3. **Drawing Inferences and Conclusions** Stephen F. Austin has been called the Father of Texas. Why do you think that is so?

Texas Test Practice

Interpreting Graphs

Study the bar graph below. Then use the information in the graph to help you answer the questions.

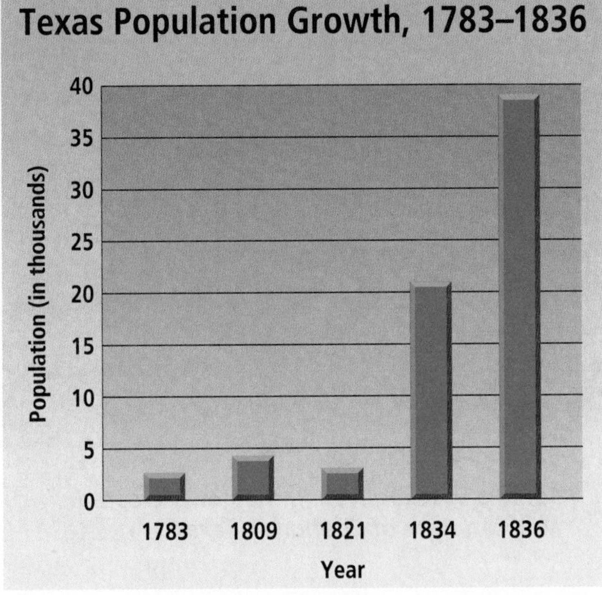

1. About how many times bigger was the Texas population in 1836 than in 1821?
   - **A** about 20 times
   - **B** about 3 times
   - **C** about 42 times
   - **D** about 10 times

2. What was the main reason for this growth?

Main Ideas and Their Support

Read the following passage from Section 4 of this chapter. Then answer the questions.

"As time passed and new settlers arrived, some Tejanos developed less favorable views of their new neighbors. Conflicts sometimes arose. These conflicts often dealt with land or property. For example, a dispute arose in 1826 between Tejano residents of De León's colony and American settlers in DeWitt's colony. Livestock that had gone missing from De León's colony was found on DeWitt's land. The dispute almost resulted in violence, but war was prevented by the intervention of two men. One was Stephen F. Austin. The other was Rafael Antonio Manchola, a son-in-law of Martín de León. Manchola was a leader of the local militia."

3. What sentence best restates the main idea of this passage?
   - **F** Livestock had gone missing from De León's colony.
   - **G** As time passed, conflicts arose between Tejanos and American settlers.
   - **H** American settlers lived in Green DeWitt's colony.
   - **J** As time passed, more settlers arrived.

4. What details in the passage support the main idea?

Interdisciplinary Connection to the Arts

Work with a small group to create a mural that transfers the information in this chapter to visual form. Subjects for your mural might include new colonization policies for Mexico, the arrival of settlers in the 1820s and early 1830s, or the reactions of the Tejano population. Provide a caption of one or two paragraphs explaining your design. When you have finished, review your work to check the grammar, spelling, and punctuation.

Internet Activity

Access the Internet to research the location of an *empresario* colony in Texas. Then analyze physical factors that affected where that colony was established. Create a chart that displays the following information about your chosen colony: the name, nearby landforms, natural resources, and climate. You may want to create a map or find images online to illustrate your chart.

CHAPTER 9

Life in Mexican Texas (1820–1835)

Texas Essential Knowledge and Skills (TEKS) 2D, 2E, 2F, 8A, 9A, 9B, 10A, 11A, 11B, 15A, 19B, 19C, 19D, 21A, 21B, 21C, 21D, 21F, 21G, 22A, 22B, 22C, 22D, 23A

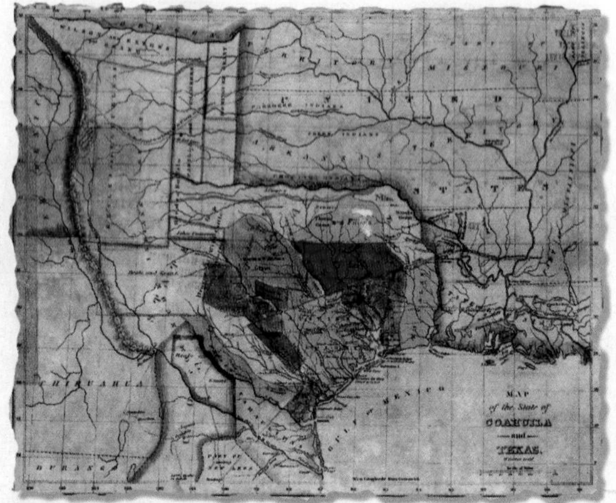

Settlers in Texas lived in the newly created Mexican state of Coahuila y Texas.

TEXAS

1822 Settler Jared Groce plants a cotton crop, possibly the first in Stephen F. Austin's colony.

1824 Mexican officials adopt the Constitution of 1824. Coahuila and Texas are merged to form one state.

1827 Stephen F. Austin receives a contract to settle an additional 100 families in Texas.

1820 — 1822 — 1824 — 1826

U.S. and WORLD

1821 The first public high school opens in Boston, Massachusetts.

1823 Charles Macintosh invents waterproof fabric, which was used in raincoats.

1825 The Erie Canal is completed.

If you were there . . .

How would you improve frontier life?

Build on What You Know

In the early 1820s *empresarios* such as Stephen F. Austin and Martín de León established colonies in Texas. Their actions and a generous colonization law for Texas led to a wave of immigration from the United States and other countries. New settlers worked hard to build lives in Texas.

To prepare cotton for market, farmers often bound their harvests in large bales.

The availability of cheap land drew thousands of Anglo settlers to Texas and other regions during the early 1800s.

1828 — 1830 — 1832 — 1834

1829 Thomas J. Pilgrim organizes a Sunday school and private boys' school in San Felipe.

1833 Mary Austin Holley's letters, describing life in early Texas, are published.

1833 Great Britain abolishes slavery throughout its empire.

1834 Texas farmers export some 7,000 bales of cotton, worth about $315,000, to New Orleans.

1834 Cyrus McCormick patents a reaping machine that allows farmers to harvest grains such as wheat three times faster.

1835 An estimated 1,000 U.S. immigrants enter Texas each month.

You Be the Historian

myNotebook

What's Your Opinion? Do you **agree** or **disagree** with the following statements? Support your point of view in your notebook.

- **Culture** The interaction between groups of people in a region can lead to a blending of cultures.
- **Citizenship** Obeying the law is an important requirement of citizenship.
- **Geography** Transportation systems affect economic growth.

Section 1

The New Texas Population

Main Ideas

1. Brought to Texas for a variety of reasons, immigrants settled in all parts of the state.
2. Rivers and climate helped people choose where to live.

Key Terms

- **G.T.T.**
- **squatters**
- **flatboats**

Why It Matters Today

The early immigrants who came to Texas had to endure long, hard journeys. Use current events sources to find information about the conditions people face on modern migrations.

TEKS: 2D, 2F, 8A, 11A, 11B, 21A, 21B, 21C, 21F, 22D

myNotebook

Use the annotation tools in your eBook to take notes on the people who lived in Texas in the 1820s and 1830s.

The Story Continues

The lone rider heard the wagon train before he saw it. Shouts and cries mixed with the thuds, clangs, and groans of the wagons and the oxen. Slowly bumping over ruts and stones, the wagons rolled into view. Weary immigrants struggled past. Some rode, while others trudged along on foot. Despite the hard journey, they kept going, eager to reach Texas.

Gone to Texas

The population of Texas grew quickly during the 1820s and 1830s. In 1820 the region had been home to only about 3,000 Tejanos. By 1834 that number had grown to about 24,000 Tejanos and new arrivals. Some of the new arrivals to the state had come from Europe or from other parts of Mexico. However, most of the settlers flooding into Texas were farmers from the southern United States. Texas was also home to thousands of American Indians, some of them immigrants from the United States, who remained independent and were not counted in the population.

Why were people so eager to move to Texas? There were many reasons. The promise of cheap land and easy payment terms drew some immigrants. Others were simply looking for reasons to leave the United States. Many immigrants were escaping debts resulting from an economic crisis that hit the country in 1819. They hoped to make a fresh start in Texas, where American creditors had no authority to collect debts. For example, both Stephen F. Austin and Jared Groce had left behind large debts when they moved to Texas.

Authorities from the United States could not follow criminals into Texas either. As a result, a number of drifters and outlaws began entering the region. Gradually, word spread through the southern United States that Texas was filling with undesirable people. Such rumors made some people hesitant to move to Texas. One man wrote to Austin about his concerns.

TEXAS VOICES

"As I contemplate becoming a resident of Texas, I feel great solicitude [concern] about the nature of the population which will inhabit the country. . . . The planters here have a most desperate [low] opinion of the population there, originating . . . from such villains as . . . have taken shelter in that province."

—Thomas White, quoted in *Texas Siftings,* by Jerry Flemmons

Analyzing Primary Sources
Identifying Bias What factors might have influenced White's opinion of Texas settlers?

In some cases, these rumors became part of popular culture. When someone left town in debt or accused of a crime, people said they had probably gone to Texas. Many overdue accounts were marked "**G.T.T.**" for "Gone to Texas."

Reading Check **Categorizing** What were the major factors that led people from the United States to move to Texas?

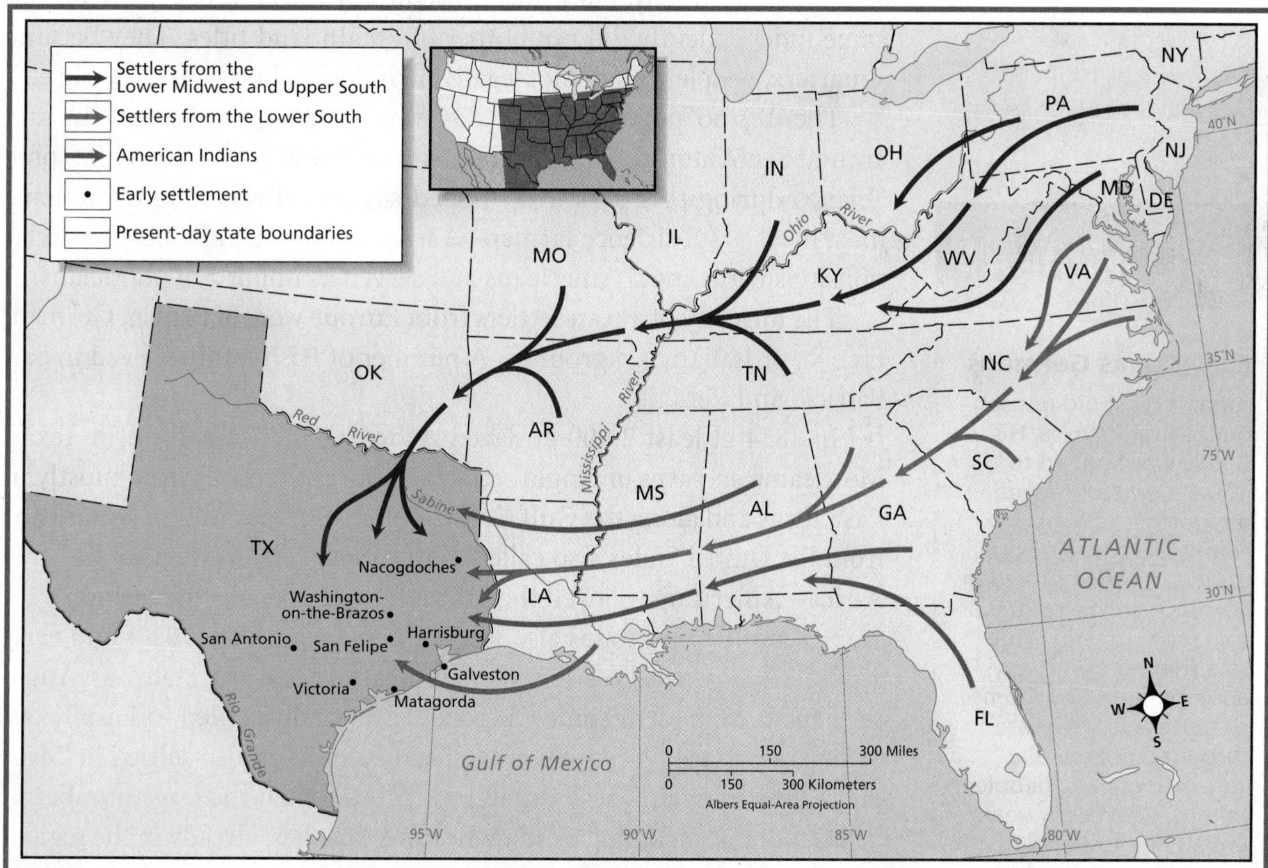

U.S Settlers Come to Texas, 1830s

Interpreting Maps Settlers from different parts of the United States came to Texas and built homesteads.
Locate To what region of Texas did each group of settlers move?

Interpreting Visuals

Getting to Texas. *Many U.S. immigrants traveled on flatboats for part of their journey.* ***How do you think geographic features such as rivers affected immigration to Texas?***

★ The People of Texas

In 1834 nearly three-fourths of the people of Texas—some 15,000— were from the United States. They mainly settled along the Gulf Coast and in East Texas. While many of these settlers came to Texas with the help of *empresarios,* a few came on their own. Mexican law allowed settlers to acquire land directly, but it was difficult. As a result, most settlers who came independently did not bother to obtain land titles. They became **squatters**, people who do not legally own the land on which they live.

The Tejano population in 1834 was about 4,000, mainly in and around San Antonio, Nacogdoches, and La Bahía–Victoria. While some Tejanos during this period developed successful ranching operations, most lived as subsistence farmers. A few established close business relationships with Anglo Americans and served as important politicians.

The majority of Texan settlers from Europe were of British, German, French, or Italian backgrounds. A number of Irish families lived in San Patricio and Refugio.

In 1834 at least 2,000 enslaved African Americans lived in Texas. Most came as slaves of Anglo settlers. As a result, slaves lived mostly in East Texas and along the Gulf Coast. About 150 free African Americans from the United States also called Texas home. Under Mexican law, free African Americans enjoyed the full rights of Mexican citizenship.

Several Indian groups also migrated to Texas in the 1820s and early 1830s. Many Cherokees left the southeastern United States as Anglo settlement expanded. Some Cherokees eventually settled in East Texas. Chickasaw, Creek, Delaware, and Shawnee Indians also settled in Texas during this period. These immigrant tribes joined the large number of Texas Indians, including Comanches and Apaches, already in the region.

Reading Check **Summarizing** What immigrant groups came to Texas, and where did they settle?

That's Interesting!

Early Texas Germans

Johann Ernst did not set out to live in Texas. His family was headed to Missouri when he read a report about Austin's colony. Intrigued, Ernst decided to try his hand in Texas. Once there, he was so happy that he wrote to a friend in Germany describing his new home. His letter was circulated throughout Germany, convincing many people to move. For many years, Ernst's home served as a hotel for new arrivals from his homeland.

Getting to Texas and Choosing Land

By 1835 an estimated 1,000 settlers from the United States entered Texas each month. Most of these new Texans traveled overland. Some came in covered wagons pulled by horses, mules, or oxen. Others rode horses with their belongings tied behind their saddles. Some even walked. For most, the fastest way to reach Texas was by boat, but water travel was more expensive than traveling overland. Those who could afford to go by water usually went to New Orleans first. Those from northern areas first floated down the Mississippi River on long, low **flatboats** to the city. There they boarded ships headed to Texas.

On reaching Texas, settlers had to decide where to live. Although *empresarios* sometimes assigned specific grants of land, most settlers made their own choices. Most preferred settling along rivers and streams that provided water for drinking and farming. Rivers and streams made travel and transportation easier. The fertile soil and mild climate of the Gulf Coast Plain and the Piney Woods were likewise appealing to many immigrants. Some settlers also chose land that resembled their old homes. For example, many people from hilly southern Tennessee settled in hilly areas in present-day Red River County.

The presence of American Indians also affected settlement patterns in Texas. Many settlers had heard stories of fierce Plains Indians such as the Apaches and Comanches. As a result, colonists avoided the lands of those groups, settling east of the Guadalupe River and south of the Old San Antonio Road instead. There, Texas Indians posed less of a threat.

Reading Check **Drawing Conclusions and Inferences** Why do you think many new Texans were drawn to areas similar to those they had lived in before?

The Big Thicket

Some people who moved to East Texas settled in an area called the Big Thicket. In the 1830s, yellow pines up to six feet in diameter covered the region. Bear, deer, panthers, and wolves roamed the area's hills and swamps. Today the Big Thicket offers one of the largest varieties of plant life in the world, including four meat-eating plants. The region is also home to some 350 bird species. **How do you think the natural resources of the area affected settler life?**

Section 1 Review

1. **Define and explain:**
   - flatboats
   - squatters
2. **Identify and explain** the significance of the following:
   - G.T.T.
3. **Locate on a Texas map:**
   - San Antonio
   - Nacogdoches
   - Victoria
4. **Categorizing** Copy the diagram below. In each segment, identify one group of people that moved to Texas and explain their reasons for moving.

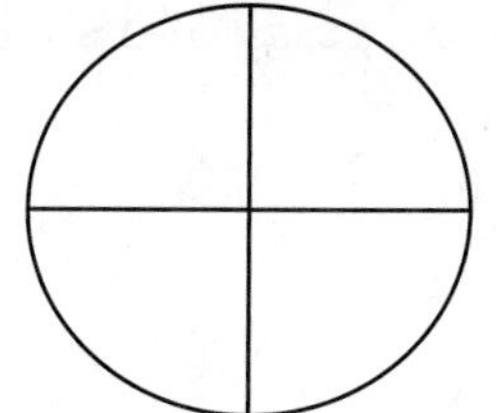

5. **Finding the Main Idea**
   a. How did settlers travel to Texas?
   b. What factors did settlers consider when choosing land, and how did this affect the development of Texas?
   c. Compare Mexican and Anglo settlement.
6. **Writing and Critical Thinking** myWriteSmart
   Summarizing Imagine that you are a Mexican official living in Texas in the early 1830s. Write a report describing the people of Texas. Consider the following:
   - where different groups settled in Texas
   - how immigration affected Texas culture

Section 2

Daily Life on the Frontier

Main Ideas

1. Early Texans made homes, clothing, and meals out of the resources around them.
2. Roman Catholicism was the official religion of Mexican Texas, but many settlers wanted to remain Protestant.
3. Education was limited in early Texas.

Key Terms

- **dogtrot cabin**
- **quilting bees**
- **buckskin**
- **venison**

Why It Matters Today

Many settlers in Texas relied on their crops for food. Use current events sources to find out how people rely on agriculture today.

TEKS: 2F, 10A, 11A, 19B, 19C, 21B, 21C, 22D

myNotebook

Use the annotation tools in your eBook to take notes on daily life in Texas during the Mexican national period.

The Story Continues

After a long journey, immigrant families often found a warm welcome in Texas. From miles around, settlers came to help them build a house. After greeting the new arrivals, they set to work. While the men cut down trees and hauled logs, the women barbecued meat and prepared cornbread. Children played games and learned to dance. Their work done, the settlers finally left as night fell.

VIDEO
Log Home

hmhsocialstudies.com

Frontier Homes

One of the first tasks for newcomers in Texas was building a house. For this chore, Texans had to rely on the building materials at hand. What those materials were depended on where a person lived. To the south and west, trees were scarce. As a result, the people who lived there—mostly Tejanos—did not have much wood to build with. Some built with adobe or stone. Others lived in jacales, small huts made of sticks and mud.

In East Texas, where trees were plentiful, Tejanos and newly arrived Anglo settlers built rough log cabins. Cut logs of pine, cedar, or oak were stacked and notched together to form walls. The space between logs was filled with clay, stones, grass, and sticks. In hot weather, people might knock out this filling to let in breezes. Of course, bugs came in as well. Long, thin boards formed the cabins' roofs, while floors were usually clay, dirt, or wood.

Most log homes were small one- or two-room cabins. A popular design was the **dogtrot cabin**, which included an open passage separating two rooms. Breezes would flow through this passage, cooling the cabin. Even prominent settlers like Stephen F. Austin lived in dogtrot cabins. One visitor described Austin's home as "a double log cabin with a wide 'passage' through the center, a porch . . . on the front with windows opening upon it, and [a] chimney at each end." As time passed, many successful settlers replaced their cabins with larger, fancier homes.

Settlers usually furnished their homes with items they made themselves. This handmade furniture was generally simple and sturdy. Some items, though, were both functional and beautiful, like the quilts that women made. Many of these quilts were made at **quilting bees**, which doubled as social occasions. Participants could chat and trade stories as they assembled their quilts.

Reading Check **Analyzing Information** What factors contributed to the design of homes in Texas during this period?

CONNECTING TO

The Arts

Texas Quilts

Because settlers could rarely obtain new fabric, they used old clothing, sacks, and scraps to make quilts. Pieces of fabric were arranged and sewn in complex patterns. The quilt below is example of a design called the Lone Star, which was popular in Texas during the Mexican period. **Why do you think quilters chose elaborate patterns for their quilts?**

Clothing in Early Texas

Just as they did for their homes, Texans used local materials to make their clothes. Cloth was hard to come by in so remote an area, so Texans of the period turned to other sources. In addition, life on the Texas frontier was rough, so clothing had to be durable and sturdy. Texas had plenty of wild deer and other animals, so leather clothing was common. Many people—men, women, and children—wore **buckskin**, or tanned deer hide. Although it was extremely strong, buckskin was very uncomfortable and often smelly, especially when it got wet. It was generally worn only as a last resort.

Although buckskin was convenient, it was not the only fabric used to make clothing. Wool was a popular choice, especially for making shirts. By the 1830s Texans had begun growing cotton, and homespun cotton fabric was soon in common use. More expensive fabrics could be imported from the United States, Mexico, or Europe.

Clothing styles differed based on people's backgrounds. Anglo settlers tended to dress much as they had in the United States, while Tejanos dressed similarly to other Mexican citizens. For working, men usually wore long shirts that could be tucked into their pants. Heavy leather boots protected their feet, while hats provided protection from the sun and extra warmth on cold days. Hat styles ranged from coonskin caps popular with some Anglo settlers to straw sombreros worn by some Tejanos. Women and girls wore dresses, often made from cotton, and bonnets or sun hats. In cold weather, people wore coats of leather or wool. Many Tejanos preferred to wear Saltillo blankets—or ponchos—and some Anglo settlers adopted this style as well.

Texans of this period enjoyed dances and other celebrations, and they liked to dress for the occasions. Wealthy men wore suits of patterned silk or wool. A popular style of the time was the frock coat, which fit tightly across the chest but flared into a skirtlike shape around the waist and thighs. It was commonly worn with a ruffled shirt and vest. Less wealthy men wore similar styles but made of less expensive cotton. Women wore fancier dresses. For those who could afford to buy them, elaborate gowns from the United States and Mexico were popular. Stylish dresses had long pleated skirts and full sleeves.

Reading Check **Summarizing** What materials were used to make clothing in Texas during the Mexican period?

★ Frontier Foods

As you would expect, most Texans had to be self-reliant for food as well as clothing. They depended on the crops they grew, livestock they raised, and game they hunted for their meals. Corn, which both Indians and Tejanos had been growing for hundreds of years in Texas, also became a staple of the new arrivals' diets. It was both easy to harvest and nutritious. As one new arrival to Texas stated, "Raising corn was a matter of life and death, since upon it depended the existence of the colony."

Luckily for the Texans, corn was also versatile. It could be—and was—prepared in many different ways. Settlers roasted or boiled corn on the cob. They dried corn kernels to make cornmeal, which could be used to make tortillas or cornbread, depending on one's background and preferences. Cornmeal batter cooked over hot coals produced johnnycakes. Tejanos also made tamales and *atole*. Corn was also useful for feeding their livestock. People even found uses for corn cobs, making items such as bottle stoppers and fishing floats.

Besides corn, Texans grew vegetables such as cabbages, peas, pumpkins, sweet potatoes, and turnips. Tejanos grew sugar cane, watermelons, and chili peppers. Indians, including the Caddo, grew squash and sunflowers. Texans gathered fruits such as berries, grapes, and peaches along with the pecans and other nuts. Because refrigeration was not available, butter, cheese, eggs, flour, and milk were rarely on hand.

The Spanish had introduced ranching to Texas early in its history. In addition, wild game was common in the area. As a result, meat was a major part of the Texan frontier diet. The meats most commonly eaten were beef, pork, and **venison**, or deer meat. Among Tejanos, *cabrito*, or goat, was also popular. Along coasts and rivers, fish was also standard fare. Meat and fish were sometimes cooked fresh, but more often they were preserved to be eaten later. Cuts of meat were smoked or salted so they would keep for long periods.

Reading Check **Evaluating** How did the Texas settlers' use of corn demonstrate their ability to adapt to and modify their environment?

A Blending of Foods

Immigrants brought their traditional recipes and cooking styles to Texas. For example, German immigrants introduced spicy sausages and sauerkraut. Settlers from the United States expanded their diets as they encountered new foods. Many settlers became fond of Mexican tortillas and tamales. Sometimes settlers combined traditional dishes to form a new tradition, such as Tex-Mex food. **How did immigrants adapt to Texas culture while maintaining their own heritage?**

Residents of San Antonio could attend churches such as the Mission Espada Church, founded in 1720. Few other parts of Texas had active places of worship.

★ Religion in Early Texas

Mexico's official religion was Roman Catholicism, and most of the Tejanos living in Texas were active in that religion. They went to mass on Sundays and holidays. Religious events such as baptisms, weddings, and saints' days were times of great celebration. Even nonreligious holidays, such as Mexican Independence Day, were celebrated with masses.

Although the Anglo settlers who came to Texas in this period had promised to become Catholic, few truly converted. Most of them were Protestant and unwilling to change their beliefs. Publicly, they stated support for the Roman Catholic Church, but privately they worshiped as they pleased. In fact, most Anglo settlements did not have any priests. Finally, Father Michael Muldoon, an Irish priest, arrived in San Felipe in 1831. He was one of the few priests any of the early U.S. settlers ever saw.

While under Mexican rule, Texas did not have any organized Protestant churches. Only the Catholic Church was legal. A fair amount of Protestant activity did exist, however. Traveling preachers and missionaries from the United States held camp meetings. Sumner Bacon, a Presbyterian, traveled through Texas giving sermons and handing out Bibles. Several Texans also organized Protestant Sunday schools. In 1829 Thomas J. Pilgrim, a Baptist, organized the first Sunday school in San Felipe. That same year, Mary Wightman began a Sunday school at Matagorda. Mexican officials usually ignored such religious activity.

Reading Check **Analyzing Information** How did Anglo settlers in Texas maintain their religious heritage?

Daily Life

Leisure Time

Settlers in early Texas enjoyed many forms of entertainment. Riders and spectators alike loved horse racing, a favorite pastime of the first Spanish settlers. Frontier Texans also enjoyed music and dancing. One man remembered a dance that lasted almost 15 hours. Weddings and balls were also popular social occasions. At home, settlers often read aloud from the Bible and other books. Storytellers told tall tales as family members gathered around. **How did settlers entertain themselves in Texas?**

Education. Students met to study in small, one-room schools. ***How does this painting reflect the way children were taught in Mexican Texas?***

★ Education on the Frontier

The Coahuila y Texas Constitution stated that public education should be available for all children. However, few settlements had money to establish schools. In addition, capable teachers were in short supply. As a result, education in early Texas was mainly limited to teaching in the home. Wealthier settlers sometimes sent their children to schools in the United States, where the education system was better established.

A few ambitious individuals did open private schools in Texas for those students whose parents could afford to pay for education. These schools were often small. Teachers often lived in the same rooms in which they taught. Frances Trask, who opened a school at Cole's Settlement in 1835, wrote of her small building that it "answers for schoolroom, parlor, bed chamber, and hall." Students paid two dollars per week to live and study with her.

Although limited by money and the availability of teachers, schools had operated in San Antonio as far back as the 1700s. Aside from the missions, small schools in San Antonio, La Bahía, and Nacogdoches operated when people could afford to pay a teacher. During the 1820s such small schools also opened in Jonesborough, San Augustine, and other settler communities. Students in these schools learned reading, writing, arithmetic, and other subjects.

By 1836 Texas had more than 20 schools. However, many children did not have access to education. Even when schools were available, the demands of farm life kept many children in the fields. In addition, enslaved African Americans were not allowed to attend school.

Reading Check **Drawing Inferences and Conclusions** Why do you think the Mexican government tried to establish public schools in Texas?

★ Section 2 Review

hmhsocialstudies.com ONLINE QUIZ

1. Define and explain:
- dogtrot cabins
- quilting bees
- buckskin
- venison

2. Summarizing
Copy the graphic organizer below. Use it to describe life in Texas during the 1820s and early 1830s.

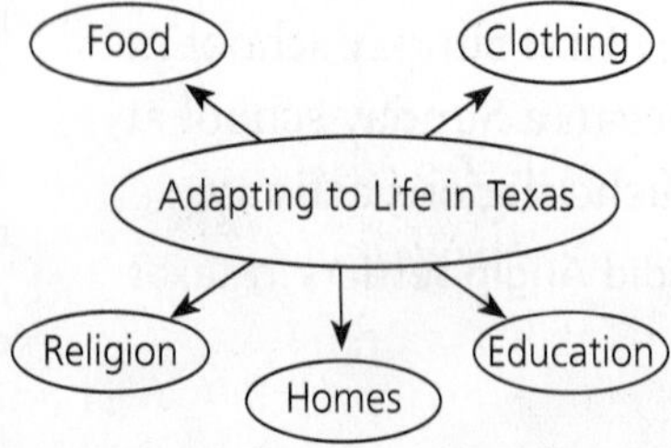

3. Finding the Main Idea

a. What were some ways in which Mexican ways of life continued to shape life in Texas even as more Anglo settlers moved here?

b. Why were public schools rare in Texas?

4. Writing and Critical Thinking *my*WriteSmart

Analyzing Information Write a letter to a family planning to move to Texas in the early 1830s. Explain how they can adapt to life there.

Consider the following:
- available resources in Texas
- culture and policies of Texas

Section 3 Cities and Trade

Main Ideas

1. During the Mexican period, Texas had a few large settlements, mostly inhabited by Tejanos.
2. In cities, people took part in business and trade.

Why It Matters Today

Settlers in early Texas traded a great deal with the United States. Use current events sources to find information about trade in the United States or Texas today.

Key Terms and People

- **William Goyens**
- **barter**
- **sawmills**
- **exports**
- **imports**

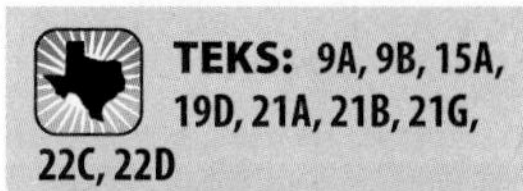

The Story Continues

Juan Seguín was only 22 when he was elected to the city council, or *ayuntamiento*, of San Antonio. The son of Erasmo Seguín, a former alcalde of the city and a friend of Stephen F. Austin, Juan Seguín was a member of one of the most prominent families in San Antonio. As a city council member, he would now help make the decisions that would shape the future of the city and people of his hometown.

myNotebook

Use the annotation tools in your eBook to take notes on life and economic activities in cities during the Mexican period.

Life in Texas Cities

Unlike Juan Seguín, most Texans during the Mexican period lived on isolated farms or in small communities. There were, however, a few larger settlements in Texas as well. Towns such as San Antonio, Goliad, and Nacogdoches were each home to more than 1,000 people, mostly Tejanos. As you might expect, life in these towns was very different from life in rural areas.

Because of their larger populations, towns needed a more structured government than small communities did. That government was the *ayuntamiento*, or city council. The constitution of Coahuila y Texas laid out the powers and responsibilities of these councils. They had to establish police forces and maintain roads. They were also responsible for providing food inspection, sanitation, and health care for their towns. All these services were paid for through taxes charged to the townspeople. One member of the *ayuntamiento* served as the alcalde.

Interpreting Visuals

San Antonio. *The Plaza de las Islas, named for the city's early Canary Islander residents, was at the heart of San Antonio. The cathedral near the plaza was the city's spiritual center.* ***Based on this image, how was life in San Antonio in the 1800s different from life there today?***

The oldest civil settlement in Texas, San Antonio was also the largest at the beginning of the Mexican period. In 1820 it was home to about 2,000 people. Most residents of San Antonio made their living farming or ranching in the fields around the city. Others ran stores or other businesses to support the ranchers and farmers. A number of businesses were owned or managed by women, often widows.

Though it was the largest town in Texas, San Antonio remained very much a frontier settlement. The streets were unpaved and muddy after rainfall. The canals that carried water through the town were open and subject to pollution. As in all cities and towns of the period, outbreaks of disease were common. There were very few stone buildings, and most people lived in either adobe houses or jacales. Many residents kept small garden plots, with which they supplemented the food available from area farms and ranches.

During the Mexican period, the population of San Antonio did not grow much. In Nacogdoches, the situation was exactly the opposite. After the Mexican Revolution, Nacogdoches had been almost abandoned. However, over the following 10 years, the population steadily increased. By 1835 nearly 1,000 people lived there. It included a mixture of Tejanos, Anglo settlers, and slaves. Most people lived in small, rough log cabins. Like most Texans of the time, they farmed for a living.

San Antonio and Nacogdoches were both established towns by the time Mexico became independent. New cities developed during this period, though, as Anglo settlement increased. For example, San Felipe, in Austin's colony, was larger than San Antonio by 1835.

Reading Check **Contrasting** How were Texas cities in the early 1800s different from cities today?

★ Business, Trade, and Transportation

Unlike small settlements, Texas towns were home to crafters and merchants. By offering their services to other townspeople, blacksmiths, carpenters, and merchants could make a living in towns. For example, **William Goyens** of Nacogdoches became wealthy by running a blacksmithing shop and other businesses. Because few people had much money, though, most business was conducted through **barter**, or trade.

Blacksmiths such as Goyens made items needed by farmers and others. These include plows, tools, and other items. Similarly, carpenters made wagons and other items. Other business owners made their livings refining products for others. A few Texans, for example, ran **sawmills**, which cut wood into usable pieces.

Texas business and trade increased during the Mexican period. However, poor transportation systems made travel and trade difficult. The roads that linked towns were little more than trails. Bumpy and dusty in dry weather, the roads became muddy, impassable swamps when it rained. Transporting goods by river was not much better. Many rivers were shallow and full of sandbars. Small boats and rafts could navigate them, but large boats had difficulties.

Some trade was carried out by ship through ports on the Gulf of Mexico. One of the busiest ports was Galveston. In the early 1830s Brazoria and Matagorda became important ports as well.

Despite obstacles in transportation, by the 1830s Texas was producing about $500,000 worth of **exports**, or items to be sold in other places. These included cattle, corn, cotton, furs, horses, pork, and salt. In return, Texas required many **imports**, or items bought from other regions. Texas imports included manufactured and luxury products.

Reading Check **Analyzing Information** What kinds of businesses could be found in Texas towns?

BIOGRAPHY

William Goyens

(1794–1856) A free African American of mixed black and white ancestry, William Goyens became a wealthy business owner in Nacogdoches. He was a blacksmith, wagon maker, and innkeeper. Goyens spoke English, Spanish, Cherokee, and Comanche. As a result, he served as a diplomat, assisting in negotiations with the Cherokees. **What contributions did Goyens make to Texas?**

★ Section 3 Review

hmhsocialstudies.com ONLINE QUIZ

1. **Define and explain:**
   - barter
   - sawmills
   - exports
   - imports
2. **Identify and explain** the significance:
   - William Goyens
3. **Locate on a map:**
   - San Antonio
   - Nacogdoches
4. **Analyzing Information**
   Copy the graphic organizer below. Use it to compare and contrast life in cities and rural areas during the Mexican period.

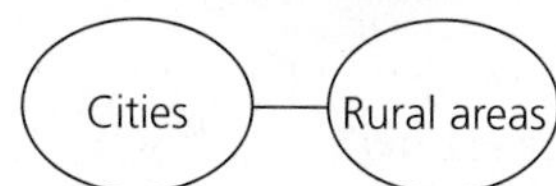

5. **Finding the Main Idea**
   a. What were the largest settlements in Texas in the period, and who lived there?
   b. How did transportation in early Texas affect business and trade?
6. **Writing and Critical Thinking** myWriteSmart
   Evaluating Study the image on the facing page. Based on this image, write a description of what life was like for residents of San Antonio in the early 1800s.
   Consider the following:
   - the buildings seen in the image
   - what actions are taking place in the image

Connecting To

Literature

Texas: Observations, Historical, Geographical, and Descriptive

Mary Austin Holley

The diaries, letters, and histories of Mary Austin Holley provide a detailed picture of life in early Texas. The cousin of Stephen F. Austin, Holley was a well-educated and sophisticated woman from Connecticut who visited Texas in 1831. While there, she wrote letters about the region to friends. In 1833 her letters were published in a book entitled Texas: Observations, Historical, Geographical, and Descriptive. *Holley visited Texas several more times and published her diary of one such trip. Holley followed this work with the book* Texas. *Published in 1836, it is the first known history of Texas written in English. The following excerpt is from an 1831 letter, in which Holley describes how settlers adapted to life in Texas.*

Writing desk from the 1800s

It is found to be easier to raise or manufacture such articles as are needed in the family, or to do without, than to obtain them from abroad, or to employ an individual to **scour**[1] the country, in search of such as may be desired. People live too far apart, to beg or borrow often. . . . If they want any article of first necessity, coffee, for instance, which is much used, they will send some of their chickens, butter, and eggs, to a neighboring family newly arrived, and propose an exchange, as most new comers bring with them some **stores.**[2] There is much of this kind of barter, **provisions**[3] being so much more plenty than money. . . .

The common concerns of life are sufficiently exciting to keep the spirits **buoyant,**[4] and prevent every thing like **ennui.**[5] Artificial wants are entirely forgotten, in the view of real ones. . . . Even **privations**[6] become pleasures: people grow **ingenious**[7] in overcoming difficulties. Many **latent**[8] faculties are developed. They discover in themselves, powers, they did not suspect themselves of possessing. Equally surprised and delighted at the discovery, they apply to their labours with all that energy and spirit, which new hope and conscious strength inspire.

Understanding What You Read

1. **Literature and History** According to Holley, what was life like for people in Texas during the 1830s?
2. **Literature and You** Based on information in this chapter, do you think this letter is a valid source about life in Texas? Why or why not?

[1] **scour:** search
[2] **stores:** goods
[3] **provisions:** goods
[4] **buoyant:** uplifted
[5] **ennui:** boredom
[6] **privations:** hardships
[7] **ingenious:** clever
[8] **latent:** hidden

Section 4

Agriculture and Society

Main Ideas

1. Farming and ranching were the main industries in Texas.
2. Conflicts arose over the issue of slavery in Texas.

Why It Matters Today

Farming and ranching were major economic activities in early Texas. Use current events sources to find information about agriculture in the state today.

Key Term

- **plantations**

TEKS: 2D, 2E, 10A, 21B, 21D, 22D

myNotebook

Use the annotation tools in your eBook to take notes on agriculture and its effects on society in Texas.

The Story Continues

Once in Texas, Austrian immigrant George B. Erath realized that he lacked several important items. Looking through his belongings, Erath selected some with which he was willing to part. Approaching other settlers, he traded his clothes for cattle and hogs. To obtain corn, he gave up his horse. Erath's partner, who was in a similar position, traded his ox for a pig and his feather bed for three cows. In Texas, livestock and corn were more important than luxuries.

★ Farming and Ranching

Agriculture dominated the Texas economy during the 1820s and 1830s. Most Texans during this time lived on small family farms. Families worked hard to prepare fields, harvest crops, and perform household tasks. Few people lived near stores, and even those who did had little cash. As a result, families had to produce many of the items they needed, such as tools and clothing.

A few wealthy Texans established **plantations**, large farms that specialized in growing one crop. One of the first plantations in Texas was established by Jared Groce, the wealthy settler who had arrived with Stephen F. Austin. Called the Bernardo Plantation, it was located south of present-day Hempstead. Like many plantations, it resembled a small community. In addition to a large house, Bernardo included a kitchen, smaller homes for visitors and a doctor, a dairy, and quarters for slaves.

Interpreting Visuals

Farming. *Farm life in this period was difficult. Each member of the family, including children, had many chores to perform.* ***What kind of chores do you think people had to do on a farm?***

Slaves were the main labor force of the plantation, both in the house and in the fields. Field slaves often worked from dawn to dusk performing backbreaking labor.

On both small and large farms, cotton became the main crop grown for profit. Although Caddos and Tejanos had grown small amounts of cotton for centuries, Anglo settlers brought large-scale cotton farming to Texas. They made the lower Brazos, Colorado, and Trinity river valleys the center of cotton production.

While cotton farming was a major economic activity for the Anglo settlers of Texas, ranching was more popular among Tejanos. First introduced to Texas by Spanish settlers, ranching had been a key component of Spanish settlement in the area. It is not surprising, then, that the descendants of these Spanish settlers would continue to run ranches during the Mexican period.

Texas is well suited to ranching. The mild climate, open prairies, and river valleys provided good pasture for livestock. In addition, ranching was a clever lifestyle choice in a region with a small population and the dangers of Indian attack. It took only a few men to tend a lot of animals, and the open range offered some safety from complete destruction.

During the 1820s and 1830s prominent Tejanos such as Martín de León and Erasmo Seguín were able to expand their ranching operations by taking over pastures that had once belonged to missions. Family, friends, and hired hands typically all lived together on the ranch, which resembled a small community. A visitor in 1834 described the Seguín ranch: "It consists of a square, palisaded [walled] round, with the houses of the families residing there forming the sides." The De León ranch covered some 22,000 acres and was home to thousands of cattle.

Reading Check **Comparing** How did the cotton farming and ranching populations of Texas differ during the Mexican period?

★ The Issue of Slavery in Texas

The introduction of large-scale cotton farming to Texas also led to the expansion of slavery. Cotton farming requires a great deal of labor. In the United States, where most Texas cotton farmers came from, that labor was performed by slaves. When these farmers moved to Texas, they brought their slaves with them.

As you may recall, some Tejanos, especially in Coahuila, were opposed to slavery. The Mexican government viewed the matter the same way. In 1829 President Vicente Guerrero—himself of African ancestry—outlawed slavery in Mexico. However, officials in Texas warned the government that the ban violated their colonization policies. As a result, slavery temporarily continued in Texas.

Even with the exception, some Texans feared that the government would one day ban slavery. They worried that the possibility of such a ban might keep new settlers from moving to the area. A letter from an Alabama farmer to Stephen F. Austin expressed these concerns.

TEXAS VOICES

"Our most valuable inhabitants here own [slaves]. I am therefore anxious to know what the laws are upon that subject. . . . Our planters are not willing to remove without they can first be assured of their [slaves] being secured to them by the laws of your Govt."

—Charles Douglas, quoted in *Westward Expansion,* by Sanford Wexler

Analyzing Primary Sources
Identifying Points of View Do you think the writer would go to Texas if he could not keep his slaves? Why or why not?

When Austin's Old 300 settled in Texas, they brought more than 400 slaves with them. By 1836 some 5,000 slaves lived in Texas—about 13 percent of the population. Although slavery was not totally outlawed in Texas, it remained a divisive issue. As time passed, tensions between Anglos and Mexican officials over slavery and other issues rose.

Reading Check **Making Generalizations and Predictions** How do you think U.S. settlers' unwillingness to adopt Mexican ways affected Texas?

★ Section 4 Review

hmhsocialstudies.com ONLINE QUIZ

1. Define and explain:
- plantations

2. Locate on a Texas map:
- Brazos River
- Colorado River
- Trinity River

3. Comparing and Contrasting
Copy the graphic organizer below. In each column, write three sentences to describe agricultural activity in Texas.

Farming	Ranching

4. Finding the Main Idea
- **a.** What factors made Texas a suitable place to develop a ranching industry?
- **b.** Why did the issue of slavery cause increasing tensions in Texas?

5. Writing and Critical Thinking myWriteSmart
Drawing Conclusions By the 1830s, some Mexican officials were concerned about the number of Anglo settlers in Texas. Write a paragraph explaining their concerns.
Consider the following:
- tensions about the issue of slavery
- differences between Tejanos and Anglos

CHAPTER 9 REVIEW

The Chapter at a Glance

Examine the following visual summary of the chapter. Then use the visual to write a one-page short story about life in Texas during the early 1800s. Use standard grammar, spelling, sentence structure, and punctuation to describe the economy, immigration, and Mexican government in Texas.

Identifying People and Ideas

Write a sentence to explain the role or significance of each of the following terms or people.

1. squatters
2. flatboats
3. dogtrot cabins
4. quilting bees
5. plantations
6. buckskin
7. barter
8. exports
9. William Goyens
10. imports

Understanding Main Ideas

Section 1

1. Why did many U.S. immigrants come to Texas in the early 1800s?
2. What different groups settled in Texas during the 1820s and early 1830s?

Section 2

3. How did Texas settlers adapt to their new environment?
4. How did Anglo settlers maintain their cultural heritage, particularly their religious beliefs, while adapting to Texas culture?

Section 3

5. Describe life in Texas cities in the 1830s.

Section 4

6. What activities were the basis of the Texas economy during the Mexican period?

You Be the Historian

Reviewing Themes

1. **Culture** What were some examples of cultural blending that developed from the interaction of Tejanos and Anglo settlers?
2. **Citizenship** Do you think that Texas settlers who broke Mexican laws were good citizens? Provide reasons for your answer.
3. **Geography** How did poor transportation networks in Texas affect the region's economy?

Thinking Critically

1. **Contrasting** How did the purposes and methods of Spanish and Anglo settlement in Texas differ?
2. **Summarizing** Describe the major characteristics of life in Texas during Mexican rule.
3. **Evaluating** How did both physical and human factors affect the settlement of immigrants from the United States in Texas?

Texas Test Practice

Interpreting Maps

Study the map below. Use the information on the map to help you answer the questions that follow.

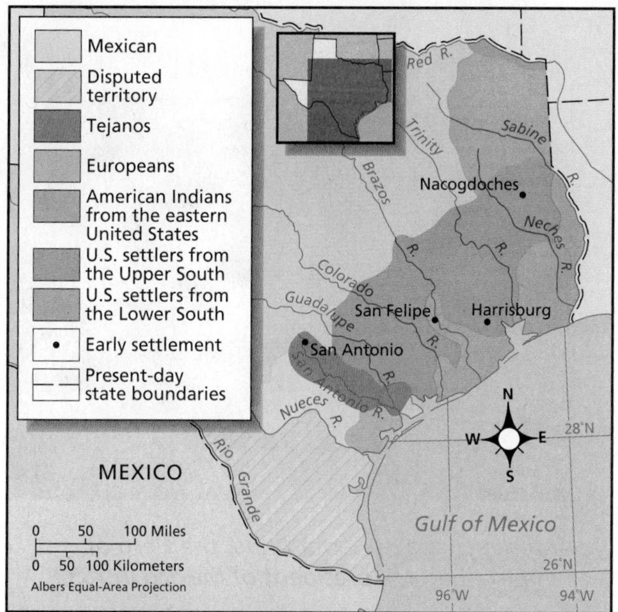

1. In 1836 what group or groups occupied the largest part of Texas?

- **A** settlers from the Upper South
- **B** settlers from the Lower South
- **C** Europeans and Tejanos
- **D** American Indians and Tejanos

2. Interpret the settlement patterns you see on this map. Why do you think people of similar backgrounds tended to live near each other?

Analyzing Primary Sources

Read the following story by Solomon Wright. Then answer the questions.

"A man moving to this promised land from Missouri drove two spans of powerful, spirited Thoroughbred horses [attached] to two brand new wagons. . . . Anybody would ask him where he was going, he'd boom out in the heartiest voice you can imagine, 'Goin' to Texas to get rich.'

After a couple of years in the alligator-swamp country, this man and his family had been shaken by so many chills and burned up by so much fever that they were as yellow as pumpkins, and just about as spirited. . . . Finally he started back to Missouri in an old shackly [rickety] wagon, each of its four wheels trying to go in a different direction, pulled by a pair of ewe-necked, rabbit-hipped prairie ponies. When anyone would ask him where he was going, he would squeak out in a weak, whiney voice, 'Goin'-back-to-Missouri.' "

3. This humorous story illustrates what serious fact about settling in Texas?

- **F** Wagons often broke down in Texas.
- **G** Failure struck many hopeful settlers.
- **H** Hard work assured success on the Texas frontier.
- **J** Prairie ponies sold well in Missouri.

4. Why do you think that East Texans enjoyed telling this sort of story?

Cooperative Learning

Work with a small group to complete the following activity. You have been chosen to find ways to improve the economy of early Texas. As a group, use a problem-solving process to identify problems, gather information, and list and consider options. Then think about the advantages and disadvantages of each option. Next, pick and implement one or two of the best solutions. Finally, write an evaluation of how effective you think those solutions would have been. Your solutions must have been workable in early Texas.

Internet Activity 

Access the Internet to research what life was like for the people who lived in Texas in the early 1800s. First, locate primary or secondary sources that describe daily life in the period. Then write an essay or build a collage or a model that demonstrates an aspect of the transportation, housing, education, diet, and entertainment of Texans during this time. Check your essay or any labels on your collage for proper grammar, spelling, sentence structure, and punctuation.

CHAPTER 10

The Road to Revolution (1825–1835)

Texas Essential Knowledge and Skills (TEKS) 1B, 3A, 3B, 8A, 9A, 10B, 17B, 17C, 21A, 21B, 21C, 21E, 21H, 22A, 22B, 22C, 22D

Antonio López de Santa Anna, the Hero of Tampico, became president of Mexico in 1833.

TEXAS

1826 The Fredonian Rebellion begins when Haden Edwards declares independence from Mexico.

1828 General Manuel de Mier y Terán begins a tour of Texas for the Mexican government.

1829 President Guerrero issues a decree ending slavery in Mexico, but an exemption is made for Texas.

1830 On April 6 Mexico issues a law that changes rules on immigration and trade in Texas.

1825 — 1826 — 1827 — 1828 — 1829 — 1830

U.S. and WORLD

1825 Bolivia wins its independence from Spain.

1827 The United States formally offers to purchase Texas from Mexico for $1 million.

1829 Spanish soldiers land at Tampico in a final attempt to reconquer Mexico. Forces led by Antonio López de Santa Anna defeat them, earning him the nickname Hero of Tampico.

If you were there . . .

Would you support war or peace?

Build on What You Know

During the 1800s thousands of American immigrants came to Texas. As they did, conflict with the Mexican government developed. By the mid-1830s, that conflict had led some Texans to believe that they should to to war for their independence.

In Mexico City, the federal government made many changes, including abolishing the Constitution of 1824, that were unpopular in Texas.

Cannons were important for defense of early settlements in Texas.

1831
The town of Gonzales receives a cannon from the Mexican government to defend citizens against American Indian attacks.

1834
Stephen F. Austin is arrested in Saltillo.

1835
Texans become concerned when the Mexican government officially abolishes the Constitution of 1824.

1831 | 1832 | 1833 | 1834 | 1835

1831
A violent slave revolt, known as Nat Turner's Rebellion, takes place in Virginia.

1832
General Santa Anna leads a revolt against President Bustamante.

1835
Alexis de Tocqueville begins publishing *Democracy in America.*

You Be the Historian

*my*Notebook

What's Your Opinion? Do you agree or disagree with the following statements? Support your point of view in your notebook.

- **Economics** Economic factors such as trade are usually the cause of conflicts between nations.
- **Constitutional Heritage** A president should be able to abolish the nation's constitution.
- **Government** New governments have more problems than old governments.

Section 1

Political Unrest in Texas

Main Ideas

1. The Fredonian Rebellion was an attempt to create an independent republic in East Texas.
2. General Mier y Terán toured Texas and concluded that American influence in the area was too strong.
3. The Law of April 6, 1830, banned American immigration to Texas.

Key Terms and People

- **Fredonian Rebellion**
- **Mier y Terán Report**
- **Law of April 6, 1830**
- **customs duties**

Why It Matters Today

In the early 1830s many Texans were unhappy with the Mexican government and began thinking about rebellion. Use current events sources to find information on protests or rebellions against governments in the world today.

TEKS: 1B, 3A, 9A, 17C, 21A, 21B, 21E, 22D

myNotebook

Use the annotation tools in your eBook to take notes on political unrest and changes in Texas.

The Story Continues

The son of a U.S. Senator from Kentucky, Haden Edwards was not a typical *empresario.* Although trained as a lawyer, Edwards was more interested in acquiring land than in practicing the law. In 1820 he moved with his wife and brother to Mississippi, where he bought a plantation. Eventually he moved to Texas with Stephen F. Austin and created his own colony near Nacogdoches.

The Fredonian Rebellion

Haden Edwards received his *empresario* contract from the Mexican government in 1825. The contract gave him permission to settle some 800 families near Nacogdoches. When he arrived, Edwards found that a number of Mexican families, Anglo settlers, and Cherokees had lived on the land for years. Some families had been living on the land for more than 100 years. They had become known as "old settlers."

Edwards's contract required him to respect the property rights of all settlers who had legal titles to their land. In this case, the only legal titles were those issued by Spain or Mexico. Edwards, however, was not happy about this rule. He declared some of the old settlers' titles to be forgeries. He also demanded that people pay him additional fees for land they had already purchased.

Edwards's actions enraged many of the old settlers. Their rage increased the following year after a questionable election. Edwards's son-in-law was elected alcalde of the settlement, but many old settlers suspected fraud. They complained to the government, which sided with the old settlers. In October 1826 the Mexican government canceled Edwards's contract, declaring that he was not fulfilling its terms.

A group of Edwards supporters took action. They arrested the new alcalde and tried to force him from office. The Mexican government sent troops to support the alcalde. In response, Edwards, his brother Benjamin, and their supporters—including some Cherokees—declared themselves free from Mexican rule. They planned to establish the republic of Fredonia. On December 21, 1826, they issued the Fredonian Declaration of Independence.

TEXAS VOICES

"The Government of the Mexican United States, have by repeated insults, treachery and oppression, reduced the . . . [people of Texas] to the dreadful alternative of either submitting their freeborn necks to the yoke . . . or of taking up arms in defence of their unalienable rights and asserting their Independence."

—Fredonian Declaration of Independence, quoted in *Documents of Texas History,* edited by Ernest Wallace

Analyzing Primary Sources
Identifying Points of View
According to this document, why did the Fredonians rebel?

Most Texans—both Tejanos and Anglo settlers alike—opposed the **Fredonian Rebellion.** Stephen F. Austin, who supported the Mexican government's decision, called out the militia. In January 1827 the Fredonians learned that Mexican troops and the militia were coming. The rebels, including Haden Edwards, fled. The republic collapsed.

Reading Check **Summarizing** What events led to the outbreak of the Fredonian Rebellion?

Interpreting Visuals

Nacogdoches. *The Fredonian rebels used the Old Stone Fort in Nacogdoches as a base. The Stone Fort Museum, shown here, is a reconstruction of the original building on the campus of Stephen F. Austin University.* ***Why do you think the rebels would have chosen such a building as their base?***

★Texas Cities★

Laredo

History: Laredo was founded in 1755 when Mexican rancher Tomás Sánchez established a settlement there. Lying on a road from Mexico to Texas, Laredo served as an important location for trade. The town prospered and grew along with Mexico's northern territories.

Population in 2012: 244,731 (estimate)

Relative location: On the Rio Grande, southwest of San Antonio

Region: Gulf Coastal Plain

County: County seat of Webb County

Special feature: Located on the Texas-Mexico border, Laredo is a center of trade and tourism.

Economy: After the arrival of railroads in the late 1800s, Laredo's importance as a trade center grew even more. Its economy was also boosted by the discovery of oil and natural gas in the 1920s. Since the passage of NAFTA, Laredo has grown as a center of import and export trade with Mexico.

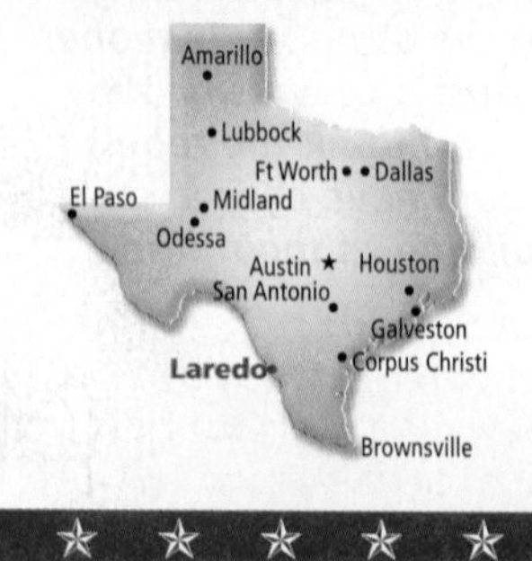

The Mier y Terán Report

The Fredonian Rebellion was a minor event, but it attracted a lot of attention. Even newspapers in the United States carried stories about the revolt. This American interest in the rebellion greatly worried the Mexican government. During the 1820s the U.S. government had made several offers to purchase Texas from Mexico, which had refused to consider such a sale. However, the repeated offers—coupled with trouble caused by American immigrants like Haden Edwards—made some Mexican officials worry about the number of Americans in Texas.

To investigate their concerns, these officials sent General Manuel de Mier y Terán with a group to tour Texas. Officially, the purpose of his trip was to examine the resources and Indians of Texas and to help determine the formal boundary with Louisiana. At the same time, the general was asked to determine how many Americans lived in Texas and what their attitudes toward Mexico were.

Mier y Terán began his inspection tour in Laredo in early 1828 and arrived in San Antonio on March 1. From there, he traveled on to San Felipe de Austin, where he met with Stephen F. Austin. The two men discussed many of the concerns with which Anglo settlers in Texas dealt. Austin also reconfirmed his own loyalty to Mexico.

The tour continued to Nacogdoches. While there, the general wrote a report to the president of Mexico. In the **Mier y Terán Report**, he noted that Mexican influence in Texas decreased as one moved northward and eastward. Around Nacogdoches, settlers from the United States outnumbered Tejanos by 10 to 1. He warned that the American influence, particularly in East Texas, was growing stronger every day.

TEXAS VOICES

"I tell myself that it could not be otherwise than that from such a state of affairs should arise an antagonism between Mexicans and foreigners. . . . Therefore, I am warning you to take timely measures. Texas could throw the whole nation into revolution."

—Manuel de Mier y Terán, quoted in *Documents of Texas History,* edited by Ernest Wallace

To help curb American influence in Texas, Mier y Terán made several recommendations to the Mexican president. First, he encouraged increasing trade between Texas and Mexico to discourage trade with the United States. Second, he argued that more soldiers needed to be sent to Texas to help keep order and to increase Mexico's control over the region. Finally, he felt that Mexico should encourage more Europeans and Mexicans to settle in Texas. Mier y Terán believed these actions would weaken Texas ties with the United States and reinforce Mexico's determination to keep Texas.

Reading Check **Finding the Main Idea** What conclusion did Mier y Terán draw, and what did he advise?

The Mexican government sent additional troops to Texas to enforce the Law of April 6, 1830.

★ The Law of April 6, 1830

In response to Manuel de Mier y Terán's report, the Mexican government passed the **Law of April 6, 1830.** This sweeping law was intended to strictly control the American presence in Texas. It banned immigration from the United States and made it illegal for settlers to bring more slaves into Texas. The law also suspended unfilled *empresario* contracts. Only a few American *empresarios,* including Stephen F. Austin and Green DeWitt, were allowed to keep their contracts. To keep unauthorized immigrants out of Texas, the government placed military bases and government offices along the borders.

Although Americans could no longer become *empresarios* under the new law, the government did not stop issuing land contracts. The government hoped to bring more Mexicans and Catholic Europeans to Texas. As a result, it issued *empresario* grants to members of these groups, making it clear that they were not to bring American families to their settlements.

In addition to restricting immigration, the Law of April 6, 1830, also began to tax all U.S. imports in Texas. These import taxes, or **customs duties**, served two purposes. Like all taxes, they raised money for the government. In addition, however, they were designed to encourage internal trade within Mexico. With the duties, goods from the United States would now be more expensive than goods from Mexico. The rest of Mexico had been paying such duties for many years. Under the new law, Texans had to pay customs duties on imports as well.

LINKING Past to Present

Trade Relations

One source of conflict between Texans and the Mexican government was customs duties. Trade still plays an important role in Texas-Mexico relations. In 1994 the North American Free Trade Agreement (NAFTA) went into effect. NAFTA removed trade barriers—such as import and export taxes—between the United States, Canada, and Mexico. As a result of NAFTA, trade between Texas and Mexico has greatly increased.
Why do you think the U.S. government agreed to the terms of NAFTA?

GLOBAL CONNECTIONS

The Antislavery Movement Abroad

In 1829 the Mexican president abolished slavery, and the Law of April 6, 1830, banned the importing of slaves to Texas. Mexico's actions reflected a growing world trend. Great Britain outlawed the buying of slaves in 1807, and the United States passed a similar law the next year. In 1823 Chile made slavery illegal. In 1833 Britain abolished slavery in the British Empire. During this time, the antislavery movement was also growing in the United States. **Why were some Texans worried about the antislavery movement?**

The Law of April 6, 1830, angered many people in Texas. They feared that the new restrictions would hurt the growing Texas economy. Immigration had led to population growth and trade, which helped the economy. Many Anglo settlers were also upset that their relatives and friends in the United States could not move to Texas.

Stephen F. Austin disliked the new law, but he tried to work with Mexican officials. He encouraged colonists to respect the law. However, Austin's own faith in the central government had been shaken by the change in its dealings with Texas. In a letter, he expressed concerns that the government was treating the people of Texas like children or slaves.

Tejanos who supported immigration, such as Erasmo Seguín, José Antonio Navarro, and Francisco Ruiz, also opposed the Law of April 6, 1830. After the law went into effect, the *ayuntamiento* of San Antonio held a special meeting. Its members, including Seguín, Navarro, and Ruiz, noted several of the advantages of having people from the United States move to Texas.

TEXAS VOICES

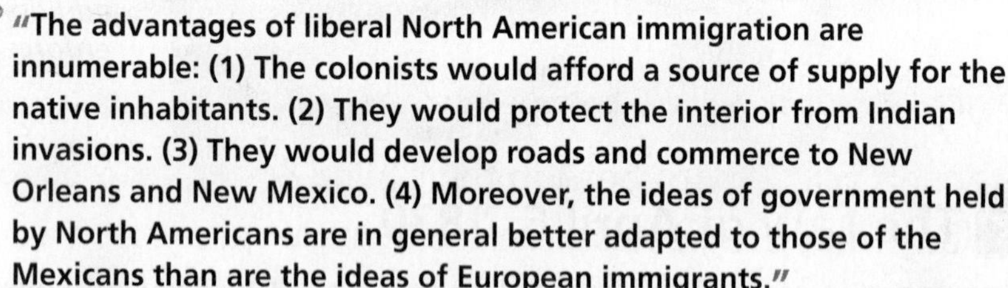

"The advantages of liberal North American immigration are innumerable: (1) The colonists would afford a source of supply for the native inhabitants. (2) They would protect the interior from Indian invasions. (3) They would develop roads and commerce to New Orleans and New Mexico. (4) Moreover, the ideas of government held by North Americans are in general better adapted to those of the Mexicans than are the ideas of European immigrants."

—The *ayuntamiento* of San Antonio, quoted in *Foreigners in Their Native Land*, edited by David J. Weber

Reading Check Evaluating How did Mier y Terán's tour of Texas and report lead to the passage of the Law of April 6, 1830?

Section 1 Review

1. **Define and explain:**
   - customs duties
2. **Identify and explain** the significance of each of the following in Texas history:
   - Fredonian Rebellion
   - Mier y Terán Report
   - Law of April 6, 1830
3. **Locate on a map:**
   - Nacogdoches
   - Laredo
4. **Identifying Cause and Effect** Copy the graphic organizer below. As you move up the ladder, describe the events that led to the Law of April 6, 1830.

Law of April 6, 1830
Mier y Terán Report
Mier y Terán Investigation
Fredonian Rebellion

5. **Finding the Main Idea**
   - **a.** How did disputes over land and other issues lead to the Fredonian Rebellion, and what was the government's response to it?
   - **b.** What steps did Mier y Terán recommend in his report?
6. **Writing and Critical Thinking** my WriteSmart
   Supporting a Point of View Imagine that you are living in Texas in the 1830s. Would you have supported or opposed the Law of April 6, 1830? Explain why or why not. Consider the following:
   - the importance of Texas to Mexico
   - the growth of the Texas economy and population

Section 2 Tensions Grow

Main Ideas

1. Tension between officials and Texans at Anahuac led to conflict.
2. The Turtle Bayou Resolutions declared Texas support for the Mexican government.

Key Terms and People

- **resolutions**
- **Turtle Bayou Resolutions**
- **Antonio López de Santa Anna**
- **Battle of Velasco**

Why It Matters Today

In the 1830s Texans were upset by the government's violation of the Constitution of 1824. Use current events sources to find information on constitutional issues today.

TEKS: 1B, 3A, 8A, 10B, 21A, 21B, 21C, 22D

myNotebook

Use the annotation tools in your eBook to take notes on growing tension between Texans and Mexican officials.

The Story Continues

Although he had been born in the United States, Juan Davis Bradburn was a loyal soldier of the Mexican army. He had joined during the revolution, winning fame and forming a close friendship with Vicente Guerrero. As a former American living in Mexico, Bradburn was fluent in both Spanish and English. Therefore he seemed to be the perfect choice to command the first customs post established under the Law of April 6, 1830.

Tension at Anahuac

Colonel Juan Davis Bradburn arrived in Texas in the fall of 1830 to enforce the Law of April 6, 1830. His troops built a fort at the mouth of the Trinity River on Galveston Bay near an important trade route and immigration point. The settlement became known as Anahuac. At this key location, troops could enforce the new trade and immigration laws.

Bradburn soon clashed with another Mexican official, Francisco Madero. As general land commissioner, Madero had been sent by the state government to Texas to issue land titles to settlers who had arrived before 1830. However, Bradburn believed that the titles Madero issued violated the national government's authority over land grants along the coast. In February 1831 Bradburn arrested Madero.

Conflicts in Texas, 1825–1835

Interpreting Maps Conflicts between Texans and Mexican officials erupted during the 1830s. Many of these conflicts were over the placement of Mexican troops in Texas and the collection of taxes on imports.

1. ***Locate*** What settlements were sites of conflict?
2. ***Evaluating*** Why do you think conflicts broke out in ports along the Texas coast?

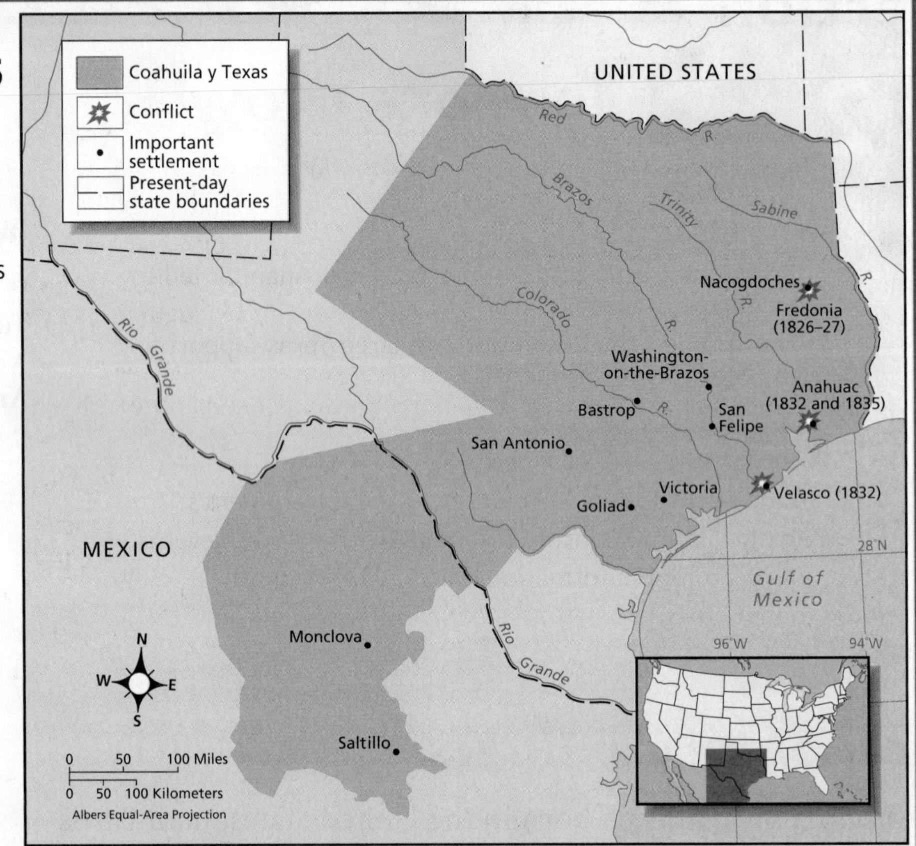

Many Texans became upset when Bradburn put Madero in jail. They became even more upset when Bradburn was ordered to disband the government of Liberty, a town that Madero had established. The government was moved to Anahuac instead. Local residents also complained that Bradburn used their slaves for projects without compensation.

The arrival of a new customs official in November 1831 further increased tensions. George Fisher demanded that all ships landing in Texas pay their customs duties at Anahuac. This rule required some shippers to travel overland from Brazoria to Anahuac to get the necessary paperwork. Stephen F. Austin, responding to complaints, wrote to Bradburn. He argued that the new customs rules were "utterly impracticable and their execution is impossible."

The tension between Mexican officials and Texan settlers came to a head in the spring of 1832. Two recently arrived settlers, William B. Travis and Patrick Jack, antagonized Bradburn. Since their arrival in Texas, they had formed a citizen militia. Officially the militia was created to defend against Indian attacks, but Bradburn was concerned about the chance of violence. Travis and Jack also pestered the commander with false rumors of a possible invasion from Louisiana. Frustrated, Bradburn arrested the two men and held them for trial. Texas settlers were enraged over the arrest.

Reading Check **Drawing Inferences and Conclusions** How did the enforcement of the Law of April 6, 1830, lead to problems at Anahuac?

The Turtle Bayou Resolutions

Patrick Jack's brother, William, rallied the people of Anahuac to support his brother. Settlers at Liberty and Brazoria also loudly demanded the prisoners' release. Some even took direct action. A force of more than 150 people marched against the fort at Anahuac. The angry Texans exchanged gunfire with Mexican troops and even captured some soldiers. Bradburn agreed to release his prisoners if the Texans would release the captured soldiers and leave. The settlers agreed to the terms, and most left. A few remained behind, which Bradburn took as a violation of the agreement. He did not release his prisoners. Some angry Texans believed he had never intended to at all.

Withdrawing from Anahuac, the settlers went to Turtle Bayou. Fearing retribution from Anahuac, they sent John Austin to retrieve cannons from Brazoria. Those who stayed at Anahuac drew up a list of **resolutions**, or statements of a group's opinions. The **Turtle Bayou Resolutions** declared that the events at Anahuac were not a rebellion against Mexico. They stated that the people were defending their rights and the constitution. Although few of the Texans present at Turtle Bayou had any real understanding of Mexican politics, the resolutions also took sides in a civil war being fought in Mexico. The settlers expressed support for General **Antonio López de Santa Anna,** who was trying to overthrow President Anastacio Bustamante.

Reading Check **Finding the Main Idea** Why did the settlers create the Turtle Bayou Resolutions, and what did they declare?

HISTORIC DOCUMENT

Turtle Bayou Resolutions

On June 13, 1832, Texans at Turtle Bayou wrote a document explaining their actions at Anahuac. These statements are called the Turtle Bayou Resolutions.

"RESOLVED [It is determined] That we view with feelings of the deepest regret, the manner in which the Gover't [government] of the Republic of Mexico is **administered**[1] by the present **dynasty**[2]—The repeated violations of the constitution—the total disregard of the law—the entire **prostration**[3] of the civil authority; and the substitution in the **stead**[4] of a military **despotism**[5] are **grievances**[6] of such a **character**[7], as to **arouse**[8] the feelings of every freeman, and **impel**[9] him to resistance. . . .

RESOLVED That the people of Texas be invited to cooperate with us, in support of the principles **incorporated**[10] in The **foregoing**[11] resolutions. — 13th June 1832. . ."

Analyizing Primary Sources

1. **Finding the Main Idea** Why were these resolutions written?
2. **Evaluating** How does this document show the importance of freedom of speech?

[1]**administered:** managed
[2]**dynasty:** ruling government
[3]**prostration:** collapse
[4]**stead:** place
[5]**despotism:** unjust government
[6]**grievances:** sufferings
[7]**character:** nature
[8]**arouse:** excite
[9]**impel:** force
[10]**incorporated:** included
[11]**foregoing:** previous

BIOGRAPHY

Antonio López de Santa Anna

(1794–1876) Antonio López de Santa Anna's long military career began in 1810. At first, he fought for Spain against Mexican independence. In 1821, though, he switched sides and supported the rebel forces. In 1832 Santa Anna led a successful revolt, and in 1833 he was elected president of Mexico. He promised to restore the Constitution of 1824. But he did not fulfill his promise, and war soon erupted. **How did Santa Anna's policies affect Texas?**

★ The Battle of Velasco

Soon after the fight at Anahuac, a Mexican force led by Colonel José de las Piedras arrived from Nacogdoches. Piedras blamed Colonel Bradburn for the conflict with the U.S. settlers. To restore the peace, Piedras recommended removing Bradburn from his post. Bradburn then resigned. With Bradburn gone, the settlers felt that the threat to their freedoms was removed. Piedras also agreed to release Travis, Jack, and other prisoners.

Unaware that the conflict at Anahuac was over, John Austin's group loaded their cannon on a ship at Brazoria. They soon reached Velasco near the mouth of the Brazos River. Colonel Domingo de Ugartechea, commander of the Mexican troops there, refused to let the rebels pass. On June 26, 1832, fighting broke out. After three days, the Mexican soldiers ran out of ammunition and had to surrender. The colonists had won the **Battle of Velasco.** However, men on both sides had been killed and wounded during the battle. After the battle, the Texans continued their journey to Anahuac. They triumphantly arrived with the cannon, only to find the conflict there settled.

However, resistance to central Mexican authority grew stronger in Texas every day. At the same time, most of the Mexican troops left the region. They went to take sides in the civil war between Santa Anna and President Bustamante. Texans anxiously waited for news from Mexico City. They hoped Santa Anna would win the fighting and restore the Constitution of 1824.

Reading Check **Making Generalizations and Predictions** How do you think events at Velasco would have been different had John Austin and his group known about the Turtle Bayou Resolutions and Piedras's trip to Anahuac?

★ Section 2 Review

hmhsocialstudies.com
ONLINE QUIZ

1. Define and explain:
- resolutions

2. Identify and explain the significance of each of the following:
- Turtle Bayou Resolutions
- Antonio López de Santa Anna
- Battle of Velasco

3. Locate on a map:
- Anahuac
- Brazoria

4. Sequencing
- Copy the graphic organizer below. Use it to show in order the steps that led to conflicts at Anahuac and Velasco.

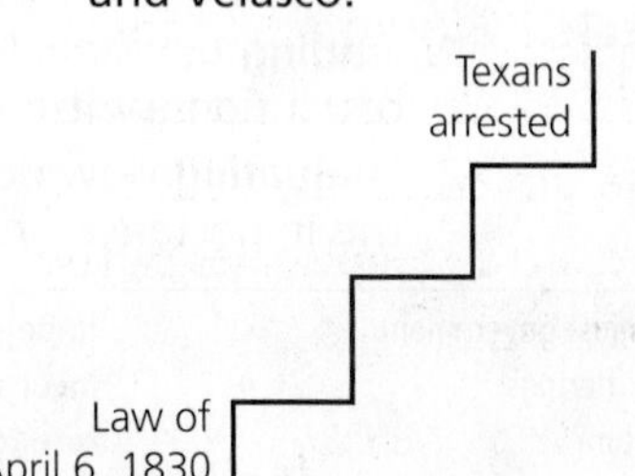

5. Finding the Main Idea

a. Based on the map in this section, in what part of Texas did early conflicts take place?

b. What led some Texans to write the Turtle Bayou Resolutions?

6. Writing and Critical Thinking myWriteSmart

Analyzing Information Imagine that you are at Velasco during the battle. Write a letter informing a friend of the causes of the conflict.

Consider the following:
- the events at Anahuac
- events in other parts of Mexico

Section 3

Conventions and Petitions

Main Ideas

1. Texans hoped that a new government in Mexico would lead to changes in Texas.
2. The Conventions of 1832 and 1833 requested changes in immigration policy and statehood for Texas.
3. Stephen F. Austin was arrested while in Mexico to present the Convention of 1833's requests.

Key Terms and People

- **reforms**
- **delegates**
- **Convention of 1832**
- **William H. Wharton**
- **Convention of 1833**

Why It Matters Today

Texans held two conventions in the early 1830s to discuss government reforms. Use current events sources to find information on a recent state, national, or international conference.

TEKS: 1B, 3A, 3B, 17B, 21A, 21B, 21D, 22D

myNotebook

Use the annotation tools in your eBook to take notes on the goals of Texans at the Conventions of 1832 and 1833.

The Story Continues

As details of the conflict between Anastacio Bustamante and Antonio López de Santa Anna filtered into Texas, people realized that Santa Anna would probably take control of the government. Stephen F. Austin wanted to assure Santa Anna that Texas supported the general. Austin met with Santa Anna supporter Colonel José Antonio Mexía in Matamoros to discuss the situation in Texas. Austin and other leaders convinced Mexía that Texas was loyal to Santa Anna and that the local disturbances were under control.

The Convention of 1832

Colonel Mexía had traveled to Texas to put down what he thought was a rebellion. Instead of fighting, he was welcomed with a party. When he returned to Mexico, Mexía gave a favorable report on Texas.

As Texans had expected, Santa Anna defeated Bustamante's forces in 1832. He was elected president of Mexico in 1833. Santa Anna was not interested in the day-to-day affairs of the government, which he left to his vice president. However, he still controlled the policies of the Mexican government.

Texans were excited about the rise of Santa Anna, who had promised to restore the Constitution of 1824. Since the passing of the Law of April 6, 1830, many Texans had been unhappy with the central government. With a new government taking power in Mexico, though, some thought that change would come to Texas as well. They called a convention in San Felipe de Austin to discuss possible **reforms**, or changes in policy, that they would like to see in Texas. Each district in Texas was asked to send **delegates**, or representatives, to San Felipe on October 1, 1832.

On that date delegates from 16 settlements began the **Convention of 1832**. The leaders of San Antonio, the largest Tejano settlement in Texas, chose not to take part in the convention. The delegates chose Stephen F. Austin as president of the convention. During the six-day convention, the delegates adopted several resolutions.

1. They asked the Mexican government to allow legal immigration from the United States.
2. They requested that Texas become a separate Mexican state instead of being joined with Coahuila.
3. They asked that customs duties be removed for three years.
4. They asked for land for public schools.

The convention chose delegates **William H. Wharton** and Rafael Manchola to present their resolutions to the state and federal governments. Partially because San Antonio refused to participate, though, the resolutions were never presented.

Reading Check **Finding the Main Idea** What did most Texans hope would happen with the Constitution of 1824, and what reforms did the Convention of 1832 propose?

Citizenship and You

Political Protest

The First Amendment to the U.S. Constitution protects the right of free speech. Participating in a convention, as Texans did in 1832 and 1833, can be one form of protest. There are many other ways to stage a protest. For example, some people hold marches or demonstrations. Many people draft petitions that express an opinion and are signed by citizens. Petitions are given to government officials or other leaders. Some people use the Internet to protest issues. There are Internet sites that keep track of the various protests occurring throughout the world. **Why do you think freedoms of speech and petition are important in a democratic society?**

★ The Convention of 1833

Stephen F. Austin realized that for reform to take place, Texans had to work together. The Convention of 1832 had lacked the backing of Tejanos in San Antonio, and so nothing had come of it. Before trying to make any more changes, Austin wanted to gain the support of the city's leaders. While he was meeting with them, though, a group of impatient Texans called for another convention.

The **Convention of 1833** met at San Felipe on April 1. Few of the 56 delegates had attended the first convention. The delegates chose William Wharton as president. He led a group that wanted to push harder for changes in Mexican policy. Among his supporters was delegate Sam Houston of Nacogdoches, a former member of the U.S. Congress and governor of Tennessee who had just arrived in Texas. Like many of the delegates, he wanted action.

Although he supported the convention, Austin was upset that it had been called in his absence. In a letter, he explained his concerns.

Mexico City was a busy commercial center when Stephen F. Austin traveled there in 1833.

TEXAS VOICES

"That measure placed me in an awkward position. . . . I went there [San Antonio] to consult with the authorities of that place. I considered that very great respect . . . was justly due to them as native Mexicans, as the capital of Texas, and as the oldest and most populous town in the country, and I knew the importance of getting them to take the lead in all the politics of Texas."

—Stephen F. Austin, quoted in *The Life of Stephen F. Austin,* by Eugene C. Barker

In the end, the convention adopted many of the same resolutions as the previous year's meeting had. Again, Texans asked that immigration from the United States be allowed. They requested that Texas be separated from Coahuila so they could have more control over their own affairs. They even wrote a constitution for the proposed state.

Stephen F. Austin, Erasmo Seguín, and James B. Miller were chosen to present the convention's proposals to Santa Anna. Neither Seguín nor Miller could make the trip, however, so Austin set out for Mexico City alone on April 22, 1833.

Reading Check **Analyzing Information** Why was the Convention of 1833 called?

★ Austin Is Arrested

The trip took Austin nearly three months. When he finally arrived, he faced one problem after another. Mexican officials were still trying to organize a new government. Santa Anna was out of the city, so Austin had to meet with Vice President Valentín Gómez Farías instead. Gómez Farías promised to present the Texans' requests to the Mexican Congress. However, the government had many other problems to handle.

That's Interesting!

Austin in Prison

Stephen F. Austin was kept in a tiny windowless cell. His food was passed through a slot in the door. When he was allowed outside his cell, he saw other prisoners but was not permitted to speak to them. He spent time writing letters to his friends. Austin pleaded with them not to take any violent action. "Such a thing would have increased my difficulty."

A disease called cholera had swept through the city, and thousands of people were sick and dying.

In September, Austin was still waiting for the Congress to discuss the proposals. He asked Gómez Farías once again to review the documents. Austin also noted that Texans might go ahead with organizing a state government without official approval. Gómez Farías thought Austin was threatening him and angrily ended the meeting. In October a frustrated Austin wrote to the local government in San Antonio. He had not yet received permission for Texas to become a separate state. Yet Austin advised Texans to meet "without a moment's delay for the purpose of organizing a local government for Texas."

When Santa Anna returned to Mexico City the following month, Austin was finally able to meet with him. Santa Anna agreed to nearly all of the resolutions of the Convention of 1833. He agreed to allow immigration from the United States and to lower taxes on U.S. imports. However, he refused to make Texas a separate state from Coahuila.

Austin left Mexico City on December 10, 1833. Although he had failed to gain permission to make Texas a state, he headed home full of hope because he had achieved his other goals. Austin's hopes were soon dashed, however. In January, when he reached Saltillo, the capital of Coahuila y Texas, Austin was arrested. Mexican officials had read his letter. The officials thought Austin had challenged Mexican authority.

Austin was taken back to Mexico City under armed guard and was put in prison without a trial. After nearly a year in prison, Austin was released on December 25, 1834. Even then, he was not permitted to return to Texas until July 1835. Back in Texas, many people worried and waited for him to return home.

Reading Check **Sequencing** List in order the events that led to Austin's arrest.

Section 3 Review

1. Define and explain:
- reforms
- delegates

2. Identify and explain the significance of each of the following in Texas history:
- Convention of 1832
- William H. Wharton
- Convention of 1833

3. Categorizing
- Copy the graphic organizer below. Use it to show what reforms Texans hoped to gain from the Conventions of 1832 and 1833.

Convention of 1832
Convention of 1833

4. Finding the Main Idea

a. How did the right to free speech, including the right to protest, shape events in Texas?

b. Why was Stephen F. Austin arrested?

5. Writing and Critical Thinking myWriteSmart

Making Generalizations and Predictions Write a paragraph explaining how you think Austin's arrest might have led to more conflict between Mexico and Texas.

Consider the following:
- why Austin went to Mexico
- what happened in Mexico City

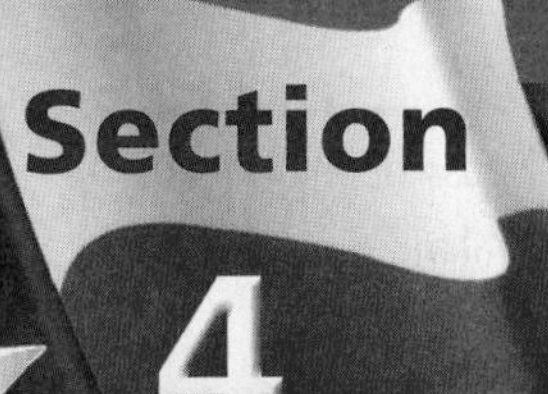

Section 4

The Move toward War

Main Ideas

1. Under Santa Anna, the Mexican government began to tighten its control of Texas.
2. Frustrated, some Texans began to call for war.

Why It Matters Today

Part of the conflict between the Mexican government and the Texans was over the question of taxes. Use current events sources to find information on a debate over taxes today.

Key Terms and People

- **Martín Perfecto de Cos**
- **faction**

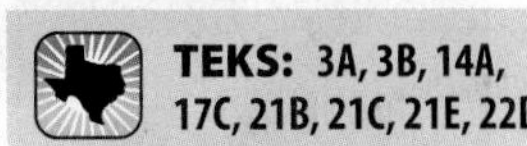

TEKS: 3A, 3B, 14A, 17C, 21B, 21C, 21E, 22D

myNotebook

Use the annotation tools in your eBook to take notes on the move toward war in Texas.

The Story Continues

Andrew Briscoe wanted to stir up trouble with the Mexican official at Anahuac. Briscoe loaded the front of his ship with bricks. He wanted it to look like it was weighed down with smuggled goods. He hoped to fool the commander at Anahuac into believing he was trying to avoid paying taxes on the goods. The commander was so irritated by the trick that he arrested Briscoe.

 Mexico Tightens Control

Briscoe's actions reflected the frustration many Texans had with the Mexican government's policies. In 1834 President Santa Anna declared that Mexico was not ready to be a republic. Despite what he had promised during the civil war, he began to strengthen the power of the central government. By creating a centralist government, he violated his pledge to restore the federal Constitution of 1824. This pledge was the reason that many Texans had supported him.

Santa Anna did honor some of the requests of the Convention of 1833. He legalized immigration from the United States and removed some customs duties. However, in January 1835 he sent more troops and customs collectors to Texas.

In the spring of 1835 Captain Antonio Tenorio began collecting customs duties at Anahuac, where taxes had not been collected since 1832. This angered Texans at Anahuac, who believed that they were paying a greater share of taxes than people at other Texas ports. Andrew Briscoe's arrest in June only increased tensions.

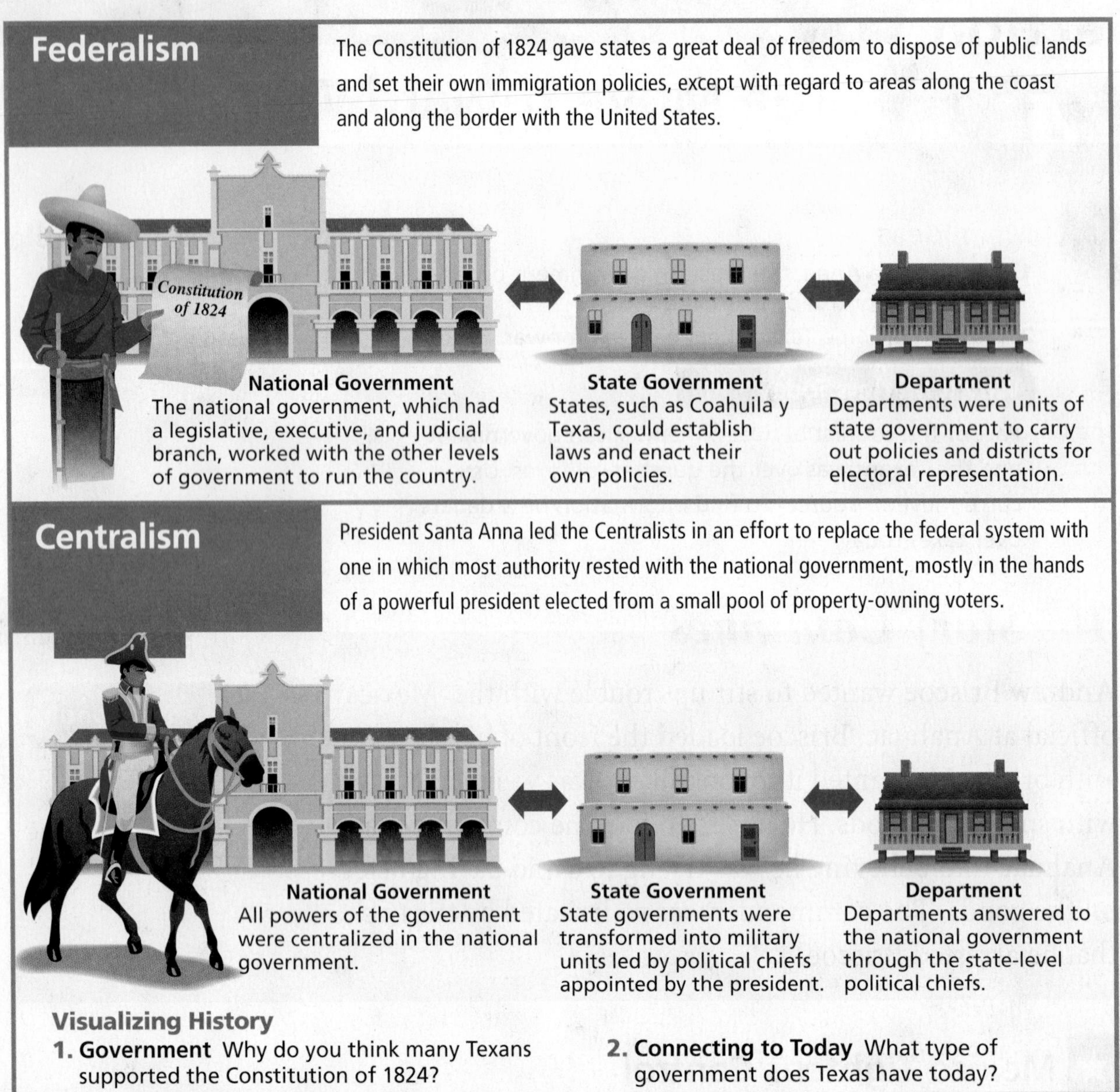

In response to Briscoe's arrest, William Travis and several supporters sailed to Anahuac. There the group fired one shot and demanded Tenorio's surrender. When he refused, Travis ordered an attack. Tenorio quickly surrendered and agreed to leave Texas.

Travis's actions disturbed many Texans, who feared that the conflict would cause problems with the Mexican government. They were right. General **Martín Perfecto de Cos**, the military commander of Texas, ordered the arrest of Travis and several other men, including Lorenzo de Zavala. Zavala was a former Mexican cabinet member and governor. He had resigned from his position and moved to Texas in 1835 after Santa Anna abandoned federalism. Cos also ordered more troops into Texas to better control the region.

Reading Check **Analyzing Information** How did Santa Anna's policies and his refusal to follow the Constitution of 1824 increase tension in Texas?

Debating War and Peace

General Cos's orders greatly concerned Texans. A military man, he planned to try his prisoners in military courts. This was legal under Mexican law, but it was unacceptable to many Anglo citizens of Texas. They had lived in the United States, where the law guaranteed trial by jury. In fact, they had successfully won the right to jury trials in 1834. But their protests did not change Cos's mind.The arrival of more troops also upset Texans.

Frustrated, Texans began debating how to respond to the growing problems with the Mexican government. One **faction**, or group, argued that Texans should remain calm. This faction wished to keep peaceful relations with the government. Another group, the war faction, argued that Texans should take action. Some members of the war faction wanted Texas to declare its independence from Mexico.

Meanwhile, the Tejanos of Texas were having debates of their own. Most Tejanos shared Anglos' frustrations with the Mexican government because they were federalists who opposed Santa Anna's centralist policies. However, some were equally frustrated with the Anglos. They felt the Anglos were less concerned with restoring federalism in Mexico than in furthering their own interests.

While the debates continued, Stephen F. Austin returned from his imprisonment in Mexico. Austin's views on the conflict with the Mexican government had changed because of his arrest. He had gone to Mexico City to work for peace. Upon his return, though, Austin urged Texans to unite against Santa Anna and declared his support for action. Austin warned that Texans had no choice but to go to war. "There is no other remedy but to defend our rights, ourselves, and our country by force of arms."

Reading Check **Evaluating** Why do you think the arrest of Austin and the conflicts in Texas led some Texans to call for war?

Section 4 Review

1. Define and explain:
- faction

2. Identify and explain the significance of the following in Texas history:
- Martín Perfecto de Cos

3. Analyzing Information
- Copy the graphic organizer below. Use it to explain how the Mexican government's actions led many Texans to call for war.

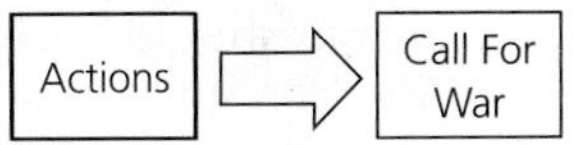

4. Finding the Main Idea

a. What is federalism, and what role did it play in the call for war in Texas?

b. How did the events at Anahuac and Austin's advice lead to a push for war with Mexico?

myWriteSmart

5. Writing and Critical Thinking

Supporting a Point of View Write a statement supporting or opposing war with Mexico. Consider the following:
- the policies of the Mexican government
- the arrest of Stephen F. Austin and other Texans

CHAPTER 10 REVIEW

The Chapter at a Glance

Examine the following visual summary of the chapter. Then use the visual to create an expanded time line that you can use as a study guide.

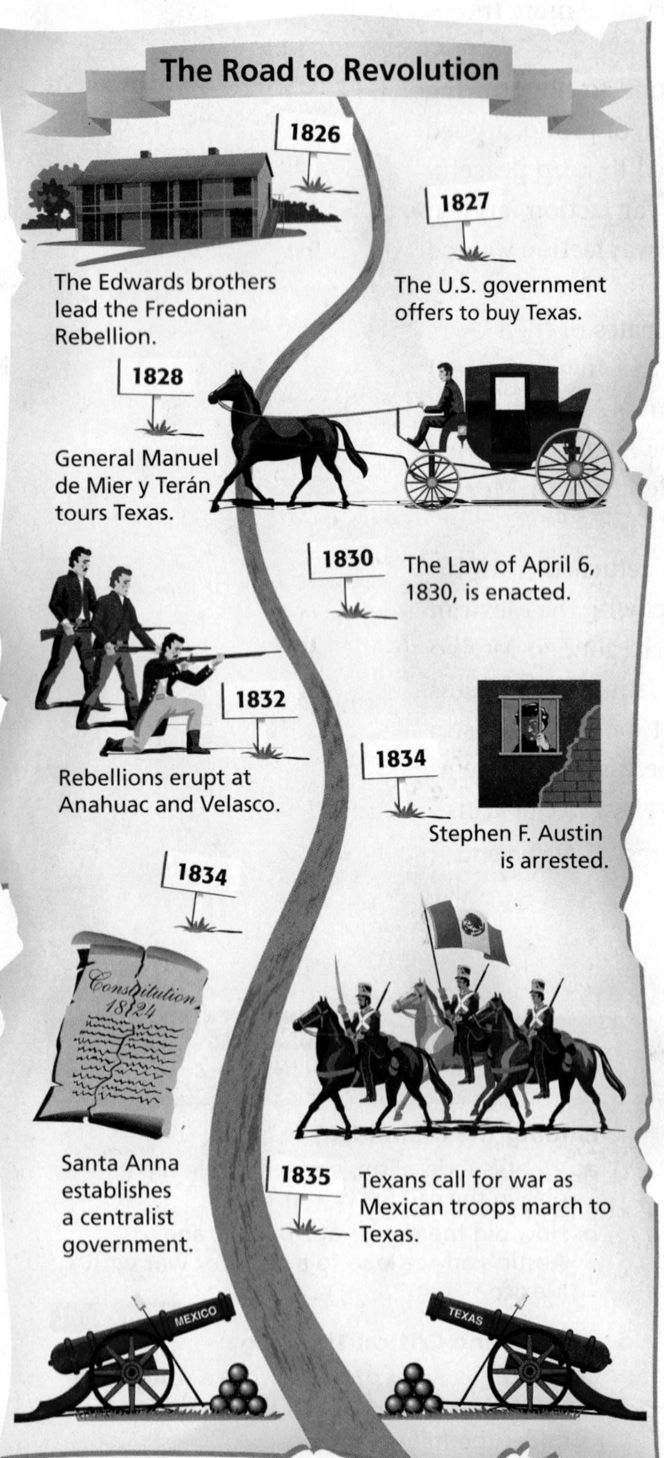

Identifying People and Ideas

Write a sentence to explain the role or significance of each of the following terms or people.

1. Fredonian Rebellion
2. Law of April 6, 1830
3. Battle of Velasco
4. Mier y Terán Report
5. customs duties
6. Martín Perfecto de Cos
7. Convention of 1833
8. Turtle Bayou Resolutions

Understanding Main Ideas

Section 1

1. What led to the Law of April 6, 1830?

Section 2

2. What caused the conflict at Anahuac?
3. What events led to the Turtle Bayou Resolutions?

Section 3

4. Describe the reforms proposed by the Conventions of 1832 and 1833.

Section 4

5. Why were Texans split over the future of Texas as a part of Mexico?

You Be the Historian

Reviewing Themes

1. **Economics** What role did regulation of trade play in the conflict between Texans and Mexico?
2. **Constitutional Heritage** How did Santa Anna's decision to set aside the Constitution of 1824 and create a centralist government affect Texas?
3. **Government** How do you think the problems facing a young nation like the Republic of Mexico affected its policies toward Texas?

Thinking Critically

1. **Making Generalizations and Predictions** What might have happened in Texas if Stephen F. Austin had not been arrested?
2. **Drawing Inferences and Conclusions** How might the Turtle Bayou Resolutions have contributed to Texans' calls for war?
3. **Supporting a Point of View** Do you think Texans should have taken up arms against the Mexican government? Explain your answer.

Texas Test Practice

Interpreting Charts

Study the pie chart below. Then use the information in the chart to answer the following questions.

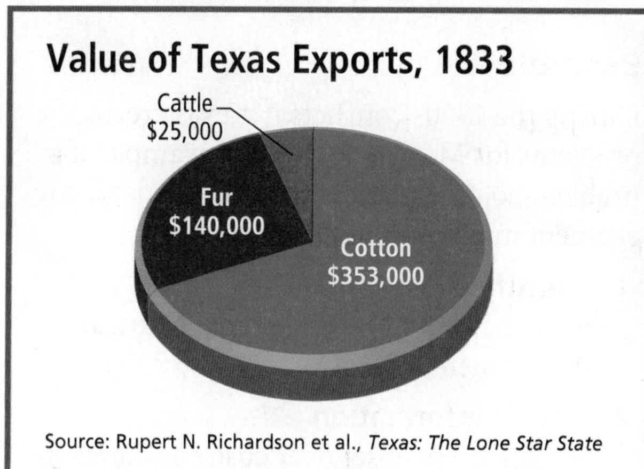

1. During the 1830s Texas had an agricultural economy. Which of the following sentences about the nature of the Texas economy is most accurate?

A The leading Texas export in 1833 was cattle.
B The leading Texas import was cotton.
C Cotton was the leading Texas export.
D People in Texas almost always wore more fur than cotton.

2. Cotton exports were about how many times more valuable than fur exports?

Analyzing Primary Sources

Read the following decree issued by the Mexican government in 1834. Then answer the questions.

"The Vice President of the Mexican United States . . . impressed by the necessity of aiding the multitude of persons whose fate has been, and still is, unfortunate . . . finds himself resolved to open its coffers [treasury] to remedy [solve the problem of] . . . such a pitiful condition. The territories situated next to the boundary line of our Republic . . . open to commerce . . . and extremely fertile, are offering, for robust [strong] Mexican arms, and industry, all kinds of things which are unavailable elsewhere. . . . The Republic finds itself plagued with families which, for one reason or another, have lost their fortune and their peace of mind. The Supreme Government invites all of them to better their fate in the peaceful pursuits of agriculture."

3. According to the Mexican government, why was the decree issued?

F to help the wealthy people of Mexico
G to help the poor farmers of Mexico
H to develop a plan that allows Texas to become an independent republic
J to make the government wealthy

4. How do you think the decree may have reflected the biases of the Mexican government at that time?

Linking to Community

Today Texas and Mexico have a good relationship, and Americans travel to Mexico by the thousands each year. Interview someone in your school or community who has been to Mexico. Or, if possible, interview someone who has lived in Mexico. Ask the person to describe the place where he or she visited or lived and what he or she did there. Present an oral report of your interview to the class. You may want to include some visuals to accompany your report.

Internet Activity: 

Access the Internet to locate one of the following major documents discussed in this chapter: the Law of April 6, 1830; the Constitution of 1824; or the Turtle Bayou Resolutions. Create a chart or table with specific information from your research that shows the effects of one of the documents and how it led to the call for revolution.

Social Studies Skills

WORKSHOP

Problem-Solving Skills

Texans in the past and present have faced difficult problems. By using appropriate problem-solving skills you will be better able to choose a solution. The following activities will help you develop and practice this skill.

Problem solving is the process of finding an effective solution to a problem. Listed below are guidelines for the problem-solving process.

1. **Identify the problem.** Identify the specific problem you are facing. Sometimes you face a difficult situation made up of several different problems.
2. **Gather information.** Conduct research on any important issues related to the problem. Try to find the answers to questions like the following: What caused this problem? Who or what does it affect?
3. **List and consider options.** Look at the problem and the answers to the questions you asked in Step 2. List and then think about your options—all the possible ways in which the problem could be solved.
4. **Examine advantages and disadvantages.** Consider the advantages and disadvantages of all the options that you have listed. Make sure that you consider the possible long-term effects of each solution. You should also determine what steps you will need to take to achieve each possible solution.
5. **Choose and implement a solution.** Select the best solution from your list, and take the steps to achieve it.
6. **Evaluate the effectiveness of the solution.** After putting your plan into action, evaluate its effectiveness. Is the problem solved? Were the results worth the effort? Has the solution created any other problems?

Example

During the 1800s conflicts in Texas created problems for Mexico. Here is an example of a problem-solving process that the Mexican government might have used.

1. **Identify the problem.** Conflicts arose between Texans and the Mexican government.
2. **Gather information.**
   - Texans are upset over customs duties.
   - Texans are upset over the arrest of fellow settlers.
3. **List and consider options.**
   - Mexico can remove customs duties and free imprisoned Texas settlers.
   - Mexico can send more troops to Texas.
4. **Examine advantages and disadvantages.**
   - If Mexico removes customs duties, the conflicts might end. But other Mexican states may not consider this fair.
   - If Mexico sends in more troops, it will show Mexico's authority over the region. But it might lead to more conflict.
5. **Choose and implement a solution.** Mexico sends troops and releases Texans.
6. **Evaluate the effectiveness of the solution.** It does not stop the conflicts.

Practicing the Skill

Chapter 8, Section 3, The Austin Colonies, discusses the challenges facing the first Anglo settlers in Texas. Imagine that you are a settler in Stephen F. Austin's colony. Use the problem-solving guidelines above to help you decide how best to solve the colony's problems. Be prepared to explain and defend your solutions.

History in Action

UNIT 3 SIMULATION

You Solve the Problem . . .

How can the government of Mexico convince people to move to Texas?

Complete the following activity in small cooperative groups. The year is 1821. Mexican officials are developing a plan to convince people to move to Texas. They ask your group to create a three-fold brochure. Follow these steps to solve your problem.

1. **Gather information** Use your textbook, websites, and other resources to find information that might influence the design of your brochure. Remember that your brochure must include information that will help the government convince people to move to Texas. Such information might include maps, charts, and graphs to show the land, plants, animals, climate, natural resources, and inhabitants of Texas. Be sure to use what you learned from this unit's Skills Workshop on Problem Solving to help you find an effective solution to this problem. You may want to divide different parts of the research among group members.

2. **List and consider options** After reviewing the information you have gathered, list and consider the options you might use to help the officials persuade people to settle in Texas. Your solution to the problem may be easier to reach if you consider as many options as possible. Be sure to record your possible options for the preparation of your brochure.

3. **Consider advantages and disadvantages.** Now consider the advantages and disadvantages of taking each option. Ask yourselves questions such as, "How will this information persuade people to settle in Texas?" Once you have considered the advantages and disadvantages, record them as notes for use in preparing your brochure.

4. **Choose, implement, and evaluate a solution.** After considering the advantages and disadvantages, create your brochure. Be sure to support your reasons why people should settle in Texas by including information you gathered. When you are ready, decide which group members will present the brochure, and then take your brochure to the Mexican government (the rest of the class).
   As an audience member, listen carefully to the words the presenter uses to describe his or her brochure. Notice any connecting words used to link ideas, because these can show how ideas are related. As each group finishes, write a brief summary of what you have heard. After all groups have finished, refer to your summaries to help you decide who made convincing presentations.

UNIT 4

Revolution and Republic

(1835–1845)

This mural of the Texas Revolution honors key figures such as Sam Houston, William B. Travis, Davy Crockett, and James Bowie.

Texas Teens

Young Texans in War

Dilue Harris, whose family had settled near present-day Houston, wrote that in 1835, when she was ten years old, settlers were "in a state of excitement during the winter." Tensions with Mexico were on the rise after a series of minor conflicts in Velasco, Anahuac, and other areas of Texas. Many settlers prepared for the worst. When war came the next year, Texans everywhere did their part to support the war effort. Even young Harris helped get ready for war. She melted lead in a pot to make bullets for settlers preparing to fight.

Texans as young as 13 volunteered to fight to defend their homes. Thinking the war would be a great adventure, teenager John Holland Jenkins of Bastrop went off to fight against Mexican forces. He took part in several battles of the Texas Revolution, fighting side by side with some of the war's great heroes. At one point, Jenkins was sent by his commanders to help his family and the other people of Bastrop escape from an approaching Mexican army. Their escape was perilous and filled with hardship.

Other young Texans became caught up in the fighting that swirled around them. Eight-year-old Enrique Esparza, son of Alamo defender Gregorio Esparza, remembered when Mexican troops arrived in San Antonio. Enrique ran home to warn his family. Enrique's family then raced to the Alamo, hoping to get inside before Mexican forces sealed off the old mission. Enrique remembered that the mission church "was shut up, when we arrived. The window was opened to permit us to enter." The troops inside quickly closed the window. The Esparzas were among the last people to enter the Alamo before Mexican forces attacked. Enrique and other young Texans met harrowing challenges in this dangerous chapter in the history of Texas. **How was life during the Texas Revolution a challenging time for Texas teens?**

In this unit you will learn about Texans' struggles for independence from Mexico. You will also learn about how Texans created a new nation.

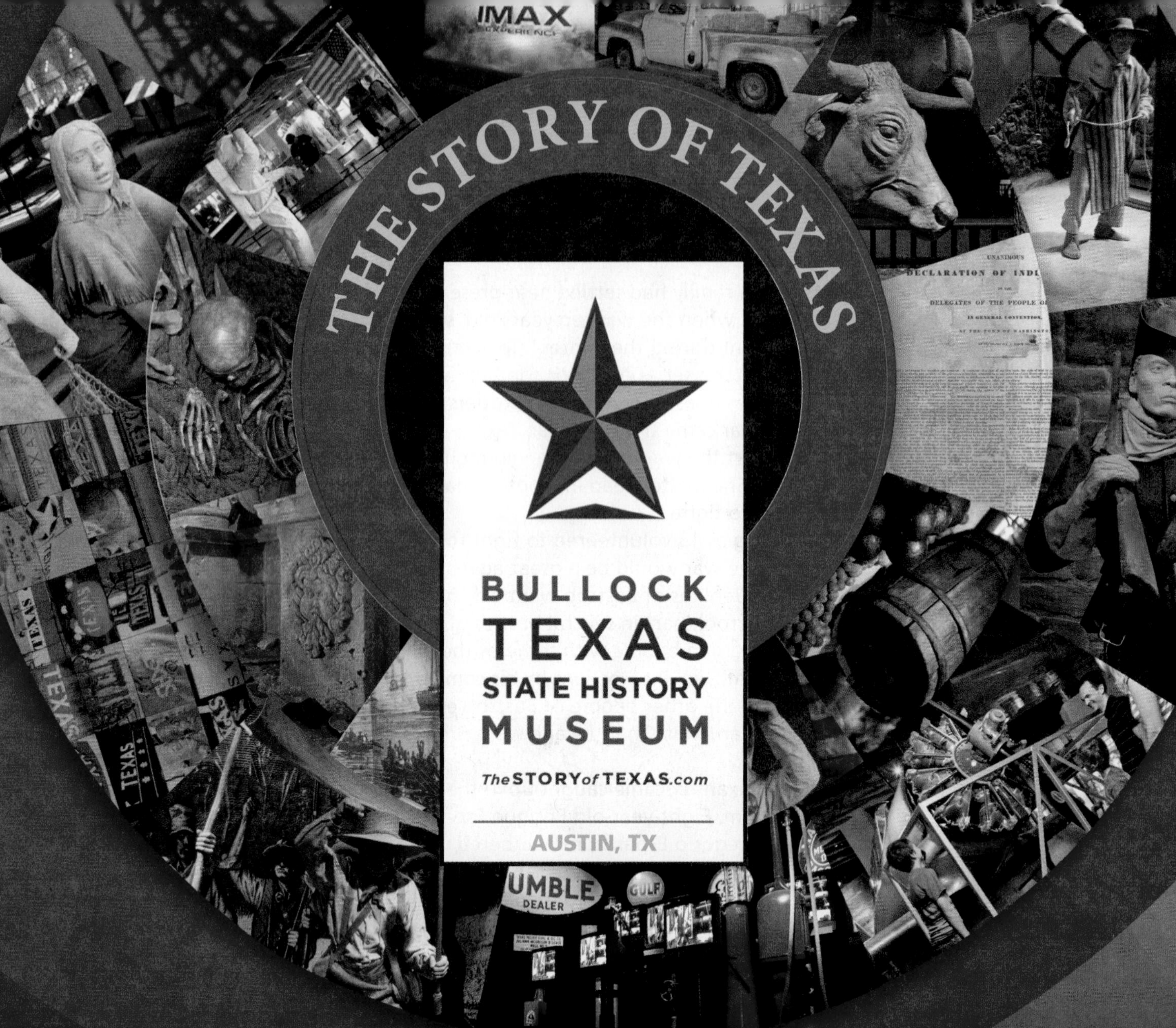

Revolution and Independence

By 1833 newcomers arriving in Texas were very independent-minded. Many were impatient with Mexico's inability to defend the Texas frontier. Some, like David Burnet, wanted Texas to separate from the Mexican state of Coahuila y Texas. These Texans were used to taking matters into their own hands, including organizing their own militia units.

Tejanos also declared their rights. At conventions in 1832 and 1833, young Tejano leaders like Juan Seguín and Ambrosio Rodríguez compiled complaints against the Mexican government. They viewed the Law of April 6, 1830, which prevented *capitalistas norteamericanos* from moving into Texas, as a threat to prosperity. Protesting *Basta ya!* (Enough!), many Tejanos joined Anglos in demanding reforms.

Tensions between settlers in Texas and the Mexican government steadily increased. When Mexican soldiers arrived at Gonzales in September 1835 to reclaim a government-issued cannon, the Texans there refused to give it back. In October the Mexicans sent a larger force. They were met with a defiant "Come and take it!" On October 2, citizens led by John Henry Moore fired at the troops, who then withdrew. The Texas Revolution had begun.

After the outbreak of hostilities, 59 delegates gathered at Washington-on-the-Brazos for the Convention of 1836. On March 2, 1836 they officially declared Texas independent from Mexico.

Exploring Museum Resources

What artifacts and documents remain from the period of the Texas Revolution and independence? What can they teach us about Texas's early history? Explore some of the resources that still exist today. You can find museum resources at

hmhsocialstudies.com

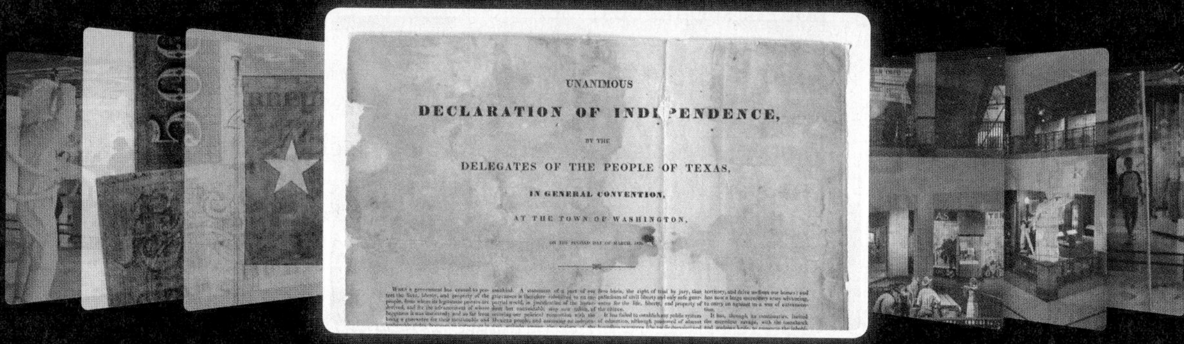

Historic Document Who wrote the Texas Declaration of Independence? Read the document and learn how it was drafted and approved.

Artifact The Lone Star Flag has been called "one of the best known symbols in the world." Find out who created this famous design and how much he was paid for his work.

Documents In 1839 Texas began to issue its own currency, known as redbacks. Go online to see some examples.

UNIT 4

Reading Social Studies

Identifying Points of View

Focus on Reading History is made up of issues, questions about what to do in a particular situation. Throughout history, people have looked at issues from all sides. Each person's view of the issue shaped what he or she thought should be done.

Understanding Points of View The way a person views an issue is called his or her **point of view**, or perspective. Points of view can be shaped by many factors, such as a person's **frame of reference**—a person's experiences or beliefs that shape how he or she sees the world. When you read a document, figuring out the author's point of view can help you understand his or her opinions about an issue. Below is a passage from the Texas Declaration of Independence. As you read it, think about the point of view of the authors.

It has sacrificed our welfare to the state of Coahuila, by which our interests have been continually depressed through a jealous and partial course of legislation, carried on at a far distant seat of government, by a hostile majority, in an unknown tongue, and this too, notwithstanding we have petitioned in the humblest terms for the establishment of a separate state government, and have, in accordance with the provisions of the national constitution, presented to the general congress a republican constitution, which was, without a just cause, contemptuously rejected.

Consider the author's frame of reference—George C. Childress, the primary author, served in the Texas army and in the Convention of 1836.

Look for emotional language—Words like *jealous, hostile,* and *contemptuously* make the author's opinion clear.

Look at the evidence— Childress lists the charges that settlers made against the Mexican government.

Put it all together to determine the author's point of view— Childress was opposed to the policies of the Mexican government and wanted a change.

You Try It!

Read the following primary source from this unit. Then answer the questions that follow.

> "Treaties of peace and [goodwill], and the maintenance of good faith with the Indians, present themselves to my mind as the most rational grounds on which to obtain their friendship. Let us [refrain] on our part from aggressions, establish commerce with the different tribes, supply their useful and necessary wants, maintain even-handed justice with them, and natural reason will teach them the [usefulness] of our friendship."
>
> —Sam Houston, quoted in *Documents of Texas History*, edited by Ernest Wallace

1. Which of the following statements best describes Houston's point of view regarding relationships between Texans and American Indians in the passage above?

a. Establishing commercial ties with American Indians is the only way to maintain peace.
b. A good relationship between Texans and American Indians is easy to achieve and maintain.
c. Texans can build peaceful relationships with American Indians through treaties and other acts of good will.
d. It is not possible for Texans and American Indians to live together peacefully.

2. What words or phrases in the passage helped you identify his point of view?

Reading Section Assessment

Read the following primary source from this unit. Then answer the questions that follow.

> ". . . I experience no difficulty in deciding on the proper policy to be pursued towards [American Indians]. It is to push a rigorous war against them; pursuing them to their hiding places without [relief] or compassion, until they shall be made to feel that flight from our borders without hope of return, is preferable to the [horrors] of war."
>
> —Mirabeau B. Lamar, quoted in *Lone Star*, by T.R. Fehrenbach

1. What was Lamar's point of view on American Indians in Texas? What words or phrases led you to this conclusion?

2. Compare the two passages on this page. How does Lamar's point of view differ from Houston's? How do you think their frames of reference differed?

Key Terms

Unit 4

Chapter 11

infantry *(p. 228)*
cavalry *(p. 228)*
provisional *(p. 232)*
casualties *(p. 239)*
noncombatants *(p. 239)*
popular sovereignty *(p. 241)*
bill of rights *(p. 242)*
petition *(p. 242)*
ad interim *(p. 242)*

Chapter 12

annexation *(p. 258)*
cabinet *(p. 259)*
expenditures *(p. 262)*
revenue *(p. 262)*
ratify *(p. 263)*
capitol *(p. 266)*
charter *(p. 266)*
homestead law *(p. 267)*
redbacks *(p. 267)*
balanced budget *(p. 271)*

Chapter 13

land speculators *(p. 287)*
circuit riders *(p. 289)*
denominations *(p. 289)*
academies *(p. 289)*

Chapter 14

foreign relations *(p. 294)*
diplomatic recognition *(p. 294)*

As you read, pay attention to how sentences and paragraphs are structured. Discuss with your teacher and classmates how the structure affects the meaning of text.

CHAPTER 11

The Texas Revolution

(1835–1836)

Texas Essential Knowledge and Skills (TEKS) 1B, 1C, 3B, 3C, 3D, 8A, 9A, 9C, 14A, 17A, 17C, 18A, 21A, 21B, 21C, 21D, 21E, 21F, 22A, 22B, 22C, 22D

During the Texas Revolution, some Mexican officers wore elaborate uniforms like this one.

TEXAS

October 2, 1835
Texas settlers attack Mexican soldiers at Gonzales, forcing them to leave.

December 9, 1835
Texas troops push Mexican troops out of San Antonio, capturing the city.

February 23, 1836
The Siege of the Alamo begins.

August 1835 | **October 1835** | **December 1835** | **February 1836**

U.S. and WORLD

September 9, 1835
In response to widespread demands for change, the British Parliament reforms local government in England.

October 27, 1835
Santa Anna, the president of Mexico, decides to personally lead the campaign to put down the Texas rebellion.

January 30, 1836
Richard Lawrence tries to assassinate U.S. president Andrew Jackson. Jackson is unharmed.

If you were there . . .

Would you support the Texas Revolution?

Build on What You Know

Different ideas about government, individual rights, and other matters had led to increasing conflict between settlers in Texas and the leaders of Mexico. During the early 1830s tensions grew, and fighting broke out. By late 1835, the first shots of the Texas Revolution had been fired.

After the Battle of San Jacinto, Santa Anna was captured and forced to surrender. Sam Houston injured his ankle during the battle.

The San Jacinto Monument, the world's tallest war memorial, honors all those who fought for Texas independence.

March 2, 1836 The Texas Declaration of Independence is adopted.

April 21, 1836 Texans win the Battle of San Jacinto, ending the Texas Revolution.

December 10, 1836 The first official Texas flag is adopted by the Texas Congress.

April 1836 | June 1836 | August 1836 | October 1836 | December 1836

March 30, 1836 Stephen F. Austin arrives in Washington to request aid for the Texas Revolution.

June 15, 1836 Arkansas is admitted as the 25th state of the United States.

August 10, 1836 Revolts erupt in several regions of Spain, forcing ruler María Cristina to restore the Constitution of 1812.

October 29, 1836 A revolt in Strasbourg led by French emperor Napoléon III fails, and he is banished from the country.

You Be the Historian

*my***Notebook**

What's Your Opinion? Do you agree or disagree with the following statements? Support your point of view in your notebook.

- **Constitutional Heritage** A constitution is necessary for good government.
- **Citizenship** Citizens should volunteer to serve their government during conflicts.
- **Geography** During a war, the geography of an area does not affect the outcome of a battle.

Section 1

The War Begins

Main Ideas

1. The Battle of Gonzales and the capture of Goliad were among the opening conflicts in the Texas Revolution.
2. The Texas army laid siege to San Antonio and fought several small battles against Mexican troops.
3. The Texas army drove the Mexican forces out of San Antonio.

Why It Matters Today

Providing the army with supplies, funds, and soldiers was a difficult task for Texas leaders in 1835. Use current events sources to learn about military funding in the United States today.

Key Terms and People

- **Battle of Gonzales**
- **Juan Seguín**
- **infantry**
- **cavalry**
- **Edward Burleson**
- **Erastus "Deaf" Smith**
- **Grass Fight**
- **Ben Milam**

TEKS: 1B, 3B, 3C, 8A, 9A, 21A, 21B, 21C, 22D

myNotebook

Use the annotation tools in your eBook to take notes on the beginning of the Texas Revolution.

The Story Continues

In 1831, *empresario* Green DeWitt wrote to officials in Bexar. He feared American Indian attacks against his colony and wanted a way to defend his people. In answer to his requests, the Mexican government sent him a small bronze cannon. DeWitt installed the cannon at Gonzales, where it could be used to fight off hostile Indians. Years later, when the Texas Revolution began, it would be used against a different foe.

The Capture of Gonzales and Goliad

By 1835, many people in Texas were upset with the Mexican government because of Santa Anna's actions. Fearing trouble, Mexican general Domingo de Ugartechea, the commander in Texas, ordered the people of Gonzales to hand over the cannon DeWitt had received four years earlier. They refused. They buried the cannon in an orchard.

In response to these actions, Ugartechea sent troops to take the cannon by force. The people of Gonzales desperately worked to keep the troops out of their town, making up excuses and stories about why they could not give up the cannon. In the meantime, they sent riders to nearby towns to ask for help in resisting the Mexican demands.

Many people responded to the call for help, and reinforcements arrived in Gonzales. The Texan militia there grew to at least 180. On October 1 the enlarged militia decided to attack the Mexican force, which included about 100 soldiers. The rebels dug up the cannon and mounted it on a wagon. To taunt the Mexican troops, they also made a flag with a picture of a cannon and the challenge *COME AND TAKE IT.*

As the rebels approached the Mexican camp on October 2, 1835, the nervous Mexicans opened fire. The Texans shot back. The fighting in the **Battle of Gonzales** was brief. No Texans were killed, but at least one Mexican soldier died. The Mexican soldiers withdrew to San Antonio.

The Battle of Gonzales is traditionally considered the beginning of the Texas Revolution. However, resistance had begun a month earlier off the mouth of the Brazos River. There, a Texas steamboat and merchant ship had attacked the Mexican coast guard vessel *Correo de México,* which had been patrolling the Texas coast looking for smugglers.

Soon after the Battle of Gonzales, a large volunteer force from towns along the coast captured the presidio at Goliad. The presidio had been left largely unguarded, because General Martín Perfecto de Cos had taken most of its soldiers to San Antonio. The rebels seized both the presidio and the town of Goliad on October 10. These attacks left no doubt that Texans were in revolt against Santa Anna's centralist government.

Reading Check **Sequencing** List in order the events that led to the Battle of Gonzales.

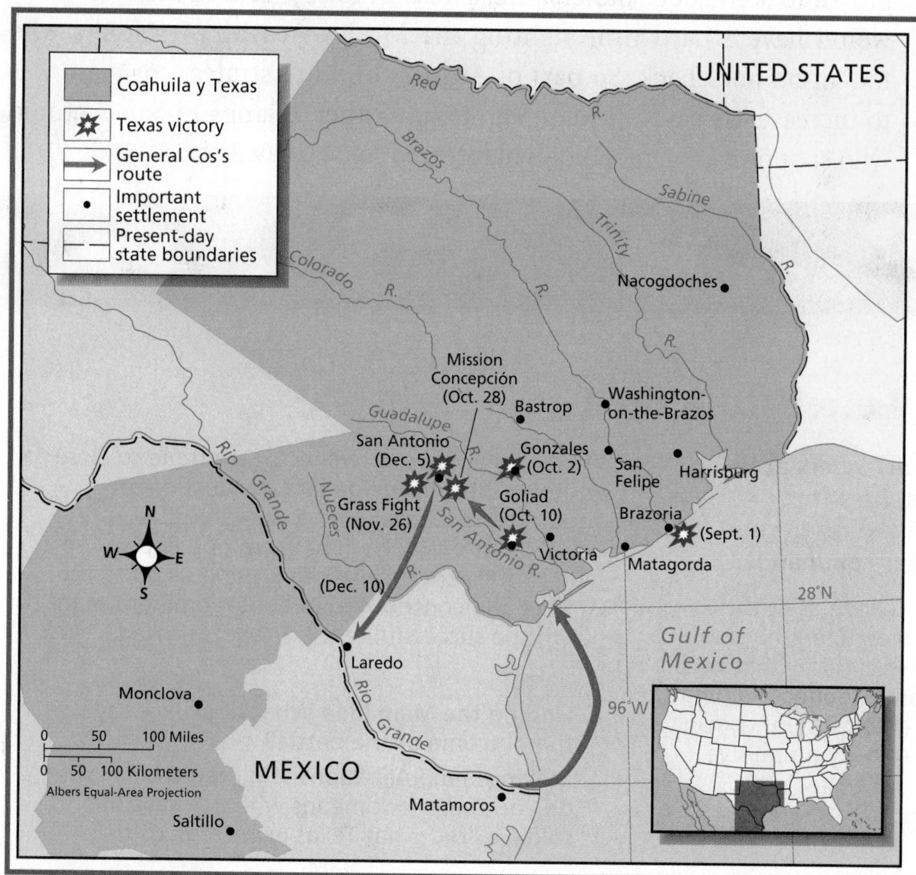

Early Conflicts of the Texas Revolution, 1835

Interpreting Map Early conflicts erupted off the coast of Brazoria and at Gonzales and Goliad. Texas soldiers then marched to San Antonio and laid siege to the city

1. ***Locate*** Where did the first conflicts of the Texas Revolution occur?
2. ***Analyzing information*** Based on this map, what conflict led to General Cos's withdrawing from Texas in late 1835?

The March on San Antonio

Motivated by their victory at Gonzales, the volunteers there planned their next step. They also began to organize themselves into a formal army. They elected officers, choosing Stephen F. Austin as their general. With their leadership in place, the army decided it would drive Cos out of San Antonio. The long, difficult march to the city began on October 12. Gunsmith Noah Smithwick described efforts to move a single cannon.

Analyzing Primary Sources
Identifying Points of View Which phrase of Smithwick's reveals his opinion of the Texas army's condition?

TEXAS VOICES

"We prodded up the oxen with our lances . . . until they broke into a trot. . . . But rapid locomotion [movement] was not congenial to them. . . . The old cannon was abandoned in disgrace at Sandy Creek before we got halfway to San Antonio."

—Noah Smithwick, *The Evolution of a State, or Recollections of Old Texas Days*

Austin set up camp on the outskirts of San Antonio in late October. There, the army found support from the city's Tejanos, many of whom had suffered after the arrival of General Cos. Leading Tejano citizens such as Erasmo Seguín had been forced to sweep the city streets. Tejano women had to bake tortillas for the Mexican troops, who also took supplies and destroyed some citizens' homes. Already opposed to Santa Anna's government, many Tejanos were further outraged by the actions of Cos and his troops. More than 100 of them—including **Juan Seguín**, the son of Erasmo Seguín—joined the Texas army.

That army, however, was ill trained and ill equipped. Although it had grown to some 600 soldiers, most were **infantry**, or foot soldiers. They would have a hard time fighting the Mexican **cavalry**—soldiers who fought on horseback. So part of Austin's military strategy, or plan, was to increase his cavalry. Juan Seguín and other Tejanos in San Antonio who supported the rebellion volunteered for the cavalry.

HISTORIC DOCUMENT

Letter from the Grass Fight

William Jack was one of the leaders at the Grass Fight. After the fight, he wrote to General Burleson to report the results and the actions of the men under his command.

"It would be unjust to particularize as to the conduct of the officers and men under my command on this occasion. Suffice it to say that each man so far as my observation extended did what Texas expected of him. The only cause of complaint arose from their impetuosity [impulsive behavior].

My feelings however will not permit me to close without noticing the gallant conduct of the aged veteran Captain Jas. Burleson [father of Edward Burleson]. He flew from one end of the field to the other constantly urging us on to the conflict and contributed in a most eminent manner to the successful result which followed."

Analyzing Primary Sources

1. **Finding the Main Idea** What does Jack say was the outcome of the battle?
2. **Making Generalizations and Predictions** What do you think Jack means when he says the soldiers "did what Texas expected" of them?

Austin was not satisfied with his camp's location. He wanted to find a location nearer the city, from which he could keep a close eye on Cos. To find a such a location, he sent a search party led by James "Jim" Bowie, a frontiersman from Louisiana. Cos had been watching, and on October 28 he sent some 400 Mexican soldiers to ambush the party near the Mission Concepción. Despite the Mexicans' larger numbers, though, the Texans won the resulting battle. Bowie's party had camped in a good defensive position behind a riverbank. Their rifles were much more accurate than the soldiers' weapons, too. The Mexican troops retreated.

Like the capture of Goliad, this victory boosted the confidence of the Texas army. Austin wanted to attack General Cos in San Antonio immediately. However, cooler heads prevailed. Other leaders reminded him about the number of soldiers and artillery in San Antonio. In addition, the Texans did not yet have a way to get through the city's walls.

Reading Check **Summarizing** How were the Texans able to drive off the Mexican attack outside of San Antonio?

BIOGRAPHY

Juan Seguín

(1806–1890) One of the great Tejano heroes of the Texas Revolution, Juan Seguín fought for both Texas and Mexico during his lifetime. He was present at the Alamo, but was away from the mission at the time of the final attack. He led a unit at the Battle of San Jacinto and accepted Mexico's surrender of San Antonio on June 4, 1836. He later served as a Texas senator and as mayor of San Antonio. After conflicts with U.S. settlers, though, Seguín resigned as mayor and moved to Mexico with his family in 1842. He fought against the United States in the Mexican War, but later returned to Texas, settling in Wilson County. He retired in Nuevo Laredo in the 1860s and died there in 1890. His body was moved to Seguin, Texas, on July 4, 1976. **How did Seguín contribute to Texas history?**

★ The Grass Fight

After the fight at Concepción, Stephen F. Austin moved his headquarters to the Old Mill just north of San Antonio. In this position, the Texas army could lay siege to San Antonio. The Mexican army in the city, however, was well supplied, and the siege seemed to have little effect. Many troops became impatient, and some decided to return home. Others fell ill as the weather grew colder. The army's leaders became discouraged.

During the siege, the Texas army underwent a change in leadership. Realizing that he was a better diplomat than a general, Austin accepted a position as a commissioner to the United States. The soldiers elected **Edward Burleson,** an experienced officer, to take command of the army.

On November 26 **Erastus "Deaf" Smith,** one of Burleson's scouts, rode into camp. He reported that more than 100 Mexican soldiers with pack animals were headed to San Antonio. A rumor quickly spread through the camp that these soldiers were carrying silver to pay the Mexican troops. Burleson sent a squad of troops led by Bowie to ambush the Mexicans and seize the silver.

Bowie's squad quickly defeated the soldiers and took their cargo. The Texans eagerly opened the bags that supposedly held silver, only to find grass for feeding horses instead. This incident became known as the **Grass Fight.** Although the Texas troops were disappointed, some of them realized that the siege was working because the Mexican forces needed feed for their starving animals.

Reading Check **Identifying Cause and Effect** Why did the Grass Fight take place, and what was the result?

Daily Life

The Home Front

The revolution disrupted the daily lives of many Texans. This was certainly true for Tejanos during the siege and capture of San Antonio. Both the Mexican and Texas armies took food, livestock, and other supplies from townspeople. During the battle, Texas troops broke down the doors of homes, tore holes in the walls and ceilings, and used the residents' furniture for cover. Many homes were left in ruins. **What types of hardships did some Tejanos suffer during the revolution?**

★ The Capture of San Antonio

After the Grass Fight, Colonel Burleson wanted to attack San Antonio, but his officers refused. Instead, he ordered a withdrawal from San Antonio to Goliad. On December 4, the day Burleson ordered the pullback, a captured Mexican officer was brought to camp. He reported that General Cos's troops were weak and disorganized. The siege and lack of supplies had worn down the Mexican soldiers. After hearing the report, Colonel **Ben Milam** shouted to the troops, "Who will go with old Ben Milam into San Antonio?" About 300 Texans answered Milam's call. They gathered that night at the Old Mill. Ben Milam and Francis W. Johnson each took command of a group for the attack on San Antonio.

The Texans attacked in the early morning hours on December 5, 1835. Fighting spread from house to house and then on to the rooftops. One Texan described the frightened citizens' reaction. "Men, women and children began to run out, in their night clothes and unarmed." On the third day of fighting, Milam was killed. Yet the battle was turning in the Texans' favor. They were forcing the Mexican troops to retreat. By December 9 the Mexican forces had been pushed out of the center of San Antonio. On December 10 Cos surrendered and agreed to lead his troops out of Texas.

The victory in San Antonio led many Texans to believe that the conflict was over. They thought that they could separate from Coahuila and form a separate state within Mexico. That would give them a greater say in their own government and a chance to live as they wished. Santa Anna had different plans for Texas, however.

Reading Check **Finding the Main Idea** What was the outcome of the siege of San Antonio?

★ Section 1 Review

1. Define and explain:
- infantry
- cavalry

2. Identify and explain the significance of:
- Battle of Gonzales
- Juan Seguín
- Edward Burleson
- Erastus "Deaf" Smith
- Grass Fight
- Ben Milam

3. Locate on a map:
- Gonzales

4. Summarizing
Copy the web diagram below. Use it to show how early victories gave confidence to the Texas troops during the Texas Revolution.

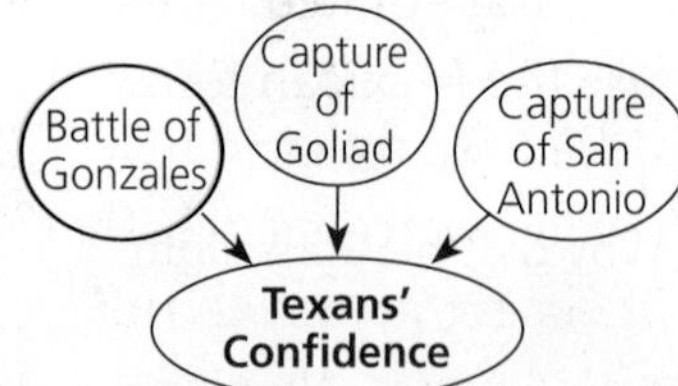

5. Finding the Main Idea
- **a.** Describe the effects of the Battle of Gonzales on Texas-Mexico relations.
- **b.** Look at the map in this section. Organize the battles on it in absolute chronological order.

6. Writing and Critical Thinking *my* WriteSmart
Drawing Inferences and Conclusions Imagine that you are a reporter covering the siege of San Antonio. Write a report that describes the events.
Consider the following:
- decisions that army officials made
- effects of geographic factors such as landforms on the battle

Section 2

The Consultation

Main Ideas

1. The Consultation met to debate the future of Texas and to form a provisional government.
2. Conflicts soon arose within the new government.

Why It Matters Today

Texans held the Consultation to discuss the formation of a government. Use current events sources to learn about new governments being formed in countries around the world today.

Key Terms and People

- **Consultation**
- **Declaration of November 7, 1835**
- **provisional**
- **Henry Smith**
- **Sam Houston**

TEKS: 3B, 3C, 17A, 17C, 21A, 21B, 21E, 22D

myNotebook

Use the annotation tools in your eBook to take notes on the decisions made and actions taken by the Consultation.

The Story Continues

Several Texas settlers had braved long distances and hard travel to reach San Felipe de Austin. Some had been delayed by the fighting in Gonzales, Goliad, and San Antonio. Others were delayed by the confusion that surrounded events. Still, they had an important mission. As delegates to the Consultation, they would debate the future of Texas.

Debating Independence

While Austin and Burleson were besieging San Antonio, another group of Texans was taking part in a convention that would have equally great consequences. Known as the **Consultation**, its purpose was to discuss Texans' plans for dealing with Mexico. Scheduled to begin in mid-October, the opening was delayed by the outbreak of battles in Texas.

Finally, on November 4, 1835, the Consultation began. No delegates from the fighting areas were present. Immediately disagreements arose. Pro-war delegates argued that Texas should declare independence from Mexico. The pro-peace group wanted to remain loyal to Mexico. Many Tejanos were torn, worried about their future in an independent Texas.

Three days after meeting, the Consultation issued the **Declaration of November 7, 1835.** In this document, they justified the fighting that had already taken place against Mexico. The Texans were not rebelling, they argued, but only fighting to defend their rights under the Constitution of 1824. As long as Mexico denied these rights, they continued, the Texan were justified in creating their own government.

HISTORIC DOCUMENT

Declaration of the People of Texas

The Consultation adopted the following statement on November 7, 1835.

"Whereas,*General Antonio Lopez de Santa Anna and other Military Chieftains have, by force of arms, overthrown the Federal Institutions of Mexico, and dissolved the Social Compact which existed between Texas and the other Members of the Mexican Confederacy—Now, the good People of Texas, availing themselves of their natural rights,*

SOLEMNLY DECLARE

1st. That they have taken up arms in defense of their rights and Liberties, which were threatened by the encroachments [advances beyond proper limits] of military despots, and in defense of the Republican Principles of the Federal Constitution of Mexico of 1824. . . .

These Declarations we solemnly avow to the world, and call GOD to witness their truth and sincerity. . . .

[P. B. Dexter], Secretary B. T. Archer, President"

Analyzing Primary Sources

1. **Finding the Main Idea** Why was the declaration issued?
2. **Drawing Inferences and Conclusions** According to the declaration, why did Texans take up arms?

The Consultation then created a **provisional**, or temporary, government. It elected **Henry Smith** governor and James Robinson lieutenant governor. Governor Smith was a member of the pro-war group and had been active in Texas politics since 1827. To help run the government, the Consultation created the General Council. In addition, the delegates chose three commissioners to travel to the United States: Stephen F. Austin, William H. Wharton, and Branch T. Archer. Their goals were to recruit volunteers for the army and to raise money.

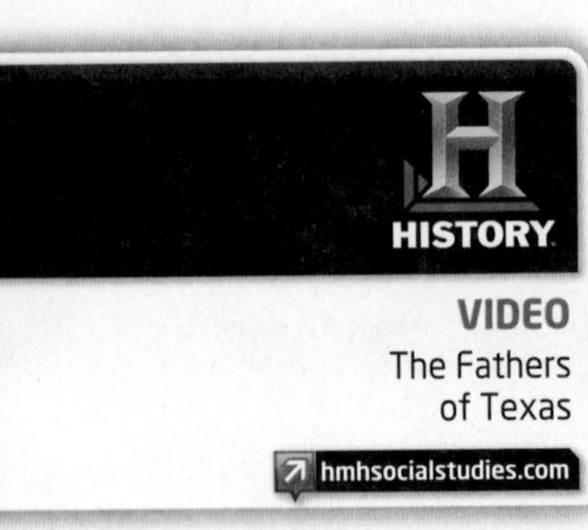

VIDEO
The Fathers of Texas
hmhsocialstudies.com

The delegates next turned to military matters. They established a professional army, modeled after the U.S. Army, with **Sam Houston** as its commander-in-chief. Houston was an experienced soldier and politician. He had served in the U.S. Congress and as governor of Tennessee. But as commander of the Texas army, Houston faced several problems. At that time, Texas forces were entirely made up of volunteers, not professional soldiers. As volunteers, they did not answer to Houston. And because the Consultation did not give him money, Houston could not pay professional soldiers. He was a commander with no army.

In addition to an army, the General Council authorized the creation of a navy. It was to protect the Texas coast and guard ships traveling from New Orleans and other eastern ports. The four-ship navy allowed supplies to reach Texas forces. It also kept Mexico from resupplying Santa Anna's army by sea. For example, in March 1836, the Mexican schooner *Pelicano* was seized with 300 barrels of gunpowder on board. The council also licensed private vessels to attack enemy ships on behalf of the government.

Reading Check **Finding the Main Idea** What were the major outcomes of the Consultation?

★ The Provisional Government

It was not long before conflict broke out among members of the provisional government. One such conflict dealt with military strategy. Some Texans in favor of independence wanted to attack Matamoros, a city across the Rio Grande. They hoped that doing so would stir federalists in other parts of northern Mexico to join the protest against Santa Anna's government. Francis Johnson and James Grant organized an army of volunteer troops for this campaign. Neither Sam Houston nor Governor Smith supported the plan. They did not think that Texas had enough resources—either money or people—to support so risky a plan. The General Council sided with Johnson and Grant. After a great deal of debate and arguments over strategy, they left for Matamoros, hoping to gather additional volunteers along the way.

Sam Houston had lived with the Cherokees for several years. For the rest of his life, he often wore Cherokee-style clothing.

Meanwhile, Houston and William Goyens of Nacogdoches went to East Texas to negotiate a peace treaty with the Cherokees. The two were well suited for the task. Houston had lived with the Cherokees in Tennessee and Oklahoma as a young man. Goyens had served as a diplomat to the Cherokees of East Texas for many years. Because of their efforts, the Cherokees agreed not to side with Mexico in the revolution.

Other efforts of the provisional government were less successful. Texas did not have clear goals or good leadership, and several conflicts emerged between members of the General Council. Disagreements also arose between Smith, who wanted immediate independence for Texas, and the council members of the pro-peace group. Despite protests from Smith, in December 1835 the General Council scheduled a new convention for March 1, 1836, to solve the government's problems.

Reading Check **Drawing Inferences and Conclusions** What caused the problems faced by the provisional government?

★ Section 2 Review

hmhsocialstudies.com
ONLINE QUIZ

1. **Define and explain:**
   - provisional
2. **Identify and explain** the significance of each of the following in Texas history:
   - Consultation
   - Declaration of November 7, 1835
   - Henry Smith
   - Sam Houston
3. **Identifying Cause and Effect** Copy the graphic organizer below. Use it to show why the Consultation met and what it hoped to accomplish.

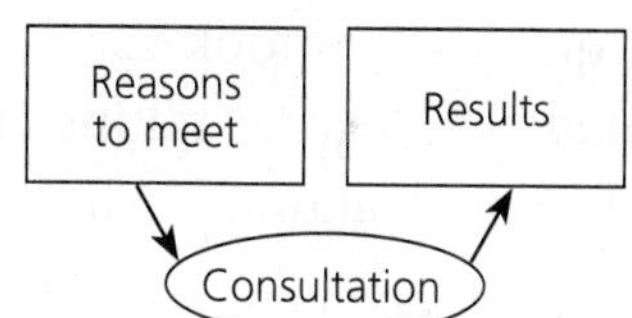

4. **Finding the Main Idea**
   - **a.** What type of government did the delegates establish?
   - **b.** How did the structure of the provisional government create problems?
5. **Writing and Critical Thinking** myWriteSmart
   Supporting a Point of View Imagine that you are a delegate. Write a letter supporting either the pro-war group's drive for independence or the peace group's position to stay part of Mexico.
   Consider the following:
   - arguments of the pro-war group
   - arguments of the peace group

Image Credit: ©Corbis

Section 3 The Siege of the Alamo

Main Ideas

1. In early 1836 Mexican forces marched into Texas, while the Texas army was disorganized.
2. The Texan army chose to make a stand against the Mexican army at the Alamo mission in San Antonio.
3. The defenders of the Alamo gave their lives in a desperate effort to hold back the Mexican army.

Key Terms and People

- **Davy Crockett**
- **José de Urrea**
- **James "Jim" Bowie**
- **William B. Travis**
- **James Bonham**
- **casualties**
- **Susanna Dickinson**
- **noncombatants**

Why It Matters Today

The battle at the Alamo became a rallying point for Texas troops throughout the Texas Revolution. Use current events sources to learn how important battles are remembered today.

TEKS: 1B, 3B, 3C, 8A, 18A, 21A, 21B, 21C, 22D

myNotebook

Use the annotation tools in your eBook to take notes on the siege of the Alamo.

The Story Continues

On January 9, 1836, Davy Crockett sat down to write a letter to his children. He had just arrived in Texas and described with enthusiasm his warm welcome. Settlers fired a cannon and held a dinner in honor of the famous frontiersman. He then looked for a place to settle and claim a piece of land. He also noted to his family that he had joined the Texas army as a volunteer and was happy with his choice. The letter would prove to be Crockett's last.

VIDEO
Davy Crockett: American Frontier Legend

hmhsocialstudies.com

The Mexican Army Advances

At the same time **Davy Crockett** was writing his letter to his children, Mexican forces were marching on Texas. Led by Santa Anna himself, these troops were determined to punish Texans for their rebellion. By February 1836 Santa Anna's army of some 6,000 soldiers was well on its way to San Antonio. At the same time, Mexican General **José de Urrea** was headed toward Goliad along the Gulf Coast with another army.

The Texas army was unprepared for an advance by the Mexican troops, and Urrea quickly overtook the Texans headed to Matamoros. Urrea easily defeated the Texans, taking many of them prisoner. The only Texans to make it to Matamoros did so in chains.

The rest of the Texas forces—those that had not been sent to Matamoros—were scattered in small groups. Colonel James Neill had just over 100 troops in San Antonio. About 400 more soldiers were in Goliad under the command of Colonel James Fannin.

Sam Houston was alarmed that the Texas army was so ill prepared and disorganized. He sent **James "Jim" Bowie** to San Antonio to evaluate the situation there. Houston recommended that the former San Antonio de Valero Mission, better known as the Alamo, be destroyed and its artillery removed. Smith disagreed, believing it was important to defend the Alamo. Its defenses had been improved several years earlier to provide protection from American Indian attacks. In addition, the Texans there had access to weapons left by Cos and his army.

In addition, the Alamo was strategically located along the Old San Antonio Road—one of the two major routes through Texas. It was along this road that the Mexican army would probably approach San Antonio. The Alamo provided the best chance to stop an army along this road, and so Smith thought that the mission would be vital to any resistance.

On January 19 Bowie arrived in San Antonio with 25 men. He examined Colonel Neill's improvements to the fort and its 21 cannons. He and Neill agreed that the Alamo and its artillery were too important to destroy. He wrote Governor Smith explaining why.

TEXAS VOICES

"The salvation of Texas depends in great measure on keeping Bexar [San Antonio] out of the hands of the enemy. . . . Colonel Neill and myself have come to the solemn resolution that we will rather die in these ditches than give them up to the enemy."

—James Bowie, quoted in *Lone Star*, by T. R. Fehrenbach

When Smith received Bowie's letter, he decided to send reinforcements to San Antonio. He ordered Colonel **William B. Travis** to raise a force and assist Bowie. However, Travis could gather only 30 soldiers. He and his troops rode in from San Felipe de Austin on February 3. Juan Seguín was also in San Antonio with a small group of volunteers.

As word spread of the rebellion, U.S. volunteers trickled into Texas. Davy Crockett led a dozen Tennessee volunteers into San Antonio a few days after Travis arrived. Although Crockett was a famous frontiersman and a former U.S. congressman, he did not want a position of authority. He told Travis, "Assign me some place and I and my Tennessee boys will defend it all right." **James Bonham** and a volunteer force from Alabama called the Mobile Grays also joined the Texas defenders. When Colonel Neill left the Alamo to care for an ill family member, he put Travis in command. Travis and Bowie argued over control, finally agreeing to share command.

Reading Check **Supporting a Point of View** Do you agree or disagree with Bowie's decision to defend the Alamo? Explain your answer.

BIOGRAPHY

William B. Travis

(c. 1809–1836) William B. Travis was born in South Carolina, but his family moved to Alabama in 1818. He later became an attorney and married Rosanna Cato. In 1830 Travis left his family and headed for Texas. He acquired land from Stephen F. Austin and set up a law practice at Anahuac. Travis became part of a rebel group that opposed the Law of April 6, 1830. After the Consultation, he became a lieutenant colonel in the Texas army. In February of 1836, he was chosen as one of the commanders at the Alamo. Upon his death he became a Texas hero. **What role did Travis play in the Texas Revolution?**

The Siege of the Alamo

In preparation for the Siege of the Alamo, Texans built up the fortifications around the old mission and placed cannons in strategic spots along the walls. However, they needed more troops to defend such a large area.

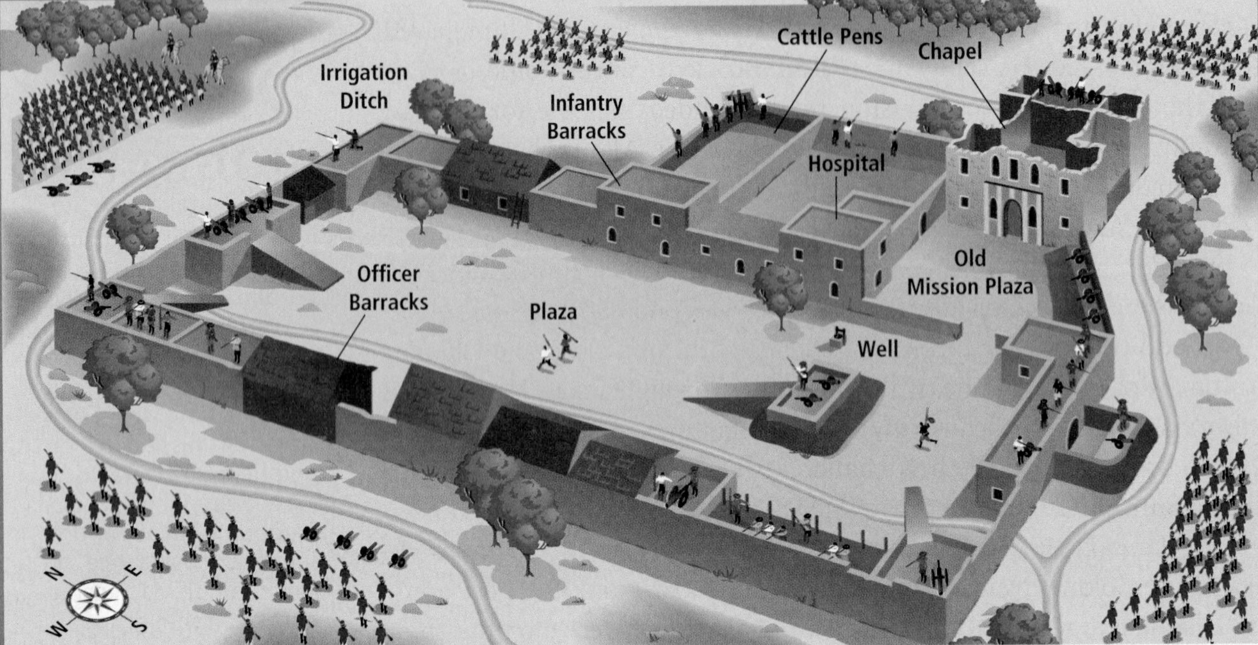

Visualizing History

1. **Science, Technology & Society** What improvements did the Texans make to the Alamo to help their chances of survival?
2. **Connecting to Today** Why do you think many Texans today consider the defenders of the Alamo heroes?

The Siege Begins

As the Mexican forces approached San Antonio, the Texas troops at the Alamo built up their defenses. Green Jameson, a 29-year-old lawyer, was in charge of strengthening the plaza walls. He and the other defenders built up some of the walls to 12 feet high and 2 feet thick. Jameson directed the building of palisades—high fences made of stakes—behind which soldiers could fight. He also worked with artillery officer Almaron Dickinson to choose locations for the fort's 21 cannons. Even with such improvements, the Alamo would be difficult to defend without more troops. It had originally been built as a mission, not a fort. The area enclosed by the two buildings and walls of the Alamo was about three acres, and would require about 1,000 soldiers to defend it properly. The Texas soldiers in the Alamo at this time numbered little more than 150.

Travis and the rest of the Alamo defenders hoped for reinforcements. Very soon, however, Travis began hearing reports that Santa Anna's army was approaching. At first, the Texans doubted the reports. Travis and Bowie had thought that the rainy weather would delay the Mexicans until mid-March. However, they were wrong. Santa Anna had pushed hard. On February 23 a lookout spotted the Mexican troops marching down the road.

VIDEO
The Alamo
hmhsocialstudies.com

As Mexican troops marched into the city, the defenders, their families, and some local residents rushed to get inside the walls of the Alamo. Expecting a siege, the defenders gathered food, ammunition, and other supplies from local citizens. General Santa Anna arrived just after the defenders were safely inside and soon demanded their surrender. The Texas rebels responded by firing a cannon shot toward the Mexican army. Santa Anna reacted swiftly. He ordered that a large blood-red flag be raised so the defenders within the Alamo could see it. This "no quarter" flag meant that Santa Anna would leave no survivors. The siege of the Alamo was underway.

On February 24, Mexican forces began firing on the Alamo. That day Travis wrote a plea "To the People of Texas and All Americans in the World." The letter was a request for aid in the face of certain death.

Cannons bombarded the Alamo for hours at a time. Bowie, who had been ill, collapsed on the second day of the siege. Travis took charge. On the fourth day of the siege, Travis ordered the Texas troops to stop returning the Mexicans' fire and save their ammunition. He was worried that Santa Anna's army would soon launch a full-scale attack.

Reading Check **Evaluating** How did Texas troops prepare for the siege of the Alamo, and was it adequate preparation in your point of view?

HISTORIC DOCUMENT

Travis's Letter

William B. Travis wrote this plea for help at the Alamo on February 24, 1836.

"Commandancy of the Alamo—

Bejar [San Antonio], Fby. 24th 1836—

To the people of Texas & all Americans in the world—

Fellow Citizens—& compatriots—

I am **besieged,**[1] by a thousand or more of the Mexicans under Santa Anna—I have **sustained**[2] a **continual** Bombardment & **cannonade**[3] for 24 hours & have not lost a man—The enemy has demanded a surrender at **discretion,**[4] otherwise, the garrison are to be put to the sword, if the fort is taken—I have answered the demand with a cannon shot, & our flag still waves proudly from the walls—I shall never surrender or retreat. Then, I call on you in the name of Liberty, of patriotism & everything dear to the American character, to come to our aid, with all **dispatch**[5]—The enemy is receiving reinforcements daily & will no doubt increase to three or four thousand in four or five days. If this call is neglected, I am determined to **sustain**[6] myself as long as possible & die like a soldier who never forgets what is due to his own honor & that of this country—

VICTORY OR DEATH

William Barret Travis

Lt. Col. Comdt.

P.S. The Lord is on our side—when the enemy appeared in sight we had not three bushels of corn—we have since found in deserted houses 80 or 90 bushels and got into the walls 20 or 30 heads of **Beeves.**[7]

Travis"

Analyizing Primary Sources

1. **Finding the Main Idea** What request does Travis make?
2. **Making Generalizations and Predictions** What effect do you think this letter had?

[1]**besieged:** under attack
[2]**sustained:** suffered
[3]**cannonade:** attack by cannons
[4]**discretion:** without demands
[5]**dispatch:** speed
[6]**sustain:** protect
[7]**Beeves:** cattle

Interpreting Visuals

The Alamo. *Fighting during the Mexican attack on the Alamo was fierce. The artist's portrayal here is fictionalized.* ***How did the artist portray the bravery of Texas soldiers?***

★ The Fall of the Alamo

Travis sent out several more requests for help. Bonham left to find aid for the Alamo, only to sneak back in on March 3. Juan Seguín also sneaked past Mexican troops to request help from Goliad. But little help arrived. On March 1, 32 volunteers from Gonzales rode into the Alamo. Led by Captain Albert Martin, they crept in under cover of early morning darkness. There would be no other help.

Historians estimate that there were about 200 soldiers defending the Alamo. Santa Anna, on the other hand, had at least 1,800 troops. Travis made one last desperate appeal for aid. On March 3 he sent a letter to Washington-on-the-Brazos.

Analyzing Primary Sources
Drawing Inferences and Conclusions What does Travis mean when he says he has to "fight the enemy on his own terms"?

TEXAS VOICES

"Colonel Fannin is said to be on the march to this place with reinforcements, but I fear it is not true, as I have repeatedly sent to him for aid without receiving any. . . . I look to the colonies alone for aid; unless it arrives soon, I shall have to fight the enemy on his own terms."

—William B. Travis, quoted in *Documents of Texas History*, edited by Ernest Wallace

In the early morning hours of March 6 the Texas defenders were awakened suddenly. They heard shouts from Mexican soldiers and the sound of music. Santa Anna's army band was playing "El Degüello." The song meant that no mercy would be shown.

At about 5:00 A.M., four columns of Mexican soldiers attacked, but they were halted by the Texas artillery. The Mexican forces regrouped, however, and the four columns of troops then overwhelmed the Texans. Mexican soldiers entered the Alamo by the hundreds. They captured a cannon, turned it inward, and opened fire. Hand-to-hand combat then followed.

As the smoke cleared, almost all the defenders were dead. Among those killed were all the leaders of the defenders, including Travis, Crockett, Bowie, and Bonham. Also among the dead were several Tejano defenders, including Juan Abamillo, Juan A. Badillo, Carlos Espalier, José María Esparza, Antonio Fuentes, Damacio Jiménez, José Toribio Losoya, and Andrés Nava. Accounts of Mexican losses vary, but there were about 600 Mexican casualties. **Casualties** are those killed, wounded, captured, or missing during battle.

Only a few Texans survived the Alamo. One of the survivors was **Susanna Dickinson**, wife of Almaron Dickinson, and her daughter Angelina. Other survivors were Ana Salazar Esparza, wife of José María Esparza, and her children. Santa Anna also spared a slave named Joe and several other **noncombatants**, or people not involved in fighting. Many of these noncombatants had entered the Alamo looking for safety from the approaching Mexican army. Despite the brutality of the attack, most—but not all—of these noncombatants survived.

General Santa Anna believed that the fall of the Alamo would convince Texans to surrender. In a letter, he wrote that he had achieved "a complete and glorious triumph." Instead, the Alamo became a symbol to many Texans that they must fight on at any cost. "Remember the Alamo!" became a rallying cry for the Texan army.

Reading Check **Analyzing Information** Why do you think that the fall of the Alamo became a symbol that inspired many Texans to fight on?

That's Interesting!

Line in the Sand

According to a famous Texas legend that arose in the 1870s, William B. Travis took his sword and drew a line on the ground on March 5. Anyone who wished to stay and defend the Alamo was asked to cross over the line. All but one of the troops did so. Some believe the one who did not was Louis Rose.

Section 3 Review

hmhsocialstudies.com ONLINE QUIZ

1. Define and explain:
- casualties
- noncombatants

2. Identify and explain the significance of each of the following:
- Davy Crockett
- José de Urrea
- James "Jim" Bowie
- William B. Travis
- James Bonham
- Susanna Dickinson

3. Sequencing Copy the diagram below. Use it to show the path of events that led to the fall of the Alamo.

The Siege of the Alamo begins.
The Alamo falls.

4. Finding the Main Idea

a. Why did Travis write his letter to the people of Texas? What was the result?

b. Based on the model and text, why were the Texans defeated at the Alamo?

c. What role did Santa Anna play at the Alamo?

5. Writing and Critical Thinking myWriteSmart

Evaluating Imagine that you are at the Alamo during the siege. Describe in a journal the traits of leadership that Texans showed. Consider the following:
- Bowie's decision to protect the Alamo
- Travis's actions

Section 4

The Convention of 1836

Main Ideas

1. The Convention of 1836 declared Texan independence.
2. The Constitution of 1836 established the first government for the Republic of Texas.

Key Terms and People

- **Convention of 1836**
- **Lorenzo de Zavala**
- **George C. Childress**
- **popular sovereignty**
- **bill of rights**
- **petition**
- **ad interim**
- **David G. Burnet**

Why It Matters Today

On March 2, 1836, convention delegates adopted the Texas Declaration of Independence. Today, March 2 is an official state holiday. Use current events sources to learn about how people around the world celebrate their nations' independence today.

TEKS: 1B, 3B, 3C, 3D, 14A, 21A, 21B, 21D, 22D

myNotebook

Use the annotation tools in your eBook to take notes on the events and results of the Convention of 1836.

The Story Continues

Rain made travel rough. But on March 1, 1836, delegates began to arrive in Washington-on-the-Brazos. At the newly built settlement, delegates found the streets full of ankle-deep mud. The convention met in a small unfurnished building. Only cloth covered its window openings, and chilly winds blew through the building regularly. In spite of the uncomfortable conditions, the delegates were determined to accomplish their task.

★ Texas Declares Independence

At Washington-on-the-Brazos, a group of prominent Texans waited anxiously for news from the Alamo. They had gathered for the **Convention of 1836**, which began on March 1, just days before the Alamo's fall. Many of the convention's 59 delegates, including Sam Houston, had served in the U.S. government. Another, **Lorenzo de Zavala,** had served in the Mexican Congress.

Although not all of the delegates had arrived yet, the convention acted quickly to declare independence from Mexico. On March 2, 1836, the delegates voted unanimously to accept the Texas Declaration of Independence. Copies of the document were sent to towns around Texas to help spread the word to the people.

Written mostly by **George C. Childress**, the declaration was modeled after the U.S. Declaration of Independence. It listed the complaints Texans had against Santa Anna's government. Because the government had denied the rights guaranteed under the Constitution of 1824, Texans could no longer tolerate being part of Mexico.

Of the 59 men who signed the Declaration of Independence, 56 were Anglos. Two, José Antonio Navarro and José Francisco Ruiz, were Tejanos and one, Lorenzo de Zavala, was Mexican. With their adoption of the declaration, the Republic of Texas was born. Texans today celebrate March 2 as Texas Independence Day.

Reading Check Summarizing What was the first significant action of the Convention of 1836, and why did the delegates take that action?

★ The Constitution of 1836

After accepting the Texas Declaration of Independence, some delegates wanted to rush to San Antonio to aid the defenders of the Alamo, which was still under siege. But Sam Houston urged the delegates to stay and create a constitution, or a plan for government, for their new republic.

Most of the delegates to the Convention of 1836 had been born in the United States. It is not surprising, then, that the Constitution they created was modeled after the U.S. Constitution. Like the U.S. government, the Texas government was to be divided into three branches—legislative, executive, and judicial. Also like in the United States, citizens would elect their leaders. Just like the United States, the Republic of Texas was based on the idea of **popular sovereignty**, the notion that the power to create or change the government comes from the people. At the same time, though, the Constitution reflected some Spanish and Mexican influence, especially in areas dealing with property ownership.

Image Credit: ©Witold Skrypczak/Alamy

Interpreting Visuals

The Birthplace of Texas. *This modern reconstruction in Washington-on-the-Brazos re-creates the building in which delegates to the Convention of 1836 wrote the Texas Declaration of Independence.* ***Why do you think Washington-on-the-Brazos has been called the birthplace of Texas?***

BIOGRAPHY

Lorenzo de Zavala
(c.1788–1836) Before moving to Texas, Lorenzo de Zavala served as a Mexican congressman and governor. In 1829 he received a colonization contract to settle 500 families in East Texas, but never built his colony. He served as a diplomat for Mexico but resigned in protest of Santa Anna's actions. As a delegate to the Convention of 1836 and admirer of the U.S. Constitution, Zavala played a key role in drafting the Texas Constitution and was elected vice president.
How was Zavala important to the Texas Revolution?

By declaring independence from Mexico, the Convention of 1836 had claimed political freedom for Texas. In the Constitution, they worked to introduce civil and religious freedom as well. The Constitution of the Republic of Texas included a **bill of rights**, or statement of basic rights that the government cannot take away from citizens. Under the new constitution, Texans who had immigrated from the United States enjoyed many of the same civil rights they previously had. For example, the constitution protected freedom of speech and protected people from unlawful arrests. Before, all Texans had been required to be Catholic, but now they could worship as they pleased. The constitution also called for a public school system and a policy of giving land to settlers.

The new Texas constitution also allowed slavery to continue and legalized the purchase of new slaves. It also enslaved African Americans who had been brought into Texas as contract laborers. Neither African Americans nor American Indians were allowed to be citizens without the permission of Congress. Any free African Americans who wanted to remain in Texas had to **petition** the government. A petition is a formal request. Among those who did so was Samuel McCulloch Jr., the first Texan casualty of the revolution. He was wounded at Goliad in 1835.

Because Texas was at war, the delegates at the Convention of 1836 created an **ad interim**, or temporary, government. New leaders would be chosen once republic-wide elections could be held. **David G. Burnet** was selected as the interim president, and Lorenzo de Zavala as vice president. They took office on March 17, 1836, at Washington-on-the-Brazos. Later that day, they fled after hearing that the Mexican army was near. The government set up again at Harrisburg, but was forced to flee again. Constantly on the move, the ad interim government had to leave the future of the Republic in the hands of Sam Houston and the army.

Reading Check **Comparing** How was the Texas Constitution similar to the U.S. Constitution?

Section 4 Review

hmhsocialstudies.com
ONLINE QUIZ

1. Define and explain:
- popular sovereignty
- bill of rights
- petition
- ad interim

2. Identify and explain:
- Convention of 1836
- Lorenzo de Zavala
- George C. Childress
- David G. Burnet

3. Locate on a map:
- Washingon-on-the-Brazos

4. Identifying Points of View
Copy the graphic organizer below. Use it to explain why the convention delegates created the documents listed below.

Document	Delegates' Purpose
Declaration of Independence	
Constitution	

5. Finding the Main Idea
a. How did the political experiences of the delegates affect the convention?
b. How did the Republic of Texas bring political, civil, and religious freedom to Texas?

6. Writing and Critical Thinking myWriteSmart
Comparing Imagine that you are reporting on the Convention of 1836. Write an article describing how the structure of the new government is a reflection of some ideas in the U.S. Constitution.
Consider the following:
- structure of the new government
- rights guaranteed in the Texas documents

THE TEXAS DECLARATION *of* INDEPENDENCE

On March 1, 1836, delegates met at Washington-on-the-Brazos to form a new government for Texas. One of the convention's first acts of business was to declare independence from Mexico. Below is the Texas Declaration of Independence, unanimously adopted on March 2.

THE DECLARATION OF INDEPENDENCE Made by the Delegates of The People of Texas in General Convention, at Washington, ON MARCH 2nd, 1836.

When a government has ceased to protect the lives, liberty and property of the people, from whom its legitimate powers are derived, and for the advancement of whose happiness it was instituted; and so far from being a guarantee for their inestimable and **inalienable** rights, becomes an instrument in the hands of evil rulers for their **suppression**. When the federal republican constitution of their country, which they have sworn to support, no longer has a substantial existence, and the whole nature of their government has been forcibly changed, without their consent, from a restricted federative republic, composed of sovereign states, to a consolidated central military **despotism**, in which every interest is disregarded but that of the army and the priesthood, both the eternal enemies of civil liberty, the ever ready **minions** of power, and the usual instruments of tyrants. When, long after the spirit of the constitution has departed, moderation is at length so far lost by those in power, that even the **semblance** of freedom is removed, and the forms themselves of the constitution discontinued, and so far from their petitions and **remonstrances** being regarded, the agents who bear them are thrown into dungeons, and mercenary armies sent forth to enforce a new government upon them at the point of the bayonet.

When, in consequence of such acts of **malfeasance** and **abdication** on the part of the government, **anarchy** prevails, and civil society is dissolved into its original elements, in such a crisis, the first law of nature, the right of self-preservation, the **inherent** and inalienable right of the people to appeal to first principles, and take their political affairs into their own hands in extreme cases, enjoins it as a right towards themselves, and a sacred obligation to their **posterity**, to abolish such government, and create another in its stead, calculated to rescue them from impending dangers, and to secure their welfare and happiness.

Exploring the Document

George C. Childress chaired the committee in charge of drafting the Texas Declaration of Independence. **How do you think Childress used the U.S. Declaration of Independence as a model for this document?**

inalienable: undeniable

suppression: holding back

despotism: dictatorship

minions: servants

semblance: likeness

remonstrances: protests

malfeasance: official's wrongdoing

abdication: giving up responsibility

anarchy: disorder

inherent: natural

posterity: future generations

Exploring the Document

Here the Declaration explains that Texans had a responsibility to call for independence. **Why do you think Texans felt that they had to demand their independence?**

Exploring the Document

Many Texas settlers were upset with Santa Anna for abandoning the Constitution of 1824. **What alternative did the Mexican government offer in the constitution's place?**

Exploring the Document

The Declaration lists the charges that the settlers made against the Mexican government. **What were some of their concerns?**

amenable: answerable

habituated: accustomed to

acquiesced: accepted

privations: hardships

incarcerated: jailed

zealous endeavor: enthusiastic efforts

procure: gain

palladium: a protecting spirit

axiom: a rule

arbitrary: unreasonable

defiance: disregard

piratical attacks: robbery

desperadoes: outlaws

confiscation: taking of goods

dictates: principles

temporal: timely or earthly

functionaries: officials

formidable: causing fear

Nations, as well as individuals, are **amenable** for their acts to the public opinion of mankind. A statement of a part of our grievances is therefore submitted to an impartial world, in justification of the hazardous but unavoidable step now taken, of severing our political connection with the Mexican people, and assuming an independent attitude among the nations of the earth.

The Mexican government, by its colonization laws, invited and induced the Anglo American population of Texas to colonize its wilderness under the pledged faith of a written constitution, that they should continue to enjoy that constitutional liberty and republican government to which they had been **habituated** in the land of their birth, the United States of America.

In this expectation they have been cruelly disappointed, inasmuch as the Mexican nation has **acquiesced** to the late changes made in the government by General Antonio Lopez de Santa Anna, who, having overturned the constitution of his country, now offers us the cruel alternative, either to abandon our homes, acquired by so many **privations**, or submit to the most intolerable of all tyranny, the combined despotism of the sword and the priesthood.

It has sacrificed our welfare to the state of Coahuila, by which our interests have been continually depressed through a jealous and partial course of legislation, carried on at a far distant seat of government, by a hostile majority, in an unknown tongue, and this too, notwithstanding we have petitioned in the humblest terms for the establishment of a separate state government, and have, in accordance with the provisions of the national constitution, presented to the general congress a republican constitution, which was, without a just cause, contemptuously rejected.

It **incarcerated** in a dungeon, for a long time, one of our citizens, for no other cause but a **zealous endeavor to procure** the acceptance of our constitution, and the establishment of a state government.

It has failed and refused to secure, on a firm basis, the right of trial by jury, that **palladium** of civil liberty, and only safe guarantee for the life, liberty, and property of the citizen.

It has failed to establish any public system of education, although possessed of almost boundless resources, (the public domain,) and although it is an **axiom** in political science, that unless a people are educated and enlightened, it is idle to expect the continuance of civil liberty, or the capacity for self government.

It has suffered the military commandants, stationed among us, to exercise **arbitrary** acts of oppression and tyranny, thus trampling upon the most sacred rights of the citizens, and rendering the military superior to the civil power.

It has dissolved, by force of arms, the state congress of Coahuila and Texas, and obliged our representatives to fly for their lives from the seat of government, thus depriving us of the fundamental political right of representation.

It has demanded the surrender of a number of our citizens, and ordered military detachments to seize and carry them into the interior for trial, in contempt of the civil authorities, and in **defiance** of the laws and the constitution.

It has made **piratical attacks** upon our commerce, by commissioning foreign **desperadoes**, and authorizing them to seize our vessels, and convey the property of our citizens to far distant ports for **confiscation**.

It denies us the right of worshiping the Almighty according to the **dictates** of our own conscience, by the support of a national religion, calculated to promote the **temporal** interest of its human **functionaries**, rather than the glory of the true and living God.

It has demanded us to deliver up our arms, which are essential to our defense—the rightful property of freemen—and **formidable** only to tyrannical governments.

It has invaded our country both by sea and by land, with the intent to lay waste our territory, and drive us from our homes; and has now a large mercenary army advancing, to carry on against us a war of extermination.

It has, through its **emissaries**, incited the merciless savage, with the tomahawk and scalping knife, to massacre the inhabitants of our defenseless frontiers.

It has been, during the whole time of our connection with it, the **contemptible** sport and victim of successive military revolutions, and has continually exhibited every characteristic of a weak, corrupt, and tyrannical government.

These, and other grievances, were patiently borne by the people of Texas, until they reached that point at which **forbearance** ceases to be a virtue. We then took up arms in defense of the national constitution. We appealed to our Mexican **brethren** for assistance: our appeal has been made in vain; though months have elapsed, no sympathetic response has yet been heard from the interior. We are, therefore, forced to the melancholy conclusion, that the Mexican people have acquiesced in the destruction of their liberty, and the substitution therefore of a military government; that they are unfit to be free, and incapable of self government.

The necessity of self-preservation, therefore, now decrees our eternal political separation.

We, therefore, the delegates, with ***plenary*** *powers, of the people of Texas, in solemn convention assembled, appealing to a candid world for the necessities of our condition, do hereby resolve and declare, that our political connection with the Mexican nation has forever ended, and that the people of Texas do now constitute a* FREE, SOVEREIGN, and INDEPENDENT REPUBLIC, *and are fully invested with all the rights and attributes which properly belong to independent nations; and, conscious of the* ***rectitude*** *of our intentions, we fearlessly and confidently commit the issue to the supreme Arbiter of the destinies of nations.*

In witness whereof we have hereunto subscribed our names.

RICHARD ELLIS,
President and Delegate from Red River.
Albert H. S. Kimble,
Secretary.
C. B. Stewart,
James Collinsworth,
Edwin Waller,
A. Brigham,
John S. D. Byrom,
Francisco Ruiz,
J. Antonio Navarro,
William D. Lacy,
William Menefee,
John Fisher,
Matthew Caldwell,
John S. Roberts,
Robert Hamilton,
Collin McKinney,
A. H. Latimer,
James Power,
Sam. Houston,
Edward Conrad,
Martin Parmer,
James Gaines,
William Clark, jun.,
Sydney O. Pennington,
William Motley,
Lorenzo de Zavala,
George W. Smyth,
Stephen H. Everett,
Elijah Stepp,
Claiborne West,
William B. Leates,
M. B. Menard,
A. B. Hardin,
John W. Bunton,
Thomas J. Gazley,
R. M. Coleman,
Sterling C. Robertson,
George C. Childress,
Bailey Hardeman,
Robert Potter,
Charles Taylor,
Samuel P. Carson,
Thomas J. Rusk,
William C. Crawford,
John Turner,
Benjamin Briggs Goodrich,
James G. Swisher,
George W. Barnet,
Jesse Grimes,
E. O. Legrand,
David Thomas,
S. Rhoads Fisher,
John W. Bower,
J. B. Woods,
Andrew Briscoe,
Thomas Barnett,
Jesse B. Badgett,
Stephen W. Blount.

emissaries: agents

contemptible: deserving scorn

forbearance: acceptance

brethren: brothers

plenary: full

rectitude: righteousness

Exploring the Document

Here the Declaration explains that Texans have carried the burden of the listed grievances. **What does the author hope Mexican citizens will do?**

BIOGRAPHY

George C. Childress
(c. 1804–1841)
George C. Childress was born and raised in Tennessee. In 1835 he volunteered for the Texas army. Childress was elected to the Convention of 1836. There he called the convention to order and served as the primary author of the Declaration of Independence. **What role did Childress play in Texas history?**

Section 5

Independence Is Won

Main Ideas

1. In the Runaway Scrape, Texans fled the Mexican army.
2. A Texan army surrendered at Goliad but was massacred a few days later at Santa Anna's orders.
3. Texas won independence at the Battle of San Jacinto.

Why It Matters Today

Many Anglo and Tejano settlers fled from Santa Anna's army to seek refuge in the United States. Use current events sources to learn about refugees to the United States today.

Key Terms and People

- **Runaway Scrape**
- **Battle of Refugio**
- **James Fannin**
- **Battle of Coleto**
- **Goliad Massacre**
- **Francita Alavez**
- **Battle of San Jacinto**

TEKS: 1B, 1C, 3B, 3C, 8A, 9A, 9C, 21A, 21B, 21C, 21E, 22D

myNotebook

Use the annotation tools in your eBook to take notes on the final battles of the Texas Revolution.

VIDEO
Independence for Texas

hmhsocialstudies.com

The Story Continues

In the spring of 1836, 10-year-old Dilue Rose Harris sadly packed up her belongings. Scouts from the Texas army had warned her family that Santa Anna's soldiers were on their way. The Harrises loaded their bed linens, clothes, and food on a sleigh pulled by oxen. They left their farm as the sun set, wondering if they would ever see their home again.

The Runaway Scrape

General Sam Houston was charged with the task of defeating Santa Anna so that Texans like the Harrises could return to their homes. During the Convention of 1836, the delegates had given Houston full command of both the regular and volunteer armies. He was no longer a commander with no army. However, Houston was still short on troops, guns, ammunition, and money. He also had to quickly organize and train his army.

On March 6 Houston left Washington-on-the-Brazos and headed to Gonzales, still unsure of the outcome at the Alamo. When Houston reached Gonzales on March 11, he was greeted with stories of the defeat. He sent out his best scouts to find out what had happened and where Santa Anna's forces were. Scouts Deaf Smith, R. E. Handy, and Henry Karnes left to investigate. The next day, the scouts escorted Susanna Dickinson and a few other survivors of the Alamo into Gonzales. Houston and the Texas army heard for the first time the details of the defenders' last stand at the Alamo.

The Texans also learned that Santa Anna was heading to Gonzales, where Houston had fewer than 400 men. With more than 700 Mexican troops advancing on them, the Texans were in danger. Houston ordered a retreat. Many civilians packed their belongings and left with the army. Houston then ordered the town of Gonzales burned so that the Mexican troops could not take any additional supplies.

Word began to spread through Texas about the Alamo. Fearing for their lives, Texans fled eastward. Anglo settlers—often accompanied by African American slaves—and many Tejanos left their farms, homes, and towns to avoid the advancing Mexican forces. This movement of settlers became known as the **Runaway Scrape.** Jeff Parson, a slave at the time, described the scene. "People and things were all mixed, and in confusion. The children were crying, the women praying. . . . I tell you it was a serious time." Conditions were made worse by heavy rains and flooding during the spring of 1836. Many died from disease and hardships during the Runaway Scrape.

Reading Check **Identifying Cause and Effect** What led to the Runaway Scrape, and how did it affect Texas?

BIOGRAPHY

Susanna Dickinson

(c.1814–1883) Susanna Wilkerson was born in Tennessee, where she later married Almaron Dickinson in 1829. Two years later the young couple moved to Gonzales. When her husband left for San Antonio with a volunteer army in October 1835, she stayed behind and took care of their home and daughter. As Mexican troops approached, she moved into the Alamo. Dickinson hid with her baby as the battle raged. After the battle Mexican troops led her to Santa Anna. She was released, but Santa Anna had her take a message to Sam Houston. It was a warning that Santa Anna was coming after the Texans.

Why did Santa Anna release Dickinson?

★ Fannin's Surrender at Goliad

Even as Texans were fleeing Santa Anna near Gonzales, people in southern regions of Texas were fleeing before another Mexican army. General José de Urrea had crossed the Rio Grande with some 550 troops. He moved up the coastline, attacking settlements along the way. He had already defeated the Texans sent to capture Matamoros, and there were few Texans to slow his progress.

While Santa Anna lay siege to the Alamo, Urrea continued toward Refugio. On March 14 he won the **Battle of Refugio,** defeating the troops who had been sent to evacuate the settlement. The Texans held out for several hours, but they eventually ran low on ammunition. Many were captured by Urrea's forces. Urrea next turned his attention to Goliad where Colonel **James Fannin** had an army.

On March 14 Fannin received an order from General Houston to withdraw to Victoria. Instead of acting immediately, Fannin waited for his troops to return from Refugio, not knowing that they had already been defeated. Meanwhile, General Urrea was hurrying to Goliad. On March 18 Urrea's advance force met Fannin and his troops in a series of brief fights. Too late, Fannin decided to leave the protection of the fort at Goliad and head northeast to Victoria.

On March 19 the Texas troops marched into an open prairie outside of Goliad during a heavy fog. When they stopped to rest their animals, Urrea and his main army surrounded them. The Texas force numbered at least 300 soldiers , and the Mexicans had 300 to 500 troops. With no choice but battle, Fannin chose to stand and fight near Coleto Creek.

During the conflict outside of Goliad, Fannin's troops were surrounded on the open prairie.

In the **Battle of Coleto,** the Texas rebels were pinned down without cover. The next morning, Mexican reinforcements arrived, giving Urrea several hundred more troops. Wounded and severely outnumbered, Fannin decided to surrender. Following the surrender, he and most of the other Texas rebels were marched back to Goliad.

The prisoners were held in Goliad for a week. Their imprisonment was not overly harsh, as one Texas recorded. "[Urrea] was not blood thirsty and when not overruled by orders of a superior . . . was disposed to treat prisoners with lenity [mercy]." Urrea wrote to Santa Anna for permission to hold the Texans as prisoners of war, rather than kill them. Santa Anna's response was swift and clear. Anyone who had taken up arms against the government of Mexico must be executed immediately.

On March 27, Mexican soldiers shot more than 400 Texans outside of Goliad. Those executed included Fannin's troops as well as Texas soldiers captured outside of Victoria. When the firing began, a few of the Texans ran and escaped. Some survived the **Goliad Massacre** during the smoky confusion. **Francita Alavez,** who was traveling with the Mexican troops, helped a few people escape. Texans later referred to her as the Angel of Goliad.

Reading Check **Summarizing** How did geographic factors and other events lead to Fannin's surrender?

BIOGRAPHY

James Fannin

(c.1804–1836) James Fannin joined the Texas army in 1835 and fought at Gonzales. Later he led Texas forces in the Battle of Concepción, in which 90 Texans defeated 400 Mexican soldiers. In December Fannin took charge of the troops at Goliad. He surrendered to General Urrea on March 20, 1836, and was executed along with many of his troops by order of General Santa Anna. In memory of Fannin and his troops, "Remember Goliad!" became a battle cry of the Texas Revolution. **How did Fannin inspire Texans?**

Houston Prepares the Troops

Upon hearing news of Goliad, some angry Texans began to demand an all-out attack on Mexican forces. The Texas army had grown to more than 1,200 men after the fall of the Alamo. Houston, however, believed that his army was still too small and untrained to defeat the larger and better-supplied Mexican army. So he continued to avoid fights. As Santa Anna moved deeper into Texas, Houston led the army eastward.

Several Texas troops openly rebelled against Houston, criticizing him for retreating from Santa Anna. They believed he was acting like a coward. Even President Burnet challenged Houston to fight. "The enemy are laughing you to scorn."

Houston ignored the criticism. When he heard that Santa Anna was approaching his base at San Felipe, he moved his army 20 miles north to Jared Groce's plantation. There Houston trained and drilled his troops. The troops also collected supplies and ammunition, some of which had come from supporters in the United States. The citizens of Cincinnati, Ohio, for example, had sent two cannons to the soldiers. The Texans named the cannons the Twin Sisters.

Houston and the Texas army left Groce's plantation on April 12, marching southeast toward Harrisburg, where they arrived six days later. That same day, Houston's scouts reported that Santa Anna and part of his army had crossed the Brazos River and were camped not far from Harrisburg. Houston made his decision. He wrote a friend, "We are in preparation to meet Santa Anna. It is the only chance of saving Texas." The stage was set for the final battle against Santa Anna.

Reading Check **Supporting a Point of View** Explain whether, in your opinion, Houston's actions after the Alamo and Goliad were or were not an example of good leadership.

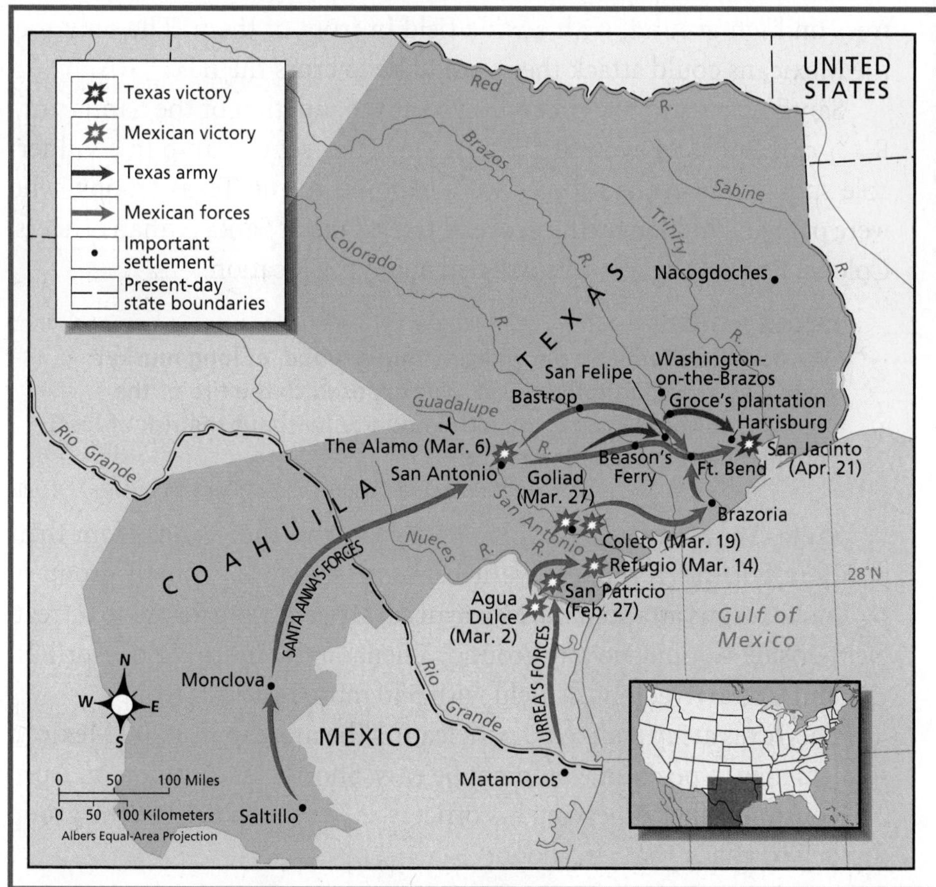

Battles of the Texas Revolution, 1835–1836

Interpreting Maps As Mexican forces marched across Texas, General Houston and his army retreated eastward.

1. ***Locate*** Where did the major battles of the Texas Revolution occur?
2. ***Evaluating*** Why do you think Texas and Mexican forces traveled through towns and river crossings such as Beason's Ferry?

Interpreting Visuals

San Jacinto. *During the Battle of San Jacinto, Texas forces crept onto the prairie that separated the Texan and Mexican camps. The Texans then launched a surprise attack crying, "Remember the Alamo! Remember Goliad!"* ***How does the artist show the confusion of battle?***

★ The Battle of San Jacinto

Houston's army moved quickly to get to Harrisburg. From there, they traveled down Buffalo Bayou to where it met the San Jacinto River near Lynch's Ferry. On April 20 the Texans camped in a grove of live oak trees on high ground, with a wide field in front of them. The only way the Mexicans could attack them would be to cross the field.

Santa Anna and his forces arrived at the junction of the San Jacinto River and Buffalo Bayou that afternoon. They set up camp in a vulnerable spot. Santa Anna's forces were exposed to the Texas troops, who were partially hidden by the grove of trees. One of Santa Anna's officers, Colonel Pedro Delgado, was worried about the location.

TEXAS VOICES

"We had the enemy on our right, within a wood, at long musket range. Our front, although level, was exposed to the fire of the enemy, who could keep it up with impunity [without the risk of loss] from his sheltered position."

—Colonel Pedro Delgado, quoted in *Texian Iliad*, by Stephen L. Hardin

Santa Anna sent a small force to try to drive the Texans from their position, but the Texans drove it back. In response, a small group of mounted Texans attacked the Mexican cavalry but were forced to retreat. Neither side would give any ground. Then, on the morning of April 21, General Cos arrived on the field with 540 more Mexican troops.

The Texas army realized that defeating the more than 1,200 Mexican soldiers now in position would not be easy. Shortly before noon on April 21, Houston called a meeting his officers. After much debate, the group decided to attack that afternoon.

KEY DATE 1836
Texas wins its independence from Mexico.

Houston assembled his approximately 900 troops—including Juan Seguín and a small group of Tejanos—at about 3:00 P.M. The Texas soldiers moved from the woods onto the prairie, unseen by the Mexican forces. Many of the Mexican soldiers, having just built new defenses and not anticipating an attack, were sleeping. Houston ordered the advance. Many Mexican troops were awakened by bullets and battle cries of "Remember the Alamo!" and "Remember Goliad!" The **Battle of San Jacinto** lasted only about 18 minutes. Surprised by the afternoon attack, many Mexican soldiers fled or tried to surrender, but the Texas troops continued firing. When the shooting stopped, 630 Mexican soldiers had been killed. Only nine Texas troops had died. Houston was among the wounded, with an ankle shattered by a rifle ball.

Sam Houston was considered a hero after the Battle of San Jacinto.

Santa Anna had disappeared during the battle. He was found the next day hiding in the marsh and taken prisoner. When the captured Santa Anna wrote his second-in-command to withdraw, the bulk of the Mexican army stopped fighting. The Texas army won not only the Battle of San Jacinto but also the war. Houston refused to let the soldiers kill the defeated Mexican general. He later explained his reasons.

TEXAS VOICES

"My motive in sparing the life of Santa Anna was to relieve the country of all hostile enemies without further bloodshed, and to secure his acknowledgment of our independence."

—Sam Houston, from an address to the citizens of Texas

The victory at San Jacinto in 1836 marked the end of the Texas Revolution. With this victory, Texas had won its independence from Mexico. The Republic of Texas was born.

Reading Check **Identifying Cause and Effect** What was the outcome of the Battle of San Jacinto?

Section 5 Review

hmhsocialstudies.com
ONLINE QUIZ

1. Identify and explain the significance of each of the following in Texas history:

- Runaway Scrape
- Battle of Refugio
- James Fannin
- Battle of Coleto
- Goliad Massacre
- Francita Alavez
- Battle of San Jacinto

2. Locate on a map:

- San Jacinto River

3. Summarizing Copy the graphic organizer below. Use it to explain the significant events in 1836 after the fall of the Alamo that led to Texas independence.

The Fall of the Alamo
Texas Independence

4. Finding the Main Idea

a. What led to the Runaway Scrape?

b. How did geographic features help the Texans win the Battle of San Jacinto?

c. In what year did Texas win independence from Mexico?

5. Writing and Critical Thinking myWriteSmart

Identifying Points of View Write a short news report explaining the Runaway Scrape and Sam Houston's leadership and how these issues affected the Battle of San Jacinto.

Consider the following:

- Houston's retreat and training of troops
- Houston's decision to attack on the afternoon of April 21

The Chapter at a Glance

Examine the following visual summary of the chapter. With a partner, take turns retelling the events of the Texas Revolution in the order in which they happened.

Identifying People and Ideas

Write a sentence to explain the role or significance of each of the following terms or people.

1. Consultation
2. Sam Houston
3. James Fannin
4. William B. Travis
5. Susanna Dickinson
6. Convention of 1836
7. Lorenzo de Zavala
8. George C. Childress
9. Goliad Massacre
10. Battle of San Jacinto

Understanding Main Ideas

Section 1

1. What events signified that Texans were rebelling against Mexico?

Section 2

2. What was the Consultation?

Section 3

3. Describe the fall of the Alamo.

Section 4

4. How did the ideas of the U.S. Constitution and Bill of Rights influence the Constitution of 1836?

Section 5

5. What was Sam Houston's strategy after the fall of the Alamo, and how successful was it?

You Be the Historian

Reviewing Themes

1. **Constitutional Heritage** Why did Texans write a constitution in 1836?
2. **Citizenship** How did Tejanos and other Texans participate in the revolution?
3. **Geography** How did the geography of Texas contribute to the outcome of several battles?

Thinking Critically

1. **Comparing** Examine both the Texans' victories and their defeats. What are some of the common elements of the victories? What are some of the common elements of the defeats?
2. **Summarizing** Why was the year 1836 significant to Texas?
3. **Supporting a Point of View** Do you think the siege of the Alamo was a tragedy or an important rallying point for Texans? Explain your answer.

Texas Test Practice

Interpreting Maps

Study the map below. Then answer the following questions.

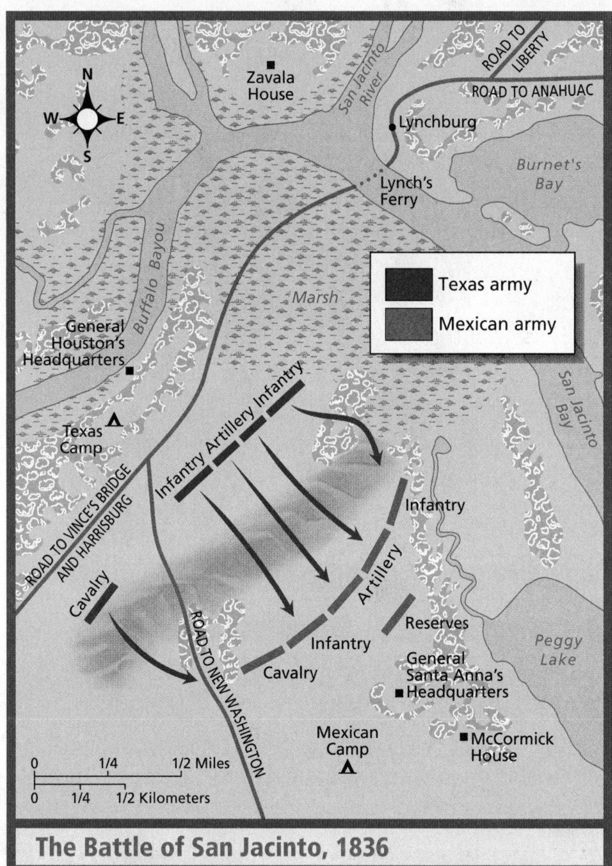

The Battle of San Jacinto, 1836

1. Which of the following statements best describes the location of the Texas forces?

- **A** near Peggy Lake
- **B** on Lorenzo de Zavala's property
- **C** in Lynchburg
- **D** near the Buffalo Bayou

2. Based on this map, how do you think geography affected the Battle of San Jacinto?

Analyzing Primary Sources

Read the following quote by Sam Houston. Then answer the questions.

"War is raging on the frontiers. Bejar [San Antonio] is besieged by two thousand of the enemy. . . . By the last report, our force in Bejar was only one hundred and fifty men strong. The citizens of Texas must rally to the aid of our army, or it will perish. . . . *Independence is declared,* it must be maintained. Immediate action, united with valor [bravery], alone can achieve the great work."

3. Which of the following statements best summarizes how Houston inspired Texans to fight?

- **F** Texans will be ashamed of themselves.
- **G** The Alamo must be avenged.
- **H** The enemy will destroy Texans if Texans do not defend themselves.
- **J** The enemy has reinforcements.

4. What events in Texas influenced Houston's comments and point of view? Give specific examples.

Cooperative Learning

Work with a small group to complete the following activity. Each person in your group should select one of the following participants in the Texas Revolution: (a) Sam Houston, (b) Antonio López de Santa Anna, (c) James Fannin, (d) William B. Travis, (e) Lorenzo de Zavala, (f) George C. Childress (g) Juan Seguín. Have each member create a biography for a news report on the important roles played by significant individuals in the Texas Revolution. Present your news report to the class.

Internet Activity 

Access the Internet to locate primary and secondary sources on the Battle of the Alamo. As you read your sources, identify any biases and the points of view of the authors of the sources. Then use what you have learned to write a short essay examining how geographic factors, transportation, communications, and other human factors affected the events. Illustrate your essay with a time line showing the events of the Alamo and events that were taking place elsewhere in Texas at the same time. Be sure to use proper grammar, spelling, and sentence structure and to cite all your sources.

CHAPTER 12

A New Nation
(1836–1845)

Texas Essential Knowledge and Skills (TEKS) 1A, 1B, 3C, 4A, 4B, 8A, 9A, 9C, 17C, 18A, 21A, 21B, 21C, 21E, 21F, 22A, 22B, 22C, 22D

Sam Houston was considered a hero after the Texas Revolution.

TEXAS

1836 Sam Houston becomes the first popularly elected president of the Republic of Texas.

1837 The Texas government begins work in Houston, the new capital.

1838 Texans elect Mirabeau B. Lamar president.

1839 Texas passes a homestead law, protecting settlers' homes from being seized to pay debts.

1840 Austin, the new capital, has 850 residents.

1836 · 1837 · 1838 · 1839 · 1840

U.S. and WORLD

1837 A financial panic leads to a depression in the United States.

1838 U.S. troops begin removing the Cherokees from Georgia to Indian Territory.

1839 The photographic process known as the daguerreotype is introduced at the Paris Academy of Sciences.

Build on What You Know

In the fall of 1835, increasing conflict between Texans and the Mexican government erupted in the Texas Revolution. With the crushing victory at the Battle of San Jacinto in April 1836, Texas won the war and became an independent nation. However, the new Republic of Texas faced many challenges.

If you were there . . .
Whom would you choose to lead Texas?

Mirabeau B. Lamar disagreed with many of Sam Houston's policies.

Edwin Waller laid out the streets and oversaw the construction of the first government buildings in the new capital of Austin.

1841
Texans again elect Sam Houston president of the Republic.

1843
The Tehuacana Creek Councils lead to peace between Texans and several Texas Indian groups.

1844
President Sam Houston sends troops into East Texas to end the Regulator-Moderator War.

1841 — 1842 — 1843 — 1844 — 1845

1841
Punch, a periodical famous for its political humor, begins publication in London, England.

1845
The U.S. Congress moves the presidential election day to the first week in November.

You Be the Historian

myNotebook

What's Your Opinion? Do you **agree** or **disagree** with the following statements? Support your point of view in your notebook.

- **Citizenship** Citizens express their points of view through voting.
- **Economics** A nation's economy is affected by events in bordering nations.
- **Government** Individuals can have a strong influence on the development of a nation.

Section 1

The Early Republic

Main Ideas

1. Under the Treaties of Velasco, Mexico would recognize Texas independence, but the treaties were not honored.
2. Texas held its first national elections in 1836.

Key Terms and People

- **Treaties of Velasco**
- **annexation**
- **Mirabeau B. Lamar**

Why It Matters Today

Because Texas was a democratic republic, its citizens elected their leaders. Use current events sources to learn about elections in other countries around the world today.

TEKS: 1A, 3C, 4A, 8A, 9C, 21B, 21C, 21E, 22D

myNotebook

Use the annotation tools in your eBook to take notes on events in the early Texas Republic.

The Story Continues

Several Texans were camped near Buffalo Bayou after fleeing their homes during the Runaway Scrape. Suddenly, a woman on the edge of the group began pointing and shouting, "Hallelujah! Hallelujah!" A man on horseback was racing toward them and yelling. "San Jacinto! The Mexicans are whipped and Santa Anna a prisoner!" Everyone laughed, hugged, and cried from happiness at the victory.

The Treaties of Velasco

With the victory at San Jacinto, Texas had become a free republic. The Republic of Texas would last 10 years, from 1836 to 1846. In 1836, some issues from the Revolution remained. Some 2,000 Mexican troops under General Vicente Filisola remained in Texas. Texans also needed to decide what to do with Mexican general and president Antonio López de Santa Anna, whom they had captured at San Jacinto. In exchange for his life, Santa Anna agreed to order the Mexican troops to leave Texas.

The Texans brought Santa Anna to Velasco, the temporary capital of Texas. On May 14, 1836, Santa Anna and Texas ad interim president David G. Burnet signed two **Treaties of Velasco**. The first treaty, which was made public, included the following terms.

1. The war between Mexico and Texas was officially ended, and Texas was independent.
2. Santa Anna would not take up arms against Texas.

3. All Mexican forces would withdraw beyond the Rio Grande.
4. Prisoners would be returned to their homes.
5. The Mexicans would return all captured property.
6. Texas leaders would promptly return Santa Anna to Mexico.

The second treaty was kept secret. It provided that, in exchange for Santa Anna's immediate release, he would try to persuade Mexican leaders to recognize Texas independence. Santa Anna also agreed to promote the Rio Grande as Mexico's border with Texas.

With the treaty signed, General Filisola immediately began to remove his troops from Texas. However, the Texans did not follow through on their part of the treaty. The Texas army refused to return Santa Anna to Mexico, instead keeping him prisoner at Velasco. In fact, the Texas government chose to send Santa Anna to Washington, DC, rather than back to Mexico. The official purpose of the Washington trip was to negotiate a lasting peace between Texas and Mexico, but nothing came of it.

Likewise, the Mexican government refused to honor the terms of the treaty. Mexican leaders stated that Santa Anna, as a prisoner of war, was no longer their president and had no authority to sign a treaty. As a result, the Mexican government refused to ratify the treaties. Although Texas had won its freedom, Mexico refused to acknowledge the fact, and would continue to refuse for many years.

Reading Check **Analyzing Information** Why did the Treaties of Velasco have little effect?

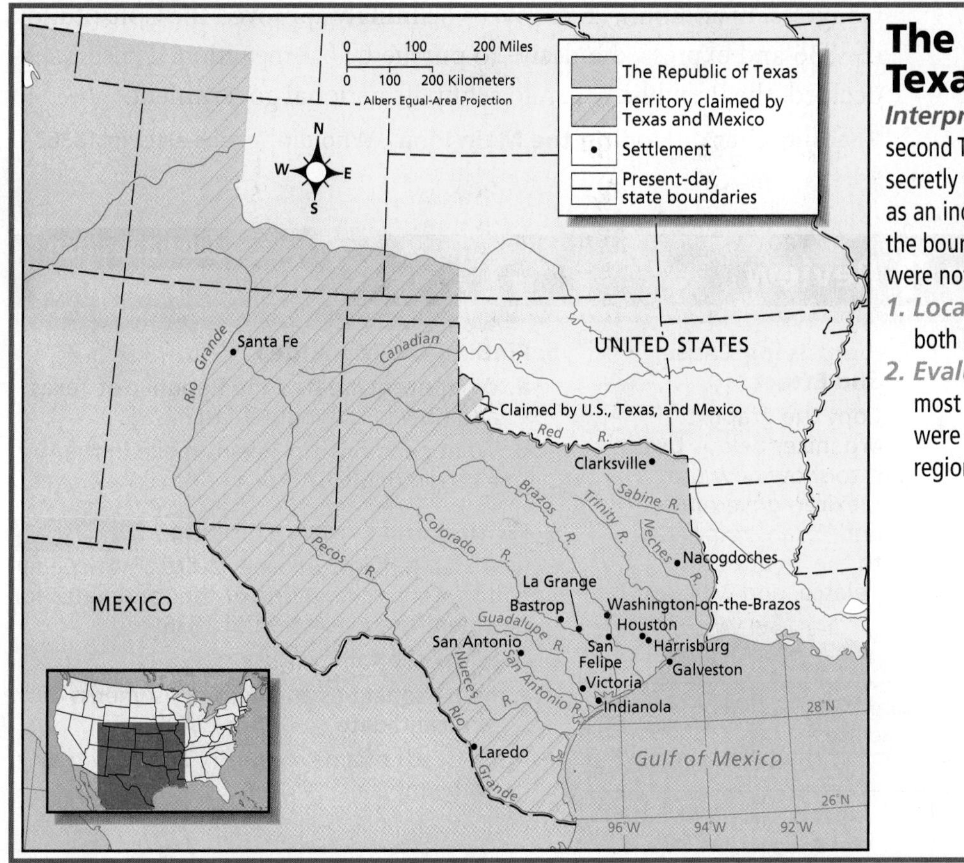

The Republic of Texas, 1836

Interpreting Maps In the second Treaty of Velasco, Santa Anna secretly pledged to recognize Texas as an independent nation. However, the boundaries of the new nation were not firmly established.

1. ***Locate*** What Texas regions did both Mexico and Texas claim?
2. ***Evaluating*** Why do you think most of the Texas settlements were located in the eastern region of Texas?

The Lone Star Flag

The first official Texas flag was adopted by the Texas Congress on December 10, 1836. It had a blue background with a gold star in the center. It was replaced by the red, white, and blue Lone Star flag in 1839. The designer of the 1839 flag is unknown. Since then, changes have been made to the specifications for the flag, but the symbol of the state of Texas has remained essentially unchanged since 1839. **How did the appearance of the Lone Star flag change during the 1830s?**

The Election of 1836

A second major challenge facing the Republic of Texas was to form a new government. The Constitution of 1836 required that elections be held to select new leaders. At the same time, Texans would decide whether to approve the Constitution of 1836 and whether to pursue **annexation** of Texas to the United States. Annexation is the formal joining of one political region to another. Burnet wrote in a letter that the election would probably "be conducted with a good deal of spirit."

Three well-known Texans ran for president—Stephen F. Austin, Sam Houston, and Henry Smith. Of the three candidates, Houston was the most popular. After all, "Old Sam Jacinto," as he became known, had led Texans to victory. Many Texans shared the view of this supporter.

TEXAS VOICES

"No person ever met Sam Houston in the early days of the Republic without being impressed with his greatness. He was then about forty-two years of age, just the prime of life. Standing largely over six feet in height, with a massive, well formed hand, . . . a large head, a piercing gray eye, [and] a mouth and nose indicating character of fine proportions."

—Francis R. Lubbock, quoted in *A Political History of the Texas Republic, 1836–1845,* by Stanley Siegel

Houston won the presidency by a large majority. For vice president, voters elected **Mirabeau B. Lamar**, another hero of San Jacinto. Texans also elected 30 representatives and 14 senators to the Republic's new Congress. In addition, voters overwhelmingly approved the Constitution of 1836 and expressed a desire to pursue U.S. annexation. These issues decided, the Republic began to set up its national government.

Reading Check **Finding the Main Idea** Who did Texans elect in 1836?

Section 1 Review

hmhsocialstudies.com
ONLINE QUIZ

1. **Define and explain:**
   - annexation
2. **Identify and explain** the significance of each of the following in Texas history:
   - Treaties of Velasco
   - Mirabeau B. Lamar
3. **Locate on a Texas map:**
   - Rio Grande
4. **Identifying Cause and Effect** Copy the graphic organizer below. Use it to show how the Mexican government and Texans responded to the Treaties of Velasco, and why.

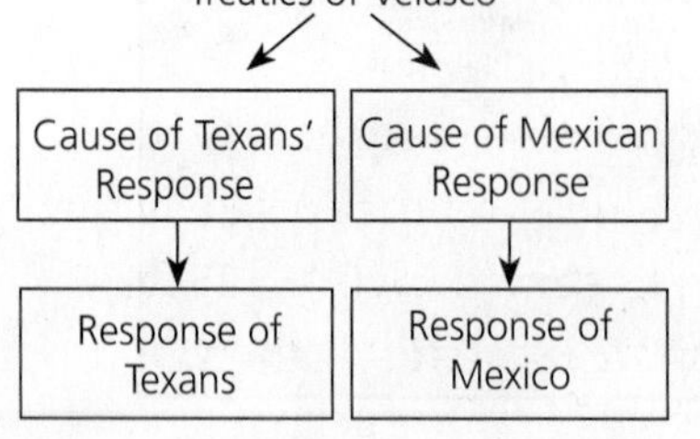

5. **Finding the Main Idea**
   a. What event created the Republic of Texas, and how long would it last?
   b. What decisions did Texans make in the election of 1836?
6. **Writing and Critical Thinking** myWriteSmart
   Identifying Points of View Write a newspaper editorial supporting one of the candidates for president in the election of 1836.
   Consider the following:
   - the personalities and accomplishments of each candidate
   - the needs of a new country and how they can be met

Section 2

Houston's First Term

Main Ideas

1. As president, Sam Houston created a cabinet to help him resolve issues facing the Republic.
2. Problems with military discipline, debt, and public land faced the first Houston administration.
3. President Houston wanted to protect the rights of American Indians in Texas.

Key Terms and People

- **cabinet**
- **Texas Rangers**
- **Texas Navy**
- **expenditures**
- **revenue**
- **ratify**
- **Chief Bowles**

Why It Matters Today

Economic problems were among the many challenges facing the Republic of Texas. Use current events sources to learn about current economic problems in Texas or the United States.

TEKS: 4A, 4B, 9A, 9C, 17C, 18A, 21A, 21B, 21D, 21E, 22D

myNotebook

Use the annotation tools in your eBook to take notes on the events of Houston's first term in office.

The Story Continues

On October 22, 1836, Sam Houston stood before the leading citizens of Texas. His sword from the Battle of San Jacinto hung at his side. The audience grew quiet as he prepared to take the oath of office. Houston spoke briefly of his plans for Texas. Then he paused, removed his sword, and grasped it in both hands. In an emotional voice, he declared that the sword was a symbol of his past position. "I have worn it . . . in defense of my country," he said. Now Houston faced new challenges as president of the Republic.

Houston's Administration

Sam Houston became the first popularly elected president of the Republic of Texas on October 22, 1836. Addressing the new Texas Congress, Houston laid out his goals for his term in office. He stressed the need for peace with American Indians and the need to stay alert and guard against an attack by Mexico. He also expressed his hope of seeing Texas annexed to the United States.

To address the challenge he faced, Houston needed the help of trusted advisers. He appointed these advisers to his **cabinet**. Many prominent veterans of the Revolution served in Houston's cabinet. Henry Smith was secretary of the treasury, and Thomas Rusk was secretary of war.

LINKING
Past to Present

The Size of the Texas Government

The Texas government has grown tremendously since the days of the Republic. Today's government includes some 250 agencies, boards, and commissions. State employees number in the hundreds of thousands. Paying for this enormous government cost more than $43 billion in 2013. In contrast, the Republic of Texas government needed only about $130,000 to operate in 1845. This amount would equal about $2.1 million today. **Why do you think state government costs so much more today?**

Stephen F. Austin was named secretary of state. However, Austin served the Republic for only a few months. As a result of overwork and exposure to cold, he developed pneumonia and died on December 27, 1836. Texans mourned the loss of the leader who had dedicated his life to Texas. President Houston issued a statement expressing the nation's loss. "The father of Texas is no more. The first pioneer of the wilderness has departed." He ordered a 30-day period of mourning to honor Austin.

With a cabinet in place, Houston and his government turned their attention to creating a court system. James Collinsworth was appointed chief justice of the Republic's Supreme Court. Below the Supreme Court were four district courts, 23 county courts, and justice courts.

Reading Check **Drawing Inferences and Conclusions** Why do you think Houston named veterans of the Revolution to his cabinet?

★ Defining Texas

When Houston took office, the Republic of Texas did not have clear boundaries. Although the Congress claimed the Rio Grande as the republic's border with Mexico, the Mexican government did not recognize this claim, and many Texans did not either. Some people south and west of the Nueces River still considered their land part of Mexico.

The republic also had no permanent capital. Velasco had been the capital at the end of the revolution, but the government had moved to Columbia after the war ended. Officials found the town too small, and in 1837, Congress named the tiny town of Houston the new Texas capital. As a result, the town grew rapidly. In January 1837 it had 12 residents and one log cabin, but within four months, some 1,500 people lived there.

As he had promised, Houston attempted to bring Texas into the United States. The U.S. government, however, was not interested in annexing Texas. It was, though, willing to recognize Texas as an independent nation in 1837.

Reading Check **Finding the Main Idea** What town became the capital of Texas during Houston's administration?

★ Houston and Army Unrest

While the Houston administration was dealing with defining Texas, a new challenge arose within the army. Volunteers from the United States had flocked to Texas, eager to take part in the Texas Revolution. Many had arrived too late to take part, but they were still eager for action. Brawls were common among the unruly troops.

Although the war had ended, some Texans in the army harbored strong feelings against Mexico. Among them was army commander Felix Huston, who wanted to invade Mexico. President Houston considered

Texas Rangers

Formed in 1835, the Texas Rangers were dedicated to protecting the people of Texas. The first Rangers rode horses and used new pistols called revolvers. Over time, the Rangers have adapted to new duties and new technologies. Today the Rangers serve as a force of special law officers charged with keeping the peace. They use modern weapons and drive vehicles with high-tech equipment. Women have served as Texas Rangers since 1993. This photograph shows a group of Rangers from around 1900, along with the wife of one Ranger. **How has the technology used by the Texas Rangers changed since their early days?**

such a move risky. He decided to replace Huston with a calmer commander, Albert Sidney Johnston. However, this decision angered Huston, who injured Johnston in a duel. With Johnston unable to take command, unrest in the army grew. One commander urged soldiers to march on the capital. He wanted the army to "chastise the President, kick Congress out of doors, and give laws to Texas." To regain control, Houston placed all but 600 troops on leave and never recalled them.

For defense and frontier protection, Houston turned to militia companies and the **Texas Rangers**. The Rangers were a defense force that tried to keep the peace along the frontier. Formed on November 24, 1835, the Texas Rangers had to be ready to ride at all times. Although Houston's actions solved some problems, conflicts with the army continued to trouble the Republic for many years.

The **Texas Navy**, which had gone into action in January 1836, also proved difficult for Houston, whose administration was unable to pay repair expenses. One ship, the *Liberty*, was seized in New Orleans and two others were almost confiscated in New York. After raiding along the Mexican coast, the *Independence* was captured by the Mexican navy on its way back to Texas from New Orleans. Defying Houston's orders to remain close to home, the *Brutus* and the *Invincible* also raided Mexican towns and took Mexican ships captive in summer 1837. The *Invincible* was forced aground by two Mexican navy ships and destroyed, and the *Brutus* was lost in a storm.

Reading Check **Finding the Main Idea** What action did Houston take to solve growing unrest in the army? What role did the Texas Rangers play?

BIOGRAPHY

Sam Houston (1793–1863) When Sam Houston first rode into Texas in 1832, he was already a well-known hero in the United States. Although he was born in Virginia, his family had moved to Tennessee in 1807. Two years later he left home to live with the Cherokees. In 1813 he joined the U.S. Army, fighting under General Andrew Jackson. His experience with the Cherokees earned him a position as an Indian agent for the U.S. government. With the support of Jackson, Houston entered politics. He represented Tennessee in the U.S. Congress and served as its governor. After again living with the Cherokees, Houston moved to Texas in December 1832. Houston served his fellow Texans—first in the military and then in politics—for some 25 years. **What experiences helped Houston become a leader in Texas?**

★ Economic Policies

In addition to these military issues, the new nation also faced economic problems. The Republic's **expenditures**, or spending, far exceeded its **revenue**, or income. When Sam Houston took office, Texas had a national debt of $1.25 million. The new government tried to pay off that debt by collecting taxes, including customs duties on imports. The Republic also sold some public lands and tried to get loans in the United States. However, the debt continued to rise as expenses increased.

To make matters worse, the United States experienced a financial crisis in 1837. The Panic of 1837 led to an economic depression. Texas, which traded heavily with the United States, soon felt the effects. Business slowed, and goods became scarce.

The Republic's limited money supply posed another economic problem. Texans manufactured few goods and therefore had to import many items. This meant that money flowed out of the Republic, but little came in. The government printed more paper notes, but it had no gold or silver to back them. People did not trust money that could not be traded for gold and silver, and so the value of the Republic's money dropped.

Reading Check **Analyzing Information** How did economic problems in the United States affect Texas?

★ Land Policy under Houston

Although the Republic had little money, it was rich in land. More than 200 million acres of public land was available to people who wanted to move onto it. The guidelines for acquiring public land were laid out in the Constitution of 1836. Heads of families living in Texas on March 2, 1836—excluding African Americans and American Indians—were given 4,606 acres at no charge. Single men aged 17 and over received 1,476 acres. Texans who had fought in the Revolution got bonus land as well. People who arrived after 1836 could also receive land, although they did not get as much as earlier settlers did. In all, the Republic distributed nearly 37 million acres of land under this land policy.

Texas officials hoped their generous land policies would help Texas recover from the devastation of the Revolution. Once land was transferred to private hands, it could be taxed to bring in revenue. To further help the economy, the government also hoped to bring more people to Texas. It tried to encourage immigration by establishing a new colonization policy in the early 1840s. Based on the Mexican *empresario* system, this policy gave agents contracts to settle immigrants in Texas. The Republic distributed another 4.5 million acres under this system.

Reading Check **Making Generalizations and Predictions** How do you think the Republic's land policy affected immigration to Texas?

Interpreting Visuals

Texas Indians. *Houston believed that American Indians and Texas settlers could live together in peace.* ***Based on this engraving, how do you think Indians' lives differed from those of settlers in Texas?***

Houston's American Indian Policy

Some of the land distributed under the Republic's land policy was already inhabited by American Indians. As Texans moved into Indian land, conflicts arose. Before long, Texans were calling on the government to remove all Indians from Texas—by force if necessary. President Houston opposed such action and supported a peaceful solution. He wanted to avoid a full-scale Indian war, which the Republic could not afford.

Houston sympathized with Indians' desire to control their land. During the Texas Revolution, he had negotiated a treaty guaranteeing the Cherokees land in East Texas. The Texas Senate refused to **ratify**, or approve, the treaty, however.

After the war, some of the Cherokees who lived north of Nacogdoches were angry that they had not received the promised titles to their land. Houston urged the Cherokees to be patient. He told them that he would do everything in his power to help them hold on to their land. Houston wrote to **Chief Bowles**, a Cherokee leader and friend. "Do not be disturbed by the troubles which are around you, but be at peace." Houston then set aside land for the Cherokees in an attempt to keep peace. This action angered Texas settlers who wanted the land for themselves. Houston's efforts at peace seemed likely to fail.

Chief Bowles agreed to help Texas officials establish peace with Plains Indians to the west, where fighting had increased. In May 1836, before Houston took office, Comanche and Kiowa forces had attacked Fort Parker, near Groesbeck. The raiders killed most of the fort's 34 residents and took five captives, including a young girl named Cynthia Parker. As Texas moved west, conflict with the Plains Indians increased.

That's Interesting!

Houston: The Raven

As a young man, Sam Houston went to live with the Cherokees. Chief Oolooteka adopted him and gave him the name Colonneh, meaning "the Raven." Later, Houston married Diana Rogers Gentry and became a citizen of the Cherokee nation. Houston admired many American Indian customs. He also enjoyed wearing Cherokee clothing, even after he moved to Texas.

BIOGRAPHY

Chief Bowles

(c. 1756–1839) Chief Bowles, whose Cherokee name was Duwali, was born in North Carolina. As U.S. settlement expanded in the South, he and his village were forced to move. In 1819 they settled in Texas. There, he served on a Cherokee decision-making council and later formed a strong friendship with Sam Houston. **Why do you think Chief Bowles chose to go to Texas?**

To reduce conflict and protect Texans on the plains, Houston and the Congress developed an American Indian policy. It established a line of forts along the frontier and encouraged trade with Indians. Houston hoped the policy would promote peace and friendship with Texas Indians. While Texas Rangers patrolled the frontier, Houston tried to negotiate and sign treaties with Texas Indians.

TEXAS VOICES

> **"Treaties of peace and amity [goodwill], and the maintenance of good faith with the Indians, present themselves to my mind as the most rational grounds on which to obtain their friendship. Let us abstain on our part from aggressions, establish commerce with the different tribes, supply their useful and necessary wants, maintain even-handed justice with them, and natural reason will teach them the utility of our friendship."**
>
> —Sam Houston, quoted in *Documents of Texas History,* edited by Ernest Wallace

Houston's goal was to make peace with each American Indian group in Texas. He was one of the few Texas leaders who believed that Indians and settlers could live together in peace. Most Texans in the Republic disagreed, preferring to remove American Indians from Texas. Some Texans thought Houston's policy was slowing westward development. Ongoing conflict between American Indians and Texas settlers over land made it difficult to maintain peaceful relations.

Reading Check **Identifying Points of View** Why did some Texans oppose President Houston's American Indian policy?

Section 2 Review

hmhsocialstudies.com
ONLINE QUIZ

1. Define and explain:
- cabinet
- Texas Rangers
- expenditures
- revenue
- ratify

2. Identify and explain the significance of each of the following:
- Texas Navy
- Chief Bowles

3. Locate on a map:
- Houston

4. Analyzing Information
Copy the graphic organizer below. Use it to show how Sam Houston's administration tried to solve the Republic's problems.

Problem	Solution/Action
Unruly army	
Debt	
Need for more people	
Conflict with American Indians	

5. Finding the Main Idea

a. What were two early actions of the Republic's Congress?

b. What economic policies did the Republic establish, and how successful were they?

6. Writing and Critical Thinking *my*WriteSmart

Evaluating Imagine that you are a member of Sam Houston's cabinet. Write a short evaluation of Houston's American Indian policy explaining why you support it. Consider the following:
- the cost of a full-scale war against American Indians
- recent conflicts with American Indians

Section 3 Lamar's Presidency

Main Ideas

1. As president, Mirabeau Lamar tried to create a public education system in Texas.
2. Lamar's administration faced great financial challenges.
3. Under Lamar, Texas adopted a harsh policy toward American Indians.

Why It Matters Today

Mirabeau B. Lamar faced many challenges during his presidency. Use current events sources to learn about the problems facing a political leader in the United States today.

Key Terms and People

- **charter**
- **Edwin Waller**
- **capitol**
- **homestead law**
- **redbacks**
- **Battle of the Neches**
- **Council House Fight**
- **Battle of Plum Creek**

TEKS: 4A, 8A, 9A, 9C, 21A, 21B, 21C, 22D

myNotebook

Use the annotation tools in your eBook to take notes on the issues and events of Lamar's presidency.

The Story Continues

Early one August morning, a few people in Linnville noticed a huge cloud of dust on the horizon. As the dust cloud neared, the residents realized that it was a Comanche raiding party. Some 1,000 Comanches swept down on the town. They captured and killed residents and stole horses. As they left, the Comanches burned the town. The raid was an angry response to a massacre that had occurred earlier at a peace conference.

Lamar in Office

Sam Houston was no longer president when the Comanche raid on Linnville occurred. In September 1838, Texans had elected new leaders. Houston could not run for re-election because, under the Republic's constitution, a president could not serve consecutive terms, or two terms in a row. But even if Houston could have run, he might not have been re-elected. Many Texans disliked his policies, particularly his American Indian policy.

Texans elected Mirabeau B. Lamar as their new president and David G. Burnet as vice president. Both men strongly disagreed with Houston's policies and personally disliked him. A hero of the Revolution, Lamar was also a poet and fiercely devoted to education.

BIOGRAPHY

Mirabeau B. Lamar

(1798–1859) A native of Georgia, Mirabeau B. Lamar came to Texas in 1835 to join the fight for Texas independence. After the war, Lamar served as vice president and then as president of the Republic. Lamar pursued an aggressive Indian policy and opposed annexation to the United States. He also faced many challenges, including a growing public debt and ongoing conflicts with Mexico. By the end of his presidency, Lamar had lost much popular support. He retired from politics and focused on his love of writing poetry. In 1857 Lamar re-entered the political world, becoming U.S. minister to Nicaragua and Costa Rica. He died in 1859, two months after his assignment ended.

What political positions did Lamar hold in the Republic?

On taking office in 1839, then, he stressed the need for a public education system. He stated that a "cultivated mind is the guardian genius of Democracy." Following Lamar's lead, the Congress passed education acts in 1839 and 1840. These acts granted each county 17,712 acres of land to support public schools. The government also set aside 231,400 acres for the future establishment of two public universities.

The first college in the Republic to receive a **charter**—a document granting permission to operate—was Rutersville College. This private college opened in 1840 in Rutersville, near La Grange. However, the Republic never actually established either a public school system or public universities, largely due to financial issues. Nonetheless, because of his efforts, Lamar is known today as the Father of Texas Education.

Reading Check **Finding the Main Idea** How did Lamar's administration try to promote public education?

★ A New Capital

During Lamar's administration, the government also selected a permanent capital for Texas. President Lamar and many members of the Congress were unhappy with Houston as the capital. Lamar thought Houston was too far east. He wanted to move the political center of Texas west, closer to the edge of Texas settlement. Lamar believed this move would strengthen the Republic's control of the region and perhaps allow the republic to expand westward.

In 1839 the Congress appointed a group to choose a site for a new capital. The group selected a site next to a village named Waterloo, located on the Colorado River. The town was renamed Austin in honor of Stephen F. Austin. Judge **Edwin Waller** arrived in Austin to lay out the streets and begin building government offices. A temporary **capitol**, or a building in which government officials meet, was soon completed. Homes and other government buildings were constructed, and businesses opened along the town's main street, Congress Avenue.

Not everyone was pleased with the new capital, however. Many Texans, including Sam Houston, claimed Austin was isolated and too far west. They feared it would be vulnerable to Mexican attack because of its location. Austin was also in Comanche territory and would therefore be exposed to Plains Indian raids. One such criticism appeared in a Houston newspaper on April 17, 1839.

Analyzing Primary Sources
Identifying Bias Why else might the writer be critical of Austin becoming the Texas capital?

TEXAS VOICES

"The location has been made at Waterloo, an inconsiderable hamlet [village]. . . . The country around this point is represented to be exceedingly fertile and beautiful, and the climate remarkably healthy. It is, however, almost entirely uninhabited, and . . . more exposed than any other point on the frontier."

—Telegraph and Texas Register.

Life in frontier Austin was difficult and dangerous. However, as more people moved to Austin, the town began to prosper. By 1840 more than 850 people lived there, including diplomats from France, Great Britain, and the United States. Eventually, most Texans became satisfied with their new capital.

Reading Check **Identifying Points of View** Why were some Texans unhappy with Austin's location?

★ Land and Economic Policies

The Lamar administration continued the land policy established by Houston. In January 1839 the Congress passed a **homestead law** that protected a family's home and up to 50 acres of land from seizure for debts. In most cases, this prevented creditors from taking a Texan's home and selling it to pay for a debt.

This protection became important, because the Republic's financial problems worsened under Lamar's administration. Public debt increased due to government spending. Military spending, for example, nearly doubled from the previous year. Part of this money went to re-outfit the Texas Navy with new ships. Public income, however did not rise.

Even as the Republic's debt grew, the value of Texas currency continued to fall. In response, the Republic issued new paper money certificates, so-called **redbacks**. The value of these redbacks dropped quickly—they were basically worthless within three years of their printing. The Republic's financial woes continued.

Reading Check **Summarizing** What were some of the Republic's financial problems during Lamar's administration?

Interpreting Visuals

Austin. *The first capitol in Austin was a rough two-room cabin. It was replaced in 1851 with the limestone building shown here.* ***Why might Texans have wanted to replace the capitol?***

Indian Battles in Texas, 1836–1845

Interpreting Maps During Lamar's presidency, conflicts between Texas troops and American Indians erupted throughout the Republic.

1. ***Locate*** Where did the conflicts between Texas Indians and soldiers take place?
2. ***Drawing Inferences and Conclusions*** How do you think these conflicts affected settlement in the different regions of Texas?

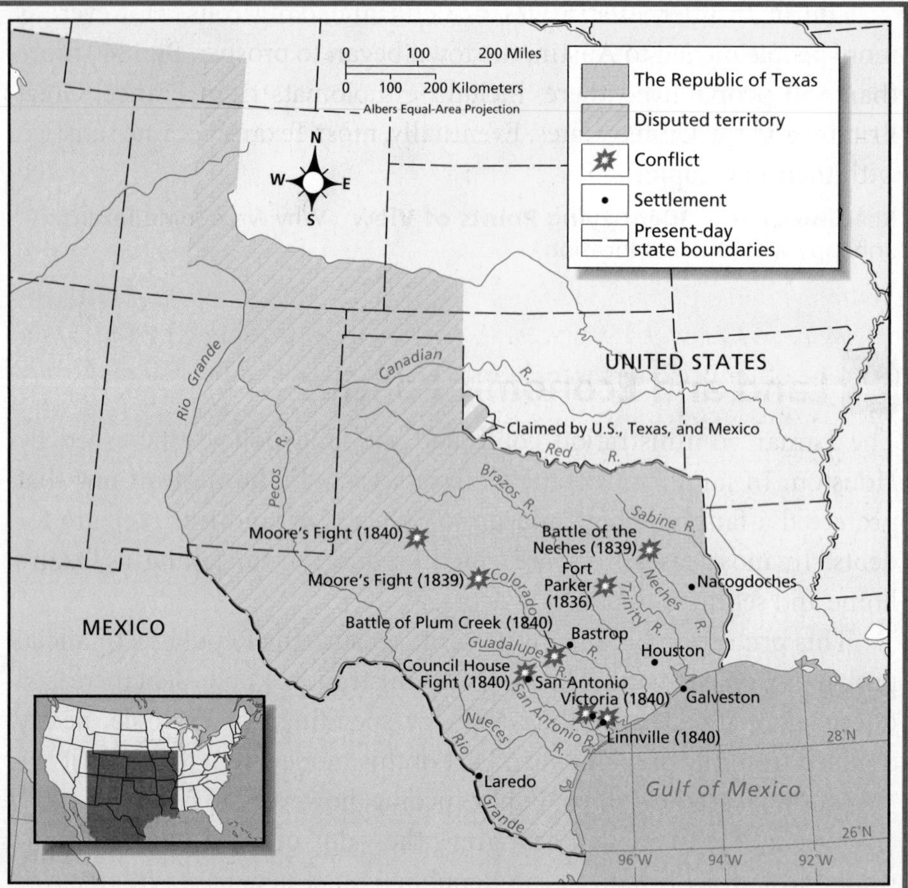

Lamar's American Indian Policy

Part of the rise in military spending under Lamar stemmed from his Indian policy. Lamar disliked Indians and wanted to remove them from Texas. Unlike Houston, he did not believe Indians had a right to their land. In his inaugural address, Lamar outlined his Indian policy.

Analyzing Primary Sources
Making Generalizations and Predictions What is Lamar's view of American Indians, and how do you think this will affect the Republic's Indian policy?

TEXAS VOICES

"The white man and the [American Indian] cannot dwell in harmony together. Nature forbids it. . . . I experience no difficulty in deciding on the proper policy to be pursued towards them. It is to push a rigorous war against them; pursuing them to their hiding places without mitigation [relief] or compassion, until they shall be made to feel that flight from our borders without hope of return, is preferable to the scourges of war."

—Mirabeau B. Lamar, quoted in *Lone Star,* by T. R. Fehrenbach

In 1839 Lamar ordered the Cherokees to leave Texas. When they refused, Lamar sent some 500 soldiers led by Kelsey Douglass to force them to go. In July fighting broke out near the Neches River. After several days of fighting in this **Battle of the Neches**, more than 100 Cherokees lay dead, including Chief Bowles. Texas forces then pursued most of the surviving Cherokees north into Indian Territory in the United States. Some other American Indians, including the Caddos and Shawnees, also left northeastern Texas during this time.

Conflict between Texans and the Comanches also worsened during this time. In January 1839 Lamar sent Colonel John H. Moore to attack the Comanches west of Texas settlements. These attacks, coupled with attacks by the Apaches and other enemies, led one group of Comanches, the Penatekas, to seek peace with Texas. They agreed to meet with Texans in San Antonio and to return any Texans they had taken captive.

On March 19, 1840, about 65 Penateka Comanches arrived at the Council House in San Antonio. The Texans there were expecting to receive many returned captives. However, the Penatekas brought only a few. The other prisoners were being held by other bands of Comanches. The Texans, not understanding Indian society, tried to take the Penatekas hostage in exchange for the other captives. Fighting between the two groups broke out in and around the Council House. By the end, of the battle 35 Comanches lay dead, including 12 chiefs, 3 women, and 2 children. At least seven Texans also died. This **Council House Fight** probably destroyed any chance of peace.

When other Comanches heard about the massacre, they were outraged. First, they put their Texan captives to death. Then a large Comanche raiding party struck the settlements of Linnville and Victoria, killing more than 20 settlers, burning houses, and stealing livestock.

Texans called for revenge against the Comanche raiders. A force of volunteers, regular soldiers, and Texas Rangers set out for battle. This force found the Comanche on August 11, 1840, and attacked. During the **Battle of Plum Creek,** more than 130 Comanches were killed. One Texan was killed, and seven were wounded.

Reading Check **Identifying Cause and Effect** What was Lamar's policy toward American Indians, and what did he hope to achieve with it?

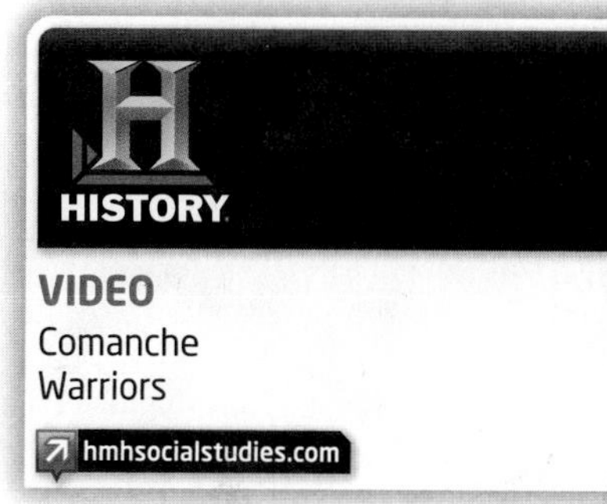

VIDEO
Comanche Warriors
hmhsocialstudies.com

HISTORIC DOCUMENT

Report on the Council House Fight

Colonel Hugh McLeod was in San Antonio and was present at the Council House Fight. His report is one of the main sources of information about the event.

"The troops now being posted, the Chiefs and Captains were told that they were *our* prisoners, and would be kept as hostages for the safety of our people, then in their hands; and they might send their young men to the tribe, and as soon as our friends were restored, they should be liberated. . . . A rush was then made to the door. Captain Howard collared one of them and received a severe stab from him in the side. He ordered the sentinel to fire upon him, which he immediately did, and the Indian fell dead. They now all drew their knives and bows, and evidently resolved to fight to the last."

Analyzing Primary Sources

1. **Sequencing** What events led to the death of the American Indian described here?
2. **Drawing Inferences and Conclusions** Do you think McLeod's account is completely trustworthy? Why or why not?

Texas settlers established small farms across the frontier.

★ The Results of Lamar's Policies

Despite this victory, many Texans still feared the Comanches. As a result, Texas leaders decided to strike farther into the frontier area known as Comanche country. In October, Colonel Moore led a force northwest in search of Comanche camps. Along the Colorado River, nearly 300 miles upriver from Austin, he found a Comanche village. The Texas force caught the Comanches by surprise and destroyed the village. Some 130 Comanches died in the conflict. Following these defeats, the Comanches moved farther west and turned their attention to raiding Mexican settlements instead.

By the end of his term, President Lamar had achieved his goal of removing the Cherokees from East Texas. The Comanches had also been pushed farther north and west, opening up vast lands for settlement. Speculators and settlers were pleased with the prospect of more land and a safer frontier. However, Lamar's new policy proved a disaster for Texas Indians. American Indians in Texas had lost much of their land and had suffered terrible losses of life.

Some Texans were also concerned about the increased warfare and the expense that went with it. Lamar's American Indian policy had cost the Republic $2.5 million. It had also led to the loss of many lives. All told, Lamar's policies had increased an already soaring national debt. During his term, the debt rose from $3.3 million to more than $8 million. One Texan wrote in 1840 that times had become "terribly severe." Once again, Texans were ready for a change.

Reading Check **Finding the Main Idea** How was Lamar's Indian policy harmful to both American Indians and the Republic?

★ Section 3 Review

hmhsocialstudies.com
ONLINE QUIZ

1. Define and explain:
- charter
- capitol
- homestead law
- redbacks

2. Identify and explain the significance of each of the following:
- Edwin Waller
- Battle of the Neches
- Council House Fight
- Battle of Plum Creek

3. Locate on a map:
- Austin

4. Summarizing
Copy the graphic organizer below. Use it to show how President Lamar dealt with the problems facing his administration.

Problem	Solution/Action

5. Finding the Main Idea
a. What did the Lamar administration do to promote education in Texas?
b. Why did the public debt continue to be a problem for the Republic?

6. Writing and Critical Thinking *my* WriteSmart
Analyzing Information Imagine that you are a U.S. official sent to Texas. Write a short report on how changes in Texas policy led to wars with American Indians.
Consider the following:
- Lamar's American Indian policy
- conflicts between Texans and American Indians during Lamar's administration

Section 4

Houston's Second Administration

Main Ideas

1. During his second term, Sam Houston tried to reduce the national debt and make peace with Indians.
2. The Regulator-Moderator War was a feud in East Texas.

Key Terms

- **balanced budget**
- **Treaty of Tehuacana Creek**
- **Regulator-Moderator War**

Why It Matters Today

In 1841 the Republic's debt had become a major national problem. Use current events sources to learn about a current nation's debt.

The Story Continues

TEKS: 1B, 4A, 17C, 21B, 21E, 22D

myNotebook

Use the annotation tools in your eBook to take notes on the highlights of Sam Houston's second presidency.

Texan James Morgan was worried about his future. He hoped to make money in a new business deal but was concerned about land prices. A piece of land that had been worth $55,000 two years earlier had sold at auction for only $800. Morgan was shocked by the price. "We're perfectly drained & times awfully hard indeed in the money way," he wrote a friend.

Houston Returns to Office

Times were hard indeed in 1841 when Texans returned to the polls to elect a new president. Sam Houston and David G. Burnet both ran for the office. Although people had turned against Houston during his first term, they chose him again to lead them. They had grown unhappy with Lamar's American Indian policy, the worthless redbacks, and the rising debt. They elected Edward Burleson as vice president.

In his second term as president, Houston struggled to reduce the growing national debt. He hoped to achieve a **balanced budget**, or one in which spending does not exceed revenue. To save money, Houston cut government jobs and salaries. He also cut the size of both the Texas army and the Texas Rangers. Houston even persuaded the Congress to sell the navy, though the sale was never carried out. As a result of these cutbacks, government spending dropped from $4.8 million during Lamar's

CONNECTING TO ECONOMICS

Money in the Republic

The so-called redbacks and other paper notes issued by the Republic of Texas were much less stable than U.S. currency. Today, the value of a dollar bill does not change wildly. In the Republic, the value of a note rose or fell drastically based on society's confidence in the government.

Technically speaking, the Republic's notes were promissory notes, or IOUs, documents that represented a promise by the government to pay the bearer a certain amount of money. Because that money was given to whoever had the note, redbacks could be traded in exchange for goods and services. However, the notes' value depended on whether people believed that the government would actually pay the full amount. As Texans' faith in the government declined, they expected to get less in return for their notes, and the value fell. In most of Texas, a one-dollar note was worth only 32 cents, and in some places it was only worth 2 cents. **Why did redbacks lose their value over time?**

presidency to a little more than $500,000. Even with this drastic reduction, though, Houston could not balance the budget. The Republic's debt continued to rise, reaching $12 million by 1845.

In an attempt to solve the nation's money-supply problems, Houston had new paper money notes printed to replace the redbacks. The government restricted how much of this money was issued to try to maintain its value. However, the value of the new money quickly fell because Texans had little faith in the money their government issued.

President Houston also returned Texas to the peaceful American Indian policy of his first term. He established more frontier trading posts to encourage trade with Texas Indians, and he signed peace treaties with various groups. Many Texas Indians began working for peace at the same time. In August 1842 the Caddos signed a peace treaty with the Texas government. They also agreed to help persuade 20 other Indian groups to attend a peace council. In March 1843 nine Indian groups—including the Caddos, Tawakonis, and Wacos—met with Texas officials. This council was held at Tehuacana Creek, south of present-day Waco. The Indians and Texas leaders agreed to stop fighting. They planned a larger peace council to be held in September at Fort Bird on the Trinity River, near present-day Dallas. There Texas officials and nine Indian groups signed a treaty to put an end to fighting.

The Comanches, still angered by the massacre at the Council House, did not attend. However, in October 1844 Houston and Chief Buffalo Hump of the Penateka Comanches met at Tehuacana Creek and signed the **Treaty of Tehuacana Creek**. Although the agreement established peace and trade between the two groups, it did not set boundaries for Comanche land. This issue later resurfaced and caused tension between Texans and the Comanches. Nonetheless, under Houston's guidance, peace between American Indians and Texans was restored.

Reading Check **Making Generalizations and Predictions** Do you think Houston's peace policy will succeed? Explain your answer.

The Regulator-Moderator War

While relations with Texas Indians were improving, violence broke out among Texans in Shelby County in East Texas. This region, known as the Redlands, bordered on the old Neutral Ground. Law enforcement was weak in the area, and as a result, many bandits and outlaws had moved there. One resident described the people who lived in the Redlands.

Houston sent troops to end the Regulator-Moderator War. Few soldiers had fine uniforms like this one, which belonged to a Texas officer.

TEXAS VOICES

"It is nothing uncommon for us to inquire of a man why he ran away from the [United] States. Few persons feel insulted by such a question. They generally answer for some crime or other which they have committed."

—W. B. DeWees, *Letters from Texas*

In 1840 a feud began between Alfred George and Joseph Goodbread over fake land certificates. An acquaintance of George's, outlaw Charles Jackson, killed Goodbread and formed a band that became known as the Regulators. In response, allies of Goodbread formed the Moderators. Both sides attacked each other and anyone else who got in their way. Violence broke out between the two groups almost immediately.

Local officials, many of whom had become involved in the feud, could not stop the violence. People were ambushed and shot. Judges were threatened, and prisoners hanged without trial. Houses were burned, and people were left homeless. Eventually, each side numbered in the hundreds.

Finally, in August 1844 President Houston sent soldiers to stop the feud. These troops arrested the leaders of each side of the conflict, ending the **Regulator-Moderator War**. Peace returned to East Texas.

Reading Check **Sequencing** Describe in order the events that led to the Regulator-Moderator War.

Section 4 Review

hmhsocialstudies.com
ONLINE QUIZ

1. **Define and explain:**
   - balanced budget
2. **Identify and explain** the significance of each of the following in Texas history:
   - Treaty of Tehuacana Creek
   - Regulator-Moderator War
3. **Identifying Cause and Effect** Copy the graphic organizer below. Use it to list reasons Sam Houston was elected to a second term. Then list the effects of this election.

Causes	Event	Effects
1.	Houston is elected to a second term as president.	1.
2.		2.
3.		3.

4. **Finding the Main Idea**
   - **a.** How did Sam Houston attempt to solve the Republic's economic problems?
   - **b.** What were the results of Houston's peace policy toward American Indians?
5. **Writing and Critical Thinking** *my*WriteSmart
   Supporting a Point of View Do you agree with Houston's decision to send in troops to put down the Regulator-Moderator War? Provide reasons to support your answer. Consider the following:
   - violence resulting from the feud
   - local officials' role in the feud

Image Credit: (tr) ©The San Jacinto Museum of History, Houston.

The Chapter at a Glance

Examine the following visual summary of the chapter. Then use the visual to create a short quiz about the major issues the Republic of Texas faced during the Houston and Lamar administrations.

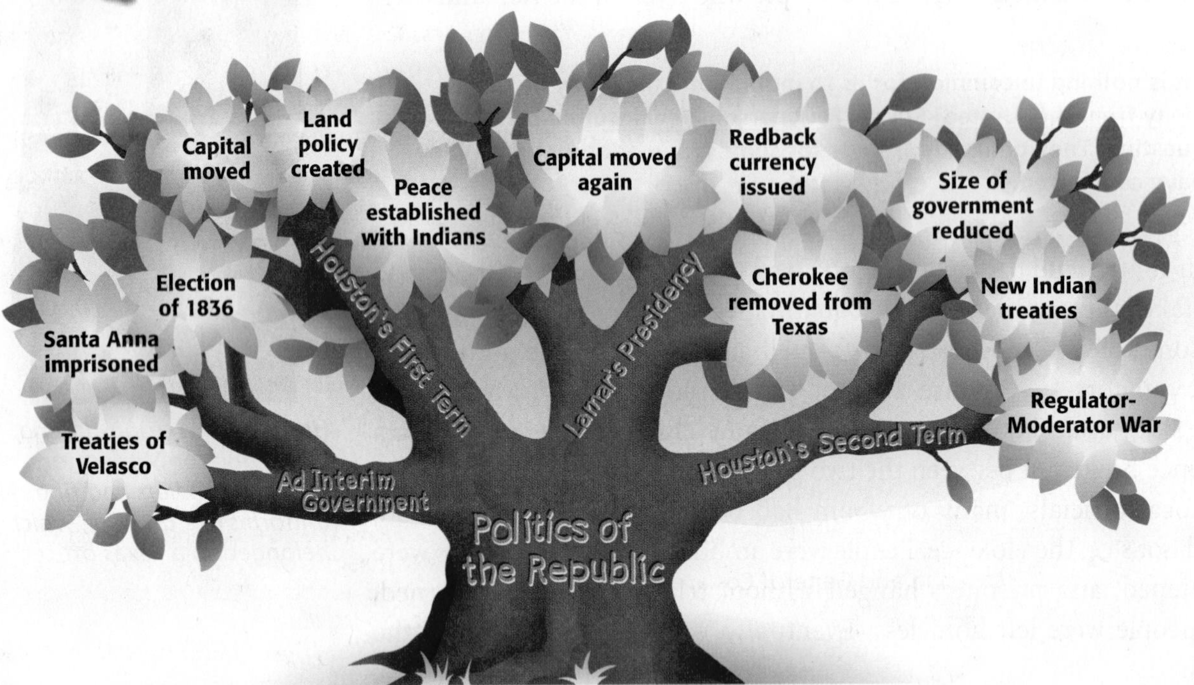

Identifying People and Ideas

Write a sentence to explain the role or significance of each of the following terms or people.

1. Treaties of Velasco
2. annexation
3. Chief Bowles
4. Mirabeau B. Lamar
5. Texas Rangers
6. redbacks
7. Battle of the Neches
8. Battle of Plum Creek

Understanding Main Ideas

Section 1

1. What were the terms of the Treaties of Velasco?

Section 2

2. What leadership qualities made Sam Houston an effective president for Texas?

Section 3

3. How did President Lamar address the need for a public education system in the Republic?
4. What conflicts with American Indians occurred during Lamar's administration, and why were such conflicts common?

Section 4

5. What policy changes did Sam Houston make during his second administration?
6. What was the Regulator-Moderator War, and how did Sam Houston end it?

You Be the Historian

Reviewing Themes

1. **Citizenship** Choose one of the early candidates for president of the Republic and explain why you would vote for that person.
2. **Economics** Analyze the impact of the U.S. economy and the Panic of 1837 on the Republic's economy.
3. **Government** How did Houston and Lamar shape the history of the Republic of Texas?

Thinking Critically

1. **Analyzing Information** Identify the major issues the Republic of Texas faced.
2. **Comparing and Contrasting** Compare and contrast the presidencies of Sam Houston and Mirabeau B. Lamar.
3. **Summarizing** Describe the defining characteristics of the Republic of Texas years.

Texas Test Practice

Interpreting Political Cartoons

Study the political cartoon below. Then use the information in the cartoon to answer the questions.

1. Which statement best describes what is occurring in this political cartoon created after the Battle of San Jacinto?

- **A** General Santa Anna and General Cos are surrendering to Sam Houston.
- **B** Houston is ordering the execution of Santa Anna.
- **C** Houston is surrendering to Santa Anna.
- **D** Houston and Santa Anna are meeting to sign a treaty.

2. What is Santa Anna doing that helps you answer question 1?

Identifying Points of View

Read the following quote from a letter that Sam Houston wrote to a council of Texas Indians. Then answer the questions.

"My brothers: The path between us . . . has become white . . . the sun gives light to our footsteps. . . . I send councillors with my talk. . . . Hear it, and remember . . . I have never opened my lips to tell [an American Indian] a lie. . . . Let the war-whoop be no more heard in our prairie—let songs of joy be heard upon our hills. In our valleys let there be laughter and in our wigwams let the voices of our women and children be heard . . . and when our warriors meet together, let them [have] peace and be happy."

3. What does this letter suggest about President Houston's point of view?

- **F** He does not like American Indians.
- **G** He is afraid that the American Indians will attack Texans.
- **H** He would like to achieve peace with American Indians.
- **J** He thinks that Texans and American Indians should go to war.

4. What words and phrases in this letter help you identify Houston's point of view?

Linking to Community

Research events that happened in your area during the period of the Republic of Texas. Then create an illustrated time line showing some of these events and the dates and the order in which the events occurred. You might look for the development of new towns, elections of local officials, the start of new businesses or schools, raids or battles, or other events. Find at least one event to contribute to the class time line.

Internet Activity

Access the Internet to locate primary and secondary sources on the Council House Fight and the Battle of Plum Creek. Transfer the information you find in these written sources into a visual form, such as an illustration, comic strip, or multimedia presentation, using computer software to help in your work if appropriate. Note any bias in the sources and make note of that bias in your presentation. Write a short summary to accompany your work. Make sure you use standard grammar, spelling, sentence structure, and punctuation in your summary.

Image Credit: (t) Library of Congress

CHAPTER 13

Life in the Republic

(1836–1845)

Texas Essential Knowledge and Skills (TEKS) 4A, 8A, 8B, 9A, 11A, 11B, 16B, 17C, 19A, 19B, 19C, 19D, 21A, 21B, 21C, 21E, 22A, 22B, 22C, 22D

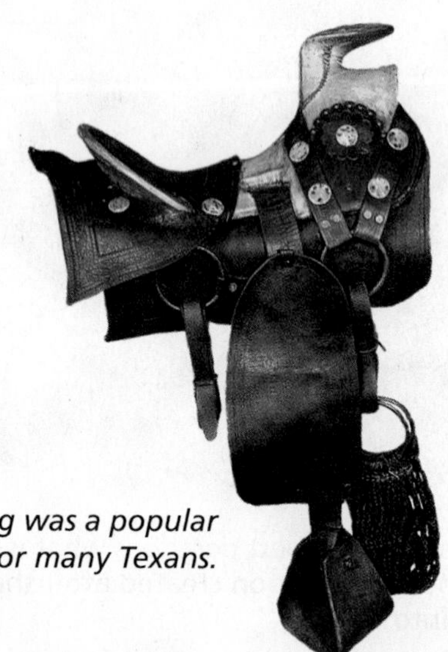

Horse racing was a popular activity for many Texans.

TEXAS

- **1838** Velasco citizens hold a horse race on the coast near the town.
- **1839** Repeated attacks and discrimination force more than 100 Tejano families to flee Nacogdoches.
- **1840** The first college chartered by the Republic, Rutersville College, is founded.

1836 — 1837 — 1838 — 1839 — 1840

U.S. and WORLD

- **1837** John Deere manufactures the steel plow.
- **1839** Tennessee produces some 45 million bushels of corn.
- **1840** The World's Anti-Slavery Convention is held in London.

If you were there . . .
Why would you have come to the Republic of Texas?

Build on What You Know

After the revolution, Texans faced new challenges. The Republic's land policy drew new immigrants from the United States and Europe to Texas, adding to the diversity of the young nation. Soon, Texans were building new towns, churches, and schools.

Steamboats helped transport people and supplies along rivers.

Prince Carl of Solms-Braunfels helped bring immigrants to Texas from Germany.

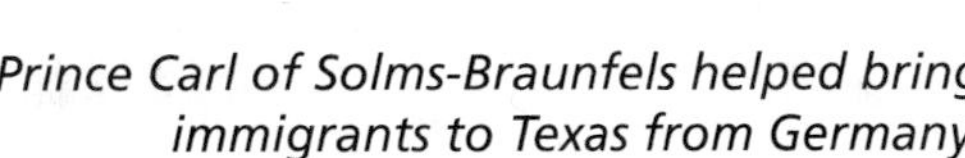

1841
William Kennedy publishes *Texas: The Rise, Progress, and Prospects of the Republic of Texas.*

1842
Snider de Pellegrini, director of a French colonization company, brings 14 settlers to Texas.

1843
Railroad lines from Paris to Rouen and Paris to Orléans are opened.

1844
Prince Carl of Solms-Braunfels comes to Texas followed by a group of German immigrants.

1845
At least 30,000 enslaved African Americans live in Texas.

1845
A severe famine in Ireland begins, eventually killing hundreds of thousands of people.

1841 1842 1843 1844 1845

You Be the Historian

myNotebook

What's Your Opinion? Do you **agree** or **disagree** with the following statements? Support your point of view in your notebook.

- **Citizenship** Citizens can change laws by creating petitions and exercising free speech.
- **Culture** Newcomers from different lands can both maintain their culture and adapt to a new culture.
- **Economics** Many immigrants move to find new economic opportunities.

Section 1 The Texans

Main Ideas

1. Immigration caused the population of the Republic of Texas to swell.
2. Most African Americans in the Republic were slaves, but even free African Americans faced challenges.
3. Tejanos and American Indians in the Republic experienced widespread discrimination.

Key Terms and People

- **Greenbury Logan**
- **Ashworth Act**
- **Córdova Rebellion**
- **José Antonio Navarro**

Why It Matters Today

During the Republic, some Texans petitioned the Republic's government to change laws to which they were opposed. Use current events sources to learn how Americans influence the government today.

TEKS: 4A, 8B, 11A, 17C, 19B, 21B, 21E, 22D

myNotebook

Use the annotation tools in your eBook to take notes on the people who lived in the Republic of Texas.

The Story Continues

One summer day in Austin, seven-year-old W. C. Walsh and a group of boys disobeyed their mothers. Instead of playing in the backyard, they sneaked off to Shoal Creek to swim. The children were having a wonderful time when they heard someone cry out. Scared, they raced home. Walsh's mother scolded him for leaving the yard. Austin during the 1830s was no place for a child to run around without supervision.

A Growing Population

Life in the new Republic presented many challenges. Texans who had fled during the Runaway Scrape returned to find much of their property destroyed. Entire towns, including Harrisburg, Refugio, and San Felipe, had been burned. To help people rebuild, the Constitution of 1836 gave land to many of the people who had lived in Texas before the Revolution.

In 1836 the population of Texas was approximately 52,700, including some 22,700 American Indians, African Americans, and Tejanos. Hoping to encourage immigration, the Republic of Texas set up a land grant policy modeled after the *empresario* system. Agents received land grants in return for bringing immigrants and establishing settlements in the Republic. The government's land policy sparked an increase in immigration to Texas, and the population grew by leaps and bounds. From 1836 to 1847, the population of Texas increased by nearly 100,000.

By far the largest group of new immigrants to the Republic came from the United States in search of land and economic opportunities. Although immigrants came from almost every state, most were from the South. Immigrants from the Lower South settled in East Texas and along the coast. People from the Upper South settled farther inland in East Texas and along the Red River in the northeast.

Reading Check Summarizing Why did many immigrants from the U.S. South come to Texas, and where did they settle?

★ African Americans

Immigrants from the American South often brought African American slaves with them to Texas. Many slaveholders were drawn to the Republic because the Constitution of 1836 ensured that slavery was legal. With the increase in U.S. immigration, the number of slaves in Texas rose from some 5,000 in 1836 to at least 30,000 by 1845.

Life for slaves was hard. Many worked long hours in cotton fields or did other farm chores. Others lived in towns as personal servants or day laborers. Slaveholders had broad control over the lives of slaves, who had no legal right to private property, to marriage, or to have a family. Almost every slave lived under threat of physical punishment.

Free African Americans also faced discrimination after the Texas Revolution. The Constitution of 1836 required free African Americans to get permission from Congress to stay in the Republic. In 1840 Congress

Interpreting Visuals

Immigration to Texas. *Many immigrants traveled to Texas in wagons like the ones shown below.* ***What transportation problems did people traveling to Texas face?***

Image Credit: ©Texas State Preservation Board

BIOGRAPHY

Greenbury Logan

(1799–date unknown)

Greenbury Logan was born into slavery in Kentucky in 1799 but was later freed. In 1831 he settled in one of Stephen F. Austin's colonies. He was wounded while fighting in the Texas Revolution. In 1837 Logan sent a petition to Congress, asking to remain in Texas. Some of the most respected men in the Republic signed his petition.

How does Logan's story demonstrate the challenges free African Americans faced in the Republic?

outlawed the immigration of free African Americans to Texas. Free African Americans already in the Republic would have to leave within two years or be sold into slavery. Even veterans of the Texas Revolution like **Greenbury Logan** risked being forced to leave. Logan had fought in the battles at Concepción and San Antonio.

The law outraged many Texans. They demanded exceptions for their friends and neighbors. In November 1840, three petitions were presented to Congress on behalf of the Ashworth family. In response, Congress passed the **Ashworth Act**, which allowed the Ashworths and all free African Americans who were in Texas at the time of the Texas Declaration of Independence to stay.

However, the free African Americans who remained in the Republic had to endure the prejudice of their neighbors. William Goyens, who had helped negotiate with the Cherokees during the war, was one example. A wealthy business owner, Goyens had to deal with repeated attempts by other townspeople to take his property. Although Goyens had the resources to challenge his persecutors in court, other free African Americans did not. Many chose to leave rather than deal with such issues. By 1850 fewer than 400 free African Americans lived in Texas.

Reading Check **Drawing Inferences and Conclusions** Why do you think petitions were made for African American veterans of the Revolution?

★ Tejanos in the Republic

Several thousand Tejanos also lived in the Republic. Most lived in the southern part of Texas along the San Antonio and Guadalupe rivers. Tejanos often faced hostility, particularly from U.S. immigrants. These immigrants saw the Tejanos as Mexican, and they thought of Mexico as an enemy. Even Tejanos who had fought in the Revolution faced discrimination. Tejanos had their property stolen. Some were forced to flee Texas completely. Juan Seguín, a hero of the revolution and mayor of San Antonio from 1840 to 1842, witnessed several conflicts between Tejanos and U.S. settlers. "At every hour of the day and night, my countrymen ran to me for protection against the assaults . . . of these adventurers."

In 1838 a group of Tejanos in Nacogdoches led by Vicente Córdova reacted to this poor treatment. Córdova, a former alcalde, had contacted officials in Mexico who wanted to drive all Anglos out of Texas. With a small group of Tejano and Indian allies, he took up arms in the **Córdova Rebellion**. President Houston ordered the rebels to return to their homes, but they declared that they would fight until their rights were protected. In response, Houston sent the army to end the rebellion. Córdova fled to Mexico, but 33 Tejanos from the Nacogdoches area were arrested and tried for treason. They were eventually released. However, resentful Anglos attacked the Tejanos, driving more than 100 Tejano families from their homes.

Despite these problems, many Tejanos remained in Texas. A few held positions of power in the San Antonio area, such as **José Antonio Navarro**, a signer of the Texas Declaration of Independence. Navarro served in the Republic's Congress and worked to protect Tejano rights.

Despite the hardships they faced, Tejanos maintained their culture. They practiced their Catholic faith, ate traditional foods, and celebrated Mexican holidays. Together with groups of Mexicans in the Rio Grande valley and other areas that would eventually become part of Texas, they helped to create a unique Texas-Mexican cultural tradition.

Reading Check **Analyzing Information** Why might Tejanos have been disappointed by life in the Republic?

José Antonio Navarro was an important figure in the Republic. He pushed for the protection of Tejano rights while serving in the Texas Congress.

★ Texas Indians

It is difficult to estimate how many American Indians lived in the Texas Republic. Bands of independent Indians were constantly on the move, especially on the Plains. They crossed back and forth from Texas into other areas. Also, new groups of American Indians were arriving in Texas throughout the 1820s and 1830s. Driven from their homes farther east by Americans, groups like the Choctaws, Coushattas, and Creeks had taken up residence in parts of East Texas during this period.

Like African Americans and Tejanos, American Indians faced discrimination in the Texas Republic. Despite Sam Houston's efforts, few Texans were interested in living peacefully with the Indians. Many, including President Lamar, viewed American Indians as enemies who had to be eliminated. Even with Houston's treaties, relations between Indians and the government were strained.

Reading Check **Finding the Main Idea** Why is it difficult to know how many American Indians lived in the Texas Republic?

★ Section 1 Review

hmhsocialstudies.com
ONLINE QUIZ

1. **Identify and explain** the significance of each of the following in Texas history:
   - Greenbury Logan
   - Ashworth Act
   - Córdova Rebellion
   - José Antonio Navarro

2. **Summarizing** Copy the graphic organizer below. Use it to show how life changed for various racial and ethnic groups after the Revolution.

   How Life Changed
   - Indians
   - Tejanos
   - African Americans

3. **Finding the Main Idea**
   a. Why did immigrants come to Texas?
   b. What do the experiences of William Goyens and José Antonio Navarro suggest about the lives of African Americans and Tejanos in the Texas Republic?

4. **Writing and Critical Thinking** myWriteSmart
   Supporting a Point of View Imagine that you live in the Republic of Texas. Write a letter to your congressperson asking for changes to the laws concerning free African Americans.
   Consider the following:
   - the effects of the Ashworth Act
   - African Americans' service in the Revolution

Section 2

European Immigration to Texas

Main Ideas

1. In the 1840s people moved to Texas from Germany, France, Ireland, and other parts of Europe.
2. The legacy of immigrants can still be seen in the names, architecture, foods, and arts of the places they settled.

Key People

- **Prince Carl of Solms-Braunfels**
- **John O. Meusebach**

Why It Matters Today

Thousands of immigrants came to the Republic of Texas. Use current events sources to learn about immigration trends today.

TEKS: 4A, 8A, 8B, 11A, 11B, 19B, 19C, 21A, 21B, 21C, 22D

myNotebook

Use the annotation tools in your eBook to take notes on the arrival and legacy of European immigrants to Texas.

The Story Continues

At about 10 P.M. in San Antonio, Théodore Gentilz and Auguste Frétellière set out with anticipation. They were going to a fandango—a dance being held by the local residents. As they neared Military Plaza, they heard the sounds of a violin. They followed the music to an adobe house. There they entered a candlelit room filled with dancers and food. Newly arrived from France, Gentilz and Frétellière had never seen such a dance.

Germans Settle in Central Texas

During the 1830s and 1840s a large number of European immigrants like Gentilz and Frétellière moved to Texas. The largest group of European immigrants to Texas were the Germans, who had first come in the early 1830s. During the years of the Republic, the number of German immigrants grew as people left Germany looking for better economic opportunities in Texas.

In 1842 a group of German businesspeople formed the German Emigration Company, or Adelsverein. Its members hoped to make a profit by encouraging Germans to settle in Texas. After acquiring land in the Hill Country, the company sent **Prince Carl of Solms-Braunfels** to Texas in 1844 followed by a group of peasants and craftspeople. Prince Carl wrote letters home about his mission.

TEXAS VOICES

"The eyes of all Germany, no, the eyes of all Europe are fixed on us and our undertaking: German princes, counts, and noblemen . . . are bringing new crowns to old glory while at the same time insuring immeasurable riches for their children and grandchildren."

—Prince Carl of Solms-Braunfels, quoted in *The Handbook of Texas*

Analyzing Primary Sources
Identifying Points of View Why does Prince Carl think his task of bringing immigrants to the Republic is so important?

Once in Texas, Prince Carl established a port for incoming settlers. The port, which was called Karlshafen by the Germans, was later renamed Indianola. In March 1845 the prince and a group of settlers established New Braunfels along the Guadalupe and Comal Rivers.

When Prince Carl returned home two months later, Baron Otfried Hans Freiherr von Meusebach replaced him. In Texas, the baron changed his name to **John O. Meusebach.** He continued the work begun by Prince Carl, and New Braunfels grew and prospered.

By 1847 the German Emigration Company had sent more than 7,000 immigrants to Texas. Some stayed in established towns such as Houston and San Antonio, while other groups moved into the Hill Country. There they formed new settlements, including Fredericksburg, Boerne, and Comfort. These and other settlements extended the western frontier of Texas.

Before they left, Prince Carl instructed new immigrants headed to Texas to "stay together and remain faithful to German culture and habits." One German settler wrote to his relatives back home asking them to bring reminders of German culture. "Be sure to bring all the sheet music that you can collect. . . . And do not fail to bring the complete works of Goethe [a German poet]." Even today many Texas Hill Country towns reflect their German heritage in their names, architecture, churches, food, and language.

Reading Check **Analyzing Information** Where did German immigrants settle, and how did they maintain their culture?

Interpreting Visuals

Fredericksburg. *German immigrants brought many of their cultural traditions to Texas. This building is a reconstruction of a church built in Fredericksburg in 1847 in an old German style.* ***What does this church suggest about the importance of their heritage to these settlers?***

Our Cultural Heritage

Little Alsace in Texas

The architecture of Castroville was distinctly European. Buildings had steep thatched roofs. The roads were often narrow lanes. The European-style construction has led Castroville to be called the Little Alsace of Texas. Many of the town's unique buildings can still be seen today. What impact did the immigrants in Castroville have on that region of Texas?

Other European Immigrants

In 1840 Texas and France signed a treaty that encouraged French immigration. A few years later, Henri Castro brought one of the first groups of French settlers to Texas. Many of them were from the province of Alsace, a mostly German-speaking area in eastern France. Castro founded the town of Castroville in 1844 near the Medina River. By 1846 Castro had helped settle more than 2,000 colonists along the river, most of whom became farmers and ranchers. The cultural traditions of these French immigrants can still be found in the architecture, churches, and customs of Castroville and nearby towns with such French names as D'Hanis, Quihi, and Vandenburg.

Irish settlers had come to Texas long before it was a republic. During the 1820s several Irishmen had received *empresario* contracts. In fact one Irish *empresario,* James Hewetson, had accompanied Stephen F. Austin on his first trip to Texas in 1821. Many Irish immigrants fought with the Texas troops at the Alamo, Goliad, and San Jacinto. Irish settlers continued to come to Texas after the Revolution, seeking economic opportunity. Irish-born Texan William Kennedy encouraged this immigration in his 1841 book, *Texas: The Rise, Progress, and Prospects of the Republic of Texas.* By 1850 there were more than 1,400 Irish settlers throughout Texas.

Some Polish and Czech immigrants had also made their way to Texas, settling in South and Central Texas. During the Revolution, Polish immigrants had fought at Goliad and San Jacinto. Polish and Czech immigration later increased as economic and political conditions pushed many from their homelands. Like other immigrants, they left their mark on the local customs of the areas in which they lived.

Reading Check **Summarizing** Why did many Europeans come to the Republic?

Section 2 Review

hmhsocialstudies.com ONLINE QUIZ

1. **Identify and explain** the significance of each of the following in Texas history:
   - Prince Carl of Solms-Braunfels
   - John O. Meusebach
2. **Locate on a map:**
   - New Braunfels
   - Fredericksburg
   - Castroville
3. **Analyzing Information** Copy the table below. Use it to explain why immigrant groups came to the Republic and where they settled.

Immigrants	Why They Came	Where They Settled
German		
French		
Irish		
Polish		
Czech		

4. **Finding the Main Idea**
   a. In what ways did new immigrants maintain their culture?
   b. How did new immigrants from Europe influence life in the Republic?
5. **Writing and Critical Thinking** *my* WriteSmart
   Identifying Cause and Effect Explain how the settlement patterns of European immigrants affected the Republic.
   Consider the following:
   - locations of European settlements
   - how this led to the development of the western frontier

Connecting To

Geography

Immigration to Texas

While most immigrants to Texas came from the United States, others came from Europe. Many Europeans faced poverty and high taxes. They found it difficult to purchase land or to make a comfortable living and came to Texas in search of new economic opportunities. Once in Texas, European immigrants formed their own communities, often located in frontier regions such as the Hill Country.

Geography **Skills**

Interpreting Thematic Maps

1. Based on this map, how would most European immigrants come to Texas?
2. How did the areas settled by people from the Upper South differ from those settled by people from the Lower South?
3. In what countries of Europe did most European immigrants originally live?

Immigration to Texas, 1836–1850

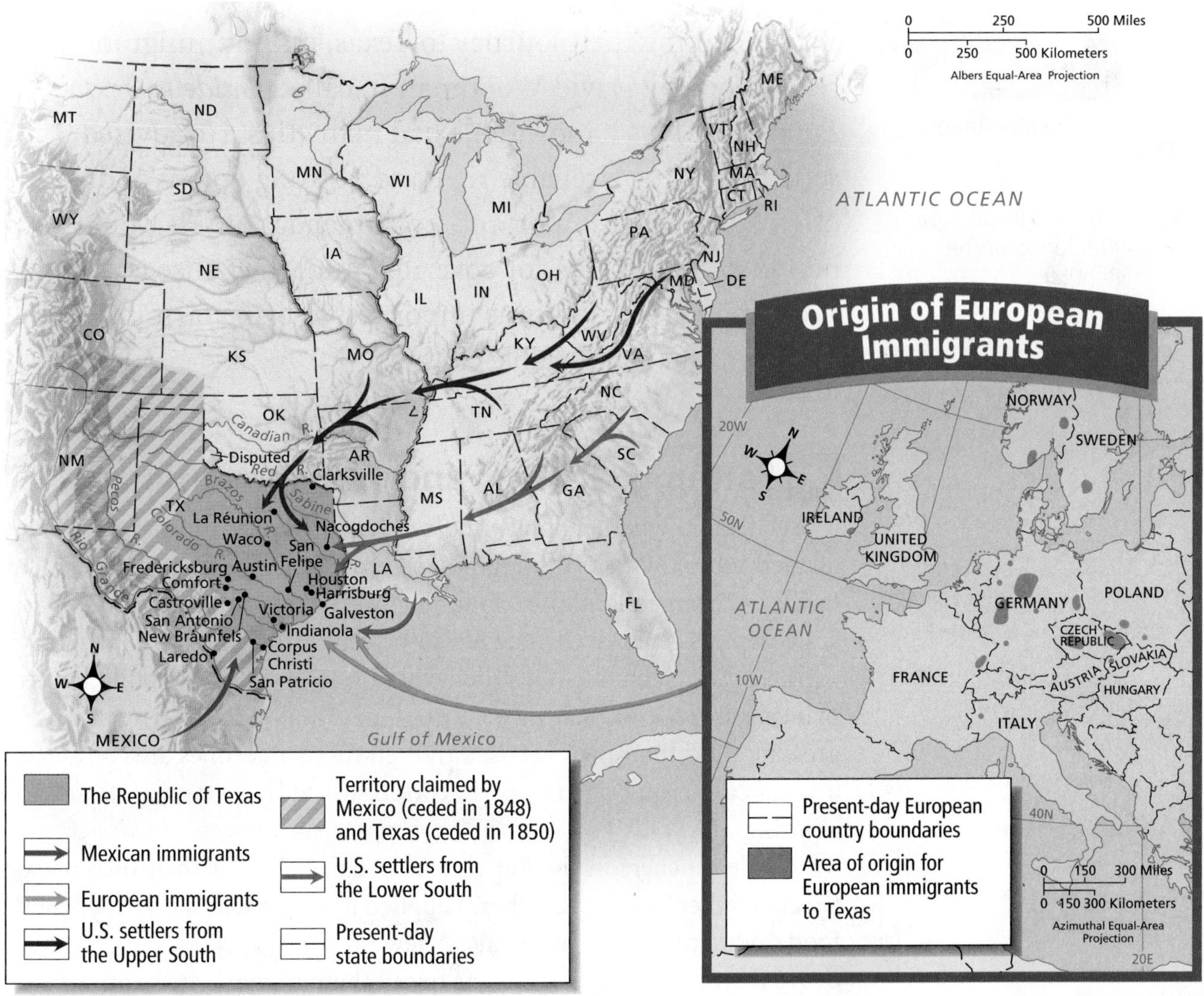

Section 3 Texas Life

Main Ideas

1. Most people in the Republic of Texas lived on farms or ranches, though some lived in towns.
2. Games, literature, and art provided leisure activities.
3. Churches and schools were social centers.

Key Terms and People

- **land speculators**
- **denominations**
- **circuit riders**
- **academies**
- **Théodore Gentilz**

Why It Matters Today

Education was a major concern for people in the Republic. Use current events sources to learn about education in the United States and other countries today.

TEKS: 4A, 9A, 19B, 19D, 21B, 22D

***my*Notebook**

Use the annotation tools in your eBook to take notes on life in Texas during the period of the Republic.

The Story Continues

Before making their journey to Texas, many immigrants read a book by David Woodman Jr. called *Guide to Texas Emigrants.* This handy guide had many tips. He advised settlers to bring a reliable rifle and a strong dog. Woodman offered one other important recommendation. "It would be best to carry tents . . . for covering, until the house is built." Woodman also said it was important to bring farming tools, a wagon, and comfortable clothing.

★ Farming, Towns, and Transportation

Most Texans, whether long-time residents or new immigrants, were farmers and ranchers, although their farms varied widely in size. Some farms were large plantations, but most were small family farms. Small-scale farmers generally owned few or no slaves; they did most farm tasks on their own. Such tasks included clearing acres of land to build homes, planting crops, and creating pastures for animals. Texas farmers mostly grew food for their own needs, although they sometimes also produced a small cash crop—such as corn, cotton, wheat, rye, or oats—to sell for a profit.

Cattle ranchers in the Republic raised animals for their own use or to sell to other Texans. Ranchers supplied townspeople and farmers with food, hides, and other materials. A few ranchers, such as Taylor White, drove their cattle to New Orleans to sell them in markets there.

As it had been in the Mexican period, ranching was popular among the Tejano population of the Republic. Tejanos continued to own ranches in southern Texas, east and south of San Antonio. Some free African Americans, such as Robert Thompson of Montgomery County, also owned ranches.

Only in towns and cities did people have jobs that were not directly tied to farming or ranching. Small towns were home to blacksmiths, carpenters, tailors, and other artisans. Doctors, shopkeepers, silversmiths, cabinetmakers, and bankers operated in the largest towns. Towns like Houston and Galveston grew quickly as immigrants moved to them. Their founders had chosen locations that were beneficial for trade. Some towns farther inland such as Dallas also began to grow.

Other new towns, though, such as Carolina, Geneva, Pompei, and Rome, were less fortunate. These towns were founded by **land speculators**—people who bought large amounts of land in hopes of making profits. Speculators would sell small lots of the land at higher prices to new settlers at higher prices than they had paid themselves. However, their attempts to make money failed when they could not attract enough settlers to buy their land. In some cases, too, people were unable to pay for land they had agreed to buy. Cash was so rare in Texas that "not a man of them can pay me a dollar," as one miserable speculator complained.

Travel during the Republic was difficult. Only a few roads connected towns in various parts of Texas. The government tried to build new roads but had limited success. Texas roads remained poor, particularly in bad weather. Travel by horseback or stagecoach was often uncomfortable and dangerous. One traveler described the road conditions. "I was obliged in the worst places to relieve the mule by getting off and leading for a mile at a time, with water to my knees and sometimes to my britches pockets."

Because the roads were so bad, some rivers were used for transporting goods and people, especially once the steamboat was introduced to Texas. The first steamboat to enter a Texas river was the *Ariel*. Henry Austin, Stephen F. Austin's cousin, had begun operating this boat on the lower Rio Grande in 1829. He traded with Mexican merchants and later took the *Ariel* up the Brazos River. By the 1840s, several steamboats traveled the Brazos, Colorado, and Trinity Rivers. These boats shipped cotton and other farm products from Texas farms and brought in needed goods to Texas settlers. Few Texas rivers were suited for steamboats, however. Floods, low water, and sandbars often prevented travel. The lack of a good transportation system slowed the growth of businesses and towns in the Republic.

Reading Check **Finding the Main Idea** How did geographic factors affect the economic development of Texas?

★Texas Cities★

Dallas

History: Dallas was founded by John Neely Bryan in November 1841. Bryan established a trading post that served the region's growing population.

Population in 2012: 1,241,162 (estimate)

Relative location: On the Trinity River in north-central Texas

Region: Blackland Prairie

County: County seat of Dallas County

Special feature: The city is home to the Dallas Market Center, the largest wholesale trade complex in the world.

Origin of name: Dallas is named for George Mifflin Dallas, a U.S. politician. At the time Texas was annexed, he was the U.S. vice president.

Economy: Dallas is one of the nation's leading financial and business centers. Many corporations moved their headquarters there after World War II, and Dallas benefited from the postwar economic boom. It soon became a major technology center.

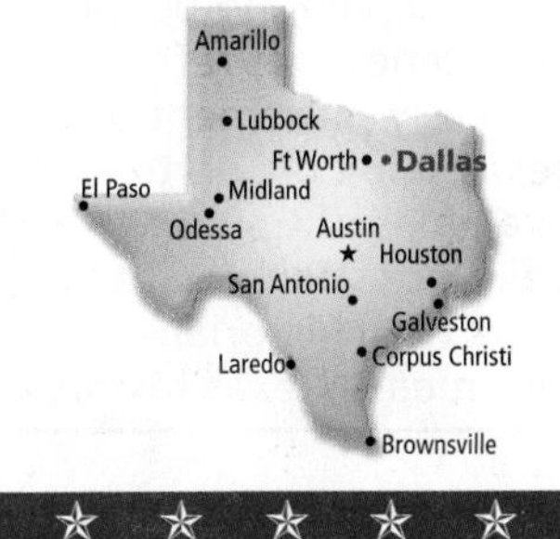

Image Credit: ©Corbis

For entertainment, Texans gathered at local dances.

★ Leisure, Literature, and Art

Life in Texas was not all work. Texans also enjoyed a number of leisure activities. Some activities combined fun with work, such as building houses for newcomers, participating in log-splitting contests, hunting, and fishing. Other activities were all fun, such as songfests. These celebrations featured popular tunes of the day, including "Yankee Doodle." Dances were one of the most popular pastimes, whether small rural affairs or elaborate plantation balls. Many Texans also enjoyed concerts, horse races, and the theater.

Some citizens enjoyed literature and art, although both were scarce in frontier Texas. Most books published in the Republic dealt with Texas history or travel in Texas. Authors on these subjects included Mary Austin Holley and William Kennedy. Some Texans also wrote poetry, including President Mirabeau B. Lamar. The most common publications in the Republic were newspapers. In 1836 Texas had only one weekly newspaper, but by 1840 more than a dozen were being published.

Artists, including portrait painters Charles Kneass and Jefferson Wright, also lived in Texas. Many of the Republic's artists were new immigrants. For example, French painter and surveyor **Théodore Gentilz** came to Texas with Henri Castro. Gentilz is known for his scenes of Texas life. Some sculptors also worked in the Republic.

Reading Check **Analyzing Information** How did Texans spend their leisure time?

CONNECTING TO

The Arts

Théodore Gentilz

Théodore Gentilz was born in Paris in 1819 and moved to Texas with Henri Castro. There Gentilz traveled the countryside looking for subjects to paint. He journeyed far into West Texas, to the Gulf Coast, and even into Mexico. He enjoyed painting people and scenes that reflected the early settlement of Texas. **Look online to find examples of Gentilz's paintings. How might his work help historians learn about early Texas history?**

★ Churches and Schools

In the towns and countryside, Texans established many churches. After Texas independence, Roman Catholicism was no longer the official state religion. Many Protestant **denominations**—organized religious groups with similar beliefs—soon built churches in the Republic. The Methodist Church was the largest denomination, followed by the Baptist Church. Presbyterians and Episcopalians were also active in Texas. Catholicism remained the dominant religion in Galveston, San Antonio, and Tejano communities along the Rio Grande. Most Czech and Polish immigrants also belonged to the Catholic Church. Jews from central and eastern Europe lived in communities across Texas. Jewish immigrants established synagogues, or Jewish houses of worship, in Galveston, Houston, and San Antonio.

Churches and temples served as the religious and social centers of most Texas communities. In addition to sermons and Sunday school, many churches sponsored revival meetings, picnics, and bazaars. **Circuit riders**, or traveling preachers, typically served regions on the frontier. They traveled to their areas on a regular basis to preach and to provide religious support to the settlers.

Churches also ran most of the Republic's schools. Rutersville College was founded by the Methodist Church in 1840. Baylor University, the oldest college in Texas still in operation, was founded by Baptists in 1845. Although President Mirabeau B. Lamar wanted Texas to establish a system of public education, funds were scarce. Houston was the only town in the Republic to establish a public school, which operated off and on throughout the 1840s. Several towns, however, did build private **academies**—schools that offered classes at the high school level.

Reading Check **Summarizing** How did churches contribute to Texas communities during the years of the Republic?

Daily Life

Texas Schoolrooms

The typical classroom in early rural Texas was very different from today's schoolrooms. Most school buildings were one-room log cabins that lacked floors or windows. One teacher wrote to her father about her schoolroom, "As to furniture no hermit's cell was ever more simply furnished." Books were few, but students learned chemistry, geography, grammar, history, and philosophy. Some students learned to read using Bibles. For Texas children, school days were long, beginning early in the morning and ending at sunset. **Why does the teacher compare her schoolroom to a "hermit's cell"?**

★ Section 3 Review

hmhsocialstudies.com ONLINE QUIZ

1. Define and explain:
- land speculators
- denominations
- circuit riders
- academies

2. Identify and explain the significance of the following in Texas history:
- Théodore Gentilz

3. Locate on a map:
- Dallas

4. Summarizing Copy the graphic organizer below. Use it to show how people made a living in Texas.

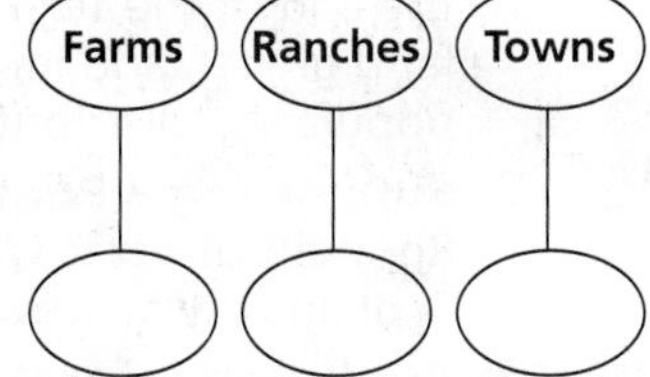

5. Finding the Main Idea

a. How did churches and schools contribute to life in the Republic?

b. What type of leisure activities and arts did Texans enjoy during the years of the Republic?

6. Writing and Critical Thinking myWriteSmart

Summarizing Write a summary explaining how geographic factors affected the economic development of Texas.

Consider the following:
- the state of the roads and rivers
- the importance of transportation

CHAPTER 13 REVIEW

The Chapter at a Glance

Examine the following visual summary of the chapter. Then convert the information from the visual into a map that you can use to describe changes in life in the Republic.

1840

Texas Daily Life

September 9, 1840

New Immigrants Come to Texas

Immigrants came to the Republic from the United States and Europe, seeking cheap land and new opportunities.

The Farm Report

Many Texans worked on small farms and ranches. Even Texans living in towns worked in businesses that were related to agriculture.

STEAMBOAT ARRIVES

Traveling over Texas roads was often difficult. With new types of transportation, travel improved a little.

Big Dance

Texans worked hard to build homes, churches, and schools, but they still found time for entertainment.

Identifying People and Ideas

Write a sentence to explain the role or significance of each of the following terms or people.

1. Ashworth Act
2. Córdova Rebellion
3. José Antonio Navarro
4. Greenbury Logan
5. Théodore Gentilz
6. John O. Meusebach
7. Prince Carl of Solms-Braunfels
8. denominations
9. circuit riders
10. land speculators

Understanding Main Ideas

Section 1

1. How did U.S. immigration change life in the Republic?
2. Did life in Texas become more diverse during the years of the Republic? Explain your answer.

Section 2

3. How did new immigrants from Europe influence the culture of Texas?
4. Where did European immigrants settle in the Republic?

Section 3

5. What was life like for the people who settled in the Republic?
6. How did churches serve communities in the Republic?

You Be the Historian

Reviewing Themes

1. **Citizenship** How do you think the actions of Texans filing petitions on behalf of the Ashworths reflected civic responsibility?
2. **Culture** How did immigrants to the Republic of Texas maintain their traditional cultures in their new home?
3. **Economics** Why did immigrants move to Texas?

Thinking Critically

1. **Drawing Inferences and Conclusions** How did the end of the Texas Revolution, the Republic's land grants, and immigration affect the population distribution in Texas?
2. **Supporting a Point of View** Do you think the Republic of Texas was a land of opportunity? Explain why or why not.
3. **Analyzing Information** Describe the defining characteristics of the Republic era.

Texas Test Practice

Interpreting Maps

Study the map below. Then use the information on the map to help you answer the questions that follow.

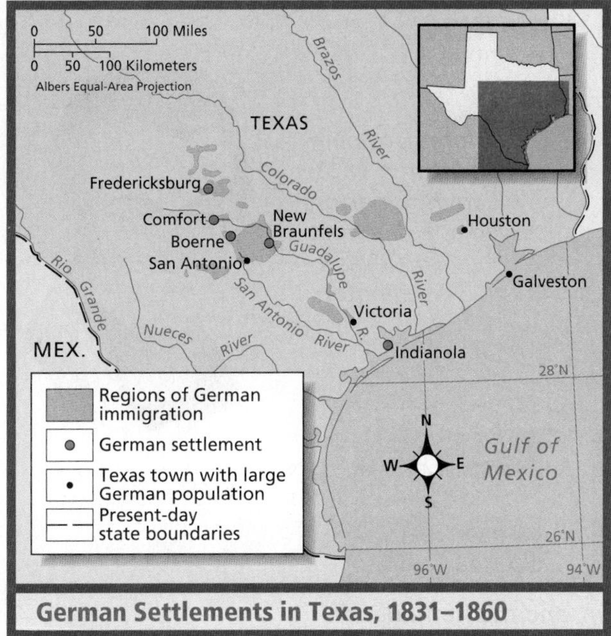

German Settlements in Texas, 1831–1860

1. In what region of Texas did German immigrants settle?
   - **A** Hill Country and Central Texas
   - **B** northeastern Texas
   - **C** West Texas
   - **D** Panhandle

2. What geographic factors influenced the German settlement patterns?

Analyzing Primary Sources

Read the following quote by Mary Austin Holley about the land owned by her brother Henry Austin. Henry Austin never earned the profit he and his sister had expected. After you read the quote, answer the questions.

"I am growing rich in Town Lots—all the town-makers, and they are not few, are ambitious to have me in their town & present me with a lot. . . . Brother will have a sale of town lots in Bolivar [on] 14 April . . . which can not fail to bring money. He expects at least $100,000. . . . He has a ware house already built, and contemplates a rail road towards Houston. . . . They say I should not know Houston it has grown so much since I was there."

3. Which of the following statements best describes the author's point of view?
   - **F** My brother's expectations for the growth of the town are too high.
   - **G** The sale of town lots will not bring in much money.
   - **H** I have already made a lot of money selling lots to new town residents.
   - **J** Texas towns are growing, and my brother and I will soon earn money selling lots in Bolivar.

4. Based on your knowledge of the chapter, why did Holley think the land in Bolivar would be profitable?

Interdisciplinary Connection to Geography

Work with a group of four or more classmates to complete the following activity. Find an online database that has statistics indicating where people lived during the Republic. Create a map that shows changes in geographic distributions of people during the period. Write a caption that describes the patterns you see. Use information from the chapter text and maps to complete the project. Based on the map, create questions for a quiz and provide an answer key.

Internet Activity 

Access the Internet to research one immigrant group that came to Texas and how that group's migration influenced Texas. Then write a newspaper article that explores how this group maintained its cultural heritage while adapting to the larger Texas culture. Also investigate any cultural activities, celebrations, or performances that celebrate that group's role in Texas. Your article should accurately reflect life in the Republic and should include information from your research. Be sure to check your article for proper grammar, spelling, sentence structure, punctuation, and citation of sources.

CHAPTER 14

Texas Faces Foreign Challenges (1836–1845)

Texas Essential Knowledge and Skills (TEKS) 1B, 4A, 4B, 8A, 9C, 17C, 19D, 21A, 21B, 21C, 21D, 21E, 22A, 22B, 22C, 22D

Before becoming a senator in 1838, William H. Wharton served as a diplomat for Texas in Washington.

Texas sought recognition from Great Britain, France, Belgium, and the Netherlands.

TEXAS

1837 The U.S. Congress authorizes a diplomat to go to Texas.

1838 William H. Wharton is elected to the Texas Senate.

1839 France becomes the first European nation to recognize Texas as an independent country.

1840 Galveston University opens its doors to five students.

1836 — 1837 — 1838 — 1839 — 1840

U.S. and WORLD

1837 Samuel Morse files for a patent for a telegraph.

1839 The Liberty Party, the first antislavery party in the United States, holds a national convention in New York.

If you were there . . .

Would you support efforts for foreign recognition?

Build on What You Know

The Texas population increased dramatically after the revolution, as land policies and other factors encouraged immigration. The Republic soon sought recognition from other nations. Tensions with Mexico, however, led to several conflicts.

In 1842 the people of Austin fought to keep the state archives from being moved to another town.

Anson Jones served as the last president of the Republic of Texas.

1841
President Mirabeau B. Lamar sends the Texas Navy to the Yucatán coast.

1842
General Adrián Woll and about 1,400 Mexican soldiers capture San Antonio.

1844
Texans elect Anson Jones president of the Republic.

1841 **1842** **1843** **1844** **1845**

1842
U.S. settlers from the Midwest flood the Oregon Trail on their way to Oregon Country.

1845
Florida becomes the 27th state to join the Union.

You Be the Historian

myNotebook

What's Your Opinion? Do you **agree** or **disagree** with the following statements? Support your point of view in your notebook.

- **Global Relations** Good relations with foreign nations can significantly benefit a country's economic and political affairs.
- **Government** The foreign policy of one administration has no effect on later presidencies.
- **Geography** The location of a nation affects its ability to remain independent.

Section 1

Foreign Recognition of Texas

Main Ideas

1. The Republic of Texas sought foreign recognition in part to ease the threat of war with Mexico.
2. Many Texans favored joining the United States.
3. Several countries recognized Texas independence.

Key Terms

- **foreign relations**
- **diplomatic recognition**

Why It Matters Today

The official recognition of Texas independence by other countries was important for a number of reasons, including improving the Republic's economy. Use current events sources to find information about ongoing diplomatic talks today.

TEKS: 4A, 4B, 17C, 21B, 21E, 22D

myNotebook

Use the annotation tools in your eBook to take notes on Texans' efforts to gain recognition of their independence.

The Story Continues

Sailors on the Texas Navy's flagship, the *Independence,* were headed home from New Orleans when trouble struck. Off the Texas coast, the *Independence* encountered two Mexican warships, and a fierce battle began. The *Independence* was soon captured, along with diplomat William H. Wharton and all the Texas sailors. It seemed that no Texans would be safe until Mexico recognized the Republic's independence.

★ The Quest for Texas Statehood

The relationship between Texas and Mexico was a key issue in the early Republic's **foreign relations**, or dealings with other countries. Mexico refused to acknowledge Texas independence. The Mexicans maintained that Texas was still a state in rebellion against its rightful government.

Texans wanted to resolve their relationship with Mexico to avoid conflicts like the one involving the *Independence*. They hoped that if other nations recognized that Texas was no longer part of Mexico, then Mexico would do the same. This would lessen the chance of war. Most important to the Republic's leaders was **diplomatic recognition** by the United States. Diplomatic recognition is the acknowledgment by one government that another government exists.

Actually, many leaders—including Sam Houston—wanted more than just recognition from the United States. They hoped that Texas could join the United States as a new state. Houston had campaigned for the Texas presidency promising that he would work for Texas statehood, and as president he tried to fulfill that promise. However, U.S. officials did not want to consider annexing Texas. In fact, they were hesitant even to recognize the Republic. U.S. President Andrew Jackson warned Congress that acknowledging Texas independence might anger Mexico. Such an action could lead to a costly war.

Another obstacle to annexation was slavery. In the early 1800s, northern and southern states were at odds over slavery. Northerners who opposed slavery argued against statehood for Texas. They refused to add another state that allowed slavery. William H. Wharton, who had been sent to Washington by President Houston, reported on the debate.

TEXAS VOICES

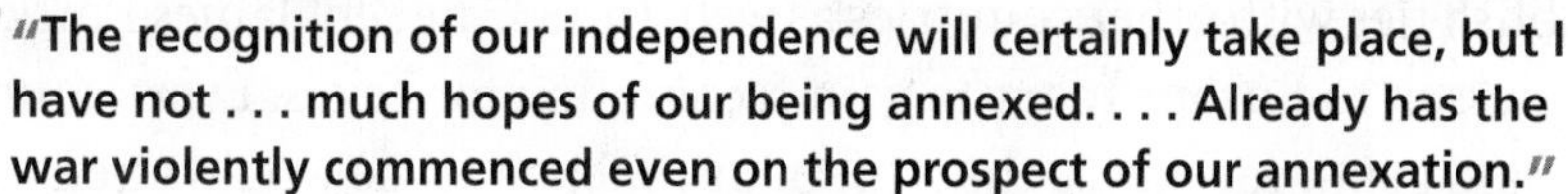

"The recognition of our independence will certainly take place, but I have not . . . much hopes of our being annexed. . . . Already has the war violently commenced even on the prospect of our annexation."

—William H. Wharton, letter to Stephen F. Austin, December 11, 1836

As the debate over annexation continued in Washington, Jackson sent Henry Morfit to Texas to learn about conditions in the Republic. Morfit's report back to the president did not support recognition. He noted that the Republic's population was too small, that the young nation had too much debt, and that it had too powerful an enemy—Mexico—to stand on its own. Americans were not sure the Republic could last.

Reading Check **Finding the Main Idea** Why was foreign recognition important to the Republic of Texas?

LINKING
Past to Present

The French Legation

After France recognized the Republic, a grand home for French diplomat Alphonse Dubois de Saligny was built in Austin. De Saligny, however, sold the mansion before it was finished. Ownership of the house was passed down through a number of hands until it was finally purchased by the state in 1949. The Daughters of the Republic of Texas restored the mansion and now run it as a museum. Today the French Legation Museum is an Austin landmark. **Why do you think the French built this grand home?**

That's Interesting!

The Pig War

In 1841, pigs found a way into the French Legation, destroying papers and clothes belonging to Alphonse Dubois de Saligny. The pigs also ate the corn set out for his prized horses. When one of de Saligny's servants killed some of the pigs, their owner attacked him. Word of the so-called Pig War spread quickly. Texas newspapers sided with the pigs, "Go it Texas! *Viva la pigs!*" When government officials refused to punish the pigs' owner to his satisfaction, de Saligny left Texas for a year.

★ Foreign Recognition

Wharton was right. Despite Morfit's report, the United States officially recognized Texas independence. In his last official act as president, Andrew Jackson appointed Alcée Louis La Branche as U.S. minister to Texas in 1837. The Republic sent Memucan Hunt as its first official representative to Washington.

As Wharton had predicted, though, the U.S. government refused to consider annexation. Many Texans were disappointed at the lost chance for statehood. The Republic's leaders, however, were more optimistic. They hoped that having official diplomatic ties with the United States would lead to foreign trade and loans, both of which were needed to improve the Republic's economy. Also, official recognition by the U.S. government might encourage immigration to Texas.

With recognition from the United States secured, Houston sought to establish ties with other countries as well. In 1837 he sent James Pinckney Henderson to Europe to try to gain recognition for Texas. Every country he could get to recognize the Republic's independence would strengthen its position.

In September 1839 France recognized Texas, becoming the first European country to do so. France sent Alphonse Dubois de Saligny as its representative to the Republic. Recognition from Great Britain, Belgium, and the Netherlands followed. Texas leaders hoped that official recognition by these nations would pressure Mexico to acknowledge Texas independence as well. When that failed, President Lamar tried both cash payments and threats of force to convince Mexico to recognize the Republic's existence. But Mexico still refused.

Reading Check **Analyzing Information** Which countries recognized the Republic of Texas as an independent country?

Section 1 Review

hmhsocialstudies.com
ONLINE QUIZ

1. Define and explain:
- foreign relations
- diplomatic recognition

2. Summarizing
Copy the chart below. Use it to show what Texas might gain from foreign recognition.

Foreign Recognition → would provide → [ ] [ ] [ ]

3. Finding the Main Idea
a. When did the United States and some European nations recognize Texas?
b. How did President Lamar try to pressure Mexico into recognizing Texas?

4. Writing and Critical Thinking *my* WriteSmart
Supporting a Point of View Imagine that you are a Texas representative in Washington. Write a speech to persuade the U.S. government to annex or recognize the Republic.
Consider the following:
- the ties between Texas and the United States
- the conditions in the Republic

Section 2

Conflict with Mexico

Main Ideas

1. President Lamar hoped to add Santa Fe to Texas.
2. The Mexican army raided several targets in Texas.
3. Mexico finally recognized the Texas Republic in 1845.

Why It Matters Today

Ongoing conflicts with Mexico made life in the Republic difficult for many people. Use current events sources to find more information about the effects of international conflicts today.

Key Terms and People

- **Santa Fe expedition**
- **Edwin W. Moore**
- **Mary Maverick**
- **Jack Coffee Hays**
- **Archives War**
- **Mier expedition**

TEKS: 1B, 4A, 8A, 21A, 21B, 21C, 21D, 22C, 22D

myNotebook

Use the annotation tools in your eBook to take notes on conflicts between the Republic of Texas and Mexico.

The Story Continues

After his capture at the Battle of San Jacinto, Mexican general Antonio López de Santa Anna was sent to Washington, DC, as a prisoner. He met President Andrew Jackson, who returned him to Mexico. Soon Santa Anna was back home at his estate in Manga de Clavo, Mexico. By 1839 he was once again running the country, and was eager to make up for the loss of Texas.

The Santa Fe Expedition

Because the Mexican government did not recognize Texas as a free country, there was no clear boundary between Texan and Mexican lands. In 1836 the Republic's Congress had established the Rio Grande as the southern and western boundaries of Texas. If you look at a map, you can see that this would mean Texas claimed about half of New Mexico, including Santa Fe. The people of New Mexico, however, remained loyal to Mexico.

When Mirabeau Lamar became president of the Republic, he wanted to secure the Republic's claim to land east of the Rio Grande. Lamar had visions of a much larger Texas than existed at the time. He also wanted access to the valuable trade moving along the Santa Fe Trail. In 1840 Lamar chose three residents of Santa Fe to act as commissioners for Texas. Their job was to convince the people of the town that they should join the Republic of Texas.

Interpreting Visuals

Santa Fe. *Some Texans wanted to gain control of Santa Fe to gain valuable trade routes along the Santa Fe Trail.* ***What does this image suggest about life in Santa Fe at that time?***

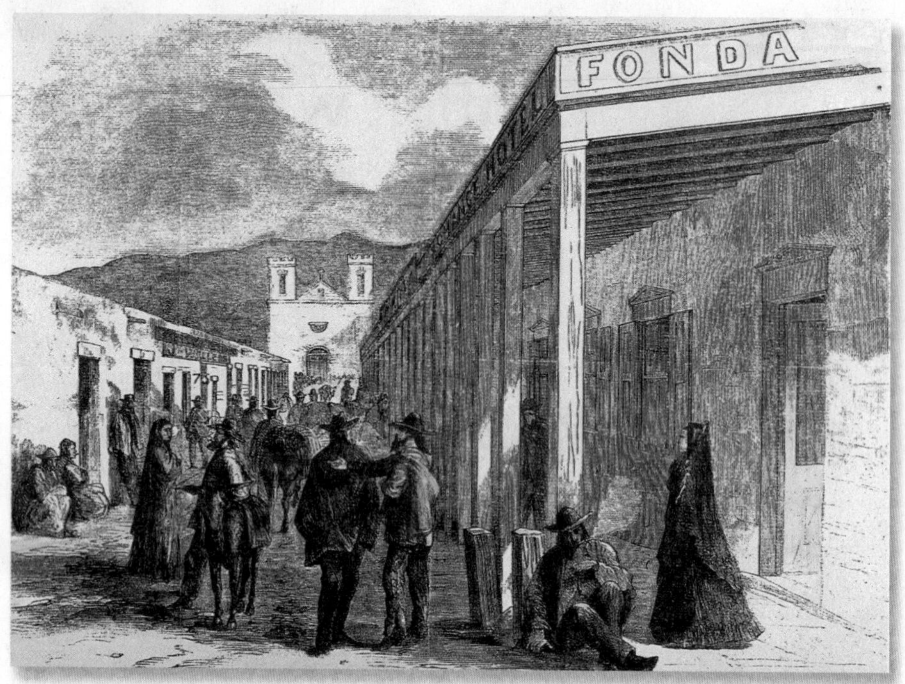

As part of his plan, Lamar also wanted to create a trade route between Texas and Santa Fe. In June 1841 he launched the **Santa Fe expedition**. It consisted of about 320 people transporting about $200,000 worth of trade goods. A number of well-known Texans, including José Antonio Navarro, accompanied the expedition, which was guarded by soldiers under the leadership of Hugh McLeod.

The expedition ran into trouble almost immediately. American Indians attacked as the Texans passed through their lands, and food and water were in short supply. When the exhausted Texans reached New Mexico in October 1841, Mexican troops were waiting for them.

The Texans were arrested and marched about 1,200 miles to Mexico City. One of the prisoners described the hardships of the march. "We had not proceeded far when some of the guard . . . shot one of the men who was lame." The Texans remained in jail until the following April.

As the only Tejano member of the expedition, José Antonio Navarro faced the worst treatment. He was a former Mexican official who had sided with the Texans in the Revolution. Therefore, he was seen as a traitor to his country. Navarro was sentenced to death and remained in prison even after the others had been released. Eventually, however, Navarro escaped and returned to Texas just in time to serve as the only Tejano delegate to the annexation convention in 1845.

Lamar's Santa Fe expedition was a failure. At least 60 Texans died, and the expedition cost Texas a great sum of money. In addition, the expedition renewed Mexican interest in Texas. It set the stage for years of conflict between the two countries.

Reading Check **Identifying Cause and Effect** What prompted Lamar to send the Santa Fe expedition, and why was it a failure?

The Texas Navy

In 1840 rebels in the Mexican state of Yucatán rebelled against the government. Hearing about the rebellion, President Lamar saw both a chance to hurt Mexico and a possible source of income. Late in 1841 he sent the Texas Navy under **Edwin W. Moore** to the Yucatán coast. Commodore Moore helped the Yucatán rebels win several battles against the Mexican government. In return, they agreed to pay Texas $8,000 a month for the use of the navy.

When Sam Houston's second term began in 1841, though, he ordered the navy home. Houston was determined to cut spending, and he ordered that the navy ships be sold at auction in Galveston. But the people of Galveston opposed the sale and would not allow people to place bids. Although the ships were not sold, they were no longer in operation.

Reading Check **Analyzing Information** Why did Lamar send the navy to Mexico?

The Archives War

Upset by Lamar's actions, the Mexican government sent armies into Texas. In March 1842, a force under General Ráfael Vásquez attacked San Antonio, Goliad, Refugio, and Victoria. In September of the same year, General Adrián Woll and 1,400 soldiers captured San Antonio. Resident **Mary Maverick** described the morning invasion in her diary, a major source of information about life in Texas during this time.

TEXAS VOICES

"We were aroused . . . by the firing of a . . . cannon [and the] tramp of a body of men. A dense fog obscured them from actual observation until they had advanced into the public square . . . when the fog disappeared discovering to us that we were surrounded on all sides by the bodies of regular [Mexican] troops."

—Samuel Maverick, quoted in *Memoirs of Mary A. Maverick*

Woll took a few dozen Texans captive and headed farther into San Antonio. A volunteer force under Ranger **Jack Coffee Hays** met Woll at Salado Creek and forced him to retreat back to Mexico. Hays is remembered today as the ideal Texas Ranger: fearless, capable, and loyal. He would later become a hero in the Mexican-American War.

President Houston took advantage of the insecurity along the frontier to call Congress into session in Washington-on-the-Brazos. In December 1842 he ordered Texas Rangers to bring the government archives there. Austin residents opposed the move, suspecting it meant their city would no longer be the capital. Led by Angelina Eberly, they fired at workers loading the documents onto wagons. This conflict, called the **Archives War,** ended with the documents back in Austin.

Reading Check **Drawing Inferences and Conclusions** What did the Mexican raids on Texas demonstrate about the Republic's security?

Daily Life

Mary Maverick's Diary

Much of what we know about life in San Antonio in the 1800s is thanks to one woman, Mary Maverick. Mary and her husband Samuel lived in San Antonio with their 10 children, four of whom would fight in the Civil War. Maverick dedicated much of her life to preserving Texas history. She published her journal as a record of her lifetime and joined both the San Antonio Historical Society and the Daughters of the Republic of Texas. **How did Mary Maverick help preserve Texas history?**

CONNECTING TO

The Arts

Frederic Remington

Artist Frederic Remington painted many scenes of the American West. In this painting, he shows Texans captured during the Mier expedition picking beans to determine who would be executed. **How did Remington portray the drama of the event?**

★ The Mier Expedition

The Mexican attack on San Antonio angered Texans. "To arms! should be shouted throughout the Republic," one newspaper declared. Many people did in fact demand war against Mexico. In November President Houston ordered General Alexander Somervell to the Rio Grande. He was to recapture the prisoners taken by General Woll.

When Somervell reached the Rio Grande, though, he realized that he did not have enough supplies or troops to complete his mission. He ordered his soldiers home, but about 300 of them disobeyed orders. They decided to invade Mexico. Led by Colonel William S. Fisher, the Texans headed toward the small Mexican town of Mier. Their action became known as the **Mier expedition**.

The Texans entered Mier on December 23 and demanded supplies, which the townspeople agreed to deliver the next day. When the supplies did not arrive, the Texans stormed the town. There, some 900 Mexican soldiers were waiting for them. After a daylong battle, about 100 Mexicans and 30 Texans were killed or wounded. Because they were running out of supplies, the Texans surrendered.

The captured Texans began a long march toward Mexico City. Almost 200 of the prisoners escaped during the march south. Wandering in the mountains without food and water, most of them either died or were recaptured. Santa Anna, who once again ruled Mexico, ordered every 10th person to be shot. The 176 prisoners drew beans from a jar

to see who would would be among the 10 percent executed. A prisoner described the scene. The beans were drawn from "a small earthen mug. The white ones signified *exemption* [no punishment], the black, *death*." The prisoners who drew the black beans were blindfolded and then shot. Of the remaining captives, 18 eventually managed to escape. At least 20 died in prison, and others were pardoned. In September 1844, Mexican officials released the last of the prisoners of the Mier expedition.

The Mier expedition was the last conflict between Mexico and the Republic of Texas. Through the efforts of Great Britain and France, peace was slowly restored between the two nations. The European countries had a specific motive in aiding Texas. They wanted the Republic to remain independent rather than join the United States, which they viewed as a rival. As a result, they were furiously trying to block any attempt to add Texas to the United States. If the Europeans could get Mexico to recognize Texas independence, they believed that the people of Texas would be less likely to seek annexation.

Great Britain and France put great diplomatic pressure on Mexico to recognize Texas. In the spring of 1845, a British diplomat presented a document to the Mexican government. By accepting the document, the government would formally acknowledge the independent Republic of Texas. In return, Texas would not join the United States.

Mexican leaders eventually decided to agree to the terms of the proposal. Like the Europeans, Mexico wished to prevent U.S. annexation of Texas. The Mexican government did not want to share a border with the rapidly growing United States. By the time it agreed to recognize Texas independence, though, it was too late. The Texans had decided in favor of annexation.

Reading Check **Finding the Main Idea** Why was the Texas agreement not to be annexed by any nation critical to Mexico?

Section 2 Review

1. Identify and explain the significance of each of the following in Texas history:

- Santa Fe expedition
- Edwin W. Moore
- Mary Maverick
- Jack Coffee Hays
- Archives War
- Mier expedition

2. Sequencing Copy the time line below. Use it to place the events of the Mier expedition in the order in which they occurred.

Sam Houston sends soldiers to the Rio Grande. — Mexican officials release the Mier prisoners.

3. Finding the Main Idea

a. How did the Santa Fe expedition increase hostilities with Mexico?

b. How did the Republic achieve peace with Mexico?

4. Writing and Critical Thinking myWriteSmart

Identifying Points of View Write an article explaining the points of view of the Texas and Mexican governments on recognition. Consider the following:

- views of the Texas Revolution
- foreign recognition of Texas

Connecting To
Geography

Conflicts with Mexico

Geographic factors played a major role in the conflicts faced by the Republic. During the Santa Fe expedition, Texans struggled across the rugged West Texas terrain. They had difficulty pulling their wagons up the 1,000-foot-high rise called the Caprock. The dry, barren area defeated the expedition even before it met any Mexican forces. Later, during the Mier expedition, Texas soldiers traveled down the Rio Grande to Mier.

Geography **Skills**

Interpreting Thematic Maps

1. Explain how geographic factors affected conflicts and foreign relations in the Republic.
2. Use the map scale to determine about how many miles the Texans marched from Austin to Mexico City.
3. What activity took place around San Antonio?

Conflicts of the Republic, 1837–1842

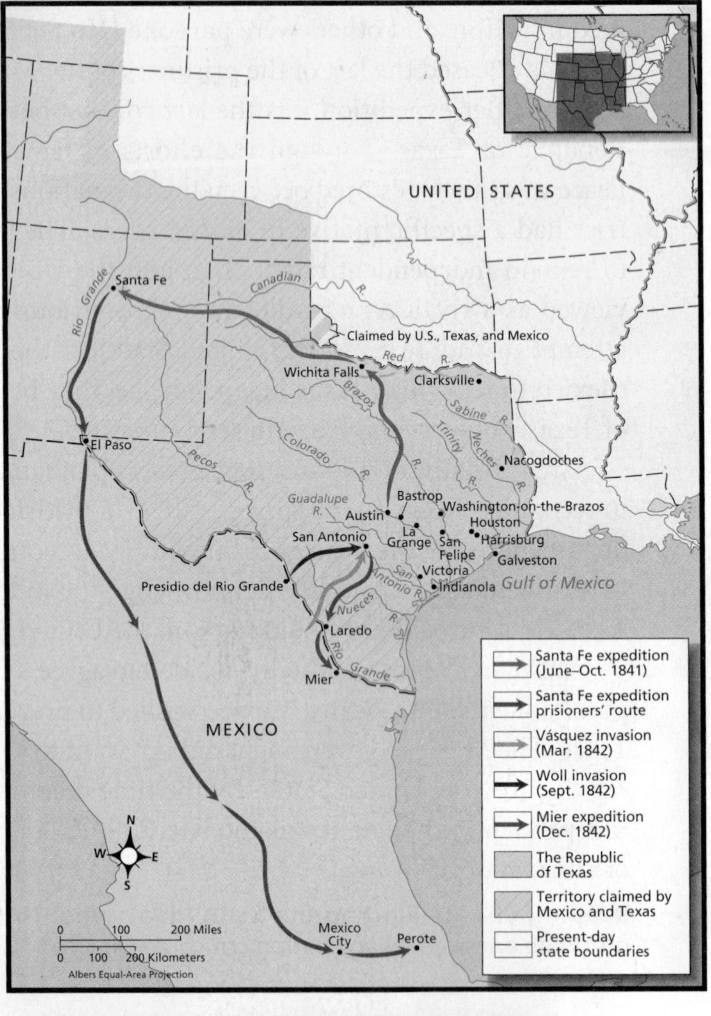

Texans on the Mier expedition traveled down the Rio Grande.

Section 3

The Last Years of the Republic

Main Ideas

1. Anson Jones was elected president of the Republic of Texas in 1844.
2. During Jones's presidency, Texans increased their calls for annexation with the United States.

Key Person

- **Anson Jones**

Why It Matters Today

Annexation to the United States was a major issue for Texas. Use current events sources to find information about major political issues facing Texas or the United States today.

TEKS: 4A, 4B, 21B, 22D

myNotebook

Use the annotation tools in your eBook to take notes on the issues of the Jones presidency.

The Story Continues

In December 1844 Sam Houston stood before the Texas Congress to give his final speech as the Republic's president. He was pleased. Under his leadership, he reminded Congress, Texas had avoided war with Mexico. The Mexicans had not invaded Texas since 1842, and all Texas prisoners but one had returned home. The economy was improving. Houston wanted the next president to continue his policies.

★ President Anson Jones

The question of who that next president would be was fiercely debated. In the election of 1844, the Republic was divided. Newspapers printed harsh criticisms of both candidates, Vice President Edward Burleson and **Anson Jones.** Jones was a doctor from Brazoria and a veteran of the Battle of San Jacinto. He had served in the Texas Congress and as secretary of state under Houston.

Jones and Houston shared similar views on most issues. As a result, Jones received Houston's support in the election. Burleson, on the other hand, had disagreed with Houston over many issues, including whether to attack Mexico. Because Burleson was at odds with Houston, he gained the support of Houston's opponents, including Mirabeau B. Lamar and his followers. As the election approached, the campaign reached a fever pitch. Voters either supported or opposed Sam Houston—there was no middle ground.

That's Interesting!

Counting the Votes

During the Texas election of 1844, presidential candidate Anson Jones was serving as secretary of state. Part of his official duties in this role included counting the votes in the presidential election in which he was the victor.

Jones easily won the election. Many Texans blamed the Republic's problems on Lamar, so his support had hurt Burleson. Kenneth Anderson was chosen as vice president. Some citizens, however, claimed that Jones would not have won on his own merits. After the election, one Texan wrote a letter about the subject.

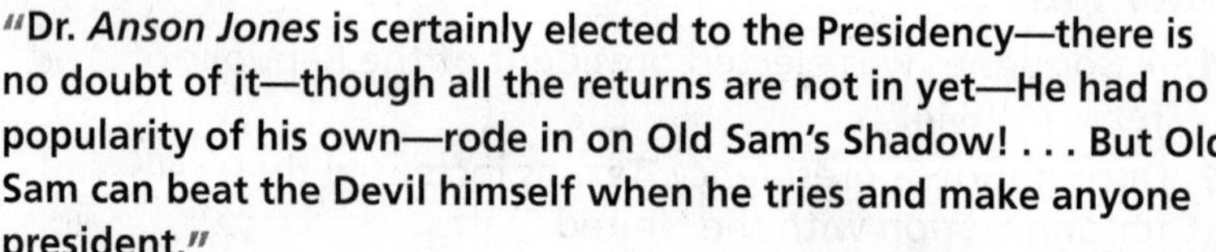

TEXAS VOICES

"Dr. *Anson Jones* is certainly elected to the Presidency—there is no doubt of it—though all the returns are not in yet—He had no popularity of his own—rode in on Old Sam's Shadow! . . . But Old Sam can beat the Devil himself when he tries and make anyone president."

—James Morgan, letter to Samuel Swartwout, September 28, 1844

As president, Jones inherited the Republic's economic problems. From its beginning, the Republic of Texas had been in debt. The debt had grown during Lamar's presidency. When Sam Houston started his second term of office, the Republic's treasury was empty. Houston had tried to limit government spending, but a partial failure of the Texas cotton crop in 1842 and 1843 prevented the economy from recovering.

Jones continued Houston's policy of limited government spending. In addition, the new president continued to work for peace with Texas Indians, a policy that was also aimed at reducing spending. As annexation to the United States became more likely, the value of Texas currency slowly began to climb. By 1845 the value of Texas currency in many parts of the Republic had become equal to that of U.S. currency. Good crop years and increased trade were also helping to improve the Texas economy.

Reading Check **Drawing Inferences and Conclusions** What signs gave Texans hope that the Republic's economy was improving?

Salaries of Texas Officials

Position	1845 Salary in 2012 Dollars	2012
President/Governor	$116,197	$150,000
Secretary of State	$34,859	$125,880
Chief Justice	$40,669	$152,500
Attorney General	$23,239	$150,000
Land Commissioner	$34,859	$145,200

Source: Texas Almanac and Laws of the Ninth Congress

Interpreting Tables As part of his plan to cut spending, Sam Houston cut the salaries of government officials. Even after adjusting for inflation, officials in the Republic made far less than officials do today. In 2012 dollars, how much more does the governor make than the president did?

Texans Debate Annexation

Although economic problems were a major concern for many Texans, President Jones was more worried about the prospects of annexation. As you have read, Texans had voted in favor of annexation in 1836. However, the U.S. government had not been willing to annex the Republic. Houston's administration had supported annexation, while Lamar's administration had opposed it.

As secretary of state, Jones had worked directly with Houston to map out foreign relations for Texas. Their ideas had included plans for the Republic's possible annexation to the United States. In 1843 a newspaper had noted that "as great a proportion [percentage] of the people [are] in favor of annexation" as had been in 1836.

During his first months in office, Jones kept silent on the issue of annexation. Many Texans wanted decisive action, and so they became frustrated with Jones. More and more, Texans called for annexation. Jones, however, wanted Texans to have the option of becoming part of their neighbor to the north or of maintaining independence. The latter option depended on peaceful relations with Mexico, so he worked to obtain Mexico's recognition.

Few Texans were interested in negotiating with Mexico, as a newspaper expressed in 1845. "The object of the Mexican government is to lie and deceive us. . . . They may dupe [trick] some of our statesmen; but they will not dupe the people of Texas." As the demand for a convention to decide the issue of annexation grew stronger, word arrived that Mexico might soon recognize the Republic. Texans debated whether their country should stay independent or continue to seek annexation.

Reading Check **Identifying Points of View** Why did President Jones want to wait on the question of annexation?

BIOGRAPHY

Anson Jones

(1798–1858) Anson Jones was born in Massachusetts. He studied medicine as a young man and began practicing in 1820. He moved to Texas in 1833. After serving in the revolution, Jones returned to his medical practice. He became interested in politics and served in a number of offices. Jones supported Houston's efforts to keep peace with Texas Indians. After serving as the last president of the Republic of Texas, Jones retired to his farm near Washington-on-the-Brazos. **What contributions did Jones make to Texas?**

Section 3 Review

hmhsocialstudies.com ONLINE QUIZ

1. **Identify and explain** the significance of the following in Texas history:
   - Anson Jones

2. **Analyzing Information** Copy the graphic organizer below. Use it to explain the choice President Jones wanted Texans to make regarding the future of the Republic.

The Future of the Republic

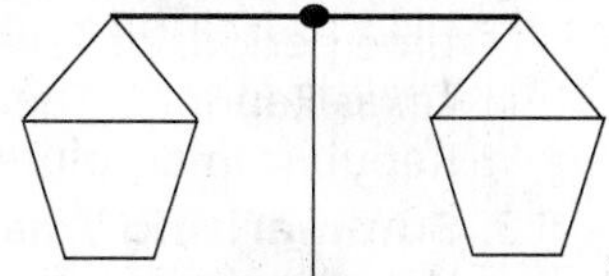

3. **Finding the Main Idea**
   a. Who won the Texas presidential election of 1844, and how did Lamar and Houston influence this outcome?
   b. In what ways had the Texas economy changed by 1844?

4. **Writing and Critical Thinking** myWriteSmart
   Making Generalizations and Predictions Write a paragraph explaining why you think Texans will or will not continue to support annexation.
   Consider the following:
   - the reasons for annexation
   - the improved economy and the possibility of recognition from Mexico

CHAPTER 14 REVIEW

The Chapter at a Glance

Examine the following visual summary of the chapter. Then use the visual to create flash cards about the chapter. Using the flash cards as a study guide, work with a partner to be sure you both comprehend the material in this chapter.

Identifying People and Ideas

Write a sentence to explain the role or significance of each of the following terms or people.

1. foreign relations
2. James Pinckney Henderson
3. Edwin W. Moore
4. Santa Fe expedition
5. Mary Maverick
6. Archives War
7. Anson Jones
8. Mier expedition
9. Jack Coffee Hays

Understanding Main Ideas

Section 1

1. Which nations were the first to recognize Texas?
2. How did President Lamar try to pressure Mexico into recognizing Texas?

Section 2

3. Describe what happened to the Santa Fe and Mier expeditions.
4. How did Texans hope to achieve peace with Mexico?
5. What role did the Texas Navy play during the Lamar administration?

Section 3

6. What was the most critical issue during the presidency of Anson Jones, and how did Texans respond to it?

You Be the Historian

Reviewing Themes

1. **Global Relations** Describe the defining characteristics of the Republic's foreign relations.
2. **Government** How did Lamar's policy toward Mexico affect events during Houston's second administration?
3. **Geography** How did geographic features like nearness to Mexico affect the Republic's foreign relations?

Thinking Critically

1. **Comparing and Contrasting** How did Houston's and Lamar's foreign policies differ? How did this affect events in their presidencies?
2. **Sequencing** Identify in absolute sequence the time periods of Texas history leading up to the Texas Republic. Then list the presidents of the Republic in absolute sequence.
3. **Summarizing** What major issues did Texas face? Why was annexation considered a good solution?

Texas Test Practice

Interpreting Graphs

Study the bar graph below. Then use the information on the graph to help you answer the questions.

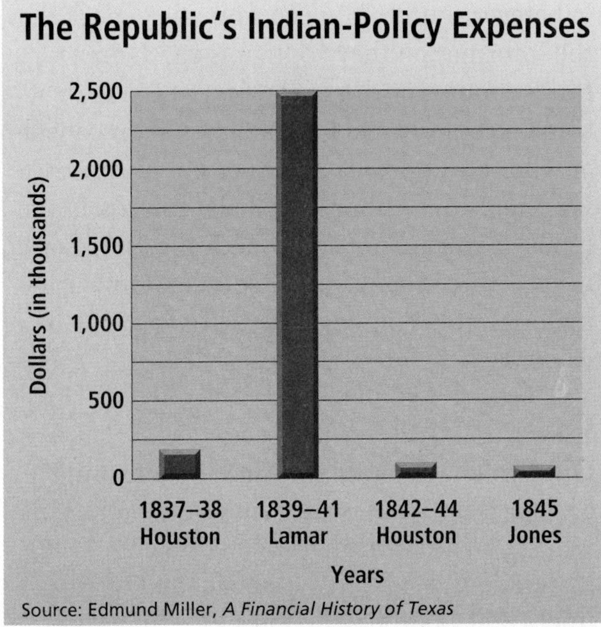

Source: Edmund Miller, *A Financial History of Texas*

1. Approximately how many times more did Lamar spend than Houston and Jones combined?

A 2
B 8
C 15
D 25

2. Organize the presidential terms on this graph in order of money spent on Indian policy, from least spent to most.

3. How does this graph reflect what you have read about Houston's and Lamar's attitudes toward American Indians? Explain your answer.

Analyzing Primary Sources

Read the following quote by Sam Houston on events following the Santa Fe expedition. Then answer the questions.

"This moment I have learned that our Santa Fe prisoners have been released, and will soon return to Texas. At this I am much rejoiced for various reasons. First, because the sufferings of our countrymen are ended, and they are again free. We have one less cause of irritation, and so much the less food for . . . agitators. When the matter is understood of their release, it may give us a squint into the affairs of Mexico."

4. What does this quote reveal about Houston's point of view toward Mexico?

F Houston wants to better understand the positions of the Mexican government.
G He has no interest in Mexico.
H He favors an invasion of Mexico.
J Relations between Texas and Mexico are peaceful.

5. What does Houston mean when he refers to "agitators"?

Cooperative Learning

Work with a small group to complete the following activity. Imagine that you and the members of your group are diplomats of the Republic of Texas. Each of you should select one of the following countries and try to convince that country to recognize Texas: a) Mexico b) Great Britain c) France d) Belgium e) the Netherlands. Prepare a presentation to the officials of the nation you have selected. You may want to prepare visuals, such as a map or poster, to make your case more convincing.

Internet Activity

Access the Internet to learn more about the debate over annexation. Locate, differentiate between, and use primary and secondary sources such as databases, biographies, and artifacts in your research. Choose which side of the debate you agree with and create a poster that supports your position. Present your poster to the class. Proofread your poster to ensure that you have used standard spelling, grammar, punctuation, and word choice in any text.

Social Studies Skills

WORKSHOP

Research Skills

Good research skills are vital for studying history. In order to learn about the past, you need to know where to look for information. You also need to know what to do with the information that you find.

Selecting Sources

There is a lot of information about Texas history out there. People have studied and written about the state in various media for more than 200 years. The list below includes a few types of primary and secondary sources you could consult to acquire information about Texas. Primary sources are created by people who actually witness events. Secondary sources are created by people who study about the events after they have already occurred.

- **Books** provide a wealth of information about historical topics, but the information may not be the most up-to-date.
- **Web sites** frequently contain historical information. However, you must examine each page carefully to determine whether it is trustworthy.
- **Databases** are collections of data. Often, the data are statistical information such as numbers and dates, which can be valuable in your research.
- **Media and news services** are vital for keeping up with current events. They can also help you keep up with recent trends in historical studies.
- **Biographies** are useful for learning the details of a person's life and actions.
- **Interviews** with historical figures can give you insight into their beliefs and thoughts.
- **Artifacts** allow you to interact with the objects used and owned by the people you are researching.

Whatever sources you use, you must check that the information they contain is valid. First, think about how the source is written. Does it sound scholarly and informative? Then consider who the author is and his or her purpose for writing. Is the author knowledgeable about the topic? If you are not sure, check the information in the source against other sources. Only use material from sources that you have decided are valid.

Using Information

Once you have found information, examine it to determine what is relevant to the project on which you are working. Take notes about that material, writing down each fact and why it is important. As you take notes, carefully record where you found each bit of information. You will need that information later so that you can cite your sources. Any time you use another person's words, thoughts, or arguments in a paper or project, you must give them credit. You can find the proper way to cite each type of source in a style manual or from your teacher.

Practicing the Skill

Conduct research online and in a library to acquire information about the Texas Revolution. Try to find at least one of each type of source listed on this page. Examine the sources you have found to learn what each contains. Then make a chart that lists your sources. Identify which are primary sources and which are secondary. Then differentiate among the various types of sources by noting what kind of material each source contains and how you might use that material in a project or paper.

History in Action

UNIT 4 SIMULATION

You Make the Decision . . .

Should Texas declare independence?

Complete the following activity in small cooperative groups. It is 1835. You and your fellow delegates have been called to a convention. Your assignment is to decide whether Texas should declare independence from Mexico. The rest of the convention is about to begin debating the issue, so you need to make a decision quickly. Follow these steps to reach your decision.

1. **Gather information.** Use your textbook and other resources to find information that might help you decide whether to declare independence. This might include your commitment to republican ideals, the actions of Santa Anna, and the views of people in your community, including Tejanos, African Americans, and recent arrivals from the United States. Be sure to use what you learned from this unit's Skills Workshop on conducting research to help you gather information. Remember that many different types of sources may have information that would be helpful in making your decision.

2. **Identify options.** After reviewing the information you have gathered, consider the options you might recommend to the convention. Your final decision may be easier to reach if you consider as many options as possible. Be sure to record your possible options for your presentation.

3. **Predict consequences.** Now take each option you and the members of your group came up with and consider what might be the outcome of each course of action. Ask yourselves questions such as, "How might Texas benefit from doing this?", "How might Mexico respond if we do this?", and "What might be the long-term effects of following this course of action?" Once you have predicted the consequences, record them as notes for your presentation.

4. **Take action to implement your decision.** After you have considered your options, plan and create your presentation. Be sure to make your decision on whether to support independence very clear to the rest of the convention. You will need to support your decision by including information you gathered and by explaining why you rejected other options. Your presentation needs to be visually appealing in order to convince the other delegates. When you are ready, decide who in your group will make which part of the presentation and take your suggestion to the convention (the rest of the class).
After you present, ask your listeners if they have any questions about what they have just heard. Listen carefully to the questions they ask and answer appropriately. In your answer, give the requested information clearly and briefly, using specific language.

UNIT 5

Early Statehood

(1845–1861)

CHAPTER 15 Texas Joins the United States (1845–1860)

CHAPTER 16 Western Expansion and Conflict (1845–1860)

CHAPTER 17 Life in a Frontier State (1845–1861)

The stagecoach was a common form of transportation across the Texas frontier in the days before the railroad.

Image Credit: Eggenhoffer, Nick, The Stagecoach, 1972, mixed media, 14x17, 82.09c.2, National Cowboy and Western Heritage Museum, Oklahoma City

Texas Teens

Young Texans on the Frontier

George Thomas Reynolds was a teenager when the Pony Express was developed. The mission of the Pony Express was to deliver mail quickly. A network of skilled horseback riders carried bags of mail across the American frontier. Riders had to be small—usually under 120 pounds—so that the 20 pounds of mail and 25 pounds of equipment they carried would not overburden the horse. As a result, many Pony Express riders were young. The youngest riders were in their early teens.

Pony Express riders traveled long distances on each shift. On longer runs, riders would change horses at stations in order to have a fresh horse. A typical rider rode a 75- to 100-mile route and received $25 a week, along with free room and board.

The routes these young men traveled were often incredibly dangerous—heading through rugged American Indian territory. There were rushing rivers to be crossed. Riders, horses, and mail could be lost in river crossings, especially when heavy rains led to floods. Extreme temperatures were also a danger. In one instance a Pony Express rider got lost while making a December delivery and froze to death.

Although he knew the work could be dangerous, George Reynolds jumped at the chance for an exciting job as a Pony Express rider. He was only 15, but he was already a good rider. In 1859 or 1860, Reynolds made his first run for the Pony Express. He left his hometown of Palo Pinto loaded down with mail that needed to be delivered to Weatherford. Reynolds had to ride 35 miles through frontier territory where raids by American Indians were common. He reached Weatherford without a problem, though. Reynolds was lucky during his adventures as a Pony Express rider. **What challenges did Texans like Reynolds face on the frontier?**

In this unit you will learn more about the Texas frontier and the early history of the Lone Star State. You will also learn about the U.S.–Mexican War, new American Indian policies, and many other changes.

Texas Takes Shape

On December 29, 1845 Texas joined the United States as the 28th state. One of the state's main resources was land—lots of it. Romantic images were printed in newspapers around the country showing Texas as a land of opportunity, rich wildlife, fertile soil, and an ideal climate. Lured by such images, thousands of Americans decided to pack up their families and start a new life on the Texas frontier. Between 1850 and 1860, the state's population nearly tripled as settlers poured in from around the United States. The young state was a land of frontier settlers, farmers, and new immigrants.

As wave after wave of settlers arrived, they kept moving farther west in search of open land. In the process, they pushed American Indians from their land. A few Indian groups were eager to trade with American settlers. But Anglo farmers' hunger for land and general hostility toward Indians resulted in increasingly violent conflicts.

During these early years of statehood, the modern borders of Texas began to take shape. Border disputes with Mexico were resolved in 1848 after the U.S.-Mexican War. The Treaty of Guadalupe Hidalgo set the Texas-Mexico border at the Rio Grande. Later, the Compromise of 1850 settled Texas's boundaries in the west and north. With these agreements, the modern shape of Texas that we recognize today was complete.

Exploring Museum Resources

The Bullock Texas State History Museum includes many resources related to Texas immigration and frontier life. These include artifacts, diary entries, and maps highlighting this early period of the state's history. Explore some of these resources online. You can find museum resources at **hmhsocialstudies.com**

Artifact Settlers on the Texas frontier were resourceful and self-reliant. What can artifacts like this candle mold teach us today about life on the Texas frontier?

Artifact Conflicts between Texas's native Indian groups and other residents were a common problem. Learn more about frontier conflicts during Texas's early statehood.

Map This map from around 1857 shows the distinctive Texas shape. Who made this map, and why? Go online to find out.

UNIT 5

Reading Social Studies

Making Generalizations and Predictions

Focus on Reading People make generalizations all the time. In fact, that statement is itself a generalization. A **generalization** is a broad statement that holds true for a variety of historical events or situations. A **prediction** is an educated guess about an outcome.

Understanding Generalizations and Predictions Making generalizations can help you see the big picture of historical events, rather than just focusing on details. When making generalizations, try not to include situations that do not fit the statement. Notice how the processes of generalizing and predicting work with the following passages.

---

(1) Many Europeans also came to Texas during this time. Most wanted to escape hardships in their homelands. Crop failures had left people starving in Ireland and parts of central and northern Europe. A series of revolutions in 1848 led many people to leave. Germans were the largest European immigrant group, with an 1860 population greater than 20,000.

(2) Polish colonists founded Panna Maria in Karnes County. Czech and Slavic immigrants also came to Texas. Hundreds of Jewish immigrants settled in cities such as Galveston and Houston. Immigrants from Italy, the Netherlands, and Belgium also arrived. Each group brought its traditional foods, celebrations, and architecture.

Example 1: Life in Europe was difficult during the mid-1800s. Many Europeans left their homelands and settled in Texas.

Example 2: People from all over Europe came to Texas, bringing with them their food, celebrations, and architecture.

Generalization: Hardships led many Europeans to immigrate to Texas. These immigrants brought with them their different cultural traditions and ways of life.

Prediction: The immigrant population of Texas will continue to increase and become more diverse. Immigrant settlements will expand to areas across the state, spreading their cultural influence.

You Try It!

Read the following passage and generalizations A, B, and C below it. Then answer the questions that follow.

Farmers and Planters

According to the 1850 census, 95 percent of Texans lived in rural areas. Agriculture in Texas continued to expand as people moved there from many other states and nations. The number of farms in the state more than doubled between 1850 and 1860.

A Agriculture was an important part of the Texas economy.

B Many people would begin to leave rural areas for cities.

C The number of farms in Texas would continue to grow.

1. Which of the generalizations above are supported by the information in the passage? Which are not? How do you know?
2. What prediction can you make about the importance of agriculture to the Texas economy in future decades?

Reading Section Assessment

Reread the passage above and review the section on Railroads on page 356 in your textbook. Use information from both passages to make generalizations and predictions.

1. Using information from both passages, create a chart like the one on the previous page that shows examples, a generalization, and a prediction about the future of agriculture in Texas.
2. How might future expansion of railroad lines affect the Texas agricultural industry and the Texas economy?

Key Terms

Unit 5

Chapter 15

manifest destiny *(p. 315)*
political parties *(p. 316)*
joint resolution *(p. 316)*
biennial *(p. 319)*
corporations *(p. 321)*

Chapter 16

offensive *(p. 333)*
Mexican Cession *(p. 334)*
Compromise of 1850 *(p. 335)*
reservations *(p. 340)*

Chapter 17

cotton belt *(p. 349)*
planters *(p. 349)*
gristmills *(p. 351)*
tanneries *(p. 351)*
oxcarts *(p. 354)*
steamboats *(p. 355)*
telegraphs *(p. 358)*
spirituals *(p. 362)*
abolition *(p. 363)*

As you read, pay attention to the pictures that appear on a page with the text. These pictures can provide context and background knowledge that will help you make sense of what you are reading.

CHAPTER 15

Texas Joins the United States (1845–1860)

Texas Essential Knowledge and Skills (TEKS) 1A, 1B, 1C, 4B, 4C, 8A, 14A, 17A, 17C, 18A, 21B, 21D, 21E, 21H, 22A, 22B, 22C, 22D

Residents of San Antonio celebrated the annexation of Texas by the United States.

TEXAS

1845 The United States annexes Texas.

1846 Thomas J. Rusk and Sam Houston become the first Texans to serve in the U.S. Senate.

1847 George T. Wood is elected governor of Texas.

1852 Work begins on the Port Isabel Lighthouse. When completed, its light could be seen from 16 miles away.

1845 — 1847 — 1849 — 1851

U.S. and WORLD

1845 Great Britain announces that it will seize all slave-carrying ships sailing to Brazil.

1848 The Seneca Falls Convention calls for equal rights for women, including the right to vote.

1850 California is admitted to the United States.

If you were there . . . *Would you support annexation?*

Build on What You Know

The Republic of Texas had finally won recognition from the United States, Mexico, and several European countries. But annexation was still on many people's minds. In the United States, the topic was a matter of fierce debate. For Texas, annexation would bring many changes.

Before becoming a U.S. senator, Thomas J. Rusk served on the Texas Supreme Court.

The Port Isabel Lighthouse was used as an observation tower and to signal sailors.

1854
The American, or Know-Nothing, Party becomes active in Texas.

1855
The Governor's Mansion is built in Austin.

1859
Sam Houston easily defeats incumbent Hardin Runnels in the election for Texas governor.

1853 | **1855** | **1857** | **1859**

1853
Commodore Matthew C. Perry of the U.S. Navy sails into Edo (now Tokyo) Bay, Japan. Perry soon signs treaties of peace and commerce with the Japanese.

1855
The Kansas Territory's legislature passes harsh pro-slavery laws that spark criticism.

Be the Historian

*my***Notebook**

What's Your Opinion? Do you **agree** or **disagree** with the following statements? Support your point of view in your notebook.

- **Geography** Most people in a nation support adding new territory.
- **Citizenship** People should organize into groups to make government respond to their demands.
- **Economics** Nations should not be allowed to go into debt.

Section 1 The Annexation of Texas

Main Ideas

1. Support for annexation in the United States was divided over the issue of slavery.
2. Texas became a state in 1845.

Key Terms and People

- **manifest destiny**
- **Jane McManus Cazneau**
- **political parties**
- **joint resolution**
- **Convention of 1845**
- **Texas Admission Act**

Why It Matters Today

During the 1840s, politicians could not agree on the issue of whether or not to annex Texas. Use current events sources to find information about an issue that politicians are debating today.

TEKS: 1B, 1C, 4B, 17A, 21B, 21C, 21D, 22D

myNotebook

Use the annotation tools in your eBook to take notes on the debates and votes that led to statehood for Texas.

The Story Continues

President John Tyler of the United States was concerned. He took office in 1841, a few years after Congress had rejected the chance to annex Texas. Since that time, Great Britain had become more involved in Texas affairs. Tyler feared that the British were working to gain a foothold in North America from which they could interfere with American matters. Perhaps it was time to reconsider Texas annexation.

The Treaty to Annex Texas

The annexation question remained a hot issue in Texas for many years. Although his initial attempt to bring Texas into the United States had failed, Sam Houston had never given up his dream. A majority of Texans still longed for statehood, too. As time had passed, support for annexation had grown in the United States as well, especially in the southern states.

Like many debates in the United States at this time, the fight over Texas annexation hinged on the issue of slavery. Pro- and antislavery factions in Congress were almost perfectly balanced. Southerners, hoping to gain more power in the government, welcomed the thought of Texas, which allowed slavery, to become a state. A New Orleans newspaper declared, "The South will almost to a man sustain the policy of . . . annexation." Northerners, afraid that they would lose influence, were strongly opposed to the idea.

U.S. president John Tyler, a southerner, favored annexation. In 1843, he sent agents to Texas to reopen negotiations. In a proposed treaty the next year, he offered to make Texas a U.S. territory—the first step toward statehood. As part of the treaty, the United States would pay off the Republic's large public debt. In exchange, Texas would give all its public lands to the federal government.

Tyler's treaty met with great opposition, both in Congress and from the American public. Northern senators protested the addition of a new slaveholding territory. Former president John Quincy Adams wrote of the treaty that "with it went the freedom of the human race." At a public rally in New York City, some 3,000 people protested the treaty. The Senate began debates about the treaty in June 1844. After three weeks of debate, the treaty was rejected.

Despite the Senate's rejection of the annexation treaty, many Americans continued to support Texas statehood. These Americans were eager to expand their country westward. They saw the West as a place of opportunity, where farming and trade would provide economic growth. They believed that the United States was meant to expand all the way across North America to the Pacific—an expansion that would include Texas. This belief became known as **manifest destiny**.

Across the country, newspaper articles began to appear supporting Texas statehood. For example, columnist Jane McManus—**Jane McManus Cazneau** after her 1849 marriage—wrote articles that helped turn northern opinion in favor of annexation.

Reading Check **Supporting a Point of View** Would you have supported annexation? Explain your answer.

BIOGRAPHY

Jane McManus Cazneau (1807–1878)
In 1833 Jane McManus Cazneau moved to Matagorda and tried to obtain a land grant. During the Revolution, she gave money to support the Texans' cause. After Texas gained its independence, she pushed for annexation in columns she wrote for the *New York Sun.* Cazneau eventually returned to Texas, where she was an early settler at the town of Eagle Pass. **Why was Cazneau an important person in Texas history?**

Interpreting Visuals

Manifest destiny. *John Gast's painting shows the westward movement of U.S. settlers across North America.* ***How does this painting show Americans' belief that they had the right to expand across North America?***

Interpreting Political Cartoons

"Texas Coming In." *This political cartoon forecasts the annexation of Texas and shows Stephen F. Austin and Sam Houston riding a boat into the United States.* ***According to this cartoon, is the United States pleased that Texas is joining the Union?***

The Annexation Resolution

The questions of annexation and manifest destiny were important issues in the U.S. presidential election of 1844. The two political parties involved in the election held differing positions on these issues. **Political parties** are groups of people who help elect government officials and influence government policies.

The Democratic Party nominated James K. Polk of Tennessee for president. Polk wanted the United States to annex Texas and expand west. His chief opponent was Whig Party candidate Henry Clay of Kentucky. At first, Clay spoke against annexation. He worried that it might result in war with Mexico. But to win votes in the South, he softened his opposition, while trying to reassure northern voters. Clay's mixed messages on the issue cost him many voters—and the election. Polk won.

Most Americans, including President Tyler, considered Polk's election a sign of the public's approval of annexation.

Analyzing Primary Sources
Identifying Points of View What conclusions did Tyler draw from Polk's election?

TEXAS VOICES

"A controlling majority of the people and a larger majority of the states have declared in favor of immediate annexation. . . . It is the will of both the people and the states that Texas shall be annexed to the Union . . . immediately."

—U.S. president John Tyler, annual message to Congress

Tyler therefore requested that the two houses of Congress pass a **joint resolution**, or formal expression of intent, for annexation. A joint resolution required only a simple majority to pass. This was less than the two-thirds majority in the Senate he would need to approve a treaty. In February 1845 Congress passed the joint resolution to annex Texas.

Reading Check **Finding the Main Idea** How did Polk's election affect the annexation of Texas?

Texas Enters the United States

KEY DATE 1845
Texas is annexed as the 28th state of the United States.

The joint resolution's terms were more favorable to Texas than the annexation treaty's had been. Texas would enter the United States as a state rather than as a territory. The new state could keep its public lands, although some would have to be sold to pay the public debt. In addition, Texas would have to turn much of its public property, such as military supplies, over to the United States.

In 1845 Texas president Anson Jones called for a convention to discuss the U.S. offer for annexation. The delegates to the **Convention of 1845** assembled in Austin on July 4, 1845, and quickly approved annexation. Then they began work on a new state constitution. You will read more about the convention and constitution in the next section.

Before Texas gained statehood, though, the people had to formally approve annexation. Texans had been proud of their independence, but there were good reasons for joining the United States. Most Texans were originally from the United States, and many still had families there. Texas and the United States also shared strong business ties. The federal government would also provide Texas with military protection and postal service. On October 13, Texas voters approved annexation by a vote of 4,254 to 267. They also approved the new state constitution. On December 29, 1845, President Polk signed the **Texas Admission Act**, making Texas the 28th state. One Texan explained.

TEXAS VOICES

"Truly we have every reason to be happy! To rejoice over the prosperity we enjoy! We are . . . united once more by the strong tie of national sympathy to all that we ever loved."

—W. B. DeWees, *Letters from an Early Settler of Texas*

Reading Check **Evaluating** Why did most Texans favor annexation?

Section 1 Review

hmhsocialstudies.com
ONLINE QUIZ

1. Define and explain:
- manifest destiny
- political parties
- joint resolution

2. Identify and explain the significance of each of the following in Texas history:
- Jane McManus Cazneau
- Convention of 1845
- Texas Admission Act

3. Categorizing
Copy the graphic organizer below. List the leaders and groups who favored or opposed annexation.

For Annexation	Against Annexation

4. Finding the Main Idea
- **a.** Why did most Texans favor annexation? Why did Americans support it?
- **b.** Beginning with the annexation treaty, identify in order the events that led to annexation.

5. Writing and Critical Thinking myWriteSmart
Comparing and Contrasting Write a paragraph comparing a northerner's and a Texan's views of annexation.
Consider the following:
- northerners' and southerners' views on slavery
- annexation's effect on the U.S. Congress

Section 2

Forming a Government

Main Ideas

1. The Convention of 1845 created a new state constitution for Texas.
2. The state constitution set up a new government and established protections for citizens and the government.

Key Terms and People

- **James Pinckney Henderson**
- **Thomas J. Rusk**
- **biennial**
- **corporations**

Why It Matters Today

In 1845, citizens of Texas gathered to create a new constitution. Use current events sources to find information about citizen involvement in government today.

TEKS: 1A, 4C, 14A, 21B, 21E, 22D

myNotebook

Use the annotation tools in your eBook to take notes on the state constitution of 1845.

The Story Continues

Texans stood, some with tears in their eyes, as the Republic's flag was lowered from the capitol for the last time. Before the flag could touch the ground, Sam Houston caught it. President Anson Jones declared, "The final act in this great drama is now performed; the Republic of Texas is no more." Many Texans looked forward to their future as U.S. citizens. When the American flag was raised, cheers erupted.

★ The Convention of 1845

On February 19, 1846, President Anson Jones formally turned the Texas government over to **James Pinckney Henderson**, the state's first governor. Texans were thrilled. Noah Smithwick remembered the event. "When the stars and stripes, the flag of our fathers, was run up . . . cheer after cheer rent [tore] the air." The Early Statehood period had begun. It would last until the outbreak of the Civil War in 1861.

Henderson took over the government under the terms of a new state constitution. It had been written the previous year at the Convention of 1845. The convention had assembled on July 4 in Austin. When it began, delegates chose **Thomas J. Rusk** as convention president. Rusk had helped write the constitution of the Republic of Texas in 1836.

The delegates to the Convention of 1845 were intelligent and able citizens. Among them were many men who had served as judges, lawyers, and legislators in the Republic of Texas or in the United States. As one newspaper reporter declared, these delegates "would rank high in any country." All but one of the delegates were originally from the southern United States. The only native Texan was José Antonio Navarro, who was also the only Tejano delegate at the convention. One delegate was missing. Sam Houston had traveled to Tennessee to pay his respects to former U.S. president Andrew Jackson, who had died in early June 1845. To honor Jackson, convention delegates wore black armbands as they formed committees to write the constitution.

The delegates used the constitutions of the United States, the Republic of Texas, and the state of Louisiana as models. They spent nearly two months working on the new state constitution. The resulting document was widely praised. It was ratified by voters in October 1845.

Reading Check **Finding the Main Idea** What was the background of many of the delegates to the Convention of 1845?

BIOGRAPHY

José Antonio Navarro (1795–1871)

José Antonio Navarro had a long and distinguished career even before he served as a delegate to the Convention of 1845. A business owner, rancher, and lawyer, he served in the Coahuila y Texas state legislature. Navarro supported Texas independence and signed the Republic's Declaration of Independence. He also helped write the Republic's constitution and served in its Congress. After statehood, he was twice elected to the Texas Senate. **How did Navarro contribute to Texas history?**

★ The Constitution of 1845

Under the new constitution, the Texas government had three branches. The governor headed the executive branch and served a two-year term. No person could serve as governor more than four years in any six-year period. The legislative branch included a senate and a house of representatives. House members served two-year terms, and senators served for four years. The state legislature met in **biennial** sessions, or every two years. The judicial branch, or court system, consisted of the supreme court—the highest state court—and district courts. Voters elected the governor and legislators. Judges were appointed by the governor until 1850 when a change in the law led to elections for judges.

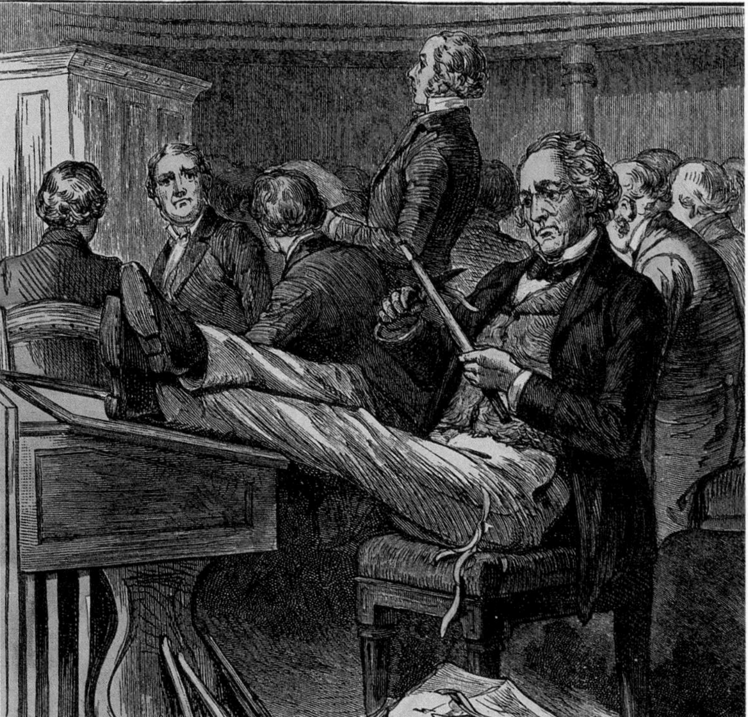

Interpreting Visuals

Texas in the Senate. *After the Constitution of 1845 was completed, Sam Houston joined the U.S. Senate.* ***What does this illustration reveal about how business was conducted in the U.S. Senate in the 1840s?***

Image Credit: (b) ©North Wind Picture Archives; (tr) ©Texas State Library and Archives Commission

The Separation of Powers

The Texas Constitution of 1845 established a separation of governing powers, in which the powers of each branch are limited. The system is similar to the one established in the U.S. Constitution.

The Executive Branch: The Texas Governor
- Administers laws
- Can sign or veto laws
- Commands state militia
- Appoints members of the executive branch
- Nominates state judges

The Legislative Branch: The Texas Legislature
- Writes state laws
- Sets the state budget
- Can propose constitutional amendments
- Can impeach judges and executive officials
- Can override executive veto

The Judicial Branch: The Texas Supreme Court
- Interprets the constitution and other laws
- Reviews lower state court decisions

Visualizing History

1. **Government** In what ways can each branch of the government check or limit the powers of the other two branches?
2. **Connecting to Today** How does the separation of powers help limit the power of government?

Although voters chose the state's leaders, not everyone could vote. Only men 21 years of age or older were allowed to cast ballots. Some delegates to the convention had wanted to limit voting to only white males, but José Antonio Navarro had fought to protect the right of Tejanos to vote. African Americans, American Indians, and women could neither vote nor hold office. The new state constitution also allowed slavery.

Although women were not allowed to vote, the constitution did set up legal protections for women, despite protests from some delegates. In the end, the delegates decided that a husband could not sell the family homestead without his wife's permission. Married women could also own property separately from their husbands. Some of these legal protections for women stemmed from old Spanish laws.

The constitution also addressed economic concerns. It banned banks, because most Texans distrusted them. After all, many banks had failed during bad economic times in the Republic. As Thomas J. Rusk explained, many people had been ruined by bank failures.

Analyzing Primary Sources
Identifying Points of View Why does Rusk dislike banks?

TEXAS VOICES

"Thousands . . . have been ruined by banks. . . . I wish by no vote of mine . . . to authorize the institution of a bank which may benefit a few individuals but will carry here as elsewhere ruin, want, [and] misery."

—Thomas J. Rusk, quoted in *Thomas J. Rusk: Soldier, Statesman, Jurist,* by Mary Whatley Clarke

In addition, **corporations**, or companies that sell shares of ownership to investors to raise money, needed the legislature's permission to operate in Texas. Any corporation that used unfair business practices could be shut down. Because debt had been such an issue for the Republic, the constitution addressed it, too. The state legislature was barred from taking on more than $100,000 in debt unless an emergency existed. It also established protection for individuals with debt. The constitution denied creditors the ability to seize a debtor's home as payment.

Reading Check **Summarizing** What were some of the main provisions of the Constitution of 1845?

★ The First State Election

The first state election was held on December 15, 1845. The major candidates had been delegates to the Convention of 1845. James Pinckney Henderson soundly won the governor's race. Albert C. Horton won the race for lieutenant governor. John Hemphill, who had served as chief justice of Texas during the Republic, remained in office. State officials took office on February 19, 1846.

The daily operations of government were transferred from the Republic to the new state government. Army posts, some public buildings, and other properties were turned over to the federal government. The state legislature met to decide who would represent Texas in the U.S. Senate. It came as no surprise that the legislators chose Sam Houston and Thomas J. Rusk. One Texan noted the appointments with approval. "These two great men placed the country before self." Within weeks, the two men left their homes for Washington.

Reading Check **Analyzing Information** Why did the Texas legislature select Sam Houston and Thomas J. Rusk as U.S. senators?

That's Interesting!

A Ban on Duels

The constitution banned anyone who took part in a duel from holding any state office. Previously, some Texans had used dueling to settle arguments. For example, in 1837 President Houston appointed Albert Sidney Johnston commander of the Texas army. Felix Huston, the commander at that time, refused to give up control and challenged Johnston to a duel. Johnston accepted the challenge and was badly wounded.

★ Section 2 Review

hmhsocialstudies.com
ONLINE QUIZ

1. Define and explain:
- biennial
- corporations

2. Identify and explain the significance of each of the following in Texas history:
- James Pinckney Henderson
- Thomas J. Rusk

3. Summarizing
Copy the web diagram below. Use it to identify the three branches of the new state government established by the Constitution of 1845.

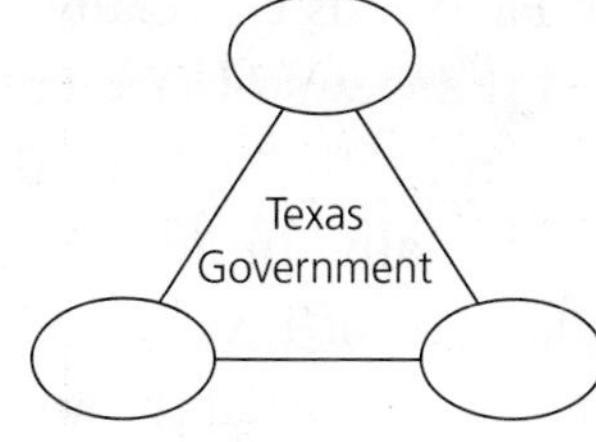

4. Finding the Main Idea

a. Who could vote and hold office under the Constitution of 1845?

b. When was the Early Statehood period in Texas, and what defined that era?

5. Writing and Critical Thinking *my* WriteSmart

Supporting a Point of View Imagine that you are a delegate to the Convention of 1845. Write a letter to the voters of Texas, explaining why you voted for or against the sections that banned banks.

Consider the following:
- Texans' experiences with banks
- the voters who elected you

Section 3

Political and Economic Issues

Main Ideas

1. Political parties became active in Texas for the first time after annexation.
2. Texas used its public lands to pay of its remaining debt, to promote education, and to improve life.

Key Terms and People

- **Democratic Party**
- **Republican Party**
- **Know-Nothing Party**
- **Elisha M. Pease**

Why It Matters Today

Texas governors in the 1840s and 1850s tried to improve conditions in the state. Use current events sources to find information about what issues the governor of Texas faces today.

TEKS: 1B, 4C, 17A, 21B, 21D, 21H, 22D

myNotebook

Use the annotation tools in your eBook to take notes on the issues leaders faced after annexation.

The Story Continues

In 1857, near the end of his career in the U.S. Senate, Sam Houston decided to run for governor of Texas as an independent candidate. Houston knew the race would be difficult, so he planned an aggressive campaign. "The people want excitement, and I had as well give it as anyone." Houston campaigned vigorously throughout the state. He traveled in a red buggy, sometimes sleeping on the ground.

★ Political Parties

Political parties had not existed in the Republic of Texas. People did band together to support particular candidates for offices, such as Sam Houston or Mirabeau Lamar, but voters had not organized into parties to promote political issues.

Parties were not active in elections for the first few years of Texas statehood either. Eventually, though, the two parties that dominated politics in the United States gained footholds in Texas as well. By the late 1840s, Texans had started to join the Democratic and Whig parties.

The Democratic Party was especially popular in Texas. Democrats generally represented the views of farmers and small business owners. The party was very strong throughout the South, where most Texas leaders came from originally. In addition, Andrew Jackson, a former U.S. president and a favorite of Texans, had been a Democrat. Like many Democrats, Jackson had supported the annexation of Texas.

The **Democratic Party** was so strong in Texas that every governor elected between 1845 and 1857 was a Democrat. This popularity led to some problems within the party, though. Because they usually had little to fear from opposing political groups, the Democrats often fought among themselves. By the 1850s the Democratic Party had split into two rival factions. One faction favored a strong central government, while the other supported the power of the states.

The other major political party in the United States was the Whig Party. Not many Texans supported the Whigs, who stood for banking and large business interests. They had opposed the annexation of Texas. These were not popular positions with most Texans.

The Whig Party collapsed in the 1850s because of divisions over slavery. In its absence, many Whigs in the North joined the newly formed **Republican Party**. Republicans believed that slavery should be banned in all states and territories of the United States. For that reason, the Republican Party had almost no support in Texas or the South.

In the mid-1850s a third party—the American Party, more commonly called the **Know-Nothing Party**—entered the U.S. political scene. This party acquired its name because when asked questions by outsiders, its secretive members answered, "I know nothing." Its members supported slavery and wanted to keep immigrants and Catholics out of government. The Know-Nothings gained some support in Texas, but most Texans were not interested in their views. Many Texans were recent immigrants or Catholics or both.

For a short time, rumors circulated that Sam Houston had joined the Know-Nothing Party. Houston denied this, saying, "Now, of the Know-Nothings I know nothing; and of them I care nothing." The appeal of the Know-Nothing Party faded quickly among Texans. By 1857 the Know-Nothing Party of Texas had disappeared.

Reading Check **Summarizing** What were the beliefs of each of the parties that challenged Democrats in Texas?

BIOGRAPHY

Elisha M. Pease

(1812–1883) One of the popular early governors was Elisha M. Pease. Pease moved to Texas in 1835. He fought in the Battle of Gonzales and helped write the Republic's constitution. Pease was governor of Texas three times. Under his leadership, the legislature created the Permanent School Fund. In addition, he led the effort to pay off the state's debt. When Pease left office, the state was debt-free and in solid financial condition.

Why is Governor Pease considered an effective leader?

★ Early Governors of Texas

About two months after James Pinckney Henderson was sworn in as the state's first governor, war broke out between the United States and Mexico. Henderson, who had served as a general in the Texas Revolution, wanted to serve his new country in the war. He asked the legislature for permission to step down from his office temporarily to rejoin the military. The legislature agreed. Henderson took command of the Second Texas Regiment in the U.S.–Mexican War and thus spent much of his term away from Texas.

Lieutenant Governor Albert C. Horton fulfilled the governor's duties during this time. When the war ended, Henderson resumed his office. However, he chose not to run for a second term in 1847.

LINKING
Past to Present

The Governor's Mansion

The Governor's Mansion in Austin is the fourth-oldest governor's mansion still in use in the United States. The early governors of Texas lived in Austin hotels or boardinghouses. In 1854 the legislature set aside $17,000 to build an executive mansion. The building was completed in 1856. Elisha M. Pease was the first governor to live in the mansion. In 1976 the mansion became a National Historic Landmark. Today visitors are welcome to tour the mansion. **Why is it important for the governor to have a residence in Austin?**

In that year Texas voters elected George T. Wood as their new governor. Wood was a plantation owner and friend of Sam Houston's. Frontier defense and disputes over the location of the state's northern and western boundaries were key issues during his administration. Wood ran for re-election in 1849 but faced strong opposition from Houston's opponents. They vowed to "move heaven and earth to defeat Wood."

Wood lost the election to Peter Hansborough Bell, a veteran of the Texas Revolution. During his two terms as governor, Bell tried to add part of New Mexico to Texas. However, he resigned from office to take a seat in the U.S. Congress. Lieutenant Governor J. W. Henderson became the governor for the remaining 28 days of Bell's term.

In 1853, Texans elected **Elisha M. Pease** to the state's highest office. Pease was an active popular governor who supported education and other reforms. He also worked to improve the state's financial situation. During his two terms, Pease paid off the state's debt. When he left office, he left Texas in excellent financial shape.

As governor, Pease also began an extensive building program in Austin. Many public buildings, including the Governor's Mansion, the General Land Office building, and the former Capitol—which burned down in 1881—were constructed as part of this program.

In 1857 Sam Houston ran for governor against Hardin Runnels. Houston campaigned hard for the office. He gave 60 speeches in little more than two months during the hot Texas summer. Even so, Houston lost in a bitter campaign—the only election he ever lost. During Runnels's term in office, conflicts between settlers and American Indians increased. Runnels proved unable to deal with the problem effectively. When Houston ran against Runnels again in 1859, he defeated Runnels easily. With that victory, Houston became the only person to serve Texas as army commander, president of the Republic, senator, and governor.

Reading Check **Sequencing** Name in order the governors of Texas during the 1840s and 1850s.

Debts and Land Issues

The first few governors of Texas, like the presidents of the Republic, faced issues of public debt and land. At the time of annexation, Texas owed some $10 million. Under the terms of the annexation agreement, the state was responsible for paying this debt.

The state tried to raise money to pay off the debt by selling public land. The state had plenty of land to sell. But with an asking price of 50 cents per acre, there were few buyers. The debt continued to rise, reaching more than $12 million by 1850.

Together, the federal government and Texas developed a plan to eliminate the debt. In the Compromise of 1850, Texas gave up its claim to 67 million acres of land in present-day Colorado, Kansas, New Mexico, Oklahoma, and Wyoming. In return, the federal government gave Texas money to help pay the debt. In this way, the debt was paid off completely by 1855.

Even without these claims, Texas had millions of acres of public land. The state gave much of it to settlers. These settlers had to live on the land and improve it in some way—typically by farming. The state also set aside land for colleges, public schools, and universities. Additional land was designated for roads, harbors, and railroads. By 1898 there was no unclaimed public land left in Texas.

Reading Check **Finding the Main Idea** How did the government use public land to improve the state?

CONNECTING TO

ECONOMICS AND MATH

The Republic's Debt

Because the Republic's government spent more than it received in revenue, the public debt grew by leaps and bounds. As the debt went unpaid and even increased, the interest mounted. Even after Texas had become a state, interest continued to increase the amount of the debt. By 1851, interest alone on the debt totaled $3.1 million.

The following chart shows how the debt accumulated by the Republic grew from 1836 to 1851. Study it and answer the questions.

YEAR	DEBT
1836	$1.25 million
1845	$9.9 million
1851	$12.4 million

Source: Handbook of Texas

Interpreting Data

1. By how many millions of dollars did the Republic's debt increase between 1836 and 1845?
2. How many times greater was the debt in 1851 than the debt in 1836?

Section 3 Review

hmhsocialstudies.com
ONLINE QUIZ

1. **Identify and explain** the significance of each of the following in Texas history:
   - Democratic Party
   - Republican Party
   - Know-Nothing Party
   - Elisha M. Pease
2. **Sequencing** Copy the time line below. Use it to show the governors between 1845 and 1859.
   - 1845 ____________
   - 1847 ____________
   - 1849 ____________
   - 1851 ____________
   - 1853 ____________
   - 1855 ____________
   - 1857 ____________
   - 1859 ____________
3. **Finding the Main Idea**
   a. What were the positions of the political parties in Texas, and what effect did they have on Texas politics?
   b. How did the state pay its debt?
4. **Writing and Critical Thinking** *my*WriteSmart
   Identifying Points of View Write a paragraph describing the Democratic and Whig positions. Explain which was more popular.
   Consider the following:
   - which party opposed slavery
   - the popularity of annexation in Texas

The Chapter at a Glance

Examine the following visual summary of the chapter. Then use the visual to create an outline of the major political and economic issues of Texas during the era of early statehood. Exchange your outline with a classmate to use as a study guide.

Texas governors adjust the state's land policy to encourage homesteading.

The U.S. government agrees to annex Texas. Texans overwhelmingly vote to join the United States in 1845. Texans adopt a new state constitution and create a new government.

After annexation, Texas governors face a large state debt and search for new solutions for the state's economic problems.

Identifying People and Ideas

Write a sentence to explain the role or significance of each of the following terms or people.

1. nominated
2. joint resolution
3. Convention of 1845
4. Texas Admission Act
5. biennial
6. corporations
7. James Pinckney Henderson
8. Thomas J. Rusk
9. Know-Nothing Party
10. Elisha M. Pease

Understanding Main Ideas

Section 1

1. Identify the different points of view of the Democratic and Whig Parties on annexation.
2. Why is 1845 a significant date in Texas history?

Section 2

3. Why did Texans create a constitution in 1845?
4. How did the Constitution of 1845 affect women?

Section 3

5. Why did Texans support the Democratic Party?
6. Use the numbers in the chart on page 325 to create a color-coded bar graph illustrating the increase of Texas's debt during early statehood.

You Be the Historian

Reviewing Themes

1. **Geography** How did westward expansion affect the debate in the United States over the annexation of Texas?
2. **Citizenship** How did political parties change politics in Texas?
3. **Economics** Why was the public debt an important issue for Texas?

Thinking Critically

1. **Identifying Cause and Effect** Why was Texas annexed to the United States? Who supported annexation, and who opposed it?
2. **Analyzing Information** Analyze the causes and events that led to Texas statehood.
3. **Identifying Points of View** Identify the different points of view of the Democratic, Whig, Know-Nothing, and Republican Parties on the issue of slavery.

Texas Test Practice

Interpreting Tables

The table below lists major political parties active in Texas in the 1800s. Use the information in it to help you answer the questions that follow.

Political Parties in Texas in the 1800s

Party	Active Dates	Platform
Democratic	Since 1832	Supported slavery and states' rights; Opposed large federal government and banks
Whig	1833-1860	Considered Congress superior to president; Supported tariffs
American (Know-Nothing)	1854–1856	Opposed immigration and naturalization; Opposed Catholicism
Republican	Since 1854	Opposed slavery; Wanted to prevent slavery from spreading
Greenback	1874–1899	Opposed monopolies and supported labor; Opposed changes in monetary policy
People's (Populist)	1892–1896	Supported agriculture; Opposed banks

1. Which party was created to oppose slavery and its spread?
- **A** Whig
- **B** Know-Nothing
- **C** Republican
- **D** Democratic

2. Based on this table, what issues do think think were important to Texans from the 1870s to the 1890s? What makes you think that?

Analyzing Primary Sources

Read the following quote by Charles Elliott, the British minister to the Republic of Texas, who was visiting the United States. Then answer the questions.

"Since I have been here [in New Orleans], I have had some good opportunity of judging of the real state of feeling in this country respecting annexation, and I am persuaded it is entirely out of the question. . . . The single . . . practicable solution for all parties concerned is the acknowledgment of her independence by Mexico, and the steady adherence to it by Texas. I was concerned, indeed, to see that some movements had been made in your [Texas] Congress . . . for they are not calculated to work good effects in Mexico, or . . . elsewhere."

3. Which of the following statements best describes the author's point of view?
- **F** Texas would benefit by being annexed by the United States.
- **G** Texas would benefit by Mexican recognition and remaining independent.
- **H** The United States would benefit by annexing Texas.
- **J** Great Britain had no opinion on what Texas should do.

4. What might have influenced Elliott's point of view on the issue of annexation?

Linking to Community

Texans elected state officials for the first time in 1845. There are many elected officials in your community. Choose one and find out what that person's responsibilities are. What are the qualifications for that person's office? What party does he or she belong to? What leadership qualities does the person bring to the office? Create a feature newspaper article that discusses your findings. Be sure to use standard grammar, spelling, sentence structure, punctuation, and citation of sources in your article.

Internet Activity

Access the Internet to research the lives and accomplishments of early Texas governors. Based on your research, create a database that includes data about when and where these governors were born, their years in office, their accomplishments, and any other information about these leaders that you find useful or interesting. When you have completed your database, use the information you collected to write a brief biography of one governor.

CHAPTER 16

Western Expansion and Conflict (1845–1860)

Texas Essential Knowledge and Skills (TEKS)
1B, 4C, 8A, 8B, 9A, 9C, 11A, 11B, 17A, 19B, 19C, 19D, 20A, 21B, 21C, 21D, 21E, 21F, 21G, 22A, 22C, 22D, 23A

Early illustrations of the Mexican War, such as this image of the Battle of Resaca de la Palma, were not very realistic.

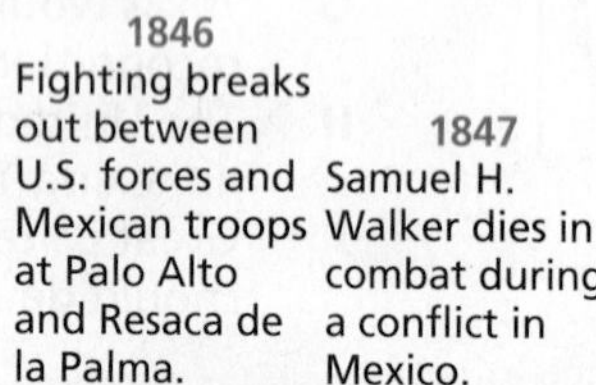

TEXAS

- **1846** Fighting breaks out between U.S. forces and Mexican troops at Palo Alto and Resaca de la Palma.
- **1847** Samuel H. Walker dies in combat during a conflict in Mexico.
- **1850** The Texas population reaches 200,000 people.

1845 — 1847 — 1849 — 1851

U.S. and WORLD

- **1846** The Bear Flag Revolt erupts as settlers in California declare independence from Mexico.
- **1848** Mexico cedes much of its territory to the United States in the Treaty of Guadalupe Hidalgo.
- **1850** Great Britain and the United States agree to build a canal in Central America to link the Pacific and Atlantic Oceans.

Build on What You Know

In 1845 Texas joined the United States and formed a new state government. Relations between the United States and Mexico grew more tense after the annexation of Texas, and war broke out in 1846. The war's outcome changed the political face of North America and the lives of Texans.

If you were there . . .
How would you resolve a border conflict?

Raids by Comanches and other American Indian groups posed a threat to many settlers on the Texas frontier.

Samuel H. Walker helped improve the design of the Colt revolver.

1853
U.S. Army troops abandon Fort Worth after settlers move farther west beyond the fort.

1853
Mexico sells the United States more than 29,000 square miles of territory along its border with present-day Arizona and New Mexico in the Gadsden Purchase.

1855
English clergyman Charles Kingsley publishes the novel *Westward Ho!*

1857
A financial panic begins in the United States.

1859
A series of clashes occurs between Texas Rangers and Mexican Americans near Brownsville.

1853 | 1855 | 1857 | 1859

You Be the Historian

myNotebook

What's Your Opinion? Do you **agree** or **disagree** with the following statements? Support your point of view in your notebook.

- **Global Relations** Nations should always respect each other's borders.
- **Citizenship** Citizens' rights are affected during wartime.
- **Geography** The expansion of new settlements into a region affects both the land and the lives of people already there.

Section 1

The U.S.–Mexican War

Main Ideas

1. The United States and Mexico went to war over issues involving Texas and California.
2. Many Texans took part in the U.S.–Mexican War.
3. The United States defeated Mexico in 1847.

Key Terms and People

- **Zachary Taylor**
- **John S. "Rip" Ford**
- **offensive**
- **Winfield Scott**

Why It Matters Today

Despite efforts from some Americans, the United States and Mexico went to war in 1846. Use current events sources to learn about peace efforts around the world today.

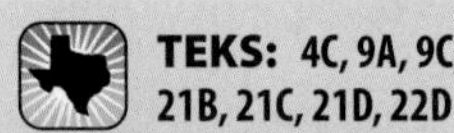

myNotebook

Use the annotation tools in your eBook to take notes on the Mexican War.

The Story Continues

U.S. lieutenant Napoleon Dana was stationed with his fellow soldiers along the Rio Grande. He had been sent there from Louisiana by the government, which expected war. There he waited, anticipating a fight with Mexico. Many of the troops were becoming anxious, eager to prove themselves in battle. Dana, who dearly missed his wife, wrote a letter home. "Here we are at a dead standstill, doing nothing. . . . I wish I had all of my glory and was on my way home again."

Fighting Breaks Out

The border conflict in which Dana took part arose from tensions between Mexico and the United States. Many Mexicans were unhappy about the annexation of Texas. They feared that annexation was just the first step and that the United States wanted to take over all of Mexico.

The conflict between Mexico and the United States was not new. For several years, Mexico had claimed that the Nueces River was the boundary between the two countries. The United States, on the other hand, maintained the old Republic of Texas claim to the Rio Grande as the boundary. In addition, the Mexican government had ordered many American settlers to leave California, which was still a Mexican territory. Many U.S. citizens also wanted to be paid for damage done to their businesses and property in Mexico.

In November 1845 President James K. Polk sent John Slidell to Mexico to settle the disputes. Slidell was authorized to purchase New Mexico and California. However, Mexican officials refused to meet with him. With conflict brewing, Polk ordered General **Zachary Taylor** and thousands of soldiers to Texas. Their mission was to protect the new state from any attack. When Taylor's troops arrived along the Rio Grande in March 1846, they discovered Mexican troops camped across the river. Taylor ordered his men to build a fort near what is now Brownsville.

In early April, a Mexican general sent a message to Taylor, ordering him to return to the east bank of the Nueces. Taylor refused. In response, Mexican cavalry crossed the Rio Grande and attacked. Several U.S. soldiers were killed or wounded, and many more were taken captive.

The next day, Taylor sent word to Washington that fighting had begun. When Polk heard this news, he asked Congress to declare war. Congress acted swiftly, and the U.S.–Mexican War was declared on May 13, 1846. The war is also called the Mexican–American War or simply the Mexican War. Even before the declaration of war reached the border, though, more fighting had broken out. On May 8 and 9, U.S. troops fought General Mariano Arista's advancing forces at Palo Alto and Resaca de la Palma near Fort Brown. Taylor won both battles.

Reading Check **Analyzing Information** What role did the Rio Grande play in the outbreak of the U.S.–Mexican War?

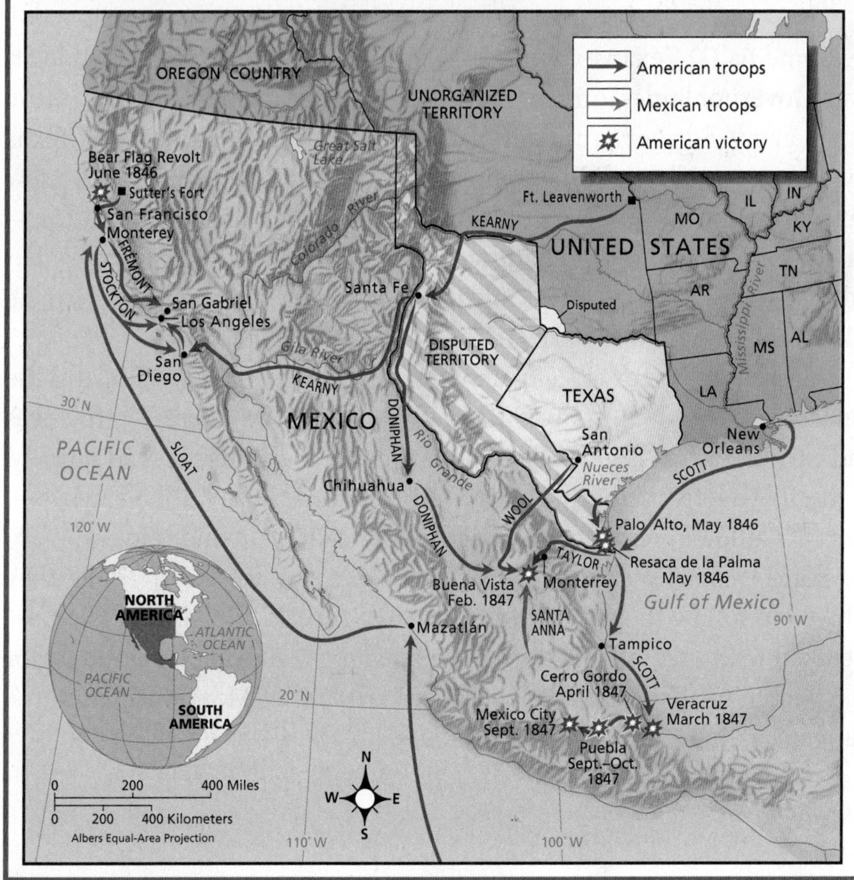

The U.S.–Mexican War, 1846–1848

Interpreting Maps After only a few months of fighting, U.S. forces had gained control of much of the territory north of Mexico City.

1. ***Place and Regions*** What region of Texas saw the most conflict during the U.S.–Mexican War?
2. ***Drawing Inferences and Conclusions*** How do you think geographic factors such as mountains, rivers, and gulfs affected the war?

Interpreting Visuals

The U.S.–Mexican War. *One of the most critical moments of the war came when General Winfield Scott captured the Mexican port of Veracruz.* ***What information about conditions during the war can you gather from this painting?***

Texans in the War

Thousands of volunteers rushed to join the army when the call for war came. In Texas, many people welcomed a chance to fight against their old rival Santa Anna. They wanted to get revenge for the suffering Texans had experienced during the Revolution. One Texas newspaper editor expressed delight at the coming of war.

TEXAS VOICES

"There is at last . . . an opportunity to pay off a little of the debt of vengeance which has been accumulating since the massacre of the Alamo. . . . We trust that every man of our army . . . will think of his countrymen martyred at the Alamo, at Goliad, and at Mier."

—Charles DeMorse, quoted in *Documents of Texas History,* edited by Ernest Wallace

Analyzing Primary Sources
Finding the Main Idea Why does DeMorse believe that Texans would support the war against Mexico?

Some 6,000 Texans volunteered to fight in the U.S.–Mexican War. Even Governor James Pinckney Henderson temporarily left office to serve in the army. Former president of Texas Mirabeau B. Lamar and Texas revolutionary Albert Sidney Johnston also volunteered. However, a few Texans, including Juan Seguín—a veteran of the Texas Revolution—fought for Mexico. Seguín had fled Texas in 1842 after being accused of aiding Mexican troops attacking Texas. When he arrived in Mexico, he was forced to fight or be arrested.

Several of the Texas Rangers who joined the U.S. forces during the war served as scouts. As one Ranger claimed, "[we] were . . . the eyes and ears of Taylor's army." The Rangers' fame as fighters spread quickly. Several Rangers, including **John S. "Rip" Ford**, Jack Coffee Hays, and Ben McCulloch, were recognized for their leadership and bravery.

Some Rangers' actions caused problems, however. At times they refused to follow the orders of U.S. Army officers. Rangers occasionally attacked Mexican villages with little reason, prompting General Taylor to threaten to throw all the Rangers in jail. Many Mexicans feared the Rangers, calling them *los diablos Tejanos*—"the Texas devils."

Reading Check **Evaluating** How did Texas Rangers participate in the war?

★ A U.S. Victory

After winning a few battles in Texas, Taylor began an **offensive**—a major troop advance—into northern Mexico. He defeated a Mexican army at Monterrey and pushed farther into Mexico. In 1847 Taylor's troops met a larger Mexican army at Buena Vista. After two days of fighting, Santa Anna's forces retreated. Texas Rangers played key roles at Buena Vista and Monterrey.

Because of his success at Buena Vista, Taylor became a national hero. President Polk was not happy about the general's new popularity, and he decided to replace Taylor as commander of the army. The new commander was **Winfield Scott.**

Scott chose to pursue a different strategy than Taylor had. He sailed to Veracruz, which had the strongest fortress in Mexico. After a long artillery battle, Scott took control of the city. He then moved inland. Santa Anna tried desperately to stop the U.S. advance, but he failed. By August 1847, Scott had reached Mexico City.

Scott ordered a massive attack on the city. Fighting took place in the streets and even on the rooftops. Finally, on September 14, 1847, Mexico City fell. U.S. troops raised the American flag over the National Palace in victory. Of the approximately 116,000 U.S. soldiers who served in the war, nearly 13,000 lost their lives. Most of these soldiers died not in battle but from disease. More than 60 Texans died in battle, and more than 270 more died from disease or accidents. The war with Mexico had cost the United States nearly $98 million. In Mexico, countless lives were lost, and much property was destroyed.

Reading Check **Sequencing** List in order the events that led to the U.S. victory in the U.S.–Mexican War.

BIOGRAPHY

Jack Coffee Hays

(1817–1883) John Coffee "Jack" Hays became one of the most famous of the Texas Rangers. According to one legend, while fighting American Indians at Enchanted Rock, Hays became separated from his men. He held off the Indians for more than an hour until he was rescued. Hays's fame grew during the Mexican War. He and the Rangers fought hand to hand with Mexican soldiers at Monterrey. Hays also fought in other important battles. He died in California in 1883. **How did Hays make a place for himself in Texas history?**

★ Section 1 Review

hmhsocialstudies.com
ONLINE QUIZ

1. Define and explain:
- offensive

2. Identify and explain the significance of each of the following in Texas history:
- Zachary Taylor
- John S. "Rip" Ford
- Winfield Scott

3. Locate on a map:
- Rio Grande
- Brownsville

4. Identifying Cause and Effect
Copy the graphic organizer below. Use it to show what problems arose between the United States and Mexico, and what the outcome was.

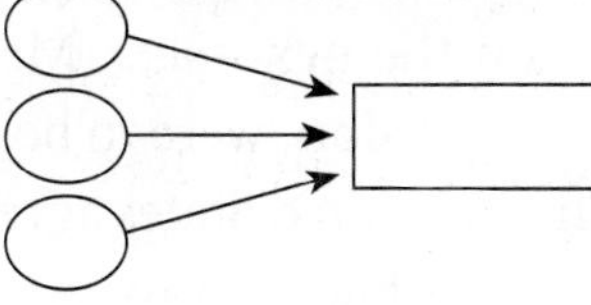

5. Finding the Main Idea

a. What issues led to the outbreak of the U.S.–Mexican War?

b. How did Texans and the Texas Rangers participate in the U.S.–Mexican War?

6. Writing and Critical Thinking my WriteSmart

Supporting a Point of View Write a story from either the Mexican or Texan perspective about the political and military events that led to the U.S.–Mexican War.

Consider the following:
- the causes of tension
- the U.S. and Mexican troops stationed along the Rio Grande

Section 2

Results of the Mexican War

Main Ideas

1. The United States gained new territory after the Mexican War, leading to debates about slavery.
2. Many Tejanos faced discrimination as a result of the Mexican War.
3. The population of Texas grew in the 1840s and 1850s, largely through immigration.

Key Terms

- **Treaty of Guadalupe Hidalgo**
- **Mexican Cession**
- **Compromise of 1850**

Why It Matters Today

At the end of the Mexican War, the United States and Mexico negotiated and signed a peace treaty. Use current events sources to learn about recent negotiations and treaties.

TEKS: 4C, 8A, 9C, 11A, 11B, 19C, 21A, 21B, 21C, 21F, 22D

myNotebook

Use the annotation tools in your eBook to take notes on changes in Texas after the Mexican War.

The Story Continues

U.S. diplomat Nicholas Trist was in Mexico City trying to work out a peace treaty. But Mexican officials were reluctant to agree to U.S. terms, and the treaty talks dragged on for months. Frustrated with the negotiations, President Polk ordered Trist to return home. With peace in sight, Trist ignored the order. Furious, Polk called Trist a scoundrel!

★ The Treaty of Guadalupe Hidalgo

After the capture of Mexico City, Mexican officials met with U.S. diplomat Nicholas Trist to discuss peace terms. Their meeting took place near Mexico City at the town of Guadalupe Hidalgo. On February 2, 1848, diplomats from the two countries signed the **Treaty of Guadalupe Hidalgo**, officially ending the Mexican War.

The terms of the treaty favored the United States. Mexico officially recognized Texas as part of the United States. It gave up all claim to the territory between the Nueces and the Rio Grande. Mexico also agreed to cede some 529,000 square miles of additional territory, including California, to the United States for $15 million. You can see this ceded territory on the map on the next page. Mexicans living in this region, known as the **Mexican Cession**, were to be granted all the rights of U.S. citizenship. In return, the United States agreed to cover the $3.25 million in claims that U.S. citizens had against Mexico.

The addition of so much territory to the United States reignited old debates about slavery. As before, the debate was split over regional lines. Legislators from pro-slavery states wanted to allow slavery in the new territories, while antislavery legislators wanted to ban it.

The Mexican Cession also raised questions about the borders of Texas. Texans claimed that the state included all land east of the Rio Grande. This would include nearly half of present-day New Mexico, including the trading city of Santa Fe. Early in 1848, the Texas legislature declared the huge disputed region to be Santa Fe County, Texas.

However, the people in this region—particularly in Santa Fe—rejected the Texas claim. Most people in Santa Fe opposed slavery and had no desire to become part of a slave state like Texas. Pro-slavery Southern members of the U.S. Congress supported the Texas claim. Northern members argued against it.

In 1850 Senator Henry Clay of Kentucky came up with a plan to resolve both the border conflict and the issue of slavery in the Texas and New Mexico. His plan was called the **Compromise of 1850.** To settle the border conflict, the federal government would pay Texas $10 million to give up its claim. Because the state government needed money to pay debts, Texas voters approved the agreement. The plan also established the present-day border between Texas and New Mexico. In addition, New Mexico and Utah became territories, and California became a state.

Reading Check **Categorizing** List what the United States gained from the Treaty of Guadalupe Hidalgo and what Mexico gained.

U.S. senator Henry Clay urged Congress to reach a compromise on slavery.

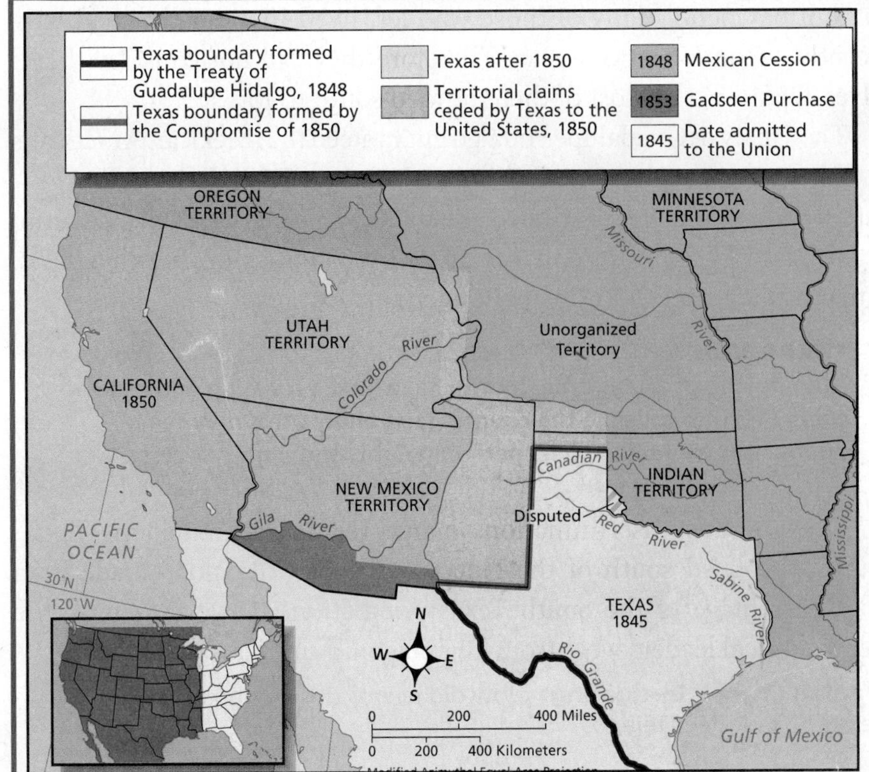

New Borders, 1853

Interpreting Maps The United States gained control of most of the Southwest through the Treaty of Guadalupe Hidalgo (1848) and the Gadsden Purchase (1853).

1. ***Locate*** What river formed the western boundary of Texas before 1850?
2. ***Evaluating*** How did the Treaty of Guadalupe Hidalgo and the Compromise of 1850 help shape the current borders of Texas?

Interpreting Visuals

Immigration. *Originally founded by German immigrants, Indianola was one of several ports of entry for immigrants to Texas.* ***What in this painting shows how transportation and geography affected immigration to Texas?***

★ Tejanos and the War

Perhaps the greatest impact of the U.S.–Mexican War was felt by Tejanos. Since the Texas Revolution, many Tejanos had been treated with suspicion and distrust by other Texans. Many questioned their loyalty. As conflicts emerged with Mexico during the 1840s, discrimination against Tejanos increased.

During the U.S.–Mexican War, many Texans viewed Tejanos as enemies because of their Mexican and Spanish ancestry. Some Tejanos, fearing that they would lose their farms and ranches because of the war, sold their property—often at low prices—and left Texas. Others were forced to leave Texas under threats of violence and had their land taken without payment. Many of those who left lived in areas that had only recently become part of Texas. Therefore they did not consider themselves Tejano at all. Most of them headed south to Mexico.

The Treaty of Guadalupe Hidalgo guaranteed that Mexican Americans would receive equal protection under U.S. law. Nonetheless, discrimination against Tejanos continued. Tejanos in some cities, such as Austin, Seguin, and Uvalde, were driven from their homes during the 1850s. A newspaper article described one such incident.

Analyzing Primary Sources
Identifying Bias What is the article's bias, and what words show the author's position?

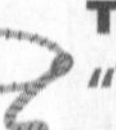

TEXAS VOICES

"The people of Matagorda County have held a meeting and ordered every Mexican to leave the county. To strangers this may seem wrong, but we hold it to be perfectly right, and highly necessary."

—Matagorda newspaper, quoted in *A Journey through Texas,* by Frederick Law Olmsted

Despite such discrimination, many Tejanos remained in Texas. Those who lived south of the Nueces—the new Tejanos—made up a large percentage of the South Texas population. However, few of the area's political leaders were from Tejano communities.

Reading Check **Evaluating** How did events during and after the Mexican War affect Tejanos?

★ New Migration to Texas

After the Mexican War, the population of Texas grew rapidly. From 212,592 people in 1850, the population swelled to 604,215 by 1860. As in the past, most new Texans were farmers from the southern United States. Many of them brought slaves when they came. As a result, the African American population in Texas nearly tripled between 1850 and 1860. However, fewer than 800 free African Americans lived in Texas during this time. The Texas population also included more than 12,000 Tejanos, mostly in the southern region of the state.

Many Europeans also came to Texas during this time. Most wanted to escape hardships in their homelands. Crop failures had left people starving in Ireland and parts of central and northern Europe. In addition, a series of revolutions in 1848 led many people to leave. Germans made up the largest European immigrant group, with a population of more than 20,000 in 1860.

The mid-1800s saw immigrants from all parts of Europe arriving in Texas. Their settlements helped push the frontier westward. Frenchman Victor Considerant established La Réunion, a colony of about 350 settlers in North Texas near the Trinity River. Polish colonists founded Panna Maria in Karnes County, while Czech immigrants settled at Cat Spring, Fayetteville, and Praha. Slavic settlers known as Wends also came to Central Texas. Hundreds of Jewish immigrants settled in cities such as Galveston, Houston, and San Antonio. The first Norwegian settlement in Texas was at Normandy. Immigrants from Italy, the Netherlands, and Belgium also arrived. Each group brought its traditional foods, celebrations, and architecture to Texas. The influence of these various cultural traditions spread across the state.

Reading Check **Analyzing Information** Why did immigrant groups come to Texas, and where did they settle?

Our Cultural Heritage

German Culture in the Hill Country

Several towns in the Hill Country show traces of their German heritage. German architecture called *Fachwerk*—part timber and part stone—can be seen in many buildings. German food is popular throughout the state. In addition, the barbecue that many Texans enjoy originated in the smokehouses of early German settlers. Texans have adopted these and other German traditions as their own. **How has the culture of German immigrants influenced Texas?**

★ Section 2 Review

hmhsocialstudies.com
ONLINE QUIZ

1. **Identify and explain** the significance of each of the following in Texas history:
   - Treaty of Guadalupe Hidalgo
   - Mexican Cession
   - Compromise of 1850
2. **Locate on a map:**
   - Nueces River
3. **Summarizing** Copy the graphic organizer below. Use it to describe the Treaty of Guadalupe Hidalgo and its effects on the border of Texas.

   Treaty → New Borders → Effects on Texas

4. **Finding the Main Idea**
   a. How did the Compromise of 1850 affect the borders of Texas?
   b. How did population growth after the Mexican War affect the state?
5. **Writing and Critical Thinking** myWriteSmart
   Identifying Cause and Effect Imagine that you are a Tejano in the 1850s. Write a diary entry about how your life has changed since the war. Consider the following:
   - why some Tejanos left Texas
   - the changing population distribution

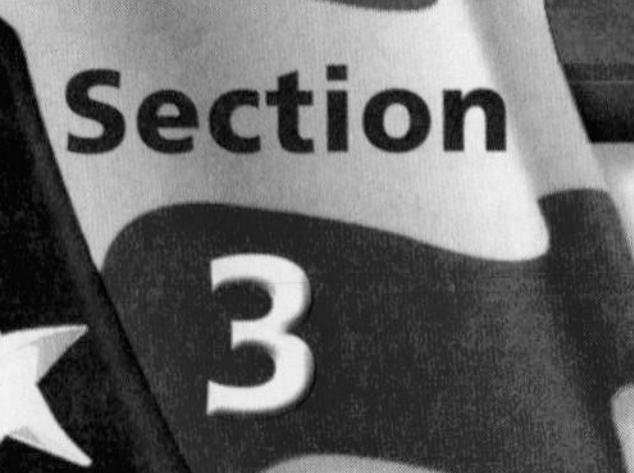

The Texas Rangers and American Indians

Main Ideas

1. The Texas Rangers protected Texans on the frontier.
2. Conflict between frontier settlers and American Indians led to the creation of reservations.
3. Texas Indians were forced to leave the state.

Key Terms and People

- **reservations**
- **Robert S. Neighbors**

Why It Matters Today

Conflicts between American Indians and settlers erupted as more settlers moved west. Use current events sources to learn about ongoing conflicts over land in various parts of the world today.

TEKS: 4C, 8A, 8B, 9A, 9C, 11B, 17A, 19D, 20A, 21B, 21C, 21D, 22D, 23A

myNotebook

Use the annotation tools in your eBook to take notes on the roles of Texas Rangers and American Indians on the Texas frontier.

The Story Continues

Texas Ranger Jack Hays had orders to establish a road from San Antonio to El Paso. To prove that the journey could be made safely, in 1848 Hays led an expedition with 71 people, including Rangers and American Indian scouts. The journey was tough. The Rangers had trouble finding water and food in this dry region of West Texas. The men even had to kill some of their horses for food. Finally, the expedition turned back for San Antonio.

Conflicts on the Frontier

One of the reasons Hays was scouting for a route to El Paso was to help people looking to settle in the West. During the 1850s, hundreds of new settlers moved westward from the United States, many of them through Texas. A newspaper reported, "For the last two weeks scarcely a day has passed that a dozen or more movers' wagons have not passed through our town." Many of these settlers moved onto the lands of American Indians, creating conflicts.

As fighting erupted, frontier settlers asked the government for protection. The federal government was responsible for solving conflicts with American Indians within the state. This task was difficult, partly because the state controlled all the public land that Indians claimed.

Texas policies encouraged settlers to move west. The state did not recognize American Indians' land rights. On the other hand, U.S. policy was to keep settlers from moving onto Indian lands. The government placed troops along the frontier to guard settlements. U.S. troops had difficulty fulfilling their task, however. Most troops sent to the frontier were infantry, or foot soldiers. They were no match for the Comanches and Kiowas, who were expert horse riders.

Texas governor George T. Wood called out the Texas Rangers to help the federal troops. The Rangers had horses and could cover land as quickly as the Comanches and Kiowas did. In addition, the Rangers had the Colt six-shooter, a powerful new weapon that could fire six shots in a row. It gave the Rangers a great advantage in frontier warfare.

The Rangers were so effective that the federal government agreed to pay them to guard the Texas frontier. The Rangers established a camp east of Laredo, where they fought several battles with the Comanches. The Rangers continued to patrol the frontier throughout the 1850s.

Reading Check **Finding the Main Idea** What role did Texas Rangers play in shaping the Texas frontier?

★ Establishing Frontier Forts

While the Rangers worked to defend settlers on the open plains, the federal government tried to protect Texans by building forts. In the 1840s the government built a line of forts from the Rio Grande to the Trinity River. Fort Brown in Brownsville and Fort Duncan near Eagle Pass guarded the south along the Rio Grande. Far to the north, Fort Worth—just west of Dallas—protected people along the Trinity. Several more forts guarded the settlements in between.

Interpreting Visuals

Texas Rangers. *The Texas Rangers protected settlers on the Texas frontier.* ***Why were the Rangers better suited than army troops to guarding the frontier?***

These forts protected both settlers and travel routes, which had become busier since the discovery of gold in California in 1848. Traffic on the roads altered American Indian life, as one Texas Indian explained.

Analyzing Primary Sources
Drawing Inferences and Conclusions How were Texas Indians affected by westward expansion?

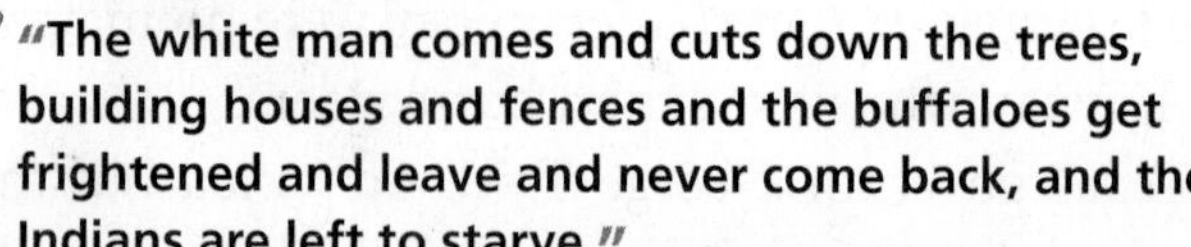

TEXAS VOICES

"The white man comes and cuts down the trees, building houses and fences and the buffaloes get frightened and leave and never come back, and the Indians are left to starve."

—Muguara, *The Evolution of a State, or Recollections of Old Texas Days,* by Noah Smithwick

Before long, settlers had moved into areas west of the original line of forts. The army abandoned those forts and built a new line of forts farther west. To the north, it built Fort Belknap along the Brazos River. In the south, it built Fort Clark. You can see these forts on the map on page 343.

The line of forts did not stop conflicts between Texans and American Indians, though. The forts were too far apart to fully protect settlers. The forts had too few troops and were often short on supplies.

Reading Check **Identifying Cause and Effect** How did settlement patterns change in the 1850s, and how did these changes lead to conflicts?

★ Texas Cities ★

Fort Worth

History: When the U.S. Army abandoned Fort Worth in 1853, settlers quickly moved to the area. During the 1870s, Fort Worth became a popular stopover for cowboys on cattle drives.

Population in 2012: 777,992 (estimate)

Relative location: In north-central Texas, 33 miles west of Dallas

Region: Grand Prairie subregion of the Central Plains

County: County seat of Tarrant County

Special feature: Known as Cowtown and Where the West Begins because of its ties to cattle trails

Origin of name: Originally an army post named for General William Jenkins Worth, who served in the Mexican War

Economy: Fort Worth's economy, which once relied on meatpacking plants, is now based on petroleum production and manufacturing, including aviation and electronics.

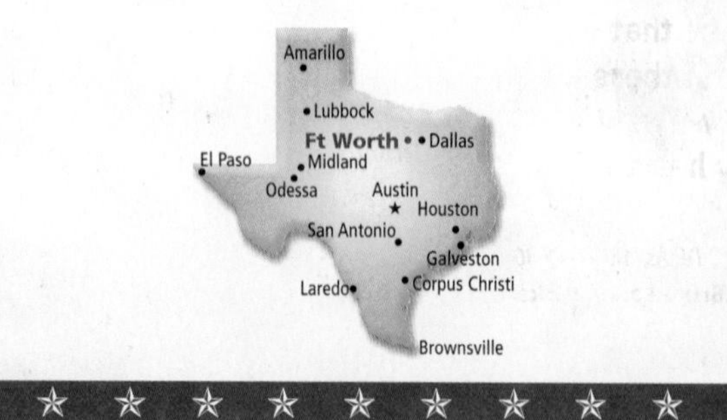

The Reservation Policy

Because of the continuing conflict on the Texas frontier, the federal government worked with the state to create a new Indian policy. The U.S. government planned to move the Texas Indians onto **reservations**—limited areas of land reserved for American Indians. The federal government would manage the reservations, while Texas would maintain ownership of the land.

The federal government, with the cooperation of the state, created two reservations in Texas in the 1850s. In 1854 the U.S. Army opened the Brazos Indian Reservation just south of Fort Belknap. About 2,000 American Indians, including Caddos, Tonkawas, and Wacos, settled there. These Indians used part of their land for farming, receiving $80,000 worth of supplies and cattle a year from the federal government.

Some 40 miles from the Brazos Indian Reservation, officials created another reservation for the Comanches. Called the Comanche Indian Reservation, it became home to about 450 Penateka Comanches. Government

The Caddos were among the Texas Indians forced to move onto reservations.

agents taught the Comanches, who were traditionally hunters, how to farm. But the Comanches did not have much luck. Drought in the mid-1850s made growing crops very difficult.

Overall, the reservations did not attract many American Indians. Many Plains Indians in particular continued to live outside the reservations. For this reason, a planned third reservation for the Lipan Apaches failed. The Apaches refused to move onto the land. They wanted to maintain their traditional way of life, hunting and following the buffalo herds. Settlers, on the other hand, wanted to build farms and homes. They refused to recognize American Indians' right to their hunting grounds and continued to move into Indian territory.

Reading Check **Analyzing Information** Why was the reservation system not successful in its goals?

★ The Removal of Texas Indians

The creation of reservations did not end conflicts in Texas. A Comanche leader recalled the Comanches' experiences.

TEXAS VOICES

"Many years ago we lived in Texas where the government opened farms and supplied us with cattle and other domestic animals which prospered and made us happy for a while, but the citizens of that county soon said, the Comanches are bad, and drove us from these homes. . . . There we had a school like you, at which twenty-five of our children attended; we have none of these now and my heart is weak."

—Tokaway, quoted in *Indian Affairs and the Frontier of Texas, 1865–1880,* by Bruce Logan Parker

LINKING
Past to Present

Fort Bliss

During the mid-1800s the U.S. government built forts across West Texas. Today most of these forts are crumbling ruins. Fort Bliss, however, remains an active military post. First established in 1854, the fort has been relocated several times. During the 1990s more than 20,000 soldiers were stationed on the base, which houses an airfield and a hospital. **How do you think the purposes and uses of Texas forts have changed over the years?**

Officials who hoped the reservation system would calm affairs between settlers and American Indians were soon disappointed. Settlers living near reservations claimed that Indians stole horses and cattle. Groups of armed Texans patrolled reservation boundaries. They sometimes killed Indians found off the reservations.

By the late 1850s some Texans were calling for an end to the reservation system. They wanted American Indians totally removed from the state, and the federal government agreed. By 1859 the Indians on the Brazos and Comanche Indian Reservations had been forced to move to Indian Territory in what is now Oklahoma.

The removal of American Indians angered some Texans. Federal Indian agent **Robert S. Neighbors** had hoped that Indians on reservations would be treated fairly. Disappointed with the policy of removal, Neighbors helped the Indians in their difficult move. After returning to Texas, Neighbors was murdered by an angry Texan at Fort Belknap.

Texas recognized the right of a few American Indian groups to remain in the state. One such group was the Alabama-Coushatta Indians of East Texas. During the Runaway Scrape, some of the Alabama-Coushattas had aided Texans fleeing east. Because of this service during the Texas Revolution—and because their land was poor and not in demand by settlers—many Texans were friendly to them. In 1854 Texas granted the Alabama-Coushattas 1,280 acres of land in Polk County. The federal government bought more than 3,000 additional acres for the reservation in 1928. In the west, reservations were established for the Tiguas near El Paso and the Kickapoos near Eagle Pass along the Rio Grande. Today these three reservations are the only ones in Texas.

Reading Check Evaluating Were U.S. policies effective in easing conflict between Texans and American Indians? How did they affect Indian life?

Section 3 Review

hmhsocialstudies.com
ONLINE QUIZ

1. Define and explain:
- reservations

2. Identify and explain the significance of the following in Texas history:
- Robert S. Neighbors

3. Locate on a map:
- Fort Worth

4. Evaluating
Copy the graphic organizer below. Use it to analyze the success or failure of the different frontier policies listed.

Policy/ Action	How Successful Was It?
Rangers	
Forts	
Reservations	

5. Finding the Main Idea
- **a.** How did the Texas Rangers change life on the Texas frontier?
- **b.** How did westward expansion affect American Indians in Texas?

6. Writing and Critical Thinking myWriteSmart
Identifying Points of View Imagine that you are trying to resolve a conflict between frontier settlers and American Indians in Texas. Write a letter that defines the issues and offers a solution to the conflict.
Consider the following:
- the westward expansion of U.S. settlers
- Texas Indians' views of U.S. settlers and opinions about reservation life

Connecting To

Geography

The Texas Frontier

As new settlers poured into Texas from elsewhere in the United States and Europe, the boundary of westward settlement moved farther west. New lines of forts were established to guard farms and settlements on the frontier. In addition, Indian reservations were established between 1854 and 1859.

Geography **Skills**

Interpreting Thematic Maps

1. What relationship exists between the line of the frontier and the location of forts?
2. Approximately how much farther from Houston was Fort Bliss than Fort Graham?

Military Posts and Indian Reservations in Texas; 1846–1860

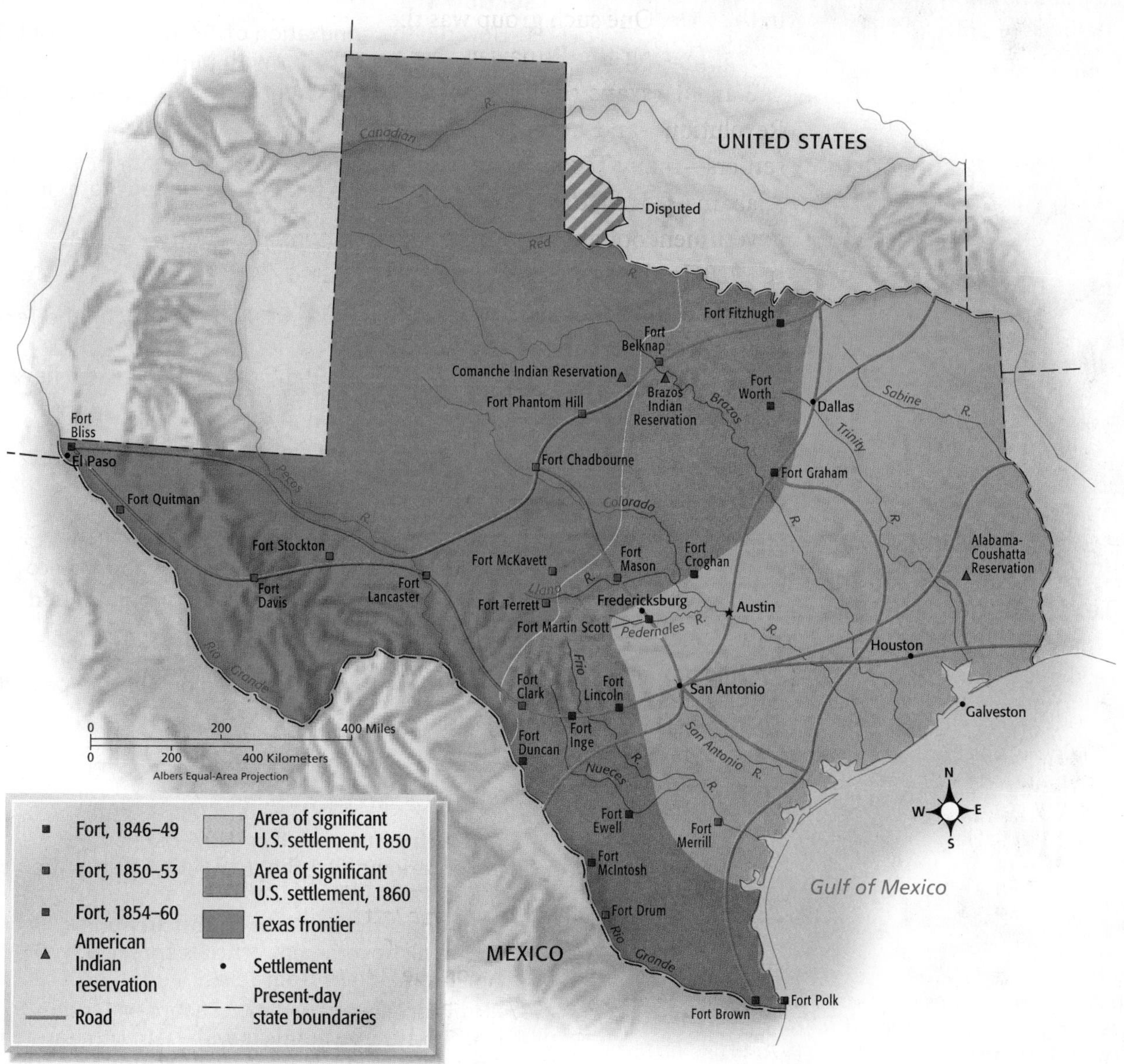

The Chapter at a Glance

Examine the following visual summary of the chapter. Then use the visual to create a thematic cause-and-effect map of the expansion of the frontier.

The Mexican War

Growing conflict between the United States and Mexico led to war. Many Texans volunteered to fight, including the Texas Rangers.

The Results of the War

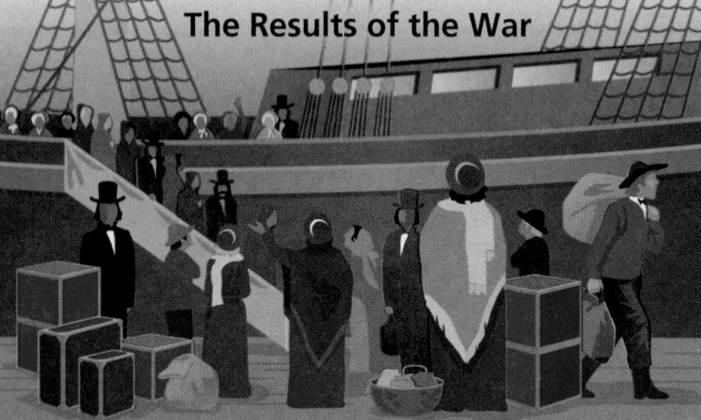

After the Mexican War and the signing of the Treaty of Guadalupe Hidalgo, new settlers from the United States and Europe came to Texas.

Texas Rangers and Indian Conflicts

As settlers moved to the Texas frontier, conflicts with American Indians increased. Officials used the Texas Rangers and a system of forts and reservations to try to stop the conflicts.

Identifying People and Ideas

Write a sentence to explain the role or significance of each of the following terms or people.

1. Zachary Taylor
2. offensive
3. Winfield Scott
4. John S. "Rip" Ford
5. Treaty of Guadalupe Hidalgo
6. Mexican Cession
7. Compromise of 1850
8. reservations
9. Robert S. Neighbors

Understanding Main Ideas

Section 1

1. How did the annexation of Texas and fears of U.S. expansion lead to war with Mexico?
2. List in absolute sequence the major events of the U.S.–Mexican War.

Section 2

3. What did Mexico cede to the United States in the Treaty of Guadalupe Hidalgo?
4. Which immigrant groups came to Texas?

Section 3

5. What role did the Texas Rangers play on the Texas frontier?
6. What problems did the reservation system have, and how did this affect Texas?

You Be the Historian

Reviewing Themes

1. **Global Relations** How did a border dispute lead to war between the United States and Mexico?
2. **Citizenship** How were Tejanos' rights limited during and after the Mexican War?
3. **Geography** How did expansion of settlements on the frontier affect the region's landscape and the lives of American Indians?

Thinking Critically

1. **Analyzing Information** How did new immigration affect the population distribution of Texas in the 1850s?
2. **Drawing Inferences and Conclusions** Why do you think government officials agreed to remove American Indians from Texas?
3. **Summarizing** How did westward expansion lead Texans into conflicts with both Mexicans and American Indians?

Texas Test Practice

Interpreting Political Cartoons

Study the political cartoon below. Then use the information to help you answer the questions that follow.

1. Which of the following statements best describes the cartoonist's view of the effects of the Mexican War on Mexico?
   - **A** Mexico was humiliated.
   - **B** Mexico was the same as before the war.
   - **C** Mexico was in some ways stronger than it was before the war.
   - **D** Mexico was disorganized.

2. Which country do you think the cartoonist supported during the war? What, if any, biases do you see reflected in the cartoon?

Making Generalizations and Predictions

Read the following passage from this chapter. Then answer the questions that follow.

During the U.S.–Mexican War, many Texans viewed Tejanos as enemies because of their Mexican and Spanish ancestry. Some Tejanos, fearing that they would lose their farms and ranches because of the war, sold their property—often at low prices—and left Texas. Others were forced to leave Texas under threats of violence and had their land taken without payment. Many of those who left lived in areas that had only recently become part of Texas. Therefore they did not consider themselves Tejano at all. Most of them headed south to Mexico.

3. Which of the following is a valid generalization that a reader might make based on this passage?
   - **F** All Tejanos fought on the side of Mexico during the Mexican War.
   - **G** The people of Texas owe a great deal to the Tejanos.
   - **H** Many Tejanos faced discrimination during and after the Mexican War.
   - **J** Tejanos were opposed to the Mexican War.

4. Based on this passage, make a prediction about the nature of relations between Tejanos and other Texans in the years that followed these events.

Interdisciplinary Connection to Literature

Imagine that you are a Texas Indian who has moved to a reservation in 1854. Write a poem that expresses the changes that you and your family have experienced. Use information about the expansion of U.S. settlement, reservations, and the removal of Indians discussed in this chapter. Create an illustration to accompany the poem. You may want to refer to Chapter 4 for more information on Texas Indians.

Internet Activity

Access the Internet to research the history of the Texas Rangers or the history of the U.S.–Mexican War. Take note of information about the authors of the sources you find and pay careful attention to the language they use so that you can evaluate the validity of the sources you have found. Then create a political cartoon with a caption that refers to an event from your research. Check your caption for proper spelling, grammar, punctuation, and sentence structure. On a separate sheet of paper, write an explanation of your cartoon.

CHAPTER 17

Life in a Frontier State

(1845–1861)

Texas Essential Knowledge and Skills (TEKS) 4C, 8A, 8B, 10A, 10B, 13A, 13B, 17C, 19B, 19D, 20A, 20C, 21A, 21B, 21C, 21D, 21E, 22A, 22B, 22C, 22D

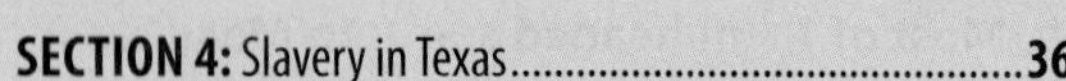

Railroads allowed Texans to ship goods quickly overland. However, building railroads was very expensive.

TEXAS

1846 Texas signs a peace treaty with the Penateka Comanches.

1847 A state census reports the state's population at more than 142,000.

1850 In her book *Texas in 1850,* Melinda Rankin describes the state and urges people to move to Texas.

1845 — **1847** — **1849** — **1851**

U.S. and WORLD

1846 The Smithsonian Institution is established.

1848 Gold is discovered in California.

1852 *Uncle Tom's Cabin,* a novel that criticizes slavery, is published and sells 300,000 copies in the United States alone in its first year in print.

If you were there . . .

Why would you move to a frontier state like Texas?

Build on What You Know

Texas was a frontier state in the 1840s and 1850s. Settlers in Texas faced many challenges, but changes and improvements were occurring rapidly. Despite the difficulties, settlers continued to move to Texas. Many settlers brought slaves with them.

Image Credit: ©Special Collections, University of Houston Libraries

The geography of Texas was particularly well suited to growing cotton.

Many stagecoaches that traveled through Texas carried both passengers and mail.

1853
After many false starts, track is finally laid for the Buffalo Bayou, Brazos, and Colorado Railway.

1856
Slaves in Colorado County acquire weapons and plan a rebellion, but the plot is discovered before it can begin.

1857
In *Dred Scott* v. *Sandford,* the U.S. Supreme Court declares that slaves are not U.S. citizens.

1858
The Butterfield Overland Mail begins taking passengers and mail by stagecoach from Missouri, through Texas, and on to California.

1859
Texas produces a record crop of more than 400,000 bales of cotton.

1860
The Pony Express is established, offering mail service from St. Joseph, Missouri, to San Francisco, California.

1853 1855 1857 1859 1861

You Be the Historian

myNotebook

What's Your Opinion? Do you **agree** or **disagree** with the following statements? Support your point of view in your notebook.

- **Government** Government should pay for a region's internal improvements.
- **Geography** Physical factors, such as climate and landforms, do not affect a region's population growth.
- **Economics** Local economies are seldom affected by national and international events.

Section 1

Earning a Living

Main Ideas

1. Most Texans in the early statehood period made their livings in agriculture or related fields.
2. Merchants and professionals could be found in towns.

Why It Matters Today

Most cotton in Texas was grown on large farms to be sold as a cash crop. Use current events sources to learn about large-scale farming today.

Key Terms and People

- **cotton belt**
- **planters**
- **Richard King**
- **Aaron Ashworth**
- **Cristóbal Benavides**
- **gristmills**
- **tanneries**

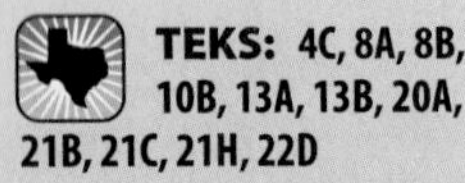

TEKS: 4C, 8A, 8B, 10B, 13A, 13B, 20A, 21B, 21C, 21H, 22D

myNotebook

Use the annotation tools in your eBook to take notes on how people made their livings in frontier Texas.

The Story Continues

On a typical day, Mathilda Doebbler Wagner was up before dawn. She started a fire in the stove and made coffee. Then Wagner rounded up the calves, milked the cows, and made breakfast for her family. After breakfast came other chores, including making butter and feeding animals. By day's end, Wagner had made two more meals and worked in the fields—all while tending a baby.

Farmers and Planters

During the early statehood period, most Texans, like Wagner, lived in rural areas. According to the 1850 census, only 5 percent of Texans lived in cities. Most of the remaining 95 percent lived and worked on farms or ranches. Agriculture continued to expand as more people moved into the state. The number of farms in Texas more than doubled between 1850 and 1860. Most of these farms were small family operations, but others were plantations covering thousands of acres.

Besides the foods their families needed to live, many Texas farmers grew a cash crop—typically cotton—to sell for profit. Sugarcane, another cash crop, was grown near the coast and along river bottoms. Among food crops, corn remained the most important, although sweet potatoes and wheat were also very popular. Farmers also raised cows for milk and dairy products and hogs for meat. Butter, chickens, and eggs could be sold to earn extra money. As the demand for wool grew, sheep became an important source of income for some farms.

The most valuable crop in Texas, though, was cotton. By the 1850s Texas was an important part of the **cotton belt**, the southern region that grew most of the cotton in the United States. Cotton production in Texas rose dramatically in the 1850s—from fewer than 60,000 bales in 1849 to more than 400,000 bales in 1859. These bales were shipped from Texas ports to northern states or to Europe to be made into cloth. The demand for—and price of—cotton rose as textile factories bought up supplies.

VIDEO
Cotton
hmhsocialstudies.com

Because cotton was so valuable, a complex economic system developed around its production. The bulk of Texas cotton was grown on plantations in East and Central Texas or along the Gulf Coast. In addition, family farms both large and small grew cotton to be sold in Texas markets. Because these farms were so focused on cotton, they did not produce much food. As a result, they depended on small farms in their areas to provide them with meat and produce.

Growing cotton required many hours of labor. Seeds had to be planted, cotton picked, and fibers separated. Much of this work was done by slaves. About one in every four families in Texas owned slaves. Most of these families owned few slaves—fewer than five—and spent much of their time in the fields alongside them. A few wealthy **planters**, or large-scale farmers, held many slaves. Large planters sometimes owned 100 or more slaves, while most smaller planters owned between 10 and 20.

Planters lived more comfortably than most people. They wore fine clothing and ate fancy dinners. Their homes ranged from fairly simple structures to huge mansions. These homes often had expensive furniture from New Orleans or Europe. Along with their wealth, planters had power and status. Although there were only about 2,000 planters in Texas in 1860, they controlled the state's economy and government.

Reading Check **Finding the Main Idea** How did Texas farmers adapt to the environment?

Interpreting Visuals

Frontier farms. *Actors at the Barrington Living History Farm in Washington-on-the-Brazos portray life on a farm from the 1840s.* ***What activities can you see being performed?***

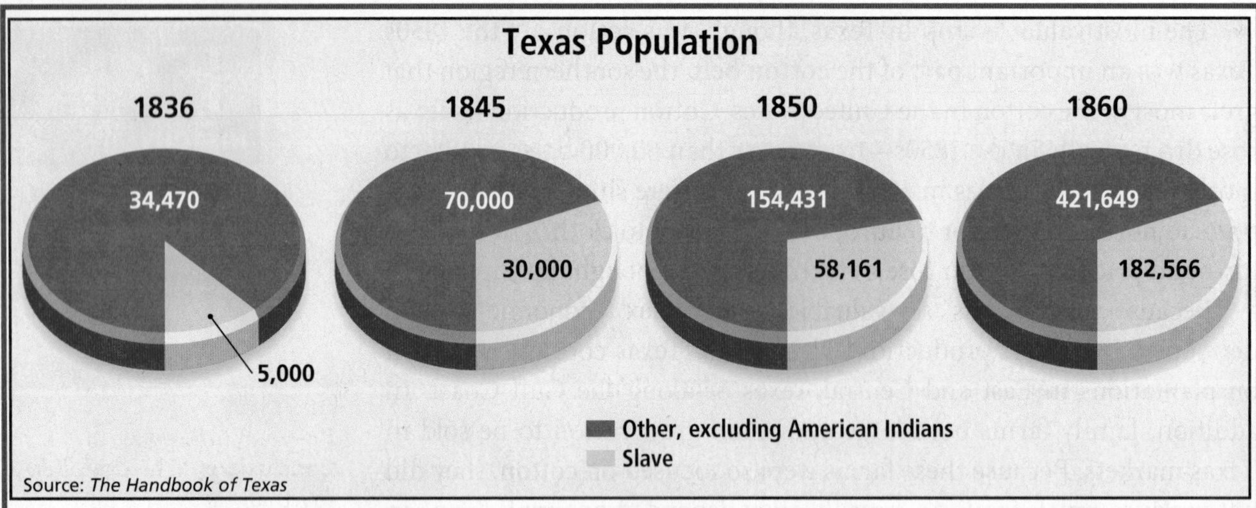

Interpreting Charts As the population of Texas grew, so did the number of slaves. What percentage of the state's population was made up of slaves in 1860?

Ranchers

After cotton, cattle was the state's second-most-valuable export. The value of beef and other products from cattle increased more than 400 percent from 1850 to 1860. Among the products cattle provided were food, hides, and tallow—animal fat used to make soap and candles. Most cattle were sold locally to the highest bidder, but some ranchers in this period began driving herds to markets in Illinois and California. Others drove cattle to the port towns of Aransas Pass, Copano, and Indianola. From there the cattle were shipped to New Orleans.

Two particularly successful ranchers were **Richard King** and Gideon Lewis. In the early 1850s, they bought thousands of acres in the Santa Gertrudis land grant. The ranch they founded—the King Ranch—soon dominated South Texas ranching. **Aaron Ashworth**, a free African American, owned a large ranch in southeastern Texas. In the Laredo area, the Benavides family were also successful ranchers. **Cristóbal Benavides**, for example, ran huge cattle- and sheep-ranching operations. Although most ranches were run by men, a few were owned by women like Sarah "Sally" Scull in South Texas.

Reading Check **Drawing Inferences and Conclusions** Why was it more profitable for ranchers to sell their cattle in other states?

The Mavericks

According to tradition, San Antonio rancher and lawyer Samuel Maverick was often paid for legal services in cattle. Maverick refused to brand his cows, so people would refer to any unbranded animal as "Maverick's." The word *maverick* eventually came to mean "unbranded cattle." Today the word also describes someone who acts independently.

Trades, Professions, and Industry

As you have read, few Texans lived in towns during this period. Most towns of the time were "mere villages, consisting of long rows of log or board houses," as one Texan noted. In 1850 the largest town in the state was Galveston. By 1860 San Antonio, with 8,235 people, had passed it in population to become the largest. Other large towns included Houston,

Jefferson, Marshall, Nacogdoches, and New Braunfels. Even though it was the state capital, Austin had fewer than 1,000 residents when Texas became a state.

Even in towns, most people were somehow involved in agriculture. Merchants provided farmers and ranchers in surrounding areas with goods. Blacksmiths, masons, carpenters, and saddle and wagon makers made products that farmers needed. Towns did provide other services as well, including hotels and laundry businesses. They were also home to various professionals, such as doctors, lawyers, ministers, and teachers. Doctors faced many challenges, as one Texan recalled.

TEXAS VOICES

"Injuries, deaths, and murders were to be expected by the frontiersman but, nevertheless, they always came as a shock. . . . Medicine and surgery were crude. It was my lot to help hold some patients for the doctor when he was amputating limbs without anesthetic [pain-killing drug]."

—James Buckner Barry, quoted in *Scalpels and Sabers,* by Sylvia Van Voast Ferris and Eleanor Sellers Hoppe

Analyzing Primary Sources
Drawing Inferences and Conclusions Why does Barry say that "medicine and surgery were crude"?

Industry was only a small part of the Texas economy. As in the rest of the South, planters in Texas preferred to invest in land and slaves rather than factories. Most of the state's industries were family-owned and tied to agriculture. The state's largest industry was flour milling, and most towns had **gristmills**—machines that ground grain into meal or flour. Cotton gins were also common, while **tanneries** were built to prepare animal hides. Lumber-rich East Texas also had a number of sawmills.

In an agricultural society like Texas, cash was scarce. Most people grew or made at home much of what they needed. The demand for most manufactured items was low, and most of the manufactured items Texans purchased came from out of state.

Reading Check **Identifying Cause and Effect** What was the basis of the Texas economy, and how did that affect Texas industry?

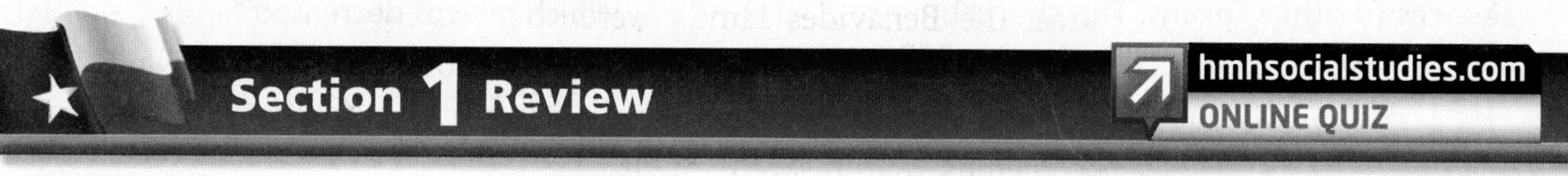

Section 1 Review

1. Define and explain:
- cotton belt
- planters
- gristmills
- tanneries

2. Identify and explain the significance of the following in Texas history:
- Richard King
- Aaron Ashworth
- Cristóbal Benavides

3. Summarizing
Copy the graphic organizer below. Use it to show how most Texans earned a living.

Farms
Ranches
Towns

4. Finding the Main Idea
a. Why did cotton planters make large profits?
b. Where did most Texans live in the 1850s?
c. How do you think geography shaped how people made their livings?

5. Writing and Critical Thinking myWriteSmart
Making Generalizations and Predictions Imagine that you are a Texan in the 1850s. Write a letter to a friend explaining why you think cotton production will increase. Consider the following:
- who is coming to Texas
- the demand for cotton

Connecting To

Economics

Free Enterprise

People moved to Texas in the 1850s hoping to earn a good living. The free enterprise economy of the United States meant that Texans had the right to exchange goods as they saw fit. They could decide for themselves what to produce, how to produce it, and whom to sell it to. In the free enterprise system, government regulation is kept to a minimum and competition flourishes.

The right to private property is a key element of free enterprise. Owning land and growing a cash crop such as cotton was often the best way to make a profit. Demand for cotton had increased rapidly in the 1850s. Cotton prices rose when demand was greater than supply. Many cotton farmers profited from these high prices. The profit motive—or the desire to make a profit—is key to the free enterprise system.

Other Texans saw opportunities to make profits in towns. They started businesses in the hopes of making money. Merchants profited by selling agricultural supplies. Tradespeople and professionals, including blacksmiths, lawyers, and doctors, provided services to other Texans. The charts below show the occupations of Texans in 1850 and 1860.

Texans buy goods from a variety of sources—from small farmers' markets to large retail stores and online sellers.

Understanding What You Read

1. **Economics and History** Analyze the impact of the free enterprise system, such as supply and demand, regulation, and profit motive, on the development of the Texas economy.
2. **Economics and You** What benefits do you think the free enterprise system offers to Texans?

Interpreting Charts

1. What occupational groups increased in popularity between 1850 and 1860? Which groups decreased?
2. How did most Texans earn a living in 1850? How do you think that has changed today?

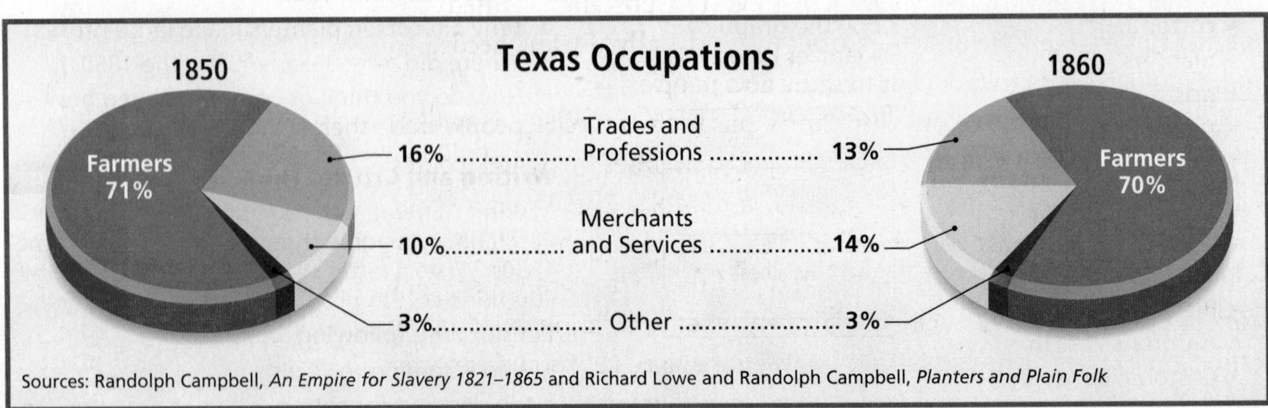

Section 2

Transportation

Main Ideas

1. Poor roads and shallow rivers made travel and transportation of goods in Texas difficult.
2. Stagecoaches, steamboats, and railroads each offered advantages and disadvantages as means of travel.

Key Terms

- **oxcarts**
- **steamboats**
- **Harrisburg railroad**

Why It Matters Today

Texans in the 1800s worked to improve transportation. Use current events sources to learn about modern advances in automobiles or other forms of transportation.

TEKS: 4C, 8A, 9A, 10A, 17C, 20A, 20C, 21B, 21C, 21D, 21E, 22D

myNotebook

Use the annotation tools in your eBook to take notes on various forms of transportation used in frontier Texas.

The Story Continues

Horses and mules did not endure the dry heat of West Texas very well. The U.S. Army soldiers stationed there wanted animals that could survive better. In an experiment, they brought 33 camels from Africa to West Texas. A Texas boy remembered his first encounter with a camel. "When my horse saw one of those things, he ran away with me. I just could not hold him." The camels were never used widely, and eventually the army sold some of them to freight companies.

Stagecoach and Freight Lines

Whether by horse, mule, or camel, transportation in early Texas was often slow. Roads were little better than in the Spanish period, turning to mud during wet weather. The lack of good transportation limited economic growth. For the state to prosper economically, Texans needed to find good ways to transport both goods and people.

Most passenger travel in Texas took place on stagecoaches, which also carried mail between towns. Stagecoach lines included routes between Houston, Austin, San Antonio, Indianola, El Paso, and other towns. But travel by stagecoach was difficult and dangerous. Rugged or muddy roads were hard on both coaches and their travelers. Passengers often found themselves repairing broken wheels, fighting bandits, or pushing the coach through streams. A typical stagecoach could carry as many as nine passengers inside and a few more outside.

Daily Life

Texas Roads

Texans—whether on foot, horseback, or stagecoach—often found travel difficult because many Texas roads were little more than trails. Roads zigzagged around obstacles and turned to mud during wet weather. Stumps in the middle of roads could shatter wagon wheels. One traveler noted, "Broken wagon parts lying along the roads give the best evidence of their condition." **How did the condition of Texas roads affect travel?**

Stagecoach service in Texas improved in the 1850s. In 1858 the Butterfield Overland Mail company began service in Texas. Its line ran from St. Louis, through Texas, and on to San Francisco. Butterfield stagecoaches ran twice a week, providing fast, reliable mail service to California. The 25-day trip cost $150 plus meals—about a year's wages for many Texans. Stations along the route kept the coaches stocked with fresh mules and water. U.S. troops at various forts provided protection, but their presence did not guarantee safety, as one customer noted. "The Comanches regard our soldiers much as they would a company of children armed with pop-guns and penny whistles."

Most stagecoaches were not large enough to move such heavy freight as food products, dry goods, and farm supplies. To transport these goods, Texans used freight wagons—heavy wagons with iron axles and large wheels. Teams of 10 to 20 horses, mules, or oxen pulled each wagon. Most freight companies were located in Gulf Coast towns, because most of the state's goods moved through Houston and Galveston. From Galveston, export goods could be shipped by water to ports outside the state.

Mexican Americans played an important role in the overland freight business, particularly in San Antonio and South Texas. Much of the freight traffic in this region was carried on **oxcarts**—large, slow, two-wheeled carts with solid wheels. Because they worked cheaper than other freighters, some Mexican American teamsters were attacked in the mid-1850s in an episode known as the Cart War. A number of carters were killed or wounded, and more had their carts destroyed.

Reading Check **Drawing Inferences and Conclusions** How did the vast distances and difficult terrain in Texas affect the state's economy?

Interpreting Visuals

Steamboats. *Although steamboats provided an alternative to wagons, river travel in Texas was limited.* ***What benefits of steamboat transportation can you see in this image?***

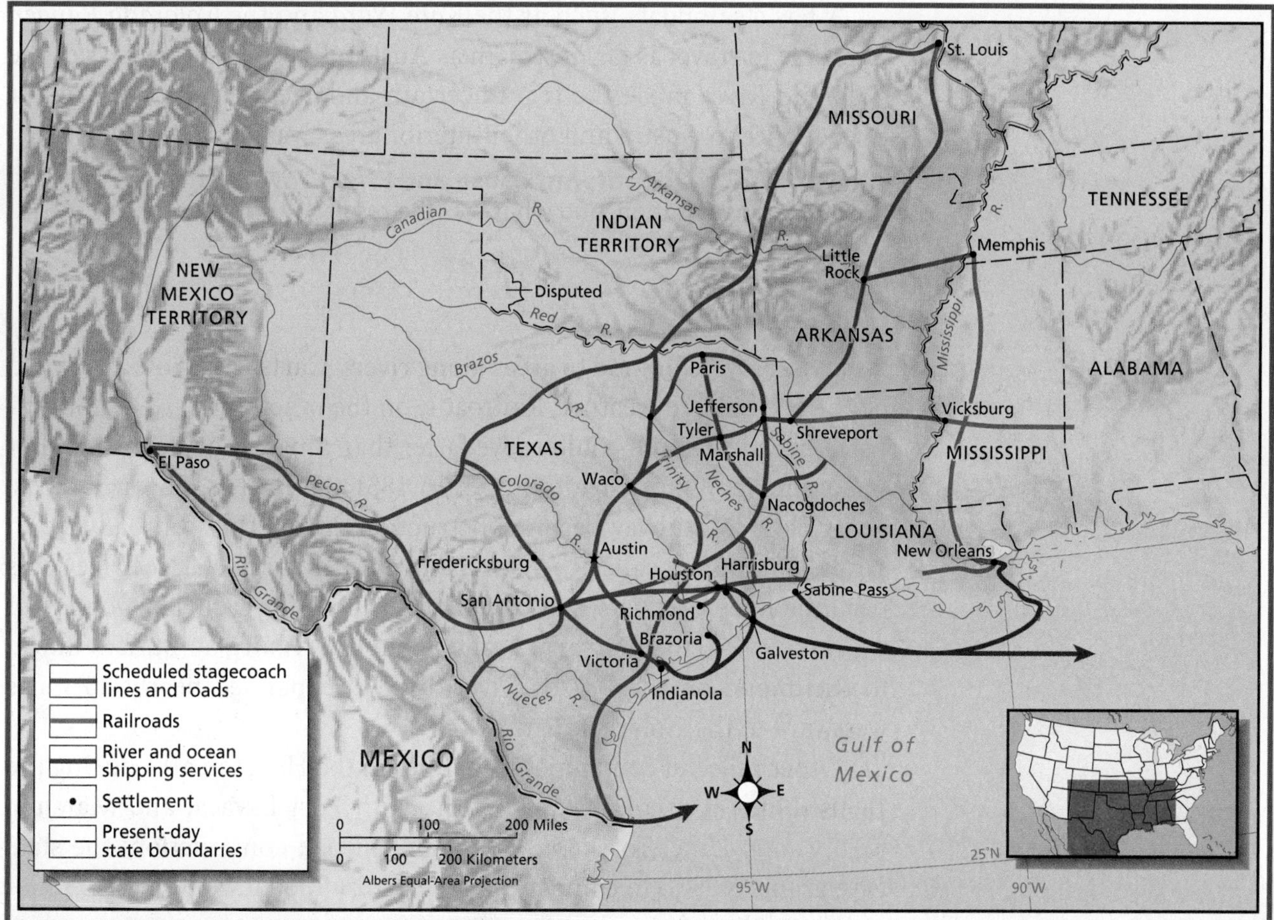

Transportation in Texas, 1860

Interpreting Maps Texas roads were in poor shape, and stagecoach line were expensive to operate. During the mid-1800s Texans began to build alternative transportation systems.

Human Systems How did transportation around Houston differ from transportation through San Antonio?

★ Steamboats

Although freight wagons could carry heavy loads, they were unreliable and slow. Wagons alone could not keep up with the Texans' needs. So Texans turned to the state's rivers to transport goods. **Steamboats**—which got power by burning wood or coal—could travel along many of the lower parts of the state's rivers. In northeastern Texas, for example, steamboats were loaded with cotton at Jefferson. They traveled along Big Cypress Bayou to Caddo Lake, and from there down the Red and the Mississippi to New Orleans. When rainfall was plentiful, boats loaded with cotton could travel the Brazos, Neches, Sabine, and Trinity Rivers.

Because of its location, Houston became a transportation center and grew to become the state's third-largest city. On Buffalo Bayou, steamboats carried goods, particularly cotton, from Houston to the busy port of Galveston. From there the goods were loaded onto larger ships for the trip to New Orleans, then the South's busiest port.

A few steamboats, such as the *Kate Ward* and the *Colorado Ranger*, were able to travel as far upstream as Austin. But the shallowness of the Colorado River made the trip uncertain and even dangerous. Regular river service to Austin and other interior areas was never established.

Reading Check **Identifying Cause and Effect** Why did Texans use rivers for transportation, and what was the result?

Railroads

Steamships were limited to areas along rivers. Carts were slow and could not be used in bad weather. Railroads, on the other hand, were not hindered by weather and could move faster than any cart or steamship. But they were very expensive to build. In 1851 the Buffalo Bayou, Brazos, and Colorado Railway began construction on the first railroad line in Texas. Commonly called the **Harrisburg Railroad**, it charged five cents per mile for passengers and one cent per mile for each 100 pounds of freight. By 1856 the line ran 32 miles from Harrisburg on Buffalo Bayou to Richmond on the Brazos River. It soon expanded nearly 80 miles westward to the Colorado River.

Other railroad companies built lines in the Houston area during the 1850s. Lines also connected Victoria with Port Lavaca, and Marshall with Caddo Lake. To encourage more railroad construction, the state gave grants of land to companies. Even so, by 1860 fewer than 500 miles of railroad lines existed in Texas.

Reading Check **Analyzing Information** What benefits did railroad technology offer over other means of transportation?

Section 2 Review

hmhsocialstudies.com ONLINE QUIZ

1. Define and explain:
- oxcarts
- steamboats

2. Identify and explain the significance of the following in Texas history:
- Harrisburg Railroad

3. Locate on a map:
- Houston
- Galveston

4. Categorizing Copy the graphic organizer below. Use it to list the advantages and disadvantages of moving people and goods by stagecoach, steamboat, and railroad.

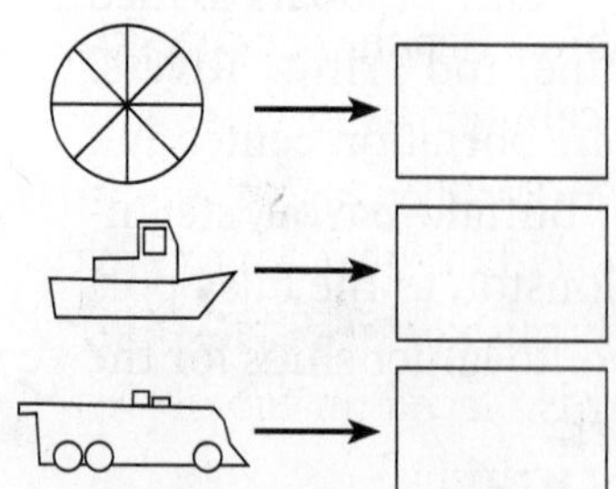

5. Finding the Main Idea

a. How did improvements in technology affect the economic development of Texas?

b. How did the locations of Galveston and Houston affect their growth?

6. Writing and Critical Thinking myWriteSmart

Supporting a Point of View Imagine that you are a Texas farmer in the 1850s. Write a newspaper editorial urging Texans to support or oppose railroad construction in the state. Consider the following:
- a railroad's ability to carry heavy loads, even in bad weather
- the state's enormous potential for cotton production

Section 3

Social and Cultural Institutions

Main Ideas

1. Frontier Texans depended on schools and churches for education, spiritual guidance, and social events.
2. Newspapers spread word of local events and issues.
3. Many Texans were active in the arts.

Key Terms and People

- **telegraphs**
- **Gail Borden Jr.**
- **Hermann Lungkwitz**

Why It Matters Today

The arts were important to many Texans on the frontier. Use current events sources to learn about a Texas writer or artist active today.

TEKS: 4C, 19D, 20C, 21B, 22D

myNotebook

Use the annotation tools in your eBook to take notes on social and cultural institutions on the Texas frontier.

The Story Continues

The Cobb sisters of Galveston were determined to keep their school open. But starting and running a school in a young state like Texas was a challenge, even in an established town such as Galveston. The two struggled throughout the 1850s to find money to keep the school's doors open. Even the local newspaper, the *Galveston News,* tried to help. The paper pleaded with the local community to support the school. "Will Galveston lose another school?" it asked.

★ Frontier Schools and Churches

Texans in the 1850s supported the idea of education. With Governor Elisha M. Pease's support, the state legislature set aside $2 million as a school fund in 1854. However, much of this money ended up being used for other purposes. For example, school funds were loaned out to support railroad construction in the state. As a result, there was little state money to build schoolhouses and pay teachers.

Some towns, like San Antonio and some German communities, did build schools. These were often one-room log cabins. Benches and desks, also cut from logs, rested on dirt floors. Some cabins had no windows and were lit by sunlight that came through the large gaps between logs. On dark winter days, children did lessons by the light of torches or lanterns. One student recalled the conditions of early schools in Texas. "Our seats . . . were long, two-foot-by-twelve-foot boards placed on top of two rocks. . . . We used our knees for desks to do our writing."

These early Texas schools combined strict discipline with a broad course of study. Even in the early grades, some schools taught students subjects like ancient world history and languages such as Latin and Greek. As time passed, more students took time off from farm work to attend school. These students often found school a welcome relief from the never-ending work at home.

Many of the early schools in Texas were opened and operated by churches. Texas churches ran schools on every level, from primary schools to colleges. Some churches also opened libraries, which made books—generally scarce on the frontier—available to Texans.

As the Texas population grew in the 1850s, church membership expanded as well. Churches provided spiritual and moral guidance and brought a social aspect to the often isolated lives of rural Texans. The most popular churches in Texas were Protestant denominations. Methodists, Baptists, Episcopalians, and Presbyterians could be found throughout the state. Many Tejanos and European immigrants remained Catholic. Several churches published newspapers to communicate with members. The *Texas Baptist,* the *Texas Presbyterian,* and the *Texas Catholic,* for example, kept people informed of church events.

Reading Check **Summarizing** How did schools and churches reflect aspects of life in Texas?

★ Newspapers

For a frontier region, Texas had a large number of newspapers—growing from 36 in 1852 to more than 80 in 1860. The *Telegraph and Texas Register,* first published in 1835, had the largest circulation of any newspaper in the state. Published in Houston, the newspaper was founded by dairy businessman **Gail Borden Jr.** and his partners. Other well-known papers were the *Galveston News,* the *Austin State Gazette,* and the *Dallas Herald.* Spanish-language newspapers were published in San Antonio and Brownsville, and the first German-language newspaper, *Zeitung,* was printed in Galveston. Most Texas newspapers were published only once or twice a week. They contained public notices, editorials, literary features, and information about local events.

Newspapers began carrying more national and world news in the 1850s after **telegraphs** were introduced. The telegraph allowed people to communicate across vast distances by sending coded signals over wires. In 1854 a telegraph line—strung from treetop to treetop—connected Galveston, Houston, Marshall, and several other towns. Texans could now receive news faster than ever.

Reading Check **Drawing Inferences and Conclusions** Why do you think that two major newspapers were based in Galveston and Houston?

BIOGRAPHY

Gail Borden Jr.

(1801–1874) A member of the Old Three Hundred, Gail Borden Jr. worked as a surveyor for Austin's colony. In the 1840s he began experimenting with ways to keep food from spoiling. Shortly before the Civil War, Borden developed condensed milk, which could be safely stored for long periods. The Union army bought all the milk that Borden could produce. The milk soon caught on among the general public as well. Borden made a fortune, much of which he used to help fund education programs. For what is Gail Borden Jr. best known?

★ Literature and Art

Besides newspapers, Texans also had access to reading material and information through libraries. Between 1850 and 1860 the number of libraries in the state rose from 12 to 132. Many of these libraries grew out of individuals' private collections. For example, Swedish settler Swante Palm donated his large book collection to the University of Texas.

Although books were relatively scarce in Texas, most families had a Bible or a McGuffey's *Reader* that they could use to teach children to read. Some books by local authors were available too. Thomas Mayne Reid wrote about Texas legends in the *Headless Horseman.* Jane McManus Cazneau published the novel *Eagle Pass,* which described life on the Rio Grande. In it, the main character describes her first view of Texas.

TEXAS VOICES

"I landed in March, in Texas, and . . . was led captive by the fresh and verdant beauty of the coast region. . . . Already green and laughing spring was holding her revels on a carpet of flowers in the bright sunshine."

—Jane McManus Cazneau, *Eagle Pass*

The first published histories of Texas also appeared in the 1840s and 1850s. Henderson Yoakum published a two-volume history in 1855. José Antonio Navarro later published his own history to refute parts of what Yoakum had written.

Artists were also captivated by Texas. Théodore Gentilz had already become known for his scenes of Texas life. Carl von Iwonski, **Hermann Lungkwitz**, and Friedrich Richard Petri were respected artists of the 1850s. Louise Heuser Wueste and Eugenie Lavender were gifted portrait artists. These artists skillfully illustrated the people and places of Texas.

Reading Check **Categorizing** Identify writers and artists of early Texas.

CONNECTING TO

The Arts

Hermann Lungkwitz

Hermann Lungkwitz was trained as a landscape painter in Germany before moving to Texas. He painted this image of the Guadalupe River in the 1860s. **How do you think immigrant artists influenced life in Texas during the 1800s?**

★ Section 3 Review

hmhsocialstudies.com
ONLINE QUIZ

1. Define and explain:
- telegraphs

2. Identify and explain the significance of the following in Texas history:
- Gail Borden Jr.
- Hermann Lungkwitz

3. Summarizing
- Copy the graphic organizer below. Use it to describe education and religion in Texas during early statehood.

Life in Texas during Early Statehood → Schools; Churches

4. Finding the Main Idea

a. What were some of the challenges faced by teachers and students in Texas?

b. What sort of information did newspapers carry during early statehood?

5. Writing and Critical Thinking *my* WriteSmart

Analyzing Information Imagine that you live in Texas in the 1850s. Write a letter to a friend describing how you spend your free time. Consider the following:
- the availability of books in Texas
- Texas writers and artists

Image Credit: Hill Country Landscape, 1862 (oil on canvas), Lungkwitz, Carl Hermann Frederick (1813-91)/Museum of Fine Arts, Houston, Texas, USA/The Bayou Bend Collection, gift of Miss Ima Hogg/The Bridgeman Art Library

Section 4 Slavery in Texas

Main Ideas

1. Slaves performed many jobs on plantations.
2. Some Texans argued against slavery.

Key Terms

- **spirituals**
- **abolition**

Why It Matters Today

Slaves in Texas—as in other southern states—had no civil rights. Use current events sources to learn about a civil rights struggle in the world today.

TEKS: 4C, 8A, 17C, 19B, 21B, 21C, 21E, 22D

myNotebook

Use the annotation tools in your eBook to take notes on slavery in Texas.

The Story Continues

Slaveholder James Johnson of Travis County saw a chance to make some money. As was common in the days of slavery, it involved breaking up a family. Nonetheless, he hired out a slave named Esther and her child to Ashbel Smith in Houston. Esther's husband, Jesse, desperate to be with his family, ran away to Houston. When Johnson caught up with him, he promised that Jesse could stay in Houston. But when Johnson instead started to take Jesse back to Travis County, Jesse ran away again.

Slave Labor

Slaves like Jesse and Esther made up much of the East Texas population. As you have read in previous chapters, most Texas slaves worked on farms. On small farms slaves performed a wide variety of tasks. On large plantations, though, most slaves had specific jobs. Most plantation slaves—men, women, and even children—worked in the fields. For them, work began at daybreak. They ate breakfast in the fields and then plowed, planted, or harvested. Men usually did the heaviest work, such as plowing. Lunch was eaten near the workplace. There was little time to stop, particularly during harvest time, because planters expected slaves to pick many pounds of cotton every day. On average, an adult male slave could pick 150 to 200 pounds of cotton per day. Besides field work, men built and repaired fences, dug and cleaned out ditches, and hauled wood. Women often worked as cooks, laundresses, or seamstresses.

By 1850, slaves made up almost 20 percent of the population of Austin, Galveston, and Houston. Slaves who lived in towns did many jobs. Men worked as carpenters or blacksmiths, while women were cooks, babysitters, or housekeepers. Slaves also helped build the state's transportation system, including its docks, railroads, roads, and warehouses. Some slaveholders hired out slaves to work for others, and a few were allowed to keep part of their wages and buy their freedom.

Interpreting Visuals

Slave life. *Picking cotton was a common job for Texas slaves.* ***What characteristics of slave life can you identify in this painting?***

Reading Check **Categorizing** What jobs did enslaved men and women on plantations and in cities do?

★ Slave Culture

The life of a slave was hard. Slaves worked at least six days a week, but most had Sunday off. They spent any spare time doing personal chores or tending to their gardens. Some slaves even worked extra jobs after completing their regular duties. They used the income to buy food, clothes, or gifts for family members.

The food and shelter available to slaves were often poor. A typical breakfast might include corn bread, coffee, and sometimes bacon. Lunch and dinner generally consisted of corn and bacon or some other type of pork. Some slaves did grow vegetables, such as sweet potatoes, to add some variety to their diets. Others trapped wild game or caught fish. Home was generally a small cabin with crude furniture. Slaves' clothing was generally made of rough, cheap fabric. Their shoes were stiff and often did not fit properly.

During their rare leisure moments, slaves visited with their families and friends, telling stories or playing games. They might hold dances, family gatherings, or picnics. Some slaveholders allowed slaves to attend a church on Sundays, while others forbade it. However, some slaves continued to worship even when it was forbidden.

CONNECTING TO
Literature

African American Folktales

Folktales are traditional stories, usually told by one person to another. Some tales passed on moral lessons, while others were told simply because they were entertaining. Folktales were popular in slave communities in Texas. J. Mason Brewer collected stories from African Americans throughout Texas. In many of these stories, a dog spirit would appear to help people in need. In one story, a woman returns from the grave in the form of a ghost dog to give her daughter medicine. **Why were folktales important to enslaved Texans?**

Music and religion were important in slave communities. They gave many African Americans strength to face the hardships of enslavement. Slaves sang songs while working in the fields, and after work they played instruments such as fiddles or banjos. Urban slaves started the first African American churches in Texas. Music was a major part of the worship service. **Spirituals**—religious folk songs—rang through black churches, carrying messages of hope and faith. One song said, "When we all get to Heaven, They'll be no slaves no more!"

Reading Check **Finding the Main Idea** Why was religion an important part of many slaves' lives?

★ Slave Escapes and Rebellions

Some Texas slaves were willing to risk their lives to escape slavery by fleeing to Mexico where slavery was illegal. Because of the likelihood of capture, however, most slaves did not try to run away. As a warning to all slaves, slaveholders severely punished those who attempted to escape. Many slaves also did not want to leave their families behind.

Some white Texans, particularly in areas with large slave populations, feared the possibility of slave rebellions. Few such rebellions ever occurred, though. One slave uprising was planned in 1856 in Colorado County. A group of slaves acquired guns, planning to rebel and escape to Mexico. Before the rebellion could take place, slaveholders learned of the plan. They hanged and whipped to death several slaves. In 1860, rumors spread that an outbreak of fire in North Texas was part of a slave plot. Although no uprising occurred, many African American and white Texans were executed for the supposed plot.

Reading Check **Analyzing Information** Why did most slaves not try to escape?

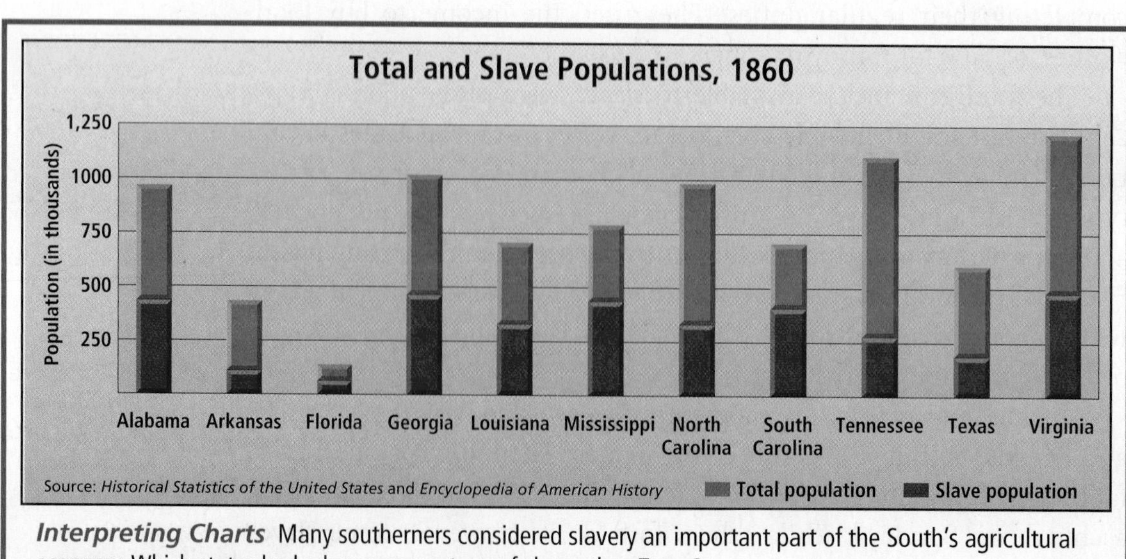

Interpreting Charts Many southerners considered slavery an important part of the South's agricultural economy. Which states had a larger percentage of slaves than Texas?

★ Debating Slavery

As you have read, planters dominated the Texas legislature during the early statehood period. To protect their livelihood, these planters passed laws to strictly control slave life. Slaves could not own property or marry, and people could be punished for hiding a runaway slave. Slaveholders and others defended the system, noting that it supported the South's economy. Without slavery, they argued, the cotton industry would fail.

Some Texans supported **abolition**, or an end to slavery. Some opposed slavery for moral or religious reasons, believing that it was wrong for one person to own another. They pointed out the cruelty of ripping families apart, a pain many slaves knew all too well. Other abolitionists opposed slavery for political reasons, arguing that it went against the ideals of democracy and freedom. In addition, a few Texans believed that slavery was hindering the state's economic progress. They wanted to diversify the state rather than continue to focus so heavily on agriculture.

Among those who opposed slavery in Texas were many Mexican Americans and European immigrants. For instance, Elise Waerenskjold, a Norwegian-born writer and journalist, spoke out against slavery. She argued that slavery could not last, because it was built on injustice.

Abolitionists were generally not welcome in Texas, and many were harassed or attacked for expressing their opinions. Stephen Andrews, a Houston lawyer, was one such abolitionist. In the 1840s he announced a plan to buy slaves so that he could give them freedom. As a result, he was forced to leave the state. Teacher and missionary Melinda Rankin, too, was forced to flee Texas.

Reading Check **Contrasting** What were some of the arguments for and against slavery?

African Traditions

Texas slaves maintained many African traditions. African Americans passed their traditions along to younger generations through songs, stories, and family history. As a result, slaves' music and dances were similar to those in Ghana, Nigeria, and other African nations. Slaves also used African farming techniques. Today some African Americans remember their heritage by celebrating Kwanzaa, a seven-day festival based in part on traditional African harvest festivals. **How did slaves maintain their African traditions?**

★ Section 4 Review

hmhsocialstudies.com
ONLINE QUIZ

1. **Define and explain:**
   - spirituals
   - abolition

2. **Summarizing**
   Copy the graphic organizer below. Use it to describe the major arguments against slavery.

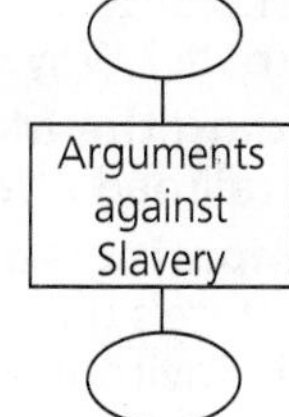

3. **Finding the Main Idea**
   - What was work and daily life like for slaves in Texas?
   - Why did most slaves not run away, and why were rebellions rare?

4. **Writing and Critical Thinking** *my* WriteSmart
   Identifying Points of View Imagine that you are an abolitionist living in Texas. Write a letter to a friend explaining why you oppose slavery.
   Consider the following:
   - the living conditions of slaves
   - the treatment slaves receive

CHAPTER 17 REVIEW

The Chapter at a Glance

Examine the following visual summary of the chapter. Then, with a partner, take turns explaining to each other what life was like in the Early Statehood period. Include specific details.

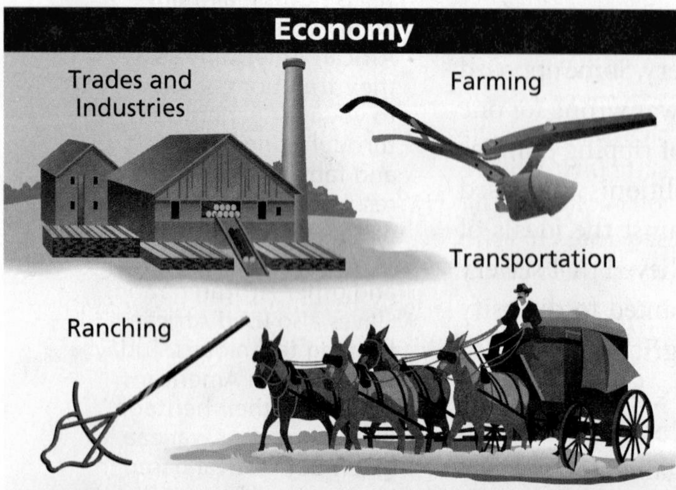

Identifying People and Ideas

Write a sentence to explain the role or significance of each of the following terms or people.

1. cotton belt
2. planters
3. Richard King
4. Aaron Ashworth
5. tanneries
6. steamboats
7. Harrisburg railroad
8. Gail Borden Jr.
9. abolition
10. Hermann Lungkwitz

Understanding Main Ideas

Section 1

1. What was the main source of income for Texans?
2. What were the major professions in Texas during the 1850s?

Section 2

3. Why did Texans need reliable transportation?
4. How did the locations of Galveston and Houston affect their growth?

Section 3

5. What role did churches and schools play in frontier Texas?

Section 4

6. Describe the daily life of enslaved African Americans in Texas.
7. Why did most Texas slaves not run away?

You Be the Historian

Reviewing Themes

1. **Government** What did the state government do to improve transportation within Texas?
2. **Geography** How did the weather and river systems affect transportation and the Texas economy in the mid-1800s?
3. **Economics** Analyze the effect of national and international markets on the production of goods and services in Texas.

Thinking Critically

1. **Identifying Points of View** Do you think that most planters would support the construction of railroads? Why or why not?
2. **Finding the Main Idea** How did the coming of the railroad affect the development of Texas?
3. **Comparing and Contrasting** How did Texans in the state's different regions adapt to and modify their environment to earn a living?

Texas Test Practice

Interpreting Maps

Study the map below. Then use the information on the map to answer the questions that follow.

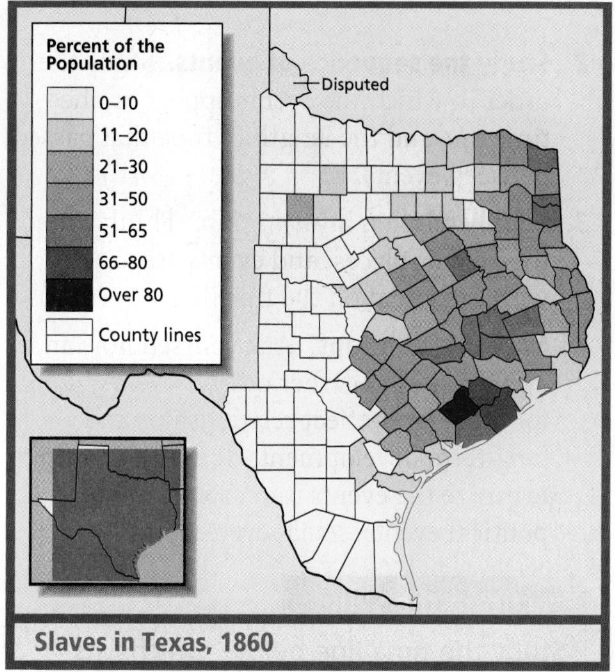

Slaves in Texas, 1860

1. Which of the following correctly describes slavery in Texas in 1860?

A Slavery was limited to West Texas.
B Few slaves lived in East Texas.
C Many slaves lived in East Texas.
D Most slaves lived along the Rio Grande.

2. Based on your interpretation of this map, in what parts of Texas were most plantations?

Analyzing Primary Sources

Read the following quote by Elise Waerenskjold. Then answer the questions.

"Let us now ask ourselves if we would be satisfied with being slaves, with being sold like animals, with being separated from our mates and our children whenever it might suit our master . . . without the slightest possibility of rising above the miserable state into which we were born, despite the fact that we might have the highest abilities and the greatest eagerness to learn. . . . I am convinced that in time slavery will be abolished either by gentle means or by force, because I believe that institutions founded on injustice cannot survive, but are doomed to fall."

3. Which of the following statements best describes the author's point of view?

F The state's booming economy was no reason to support slavery.
G She supports the institution of slavery.
H The African slave trade should be banned.
J Considering life from a slave's point of view reveals the injustice of slavery.

4. When interpreting a primary source, historians examine the historical context in which the source was written. What might have influenced the author's point of view?

Cooperative Learning

Work with a small group to complete the following activity. Each person in your group should select a Texas historical figure, such as an artist, business-person, farmer, or rancher, from the mid-1800s to research. Find out when and where the person was born, and how he or she contributed to Texas. Write a brief account about the person. You might want to include an illustration of the person or an aspect of his or her life. Then combine the results of your research with the other students in your group to create a "who's who" of frontier Texas.

Internet Activity 

Access the Internet to learn more about the physical and human geographic factors necessary for growing cotton. Consider the types of soil and climate in which cotton thrives, as well as the labor, storage, and processing needed after the cotton is grown. Then examine the conditions and factors in Texas. Create a written presentation based on your findings, explaining why cotton became a major industry in Texas and how it affected the state's economic development. Check your presentation for standard spelling, grammar, sentence structure, punctuation, and citation of sources.

Social Studies Skills

WORKSHOP

Interpreting Time Lines

Time lines display events in chronological order, or the sequence in which the events occurred. Knowing the chronological order of historical events is essential to understanding their significance. Time lines allow you to see relationships between events and help you to remember important dates.

Sequence in a Time Line

Time lines are usually read from left to right, with the oldest dates on the left. Marker dates on the time line indicate the time period that it covers. Each event on the time line has an arrow or line to show when it occurred in relation to the marker dates. These entries are thus listed in chronological order. Seeing this order may suggest a relationship between events that you may otherwise not see.

B.C. and A.D. Some time lines contain the abbreviations B.C. and A.D. The letters B.C. stand for "before Christ" and indicate dates that happened before the birth of Jesus of Nazareth. The letters A.D. stand for "anno Domini," which means "in the year of the Lord." It indicates events that happened after Jesus was born. When you read dates marked B.C. or A.D., remember that B.C. date numbers get smaller as time passes. A.D. date numbers get larger.

How to Read a Time Line

1. **Determine its framework.** Note the years covered and the intervals of time into which the time line is divided.
2. **Study the sequence of events.** Study the order in which the events appear on the time line and the length of time that passed between events.
3. **Supply missing information.** Think about the people, places, and events associated with each item on the time line.
4. **Note relationships.** Ask yourself how an event relates to earlier or later events. Look for cause-and-effect relationships and long-term developments. It may also help to organize the events into categories, such as political events, social events, and so on.

Practicing the Skill

Study the time line below, which lists events in the history of Texas during the early statehood period. Then answer the following questions.

1. What time period does the time line cover?
2. How much time passed between the signing of the peace treaty with the Penateka Comanches and the publication of Melinda Rankin's book?
3. Organize the events on this time line by type. Which are social? Literary?
4. Create your own time line about a period in Texas history. List significant events and individuals.

TEXAS

1846 — Texas signs a peace treaty with the Penateka Comanches.

1847 — A state census reports the state's population at more than 142,000.

1850 — In her book, *Texas in 1850*, Melinda Rankin describes the state and urges people to move to Texas.

1845 1847 1849 1851

History in Action

UNIT 5 SIMULATION

You Make the Decision . . .

Should Texas join the United States?

Complete the following activity in small cooperative groups. It is 1845. Texans are debating whether their nation should join the United States. Your community has asked you to serve on a committee to develop a flyer that will identify reasons why Texas should or should not join the Union. Follow these steps to reach your decision.

1. **Gather information.** Use your textbook and other resources to find information that might help you decide whether Texas should join the United States. Using what you learned from this unit's Skills Workshop on Interpreting Time Lines, create a time line to help you focus your research. You may want to divide up different parts of the research among group members.

2. **Identify options.** After reviewing the information you have gathered and the time line you created, consider the options you might recommend for the future of Texas. Should it join the United States or remain independent? Be sure to record your possible options for the preparation of your flyer.

3. **Predict consequences.** Now consider each option you and the members of your committee came up with. List the possible outcomes of each proposed course of action. Ask yourselves such questions as, "How would Texas benefit from joining or not joining the United States?" "What impact would it have on the people of Texas?" Once you have predicted the consequences, record them as notes for the preparation of your flyer.

4. **Take action to implement your decision.** After you have considered your options, plan and create your flyer. Be sure to make your decision very clear. You will need to support your decision by including information you gathered and by explaining why you rejected the other option. Your flyer needs to be visually appealing to convince the committee as well as the voters. It also needs to use standard grammar, spelling, and sentence structure. When you are ready, decide which committee members will present each part of the flyer, and then take your flyer to the community board (the rest of the class).

   As you present, think carefully about the words you are using. Try to use both vocabulary words from this unit and general academic vocabulary terms in your presentation.

UNIT 6

Texas in the Civil War and Reconstruction

(1861–1880)

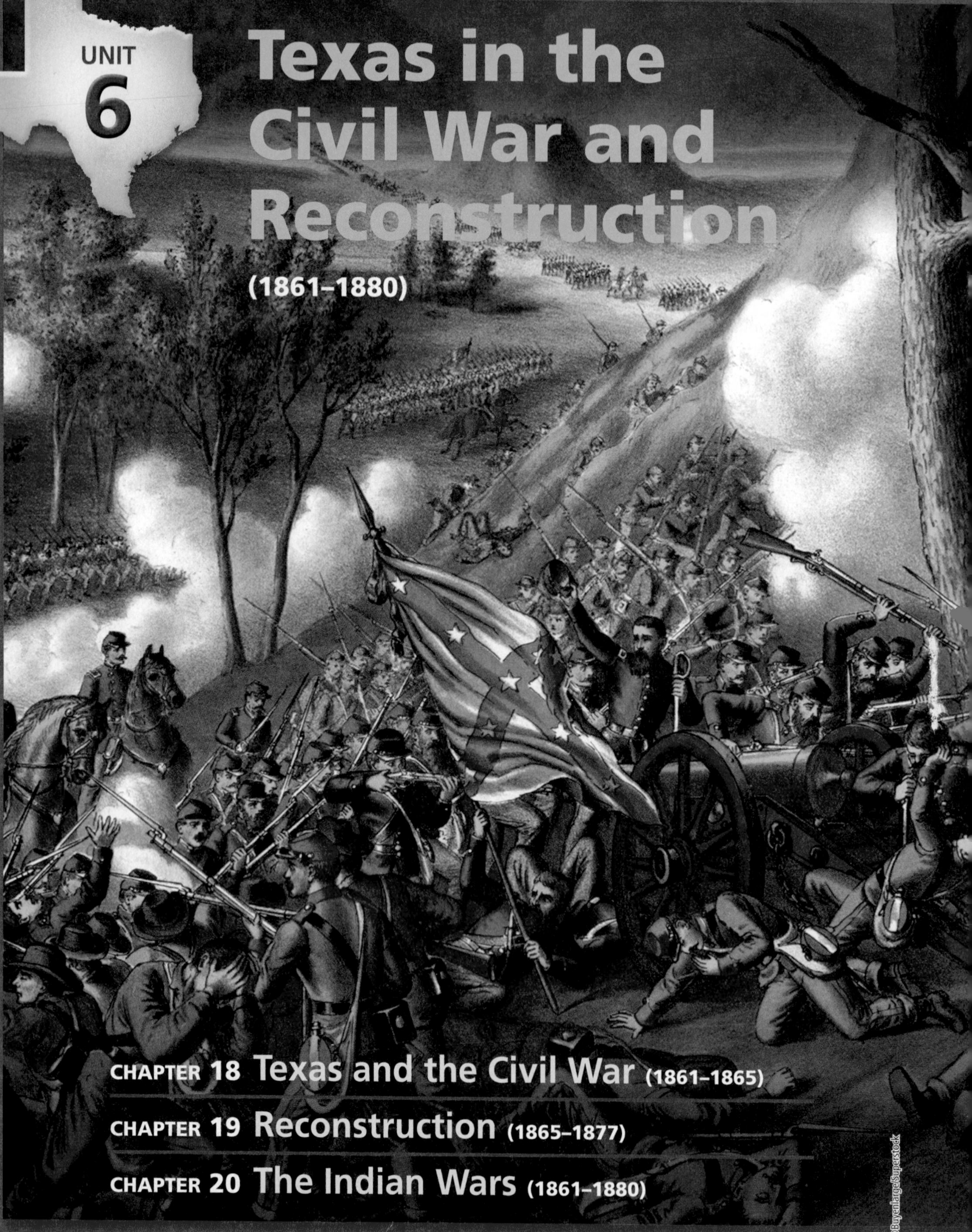

CHAPTER 18 Texas and the Civil War (1861–1865)

CHAPTER 19 Reconstruction (1865–1877)

CHAPTER 20 The Indian Wars (1861–1880)

Texans took part in many Civil War battles, including the Battle of Missionary Ridge.

Image Credit: ©Buyenlarge/Superstock

Texas Teens

Young Soldiers

During the Civil War, 17-year-old Hugh Cooke of Waller County was angry that his commander thought Cooke was too young to fight. "Cap'n, come here. They've got me here holding horses; I didn't come here to hold horses. I came here to shoot Yankees." Cooke soon got his wish. At the beginning of the war, many young Texans shared Cooke's enthusiasm for fighting. Henry Elms was 17 when he signed up for the Confederate army at Victoria. Late one night as his unit attacked a large Union force in a heavily wooded area, they "raised a regular Texas Yell . . . and started forward through the brush." The fire of weapons flashed like lightning in the woods, revealing the position of the Union soldiers. Elms's unit won the battle.

As the war dragged on, soldiers began to miss their homes. One Texas teen, William Randolph Howell, wrote home as he lay sick in a field hospital. "Still remain at hospital. . . . My health improving slowly. Get a horse and prepare to go home. GLORIOUS THOUGHT!"

Teenagers who remained at home during the war faced challenges of their own. C. W. Ackerman and his 13-year-old brother were left to take care of the family farm while their father was away running a flour mill. One day, some Confederate soldiers came around gathering horses for use by the army. Ackerman begged the soldiers to let him keep his. "After frightening me real good they told me I could keep my horse." Ackerman was lucky—he was the only person in the area with a horse. Another young Texan who stayed behind when his father left for the war was not worried. "Mother was a fearless woman and the best marksman with a rifle I ever saw, so we felt able to take care of ourselves." **How did Texas teens play a role in the Civil War?**

In this unit you will learn about the experiences of Texans during the Civil War and Reconstruction. You will also learn about the westward expansion of the frontier and its effects on American Indians in Texas.

Cotton and Conflict in Texas

In 1860 cotton was the leading cash crop in Texas. Hundreds of thousands of cotton bales were shipped from Texas ports like Galveston to northern states or to Europe to be manufactured into cloth. Cotton was so valuable that it became known as "white gold." The booming cotton trade allowed some Texans to build vast fortunes and large plantations, especially in the central and eastern parts of the state where conditions were ideal for cotton growing.

These landowners saw the institution of slavery as an essential part of the cotton industry and, as a result, the Texas economy. Enslaved African Americans provided the labor for cotton production, working from sunrise to sunset, six days a week. Slaves resisted the system as best they could by maintaining communities in spite of the inhuman conditions, committing acts of disobedience, or attempting escape.

After statehood, most Texans were keenly aware of the bitter slavery debate between Northern and Southern states. They concluded that slavery was essential to the Texas economy and their personal prosperity.

After the 1860 election of President Abraham Lincoln, Texans voted overwhelmingly to secede from the Union. Texas then joined the Confederate States of America. Governor Sam Houston had argued passionately to keep Texas in the Union. When he refused to take an oath of loyalty to the new Confederacy, he was removed from office. The United States was on the brink of civil war.

Exploring Museum Resources

The Bullock Texas State History Museum includes many resources related to the cotton economy, slavery, and the Civil War. Explore some of these resources online. You can find museum resources at hmhsocialstudies.com

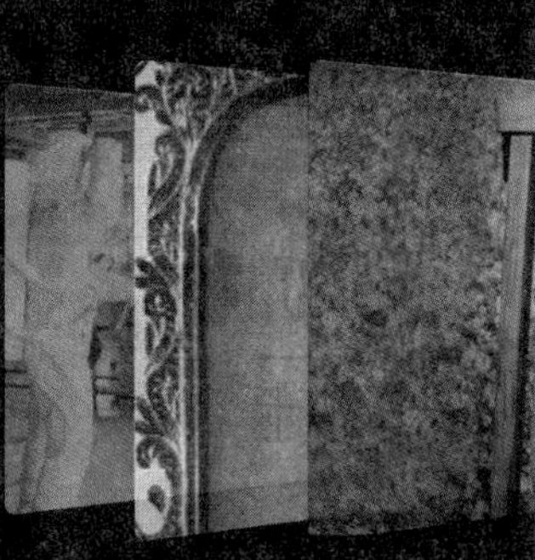

Artifact How did enslaved African Americans preserve their artistic traditions in artifacts like this jug? Go online to find out.

Artifact Cotton scales like this one indicate the importance of cotton in the Texas economy. How were scales like this used?

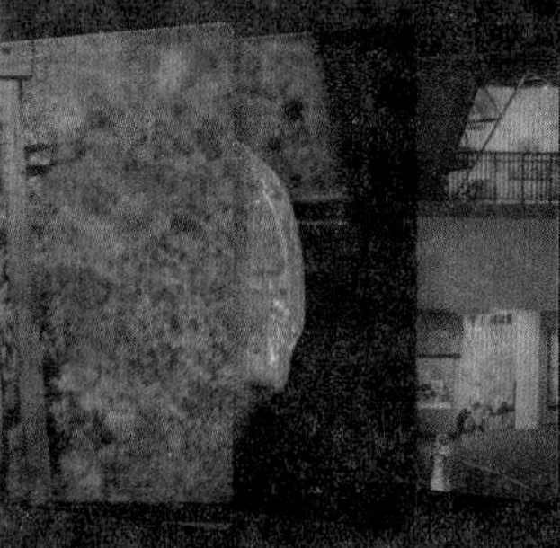

Photograph Many Texans fought in the Civil War. Go online to learn more about their experiences.

UNIT 6

Reading Social Studies

Using Context Clues

Focus on Reading When you are reading your textbook, you may often come across a word you do not know. If that word is not defined as a key term, how do you find out what it means? One way to find the meaning is to use **context clues**. *Context* means "surroundings." Authors often include clues to the meaning of a difficult word in its context. You just have to know how and where to look.

Understanding Context Clues Some helpful strategies for identifying context clues are looking at the words and sentences around a new word. Look for a word or phrase nearby that seems to have a similar meaning and see if they give you clues about the new word's meaning.

Clue	How It Works	Example	Explanation
Direct Definition	Includes a definition in the same or a nearby sentence	We are primarily immigrants—people who came here from other lands—or descendants of immigrants.	The phrase *people who came here from other lands* defines the word *immigrants*.
Restatement	Uses different words to say the same thing	Most of them went to live in urban areas, or cities.	The word *cities* is another way to say *urban areas*.
Comparisons or Contrasts	Compares or contrasts the unfamiliar word with a familiar one	As the population continued to grow rapidly and people moved to the cities, urban areas became more crowded.	The phrase *As the population continued to grow rapidly and people moved to the cities* indicates that urban areas are the same as cities.

You Try It!

Read sentences A and B, then answer the questions below.

A The United States has been an inspiration to other nations because of its basic values: equality, liberty, and justice for all people. These values are the foundation of many of your important rights and freedoms.

B The law gives preference to three groups of people: (1) husbands, wives, and children of U.S. citizens; (2) people who have valuable job skills; and (3) aliens. Aliens are permanent residents of the United States who are still citizens of another country.

1. In example A, what does the term *values* mean? What clues did you find in the example to figure that out?

2. In example B, where do you find the meaning of *aliens*? What does this word mean?

Reading Section Assessment

The following sentences are taken from the unit you are about to read. Read them and answer the questions.

A These strategies resulted in three theaters, or regions, of war.

B The Texas legislature, like others in the South, passed Black Codes. These laws denied African Americans civil rights, or the individual rights guaranteed by the U.S. Constitution.

C Coke won in a landslide—receiving 85,549 votes to 42,663 for Davis.

1. In example A, how do you know the meaning of *theater*?

2. In example B, what is the meaning of the term *Black Codes*? How do you know?

3. What does *landslide* mean in example C? What clues helped you determine its meaning?

Key Terms

Unit 6

Chapter 18

states' rights *(p. 372)*
secede *(p. 374)*
sovereignty *(p. 375)*
regiments *(p. 377)*
cotton diplomacy *(p. 378)*
ironclads *(p. 380)*
cottonclads *(p. 382)*
draft *(p. 387)*
martial law *(p. 388)*

Chapter 19

freedpeople *(p. 397)*
Reconstruction *(p. 397)*
suffrage *(p. 398)*
civil rights *(p. 399)*
impeach *(p. 402)*
bonds *(p. 405)*
scalawags *(p. 405)*
carpetbaggers *(p. 405)*
segregation *(p. 409)*
tenant farmers *(p. 411)*
sharecroppers *(p. 411)*

Chapter 20

commissioners *(p. 416)*
buffalo guns *(p. 423)*
buffalo soldiers *(p. 428)*

Before you read, discuss with your teacher and classmates the meaning of the terms listed above. Be sure to request assistance if you need to. Based on this list of words, what do you already know about the topic you will read about? Background knowledge can improve your understanding of the material you read.

CHAPTER 18

Texas and the Civil War
(1861–1865)

Texas Essential Knowledge and Skills (TEKS) 1A, 1B, 1C, 5A, 5B, 8A, 8B, 9A, 9B, 9C, 13A, 16B, 17A, 17C, 18B, 20A, 21A, 21B, 21C, 21D, 21E, 21F, 21H, 22A, 22B, 22C, 22D

Confederate troops regained control of Galveston in 1863.

TEXAS

- **February 1861** Texans vote, by more than three to one, to secede from the United States.
- **October 1861** Troops leave San Antonio for New Mexico, planning to capture the Southwest for the Confederacy.
- **October 1862** Union forces capture Galveston.
- **January 1863** President Lincoln issues the Emancipation Proclamation.

January 1861 | July 1861 | January 1862 | July 1862 | January 1863

U.S. and WORLD

- **April 1861** The Civil War begins when Confederate forces open fire on Fort Sumter in South Carolina.
- **July 1861** Union and Confederate armies clash in the First Battle of Bull Run, the first major battle of the war.
- **April 1862** The Battle of Shiloh is fought.

If you were there . . .
Would you vote to leave the Union?

Build on What You Know

In the 1850s slavery was firmly established in Texas and the South. Many northerners questioned whether slavery should be allowed anywhere in the United States. Soon, the whole nation was at war over issues that had divided the North and the South.

Thousands of Texans volunteered for the Confederate army.

During the Union advance on Brownsville, many Texans fled the community.

September 1863
A Union attempt to invade Texas is turned back at Sabine Pass.

November 1863
Union troops capture Brownsville.

April 1864
In a battle near Mansfield, Louisiana, Confederate forces stop a Union invasion of northeastern Texas.

May 1865
The last land battle of the war is fought at Palmito Ranch, Texas.

July 1863 — January 1864 — July 1864 — January 1865

July 1863
Union forces win major battles at Gettysburg, Pennsylvania, and Vicksburg, Mississippi.

September 1864
Union army troops under General William Tecumseh Sherman capture Atlanta.

April 1865
General Robert E. Lee surrenders at Appomattox Courthouse.

You Be the Historian

myNotebook

What's Your Opinion? Do you **agree** or **disagree** with the following statements? Support your point of view in your notebook.

- **Economics** War is always economically destructive for those who participate in it.
- **Citizenship** Citizens should be allowed to oppose a war even if their government has decided to fight in it.
- **Geography** A region's geography has little effect on how battles are fought there.

Section 1

Slavery and States' Rights

Main Ideas

1. The United States divided along sectional lines because of regional economic differences.
2. Many Texans supported secession because of states' rights.

Key Terms

- **states' rights**
- **Kansas-Nebraska Act**
- ***Dred Scott* decision**
- **secede**
- **Unionists**
- **Confederate States of America**
- **sovereignty**

Why It Matters Today

Northerners and southerners disagreed about many issues. Use current events sources to learn about an issue that is important to a particular region today.

TEKS: 1B, 1C, 5A, 5B, 8A, 16B, 17A, 17C, 21A, 21B, 21C, 21D, 21E, 21F, 21H, 22A, 22B, 22C, 22D

myNotebook

Use the annotation tools in your eBook to take notes on how slavery and the issue of states' rights affected Texans.

The Story Continues

After years of living as slaves, Dred and Harriet Scott faced a decision. They had lived in free territory for several years, and had recently been returned to the slave state of Missouri. White friends of the Scotts urged them to sue for their freedom. The Scotts decided to do so, believing that their residence in free territory had made them free. Dred Scott's case led to a landmark U.S. Supreme Court ruling.

★ Growing National Divisions

Slavery was one of the issues that divided the nation along sectional, or regional, lines. The North's population was growing as immigrants came to work in its factories. In contrast to the North's increasingly industrial economy, the South's agricultural economy was dominated by slave-based cotton production. Sectionalism was the result of growing economic and social differences between the North and the South. For example, the North wanted tariffs to protect its industries, while the South opposed tariffs because they increased the cost of imported items. During the tariff dispute, some southerners argued that states had a right to ignore tariffs and other federal laws. Under this **states' rights** argument, state power was greater than federal power.

As the United States expanded westward, Congress debated whether territories would enter the Union as free or slave states. This would affect the balance of power in Congress. After much debate, Texas

entered the Union in 1845 as a slave state. Then, under the Treaty of Guadalupe Hidalgo of 1848, the United States gained vast stretches of land from Mexico. In the Compromise of 1850, Congress created a way for the new territories to become states. The compromise included a Fugitive Slave Act, which made it a crime to assist runaway slaves. The act angered northerners and—along with Harriet Beecher Stowe's 1852 antislavery novel *Uncle Tom's Cabin*—greatly increased support for the abolition movement.

Interpreting Visuals

Slavery in the South. *Slaves spent many hours working in fields to produce cotton and other cash crops.* ***What characteristics of slave life does this image show?***

In 1854 Congress passed the **Kansas-Nebraska Act.** This act allowed the Kansas and Nebraska Territories to decide whether to be free or slave states. Many northern members of the Whig Party were angry because this violated the 1820 Missouri Compromise, which prohibited slavery north of the 36°30' N line. They helped form the Republican Party in 1854 to stop the spread of slavery. Sam Houston, then serving in the U.S. Senate, was one of the few southerners who opposed the Kansas-Nebraska Act. Houston's stance on the issue was unpopular in Texas.

In 1857 the U.S. Supreme Court dealt antislavery forces a blow with the ***Dred Scott* decision**. The Court ruled that African Americans were not citizens and therefore could not sue in federal court. The Court also ruled that Congress could not ban slavery in any federal territory. The ruling shocked many northerners. Sectional tensions increased in 1859 when an abolitionist named John Brown led a raid on a federal armory in Harpers Ferry, Virginia, intending to provoke a slave revolt. He and his followers were hanged for treason.

Reading Check **Summarizing** Explain why divisions arose between the North and the South.

The Union and the Confederancy, 1861

Interpreting Maps Texas joined the southern states that formed the Confederate States of America.

1. ***Human Systems*** List the states that made up the Confederacy.
2. ***Drawing Inferences and Conclusions*** What do you think Texas had in common with other Confederate states?

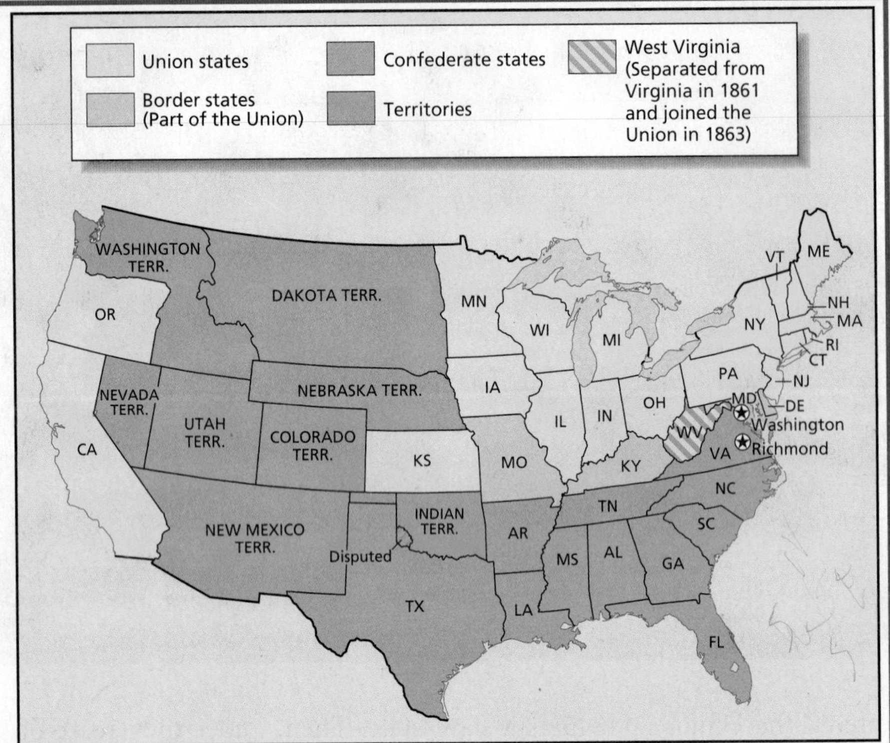

VIDEO
The South Secedes
hmhsocialstudies.com

Texas Joins the Confederacy

In 1860 Republican Abraham Lincoln won the presidential election. He received no electoral votes from the South because many southerners feared that he would support abolition. After the election, South Carolina chose to **secede**, or formally withdraw, from the Union. Mississippi, Florida, Alabama, Georgia, and Louisiana also seceded.

Many Texas leaders called for a special meeting of the legislature to consider secession. This angered **Unionists**—people who wanted to stay in the Union and work out differences over slavery. About one out of four Texans were Unionists, including Sam Houston, Elisha M. Pease, David G. Burnet, Andrew J. Hamilton, and James W. Throckmorton. Houston, who had won the governor's election in 1859, urged Texans to stay in the Union.

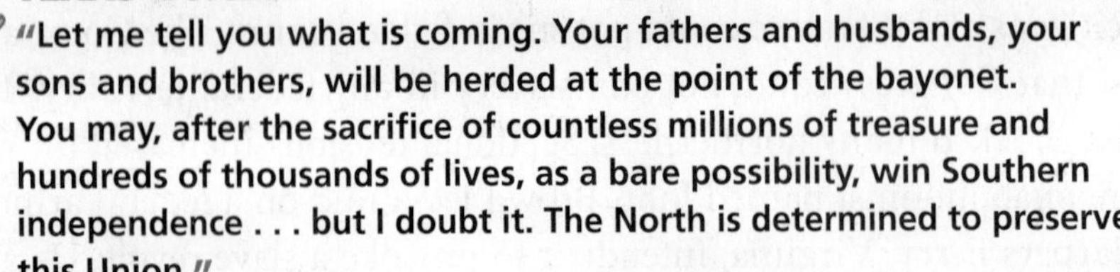

TEXAS VOICES

"Let me tell you what is coming. Your fathers and husbands, your sons and brothers, will be herded at the point of the bayonet. You may, after the sacrifice of countless millions of treasure and hundreds of thousands of lives, as a bare possibility, win Southern independence . . . but I doubt it. The North is determined to preserve this Union."

—Sam Houston, quoted in *The Raven,* by Marquis James

Houston tried to delay the legislative meeting, hoping the calls for secession would fade. Pro-secession leaders ignored him. They organized a secession convention to meet on January 28, 1861, adopting an ordinance, or order, of secession on February 1. The delegates voted 166 to 8 to leave the Union. They then scheduled a statewide vote on the issue. On February 23, 1861, Texans voted for secession by 46,153 to 14,747. A majority of people voted against it in only a few counties. On March 2, 1861, Texas became the seventh state to secede from the United States.

Reading Check **Analyzing Information** Describe the actions taken by the state's pro-secession leaders to have Texas join the Confederacy.

Serving during the War

On the brink of the Civil War, Texans had to decide where their civic duty lay—with their state or with their country. Thousands of Texans served in the Confederate army. Others joined the Union army. Those who were neutral sometimes provided aid to the wounded of both sides. After the war, veterans of both armies assumed leadership positions in the state. Edmund J. Davis, who had organized a Union cavalry unit and eventually became a brigadier general, won election as governor in 1869. Today Texans fulfill their civic duties in many ways. **How do people in your community serve Texas and the nation?**

★ The Confederacy

In February 1861 Texas sent seven delegates to Montgomery, Alabama. There representatives from the seceding states formed a government called the **Confederate States of America**, or the Confederacy. The representatives wrote a constitution that was similar to the U.S. Constitution. It differed in several ways, however. The Confederate constitution emphasized the **sovereignty**, or supremacy, of the states and the right of people to hold slaves. The delegates elected a president, Jefferson Davis of Mississippi, and other officials to run the Confederacy. They chose Texan John H. Reagan as postmaster general.

On March 5, 1861, the Texas Secession Convention reassembled to write a new state constitution. The new document was basically the 1845 constitution with references to the Confederacy replacing references to the United States. When Governor Houston refused to take an oath of allegiance to the Confederacy, the delegates removed him from office. He was replaced with Lieutenant Governor Edward Clark. Sam and Margaret Houston left Austin and retired to Huntsville, where he died on July 26, 1863.

Reading Check **Finding the Main Idea** Why was Sam Houston removed from the governor's office in 1861?

★ Section 1 Review

hmhsocialstudies.com
ONLINE QUIZ

1. Define and explain:
- states' rights
- secede
- sovereignty

2. Identify and explain the historical significance of:
- Kansas-Nebraska Act
- *Dred Scott* decision
- Unionists
- Confederate States of America

3. Sequencing
Copy the time line below. List in order the events of 1861 that led to the secession of Texas.

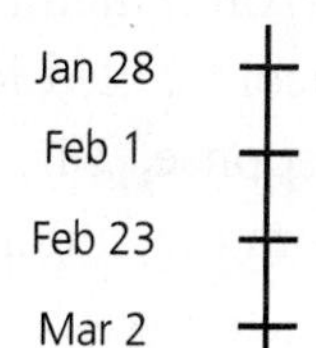

4. Finding the Main Idea

a. Why was the United States divided along sectional lines?

b. Explain the reasons for Texas' secession and its involvement in the Civil War.

5. Writing and Critical Thinking myWriteSmart

Identifying Points of View Imagine that you live in Texas in the 1850s. Write a letter to a friend explaining how Texans are reacting to sectional tensions. Consider the following:
- the Texas economy
- Texans' support of slavery

Section 2

The Civil War Begins

Main Ideas

1. Texans responded swiftly to the Confederate call to arms to join the Civil War.
2. Texas prepared for the war by establishing new industries.
3. The South's experienced military leaders were an important resource during the first half of the war.

Key Terms and People

- **regiments**
- **Albert Sidney Johnston**
- **Thomas Green**
- **cotton diplomacy**
- **ironclads**

Why It Matters Today

The North and the South debated their differences for years before going to war. Use current events sources to learn about peace talks today. Record your findings in your journal.

TEKS: 1B, 1C, 5A, 5C, 9C, 13A, 17C, 20A, 21A, 21B, 21C, 21D, 21E, 22A, 22B, 22D

myNotebook

Use the annotation tools in your eBook to take notes on early events of the Civil War.

The Story Continues

People gathered on balconies and rooftops overlooking Charleston Harbor. They watched Fort Sumter, wondering if the federal soldiers inside would surrender without a fight. The soldiers within the fort waited in the early morning darkness. They wondered if Confederate forces would actually fire upon them. They soon found out—at 4:30 A.M. cannons on the shore opened fire. Soon, as a Union soldier noted, "shot and shell went screaming over Sumter as if an army of devils were swooping around it."

★ A Call to Arms

The Confederate attack on Fort Sumter in April 1861 marked the beginning of the Civil War. A civil war is a war between factions, or opposing groups, within the same country. The news of war "fell on the land like a thunderbolt," one person remembered. The day after Fort Sumter surrendered, President Lincoln called for 75,000 volunteers to help put down the rebellion. In response, Virginia, Arkansas, Tennessee, and North Carolina seceded from the Union.

KEY DATE 1861
The Civil War begins with the Confederate attack on Fort Sumter in South Carolina.

Thousands of Texans responded to the Confederate call to arms. Even many Texas Unionists supported the Confederacy once the war began. "The North will never subdue [conquer] the South. Never, never!" vowed one Texas volunteer. By the end of 1861, some 25,000 Texans were in the Confederate army. Confederate president Jefferson Davis welcomed the first Texas troops in 1861.

TEXAS VOICES

"Texans! The troops from other States have their reputation to gain, but the sons of the defenders of the Alamo have theirs to maintain. I am sure you will be faithful to the trust."

—Jefferson Davis, address to Texas troops

Analyzing Primary Sources
Identifying Points of View Why did Davis think that the Texan volunteers were different from soldiers of other southern states?

Texas troops soon gained a reputation for spirit and daring in battle. Texans usually joined **regiments**—units of around 1,000 soldiers—from their hometowns or counties. The units took the names of the people who organized them. Terry's Texas Rangers, a cavalry unit organized by B. F. Terry, fought in battles throughout the Civil War. Hood's Texas Brigade, under the command of John Bell Hood, became a lead unit in the Army of Northern Virginia. It fought in some of the most important battles of the war. Ross's Texas Brigade, headed by Lawrence "Sul" Ross, fought in Georgia, Mississippi, and Tennessee.

Texas also contributed many officers to the Confederacy. **Albert Sidney Johnston** was the second-highest-ranking officer in the army until his death in battle. Unionist James W. Throckmorton became a brigadier general. Texan **Thomas Green** was another key Confederate officer who would later rise to the rank of brigadier general.

Reading Check **Making Generalizations and Predictions** How do you think the war will affect Texans?

Interpreting Visuals

Terry's Texas Rangers. *Texas volunteers were known for their fighting skills and daring in battle.* ***What particular skills does this painting of Terry's Texas Rangers show?***

★Texas Cities★

Brownsville

History: Spanish settlers arrived in the area of Brownsville in the late 1700s. In 1846 the U.S. Army established a post there. During the Civil War, Brownsville prospered as an important trading post.

Population in 2012: 180,097 (estimate)

Relative location: Southern edge of the South Texas Plains

Region: South Texas Plains

County: County seat of Cameron County

Special feature: Brownsville has a twin city—Matamoros—across the Rio Grande in Mexico.

Origin of name: Originally a fort named Fort Brown, established at the beginning of the Mexican War

Economy: Brownsville's economy is based on agriculture, shipping, tourism, and the manufacture of a variety of goods, including transportation equipment, metal goods, and petrochemicals.

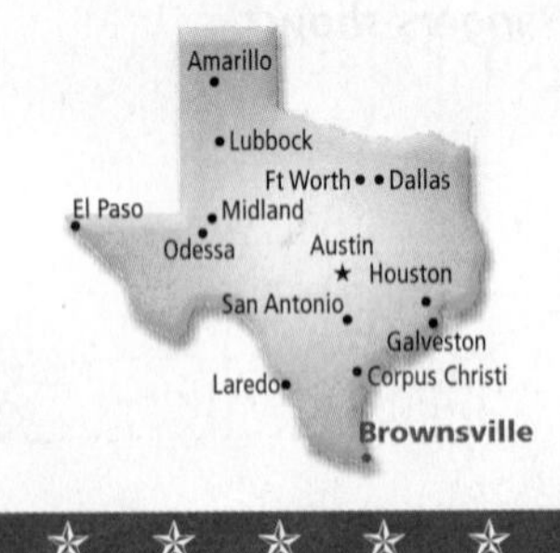

Texas Readies for War

Many of the Texas troops were ill-equipped, reporting with a variety of weapons, uniforms, and supplies. One Texas soldier remembered that "most of our blankets were pieces of carpets taken from floors." The Texans needed all the supplies they could get. Even before the state had officially seceded, the Texas government moved to seize federal property. In February 1861 a force led by Ben McCulloch surrounded the U.S. commander's headquarters in San Antonio. U.S. Army general David E. Twiggs quickly surrendered all federal property in Texas. Without firing a shot, the Texas militia captured more than $1 million in military supplies.

Texans also established new industries to get ready for the war. Thomas Anderson ran a gunpowder mill near Austin. A factory in Tyler made cannons and ammunition, while iron foundries opened in Jefferson and Rusk. Prisoners at Huntsville made 3 million yards of cloth during the war. Texas businesses made saddles, tents, uniforms, and wagons. The state's plentiful resources of cattle, cotton, and food crops such as corn were also a great help to the Confederacy.

Reading Check Summarizing How did preparation for war affect the Texas economy?

Resources and Strategies

The North had a number of advantages at the beginning of the conflict. With a larger population, it could recruit more soldiers. Because the North had more railroads, it could move troops and supplies more easily. The North had far more factories than the South did, so it could produce more weapons and supplies. The North also had an established government ready to conduct and raise money for the war.

The South did have some advantages. It had experienced military leaders, many of whom had served in the U.S. Army during the Mexican War. Many southerners, particularly Texans, were experienced in riding horses and using firearms. By the end of 1861, two thirds of Texans serving in the Confederate army were in the cavalry. A British observer noted Texans' preference for fighting on horseback. "No Texan walks a yard if he can help it."

At the beginning of the war, the Confederacy planned to stay on the defensive and wear down the Union's will to fight. The South hoped to maintain its ability to fight by getting war supplies from Europe. Southern leaders tried to gain foreign support, particularly from Great Britain, through the use of **cotton diplomacy**. The Confederacy withheld cotton shipments to British textile mills, hoping to force Britain to offer help. This strategy failed, partly because European storehouses had been fully stocked before the war.

The North faced the difficult task of having to conquer large amounts of enemy territory. The Union used a naval blockade to cut off southern seaports and prevent the Confederacy from importing war supplies. The blockade eventually extended from Virginia to Florida on the Atlantic coast and from Florida to the southern tip of Texas on the Gulf Coast. At the same time, Union forces planned to take control of the Mississippi River and cut the Confederacy in two. This would separate the important food-producing areas of Arkansas, Texas, and most of Louisiana from other southern states. Union forces also planned to capture Richmond, Virginia, the capital of the Confederacy.

These strategies resulted in three theaters, or regions, of war. The first theater was in the East, centered around Washington and Richmond. A second developed in Tennessee and Mississippi, and the third was west of the Mississippi River. Texans fought in all three theaters.

Reading Check **Evaluating** How do you think the northern strategy of taking control of the Mississippi River would affect Texas?

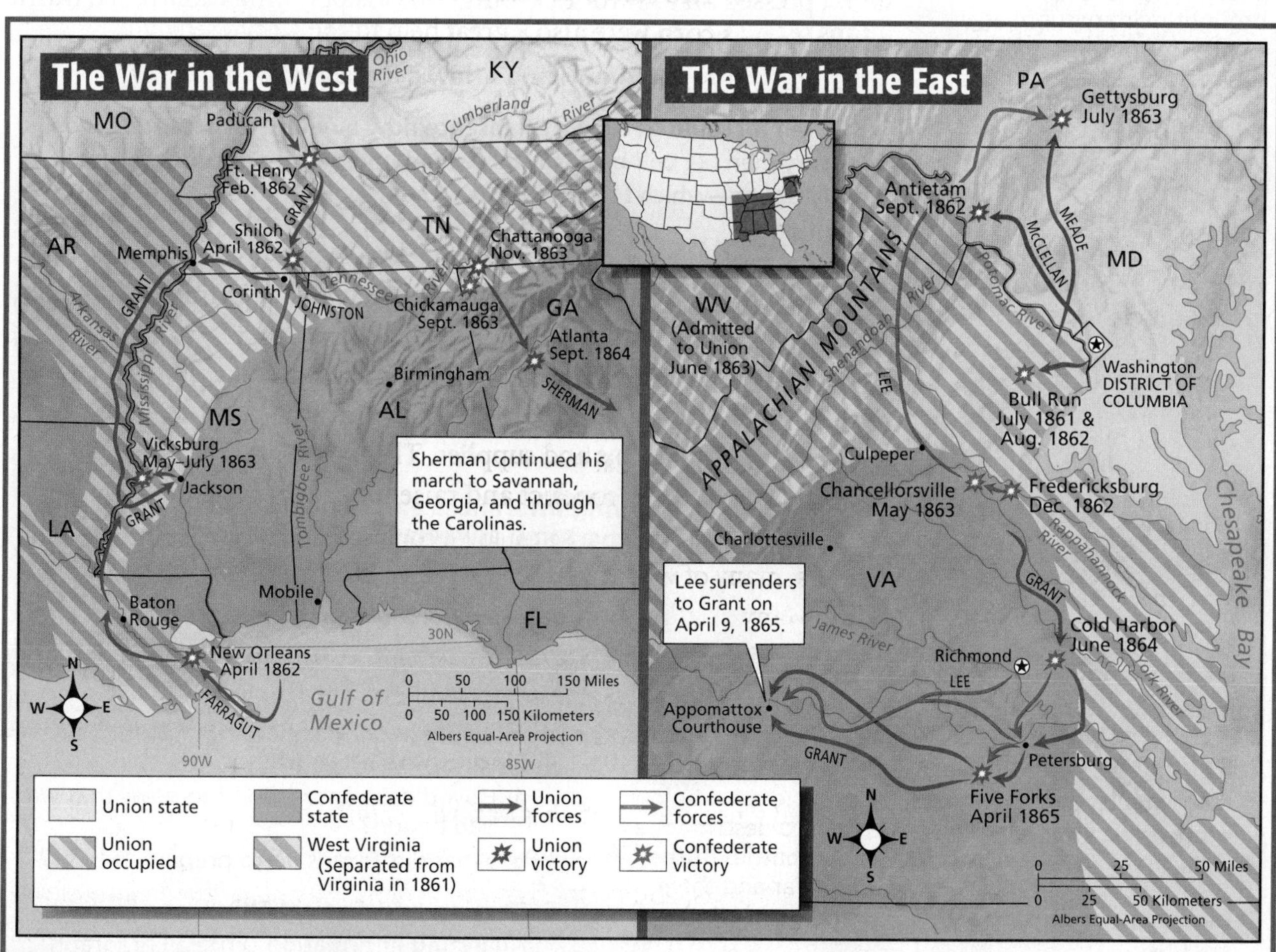

Major Battles of the Civil War

Interpreting Maps Union forces tried to divide the Confederacy by gaining control of the Mississippi River. Meanwhile, Union forces in the East tried to capture the Confederate capital.

Physical Systems How did rivers affect the location of battles?

GLOBAL CONNECTIONS

Global Trade and the Civil War

Before the Civil War, the South had traded with European nations for many items it did not produce. The Union blockade greatly limited the South's ability to obtain supplies during the war. Texas, however, bordered Mexico, and the Union navy could not block Mexican ports. Texans took cotton across the Rio Grande to trade for supplies. Hundreds of ships from Europe brought military supplies to Mexico to trade for the cotton. **How did the location of Texas affect the South in the Civil War?**

★ The Major Battles of the Civil War

The major battles of the war took place east of the Mississippi River. In July 1861 a Union army marched south to capture Richmond. Confederate forces stopped the advance at the First Battle of Bull Run. Confederate troops held off Union attacks the following year, eventually driving most Union troops from Virginia. In late September 1862 General Robert E. Lee's army clashed with a Union force in Maryland. The Battle of Antietam was an important Union victory. In late June 1863 Lee moved north again and battled Union forces at Gettysburg, Pennsylvania on July 1–3. They suffered heavy losses and retreated on July 4. The Battle of Gettysburg was a turning point—Lee was on the defensive for the rest of the war.

Meanwhile, Confederate and Union armies battled for control of the Mississippi River valley. Union general Ulysses S. Grant gained the upper hand in April 1862 in the Battle of Shiloh. It was a costly battle for both sides. General Albert Sidney Johnston of Texas was among those killed. Grant pressed on toward Vicksburg, Mississippi, which controlled traffic on the river. A Texas soldier noted the town's importance.

TEXAS VOICES

"Even if I could get leave of absence now I would not accept it when every man . . . will be so much needed in the coming contest before Vicksburg—which I regard as the hinging point in the destiny of our nation."

—J. C. Bates, quoted in *A Texas Cavalry Officer's Civil War,* edited by Richard Lowe

Grant began the six-week Siege of Vicksburg, supported by a fleet of **ironclads**—ships heavily armored with armored plates. When the town surrendered on July 4, 1863, the Confederacy was split in two. It became very difficult to get supplies from Arkansas, Louisiana, and Texas to the battlegrounds in the East.

Reading Check Drawing Inferences and Conclusions In addition to Gettysburg, what other battle could be considered a turning point, and why?

★ Section 2 Review

hmhsocialstudies.com ONLINE QUIZ

1. Define and explain:
- regiments
- cotton diplomacy
- ironclads

2. Identify and explain the historical significance of:
- Albert Sidney Johnston
- Thomas Green

3. Summarizing
Copy the chart below. Use it to describe the major battles of the Civil War and their significance.

Battle	Significance

4. Finding the Main Idea

a. How did Texans respond to news that war had begun?

b. What did Texans do to prepare for war?

5. Writing and Critical Thinking myWriteSmart

Analyzing Information Write a paragraph describing each side's main strategies in the Civil War.

Consider the following:
- cotton diplomacy
- the blockade

Section 3

Campaigns in Texas and the Southwest

Main Ideas

1. By fighting in and around Texas, the Confederacy hoped to avoid Union occupancy.
2. Geographic features affected the outcome of the military campaigns fought in the region.

Why It Matters Today

Many Texans served in the military during the Civil War. Use current events sources to learn about men and women who serve in our nation's military today.

Key Terms and People

- **Henry H. Sibley**
- **Battle of Glorieta Pass**
- **cottonclads**
- **Battle of Galveston**
- **Richard Dowling**
- **Davis Guards**
- **Battle of Sabine Pass**
- **Santos Benavides**
- **Red River Campaign**

TEKS: 1B, 5A, 8A, 9A, 9B, 9C, 18B, 21A, 21B, 21C, 21D, 21E, 22A, 22C, 22D

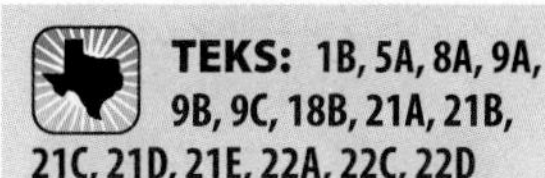

Use the annotation tools in your eBook to take notes on the campaigns fought in and around the Southwest.

The Story Continues

Texan Val C. Giles shivered in the darkness. He was on guard duty, watching a Virginia swamp where many soldiers had died that day in battle. As he thought about his fallen comrades, something terrifying happened. He recalled, "The biggest ghost I had ever seen" slowly rose out of the swamp. He thought that it must be a dead soldier. Only later did he learn that the "ghost" was merely swamp gas.

The New Mexico Campaign

While many Texans served in the eastern theater of the Civil War, some served closer to home. Shortly after the war began, Texas forces led by Colonel John R. Baylor marched into New Mexico Territory and claimed the area. In the fall of 1861, General **Henry H. Sibley** took three Texas regiments to seize the Southwest—from New Mexico to California—for the Confederacy. The region had great wealth from its gold and silver mines as well as ports on the Pacific Ocean.

Sibley's 2,000 troops won a battle against 2,500 Union soldiers at Valverde, New Mexico. The Texas force then seized Albuquerque and Santa Fe. Gradually the army was weakened by disease and lack of food and water. One soldier remembered the march through the desert region. "We had suffered a lot, had gone hungry, and did not have enough water. We sweated during the day and froze at night." Union troops met part of Sibley's force in the **Battle of Glorieta Pass** in New Mexico, on March 28, 1862. A Texas soldier recalled the battle.

Analyzing Primary Sources
Finding the Main Idea Why did the Texans retreat after the Battle of Glorieta Pass?

TEXAS VOICES

"We were under fire 6 hours, compelling [forcing] the enemy to retreat 3 miles and we won the battle. . . . On the day of the battle the enemy sent 200 men around to our camp and burned all our wagons together with all our clothing and provisions."

—Julius Eggeling, quoted in *Westward the Texans,* edited by Jerry D. Thompson

Stranded without supplies, Sibley and his small army had to retreat to Texas. Union forces occupied El Paso and kept control of the Southwest for the rest of the war.

Reading Check **Identifying Cause and Effect** What was the climate of New Mexico like, and how did that affect the Confederates' attempt to capture the region?

BIOGRAPHY

Richard Dowling
(1838–1867) Richard Dowling of Houston joined the Confederate army and became a skilled artillery commander. In 1863 he was given command of Fort Griffin, which guarded Sabine Pass. Dowling knew that his men needed to be excellent shots to prevent Union vessels from simply steaming past the fort. When Union ships did attack, firing as they came, Dowling's men were ready. In his report of the fighting, Dowling praised his men. "All my men behaved like heroes; not a man flinched from his post. Our motto was 'victory or death.'"
Why was Dowling a good choice to command the fort?

★ The Battle of Galveston

The Union navy had blockaded Texas ports by the summer of 1862. When a Union fleet sailed into Galveston Harbor in October, the small Confederate force there retreated. Galveston was vital to the Confederacy. If left in Union control, northern forces could easily sweep into Texas. General John B. Magruder, the commander of Confederate forces in Texas, made plans to recapture it.

Magruder's men converted two steamboats to gunboats, lining the sides with cotton bales for protection. Some soldiers doubted that these **cottonclads** would help much. Nonetheless, troops commanded by Colonel Tom Green boarded the *Neptune* and the *Bayou City* to attack Union ships in the harbor. At the same time, soldiers were preparing to attack the Union forces from the mainland. The **Battle of Galveston** began in the early morning hours of January 1, 1863. A Texan on the *Bayou City* remembered the events.

TEXAS VOICES

"The *Harriet Lane* [a Union ship] ran up beside us and I was ordered to cut the stays. When I cut them, the stage planks fell on the *Harriet Lane*. . . . Commodore Smith went aboard the hostile ship and after a moment's feeble resistance, she struck her colors and surrendered."

—M. L. Clark, quoted in *Reminiscences of the Boys in Gray, 1861–1865,* edited by Mamie Yeary

The remaining Union ships fled. Meanwhile, Confederate land forces overran the Union troops in Galveston, capturing several hundred soldiers. The Confederacy once again controlled the key Texas port.

Reading Check **Sequencing** List in order who controlled Galveston and the approximate dates of their control.

★ The Battle of Sabine Pass

The Union did not intend to leave Galveston in Confederate hands. In September 1863, Union troops set sail from New Orleans, which had been captured by the North in April 1862. General William B. Franklin and about 4,000 troops planned to invade Texas through Sabine Pass, march overland to Houston, and then capture Galveston. Confederate lieutenant **Richard Dowling** and about 45 soldiers in an all-Irish unit known as the **Davis Guards** were to protect the pass. They manned a small post called Fort Griffin, surrounded only by trenches and earthen mounds. The fort had six cannons, which the soldiers had used to practice hitting targets in the pass.

Union forces attacked on September 8, 1863. General Franklin planned to use gunboats to destroy Fort Griffin's cannons so that his troops could land. Union forces shelled the fort for more than an hour. The David Guards held their fire until the gunboats were close by. Dowling then ordered his men to fire. The Confederate gunners fired fast and accurately. They quickly crippled two gunboats and halted the Union attack. The rest of the Union ships turned back, but not before the Guards captured more than 300 Union soldiers. The victory excited people in Texas and the rest of the South. The Confederacy had lost two major battles that summer, and the **Battle of Sabine Pass** helped restore southern confidence. Lieutenant Dowling and the Davis Guards received special medals for their actions.

Reading Check **Summarizing** Why was Sabine Pass a strategic location, and how did holding it affect events in Texas?

Interpreting Visuals

Sabine Pass. *Sabine Pass is the outlet of the Sabine River into the Gulf of Mexico.* ***Based on this illustration of the Battle of Sabine Pass, how do you think geographic factors affected the battle?***

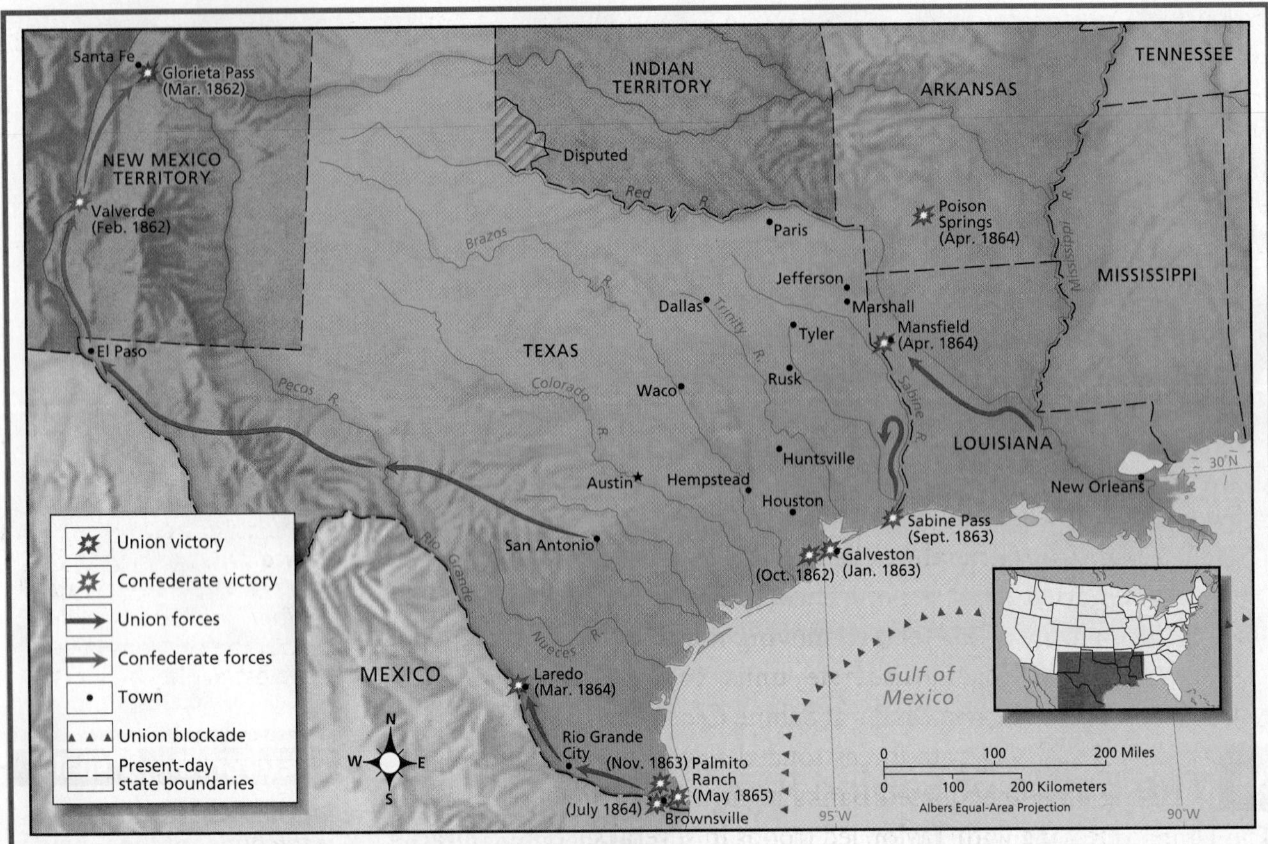

The Civil War in Texas, 1862–1865

Interpreting Maps Union forces targeted Texas ports to limit Confederate trade.
Locate What Texas towns experienced conflict during the Civil War?

★ The Coast and South Texas

Despite the Confederate victories at Galveston and Sabine Pass, Union forces once again attacked Texas. Two months after the Battle of Sabine Pass, Union forces commanded by General Nathaniel Banks captured Brazos Island off the mouth of the Rio Grande. They wanted to take Brownsville and stop trade between Texas and Mexico. Texans like Sarah "Sally" Scull led wagon trains loaded with cotton across the border to Matamoros. From there, Texans shipped the cotton overseas and purchased supplies for the Confederacy. The Union wanted to cut off this supply route. This route was important as the blockade tightened. Ships known as blockade-runners sometimes slipped past the Union navy, but they could not carry on regular trade.

Union troops captured Brownsville in early November 1863. Banks then split his forces. One group of troops moved north up the coast, capturing Matagorda Island and occupying Indianola. Colonel Edmund J. Davis of Texas, leading the other column of Union troops, captured Rio Grande City. But his attack on Laredo failed. Texas troops led by Colonel **Santos Benavides**, the highest-ranking Mexican American to serve in the Confederate army, turned back the attack. After Union forces were called away from Brownsville, Colonel John S. Ford quickly recaptured the town for the Confederacy. Although Union troops controlled Brazos Island, none remained on the mainland of the lower Texas coast.

Reading Check **Finding the Main Idea** What geographic feature made South Texas strategically important, and what was the goal of Union forces attacking the region?

★ The Red River Campaign

The Union troops had left Brownsville to take part in the **Red River Campaign**. Union leaders wanted to invade northeastern Texas from Louisiana along the Red River. They planned to attack in the spring, when the river was usually deep enough for boats.

In March 1864 General Banks and 27,000 men began moving up the river, supported by a fleet of ironclads. Banks hoped to link with a smaller Union army of 15,000 men moving south from Arkansas.

On April 8, 1864, Confederate units commanded by General Richard Taylor intercepted Banks at Sabine Crossroads near Mansfield, Louisiana. The Confederate forces totaled fewer than 9,000 men, but in a stunning blow they forced Banks to turn back. Brigadier General Tom Green, fighting with Taylor, led troops in several successful attacks against Banks during the battles of Pleasant Hill and Mansfield.

Meanwhile, unusually low water levels on the Red River slowed the Union gunboats. They narrowly escaped destruction while retreating. The Union army moving south from Arkansas had no better luck. On April 18, Confederate forces defeated it at Poison Springs, Arkansas. Confederate troops had again turned back Union attacks in Texas.

Reading Check **Analyzing Information** How did the depth of the Red River affect General Banks's invasion of Texas?

Daily Life

Camp Life

"I am sick of war," a Texas officer wrote to his wife in 1863. Many soldiers probably agreed with this officer. Soldiers spent far more time sitting in camp than fighting. Soldiers had to live with bad weather, disease, poor food, and a lack of supplies. Texans were quite creative, however, at getting food, as noted by General Lee. "When you Texans come about the chickens have to roost mighty high."

What problem did Texas soldiers face in camp?

★ Section 3 Review

hmhsocialstudies.com ONLINE QUIZ

1. Define and explain:
- cottonclads

2. Identify and explain the historical significance of:
- Henry H. Sibley
- Battle of Glorieta Pass
- Battle of Galveston
- Richard Dowling
- Davis Guards
- Battle of Sabine Pass
- Santos Benavides
- Red River Campaign

3. Analyzing Information Use the graphic organizer to list three of the Confederacy's goals for fighting in and around Texas.

Confederacy's Goals for Texas
1. ____________
2. ____________
3. ____________

4. Finding the Main Idea

a. What battles were fought in and near Texas, and what was their significance?

b. What effects did geographic factors have on military campaigns in the region?

5. Writing and Critical Thinking myWriteSmart

Supporting a Point of View Imagine that you are a Union or Confederate officer. Write a memo to your superior explaining why controlling Brownsville is important. Consider:
- trade and transportation routes to Mexico
- the use of Brownsville as a launching point for an invasion of Texas

Section 4

The Texas Home Front

Main Ideas

1. Texans endured many hardships during the Civil War.
2. Unionists lost some of their civil rights during the war.

Why It Matters Today

The Civil War affected many people, even those who did not fight in it. Use current events sources to learn about a person who has been affected by war today.

Key Terms and People

- **draft**
- **Francis Lubbock**
- **martial law**

TEKS: 5A, 5B, 5C, 9A, 13A, 17A, 21A, 21B, 21C, 22A, 22C, 22D

myNotebook

Use the annotation tools in your eBook to take notes on life on the home front for Texans during the Civil War.

The Story Continues

While her husband was in the army, Rebecca Adams ran the family's plantation and cared for nine children. Adams somehow found time to knit rabbit-fur gloves for her husband, Dr. Robert Adams. She summed up her situation in a letter to him. "I had to attend to your part of the work and mine too."

The Wartime Economy and the Draft

Although Texas suffered less than other Confederate States because few battles were fought in the state, Texans experienced many hardships. Goods became scarce and very expensive. Many newspapers stopped operation because of a lack of paper. Shortages were also created because supplies, particularly medicines, were sent to Confederate armies. Texans adapted to the wartime shortages, using thorns for pins and wallpaper as writing paper. When coffee became scarce, people used corn, okra, parched peanuts, or sweet potatoes to make drinks. Texans also made more homespun clothing.

To feed the army, farmers grew more corn and wheat and less cotton. Crop production also increased as slaveholders in other states sent slaves to Texas to prevent their being freed by Union occupation forces. Women and children ran farms and plantations, as did men who were unable to serve in the army. Women on the home front also worked in small factories, made items at home, and organized special groups to support the war effort. These groups made uniforms, bandages, and medical supplies. They also provided aid to the families of soldiers.

Political activity in Texas also focused on the war effort. All officeholders strongly supported the Confederacy. **Francis R. Lubbock**, who had been elected governor in 1861, worked to improve the state's military capabilities. After his term ended, Lubbock joined the Confederate army in 1863 as a lieutenant colonel. Pendleton Murrah was elected governor of Texas in 1863. Like Lubbock, Murrah struggled with state debts, defending the frontier against raids by American Indians, and raising troops for the Confederacy.

Although thousands of men had volunteered at the beginning of the war, they were not enough. In April 1862 the Confederate Congress passed a **draft,** or requirement of military service. All white males between the ages of 18 and 35 had to serve. The age limits were later broadened to 17 and 50. However, there were several loopholes in the law. People with certain key jobs were exempt. During his governorship, Lubbock had been strongly opposed to draft exemptions. Men could also buy their way out of service or provide a substitute. Because of these loopholes, some southerners complained that the conflict was a "rich man's war, poor man's fight." Even with a draft, the Confederacy struggled throughout the war to put enough soldiers in the field.

Reading Check **Analyzing Information** Why do you think the Confederacy had to pass a draft law?

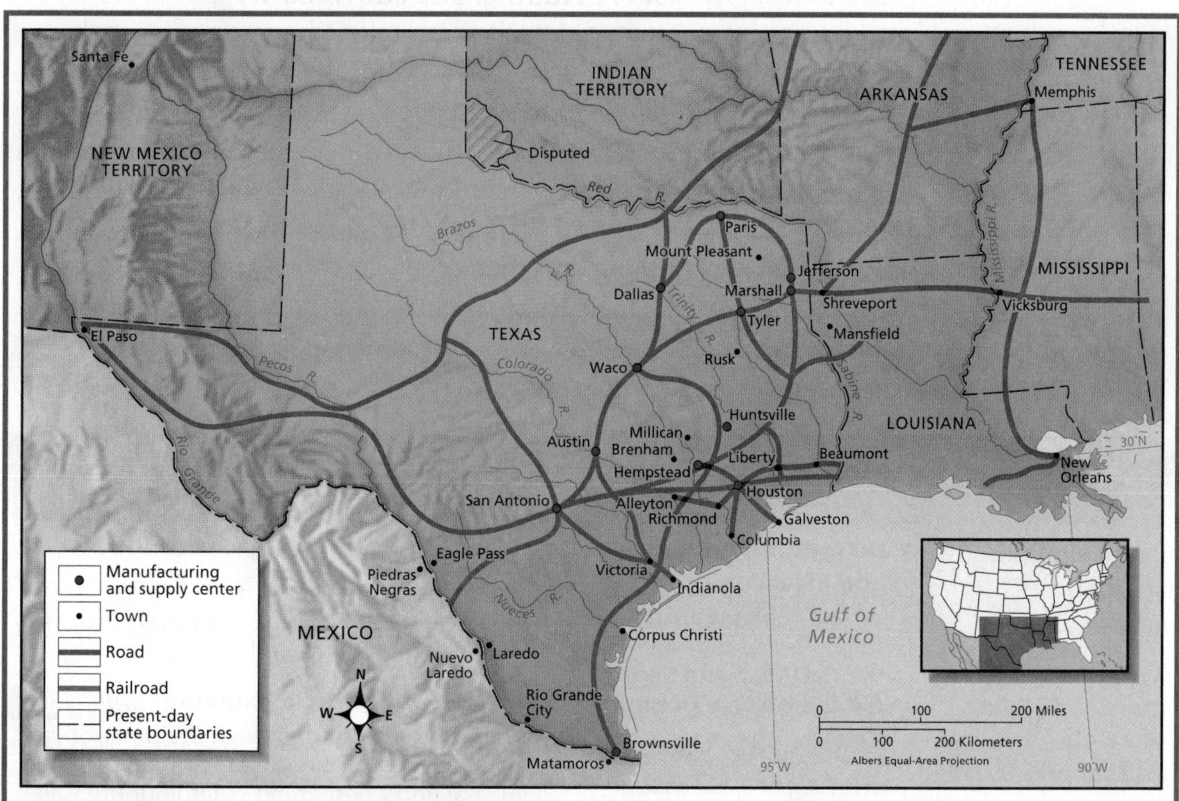

Civil War Trade, 1861-1865

Interpreting Maps Texas supplied the Confederacy with military goods and agricultural exports such as cotton.
Places and Regions In what region were most manufacturing and supply centers located?

★ Unionists in Texas

The Confederate draft sparked fierce opposition from some Unionists. Although many had joined the southern war effort, some refused to fight for either side. Many German Americans and Mexican Americans remained neutral. Some recent immigrants to Texas also agreed with the Unionist cause and had opposed secession. After the draft was passed, however, Texans had to choose sides. Some Unionists fled Texas to avoid the draft.

Confederate officials regarded many Texas Unionists as potentially dangerous traitors. Officials placed some areas with a large Unionist population under **martial law**, or rule by armed forces. Some Unionists were violently attacked. In August 1862 about 60 German Texans attempted to flee to Mexico rather than be drafted into the Confederate army. The Texas militia caught and attacked them near the Nueces River, killing many. When German communities in Central Texas organized to protest, Confederates hanged 50 protesters.

Confederate leaders also worried about Unionists in North Texas. On October 1, 1862 Confederate troops led by Colonel James G. Bourland arrested more than 150 suspected Unionists and formed a court to try the accused people. A member of the jury remembered the events. "There were crowds in sight in every direction, armed, pressing forward prisoners under guard. . . . The mind of almost every man I saw seemed to be unhinged, and wild excitement reigned supreme." A mob soon took over.

By the time the violence had ended, 40 suspected Unionists were hanged in Gainesville in Cooke County. This became known as the Great Hanging at Gainesville. Men were also killed in neighboring counties. Violence against Unionists revealed how deep the feelings about the war ran.

Reading Check Summarizing What happened to some Unionists in Texas?

Section 4 Review

hmhsocialstudies.com ONLINE QUIZ

1. **Define and explain:**
   - draft
   - martial law
2. **Identify and explain** the historical significance of:
   - Francis Lubbock
3. **Identifying Cause and Effect** What problems arose for Unionists during the Civil War, and how did these issues affect them?

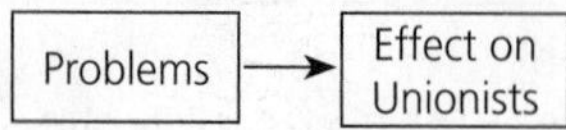

4. **Finding the Main Idea**
   a. What was life like in Texas during the war?
   b. Why did the Confederate government start drafting men into military service?
5. **Writing and Critical Thinking** myWriteSmart
   Analyzing Information Imagine that you are living in Texas during the Civil War. Write a journal entry describing what your life is like. Consider the following:
   - what you eat
   - what you wear

Section 5

The End of the War

Main Ideas

1. Decisive Union victories in 1863, 1864, and 1865 ended the Civil War.
2. The Texas economy was badly damaged by the Civil War.

Key Terms

- **March to the Sea**
- **Emancipation Proclamation**

Why It Matters Today

The Civil War left much of the South in ruins. Use current events sources to learn more about a nation or group today that is rebuilding after a war.

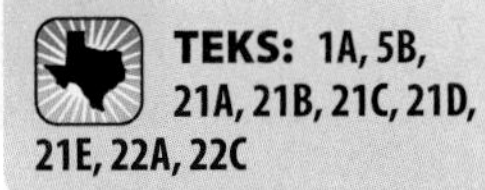

myNotebook

Use the annotation tools in your eBook to take notes on the effects of the Civil War on Texas.

The Story Continues

The Union advance had become unstoppable. General William T. Sherman's army pushed relentlessly through the South toward the Atlantic coast, destroying whatever lay in its path. After one battle, Texan Oscar Alexander rode out to look at the Georgia countryside. An elderly woman on crutches looked up at Alexander. "I do not know where those two little children and I are going to stay," she said. Alexander had no response. All he could see in every direction was the smoke of burning houses.

★ The War Draws to a Close

After the Battle of Gettysburg and fall of Vicksburg in July 1863, Union forces moved steadily into the South. In 1864 President Lincoln ordered General Ulysses S. Grant to take command in the eastern theater. Grant moved his army into eastern Virginia and engaged General Lee's troops in a series of battles. Lee's army was now on the defensive. Both sides suffered heavy losses, but Grant's army greatly outnumbered the Confederate forces. He continued to drive toward Richmond.

Meanwhile, Union general William Tecumseh Sherman led an army south from Tennessee toward Atlanta, an important railroad center. After capturing Atlanta in September 1864, Sherman set out across Georgia to Savannah. As he marched through the state, his army destroyed crops, livestock, railroads—any resources that could help the South. General John Bell Hood of Texas was unable to stop Sherman.

Interpreting Visuals

Surrender. *General Lee surrenders to General Grant at Appomattox Courthouse, Virginia, marking the end of the Civil War.* ***How does the artist show the importance of this event?***

Sherman completed his **March to the Sea** when he reached Savannah in December. A Texas soldier remembered the ruin that Sherman's army left behind. "On Gen. Sherman's 'destruction' to the sea . . . the Yanks had burned and destroyed everything." While Sherman marched north through the Carolinas, Grant was pursuing Lee. In April 1865, Union forces surrounded Lee's army near the town of Appomattox Courthouse, Virginia. With few options left, Lee met with Grant on April 9 and agreed to the Union's terms of surrender.

Reading Check **Analyzing Information** Why did Sherman destroy property on his March to the Sea?

★ Battle at Palmito Ranch

Word of Lee's surrender reached Confederate troops in the Brownsville area by May 1865. Hundreds of soldiers left their posts for home. But many stayed when General E. Kirby Smith, the commander of the western Confederate states, urged the soldiers to continue the war.

On May 12, Union troops moved inland to occupy Brownsville. The next day—more than a month after General Lee's surrender—Union and Confederate forces clashed at Palmito Ranch near Brownsville. Led by Colonel John S. Ford, the Confederate troops defeated the Union forces and captured more than 100 prisoners. A few days later, Union officers met with Ford to arrange a truce. The last land battle of the Civil War was a Confederate victory, but the South had already lost the war.

Reading Check **Supporting a Point of View** Do you agree or disagree with the soldiers' decision to continue fighting after Lee surrendered? Explain your answer.

★ Consequences of the War

The Emancipation Proclamation freed all slaves in areas "in rebellion against the United States."

About 620,000 Americans lost their lives in the Civil War, making it the deadliest conflict in U.S. history. Some 90,000 Texans served, and thousands were killed or wounded. Many soldiers suffered serious injuries such as the loss of an arm or leg. One Texas soldier remembered how he felt after the war. "I came home in May, 1865, not . . . scrappy as I started out, but . . . well versed [familiarized] in hardships, privations [loss], dangers and the art of war. . . . All I wanted in this life was some old clothes and something to eat."

Although Texas suffered few battles, the war left the state's economy in shambles. The cotton trade had nearly stopped. The deaths of many men placed hardships on Texas businesses, farms, and plantations. Fields needed to be plowed, and businesses needed to be reopened. Much work needed to be done to rebuild the state. When Governor Murrah and other officials fled to Mexico at the end of the war, the state's government had collapsed. No one seemed to know who was in charge. It took some time before Union forces could move in and restore order.

Enslaved Texans saw the war as a struggle for freedom. African American William Adams remembered, "We sure didn't want the South to win." After the war African Americans in Texas wondered about their future. The quarter million slaves in Texas did not learn of their freedom until after the war's end, on June 19, 1865. More than two years before, President Lincoln had issued the **Emancipation Proclamation**, stated that slaves were free in those areas rebelling against the United States. As the Union army advanced into a Confederate state, slaves were freed.

Reading Check **Summarizing** How did the Civil War affect the Texas economy?

★ Section 5 Review

hmhsocialstudies.com
ONLINE QUIZ

1. Identify and explain the historical significance of:
- March to the Sea
- Emancipation Proclamation

2. Summarizing
- Copy the graphic organizer below. Use it to show the effects of the Civil War on Texas.

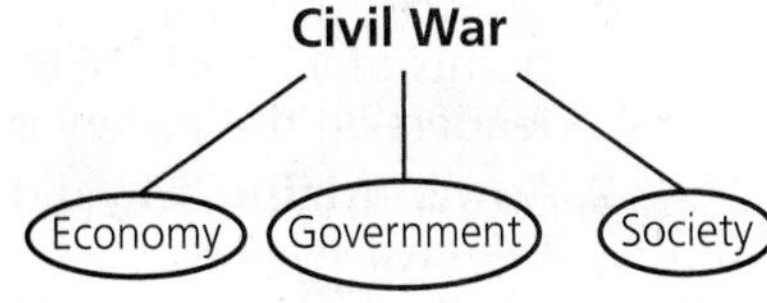

3. Finding the Main Idea

a. Describe the final events and battles of the Civil War.

b. Why do you think some Texas soldiers continued to fight even after Lee surrendered?

4. Writing and Critical Thinking myWriteSmart

Making Generalizations and Predictions Imagine that you are a Confederate or Union soldier who has returned to Texas after the war. Write a letter to a friend explaining what you think is in store for Texas.

Consider the following:
- the condition of the state's economy
- the condition of the state's government

CHAPTER 18 REVIEW

The Chapter at a Glance

Examine the following visual summary of the chapter. Then use the visual to write a one-page story about the role of Texas in the Civil War. Use standard grammar, spelling, sentence structure, and punctuation to describe the battles in and near Texas and life on the Texas home front during the war.

Texas in the Civil War

Texans voted to secede from the Union and join the Confederacy.

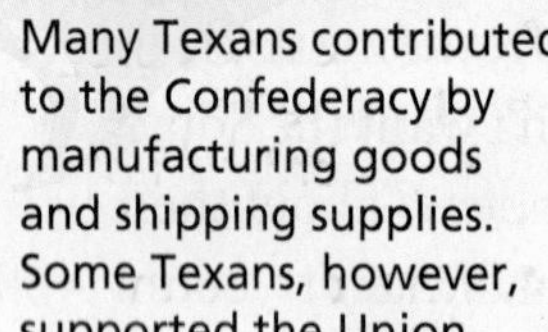

Many Texans contributed to the Confederacy by manufacturing goods and shipping supplies. Some Texans, however, supported the Union.

Fighting during the Civil War spread to Texas. Conflicts erupted along the Texas coast at places such as Galveston and Sabine Pass.

The war took a heavy toll on both sides. Many Texans were killed or wounded in the fighting.

Identifying People and Ideas

Write a sentence to explain the role or significance of each of the following terms or people.

1. secede
2. states' rights
3. Unionists
4. regiments
5. Battle of Sabine Pass
6. Red River Campaign
7. Francis R. Lubbock
8. draft
9. Emancipation Proclamation

Understanding Main Ideas

Section 1

1. Why did Texas secede from the Union?

Section 2

2. What significant events took place in Texas in 1861?
3. What were the North's and the South's strategies for fighting the war?

Section 3

4. How did geographic factors affect the military campaigns at Sabine Pass and the Red River?

Section 4

5. How did the Civil War affect life in Texas?

Section 5

6. How did the Civil War affect the Texas economy?

You Be the Historian

Reviewing Themes

1. **Economics** Why did Texas suffer less from the war than other areas of the South did?
2. **Citizenship** How did some Texas Unionists lose their civil rights during the war?
3. **Geography** Why did the Union forces most often invade Texas by attacking coastal ports?

Thinking Critically

1. **Identifying Points of View** What were the points of view of abolitionists and southern leaders on the slavery issue?
2. **Summarizing** Why did Texas become involved in the Civil War?
3. **Analyzing** List the political, economic, and social effects of the Civil War on Texas.

Texas Test Practice

Interpreting Maps

Study the map below. Then use the information on the map to answer the questions that follow.

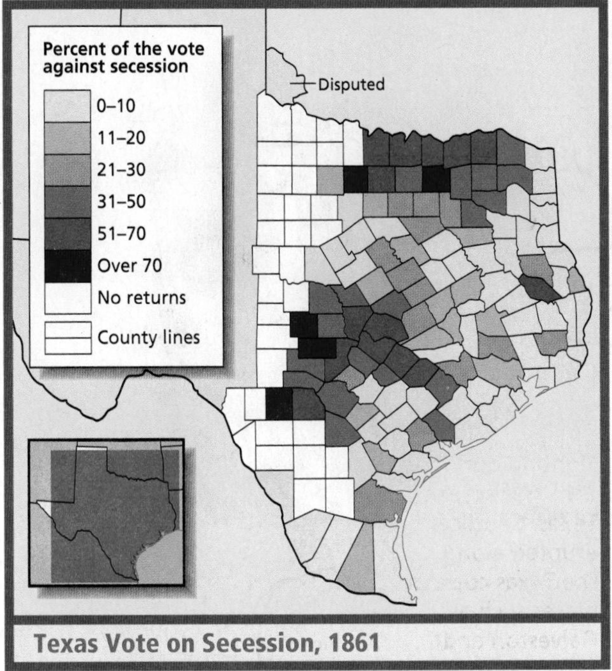

Texas Vote on Secession, 1861

1. Which of the following statements describes the pattern of voting on the secession issue?
   - **A** Few slaves lived in East Texas.
   - **B** Most plantations were in North Texas.
   - **C** Cotton grew well in the Hill Country.
   - **D** White Texans in good cotton-growing regions were likely to vote for secession.

2. Why do you think many counties in North Texas opposed secession?

Analyzing Primary Sources

Read the following quote by Texas soldier Ralph Smith. Then answer the questions.

"In great battles with thousands on each side . . . privates are like little screws in the wheel of a giant machine. All I remember for the first few minutes . . . was a terrible noise[,] great smoke, incessant [continual] rattling of small arms, infernal [terrible] confusion and then I realized that the whole line of the enemy was in disorderly retreat."

3. Which of the following statements best describes the author's point of view?
   - **F** His memory of the first few minutes of the battle is very clear.
   - **G** Individual soldiers often do not make a significant difference in large battles.
   - **H** He was always able to keep track of the battle's progress.
   - **J** He believes the enemy retreated in an orderly fashion.

4. What do you think Smith meant when he described privates as screws in a giant machine?

Cooperative Learning

Work with a small group to complete the following activity. Each person in your group should select a significant individual such as the following: a) John Bell Hood b) John Reagan c) Francis Lubbock d) Thomas Green e) John Magruder. You may want to select someone who lived in your county. Each member should research information about the person. Then work with your group to create a time line that shows the person's activities before, during, and after the war.

Internet Activity 

Conduct online research to learn more about the role of Texas in the Civil War. Then create a collage, diorama, or model that shows how the Civil War affected politics, the economy, and society in Texas. Write captions explaining your creation. Be sure to use standard grammar, spelling, sentence structure, and punctuation.

CHAPTER 19

Reconstruction

(1865–1877)

Texas Essential Knowledge and Skills (TEKS) 1A, 1B, 5B, 6A, 8B, 9C, 10B, 12A, 16B, 17A, 17C, 18B, 19A, 21A, 21B, 21C, 21D, 21E, 21F, 21G, 22A, 22B, 22C, 22D

The Emancipation Proclamation was issued in 1863 but did not take effect in Texas until after the Civil War.

TEXAS

1865 The Emancipation Proclamation goes into effect in Texas, freeing the state's slaves.

1868 African American George T. Ruby is elected as a delegate to the Republican National Convention.

1869 Republican Edmund J. Davis is elected governor.

1865 — 1867 — 1869

U.S. and WORLD

1865 The Thirteenth Amendment, abolishing slavery, is put into effect.

1867 The U.S. Congress removes control of Reconstruction from the president.

1868 Ulysses S. Grant is elected president.

1870 The Fifteenth Amendment gives African American men the right to vote.

If you were there . . .

How would you restore the Union?

Build on What You Know

The Civil War had divided the country and badly damaged the South. The country needed to reunite and to help the millions of newly freed African Americans adjust to life after slavery. Leaders from the North and the South worked to rebuild the nation.

The 1873 election led to conflict between Republicans and Democrats in which armed supporters took over parts of the state capitol.

Most early public schools in Texas were small buildings attended by primary, elementary, and advanced students.

1871
A public school system is created in Texas.

1872
The General Amnesty Act allows most former Confederates to once again hold public office.

1874
The Democratic Party regains full control of state government.

1874
Republicans lose control of the U.S. House of Representatives.

1876
Texas adopts a new constitution.

1877
The Compromise of 1877 ends Reconstruction throughout the South.

1871 — 1873 — 1875 — 1877

You Be the Historian

myNotebook

What's Your Opinion? Do you **agree** or **disagree** with the following statements? Support your point of view in your notebook.

- **Government** People who participate in a rebellion should be harshly punished.
- **Citizenship** People who have been on different sides in a war can work together to rebuild a country.
- **Economics** War always leads to dramatic changes in a nation's economy.

Section 1 Presidential Reconstruction

Main Ideas

1. After Emancipation, many former slaves left the plantations to look for family or find work.
2. In order to rejoin the Union, Texas had to write a new constitution, abolish slavery, and declare secession illegal.
3. The lives of freedpeople in Texas remained restricted under the Black Codes.

Key Terms and People

- **Juneteenth**
- **freedpeople**
- **Reconstruction**
- **Thirteenth Amendment**
- **Freedmen's Bureau**
- **suffrage**
- **Black Codes**
- **civil rights**

Why It Matters Today

The federal government helped former slaves after the Civil War. Use current events sources to learn more about a government program that helps citizens today.

TEKS: 5B, 6A, 10B, 17C, 18B, 21A, 21B, 21C, 21D, 21E, 21F, 22A, 22B, 22C, 22D

myNotebook

Use the annotation tools in your eBook to take notes on emancipation and presidential reconstruction in Texas.

The Story Continues

One day after the Civil War ended, Tempie Cummins's mother was eavesdropping on their slaveholder. She heard him say that slaves in Texas had been freed. He also vowed to keep his slaves until "he had made another crop or two." Tempie's mother immediately told the other slaves that they were free and that they should quit working. The slaveholder chased her and shot at her, but she escaped with Tempie.

Emancipation

U.S. troops took control of Texas at the end of the Civil War. When Union general Gordon Granger landed at Galveston in 1865, he issued a proclamation freeing Texas slaves. That day, June 19, is celebrated as **Juneteenth**. One former slave remembered hearing the news.

TEXAS VOICES

"We were working one day when somebody . . . came by and told us we were free, and we stopped working. . . . The boss man came up, and he said he was going to knock us off the fence if we didn't go back to work. . . . He called for his carriage, and said he was going to town to see what the government was going to do. Next day he came back and said, 'Well, you're just as free as I am.'"

—Anonymous, quoted in *Black Texas Women: A Sourcebook,* by Ruthe Winegarten

As the news of emancipation spread, many **freedpeople**, or former slaves, left the plantations. For many it was the first time they had the freedom to travel. During the summer and fall of 1865, Texas roads were crowded with former slaves loaded down with their possessions. Many freedpeople rushed to courthouses to legalize their informal slave marriages. Others searched for family members from whom they had been separated. Some gathered at military posts and towns, hoping to find paying jobs and military protection. Many who had been sent to Texas during the war returned to their prewar homes.

Reading Check **Summarizing** How did the end of the Civil War affect Texas slaves?

Juneteenth

In 1863 the Emancipation Proclamation had declared all slaves in the rebelling states free. Because Union forces did not control Texas at that time, the Proclamation had no practical effect in the state until General Gordon Granger read his order in Galveston. Since 1865, June 19 has been celebrated in Texas as a day of freedom. Since 1979 Juneteenth has been a state holiday and its celebration has been spreading across the nation. **Why do African Americans celebrate Juneteenth?**

★ The Freedmen's Bureau

The U.S. government wanted to help freedpeople and bring the southern states back into the Union. **Reconstruction**—the process of reuniting the nation and rebuilding the southern states—lasted from 1865 to 1877. In February 1865 the U.S. Congress had proposed the **Thirteenth Amendment**, which abolished slavery. In March, Congress created the **Freedmen's Bureau** to provide help and legal aid to freed people. Because they had no land and few job opportunities, many freedpeople returned to their old plantations for work. Bureau agents tried to regulate freedpeople's employment contracts with landowners.

In addition, the bureau and churches helped African Americans open many schools in Texas. By 1870 more than 9,000 African Americans were enrolled in 150 schools. As a result, illiteracy—or the inability to read or write—among African Americans dropped from 95 percent in 1865 to 75 percent in 1880. A reporter toured one school.

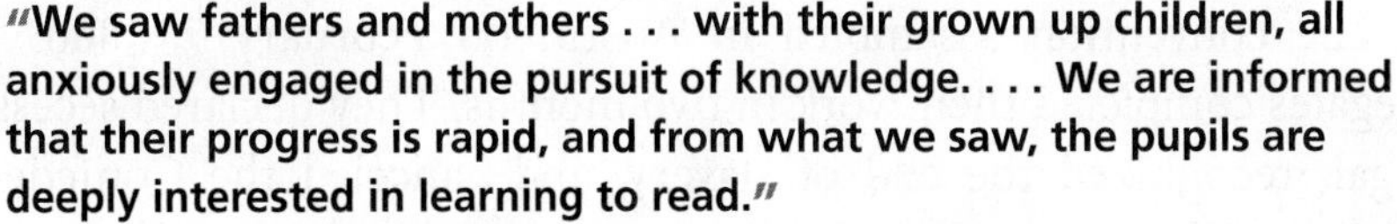

TEXAS VOICES

"We saw fathers and mothers . . . with their grown up children, all anxiously engaged in the pursuit of knowledge. . . . We are informed that their progress is rapid, and from what we saw, the pupils are deeply interested in learning to read."

—*Flake's Bulletin,* quoted in *Republicanism in Reconstruction Texas,* by Carl H. Moneyhon

Analyzing Primary Sources
Drawing Inferences and Conclusions Why were adult African Americans in school alongside their children?

However, with only a few dozen agents assigned to Texas at any one time, bureau agents were limited in what they could achieve. There was also a limited number of federal troops assigned to support the agents' activities. Many Texans opposed the bureau's efforts to help freedpeople. One agent noted that former Confederates "seem to take every opportunity to vent their rage and hatred upon the blacks. They are frequently beaten unmercifully." Bureau agents tried to protect freedpeople from such violence and to help them adjust to freedom.

Reading Check **Analyzing Information** Why might new educational opportunities for African Americans be considered an important social effect of Reconstruction in Texas?

Daily Life

African American Schools

Reconstruction schools offered the first chance for freedpeople to get an education. But schools faced many challenges. The Freedmen's Bureau had difficulty recruiting teachers, and schools were often short of supplies. In September 1865 a Galveston teacher complained that he had 250 students but no books. Some schools were held in local churches. A teacher in Chambers County taught school in a grove of trees. **What challenges did black schools face during Reconstruction?**

★ President Johnson's Plan

While the bureau was helping freedpeople, leaders in the federal government were debating how Reconstruction should proceed. Some people wanted to punish the South. Others, like President Abraham Lincoln, did not want to increase feelings of bitterness. Before the war ended he proposed a plan to reunite the country quickly. After Lincoln was assassinated in April 1865, Andrew Johnson became president.

Like Lincoln, Johnson wanted Reconstruction to proceed quickly. Under his plan, voters in the former Confederate states had to take oaths of loyalty to the United States. High-ranking Confederate officials and wealthy property owners needed to apply for a presidential pardon. Afterward, they could take part in government once again.

Before a state could rejoin the Union, it had to create a provisional government. The state had to write a new constitution that declared secession illegal and abolished slavery. After ratifying the new constitution, voters would elect a governor and legislature. The legislature then had to ratify the Thirteenth Amendment. Once a state's representatives had been seated in the U.S. Congress, the state would be fully restored to the Union. Johnson's Reconstruction plan was acceptable to many Texans.

Johnson appointed Unionist Andrew J. Hamilton as provisional governor of Texas in June 1865. Hamilton had previously represented Texas in the U.S. Congress from 1859 to 1861. When war broke out, he had gone north and become a general in the Union army. Nonetheless, many Texans welcomed him back to Austin in August 1865. Governor Hamilton soon appointed government officials, selecting Unionists as well as some former Confederates. In November he called an election to select delegates to a constitutional convention. Former Confederates, but not African Americans, could vote in the election.

The convention assembled in Austin on February 7, 1866. The delegates completed their work in two months. They declared secession illegal, recognized the end of slavery, and canceled the Confederate war debt. The remainder of the constitution was similar to the 1845 constitution. Debate was heated, however, over the status of freed people. The delegates failed to give African Americans equal rights. For example, black Texans could not testify in court cases involving white Texans or hold office. Nor were they granted **suffrage,** or voting rights. In June 1866, Texas voters approved the new constitution and elected government officials. James W. Throckmorton won the governor's race over Elisha M. Pease, a former governor. Former secessionists easily won control of the legislature. When it met on August 6, 1866, the legislature refused to ratify the Thirteenth Amendment.

Reading Check **Finding the Main Idea** Why did Governor Hamilton call a constitutional convention?

The Black Codes

The Texas legislature, like others in the South, passed **Black Codes**. These laws denied African Americans' **civil rights**. Civil rights are the individual rights guaranteed to people by the U.S. Constitution. Many Black Codes restricted African Americans' freedom of movement and work.

For example, African Americans had to sign labor contracts that strongly favored their employers. In addition, they could be jailed simply for not having jobs. Some large landowners in Texas argued that such laws were needed to ensure that enough workers were available to harvest the state's crops.

African Americans also had to deal with threats and violence. Between 1865 and 1868, some 468 freedpeople in Texas were murdered—90 percent of them by white men. Bringing the murderers to justice was difficult, as one Texas judge noted.

Even after the Civil War, freedpeople who fell into debt could be auctioned as servants to pay off the debt.

TEXAS VOICES

"I regard it as almost an impossibility under existing arrangements to convict a white man of any crime . . . where the proof . . . depends upon the testimony of a black man, or where the violence has been against a black man. . . . I can suggest no means by which I think the civil courts can remedy the evil without a change in the public sentiment of the country."

—James J. Thornton, quoted in *Reconstruction in Texas,* by Charles William Ramsdell

Reading Check **Comparing and Contrasting** How was life similar and different for African Americans under the Black Codes and slavery?

Section 1 Review

hmhsocialstudies.com
ONLINE QUIZ

1. Define and explain:
- freedpeople
- suffrage
- civil rights

2. Identify and explain the historical significance of:
- Juneteenth
- Reconstruction
- Thirteenth Amendment
- Freedmen's Bureau
- Black Codes

3. Sequencing
Copy the graphic organizer below. Use it to show, in order, the steps Texas had to take to be readmitted to the Union under President Johnson's plan.

4. Finding the Main Idea

a. How did the Freedmen's Bureau assist freedpeople in Texas?

b. In what ways were African Americans in Texas denied their civil rights after the Civil War?

5. Writing and Critical Thinking myWriteSmart

Analyzing Information Imagine that you are living in Texas when General Granger announces the Emancipation Proclamation. Write a letter depicting freedpeople's response. Consider the following:
- activity at military posts and courthouses
- activity on the state's roads

Section 2

Congressional Reconstruction

Main Ideas

1. Congress took control of reconstruction because freedpeople were being denied their rights.
2. Texas and other southern states wrote new constitutions in order to gain readmission to the Union.

Why It Matters Today

Congress and the president disagreed about how Reconstruction should be handled. Use current events sources to learn about an issue that Congress and the president are debating today.

Key Terms and People

- **Radical Republicans**
- **Civil Rights Act of 1866**
- **Fourteenth Amendment**
- **Reconstruction Acts**
- **impeach**
- **Edmund J. Davis**
- **George T. Ruby**
- **Union League**
- **Fifteenth Amendment**

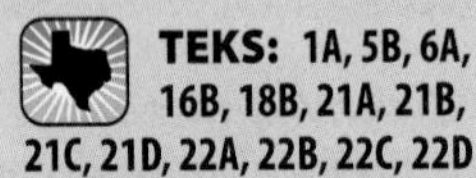

myNotebook

Use the annotation tools in your eBook to take notes on Congressional Reconstruction in Texas.

The Story Continues

Allen Manning was frustrated. He and other African Americans had finally won their freedom. But many of the same people who controlled Texas before the war were regaining power. He wondered if life would truly become better for black Texans. To Manning, it seemed that many white Texans could not "get over us being free."

Radical Republicans React

The Black Codes raised new concerns in the U.S. Congress about President Johnson's Reconstruction plan. In addition, southern states had elected many of the people who had led the rebellion. For example, U.S. senator Oran M. Roberts had served as president of the Texas Secession Convention in 1861. As large-scale landowners took control of the South's politics, they passed laws that suited them economically and politically. Not only were African Americans denied equal rights but violence against them was occurring throughout the South.

Many **Radical Republicans** believed the U.S. Congress needed to take a greater role in Reconstruction. They thought that loyal southern state governments could be created only with the participation of Unionists and African Americans. As Radical Republicans gained power and influence, they passed the **Civil Rights Act of 1866**. This act gave citizenship to African Americans and guaranteed them basic rights. President Johnson vetoed the act, arguing that it gave too much power to the federal government. He also rejected the principle of equal rights for African Americans. Congress overrode Johnson's veto. This marked a serious split between Congress and the president. Congress took an additional step to ensure that the act would not be overturned by a later Congress. In the summer of 1866, Republicans proposed the **Fourteenth Amendment** to guarantee citizenship and equal rights to African Americans. The Texas legislature and most other southern states refused to ratify it.

Reading Check **Identifying Cause and Effect** Who returned to power in the South, and how did this affect the actions of the U.S. Congress?

★ The Reconstruction Acts

The 1866 elections gave the Republicans strong majorities in both houses of the U.S. Congress. Republicans now had enough votes to override any presidential veto. Congress passed a series of **Reconstruction Acts** beginning in March 1867. These acts marked the beginning of Congressional Reconstruction. The new southern state governments were once again declared provisional. Congress divided the South into five military districts, with each placed under the command of an army officer. Southern states would have to do more than Johnson's plan had

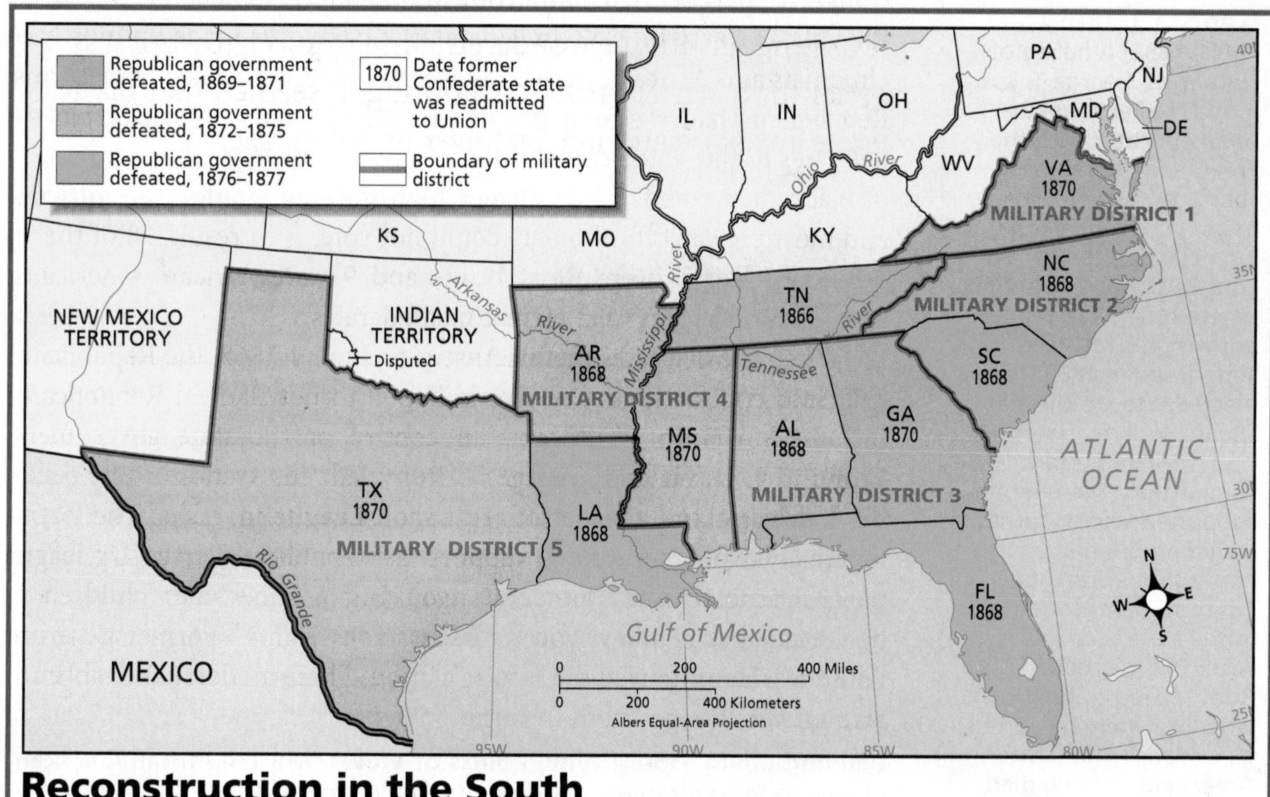

Reconstruction in the South

Interpreting Maps The Reconstruction Acts established five separate military districts to control the South.

Places and Regions In which military district was Texas located?

required to rejoin the Union. The states had to write new constitutions guaranteeing rights for African Americans, including suffrage for black men. The states also had to ratify the Fourteenth Amendment.

Texas and Louisiana made up the Fifth Military District, commanded by General Philip Sheridan. In July 1867 Congress gave military commanders wide authority to remove uncooperative southern leaders from office. That month Sheridan removed Governor Throckmorton, calling him "an impediment [obstacle] to Reconstruction." Sheridan appointed Elisha M. Pease to replace Throckmorton. Pease, a former two-term governor, was respected by most Texans. Over the next few months the military removed hundreds of other state and local officials.

President Johnson tried to block Congressional Reconstruction, prompting the House to **impeach** him. To impeach is to bring charges of wrongdoing against a public official. Johnson avoided being removed from office by one vote in the Senate, but his power had been broken. Ulysses S. Grant, who was more supportive of Congressional Reconstruction, won the 1868 presidential election.

Reading Check **Finding the Main Idea** What was the significance for Texas of the Republicans' success in the 1866 elections?

The Texas Republican Party

Congressional Reconstruction led to the development of the Texas Republican Party in 1867. In general, the party was made up mostly of Unionists and African Americans as well as many Mexican Americans. Republicans had a strong turnout in the February 1868 election for delegates to the state's constitutional convention. More than 80 percent of black men voted, while former high-ranking Confederate officials and most prewar officeholders could not vote. As a result, 78 of the 90 original delegates were Republicans and 9 were African Americans. Only a few delegates were former Confederates.

When the delegates met in Austin on June 1, 1868, the Republicans split into two factions. One group hoped to put Radical Republicans, including African Americans, in control of the state government. **Edmund J. Davis** and **George T. Ruby** led this faction. Ruby was a black delegate and a leader of the **Union League** in Texas. The league urged African Americans to support the Republican Party. One league pamphlet noted that Democrats would "not allow your children to be educated nor [allow] you to discuss your rights." Former governor Andrew J. Hamilton led the second faction. These moderate Republicans favored few changes from the past.

Reading Check **Identifying Points of View** Why did African American leaders in Texas try to rally support for the Republican Party?

BIOGRAPHY

George T. Ruby
(1841–1882) A native of New York, George T. Ruby moved to Texas in 1866 as an educator with the Freedmen's Bureau. He soon became involved in politics. In 1868 Ruby won election to the constitutional convention, where he pushed for equal rights for African Americans. In 1869, Texans elected Ruby to the state senate, where he served on several important committees. There he supported several causes, including bringing African American and white students together in the state's schools. After Reconstruction, Ruby moved to New Orleans, where he edited a newspaper for African Americans until he died of malaria. **How did George T. Ruby contribute to Texas?**

★ The Constitution of 1869

The Constitutional Convention of 1868–69 was controlled largely by Radical Republicans. The delegates finished their work on the constitution in February 1869. The new Texas constitution gave equal rights to African Americans, including the right to vote. That same year the U.S. Congress proposed the **Fifteenth Amendment**, which gave suffrage to African American men.

In contrast to past constitutions, the new constitution gave the governor the power to appoint many state officials and judges. The governor's term of office was lengthened from two to four years, and the legislature was to meet every year. The constitution also made important changes in public education. The sale of public lands and a tax of one dollar per voter was to fund schools. In addition, one fourth of state revenue was to be set aside for schools. For the first time, attendance at school was required by law.

Texas voters approved the constitution by a wide margin. In the same election, Edmund J. Davis defeated Andrew J. Hamilton in a close race for governor. The Radical Republicans in the U.S. Congress now had a supporter in the Texas governor's office. Republicans also controlled the newly elected Texas legislature, which quickly ratified the Fourteenth and Fifteenth Amendments. This paved the way for Texas to be restored to the Union. In March 1870 President Grant signed an act of Congress admitting Texas senators and representatives. The next month, control of Texas was returned to the state government.

Reading Check **Contrasting** How did the rights of African Americans differ under the Texas constitutions of 1866 and 1869?

Your Vote Counts

Black Texans first registered to vote in 1867. About 98 percent of black men registered to vote that year. Later amendments to the U.S. Constitution gave the right to vote to women and younger people. More Texans have the power to vote today than at any time in the state's history. **What was one way African Americans fulfilled their civic responsibilities?**

★ Section 2 Review

hmhsocialstudies.com
ONLINE QUIZ

1. Define and explain:
- impeach

2. Identify and explain the historical significance of:
- Radical Republicans
- Civil Rights Act of 1866
- Fourteenth Amendment
- Reconstruction Acts
- Edmund J. Davis
- George T. Ruby
- Union League
- Fifteenth Amendment

3. Summarizing
Copy the graphic organizer below. Use it to list four major provisions of the Constitution of 1869.

4. Finding the Main Idea

a. Why did the Radical Republicans take control of Reconstruction away from President Johnson?

b. What did southern states have to do to be readmitted to the Union under Congressional Reconstruction?

5. Writing and Critical Thinking myWriteSmart

Making Generalizations and Predictions Imagine that you are a newspaper editor in 1869. Write an editorial discussing how the new constitution and military control of the state will affect Texans. Consider the following:
- who had the right to vote
- the military's role in Texas

Section 3

The Davis Administration

Main Ideas

1. The Davis administration improved education and transportation in Texas but increased the state debt.
2. Reconstruction ended in Texas in 1874 when Republicans lost political power.

Key Terms and People

- **Ku Klux Klan**
- **bonds**
- **scalawags**
- **carpetbaggers**
- **Richard Coke**

Why It Matters Today

Texans during Reconstruction struggled to pay for Governor Edmund J. Davis's programs. Use current events sources to learn about how citizens pay for government programs today.

TEKS: 1A, 1B, 5B, 6A, 17C, 21A, 21B, 21C, 21D, 21E, 22A, 22B, 22C

myNotebook

Use the annotation tools in your eBook to take notes on the Davis administration and the end of Reconstruction in Texas.

The Story Continues

The First Texas Cavalry of the Union army was together again. This time they had gathered to celebrate, not to fight. The men, thrilled at their former leader Edmund J. Davis's victory in the governor's race, threw him a barbecue. Many Texans were there—"all the world hereabouts," according to the *Galveston News.* The time for celebration was short, however, as the Republicans turned to the business of rebuilding the state.

The Davis Administration's Policies

Governor Edmund J. Davis had the support of the legislature that assembled in April 1870. It was dominated by Republicans, 11 of whom were African American. Senators Matthew Gaines and George T. Ruby led the legislative effort to stop the widespread crime in the state, particularly the actions of the **Ku Klux Klan**. This secret society had been threatening and murdering African Americans to keep them from expressing their political views. The legislature created a state militia and police force, which soon took action. As the police made arrests, crime dropped, and the influence of the Ku Klux Klan lessened.

The Republicans also tackled an important social issue—education. Davis wanted African Americans to be treated equally by the law. "I do not want to see white or black named in any law whatsoever." The legislature created free public schools for all the state's children. Money from public land sales and state and local taxes helped pay for school expenses. A state board of education and a superintendent of education oversaw the state's schools. Schools had a common course of study, teacher certification, and a central administration. Enrollment grew rapidly, with almost 130,000 students in the public schools during the 1872–73 school year.

The legislature also tried to help Texas recover economically after the war. To improve the state's transportation system, the legislature set aside money for roads and bridges. The state also issued **bonds** to help pay for railroad lines. Bonds are certificates that represent money the government has borrowed. The administration raised taxes to pay for schools, roads, and the larger central government.

Reading Check **Analyzing Information** How did Reconstruction affect the state socially and economically?

Historically Black Colleges

Two of the oldest historically black colleges in the nation are in Texas. Wiley College in Marshall, founded in 1873, is the oldest historically black college west of the Mississippi River. Paul Quinn College, founded in Austin and now in Dallas, was also established during Reconstruction.

Opposition to Reconstruction

Many Texans opposed these policies. They referred to Texans who supported the Republicans as "**scalawags**," or "mean fellows." The few northerners who had come to Texas after the war were sometimes called "**carpetbaggers**" because some carried all they owned in bags made of carpet. An Illinois man explained why he moved to Texas. "I am going to introduce new ideas here in the farming line, and show the beauties of free over slave labor."

In the political arena, Democrats opposed Edmund J. Davis and the Radical Republicans at every opportunity. They clashed over the state police, the militia, and taxes. Democrats called many of the new laws Obnoxious Acts—obnoxious means very unpleasant. When Democrats complained of the rising state debt, Davis defended the spending. "If you have no government it will cost you nothing. If you have public schools and law and order, you must pay for it." Democrats also accused the Davis administration of taking money by fraud.

Democrats were also angered when Davis used the state police to guard voters in the 1872 elections. Davis's opponents claimed he was trying to frighten Democratic voters. In this election the Democrats regained control of the legislature.

Reading Check **Drawing Inferences and Conclusions** How did the policies of Davis's administration affect the state's economy?

Interpreting Political Cartoons

Reconstruction. *In this political cartoon, the South is shown carrying President Grant, who rides in a heavy carpetbag.* ***How does this political cartoon reflect the southern point of view?***

LINKING Past to Present

Party Politics
Before the Civil War, the Democratic Party dominated Texas politics. This ended when Radical Republicans rose to power. Supported overwhelmingly by freed people, the Republicans in Texas brought a temporary halt to the Democrats' control. With the end of Reconstruction, the Democratic Party regained control of Texas politics. Both parties are now represented in state government. **How did Reconstruction affect Texas politics?**

★ The End of Reconstruction

In the 1873 election for governor Edmund J. Davis had the support of Radical Republicans. Most white Texans supported Democrat **Richard Coke**, a former Confederate officer. Coke won in a landslide—receiving 85,549 votes to 42,663 for Davis. Democrats also won the legislature. Some Republicans argued that the polls had closed too early. They brought the issue to the Texas Supreme Court, which ruled that the election was unconstitutional. Nonetheless, Democrats demanded control of the government. Davis was unsure what to do. He had been ready to turn the office over to Coke, but he did not want to ignore the court's ruling. Coke, meanwhile, "intended to become governor . . . no matter what it cost him or the state," according to one observer.

Davis allowed the legislature to meet, but he feared that the Democrats might take the governor's office by force. So he called in armed supporters to guard the first floor of the Capitol. Democratic leaders then brought in armed supporters to guard the legislative chambers on the second floor. When Davis learned that the federal government would not help, he stepped down. He turned the office over to Coke on January 19, 1874. This marked the end of Reconstruction in Texas.

Reconstruction was ending in other parts of the South as the Radical Republicans' power faded. The party was hurt by scandals in President Grant's administration and a financial panic in 1873. In the 1876 presidential election, Republican Rutherford B. Hayes ran a close race against Democrat Samuel J. Tilden. Each candidate claimed to have won. In the Compromise of 1877, Democrats agreed to accept Hayes. In exchange for the Democrats' support, Hayes ended the involvement of federal troops in the South's political affairs. Reconstruction was over.

Reading Check **Identifying Cause and Effect** What happened in the election of 1876, and how did it affect Reconstruction in Texas?

★ Section 3 Review

hmhsocialstudies.com ONLINE QUIZ

1. **Define and explain:**
   - bonds
   - scalawags
   - carpetbaggers
2. **Identify and explain** the historical significance of:
   - Ku Klux Klan
   - Obnoxious Acts
   - Richard Coke
3. **Summarizing** Copy the graphic organizer below. Use it to show the economic and social effects of Reconstruction in Texas.

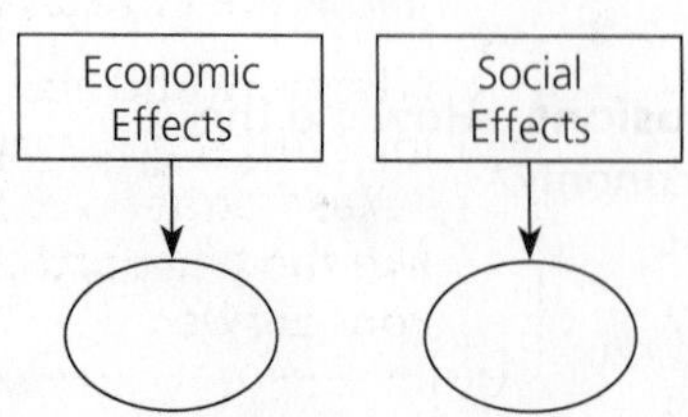

4. **Finding the Main Idea**
   a. What were the major policies and criticisms of the Davis administration?
   b. What brought about the end of Reconstruction in Texas?
5. **Writing and Critical Thinking** myWriteSmart
   Supporting a Point of View Write a short speech for Governor Davis that strongly defends his policies.
   Consider the following:
   - crime in Texas
   - internal improvements in Texas

Connecting To Literature

Old Yeller

Fred Gipson

Fred Gipson grew up in the Hill Country near Mason. His novel Old Yeller *tells the story of 14-year-old Travis, who protects the family while his father is away in the late 1860s. Settlers on the Texas frontier faced many day-to-day challenges as the state went through Reconstruction. Old Yeller is a stray dog taken in by Travis. In this excerpt, a bear is chasing Travis's younger brother Arliss, who somehow managed to grab onto the bear's cub.*

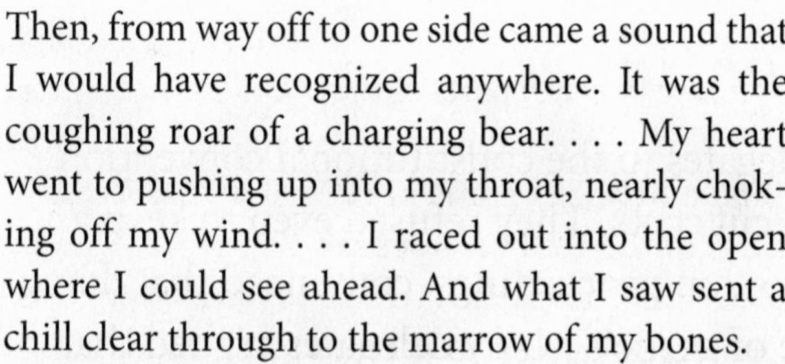

Then, from way off to one side came a sound that I would have recognized anywhere. It was the coughing roar of a charging bear. . . . My heart went to pushing up into my throat, nearly choking off my wind. . . . I raced out into the open where I could see ahead. And what I saw sent a chill clear through to the marrow of my bones.

There was Little Arliss . . . holding onto the hind leg of a little black bear cub no bigger than a small coon. . . . Little Arliss was holding on for all he was worth, scared now and screaming his head off. Too scared to let go. . . .

Now the she bear was charging across the shallows in the creek. She was knocking sheets of water high in the bright sun, charging with her fur up and her long teeth bared, filling the canyon with that awful coughing roar. And no matter how fast Mama ran or how fast I ran, the she bear was going to get there first! . . .

Then, just as the bear went lunging up the creek bank toward Little Arliss and her cub, a flash of yellow came streaking out of the brush.

It was that big yeller dog. He was roaring like a mad bull. He wasn't one-third as big and heavy as the she bear, but when he piled into her from one side, he rolled her clear off her feet. They went down in a wild, roaring tangle of twisting bodies and scrambling feet and slashing fangs. . . . I didn't wait to see more. Without ever checking my stride, I ran in and jerked Little Arliss loose from the cub. I grabbed him by the wrist and yanked him up out of that water and slung him toward Mama like he was a half-empty sack of corn. I screamed at Mama. "Grab him, Mama! Grab him and run!" Then I swung my chopping axe high and wheeled, aiming to cave in the she bear's head with the first lick.

But I never did strike. I didn't need to. Old Yeller hadn't let the bear get close enough. . . . The minute Old Yeller saw we were all in the clear and out of danger, he . . . lit out for the house. The bear chased him for a little piece, but at the rate Old Yeller was leaving her behind, Mama said it looked like the bear was backing up.

Understanding What You Read

1. **Literature and History** What does the fact that Old Yeller saved Arliss's life tell you about life in Texas at that time?
2. **Literature and You** Do you think Gipson included this passage to suggest that the Texas frontier was too dangerous for families like the one portrayed in *Old Yeller?* Explain your answer.

Section 4

Texas after Reconstruction

Main Ideas

1. Texas politics changed with the Constitution of 1876 and one-party rule.
2. African Americans were denied equal rights after Reconstruction.
3. After Reconstruction, many Texas farmers became sharecroppers and tenant farmers.

Key Terms and People

- **Redeemers**
- **segregation**
- **Jim Crow laws**
- **tenant farmers**
- **sharecroppers**

Why It Matters Today

Texans wrote a new constitution in 1876. Use current events sources to learn about how laws are made in Texas today.

TEKS: 1C, 5B, 6A, 10B, 17C, 21A, 21B, 21C, 21D, 21E, 21F, 22A, 22B, 22C, 22D

myNotebook

Use the annotation tools in your eBook to take notes on the changes that took place in Texas after Reconstruction.

The Story Continues

The Democratic delegates to the constitutional convention were determined to cut costs. They refused even to keep a journal of the convention proceedings, convinced that doing so would be a waste of money. Many delegates argued that state officials earned too much. But they could not agree on what the governor's salary should be. Was $5,000 a year, as provided in the Constitution of 1869, too high? Delegate J. L. German, a teacher, thought so. "The position should not be one that men would aspire to [desire] for the sake of money," he argued. "But rather for the honor attached to it."

The Texas Constitution of 1876

Democrats soon called for another constitutional convention, and in 1875 delegates met to write a new constitution. Of the 90 delegates, 15 were Republicans. Six of the Republicans were African American. Under the new constitution, the governor's term again became two years rather than four. The governor's power to appoint officials was reduced, and the legislature was again scheduled to meet once every two years instead of every year.

KEY DATE 1876
Delegates to the constitutional convention pass the Texas Constitution of 1876, which remains the foundation of our state government today.

To limit government spending, the constitution did not let the legislature go into debt for more than $200,000. Many spending proposals had to be approved by Texas voters. The issue of education prompted considerable debate. Delegate Richard Sansom called for reduced support for public schools because Texans had complained about taxes. Most delegates agreed, and the new constitution dramatically cut back public school funding. Texas voters approved the constitution in February 1876. The Constitution of 1876 is still the state's basic law.

In addition to writing a new constitution, the Democrats immediately began to reverse the policies of the Davis administration. They removed Republican officials and cut government spending. Richard Coke's victory marked the beginning of 100 years of Democratic control in Texas. During this period of one-party rule, Democrats in Texas won nearly all state and local offices. Democrats continued to limit taxes and government spending, including education spending. School attendance was no longer required, and local authorities were allowed to take control of schools.

Reading Check **Finding the Main Idea** What was the Democrats' goal in writing the Constitution of 1876?

BIOGRAPHY

Richard Coke

(1829–1897) A native of Virginia, Richard Coke moved to Waco in 1850. Coke attended the Secession Convention and fought for the Confederacy. After the war he served on the Texas Supreme Court. He was removed from office by federal military authorities in 1867. As governor he reversed many policies put in place by the Radical Republicans. Coke was reelected governor in 1876 but resigned that year to take a seat in the U.S. Senate. **What positions did Richard Coke hold in Texas government?**

★ Segregation and Jim Crow

African Americans' political power, which had peaked during the years of Radical control, fell along with the influence of the Republican Party in Texas. Nonetheless, African Americans remained active in the Republican Party throughout the late 1800s. In counties with large numbers of African Americans, local offices were sometimes won by black Republicans.

Before 1897, at least one African American served in every Texas legislature but one. During these years, African American Norris Wright Cuney led the Republican Party in Texas. He was a delegate to every Republican national convention between 1872 and 1892.

As African Americans' political power declined, they once again lost many of their civil rights. After Reconstruction ended, many Texas and other southern leaders—mostly Democrats—tried to "redeem," or restore, the South to its prewar days. These "**Redeemers**" limited the size of state government and cut back on political participation by African Americans. They also supported social separation of the races.

At first this separation was customary and informal. However, Redeemer lawmakers began passing laws to enforce **segregation**, the forced separation of people of different races. These laws became known as **Jim Crow laws**. The name *Jim Crow* came from the racist song "Jump Jim Crow." It was made famous by white performer Thomas Rice, who wore blackface in his act. His act was so popular in the South that, for many, the term became synonymous with African American.

The character Jim Crow, representing all African Americans, is forced to leave a whites-only railway car in this cartoon from the 1850s.

It became illegal for African Americans—and in some cases Mexican Americans—to eat in the same restaurants as white Texans. Nor could they stay in the same hotels, attend the same schools, or ride in first-class railcars. One white southerner described segregated areas as "in every instance . . . the most uncomfortable, uncleanest, and unsafest place[s]." Norris Wright Cuney's daughter Maud remembered when her mother tried to take a seat in a first-class railcar.

Analyzing Primary Sources
Drawing Inferences and Conclusions Why did the conductor believe it necessary to lock the door?

TEXAS VOICES

"My uncle Joseph had gone to the depot with mother to see her off to Houston. . . . The conductor of the first-class coach saw them coming, and, . . . he quickly locked the door of the coach, as he knew from experience that no argument or force could compel [force] mother to enter a second-class car. . . . Mother looked around and then innocently turning to Uncle Joseph, said: 'Well Joe . . . I see but one means of entrance and that is the window, so give me your hand. . . .' She got in the window and took her seat."

—Maud Cuney Hare, *Norris Wright Cuney: A Tribune of the Black People*

The Jim Crow system in Texas not only instituted segregation but also denied African Americans equal rights, equal opportunity, and equal protection under the law. African Americans challenged these laws in court. In 1883, however, the U.S. Supreme Court ruled that the Fourteenth Amendment applied only to the actions of state governments. This allowed private businesses and individuals to continue practicing discrimination and segregation.

Reading Check **Summarizing** How did the end of Reconstruction affect African Americans in Texas?

★ The Growth of Tenant Farming

With Reconstruction over, large landowners once again returned to political power. Agriculture continued to be the most important part of the economy. But many Texans—particularly freedpeople—could not afford land. Many of them became **tenant farmers**, or people who rent land to grow crops. A landowner would usually receive a part of a tenant farmer's crop as payment for using the land.

Farmers who lacked land and necessary supplies, such as mules, plows, and seed, promised a larger part of the crop in return for these items. These farmers were called **sharecroppers**. To make a profit, landowners made tenant farmers grow the most valuable cash crop—cotton.

A tenant farmer who was unable to grow enough cotton to cover the land rental would have to take out more loans. These loans often had very high interest rates, which made them difficult to pay back. Most farmers did not make enough in a year to pay back a single loan. To make matters worse, another bad crop would force the farmer to borrow even more money. As a result, many people never repaid their loans.

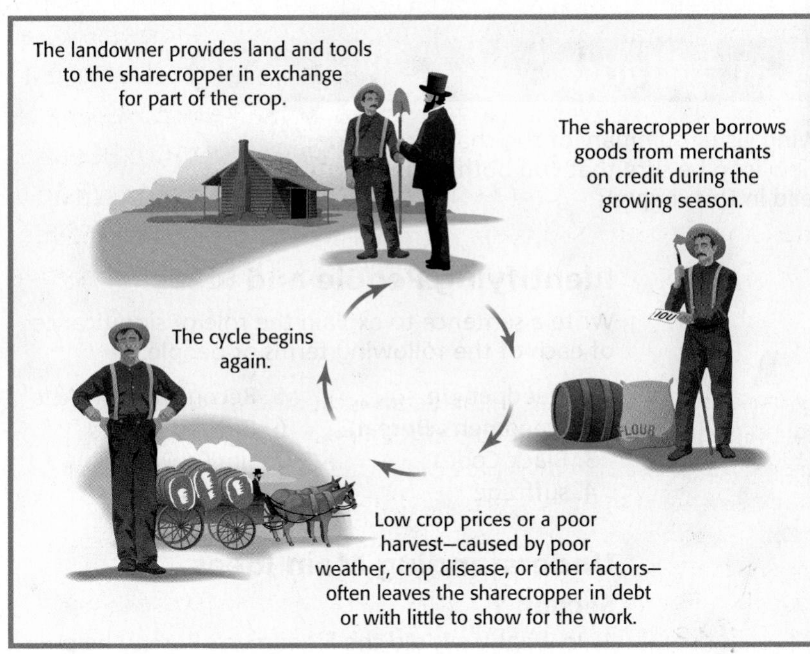

The Sharecropping Cycle

Many Texans who could not afford land became sharecroppers or tenant farmers. Because of debt, it was hard to get out of the sharecropping cycle.

Visualizing History

1. **Geography and Economics** How do you think geographic factors influenced the sharecropping system?
2. **Connecting to Today** How do you think debt and geographic factors affect farmers today?

As long as they owed money, tenant farmers and their children could not leave the land. They had to keep working for the landowner. This system gave landowners a great deal of power over tenant farmers.

Many Texans worked as tenant farmers during Reconstruction. The highest numbers were in counties where slavery had flourished before the Civil War. For example, about three fourths of farmers worked as tenant farmers in Fort Bend County. Both white and black Texans were tenant farmers, but the percentage was far higher among African Americans. By 1880, about 40 percent of all Texas farmers worked as tenant farmers.

Reading Check **Finding the Main Idea** What were the economic effects of Reconstruction on farming?

Section 4 Review

hmhsocialstudies.com
ONLINE QUIZ

1. **Define and explain:**
   - segregation
   - tenant farmers
   - sharecroppers
2. **Identify and explain** the historical significance of:
   - Redeemers
   - Jim Crow laws
3. **Comparing and Contrasting** Copy the graphic organizer below. Use it to show the differences between the 1869 and 1876 constitutions.

	1869	1876
1. Public schools		
2. Governor's term		
3. Legislature's term		
4. Debt		

4. **Finding the Main Idea**
   - **a.** Explain how the Constitution of 1876 and one-party rule changed Texas politics.
   - **b.** How did Jim Crow laws affect the rights of black Texans?
5. **Writing and Critical Thinking** myWriteSmart
   Analyzing Information Imagine that you are a tenant farmer in Texas in the 1870s. Write a letter to a friend describing some of the challenges you face.
   Consider the following:
   - why you grow cotton
   - how you obtained the tools and supplies you need

CHAPTER 19 REVIEW

The Chapter at a Glance

Examine the following visual summary of the chapter. Working with a partner, review it to be sure that you both understand the material you read in this chapter.

Reuniting the Nation

With the end of the Civil War, slaves were emancipated in Texas. African Americans received new rights including suffrage and citizenship. However, many of these rights were not enforced.

The Reconstruction Acts placed Texas in a military district. Texans elected pro-Union Republicans such as Edmund J. Davis. Eventually, Democrats returned to power, and Texas became a one-party state.

The Compromise of 1877 ended Reconstruction. Segregation was enforced in Texas and the South through Jim Crow laws.

Identifying People and Ideas

Write a sentence to explain the role or significance of each of the following terms or people.

1. freedpeople
2. Freedmen's Bureau
3. Black Codes
4. suffrage
5. Reconstruction Acts
6. Richard Coke
7. Jim Crow laws
8. segregation

Understanding Main Ideas

Section 1

1. In what ways did the Freedmen's Bureau help African Americans in Texas?
2. How did the Black Codes restrict the rights of freedpeople?

Section 2

3. What were the major provisions of the Texas Constitution of 1869?
4. What did Texas have to do under Congressional Reconstruction to be readmitted to the Union?

Section 3

5. What were the Republicans' major actions during Edmund J. Davis's administration?
6. What brought Reconstruction in Texas to a close?

Section 4

7. How did Jim Crow laws affect African Americans?

You Be the Historian

Reviewing Themes

1. **Government** In what ways was Congressional Reconstruction more demanding of southern states than Presidential Reconstruction?
2. **Citizenship** What role did Texas leaders who had supported or opposed secession play during Reconstruction?
3. **Economics** How did Reconstruction affect Texas economically?

Thinking Critically

1. **Identifying Points of View** What were the positions of the Texas Republican and Democratic Parties on suffrage for African Americans?
2. **Summarizing** What were the major political and social effects of Reconstruction in Texas?
3. **Drawing Inferences and Conclusions** What were the defining characteristics of the Civil War and Reconstruction era in Texas?

Texas Test Practice

Interpreting Political Cartoons

Study the political cartoon below. Then use the information in the cartoon to help you answer the questions.

1. Which sentence best explains why the knife has the words "For Reconstruction" on it?
   - **A** Texans wanted to undo Reconstruction policies.
   - **B** Texans supported Reconstruction policies.
   - **C** Texans sold many weapons.
   - **D** Texans liked to hunt.

2. What bias did the artist have that may have influenced this cartoon?

Analyzing Primary Sources

Read the following quote by former slave Felix Haywood about when he was freed. Then answer the questions.

"Everybody went wild. We all felt like heroes, and nobody had made us that way but ourselves. . . . We thought we were going to get rich like the white folks, because we were stronger and knew how to work . . . and we didn't have to work for them any more. But it didn't turn out that way. We soon found out that freedom could make folks proud but it didn't make them rich."

3. Which of the following statements best describes the author's point of view?
   - **F** He was pleased that many freedpeople were able to earn a good living.
   - **G** He was proud that African Americans won their freedom but disappointed in their economic opportunities.
   - **H** He expected white Texans to help freedpeople.
   - **J** He believed freedpeople would succeed because of their work experience.

4. What do you think Haywood meant when he said freedpeople "felt like heroes"?

Cooperative Learning

Working with a partner, create a large poster-size time line of the Civil War and Reconstruction era in Texas. Include as many major events, issues, and people of the era as possible. Illustrate your time line with colorful drawings of people and symbols to better explain the era. Write captions to help describe the events and people that you have included on your time line. Be sure to use standard grammar, spelling, sentence structure, and punctuation.

Internet Activity 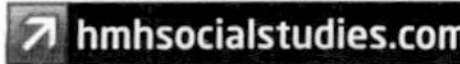

Conduct Internet research to analyze some of the political, economic, and social effects of Reconstruction in Texas. Then write an editorial in which you support the election of either Edmund J. Davis or Richard Coke. Be sure to support your answer. Identify any bias you discover in the sources used for your editorial.

CHAPTER 20

The Indian Wars
(1861–1880)

Texas Essential Knowledge and Skills (TEKS) 1B, 5B, 6A, 8A, 8B, 9A, 9B, 9C, 10B, 11C, 11D, 17C, 19A, 19B, 20A, 20C, 20D, 21A, 21B, 21C, 21D, 21E, 21H, 22A, 22B, 22C, 22D

Artist George Catlin painted images of the Comanches like this portrait of Little Spaniard.

TEXAS

- **1861** The Texas Frontier Regiment is established.
- **1864** Colonel Christopher "Kit" Carson leads an attack against Plains Indians in the Panhandle.
- **1868** Fort Richardson is established near Jacksboro.

1861 — 1863 — 1865 — 1867 — 1869

U.S. and WORLD

- **1865** U.S. negotiators sign the Treaty of the Little Arkansas with Comanche and Kiowa leaders.
- **1867** Railroads cut through the Great Plains, dividing the buffalo into northern and southern herds.
- **1870** The Illinois Central Railroad extends its line west, reaching Sioux City, Iowa.

Build on What You Know

Many of the soldiers stationed in Texas during Reconstruction guarded the frontier. Tensions between Texans and American Indians had increased as more and more settlers moved westward. Soon wars erupted on the frontier between the U.S. Army and American Indians in Texas.

If you were there . . .
Would you move to the Texas frontier?

Buffalo hunting was an important part of the lives of Plains Indians in Texas.

Quanah Parker led the Comanches in battles against U.S. forces.

1874
Plains Indians attack a group of buffalo hunters in the Battle of Adobe Walls.

1875
Comanche leader Quanah Parker surrenders, ending the Red River War.

1879
Apache leader Victorio launches raids along the Texas-Mexico border.

1871 — 1873 — 1875 — 1877 — 1879

1871
Manufacturers begin to use buffalo hides to produce leather for industrial purposes.

1875
A gold rush in the Black Hills of Dakota Territory leads to war between the Sioux and the United States.

1879
War breaks out between the British and the Zulu in South Africa.

You Be the Historian

*my*Notebook

What's Your Opinion? Do you **agree** or **disagree** with the following statements? Support your point of view in your notebook.

- **Geography** Groups moving into a region usually have little effect on people already living there.
- **Science, Technology & Society** As humans rely more on machines, they have less need for animals.
- **Culture** Groups rarely try to maintain their traditional values as their ways of life change.

Section 1

Changes in Indian Policy

Main Ideas

1. The Civil War and Reconstruction affected relations between American Indians and settlers in Texas.
2. The federal government took several steps to end American Indian raids in Texas.

Key Terms and People

- **commissioners**
- **Treaty of the Little Arkansas**
- **Satanta**
- **Treaty of Medicine Lodge**

Why It Matters Today

During the 1800s Texas and federal officials debated American Indian policy. Use current events sources to learn about American Indian policies today.

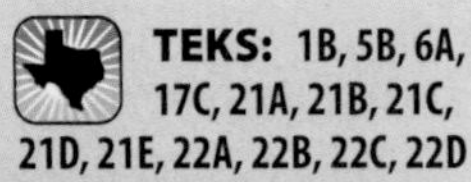

TEKS: 1B, 5B, 6A, 17C, 21A, 21B, 21C, 21D, 21E, 22A, 22B, 22C, 22D

myNotebook

Use the annotation tools in your eBook to take notes on Texas American Indian policy and relations.

The Story Continues

Mary and Britton Johnson wanted to build a new life in Young County. Their hopes were dashed in October 1864, when some Kiowas and Comanches attacked the settlement along Elm Creek. Johnson's son was killed and his wife and two daughters were taken captive. He rode into Indian Territory, determined to get them back. After some negotiation, Johnson managed to pay for their return.

★ American Indian Relations

The raid along Elm Creek was not an unusual event in the early 1860s. Many settlements were open to attack when soldiers and militias left to fight in the Civil War. Some Plains Indians took advantage of their absence to reclaim lost lands. The Comanches, for example, raided the area between Gainesville and Fredericksburg.

When the Civil War ended, federal troops arrived in Texas. However, there were not enough troops to protect the scattered frontier settlements. To try to ensure peace, federal **commissioners**—government representatives—met with leaders of the Comanches, Kiowas, and other groups in October 1865. In the **Treaty of the Little Arkansas**, Comanche and Kiowa leaders agreed to settle on a reservation that would include much of modern Oklahoma and the Texas Panhandle. In addition, the government would pay the Indians annual stipends. However, this reservation was never created, and peace did not last.

As settlers continued to move westward, some Comanches and Kiowas renewed their attacks. Governor James W. Throckmorton estimated that American Indians killed 162 Texans and captured 43 more between 1865 and 1867. As a result, many settlers, including more than half the population of Denton, Wise, and Young Counties, moved away to safer areas. The frontier line slowly crept back to the east.

Reading Check **Identifying Cause and Effect** What happened on the Texas frontier during the Civil War and Reconstruction?

Interpreting Visuals

Indian council. *Plains Indian chiefs and U.S. officials met to discuss peace.* ***Based on this image, how were these meetings conducted?***

★ The Treaty of Medicine Lodge

In 1867 the federal government sent commissioners to negotiate a new peace treaty with Comanches, Kiowas, and other Plains Indians. They met at Medicine Lodge Creek in Kansas. The commissioners offered some 3 million acres of land for a reservation in Indian Territory. Those who moved to the reservation had to stop raiding and take up farming.

Kiowa chief **Satanta** bitterly opposed the offer of a reservation. He argued that the Panhandle belonged to the Kiowas and the Comanches. At the meeting, Satanta spoke out against the reservation system.

TEXAS VOICES

"I have heard that you intend to settle us on a reservation near the mountains. I don't want to settle. I love to roam over the prairies. There I feel free and happy, but when we settle down we grow pale and die. . . . A long time ago this land belonged to our fathers; but when I go up to the river I see camps of soldiers on its banks. These soldiers cut down my timber; they kill my buffalo; and when I see that, my heart feels like bursting."

—Satanta, quoted in *Bury My Heart at Wounded Knee,* by Dee Brown

Interpreting Visuals

The meeting at Medicine Lodge. *During the meeting, U.S. officials encouraged the Plains Indians to move to reservations.* ***Based on this illustration, who participated in this meeting?***

Some Indian leaders disagreed with Satanta and chose to accept the government's offer. Kiowa leader Kicking Bird and Comanche chief Horseback, for example, argued that the survival of their people depended on moving to the reservations. They and other Plains Indians who shared their opinions agreed to the **Treaty of Medicine Lodge.**

Under this treaty, several thousand moved to Indian Territory. Among them were several bands of Comanches, Apaches, and Kiowas. In addition to land, the government promised to provide buildings, schools, farming tools, and a total of $25,000 a year for 30 years to the Indians living on the reservations.

Not all Plains Indians were agreeable to the terms of the treaty, though. They chose to remain on the plains, determined to maintain their hunting grounds. Ten Bears, a Texas Comanche chief, echoed Satanta's sentiments, expressing his disdain for reservation life and the promises of the government.

TEXAS VOICES

"You said that you wanted to put us upon a reservation, to build us houses and make us medicine lodges. I do not want them. I was born upon the prairie, where the wind blew free. . . . I know every stream and every wood between the Rio Grande and the Arkansas. I have hunted and lived over that country. I live like my fathers before me and like them I lived happily."

—Chief Ten Bears, quoted in *Documents of Texas History,* edited by Ernest Wallace

Reading Check **Summarizing** What were the terms of the Treaty of Medicine Lodge?

★ The Peace Policy

In 1869 President Ulysses S. Grant established a Board of Indian Commissioners to carry out the terms of the peace treaty. Grant appointed many Quakers, members of a Protestant sect called the Society of Friends, to act as American Indian agents. The Quakers believed in religious tolerance for all peoples and in nonviolence. Many Quakers and Christian missionaries became active in Indian affairs in hopes of preventing war on the frontier by helping American Indians adjust to reservation life. The government hoped to teach the Plains Indians to make a living by farming, and agents arranged for the construction of schools and churches on the reservations. Lawrie Tatum, a Quaker, was the Indian agent for the Comanches and Kiowas at the reservation in Indian Territory.

There were serious problems with the reservation system. Although the government hoped that the Plains Indians would become farmers rather than buffalo hunters, the land the government set aside for them had poor soil. The few Indians who tried farming thus had trouble growing enough food to survive. Government food supplies failed to make up the difference. In addition, goods sent by the government to the reservation were sometimes sold illegally by contractors and never reached their proper destination. Some buffalo hunters entered the reservation, further threatening the Indians' food supply. As a result, American Indians living on reservations lacked basic supplies and often went hungry.

Reading Check **Summarizing** Explain how the Treaty of Medicine Lodge affected Plains Indians in Texas.

BIOGRAPHY

Satanta (c.1820–1874)
When Kiowa leader Satanta was born, Plains Indians were at the height of their power. Over the course of his life, he watched the Kiowas suffer military defeat and confinement to reservations. Satanta used both diplomacy and warfare to protect the Kiowas. He never adjusted to reservation life. Satanta was re-arrested and died in a prison at Huntsville. **What changes did Satanta see on the Texas frontier during his life?**

★ Section 1 Review

hmhsocialstudies.com
ONLINE QUIZ

1. Define and explain:
- commissioners

2. Identify and explain the historical significance of:
- Treaty of the Little Arkansas
- Satanta
- Treaty of Medicine Lodge

3. Sequencing
Copy the graphic organizer below. Use it to explain in order the significant events on the Texas Plains during the 1860s.

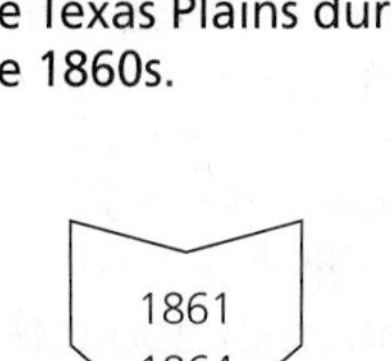

4. Finding the Main Idea

a. How did the Civil War and Reconstruction affect the Texas frontier?

b. Explain how the federal government hoped to achieve peace in Texas and protect western settlement.

5. Writing and Critical Thinking 

Supporting a Point of View Imagine that you live in Texas in the 1860s. Write a letter to Congress supporting or opposing the federal government's American Indian policies. Consider the following:
- the effects of westward expansion on American Indians
- the success of previous treaties in achieving peace

Section 2

War on the Plains

Main Ideas

1. The Salt Creek Raid affected military policy toward American Indians on the frontier.
2. The spread of railroad lines west and the slaughter of the buffalo greatly affected life for Plains Indians.

Key Terms and People

- **Salt Creek Raid**
- **Quanah Parker**
- **Cynthia Parker**
- **buffalo guns**

Why It Matters Today

The Plains Indians relied heavily on the buffalo for clothing, food, and shelter. Use current events sources to learn about how American Indian life today.

TEKS: 1B, 6A, 8A, 9A, 9C, 20A, 20C, 21A, 21B, 21C, 21D, 21H, 22A, 22B, 22C, 22D

myNotebook

Use the annotation tools in your eBook to take notes on how the destruction of the buffalo affected Plains Indians.

The Story Continues

Fannie Beck's parents were away at the funeral of her cousin, Jesse, who had been killed by Texas Indians while hunting. Fannie and her brother Milton had been left overnight to watch the younger children. They huddled together by the fire. "We suffered an agony of fear every time Sue, the baby, stirred. . . . We didn't want her to cry and let the Indians know there was a houseful of unprotected children."

The Salt Creek Raid

After the Treaty of Medicine Lodge, tensions between Plains Indians and settlers remained high. Indians living on the reservation were frustrated with the quality of life there. Other American Indians were upset by the continued westward movement of U.S. settlers into their hunting grounds. Some of these Indians began to attack Texas settlements. In July 1870 a large group of Kiowas attacked a stagecoach carrying mail near Fort Richardson. U.S. Army troops chased the raiders but were defeated in battle by the larger Kiowa force. Then in August a Kiowa leader named White Horse led a series of attacks. The Texas legislature complained to federal officials about these and other attacks.

In 1871 the U.S. Army sent General William Tecumseh Sherman to investigate Texans' complaints. Sherman doubted that American Indians posed a serious threat in Texas. However, early in May some 100 Kiowas and Comanches crossed into Texas. Led by Big Tree, Satank, and Satanta, they attacked a wagon train near Salt Creek on May 18, killing seven men. A wounded survivor of this **Salt Creek Raid** made his way to Fort Richardson and reported the raid to Sherman. The general sent troops after the raiders and then traveled to Fort Sill near Indian Territory.

When the raiders came to the Indian Territory reservation for food supplies, Lawrie Tatum asked them about the attack. Satanta responded, "If any other Indian comes here and claims the honor of leading the party he will be lying to you, for I did it myself." Satanta defended the raid by charging that the government had not treated the Indians fairly. He also accused Tatum of stealing supplies. The hardships of reservation life would result in more attacks, warned Satanta.

When Sherman learned of Satanta's statements, he had Big Tree, Satank, and Satanta arrested in a tense confrontation at Fort Sill. Satank was later killed while trying to escape. Big Tree and Satanta were tried for murder and sentenced to death. Tatum and other supporters of the peace policy worried that hanging the men would only make matters worse on the frontier. Texas governor Edmund J. Davis shared this concern, and he changed the death sentence to life in prison. Big Tree and Satanta were released from prison on parole, or let go under condition of good behavior, in 1873.

Reading Check **Summarizing** What significant events occurred on the Texas frontier in the early 1870s?

General Sherman's Near Miss

On May 17, 1871, General Sherman's wagon train was on its way to Fort Richardson. Unknown to Sherman, a group of Kiowas and Comanches considered attacking the wagon train. Instead, they attacked the next wagon train in the Salt Creek Raid.

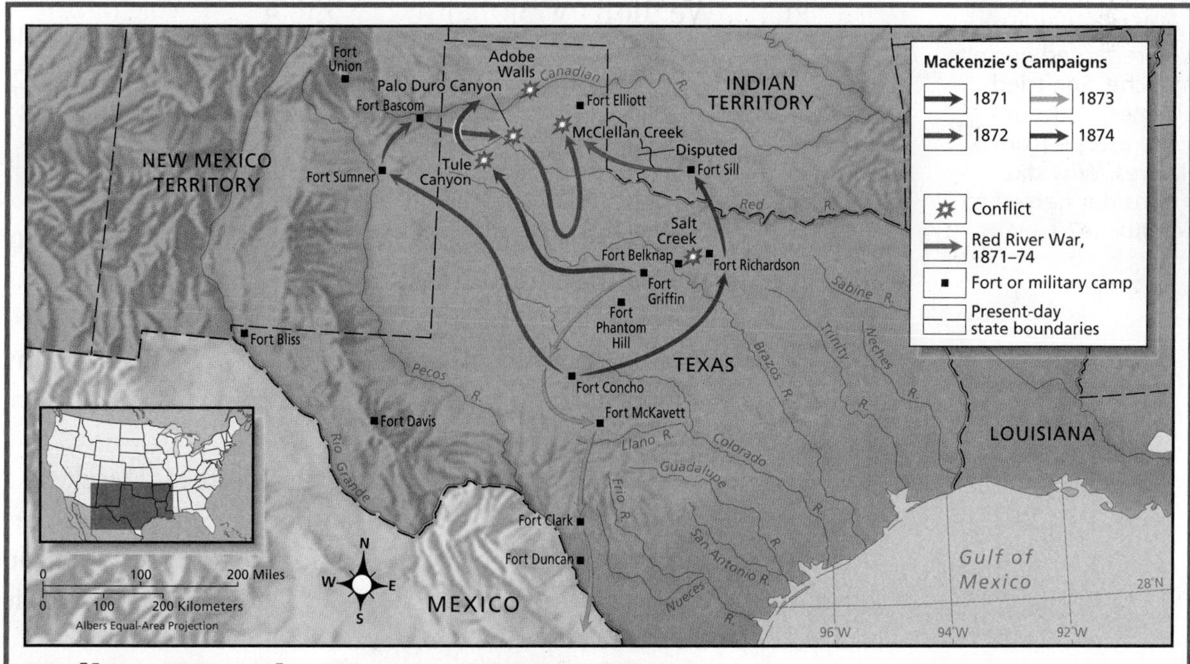

Indian Wars in Texas, 1871–1874

Interpreting Maps During the 1870s military campaigns forced the remaining American Indians out of Texas.

Locate In what region did most of the conflicts occur?

BIOGRAPHY

Cynthia Parker

(c.1825–1871) On May 19, 1836, Comanche raiders attacked Parker's Fort in what is now Limestone County. The Comanches captured five settlers, including Cynthia Ann Parker, who was then 10 or 11 years old. Parker remained with the Comanches for almost 25 years. During that time, she married Peta Nocona and had three children. Her son Quanah Parker became one of the most important Comanche leaders of his time. In 1860, Texas Rangers attacked a Comanche camp and captured Cynthia Parker. Relatives forced Parker to settle with them. Parker, however, regarded herself as Comanche. She tried several times, without success, to escape from her relatives. **Why did Parker consider herself to be a Comanche?**

★ Mackenzie's Raids

In response to the Salt Creek Raid, the U.S. War Department planned a series of attacks against Plains Indians who refused to live on reservations. Colonel Ranald S. Mackenzie—whom Ulysses S. Grant had called the most talented young officer in the U.S. Army—led the campaign. He commanded the 4th Cavalry regiment, which was stationed at several posts along the Texas frontier in the 1860s and 1870s.

Mackenzie and his troops, called Mackenzie's Raiders, achieved great fame fighting on the Texas frontier. The *Galveston News* expressed support for their actions, a view shared by many Texans.

TEXAS VOICES

"Go into the heart of their country. . . until the Indians are caught. . . . Lay waste [destroy] their villages, burn everything within reach, kill every warrior found in fighting trim [equipped to fight], and so utterly desolate [ruin] their regions that by sheer weakness they will never be able to send another war party to our border."

—*Galveston News,* March 14, 1873

Mackenzie began his raids in the fall of 1871, traveling northwest from Camp Cooper on the Clear Fork of the Brazos River. Mackenzie's troops were guided by Tonkawa Indian scouts. At Blanco Canyon, Mackenzie's troops fought a battle against a Comanche group led by **Quanah Parker**. Parker was the son of **Cynthia Parker**, a captured settler, and Peta Nocona—a Comanche. Forcing the Comanches to flee, Mackenzie pursued them deeper into the Panhandle. However, the Comanches escaped during a heavy snowstorm.

Following several Indian raids in the spring of 1872, Mackenzie renewed his attacks on the Comanches. He also crossed the Panhandle into New Mexico, chasing cattle thieves. On September 29, 1872, Mackenzie's troops defeated a Comanche force at McClellan Creek, near present-day Pampa. They killed many Comanches, destroyed their village, and took some 120 women and children prisoner.

Quanah Parker led an attack on Mackenzie's camp the following night and stampeded the animals that the Texans had captured. But he could not free the Comanche prisoners. Mackenzie kept the prisoners at Fort Concho to pressure the others to surrender. As a result, many Comanches abandoned life on the plains and moved to the reservation. It was a major victory for Mackenzie.

With the raids temporarily halted in northwest Texas, Mackenzie and the 4th Cavalry headed for the Mexican border. Stationed at Fort Duncan near Eagle Pass, Mackenzie led the effort to stop Kickapoo and Lipan Apache raids along the Rio Grande. By the end of 1873, Mackenzie had brought a stop to most of the border raids.

Reading Check **Sequencing** Describe in order the actions Colonel Mackenzie took against the Comanches.

Interpreting Visuals

Buffalo. *During the late 1800s the buffalo were hunted to nearly extinction.* ***How did buffalo hunters' means of hunting differ from those of American Indians?***

★ The Slaughter of the Buffalo

Other events also threatened Plains Indians. For generations, they had depended on the buffalo. By the 1870s the survival of the buffalo—and the Plains Indians' way of life—was at serious risk. As American railroad companies built lines across the Great Plains, non-Indian hunters killed hundreds of buffalo to feed the rail crews.

Once railroads reached towns in Kansas, buffalo hides could be moved quickly and cheaply to eastern cities. The buffalo hide industry began in 1871 when J. Wright Mooar shipped 56 hides to his brother John in New York City. John sold the hides to a tanning firm, which soon ordered 2,000 more.

A new method for tanning buffalo hides into high quality leather led to a sharp rise in demand and price. With an average hide worth more than three dollars on the market, buffalo hunters swarmed onto the plains to make their fortune.

Most buffalo hunters used a method called still hunting. In the early morning, hunters would sneak downwind of a herd and set up powerful rifles known as **buffalo guns**. These guns had telescopes, allowing hunters to slowly pick off members of the herd from a distance. One Texan later recalled, "A remarkably good hunter would kill seventy-five to one hundred [buffalo] a day."

CONNECTING TO

MATH

The Buffalo Population

Scholars have had great difficulty determining the size of the buffalo population over time. Historians agree that during the late 1800s the herds were nearly wiped out. The following are estimates of the population.

YEAR	BUFFALO POPULATION
1800	30 million
1850	20 million
1889	835
2000	200,000
2013	400,000

Interpreting Data

1. Use the information above to create a graph showing the buffalo population from 1800 to 2000.
2. By what percentage did the buffalo population decrease from 1800 to 1850?
3. By how much did the buffalo population grow between 1889 and 2013?

Under the terms of the Treaty of Medicine Lodge, buffalo hunters were not allowed onto Indian hunting grounds south of Kansas. These lands were reserved exclusively for Indian use. The U.S. Army was supposed to patrol the Kansas–Indian Territory border to enforce this provision of the treaty, but it failed to do so. As a result, by 1873 hunters were illegally pouring into Texas.

Contrary to their assigned role, many military officials actually encouraged hunters to follow the buffalo herds. They supported the extermination, or complete destruction, of buffalo on the Plains. General Philip Sheridan, who commanded the region including Texas, believed that killing off the buffalo would force Plains Indians onto reservations. In 1875 he urged the Texas legislature to allow the hunters to continue the slaughter. "Let them [hunters] kill, skin, and sell until the buffaloes are exterminated. Then your prairies can be covered with speckled cattle."

Between 1872 and 1874, hunters killed an estimated 4.3 million buffalo. The buffalo hunters' activities—particularly their practice of taking the hides and leaving the meat to rot—outraged Plains Indians. As a Comanche named He Bear explained, "Just as it makes the white man feel to have his money carried away, so it makes us feel to see others killing and stealing our buffaloes."

Reading Check **Finding the Main Idea** What technological advances helped lead to the slaughter of buffalo herds in the late 1800s?

Section 2 Review

hmhsocialstudies.com ONLINE QUIZ

1. **Define and explain:**
   - buffalo guns
2. **Identify and explain** the historical significance of:
   - Salt Creek Raid
   - Quanah Parker
   - Cynthia Parker
3. **Analyzing Information** Copy the graphic organizer below. Use it to explain how the destruction of the buffalo affected American Indians.

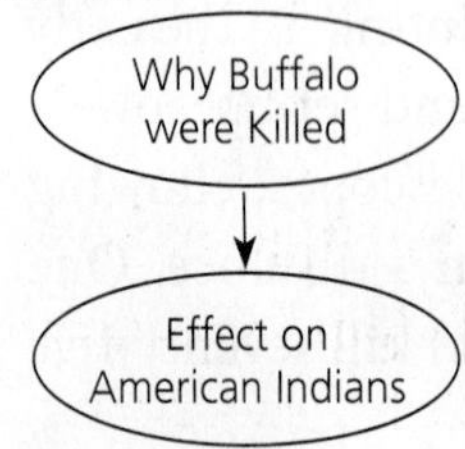

4. **Finding the Main Idea**
   a. How did the Salt Creek Raid affect the military's policy toward American Indians on the frontier?
   b. What role did Colonel Mackenzie play in Texas?
5. **Writing and Critical Thinking** myWriteSmart
   Identifying Points of View Imagine that you are a Plains Indian. Write a poem that describes the importance of the buffalo. Consider the following:
   - how Indians used the buffalo
   - the effect that hunters had on buffalo herds

Section 3

The Red River War

Main Ideas

1. The attack on Adobe Walls led to war between the Plains Indians and the U.S. government.
2. The Battle of Palo Duro Canyon marked the end of the era of American Indian control over the Texas Plains.

Key Terms

- **Battle of Adobe Walls**
- **Battle of Palo Duro Canyon**

Why It Matters Today

American Indians and U.S. Army soldiers fought in many regions of Texas. Use current events sources to learn about the U.S. Army today.

TEKS: 1B, 6A, 9A, 9C, 20A, 21A, 21B, 21C, 21D, 22A, 22D

myNotebook

Use the annotation tools in your eBook to take notes on the effects of Red River War.

The Story Continues

The summer sun had not yet risen. Arapahos, Cheyennes, Comanches, and Kiowas waited in the dark. In the distance stood Adobe Walls, a trading post that served buffalo hunters on the Texas plains. Isatai, a powerful medicine man, promised that "those white men can't shoot you. . . . I will stop all their guns." With that, the Indians rode at full speed toward the settlement.

★ The Battle of Adobe Walls

By the spring of 1874, the situation had become desperate for Plains Indians. They were starving on the reservations, and the buffalo were being slaughtered by white hunters. Little Robe, a Cheyenne, reminded reservation agents of the importance of the buffalo.

TEXAS VOICES

"Your people make big talk and sometimes make war, if an Indian kills a white man's ox to keep his wife and children from starving; what do you think my people ought to say when they see their [buffalo] killed by your race?"

—Little Robe, quoted in *The Buffalo War*, by James L. Haley

Isatai called for a war to drive out the buffalo hunters. In response, several Plains Indians leaders met in June 1874. Quanah Parker led the Comanches, and Lone Wolf led the Kiowas. Encouraged by Isatai, they targeted the trading post at Adobe Walls in the Texas Panhandle.

On June 27 about 700 Indians attacked Adobe Walls. Only 28 men and one woman were at the trading post, but they had an important advantage—buffalo guns. These powerful weapons could shoot long

VIDEO
Quanah Parker: The Last Comanche

hmhsocialstudies.com

Quanah Parker, last chief of the Comanches, fought hard to protect his people's land. However, within a year after the defeat at Adobe Walls, Parker and the Comanches were forced onto a Kiowa-Comanche reservation in southwestern Oklahoma.

distances. Despite repeated attacks, the hunters held their ground at the **Battle of Adobe Walls**. Four defenders died in the battle, while Indian casualties are estimated at 12 to 30. Although the attack failed, Plains Indians remained determined to protect their hunting grounds. They began a widespread war against buffalo hunters and settlers, launching attacks in Colorado, Kansas, New Mexico, Oklahoma, and Texas.

Reading Check **Sequencing** Explain in order the events leading to American Indian attacks on the Texas frontier.

★ The Battle of Palo Duro Canyon

After the attack at Adobe Walls and other American Indian raids, U.S. officials ordered General William Tecumseh Sherman to attack raiding Indians "wherever found. . . . The Reservation lines should be no barrier." Generals Sherman and Philip Sheridan organized a military campaign to kill or remove remaining American Indians in the Panhandle.

In August 1874 the army began a major offensive known as the Red River War. Some 3,000 troops in five different groups headed toward the Indian villages along the upper parts of the Red River. They were joined by the Frontier Battalion of the Texas Rangers, commanded by Major John D. Jones. Colonel Nelson Miles led a force of 750 soldiers into Texas from Fort Dodge in Kansas. These soldiers fought continuously against some 600 Cheyenne, who finally escaped in late August.

Major William Price led troops eastward from Fort Union in New Mexico Territory. Price defeated a band of Indians near Sweetwater Creek in the eastern Panhandle. Meanwhile, Colonel John Davidson and Lieutenant Colonel George Buell commanded two other military forces patrolling the region. Both forces destroyed many American Indian villages. The soldiers forced hundreds of Indians, mainly women and children, onto reservations, where supplies were already short.

Colonel Ranald S. Mackenzie struck the final blow to the Texas Plains Indians. In August, Mackenzie's forces marched north from Fort Concho. Mackenzie learned that many Comanches, Kiowas, and a few Cheyennes were camping in Palo Duro Canyon, which had provided safe shelter to Indian families for centuries.

Just before dawn on September 28, 1874, Mackenzie and about 500 troops quietly worked their way down into the canyon. The soldiers surprised the Indian villages and killed three Comanches. Panic-stricken, women and children fled out onto the plains. The **Battle of Palo Duro Canyon** took a terrible toll on the Comanches. In their haste to escape, the Comanches left behind most of their supplies—including more than 1,400 horses. Mackenzie had most of the horses shot to prevent the Comanches from recapturing them. He also ordered his men to burn the villages in the canyon. Lacking clothing and horses, few Indians could hope to survive the winter in the Panhandle. They had no choice but to move to the reservations in Indian Territory.

The battle marked a turning point in the Red River War. The era of American Indian control of the Texas Plains had come to an end. Indian leaders advised the Cheyennes to accept reservation life.

TEXAS VOICES

"... we want them to travel in the white man's road. The white men are as many as the leaves on the trees and we are only a few people, and we should do as the white man wants us to, and live at peace with him."

—Grey Beard and Minimic, quoted in *The Military Conquest of the Southern Plains*, by William H. Leckie

Analyzing Primary Sources
Drawing Inferences and Conclusions Why did Grey Beard and Minimic advise the Cheyennes to adopt the ways of white Americans?

Reading Check **Identifying Cause and Effect** What was the outcome of the Battle of Palo Duro Canyon, and how did it affect Texas Plains Indians?

Section 3 Review

hmhsocialstudies.com
ONLINE QUIZ

1. **Identify and explain** the historical significance of:
   - Battle of Adobe Walls
   - Battle of Palo Duro Canyon

2. **Identifying Cause and Effect**
   - Copy the graphic organizer below. Use it to explain the main events of the early 1870s and how they led to the Red River War.

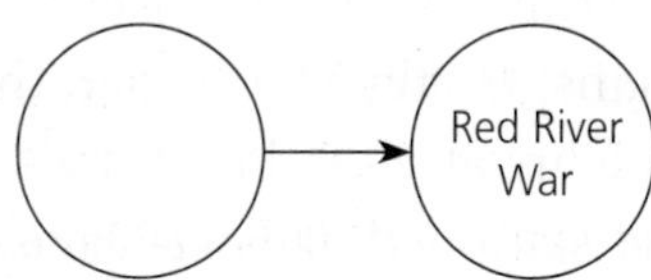

3. **Finding the Main Idea**
   a. How did the Battle of Adobe Walls affect Plains Indians on the frontier?
   b. How did Mackenzie and his troops win the Battle of Palo Duro Canyon?

4. **Writing and Critical Thinking** myWriteSmart
   Drawing Inferences and Conclusions Write a short report explaining why some Plains Indians groups in Texas believed it was necessary to attack the buffalo hunters and settlers.
   Consider the following:
   - life on the reservations
   - the effect of hunters on the buffalo

Section 4

The Indian Wars End in Texas

Main Ideas

1. The Indian raids stopped when the Mexican army joined the United States on the chase.
2. The American Indian population had decreased greatly by the 1880s.

Key Terms and People

- **Victorio**
- **buffalo soldiers**
- **Henry O. Flipper**

Why It Matters Today

Texas Indians were forced onto reservations during the Red River War. Use current events sources to learn about people who are forced to relocate because of war or natural disaster today.

TEKS: 6A, 8B, 9A, 9B, 9C, 10B, 19A, 19B, 21A, 21B, 21C, 21D, 21E, 22A, 22B, 22C, 22D

*my*Notebook

Use the annotation tools in your eBook to take notes on how reservations changed the lives of American Indians.

The Story Continues

Victorio never forgot what the U.S. Army had done to his mentor, Mangas Coloradas. Under a flag of truce, soldiers had killed the Apache chief. Now an Apache chief himself, Victorio would never trust the U.S. Army. When troops ordered Apache families to move to a hot barren reservation in Arizona, Victorio led many of them to Mexico.

★ Fighting on the Rio Grande

The departure of the group led by **Victorio** marked the beginning of one of the last Indian wars in the United States. Victorio and other American Indians began raids into Texas from Mexico. The Apaches could easily attack travelers on the miles and miles of lonely roads of the Trans-Pecos region. In response to the raids, the U.S. Army ordered more troops to the Rio Grande area. Stopping the raids was not an easy task—the army chased Victorio for two years. Troops following the Apaches had to carry their own food and water to survive in the dry rugged area.

Most of the some 2,500 troops stationed along the border served in the 9th and 10th Cavalries as well as in the 24th and 25th Infantry Regiments. Although white officers commanded these regiments, all the troops were African American. They were called "**buffalo soldiers**" by American Indians. **Henry O. Flipper**, the first black graduate of the U.S. Military Academy at West Point, took part in a campaign against the Apaches while stationed at Fort Davis. Troops from this fort and

Fort Bliss sometimes trailed the Apaches for weeks, only to find they had crossed the Rio Grande back into Mexico. The raids were not stopped until the Mexican army became active in the chase. Victorio died in 1880 while being pursued by Mexican troops.

Reading Check **Analyzing Information** What problems did the climate create for the U.S. Army in the Trans-Pecos region?

BIOGRAPHY

Henry O. Flipper

(c.1856–1940) Henry O. Flipper was born into slavery in 1856. In 1878 he became the first African American to graduate from the U.S. Military Academy. After graduating, Flipper served as a second lieutenant in the 10th Cavalry. He worked as an army engineer, supervising the construction of roads and telegraph lines in Texas. Today West Point offers an award named after Flipper to students who succeed in the face of severe obstacles. **What role did Flipper play in the development of Texas?**

Reservation Life

As Apache resistance was overcome, most Texas Indians were facing the challenge of living on reservations in what is now Oklahoma. When they moved onto the reservation, Plains Indians had to give up their traditional way of life—hunting buffalo—and take up farming. Their efforts to farm and ranch often failed. They usually received poor land, and they had little experience raising crops using the techniques taught by the reservation agents. When government officials did not supply food, Indians often faced starvation. General Nelson Miles described conditions on the reservations. "[Indians] were sometimes for weeks without their rations." Few American Indians prospered on the reservations.

Indians on the reservations faced other challenges to their traditional ways of life. In 1883 the federal government banned many American Indian religious practices, including the Sun Dance. When some Kiowas planned the dance in 1889, soldiers stopped the event. Indians often had to hold traditional celebrations and ceremonies in secret. Many Indians continued to use their own languages as well as English. Indians also preserved many of their customs, myths, and styles of dress, despite government officials' efforts to eliminate these traditional aspects of the Indians' lives.

Soldiers from Fort Davis patrolled far western Texas. Today, reenactors demonstrate what life was like at the fort.

Our Cultural Heritage

American Indian Celebrations

Throughout the United States, American Indians celebrate their cultural heritage. Texans can learn about this heritage at places such as the Alabama-Coushatta Reservation in Polk County. Many American Indians hold gatherings called powwows, which attract many visitors. People attend the powwows to watch the festivities and sometimes participate in activities such as singing and dancing. **What activities celebrate American Indian culture in Texas today?**

Quanah Parker, who had surrendered and moved to the reservation in 1875, worked to better relations between the federal government and American Indians. On occasion Parker went to Washington, D.C., to negotiate on behalf of American Indians. Parker managed to live successfully in the cultures of American Indians and white Americans alike. He once remarked about his mother, "If she could learn the ways of the Indian, I can learn the ways of the white man." Parker continued to try to improve the lives of the Comanches until his death in 1911.

Quanah Parker and other Indians on reservations shared the land they farmed. Some government officials believed that the Indians would be better off if they owned the land they worked. The Dawes General Allotment Act of 1887 divided up reservation lands in Oklahoma and promised Indians U.S. citizenship. Some of the reservation lands were allotted, or divided, among individual families. This division of lands dissolved some of the unity within the Kiowa tribe, as well as other Texas Indians. In addition, many Indians did not receive enough land to support themselves.

After dividing the reservations, the government sold the remaining lands. As a result, Indians lost an enormous amount of land. The act also failed to grant Indians full citizenship as promised. All American Indians were not granted citizenship until 1924.

The difficulties of reservation life, military attacks, and the slaughter of the buffalo took a terrible toll on Texas Indians. By the 1880s their population had been greatly reduced. Most had either been killed or moved out of the state. This opened vast stretches of land on the Texas plains to farming and ranching. Settlers quickly moved onto lands that Texas Indians had called home for hundreds of years.

Reading Check **Analyzing Information** How did the Indian wars affect migration patterns in Texas?

Section 4 Review

hmhsocialstudies.com ONLINE QUIZ

1. Identify and explain the historical significance of:
- Victorio
- buffalo soldiers
- Henry O. Flipper

2. Summarizing
- Copy the graphic organizer below. Use it to show how living on reservations changed the lives of American Indians.

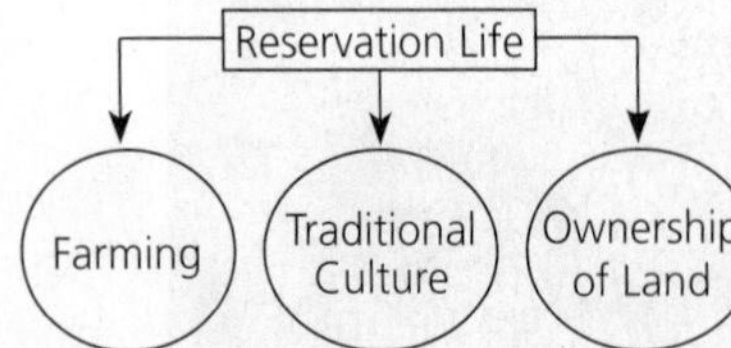

3. Finding the Main Idea

a. Why did the Apache raids along the Rio Grande stop?

b. What effect did the Indian wars have on migration patterns?

4. Writing and Critical Thinking myWriteSmart

Supporting a Point of View Imagine that you live in the 1870s. Write an editorial explaining how you think the reservation system will affect American Indians in the future.

Consider the following:
- farming on the reservations
- government policy toward American Indian cultures

Connecting To

Geography

The Expanding Texas Frontier

Most American Indians had been removed from East Texas during the years of the Republic. In the 1860s settlement along the Texas frontier slowed. American Indian raids prevented white settlers from claiming new lands. During the 1870s, however, settlement along the frontier boomed as American Indians were removed from the land.

Geography **Skills**

Interpreting Thematic Maps

1. About what percent of Texas was frontier land in 1860?
2. How did the location of forts relate to the lines of frontier settlement?
3. Why did frontier settlement increase in the 1870s?

Settlement of the Texas Frontier, 1880

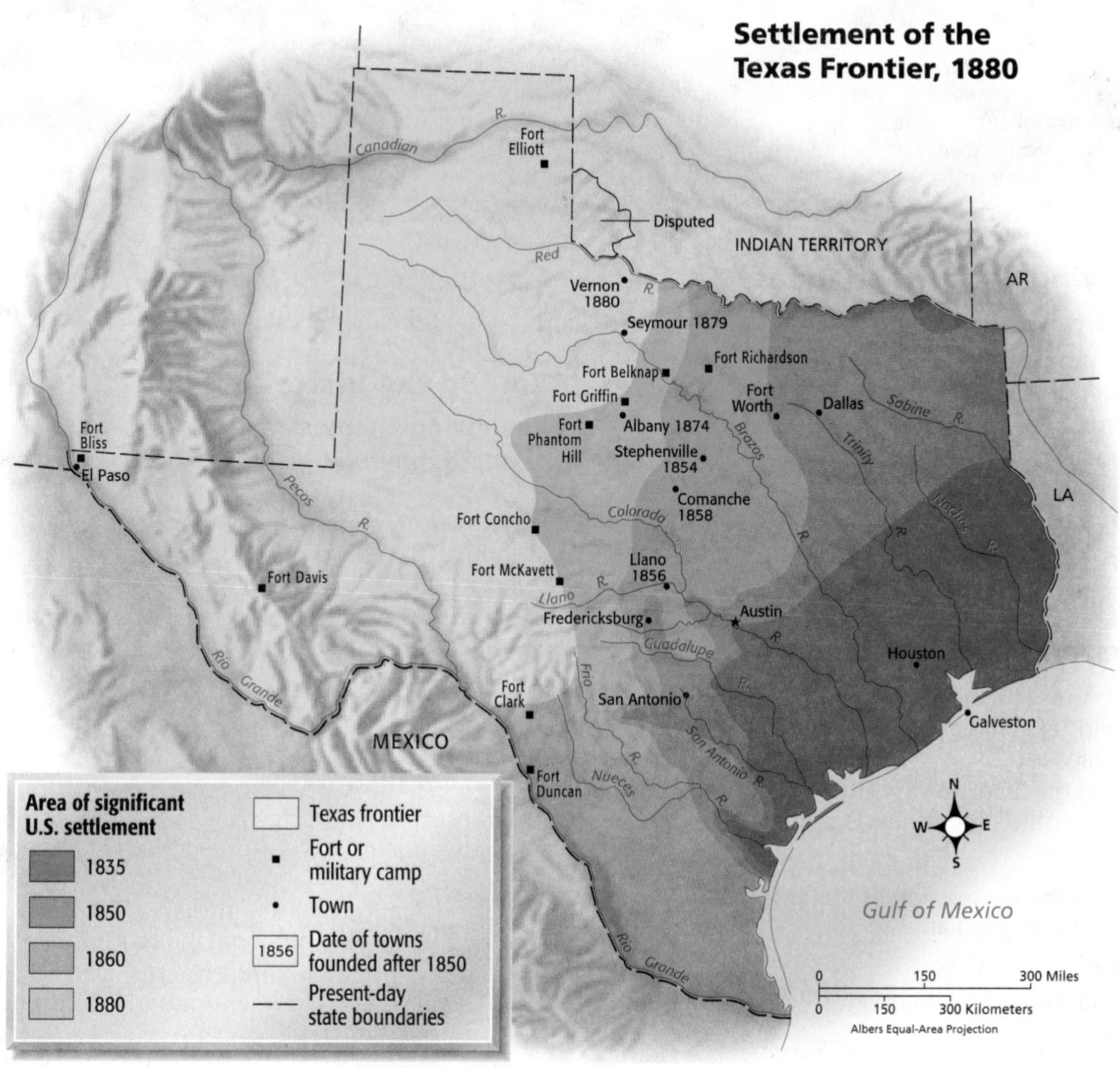

The Chapter at a Glance

Examine the following visual summary of the chapter. Then use the visual to create a chart that shows the causes of conflicts on the Texas frontier and their effects.

During the Civil War, American Indian raids increased on the Texas frontier until some Plains Indians signed a treaty and agreed to move onto reservations.

The U.S. Army began a campaign to remove all Plains Indians to reservations. The killing of the buffalo herds also threatened Plains Indians.

With most Indians driven out of Texas, settlers began moving farther west.

Identifying People and Ideas

Write a sentence to explain the role or significance of each of the following terms or people.

1. Treaty of the Little Arkansas
2. Satanta
3. Salt Creek Raid
4. Treaty of Medicine Lodge
5. Quanah Parker
6. Cynthia Parker
7. buffalo guns
8. Battle of Palo Duro Canyon
9. buffalo soldiers
10. Victorio

Understanding Main Ideas

Section 1

1. Why did Texas Indians increase their raids during the Civil War?
2. Why did the Treaty of the Little Arkansas fail to resolve conflicts on the Texas plains?

Section 2

3. Why was the destruction of the buffalo a serious threat to Plains Indians?

Section 3

4. Why did American Indians attack Adobe Walls?

Section 4

5. What were conditions like on the reservations?

You Be the Historian

Reviewing Themes

1. **Geography** How did westward expansion affect American Indians?
2. **Science, Technology & Society** How did industrial development contribute to the destruction of the buffalo?
3. **Culture** How did American Indians maintain some of their traditional values even while living on the reservation?

Thinking Critically

1. **Evaluating** How effective was the reservation policy at dealing with conflicts between settlers and American Indians?
2. **Summarizing** What events led to the decline of the American Indian population in Texas?
3. **Identifying Cause and Effect** How did the Civil War affect settlement patterns on the Texas frontier?

Texas Test Practice

Interpreting Graphs

Study the graph below. Then use the information on the graph to help you answer the questions that follow.

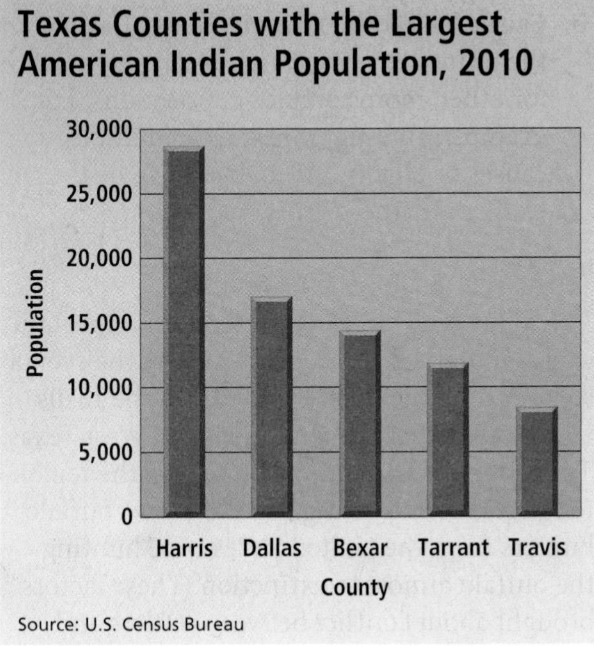

1. What is the difference in the American Indian populations between Dallas and Travis counties?

A 12,000
B 5,000
C 17,000
D 7,000

2. Based on this graph, what conclusions can you draw about the population distribution of American Indians in Texas?

Analyzing Primary Sources

Read the following quote from a 1867 government committee report on the status of American Indians. Then answer the questions that follow.

"The Indians everywhere, with the exception of the tribes within the Indian Territory, are rapidly decreasing in numbers from various causes . . . by disease; . . . by wars . . . by the steady and restless emigration of white men into the territories of the west, which, confining the Indians to still narrower limits, destroys that game [wildlife], which in their normal state, constitutes [provides] their principal means of subsistence [food]."

3. According to the report, which of the following is a cause of American Indians' decline?

F Indians selling their lands
G the government policy of signing treaties with Indians
H the growing number of white settlers in Indian homelands
J drought that ruins crops on the Plains

4. When interpreting a primary source, historians examine the historical context in which the source was written. What recommendations do you think the committee made regarding the future of American Indians?

Cooperative Learning

Work with a small group to complete the following activity. Create a colorful illustrated map showing where American Indians lived in Texas before 1880 and today. Each person in your group should create questions about geographic distributions and patterns for the map's legend. Be sure to ask questions about how migration and settlement have affected American Indians in Texas.

Internet Activity: 

Use the internet to research traditional cultural practices of an American Indian group living in Texas. Take note of the group's traditional celebrations, styles of dress, myths, and customs. Create a painting or thematic model that you can use to show the class what you have learned about the American Indian group.

Social Studies Skills

WORKSHOP

Identifying Cause and Effect

Identifying and understanding cause-and-effect relationships is crucial to the study of history. To investigate why events happen and what else may have happened because of these events, historians often ask several questions. These questions include the following: What immediate activities may have triggered the event? What past activities may have led up to the event? Who was involved?

How to Identify Cause and Effect

1. **Look for clues.** Certain words and phrases are immediate clues. They reveal the existence of a cause-and-effect relationship in history. The following chart lists some examples of clue words and phrases.

Clue Words and Phrases

Cause	Effect
because	aftermath
brought about	as a consequence
gave rise to	as a result of
inspired	depended on
led to	originating from
produced	outcome
provoked	proceeded from
spurred	resulting in
the reason	this led to

2. **Identify the relationship.** Read closely to identify how historical events may be related. Writers do not always state the link between cause and effect. Therefore, you must read very carefully. You may sometimes have to infer, or draw your own conclusions about, the cause or the effect of an event.

3. **Check for complex connections.** Beyond the immediate cause and effect, check for other, more complex connections. For example, an event might have multiple causes or effects. Effects may also be the cause of further events.

Example

The following flowchart presents an important cause-and-effect relationship among the events surrounding the Red River War. In the 1870s and 1880s settlers began to move to West Texas. Texas Indians had hunted buffalo in the region for generations. During the late 1800s, buffalo hunters from the United States were hunting the buffalo almost to extinction. These factors brought about conflict between settlers and Plains Indians.

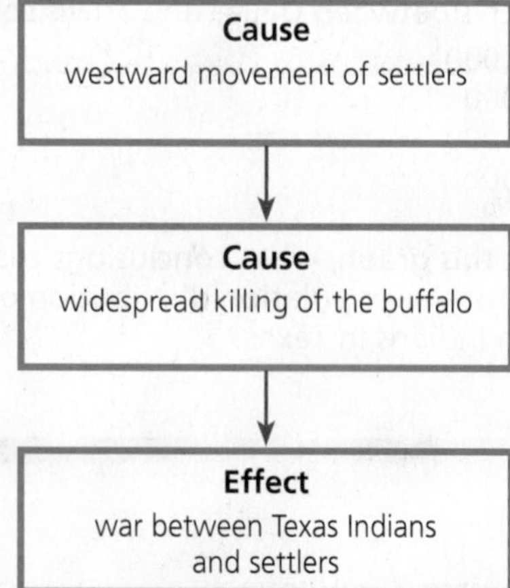

Practicing the Skill

Reread Chapter 19, Section 2, of your textbook, which discusses the causes of Congressional Reconstruction. Draw a diagram like the one above, showing the relationships between the important events leading up to Congressional Reconstruction.

History in Action

UNIT 6 SIMULATION

You Make the Decision . . .

Should Texas support the Union or the Confederacy?

Complete the following activity in small cooperative groups. The day is April 12, 1861. The Confederates have opened fire on Fort Sumter in Charleston Harbor. The people in Texas have strong feelings on both sides of the conflict. The Texas legislature has asked you to make a recommendation about which side of the Civil War Texas should support—the Union or the Confederacy. Follow these steps to reach your decision.

1. **Gather information.** Use your textbook and other resources to find information that might help you decide whether to support the Union or the Confederacy in this conflict. Be sure to use what you learned from this unit's Skills Workshop on Identifying Cause and Effect to help you make an informed decision. You may want to divide up different parts of the research among group members.

2. **Identify options.** After reviewing the information you have gathered, consider the options you might recommend to the legislature. Your final decision may be easier to reach if you consider as many options as possible. Be sure to record your possible options for your presentation.

3. **Predict consequences.** Now take each option you and your group came up with and consider what might be the outcome of each course of action. Ask yourselves questions such as, "What would be the consequences of supporting the Union or the Confederacy?" Once you have predicted the consequences, record them as notes for your presentation.

4. **Take action to implement your decision.** After you have considered your options, you should plan and create your presentation. Be sure to make your decision on whether to support the North or the South very clear. You will need to support your decision by including information you gathered and by explaining why you rejected other options. Your presentation needs to be visually appealing to gain the support of the legislature. When you are ready, decide which group members will make each part of the presentation, and then take your decision to the legislature (the rest of the class).

As an audience member, listen carefully as other groups make their presentations. Take notes about what each group is saying. If you are unclear about what a group has said or if you want more details about its proposal, ask the group members for more information. After the class has asked its questions, vote on whether you would accept the group's proposal.

UNIT 7

Cotton, Cattle, and Railroads

(1860–1920)

Cowboys and their herds roamed the plains of West Texas.

Texas Teens

Young Cowhands

Teenagers played a crucial role in the growth of the state's cattle industry. With so many men in the military, the numbers of Texas cattle that roamed free on the frontier grew rapidly during the Civil War. When the war ended, ranchers needed help gathering, herding, and caring for these cattle. Teenagers such as L. B. Anderson of Seguin participated in roundups, spent many years working on ranches, and went on cattle drives.

As parts of western Texas were opened up for ranching, many young Texans found work on cattle ranches. These were mostly young men, but occasionally, young women also participated in the ranch work. These teens did many jobs, including roping and herding cattle, mending fences, breaking horses, and maintaining the ranch's equipment.

Ranchers also needed people who could tolerate the hardships of driving cattle over hundreds of miles to northern stockyards. Many young Texans jumped at the chance for adventure. Cowhands faced a variety of dangers, including cattle thieves, bad weather, and stampedes. S. H. Woods, a 16-year-old from Alice, remembered a stampede. "About 10 o'clock at night we were greeted with a terribly loud clap of thunder. . . . That started the ball rolling. Between the rumbling, roaring and rattling of hoofs, horns, thunder and lightning, it made an old cow-puncher long for . . . some dug-out on the banks of some little stream."

For many young Texans, the excitement of life on the trail more than made up for the dangers. J. M. Custer recalled, "We endured many hardships . . . but, just the same . . . the world is better for it." **Why did some Texas teens want to be cowhands?**

In this unit you will learn about the Texas cattle industry. You will also learn about the expansion of farming and railroads into the Texas frontier and how the Texas oil boom began.

Vaqueros and Cowboys

The first ranchers in Texas came with Spanish missionaries to the San Antonio River valley. By the 1730s, they were raising small herds to feed mission residents. In time, Spanish settlers established ranches throughout southern Texas. They realized that the climate and terrain offered plenty of grasslands and water—ideal conditions for raising cattle, horses, sheep, and goats.

On the ranches, horsemen called vaqueros earned a reputation for their horse-riding and cattle-herding skills. Vaqueros adapted to the challenges of ranching in Texas. They modified their clothing, saddles, ropes, and brands to suit their needs. Whether chasing animals across the open range or driving cattle for hundreds of miles to markets in Mexico and New Orleans, vaqueros became known for their bravery and herding skills. They were the first Texas cowboys, and they established a proud tradition.

As Anglo settlers arrived in Texas, they were influenced by the established Spanish ranching customs. Over time, some former cowboys began to establish their own ranches, expanding the ranching industry across Texas. As ranching in Texas spread and grew, it evolved as a unique blend of Spanish and American traditions and practices. A new breed of cattle evolved along with it. Known as the longhorn, it developed from Spanish breeds that mixed with English cattle brought by U.S. settlers. The longhorn became the best-known breed of Texas cattle.

Exploring Museum Resources

The Bullock Texas State History Museum has more information on how ranching evolved from Spanish colonial times to today. Visitors can learn about the obstacles cowboys faced as they traveled along cattle trails or explore the cowboy identity and lifestyle, historically and as it has been portrayed in the movies and other media. Explore some of these resources online. You can find museum resources at **hmhsocialstudies.com**

Photograph Go online to learn more about vaqueros, the first Texas cowboys.

Photograph How did longhorn cattle develop in Texas, and why were they so well suited to the Texas climate?

Photograph The cowboy is widely recognized as a symbol of Texas. How has the idea of the cowboy been romanticized through stories and film?

UNIT 7

Reading Social Studies

Organizing Information

Focus on Reading How are books organized in the library? How are groceries organized in the store? Clear organization helps us find the product we need, and it also helps us find facts and information.

Understanding Structural Patterns Writers often use structural patterns to organize information in sentences or paragraphs. A structural pattern is simply a way of organizing information. Recognizing those patterns will make it easier for you to understand social studies texts. When you are presented with information, it can sometimes help you understand it if you reorganize that information into another form. For example, you could take events listed chronologically in a time line and categorize them as political, military, and so on. Organizing information can help you make sense of outlines, reports, databases, graphs, charts, time lines, maps, and other sources.

Patterns of Organization

Pattern	Clue Words	Graphic Organizer
Cause-effect shows how one thing leads to another.	as a result, because, therefore, led to	Cause → Effect; Cause → Effect; Cause → Effect
Chronological Order shows the time sequence of events or actions.	after, before, first, then, not long after, finally	First → Next → Next → Last
Compare-contrast points out similarities and/or differences.	although, but, however, on the other hand, similarly, also	Similarities / Differences 1. / 1. 2. / 2.
Listing presents information in categories such as size, location, or importance.	also, most, important, for example, in fact	Category • fact • fact • fact • fact

You Try It!

The following passages are from the unit you are about to read. As you read each set of sentences, ask yourself what structural pattern the writer used to organize information. Read passage A and answer the questions that follow.

(A) The Texas cattle industry slowly expanded in the 1840s. For example, Aaron Ashworth of Jefferson County had ranch holdings worth more than $30,000. Some Texans began driving cattle to out-of-state markets. James Taylor White began to drive cattle from Liberty County to market in New Orleans, and in 1846 Edward Piper took a herd of Texas cattle to Ohio.

(B) Many Texans eagerly awaited the arrival of rail lines, hoping they would spur economic growth. The state's economic development had been slowed by its transportation problems. Most Texas rivers were either too shallow or too unreliable for shipping goods, and dirt roads turned to mud during wet weather. As a result, moving people and goods was time-consuming and expensive. Railroads promised cheap, fast, and reliable transportation.

(C) Some Texas oil companies began to use a business strategy called vertical integration—owning the businesses involved in each step of a manufacturing process. For example, the Texas Company began by purchasing and transporting oil from Spindletop. As its profits grew, the company expanded into oil drilling, production, and refining. The company also bought items it needed for its business, such as barges and railroad tanker cars.

What structural pattern did the writer use to organize the information in passage A? How can you tell?

Reading Section Assessment

Use passages B and C to answer the questions below.

1. What structural pattern did the writer use to organize the information in passage B? How can you tell?
2. What structural pattern did the writer use to organize the information in passage C? How can you tell?

Key Terms

Unit 7

Chapter 21

brands *(p. 441)*
cattle drives *(p. 441)*
rustlers *(p. 441)*
longhorn *(p. 442)*
stockyards *(p. 443)*
open range *(p. 444)*
remuda *(p. 447)*
wrangler *(p. 447)*
range wars *(p. 455)*

Chapter 22

transcontinental railroad *(p. 463)*
junctions *(p. 465)*
dry farming *(p. 467)*
threshers *(p. 468)*
commercial farming *(p. 469)*
boll weevil *(p. 470)*
labor unions *(p. 473)*
strike *(p. 473)*

Chapter 23

petroleum *(p. 478)*
fossil fuel *(p. 478)*
derricks *(p. 479)*
refinery *(p. 479)*
boom-and-bust cycle *(p. 481)*
wildcatters *(p. 483)*
horizontal integration *(p. 485)*
vertical integration *(p. 485)*
boomtowns *(p. 486)*
philanthropy *(p. 489)*

As you read, think about how the ideas are presented in the text. Look for signal words, and ask yourself why the writer chose to organize the information in this way.

CHAPTER 21

The Cattle Kingdom
(1860–1890)

Texas Essential Knowledge and Skills (TEKS) 1B, 5B, 6A, 6B, 6C, 6D, 8A, 9B, 9C, 10A, 10B, 13A, 13B, 17C, 19C, 20C, 20D, 21A, 21B, 21C, 21D, 21E, 21H, 22A, 22C, 22D

After the long drive from Texas to Abilene, Kansas, cattle were loaded on railcars and shipped to eastern markets.

TEXAS

1863 The Texas cattle population increases rapidly during the Civil War.

1869 Texas cowboys move a herd of 15,000 cattle to market. It is the largest single herd of the era.

1873 Ranchers begin to ship thousands of cattle from Denison after the Missouri-Kansas-Texas Railroad extends a line there.

1860 — 1864 — 1868 — 1872

U.S. and WORLD

1863 People rush to what is now Montana after gold is discovered there.

1867 The Kansas Pacific Railroad establishes a shipping point for cattle in Abilene, Kansas.

1873 The U.S. economy suffers a downturn, causing a temporary decline in the value of cattle.

If you were there . . .
Would you become a cattle rancher?

Build on What You Know

Many U.S. settlers moved to the Texas frontier during the 1860s. These new settlers competed with American Indians for control of the land. As the frontier moved west, Texans drove cattle to out-of-state markets to sell them. Soon the state had a booming cattle industry.

Image Credit: ©North Wind Picture Archives

Cattle stampedes were one of the many dangers cowboys faced.

This barbed-wire sample board advertises different types of wire.

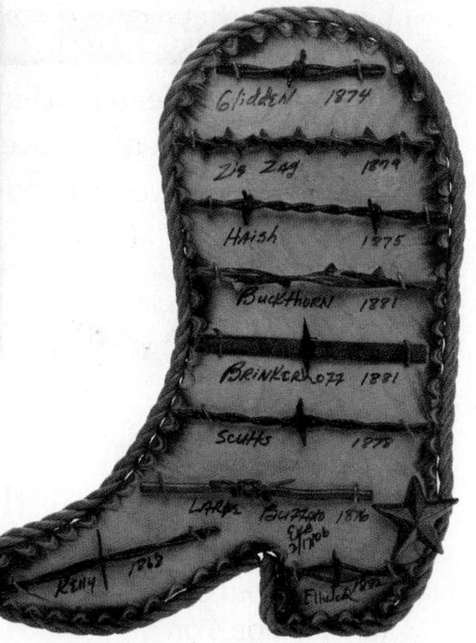

1876
About 2,700 animals die during a cattle stampede near the Brazos River.

1882
A ranch in the Panhandle purchases enough barbed wire to fence 250,000 acres.

1876 — **1880** — **1884** — **1888**

1876
Wyatt Earp and Bat Masterson work as law officers in the cattle town of Dodge City, Kansas.

1880
Up to 21,000 cattle go through the Union Stockyards in Chicago every day.

1886
Cowboys in Wyoming Territory stage a labor strike to protest a pay cut.

You Be the Historian

myNotebook

What's Your Opinion? Do you **agree** or **disagree** with the following statements? Support your point of view in your notebook.

- **Culture** A region's culture is always dominated by its most important industries.
- **Economics** Events in one region rarely affect other regions economically.
- **Science, Technology & Society** New technologies negatively affect existing industries.

Section 1

Early Cattle Ranching

Main Ideas

1. The Texas cattle industry grew from the ranchos established by the Spanish in the 1700s.
2. The longhorn was uniquely suited for the hot, dry Texas climate.
3. The Civil War increased demand for Texas cattle.

Key Terms

- **brands**
- **cattle drives**
- **rustlers**
- **longhorn**
- **Texas fever**

Why It Matters Today

People have been ranching in Texas for about 300 years. Use current events sources to learn more about the modern-day livestock industry.

TEKS: 1B, 5B, 6B, 9C, 10B, 13A, 13B, 21A, 21B, 21C, 22A

myNotebook

Use the annotation tools in your eBook to take notes on early cattle ranching in Texas.

The Story Continues

In the late 1870s brothers James and Bob Cator moved to the Panhandle and bought a herd of cattle. There were already many ranches in the area, and cattle herds often intermingled. To keep their animals separated, many ranchers built fences. When heavy blizzards struck the Panhandle in 1885, though, these fences kept the herds from moving south to escape the weather. Thousands of cattle—entire herds—died in an event known as the Big Die-Up. The Cator brothers and many other ranchers suffered huge losses.

VIDEO
Cattle Ranching
hmhsocialstudies.com

Spanish Beginnings

Ranching had been established in Texas long before the 1870s. The Spanish had established cattle ranchos, or ranches, in Mexico in the 1500s. By the early 1700s the Spanish were moving herds and flocks north onto pastures in the San Antonio and Guadalupe River valleys. These regions had a good climate and water supply, as well as plentiful grasses. Beginning in the 1750s a new ranching frontier was opened along the lower Rio Grande valley. Tomás Sánchez de la Berrera y Garza owned one of the largest ranches, which was located near Laredo. Martín de León owned another huge cattle ranch in present-day Victoria County. Rosa María Hinojosa de Ballí, who was the first cattle queen of Texas, controlled more than one million acres at the time of her death in 1803.

As the number of cattle ranches grew, disputes sometimes arose when ranchers lost track of which cattle they owned. The Spanish government began ordering cattle owners to put **brands**, or identification marks made with hot metal, on their cattle. For example, Martín de León's brand was EJ, which stood for Espíritu de Jesús, or "Spirit of Jesus." Tejano ranchers staged the first **cattle drives** in Texas, herding groups of cattle south of the Rio Grande to supply beef to Spanish military outposts. During the Revolutionary War, cattle from Texas supported Spanish and American armies in the Mississippi River valley and Gulf regions. Cattle ranching soon became an important part of the region's economy.

As U.S. settlers arrived in the early 1800s, ranching spread to other areas. Each region had its advantages. East Texas was relatively close to the cattle markets in New Orleans, while Central and South Texas had rich prairie grasses and moderate climates. After seeing the lush prairies, some U.S. settlers decided to become ranchers rather than farmers.

The Texas cattle industry slowly expanded in the 1840s. For example, Aaron Ashworth of Jefferson County had ranch holdings worth more than $30,000, or about $700,000 in today's dollars. Some Texans began driving cattle to out-of-state markets. James Taylor White began to drive cattle from Liberty County to market in New Orleans, and in 1846 Edward Piper took a herd of Texas cattle to Ohio. After gold was discovered in California, some Texans drove a number of cattle west to help feed the growing population of miners.

Despite the growth of the cattle industry, ranchers faced several challenges. Cattle **rustlers**, or thieves, threatened the herds. A bigger hurdle was access to markets. The demand for cattle within Texas was limited because of the region's fairly small population. Ranchers could herd their stock to sell outside of Texas, but it was a difficult and often dangerous process.

Reading Check **Sequencing** Describe in order the development of the cattle industry in Texas from its Spanish beginnings.

Interpreting Visuals

Ranch life. *Ranchers had to protect their herds from dangerous animals such as bears.* ***What tools and techniques are these vaqueros using?***

Vaqueros and Cowboys

Vaqueros were the first cowboys in Texas. Most were skilled ropers and riders. Over time, Spanish practices combined with the practices of U.S. settlers to create a Texas cowboy tradition. It's not uncommon to see Texans wearing cowboy fashions, particularly boots and hats. Museums and events around the state celebrate vaqueros and cowboys. For example, the Texas Cowboy Reunion in Stamford features wild-horse races. **How have cowboys influenced the culture of Texas?**

The Longhorn

During the 1800s longhorn beef fed thousands of Texans. Cowboys munched on jerky, or beef that has been dried in the sunshine. Other Texans ate beefsteaks fried in tallow, or grease. A poem described the longhorn's role in Texas history.

"Other states are carved
or born;
Texas grew from hide and
horn.
Other states are long or
wide;
Texas is a shaggy hide."

How did Texas grow "from hide and horn"?

The Texas Longhorns

During the mid-1800s the **longhorn** appeared in Texas. This new breed of cattle developed as Spanish breeds mixed with English cattle brought by U.S. settlers. The longhorns were well suited to life in Texas, thriving on its native grasses. These lean strong animals could endure hot weather as well as cold. They even ate prickly pear cacti during droughts and could survive on little water. In addition, longhorns were resistant to the cattle disease commonly called **Texas fever**.

While older longhorns weighed up to 1,600 pounds, some people said the longhorn had too little meat. They called it "8 pounds of hamburger on 800 pounds of bone and horn." However, long legs allowed longhorns to travel great distances, and their horns protected them from mountain lions, wolves, and other predators. Mature animals had enormous pointed horns—some were five or more feet across. Early Texas settlers displayed these horns on their walls. They made buttons, cups, decorations, furniture, and household utensils from the horns. They even stored gunpowder in hollowed-out horns. Few animals were as useful to people on the Texas frontier as the longhorn was.

The longhorns became more valuable as cattle ranching grew in the late 1850s. When the Civil War broke out, the demand for Texas beef increased rapidly. The Confederate army needed to feed the troops. However, as the war dragged on, Texans found it difficult to move their cattle to the front. By 1863 the Union army had blocked trade from Confederate states, including Texas. As a result, the number of cattle in Texas grew rapidly. By the end of the Civil War, about 5 million cattle roamed the state. Many of these animals were mavericks, or unclaimed cattle. After the war, Texans looked for new markets to sell their cattle.

Reading Check **Finding the Main Idea** Why were longhorn cattle important to the Texas cattle industry?

Section 1 Review

hmhsocialstudies.com
ONLINE QUIZ

1. Define and explain:
- brands
- cattle drives
- rustlers
- longhorn
- Texas fever

2. Analyzing Information
Use a chart to explain how the Texas cattle industry developed from its beginnings through the Civil War.

Cattle Ranching in Spanish Texas
↓
Early Ranching in Texas
↓
Ranching during the Civil War

3. Finding the Main Idea

a. How did physical factors influence the development of cattle ranching in Texas?

b. How did the migration of U.S. settlers to Texas affect the cattle industry?

4. Writing and Critical Thinking myWriteSmart

Drawing Inferences and Conclusions Imagine that you are an economist. Explain how free enterprise affected the Texas cattle industry. Consider the following:
- demand for cattle
- supply of cattle

Section 2

Texas Cattle Trails

Main Ideas

1. The growing market for beef was profitable for many Texas ranchers.
2. Some of the most well-traveled trails included the Sedalia, Chisholm, Western, and Goodnight-Loving trails.
3. Life on the trail was difficult and often dangerous.

Why It Matters Today

Texas cattle drivers had an on-the-move occupation. Use current events sources to learn more about jobs that involve travel today.

Key Terms and People

- **stockyards**
- **open range**
- **Sedalia Trail**
- **Chisholm Trail**
- **Western Trail**
- **Charles Goodnight**
- **remuda**
- **wrangler**

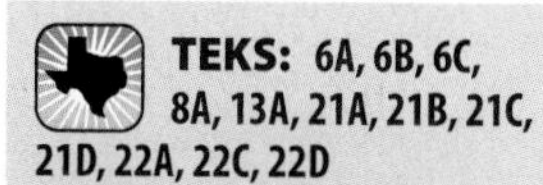

The Story Continues

Abilene was just a dusty Kansas town until a businessman named Joseph McCoy decided to build a cattle market there. He formed a giant Wild West show that traveled by train to advertise his operations. The show featured trick riders and ropers as well as a 2,300-pound buffalo. Every time the train stopped, the performers and animals went into action. The show thrilled spectators. As word spread, many cattle buyers from the northeastern United States came to Abilene.

myNotebook

Use the annotation tools in your eBook to take notes on Texas cattle trails and the expansion of the beef industry in Texas.

The Cattle Drives

Demand for beef outpaced supply in the Northeast. The region had a large population, and its cattle supply had been greatly reduced by the Civil War. But in Texas the supply of cattle was greater than the demand for beef. As a result, cattle that sold for $3 or $6 a head in Texas sold for $38 in Kansas or $80 in New York.

Such high prices convinced Texas ranchers that they could make large profits by raising more cattle. However, ranchers could not drive longhorns to eastern markets because of the distance and the many populated farm areas the herds would have to cross. By 1865, **stockyards**, or huge holding pens, and packing houses were opening in Chicago.

Longhorns could endure heat and cold and were resistant to diseases such as Texas fever, making the breed well suited to life in Texas and on the trail.

Soon, more beef-processing plants were built farther west, in St. Louis and Kansas City. These plants were built to prepare the beef for shipment to cities in the North and East. Railroads connected cities in midwestern states such as Missouri with the larger cities in the Northeast. To reach these additional markets, Texas ranchers needed a way to get their cattle to the nearest railroad lines.

Cattle drives provided the answer. During the fall and winter, cattle grazed on the **open range**, or unfenced lands, of Texas. One rancher wrote, "Cattle are permitted to range . . . over a large surface of the country, thirty, forty, and even fifty miles in extent [size]." As spring approached, cowboys gathered cattle together in a roundup. Cowboys caught as many mavericks as possible and branded them to establish ownership of the animals. When the grass turned green in the spring, cowboys drove the cattle north. Along the way, the cattle grazed on the open range.

During one large cattle drive in 1866, cowboys moved about 260,000 cattle north over the **Sedalia Trail**, which became known as the Shawnee Trail. This trail led from South Texas through Indian Territory to Sedalia, Missouri. Toward the end of the trail, problems arose. In Missouri and eastern Kansas, there was little open range left—much of the land was farmed. As the huge herds passed through, farmers' crops were sometimes trampled. The longhorns also infected many other cattle by giving them ticks that carried Texas fever. Farmers became angry as their cattle died. Kansas and Missouri had already passed laws in an attempt to stop the cattle drives, and farmers began to turn back the Texas herds. The future of Texas cattle drives seemed uncertain.

Reading Check **Identifying Cause and Effect** Why was there a national market for beef, and how did demand affect the Texas cattle industry?

★ The Chisholm and Western Trails

Entrepreneur Joseph McCoy stepped in with a solution. McCoy knew that rail lines were moving farther west—by early 1867 tracks were being built in Kansas. State legislators there passed a law allowing cattle drives west of farm areas. McCoy arranged for the building of a cattle market complete with holding pens and loading chutes in Abilene, Kansas. McCoy made many improvements to the small town. Before he began, Abilene was, in McCoy's words, "a very small dead place, consisting of about one dozen log huts." McCoy even bargained with the Kansas Pacific Railroad to get special rates for shipping cattle to Chicago. To drum up business, McCoy sent scouts southward to urge Texas ranchers to bring their cattle to Abilene.

In 1867, Texas cowboys herded about 35,000 longhorns over the **Chisholm Trail**. The route to Abilene was named after Jesse Chisholm, a fur trader. The child of a Cherokee woman, Chisholm blazed the original trail in the mid-1860s to trade with American Indians. His trail went through Indian Territory to Kansas. The Chisholm Trail was an ideal route for the Texas cattle drives because it was not near farms. Over the next few years, even more cowboys used this trail to move their herds to Abilene.

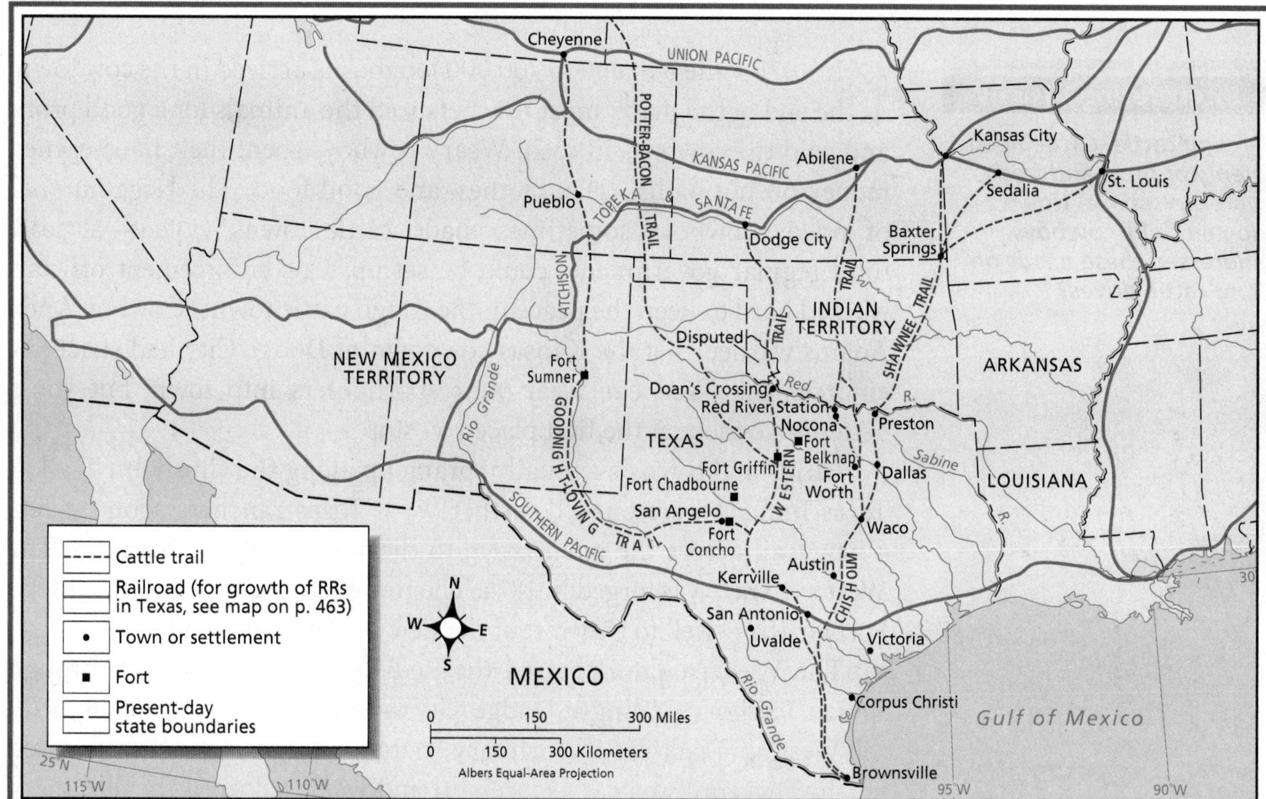

The Cattle Kingdom of Texas, 1865–1890

Interpreting Maps The use of cattle trails and railroads allowed Texas ranchers to sell their livestock in national markets.

Human Systems How did railroad technology and cattle drives encourage an interdependence between Texas ranching and out-of-state cattle markets?

Interpreting Visuals

Driving cattle. *Cattle need plenty of grass and fresh water to survive.* ***How do you think cowboys addressed these needs on long cattle drives?***

In 1871 some 600,000 to 700,000 longhorns arrived in the cow town. At the end of the drive, most ranchers sold the animals for a good profit and paid the cowboys in cash. Weary cowboys spent their hard-earned money on hot baths, clean clothes, and good food. The large number of rowdy cowboys sometimes made cattle towns violent—at least until regular governments could be set up. Law-enforcement officials worked hard to keep the peace in the rough cattle towns. Cowboy Andy Adams warned that the Kansas cow town of Dodge City had strict law enforcement. "You can wear your six-shooters into town, but you'd better leave them at the first place you stop."

Farms and towns eventually sprang up along the Chisholm Trail as Texas Indians were pushed farther west. Texas ranchers soon needed a new trail across the open range to the west of settled territory. The **Western Trail** was forged in 1874. The route ran north from Kerrville to Fort Griffin—well to the west of the new settlements.

The Western Trail crossed the Red River and continued through Indian Territory, ending at Dodge City in southwestern Kansas. By 1879 the Western Trail was the primary route for Texas cattle being moved north. This trail was very successful and was used until the closing of the open range.

Reading Check **Analyzing Information** Why did Texas ranchers stop using the Chisholm Trail and begin using the Western Trail?

★ The Goodnight-Loving Trail

Not all of the cattle drives ended at railroad stockyards in Kansas. Ranchers also saw opportunities to profit by supplying cattle to military posts, mining camps, and American Indian reservations. **Charles Goodnight** and Oliver Loving were two cattlemen who looked beyond the eastern markets. In 1866 Goodnight and Loving combined their herds and set out for Fort Sumner, New Mexico. Their route became known as the Goodnight-Loving Trail. The trail ran from Young County west of Fort Worth, through San Angelo, across West Texas, north through New Mexico, and into Colorado.

Over time, this trail became one of the most-traveled routes in the Southwest. Ranchers stopped using the trail when railroads came to Texas and eliminated the need for long cattle drives to rail lines. Cowboy H. P. Cook participated in many drives to American Indian reservations in the West. He described his experiences on one trip:

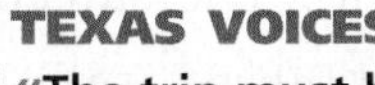

TEXAS VOICES

"The trip must have taken about six weeks going and returning. It was really tough, sleeping on the ground this trip, it was so wet and cold. I had just a couple of cotton quilts, and by morning there wasn't a dry thread in them, it was so wet. I used my saddle for a pillow. We would move the fire over and flop down on the ground where the fire had been, which would stay warm for a while."

—H. P. Cook, quoted in *Texas Cowboys*, edited by Jim Lanning

Reading Check **Finding the Main Idea** Why did Goodnight and Loving blaze a cattle trail?

BIOGRAPHY

Charles Goodnight

(1836–1929) Born in Illinois, Charles Goodnight moved with his family to Texas at age nine. As a young man, Goodnight entered the cattle business, managing a herd of wild cattle. In 1860 he served as a scout for the Texas Rangers. During the Civil War, he served in the Frontier Regiment, patrolling the Texas Panhandle. The knowledge he gained about the region was useful when he helped establish the JA Ranch. Goodnight soon became one of the most successful ranchers in Texas. **How did Goodnight's experiences help his ranching career?**

★ Life on the Trail

A typical cattle drive had 8 to 12 cowboys to care for 2,000 to 3,000 cattle. Mary Bunton, one of the few women to go on a trail drive, remembered the sight of so many cattle on the move. "I would turn in my saddle and look back, and it would look as if the entire face of the earth was just a moving mass of heads and horns."

All those cattle did not belong to just one rancher. Cowboys usually represented many ranchers and supervised many herds on each cattle drive. Some ranchers drove their own cattle, but most hired a drover, or a cattle drive operator. John Henry Stephens, a well-known drover, made large sums of money herding other people's cattle to market. Cattle-herding outfits also included a trail boss, or a drive leader.

Each cowboy used several horses in relays of two or three, so that a fresh mount was always available when needed. The herd of these animals was known as the **remuda**, the Spanish word for "remount." A professional horse handler called a **wrangler** cared for the crew's horses.

CONNECTING TO

Literature

Andy Adams and Cowboy Stories

Some cowboys wrote about their adventures on cattle drives. Andy Adams wrote *The Log of a Cowboy,* in which he recalled a common but dangerous event—a stampede. "The cattle jumped from the bed ground and were off like a shot." The cowboys managed to calm the cattle, but their horses were a different matter. "The horses . . . gave us a long, hard run." **What does *The Log of a Cowboy* reveal about the cowboys' way of life?**

The camp cook was another important member of the drive crew. Good food meant happy cowboys. The cook traveled ahead of the herd and had meals prepared when the rest of the outfit arrived. The cook's supplies were carried in the chuck wagon, or the covered supply wagon. A day on the trail began before sunrise. After a hot breakfast of bacon, beans, and biscuits, the cowboys would choose their horses from the remuda and start to move the cattle.

Two highly experienced cowboys called point men guided the herd, while other cowboys rode on the sides of the herd. Drag men traveled behind the herd. This was the drive's worst position because drag men "ate" dust the whole trip.

On a good day, the herd would move 15 to 18 miles. After hours in the saddle—about 5:00 P.M. or later—the crew stopped for the night. The dinner menu was usually beef or pork, but sometimes included "son-of-a-gun" stew. This thick soup was made from cow brain, heart, kidneys, liver, and tongue.

Trail drives were difficult and often dangerous. The sunshine was hot, and water was sometimes in short supply. Prairie fires swept across the plains, sometimes moving fast enough to overtake a cowboy on a galloping horse. Cowboys encountered bad weather, and rustlers tried to steal the livestock. In his diary, one cowboy described an unpleasant cattle drive.

Analyzing Primary Sources
Making Generalizations and Predictions Why might cowboys like George Duffield have continued to go on cattle drives despite the hardships?

TEXAS VOICES

"Awful night . . . not having a bit to eat for 60 hours . . . Tired. . . . Oh! what a night—Thunder Lightning & rain—we followed our Beeves [cattle] all night as they wandered about. . . . We Hauled cattle out of the Mud with oxen half the day. . . . My back is Blistered bad. . . . Found a Human skeleton on the Prairie to day."

—George Duffield, quoted in *The Cowboys,* by William H. Forbis

Reading Check **Categorizing** Who made up a typical cattle-driving crew, and what were their responsibilities?

Section 2 Review

hmhsocialstudies.com
ONLINE QUIZ

1. Define and explain:
- stockyards
- open range
- remuda
- wrangler

2. Identify and explain the historical significance of:
- Sedalia Trail
- Chisholm Trail
- Western Trail
- Charles Goodnight

3. Categorizing
Use a graphic organizer like the one below to show the four main trails and where they began and ended.

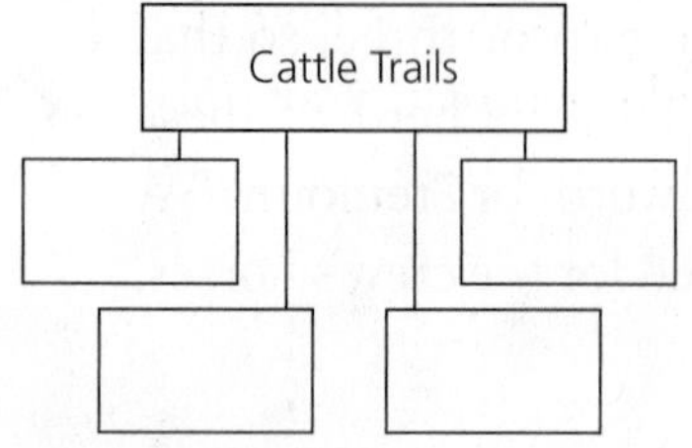

4. Finding the Main Idea

a. How did national demand for beef affect the cattle industry in Texas?

b. Explain how expansion on the frontier and railroads affected the different cattle trails.

5. Writing and Critical Thinking myWriteSmart

Summarizing Imagine that you are a cowboy on a cattle drive. Write a letter to a friend describing the realities of life on the trail.
Consider the following:
- your daily routine
- the many dangers on the trail

Section 3

Ranches, Ranchers, and Cowboys

Main Ideas

1. Ranching was a major industry in both South Texas and in the Panhandle.
2. Cowboys and ranchers had to fill many roles on a ranch.
3. Western novels and shows helped spread the myths of a carefree cowboy life.

Why It Matters Today

Cowboys worked hard on Texas ranches. Use current events sources to learn more about modern-day cowboys or other farmworkers.

Key Terms and People

- **Cattle Kingdom**
- **King Ranch**
- **windmills**
- **JA Ranch**
- **XIT Ranch**

TEKS: 6A, 6B, 9B, 10A, 10B, 19C, 20C, 21A, 21B, 22A, 22D

myNotebook

Use the annotation tools in your eBook to take notes on ranching and cowboy culture in Texas.

The Story Continues

Molly Goodnight, the wife of Texas rancher Charles Goodnight, loved to entertain. But visitors were rare on the isolated JA Ranch in the Panhandle. One evening a visiting cowboy brought three live chickens as a gift. He wanted Mrs. Goodnight to cook them, but she decided to keep them as pets. In a letter to her sister, she wrote, "You've no idea how much company a chicken can be."

★ Ranching in South Texas

During the 1800s the cattle ranches that arose on the open range from Texas to Canada formed the **Cattle Kingdom**. The **King Ranch** in South Texas was one of the most important cattle operations in the state. Richard King and Gideon Lewis established the ranch in Nueces County in the early 1850s. King died in 1885, leaving his wife to run the ranch.

Henrietta King and her son-in-law, Robert Kleberg, built the King Ranch into a thriving operation. By 1925 it included more than 1 million acres of land. King used her wealth to develop South Texas. She gave land for the towns of Kingsville and Raymondville, and she donated land and money for churches and schools. King also helped establish Texas A&M University–Kingsville.

★ Texas Cities ★

Amarillo and Lubbock

History: Businesspeople established Amarillo in 1887. It boomed as a large cattle-shipping location. Ranchers and farmers settled the general area of present-day Lubbock in the 1870s. The town was formed in 1890.

Amarillo population in 2012: 195,250 (est.)

Lubbock population in 2012: 236,065 (est.)

Relative location: Northwest Texas

Region: Panhandle

County: Amarillo is the county seat of Potter County, and Lubbock is the county seat of Lubbock County.

Origin of Name: Spanish herders called the area Amarillo *amarillo,* or "yellow," to describe the local soil and flowers. The county of Lubbock was founded in 1876 and named for Thomas S. Lubbock, a Texas Ranger and Civil War veteran.

Economy: Amarillo relies on ranching, oil, and manufacturing. Lubbock has industrial, technological, and agricultural businesses. Lubbock is the home of Texas Tech University. Lubbock is also a leading cotton producer.

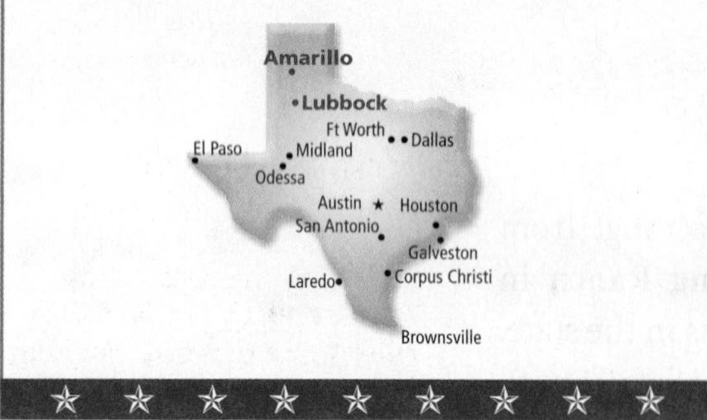

Other large ranches developed in South Texas, where the climate was well suited to cattle ranching. Manuel Guerra owned a large ranch in Starr County. Like King and other big ranchers, Guerra was an important leader in South Texas. Another successful South Texas rancher, Margaret Borland, owned more than 10,000 cattle by 1873. That same year she led a trail drive to Kansas. Borland is believed to be the only woman ever to head up a trail drive.

Reading Check **Analyzing Information** How did cattle ranchers like Henrietta King affect the social development of Texas towns?

★ Ranches in the Panhandle

By the early 1880s cattle ranching was a thriving and profitable industry in many parts of Texas. As Plains Indians were removed from West Texas, the Panhandle was opened up for ranching. The grass that covered the plains provided plenty of food for the cattle. In addition, the region's flat open land was well suited for cattle ranching because it allowed ranchers to keep close watch on the livestock. Although there were not enough rivers to water the cattle, the Ogallala Aquifer lay underneath the region. Ranchers adapted to the environment by using **windmills** to reach this huge supply of water. Windmills operate on a simple principle. The wind blows against a vane that turns the blades into the breeze. The wind then hits the blades, creating power to operate a pump. This power brings underground water to the surface.

In the mid-1870s Charles Goodnight and John Adair established one of the first ranches in the Panhandle—the **JA Ranch** in Palo Duro Canyon. Goodnight and Adair had moved their herd into the canyon soon after Colonel Ranald Mackenzie and his forces cleared out the Comanches and Kiowas during the Battle of Palo Duro Canyon in 1874.

Palo Duro Canyon had a good supply of grass and offered shelter from the harsh winds that swept across the region. The JA Ranch became large and successful. By the mid-1880s it covered more than 700,000 acres and supported about 40,000 cattle. Other pioneers also established ranches in the Panhandle. Thomas Sherman Bugbee built the Quarter Circle T Ranch in

Hutchinson County. Another large ranch, the Matador, was founded in 1878. These ranches helped bring prosperity to the Panhandle.

Corporations, often funded by investors from the northern United States and from Great Britain, moved into the Panhandle along with the ranchers. The **XIT Ranch** was established in 1885 when the state gave the land to the Capitol Freehold Land and Investment Company. This company was funded by investors from Chicago and Britain. In return, the investors agreed to construct a new state capitol building to replace the one that had burned in 1881. The new capitol was completed in Austin in 1888 and is still the seat of Texas government.

Over time, the XIT Ranch became one of the largest and most famous ranches in Texas. The XIT covered about 3 million acres, extending nearly 200 miles along the Texas–New Mexico border—an area almost the size of Connecticut. At its peak, the XIT employed about 150 cowboys to care for roughly 150,000 cattle.

Reading Check **Summarizing** Why did ranching develop in the Panhandle, and what are some of ranching's political legacies?

The XIT Ranch

The ranch took its name from the XIT brand that a drover created. The block letters made it difficult for cattle rustlers to change. Some people disagree with this story about the ranch's name, however. They claim—because the roman numeral X stands for 10—that XIT stood for "ten In Texas," or the 10 counties that contained the ranchland. Other people argue that it stood for "biggest in Texas."

★ Ranchers and Cowboys

Most Texas ranches were located far from towns. Ranchers had to rely on their own resources to solve the many challenges they faced. Mary Jaques outlined the skills needed by ranchers. "The ideal ranchman must be butcher, baker, carpenter, . . . blacksmith, plain cook, milker." Female ranchers handled many tasks. In addition to herding and branding livestock, they raised children and operated households. Mrs. C. C. West helped manage a sheep ranch in West Texas. She remembered "living under a tree, herding sheep with my babe in my arms and using one big skillet for a whole kitchen outfit."

Image Credit: E.E. Smith Photo Collection, Library of Congress

Interpreting Visuals

Ranch life. *Cowboys who worked on Texas ranches had many jobs, including training horses and branding cattle.* ***What traditional cowboy clothing are these ranch workers wearing?***

CONNECTING TO

The Arts

Western Artists

In this painting, *Roping a Steer,* artist and former cowboy Edward Borein shows a cowboy at work. Roping cattle was an essential skill for cowboys. **How does this painting capture the difficulty of roping a running steer?**

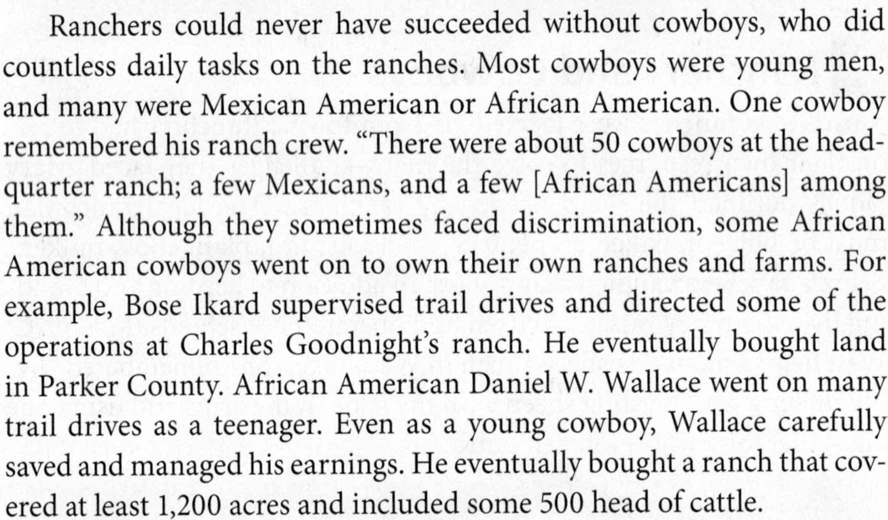

Ranchers could never have succeeded without cowboys, who did countless daily tasks on the ranches. Most cowboys were young men, and many were Mexican American or African American. One cowboy remembered his ranch crew. "There were about 50 cowboys at the headquarter ranch; a few Mexicans, and a few [African Americans] among them." Although they sometimes faced discrimination, some African American cowboys went on to own their own ranches and farms. For example, Bose Ikard supervised trail drives and directed some of the operations at Charles Goodnight's ranch. He eventually bought land in Parker County. African American Daniel W. Wallace went on many trail drives as a teenager. Even as a young cowboy, Wallace carefully saved and managed his earnings. He eventually bought a ranch that covered at least 1,200 acres and included some 500 head of cattle.

Texas cowboys wore clothes and used tools that were suited to the state's environment. Some cowboys wore the familiar cowboy hat, while others wore the vaqueros' broad felt hat. Many cowboys wore sombreros to protect themselves from the harsh sunlight and rain. Cowboys relied on leather chaps, from the Spanish *chaparreras,* worn over their pants to protect them from thorny brushes. All cowboys used a long light rope called a lariat, from the Spanish *la reata*. Cowboys sometimes called their ropes "lassos" instead of lariats. The word *lasso* came from the Spanish word *lazo.* These and other terms reflect the Spanish heritage of ranching in Texas.

VIDEO
Cowboy Tech

hmhsocialstudies.com

Reading Check **Finding the Main Idea** Identify examples of Spanish influence on vocabulary that originated in Texas cattle ranching.

★ Cowboy Culture

Over time, cowboys became an important part of American popular culture. Inexpensive novels featured countless cowboy heroes such as Arizona Joe, Denver Dan, and Fancy Frank. The novels glorified cowboy life. Wild West shows were also popular, using colorful posters to attract large crowds. Some people believed that western novels and shows accurately portrayed cowboy life. According to the myths, cowboys were fearless, happy, and worry free. They spent their days roaming through rugged but gorgeous landscapes.

The realities of cowboy life were far different from the myths. Cowboys faced many dangers, including blizzards, floods, and stampedes. These hazards injured and killed many cowboys. Cowboys also worked hard for hours on end. During trail drives, some cowboys rode 24 hours at a stretch and slept in their saddles. For their work most cowboys earned salaries of about $300 per year. Cowboy Charles Siringo worked for the Rancho Grande Company for two years without receiving a regular paycheck. After subtracting his purchases at the ranch store, he earned just 75 cents for two years. Some, like Siringo, found it very difficult to make ends meet after buying what they needed for work.

TEXAS VOICES

"We had unlimited credit at the company store. My credit was stretched almost to the breaking point in purchasing a cowboy outfit, such as saddle, bridle, spurs, pistol, bowie-knife, bedding, sombrero, silk handkerchiefs, slicker, high-heel boots, etc."

—Charles Siringo, *A Lone Star Cowboy*

Reading Check **Contrasting** How did the myths differ from the realities of the cowboy way of life?

CONNECTING TO Music

Cowboy Songs

Cattle were nervous creatures, particularly at night, so cowboys sang to help keep them calm and peaceful. Some trail bosses even auditioned cowboys before hiring them. Cowboy songs were often slow and sad. Cattle seemed to like these soothing tunes. "The Old Chisholm Trail" was one popular song.

"I'm up in the mornin'
afore daylight
And afore I sleep the
moon shines bright.
Oh, it's bacon and beans
most every day–
I'd as soon be a-eatin'
prairie hay."

Why might the "The Old Chisholm Trail" have been soothing to cowboys as well as their cattle?

★ Section 3 Review

hmhsocialstudies.com ONLINE QUIZ

1. **Define and explain:**
   - windmills
2. **Identify and explain** the historical significance of:
   - Cattle Kingdom
   - King Ranch
   - JA Ranch
   - XIT Ranch
3. **Categorizing** Use a graphic organizer to identify some of the myths and realities of cowboy life that became part of Texas culture.

Myths

Realities

4. **Finding the Main Idea**
   a. In what parts of the state was ranching a big industry, and why did ranches develop there?
   b. List examples of the Spanish influence on vocabulary related to cattle ranching in Texas.
5. **Writing and Critical Thinking** *my*WriteSmart
   Analyzing Information Write an advertisement that encourages ranchers to establish operations in the Panhandle. Consider the following:
   - the availability of land and water
   - innovations such as the windmill

Section 4

The Closing of the Open Range

Main Ideas

1. The use of barbed wire led to the closing of the open range and to range wars.
2. Overgrazing and heavy use of ranch land helped contribute to the decline of the Cattle Kingdom.

Key Terms and People

- **Joseph F. Glidden**
- **barbed wire**
- **range wars**

Why It Matters Today

Technological innovations changed the Texas frontier. Use current events sources to learn more about new technology and scientific discoveries that affect the world today.

TEKS: 6A, 6B, 6D, 8A, 8B, 9C, 10A, 17C, 20C, 20D, 21B, 21C, 21E, 21H, 22A, 22C, 22D

myNotebook

Use the annotation tools in your eBook to take notes on the decline of the Cattle Kingdom and the close of the open range in Texas.

The Story Continues

John Warne Gates, an eager salesman, saw a golden opportunity to increase sales of barbed wire in Texas. In 1878 he held a demonstration in downtown San Antonio to advertise his product. Gates fenced a holding pen with barbed wire and stocked it with a herd of wild longhorns. Although the longhorns were strong and mean, the barbed wire held them back. The crowds were very impressed, and sales of barbed wire in Texas skyrocketed.

★ Fencing the Open Range

Farmers moving into West Texas wanted to fence their land to protect their crops from stray cattle. Some ranchers also tried to fence in their land. But building long fences was difficult because wood was scarce on the open plains. **Joseph F. Glidden**, a farmer in De Kalb, Illinois, answered this challenge. In 1873 he developed **barbed wire**, a type of wire fencing designed with sharp points, or barbs, at intervals along its length. The wire was strung between fence posts, and the barbs kept cattle off the fences without hurting the animals. Glidden quickly opened a factory to make his product. Soon, inexpensive barbed wire was readily available. The sharp wire fences even survived the strong Texas winds. One advertisement described barbed wire as "light as air . . . and cheap as dirt."

Many people, particularly small-scale ranchers, disliked the idea of fencing the range. Over time, however, the idea became more popular. The new invention made large-scale fencing both easy and inexpensive. By the end of the 1880s, there were barbed-wire fences in nearly every Texas county. This marked the end of the open range in Texas and the close of the frontier.

Reading Check **Identifying Cause and Effect** What innovation was widely used in the 1880s, and how did it affect the use of land?

★ The Range Wars

Widespread fencing led to conflict in Texas in the early 1880s. Owners of small properties complained that they were being surrounded by the fences of giant cattle companies. Fencing became so extensive that public roads were blocked and mail delivery was interrupted. Many large ranchers fenced off water sources even though they did not own the land. Ranchers who let their cattle roam free complained that fencing cut their cattle off from water sources.

This issue became critical when Texas was hit by a drought in 1883 and cattle began to die of thirst. Under the cover of darkness, ranchers would snip the barbed-wire fences. Before long, **range wars** broke out. A Gainesville farmer found a note that read, "If you don't make gates, we will make them for you."

In Coleman County, cutters destroyed 500 miles of barbed-wire fences. Other ranchers, usually wealthy cattle operators, struck back. They hired guards to protect their fences, and gunfights sometimes broke out. After seeing several of her fences destroyed, rancher Mabel Day brought the issue of fence cutting before the state legislature.

Fence cutting soon became an important political issue. In 1884 Governor John Ireland called an emergency session of the legislature. After heated debate, it passed a law making fence cutting illegal. The law also required a gate in every three miles of fence to allow passage for roads and railroads. In addition, the law banned people from fencing land they did not own or lease. The governor sent out the Texas Rangers to enforce the law.

Cattle ranchers also came into conflict with sheep ranchers. The Spanish had introduced sheep ranching to Texas in the early 1700s. By the time of the range wars, most sheep ranching in Texas took place in the state's southern and western regions. In general, sheep were raised for their wool rather than for meat. Many cattle ranchers resented the presence of sheep ranchers in Texas. They were angry because sheep ate grass all the way to the root, making land useless for cattle.

Reading Check **Analyzing Information** How did the ranchers' use of fencing spark a political controversy?

Interpreting Visuals

Sheep ranching. *As sheep ranching expanded in the late 1800s, many Mexican Americans worked as* pastores, *or herders, on Texas ranches.* ***In what ways do you think sheep ranching is similar to and different from cattle ranching?***

CONNECTING TO

SCIENCE AND TECHNOLOGY

Barbed Wire and Windmills

Barbed wire consists of two wires. The first wire is long. The second is cut into short sharp pieces that are twisted around the long portion. The wire is very effective at keeping livestock in or out of fields. Inventors tinkered with windmills by adding a vane to allow the windmill's wheel to turn into the wind. This ensured that the wheel would turn whenever a breeze was present, continuously pumping water. **How did these technical innovations affect Texas?**

★ Legacy of the Open Range

Toward the end of the 1880s the open range began to disappear. After the introduction of windmills, farmers and their crops were expanding onto the plains. Sheep ranching was also expanding in the late 1800s. Greater demand for woolen textiles in New England led to a rise in wool prices. Texas ranchers, particularly in regions with dry climates and more-rugged land, began to turn to sheep herding. Many cattle ranchers resented these changes.

The cattle industry changed in other ways as well. Severe winters in the 1880s caused the death of thousands of open-range cattle and thus cut down on the number of cattle drives. Many ranches went out of business. A number of ranchers had expanded too quickly and allowed overgrazing of their land to occur. Years of heavy use had stripped the grass and damaged the soil itself. Some cattle operators sold their land to farmers. These new trends limited job opportunities for cowboys. In addition, the extension of railroad lines to Texas eventually ended the need for long cattle drives. Newly invented refrigerator cars could move processed beef to eastern cities. Large ranches remained, but the era of the open range was over.

Despite the decline of the cattle era, the industry created an important legacy in Texas. Throughout the world, people associate Texas with cowboys and cattle ranchers, and many Texans still raise and sell cattle. In addition, tourists visit Texas to watch rodeos and tour cattle operations such as the King Ranch. Cattle ranching continues to contribute to the state's economy. In 2010, for example, the total value of cattle production in the state was over $6 billion.

Reading Check Summarizing What two technological innovations came to the open range, and how did they affect the cattle industry?

Section 4 Review

1. **Define and explain:**
   - barbed wire
   - range wars
2. **Identify and explain** the historical significance of:
   - Joseph F. Glidden
3. **Identifying Cause and Effect** Copy the graphic organizer below. Use it to explain what innovations came into use in the 1870s and 1880s and how they influenced the development of Texas.

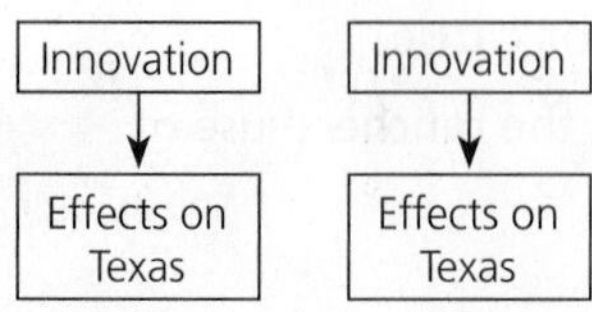

4. **Finding the Main Idea**
   - **a.** How did the development of the railroad affect the Texas cattle industry?
   - **b.** How did ranchers' use of land contribute to the decline of the Cattle Kingdom?
5. **Writing and Critical Thinking** *my* WriteSmart
   Supporting a Point of View Imagine that you are a Texas rancher who either supports or opposes fencing the open range. Write a letter to your neighbor expressing your viewpoint.
   Consider the following:
   - the economic consequences of fencing
   - the political consequences of fencing

Connecting To

Geography

The Texas Ranching Industry

Cattle and sheep ranching were important to the state's economy in the 1800s. These industries are still important in Texas. Today there are more than 130,000 cattle ranches and 7,000 sheep and lamb ranches in Texas.

Ranching in Texas

Geography **Skills**

Interpreting Thematic Maps

1. In what region of Texas are most cattle raised?
2. In what region of Texas are most goats and sheep raised?
3. Use the information in the table to create a bar graph showing the growth in the cattle population in Texas.
4. What was the increase in the number of cattle in Texas between 1840 and 1850?
5. How many more cattle were raised in Texas in 2010 than in 1860?

The Cattle Boom in Texas

YEAR	NUMBER OF CATTLE
1840	124,397
1850	917,524
1860	3.8 million
2010	13.3 million

CHAPTER 21 REVIEW

The Chapter at a Glance

Examine the following visual summary of the chapter. Then use the visual to create flash cards about the chapter. Use the flash cards to drill with a partner.

The use of barbed wire and windmills closed the open range and allowed farming to develop in West Texas.

Once stockyards were established along rail lines, ranchers could ship their cattle to eastern markets.

Cowboys and vaqueros rounded up cattle and drove them along trails to markets out of state.

The Spanish introduced ranching to Texas.

Identifying People and Ideas

Write a sentence to explain the role or significance of each of the following terms or people.

1. brands
2. cattle drives
3. longhorn
4. Texas fever
5. Chisholm Trail
6. Charles Goodnight
7. remuda
8. XIT Ranch
9. Joseph F. Glidden
10. range wars

Understanding Main Ideas

Section 1

1. How was the Texas cattle industry affected by the migration of U.S. settlers to Texas?
2. How did physical factors influence the development of ranching in Texas?

Section 2

3. Which cattle trails did Texas cowboys use, and what were cattle drives like?

Section 3

4. How did the innovation of the windmill affect the development of the Texas Panhandle?
5. Describe the Spanish influence on the vocabulary of Texas cattle ranching.

Section 4

6. How did barbed wire lead to political conflict in Texas?

You Be the Historian

Reviewing Themes

1. **Culture** Describe some myths and realities of cowboy life.
2. **Economics** How did demand for beef in the eastern United States affect the Texas cattle industry?
3. **Science, Technology & Society** How did the invention of windmills and barbed wire affect the Texas cattle industry?

Thinking Critically

1. **Sequencing** Trace in order the development of the Texas cattle industry from its Spanish beginnings to the Cattle Kingdom.
2. **Analyzing Information** In what ways did cattle ranchers adapt to and modify the environment, and what were some of the consequences?
3. **Summarizing** What were some of the defining characteristics of the cattle era in Texas history?

Texas Test Practice

Interpreting Maps

Study the map below. Then use the information on the map to help you answer the questions that follow.

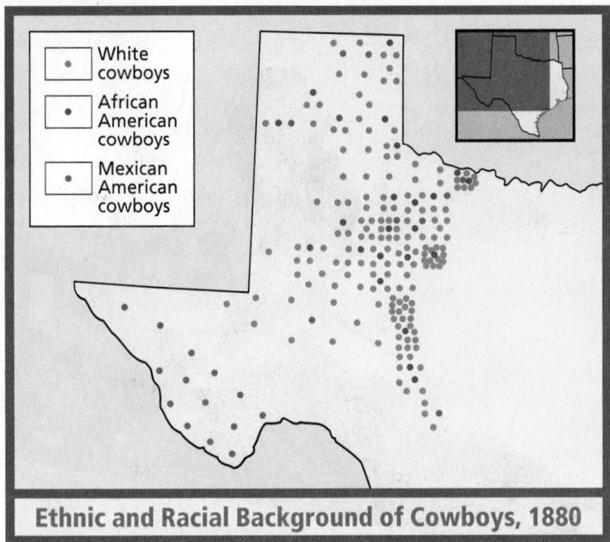

Ethnic and Racial Background of Cowboys, 1880

1. Which group of cowboys worked mostly in the far west region of Texas?

A white cowboys
B African American cowboys
C Mexican American cowboys
D All of the above

2. Why do you think these cowboys worked in that region of Texas?

Analyzing Primary Sources

Read the following song written by cowboy E. C. "Teddy Blue" Abbott. Then answer the questions.

"As I was out walking one morning for pleasure,
I spied a cowpuncher come riding along.
His hat was throwed back and his spurs were a-janglin',
And as he rode by he was singing this song:

'Whoopee ti yi yo—git along along little dogies,
It's your misfortune, and none of my own.
Whoopee ti yi yo—get along little dogies,
You know that Wyoming will be your new home.'

Early in the springtime we'll round up the dogies,
Slap on their brands, and bob off their tails;
Round up our horses, load up the chuck wagon,
Then throw those dogies upon the trail."

3. Which of the following events was E. C. "Teddy Blue" Abbott describing?

F a cattle drive
G a group of calves going to their mothers
H a line of dogs beginning to hunt foxes
J a Wild West show

4. What do you think the cowpuncher meant when he sang, "It's your misfortune, and none of my own"?

Cooperative Learning

Work with a small group to research primary and secondary sources on cattle ranching. These resources may include databases, media and news services, biographies, interviews, and artifacts. Use the sources to create an oral or multimedia presentation about the Texas cattle industry in the 1800s. Consider the myths and realities of cowboy life, technological innovations, cattle drives, and the political, economic, or social effects of the industry. Deliver your presentation to the class.

Internet Activity

Conduct internet research on the King Ranch and boom-and-bust cycles in the ranching industry today. Create an illustrated time line that shows how the King Ranch has changed since it was founded. Be sure to trace the cycles of boom and bust and its effects on ranching. Use the time line to create a quiz and answer key about ranching in Texas.

CHAPTER 22

Railroads and Farming

(1870–1900)

Texas Essential Knowledge and Skills (TEKS) 1A, 6A, 6C, 6D, 7B, 8A, 9A, 9B, 9C, 10A, 10B, 11A, 12A, 12B, 13A, 13B, 20A, 20C, 20D, 20E, 21A, 21B, 21C, 21D, 21H, 22A, 22D

Early Texas locomotives provided a reliable and inexpensive form of transportation.

TEXAS

1870 Texas has 583 miles of rail lines.

1876 The Texas legislature passes a law that allows the state to fund railroads with land grants.

1881 The Texas and Pacific Railway meets the Southern Pacific line near El Paso, forming the first transcontinental railroad route through Texas.

1870 — 1874 — 1878 — 1882

U.S. and WORLD

1875 The Huber Manufacturing Company, which builds threshers and other farm machinery, is incorporated.

1880 American farmers grow almost $325 million worth of cotton.

1882 Thomas Edison installs electrical power plants in New York City and London.

If you were there . . .

How would the growth of railroads change your life?

Build on What You Know

Soon after cattle ranchers settled on the Texas frontier, railroads and farmers began to press westward. The growth of farming and railroads helped spur economic progress in Texas. New businesses and technologies boomed in Texas and changed life in the state.

Railroad conductors relied on watches to keep trains on time.

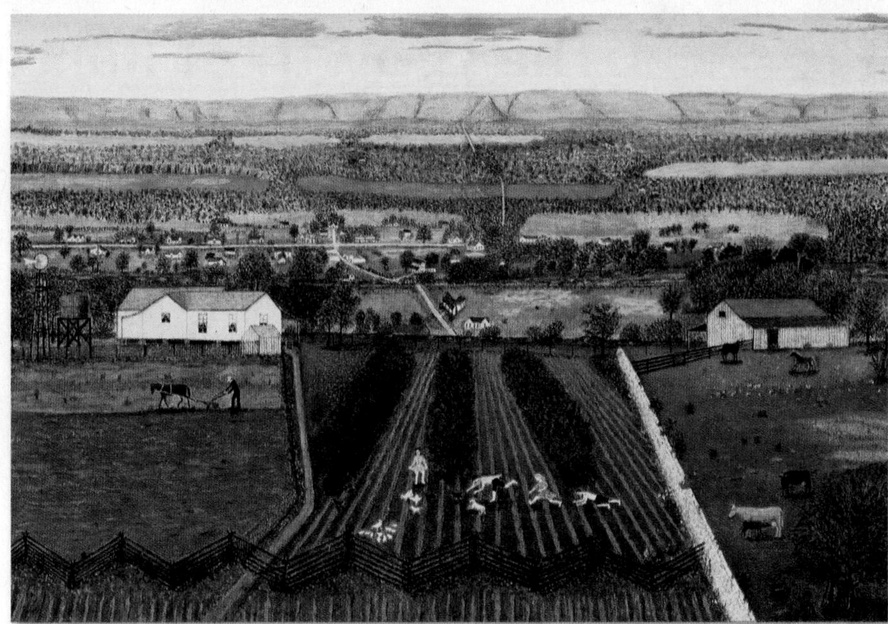

With new technology such as the windmill, Texas farms became more productive.

1886
The Knights of Labor begin a major strike against Jay Gould's railroad company.

1889
There are more than 8,000 miles of railroad track in Texas.

1891
The Texas Railroad Commission is established to regulate railroads in Texas.

1900
Texas has more than 350,000 farms, and almost half of all farmers are tenant farmers.

1886 — 1890 — 1894 — 1898

1886
A labor rally in Chicago's Haymarket Square erupts in violence.

1892
The first gasoline-powered tractor is developed in Waterloo, Iowa.

1900
There are more than 5.7 million farms in the United States.

You Be the Historian

*my*Notebook

What's Your Opinion? Do you **agree** or **disagree** with the following statements? Support your point of view in your notebook.

- **Geography** The settlement of frontier land is only possible with new technologies.
- **Science, Technology & Society** The growth of industries is dependent on new transportation technologies.
- **Economics** Only in recent times has national and international demand for agricultural goods driven local economies.

Section 1

The Growth of Railroads

Main Ideas

1. Rail travel was faster and more reliable than other forms of transportation in Texas.
2. Railroads brought trade and businesses to many towns.
3. The expansion of railroads led to the development of the Texas frontier.

Key Terms

- **transcontinental railroad**
- **junctions**

Why It Matters Today

Railroads brought an economic boom to many towns. Use current events sources to learn about transportation in Texas today.

TEKS: 6A, 6C, 8A, 9A, 9B, 11A, 12A, 12B, 20A, 20C, 21B, 21C, 21H, 22A

myNotebook

Use the annotation tools in your eBook to take notes on the growth of railroad transportation in Texas.

The Story Continues

On Christmas morning in 1871, hundreds of people gathered outside of Austin. They hoped to get a glimpse of the first locomotive to enter the capital city. By mid-afternoon the crowd had moved to the downtown terminal. Officials hammered in the last spike of the railroad line as Austinites cheered. The crowd celebrated the completion of the rail line connecting Austin with Houston and Galveston.

★ New Railroad Lines

Many Texans eagerly awaited the arrival of rail lines, hoping they would spur economic growth. The state's economic development had been slowed by its transportation problems. Most Texas rivers were either too shallow or too unreliable for shipping goods, and dirt roads turned to mud during wet weather.

As a result, moving people and goods was time-consuming and expensive. Railroads promised cheap, fast, and reliable transportation. A 35-mile trip that took a day and a half to travel by horse took less than two hours by rail. It was also cheaper to ship goods by railroad than by wagon. In the 1870s wagon freight rates averaged $1 for every 100 pounds shipped 100 miles, while railroad rates were less than 50 cents for the same amount over the same distance.

In 1861 there were about 470 miles of rail lines in Texas. However, the Civil War interrupted plans for new railroad construction. At the end of the decade, Texas continued to lag behind the rest of the country, which had almost 53,000 miles of track in 1870. The United States even had a **transcontinental railroad**—one that runs across a continent.

Community leaders in Texas offered to fund, or help pay for, railroad construction. Many cities issued bonds to help pay for rail construction. A bond is a certificate that represents money owed by an entity such as the government to the person who purchased the bond. San Antonio had issued the first Texas railroad bonds in 1850. Between 1850 and 1876, Texas cities and counties issued about $2.4 million in railroad bonds.

The Constitution of 1876 banned these local bonds but allowed the legislature to pass a general land grant law. For every continuous mile of track completed, a company could receive 16 square miles of land. The railroads were required to sell the land to finance surveying and construction of their lines. Texas eventually gave more than 32 million acres of land to more than 40 railroad companies.

Reading Check **Comparing and Contrasting** List the advantages of railroads over other forms of transportation in Texas.

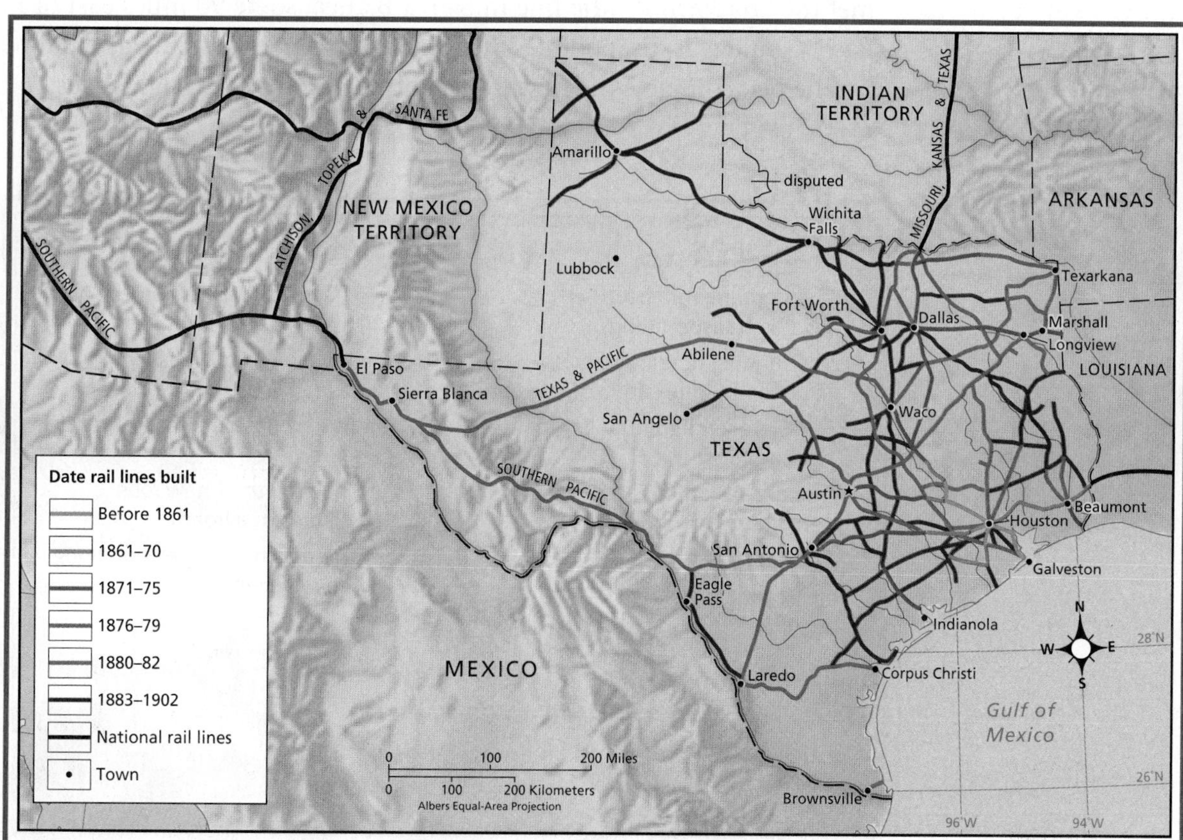

The Growth of Railroads, 1860–1902

Interpreting Maps Railroads allowed Texas farmers to ship goods to markets faster and at less cost and carried imports of construction materials and supplies to western parts of the state.

Environment and Society How do you think railroads affected the development of the Texas frontier?

The Railroad Boom

Land grants and other forms of government aid helped create a Texas railroad boom. In the early 1870s the Houston and Texas Central Railway (H&TC) built a line from Galveston to Dallas and Denison. At Denison, it met the Missouri, Kansas, and Texas line, which provided service north to St. Louis, Missouri. Between 1876 and 1879, railroad companies laid more than 750 miles of track in Texas.

During the boom, railroad companies began a race west. The Southern Pacific was building a rail line from California to Texas. Other railroad companies competed to meet the Southern Pacific first. The company with the most miles of track would profit by receiving the largest government land grants and the biggest share of business. The Galveston, Harrisburg, and San Antonio Railway Company (GH&SA) had already built a line from Galveston to San Antonio. The line eventually earned the nickname the Sunset Route. In 1881 GH&SA work crews started building a line west from San Antonio toward El Paso. However, the Texas and Pacific Railway (T&P) had a jump on the GH&SA. Jay Gould, a national-railroad owner, had bought the T&P and begun construction on a westward route. In December 1881 the T&P met the Southern Pacific line in Sierra Blanca, some 90 miles east of El Paso. Gould was disappointed that his line did not reach El Paso, but he had helped complete the first transcontinental route through Texas.

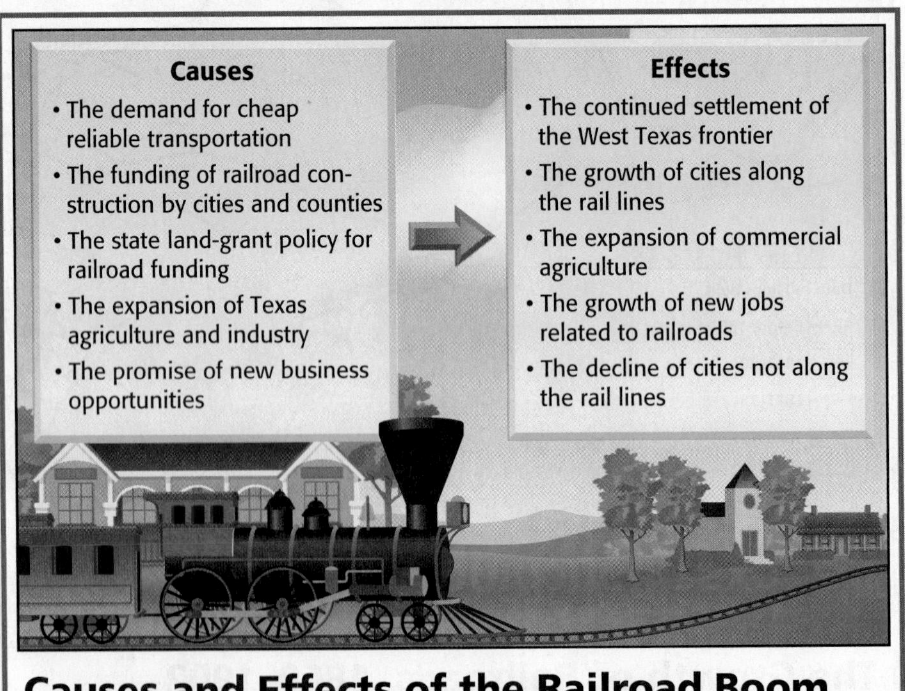

Causes and Effects of the Railroad Boom

Interpreting Charts The railroad boom was spurred by public funding and demand. The boom affected the economic development of Texas. How did the railroad industry affect city growth?

Texas railroad companies also encouraged trade between Texas and Mexico by running lines to the Mexican border. In the early 1880s the International and Great Northern Railway extended its line from San Antonio to Laredo. The Panhandle was one of the last regions to receive rail service. The Fort Worth and Denver City Railway (FW&DC) began construction north of Fort Worth in 1881. New towns such as Amarillo emerged along the railroad stops in the Panhandle. Many of these towns boomed with the business that the railroads brought. Between 1879 and 1889, railroad crews laid 6,000 miles of track in Texas.

Reading Check **Drawing Inferences and Conclusions** Why did railroads compete to build lines in Texas, and how did they help expand settlement on the Texas frontier?

GLOBAL CONNECTIONS

Immigrant Labor

Many Chinese immigrated to the United States and found work building railroads. The first group of Chinese to arrive in Texas, some 250 people, came in 1870. More Chinese immigrated after a three-year drought struck China in 1876. In 1881 approximately 2,600 Chinese workers arrived to build the Southern Pacific line east from El Paso. U.S. railroad companies, including the Southern Pacific, also encouraged Mexican immigration to help fill their labor needs, and the majority of railroad workers in Texas were Mexican immigrants. **Why did some Chinese and Mexican immigrants come to Texas in the late 1800s?**

★ The Effects of the Rail Boom

The arrival of railroads greatly affected Texas. New cities were born, new areas were settled, and Texas became more connected to the rest of the country. Farm goods raised in Texas could be shipped out of state more easily, and goods produced elsewhere could be purchased in Texas. Towns such as Abilene, Big Spring, Eastland, and Sweetwater were established or grew with the arrival of the Texas and Pacific Railway (T&P). Cities grew rapidly at **junctions**, or the meeting places of two or more lines. These cities included Dallas, Houston, San Antonio, Galveston, Waco, El Paso, and Austin. Railroad-car repair shops and many other railway-related businesses appeared in these towns. Farmers and ranchers brought their crops and cattle to ship from cities along the railroad.

The economic boom in railroad towns attracted new residents. For example, Fort Worth grew up around a busy railroad junction. One local newspaper reported on the city's population boom.

TEXAS VOICES

"Work on the T&P . . . has already produced a good effect on the businesses of our town. It has infused [brought in] a new life and vigor [energy] into our people which reacts on those coming here with good results. Vacant houses are filling up; hotels are crowded."

—*Fort Worth Democrat,* quoted in *How Fort Worth Became the Texasmost City,* by Leonard Sanders

Analyzing Primary Sources
Drawing Inferences and Conclusions According to this newspaper, what effects were railroads having on Fort Worth?

Towns that were bypassed by new rail lines often experienced drops in population and economic activity. For example, Jefferson was the sixth-largest Texas city in 1870. Tons of cotton and other farm products were shipped from Jefferson to New Orleans by water. But in 1873 the T&P built a rail line from Texarkana to Marshall, bypassing Jefferson. Jefferson declined in importance as goods were increasingly sent by rail.

Reading Check **Identifying Cause and Effect** How did railroads encourage business in some Texas cities, and what effects did this have on city populations?

CONNECTING TO

ECONOMICS AND MATH

The Railroad Boom

The growth of railroads allowed farmers to get goods to markets faster and at lower cost. The agricultural economy of Texas grew as more railroads were constructed. While there are fewer miles of track today, railroads remain an important method of transportation. Shipping by rail is cheaper and less harmful to the environment than other methods, such as shipping by truck.

YEAR	MILES	YEAR	MILES
1860 –	470	1940 –	17,057
1870 –	583	1950 –	16,296
1880 –	2,440	1960 –	15,445
1890 –	8,710	1970 –	14,683
1900 –	9,971	1980 –	13,075
1910 –	14,339	1990 –	11,541
1920 –	16,383	2000 –	10,749
1930 –	17,569	2011 –	10,425

Interpreting Data

1. Use the information in the table to create a line graph of the miles of tracks in Texas from 1890 to 1990.
2. How many more miles of rail lines were operating in 1900 than in 1870?

★ Farmers Move West

Railroads played a major role in opening the Texas frontier to farming. As railroad companies built tracks through West Texas, settlers followed these lines and purchased land near railroad stops. Railroad companies encouraged this settlement, hoping to make money by selling parcels of land grants to farmers. The farmers would then raise crops or livestock and ship their goods over the companies' rail lines.

Railroad companies advertised the region's rich farmland, sending brochures out to all parts of the country. To ease farmers' concerns about the West Texas climate, some companies created demonstration farms with a wide variety of crops. The companies then brought potential land buyers to see what crops could be grown in the region. Partly as a result of such efforts, people began flocking to the frontier to find inexpensive land. The population of West Texas boomed. For example, the population of Jack County jumped from 694 in 1870 to more than 6,600 in 1880. Even a New Orleans newspaper commented on this trend. "Farmers are pouring into western Texas so fast that ranchmen have just time enough to move their cattle out and prevent their tails being chopped off by the advancing hoe." The number of farms in Texas rose from some 61,000 in 1870 to 350,000 in 1900.

Reading Check **Evaluating** How did railroads contribute to the settlement and development of West Texas?

★ Section 1 Review

1. **Define and explain:**
   - transcontinental railroad
   - junctions
2. **Locate on a Texas map:**
   - Fort Worth
   - El Paso
   - Amarillo
3. **Identifying Cause and Effect**
   Copy the graphic organizer below. Use it to trace the development of the railroad boom and its effects on Texas.

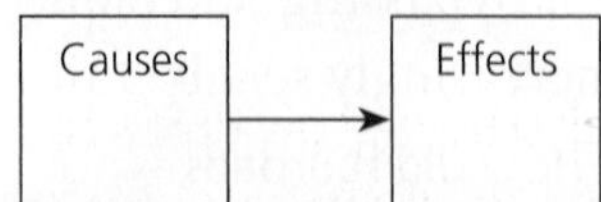

4. **Finding the Main Idea**
   a. Compare the types and uses of new transportation technology in Texas in the late 1800s.
   b. How did the railroad have both positive and negative effects on urban growth?
5. **Writing and Critical Thinking** myWriteSmart
   Drawing Inferences and Conclusions Write a short memo describing how railroads affected the development of the Texas frontier. Consider the following:
   - the rail lines into the frontier
   - the rail lines that connected Texas with U.S. and Mexican railroads

Section 2

Changes in Farming

Main Ideas

1. New farming technology helped Texans adapt to life on the frontier.
2. The commercial cotton-farming boom had both positive and negative effects for Texans.

Why It Matters Today

In the late 1800s, Texans experienced a major farming boom that was followed by a bust in crop prices. Use current events sources to learn about boom-and-bust business cycles today.

Key Terms and People

- **dry farming**
- **threshers**
- **commercial farming**
- **Dora Nunn Roberts**
- **boll weevil**

TEKS: 6D, 7B, 10A, 10B, 13A, 13B, 20A, 20C, 20D, 20E, 21B, 21C, 21H, 22A, 22D

myNotebook

Use the annotation tools in your eBook to take notes on changes in farming in Texas during the late 1800s.

The Story Continues

In 1891 General Robert St. George Dyrenforth began a series of government-sponsored experiments in West Texas. He believed that a big explosion in the sky might lead to rain in the dry region. Dyrenforth hauled more than 60 balloons, 100 kites, and thousands of pounds of explosives to a rural area outside of Midland. He then sent large balloons filled with hydrogen and loaded with dynamite into the air. The explosions produced gray clouds of smoke but little rain. After further experiments also failed, Dyrenforth returned $5,000 to the U.S. government and earned the nickname Major Dry-henceforth.

★ New Farming Technology

Although West Texas was dry, many farmers had moved into the region during the late 1800s because the land there was inexpensive. Farmers soon learned that certain crops grew well in West Texas. Instead of growing corn like some East Texas farmers, West Texas farmers turned to wheat and other grains such as sorghum.

Even so, farmers needed new techniques to help them grow crops in the dry climate. Many farmers practiced **dry farming** techniques such as terracing to keep moisture in the soil. Farmers built terraces, or small ridges, to catch runoff from rainfall and to help stop soil erosion.

Interpreting Visuals

Railroads and farming. *Railroad junctions, like this Houston depot, were busy with farmers bringing their cotton and other goods to be shipped to out-of-state markets.* ***How do you think the national demand for cotton affected the local market in Houston?***

The soil in the Panhandle and some areas of West Texas was quite rich but was often very hard on the surface. John Deere's deep steel plow—widely used by 1845—helped West Texas farmers break through the hard soil. This type of plow left a layer of loose soil on top to allow crops to better absorb moisture from the air. During the 1880s a few farmers, following the lead of ranchers, began to use windmills to pump water from aquifers for crop irrigation.

Texans also began to use new mechanical farm tools. Farmers began using horse-drawn plows that could plow several rows at once. Two-row planters also made planting faster and less difficult. **Threshers**—machines that separate grain or seeds from plants—made harvesting crops faster and easier. In the late 1800s a few Texas farmers even began to use steam-powered threshers and tractors. Steam-powered machines were rare and often attracted public interest. One Abilene newspaper reported the arrival of a steam-powered thresher. "The steam thresher received by T. & B. Gardner last week was a considerable source of amusement and curiosity while it remained in town." Although often amazed by these new machines, farmers used them to increase production.

Reading Check **Analyzing Information** How did new technology compare to past technologies and help farmers adapt to farming in West Texas?

★ Commercial Farming

New machinery, the increase in the number of farms, and the availability of railroads to ship products all encouraged agricultural growth in Texas. The increase in the state's agricultural production resulted in a boom in **commercial farming** during the late 1800s. Commercial farming is the large-scale growing of crops to sell for profit. Because cotton brought larger profits per acre than other crops, some Texas farmers began to grow only cotton. It grew well in the state's drier western regions as well as in East Texas. In 1880, Texas farmers produced about $57 million worth of cotton. Texas had just a few textile mills in the late 1800s, so much of this cotton was shipped out of state. Railroads provided a cheap way to ship cotton to national markets. This contributed to the boom in commercial cotton farming. The development of cottonseed oil further spurred cotton production. Cottonseed oil was used in cooking products, cosmetics, and roofing material.

Railroads also opened up new areas to commercial farming. Spur lines were extended off main lines into regions where cotton could be grown. Railroad companies offered lower rates for shipping cotton and built large cotton loading platforms at each railroad stop. From 1874 to 1878, the number of cotton bales shipped on the Texas and Pacific Railway more than tripled. Railroad companies also transported other crops, including fruits, rice, and vegetables.

As commercial farming boomed, the value of Texas agricultural goods shot up. In East Texas their value rose from more than $10 million to almost $40 million during the late 1800s. West Texas experienced an even more dramatic shift, increasing from $574,000 to more than $8 million during that same period. This rise in value was the result of increased crop production rather than a rise in farm prices.

Reading Check **Finding the Main Idea** What geographic and other factors led to the boom in commercial farming of cotton in Texas?

★ Farming Troubles

The boom in commercial farm production eventually led to a bust in prices. As farmers grew more crops, supply began to exceed demand, and thus prices fell. This is the economic law of supply and demand. If supply is more than demand, prices fall. But if demand is greater than supply, prices rise. For example, between 1874 and 1897 national production of wheat rose by 250 million bushels. The price fell from 94 to 63 cents per bushel.

CONNECTING TO

ECONOMICS

King Cotton in Texas

Cotton production expanded rapidly during the late 1800s. Overproduction of cotton eventually led to a drop in prices.

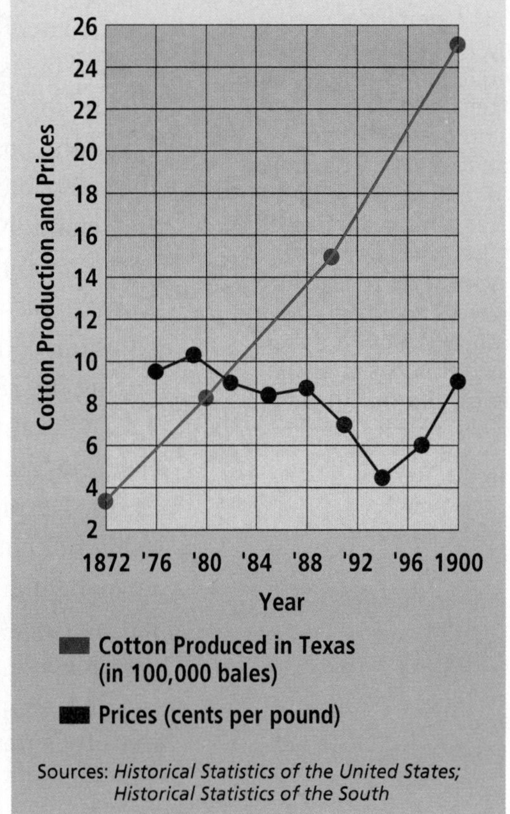

Sources: *Historical Statistics of the United States; Historical Statistics of the South*

Interpreting Graphs

1. How many more bales were produced in 1900 than in 1880?
2. In general, what happened to the price of cotton as production increased? Why did this happen?
3. Based on this chapter, what historical and geographic factors might have led to the rise in cotton production?

BIOGRAPHY

Dora Nunn Roberts (1863–1953) Born in Alabama, Dora Nunn moved to Texas and married Andrew Griffin. The couple settled in Howard County in 1884. The family used a windmill to pump water and irrigate vegetables. After her husband died, Nunn married John Roberts. When he died, she managed the farm. After oil was discovered on her property, she made large donations to several Texas colleges and hospitals. **How did Dora Nunn Roberts adapt to life on the frontier?**

Around this same period, national cotton production increased from more than 3.8 million to about 10.9 million bales. Cotton prices also fell from 11 to 6 cents per pound. Railroads had integrated Texas with the national and international markets for cotton. Therefore, the price of a bale of cotton in Texas was determined by the quantity of cotton produced in all parts of the world. Texas farmers were now vulnerable to supply and price changes in world markets.

The drop in prices hit farmers hard because the cost of farming was on the rise. Prices for farmland rose once most of the inexpensive land on the Texas frontier had been purchased. Some of the best farmland rose in cost from $10 an acre in 1870 to more than $500 in 1900.

Many migrants, freedpeople, and immigrants from Mexico and Europe could not afford to buy land. Instead they worked as farm laborers, tenant farmers, or sharecroppers. Between 1880 and 1900 the number of tenant farms in Texas tripled. Texas farmers such as **Dora Nunn Roberts** also struggled to survive a lengthy drought in the 1880s. In addition, cotton farmers suffered from crop-destroying pests and weeds during the 1890s.

For example, the **boll weevil,** a type of beetle, first infested cotton fields in the Rio Grande valley and then quickly spread throughout Texas. Despite the pest problems, many farmers refused to grow anything but cotton. Farm organizations and scientists tried to encourage farmers to diversify and grow a variety of crops. However, even with the falling prices, farmers still made more money on cotton than on other crops.

Reading Check **Drawing Inferences and Conclusions** How do you think the interdependence of Texas and national and international markets and the economic law of supply and demand affected Texas farmers?

Section 2 Review

1. Define and explain:
- dry farming
- threshers
- commercial farming
- boll weevil

2. Identify and explain the historical significance of:
- Dora Nunn Roberts

3. Summarizing Copy the graphic organizer below. Use it to explain how railroads and farming led to the interdependence between the Texas economy with national and international markets.

Farming and Railroads	International Markets

4. Finding the Main Idea

a. Compare the new types of farming technology. How did they help Texans adapt to and modify their environment?

b. Why did a boom in cotton farming occur, and what were its effects?

5. Writing and Critical Thinking *my* WriteSmart

Categorizing Imagine that you visited Texas in 1870 and in 1900. Write a letter explaining the positive and negative effects of the commercial agricultural boom. Consider the following:
- the value of farm goods and changes in farming costs
- the effects of the law of supply and demand on farmers

Section 3

Agricultural Industries and Workers

Main Ideas

1. In the late 1800s, lumber, flour milling, and cottonseed oil were major industries in Texas.
2. Labor unions in Texas had some success, but public support decreased greatly by the end of the century.

Key Terms

- **labor unions**
- **Knights of Labor**
- **strike**

Why It Matters Today

New inventions helped Texas industries grow and become even more productive. Use current events sources to learn more about recent inventions.

TEKS: 6A, 13A, 20C, 20D, 21A, 21B, 21D, 22A

myNotebook

Use the annotation tools in your eBook to take notes on major industries in Texas and the problems labor unions faced at the end of the 19th century.

The Story Continues

In 1876 a newspaper owner named Colonel A. H. Belo left his Galveston home for an exhibition in Philadelphia. He was eager to see all the new inventions that would be on display there. At the exhibition Belo and many others saw Alexander Graham Bell's new invention—the telephone. Thoroughly impressed, Belo decided that he had to have one. The telephones that he had installed at his home and at his office at the *Galveston News* were among the first in the United States.

★ Leading Industries

New inventions like the telephone helped newspapers report on the state's expanding industries. The most important Texas industries continued to be ones that helped turn farm goods into products. Flour milling was the state's leading industry after agriculture. By 1870 there were more than 530 flour mills in Texas, and mills in Dallas County alone produced nearly $3 million worth of flour.

By the 1890s lumber had overtaken flour milling in value. Between 1870 and 1900 the production of lumber in Texas increased more than eightfold to more than $16 million. Much of the cutting and processing of timber in sawmills was done in the Piney Woods region. The growth of railroads created greater demand for lumber. Railroads used timber for rail ties and bridges and for fuel. Railroads also provided cheap transportation for timber products, which were used for building

The Lutcher and Moore Lumber Company in Orange, Texas, operated from 1877 until the 1930s and was a major employer in the town.

in the treeless frontier of western Texas and in other parts of the United States. Timber was also transported to port cities such as Galveston, where it could be shipped by boat to national and international markets. International demand for Texas lumber boosted the state's economy. One Texas businessman recognized this trend.

TEXAS VOICES

"Three large [lumber] mills at Beaumont . . . [have] built up an enormous trade. . . . They will go after the foreign trade harder than ever, when they have a surplus of stock and they expect to bring to Texas for the enrichment [benefit] of this section [region] and especially of the toilers [laborers] who seek their fortunes in this business, the trade and the cash of other countries."

—Jerome Swinford, quoted in *The Road to Spindletop,* by John Stricklin Spratt

Analyzing Primary Sources
Identifying Points of View How does Swinford think international trade will affect the lumber industry in Texas?

Other industries also developed. By 1900 Texas was the number-one producer of cottonseed oil for the U.S. market. Meatpacking was another leading Texas industry. Stockyards and meatpacking plants were built near railroad junctions to take advantage of refrigerated railroad cars that could transport beef across great distances.

The mining industry in Texas developed in the 1880s, when railroad locomotives began to use coal instead of wood as fuel. Coal burned more efficiently, and trains could run faster with this fuel. Railroads in Texas continued to grow as the 1800s drew to a close.

Reading Check **Analyzing Information** How did the growth of railroads affect Texas industries and the use of natural resources?

★ Industrial Workers

Although these growing industries created new job opportunities, most Texans still worked in agriculture. In 1900 less than 2 percent of the population worked in manufacturing. Wages and hours for industrial workers varied from job to job. Some workers joined **labor unions**—organizations that supported the interests of workers. Unions pushed for improvements in the hours, wages, and working conditions of laborers.

The first national labor union arrived in Texas in 1882. The **Knights of Labor** organized to support skilled and unskilled workers of almost every trade, including large numbers of farmers. Unlike most national unions, membership in the Knights was open to women and African Americans. Local chapters of the group were established in several cities, including Houston, Galveston, Waco, Fort Worth, and Austin. There were more than 300 local Knights groups in Texas by the mid-1880s.

In Texas the Knights organized railroad workers. The railroad union led a successful **strike** against Jay Gould's Wabash Railroad in 1885. A strike occurs when workers refuse to do their job until a company meets their demands. In 1886 the Knights were defeated in the Great Southwest Strike against Gould's Texas and Pacific Railroad. This defeat led to violence in Fort Worth. Labor unrest continued until Governor John Ireland sent the state militia and Texas Rangers to restore order. Texans, as well as people around the country, were upset by the violence, and many believed that strikes and other labor actions threatened the production and transportation of goods. As a result, support for unions decreased in Texas.

Reading Check **Identifying Cause and Effect** Why did labor unions grow in Texas, and what led to their decline?

Mutualistas

Because of discrimination and segregation, many Mexican American workers formed their own mutual aid societies. These *mutualistas* were modeled after the ones that developed in Mexico in the 1870s. These organizations were a source of support for workers and provided social services and allowed for the exchange of ideas. Some *mutualistas* also functioned as trade unions.

★ Section 3 Review

hmhsocialstudies.com ONLINE QUIZ

1. **Define and explain:**
   - labor unions
   - strike
2. **Identify and explain** the significance of:
   - the Knights of Labor
3. **Categorizing** Copy the graphic organizer below. Use it to describe how agricultural industries contributed to the growth of the Texas economy.

Industry	Effect on Agriculture	Effect on Economy
Flour milling		
Lumber		
Cottonseed oil		

4. **Finding the Main Idea**
   - **a.** What were the leading manufacturing industries in Texas for 1870 and 1890?
   - **b.** List two reasons why labor unions did not succeed in Texas.
5. **Writing and Critical Thinking** myWriteSmart
   Analyzing Information Imagine that you are traveling through Texas in 1870 looking for industries in which to invest money. Write a memo to other investors on the effect of national and international markets on Texas.
   Consider the following:
   - the growth of railroads
   - the demand for natural resources

The Chapter at a Glance

Examine the following visual summary of the chapter. Then use the visual to pose and answer questions about how Texas industries were affected by geographic factors and natural resources.

Identifying People and Ideas

Write a sentence to explain the role or significance of the following terms or people.

1. transcontinental railroad
2. junctions
3. dry farming
4. thresher
5. commercial farming
6. strike
7. Dora Nunn Roberts
8. boll weevil
9. labor unions
10. Knights of Labor

Understanding Main Ideas

Section 1

1. How did the railroad boom affect the growth of Texas towns and local economies?
2. How did railroads become a factor in settling the West Texas frontier?

Section 2

3. Identify ways that Texans used new farming technologies to adapt to and modify their environment.
4. Analyze the impact of supply and demand in international markets on Texas farmers.

Section 3

5. What goods did Texas industries supply for national and international markets?

You Be the Historian

Reviewing Themes

1. **Geography** How did physical factors of Texas geography and human factors lead to the growth of agriculture and industry in Texas?
2. **Science, Technology & Society** How did the development of the railroad help the growth of Texas industries and cities?
3. **Economics** How was the Texas economy affected by the national and international demand for farm and industrial goods?

Thinking Critically

1. **Drawing Inferences and Conclusions** How do you think new technology in Texas made the state more connected with the United States and the rest of the world? What were the effects?
2. **Identifying Cause and Effect** What factors led to the development of the West Texas frontier, and how did this affect the social, political, and economic life of the area?
3. **Summarizing** What were some of the defining characteristics of the era of cotton, cattle, and railroads in Texas?

Texas Test Practice

Interpreting Graphs

Study the table below. Then use the information in the table to answer the following questions.

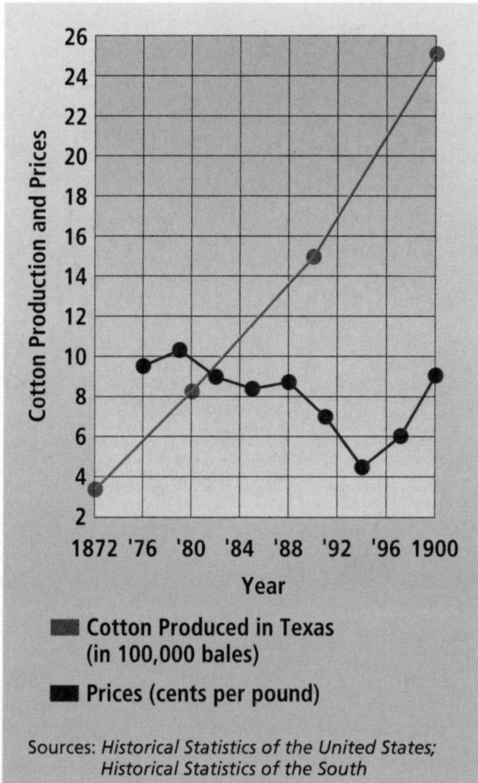

1. How did the price of a pound of cotton change between 1888 and 1894?

- **A** increased by about 4 cents
- **B** decreased by about 8 cents
- **C** decreased by about 4 cents
- **D** increased by about 2 cents

2. Based on what you have read in this chapter, what historical and geographic factors might have led to the rise in cotton production?

Analyzing Primary Sources

Read the following quote by a Texas newspaper editor who urged farmers to diversify their crops and thus avoid relying too heavily on cotton. Then answer the questions.

"Diversity in farming has so many advantages that it should find favor in the practice of every sensible agriculturalist [farmer]. It puts on the home table a great variety and prevents the necessity of many purchases; distributes both the labor and cash receipts pretty evenly throughout the year; prevents the overstocking in any single department, and so tends to keep up prices; is favorable to the rotation of crops, the advantage of which all appreciate; and finally is an insurance against heavy loss by distributing among many products the risks of failure of one."

3. Which of the following is not a reason the editor gives in support of crop diversification?

- **F** Crop rotation provides a number of advantages.
- **G** It helps protect the farmer against losses from droughts.
- **H** Diversification provides the farmer with a variety of foods.
- **J** It helps protect farmers by distributing the risk of failure among many crops.

4. Why do you think some Texas farmers would not want to diversify their crops?

Linking to Community

Many Texans today work on farms or in industries related to agriculture. Interview someone in your community who works on a farm or in an agricultural industry. Ask that person what role new machinery or technology plays in his or her work. How has that person adapted to the region's environment? How have geographic and human factors influenced his or her work? Create a model or collage of a machine or other type of technology the person uses in his or her work.

Internet Activity

Use the Internet to research the coming of the railroads to Texas. Then create an advertisement promoting a new railroad line. Be sure your advertisement points out the social impact and economic benefits that the new line will bring to the area's residents. You may want to include a poster with maps and colorful illustrations with your presentation.

CHAPTER 23

The Oil Boom

(1890–1920)

Texas Essential Knowledge and Skills (TEKS) 1A, 1B, 1C, 6A, 7A, 7B, 8A, 8B, 9A, 9B, 10A, 10B, 12A, 12B, 13B, 13C, 15B, 15C, 17C, 20A, 20C, 20D, 21A, 21B, 21C, 21E, 22A, 22D

When the Spindletop well struck oil, a huge plume of oil erupted from the ground.

TEXAS

- **1890** Texas Normal College and Teachers' Training Institute, now called the University of North Texas, opens in Denton.
- **1894** Drillers strike oil in Corsicana.
- **1901** The Spindletop well strikes oil, producing more than 17 million barrels of oil the next year.
- **1905** A large oil strike is made in the Humble oil field in Harris County.

1890 — 1894 — 1898 — 1902

U.S. and WORLD

- **1890** American inventor John Lambert builds the first automobile that uses an internal combustion engine.
- **1896** B. F. Goodrich Company manufactures the first automobile tires.

If you were there . . .
Would you work in the oil industry?

Build on What You Know

Texans witnessed many economic changes in the late 1800s. The growth of industry, commercial farming, and railroads affected the way Texans lived and worked. As the new century approached, Texans would witness another major economic change—the growth of the oil industry.

Oil from the Santa Rita No. 1 helped fund Texas universities during the 1920s and 1930s.

The popularity of the automobile guaranteed the Texas oil industry millions of customers.

1906

1908
Oil is discovered at Goose Creek along Galveston Bay.

1908
The Ford Motor Company introduces the Model T, one of the most popular cars in American history.

1910

1911
The U.S. Supreme Court orders the Standard Oil Company to break up into several smaller companies.

1914

1914
The Houston Ship Channel opens, and Houston soon becomes an important oil-refining center.

1918

1917
A French inventor builds a gyroplane—a flying craft much like a helicopter.

1919
An application is filed to drill for oil on state-owned land in West Texas. Several years later the Santa Rita No. 1 strikes oil.

You Be the Historian

*my*Notebook

What's Your Opinion? Do you **agree** or **disagree** with the following statements? Support your point of view in your notebook.

- **Science, Technology & Society** The uses for natural resources do not change over time.
- **Culture** The rapid growth of industry affects all aspects of social life, including urban growth, education, and the arts.
- **Economics** National markets always influence local businesses and industries.

Section 1

The Birth of the Oil Industry

Main Ideas

1. The Texas oil industry began with the discovery of a major oil field in Corsicana.
2. The Spindletop strike marked the beginning of the oil boom in Texas.

Key Terms and People

- **petroleum**
- **fossil fuel**
- **derricks**
- **refinery**
- **Pattillo Higgins**
- **Anthony F. Lucas**
- **Spindletop strike**
- **boom-and-bust cycle**

Why It Matters Today

During the 1800s Americans searched for new energy sources. Use current events sources to learn about different sources of energy available today.

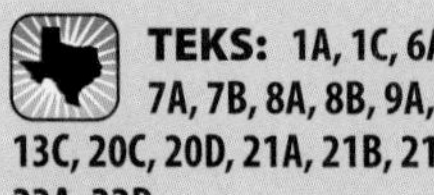

TEKS: 1A, 1C, 6A, 7A, 7B, 8A, 8B, 9A, 13C, 20C, 20D, 21A, 21B, 21C, 22A, 22D

myNotebook

Use the annotation tools in your eBook to take notes on the discovery of oil at Spindletop and the beginning of the oil industry in Texas.

The Story Continues

Spindletop was a small hill just outside Beaumont. Although it was only 12 feet high, people often called it Big Hill. One day Pattillo Higgins took a Sunday school class on an outing to Big Hill. He happened to notice gas bubbles in the spring at the top of the hill. When Higgins poked his cane into the ground, gas escaped. This visit convinced Higgins that there was oil under Big Hill.

★ The Search for Oil

The demand for oil had risen dramatically after scientists developed kerosene in the mid-1800s. Kerosene was a new form of fuel for lighting that could be made from coal or **petroleum**. Commonly called oil, petroleum is a dark, thick, liquid **fossil fuel**. A fossil fuel is a fuel formed underground from plant or animal remains. Compared to other fuels, such as whale oil, kerosene was less expensive and less dangerous to use. The first major U.S. oil strike occurred in the late 1850s. An oil company sent Edwin Drake to northwestern Pennsylvania to search for oil. He drilled holes to try to reach petroleum deep underground but had little luck. One day when the drill reached 69 feet, a black liquid oozed out of the well. Local farmers ran through a nearby town shouting, "The Yankee has struck oil!"

Drake's success led others to search for oil. In Texas a Civil War veteran named Lyne T. Barret drilled for oil outside Nacogdoches in 1866. He struck oil at 106 feet. His oil well was soon producing 10 barrels of oil a day. However, Barret could not raise the money necessary to continue drilling and had to shut the well down. Other Texans accidentally discovered oil. George Dullnig, a rancher in Bexar County, struck oil while drilling for water in 1886. Dullnig drilled two more wells but did not find enough oil to continue drilling. Other efforts at finding oil in Texas met with little success. Texas produced only 48 barrels of oil in 1889, compared to the 35 million barrels of oil produced in the rest of the United States.

It was not until 1894, when drillers in Corsicana searching for water struck oil, that the Texas oil industry truly began to grow. The Corsicana landscape was soon dotted with **derricks**, or towers that support oil-drilling equipment. During 1896 the Corsicana oil field produced 1,450 barrels of oil. Just four years later, Texans took more than 839,000 barrels of oil out of the oil field.

To process the oil, business leaders constructed a **refinery**. A refinery is a factory where crude oil is refined, or made pure, and then made into various products. The oil refined at Corsicana was used to lubricate machinery and provide kerosene for lamps.

Reading Check **Identifying Cause and Effect** What scientific innovation occurred in the mid-1800s, and how did that affect Texas?

Interpreting Visuals

Spindletop. *The Spindletop strike led to an oil boom in the Gulf Coast region.* ***How does this image of the Spindletop oil field six years after the first strike reflect the oil boom?***

BIOGRAPHY

Anthony F. Lucas (1855–1921) In 1879 Austrian Antonio Francisco Luchich came to the United States, eventually changing his name to Anthony Francis Lucas. He worked as a mining engineer in Colorado and Louisiana before arriving in Texas in 1899. While drilling at Spindletop, Lucas and his wife lived in a shack and used boxes and crates for furniture. Spindletop made Lucas a wealthy man—he received $400,000 for his work there. **What role did Lucas play in the Spindletop strike?**

The Spindletop Strike

The success at Corsicana was quickly overshadowed by a discovery at an oil field near Beaumont. **Pattillo Higgins**, a brick-factory owner, believed that oil would be found under a salt dome at a place called Spindletop Hill, or Big Hill. Salt domes are underground formations that often trap oil and natural gases. In 1892 Higgins and some friends worked together to form the Gladys City Oil, Gas, and Manufacturing Company. Although the company drilled three wells at Spindletop, it did not strike oil. But Higgins refused to give up.

Higgins ran an advertisement calling for a drilling engineer. In 1899 an engineer named **Anthony F. Lucas** responded to Higgins's ad. Lucas was an expert on salt domes, and he agreed that oil was probably beneath the Spindletop dome. He started drilling there in June 1900. At 575 feet, Lucas found traces of oil, but his equipment was not strong enough to continue. After finding business leaders willing to invest in new equipment, Lucas continued drilling. A man who worked at Spindletop described the big oil strike that occurred on January 10, 1901.

TEXAS VOICES

"All of a sudden, a chunk of mud came out of the six-inch hole . . . with an explosion just like a cannon popping off. . . . I walked over and looked down in the hole there . . . this frothy oil was coming up . . . each flow a little higher and a little higher and a little higher. Finally it came up with such momentum that it just shot up clear through the top of the derrick."

—Al Hamill, quoted in *Tales from the Derrick Floor*, by Mody C. Boatwright and William A. Owens

The giant plume of oil shooting into the air at Spindletop could be seen from more than 10 miles away. People came from miles around to see it. Over the next nine days some 800,000 barrels of oil shot out of the Spindletop well before workers could cap the gusher. Word of the strike quickly spread around the world, with newspapers calling it the great gusher in Texas. The **Spindletop strike** marked the beginning of the Texas oil boom and the age of oil in Texas.

Reading Check **Finding the Main Idea** What was the significance of the strike at Spindletop?

KEY DATE 1901
The discovery of oil at Spindletop near Beaumont was the beginning of the modern oil industry.

Boom and Bust after Spindletop

The discovery of oil at Spindletop led to a boom in the Texas economy and created many jobs. Hundreds of oil companies formed to drill new wells, and the population of Beaumont swelled by nearly 40,000 people. By 1902 more than 500 oil companies were operating there. The *Galveston Daily News* reported on the growth and excitement in Beaumont. "The town continues to fill up. The street resembles a great holiday event. . . . Physicians are becoming real estate men. The lumber industry is forgotten in the wild rush for oil land. . . . Throngs of people frequent the streets until late at night and everything is oil."

Spindletop oil production peaked in 1902 at more than 17 million barrels of oil. That year, nearly 20 percent of the oil produced in the United States came from Spindletop. The discovery of this huge oil field soon affected oil prices. With large quantities of oil being produced, the supply of oil outpaced the national demand. As a result, the price of oil dropped. By 1902 oil prices had hit an all-time low of three cents a barrel. These changes in price were part of a **boom-and-bust cycle**, or alternating periods of growth and depression in an industry or economy. The boom and bust at Spindletop was the first such cycle the Texas oil industry would experience.

The rush of companies drilling oil at Spindletop soon led to the depletion of the field. By 1904 Spindletop was producing only 10,000 barrels of oil a day. Most of the new companies that had formed went out of business when their wells dried up. Of those Texas companies that survived, several grew into major businesses. J. S. Cullinan, who owned the Corsicana refinery, founded the Texas Fuel Company in Beaumont in March 1901. The company soon changed its name to the Texas Company—later Texaco—and grew rapidly. By 1905 it owned oil wells and a refinery as well as railroad cars and pipelines for transporting oil.

Another Spindletop oil company, the J. M. Guffey Petroleum Company, was formed in May 1901. Its owners also founded the Gulf Refining Company. The two companies struggled for several years until merging in 1907 to become the Gulf Oil Corporation. The Magnolia Petroleum Company and the Humble Oil Company, both founded in 1911, also became major businesses.

The oil companies that survived the early boom were important to the Texas economy. They employed thousands of Texans, which in turn helped boost many of the state's other businesses.

Reading Check **Evaluating** How did the Spindletop oil boom affect the local economy and national oil prices?

Daily Life

Life in the Oil Fields

Working in the Texas oil fields was rough, dirty, and dangerous. Laborers usually worked 12-hour shifts. O.G. Lawson recalled that workers were sometimes burned by "gas wells that they had no way of controlling." Gases escaping from wells could hurt or kill. **What was life like for workers in the oil industry?**

Section 1 Review

hmhsocialstudies.com ONLINE QUIZ

1. Define and explain:
- petroleum
- fossil fuel
- derricks
- refinery
- boom-and-bust cycle

2. Identify and explain:
- Pattillo Higgins
- Anthony F. Lucas
- Spindletop strike

3. Identifying Cause and Effect
Use a graphic organizer to describe causes of each event below.

Boom and Bust
Spindletop produces 17 million barrels
Oil prices drop
Spindletop strike

4. Finding the Main Idea
a. Trace the rise of the Texas oil industry.
b. How did the oil boom affect national oil markets and local communities?

5. Writing and Critical Thinking *my*WriteSmart
Making Generalizations and Predictions You are a reporter present at the Spindletop strike. Write a short newspaper article on the event. Consider the following:
- the people and events that led to the strike
- how the strike will affect the future

Connecting To

Geography

Oil and Natural Gas Fields

While the Spindletop oil strike brought a surge of drilling to the Gulf Coast, oil fields were later discovered in many regions of Texas. Oil was soon discovered in North Texas, the Panhandle, and the Permian Basin. Natural gas was also found in these regions. These natural resources spurred Texas industries and economic growth.

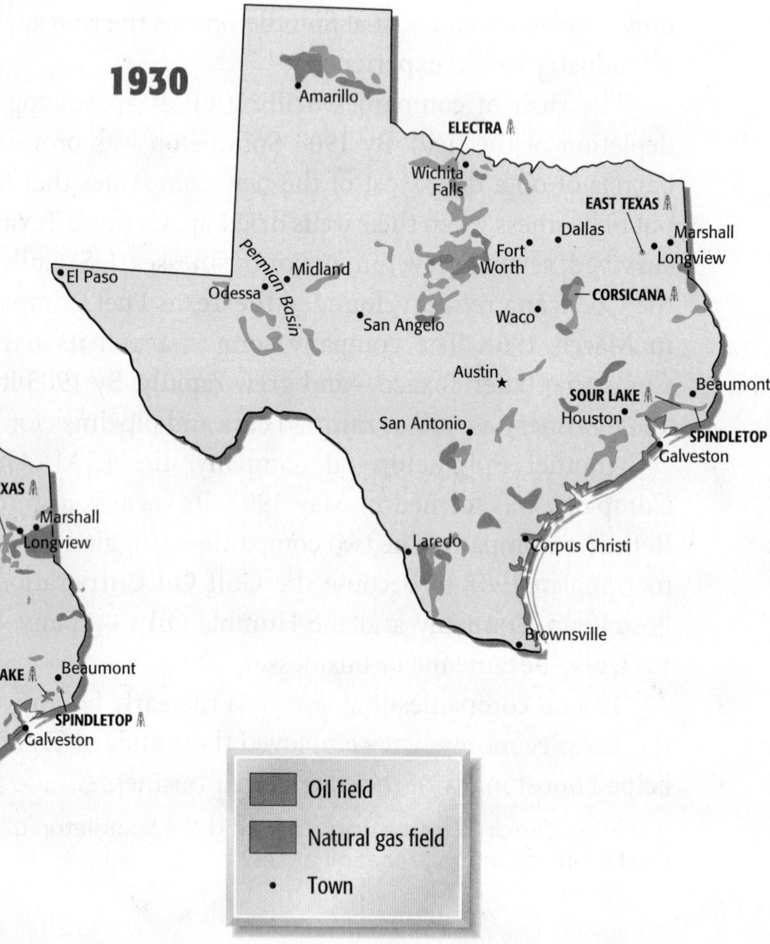

Geography **Skills**

Interpreting Thematic Maps

1. Which region of Texas had the fewest oil fields in 1930?
2. Which region had the most natural gas fields in 2011?
3. Based on these maps, what conclusions can you draw about changes in the oil and natural gas industry, and how those changes affected regional economies in Texas?

Section 2

The Growth of the Oil Industry

Main Ideas

1. After Spindletop, oil fields quickly sprung up in many regions of Texas.
2. New business ideas such as horizontal and vertical integration changed the oil industry.

Why It Matters Today

The oil industry was important to the Texas economy in the early 1900s. Use current events sources to learn about the oil industry today.

Key Terms

- **wildcatters**
- **natural gas**
- **vertical integration**
- **horizontal integration**

TEKS: 1B, 7A, 7B, 8A, 8B, 9A, 9B, 10A, 10B, 13B, 13C, 20D, 21B, 21C, 22A, 22D

myNotebook

Use the annotation tools in your eBook to take notes on the growth of the oil industry in Texas.

The Story Continues

The Spindletop strike brought thousands of people to the Beaumont area, lured by the dream of huge profits. Soon it seemed as if everyone owned an oil company. In Beaumont a newspaper reporter saw two men looking at a map. The next day he learned that the newcomers had formed the What-Not Oil Company. This new company was just one of the hundreds that appeared in Beaumont in 1901.

★ Wildcatters and New Oil Fields

Some of these companies were owned by **wildcatters**—independent oil operators who searched for new fields. These entrepreneurs saved and borrowed money to invest in the oil business. In hopes of finding oil fields, wildcatters competed with one another to find salt domes in the Gulf Coast Plain. They found salt domes some 20 miles outside Beaumont at Sour Lake. Drilling began there in 1893, but the first big strike did not occur until 1902. That year a gusher produced as many as 50,000 barrels a day. By 1903 there were some 150 wells at Sour Lake. Overdrilling soon led to a drop in underground pressure, making further oil drilling difficult. By the end of 1903, more than half of the wells at Sour Lake were abandoned. Other Gulf Coast oil fields faced a similar drop in oil production when they were overpumped.

Oil production extended beyond the Gulf Coast to North Texas. In 1903 North Texas rancher W. T. Waggoner struck oil. He later complained that he was only drilling for water. "I wanted water, and they

Vertical and Horizontal Integration

Many corporations used horizontal and vertical integration to increase their business. Some large oil companies owned smaller companies that made products for each step of the oil-production process. Oil companies also bought many refineries or oil fields.

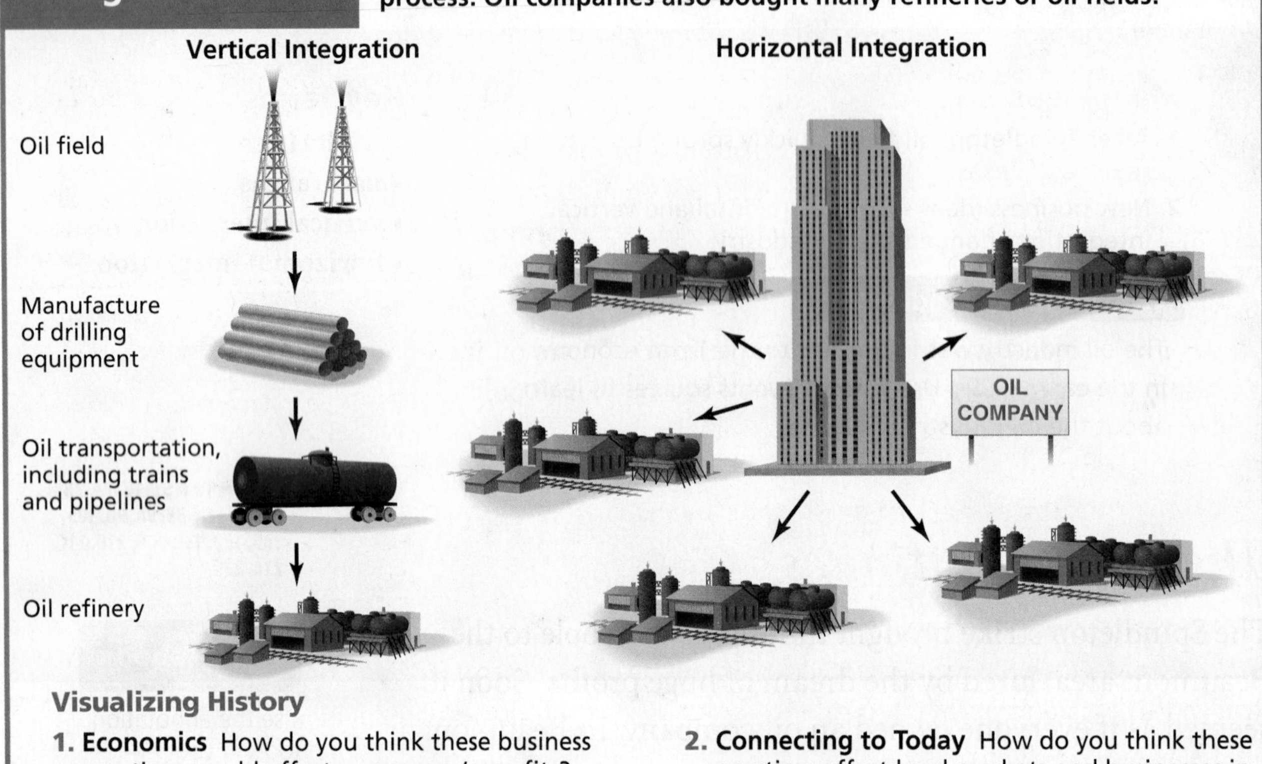

Visualizing History

1. **Economics** How do you think these business practices would affect a company's profits?
2. **Connecting to Today** How do you think these practices affect local markets and businesses in Texas today?

got me oil. I was mad, mad clean through." This Electra oil field made Waggoner a wealthy man, however. Other major North Texas oil fields included Wichita Falls and Burkburnett. In 1919 the Burkburnett field produced some 31.6 million barrels of oil.

After their success in North Texas, oil companies began drilling in the Panhandle. The first successful strike there took place in 1921. Six years later, Panhandle oil fields produced some 39 million barrels of oil in a single year. Oil was also discovered in the Permian Basin region of West Texas in 1921. During the 1920s several large oil fields were discovered in the area, including the Yates, Hobbs, and Big Lake oil fields. South and Central Texas were also the sites of oil production. However, these regions never produced the amount of oil that made other parts of the state famous. An oil strike deep in the heart of East Texas gave the oil industry its greatest surprise. Geologists had claimed that there was very little oil in East Texas north of the Gulf Coast. But a wildcatter's 1930 strike proved them wrong—the East Texas oil field turned out to be one of the largest in the world.

Reading Check **Sequencing** Identify in order where and when oil was discovered in the major regions of Texas.

★ Oil Business Is Big Business

Texas oil fields produced more than just oil. **Natural gas**—a gas that can be used as a fuel—was also abundant. However, there was no way to get it to market safely in the early years of the oil industry. As a result, gas coming out of oil wells was allowed to burn. In the 1890s scientists invented a leakproof pipeline that could safely move natural gas about 100 miles. The first Texas gas pipeline stretched 19 miles between the Petrolia oil field and Wichita Falls. Further advances in pipeline technology during the 1920s and 1930s expanded the distance gas could be shipped. This new pipeline technology opened the market for Texas natural gas.

As more oil and gas fields were discovered, the Texas oil industry grew into a big business. In 1915, Texans sold more than 13 million dollars' worth of oil. Some Texas oil companies began to use a business strategy called **vertical integration**—owning the businesses involved in each step of a manufacturing process. For example, the Texas Company began by purchasing and transporting oil from Spindletop. As its profits grew, the company expanded into oil drilling, production, and refining. The company also bought items it needed for its business, such as barges and railroad tanker cars. By streamlining the processes of drilling, transporting, and refining oil, the Texas Company was able to develop into a huge corporation.

Most large oil companies also practiced **horizontal integration**—owning many business in a particular field. The larger oil corporations would run many refineries, sharing supplies and resources to make their businesses more efficient.

Reading Check **Drawing Inferences and Conclusions** How did oil companies expand to control a large part of the oil industry?

CONNECTING TO ECONOMICS

Wildcatters

Motivated by the potential profits, wildcatters bought land, hired oil workers, and drilled wells. Wildcatters worked hard, hoping that their investments would pay off. However, wildcatting was risky and expensive. Many wildcatters went bankrupt after drilling a few wells. While most wildcatters did not strike oil, some became wealthy. Pattillo Higgins could be considered one of the earliest successful wildcatters. **How did the free enterprise system, particularly the desire for profit, motivate wildcatters in Texas?**

★ Section 2 Review

hmhsocialstudies.com
ONLINE QUIZ

1. Define and explain:
- wildcatters
- natural gas
- vertical integration
- horizontal integration

2. Locate on a Texas map:
- Wichita Falls
- Permian Basin

3. Sequencing
Copy the graphic organizer below. Use it to trace the discovery of oil in the various regions of Texas.

Region	When oil was discovered
Gulf Coast	
North Texas	
Panhandle	
Permian Basin	
East Texas	

4. Finding the Main Idea

a. What role did wildcatters play in the oil boom?

b. Explain how new business strategies affected the oil industry.

5. Writing and Critical Thinking *my WriteSmart*

Evaluating Imagine that you are a wildcatter traveling from region to region in 1919. Create a journal entry describing what businesses in the oil-production process you would want to own. Consider the following:
- the steps of oil production
- getting oil to market

Section 3

Effects of the Oil Boom

Main Ideas

1. The oil boom caused Texas towns to grow rapidly.
2. New technologies fueled the growth of the oil industry.
3. The oil industry affected the politics, economy, and social life of Texas.

Why It Matters Today

During the early 1900s oil production created boomtowns. Use current events sources to learn about how industry affects city growth today.

Key Terms

- **boomtowns**
- **internal combustion engines**
- **Texas Railroad Commission**
- **Permanent University Fund**
- **philanthropy**

TEKS: 6A, 7B, 9A, 9B, 12A, 12B, 13B, 13C, 15B, 15C, 17C, 20A, 20C, 20D, 21B, 21C, 21E, 22A, 22D

myNotebook

Use the annotation tools in your eBook to take notes on the effects of the Texas oil boom.

The Story Continues

Lured into the Texas oil business by the dramatic events at Spindletop, Howard Hughes Sr. encountered a problem faced by all oil producers. Drill bits could not cut through hard rock. Unlike others, though, Hughes came up with a solution. He outlined the basic design of the Hughes Rock Bit, which could cut through rock 10 times faster than other bits.

Boomtowns

Like Hughes, thousands of people were drawn to Texas by the promise of spectacular fortunes to be made in the oil business. Before Spindletop, Beaumont had 9,000 residents. Within two years it had swelled to a city 50,000. Nearby Sour Lake grew from a small village to a city of 10,000 people within a matter of months. Such fast growing towns were called **boomtowns** because they grew along with economic booms. Boomtowns were busy places where everyone was trying to make money. A Texas schoolteacher described life in her boomtown.

TEXAS VOICES

"In McCamey, they worked twenty-four hours a day. Everything stayed open twenty-four hours, the eating places and all, because the men worked night shifts and day shifts. I've seen my brother-in-law stay up twenty-four hours at the lumberyard. Businessmen had their living quarters at their place of business. They worked Sunday. It was no different from any other day."

—Allie V. Scott, quoted in *Life in the Oil Fields*, by Roger M. Olien and Diana Davids Olien

Thousands of Texans arrived at these boomtowns seeking work in the oil industry. Among them were many young farm workers looking for a new type of work. Some moved from town to town, following news of oil strikes. Relatively few women and children lived in these towns.

Because most people were more concerned with drilling oil than city planning, most Texas boomtowns were crowded, dirty, and rough places. Oil-field workers often lived in tents or wooden shacks. The dirt streets of these towns became rivers of mud when it rained. New businesses opened to serve the growing population. Some, such as stores and hotels, were typical of any town. Others were geared more to workers, offering gambling and drinking. Such activities often led to violence, making some boomtowns dangerous places to live.

Reading Check **Drawing Inferences and Conclusions** How did the development of the oil industry lead to urban growth in Texas?

Interpreting Visuals

Boomtowns. *People flocked to boomtowns seeking jobs in the oil business.* ***What other type of work do you think people found in Texas boomtowns?***

★ Automobile and Petrochemical Industries

Oil companies grew at a time when electricity was replacing kerosene for lighting homes and industries. Fortunately for oil producers, though, new uses for petroleum were being discovered. Because it was cheaper than coal, oil quickly replaced coal as the fuel for steam engines. The use of **internal combustion engines** to power automobiles and other vehicles was also increasing. Instead of steam, these engines used either gasoline or diesel—oil by-products—for power.

★Texas Cities★

Midland and Odessa

History: Odessa was established in 1881 as a stop on the Texas and Pacific Railway. Farming families established Midland in 1884. Both cities grew slowly until the oil boom of the 1920s.

Midland population in 2012: 119,385 (est.)

Odessa population in 2012: 106,102 (est.)

Relative location: In the Permian Basin of West Texas

Region: Southern edge of the High Plains where the Edwards Plateau meets the Mountains and Basins region

County: Midland is the county seat of Midland County, and Odessa is the county seat of Ector County.

Origin of name: Midland was named for its location midway between Dallas and El Paso; Odessa was named after a Russia city.

Economy: The major source of income and jobs for both cities is the petroleum industry. Banking, farming, and ranching are also important.

Before the development of the internal combustion engine, oil producers had not made much gasoline because demand for it was low. This situation changed as more Americans began to buy cars. Between 1895 and 1906 the number of registered cars in the United States rose from 5 to some 619,000. By 1916 Texans were driving about 195,000 of the 3.4 million cars in the United States.

As Americans continued to purchase cars and drove longer distances, the demand for gasoline grew across the country. Between 1916 and 1920, gasoline production in the United States rose from 49 million barrels to more than 116 million barrels per year. By producing gasoline, the Texas oil industry helped keep Americans traveling the nation's roads and highways.

The growing popularity of the automobile guaranteed the Texas oil industry millions of customers. In addition, scientists continued to develop new uses for petroleum. Petrochemicals, products made from oil and gas, became an important part of the Texas economy. Petrochemical products include synthetic rubber, plastics, and carbon black, which is used to make ink, tires, and other products.

Reading Check **Analyzing Information** How did the development of new technologies affect the use of fossil fuels such as oil in Texas?

★ The Effects of the Oil Boom

While the oil boom boosted the state's economic growth, it also affected Texas in many other ways. The oil boom attracted many young farm workers to jobs in the oil fields. Most drilling and production jobs were reserved for white workers. Despite facing discrimination in the oil fields, some African American and Mexican American workers found jobs as teamsters, hauling goods to and from the oil fields. Many oil workers lived a very mobile life, moving from town to town as they followed new oil strikes.

The oil boom also affected Texas politics and the environment. State officials began to pass restrictions designed to control parts of the oil industry. In 1899 the legislature passed laws concerning abandoned wells and the protection of groundwater from oil pollution. Some 20 years later, the legislature made it illegal to waste oil and natural gas. In 1917 the legislature gave the **Texas Railroad Commission**, an agency originally created to regulate railroads, authority to enforce laws concerning the petroleum industry. The commission set standards for spacing between wells and for pipeline transportation of oil and gas. These rules helped prevent overdrilling.

The state government also began collecting taxes on oil production in 1905, taking in more than $101,000 in taxes that year. By 1919 the amount of money collected from taxes on oil production rose to more than $1 million.

This money helped fund the state government and education programs for Texas children. Higher education in Texas also benefited from the state's oil production. In 1876 the Texas legislature had set aside some 1 million acres of land in West Texas for the **Permanent University Fund**. Texas universities received money from the sale or use of this land. However, many people considered the land worthless until the Santa Rita No. 1 oil well struck oil in 1923.

Income from oil production went into the Permanent University Fund, which grew by more than $2,000 a day in 1925. The University of Texas system and the Texas A&M system continue to share the money in this fund. Their campuses have become two of the most important education centers in the state.

Texas has also benefited from oil producers' **philanthropy**—the giving of money or gifts. Many of the wildcatters who became wealthy gave generous gifts to public institutions that still influence life in Texas. Wildcatters such as Hugh Roy Cullen gave large gifts to the University of Houston, Texas Medical Center, and many charitable organizations. Oil producers Sid Richardson and Walter William Fondren both gave money and gifts to Texas schools, hospitals, and other social institutions.

Other oil producers have given generously to the arts in Texas. For example, John and Dominique de Menil established a collection of more than 10,000 works of art for public display. Oil producers have provided many jobs and spurred related industries in Texas. They have also had a major effect on the state's social life through their philanthropy and education funding.

Reading Check **Summarizing** What are some ways in which the oil boom affected the politics, economy, and society of Texas?

CONNECTING TO

SCIENCE AND TECHNOLOGY

Oil Drilling

The first oil wells were drilled with a heavy drill bit attached to a long cable. This cable was lowered into the hole. The bit was lifted up and down to push farther and farther into the rock. Workers also used the cable to pull dirt and rock out of the hole. Rotary drilling quickly became the preferred method. In rotary drilling the drill bit turns or spins as it pushes downward. As the bit turns, workers shoot drilling mud into the well to prevent gushers and explosions. It also carries loose rock to the top of the well, so that workers do not have to stop as often. **How is oil-drilling technology different now than in the past?**

Section 3 Review

1. Define and explain:
- boomtowns
- internal combustion engines
- philanthropy

2. Identify and explain the historical significance of:
- Texas Railroad Commission
- Permanent University Fund

3. Locate on a map:
- Midland
- Odessa

4. Categorizing
Copy the graphic organizer below. Use it to show how the oil industry affected the economy, politics, and social life of Texas.

Social Life
Economic Effects
Political Effects

5. Finding the Main Idea

a. In what ways did the oil industry contribute to urban growth in Texas?

b. How did new technological developments such as the internal combustion engine, the automobile, and petrochemicals affect the demand for and use of oil?

6. Writing and Critical Thinking myWriteSmart

Supporting a Point of View Write a letter to a member of Congress supporting a position for or against taxation and government regulation of the oil industry.

Consider the following:
- wildcatters and the spirit of free enterprise
- the Permanent University Fund and taxes collected on oil production

The Chapter at a Glance

Examine the following visual summary of the chapter. Sketch a map that illustrates where these events of the oil boom occurred. Be sure to record the date of each event on the map.

The Oil Boom

- **1925** Texas oil fields produce more than 144 million barrels of oil.
- **1916** Texans own more than 195,000 cars.
- **1902** Oil is discovered at Sour Lake, leading to a rush of drilling there.
- **1901** Anthony F. Lucas strikes oil at Spindletop, leading to a boom in drilling and the rapid growth of nearby towns such as Beaumont.
- **1894** Drillers searching for water discover oil in Corsicana.
- **1866** Lyne T. Barret drills for oil outside Nacogdoches.

Identifying People and Ideas

Write a sentence to explain the role or significance of each of the following terms or people.

1. petroleum
2. Pattillo Higgins
3. Anthony F. Lucas
4. Spindletop strike
5. wildcatters
6. natural gas
7. vertical integration
8. boomtowns
9. internal combustion engines
10. Permanent University Fund

Understanding Main Ideas

Section 1

1. List in chronological order the events that led up to the discovery of oil at Spindletop.
2. In what ways did the Spindletop strike lead to a boom-and-bust cycle in the oil industry?

Section 2

3. Compare the levels of oil production in various regions of Texas.

Section 3

4. How did new technology such as the automobile affect the use of natural resources in Texas?
5. How did the oil boom affect education in Texas?
6. How did the growth of the oil industry affect sources of revenue for the state?

You Be the Historian

Reviewing Themes

1. **Science, Technology & Society** How did technological advances lead to the oil boom and contribute to the growing use of the state's natural resources?
2. **Culture** In what ways did the oil boom affect Texas society and urban growth?
3. **Economics** How did the national demand for oil affect local businesses in Texas, and how did Texas oil discoveries affect the national oil market?

Thinking Critically

1. **Evaluating** How did geographic factors such as natural resources affect the economy and politics of Texas?
2. **Drawing Inferences and Conclusions** What role did the desire for profit play in the growth of the oil industry in Texas?
3. **Summarizing** Describe the defining characteristics of the era in Texas history known as the Age of Oil.

Texas Test Practice

Interpreting Graphs

Study the graph below. Then use the information on the graph to answer the questions that follow.

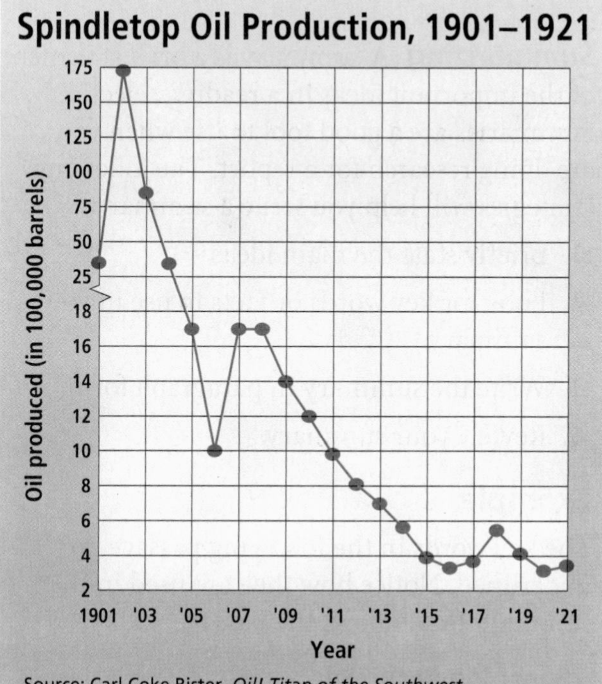

1. Approximately how much did Spindletop oil production change between 1902 and 1910?

A dropped 16 million barrels
B rose 16 million barrels
C dropped 18 million barrels
D rose 18 million barrels

2. Based on your reading of the chapter, what do you think may have caused the change?

Organizing Information

Read the passage below. Then answer the questions.

"Higgins ran an advertisement calling for a drilling engineer. In 1899 an engineer named Anthony F. Lucas responded to Higgins's ad. Lucas was an expert on salt domes, and he agreed that oil was probably beneath the Spindletop dome. He started drilling there in June 1900. At 575 feet, Lucas found traces of oil, but his equipment was not strong enough to continue. After finding business leaders willing to invest in new equipment, Lucas continued drilling. Finally, a big oil strike occurred on January 10, 1901."

3. What structural pattern does the author use to organize the information in the passage above?

F cause-effect
G chronological order
H compare-contrast
J listing

4. Which words help you understand the author's structural pattern?

Interdisciplinary Connection to the Arts

Imagine that you are an artist hired by the city of Beaumont to design a mural to celebrate the Spindletop strike. Choose images that reflect the events, individuals, and issues surrounding Spindletop and this period in Texas history. Include a brief artist's statement with your mural explaining the economic, social, and political impact of the oil industry on the industrialization of Texas.

Internet Activity 

Use the Internet to research the impact of the oil industry on local Texas communities. Then create a poster or model that illustrates products made from petrochemicals, analyzes technological innovations in the oil industry, or evaluates the effects of those innovations on the use of resources such as fossil fuels, water, and land.

Social Studies Skills

WORKSHOP

Study Skills

Taking notes and summarizing are key study skills. The following activities will help you develop and practice these skills.

Taking Notes

Taking notes helps you identify the main points of what you are studying. Write your notes in your own words. Your notes should include the main idea of each topic, interesting and supporting details, examples, and key vocabulary words. You should be able to use your notes to write a detailed summary. Try to use the following steps when taking notes:

- Identify your subject or main topic.
- Identify the main ideas.
- Note interesting and important details.
- Identify key vocabulary terms.
- Review your notes shortly after you write them.

Example

In the following example, all important words have been underlined. Looking just at the underlined words, you can learn a lot. To grasp the basic information contained in this section, you need only those words that are underlined.

Texas Agriculture

Many Texans eagerly awaited the arrival of new rail lines, hoping they would spur economic growth. The economic development of Texas had been slowed by its transportation problems. Most Texas rivers were either too shallow or too unreliable for shipping goods, while roads turned to mudholes during wet weather. Moving people and goods was time-consuming and expensive. Railroads promised cheap, fast, and reliable transportation.

Summarizing A summary is a brief statement of the important ideas in a reading selection. Summaries are a good tool to use when you are doing research for a report. The following strategies will help you write a summary.

1. Briefly state the main ideas.
2. Look for key words or facts to use in your summary.
3. Write the summary in paragraph form.
4. Review your summary.

Example

The key words in the following passage are underlined. Notice how they are used in the summary that follows the passage.

Ranching in the Panhandle

As Plains Indians were removed from West Texas, the Panhandle was opened up for ranching. The region's flat, open land was well suited for cattle ranching because it allowed ranchers and cowboys to keep close watch on the livestock. In addition, the grass that covered the Plains provided plenty of food for the cattle.

Summary The Texas Panhandle was opened up for ranching as the Plains Indians were removed from the region. The Panhandle's grasslands were well suited for cattle ranching.

Practicing the Skill

1. Look at Chapter 23, Section 2. Read the subsection titled Wildcatters and New Oil Fields. On your own paper, take notes by writing down the key words from each paragraph.
2. Now look at Chapter 22, Section 2. Read the subsection titled Commercial Farming. Use the strategies outlined above to write a short summary of each paragraph.

History in Action

UNIT 7 SIMULATION

You Solve the Problem . . .

How will you move Texas cattle to market?

Complete the following activity in small cooperative groups. It is 1866. You and your family own a cattle ranch. You would like to prepare a brochure to encourage other ranchers in the area to sell their cattle in out-of-state markets. Follow these steps to solve your problem.

1. **Gather information.** Use your textbook and other resources to find information that might influence your plan of action for moving Texas cattle to market. Remember to include in your brochure information that will show ranchers how they can get their cattle to market. Be sure to use what you learned from this unit's Skills Workshop on Taking Notes and Summarizing to help you find an effective solution to this problem. You may want to divide up different parts of the research among group members.

2. **List and consider options.** After reviewing the information you have gathered, list and consider the options you might recommend for successfully moving Texas cattle to market. Your final solution to the problem may be easier to reach if you consider as many options as possible. Be sure to record your possible options for the preparation of your brochure.

3. **Consider advantages and disadvantages.** Now consider the advantages and disadvantages of taking each option. Ask yourselves questions such as "Will this information persuade other ranchers to move cattle to markets?" and "Will this information convince the ranchers that a profit can be made by using this method?" Once you have considered the advantages and disadvantages, record them as notes for use in preparing your brochure.

4. **Choose, implement, and evaluate a solution.** After considering the advantages and disadvantages, you should create your brochure. You will need to support your proposed solution on how to move Texas cattle to market by including information you gathered and by explaining why you rejected other options. When you are ready, decide which group members will present the brochure, and then take your brochure to the ranchers (the rest of the class).
After you present, ask your listeners if they have any questions about what they have just heard. Listen carefully to the questions they ask and answer appropriately. In your answer, give the requested information clearly and briefly, using specific language to address your listeners' needs.

UNIT 8

Prosperity and the Great Depression

(1870–1939)

During the 1920s, Houston grew to a city of almost 300,000 people. Automobiles and skyscrapers changed the look and feel of the city.

Texas Teens

Young Relief Workers

Benito Rodriguez was not even a teenager when the Great Depression struck Texas. Many people were out of work, and Texas youth had to do whatever they could to help their families. Rodriguez found one way to help—he joined the Civilian Conservation Corps (CCC).

The CCC was designed to put unemployed young people to work in the nation's forests and parks, employing more than 3 million young people at the height of the depression. Between 1933 and 1942, the CCC employed about 50,000 Texans.

Although the CCC was only supposed to take young men between 17 and 25, Rodriguez enrolled early, at the age of 16. He worked for $30 a month and, as was required, sent $25 of that home. This much needed money allowed his family to purchase necessities. The government provided room, board, clothing, and tools for CCC workers.

The CCC performed many tasks, but one of the most long-lasting was the work they performed in the national and state parks systems. The CCC helped develop 800 state parks and plant 2 to 3 billion trees across the country. At Indian Lodge in Davis Mountains State Park, the CCC built the lodge and its furnishings. The CCC also built stone structures at Caddo Lake State Park and constructed buildings and trails, as well as planted trees, at Lake Brownwood State Park. Some CCC city and county parks still remain.

The CCC left a legacy of education by training teenage workers in Texas. One CCC worker explained that "getting up at 4 in the morning" gave him discipline. **How did some Texas teens help their families during the depression?**

In this unit you will learn more about the Great Depression in Texas. You will also learn about reform movements in Texas, changes in rural and urban life, and Texans' involvement in world affairs.

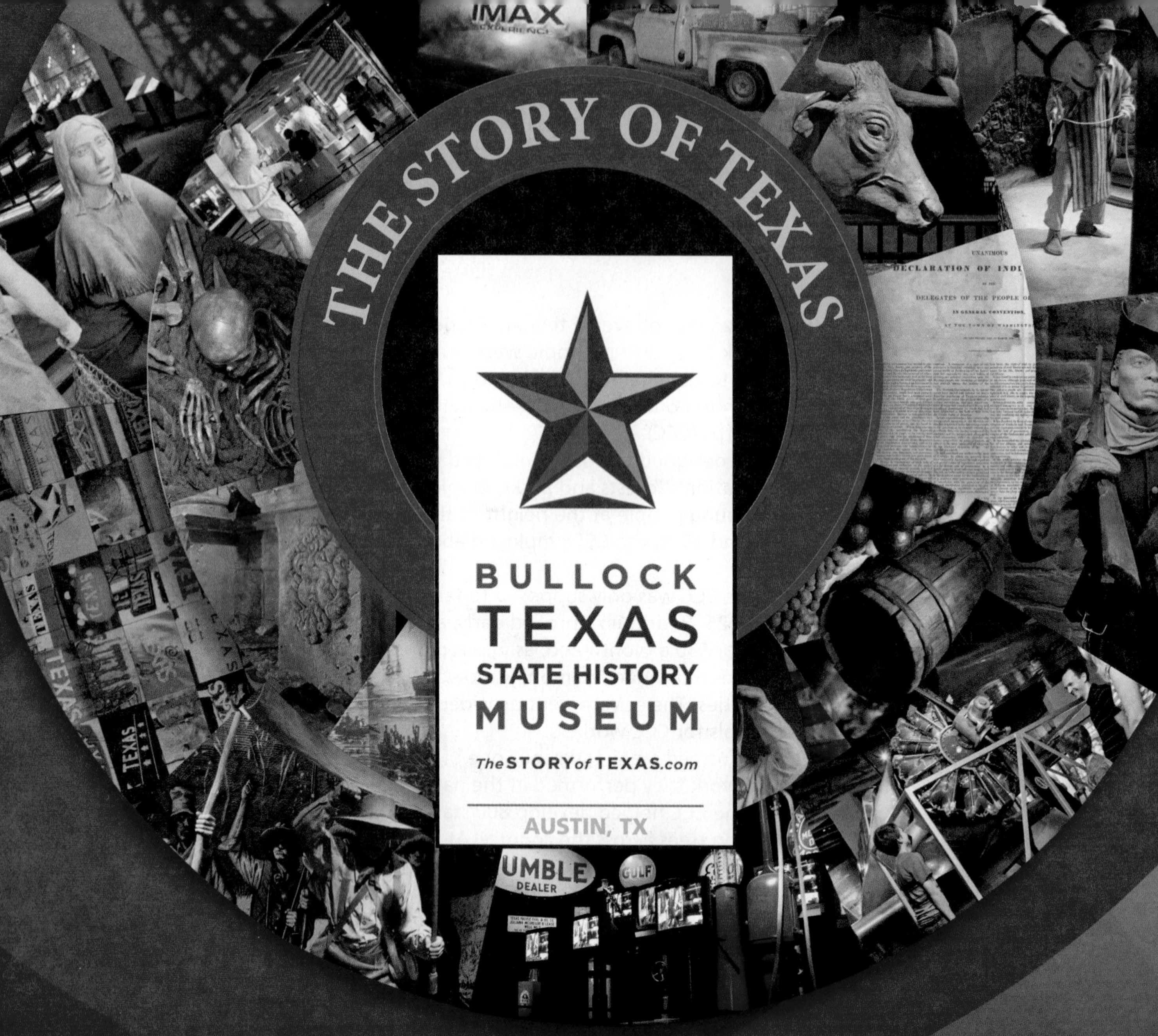

Texas in the 20th Century

The beginning of the 20th century was a time of great change in Texas. One major change was the birth of the oil industry. In 1901 Texans struck oil at Spindletop. Over the next 40 years, Texas became the center of U.S. oil production. The booming industry led to the growth of new jobs, businesses, and communities, attracting workers from Texas farms and ranches to jobs in factories and offices. In the process, Texas was transformed from a mostly rural state to a mostly urban one. The oil industry brought tremendous wealth to the state and helped fund the construction of new roads, ports, universities, and other facilities.

Another important change was the expansion of voting rights for women. Under the 1876 Texas Constitution, women were excluded from voting. Strong-willed Texas women such as Rebecca Henry Hayes, Annette Finnegan, and Minnie Fisher Cunningham organized mass meetings, circulated petitions, and lobbied members of the Texas Legislature for change. With such efforts, women won the right to vote in the state's 1918 primary elections. Texas also became the first state in the South to ratify the 19th Amendment to the U.S. Constitution granting women the right to vote.

By 1936 Texas had changed dramatically. That year, Texans held a World's Fair in Dallas to celebrate the 100th anniversary of Texas independence. The Texas Centennial highlighted the remarkable history and development of the Lone Star State and helped promote the state's image around the country, and the world.

At the Bullock Texas State History Museum visitors can explore the beginnings of the modern oil industry in Texas, learn about the social changes that led to the expansion of voting rights for women, and follow the development of the Texas identity as expressed during the Texas Centennial. Explore some of these resources online. You can find museum resources at

hmhsocialstudies.com

Photograph What challenges did people face as they tried to locate and drill for oil in Texas? Go online to find out.

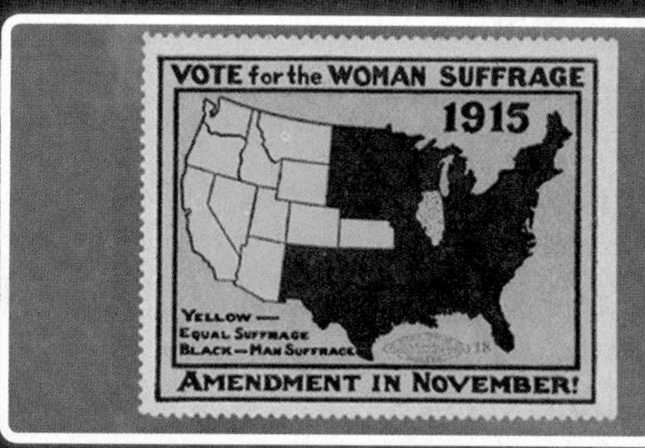

Artifact How were stamps like this one used to promote women's suffrage in the United States? Explore the artifact to learn more.

Art What kinds of events and displays were included in the Texas Centennial in 1936? Go online to find out.

UNIT 8

Reading Social Studies

Evaluating Sources

Focus on Reading **Primary sources** are materials created by people who lived during the times they describe. Examples include letters, diaries, and photographs. Accounts written later by someone who was not present are known as **secondary sources**. They are designed to teach about or discuss a historical topic. This textbook is an example of a secondary source.

Assessing Primary and Secondary Sources Together, the two types of sources can present a good picture of a historical period or event. However, they must be used carefully to make sure that the picture they present is accurate. Checklists like the ones below can help you judge which sources are reliable.

Checklist for Primary Sources

- √ Who is the author? Does he or she seem trustworthy?
- √ Was the author present for the event described in the source?
- √ How soon after the event occurred was the source created?
- √ Can the information in the source be verified in other primary or secondary sources?

Historians in the past were not always careful about what they included in their books. Some included rumors, gossip, or hearsay.

The more time that passed between the event and the creation of the source, the greater the chance of errors or distortion in the description.

Checklist for Secondary Sources

- √ Who is the author? Why is he or she qualified to write about this subject?
- √ Where did the author get his or her information?
- √ Is the information in the source documented properly?
- √ Has the author drawn valid conclusions from his or her sources?

Not everyone who writes about history is a good historian. Try to use sources by qualified writers.

Good historians will always tell you where they get their information. If they don't cite their sources, you can't always trust that it is true or accurate.

You Try It!

The passage below is found in the unit you are about to read. Read it, and then answer the questions below.

> "We were told . . . to go to work and raise a big crop, that was all we needed. We went to work and plowed and planted; the rains fell, the sun shone, nature smiled, and we raised the big crop that they told us to; and what came of it? Eight cent corn, ten cent oats, two cent beef and no price at all for butter and eggs—that's what came of it. Then the politicians said that we suffered from over-production."
>
> —Anonymous farmer, quoted in *The Populist Revolt* by John D. Hicks

1. Would this be a good source to use to learn more about farming in early Texas? Why or why not? What other things might you learn about by evaluating this source?
2. Where else might a historian look to verify the information found in this source?

Reading Section Assessment

The passage below is from this unit. Read it and answer the questions that follow.

Texas Farmers Face Hardships

Farmers also faced other problems, such as foreign competition, high interest rates, and droughts. When they tried to overcome these obstacles by growing more crops, the result was further overproduction. Prices fell still more. This cycle, which had troubled farmers for many years, became particularly severe in the 1870s. Even as they earned less, farmers had to pay more for many of the goods and services they needed to operate. Some farmers borrowed money from merchants based on how much they expected to earn from their crops. Then they had to pay the money back with interest.

1. Is the passage above a primary or secondary source? Does it appear to be reliable? How can you tell?
2. Does the information presented in this source support the information presented in the first passage? Why or why not? Where else might you look to find more information to verify the information in the passage?
3. According to both of the passages, what was life like for farmers in Texas at the time?

Key Terms

Unit 8

Chapter 24

cooperative stores *(p. 499)*
pooling *(p. 500)*
platform *(p. 502)*
monopoly *(p. 503)*
trusts *(p. 503)*
progressives *(p. 507)*
commission plan *(p. 508)*
temperance movement *(p. 511)*
prohibition *(p. 511)*
poll tax *(p. 513)*

Chapter 25

suburbs *(p. 523)*
ragtime *(p. 525)*
refugees *(p. 529)*
neutral *(p. 530)*

Chapter 26

demobilization *(p. 536)*
primary election *(p. 539)*
white primary *(p. 539)*
blues *(p. 542)*
consumer goods *(p. 542)*
stocks *(p. 544)*
soup kitchens *(p. 546)*
breadlines *(p. 546)*
scrip *(p. 546)*
proration *(p. 546)*
centennial *(p. 554)*

As you read, ask your teacher or classmates for assistance with difficult words, meanings, or sentence structures.

CHAPTER 24

Texas in the Age of Reform

(1870–1920)

Texas Essential Knowledge and Skills (TEKS) 6A, 6B, 6C, 7C, 9A, 10B, 13A, 13B, 17A, 17C, 18B, 21B, 21C, 21E, 22A

The opening of Texas A&M University and the University of Texas gave Texans new educational opportunities.

TEXAS

1876 Texas A&M University opens as an all-male military institution.

1883 The University of Texas formally opens.

1889 The Texas legislature passes the Antitrust Act of 1889

1892 A leading association of farmers endorses the Populist Party.

1870 — 1876 — 1882 — 1888 — 1894

U.S. and WORLD

1881 The Knights of Labor, the first union to allow female members, establishes a local women's chapter in Philadelphia.

1886 A riot erupts in Chicago's Haymarket Square during a nationwide strike by unions.

1891 More than 1,400 delegates from 33 states and territories gather in Cincinnati to form the Populist Party.

If you were there . . .
What social problem would you work to solve?

Build on What You Know

The Texas oil boom led to a rapid growth of oil-related industries, and big business grew powerful. Texans on farms and in the cities demanded that their government ensure fair treatment from big business. Across Texas, reformers took up the call for change.

The Galveston Hurricane of 1900 was the deadliest hurricane in U.S. history. It destroyed the city and killed an estimated 6,000 to 8,000 people.

Some progressives in Texas wanted prohibition, or a ban on alcohol.

1900 A hurricane hits Galveston, killing some 6,000 to 8,000 people.

1901 New Zealand passes a third Factory Act designed to protect the rights of workers.

1909 The National Association for the Advancement of Colored People (NAACP) is founded.

1911 Jovita Idar becomes the first president of the League of Mexican Women.

1918 Texas ratifies the Eighteenth Amendment to the U.S. Constitution, which bans the sale or manufacture of alcohol.

1920 The Nineteenth Amendment is adopted, granting women the right to vote.

1900 | 1906 | 1912 | 1918

You Be the Historian

myNotebook

What's Your Opinion? Do you **agree** or **disagree** with the following statements? Support your point of view in your notebook.

- **Economics** Free enterprise is harmed by government regulations.
- **Government** People are rarely able to bring about changes in government to correct social or economic problems.
- **Citizenship** People must work in groups to bring about social change.

Section 1

Farmers and Reform

Main Ideas

1. Texas farmers faced serious economic challenges in the late 1800s as crop prices fell and farmers' debts grew.
2. The Grange and the Southern Farmers' Alliance worked for economic reforms to improve the lives of farmers.
3. Dissatisfaction with the Democratic Party led some farmers to help form the Populist Party in 1891.

Why It Matters Today

During the late 1800s Texas farmers joined organizations to push for reform. Use current events sources to find information about an organization seeking reforms today.

Key Terms and People

- **Grange**
- **cooperative stores**
- **Southern Farmers' Alliance**
- **pooling**
- **Populist Party**
- **Populists**
- **platform**

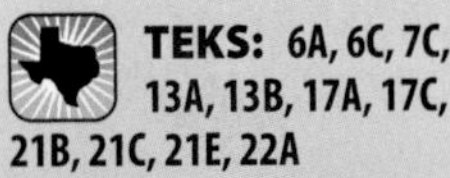

TEKS: 6A, 6C, 7C, 13A, 13B, 17A, 17C, 21B, 21C, 21E, 22A

myNotebook

Use the annotation tools in your eBook to take notes on how Texas farmers worked for reform.

The Story Continues

Farmers in Lampasas County were worried and angry. Crop prices remained low, and the only thing that seemed to grow each year was their debt. In 1877 some farmers gathered at J. R. Allen's farm to come up with a plan of action. They wanted to improve their economic situation, but how could they push for the reforms they so desperately needed?

Texas Farmers Face Hardships

Many farmers in Texas and other parts of the United States faced serious hardships in the late 1800s. The movement of farmers and railroads into the Plains sparked a boom in farm production, but the supply of crops outpaced the demand. This, combined with problems in the national economy, caused prices to fall. One rural man noted the difficulties farmers faced.

TEXAS VOICES

"We were told . . . to go to work and raise a big crop, that was all we needed. We went to work and plowed and planted; the rains fell, the sun shone, nature smiled, and we raised the big crop that they told us to; and what came of it? Eight cent corn, ten cent oats, two cent beef and no price at all for butter and eggs—that's what came of it. Then the politicians said that we suffered from over-production."

—Anonymous farmer, quoted in *The Populist Revolt*, by John D. Hicks

The Grange supported farmers by forming cooperatives, opening schools, and offering other aid.

Cotton farmers were particularly vulnerable to the changing national market. In the 1880s, cotton was selling for less than 10 cents a pound. Yet on most farms, it cost 8 cents a pound just to produce the cotton.

Farmers also faced other problems, including foreign competition, high interest rates, and droughts. When they tried to overcome these obstacles by growing more crops, the result was further overproduction. Prices fell still more. This cycle, which had troubled farmers for many years, became particularly severe in the 1870s.

Even as they earned less, farmers had to pay more for many of the goods and services they needed to operate. Some farmers borrowed money from merchants to make ends meet. These farmers estimated how much they expected to earn from their crops in that year, planning to borrow only what they could pay back after selling their harvest. However, they had to pay the borrowed money back with interest. One observer said that merchants charged rates ranging "from 25 percent to grand larceny [great theft]." And if crops failed or a harvest was smaller than expected, the farmers could not pay their loans at all. As crop prices continued to drop, farmers struggled to make ends meet.

Reading Check **Summarizing** What challenges did Texas farmers face?

The Grange

As their problems mounted, many farmers joined together to work on solutions. In the late 1860s farmers had established the Patrons of Husbandry—commonly called the **Grange**. It promoted cooperation and social activities among farmers as well as education for rural families. Wherever Grange leaders went, they encouraged farmers to join.

As the organization grew and spread, it began opening **cooperative stores**—businesses owned by and operated for the benefit of the organization's members. The Grange bought large amounts of goods such as seeds, fertilizers, and clothing. This lowered individuals' costs for buying such items, and the savings were then passed on to the members.

Getting Involved in Government

Many Texans in the late 1800s tried to reform society. They demanded that government take an active role in improving their lives. Texans still work with government to meet today's challenges. Voting, organizing into political groups, and meeting with government officials are just a few ways people can try to change society. Teenagers can get involved by learning about the government of Texas. **What can Texans do to get involved in the state's government?**

Interpreting Visuals

The Grange. *Members of the Grange met regularly to discuss issues, sing songs, and listen to speakers.* ***What aspects of the daily life of Grange members are portrayed in this poster?***

The Grange also focused on lowering railroad shipping rates. The expansion of rail lines had allowed farmers to move farther west and ship goods across great distances to national markets. However, the railroads charged more and more for their services. The Grange tried to end the railroads' policy of charging more for short hauls than for longer ones. For example, it might cost more to ship cotton from Austin to Waco than from Austin to New Orleans. This was a problem for small farmers who shipped goods only within the state. Railroads claimed that long hauls were more profitable, so they set rates to encourage this type of business. The lack of competition allowed railroads to charge high rates for local hauls.

After pressure from the Grange to change these unfair practices, the state passed several laws to regulate, or control, railroads. In 1879 the legislature set maximum freight charges, and in 1882 it reduced fares for passengers using railroads in Texas. In 1883 a new law required railroads to charge the same rates for the same services. However, these laws proved hard to enforce because Texas had no government agency to regulate the railroad companies.

Reading Check **Identifying Cause and Effect** Why did Texas pass legislation regulating railroads, and what was the result?

★ The Southern Farmers' Alliance

In 1877 former Grange members and other farmers in Texas formed the National Farmers' Alliance and Industrial Union, or **Southern Farmers' Alliance**. This organization was more politically active than the Grange. The Southern Farmers' Alliance spread to other states, eventually claiming about 3 million members nationwide. The Alliance took some ideas from the Grange, such as forming trade agreements with merchants and setting up cooperative stores. However, merchants who did not take part in the Alliance system were often hostile to it. These retailers often dropped their prices to compete with the Alliance cooperatives. The Alliance stores also struggled because they sold goods for cash rather than for credit. Farmers who were heavily in debt had little cash on hand.

The Alliance also tried to help farmers market their goods more effectively. Through the Farmers' Alliance Exchange of Texas, members could sell crops at one location and bypass costly middlemen. However, the Exchange struggled financially and ended within two years.

Like the Grange, the Alliance wanted railroads to be regulated. It called for a law governing interstate trade to regulate companies operating between different states. Alliance members also wanted to prevent railroad companies from **pooling**—combining efforts to prevent competition between companies. In addition, the Alliance objected to the state's practice of granting land to railroad companies that then sold the land to settlers for high prices.

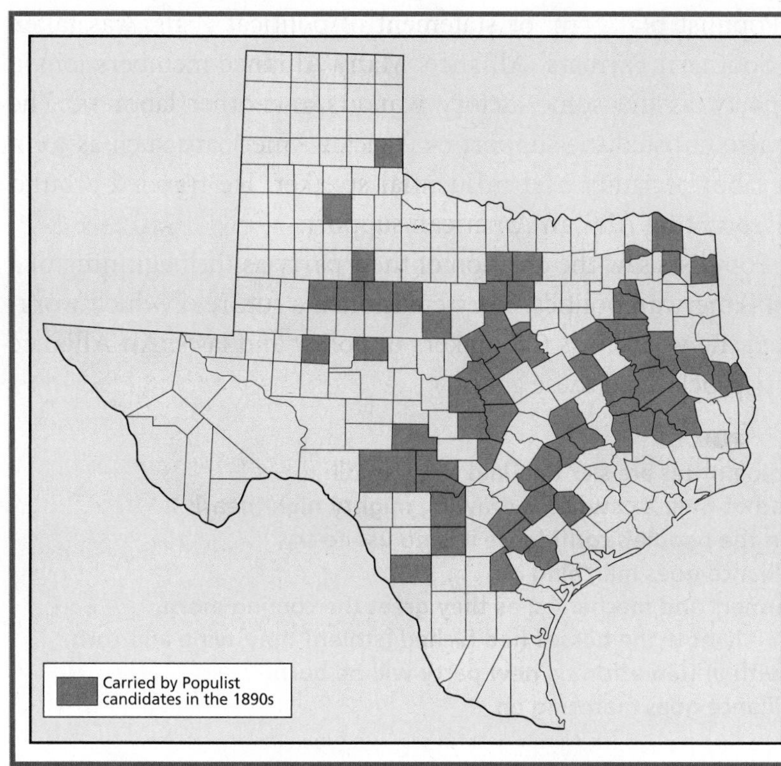

Populism in Texas, 1890s

Interpreting Maps

Populist candidates won the support of many Texas farmers and ranchers by pushing for the regulation of transportation and other issues.

1. Places and Regions In which regions of Texas were Populists most successful?

2. Evaluating What positions in the Populist platform might have appealed to those counties' residents?

In 1889 Texan Charles W. Macune, the president of the Southern Farmers' Alliance, laid out a bold plan to help farmers. He believed that crop prices would rise and that the farmers' situation would improve if the government put more currency into circulation. Macune and an Alliance committee proposed that farmers deposit and store their crops in U.S. government warehouses until prices went up. The government would give low-interest loans based on the value of the crops deposited. Farmers could repay the loans later after selling their crops at higher prices. This plan, known as the subtreasury plan, had much support within the Alliance. It gave farmers hope that they would soon receive help. However, the Democratic Party refused to support the subtreasury plan, and it never went into effect.

Reading Check **Analyzing Information** What action did the Southern Farmers' Alliance want the government to take to help farmers?

★ The Populists

Southern farmers had traditionally voted for Democratic Party candidates. However, the Democrats' failure to back the subtreasury plan prompted Alliance members to help form the People's Party—commonly called the **Populist Party**—in 1891. Its members were known as **Populists**. The Populists wanted to reduce the influence of big business on government. They called for government ownership of railroads and the telephone and telegraph system. They also demanded an eight-hour workday and an increase in the money supply.

Despite his loss in 1896, William Jennings Bryan ran for president again in 1900, pushing for many of the same reforms he had in the previous election.

This Populist **platform**, or statement of political goals, was taken from the Southern Farmers' Alliance. Many Alliance members joined the new party, as did some factory workers and other laborers. The Populists also enlisted the support of African Americans such as John Rayner, a labor recruiter and influential speaker. He traveled around East Texas, building African American support.

Some Populists saw the creation of their party as the beginning of a new era in American politics. They envisioned a future in which workers replaced the wealthy as the makers of policy and laws. An Alliance song boldly proclaimed these goals.

TEXAS VOICES

"The old parties are sick and laid away to die
The end of their existence is drawing mighty nigh [near];
To gain the people's confidence it is no use to try,
The Alliance goes marching on. . . .
The farmers and mechanics, as they greet the coming morn,
See plainly how the bosses had filched [stolen] their wine and corn.
Now with united efforts a new party will be born.
The Alliance goes marching on."

—"The Alliance Goes Marching On," from *The Alliance and Labor Songster*, edited by Leopold Vincent

In the 1890s the Populists ran candidates for national and state offices. Texas voters elected 22 Populists to the Texas House of Representatives in 1894. In 1896 both the Populists and the Democrats nominated William Jennings Bryan of Nebraska for president. Bryan ran as the Democratic candidate and lost despite winning Texas and many other states. The Populist Party faded from the political scene as members argued about policy issues. The Democrats also weakened the party by adopting some of the Populists' programs. Through it all, Texas farmers continued to face economic problems.

Reading Check **Finding the Main Idea** What civic responsibility were Alliance members fulfilling when they formed the People's Party?

Section 1 Review

1. Define and explain:
- cooperative stores
- pooling
- platform

2. Identify and explain the significance of each in Texas history:
- Grange
- Southern Farmers' Alliance
- Populist Party
- Populists

3. Identifying Cause and Effect
Copy the graphic organizer below. Use it to show the causes and effects of the boom-and-bust cycle of farming in Texas.

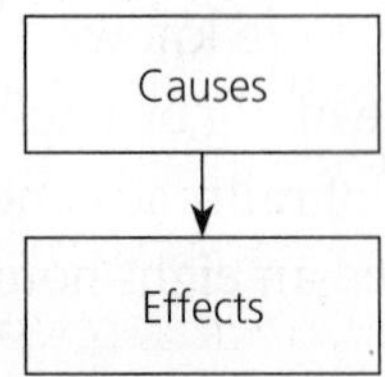

4. Finding the Main Idea

a. How did the national market for crops and world competition affect Texas farmers?

b. What did the Grange and the Southern Farmers' Alliance hope to achieve?

5. Writing and Critical Thinking myWriteSmart

Supporting a Point of View You are a member of the People's Party. Write a speech in which you argue for one Populist position. Consider the following:
- farmers' problems with debt, railroad rates, and high prices for goods
- reasons your organization was formed

Section 2 Government in the Reform Age

Main Ideas

1. Big businesses in Texas used trusts and monopolies to increase their power and wealth, and citizens demanded change.
2. Texas political leaders such as Lawrence Ross, James Hogg, and James Ferguson worked to reform unfair business practices.

Why It Matters Today

During the late 1800s and early 1900s, some Texans worried about the influence of big business on politics. Use current events sources to find information about big business and government policies today.

Key Terms and People

- **trusts**
- **monopoly**
- **Lawrence Sullivan "Sul" Ross**
- **James Stephen Hogg**
- **Hogg Laws**
- **James E. Ferguson**

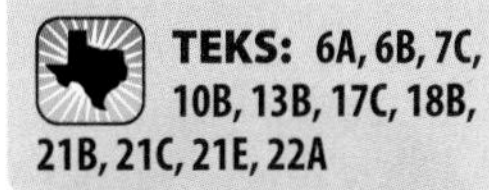

myNotebook

Use the annotation tools in your eBook to take notes on Texas government in the reform age.

The Story Continues

When the railroad foreman at Marshall was late for work, the Texas and Pacific Railway fired him. In response, the foremen's union launched a strike against the railroad company. Only a year before, the union had carried out a successful strike for better wages against another railroad company. But the management of the Texas and Pacific was determined to break the union this time. Violence broke out, and the governor sent in troops. Soon the strike was crushed, and the workers returned to their jobs.

★ Regulating Big Business

By the late 1800s many railroad companies, oil companies, and other businesses that operated in Texas had become large and powerful. They provided many new jobs, products, and services in the state. But many Texans worried that the companies had become too powerful. Some businesses had formed **trusts**—legal arrangements in which one board of trustees controls a number of companies. A **monopoly**—sole economic control of a field of business—could be more easily created by using a trust. A monopoly eliminates competition, giving one corporation the ability to control prices. Because of monopolies, Texans often had to pay higher prices for the goods they needed. Some people argued that this lack of competition violated the principles of free enterprise. These Texans wanted government policies that would regulate the power of these corporations. Government regulation met with opposition, however, because others argued that it also limited free enterprise.

Reading Check **Identifying Cause and Effect** What new business practices arose in the late 1800s, and how did they affect free enterprise?

★ Governor Sul Ross

One Texas leader who contributed to new reforms was **Lawrence Sullivan "Sul" Ross**, a Democrat who became governor in 1887. Ross was a former Texas Ranger, Confederate general, farmer, and state senator who was very popular in the state. Under his leadership, the Texas legislature passed new laws related to water and grazing rights on public lands, a source of conflict between farmers and ranchers. Other reforms created a fairer system for assessing the value of property for tax purposes and required that local taxes support public schools. During Ross's governorship, Texas experienced a boom in industrial and agricultural growth. In fact, Ross's reforms were so successful he became the only governor in Texas history to call a special session of the legislature to decide what to do with a treasury surplus.

Another Texan who believed in reform was **James Stephen Hogg**, a Democrat who was elected attorney general of Texas in 1886. Hogg served as attorney general while Ross was governor. Hogg brought lawsuits against companies with unfair business practices. He went after insurance companies that were engaging in illegal activities, forcing many of them to stop operating in Texas. He then broke up the Texas Traffic Association, a railroad organization that eliminated competition and drove up shipping rates through pooling. Hogg and many Texans believed these practices violated the spirit of free enterprise.

In 1887 the federal government passed an act that created the Interstate Commerce Commission. This federal agency regulated railroads. The act also made pooling illegal and prohibited railroads from charging more for short hauls than for long ones over the same line. Hogg helped write state antitrust legislation that further regulated railroads. The Antitrust Act of 1889 regulated monopolies and trusts that were dominating the market in Texas. It targeted railroads by making it illegal to fix prices or restrain competition. The state won court cases against many railroads and other industries that violated the Antitrust Act. Price-fixing—setting prices artificially and against free-market operations—decreased in the railroad industry, but problems still existed. For example, rates for rural communities were still high. Many Texans demanded more regulation.

Reading Check **Summarizing** How did Sul Ross contribute to reform?

BIOGRAPHY

James Stephen Hogg (1851–1906) Born in Rusk, James Stephen Hogg was the first governor of Texas born in the state. As a young man, Hogg worked in the newspaper business and as a lawyer. He began his political career in 1876. He served as county attorney, district attorney, attorney general, and governor. After his terms as governor, Hogg returned to his law practice. He never ran for elected office again, but he continued to be politically active until his death.

How did James Stephen Hogg contribute to Texas politics?

Hogg as Governor

James Hogg's reforms as attorney general were popular with Texas voters. He was also personally popular. He had a reputation as a plain-speaker, a politician who spoke to the common people in a way they could understand. Huge crowds gathered to hear him deliver campaign speeches in his loud, booming voice, sometimes for hours at a time. In 1890 he was elected governor by a landslide. He was the first governor since annexation born in Texas.

Hogg's administration pushed for a number of laws regulating business, which together became known as **Hogg Laws**. At the time, Texas had no agency that could effectively enforce public-interest laws. In 1891 Hogg tackled this issue by creating the Texas Railroad Commission to oversee railroads in the state. He appointed former U.S. senator John H. Reagan head of the commission. Although many Texans had supported the creation of the agency, some feared it would slow economic growth. They thought railroads would invest less in new tracks and lines in the state because of its oversight.

TEXAS VOICES

"There can be no doubt that the creation of a railroad commission in answer to the demand of an anti-railroad sentiment [feeling], speaking through politicians and demagogues [bad leaders], would put a stop to investments in railroads."

—*Fort Worth Gazette*, August 30, 1889

Governor Hogg also promoted other reforms, particularly for the public school system. He supported teacher-training schools and universities, as well as teacher-training scholarships. The governor also tried to reform the prison system and to change laws regarding corporate landholdings. Hogg's reforms proved popular, and he was re-elected.

While Hogg was governor, a controversy concerning the state's border broke out. The Texas legislature had passed an act to form Greer County in 1860. However, the U.S. government claimed the area as part of its territory. The dispute stemmed from two major mistakes on a map created in 1819. Finally, in 1891, the U.S. attorney general filed suit against the Texas claim. The U.S. Supreme Court ruled that the disputed land belonged to the federal government.

Under Hogg and other party leaders such Edward M. House, the Democrats dominated Texas politics. Charles Culberson, who had been attorney general during Hogg's administration, became governor in 1895. Culberson also pursued a reform agenda. Other reform-minded leaders such as Thomas M. Campbell also worked on public interest issues. During his terms as governor from 1907 to 1911, Campbell helped enact railroad regulations, antitrust laws, and pure food and drug laws.

Reading Check **Summarizing** How did reform affect Texas businesses?

CONNECTING TO

GEOGRAPHY

The Greer County Dispute

The conflict grew out of the 1819 Adams-Onís Treaty, which was accompanied by a map with the boundaries separating Spanish and U.S. territories. However, the map had two major mistakes. As a result, Texas and the U.S. government both claimed the same area along the upper Red River. The U.S. Supreme Court ruled in 1896 that what Texas called Greer County was actually federal land. The land eventually became part of Oklahoma Territory in 1906. **Where was the disputed region located?**

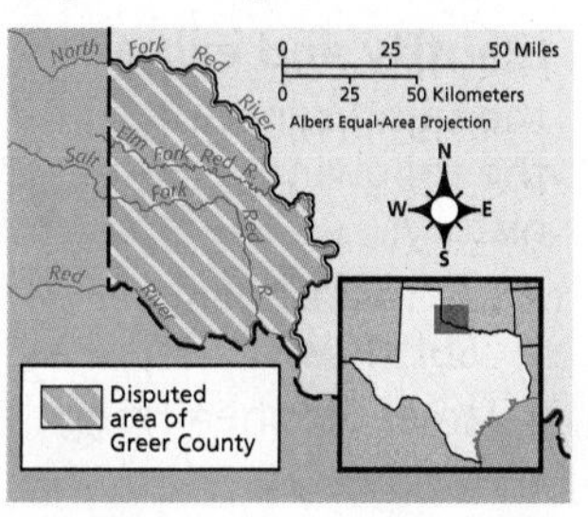

Governor James Ferguson supported reforms that would benefit Texas farmers.

★ Farmer Jim

James E. Ferguson was another influential member of the Texas Democratic Party. He gained the support of the state's poor citizens, particularly its tenant farmers, by working for reforms. Because of his support for Texas farmers and poor people, Ferguson was nicknamed Farmer Jim. One of his admirers wrote, "He swayed them [rural voters] like the storm sways the slender pines." Those opposed to Ferguson, in contrast, said that he was dishonest and stirred up people for his own benefit. Most Texas voters seemed to like Ferguson, however, and he was elected governor in 1914 and 1916.

Several important reforms were passed during Ferguson's first term. The legislature passed a law limiting the rent landowners could charge tenant farmers. Although it was later struck down by the courts, the law represented a bold effort to help farmers. Another new law provided aid to rural schools and more funds to colleges. The most important law passed during Ferguson's second term established a highway department in 1917 to improve Texas roads.

As governor, Ferguson developed some powerful enemies who accused him of misusing state funds. In his second term he vetoed most of the funding for the University of Texas because school officials did not fire certain faculty members as he requested. Many Texans disapproved of the veto, and some wanted him removed from office. The Texas House of Representatives impeached the governor in 1917, filing 21 charges against him. The Senate found the governor guilty of 10 charges, including using state funds for personal benefit. Ferguson left office, and Lieutenant Governor William P. Hobby became the new governor.

Reading Check **Analyzing Information** How successful was Ferguson in enacting reform legislation?

★ Section 2 Review

hmhsocialstudies.com
ONLINE QUIZ

1. Define and explain:
- trusts
- monopoly

2. Identify and explain the significance of the following in Texas history:
- Lawrence Sullivan "Sul" Ross
- James Stephen Hogg
- Hogg Laws
- James E. Ferguson

3. Categorizing Copy the chart below and use it to show the reforms backed by James Stephen Hogg.

Hogg in Office	Effect on Texas
Attorney General	
Governor	

4. Finding the Main Idea

a. How was the free-enterprise system in Texas affected by the rise of big business?

b. What contributions to reform did Sul Ross make?

5. Writing and Critical Thinking myWriteSmart

Analyzing Information You are a Texan in the late 1800s. Write a newspaper editorial defending or opposing government regulation of corporations and its effect on the free-enterprise system. Consider
- how regulation will change business
- how regulation will affect consumers

Section 3

The Progressive Movement

Main Ideas

1. Beginning in the early 1900s, the progressive movement worked to reform and improve society.
2. Progressive reforms focused on areas such as working conditions, health and safety, and education.

Key Terms

- **progressives**
- **Seventeenth Amendment**
- **Galveston Hurricane of 1900**
- **commission plan**

Why It Matters Today

To force changes in working conditions, union members have occasionally gone on strike. Use current events sources to find information about a recent labor dispute in Texas or another state.

TEKS: 6A, 6C, 7C, 9A, 13B, 21B, 21C, 22A

myNotebook

Use the annotation tools in your eBook to take notes on how progressives worked to improve society.

The Story Continues

Elizabeth Gaertner moved to Galveston from New York City as a young girl. After marrying a successful merchant, Alphonse Levy, she raised a family and joined some local clubs. Gaertner was fortunate to live in a comfortable home, but she was concerned about some of the less fortunate people around her. She became active in her community. Gaertner was one of the many women working to solve social problems in Texas.

★ Government Reform

In the early 1900s reformers known as **progressives** worked to improve society. *Progressive* means "forward-looking" or "related to progress." Progressives tackled many issues, such as election reform. In 1905 the Texas legislature passed the Terrell Election Law, named after its sponsor Alexander W. Terrell. The law established primary elections to choose candidates for all state, district, and county races. Candidates who won the primaries would represent their party in the later general elections. The law also attacked election fraud—for example, by requiring the use of official ballots.

In the federal government, too, progressives were working to improve the election process. The passage of the **Seventeenth Amendment** to the U.S. Constitution in 1913 allowed American voters—rather than the state legislatures—to vote directly for U.S. senators. Reformers believed this change would give people a greater say in the government.

That's Interesting!

The Great Storm

After the disastrous 1900 hurricane, Galveston residents struggled to rebuild. One of their efforts involved raising the city to a greater height above sea level. To do this, they pumped sand into the city from the ocean floor. Any buildings that had survived the hurricane were then jacked up and placed on new foundations. In addition, a 17-foot-high seawall was built along the beach for protection.

Another of the progressives' goals was to make local government more efficient. A major natural disaster in Galveston in September 1900 spurred this reform effort. On September 8 newspapers reported a huge hurricane was moving toward the city. Residents, though, went on about their business. After all, they had lived through hurricanes before. While observing the ocean early that Saturday morning, however, Galveston weather reporter Isaac Cline began to worry. This storm seemed different from others he had witnessed.

TEXAS VOICES

"Unusually heavy swells [waves] from the southeast . . . overflowing low places [in the] south portion of the city three to four blocks from beach. . . . Such high water with opposing winds never observed previously."

—Isaac Cline, quoted in *Texas: An Album of History,* by James L. Haley

The **Galveston Hurricane of 1900** hit later that day. Waves battered Galveston, drowning people and destroying buildings. Some 6,000 to 8,000 people lost their lives, and half the city lay in ruins.

Many people in Galveston felt that the city government could not cope with the disaster. To rebuild the city, a new form of local government called the **commission plan** was established. Under this plan, voters elect a mayor and four city commissioners. Each commissioner supervises different city services. The new government of Galveston oversaw the rebuilding of the city, including the construction of a six-mile seawall to protect the island. Progressives liked the commission plan because it was efficient. In choosing commissioners, more emphasis was placed on knowledge of city services and less on politics. The commission plan was a major reform of the progressive movement, and it was soon adopted by other U.S. cities.

Reading Check **Analyzing Information** How did geographic factors such as weather lead to a reform in the structure of local government in Texas?

Interpreting Visuals

The great storm. *The Galveston Hurricane of 1900 left the city in ruins.* ***Based on this photo, what challenges do you think the city faced in rebuilding efforts?***

Workplace and Health Reform

Progressives also tried to help improve conditions for Texas workers. Many workers, especially those who worked in factories, labored long hours but earned little for their efforts. The conditions in which they worked could be very dangerous, and accidents were common. Along with unions, progressives fought for higher wages, better working conditions, and a shorter workweek for factory workers.

Progressives also opposed child labor. Many children during this period worked in factories, and they risked serious illness from long hours and poor conditions. Many received little education or exercise. Texas passed its first child labor law in 1903. Laws that regulated child labor more strictly soon followed.

Progressives also worried about unregulated food and drugs. Eating poorly processed food or taking unsafe medications made many people sick each year. Progressives such as the members of Texas Federation of Women's Clubs backed candidates who favored food and drug regulation. The clubs helped elect progressive candidate Thomas M. Campbell as governor in 1906.

During Campbell's administration, the legislature passed laws to regulate the food and drug industries and created the Dairy and Food Commission to set health standards. These laws led to increased costs for businesses that had to meet the higher standards. However, most Texans agreed that the benefits outweighed the costs because the laws helped improve the lives and health of many in the state.

Reading Check **Finding the Main Idea** What social reforms and government regulations did progressives pursue?

★ Education Reform

Many progressives, particularly women, also tried to improve Texas schools. Texas ranked near the bottom in the nation for its education system. About 15 percent of Texas children older than 10 could not read or write. Teachers were often untrained, and schools lacked the proper resources and facilities.

In the late 1800s and early 1900s the state established several schools to train teachers. These schools were called normal schools, because they were designed to teach the basic standards, or norms, required to be an effective teacher. Normal schools established in this period included Sam Houston Normal Institute in Huntsville—now Sam Houston State University—and Southwest Texas State Normal School in San Marcos—now Texas State University. The state also established medical schools such as the University of Texas Medical School at Galveston.

During the early 1900s the legislature passed a number of laws to improve the public school system. Under the new laws, rural schools could borrow money and raise tax rates. More local funds could also be used to provide free textbooks. In addition, the legislature raised teachers' salaries and lengthened school terms.

★ Texas Cities ★

Galveston

History: The city of Galveston was founded in 1836. With its good natural harbor and growing trade, the city had a booming local economy. Galveston was also a major arrival point for immigrants arriving in Texas.

Population in 2012: 47,762 (estimate)

Relative location: Located on the eastern end of Galveston Island, some 50 miles southeast of Houston.

Region: Gulf Coastal Plain

County: County seat of Galveston County

Special feature: Located on an island, the city is a popular destination for tourists and beachgoers.

Origin of name: The city was named after Galveston Bay, which was named by explorer José de Evia in 1785. Evia named the bay in honor of Bernardo de Gálvez, then the viceroy of New Spain.

Economy: Galveston's economy today is largely based on tourism and shipping. The city's port is still active, and many people travel to Galveston for recreation.

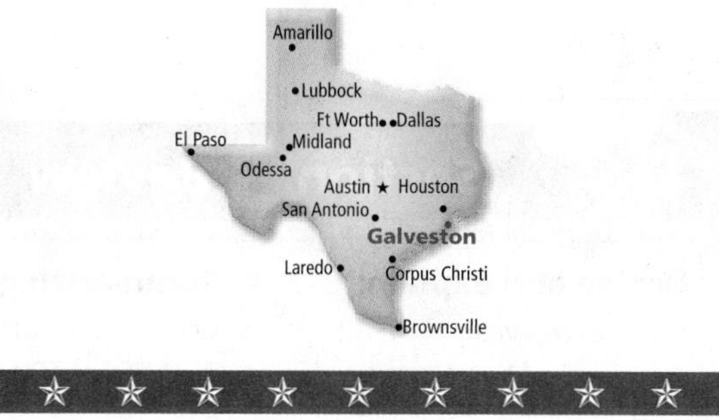

These reforms helped some 1 million Texas children attend school by 1910. The number of children in school increased after the legislature passed a law in 1915 requiring school attendance. As a result of these reforms, more women gained access to education in the late 1800s than ever before. By 1890 more girls than boys attended Texas schools. Some women went on to get a higher education. Several colleges, including the University of Texas, began allowing women to attend. The Girls' Industrial College—now Texas Woman's University—opened in 1903.

As educational opportunities for women increased, so too did their job prospects, particularly in the field of education. So many women became teachers that by 1900 they outnumbered men in teaching positions in Texas.

Education reform did not reach all Texans, however. African American and Mexican American students generally did not benefit from Progressive Era changes in education. The Constitution of 1876 had established separate schools based on race. However, these separate facilities were not equal. Facilities for white children were better funded and better supported. The schools that African American and Mexican American students attended often lacked adequate funding for facilities and supplies. Prairie View Normal Institute—now known as Prairie View A&M University—had been founded for African Americans, but it struggled for decades to obtain enough funding to meet its students' basic needs.

African Americans seeking to earn law or medical degrees had to attend out-of-state schools. Mexican Americans also faced widespread discrimination in education. The fight to make public schools serve all Texans was only just beginning.

Reading Check Categorizing List some of the successes and some of the failures of education reform in the Progressive Era.

Section 3 Review

hmhsocialstudies.com
ONLINE QUIZ

1. Define and explain:
- progressives
- commission plan

2. Identify and explain:
- Seventeenth Amendment

3. Locate on a Texas map:
- Galveston

4. Summarizing
Copy the chart below and use it to show progressive reforms in the workplace, society, and education.

Progressive Reforms in Texas	
Workplace	
Society	
Education	

5. Finding the Main Idea
- **a.** How did reformers change the state's political system?
- **b.** How did the structure of local government change in Texas during the Progressive Era?

6. Writing and Critical Thinking myWriteSmart
Evaluating Choose an issue that progressives were attempting to reform. Then write a paragraph in which you analyze progressives' success in reform regarding the issue.
Consider the following:
- reforms proposed
- how these reforms affected life in Texas

Section 4

Women and the Progressive Movement

Main Ideas

1. Progressives in Texas and other states worked to ban the sale of alcohol.
2. Suffrage, or the right to vote, was a major goal for women in the progressive movement.

Why It Matters Today

During the Progressive Era, women became increasingly involved in politics. Use current events sources to learn about women who are active in politics today.

Key Terms and People

- **temperance movement**
- **prohibition**
- **Eighteenth Amendment**
- **Annie Webb Blanton**
- **Jane McCallum**
- **Nineteenth Amendment**
- **Jovita Idar**
- **poll tax**

TEKS: 6A, 6B, 6C, 7C, 17A, 21B, 21C, 22A

The Story Continues

After the Civil War, Carry Moore met and married physician David Gloyd. Less than a year later, though, the couple separated, because Gloyd was an alcoholic. Moore remarried in 1877 and took the name Carry Nation. She and her new husband moved to Texas for a time in 1879. Later, Nation became a strong opponent of alcohol sales, campaigning to have it made illegal. At times, Nation and others who shared her beliefs even used hatchets to destroy furniture and bottles in saloons while singing hymns.

myNotebook

Use the annotation tools in your eBook to take notes on women and the progressive movement.

The Temperance Movement

Like Carry Nation, many Texans worried about the effects alcohol abuse had on families. This led to the growth of the **temperance movement**, a social reform effort that encouraged people to drink less alcohol. Support for **prohibition**—a ban on the manufacture, distribution, and sale of alcohol—increased during the late 1800s and early 1900s.

Many men and women supported prohibition as part of their religious beliefs. They believed drinking was immoral and that if people did not drink alcohol, society as a whole would improve. Organizations such as the Woman's Christian Temperance Union and the Anti-Saloon League pushed for prohibition. By 1895 more than half of the state's counties had placed limits on the production and sale of alcohol and 53 had banned alcohol sales outright.

VIDEO
America Goes Dry with Prohibition
hmhsocialstudies.com

Prohibition became an even more important political issue in the early 1900s. The *Dallas Morning News* described prohibition as the "paramount [dominant] . . . issue in our politics." Candidates often ran for election chiefly on the prohibition issue. In 1917 U.S. senator Morris Sheppard of Texas sponsored a constitutional amendment for national prohibition. The **Eighteenth Amendment** won the support of enough state legislatures—including the Texas legislature—to be ratified in 1919. As a result, the manufacture and sale of alcohol became illegal throughout the nation in 1920.

Reading Check **Analyzing Information** How did prohibition affect the Texas Democratic Party?

Preserving the Alamo

Texas women took up many causes, such as preserving the state's historic structures. In the early 1900s, Adina de Zavala and Clara Driscoll worked with the Daughters of the Republic of Texas to save the Alamo. The old mission had been purchased by a wholesale grocery company and fallen into poor condition. Driscoll used her personal fortune to buy the Alamo property, helping to save it for future generations.

★ The Suffrage Movement

Women played a key role not only in prohibition but also in most progressive reforms. They fought to protect working mothers' rights and for new laws limiting child labor, ensuring food safety, and requiring school attendance. Some women even held political office. In 1918 **Annie Webb Blanton** became the first woman to win election to a Texas state office. She served as the state's superintendent of public instruction. As state superintendent, she helped establish a system of free textbooks, revise the teacher certification process, and improve rural education.

An overriding issue for women of the time was the effort to gain the right to vote. In 1913 Eleanor Brackenridge was chosen president of the Texas Woman Suffrage Association, later known as the Texas Equal Suffrage Association. Minnie Fisher Cunningham, Annie Webb Blanton, and **Jane McCallum** were other important suffrage leaders in Texas. Association leaders believed that "no state can be a true democracy in which one half of the people are denied the right to vote." They campaigned across Texas in favor of voting rights for women. However, the suffragists faced strong opposition in the state. Cunningham and the other suffrage leaders struggled to convince Texans that women should be allowed to participate in the state's politics.

Women in other states were also working for suffrage. Finally, in 1919 the U.S. Congress proposed the **Nineteenth Amendment** to the U.S. Constitution, granting women the right to vote. The Texas legislature ratified the amendment in June 1919, and in 1920 women across the nation were able to vote.

Jane McCallum and other leaders went on to work with the Women's Joint Legislative Council. This group focused on education, prison reform, and child-labor issues. Nicknamed the Petticoat Lobby, this group was an influential force in Texas politics for years to come.

Reading Check **Summarizing** How did Texas women exercise their civic responsibilities in the early 1900s?

★ Limits of Reform

African American and Mexican American women in Texas also fought for reforms. In many cases, however, they were not welcomed by white reformers. For example, many women's suffrage groups were white only. Nonetheless, Christia Adair, a black Texan, worked for women's suffrage and equal rights for all black Texans. In South Texas, **Jovita Idar** organized people to support women's rights as well as rights for Mexican Americans in Texas. She also campaigned for education for poor children. Like many Texas women, Idar played an active role in reform efforts during the Progressive Era. Despite the efforts of Adair, Idar, and others, measures were passed in Texas denying suffrage to members of minority groups. Voting in local Democratic primary elections was restricted to white Texans only. In 1902 Texas began to require a **poll tax**, a tax on voting. As a result, poor Texans, many of whom were African American and Mexican American, could not afford to vote.

African Americans in Texas were denied the benefits of reform in other areas as well. The state legislature and city governments passed more Jim Crow laws during the early 1900s. Between 1910 and 1925, several Texas towns imposed segregated housing laws. Public facilities, restaurants, and hotels—even drinking fountains—were segregated. African Americans also faced racial violence. Increased racial hostility sometimes led to the lynching—or killing by a mob—of black citizens. Many years would go by before laws were passed to help protect the rights of African Americans and Mexican Americans in Texas.

Reading Check **Finding the Main Idea** What were some of the limits of reform?

BIOGRAPHY

Jovita Idar (1885–1946)
As a young woman, Jovita Idar of Laredo worked for her father's newspaper, *La Crónica*. The newspaper became a political tool for Mexican Americans. Idar helped establish the League of Mexican Women and served as its first president. After her marriage in 1917, Idar moved to San Antonio. There she was active in community service and served as an interpreter for Spanish-speaking patients in a hospital. How did Jovita Idar exercise her civic responsibilities in her lifetime?

★ Section 4 Review

hmhsocialstudies.com
ONLINE QUIZ

1. **Define and explain:**
   - temperance movement
   - prohibition
   - poll tax
2. **Identify and explain** the significance of the following:
   - Eighteenth Amendment
   - Annie Webb Blanton
   - Jane McCallum
   - Nineteenth Amendment
   - Jovita Idar
3. **Analyzing Information**
   Copy the graphic organizer below. Use it to show how activists in Texas affected national progressive reforms.

Eighteenth Amendment
Nineteenth Amendment

4. **Finding the Main Idea**
   a. Explain the different points of view held by members of the Democratic Party on prohibition. How did differing points of view affect the party?
   b. Who did not benefit from the progressives' reforms?
5. **Writing and Critical Thinking** *my*WriteSmart
   Summarizing Write an editorial on the achievements and the limitations of the effort to expand democracy in the Progressive Era.
   Consider the following:
   - the Nineteenth Amendment
   - the poll tax and Jim Crow laws

CHAPTER 24 REVIEW

The Chapter at a Glance

Examine the following visual summary of the chapter. Then use the visual to create an outline of the chapter you can use to study with a classmate.

Farmers and Populism

- Regulate railroad companies
- Form cooperative stores
- Government ownership of railroads and telegraphs
- Reduce influence of big business on government

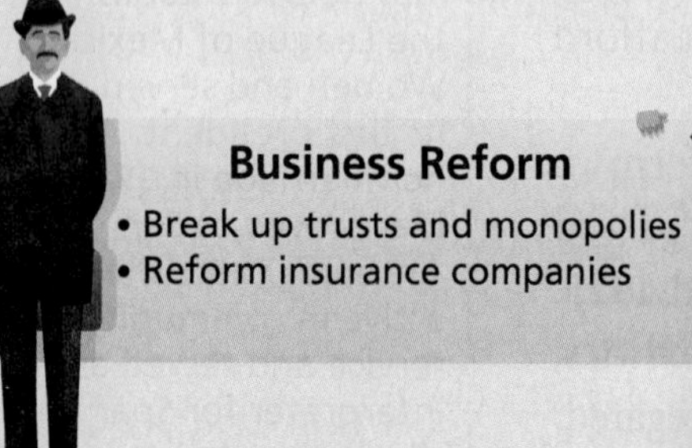

Business Reform

- Break up trusts and monopolies
- Reform insurance companies

City Government

- Establish a commission plan for local government
- Support efficient government

Education and Health

- Reform school funding
- More colleges to train teachers
- Regulate food and drugs

Women's Rights and Temperance

- Ban the production and sale of alcohol
- The right to vote for women

Identifying People and Ideas

Write a sentence to explain the role or significance of each of the following terms or people.

1. Grange
2. Populists
3. monopoly
4. James Stephen Hogg
5. James E. Ferguson
6. progressives
7. commission plan
8. prohibition
9. Lawrence Sullivan Ross
10. Nineteenth Amendment

Understanding Main Ideas

Section 1

1. Explain the effect of the national agricultural market on Texas farmers' lives in the late 1800s.
2. What effect did railroad companies' practices have on farmers' lives?
3. What were the policies of the Populist Party?

Section 2

4. How did trusts and monopolies affect Texas?
5. What reforms did James Stephen Hogg fight for as attorney general and governor?

Section 3

6. What social, educational, and governmental reforms did the progressives support?

Section 4

7. What role did women play in the progressive movement, and what right did they gain?

You Be the Historian

Reviewing Themes

1. **Economics** How did government regulations in the late 1800s and early 1900s try to protect business competition?
2. **Citizenship** How did farmers, laborers, and women work to solve problems during the late 1800s and early 1900s?

Thinking Critically

1. **Comparing** How did the impact of the Populists compare with that of the Progressive Movement?
2. **Summarizing** Describe some of the defining characteristics of the Progressive Era.
3. **Sequencing** List in order and by date significant reforms achieved by women.

Texas Test Practice

Interpreting Maps

Study the map below. Then use the information on the map to answer the questions that follow.

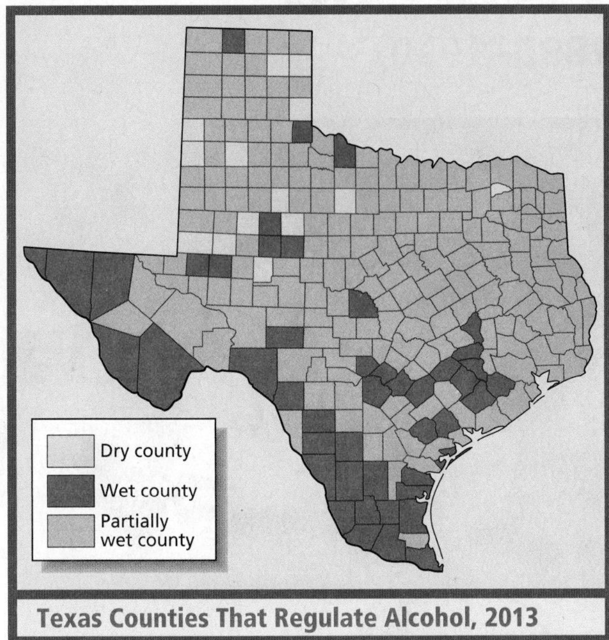

Texas Counties That Regulate Alcohol, 2013

1. Some Texas counties have laws banning the sale of alcohol. These counties are called dry counties. What region had the most dry counties in 2013?
   - **A** the Rio Grande valley
   - **B** the Panhandle
   - **C** the Gulf Coast
   - **D** West Texas

2. How do you think this map reflects the legacy of the temperance movement in Texas?

3. Make a list of ten counties with which you are familiar, or look up ten counties in the atlas at the back of this book. Based on the information in this map, organize your list into a table of dry, wet, and partially wet counties.

Analyzing Primary Sources

Read the following quote from the platform of the Populist Party of Texas. Then answer the questions.

"We demand the most rigid, honest, and just national control and supervision of the means of public communication and transportation, and if this control and supervision does not remove the abuses now existing, we demand the government ownership of such means of communication and transportation."

3. Which of the following statements best describes the party's point of view?
   - **F** Private ownership of railroads is the best policy for Texas.
   - **G** Government should not interfere with how railroad companies decide to conduct their business.
   - **H** The government should take control of railroads if railroads are unsupervised.
   - **J** Free enterprise supports government ownership of railroads.

4. Why do you think the platform of the Populist Party singles out transportation for reform?

Interdisciplinary Connection to Literature

Imagine that you are a farmer in Texas during the late 1800s and early 1900s. Write a poem or song in which you express your fears about your livelihood and your hopes for the future. Be sure to include the sources of your problems such as the effects of international and national markets, overproduction of crops, falling crop prices, debt, and droughts. Create an illustration to accompany your poem or song. The illustration should include images from your everyday life as a farmer in Texas.

Internet Activity 

Use the Internet to research how the Galveston Hurricane of 1900 affected the political, economic, and social development of Texas. Then locate primary and secondary sources to create a pamphlet that shows the various ways in which the hurricane changed Galveston's people, infrastructure, and government.

CHAPTER 25

Texans at Home and Abroad

(1890–1920)

Texas Essential Knowledge and Skills (TEKS) 6A, 7B, 7E, 11A, 11B, 11C, 12A, 12B, 19A, 19B, 19D, 20C, 20D, 21A, 21B, 21C, 21D, 21H, 22A, 22D

Lieutenant Colonel Theodore Roosevelt sits at an officer's table during the training of the Rough Riders in San Antonio.

TEXAS

1894 The first football game is played between the University of Texas and Texas A&M.

1898 Teddy Roosevelt organizes and trains the Rough Riders in San Antonio.

1902 The Corsicana Oilers set a baseball record by defeating the Texarkana team 51 to 3.

1890 — 1894 — 1898 — 1902

U.S. and WORLD

1895 Cuban rebels revolt against Spanish rule.

1898 The United States declares war on Spain.

1904 The United States begins construction on the Panama Canal to provide a shorter route from the Atlantic Ocean to the Pacific Ocean. It takes 10 years to build.

If you were there . . .

Would you move from a farm to a city for a job?

Build on What You Know

In the late 1800s the economy of Texas and the daily lives of Texans were changing. By 1900 industrialization, the oil boom, and the progressive movement had reshaped the state. In addition, many people from all over the world were moving to Texas.

The Austin Baseball Club was one of the founding teams of the State Base Ball League.

The Houston Ship Channel and the city's bayous increased trade and spurred the growth of Houston.

1906 | **1910** | **1914** | **1918**

1907 The first Neiman Marcus department store opens in Dallas.

1911 Mexican dictator Porfirio Díaz is overthrown.

1914 The Houston Ship Channel is completed, leading to the growth of industry in the Houston area.

1917 The United States declares war on Germany and enters World War I.

1918 Texas troops are sent to France to fight in World War I.

You Be the Historian

*my*Notebook

What's Your Opinion? Do you **agree** or **disagree** with the following statements? Support your point of view in your notebook.

- **Geography** Conflicts within a country rarely affect neighboring nations.
- **Economics** Immigrants are only attracted to a country or state because of jobs.
- **Global Relations** It is important for citizens to support their country's actions in other parts of the world.

Section 1

From Farm to City

Main Ideas

1. New farm technology changed life for many rural Texans in the early 1900s.
2. Industry spurred population growth in Texas cities.
3. Job opportunities drew many immigrants to Texas.

Key Terms and People

- **Houston Ship Channel**
- **Federal Reserve System**
- **Carrie Marcus Neiman**

Why It Matters Today

Four out of five Texans lived in rural areas in 1900. Use current events sources to find information about city growth today.

TEKS: 6A, 7B, 11A, 11B, 11C, 12A, 12B, 19D, 20D, 21B, 21D, 22A

myNotebook

Use the annotation tools in your eBook to take notes on the causes of city growth in Texas during the early 1900s.

The Story Continues

Like many farm children, Maggie Washington was doing adult work while still a child herself. Growing up in rural Navarro County in the early 1900s, Maggie did all of her family's housework. On top of her chores, she also took care of her baby sister. Maggie later explained, "When I was six years old I was keeping house like a woman. I had the babies to care for, the food to cook, clothes to wash and iron."

Life in Rural Texas

Like Maggie Washington, most family members in rural Texas helped with farm work during the early 1900s. Texas farm families worked hard year-round. Crops had to be planted before spring and harvested before winter. Fields required constant attention to keep them clear of weeds. At the same time, family members raised livestock, fixed fences, and took care of one another.

Life on Texas farms offered few luxuries. Before the 1930s few rural homes had electricity. Most farmers used kerosene lamps for light and outdoor pumps for water. Because less than 10 percent of Texas farmers had indoor plumbing in the 1920s, most farms had outhouses. However, mechanical farm machinery such as threshers, binders, and reapers had become more common in Texas. More farmers used gasoline-powered tractors to do field work. Some farmers also used gasoline-powered or electric pumps instead of windmills to pump water for irrigation.

Farm production increased as new tractors and other machines made farming more efficient. The resulting surplus of agricultural products led to a drop in the prices of farm goods. With prices falling, it became hard for many farmers to pay their debts. The numbers of sharecroppers and tenant farmers rose. Texas newspapers published reports on these issues. "There is something rotten in Texas when more than half of our farm families are landless tenants." The struggles of farm life led many rural families to move to cities for new opportunities.

Reading Check **Summarizing** How did new technology change farm life and lead to both a boom in production and a bust in farm prices?

Some Texas farmers began using gasoline-powered tractors during the early 1900s.

Industry and the Growth of Cities

Although half of the nation lived in cities in 1920, only about one third of Texans lived in cities. Between 1910 and 1920, the populations of San Antonio, Dallas, and Houston each nearly doubled. This urbanization, or the growth of cities, was directly tied to the development of industry. Cattle markets, oil, railroads, textiles, and other industries created jobs that attracted people to Texas cities. During the 1910s the number of Texans who worked in industry rose from almost 12 to nearly 16 percent. At the same time, the number of Texans involved in agriculture declined by about 24 percent.

Connecting To Literature

O. Henry and the Modern Short Story

William Sydney Porter came to Texas in 1882. He worked on a ranch and had several other jobs. Porter began publishing short stories in the 1890s, using the name O. Henry. His Texas stories were humorous tales about cowboys, ranchers, and Texas Rangers. This excerpt from The Heart of the West *tells the story of a drifter named Curly who comes to San Antonio.*

Curly stood a few moments in the narrow, mesquite-paved street. San Antonio puzzled and disturbed him. Three days he had been a non-paying guest of the town, having dropped off there from a box car of an I. & G. N. freight, because Greaser Johnny had told him in Des Moines that the Alamo city has **manna**[1] fallen, gathered, cooked and served free with cream and sugar. Curly had found the tip partly a good one. There was hospitality in plenty . . . [but] the town itself was a weight upon his spirits after his experiences with the rushing, business-like, systematized cities of the North and East. . . . The winding, doubling streets, leading nowhere, **bewildered**[2] him.

[1]manna: food from heaven [2]bewildered: confused

Understanding What You Read

1. **Literature and History** Why does O. Henry describe San Antonio as a weight upon Curly's spirits?
2. **Literature and You** What do you think it would have been like to live in San Antonio in the early 1900s?

Camp Travis in San Antonio, built during World War I, served as a military training facility.

City growth was concentrated in the more populated eastern half of the state, which had ports and markets for farm goods. Houston's location near the Gulf of Mexico had helped spur its growth. In 1914 the Buffalo Bayou, a waterway between Houston and the Gulf, was deepened and widened to allow larger ships to travel on it. The new **Houston Ship Channel** gave the city a direct link to the Gulf. Texans built oil refineries and factories near the channel to take advantage of this new transportation route. The region boomed with new residents seeking jobs in factories, on docks, and in freight yards. These jobs attracted many rural Texans, including African Americans, to Houston.

In 1914 the federal government built a district bank of the **Federal Reserve System** in Dallas. Federal Reserve banks distribute money to other banks and help regulate the banking industry. The Federal Reserve Bank brought new finance-related businesses to Dallas. The city was one of the largest cotton markets in the world. The cotton trade made some Dallas residents quite wealthy. By 1907, in fact, Dallas had enough successful shoppers to support specialty stores such as Neiman Marcus. Founded by siblings Herbert Marcus and **Carrie Marcus Neiman**, the store specialized in high-quality ready-to-wear clothing for women.

Meanwhile, San Antonio served as an important military center. Businesses sprang up to provide services for the troops stationed at the city's bases, and modern conveniences, such as streetlights, were built. Between 1900 and 1920 San Antonio was the largest city in Texas.

VIDEO
Neiman Marcus: Last of the Merchant Kings
hmhsocialstudies.com

Although a lack of water and timber slowed settlement in West Texas and the Panhandle, a few commercial centers grew up in the region, including Lubbock and Amarillo. Such centers served the needs of the rural population who lived nearby. In all of West Texas, only El Paso had a population above 50,000 by 1920. It grew in part because of railroad connections with Mexico and the American Southwest.

Reading Check Identifying Cause and Effect How did different industries contribute to the growth of Texas cities?

Migration and City Growth

The booming oil industry, the expansion of commercial farming, and industrial jobs attracted many people to Texas. Continuing the trend of the 1800s, the largest group of new Texans came from other southern states. The majority of immigrants came from Mexico—almost 180,000 Mexicans arrived between 1900 and 1920. By 1930 nearly 700,000 Mexican Americans lived in the state, many of them settling in San Antonio and cities along the Rio Grande. Many of these immigrants lived in Mexican American communities and traveled to farms when labor was needed.

The German American population in Texas also grew—reaching more than 170,000 by 1910. Many German immigrants hoped to start their own farms in the rolling farmland of the Hill Country. Other European newcomers included Czechs, Irish, Italians, and Poles. Many of these groups settled in Central Texas and took up farming. Because of limits on Asian immigration, few Asians immigrated to Texas during the early 1900s. Although some Chinese Americans from California came to work on Texas railroads, in 1900 only about 800 lived in Texas.

Galveston was the main port of entry for immigrants from Europe. When one group of Jewish immigrants from Russia arrived in Galveston, their spokesperson thanked the mayor for greeting them.

TEXAS VOICES

"We are overwhelmed that the ruler of the city should greet us. We have never been spoken to by the officials of our country except in terms of harshness, and although we have heard of the great land of freedom, it is very hard to realize that we are permitted to grasp the hand of the great man. We will do all we can to make good citizens."

—Anonymous Russian immigrant, quoted in *Galveston Daily News*, July 2, 1907

Reading Check **Finding the Main Idea** Why did migrants and immigrants come to Texas, and where did they settle?

BIOGRAPHY

Carrie Marcus Neiman (1883–1953)

Carrie Marcus Neiman was the daughter of German Jewish immigrants. She began her career as a salesperson at a Dallas women's clothing store in the early 1900s. In 1905 she married Abraham Lincoln Neiman. Together with her brother and husband, Neiman cofounded the Neiman Marcus department store. As head buyer, her eye for fashion was central to the store's success. She oversaw the growth of Neiman Marcus from a local store to a national chain. **How did Carrie Marcus Neiman contribute to the growth of Texas business in the early 1900s?**

Section 1 Review

hmhsocialstudies.com
ONLINE QUIZ

1. **Identify and explain** the historical significance of:
   - Houston Ship Channel
   - Federal Reserve System
   - Carrie Marcus Neiman

2. **Summarizing** Use a graphic organizer to list the factors that pulled people to Texas cities. Also list the difficulties of farm life that pushed Texans off of farms.

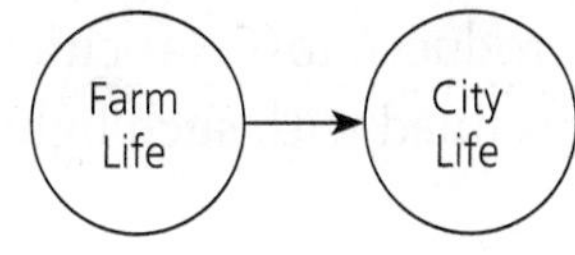

3. **Finding the Main Idea**
   a. How did new technology change life on Texas farms in the early 1900s?
   b. How did the population trends of Texas change in the early 1900s? Why was this?

4. **Writing and Critical Thinking** myWriteSmart
   Evaluating Write a letter to a friend explaining how Texas changed between 1900 and 1920. Consider the following:
   - what opportunities attracted immigrants
   - where immigrants settled

Section 2

Urban Life in Texas

Main Ideas

1. New technologies affected life in Texas cities during the early 1900s.
2. Automobile traffic and housing shortages were some of the problems faced by Texans living in urban areas.
3. Texans enjoyed new forms of leisure, entertainment, and art in the early 1900s.

Key Terms and People

- **suburbs**
- **Adina Emilia De Zavala**
- **Texas Highway Department**
- **Texas Department of Health**
- **Texas Water Commission**
- **ragtime**
- **Scott Joplin**
- **O. Henry**
- **Elisabet Ney**

Why It Matters Today

During the early 1900s city life presented many challenges. Use current events sources to find information about the challenges of urban life today.

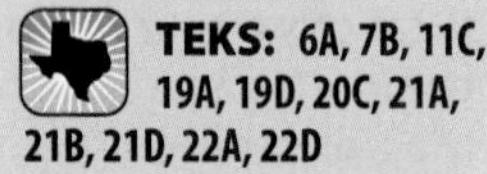

TEKS: 6A, 7B, 11C, 19A, 19D, 20C, 21A, 21B, 21D, 22A, 22D

myNotebook

Use the annotation tools in your eBook to take notes on urban life in Texas during the early 1900s.

The Story Continues

In 1902 young Jesse Illingsworth of Dallas made one of the first long-distance car trips in Texas. Illingsworth stood out with his gloves, goggles, and racing cap. It took him three days to make the 40-mile trip from Terrell to Dallas. He was unable to drive at night because the car had no headlights. Illingsworth sent scouts ahead on horseback to warn other travelers that a car was coming. He did so to avoid spooking travelers' horses with the racket of his engine.

Urban Technology

The availability of new technologies made city life different from country life. In 1878 Colonel A. H. Belo installed the first telephone line in Texas, between his house and his office at the *Galveston News*. Telephone switchboards soon opened in several Texas cities. By 1906 more than 100,000 Texans had telephones.

Electric power came into use more slowly than the telephone, which worked on its own system. The first electric power plant in Texas was built in Galveston during the early 1880s. In the next decade, steam and hydroelectric, or water-powered, plants were built. These power plants provided electricity for industries, lighting, and transportation. Electric streetlights were introduced to Texas cities in the early 1900s. Elm Street in central Dallas was lined with such lights in 1911.

Electricity also played a role in the development of new forms of mass transit, or public transportation. By 1920 Texas had more cities with electric streetcars than any state west of the Mississippi River. Streetcars led to the development of the first Texas **suburbs**, or residential neighborhoods built outside of a central city. Streetcars provided efficient transportation, so people could live in suburbs and work in cities. Texans began to move to suburbs for fresh air and a lifestyle that was more like that in the country.

Texas cities grew not only outward but also upward. Texans began to construct taller buildings to make room for new industries and the growing population. Skyscrapers, or multistory buildings, became common after the development of steel frames and elevators. The tallest building in Texas in the early 1900s was the 20-story Amicable Building in Waco. Skyscrapers such as the Rice Hotel in Houston were built to catch breezes coming off the Gulf of Mexico. As new buildings were rising, Texans such as **Adina Emilia De Zavala** worked hard to keep the state's historic buildings from being torn down.

The new technology that eventually had the greatest effect on Texas cities was the automobile. In 1900, however, cars were rare and not very practical. Except for a few streets paved with bricks or wood, most cities had bumpy dirt roads and few bridges. In 1900 a 10-block stretch of Main Street was the only paved road in Dallas. Even the largest urban areas in Texas were still "walking cities"—small enough so people could walk wherever they needed to go.

Reading Check **Analyzing Information** How did new transportation technologies affect the development of Texas?

BIOGRAPHY

Adina Emilia De Zavala (1861–1955)

Adina Emilia De Zavala helped preserve Texas history while cities were changing life in the state. During the early 1900s she tried to prevent the destruction of parts of the Alamo. She even barricaded herself inside the Alamo for three days in protest. De Zavala helped organize the Texas Historical and Landmarks Association, and she fought for the preservation of other historic sites. **How did De Zavala try to preserve the state's cultural heritage?**

Powerlines began to appear lining the streets of Dallas and other cities in the early 1900s. Paved streets were still rare, though.

Interpreting Visuals

Changing cities. *New technologies changed the face of Texas cities, including Austin, in the 1910s.* ***What new technologies do you see in this photo?***

★ Urban Problems and Reform

The new urban technologies and the growth of cities caused some problems for city residents. Cars were considered dangerous. For example, drivers in Fort Worth were required by law to warn pedestrians by sounding their horn each time they came to an intersection. Texans had to pave roads, build bridges, and pass safety laws to manage increasing traffic. The first speed limit, 18 miles per hour, was passed in 1907. In 1917 the state government formed the **Texas Highway Department** to help build and maintain highways. As roads improved and cars became less expensive, automobile use expanded rapidly. This contributed to the changing life in Texas cities as streets became even busier with automobile traffic.

The booming Texas cities also faced housing shortages. Dallas had grown so fast—almost doubling in size between 1900 and 1910—that new residents had trouble finding housing. Some people even had to live in tents. Poorer city dwellers often lived in older homes, which they sometimes shared with several families. A survey of Austin in 1917 found people "crowded together in small huts, one and two families in a one-room shanty [cabin]."

Rapid urban growth made it difficult for cities to provide services such as electricity, garbage collection, sewers, police, health care, and fire protection. As a result, public health was a major concern. Lack of sewage as well as garbage disposal services led to high death rates from disease. Progressive reformers pushed for changes in these conditions. In 1903 the agency that became the **Texas Department of Health** was formed to help prevent disease. Dr. William Brumby, the head of the department in 1908, explained its mission.

TEXAS VOICES

"[Our mission] is to preserve water supply by preventing pollution; to guard the neighbors by draining all premises; to protect the community by exterminating rodents; to promote the general welfare by proper sanitary law."

—Dr. William Brumby, quoted in *The Handbook of Texas*

That's Interesting!

Moving the Bank

When the city of San Antonio decided to pave and widen Commerce Street in 1913, the Alamo National Bank refused to close its doors. When the construction crew came, the five-story stone building was simply jacked up, put on wheels, and moved back from the road. The employees inside continued business as usual while the building was moved.

Some cities grew so fast that their water supplies could not meet the demand. For example, in 1910 a water shortage in Dallas forced residents to buy water from people who had wells. To solve these problems, cities began building more dams on creeks and rivers to create reservoirs. The **Texas Water Commission** was formed in 1913 to help cities and counties manage water resources.

Because many city buildings were built of wood, fire was also a serious threat. Without fire trucks and fire hydrants, volunteer firefighters could not keep fires under control. In 1912 a fire burned down much of the northern part of Houston. No one died, but the fire reduced 46 blocks to ashes. To prevent such fires, city governments began replacing volunteers with full-time firefighters. The first fire truck in Texas was purchased by Big Spring in 1909. This West Texas town bought the truck—which had a hose, pump, and water tank—after experiencing several fires. Like Big Spring, many Texas towns had to find solutions to problems created by growth and new technology.

Reading Check **Summarizing** How did changes in population distribution, such as urban growth, affect Texas cities?

★ Sports, Leisure, and the Arts

During the early 1900s Texans looked for new ways to relax to escape the fast pace of city life and the hard work of rural life. Texans loved sports. Horse racing had long been a favorite Texas pastime. Professional baseball came to Texas in 1888 when the Texas League of Professional Baseball Clubs was formed. The best team in the league's early years was the Corsicana Oilers. Their 51-to-3 defeat of the Texarkana team in 1902 set a professional baseball record. Football, one of the most popular sports in the state today, was new to Texas in the 1890s. The state's oldest college football rivalry began in 1894 when the University of Texas beat Texas A&M 38 to 0. Many Texans also enjoyed boxing. Jack Johnson of Galveston became the first African American world heavyweight boxing champion. He won the heavyweight title by defeating Tommy Burns in 1908.

While sports were becoming more popular, Texans also enjoyed a good show. Children and adults alike loved the circus. Mollie Bailey, who was called the Circus Queen of the Southwest, ran one of the most popular circuses in the state. Her show was billed as "A Texas Show for Texas People." Bailey's circus traveled from town to town, entertaining crowds with dozens of acrobats and animal acts.

Nearly every town had a concert hall or theater where traveling shows performed. Local concert halls often featured **ragtime**, a new form of popular music. One of the earliest and best-known ragtime musicians was **Scott Joplin** of Texarkana. Ragtime musicians toured the state and played in vaudeville shows, which featured music, comedy, dance, and

CONNECTING TO

Music

Scott Joplin

Scott Joplin was born into a family of former slaves in Linden, Texas, in 1868. By the age of seven, Joplin could play the banjo and was learning the piano. As a young man, he helped develop a new type of music known as ragtime. Two of his best-known works are "The Maple Leaf Rag" and "The Entertainer." Although Joplin never made much money, he published many works. Joplin is now recognized as a pioneer in American music. **How did Scott Joplin contribute to Texas culture?**

CONNECTING TO

The Arts

Elisabet Ney

Elisabet Ney studied sculpture in Munich, Germany, before she immigrated to Texas in 1872. Ney was one of the first professional sculptors in Texas. Her work reflects a classical style that presents humans realistically and according to scale. She made sculptures of many Texas heroes. **How do you think this sculpture reflects Ney's classical style?**

acrobatics acts together in one place. The first movies in Texas were shown in cities during the early 1900s. In Fort Worth, the first movie house used bedsheets for a screen, and admission was five cents. San Antonio was home to one of the state's first film studios—Star Film Ranch. Silent movies filmed at Star included *Cyclone Pete's Matrimony* (1910) and *The Immortal Alamo* (1911).

Many Texans also read books for leisure and entertainment. Books about frontier times in Texas were particularly popular. Among the most celebrated Texas authors was Charles A. Siringo. One of his most popular books, *A Texas Cowboy*, told the story of his experiences on the Chisholm Trail. Siringo also wrote a biography of the outlaw Billy the Kid. His books helped establish the romantic myth of the Old West. William Sydney Porter, known as **O. Henry**, became famous for short stories about Texas cowboys. Texas artists also portrayed the state's past. For example, sculptor **Elisabet Ney** specialized in statues of early Texas heroes. Today her statues of Sam Houston and Stephen F. Austin can be seen in the Capitol in Austin.

To encourage interest in the arts and culture, Texas citizens paid for the construction of libraries and museums in cities across the state. During the late 1800s only the largest Texas towns, such as Houston, El Paso, and San Antonio, had libraries. However, with funding from wealthy businessman Andrew Carnegie, a national public library-building boom began. Between 1898 and 1917 Carnegie gave some $645,000 for the construction of 32 libraries in Texas. One of the first museums in Texas was established in 1879 by the Sam Houston Normal Institute to preserve its collection of Sam Houston's documents and materials.

Reading Check **Drawing Inferences and Conclusions** How did Texas artists, musicians, and writers contribute to life in the state in the early 1900s?

Section 2 Review

1. Define and explain:
- suburbs
- ragtime

2. Identify and explain the historical significance of:
- Adina Emilia De Zavala
- Scott Joplin
- O. Henry
- Elisabet Ney

3. Analyzing Information
Copy the graphic organizer below. Use it to show the problems of city life and reforms.

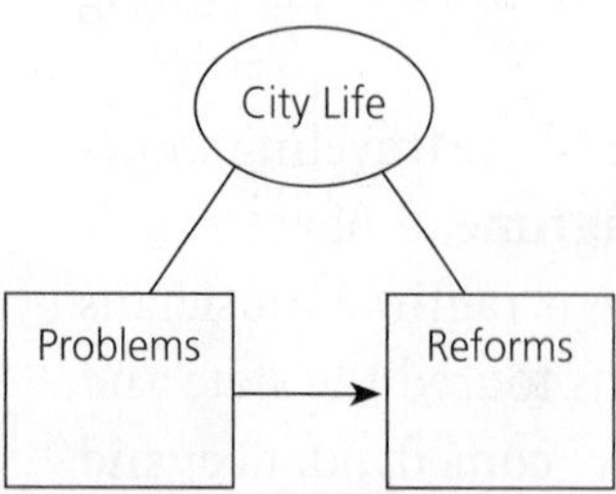

4. Finding the Main Idea

a. How did new technology change city life and encourage the development of Texas?

b. What did Texans do for leisure and entertainment during the early 1900s?

5. Writing and Critical Thinking *my*WriteSmart

Summarizing Imagine that you are living in Dallas in the early 1900s. Write a journal entry describing how the changing population distribution has altered city life. Consider the following:
- the growing populations of cities
- transportation and health issues

Image Credit: ©Bob Daemmrich/Alamy

Section 3

Texas and World Events

Main Ideas

1. Texas served as a military training ground during the Spanish-American War.
2. The Mexican Revolution and raids along the Texas-Mexico border led to conflicts in South Texas.
3. World War I had great social and economic effects on Texas.

Why It Matters Today

During the early 1900s many Mexicans immigrated to Texas. Use current events sources to find information about Mexican immigration today.

Key Terms and People

- **Theodore Roosevelt**
- **Rough Riders**
- **Battle of San Juan Hill**
- **Francisco "Pancho" Villa**
- **refugees**
- **John J. "Black Jack" Pershing**
- **Plan de San Diego**
- **neutral**

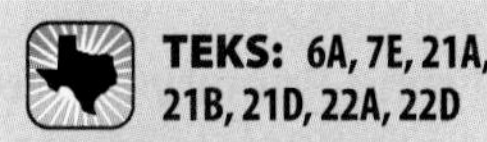

myNotebook

Use the annotation tools in your eBook to take notes on Texas's role in world events and conflict during the early 1900s.

The Story Continues

Texas soldiers of the 1st U.S. Volunteer Cavalry were on a mission. Their orders were to capture the port of Santiago de Cuba. First, however, they had to take San Juan Hill and Kettle Hill. The soldiers were scared but well trained. The cavalry unit joined forces with the African American 9th and 10th Cavalries and other regulars to capture Kettle Hill. The soldiers charged up the hill in the tropical heat against fierce gunfire. They captured the hill from the Spanish forces, but at the cost of hundreds of U.S. casualties.

The Spanish-American War

In 1895, Cubans revolted against Spain. Many Americans supported their fight for independence. When the U.S. battleship *Maine* exploded in Havana Harbor in 1898, some Americans blamed Spain. Newspapers called for war, crying "Remember the *Maine*!" In April 1898 the U.S. government declared war on Spain. Some 10,000 Texans, many still of school age, showed up at recruiting stations volunteering to fight. Soldiers from all over the country learned about weapons and conducted drills on Texas army bases. Texas' military background and access to ports made it an ideal training ground for the war.

Interpreting Visuals

The Spanish-American War. *During the conflict Texas soldiers fought alongside "buffalo soldiers" from the 9th and 10th Cavalries.* ***How do you think geographic factors affected the fighting in Cuba?***

When Lieutenant Colonel **Theodore Roosevelt** came to Texas to recruit troops, both cowboys and college students joined his 1st U.S. Volunteer Cavalry. This outfit, known as the **Rough Riders**, trained in San Antonio. Roosevelt was proud of his recruits, particularly the Texans.

Analyzing Primary Sources
Identifying Points of View What was Theodore Roosevelt's general opinion of his Texas troops?

TEXAS VOICES

"We drew a great many recruits from Texas. . . . They were splendid shots, horsemen, and trailers [scouts]. They were accustomed [used] to living in the open, to enduring great fatigue [tiredness] and hardship."

—Theodore Roosevelt, *The Rough Riders*

The Rough Riders were the first U.S. troops to land in Cuba. They became famous for helping to defeat Spanish troops in the **Battle of San Juan Hill**. Other U.S. forces fought in Cuba, the Philippines, and Puerto Rico. U.S. forces defeated Spain and gained control of these islands. With its victory in the Spanish-American War, the United States expanded its role in world affairs. As a result, Texas continued to be a major training ground for U.S. troops.

Reading Check **Analyzing Information** What geographic features of Texas made the state a good place to train troops for battle in Cuba?

★ The Mexican Revolution

Closer to home for Texans was the conflict that erupted in Mexico as rebels overthrew President Porfirio Díaz. Although he had been elected, Díaz had since ruled as a dictator for many years. Democratic reformers, such as Francisco Madero, were arrested. After getting out of jail in 1910, Madero headed to San Antonio to organize a revolution. He joined with other rebels, including **Francisco "Pancho" Villa**, and attacked Mexican forces. At times the fighting was close to the Texas border.

The Mexican Revolution forced Díaz to leave office in May 1911. Madero then became president. However, the fighting continued. The violence increased after General Victoriano Huerta—a Díaz supporter—had Madero assassinated on February 22, 1913.

For the next several years, Mexican leaders fought for control. While Emiliano Zapata led forces in southern Mexico, Villa led forces in the north. The former governor of Coahuila, Venustiano Carranza, also led a force against Huerta. More than 1.5 million Mexicans were killed in the revolution, and many more lost their homes and land. Many became **refugees**—people forced to leave their homeland due to war or persecution. Thousands came to Texas, settling in the Valley and San Antonio.

Fearing that violence would spill over the border, U.S. leaders closely watched the events in Mexico. Some worried that the war would hurt the American businesses that had invested some $1 billion in Mexico. In April 1914 President Woodrow Wilson sent U.S. Marines to seize Veracruz, Mexico's main port. Wilson hoped to prevent the arrival of a German ship loaded with weapons for Huerta. After negotiations, Huerta left office and Carranza became president. But civil war broke out again, and violence continued in Mexico until the 1920s.

Reading Check **Evaluating** What was a major social effect of the Mexican Revolution on Texas?

★ Border Troubles

Pancho Villa was angered by U.S. recognition of his rival, Carranza, as president. In 1916 Villa's forces stopped a train headed south from El Paso and shot 18 American passengers. In March, they raided Columbus, New Mexico, leaving 17 citizens dead. In response to these raids, President Wilson sent General **John J. "Black Jack" Pershing** and some 15,000 U.S. troops from Fort Bliss into northern Mexico to capture Villa. The U.S. troops searched the rough landscape but failed to find Villa. Pershing's expedition returned home in January 1917.

The Mexican Revolution also led to conflicts in South Texas, where many migrants from the American Midwest had recently moved. Clashes broke out with many Mexican American families who had lived on the land for generations. In addition, some Mexican Americans—inspired by the Mexican Revolution—began to talk about rebelling against Texas. In early 1915, Mexican radicals had drafted a document called the **Plan de San Diego.** It called for Mexican Americans to take control of South Texas and other territories Mexico had lost in the U.S.-Mexican War.

From 1915 to 1917, supporters of the rebellion raided the property of many new residents in the Rio Grande valley. They killed 21 people and caused millions of dollars in property damage. Some angry citizens and Texas Rangers killed about 300 Mexicans and Mexican Americans in revenge. The conflicts on the border led to greater distrust between Mexican Americans and other Texans.

Reading Check **Summarizing** How did the Mexican Revolution and the migration of people from the Midwest to South Texas lead to conflict there?

CONNECTING TO

Literature

Jovita González de Mireles

Jovita González de Mireles was born in 1903 on a ranch in South Texas. González de Mireles was a public school teacher who became known for her novels, folk songs, and folktales about Tejano culture. Her novel *Dew on the Thorn* explores the relations between Mexican Americans and other Texans. One character declares that her family will stay on their land. "This land is ours. . . . It was blessed by the blood of our ancestors who fought and suffered for it and conquered it, that we, their children, might have a home!" **How has González de Mireles's work helped Tejanos maintain their cultural heritage?**

Interpreting Visuals

World War I. *This Fort Worth parade honored returning Texas troops in 1918.* ***What does this photograph reveal about life in Fort Worth in the early 1900s?***

Texans and World War I

While the Mexican Revolution was being fought, World War I erupted in Europe in 1914. The Allied Powers—Great Britain, France, and Russia—battled the Central Powers. These were Germany and its allies—Austria-Hungary and Turkey. Most Americans wanted to remain **neutral**—not aligned with either side in a conflict—but this was difficult. In 1915, German submarines sank the British passenger ship *Lusitania,* killing 1,198 passengers, including 128 Americans. The German government also tried to ally itself with Mexico, promising to help it regain territory lost to the United States—including Texas. These actions greatly angered most Americans.

The United States declared war on Germany on April 6, 1917. More than 2 million Americans, including nearly 200,000 Texans, went to fight. Before going to Europe, many U.S. soldiers trained in Texas. The army sent them to Camp MacArthur in Waco, Camp Logan in Houston, and Camp Travis in San Antonio. Military pilots trained at Hicks Field in Fort Worth and at Kelly Field in San Antonio. Katherine and Marjorie Stinson owned the Stinson School of Flying in San Antonio, where some pilots were trained.

Once they arrived in Europe, soldiers spent weeks living in trenches, often ankle-deep in mud. These long shoulder-deep holes were dug in the ground to protect soldiers from bullets and artillery shells. Soldiers also faced German machine guns, artillery, and poison gas. In October 1918 one U.S. company was stopped by heavy machine-gun fire. Using hand grenades captured from the enemy, Texan Samuel M. Sampler attacked the German trenches. The young Texan single-handedly captured 28 German soldiers. Sampler was one of four Texans to win the Congressional Medal of Honor in World War I.

Other Texans played important roles in President Wilson's government during the war. Edward M. House of Austin was a close adviser to the president on matters of foreign policy. Albert Sidney Burleson and Thomas Watt Gregory served as the postmaster general of the United States and the U.S. attorney general, respectively. President Wilson asked Jesse Jones of Houston to serve as the director of general military relief for the American Red Cross.

Back home, Texans showed their support for the war effort. They bought Liberty bonds, which the U.S. government issued to pay for the war. Texans also observed meatless Mondays and wheatless Wednesdays, so that more food would be available for soldiers.

Texans stepped up agricultural production. Farmers borrowed money for more land and equipment, which led to a farming boom. Texas oil and lumber production also boomed to meet military needs. Businesses near military bases provided goods and services to troops stationed there. As the Texas economy expanded during the war, the state reached almost full employment. Women took on more responsibilities, working in the fields as well as in businesses.

Because the war was with Germany, some Texans accused German Americans of being unpatriotic and of not supporting the United States. These feelings ran high. Even the name of the popular German food sauerkraut was changed to "liberty cabbage." The war ended when Germany surrendered in November 1918. Texas soldiers came home, and the nation returned to a peacetime economy.

Reading Check **Finding the Main Idea** How did World War I affect the Texas economy?

GLOBAL CONNECTIONS

The Political Origins of World War I

In 1914, Europe was divided between two major alliances: the Central Powers and the Allied Powers. A conflict erupted when Gavrilo Princip, a Serb, assassinated Austrian archduke Franz Ferdinand in Sarajevo in June 1914. In response, Austria-Hungary declared war on Serbia. Russia then declared war on Austria-Hungary. Germany, an ally of Austria-Hungary, declared war on Russia and its allies France and Britain. Soon, much of Europe was drawn into the war. **What were some of the causes of World War I?**

Section 3 Review

hmhsocialstudies.com
ONLINE QUIZ

1. Define and explain:
- refugees
- neutral

2. Identify and explain the historical significance of the following:
- Theodore Roosevelt
- Rough Riders
- Battle of San Juan Hill
- Francisco "Pancho" Villa
- John J. "Black Jack" Pershing
- Plan de San Diego

3. Evaluating
Copy the graphic organizer below. Use it to show how events in Mexico and along the border affected Texas.

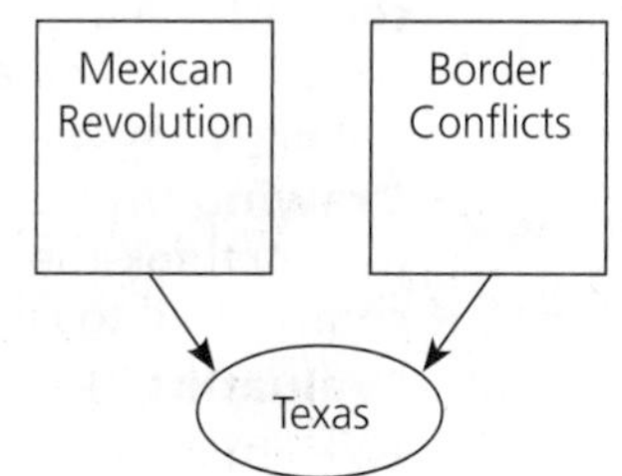

4. Finding the Main Idea
- **a.** What effect did the Spanish-American War have on Texas?
- **b.** How was the Texas agricultural industry affected by World War I?

5. Writing and Critical Thinking myWriteSmart
Evaluating Imagine that you lived in Texas during World War I. Write a letter to a friend explaining how the war affected your hometown. Consider the following:
- the social, economic, and political effects
- Texans who fought in the war

The Chapter at a Glance

Examine the following visual summary of the chapter. Then use the visual to write a series of questions about the material you have read. Working with a partner, take turns asking and answering the questions you have written.

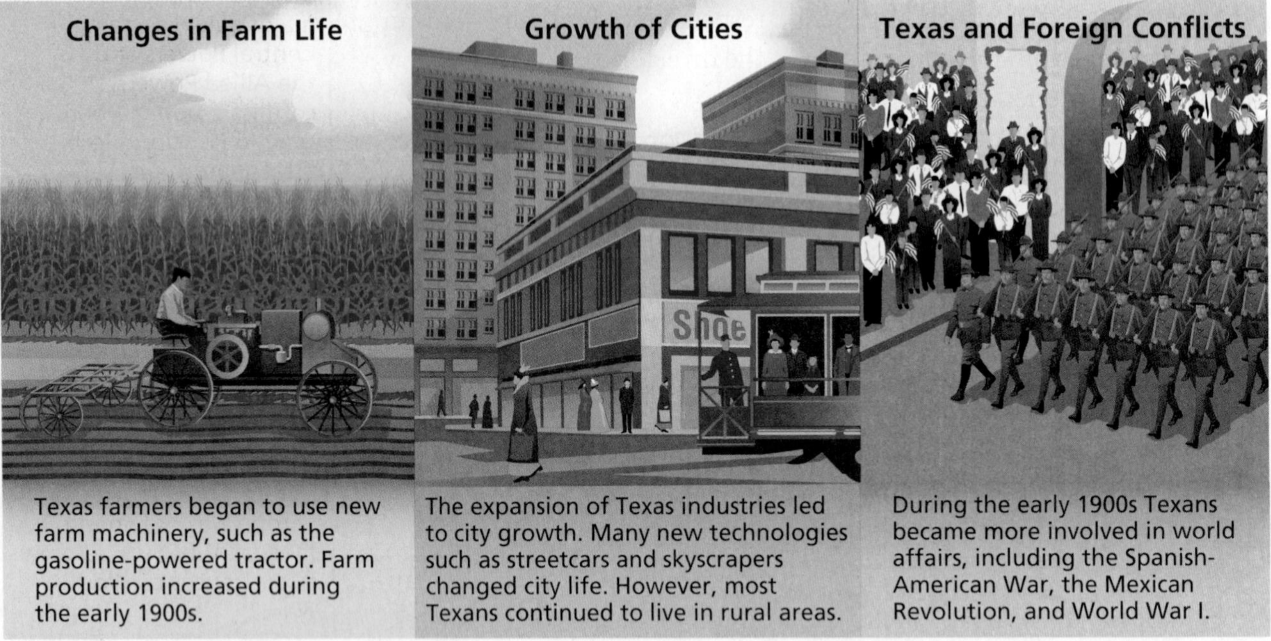

Texas farmers began to use new farm machinery, such as the gasoline-powered tractor. Farm production increased during the early 1900s.

The expansion of Texas industries led to city growth. Many new technologies such as streetcars and skyscrapers changed city life. However, most Texans continued to live in rural areas.

During the early 1900s Texans became more involved in world affairs, including the Spanish-American War, the Mexican Revolution, and World War I.

Identifying People and Ideas

Write a sentence to explain the role or significance of each of the following terms or people.

1. Houston Ship Channel
2. ragtime
3. suburbs
4. Scott Joplin
5. O. Henry
6. Elisabet Ney
7. refugees
8. Rough Riders
9. Francisco "Pancho" Villa
10. Plan de San Diego

Understanding Main Ideas

Section 1

1. How did new technologies affect agricultural development in Texas?
2. What economic factors led to increased urbanization in Texas?

Section 2

3. How did new technologies contribute to the urban development of Texas?
4. How did the changing population distribution in Texas affect cities during the early 1900s?

Section 3

5. How did the Mexican Revolution affect Texas?
6. How did World War I affect the economy and society of Texas?

You Be the Historian

Reviewing Themes

1. **Geography** How did its shared border with Mexico affect events in Texas during the early 1900s?
2. **Economics** How did the state's economy affect immigration and migration to Texas?
3. **Global Relations** What role did Texas play in the Spanish-American War and in World War I?

Thinking Critically

1. **Comparing and Contrasting** Compare and contrast the uses of technology on farms and in cities before and after the new developments of the early 1900s.
2. **Drawing Inferences and Conclusions** How do you think the use of machines in farming contributed to city growth?
3. **Evaluating** How did immigration and migration to Texas lead to political conflict?

Texas Test Practice

Interpreting Graphs

Study the bar graph below. Then use the information in the graph to help you answer the questions that follow.

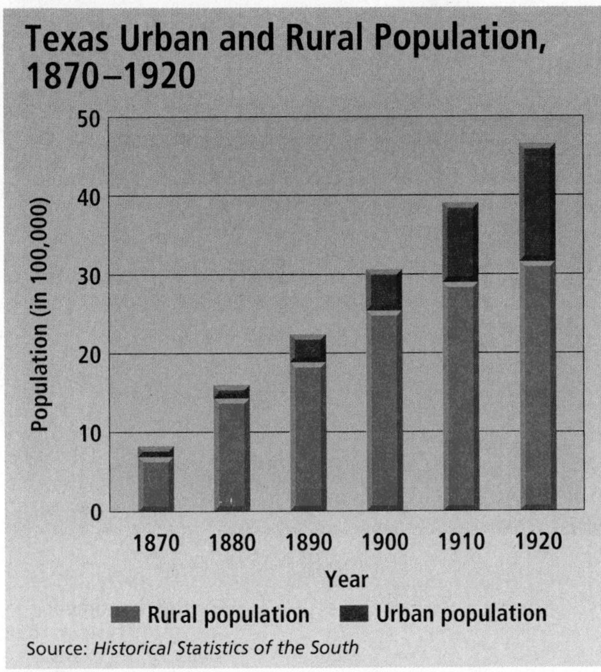

1. Approximately how many more people lived in urban areas of Texas in 1920 than in 1870?

- **A** 1.4 million
- **B** 25 million
- **C** 1 million
- **D** 4 million

2. What factors do you think may have contributed to this change in population distribution?

Analyzing Primary Sources

Read the following lyrics to a popular song from the late 1800s. Then answer the questions.

"Come, boys, I have something to tell you,
Come near, I would whisper it low;
You are thinking of leaving the homestead.
Don't be in a hurry to go.
The city has many attractions,
But think of the vices [bad habits] and sins,
When once in the vortex [whirl] of fashion,
How soon the course downward begins.
(Chorus:)
Stay on the farm, stay on the farm,
Though profits come in rather slow,
Stay on the farm, stay on the farm;
Don't be in a hurry to go."

3. What problems does the author of this song see with city life?

- **F** Its profits come in slowly.
- **G** Everyone is in a hurry.
- **H** It is full of dangers.
- **J** Everyone talks too loudly.

4. What change in the population distribution does this song characterize as a negative trend?

Cooperative Learning

Work with a small group to complete the following activity. Each person should select one of the following themes: a) immigration and geographic patterns, b) the Spanish-American War and World War I, c) new technology, d) the growth of Texas cities. Each member should pose questions and create answers based on the theme chosen. Combine the questions and answers and hold a quiz show about the chapter.

Internet Activity

Use the Internet to research events of the Mexican Revolution and its impact in Texas. Some refugees wrote *corridos*—or ballads—about their experiences. Create your own *corrido* with the information you have found. Include a short explanation of how Mexican Americans have maintained their cultural heritage while adapting to and contributing to the larger Texas culture.

CHAPTER 26

Boom and Bust
(1920–1939)

Texas Essential Knowledge and Skills (TEKS) 1B, 1C, 6A, 7A, 7B, 7C, 7D, 7E, 8A, 9A, 9C, 10A, 10B, 13A, 13B, 13C, 18B, 19A, 19D, 20B, 21A, 21B, 21C, 21D, 21H, 22A, 22C, 22D

Ma Ferguson was a popular governor despite charges of corruption in her administration.

TEXAS

- **1920** Governor William Hobby breaks a dockworkers' strike in Galveston.
- **1924** Texans elect Miriam A. "Ma" Ferguson as the state's first female governor.
- **1926** Automobile registrations reach 1 million.
- **1928** For the first time in the state's history, the majority of Texans vote for a Republican presidential candidate—Herbert Hoover.

1920 1922 1924 1926 1928

U.S. and WORLD

- **1920** The Nineteenth Amendment is ratified, giving women the right to vote.
- **1922** Americans spend some $60 million on radios.
- **1924** Jazz music reaches a wider audience with the first public performance of George Gershwin's *Rhapsody in Blue*.
- **1926** The United States imports some $4.4 billion worth of goods.
- **1929** The U.S. stock market crashes, leading to business failures and massive unemployment.

If you were there . . .
How would you help others during an economic depression?

Build on What You Know

Texas had become increasingly urbanized during the early 1900s. The Texas economy had expanded to meet the military's needs during World War I. But the postwar period brought social unrest and economic troubles. Although some enjoyed boom times in the 1920s, hard times lay ahead.

During the Great Depression the U.S. government established programs to help farmers.

Republican Herbert Hoover won the majority of Texas votes for president in 1928.

The Texas Centennial was celebrated with a world's fair in Dallas.

1930

1932

1932
Some 300,000 Texans are unemployed.

1932
U.S. voters choose Democrat Franklin D. Roosevelt to be their next president.

1934

1934
James V Allred is elected governor of Texas.

1934
The Federal Farm Bankruptcy Act extends credit to farmers in danger of losing their farms.

1936

1936
Texas celebrates the 100th anniversary of the Texas Revolution.

1936
The U.S. government creates a program to promote soil conservation.

1938

1938
Texans elect W. Lee "Pappy" O'Daniel as governor.

1938
The Fair Labor Standards Act sets a minimum wage for some American workers.

You Be the Historian

*my*Notebook

What's Your Opinion? Do you agree or disagree with the following statements? Support your point of view in your notebook.

- **Economics** War affects industries but not the agricultural economy.
- **Geography** Farmers change the environment, without any environmental consequences.
- **Citizenship** To fight for equal rights is an act of civic responsibility.

Section 1

The Transition to Peace

Main Ideas

1. Demobilization following World War I slowed the Texas economy and caused labor unrest.
2. Texas made some progress toward protecting Texans' civil rights in the post-World War I era.
3. Miriam A. "Ma" Ferguson was both a popular and a controversial governor.

Why It Matters Today

Civil rights organizations became active in Texas during the 1920s. Use current events sources to learn about civil and human rights organizations today.

Key Terms and People

- **demobilization**
- **Miriam A. "Ma" Ferguson**
- **National Association for the Advancement of Colored People**
- **primary election**
- **white primary**
- **League of United Latin American Citizens**

TEKS: 1B, 6A, 7C, 7D, 7E, 13A, 18B, 21B, 21E, 22A, 22D

myNotebook

Use the annotation tools in your eBook to take notes on the economic effects of World War I and early civil rights efforts in Texas.

The Story Continues

On March 19, 1920, a national dockworkers' strike that had swept down the East Coast reached Galveston. For several days, residents listened nervously to reports of beatings and even shootings by striking workers. Governor William Hobby took action and declared martial law. National Guard troops shut down the city and watched as workers loaded 8,700 tons of freight that had been sitting on the docks.

Demobilization and Labor Unrest

The dockworkers were struggling to make ends meet in the slowing U.S. economy that followed World War I. During the war, farms and factories had increased production to keep up with the U.S. military's needs. Many Texans had moved from farms to cities to take jobs in industries that were offering high wages to attract workers. When the war ended, the United States began the process of **demobilization**, or moving from a wartime to a peacetime economy. Soldiers returning home needed jobs, often displacing female and African American workers who had taken jobs in industry during the war. As military spending was cut, the economy slowed and competition for jobs increased. Some businesses laid off workers or reduced wages, creating hardships for many workers. In 1919 some 4 million American workers went on strike for higher wages and better working conditions.

Some African Americans who had served in World War I returned home to find discrimination and a slowing economy.

Texas had its share of labor troubles. Two years after the Galveston dockworkers' strike, a railroad strike in Denison and other towns led Governor Pat Neff, whom Texans had elected in 1920, to declare martial law. Order was soon restored, and the workers returned to their jobs.

Labor issues were not the only challenges Texans encountered. During World War I various groups had faced discrimination. Because the United States was fighting Germany, some Americans turned against everything German. For example, in 1919 Governor Hobby blocked funding for the German department at the University of Texas.

Racial tension had also increased. Some 31,000 African Americans from Texas had served in World War I. When black soldiers were serving their country began to demand equal rights, though, many white Texans responded angrily. A riot in Houston involving African American soldiers and local residents resulted in 20 deaths. On questionable evidence, 19 soldiers were hanged for their part in the conflict.

Violence also increased with the formation of a new Ku Klux Klan in the early 1920s. Wearing hoods to hide their identities, Klan members threatened, attacked, and sometimes murdered people whom they disliked. They targeted African Americans, Jews, Roman Catholics, and recent immigrants. The Klan became a powerful political force in Texas. It helped elect mayors, members of the legislature, and U.S. senator Earle Mayfield. Many law enforcement officials had Klan connections. As one black Texan recalled, "A person couldn't trust nobody. Even the law was hooked up with them a lot of the time." In the mid-1920s internal disagreements and growing opposition to the Klan led to a decline in its power and influence in Texas.

Reading Check **Analyzing Information** What challenges did Texans face after World War I?

BIOGRAPHY

Miriam A. "Ma" Ferguson (1875–1961)

Miriam Amanda Wallace was born in Bell County, Texas. In 1899 she married James Ferguson, who became governor of Texas in 1915. At first, Miriam Ferguson showed little interest in politics. She ran for governor in 1924 only because her husband could not. After a controversial first term, Ferguson was defeated in her 1926 re-election campaign. However, Texans elected her as governor again in 1932. Ferguson limited state spending while increasing state aid to Texans during the 1930s. Ferguson ran for a third term in 1940. **What actions did Ferguson take in her second term?**

★ The Ferguson Administration

The influence of the Ku Klux Klan was a major issue in the 1924 governor's election. Candidate **Miriam A. "Ma" Ferguson** took a strong stand against the Klan. During the campaign she also promised Texans "two governors for the price of one." James E. Ferguson, her husband and campaign manager, had been governor from 1915 to 1917. Because he had been impeached and removed from office, he could not run for governor again.

Nonetheless, the Fergusons were popular among many Texans. Reporters referred to Miriam Ferguson as Ma, and James Ferguson as Pa. Miriam Ferguson won the election, becoming the first female governor of Texas and the second female governor in U.S. history.

Miriam Ferguson was a controversial governor. Critics accused her husband of using his wife's influence to sell pardons to raise money. She pardoned more than 1,000 prisoners, many more than other Texas governors had pardoned. Unlike other governors of the 1920s, Ferguson did little to help education. For example, William Hobby's administration had led the effort to have the state provide students with free textbooks. Governor Neff had signed a bill creating Texas Technological College, now Texas Tech University, which opened in Lubbock in 1925.

Critics also accused the Fergusons of giving Highway Department contracts to friends instead of to the lowest bidder. In one lawsuit, Texas attorney general Dan Moody charged that the state was paying $7 million for work worth only $2 million. As a result of Moody's actions, several highway contracts were changed or canceled. In 1926 Ferguson lost her bid for re-election to Moody. At age 33, Moody became the youngest governor ever elected in Texas. He reorganized the highway department and reformed the prison system. He also appointed Jane McCallum, a reformer active in child care, education, and women's rights, as secretary of state. Moody easily won re-election in 1928.

Reading Check **Finding the Main Idea** How was the election of Miriam Ferguson a first in Texas history?

★ Early Civil Rights Efforts

Many Texans were becoming politically active by joining civil rights organizations such as the **National Association for the Advancement of Colored People** (NAACP). Founded in New York City in 1909, the NAACP opened its first Texas chapter in El Paso in 1915. The state soon had 31 NAACP chapters claiming some 7,000 members. However, many Texans violently opposed the NAACP's efforts. By 1923 only five Texas chapters remained in operation. Only in the late 1930s did the NAACP again become an important force in Texas.

In the 1920s many politically active African Americans centered their efforts on gaining voting rights. Texas had used a variety of methods—including a poll tax—to stop African Americans from voting. In 1923 a new law barred black Texans from voting in the Democratic **primary election**, which selected candidates to run in the later general election. Because the Republican Party was weak in Texas, this **white primary** effectively prevented African Americans from voting. When Lawrence A. Nixon, a black doctor from El Paso, was not allowed to vote in a Democratic primary in 1924, he filed suit against the state. The U.S. Supreme Court struck down the Texas law in 1927. The Texas legislature then gave the Democratic State Committee the power to exclude African Americans from primary elections. This move barred black Texans from voting for years to come.

African Americans faced discrimination in other areas. Teacher Lula Byars described her school. "I remember . . . nailing a piece of cardboard over the window to keep the cold wind out." African American newspapers such as the *Dallas Express* and the *San Antonio Register* called for an end to discrimination. Clifford Richardson of the *Houston Informer and Texas Freeman* and other black editors wrote editorials condemning racial violence.

Mexican Americans also struggled for equal rights. They were discriminated against in hotels, restaurants, and schools. In some counties, Mexican Americans could not vote in the Democratic primary. As one woman later recalled, "We Mexicanos had to fight for everything we ever had, even the right to go to school." To fight for their rights, Mexican Americans organized the **League of United Latin American Citizens** (LULAC) in Corpus Christi in 1929. It soon became the best-known Mexican American civil rights organization in the nation.

Reading Check **Summarizing** Describe the civil rights efforts of various groups in Texas during the 1920s.

Civil Rights Organizations

NAACP

- Founded in New York in 1909
- First Texas chapter begun in El Paso in 1915
- Called for economic and educational equality for African Americans

LULAC

- Founded in Corpus Christi in 1929
- Worked to end unfair treatment toward Mexican Americans
- From Texas, spread to become a national organization

Section 1 Review

hmhsocialstudies.com
ONLINE QUIZ

1. Define and explain:
- demobilization
- primary election
- white primary

2. Identify and explain the historical significance of:
- Miriam A. "Ma" Ferguson
- NAACP
- LULAC

3. Sequencing
Use the chart below to discuss significant actions of 1920s Texas governors in the order in which they occurred.

Neff → Ferguson → Moody

4. Finding the Main Idea

a. Describe civil rights efforts in Texas after World War I.

b. What problems arose during Miriam Ferguson's administration?

5. Writing and Critical Thinking myWriteSmart

Summarizing Write a paragraph explaining how World War I affected Texans economically, socially, and politically.

Consider the following:
- the wartime boom and demobilization
- civil rights efforts

Section 2

Economic and Cultural Change

Main Ideas

1. Oil discoveries and production fueled economic growth in Texas in the 1920s.
2. Overproduction of cotton and poor weather conditions hurt Texas farmers after the war.
3. The Jazz Age brought new forms of entertainment such as music and movies to Texans.

Key Terms and People

- **C. M. "Dad" Joiner**
- **Howard Hughes Sr.**
- **blues**
- **consumer goods**

Why It Matters Today

Consumer goods became an important part of the Texas and U.S. economies during the 1920s. Use current events sources to learn about how a consumer item affects people today.

TEKS: 1C, 7A, 7B, 7D, 9A, 13A, 13B, 13C, 19A, 20B, 21A, 21B, 22A, 22D

myNotebook

Use the annotation tools in your eBook to take notes on economic and cultural change in Texas during the 1920s.

The Story Continues

The oil workers could not decide where to place the old rig to begin drilling. Mrs. Daisy Bradford, who owned the land, suggested moving downhill. At the bottom of the hill, Mrs. Bradford shouted, "Stop boys. Drill right there." Although she did not know it, Mrs. Bradford had chosen a spot that would yield one of the greatest oil strikes in Texas history.

★ Economic Growth

The strike Mrs. Bradford accidentally helped locate was made by a wildcatter named **C. M. "Dad" Joiner**, who had leased land from her in East Texas. In October 1930 his third well—the Daisy Bradford No. 3—"blew in," opening one of the largest oil fields in the world. The East Texas oil field extended from Henderson and Kilgore to Longview and Gladewater. By midsummer 1931 this oil field produced some 900,000 barrels of oil per day. In 1933 it accounted for more than 20 percent of U.S. oil production.

Joiner's strike was part of the continuing Texas oil boom that had started with Spindletop. New fields were discovered during and just after World War I at Ranger and Burkburnett. Other fields opened at Big Spring, Borger, and Mexia, and a discovery in Nueces County led Corpus Christi to become a major port for oil products.

Oil discoveries made fortunes for a number of other Texans, including **Howard Hughes Sr.**, H. L. Hunt, Clint Murchison, and Sid Richardson. Hughes had developed a drill bit that could drill through very hard rock, allowing producers to reach previously unavailable oil reserves. Oil production in Texas increased as a result of this technological innovation. His son, Howard Hughes Jr., used the family wealth to become a leader in the aviation and filmmaking industries. Some Texans grew wealthy in the oil fields, but the work was hard, as one oilman recalled.

TEXAS VOICES

"When I went to work for the Magnolia Petroleum Company in '27, we worked eighty-four hours a week. We worked seven twelve-hour days with an occasional day off once or twice a month. . . . Most of the work was done with shovels, teams [of mules], and wagons, and a few trucks. And it took lots of men and lots of man-hours to do the work that we can do in a few hours today."

—Bruce Turner, quoted in *Tales from the Derrick Floor,* by Mody C. Boatright and William A. Owens

Cotton mills and clothing manufacturers also employed many Texans. Meatpacking and other industries that processed farm and ranch products continued to be important to the Texas economy.

Reading Check **Analyzing Information** What influence do you think Texas oil production had on local and national markets?

Hard Times for Farmers

Despite this industrial growth, most Texans still worked in agriculture. Farmers had expanded production to meet the military's demands during World War I. New irrigation methods, such as advanced windmills, made it possible to grow cotton and wheat in areas that were once too dry for farming, such as the Panhandle. As one farmer noted, "This land we're standing on is just a crust over a great big underground lake [Ogallala Aquifer]."

With its flat, treeless land, the Panhandle was well suited for large farm machines. Irrigation and mechanization increased West Texas cotton production from 51,000 bales in 1918 to 1.1 million in 1926. As farming boomed, Panhandle ranches were divided into small farms. By 1924, more than 2.3 million acres were being farmed in the Panhandle, up from just 45,000 acres in 1909.

As farming increased in the Panhandle, many ranchers moved their herds to the south and east. Central Texas, the Gulf Coast, and the Pecos River region became important ranching centers. In much of these areas topsoil was thin and rainfall was spotty, making farming difficult. Conditions were better for farming in some parts of South Texas. Farmers there planted vast citrus-fruit orchards that produced oranges, grapefruits, lemons, and limes.

BIOGRAPHY

C. M. "Dad" Joiner

(1860–1947) Born in Alabama, Columbus Marion Joiner served in the Tennessee legislature before moving to Oklahoma Territory in 1897. Although trained as a lawyer, he became involved in the oil business. In 1926 he moved to Texas to search for oil. In Rusk County, Joiner struck oil on his third try in 1930. He earned the nickname "Dad" for being the "father" of the East Texas oil field he had discovered. By 1938 Joiner was worth some $3 million. Joiner faced many legal problems, however, and lost much of his wealth. **How did C. M. "Dad" Joiner contribute to the economic development of Texas?**

★Texas Cities★

Corpus Christi

History: In 1839 Henry L. Kinney established a trading house and ranch on the site of present-day Corpus Christi. Tourism and industry increased, and Corpus Christi grew rapidly.

Population in 2012 : 312,195 (estimate)

Relative location: On the Gulf Coast at the mouth of the Nueces River

Region: Southern edge of the Gulf Coast Plain

County: County seat of Nueces County

Special feature: Largest city on the coastal bend

Origin of name: Legend has it that Álvarez de Pineda named the nearby bay Corpus Christi because he arrived there on the festival day of Corpus Christi, which is Latin for "body of Christ."

Economy: Corpus Christi is a major port city. Ocean freighters and oil supertankers serve the entire South Texas area through Corpus Christi Bay. Industries include fishing, oil refining, and tourism.

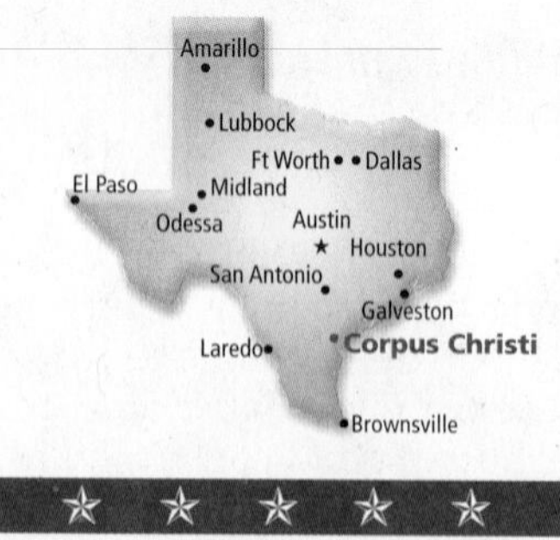

The prosperity that most farmers enjoyed during World War I did not last. Growth in the use of synthetic, or artificial, fabrics hurt demand for cotton. Farmers soon grew more cotton than Americans wanted to buy. Overproduction meant lower prices and profits. In April 1920, cotton sold for 42 cents a pound. A year later, it sold for less than 10 cents a pound. Even as farmers received less money for their crops, the cost of operating farms was rising. Farmers had to invest in farm machinery, and land prices in the Panhandle increased. Although machinery was a part of the farming process, harvesting cotton was still done by hand. A large Mexican migrant-labor force was employed to carry out much of this work. Entire families worked in the harvest, including school-age children.

One West Texas farmer recorded his thoughts about the cotton crisis in his diary.

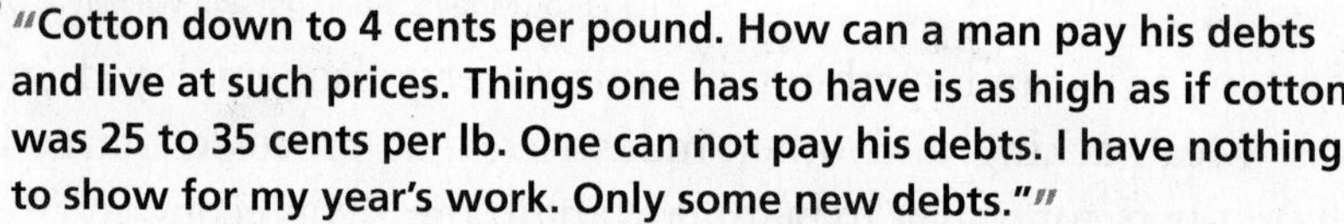

TEXAS VOICES

"Cotton down to 4 cents per pound. How can a man pay his debts and live at such prices. Things one has to have is as high as if cotton was 25 to 35 cents per lb. One can not pay his debts. I have nothing to show for my year's work. Only some new debts."

—William G. DeLoach, *Plains Farmer,* edited by Janet M. Neugebauer

Reading Check **Identifying Cause and Effect** Describe the boom-and-bust cycle of farming during and following World War I, and explain why it occurred.

★ The Jazz Age in Texas

While cotton farmers were experiencing hard times, many Texans were enjoying the social changes brought by the 1920s. The decade has several nicknames including the "Jazz Age" and the "Roaring Twenties." Jazz arose from the **blues**, a musical form with lyrics that often reflected the difficulties people faced in life. African American artists created jazz, which soon became associated with the decade's energy and excitement. Dances such as the bunny hug, the Charleston, and the fox-trot also became popular in the 1920s. In addition, families and friends liked attending baseball and football games. The development of a new technology—the radio—changed entertainment in Texas. Texans listened to music, news reports, and sports broadcasts. By the end of 1922 Texas had 25 commercial radio stations operating.

Texans also loved going to the movies, particularly westerns. Early films were in black and white and had no sound. A piano player or a phonograph typically provided music to accompany the scenes on the movie screen. It was not until 1927 that a movie with sound, *The Jazz Singer,* was released. *Wings,* one of the five major movies filmed in Texas during the 1920s, won the first Academy Award for best motion picture.

Texans had more leisure time partly because of **consumer goods**—items intended for personal use—that made household tasks much easier. Electric sewing machines and household appliances such as refrigerators, toasters, and vacuum cleaners became more common in the 1920s. The demand for these and other consumer goods also led to the growing popularity of large department stores in cities such as Dallas and Houston.

One of the most popular consumer goods was the car. In 1916, Texans registered some 195,000 cars, a number that grew to 1 million just 10 years later. The automobile industry's growth boosted both demand for oil products and the Texas economy. Automobiles, trucks, and buses brought other economic changes to Texans. By using trucks to haul products to markets, farmers became less reliant on railroads. Bus lines competed with railroads for passengers.

The popularity of cars soon created a need for more roads. In 1922 Governor Pat Neff called for "a big road building program for this State, not a little, sickly, puny one." The following year the Texas Highway Department received money from a tax on gasoline to build roads. Road construction moved slowly, however—in 1930 only 7,300 miles of paved roads crossed Texas.

Despite these advances, not all Texans were pleased with the changes the Jazz Age was bringing. Some worried that the automobile was destroying traditional values. Young people were more likely to drive around in the family car than to spend time with other family members. Texans also worried that people were drinking too much alcohol. As a result, many Texans supported prohibition, which was in effect throughout the 1920s until its repeal in 1933.

Reading Check **Summarizing** How did life in Texas change during the Jazz Age?

CONNECTING TO

Music

Texas Blues

The blues is a form of music that African Americans living in the South created in the late 1800s. Blues singers and performers drew upon both African and American musical traditions to create music that told of the suffering African Americans endured. Several Texans contributed to the development and popularity of the blues. Blind Lemon Jefferson performed in the Dallas area, and his records were popular in northern states. One of the most famous Texas bluesmen, Robert Johnson, came from Mississippi, but recorded his music in Dallas and San Antonio. **How does the blues reflect the cultural diversity of Texas?**

Section 2 Review

hmhsocialstudies.com
ONLINE QUIZ

1. Define and explain:
- blues
- consumer goods

2. Identify and explain the historical significance of:
- C. M. "Dad" Joiner
- Howard Hughes Sr.

3. Locate on a map:
- Corpus Christi

4. Summarizing
Use a graphic organizer like the one below to identify industries that boomed during the 1920s.

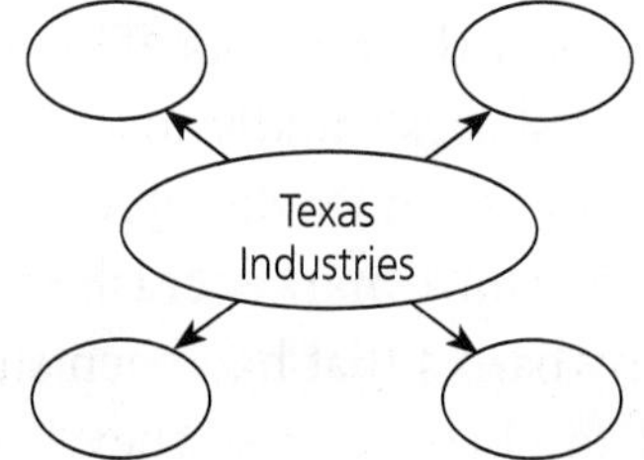

5. Finding the Main Idea

a. How did new forms of entertainment and demand for consumer goods change life in Texas?

b. What effect did the demand for automobiles have on the Texas oil industry?

6. Writing and Critical Thinking 

Evaluating Imagine that you are a Texas farmer in the 1920s. Write a diary entry describing how the boom-and-bust cycle of Texas agriculture has affected you. Consider the following:
- the boom during World War I
- the fall in cotton prices in the 1920s

Section 3

The Great Depression

Main Ideas

1. The Great Depression was a time of great hardship for Texans.
2. The Texas oil industry suffered during the depression.
3. Many Texas farmers were forced to abandon their farms in the Dust Bowl.

Key Terms and People

- **stocks**
- **Great Depression**
- **Ross Sterling**
- **soup kitchens**
- **breadlines**
- **scrip**
- **proration**
- **Dust Bowl**

Why It Matters Today

The U.S. economy greatly affected the lives of Texans during the 1920s and 1930s. Use current events sources to learn about the U.S. economy today.

TEKS: 7E, 8A, 9C, 10A, 10B, 13A, 13B, 13C, 21A, 21B, 21C, 21D, 21H, 22A, 22C, 22D

myNotebook

Use the annotation tools in your eBook to take notes on the effects of the Great Depression and the Dust Bowl in Texas.

The Story Continues

At stockbrokers' offices throughout the United States, cards displaying the latest stock prices from the New York Stock Exchange were posted outside. On one day in October 1929, they could not keep up with the changing prices. At the end of the day, the reporting of stock prices had fallen more than an hour behind. Investors had no idea what the values of their stocks were. They did know one thing for certain—prices were falling faster than anyone had ever seen before.

An Economic Crisis

Companies sell **stocks**—shares of ownership—to raise money. Many people buy stocks hoping to sell them later and make a profit. During the 1920s the price of many stocks rose steeply. Many Americans began to speculate. Speculating involved taking out loans to buy stock and being unable to repay those loans when stock prices went down. Then in late October 1929 a panic spread at the New York Stock Exchange as people rushed to sell their stocks. This panic led to a stock market crash. Thousands of shares rapidly lost their value. Many people who had invested their savings in stocks were left with nothing.

The effects of the stock market crash were soon felt throughout the United States. Many banks that had been successful in Texas and other states were forced to close because they had made too many loans to people who now could not repay them. People who had savings in these banks sometimes lost all of their money. As people lost their savings, they bought less. Businesses began laying off workers to reduce expenses. Workers who were unemployed, or without work, could not buy as much food, clothing, or other goods as they once had. When demand for these goods fell, business was hurt even more. As this cycle continued, the economic slowdown became a depression.

During the first year of the depression, many people believed the economy would improve quickly. A Houston newspaper editor dismissed the stock market crash. "The changes in stock prices are purely an affair of and for the stock speculators." This optimistic spirit did not last long, however. The global economic slowdown in the 1930s was so severe that it became known as the **Great Depression.** Millions of people throughout the world became unemployed. By 1933 some 15 million American workers were unemployed and millions of families were on relief, or public assistance. Thousands of families lost their homes, and many people had to beg for money on the streets.

Governor **Ross Sterling** announced in 1932 that some 300,000 Texans were unemployed. African Americans and Mexican Americans were hit particularly hard. They were often the first to be laid off from work so that white employees could keep their jobs. As a result, many Mexican immigrants returned to Mexico. Some Mexican Americans were forced to leave the country. Two San Antonio women later described life during the depression.

TEXAS VOICES

"Some of us had lost our homes which were nearly paid for, had sold our furniture, piece by piece, our jewelry, and even most of our clothes, hoping against hope that something in the way of a job would materialize [appear]."

—Stella Boone and Ethel Stringer, quoted in *Women of the Depression,* by Julia Kirk Blackwelder

Reading Check **Finding the Main Idea** How were the banking industry and the production of goods and services in Texas affected by the boom-and-bust cycle after the stock market crashed?

That's Interesting!

Hoover Hogs

The nine-banded armadillo is the only species of armadillo found in North America. During the Great Depression, some Texans were so poor that they ate armadillos. They referred to these animals as Hoover hogs, after President Hoover. Texans made armadillo shells into souvenirs ranging from baskets to lamp shades. In 1981 the armadillo was made the state mascot by executive decree.

Image Credit: ©Smithsonian American Art Museum, Washington, DC/Art Resource, NY

Interpreting Visuals

Effects of the depression. *This painting, entitled* Prayer for Rain, *shows a depression-era family being forced to move.* ***Based on the landscape, how do you think the family's harvest might have affected their situation?***

The Great Depression left many Texans out of work and seeking relief.

The Depression in Texas

The depression was somewhat less severe in Texas than it was in many other states. Most Texas farmers could at least feed their own families, and the oil industry continued to provide many jobs. Texans' need for assistance grew as the depression continued. Churches and private organizations tried to help as many people as possible, setting up **soup kitchens** and **breadlines** to give out food. Charitable organizations also donated clothing and provided shelters. Basic necessities were scarce, as one Texan recalled.

The Red Cross helped some 3,000 people in Dickens County—a county of fewer than 9,000 residents. However, charitable organizations could not assist everyone who needed aid. As the depression deepened, many Texans and other Americans grew frightened and angry.

Local governments also struggled to deal with the Great Depression. To reduce spending, many cities and counties cut jobs. African Americans and Mexican Americans were often let go first or put at the back of the line for public assistance programs. One Texan complained, "This thing of cutting salaries and laying off employees, is one of the main things that has brought on this depression era." Local governments also issued **scrip**, or paper notes, to save money. These paper notes were a promise to pay at a later date. For example, teachers in San Antonio received scrip for their salary. Such measures did little to help the Texas economy or to boost confidence.

President Herbert Hoover and Governor Ross Sterling—like many Texans—opposed government programs such as unemployment relief because they claimed that it would destroy individuals' self-reliance. They supported limited government aid to businesses. They believed that once businesses had recovered, new jobs would be created and the economy would revive. However, Texan and American citizens grew increasingly unhappy with these policies as the depression continued.

Reading Check **Summarizing** How did the Great Depression affect Texans?

CONNECTING TO

ECONOMICS AND MATH

Texans at Work

Texans worked in a variety of industries during the Great Depression. Create a pie chart of the jobs Texans had in 1930.

INDUSTRY	NUMBER EMPLOYED
Agriculture	838,571
Manufacturing and mechanical	386,184
Trade	260,399

Interpreting Data

1. How many more people worked in agriculture than in the second leading Texas industry?
2. How do you think life in Texas was affected by the types of work Texans did during the Great Depression?

A Crisis in the Oil Industry

As the depression deepened, the Texas oil industry faced a crisis. The East Texas oil discovery led to overproduction. The price of oil dropped from more than $1 per barrel to a dangerously low 8 cents per barrel. These low prices threatened to ruin profits and the Texas oil industry.

Governor Ross Sterling tried to get oil companies to limit production, but had little success. In August 1931 he declared martial law in four East Texas counties. He sent in the National Guard to enforce **proration**, or the proportionate division of oil production. Under proration, each well could produce only a certain amount of oil each day. Oil

The Causes of the Dust Bowl

The Dust Bowl was caused by both physical and human factors. The drought and dust storms resulted in millions of dollars in damage.

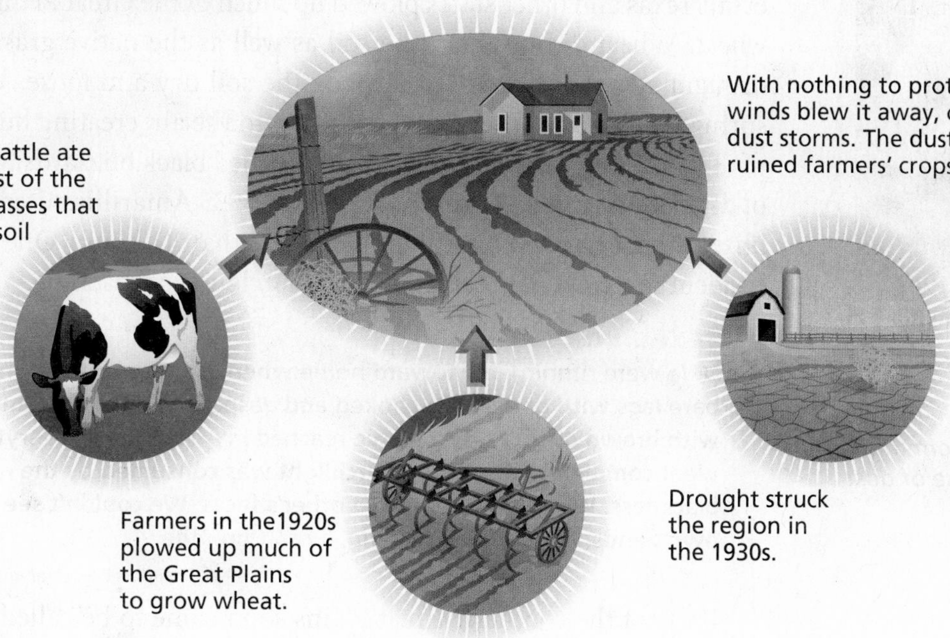

Grazing cattle ate away most of the native grasses that held the soil in place.

With nothing to protect the dry soil, winds blew it away, creating huge dust storms. The dust and drought ruined farmers' crops and killed cattle.

Farmers in the1920s plowed up much of the Great Plains to grow wheat.

Drought struck the region in the 1930s.

Visualizing History

1. **Geography** How did physical factors combine with human factors—like farming and ranching practices—to cause the Dust Bowl?
2. **Connecting to Today** What measures would you recommend to help people who change the environment avoid another Dust Bowl?

producers argued that the state government had no right to tell them how to use their property. In response, the state legislature passed laws granting the Railroad Commission more authority to regulate the oil industry.

Opposition existed to these economic controls, however, and some Texas companies produced "hot," or illegally produced, oil. State and federal laws were later able to help prevent overproduction, which eventually increased stability in the wake of the hot oil controversy.

Reading Check **Analyzing Information** How did the boom-and-bust economic cycle affect the Texas oil industry?

★ The Dust Bowl and Farmers

Although Texas farmers could grow much of their own food, the depression hit them hard economically. Farmers had experienced difficult times during the 1920s, but life grew even harder during the 1930s. Crop prices continued to drop. In 1932, cotton sold for less than six cents a pound. Prices fell so low that some farmers burned their crops. As one newspaper noted, "There is no waste in burning something that . . . is hardly worth hauling to town."

Many farmers were forced to move from the Panhandle because of dust storms.

An environmental disaster made matters worse. Ranching and farming were changing the environment. Cattle grazing had already damaged the native grasses that held the soil in place. In the 1920s farmers in Texas and other states plowed up much of the Great Plains to grow wheat. Wheat did not hold the soil as well as the native grasses. Then drought struck in the 1930s, leaving the soil dry and loose. When the spring winds came, they lifted the soil into the air, creating huge clouds of dust. The worst of these storms were called black blizzards, with walls of dirt reaching more than a mile high. In 1935 Amarillo suffered a black blizzard that blocked out the sun for more than 11 hours. One Amarillo resident remembered seeing a huge dark cloud approaching.

TEXAS VOICES

"We were running . . . toward home when the wind hit, pelting our bare legs with gravel. We choked and gasped . . . as the air thickened with brown dust. . . . Just as we reached my front porch everything went completely black. The porchlight was consumed by the blackness. We couldn't see each other's faces. We couldn't see our own hands. I remember gasping, 'I can't breathe.'"

—Pauline Robertson, *Panhandle Pilgrimage*

Analyzing Primary Sources
Evaluating Based on this eyewitness account, how did changes to the environment affect the Panhandle?

Parts of the southern Great Plains soon came to be called the **Dust Bowl**. Drought and dust ruined crops, and thousands of cattle died. Many cattle ranchers struggled financially during this time. One third of Panhandle farm families received charity or relief. About 90 percent of the local farmers had to take out crop loans to be able to buy necessities.

Reading Check **Finding the Main Idea** How did weather affect the Panhandle and Texas farmers and ranchers during the Great Depression?

Section 3 Review

1. Define and explain:
- stocks
- soup kitchens
- breadlines
- scrip
- proration

2. Identify and explain the historical significance of:
- Great Depression
- Ross Sterling
- Dust Bowl

3. Analyzing Information
Copy the graphic organizer below. Use it to show the effects of the Great Depression on the Texas economy.

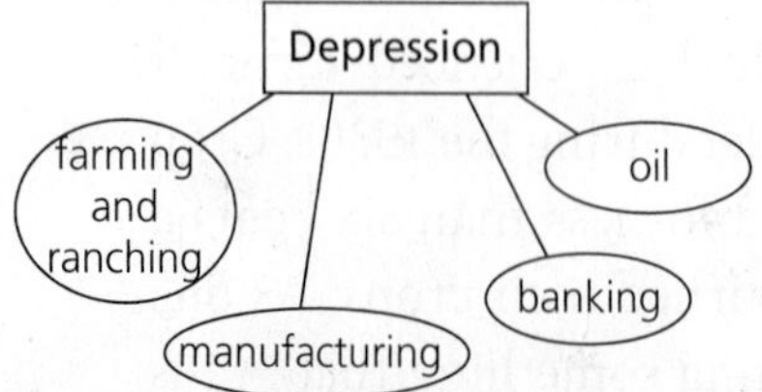

4. Finding the Main Idea
a. How did government regulation affect the Texas oil industry?
b. How did Texas farmers and ranchers modify the environment during the 1920s, and what were the consequences of these modifications?

5. Writing and Critical Thinking myWriteSmart
Analyzing Information Imagine that you live in Texas during the 1930s. Write a letter to a friend in New York describing how Texans have responded to the Great Depression.
Consider the following:
- the social effects of the Great Depression
- the environmental crisis that created the Dust Bowl

Connecting To

Geography

Drought and Farming in Texas

Drought has long been a problem for Texas farmers and ranchers. In the 16th century, Spanish explorer Álvar Núñez Cabeza de Vaca provided the first recorded information about a drought in West Texas. The map shows the regions of Texas affected by drought in the 1930s. The chart shows years of drought in different regions of Texas. Between 1920 and 1940 the only region that had no years of drought was the Low Rolling Plains. Crops failed during this time, and the state's cattle industry suffered. Texans endured droughts again in the 1950s, 1980s, 1990s, and 2010s. In addition to having trouble with water, ranchers had trouble obtaining enough feed for their cattle because of the effects of erosion.

The Dust Bowl, 1903s

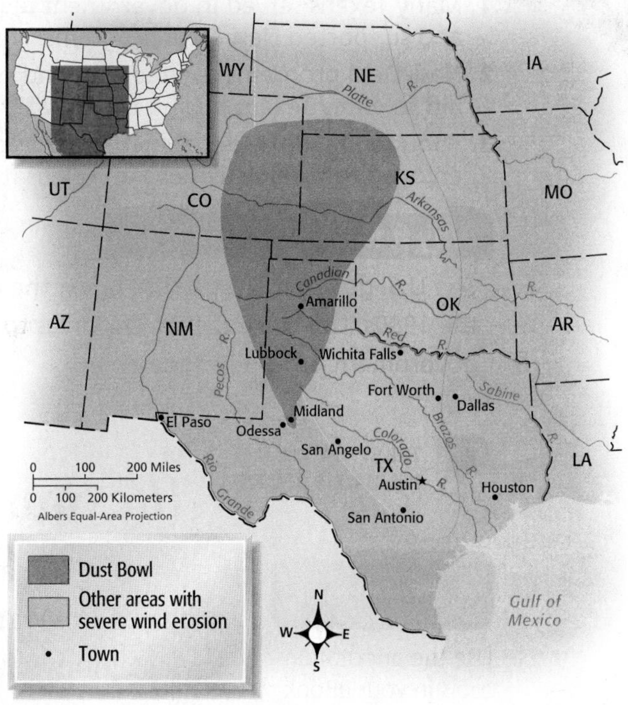

Geography Skills

Interpreting Thematic Maps and Graphs

1. What region of Texas was most affected by the drought and erosion that led to the Dust Bowl?
2. Which regions suffered the greatest number of drought years?
3. How do you think years of drought affected the cattle industry?
4. Organize the cities on this map into lists of those affected by the Dust Bowl, those affected by other wind erosion, and those not affected.

Drought in Texas, 1920–1940

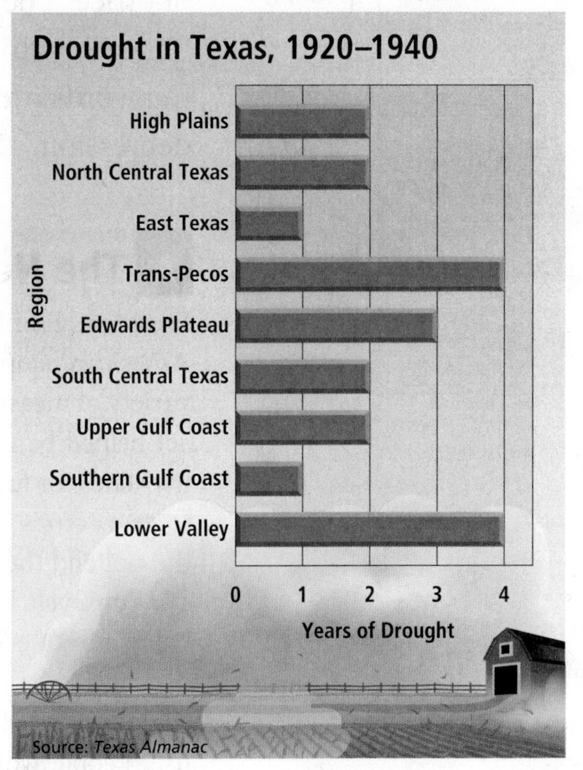

Source: *Texas Almanac*

Section 4

Texas and the New Deal

Main Ideas

1. Many Texans served in government leadership positions and supported New Deal programs.
2. New Deal programs created jobs and provided financial aid to many Texans during the Great Depression.
3. Though life in the depression era was difficult, Texans enjoyed cultural activities and celebrated a centennial.

Key Terms and People

- **New Deal**
- **Social Security**
- **John Nance Garner**
- **Sam Rayburn**
- **James V Allred**
- **J. Frank Dobie**
- **centennial**

Why It Matters Today

The U.S. government tried to boost the economy in the 1930s. Use current events sources to learn about government programs today.

TEKS: 13A, 18B, 19A, 19D, 21A, 21B, 22A, 22D

myNotebook

Use the annotation tools in your eBook to take notes on life in Texas during the New Deal era.

The Story Continues

A young Texan named Lyndon Baines Johnson stood in the crowd on March 4, 1933. The sky over Washington, D.C., was cloudy, but the rain of the past few days had stopped. The audience watched Franklin D. Roosevelt take the oath of office. The new president told the American people, "The only thing we have to fear is fear itself." His comforting words provided hope to a nation battered by years of depression.

The New Deal

President Franklin D. Roosevelt had promised "a new deal for the American people." Roosevelt and his advisers asked Congress to pass a variety of measures—called the **New Deal**—to fight the depression. One act helped banks remain open, while another program gave money to the states for food and other aid to people. Another act paid farmers not to grow crops in order to cut down on overproduction. The New Deal did not end the depression, but it gave hope to millions of Americans.

Roosevelt believed that if workers had money to spend it would help spur an economic recovery. Business would benefit and the whole economy would improve. New Deal programs created jobs by funding public works—government-sponsored building projects for public use. People worked for New Deal agencies such as the Public Works

Interpreting Visuals

Hard times. *Many teenagers tried to find jobs to support their families during the depression.* ***How have these Texas boys managed to earn some money during the Great Depression?***

Administration (PWA) and the Works Progress Administration (WPA). Workers constructed schools, dams, parks, and roads. These programs became so well known that many people wrote directly to Roosevelt looking for work. Lulu Gordon of San Antonio wrote, "I am willing to do any kind of work because I have to support myself and my children. . . . Please give me some work."

Roosevelt also wanted to provide Americans with economic security for the future. In 1935 Congress created the **Social Security** system. This program provided payments to retired citizens and benefits for unemployed workers. The Social Security system collected the money it needed for its payments from employers and from workers.

Several Texans served under Roosevelt and helped with his New Deal efforts. **John Nance Garner** of Uvalde served as vice president from 1933 to 1941. He had previously been Speaker of the U.S. House of Representatives. Under President Hoover, Jesse Jones of Houston had headed a government agency that loaned money to businesses. President Roosevelt then appointed Jones to head all government lending programs and to the position of secretary of commerce. Lyndon Baines Johnson of Johnson City served as state director of the National Youth Administration (NYA), which employed young people between the ages of 16 and 25. Johnson was only 27 years old when he became the NYA director. An NYA official complimented Johnson's service. "You have the best Youth Director in the nation in Lyndon Johnson."

Among the well-known Texans in the U.S. Congress was **Sam Rayburn** of Bonham. Rayburn held a seat in Congress for almost 50 years and served for many years as Speaker of the House. Rayburn was generally a loyal supporter of Roosevelt. Like Rayburn, other members of Congress from Texas usually supported New Deal programs.

Reading Check **Summarizing** Which Texans played a role in the New Deal, and what were their contributions?

BIOGRAPHY

Sam Rayburn (1882–1961) Born in Tennessee but raised in Bonham, Texas, Sam Rayburn won a seat as a Democrat in the Texas House of Representatives in 1906. In 1912, voters elected him to the U.S. House of Representatives. Rayburn was re-elected 24 times, serving from 1913 until his death in 1961. In Congress, Rayburn promoted the New Deal. Both Democrats and Republicans respected Rayburn for his abilities at effective compromise. He served as Speaker of the House in every Democrat-controlled Congress from 1940 until 1961. **How did Sam Rayburn serve Texas?**

Interpreting Visuals

New Deal programs. *During the Great Depression, the Works Progress Administration funded public works including murals, such as this one at the post office in Rockdale, Texas.* ***How does this mural show aspects of depression-era life in Texas?***

★ New Deal Programs in Texas

Several New Deal agencies offered assistance to Texans during the Great Depression. In 1934 some 13 percent of Texans received aid. The Federal Emergency Relief Administration provided millions of dollars to assist Texans. The Civilian Conservation Corps (CCC) created jobs for some 100,000 Texans. CCC workers built and repaired bridges, dams, and state parks. Workers received $30 a month but were required to send $25 of their pay back home to their families. The families could then spend the money in their local economies. By January 1938, Texans had received some $23 million from family members in the CCC. Other Texans found jobs with the Works Progress Administration (WPA). The WPA aided in the construction of dams along the Colorado River. NYA workers in Texas built many highway rest stops—an idea that soon spread throughout the nation. As a result of these jobs, Texans had money to spend on goods and services, thereby helping the state's small businesses.

The Rural Electrification Administration (REA) helped Texas farms gain access to electricity. This program was important to Texans because fewer than 10 percent of Texas farms had electricity in 1935. By 1965, 98 percent of Texas farms had electricity. The federal government also helped Texas farmers by purchasing farmland to keep it out of production and allow it to recover. Agents of the Soil Conservation Service taught farmers how to plant trees and grass to prevent soil from blowing away. They also advised farmers to plow in the direction of the natural shape of the land. That way the ridges and furrows would prevent further erosion by water and wind.

Many Texans welcomed the federal assistance, but as the depression continued some people began to criticize the New Deal. They feared that the rapid expansion of government would threaten individual liberty.

Reading Check Drawing Inferences and Conclusions How did New Deal programs affect the production of goods and services in Texas?

Texas Politics during the New Deal

Miriam Ferguson, who had been elected governor again in 1932, supported New Deal policies. In 1933 she convinced Texans to approve $20 million in bonds for relief aid. She also issued an order creating the Texas Relief Commission to assist Texans.

Ferguson chose not to run for office in 1934, opening the way for Texas attorney general **James V Allred** of Wichita Falls to win election as governor. Allred worked hard to bring New Deal programs and federal money to Texas, and he was re-elected in 1936. He once declared, "I'm gonna grab all I can for the State of Texas." Allred also helped create a state old-age pension program and a retirement plan for public school teachers. In addition, during Allred's administration the Texas Unemployment Compensation Commission—now known as the Texas Workforce Commission—was established. This commission gives Texans information about available jobs and distributes payments to unemployed workers.

In 1938 a candidate with a style unlike anyone else's ran for governor. W. Lee O'Daniel was the sales manager of a flour-milling company in Fort Worth. During the late 1920s O'Daniel had begun airing a radio show that featured a country music group called the Light Crust Doughboys. The show opened with the words, "Please pass the biscuits, Pappy!" Soon the show's host was known as Pappy Lee O'Daniel. In May 1938 O'Daniel announced that he had received some 54,000 letters in one week urging him to run for governor. Much to the surprise of political experts, O'Daniel ran a successful campaign. Texas journalist Robert Hicks described an O'Daniel campaign rally.

TEXAS VOICES

"The rally opens with hillbilly songs, then the candidate tells the crowd that the singing is over, and anyone who came for the show can leave. But no one does. He admits that when he first started talking about running [for governor] he was simply looking for a new way to help sell his flour. But when the people became serious about it he did so too. O'Daniel is as mystified [bewildered] as his opponents in regard to his large crowds."

—Robert Hicks, quoted in *Texas after Spindletop*, by Seth S. McKay and Odie B. Faulk

Texans elected O'Daniel by a wide margin in 1938. Some 100,000 people jammed Memorial Stadium in Austin to watch O'Daniel take the oath of office. Pappy O'Daniel's lack of political experience began to show after he took office, however. He had a poor relationship with the legislature, and few of his proposed programs became law. Nevertheless, Texans re-elected him in 1940. O'Daniel gave up the governor's office in 1941 to take a seat in the U.S. Senate. By that time, the depression was nearing its end.

Reading Check **Analyzing Information** Identify the accomplishments of the Texas governors elected during the 1930s.

LINKING Past to Present

Social Security

When Congress passed the Social Security Act in 1935 as part of the New Deal, it was intended to help Americans deal with the depression. Since that time Social Security benefits have continued to help Texans and other Americans. Social Security provides financial assistance to retired persons, people with disabilities, and families of deceased workers. **How does Social Security help Texans?**

Analyzing Primary Sources
Identifying Points of View Why did Hicks claim that O'Daniel was "mystified" by his popularity?

CONNECTING TO

Music

Western Swing

During the 1930s a new style of music appeared in Texas. Western swing featured traditional country music instruments such as the fiddle and the guitar. James Robert "Bob" Wills, a fiddle player, was the most influential western swing musician of the 1930s. Wills borrowed from the various musical traditions that he heard growing up in Texas. Mexican ballads, the blues of black Texans, and the sounds of rural southern music all inspired his music. In 1934 Wills formed a new band, the Texas Playboys. It became the most popular western swing band in the United States. **How does western swing reflect how the diversity of Texas has blended to form a unique Texas culture?**

★ Life and Culture during the Depression

Life during the depression was difficult for many Texans. In 1934 journalist Lorena Hickok toured Texas. She noted, "I've been out on this trip now for a little more than two weeks. In all that time I've hardly met a person who seemed confident and cheerful." Music provided a welcome distraction to Texans. African American musicians such as Huddie Ledbetter and Aaron "T-Bone" Walker played the blues. Mexican American artists such as Narciso Rodríguez became known as the father of Texas-Mexican conjunto music. He helped make conjunto popular. Conjunto blends elements of traditional Mexican, German, and Czech music.

Bob Wills and his band the Texas Playboys offered a new kind of dance music called western swing. Other musicians such as Woody Guthrie, who lived in the Panhandle from 1929 to 1937, wrote songs about the experiences of Texans in the depression.

Texans also enjoyed other forms of music during the depression. Some Texans attended symphonies in Dallas, Houston, and San Antonio. Many Texans went to the movies. Texans also read the works of **J. Frank Dobie**, whose stories and collections of folktales captured many aspects of life in Texas. Another bright spot came in 1936, when Texas celebrated its **centennial**, or 100th birthday since independence. With federal assistance, the state spent $25 million to stage a world's fair in Dallas to mark the occasion. President Roosevelt visited the fairgrounds. The centennial provided an opportunity for Texans to enjoy the efforts of the many organizations that worked to preserve the state's historic buildings and sites.

Reading Check **Summarizing** What kind of celebrations, cultural activities, and performances did Texans enjoy during the depression?

★ Section 4 Review

hmhsocialstudies.com ONLINE QUIZ

1. Define and explain:
- New Deal
- Social Security
- centennial

2. Identify and explain the historical significance of:
- John Nance Garner
- Sam Rayburn
- James V Allred
- J. Frank Dobie

3. Categorizing
Copy the graphic organizer below. Use it to identify the significant achievements of Texas leaders during the depression.

Texan	Achievements
Garner	
Johnson	
Rayburn	
Allred	

4. Finding the Main Idea

a. Explain how New Deal programs affected the production of goods and services in Texas.

b. How did New Deal programs affect rural Texans?

5. Writing and Critical Thinking myWriteSmart

Summarizing Write a paragraph describing Texas politics and culture during the Great Depression. Consider the following:
- accomplishments of governors of Texas during the depression
- diversity of music, movies, and celebrations in Texas

Connecting To

Literature

"Mustang Gray"

J. Frank Dobie

J. Frank Dobie was born on a ranch in Live Oak County. He joined the faculty of the University of Texas in 1914, but left the university for a year to manage his uncle's ranch. The western tales he heard from the ranch hands sparked his interest in the folklore of Texas and the American Southwest. By the 1930s, Dobie's writings and folktales were recognized in Texas and across the United States. His short story "Mustang Gray" tells the story of Mayberry B. Gray's efforts to capture a mustang.

Not long after coming to Texas, [Gray] was a-ranging after buffalo, far away from the settlements, when his horse fell, throwing him to the ground. He held to the reins, but the charge of a buffalo **mortally**[1] shot so frightened the horse that he jerked away and ran out of sight. After trailing him for a long time and finding his tracks mingled with those of wild horses, Gray came back to the slain buffalo for a meal. He took some of the meat to a pond nearby, built a fire, and cooked it.

Tracks . . . told him that mustangs were watering here. If he but had a rope, he might catch one. He climbed a tree over the main horse trail for a look. Before long he saw a band of mustangs galloping to water. Some of them, including a heavy-set stallion, passed beneath him. . . .

After the mustangs had water and left, Gray came down from the tree with a plan. If he attempted to walk back to the settlements, he would certainly suffer from thirst. Walking was against his principles anyhow. . . .

Animals have regular hours for watering, and when the time approached on the fourth day for the mustangs to come to the pond, Gray was ready for them. Having tied one end of the **reata**[2] to a low, stout branch, he took the other up the tree to an open space immediately over the trail and made it into a loop. He knew that he would have but one throw at one mustang. He wanted the heavy-set stallion. He did not miss.

The stallion jerked himself flat, but got up. For hours he plunged, ran, jerked, snorted but gradually as the man talked to him in low tones and moved gently, he calmed down. It was the next day before he tremblingly allowed a hand on his neck. . . . The taming process went on until Gray . . . got the stallion to stand until he was firmly seated. Then, headed towards the settlements, he pulled the bandanna free. For many miles the prairie was open. The mustang ran until he was completely exhausted. That evening Gray watered him and hobbled him short. The next morning he had comparatively little trouble keeping him under control. Riding bareback, he came to the camp of men who knew him. They dubbed him Mustang Gray, a name still attached to a place as well as to legend and song.

[1]**mortally:** fatally [2]**reata:** rope

Understanding What You Read

1. **Literature and History** Why did Gray need to capture the mustang?
2. **Literature and History** What does this story reveal about the dangers of hunting on the Texas frontier?
3. **Literature and You** What folktales and stories are told in your community?

CHAPTER 26 REVIEW

The Chapter at a Glance

Examine the following visual summary of the chapter. Create an outline of the major events of the boom era of the 1920s and the depression era in Texas. Then compare your outline with a classmate's.

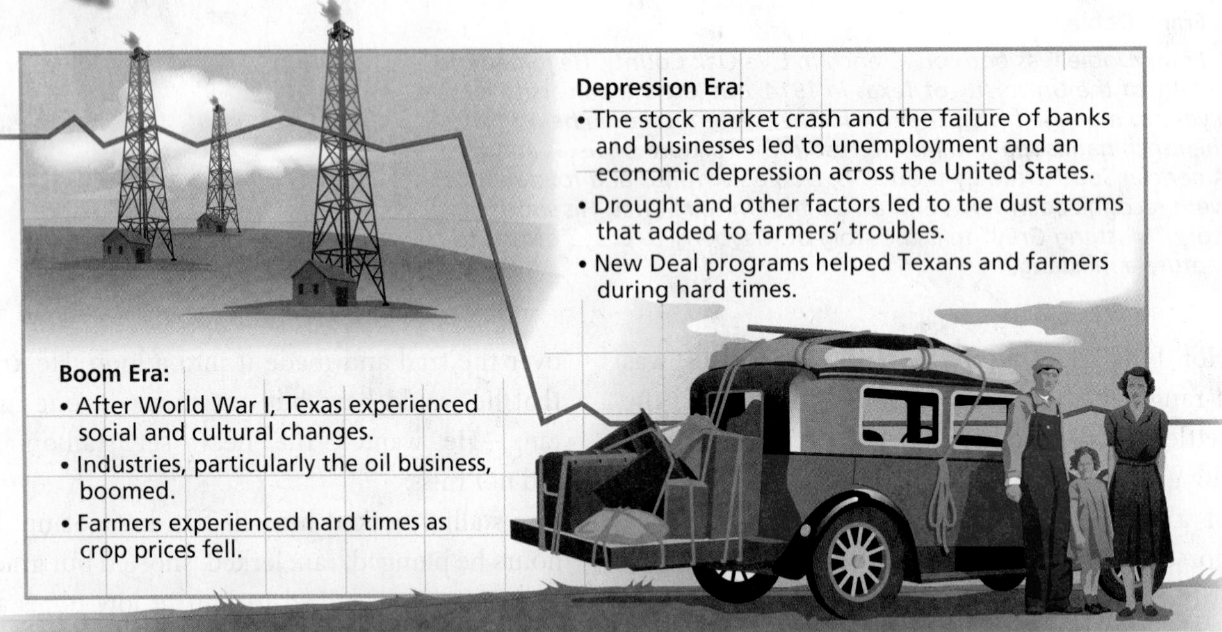

Identifying People and Ideas

Write a sentence to explain the role or significance of the following terms and people.

1. demobilization
2. Miriam A. "Ma" Ferguson
3. blues
4. consumer goods
5. Great Depression
6. Dust Bowl
7. proration
8. New Deal
9. John Nance Garner
10. Sam Rayburn

Understanding Main Ideas

Section 1

1. What problems arose while Miriam Ferguson was governor?
2. What was the white primary, and how did it influence civil rights efforts in Texas?

Section 2

3. How did the geographic distribution of farming and ranching change during the 1920s?
4. What was life like in Texas during the Jazz Age?

Section 3

5. How did government regulation affect East Texas oil producers during the Great Depression?
6. How did weather affect the Panhandle and Texas farmers and ranchers during the Great Depression?

Section 4

7. How did Texans contribute to the New Deal?
8. How did New Deal programs help the Texas economy?

You Be the Historian

Reviewing Themes

1. **Economics** How did World War I contribute to the boom-and-bust cycle of Texas agriculture?
2. **Geography** How did farmers in the Panhandle adapt to and modify the environment, and what were the consequences of the modifications?
3. **Citizenship** What steps did Texans take to fight for equal rights in the 1920s?

Thinking Critically

1. **Drawing Inferences and Conclusions** Many Texas businesses experienced boom-and-bust cycles during the depression. What part of this economic cycle did banking and ranching experience during this time?
2. **Analyzing Information** Describe some of the defining characteristics of the Great Depression era of Texas history.
3. **Summarizing** What effect did the New Deal have on farming and ranching in Texas?

Texas Test Practice

Interpreting Artifacts

Study the poster below. Then use the information in the poster to help you answer the questions that follow.

1. Based on the poster, who is eligible for Social Security benefits?
   - **A** government employees
   - **B** retired workers
   - **C** CCC workers
   - **D** agricultural workers

2. Why might the government offer financial assistance to citizens?

Evaluating Sources

Read the following passage from this chapter. Then answer the questions.

"When I went to work for the Magnolia Petroleum Company in '27, we worked eighty-four hours a week. We worked seven twelve-hour days with an occasional day off once or twice a month. . . . Most of the work was done with shovels, teams [of mules], and wagons, and a few trucks. And it took lots of men and lots of man-hours to do the work that we can do in a few hours today."

3. Where else might you look to verify the information presented in the passage above?
   - **F** a textbook
   - **G** a diary
   - **H** a photograph
   - **J** all of the above

4. Is the passage above a primary or a secondary source? Does it appear to be reliable? Why or why not?

Linking to Community

The Great Depression remains a vivid memory for many Americans who lived during the 1930s. Interview a member of your community who lived through the Depression. Ask the person what kind of work his or her family did to make enough money to survive. Prepare a scrapbook of that individual's life and your community during the Depression. You may want to include images of the era in your scrapbook.

Internet Activity 

Use the Internet to research the Great Depression and to analyze the impact of national and international markets on the production of goods and services in Texas. Then create a chart that has the following information: the cause of the Depression, whether the cause was national or international, and ways people attempted to solve challenges presented by the Depression.

Image Credit: Library of Congress Prints and Photographs Division [LC-USZC4-4890]

Social Studies Skills

WORKSHOP

Using Primary and Secondary Sources

When studying the past, you will use two main types of sources. *Primary sources* are created by people who actually took part in or witnessed events. Common examples of primary sources include diaries, journals, artifacts, paintings, photographs, interviews, letters, oral histories, and legal documents. Sources that comment on recent events, such as newspaper reports, editorials, and political cartoons are also considered primary sources. The same is true for personal memoirs and autobiographies, even if they were created late in a person's life. Primary sources allow you to discover how people living in a period felt about what was happening around them. This makes them valuable historical tools that allow a close-up look at the past.

Secondary sources, on the other hand, are descriptions or interpretations of historical events written after the events have occurred. These sources are written by persons who did not take part in or witness the events. Biographies, encyclopedias, history books, databases, and other reference works are examples of secondary sources. Writers of secondary sources have the advantage of knowing the long-range consequences of events. This knowledge helps shape their viewpoints. Because the writers of secondary sources are removed from the action taking place, they can be more impartial, which can help a reader discover what actually happened. However, these sources will not reveal as clearly the feelings and motivations of the people involved in events. That is why the best way to study the past is to use both primary and secondary sources together.

How to Study Primary and Secondary Sources

1. **Study the material carefully.** Consider the nature of the material. Is it verbal, visual, or oral? Is it based on firsthand information or on the accounts of others? In other words, is it a primary or secondary source? Note the major ideas and supporting details.
2. **Consider the audience.** Ask yourself: For whom was this message originally meant? Whether a message was intended, for example, for the general public or for a specific private audience may have influenced its style or content.
3. **Check for bias.** Watch for certain words or phrases that signal a one-sided view of a person or event. Both primary and secondary sources can contain bias, depending on the attitudes of the creator.
4. **When possible, compare sources.** Study more than one source on a topic if you can. Comparing sources gives you a more complete and balanced account.

Practicing the Skill

Select a topic discussed in Unit 8. Write a brief report on this topic, using one primary source and one secondary source. Explain why each source is considered primary or secondary. Your sources may include databases, media and news services, biographies, interviews, or artifacts. Be sure to check for bias and evaluate the validity of the sources by comparing the sources to each other, analyzing the language used in the sources, or researching the authors.

History in Action

UNIT 8 SIMULATION

You Solve the Problem . . .

How can Texas farmers raise crop prices?

Complete the following activity in small cooperative groups. It is the late 1800s. You and your fellow Texas farmers want to work with other farmers to find a way to earn more money. You and the other farmers in your group decide to make a presentation to encourage other farmers to join the Southern Farmers' Alliance. Follow these steps to solve your problem.

1. **Gather information.** Use your textbook and other resources to find information that might influence your plan of action for convincing farmers to join the Southern Farmers' Alliance. Remember that your presentation must include information that farmers will need to persuade them to join the Alliance. Be sure to use what you learned from this unit's Skills Workshop on Using Primary and Secondary Sources to help you find an effective solution to this problem. You may want to divide up different parts of the research among group members.

2. **List and consider options.** After reviewing the information you have gathered, list and consider the options you might recommend for successfully convincing Texas farmers to join the Alliance. Your final solution to the problem may be easier to reach if you consider as many options as possible. Be sure to record your possible options for the preparation of your presentation.

3. **Consider advantages and disadvantages.** Now consider the advantages and disadvantages of taking each option. Ask yourselves questions such as, "How will joining the Alliance help bring about political changes that will help us?" Once you have considered the advantages and disadvantages, record them as notes for use in preparing your presentation.

4. **Choose, implement, and evaluate a solution.** After considering the advantages and disadvantages, prepare a presentation. Be sure to support your reasons by including information you gathered and by explaining why you rejected other options. When you are ready, decide which group members will make each part of the presentation, and then take your solution to the farmers (the rest of the class).

   As you present, think carefully about the words you are using. Try to use vocabulary words from this unit as well as academic vocabulary terms in your presentation.

UNIT 9

The Modern Era

(1939–PRESENT)

The first space shuttle launch began a new era of space exploration during the 1980s.

Image Credit: NASA

Texas Teens

Young Scientists

Millions of students across the nation eagerly watched as the National Aeronautics and Space Administration (NASA) launched its *Apollo 11* spacecraft to the moon in 1969. They listened excitedly as astronauts spoke to flight controllers at the NASA Mission Control in Houston. The phrase *This is Houston* became famous. The interest created by the space race inspired many Texas students to study science and math. Some of these students have taken their interest in science and technology and created their own businesses.

To encourage this interest in science and math, NASA runs the Reduced Gravity Education Flight Program. This program gives science and math students from colleges across the country an opportunity to conduct research in low-gravity conditions—the same type of conditions that astronauts experience in space. Teams of students submit proposals for experiments they would like to conduct. Those teams whose proposals are accepted construct their experiments and travel to Houston. There they are given an opportunity to fly on a reduced gravity aircraft. While in flight, they conduct their experiment. Afterward, they report the results to NASA officials.

In addition to providing students with a rare opportunity to conduct hands-on research, the Reduced Gravity Education Flight Program also benefits NASA. The experiments that students conduct help fill gaps in our current knowledge about space travel and the effects of low gravity on people and objects. In 2012, for example, a group of students from the University of Houston–Clear Lake helped test new methods for controlling robots in low-gravity situations. NASA officials hope to use the information gained by the test to determine the best ways to use robots on future space missions. **How are young Texans helping shape the future of space exploration and research?**

In this unit you will learn more about Texas scientists. You will also learn about the many changes in Texas since World War II, including urban growth, civil rights movements, a changing economy, and the emergence of a two-party political system.

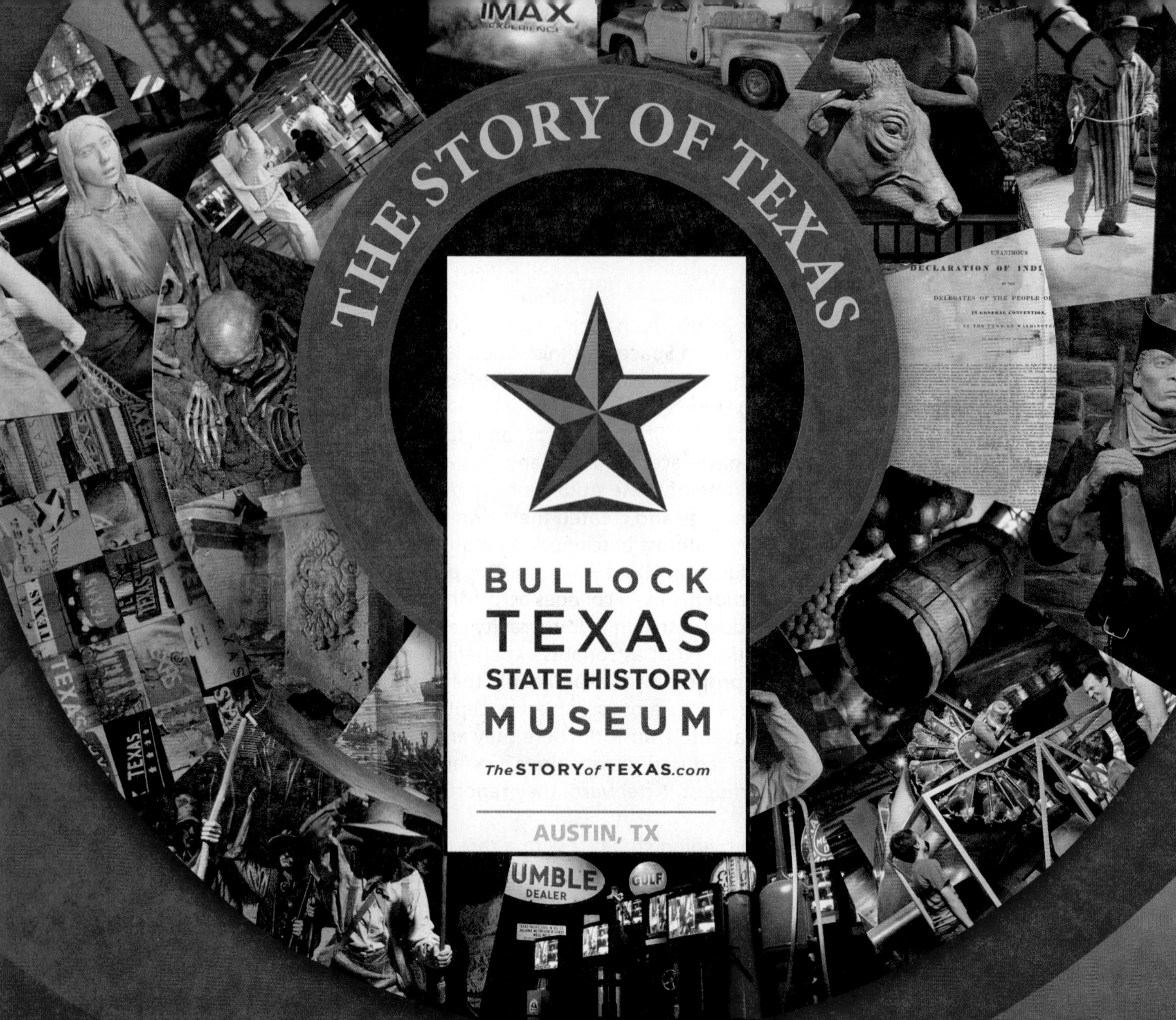

Texas Technology

In the second half of the 20th century, advances in technology helped Texas become an economic, political, and industrial leader in the United States. Texans achieved milestones in transportation, aerospace, engineering, space exploration and other fields, and new technologies helped power the Texas economy into the 21st century.

Texas became a center of military aircraft production and training during World War II. At the start of the war, the United States urgently needed new pilots. Most new recruits had rarely flown an aircraft. They needed planes to learn how to fly. A sprawling factory was built in Dallas. It produced the AT-6, also known as the *Texan*. The AT-6 was one of the most important aircraft trainers of all time.

Texas technology took another huge step in the early 1950s. In 1952 Texas Instruments created the first commercial transistor. This led to transistors made of silicon, which led to the invention of the integrated circuit. Integrated circuits made electronic equipment run faster and more smoothly and allowed electronics to get smaller, which led to a revolution in computing technology.

Texas also helped lead advancements in space exploration. In 1961 the National Aeronautics and Space Administration (NASA) made Houston headquarters for its astronauts. The Johnson Space Center in Houston monitors and supports space missions. In July 1969, Houston supported the *Apollo 11* mission, resulting in the world's first moon landing.

Exploring Museum Resources

At the Bullock Texas State History Museum, you can explore advances Texas has made in transportation, space exploration, medicine, and computing technology and learn about the people who have made important contributions to these fields. You can find museum resources at hmhsocialstudies.com

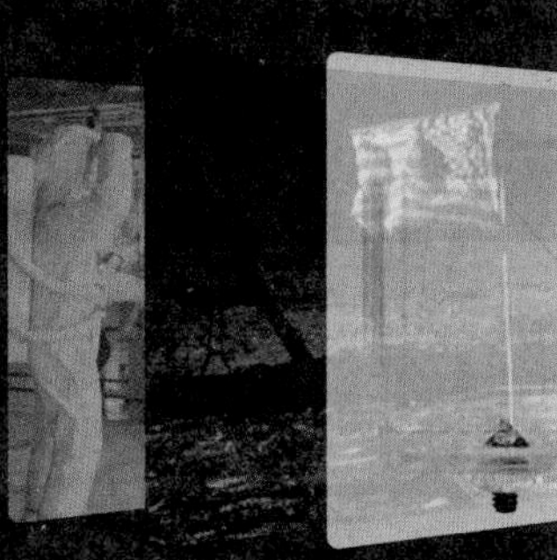

Photograph What made the AT-6 such a good plane for pilot training? Go online to find out.

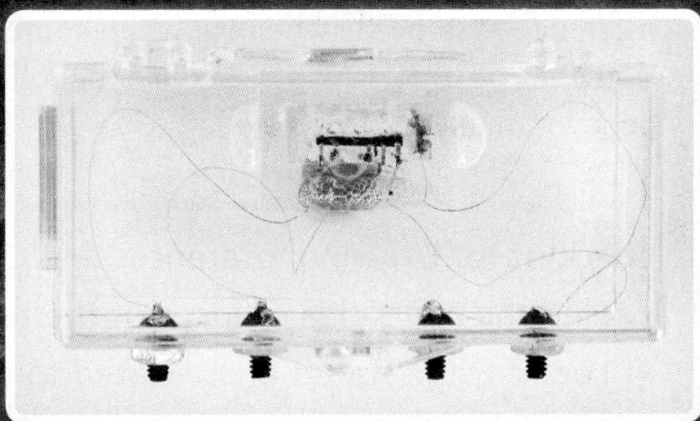

Artifact Who designed this integrated circuit, and how did it lead to the beginning of the Information Age?

Photograph Learn about one of the most significant achievements in history—the *Apollo 11* moon landing.

UNIT 9

Reading Social Studies

Drawing Inferences and Conclusions

Focus on Reading Unstated information can be just as important as what is stated in a text. To understand what is not stated, you need to make an inference. An **inference** is a conclusion reached on the basis of evidence and reasoning. In other words, it is a result based on some knowledge or information.

Understanding Inferences and Conclusions You make inferences all the time. For example, if you walk into a classroom where all of the students are quietly filling out a paper, you might infer that they are taking a test. Although no one actually told you that the students were being tested, you know from past experience that classrooms are quiet during a test. You drew a conclusion based on the limited information you had—quiet room, students filling out papers—plus your prior knowledge about the topic. Making inferences can be very helpful when some of the information about a topic is unstated. Use the following checklist to help you make inferences.

Checklist for Drawing Inferences and Conclusions

- √ Find the main idea or ideas of the text.
- √ Look for the stated facts related to that topic.
- √ Consider what you already know about the topic.
- √ Look for additional information in the text or elsewhere to prove or disprove your inference.
- √ Use the stated facts and what you already know to draw a logical inference or conclusion.

You Try It!

The passage below is from the unit you are about to read. Read the passage, then answer the questions below.

World War II opened some economic doors to African Americans. Many black Texas moved to cities to work at new jobs. However, such moves sometimes met resistance—and sometimes violence—as seen in Beaumont in 1943. Thousands of people had moved to the city to work in its shipyards. Competition for work and for housing led to tensions between black and white workers. When a white woman claimed to have been attacked by a black man, it sparked a massive riot involving more than 2,000 people. Two people lost their lives, and several black-owned businesses were burned.

1. What facts are stated in the passage?

2. What is one conclusion you might draw from the passage?

Reading Section Assessment

The following passage is from the unit you are about to read. Read it and then answer the questions below.

President Johnson and Civil Rights

In his first address to Congress, President Johnson urged passage of a civil rights law. He believed that the federal government needed to take action to ensure the rights of all Americans.

Congress soon passed the Civil Rights Act of 1964, which banned segregation in public places. It also outlawed discrimination in the workplace on the basis of race, sex, religion, or national origin.

1. What facts are stated about President Johnson's interest in civil rights?
2. What can you infer about Johnson's stance on education by reading the passage? What is a conclusion you might draw?

Key Terms

Unit 9

Chapter 27

victory gardens *(p. 566)*
aerospace *(p. 568)*
tidelands *(p. 571)*
commute *(p. 574)*
desegregate *(p. 578)*
nonviolent resistance *(p. 578)*

Chapter 28

Great Society *(p. 587)*
sit-ins *(p. 590)*
Chicano movement *(p. 593)*
scandal *(p. 604)*

Chapter 29

two-party system *(p. 610)*
bipartisanship *(p. 615)*
terrorism *(p. 617)*
deportation *(p. 620)*
infrastructure *(p. 621)*
desalinization *(p. 622)*
Cinco de Mayo *(p. 625)*
biomass *(p. 630)*
wind farms *(p. 630)*
globalization *(p. 631)*

As you read, pay attention to the headings and pictures that appear around the text. These headings and pictures can provide context that will help you understand what you read.

CHAPTER 27

World War II and the Cold War

(1939–1960)

Texas Essential Knowledge and Skills (TEKS) 1B, 7D, 7E, 7F, 8A, 9C, 11C, 12A, 12B, 12C, 13A, 16A, 18A, 18B, 19D, 21A, 21B, 21C, 21D, 22A, 22B, 22C, 22D

Texan Audie Murphy earned many medals and honors for his service in World War II.

TEXAS

1941 Large numbers of Texans volunteer for military service in World War II.

1944 The U.S. Supreme Court declares the Texas white primary unconstitutional.

1945 Texan Audie Murphy receives the Medal of Honor for stopping a German tank attack in France.

1939 — 1942 — 1945 — 1948

U.S. and WORLD

1939 Germany invades Poland, leading to World War II.

1941 Japanese forces attack U.S. Navy ships at Pearl Harbor.

1944 Allied troops launch D-Day, an invasion on the European continent.

1947 President Harry S Truman announces that the United States will help other nations that are fighting communism.

If you were there . . .

Would you volunteer to fight in World War II?

Build on What You Know

As Texans were struggling through the Great Depression, trouble was brewing in Europe and Asia. In the late 1930s a second world war broke out after nations in Europe and Asia threatened their neighbors. War brought many changes to Texas.

Lubbock native Buddy Holly was an early rock 'n' roll star.

As Texas cities grew in population and size, more people moved into suburbs and used automobiles for transportation.

Lubbock native Buddy Holly was an early rock 'n' roll star.

1951
More than 3 million automobiles are registered in Texas.

1954
Allan Shivers successfully runs for a third term as governor.

1957
Texas women call for an equal rights amendment to the state constitution.

1957
The Soviet Union launches *Sputnik*, the first artificial satellite.

1959
Texas musician Buddy Holly is killed in a plane crash.

1960
The U.S. Supreme Court rules that Texas owns Gulf coastal tidelands up to a 10.35-mile limit.

1960
The Soviets shoot down a U.S. spy plane.

1951 — 1954 — 1957 — 1960

You Be the Historian

myNotebook

What's Your Opinion? Do you **agree** or **disagree** with the following statements? Support your point of view in your notebook.

- **Economics** A war can transform and improve a nation's economy.
- **Constitutional Heritage** Individuals must sometimes struggle to protect their constitutional rights.
- **Science, Technology & Society** Industrial development always affects population distribution.

Section 1 World War II

Main Ideas

1. Millions of Texans served in World War II.
2. Texans and Texas industries supported the war effort.
3. Forces from Texas helped bring about Allied victory.

Why It Matters Today

Democratic nations went to war to preserve their freedoms in World War II. Use current events sources to learn about a nation's efforts to guard the freedoms of its citizens.

Key Terms and People

- **Dorie Miller**
- **Chester W. Nimitz**
- **Oveta Culp Hobby**
- **Audie Murphy**
- **victory gardens**

TEKS: 7D, 7E, 13A, 21B, 22D

myNotebook

Use the annotation tools in your eBook to take notes on Texans' roles in World War II.

The Story Continues

December 7, 1941, dawned like any other day for Texan Dorie Miller. A sailor in the U.S. Navy, Miller was hard at work on board the USS *West Virginia* in Pearl Harbor, Hawaii, when a loud explosion rocked the ship. Miller raced to the main deck and could not believe what he saw. The skies were filled with Japanese warplanes. With bombs exploding around him, he helped his wounded captain to safety. Running back to the deck, Miller did his best to defend his ship by firing a machine gun at the attacking planes.

Texans in the War

The attack on Pearl Harbor that **Dorie Miller** witnessed pulled the United States into another global conflict. World War II had begun in Europe just over two years earlier, when German forces invaded Poland. Great Britain, France, and their allies had declared war on Germany and its ally Italy. Meanwhile in Asia Japanese forces were trying to conquer China and other parts of East Asia.

For the first years of the war, the United States remained neutral, though it did send supplies to Great Britain and France. After the attack on Pearl Harbor, which sank or damaged 19 U.S. naval ships, the United States declared war on Japan. In response, Germany and Italy—Japan's allies—declared war on the United States. Less than 25 years after World War I, the United States was involved in another global war.

Interpreting Visuals

Texas military bases. *During World War II, soldiers, sailors, and pilots from all over the United States came to Texas military bases, such as the Naval Air Station in Corpus Christi.* ***For what role are these men training?***

After the Pearl Harbor attack, thousands of Texans rushed to enlist in the armed forces. Some 750,000 Texans served in the armed forces during World War II—about 7 percent of all Americans who took part in the war. Of those 750,000, about 75 percent joined the army. The rest served in the navy, marines, or coast guard. About 80,000 of the Texans in World War II were African Americans, including Dorie Miller about whom you have already read. Thousands more were Hispanic.

Many Texans served as officers. Some 150 generals and 12 admirals were from Texas. Fleet Admiral **Chester W. Nimitz** of Fredericksburg commanded the U.S. fleet in the Pacific. In Europe, Lieutenant General William Simpson of Weatherford commanded the Ninth Army, which fought its way across northern France and Germany. In addition, Colonel James Earl Rudder from Brady played key roles in the D-Day Invasion and the Battle of the Bulge.

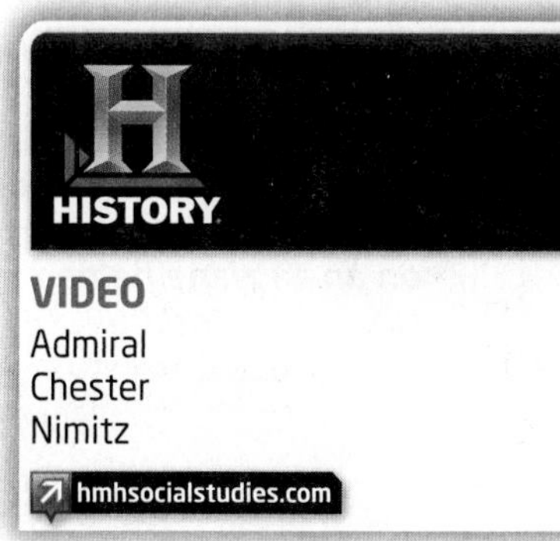

VIDEO
Admiral Chester Nimitz

hmhsocialstudies.com

About 12,000 of the Texans who served in the military in World War II were women. Although women could not take part in actual fighting, they could serve in noncombat military positions in the war. They served mostly in auxiliary, or support, organizations. One such organization was the Women's Auxiliary Army Corps, or WAAC, run by **Oveta Culp Hobby** of Houston. Members of the WAAC—the first women besides nurses ever to serve with the army—were trained mostly in operations and management tasks. About 8,000 female Texans joined the WAAC, and another 4,000 served in Women Accepted for Volunteer Emergency Service (WAVES), an auxiliary unit of the navy. At Avenger Field in Sweetwater, about 1,000 women trained for the Women's Airforce Service Pilots (WASPs). WASPs flew planes, gave instruction to pilots, and tested damaged planes.

Thousands of Texans won distinction for their efforts in World War II. Thirty-three Texans—five of them Mexican American—received the Medal of Honor, the country's highest military honor. José Mendoza López, for example, was honored for saving his company at the Battle of the Bulge. **Audie Murphy** of Hunt County was the nation's most decorated soldier of the war, with 33 awards and medals. Dorie Miller, born in Waco, was the first African American ever to receive the Navy Cross.

Reading Check Summarizing How did Texans serve in World War II?

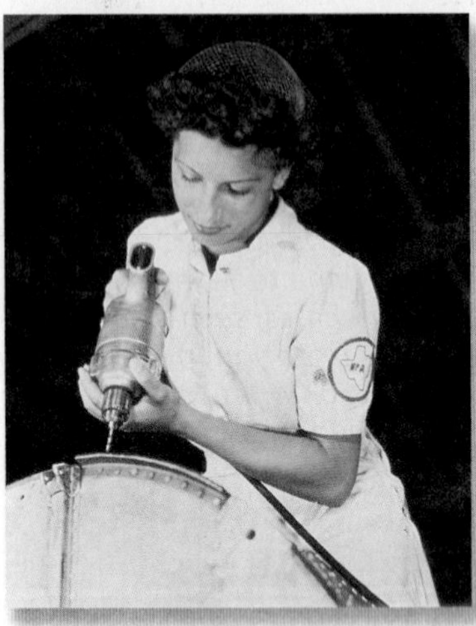

Interpreting Visuals

Factory work. *Women found jobs in Texas factories operating punch presses, working on assembly lines, and riveting metal parts.* ***How do you think this woman's work on an airplane helped the U.S. war effort?***

★ The Texas Home Front

While many Texans were fighting in Europe and the Pacific, millions more took part in the war effort from home. Texas was a major center for training during the war. About 1.2 million army soldiers and 200,000 pilots trained at the state's 15 army camps and 40 airfields. With four air bases, San Antonio became the world's largest aviation training center. The Naval Air Station in Corpus Christi was also a major aviation training center. The navy also had bases at Beeville, Grand Prairie, and Kingsville. In addition, thousands of German, Italian, and Japanese prisoners of war were housed at camps across Texas.

Many Texas businesses provided needed supplies and services to nearby military bases. Industry and agriculture also geared up to meet the demands of the military overseas. Texans built aircraft at plants in Fort Worth, Garland, and Grand Prairie. They built ships in ports across the state. The chemical, oil, and steel industries also expanded production to meet war needs. This expanded production led to the creation of thousands of new jobs, ending the Great Depression in Texas.

The growing economy also led to social change. Some 500,000 Texans, including many African Americans, moved from rural areas to cities to work in booming industries. In addition, many Mexicans moved to Texas to assist with the war effort. As Texas men enlisted, women took over factory jobs. They built planes and ships, operating heavy machinery and working jobs that had traditionally been considered "unladylike." As Governor Coke R. Stevenson stated, "No Texas wife or mother will neglect a single detail in any plane or tank or truck or ship which might preserve the life of husband or son.'"

Like other Americans, Texans made sacrifices for the war effort. Many goods valued by the military, such as gasoline, meat, rubber, and sugar, were in short supply. The government rationed, or set aside for each family, a specific amount of these goods. In addition to reducing their own use of scarce items, Texans found ways to help the military. To help feed troops, Texas farmers devoted more land than usual to food crops rather than to cotton. Some Texans planted **victory gardens**, or small vegetable gardens, to grow extra food. Texans also purchased war bonds to finance the war. In a speech, Audie Murphy applauded such efforts.

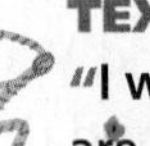

TEXAS VOICES

"I would like to . . . pay a tribute to the Mothers and Fathers who are here. For, it is they who perhaps suffer most in time of war. Too, I would like to express my gratitude for the swell job you have done on the home front. You have given us everything we asked for in the way of tools for modern warfare."

—Audie Murphy, quoted in *No Name on the Bullet,* by Don Graham

Reading Check **Identifying Cause and Effect** How did World War II affect Texas economically and socially?

Young Texans Help the War Effort

Young Texans took on extra responsibilities during the war. Some schools adjusted their schedules so that students could have more time to plant and harvest. Other young Texans searched their towns for scrap metal that could be used by the military.

★ Victory for the Allies

Supported by their friends and family on the home front, Texas soldiers fought in Europe, North Africa, and the Pacific. The first U.S. division to invade Europe was the 36th Infantry Division, based in Brown County. The division had arrived in North Africa in 1943. From there it invaded Italy and southern France, helping bring about Italy's surrender.

The 90th Infantry, based at Abilene, took part in the famous D-Day invasion of June 6, 1944. On that date, Allied troops invaded France to drive out the Germans. The soldiers of the 90th Infantry suffered heavy casualties as they fought their way across Europe. The Second Infantry, based at Fort Sam Houston in San Antonio, also took part in D-Day. Both divisions were still actively fighting in Europe when Germany surrendered in 1945.

The U.S. government required citizens to ration goods, encouraged them to grow vegetables, and urged them to buy bonds to help the war effort.

The war in Europe ended with Germany's surrender, but the war in the Pacific continued. Many Texas units, including the 103rd Infantry Division and 144th Infantry Regiment, saw extensive action in the Pacific. Along with other Allied forces, these units moved steadily toward Japan, capturing key islands on the way. This island-hopping strategy allowed the Allies to move into position to invade and bomb Japan. After American planes dropped atomic bombs on the Japanese cities Hiroshima and Nagasaki, Japan surrendered on September 2, 1945. World War II was over.

World War II was incredibly destructive. Some 50 million people died worldwide as a result of the war—more than half of them civilians. Of the more than 400,000 Americans who died, 23,000 were from Texas. With the fighting over, it was time for Texans and people around the world to turn to the task of rebuilding their lives.

Reading Check **Analyzing Information** How did troops based in Texas contribute to the war effort?

★ Section 1 Review

hmhsocialstudies.com
ONLINE QUIZ

1. Define and explain:
- victory gardens

2. Identify and explain the significance of each of the following:
- Dorie Miller
- Chester W. Nimitz
- Oveta Culp Hobby
- Audie Murphy

3. Locate on a map:
- Corpus Christi

4. Categorizing
Copy the graphic organizer below. Use it to explain the ways in which World War II affected the Texas economy.

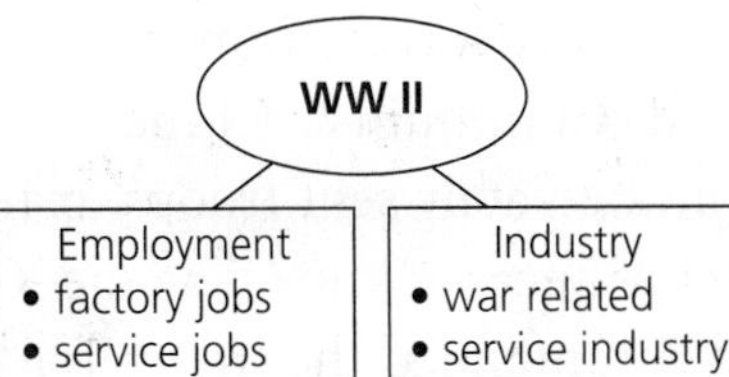

5. Finding the Main idea
- **a.** What roles did Texans play in World War II?
- **b.** How did Texans at home support the efforts of troops overseas?

6. Writing and Critical Thinking myWriteSmart
Making Generalizations and Predictions
Imagine that you live in Texas in 1943. Write a paragraph describing how you and your friends are helping the war effort.
Consider the following:
- what kind of work you do
- victory gardens and rationing

Section 2

Postwar Peace and Politics

Main Ideas

1. Government programs passed after World War II benefited Texans.
2. The postwar economic boom benefited Texas greatly.
3. In the 1950s, Texas passed education laws and won a dispute with the federal government.

Key Terms and People

- **Cold War**
- **aerospace**
- **Texas Education Agency**
- **GI Bill of Rights**
- **Allan Shivers**
- **conservatism**
- **tidelands**

Why It Matters Today

Many military bases opened in Texas during and after World War II. Use current events sources to learn about the status of military bases in Texas today.

TEKS: 7E, 7F, 9C, 13A, 18A, 18B, 21B, 21D, 22D

myNotebook

Use the annotation tools in your eBook to take notes on changes in Texas after World War II.

The Story Continues

Salvador Guerrero of San Angelo was part of the D-Day invasion during World War II. When he returned home after the war he had trouble finding a good job. A friend told Guerrero about a job in Monahans. The job paid well and seemed to offer a bright future. Soon, however, Guerrero heard about an even better job in Odessa. He moved his family there to start work at a weekly salary of $75.

★ The Cold War and the Economy

The booming postwar Texas economy in which Guerrero found work was partly the result of international tensions. After World War II, the Soviet Union established Communist governments in Eastern Europe. The Soviets wanted to spread communism around the world. The United States, however, was opposed to the spread of communism. American leaders acted quickly to limit the spread of Soviet influence. As a result, tensions grew between the two countries. This struggle for global power and influence became known as the **Cold War**.

In 1950 Communist forces from North Korea—supported by the Soviet Union and Communist China—invaded South Korea. The United Nations immediately sent troops, primarily U.S. soldiers, to aid South Korea in what became known as the Korean War. Walton Harris Walker of Belton commanded the troops for the first part of the war.

Texas bases and military installations that had closed after World War II were quickly reopened, including Avenger Field, Dyess Air Force Base, and Harlingen Air Force Base. Just as they had in World War II, Texas industries churned out much-needed war supplies.

The war in Korea lasted several years. Eventually, however, Dwight D. Eisenhower, who had been elected president in 1952, helped bring about peace. After intense negotiations, the war ended in 1953. Some 1.8 million U.S. soldiers—many of them Texans—had fought in the war, and some 54,000 lost their lives.

Among the Texans who fought in Korea was Benito Martinez of Fort Hancock. While alone at a post to monitor enemy activity, he was attacked by a large hostile force. He single-handedly defended his position for hours despite overwhelming odds. Although he died in the attack, his efforts slowed the enemy enough to allow the American forces to organize a defense. A fellow soldier recalled, "Even though he knew he would probably die, he was determined to stay on his position and fight off the enemy." Martinez was awarded the Medal of Honor for his valor, or courage, in the battle.

National military spending increased during and after the Cold War. As a result, Texas industries boomed. Because much of the state's industry produced goods and services for the military, the Texas economy grew during the Cold War.

By 1955 Texas led the United States in the production of helium, oil, petrochemicals, and sulfur. The **aerospace** industry, which manufactured airplanes and missiles, thrived due to increased civilian travel and military demands. Missile research was carried out at Texas plants owned by Boeing and General Dynamics Corporation. The electronics industry also benefited from military research. Many military bases in Texas continued to be major training installations during the 1950s.

Reading Check **Analyzing Information** How did the Korean War and the Cold War affect the Texas economy?

GLOBAL CONNECTIONS

The Cold War

After World War II, many Americans worried that the Soviet Union planned to expand its influence beyond Eastern Europe. The Soviets resented America's efforts to stop the spread of communism. Suspicion on both sides led to the Cold War, which lasted more than 40 years. The two countries came close to outright war on several occasions, leading to widespread fears of nuclear war. **Why did Americans not trust the Soviet Union?**

Aircraft manufacturing became a major industry in Texas during World War II and the Cold War.

BIOGRAPHY

Oveta Culp Hobby

(1905–1995) Oveta Culp was born in Killeen and became interested in politics at an early age. After graduating from the University of Texas School of Law, she served as an advisor to the Texas legislature and married former governor William Hobby. During the 1930s she was president of the League of Women Voters of Texas and became publisher of the *Houston Post.* After World War II she was appointed to several federal positions, heading the Federal Security Agency and the Department of Health, Education, and Welfare. **How do you think Oveta Culp Hobby inspired other Texas women?**

★ Postwar Politics

After World War II, Texans played key roles in the federal government. After Dwight D. Eisenhower was elected president in 1952, he named Oveta Culp Hobby to his cabinet. Hobby, who had run the WAAC in World War II, was head of the Department of Health, Education, and Welfare from 1953 to 1955. Texan Sam Rayburn served as Speaker of the House of Representatives. Under Eisenhower, the country—and Texas—prospered due to an economic boom. Under Governor Coke R. Stevenson, who served from 1941 to 1947, the state paid off its debt.

Within Texas, politics were changing rapidly. The period after World War II saw a rise in conservatism in Texas. **Conservatism** is an approach to politics that supports gradual, rather than rapid, change. Conservatives generally favor keeping systems and programs that have worked in the past rather than creating new ones. They also support lower taxes, limited government regulation of business, and strong national defense. Conservative Democrats like Stevenson wanted to limit state spending, while more liberal members of the party hoped to create programs to support the rights of women, the working class, and minorities. The rise of conservative politics was a key characteristic of this era in Texas history, the era of Conservatism and Civil Rights. (You will read about the civil rights movement later in this chapter.)

Despite their differences, political leaders in Texas pulled together to support education. Conservative Beauford Jester, elected governor in 1946 and 1948, made education a priority. He signed laws that set the school year at nine months and funded teachers' salaries. In addition, they created the educational framework used today. An elected board of education sets educational policy. The state Department of Education—now called the **Texas Education Agency**—sets and reviews standards for schools and teachers. It also reviews and approves textbooks.

Education in Texas also got a boost from federal laws. In 1944 Congress passed the **GI Bill of Rights**. Under this new law, veterans could receive money to attend college. Coupled with state laws that helped veterans with tuition at state universities, it led to a dramatic increase in college enrollment. In addition to paying for college, the GI Bill provided veterans loans to buy homes or create businesses.

When Jester died in 1949, **Allan Shivers** became governor. Shivers helped expand government services by pushing tax increases through the legislature. This gave the state government money to fund schools, pay teachers' salaries, and fund retirement benefits for state employees. During this time the legislature also allowed women to serve on juries and grand juries for the first time.

Reading Check **Summarizing** Describe the important laws passed during the terms of governors Jester and Shivers.

★ The Tidelands Dispute

Governor Shivers is perhaps best known for his efforts to defend the state's ownership of **tidelands**—underwater lands bordering the coast. Texas claimed ownership of the tidelands extending three leagues—or 10.35 miles—from the shoreline. When oil was discovered in the tidelands, however, the federal government claimed that it owned the land.

Several states, including Texas, protested the federal claim. U.S. senator Lyndon B. Johnson from Texas declared his "determination to do all that [he] can to keep the tidelands of Texas away from federal control." The issue was particularly important to Texas education. Revenue from oil drilling on the tidelands was a major source of money for the Permanent School Fund.

The state of California sued the federal government for control of the tidelands, but the Supreme Court decided in the government's favor. Texans, however, argued that their claim was different from other states' claims. Texas, they argued, had owned the tidelands as an independent country, before it joined the Union. Shivers and others argued that the government had agreed to the state's boundaries—including the tidelands—when Texas joined the Union. In 1960 the U.S. Supreme Court ruled that Texas had clear title to some 2.4 million acres of tidelands. The Permanent School Fund has since received hundreds of millions of dollars in oil-related revenue from these tidelands.

In addition to Shivers, a key figure in the state's victory was Attorney General Price Daniel. He became governor in 1957 and served three terms. During his time in office the state passed its first sales tax, or tax paid by consumers when they buy certain goods.

Reading Check **Finding the Main Idea** What led to the tidelands dispute between Texas and the federal government?

1. Define and explain:
- Cold War
- aerospace
- tidelands

2. Identify and explain the significance of the following in Texas history:
- Texas Education Agency
- GI Bill of Rights
- Allan Shivers

3. Identifying Cause and Effect Copy the graphic organizer below. Use it to describe the Cold War and how it affected Texas.

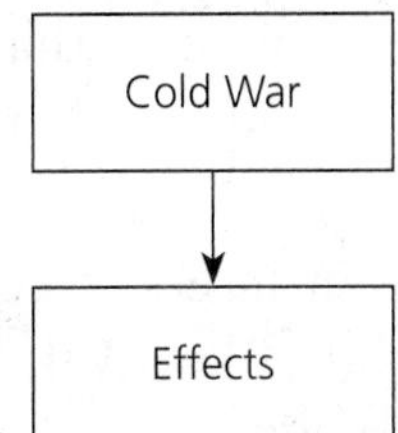

4. Finding the Main Idea
- **a.** How did Texas veterans benefit from the GI Bill?
- **b.** What changes occurred in Texas politics after World War II?

5. Writing and Critical Thinking myWriteSmart
Comparing and Contrasting Imagine that you are a lawyer representing Texas in the tidelands dispute. Write a paragraph explaining how the claim of Texas is similar to and different from that of other states.
Consider the following:
- the issues involved in the tidelands controversy
- the historical claims of Texas

Section 3

The Urbanization of Texas

Main Ideas

1. The growth of industries and the creation of jobs led to urbanization in Texas.
2. American culture changed in the 1950s as people moved to suburbs and new art forms developed.

Key Terms and People

- **commute**
- **Robert Rauschenberg**
- **Katherine Anne Porter**
- **Buddy Holly**
- **Horton Foote**
- **Babe Didrikson Zaharias**

Why It Matters Today

Texas cities grew rapidly in the 1950s. Use current events sources to learn about the effects of growth of Texas cities today.

TEKS: 7E, 8A, 9C, 12A, 12B, 12C, 19D, 21B, 21C, 22D

myNotebook

Use the annotation tools in your eBook to take notes on the urbanization of Texas.

The Story Continues

Lubbock High School student Buddy Holly wanted to be a rock 'n' roll star. His parents had encouraged his musical talents, and he had performed publicly since he was five. He was already a regular on Lubbock radio station KDAV's *Sunday Party*. Not long after graduating from high school, Holly signed a recording contract. His song "That'll Be the Day" became a huge hit. Soon he and his band were playing concerts at packed houses across the country.

Urban Growth

Buddy Holly's career began during a time of major change in Texas. During World War II some 450,000 people had moved to Texas to take advantage of the state's economic growth. Most of these people settled in urban areas. By 1950 some 7.7 million people lived in Texas, a 20 percent increase over its population just a decade earlier. In 1960 the state's population reached 9.6 million.

As the population grew, Texas underwent urbanization. The process occurred more slowly in Texas than in the United States as a whole. However, the shift from rural to urban in the 1940s was still dramatic. Between 1940 and 1950 the number of Texans living in urban areas increased from 45 percent to 60 percent. Houston became the fastest-growing urban area in the nation. At the same time, the rural population of Texas dropped by 600,000, in part because many African Americans left rural communities to seek better jobs in cities or in the North.

Industries that had grown rapidly during World War II continued to draw people to cities. Aircraft manufacturers, electronics firms, oil refineries, and ship manufacturers all still needed workers. New businesses opened rapidly. In Dallas in 1949, for example, an average of five new businesses opened every day, and 13 new manufacturing plants began operations each month. With the growing population of cities, more people began to find jobs in service industries to cater to other city residents. Such industries included health care, banking, construction, plumbing, and retail sales.

The growth of industries also dramatically changed the look of Texas cities. What had once been quiet towns were rapidly turning into major cities, with skyscrapers towering over the surrounding landscape. When it was completed in 1954, the Republic National Bank Building in Dallas was the tallest building west of the Mississippi. It was 36 stories tall. Before long, both Dallas and Houston had taller buildings.

Reading Check **Finding the Main Idea** What major industries contributed to the urbanization of Texas?

★ Transportation

The popularity of the automobile promoted urbanization in Texas. Between 1945 and 1950, the number of cars in Texas rose from some 1.7 million to 3 million. To handle these cars, Texans built thousands of miles of new roads. In 1940 Texas had only 19,000 miles of paved roads. By 1950, that had grown to 34,000 miles. These roads linked Texas cities to one another. Cities such as Dallas and Houston also built four-lane expressways to speed the movement of traffic. Such expressways became part of the interstate highway system that Congress authorized in 1956.

Rural Texans also benefited from the spending to build roads. In 1945 the state began paving rural roads to help farmers get their goods to market. The program proved popular, and in 1949 the state government agreed to spend $15 million a year to upgrade rural farm-to-market roads.

Texas air transportation also expanded. As early as 1927, airlines had begun offering passenger service to Texans. Because of its central location, Dallas became a stopover for many coast-to-coast flights. By the late 1950s, Love Field in Dallas was one of the nation's busiest airports. Texas also served as a gateway for people traveling to and from Latin America. Brownsville was a hub for many of these flights. In addition, an increasing number of Texas businesses bought private airplanes. Although not as common as it is today, air transportation during the 1950s was increasingly important.

Reading Check **Analyzing Information** How did improvements in transportation affect the development of Texas?

CONNECTING TO

Music

Buddy Holly and Rock 'n' Roll

One of the most popular early rock 'n' roll musicians was Lubbock native Buddy Holly. He taught himself how to play guitar and in 1957 formed a band, The Crickets, with two friends. Their second record, "Oh Boy!" sold nearly 1 million copies. Buddy Holly and The Crickets toured widely and appeared on popular TV shows. In 1959 Holly died in a plane crash. Artists including the Beatles and Bruce Springsteen have pointed to Holly as an important influence. **What influence did Holly have on music in the United States?**

Connecting To Literature

Katherine Anne Porter

Texas author Katherine Anne Porter is a nationally known fiction writer. Born in Indian Creek, Porter grew up in San Antonio, Kyle, and Victoria. Many of Porter's stories focus on family life and are set in Central Texas. She won the 1966 Pulitzer Prize for The Collected Stories of Katherine Anne Porter. *In this excerpt from a collection of essays, Porter describes how the area in which she grew up helped shape her writing.*

I write about Mexico because that is my familiar country. I was born near San Antonio, Texas. My father lived part of his youth in Mexico, and told me enchanting stories of his life there; therefore the land did not seem strange to me even at my first sight of it. . . . I have been accused by Americans of a taste for the exotic. . . . Maybe so, for New York is the most foreign place I know, and I like it very much. But in my childhood I knew . . . the German colonists in Texas and the Mexicans of San Antonio country, until it seemed to me that all my life I had lived among people who spoke broken, laboring tongues, [and] who put on with terrible difficulty. . . . I have never thought of these people as any other than American. . . . All the things I write of I have first known, and they are real to me.

Understanding What You Read

1. **Literature and History** How does Porter's writing reflect the history of cultural groups in Texas?
2. **Literature and You** How do different culture groups in your community maintain their culture while adapting to a larger Texas culture?

★ 1950s Culture

Economic prosperity after World War II allowed many Texas families to buy their own homes, often for the first time. By 1960 tens of thousands of Texans lived in suburbs. Most Texans living in the suburbs chose to **commute** to their jobs, meaning they lived in one area but drove elsewhere to work. As a result, the car was central to suburban life. Rather than going to town to shop, people in the suburbs drove to roadside shopping malls. Fewer than 10 such malls existed in the United States in 1946, but by the late 1950s, there were some 4,000.

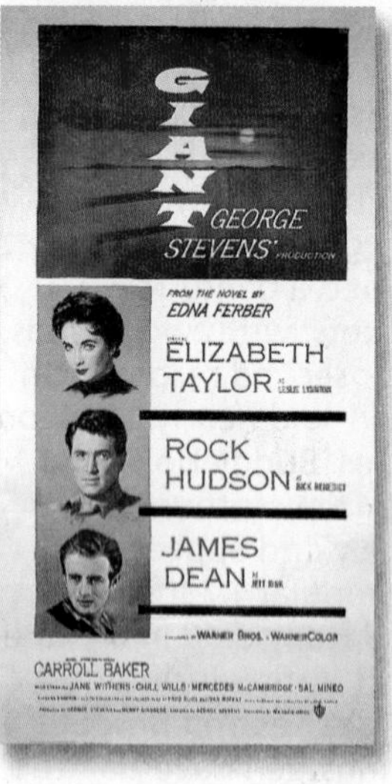

The movie Giant *was filmed near the West Texas community of Marfa.*

During the 1950s wages for many Texans in the suburbs and elsewhere increased even as their work hours declined. With more leisure time, many Texans went to art galleries, concerts, theater productions, and the movies. Texans such as **Robert Rauschenberg** became well-known artists. Movies about Texas and the American West were very popular. The hit movie *Giant*, starring James Dean, Rock Hudson, and Elizabeth Taylor, showed wildcatters and life on an enormous Texas ranch. Texas literature also grew in popularity as writers such as **Katherine Anne Porter** published works about Texas.

Texans also enjoyed a new form of communication and entertainment that arrived in the late 1940s—television. The first Texas television station was WBAP-TV in Fort Worth. In 1950 the Dallas–Fort Worth area had three stations, San Antonio had two, and Houston had one. The nation's first educational station, KUHT, began broadcasting in Houston in 1953. Although few Texans owned TV sets in 1950, television soon became a common feature in every Texas home. People began receiving much of their news and entertainment from television. Texan **Horton Foote**, who became an award-win ning screenwriter and playwright, got his start writing for television in 1948.

Television allowed Texans to see performances of a new kind of music that was popular with American teenagers. Rock 'n' roll had roots in African American blues music. In the 1950s white performers such as Elvis Presley brought this music to teenagers. The young people of America loved it. Texans such as **Buddy Holly**, Roy Orbison, and J. P. Richardson, known as the "Big Bopper," became popular artists.

Texans also entertained themselves by playing or watching sports. They formed teams for children and adults in baseball, football, and softball. Fans turned out to support high school and college teams across Texas. In addition, the first professional sports teams in Texas were organized in the postwar years. Texas women formed the first two organizations of female athletes in the United States, the Women's Professional Rodeo Association (WPRA) in 1948 and the Ladies Professional Golf Association (LPGA) in 1949. One founding member of the LPGA was **Babe Didrikson Zaharias**. A native of Port Arthur, Zaharias had won several medals in track and field at the 1932 Olympics before taking up golf. As a golf champion she became a national celebrity, and she was later named one of the top athletes of the twentieth century.

Reading Check **Summarizing** How did many Texans spend their leisure time in the 1950s?

CONNECTING TO

The Arts

Horton Foote

Born in Wharton, Texas, Horton Foote became one of the country's best-known writers of movies and plays. He began his career writing for television shows in 1948, but later turned to film. Foote was honored many times in his long career. In 1962 he won an Academy Award for his screenplay of *To Kill a Mockingbird,* based on a novel by Harper Lee. In 1995, he received a Pulitzer Prize for his play *The Young Man from Atlanta.* **What contributions did Horton Foote make to the arts?**

Section 3 Review

hmhsocialstudies.com ONLINE QUIZ

1. **Define and explain:**
   - commute
2. **Identify and explain:**
   - Robert Rauschenberg
   - Katherine Anne Porter
   - Buddy Holly
   - Horton Foote
   - Babe Didrikson Zaharias
3. **Summarizing** Copy the graphic organizer. Use it to list the major industries that contributed to urbanization and to describe the jobs Texans had in those industries.

4. **Finding the Main Idea**
   a. What economic factors led to the urbanization of Texas?
   b. How did transportation improvements affect the urbanization of Texas?
5. **Writing and Critical Thinking** myWriteSmart
   Analyzing Information Imagine that you are a young person growing up in the 1950s. Write a letter to a friend describing what you and your friends do for fun.
   Consider the following:
   - movies, television, and music
   - sports that you and your friends play

Connecting To Geography

Trade and Interstate Highways

The United States and Mexico have been trading partners for decades. The pie graphs below show the value of exports from the United States to Mexico in the years 2000 and 2012. Much of this trade is carried out over the highways of Texas.

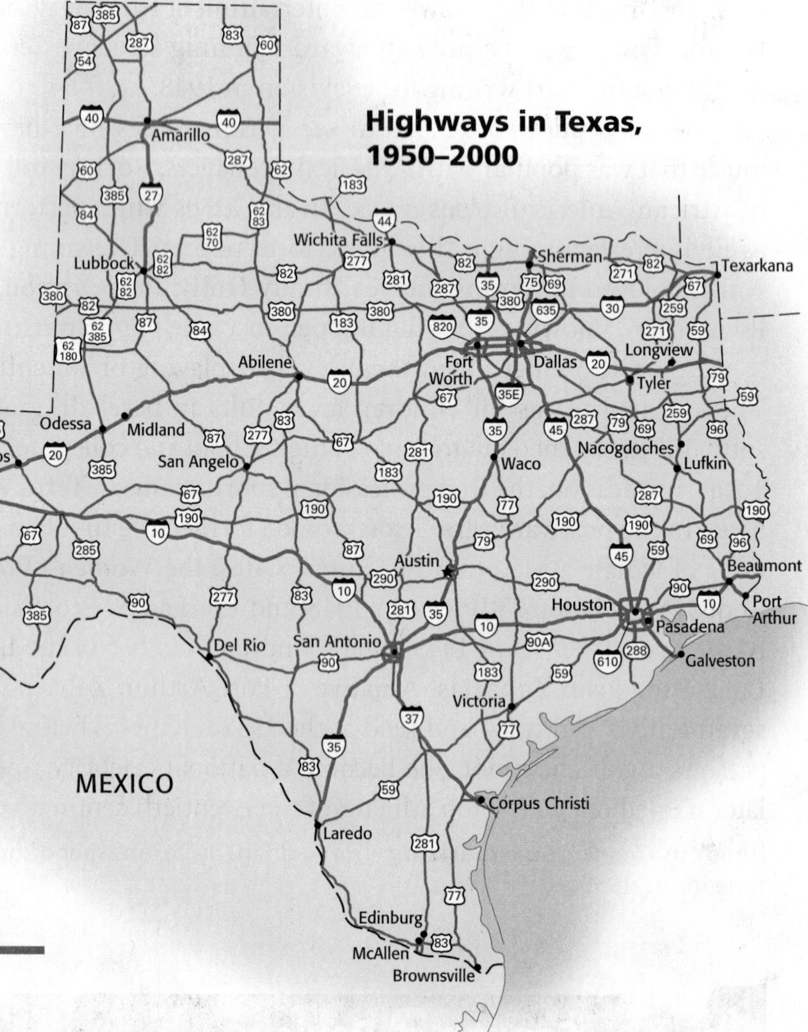

Geography Skills

Interpreting Thematic Maps and Charts

1. Which highways on the map are probably important trade routes between the United States and Mexico?
2. What Texas cities are located on interstate highways where they cross the border between the United States and Mexico?
3. What means of transportation carries the greatest value of exported goods into Mexico from the United States?

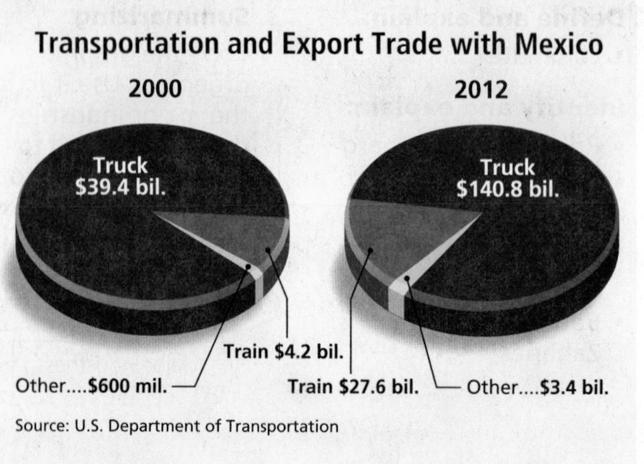

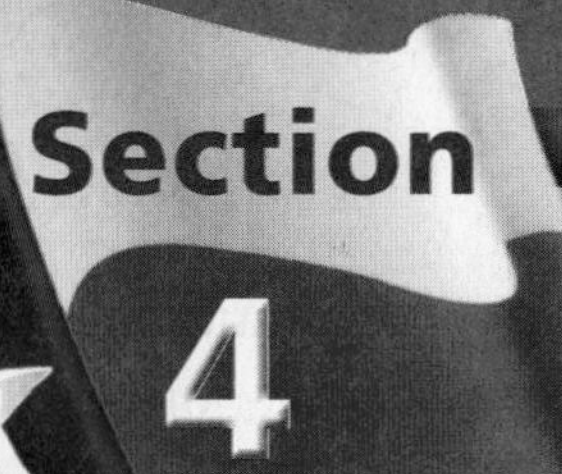

The Search for Equal Rights

Main Ideas

1. Through legal action and peaceful demonstrations, African Americans in Texas gained many civil rights.
2. Hispanic Texans also took steps to secure civil rights.
3. Women worked for equality in the 1950s.

Why It Matters Today

Many Texans struggled for decades to be treated equally under the law. Use current events sources to learn about continuing civil rights efforts in the United States today.

Key Terms and People

- **Lulu Belle Madison White**
- **desegregate**
- **nonviolent resistance**
- **James L. Farmer Jr.**
- **Hector P. García**
- **American GI Forum**
- **Heman Sweatt**
- **Benjy Brooks**

TEKS: 1B, 7D, 7E, 11C, 12A, 16A, 21B, 22D

myNotebook

Use the annotation tools in your eBook to take notes on the struggle for civil rights in Texas.

The Story Continues

Dorothy Robinson was angry. When she rode the train from California to Texas in 1944, she had not been allowed in the dining car because she was African American. She later recalled, "White prisoners-of-war (Germans, I suppose) were marched under guard through my coach to enjoy a meal in the dining car to which I had been denied admittance."

★ African-American Rights

The discrimination that Dorothy Robinson experienced on her train ride was all too familiar to African Americans of her era. Even the thousands of African Americans who fought for their country during World War II were not free from its effects. African-American soldiers—who made up more than 10 percent of all troops from Texas—could serve only in segregated units.

As you have read, World War II opened some economic doors to African Americans. Many black Texans moved to cities to work at new jobs. However, such moves sometimes met resistance—and sometimes violence—as seen in Beaumont in 1943. Thousands of people had moved to the city to work in its shipyards. Competition for work and for housing led to tensions between black and white workers. When a white woman claimed to have been attacked by a black man, it sparked a massive riot involving more than 2,000 people. Two people lost their lives, and several black-owned businesses were burned.

Interpreting Visuals

Nonviolent resistance. *During the 1950s Texans took action to end segregation by protesting and boycotting businesses that banned African Americans.* ***How are the people in the photo trying to end segregation?***

Thankfully, instances of violence like the Beaumont riots were rare in Texas. However, African Americans still had to deal with Jim Crow laws that restricted their right to vote and denied them opportunities for education and jobs. In addition, Texas law supported the segregation of public facilities. African Americans had to use different bathrooms and public parks—in some areas they even had to use separate water fountains. These public facilities were rarely equal.

Organizations like the National Association for the Advancement of Colored People (NAACP) tried to stop such discrimination. In the 1930s and 1940s, for example, the NAACP campaigned to eliminate the white primary in Texas. With support from the NAACP, Lonnie Smith, a black dentist from Houston, filed a lawsuit seeking the right to vote in the Democratic primary. In the 1944 case *Smith* v. *Allwright,* the U.S. Supreme Court sided with Smith. The decision struck down the white primary system in Texas and the rest of the country.

Black Texans responded enthusiastically to the defeat of the white primary. African-American organizations like the Democratic Progressive Voters League organized registration drives among black Texans. As a result, the number of African Americans registered to vote in Texas rose from 30,000 in 1940 to 100,000 in 1947.

One of the major figures in the fight to overturn the white primary system was **Lulu Belle Madison White**. She served as head of the Houston chapter of the NAACP from 1939 to 1949, when she became the organization's state director. Under her leadership, the Houston chapter became the largest in the South. White urged other members to continue the struggle for civil rights.

TEXAS VOICES

"If we can work together just a little harder—all our aims and objectives will be reached. . . . The enemies of democracy are concentrating their efforts to destroy our most effective Civil Rights—the right to vote and to be candidates for office—the right to jobs at equal pay—and the equal right to education. Only a united effort can meet this attack."

—Lulu Belle Madison White, quoted in *Black Texas Women: A Sourcebook*

African Americans did win some federal rights in the 1940s. In 1948, for example, President Truman ordered the military to **desegregate**, or stop the practice of separating people by race. That same year, Truman also banned racial discrimination in hiring federal employees.

Despite these gains, African Americans in the United States were still denied some basic civil rights. To call attention to their lack of rights, people in Texas—as in other parts of the country—held demonstrations and marches. They were following a policy of **nonviolent resistance**, or the use of peaceful means to achieve a goal. Much of the inspiration for this nonviolent resistance came from a young pastor in Alabama named Martin Luther King Jr. King inspired thousands of Texans of all backgrounds to work for equality for all people.

Texans also helped lead the struggle to end discrimination. Marshall native **James L. Farmer Jr.** was a cofounder of the Congress of Racial Equality (CORE) in Chicago in 1942. Like King, Farmer and other members of CORE called for nonviolent resistance to Jim Crow laws. CORE initially did most of its work in northern states. Later, however, CORE members worked in the South to train civil rights protesters.

Reading Check **Summarizing** How did civil rights leaders try to end discrimination?

★ The American GI Forum

Mexican American veterans in Texas also faced discrimination despite their service in the war. To fight that discrimination **Hector P. García** of Corpus Christi—a highly decorated U.S. Army surgeon who had been denied the right to work in Texas hospitals because he was Mexican American—founded the **American GI Forum** in 1948. Its purpose was to protect the rights of Mexican Americans. The GI Forum focused mostly on helping veterans with education and health care.

The American GI Forum received national attention in 1949. That year the family of Felix Longoria, who had been killed in the Philippines during the war, tried to hold a memorial service for him. When a funeral home in Three Rivers refused to permit the family use the whites-only chapel, they contacted García. He used the GI Forum to inform political leaders about the developing controversy.

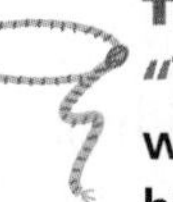

TEXAS VOICES

"The denial was a direct contradiction of those same principles for which this American soldier made the supreme sacrifice in giving his life for his country, and for the same people who deny him the last funeral rites deserving of any American hero regardless of his origin."

—Hector P. García, quoted in American Forces Information Services Web site

Senator Lyndon B. Johnson of Texas arranged for Longoria's remains to be buried with honors in Arlington National Cemetery.

The Longoria affair motivated many Mexican Americans to take action. The GI Forum, along with LULAC, filed desegregation lawsuits. The GI Forum, represented by Laredo-born lawyer Gus Garcia, was a key player in the 1954 Supreme Court case *Hernandez* v. *Texas*, in which the Court declared that the Fourteenth Amendment protected the rights of all minority groups. In a series of court cases, the Forum worked to end segregation of Mexican American children in Texas schools. This goal was legally achieved in 1957. However, local officials in some places used a variety of measures to underfund and isolate schools for "Mexicans." In 1958 the GI Forum became a national organization and continued its efforts nationwide.

Reading Check **Finding the Main Idea** How did Hector P. Garcia, Gus Garcia, and the American GI Forum assist Mexican Americans in Texas?

BIOGRAPHY

Hector P. García

(1914–1996) Born in Mexico, Hector P. García and his family moved to Texas in 1918. García attended the University of Texas Medical School, receiving his degree in 1940. Because Texas hospitals denied him the opportunity to practice medicine, he moved to Nebraska. After the Pearl Harbor attack, he joined the U.S. Army. In addition to his civil rights work, García served as an adviser to several U.S. presidents and received many awards for public service. In 1984 President Ronald Reagan awarded him the Medal of Freedom. García died in Corpus Christi in 1996.

How did García serve his country?

Despite an official end to segregation in schools, many Texans fought against integration. Protesters in 1956 blocked African-American students from entering Texarkana College.

★ Desegregating Public Schools

These court victories for Mexican Americans did not change the situation of African Americans, who had to wage their own battle against Jim Crow laws. Under the policy of "separate but equal" facilities, African Americans were still forced to attend schools separate from white students. Although the schools were separate, they were not equal. Schools for minority students were typically of much poorer quality.

In 1946 **Heman Sweatt** applied to the University of Texas School of Law. The school denied his application but created a separate law school for African Americans. With the backing of NAACP leaders, including Lulu Belle Madison White, Sweatt filed a lawsuit against the university. He argued that he would receive a better education at the regular law school. In *Sweatt* v. *Painter,* the U.S. Supreme Court ruled that segregated facilities in professional schools violated the Constitution.

The *Sweatt* decision led the way for *Brown* v. *Board of Education,* which eventually ended segregation in public schools. In its 1954 decision, the U.S. Supreme Court ruled that separate educational facilities are by definition unequal. This was a major victory for minority groups. However, the decision shocked and angered many white Texans. In 1956 a court ordered the Mansfield school district south of Fort Worth to desegregate. In response, a mob formed around the school. Governor Allan Shivers sent Texas Rangers to stop the court order from going into effect, and the federal government took no action to enforce it. Encouraged by their success, the Texas legislature passed laws that kept most Texas schools segregated until the 1960s.

Reading Check Sequencing Describe in order the events leading to the desegregation of Texas public schools.

New Opportunities for Women

Texas women also fought for recognition of their civil rights in the 1950s. Many women had gone to work during World War II, and some wanted to continue working when the war ended. They began to express their dissatisfaction at the limited opportunities available to them. Leaders such as Oveta Culp Hobby believed that women deserved to be treated equally. Hobby was the first woman to win the U.S. Army's Distinguished Service Medal. She also served in President Eisenhower's cabinet as secretary of health, education, and welfare.

In the 1950s women began attending Texas colleges and universities in greater numbers. Many pursued professional careers. In 1956 Hattie Briscoe became the first black woman to graduate from St. Mary's School of Law in San Antonio. She graduated at the top of her class, but no law firms would hire a black woman. Briscoe opened her own firm. **Benjy Brooks** from Lewisville earned a degree from the University of Texas Medical Branch in Galveston. In 1960 she became the first female pediatric surgeon in Texas.

Working women demanded pay equal to what men earned in similar jobs. Gladys Humphrey recalled working in a meatpacking plant. "Sometimes our jobs were just as hard and complicated as the men but women never made quite the same wage." Women did not gain equal pay, but they laid the foundation for later achievements. In 1957 a group of women led by Dallas attorney Hermine Tobolowsky proposed that the state constitution be amended to guarantee the equal rights of all Texans, regardless of sex. Over the next 15 years, Tobolowsky appeared before the state legislature more than 20 times to argue for the amendment. Finally in 1972, voters approved the Texas Equal Rights Amendment.

Reading Check **Finding the Main Idea** How did women in Texas seek to gain equal rights during the 1950s?

BIOGRAPHY

Lulu Belle Madison White (1907–1957)

A native of Elmo, Lulu Madison moved to Houston and married business owner Julius White. She also joined the Houston chapter of the NAACP. An active opponent of white primaries, White worked to get other African American women involved in the campaign to end them. After several years as a teacher, White became the Houston NAACP's Youth Director. In 1939 she became the first female president of the chapter, and in 1949 became the state director of the NAACP. **For what achievements is Lulu Belle Madison White known?**

Section 4 Review

hmhsocialstudies.com
ONLINE QUIZ

1. **Define and explain:**
   - desegregate
   - nonviolent resistance

2. **Identify and explain** the significance of:
   - Lulu Belle Madison White
   - James Farmer
   - Hector P. García
   - American GI Forum
   - Heman Sweatt
   - Benjy Brooks

3. **Analyzing Information**
   Copy the table below. Use it to trace the key developments of the civil rights movement in the 1940s and 1950s.

Event	Significance

4. **Finding the Main Idea**
   a. What organizations struggled for civil rights, and what were their achievements?
   b. How did Texas women pursue equal rights during the 1950s?

5. **Writing and Critical Thinking** myWriteSmart
   Analyzing Information Write a newspaper story that explains the effect of the *Brown* v. *Board of Education* decision in Texas.
   Consider the following:
   - the Supreme Court's ruling
   - the crisis in Mansfield

The Chapter at a Glance

Examine the following visual summary of the chapter. Then use the visual to create a time line that shows some of the changes occurring in Texas in the 1940s and 1950s.

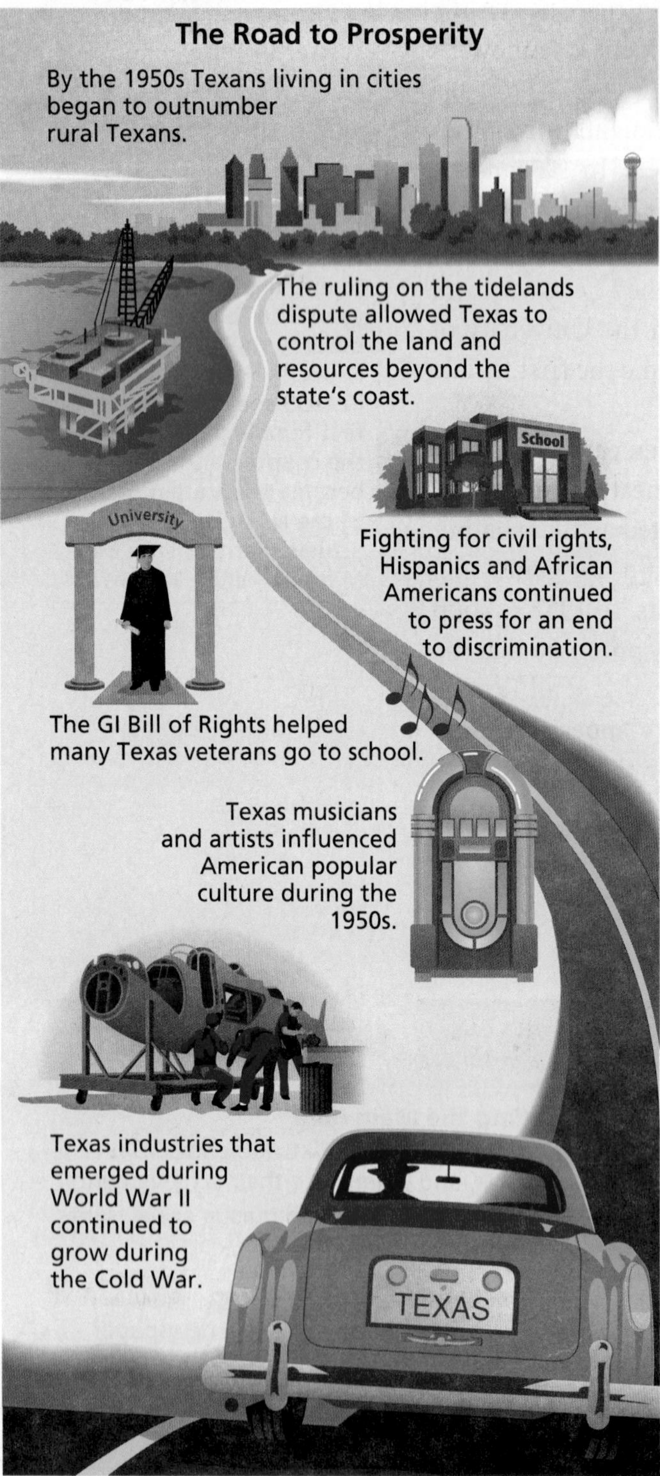

Identifying People and ideas

Write a sentence to explain the role or significance of each of the following terms or people.

1. Dorie Miller
2. Audie Murphy
3. Chester W. Nimitz
4. Oveta Culp Hobby
5. Cold War
6. Lulu Belle Madison White
7. James L. Farmer Jr.
8. Hector P. García
9. Benjy Brooks

Understanding Main Ideas

Section 1

1. How did World War II affect the lives of Texans?

Section 2

2. What effect did the Korean War have in Texas?
3. How might Texas have changed had the federal government won control of the tidelands?

Section 3

4. How did the distribution of the Texas population change in the 1940s and 1950s, and how did that change affect life in Texas?
5. What major industries attracted Texans to urban areas in the 1940s and 1950s, and what new jobs did people find there?

Section 4

6. How were civil rights efforts among African Americans, Mexican Americans, and women similar? How were they different?

You Be the Historian

Reviewing Themes

1. **Economics** How did World War II affect local and state economies in Texas?
2. **Constitutional Heritage** How did civil rights leaders in Texas end the white primary?
3. **Science, Technology & Society** What factors led to urbanization in the 1940s and 1950s?

Thinking Critically

1. **Analyzing Information** What defined the Conservatism and Civil Rights era in Texas?
2. **Summarizing** What roles did Oveta Culp Hobby and Benjy Brooks play in the push for equality?
3. **Finding the Main Idea** What was life in Texas like in the Great Depression and World War II?

Texas Test Practice

Interpreting Graphs

Study the graph below. The graph shows changes in the Texas rural and urban populations from 1920 to 1970. Use the graph to answer the questions below.

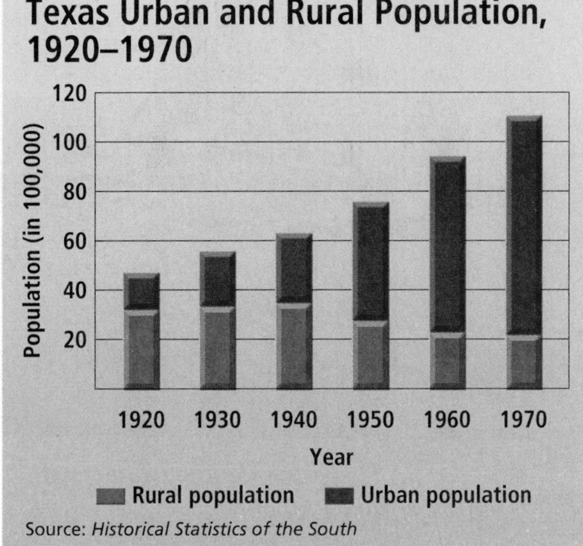

1. Between what years did the rural portion of the total Texas population decrease?
   - **A** 1940–70
   - **B** 1930–40
   - **C** 1920–40
   - **D** It never decreased.

2. Interpret the information from the graph to draw a conclusion about the change in population distribution that occurred in Texas between 1920 and 1970.

Analyzing Primary Sources

Elmer Kelton was the son of a foreman who worked on a ranch near Crane, Texas. Kelton remembered that when ranch hands learned of the attack on Pearl Harbor, many of them joined the military. Read his description of the effect of the war on ranching in Texas. Then answer the questions.

"The ranching industry changed drastically during and after the war. The severe manpower shortage led to technological innovations that forever reduced the labor needs on ranches as well as farms. Another was the ranches' much heavier dependence upon family men than on the bachelor cowboys of an earlier era. Family men as a group were less likely to drift over the hill to see what was on the other side."

3. What was the main effect of World War II on ranching, according to Kelton?
   - **F** the loss of land to military training centers
   - **G** the decline of family-owned ranches
   - **H** a manpower shortage that led to technological developments
   - **J** a reduced demand for beef

4. Oral histories can reveal information about the ways that social change affects the lives of individuals. How did World War II change the lives of ranching families?

Interdisciplinary Connection to the Arts

The Cold War was a time of strong opinions and feelings. Many works of art created during this time reflect people's opinions about such subjects as communism. Find examples of art created during the 1950s and 1960s. Include written art, such as novels, stories, and poems; visual art, such as paintings, posters, and photographs; and audio art, such as songs or speeches. Analyze any signs of bias you see expressed in the works you have selected. Then write a paragraph about what this bias can tell us about American life in the period.

Internet Activity

Access the Internet to find online databases with which to analyze the political, economic, and social impact of World War II and the Cold War on Texas. Then use computer software to create databases and graphs that show the effects of World War II and the Cold War during the decades covered in the chapter. Write a short paragraph that summarizes the statistical information you included in your graph. Check your paragraph for standard spelling, punctuation, sentence structure, and grammar.

CHAPTER 28

Texas in Transition

(1960–1980)

Texas Essential Knowledge and Skills (TEKS) 1B, 7B, 7D, 7F, 8B, 9A, 9C, 11A, 11C, 12A, 12B, 12C, 13A, 13C, 16A, 17B, 17C, 18A, 18B, 19A, 19B, 20A, 20B, 20C, 20E, 21A, 21B, 21C, 21E, 22A, 22B, 22C, 22D

Astronauts on the Moon kept in contact with Mission Control in Houston.

TEXAS

1961 Henry B. González is elected to the U.S. House of Representatives, and John Tower is elected to the U.S. Senate.

1963 Lyndon B. Johnson becomes president of the United States after President John F. Kennedy is assassinated.

1967 Texas singer Janis Joplin's career takes off after a performance at the Monterey International Pop Festival.

1960 — 1963 — 1966

U.S. and WORLD

1962 A crisis erupts between the United States and the Soviet Union over Soviet missiles in Cuba.

1965 Civil rights leader Martin Luther King Jr. and about 800 other protesters are arrested in Selma, Alabama.

1966 Leaders of the women's movement in the United States found the National Organization for Women.

If you were there . . .
How would you promote equal rights?

Build on What You Know

Life changed for many Texans in the post–World War II years. Cities in Texas grew rapidly, and new business opportunities developed. However, some members of the population, particularly those belonging to minority groups, benefited less from these changes.

La Raza Unida Party helped Hispanic activists run for political office in Texas.

Representative Barbara Jordan gained national attention for her powerful speaking and her devotion to fighting for equal rights for all Americans.

1969 The National Aeronautics and Space Administration sends the *Apollo 11* mission to the Moon.

1970 Members of the Chicano movement and the Mexican American Youth Organization form La Raza Unida Party.

1972 Barbara Jordan is elected to the U.S. House of Representatives.

1974 *Austin City Limits* goes on the air with Willie Nelson as its first guest musician.

1980 The Texas population reaches 14 million.

1969 — 1972 — 1975 — 1978

1970 Four Kent State University students are killed by the Ohio National Guard during a Vietnam War protest.

1973 The Organization of Petroleum Exporting Countries (OPEC) cuts off oil supplies to the United States, leading to a jump in oil prices.

1975 The Vietnam War comes to an end.

1980 Eleven European countries form the first commercial firm to market the launching of satellites.

You Be the Historian *my*Notebook

What's Your Opinion? Do you **agree** or **disagree** with the following statements? Support your point of view in your notebook.

- **Citizenship** Citizens have a responsibility to defend everyone's rights.
- **Science, Technology & Society** New technological developments can be beneficial to a state's economy.
- **Geography** Geographic factors have substantial effects on the development of a society.

Section 1

A Texas President

Main Ideas

1. Lyndon B. Johnson served in many elected positions before he became president of the United States.
2. The Great Society included programs to improve health care, education, and other aspects of American life.
3. The Vietnam War had significant effects in Texas.

Key Terms and People

- **Lyndon B. Johnson**
- **Great Society**
- **Head Start**
- **Economic Opportunity Act**
- **Tonkin Gulf Resolution**

Why It Matters Today

During the 1960s U.S. leaders expanded the use of government resources to try to help Americans. Use current events sources to find information about U.S. government social programs today.

TEKS: 7F, 11A, 17C, 18A, 18B, 21B, 21E, 22D

myNotebook

Use the annotation tools in your eBook to take notes on the events and issues of the Lyndon Johnson presidency.

The Story Continues

In November, 1963, President John F. Kennedy traveled to Texas with his vice president, Texan Lyndon Johnson. Kennedy had been elected in 1960, when at 43 he was the youngest person ever elected president of the United States. He was in Texas in part to raise money for his re-election campaign. Kennedy arrived in Dallas on November 22. As his motorcade passed through downtown Dallas on its way to the airport, cheering crowds lined the streets.

VIDEO
LBJ's Management Style

hmhsocialstudies.com

A Texan in the White House

President Kennedy believed that the United States stood "on the edge of a New Frontier." His administration planned to cut taxes, reduce unemployment, protect African Americans' civil rights, and increase international trade. On November 22, 1963, Kennedy was in Dallas with Texas governor John Connally and Vice President **Lyndon B. Johnson.** As the presidential motorcade passed through downtown Dallas, shots rang out. The president and Governor Connally were hit. Although the governor survived, Kennedy died a short time later at a Dallas hospital. At 1:38 p.m. CST on the day of the assassination, Johnson was sworn in as the new president. He is the only U.S. president ever to take the oath of office in Texas.

Johnson—who later became known as LBJ—was born near Stonewall, Texas, in 1908 and grew up in nearby Johnson City. He attended Southwest Texas State Teachers College in San Marcos. After earning a teacher's certificate, Johnson taught school and served as a principal. Ambitious and hardworking, Johnson became involved in politics during his college and teaching years. In 1935 he became director of the Texas division of the National Youth Administration. Johnson was a strong supporter of the New Deal and President Franklin Roosevelt.

Johnson was elected to the U.S. House of Representatives in 1937 and to the U.S. Senate in 1948. He became one of the most skilled politicians in the national government. As senator, he was expert at getting bills that he supported passed. Abe Fortas, a close friend and former U.S. Supreme Court justice, once described Johnson's personality

TEXAS VOICES

"He was a very emotional man and a very sensitive man, a man of enormous power, power that was communicated to others. There was a physical element in his communication of power. There was also an element of his own dedication and his own intense commitment to achieve a chosen objective. Johnson was fervently result-oriented."

—Justice Abe Fortas, quoted in *The Johnson Presidency*, by Kenneth W. Thompson

As a Democrat, Johnson became majority leader in the Senate in 1955. This leadership position is held by a member of the party that has the majority of seats. In this powerful position, Johnson influenced policy in a number of areas, including civil rights and space exploration. These issues would become central to his presidential administration.

Reading Check **Finding the Main Idea** What characteristics did Lyndon B. Johnson have that led to his becoming a political success?

BIOGRAPHY

Lyndon B. Johnson (1908–1973) Lyndon Baines Johnson was born on a farm in the Texas Hill Country. His interest in politics began at an early age—his father had served in the Texas legislature. Johnson's experiences teaching poor Mexican and Mexican American students in Cotulla helped spur his belief in government programs to help the needy. As president, he worked to improve the lives of poor Americans. After retiring from public office in 1969, Johnson returned home to his ranch near Johnson City. He died in 1973 and was buried in his beloved Hill Country. **What early experience contributed to Johnson's belief in government programs to help Americans?**

★ The Great Society

When Lyndon Johnson became president, he took up and expanded many of John F. Kennedy's plans. President Johnson believed that the United States should provide equal rights, education, jobs, and decent housing for all its citizens. These issues were the basis for Johnson's re-election campaign in 1964, and he won the election by a landslide.

Using this popular support, Johnson launched a program that he called the **Great Society**. This program included a number of sweeping reforms designed to improve the lives of Americans. His first goal was to eliminate poverty and racial injustice. In 1964 and 1965 the Johnson administration introduced bill after bill to Congress to support this goal. By the time Johnson left office in 1969, more than 200 of his proposed bills had been signed into law. For example, as part of the Great Society Johnson and Congress created two programs, Medicare and Medicaid, designed to improve health care for older and disabled Americans.

Interpreting Visuals

Head Start. *The Head Start program provides early childhood education to low-income students. Lady Bird Johnson visited this Head Start class in 1968.* ***Why was education so important to Lyndon Johnson?***

As a former teacher, Johnson was deeply concerned with improving education in America. He had spent much of his career teaching poor children in rural Texas. During that time he had become convinced that education was necessary for overcoming poverty. Early in his second term Johnson signed the Elementary and Secondary Education Act (ESEA), which provided funding for public schools. To signify the importance of education in his own life, Johnson signed the bill into law at his old elementary school in Johnson City with his first grade teacher sitting by his side.

Another part of Johnson's focus on education was the creation of the **Head Start** program. This program was designed to provide early childhood eduction and nutrition information to low-income students and their families. Created in 1965, Head Start is still active today. By 2005 more than 22 million students had taken part in Head Start programs.

The **Economic Opportunity Act** launched another Great Society program. Part of this act provided funds for job training and created community action programs. The act also provided funds for the Job Corps, which trained young people for employment. In addition, Congress passed a new immigration act that allowed more people from Latin America and Asia to come to the United States. Partly as a result of this act, Hispanic and Asian immigration increased. This immigration contributed significantly to the growth of Texas in the 1960s and 1970s.

Although many Americans supported Johnson's Great Society programs, some people argued that the federal government was spending too much on social programs. Others thought that these acts gave the federal government too much power over the states.

Reading Check **Supporting a Point of View** Do you believe that the Great Society's programs benefited Texas and the United States? Explain your answer.

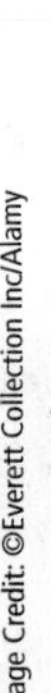

★ The Vietnam War

At the same time as President Johnson was working for change in the United States, conflict was brewing in Southeast Asia. The government of South Vietnam was fighting communist forces backed by North Vietnam. Previously, presidents Eisenhower and Kennedy had sent military advisers to South Vietnam to help train its military forces.

Then in 1964 a confrontation occurred involving U.S. naval forces in the Gulf of Tonkin, off the coast of North Vietnam. Johnson saw this confrontation as an act of war by North Vietnam. Upon his request, Congress passed the **Tonkin Gulf Resolution**, which gave the president the authority to order troops into combat. Soldiers and weapons were sent to Vietnam by the thousands. Some 150,000 Texans served in Vietnam during the war. As industrial production increased to meet the war needs, the booming defense industry boosted the Texas economy.

Casualties in Vietnam mounted quickly, and so did opposition to the war. Some Americans criticized President Johnson's handling of the war. Others demanded that he bring U.S. troops home. On college campuses across the country, students demonstrated against the war. Protesters followed Johnson everywhere, including in his home state. Worried about the division in the country over the war and about his own health, Johnson announced that he would not run for re-election.

Johnson had little success in ending the war, which continued into the 1970s. In all, 58,000 Americans died in the war, more than 3,400 of them Texans. In Vietnam and other Southeast Asian countries, millions were killed. Thousands more became refugees. Many of these refugees settled in Texas, forming large Vietnamese American communities in Houston and other cities.

Reading Check **Identifying Cause and Effect** How did war in Vietnam affect the economy and society in Texas?

About 500,000 U.S. soldiers, including some 150,000 Texans, fought in the Vietnam War.

★ Section 1 Review

hmhsocialstudies.com ONLINE QUIZ

1. Define and explain:
- Great Society

2. Identify and explain the significance of the following in Texas history:
- Lyndon B. Johnson
- Head Start
- Economic Opportunity Act
- Tonkin Gulf Resolution

3. Analyzing Information
Copy the graphic organizer below. Use it to show what leadership qualities President Johnson had and what goals they helped him achieve.

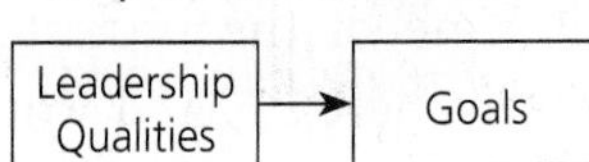

4. Finding the Main Idea
a. Explain the Great Society and its programs.
b. What social, political, and economic effects did the Vietnam War have on Texas?

5. Writing and Critical Thinking myWriteSmart
Supporting a Point of View Imagine that you are a reporter living in Texas during the 1960s. Write an editorial describing how successful you think Johnson's leadership is.
Consider the following:
- domestic policy
- foreign policy

Section 2

The Civil Rights Movement

Main Ideas

1. The civil rights movement arose in the 1960s to secure equal rights for African Americans.
2. Through the efforts of politicians and activists, Hispanic Americans won many civil rights.
3. Texan women also worked to gain equal rights.

Key Terms and People

- **sit-ins**
- **Barbara Jordan**
- **Henry B. González**
- **Raymond L. Telles**
- **Chicano movement**
- **La Raza Unida Party**

Why It Matters Today

During the 1960s, African Americans, Mexican Americans, and women became increasingly involved in politics. Use current events sources to find information about the continuing efforts of people and groups to gain equal rights today.

TEKS: 1B, 7D, 16A, 17B, 18A, 18B, 21B, 21C, 21D, 22D

myNotebook

Use the annotation tools in your eBook to take notes on the civil rights movement of the 1960s.

The Story Continues

Christia Adair of Houston was tired of segregation. One day while shopping in a department store she asked a clerk if she could try on an item in the fitting room. The clerk tried to steer her toward an alteration room because African Americans were not allowed in the store's fitting rooms. Adair insisted that she only wanted to try the item on and that it did not need alterations. The clerk called the manager who said, "Show the customer to the fitting room."

Police challenge participants in a Houston sit-in.

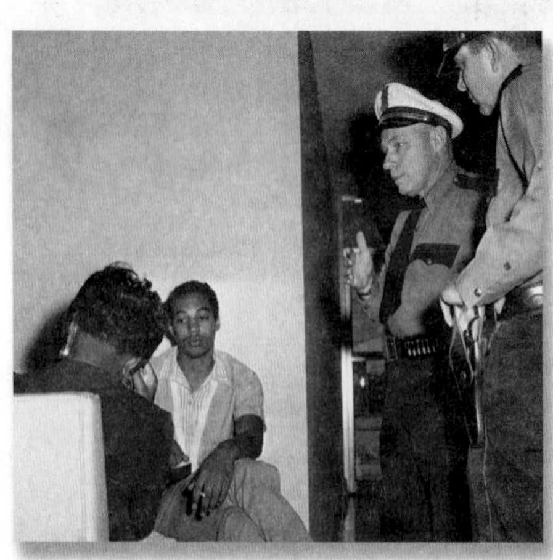

Nonviolent Protest

The movement for civil rights that had begun after World War II picked up speed during the 1960s. African Americans across the nation began to practice nonviolent resistance to end discrimination and segregation. Protesters staged boycotts and **sit-ins**—protests that involve sitting down in a public facility and refusing to leave—to bring an end to segregation.

A number of Texas students held sit-ins at lunch counters and other dining facilities. A group in Kingsville forced the integration of a local drive-in restaurant. One of the protesters recalled, "We started just parking our cars up in there . . . and wouldn't move. . . . [Finally] they started serving us." Despite the peaceful nature of these protest, some participants were threatened with arrest or even violence.

Texans also worked to integrate other facilities. In 1962 a group of Austin mothers protested an ice rink that would not allow African Americans to skate. Members of the Mothers Action Council and their children marched every day for a year until the skating rink owners changed their policy. Press coverage of civil rights protests often helped the movement.

Texan James Farmer was a national leader of the civil rights movement. Through his organization, the Congress of Racial Equality (CORE), Farmer led civil rights protests. He also organized activists on bus rides—called Freedom Rides—through the South. Black and white activists rode together on buses to segregated bus stations in the South. White riders planned to use facilities set aside for African Americans in bus stations. Black riders would use white-only facilities. In many places, the riders were met with hostility and threats.

The Freedom Rides were concentrated mostly in the Southeastern United States. However, a few rides took place in Texas as well. In August 1961 a group of Freedom Riders sat down to dinner together in the segregated bus station in Fort Worth. A month later, another group rode to a bus station in Houston. When 11 black and white riders tried to sit together to eat, however, they were arrested and fined.

When Martin Luther King Jr. led peaceful demonstrations throughout the South, he drew national attention to the civil rights movement. In 1963 King and thousands of Americans participated in a March on Washington in support of civil rights. Some 900 Texans of all races participated in a march on the state Capitol. Like those in the national march, these protesters pushed for an end to discrimination and segregation.

Reading Check **Drawing Inferences and Conclusions** How did the right to free speech, press, and assembly affect the civil rights movement?

BIOGRAPHY

James Farmer

(1920–1999) James Farmer of Marshall attended Wiley College and Howard University. After helping to found CORE in 1942, Farmer dedicated his life to the civil rights movement. He served as national director of CORE from 1961 to 1966. After leaving CORE, Farmer directed an adult literacy project and worked in the Department of Health, Education, and Welfare. Farmer also published the books *Lay Bare the Heart* and *Freedom—When?* **How did Farmer fulfill his civic responsibilities?**

★ President Johnson and Civil Rights

As a Senator, Johnson had worked to ensure that all residents of his district had the same rights, regardless of race. As president, he wanted to to the same for the whole country. In his first address to Congress, President Johnson urged passage of a civil rights law. He believed that the government needed to take action to ensure the rights of all Americans.

TEXAS VOICES

"We have talked long enough in this country about equal rights. We have talked for 100 years or more. It is time now to write the next chapter—and to write it in the books of law. I urge you . . . to enact a civil rights law so that we can move forward to eliminate from this Nation every trace of discrimination and oppression that is based upon race or color."

—President Lyndon B. Johnson, Address to Joint Session of the House and Senate, November 27, 1963

President Lyndon B. Johnson signed the Civil Rights Act of 1964 into law in front of legislators and other officials.

Congress soon passed the Civil Rights Act of 1964, which banned segregation in public places. It also outlawed discrimination in the workplace on the basis of race, sex, religion, or national origin. One year later Congress passed the Voting Rights Act of 1965, which gave the federal government the power to protect the voting rights of all citizens. This act outlawed literacy tests as a requirement for voting. It also gave the government the power to oversee election processes in parts of the South that had traditionally kept African Americans from voting.

With the successes of the civil rights movement, African Americans gained more positions in the government. In Texas, African Americans began to win state offices for the first time since Reconstruction. In 1966 **Barbara Jordan** of Houston was elected as a state senator. Jordan was elected to the U.S. House of Representatives in 1972, becoming the first African American to represent Texas in the U.S. Congress.

Reading Check **Finding the Main Idea** What effects did the Civil Rights Act of 1964 and the Voting Rights Act of 1965 have on society?

★ Hispanic Rights

During the 1960s Hispanic Americans also pushed for civil rights through protests, marches, and political organizations. The Political Association of Spanish-Speaking Organizations, the American GI Forum, and the League of United Latin American Citizens (LULAC) led the movement for equal rights for Hispanic Americans. With leadership from Hector P. García and Albert Peña Jr., these groups hoped to spur Hispanic voters to become more active and to make their concerns known to lawmakers.

In 1956 Democrat **Henry B. González** had become the first Mexican American elected to the Texas Senate in the 1900s. As a state senator he was a fierce opponent of segregation. In 1957 González and a fellow senator spoke for 36 straight hours to block passage of several bills. These bills would have kept Texas schools segregated, despite the Supreme Court's ruling in the case *Brown* v. *Board of Education*. Because of their efforts, nearly all of the bills were killed. In 1961 González was elected to the U.S. House of Representatives, where he served for 37 years. He was the first Mexican American to represent Texas in the U.S. Congress.

Mexican Americans were also elected to city, county, and state offices in Texas. In 1957 **Raymond L. Telles** was elected mayor of El Paso—the first major American city to elect a Hispanic mayor. Telles later held several national positions, including the ambassadorship to Costa Rica. He also served as an adviser to President John Kennedy.

Because of new laws and the work of civil rights organizations during the 1960s, large numbers of Hispanic Americans registered to vote. Despite many gains, Hispanic Americans still faced discrimination by local officials. Schools that served the Mexican American population were often poor and continued to be segregated in reality, if not by law.

Reading Check **Analyzing Information** Who were the early leaders of the Hispanic rights movement, and what successes did they have?

BIOGRAPHY

Henry B. González

(1916–2000) Henry B. González was a political role model for many Mexican Americans. Born in San Antonio to Mexican immigrants, he attended St. Mary's University Law School, where he earned a law degree. His first political office was as a member of the San Antonio City Council. His 1958 run for the Democratic Party's nomination for governor of Texas encouraged Mexican Americans to become more involved in Texas politics. In 1994 González received the Profile in Courage award from the John F. Kennedy Library. **How did Henry B. González contribute to Texas history?**

★ The Chicano Movement

Many Hispanic Americans were also concerned about their economic situation. Poverty was a persistent problem, particularly among farm laborers known as *campesinos*. In June 1966, farm laborers in Texas went on strike to demand a minimum wage. They marched 290 miles, from the Rio Grande valley to Austin. Their call for change was part of a growing national effort known as the **Chicano movement**, or *el movimiento*. The movement took inspiration from César Chávez, a Mexican American who had organized migrant farm workers in California. The success of the Chicano movement increased cultural pride in Mexican American communities and established Mexican Americans as a political force.

Students also became active in the Chicano movement. For example, Mexican American students in Crystal City walked out of school in 1969 to protest discrimination. Severita Lara described how the protests began at the school, which had an 85 percent Hispanic student body.

TEXAS VOICES

"In all of our activities, like for example, cheerleaders . . . there's always three Anglos and one mexicana. . . . We started questioning. Why should it be like that? . . . [We] started looking at other things."

—Severita Lara, quoted in *Chicano!* by F. Arturo Rosales

In January 1970 the students returned to school after they won broad changes and the school board promised reforms.

Analyzing Primary Sources
Identifying Points of View Considering that 85 percent of the school was Hispanic, why might Lara find the number of Hispanic cheerleaders important?

Registered Voters in Texas, 1970-1980

Interpreting Charts During the 1970s the number of registered voters rose with the growth of population and changes in voting rights laws. By how much did the number of voters increase between 1970 and 1980?

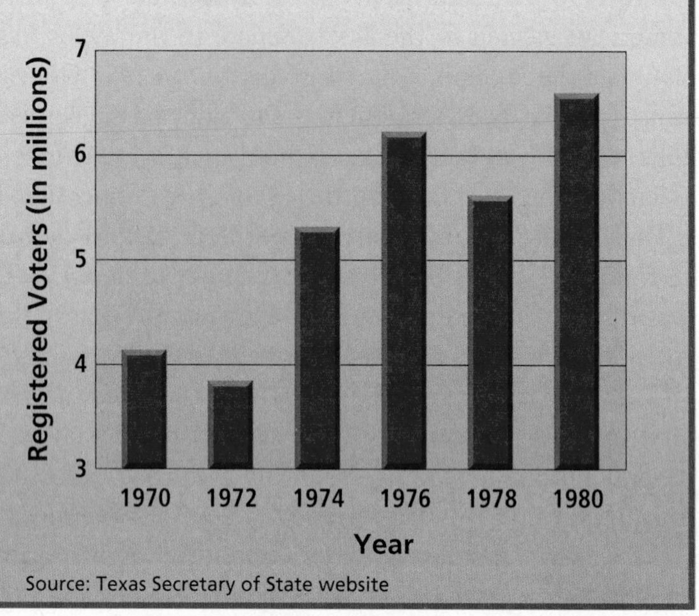

The students of Crystal City were supported in their protests by the Mexican American Youth Organization (MAYO), which had been founded by José Angel Gutiérrez and Mario Compeán in 1967. In 1970 Gutiérrez helped form a new political party, called **La Raza Unida Party** (RUP). The RUP hoped to highlight issues affecting Hispanic Americans and to elect more Hispanic Americans to political office. Through such elections, party leaders wanted to create government policies to improve the lives of local Mexican Americans.

The RUP achieved some success in Texas. In Crystal City, Gutiérrez and other RUP members won election to the school board and city council. Among those elected were several Hispanic American women. Party leader Marta Cotera explained that women "were very much in evidence as . . . candidates, [and] as organizers in leadership position[s]." Following its early successes, the movement began to decline in the mid-1970s. RUP members disagreed over policy, and fundraising became more difficult. RUP disappeared after 1978. Hispanic participation in the political process had greatly increased.

La Raza Unida Party leaders traveled across the country to speak about Hispanic participation in government.

This increased participation was largely the result of new federal laws. For example, a 1975 extension to the Voting Rights Act required that, in areas with large immigrant populations, ballots be provided in the voters' preferred language. This new extension, championed by Texas Representative Barbara Jordan, meant that people who were more comfortable speaking Spanish than English could vote more easily. The availability of Spanish ballots helped more Hispanic candidates win elections in many regions.

Reading Check Summarizing What role did La Raza Unida Party play in the struggle for Hispanic Rights?

★ The Women's Movement

During the 1960s and 1970s, women's groups also made political gains. In 1966 author Betty Friedan and other feminists founded the National Organization for Women (NOW). NOW's statement of purpose declared that "the time has come for a new movement toward true equality." NOW chapters sprang up across Texas. Members pushed for new legislation and filed lawsuits on behalf of women who claimed workplace discrimination. They also staged marches, protests, and other demonstrations.

The Texas Women's Political Caucus, founded in 1971, worked to get more women elected to political office. The organizers of this group included Liz Carpenter and Jane Wells. When the caucus was founded, there were only two women in the state legislature: Barbara Jordan and Frances Farenthold. Women made significant political gains the following year. Five women were elected to the state legislature, and Jordan was elected to Congress. In addition, Farenthold made a serious bid for governor. On the national level, the Republican Party chose Texan Anne Armstrong as speaker and co-chair of the National Republican Committee. She was the first woman co-chair and the first female to give a keynote address at a national party convention.

By the mid- to late 1970s, women were making successful bids for local office as well. For example, Carole Keeton McClellan (later Strayhorn) became the first female president of the Austin school board and was mayor of Austin from 1977 to 1983. She later served on the Railroad Commission and as state comptroller. By 1980 many more women had been elected to political office.

Reading Check **Sequencing** Trace in order the development of the women's rights movement in Texas.

BIOGRAPHY

Barbara Jordan

(1936–1996) In 1973, with President Johnson's support, Barbara Jordan of Houston became the first African American woman to represent Texas in the U.S. Congress. There, she took an important role in the Watergate hearings in 1974. Jordan was listed in *Time* magazine as one of several Women of the Year in 1975. After leaving office, Jordan became a professor of public service in the Lyndon B. Johnson School of Public Affairs at the University of Texas. She remained in public service until her death on January 17, 1996. **How did Barbara Jordan demonstrate effective leadership?**

★ Section 2 Review

hmhsocialstudies.com
ONLINE QUIZ

1. Define and explain:
- sit-ins

2. Identify and explain the significance of each of the following in Texas history:
- Barbara Jordan
- Henry B. González
- Raymond L. Telles
- Chicano movement
- La Raza Unida Party

3. Sequencing Copy the graphic organizer below. Use it to compare developments in the civil rights movement for groups in Texas.

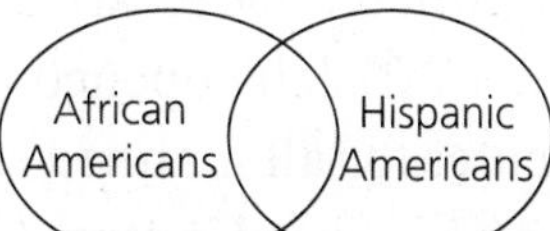

4. Finding the Main Idea

a. What were some of the key events in the Hispanic civil rights movement?

b. How did President Lyndon Johnson contribute to the civil rights movement?

5. Writing and Critical Thinking myWriteSmart

Summarizing Write a short article for a Web site comparing and contrasting the struggles for civil rights in Texas by African Americans and Hispanic Americans.

Consider the following:
- the goals of African Americans
- the goals of Hispanic Americans

Image Credit: (tr) ©Wally McNamee/Corbis

Section 3

New Technology and the Space Race

Main Ideas

1. The aerospace and defense industries in Texas grew in the 1950s and 1960s.
2. The high-tech and medical industries have attracted people and businesses to Texas.

Key Terms and People

- **National Aeronautics and Space Administration**
- **Manned Spacecraft Center**
- **Walter Cunningham**
- **Michael DeBakey**
- **Denton Cooley**

Why It Matters Today

The defense industry developed new technology during the 1960s. Use current events sources to find information about advances in today's weapons technology.

TEKS: 7F, 13A, 13C, 20A, 20B, 20C, 20E, 21B, 22D

myNotebook

Use the annotation tools in your eBook to take notes on new industries and technologies that developed in Texas.

The Story Continues

In 1961, part of the U.S. space program was moving from Virginia to Houston. Gene Kranz had 30 days to find new housing for himself and his family. But Kranz was in the middle of research and did not want to go to Houston. He called in his newest employee, Dutch, and told him to "scout around and find the best place to live." Dutch went and picked out houses for 10 families in southwest Houston, an area that later became known as Flight Controller Alley.

★ Texas in the Space Age

As a leader in aircraft and weapons production, Texas was a logical choice to become a center for the nation's developing space program. The launching of the Soviet *Sputnik* satellite in 1957 had prompted the creation of the **National Aeronautics and Space Administration** (NASA) in 1958. NASA took charge of the U.S. space program and worked to make U.S. goals in space a reality.

In 1961 NASA chose Houston as the headquarters for its astronauts. There it built the **Manned Spacecraft Center** on 1,000 acres of former ranchland. The center officially opened that same year and became the Mission Control Center for all manned space flights. From the moment a rocket lifts off, the Mission Control Center monitors the flight and helps solve any problems.

The astronauts at Houston attracted worldwide attention as the space race intensified. After the Soviet Union sent the first human into space in 1961, President Kennedy announced his goal "of landing a man on the moon and returning him safely." On May 5, 1961, Alan Shepard Jr. became the first American to enter space.

VIDEO
Mission to the Moon

hmhsocialstudies.com

In 1968 NASA launched the *Apollo 7* mission, the first manned flight of the Apollo program. Astronaut **Walter Cunningham** was the lunar module pilot on the flight. On July 16, 1969, NASA sent *Apollo 11* into space and achieved what many had thought impossible. As the craft set down on the Moon's surface four days later, astronaut Neil Armstrong uttered the now famous line, "Houston, the Eagle has landed."

The Manned Spacecraft Center—renamed the Lyndon B. Johnson Space Center in 1973—researched, developed, and built the first space shuttle, *Columbia.* It was launched into space in 1981. As the heart of the U.S. space program, the center brought many jobs to the Houston area. It had thousands of employees and was a primary site for research and development of manned spacecraft. The space center was also home to space station research, astronaut training, and aerospace medicine.

In 2004 the federal government announced the end of the space shuttle program. However, the Johnson Space Center remains in operation. Among other projects, it is the main NASA headquarters for the International Space Station—an international project launched in 1998—and a major science education center.

Reading Check **Analyzing Information** How did the aerospace industry affect the economic development of Texas?

★ The Defense Industry

The defense industry in Texas grew along with the space industry. Texas had been a center of military aircraft and weapons production since World War II. As the Cold War continued, the push for new weapons technology grew, and the defense industry expanded. Several Texas firms, including General Dynamics Corporation and Texas Instruments, had U.S. government defense contracts to build weapons systems. By 1965 General Dynamics was the number one weapons exporter in

Helicopters were one of many products developed by the booming aerospace and defense industries in Texas.

CONNECTING TO

ECONOMICS

The Texas Aerospace Industry

Aircraft manufacturing began in Texas in the early 1940s. By the 1960s it was one of the state's leading industries. As a center for the manufacture and testing of rockets for the military, Texas was known for aerospace technology even before it was chosen as home for the Manned Spacecraft Center. Texas companies created products to support NASA projects, while educational facilities such as Rice University assisted NASA in its space research. Today Texas remains one of the world's leading centers of aerospace research and manufacturing.

1. **Economics and History** How did the aeronautics and aerospace industries affect the development of Texas?
2. **Economics and You** How do you think the Texas aerospace industry has affected local, national, and international markets?

the nation. Texas also ranked second of all states in aircraft production during the 1960s. In addition, the state continued to be home to many military bases and personnel during the 1980s. By adding millions of dollars to the Texas economy, the defense industry—both military bases and weapons production—had become critical to the state's economy.

Reading Check **Finding the Main Idea** How did the development of new weapons technology during the Cold War affect the economy of Texas?

★ High-Tech Industries

As a leader in defense and space research, Texas rapidly became a leader in other high-tech industries in the 1950s and 1960s as well. Texas companies manufactured a variety of electronic devices, including transistors, television sets, and computers. Firms were drawn to Texas because of affordable labor and good climate. By the late 1950s, Dallas, Fort Worth, and Houston had become centers for the electronics industry.

Technological developments in communications, radar, and other systems led to even greater growth in the industry. By 1963 nearly 300 businesses in Texas produced electronic devices. Firms such as Texas Instruments, Tracor, and Tandy grew as their sales reached millions of dollars a year. Several Texas companies became world leaders in the electronics industry, shipping billions of dollars worth of products to national and international markets.

As computer technology became more advanced, computers became important to the daily operations of businesses all over the world. The Texas high-tech industry began to design and manufacture semiconductors and microchips to meet the national and international demand for computers. The demand for these goods boosted and expanded the high-tech economy in Texas. Austin became another Texas high-tech research center as companies such as IBM built facilities there during the 1960s and 1970s.

Reading Check **Drawing Inferences and Conclusions** How do you think scientific discoveries and high-tech industries in Texas made the state more interdependent with the world?

★ Medical Technology

Scientific research in medicine also spurred the Texas economy. With the development of medical centers such as the Texas Medical Center in Houston, the state has been at the forefront of medical research and treatment. Texas doctors and scientists studied treatments for cancer, evaluated new drugs, and developed other medical innovations. Texas doctors such as **Michael DeBakey** and **Denton Cooley** helped revolutionize the treatment of heart disease. In 1964 DeBakey performed the first arterial bypass operation to repair a damaged heart. In 1968 Cooley placed the first artificial heart in a patient.

As a center for medical research, Texas has attracted patients seeking quality health care from all over the world. Medical technologies that were developed in the state, such as the artificial heart, have been used throughout the world to treat patients. As a result of these scientific and medical advances, many medical technology companies have located their operations in Texas.

The booming Texas high-tech and medical technology industries affected not only the markets in which they operated but also the cities in which they were based. The population of these cities grew rapidly. As the population and economy expanded in Texas cities, world-class buildings and new sports arenas were built, including the Houston Astrodome. Museums and other attractions were established or improved. People moved to Texas in increasing numbers to take advantage of not only the jobs in these industries but also the quality of life that a growing economy helped provide.

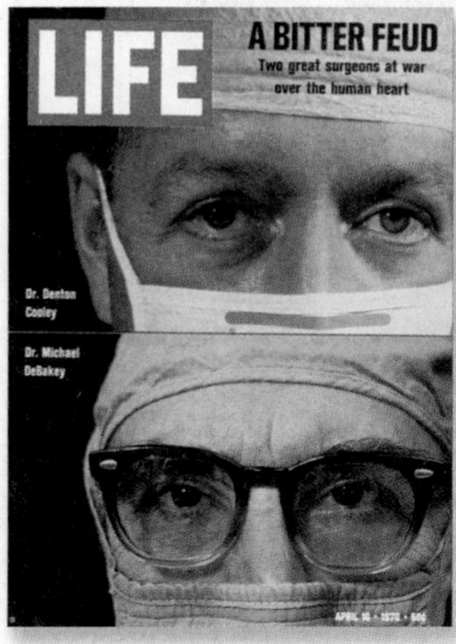

Texas heart surgeons Michael DeBakey and Denton Cooley became internationally known in the 1960s.

Reading Check **Analyzing Information** How has the medical technology industry affected markets in Texas, the United States, and the world?

★ Section 3 Review

1. Identify and explain the significance of each of the following:
- National Aeronautics and Space Administration
- Manned Spacecraft Center
- Walter Cunningham
- Michael DeBakey
- Denton Cooley

2. Locate on a map:
- Houston

3. Summarizing Copy the graphic organizer below. Use it to show how new technology has affected the development of Texas.

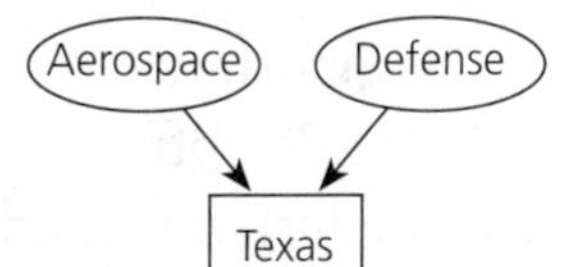

4. Finding the Main Idea

a. Explain how world events led to the growth of the Texas defense industry.

b. How was the development of Texas affected by the high-tech and medical industries?

5. Writing and Critical Thinking myWriteSmart

Analyzing Information Imagine that you are an economist living in the 1960s. Write a short speech on how technology has led to an increasing interdependence among Texas, the United States, and the world.

Consider the following:
- the military weapons produced in Texas
- the booming high-tech industries

Section 4

Texas in the 1970s

Main Ideas

1. Population increases led to rapid growth for Texas cities and many industries in the 1970s.
2. An international increase in oil prices led to a boom in the Texas oil industry.
3. Texas politics changed in the 1970s as the Republican Party gained support throughout the state.

Key Terms and People

- **John Tower**
- **scandal**
- **William Clements**

Why It Matters Today

During the 1970s the Texas economy thrived as a result of high oil prices and booming industry. Use current events sources to find information about major Texas industries today.

TEKS: 7B, 7F, 8B, 9A, 9C, 11C, 12A, 12B, 12C, 13A, 19A, 19B, 21B, 21C, 22D

myNotebook

Use the annotation tools in your eBook to take notes on changes in Texas in the 1970s.

The Story Continues

In the 1950s a writer described the landmarks that dominated the Austin skyline: "From a point of higher ground, one can see the [University of Texas] tower and the Capitol building." By the early 1970s, these old buildings were being dwarfed by a new arrival—a skyscraper. The new building was a sign of the times. During the mid-1970s and early 1980s, Austin would become known for the thousands of newcomers flocking there to join a high-tech revolution.

The Sunbelt and Urban Growth

Austin was part of a new trend of growth in the Sunbelt—the South and Southwest—that had begun in the mid-1900s. The Sunbelt offered employment opportunities, a mild winter climate, and an appealing standard of living. With the development of air conditioning, even the hot Texas summer was no longer a major drawback.

Quality of life was an important factor in the Sunbelt migration. As one person wrote, "The Sun Belt offers both more 'sun' and more 'fun.' Outdoor living, informal entertaining, and golf year round—all afford the new lifestyles which Americans have adopted." Between 1940 and 1980, the population of the Sunbelt grew by more than 110 percent. In 1980 about one third of the U.S. population lived in this region.

Much of this growth took place in Texas. During the 1970s oil and gas companies and other successful industries drew people by the hundreds of thousands. Most of these new Texans moved to cities. Houston and Dallas in particular grew rapidly, as industry boomed there.

Reading Check **Finding the Main Idea** Why did so many people move to Texas in the 1970s, and where did they settle?

★ New Jobs and City Life

As the population of Texas cities continued to grow, the economy entered a cycle of expansion. Most newcomers moved to cities because jobs and housing were plentiful. These newcomers added to the growing labor force in Texas. The prospect of a large labor pool of highly educated workers attracted new business to Texas cities. During the 1970s and 1980s several major national companies moved their headquarters to Texas. These businesses in turn attracted more job-seekers to the state.

The increase in city populations also created new demands for a variety of services, from restaurants to utilities. The new industries attracted national and international business to Texas cities. This increased the demand for hotels, airports, and other services. The number and size of service industries grew to meet the rising demand, thus creating jobs for Texans. Manufacturing jobs, particularly in high-tech fields, increased. The number of manufacturing jobs more than doubled in Dallas, Fort Worth, and Houston.

The growth of industries and jobs led to a growing demand for new houses, offices, and other buildings. As a result, the real estate and construction markets boomed in Texas. Construction cranes dominated the landscape in major cities. New tax laws made it easier for Texas banks and financial institutions to loan money to finance new construction. As a result, the banking industry also expanded rapidly. Texas cities grew at an unheard-of rate, both in numbers of buildings and in population.

CONNECTING TO

SCIENCE AND TECHNOLOGY

Keeping Cool

Home-cooling technology dates back to the early Spanish settlers who built houses of adobe, or sun-dried brick. The adobe cooled down at night and stayed cool inside until afternoon. Texans began making simple devices to cool their homes as early as the late 1800s. These usually involved air blown over ice in various ways. Gradually, the machines became more complex, and by the 1940s Texas had become a national center for the manufacture of air-conditioning equipment. **How might new air-conditioning technology contribute to Sunbelt migration?**

Sunny climate and growing industries attracted people to Texas cities such as Dallas.

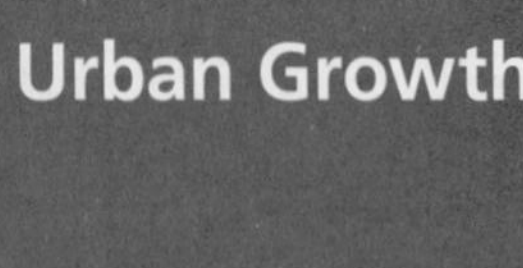

Urban Growth

Texas cities began to grow rapidly during the mid- and late 1900s. This growth was encouraged by several factors, including the region's sunny climate, improved transportation, economic opportunities, and air conditioning.

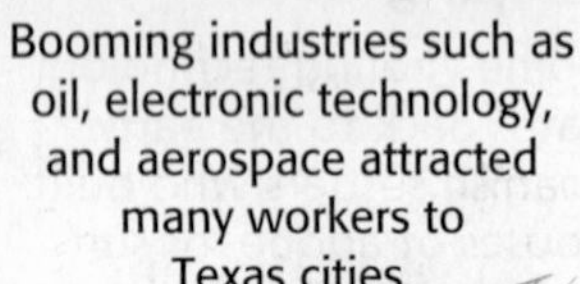

Booming industries such as oil, electronic technology, and aerospace attracted many workers to Texas cities.

The sunny climate attracted many companies and people to Texas.

The development of efficient air conditioning made life during hot Texas summers more enjoyable. This led to even more migration to Texas.

The expansion of the highway system and the affordability of cars led to the growth in city size in Texas.

Visualizing History

1. **Geography** What geographic factors aided the growth and development of Texas?
2. **Connecting to Today** How do you think these factors affect the economy of Texas today?

As Texas cities grew, many people chose to live in new housing developments outside the central city. However, many of these people still worked downtown. State and city leaders responded by building new freeway systems that allowed Texans to commute more easily from suburbs into cities. New public transportation systems such as buses to help people travel throughout the growing urban areas.

Increased immigration also changed Texas cities. Between 1970 and 1980 the Mexican American population grew by nearly a million people, totalling more than 20 percent of the population. Before World War II, most of the Mexican American population in Texas had lived in rural areas, mostly farming communities in South Texas. As industrialization and urbanization created new jobs in cities, though, more Mexican Americans chose to move to urban areas. Houston, Dallas, and other cities soon had large Mexican American communities.

At the same time, thousands of people moved to Texas from Asia. Many Vietnamese immigrants, for example, moved to the state during and after the Vietnam War. Most of these Vietnamese Americans settled in coastal areas or in large cities, including Houston, Dallas, and Austin. In those cities, the new immigrants established communities in which they could maintain familiar customs and traditions.

Reading Check **Evaluating** What led to the Texas real estate boom?

★ The Oil Boom and Bust

Booming industries sparked rapid population growth in Texas. One of the most important industries that experienced a major boom in the 1970s was the oil business. In 1973 the Organization of Petroleum Exporting Countries (OPEC) banned oil shipments to the United States for political reasons. Although the situation lasted only a few months, it drove up world oil prices substantially. While much of the U.S. economy was hurt by the higher gas prices, Texas businesses that produced and sold oil and natural gas benefited greatly.

The spike in the price of oil produced a boom in the Texas oil industry. With the rising prices, profits for oil companies grew. Oil companies expanded production to meet the high demand. This created many new jobs in the industry, and salaries of oil workers grew to almost three times their earlier level. Offshore oil drilling also increased. With the boom in production, Texas was supplying more oil to national and international markets.

This boom came to a halt in 1982 when oil prices dropped. More than 200,000 jobs were lost in Houston alone. The oil bust of the 1980s also hurt other businesses in Texas, such as service industries that catered to the oil industry. The bust also led to a slowdown in the Texas real estate market.

Reading Check **Analyzing Information** How did the international market for oil and boom-and-bust cycles affect Texas?

★ Politics in the 1970s

Texas government changed along with the state's population and economy. With the successes of the civil rights movements of the 1960s, Texans of all backgrounds became involved in deciding the direction of state government. U.S. Supreme Court decisions in the 1960s also brought changes to the makeup of the state legislature. Because of these decisions, large cities—which often had large minority populations—gained additional representation in the legislature.

Another major change in Texas during the 1970s was the growth of the Republican Party. Texas had been led primarily by the Democratic Party state since Reconstruction. After World War II, however, some Texans felt that the Democrats were becoming too liberal. At the same time, the Republic Party was beginning to support more conservative viewpoints. As a result, Republicans gained some support in Texas in the 1950s. For example, a majority of Texans had supported Republican Dwight Eisenhower in the 1952 and 1956 presidential elections. In 1961 **John Tower** became the first Republican elected to the U.S. Senate from Texas since Reconstruction. Republican Richard Nixon carried Texas in the 1972 presidential election.

Our Cultural Heritage

The Chinese Lunar New Year

Among those who moved to Texas's growing cities were many Asian immigrants. They and their descendants have maintained their cultural traditions, including holidays and festivals. For example, many Chinese Americans and Vietnamese American hold banquets and shoot off firecrackers for the Chinese Lunar New Year. Family celebrations usually involve a dinner, staying up until the New Year arrives, and sealing the doors with red paper for good luck. **How have Chinese immigrants contributed to Texas culture?**

Chinese dragon dancers in Austin

The Democrats still held the state's executive office, however. They had won every election for governor in Texas for nearly 100 years. However, support for Democratic governors was shaken in the early 1970s. In 1971, Governor Preston Smith, a Democrat, was caught up in a political **scandal**—a publicized event in which officials are disgraced for wrongdoing. Several government officials were convicted of accepting bribes from Frank Sharp, a Houston businessman. In exchange for the bribes, these officials had passed legislation favorable to Sharp. As a result of this, the legislature passed several reforms. Elected officials had to report how they acquired and spent donations to their campaigns. The laws also required records to be opened to the public.

The scandal ruined Smith's chances for re-election, and Dolph Briscoe was elected governor in 1972. Soon afterward, the governor's term in office was lengthened from two years to four. When Briscoe was re-elected in 1974, he became the first Texas governor to serve a four-year term.

Briscoe ran for re-election in 1978 but lost the Democratic nomination to John Hill. Many people thought that Hill could not lose, because Texas had not had a Republican governor since 1874. They were wrong. Republican **William Clements** won by nearly 17,000 votes. Clements described his political style.

TEXAS VOICES

"They talk about how I'm direct, I'm abrupt, so forth and so on. Nonsense. I'm certainly straightforward, there's no question about that. You know, I don't have time to willynilly around the issues and blow a lot of smoke about this and that and so forth."

—Governor William Clements, quoted in *The Texas Governor's Mansion*, by Jean Daniel, Price Daniel, and Dorothy Blodgett

Reading Check Summarizing How and when did the Republican Party begin to gain support in Texas?

Section 4 Review

hmhsocialstudies.com ONLINE QUIZ

1. Define and explain:
- scandal

2. Identify and explain the significance of each of the following in Texas history:
- John Tower
- William Clements

3. Analyzing Information
Copy the graphic organizer below. Use it to show why people moved to Texas, where they settled, and how the new population distribution affected Texas.

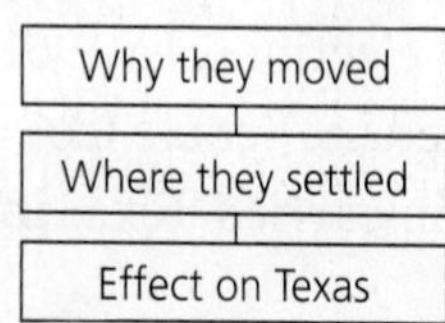

4. Finding the Main Idea
a. Describe the effect of high oil prices on international markets and booming industry on Texas.
b. Trace the development of changes in Texas politics in the 1970s.

5. Writing and Critical Thinking myWriteSmart
Summarizing Write a paragraph describing the effects of the Sunbelt migration on Texas in the 1970s.
Consider the following:
- economic growth
- effects on society

Boom-and-Bust Cycles in Oil

The Texas oil and gas industry experienced a dramatic boom-and-bust cycle during the 1970s and 1980s. The years from 1973 to 1982 were the boom period, fueled by high prices for oil and natural gas. The initial cause of the increased prices was an OPEC ban on the sale of oil to the United States. The ban created an energy shortage in the United States and drove up prices. But oil prices dropped in 1982, leading to a bust in the oil industry. By September 1982, 17 Dallas-area oil companies had gone out of business.

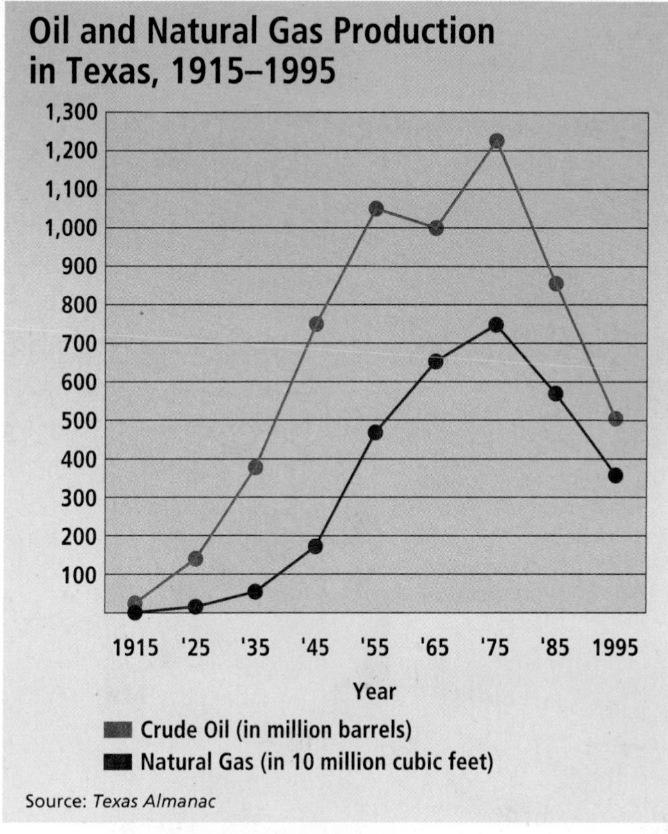

Interpreting Charts

1. By how much did the production of oil increase between 1925 and 1975?
2. How much did production drop after 1975?
3. How did international markets affect production of oil and natural gas in Texas?
4. How do you think a state or nation can avoid serious effects of a boom-and-bust cycle in its economy?

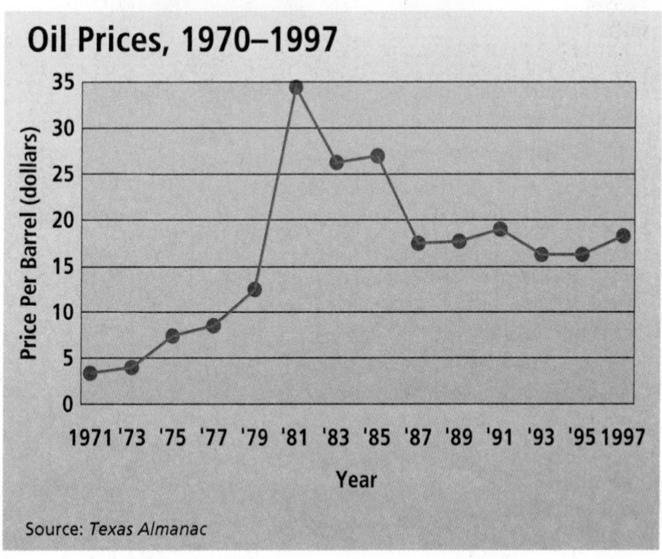

The Chapter at a Glance

Examine the following visual summary of the chapter. Then use it to create a time line that includes the significant individuals and time periods discussed in the chapter.

Texas in the 1960s–1970s

Identifying People and Ideas

Write a sentence to explain the role or significance of each of the following terms or people.

1. Lyndon B. Johnson
2. Great Society
3. sit-ins
4. Raymond L. Telles
5. Barbara Jordan
6. Henry B. González
7. Chicano movement
8. John Tower

Understanding Main Ideas

Section 1

1. Describe the leadership qualities of President Lyndon B. Johnson.

Section 2

2. How was the women's rights movement similar to the civil rights movement for African Americans?
3. What steps did African Americans take in the 1960s to secure civil rights?

Section 3

4. What effect did aerospace technology have on the development of Texas?

Section 4

5. How did Sunbelt migration lead to new jobs in Texas cities?

You Be the Historian

Reviewing Themes

1. **Citizenship** How do you think Texans who participated in the civil rights and equal rights movements exercised civic responsibilities?
2. **Science, Technology & Society** How did the development of new technologies affect the growth of Texas from the 1960s to the 1980s?
3. **Geography** How did geographic factors affect the political, economic, and social development of Texas during the 1970s?

Thinking Critically

1. **Analyzing Information** How did the boom in the aerospace, high-tech, and oil and gas industries affect the development of Texas?
2. **Summarizing** Trace the development of the Hispanic rights movement.
3. **Identifying Cause and Effect** How were oil and gas prices affected by international events?

Texas Test Practice

Interpreting Maps

Study the map below. Use the information on the map to help you answer the questions that follow.

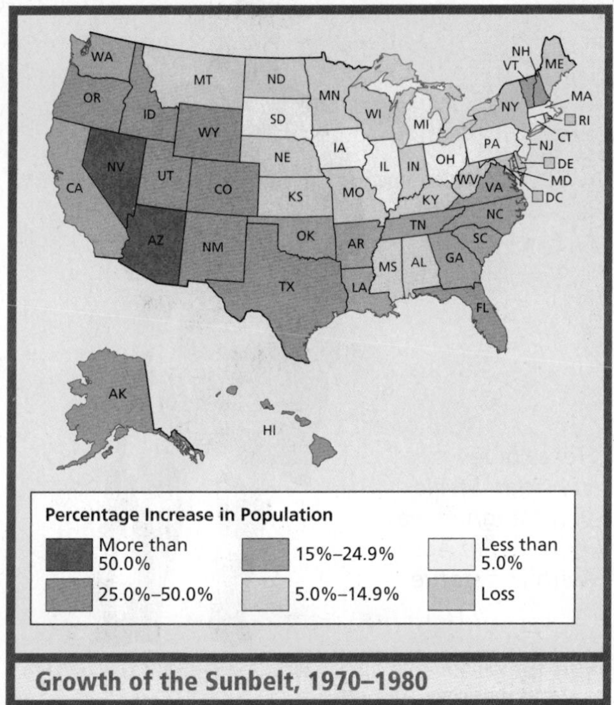

Growth of the Sunbelt, 1970–1980

1. What geographic pattern is shown on this map?

- **A** New England grew fastest in the 1970s.
- **B** Texas was the fastest-growing state.
- **C** The Southwest was one of the fastest-growing regions.
- **D** Texas was the slowest-growing state.

2. What geographic factors, such as climate and weather, contributed to the Sunbelt's growth?

Analyzing Primary Sources

When Barbara Jordan began her campaign for a seat in the U.S. House of Representatives, Lyndon B. Johnson urged people to vote for her. Read the quote by Johnson. Then answer the questions.

"Barbara Jordan proved to us that black is beautiful before we knew what that meant. She is a woman of keen intellect and unusual legislative ability, a symbol proving that We Can Overcome. Wherever she goes she is going to be at the top. Wherever she goes all of us are going to be behind her. Those with hurting consciences because they have discriminated against blacks and women can vote for Barbara Jordan and feel good."

3. What leadership traits did Johnson say Jordan had?

- **F** She could convince people to vote for her.
- **G** She was a native Texan.
- **H** She was a friend of Johnson's.
- **J** She was a symbol of people's ability to overcome.

4. What role do you think bias may have played in Johnson's praise of a fellow Democrat?

Cooperative Learning

Work with a small group to complete the following activity. Imagine that you and your group are members of the Texas Chamber of Commerce and that you want to encourage companies to relocate to Texas. Each person in your group should select one of the following industries: a) aerospace, b) high-tech, c) medical, d) defense. Work together to prepare a colorful brochure that should convince companies to move to Texas. You might want to include visuals such as charts, diagrams, graphs, or maps to make your case more convincing.

Internet Activity

Access the Internet to research the changes in the types of jobs that have resulted from urbanization, such as the growth of service industries. Then create a database and generate a graph that illustrates the data you have found. You may wish to use computer software to help you create your graph. On a separate sheet of paper, write a paragraph telling how the growth of Texas cities affects the state's economy. Check your paragraph for standard grammar, spelling, sentence structure, and punctuation and for proper citation of sources.

CHAPTER 29

Contemporary Texas
(1980–Present)

Texas Essential Knowledge and Skills (TEKS) 7B, 7F, 9C, 10B, 11A, 11B, 11C, 12B, 13A, 13C, 17A, 18A, 18B, 19A, 19B, 19D, 20A, 20C, 20D, 20E, 21A, 21B, 21C, 22A, 22B, 22C, 22D

Texas blues musician Stevie Ray Vaughan was honored in Austin with this statue.

TEXAS

1986 Texas writer Larry McMurtry receives the Pulitzer Prize for his novel *Lonesome Dove*.

1990 Texas musician Stevie Ray Vaughan is killed in a helicopter crash.

1995 George W. Bush takes office as governor.

1980 1984 1988 1992 1996

U.S. and WORLD

1980 Republican Ronald Reagan is elected president of the United States.

1988 Vice President George H. W. Bush is elected president of the United States.

1994 The North American Free Trade Agreement (NAFTA) among Canada, Mexico, and the United States goes into effect.

As a Texan . . .
What do you think your state will be like in the future?

Build on What You Know

By 1980 Texas had seen many changes, including the civil rights movement and the growth of the Republican Party. The development of new technologies that brought the state into the space age also brought opportunities and challenges as Texas entered the new century.

Republican George W. Bush became president of the United States in 2001.

AT&T Stadium in Arlington, completed in 2009, is the home of the Dallas Cowboys football team.

2000 Rick Perry becomes the 47th governor of Texas.

2000 Vicente Fox Quesada is elected president of Mexico.

2001 George W. Bush becomes president. On September 11, terrorists attack the World Trade Center and the Pentagon.

2002 Republicans gain control of the Texas House of Representatives.

2005 Iraq holds its first elections since the overthrow of Saddam Hussein.

2006 Texas becomes the national leader in wind power generation.

2008 Barack Obama is elected the first African American president of the United States.

2009 Cowboys Stadium, later renamed AT&T Stadium, opens in Arlington.

2011 Texas receives its lowest ever recorded rainfall.

2011 Osama bin Laden is killed by American forces in Pakistan.

2000 — 2004 — 2008 — 2012 — Present

You Be the Historian

myNotebook

What's Your Opinion? Do you **agree** or **disagree** with the following statements? Support your point of view in your notebook.

- **Science, Technology & Society** Advances in technology always improve people's lives.
- **Global Relations** Events that occur in one country can have effects in countries far away.
- **Culture** Ethnic groups are rarely able to maintain traditional celebrations and activities while living within a larger culture.

Section 1 Political and Economic Change

Main Ideas

1. Republicans, women, and members of minority groups won state offices in the 1970s and 1980s.
2. The Texas oil industry crashed in the 1980s.

Key Terms and People

- **two-party system**
- **Ann Richards**
- **Kay Bailey Hutchison**
- **Raul A. Gonzalez Jr.**
- **budget surplus**
- **savings and loan associations**

Why It Matters Today

Both Democrats and Republicans served as governor in Texas during the 1970s and1980s. Use current events sources to learn more about political parties in Texas today.

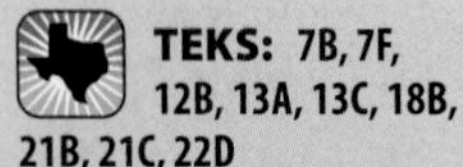

TEKS: 7B, 7F, 12B, 13A, 13C, 18B, 21B, 21C, 22D

myNotebook

Use the annotation tools in your eBook to take notes on changes in politics and economy in the 1970s and 1980s.

The Story Continues

Bill Clements faced a difficult challenge in 1978. He was the Republican candidate for Texas governor, but no Republican had held the office in more than 100 years. Nevertheless, Clements campaigned hard, crisscrossing the state to urge Texans to vote for him. To the shock of many political observers, Clements won the election.

★ Changes in State Politics

The election of Bill Clements in 1978 marked a turning point in state politics. For the first time since Reconstruction, the Republican Party had gained enough support to challenge Democratic control of Texas. The state was experiencing the reemergence of a **two-party system**—a political system in which two parties of comparable strength compete for political office—rather than one in which one party dominates elections. In the four elections for governor from 1978 to 1990, for example, Republicans won two, and Democrats won two. This political shift is one of the defining characteristics of the Contemporary Texas era.

The popularity of the Republican Party grew in part because it had developed a reputation as the party of business. Republican candidates promised to bring a no-nonsense business approach to government. Clements, for example, pledged to boost the economy by lowering taxes and reducing government regulation of business. Although he lost a reelection bid in 1982 to Democrat Mark White, Clements was elected to a second term as governor in 1986.

The growing popularity of the Republican Party was also seen in the makeup of the Texas Legislature. In 1961 only two Republicans had held seats in the 181-seat Legislature. By 1977 there were 21 Republicans in the Legislature, and that number would continue to grow. Likewise, the number of Republicans from Texas elected to Congress increased.

While the Texas Republican Party was gaining in strength, women and members of minority groups were also becoming more prominent in state politics. In 1982 **Ann Richards**, a Democrat, was elected state treasurer. With her victory, Richards became the first woman elected to a statewide office since Ma Ferguson in 1932. A few years later, **Kay Bailey Hutchison** won the same office, becoming the first Republican woman ever elected to state office. In 1993 she became the first woman to represent Texas in the U.S. Senate.

Hispanic Texans also held some major political positions in the 1980s. **Raul A. Gonzalez Jr.**, for example, became the first Hispanic Texan to hold a major state office. In 1984 he was appointed by Governor Mark White to the state Supreme Court. Judith Zaffirini became the first Mexican American woman elected to the Texas Legislature in 1986.

Reading Check **Summarizing** How did the nature of Texas politics change in the late 1970s and 1980s?

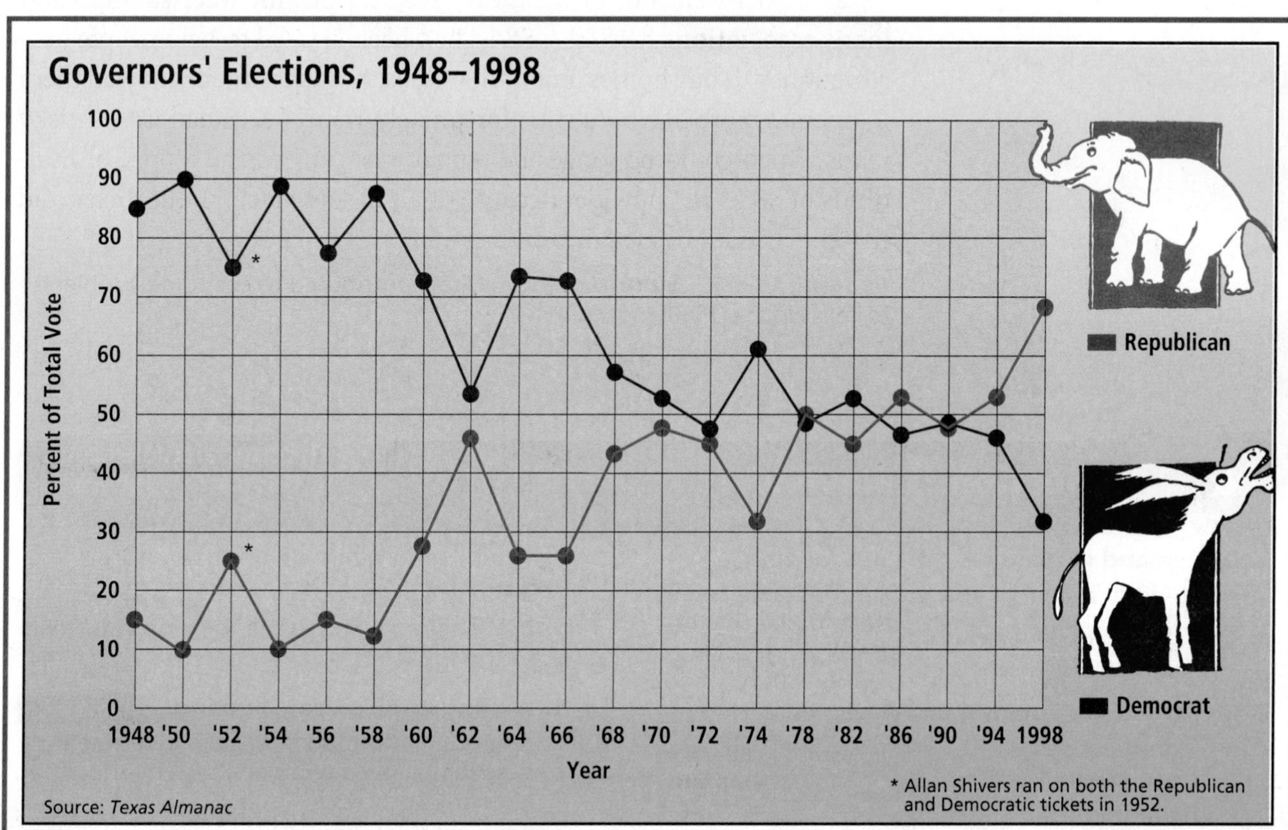

Interpreting Graphs The rise of the two-party system in Texas during the late 1900s led to greater competition between Republican and Democratic Party candidates. What years did Republican candidates defeat Democratic candidates?

★ Boom and Bust in the 1980s

As you read in the previous chapter, the 1970s were a boom time for the Texas oil industry. The price of oil skyrocketed internationally, and oil production in the state increased. The boom continued into the early 1980s: by 1981 the oil industry was responsible for some 25 percent of all economic activity in the state. Money from oil poured into the state, creating a **budget surplus**, meaning that the state's income exceeded its expenses. The state used its extra money to fund education and public works. Many oil workers also had money to spare during this time. Many invested heavily in real estate, causing real estate prices to rise.

In the mid-1980s, however, circumstances changed. The price of oil dropped, in part due to international overproduction. As prices dropped, so did oil companies' profits. Companies reduced oil production in the state, and between 1982 and 1994 one third of workers in the Texas oil industry lost their jobs. With the loss of income from oil, the state had to cut back on services or seek new ways of paying for them.

The downturn in the oil industry soon affected other businesses in the state. With the collapse of the oil industry, real estate prices fell. Texas banks—which had profited from the strong real estate market—were hit particularly by the price drop. Defaulted, or unpaid, loans to oil companies made matters worse. Between 1985 and 1992, some 470 Texas banks went out of business. Even harder hit were **savings and loans associations**, or S&Ls. S&Ls had been created to help people borrow money to buy homes, but in the 1980s the government allowed them to operate more like banks. Unfortunately, many S&Ls had issued risky loans which could no longer be repaid, resulting in the failure of hundreds of S&Ls nationwide. Because of all of these factors, the Texas and national economies fell into a recession.

Reading Check **Summarizing** What contributed to economic problems in Texas in the 1980s?

Section 1 Review

hmhsocialstudies.com
ONLINE QUIZ

1. Define and explain:
- two-party system
- budget surplus
- savings and loan

2. Identify and explain the significance of each of the following:
- Ann Richards
- Kay Bailey Hutchison
- Raul A. Gonzalez Jr.

3. Categorizing
Copy the table below. Use it to identify the effects of the oil bust of the 1980s on various industries.

Industry	Effects of oil bust

4. Finding the Main Idea
a. How did the two-party system develop?
b. What happened to the Texas oil industry in the 1980s?

5. Writing and Critical Thinking myWriteSmart
Analyzing Information Write a paragraph describing how a two-party system affects the legislative process in Texas.
Consider the following:
- bipartisanship
- the makeup of the state government

Section 2 Texans in the White House

Main Ideas

1. Texans George H. W. Bush and George W. Bush both served as president of the United States.
2. Texas governors during the 1990s and 2000s focused on economic and social issues.
3. During George W. Bush's presidency, the United States launched the War on Terror.

Why It Matters Today

The effects of terrorist attacks and the War on Terror continue to affect American life and U.S. foreign policy. Use current events sources to learn about the latest issues and events stemming from the fight against terrorism.

Key Terms and People

- **George H. W. Bush**
- **James A. Baker III**
- **George W. Bush**
- **bipartisanship**
- **Bob Bullock**
- **Rick Perry**
- **terrorism**

TEKS: 7F, 13A, 13C, 18A, 18B, 21B, 22D

The Story Continues

On January 20, 1989, George H. W. Bush stood on a platform in Washington, DC, with Chief Justice William Rehnquist. With one hand on his family Bible and his wife, Barbara, by his side, he took the oath of office to become the 41st president of the United States of America. Afterward he addressed the assembled crowd, calling on all Americans to work together to improve the country and the world.

myNotebook

Use the annotation tools in your eBook to take notes on the achievements of Texas leaders in the 1990s and 2000s.

President George H. W. Bush

George H. W. Bush, a former Texas oil executive, was elected president in 1988. By the time of his election, Bush had already had a long political career. He had represented Texas in Congress, served as the U.S. ambassador to the United Nations, and served two terms as vice president of the United States. A former navy pilot, Bush had also served as the head of the Central Intelligence Agency in the 1970s.

Upon becoming president, Bush brought several Texans into his administration. One was Houston lawyer **James A. Baker III,** who was named secretary of state. Baker had previously served as chief of staff under President Ronald Reagan. In that position, he had held a great deal of influence in policy making.

As president, Bush wanted to focus on domestic issues. He created policies to fight the trade and use of illegal drugs. In 1990 he signed the Americans with Disabilities Act (ADA), which guaranteed people with disabilities equal access to public places, transportation, and jobs.

President George H. W. Bush meets with U.S. troops during Operation Desert Shield before the Persian Gulf War.

Events overseas largely overshadowed Bush's domestic policies, though. During his presidency, the Soviet Union broke apart and the Cold War ended. Also during this time, a crisis arose in the Middle East. On August 2, 1990, Iraq invaded Kuwait, its neighbor to the south. Iraq's action threatened much of the world's oil supply. Bush and other world leaders quickly demanded that Iraqi forces withdraw from Kuwait. When Iraq refused, the United States and some 30 other nations formed a military coalition, or alliance, to drive Iraqi forces out of Kuwait. In January 1991 the international coalition launched Operation Desert Storm. Forces from the United States and other coalition nations swept through Kuwait, quickly freeing the nation from Iraqi control.

Many Americans approved of the way Bush handled the war, but a downturn in the economy became a major issue in the 1992 presidential race. Bush was defeated in that election by Democrat Bill Clinton, who went on to serve two terms as president.

Reading Check **Finding the Main Idea** What were some key events of George H. W. Bush's presidency?

State Politics Since 1990

While George H. W. Bush was in the White House, the growing power of the Republican Party in Texas was put to the test. In 1990 the Democrats nominated Ann Richards, the state's treasurer since 1983, for governor. Republicans chose Clayton Williams, a businessman from Midland. Richards won the election, which featured the highest voter turnout for a governor's race since 1970.

Richards was very popular with the public, known for her sense of humor and charisma. As governor, Richards worked to support the state's businesses. Through her efforts, the Texas economy grew slightly, even as the U.S. economy was in decline. She worked to reform the state's prison system, proposed laws to protect the environment, and looked for new ways to finance education in the absence of oil money. She also called for more women and members of minority groups to participate in state government.

Richards ran for governor again in 1994. This time, the Republican Party nominated **George W. Bush**, the son of George H. W. Bush. Bush had worked in the Texas oil industry and was a part owner of the Texas Rangers baseball team. Like Richards, Bush was charismatic and popular with many people. He won after a vigorous campaign.

In his campaign, Bush called for improvements to the economy and schools, lower property taxes, and stronger criminal laws. Thanks to a budget surplus, he was able to accomplish many of his goals. He proposed a huge tax cut, reducing the amount Texans had to pay the state by some $2 billion. He increased funding for organizations working to fight alcohol and drug abuse and domestic violence. Bush also worked to increase teacher salaries and improve the quality of education for students in Texas.

During Bush's term in office, the Texas Legislature was controlled by Democrats. However, Bush needed help from the Legislature to pass his agenda. As a result, he encouraged **bipartisanship,** or cooperation between parties. Bush himself developed a strong working relationship with Democratic leaders such as **Bob Bullock,** who was lieutenant governor from 1991 to 1999. Bullock had served in the Texas government in various positions since the 1960s as a legislator, secretary of state, and comptroller. He had also worked for many years with the Texas Historical Commission. After serving two terms, Bullock chose not to run for re-election in 1998.

Bush easily won re-election in 1998. Less than a year afterward, though, he decided to run for president in 2000. He won the election and resigned as governor to assume his new office. As a result, Lieutenant Governor **Rick Perry,** a Republican, became the new governor of Texas. After finishing Bush's term, Perry was re-elected in 2002, 2006, and 2010. He chose not to run again in 2014. In total, Perry was governor of Texas for 14 years, making him the longest-serving governor in the state's history.

As governor, Perry focused largely on economic issues. A strong supporter of business, he invited companies to relocate to or build new operations in Texas. Perry also worked to keep taxes low, resisting efforts by some legislators to create new taxes. For example, he opposed attempts to create a state income tax in Texas. Perry also supported states' rights, protesting federal policies that he saw as interference in the state. As a result, he argued strongly against many federal policies, especially those of President Barack Obama, who was elected in 2008.

Unlike Bush, Perry did not have to work with a Legislature dominated by the opposing party for much of his term. In 1996 the Republican Party had won control of the Texas Senate for the first time since Reconstruction. Although Democrats had held a small majority in the House of Representatives, the Republicans took over the House in 2002. As a result, Perry had little trouble passing legislation that supported Republican policies. In addition, Republicans have held every major office in the state's executive branch since 1994.

Reading Check **Analyzing Information** What goals did Ann Richards, George W. Bush, and Rick Perry set for Texas?

Bob Bullock and the Story of Texas

Bob Bullock loved to read about Texas history. He wanted the state to build a museum that would be "as great as this state is." Bullock convinced state legislators to approve funding for just such a museum. He considered this one of his crowning achievements. The museum—the Bullock Texas State History Museum—opened in April, 2001.

BIOGRAPHY

George W. Bush

(1946–) George Walker Bush was born in Connecticut but grew up in Midland and Houston. In 1994, he defeated Ann Richards in the race for governor of Texas. Bush was re-elected in 1998. During his successful run for the presidency in 2000, Bush called for "compassionate conservatism." His father, former president George H.W. Bush, watched as his son took the oath of office. **What elected office did Bush hold before becoming president?**

★ The Diversifying Texas Economy

During the Richards, Bush, and Perry administrations, Texans worked to diversify the state's economy. This effort was partially in response to the oil bust of the 1980s. At the same time, there was a growing need for new products in both national and international markets.

In 1983, Texas had received more than 25 percent of its income from oil activities. By 1993 that figure had dropped to 7 percent. Many Texans had turned from oil to other industries, such as manufacturing, retail trade, and new high-tech industries. Many Texans had also found work in service industries such as sales and tourism. In addition, the Texas banking industry revived. Texas also developed one of the nation's leading medical technology industries.

High-tech industries such as computers, electronics, and telecommunications experienced dramatic growth in the late 1980s and 1990s. The Dallas–Fort Worth area became a telecommunications and transportation center. Some 500 telecommunications companies in the region employed more than 70,000 people. The growth of communications technologies and the birth of the Internet further spurred the Texas economy. Austin, San Antonio, and Dallas became centers for high-tech manufacturing and computer-related industries.

The 1990s also witnessed the growth of international trade from Texas. In 1994 the North American Free Trade Agreement (NAFTA) took effect. Under this agreement, trade among the United States, Mexico, and Canada became easier. Because of its location, Texas became a major center for trade with Mexico.

The state's diversified economy allowed many Texans to enjoy a high standard of living. It also enabled Texas to compete with other regions of the United States and the world. In 2012 state officials announced that if Texas were a nation, it would be the world's 14th-largest economy.

Reading Check **Analyzing Information** What industries developed in Texas in the 1990s and 2000s?

★ George W. Bush as President

In 2000 Governor George W. Bush of Texas, ran for president against Vice President Al Gore. The race was extremely close. On election night, the voting in some states was so close that no winner could be declared. It soon became clear that Florida's 25 electoral votes would determine the outcome of the election. The popular vote in Florida was so close that state law required the votes to be recounted. A machine recount found that Bush had received a few hundred more votes than Gore. But Gore supporters wanted the votes in four counties to be counted by hand. The Bush campaign challenged this manual recount in court.

After several weeks of debate and suspense, the U.S. Supreme Court ruled that manual recounts could not ensure that all votes would be counted in the same way. Therefore, they ordered the recount to stop. Florida's electoral votes went to Bush, making him the winner of the election. Gore conceded defeat.

Rescue workers dig through the wreckage of the World Trade Center after its collapse.

George W. Bush was sworn into office on January 20, 2001. He soon appointed a number of Texans to key posts, including Rod Paige of Houston as secretary of education. During his two terms in office, Bush enacted many new domestic policies. He reduced taxes on individuals and businesses in an effort to promote economic growth. He also issued an education reform plan called No Child Left Behind. This act created a national set of standards for every student and every school to meet. It also raised funding for schools.

Despite plans for educational and economic reform, President Bush was soon faced with the challenge of confronting **terrorism**—the use of fear or terror to advance political goals. On September 11, 2001, terrorists took control of four commercial airliners and used them as weapons to attack sites in Washington, D.C., and New York City. The hijackers flew an airplane into each of two towers that made up the World Trade Center, an important business center in New York. The resulting fires caused the buildings, among the tallest in the nation, to crumble to the ground. About 2,500 people were killed in the collapsing buildings. Another airplane was flown into the Pentagon, the headquarters of the Department of Defense outside of Washington. A fourth hijacked airplane crashed in a Pennsylvania field.

HISTORIC DOCUMENT

President Bush's Address to the Nation

On September 20, 2001, President George W. Bush addressed Congress and the American people. The following is an excerpt from his speech.

"Tonight we are a country awakened to danger and called to defend freedom. Our grief has turned to anger, and anger to resolution [determination]. Whether we bring our enemies to justice, or bring justice to our enemies, justice will be done. . . .

Every nation, in every region, now has a decision to make. Either you are with us, or you are with the terrorists. From this day forward, any nation that continues to harbor or support terrorism will be regarded by the United States as a hostile regime. . . .

This is the world's fight. This is civilization's fight. This is the fight of all who believe in progress and pluralism, tolerance and freedom. We ask every nation to join us. . . .

The advance of human freedom—the great achievement of our time, and the great hope of every time—now depends on us. Our nation—this generation—will lift a dark threat of violence from our people and our future. We will rally the world to this cause by our efforts, by our courage. We will not tire, we will not falter, and we will not fail."

Analyzing Primary Sources

1. **Analyzing Information** What did President Bush call on other nations to do?
2. **Evaluating** How did the president say the United States would react to terrorist acts?

U.S. officials soon determined that the hijackers were members of a fundamentalist Islamic terrorist group called al Qaeda. The group was led by a wealthy Saudi Arabian exile, Osama bin Laden. Bin Laden and his followers were based in Afghanistan. The Taliban, an extreme Islamic group, ruled the country. After Taliban leaders refused to turn over bin Laden, the United States took military action. In October 2001 the United States attacked Afghanistan and drove the Taliban from power. However, they failed to find and capture bin Laden. The United States then began helping Afghanistan to rebuild and establish a democratic government.

After the attack on Afghanistan, President Bush argued that Saddam Hussein, the dictator of Iraq, posed an immediate threat to U.S. security. When the Persian Gulf War ended in 1991, Saddam had agreed to give up Iraq's weapons of mass destruction—chemical, biological, or nuclear weapons that can kill thousands. However, Saddam failed to fully cooperate with U.N. weapons inspectors.

VIDEO
9/11 Watershed Event

hmhsocialstudies.com

In March, 2003, the United States and a coalition of allies launched a ground attack on Iraq. Saddam's government collapsed, and Saddam was eventually captured. In 2006 an Iraqi court sentenced Saddam to death, and he was executed a short time later. As in Afghanistan, U.S. officials began working with Iraqis to establish a democratic government.

After Bush left office in 2008, the policies he had begun in Iraq and Afghanistan continued for many years. In 2011, U.S. special forces tracked down Osama bin Laden at a camp in Pakistan. During a raid on the camp, bin Laden was killed. U.S. troops remained in Iraq until 2011, when they were withdrawn by President Barack Obama. Troops remained in Afghanistan a few years longer. In 2011 Obama announced that all U.S. forces would leave Afghanistan by 2014.

Reading Check **Analyzing Information** What issues did George W. Bush face as president?

Section 2 Review

hmhsocialstudies.com
ONLINE QUIZ

1. Define and explain:
- bipartisanship
- terrorism

2. Identify and explain the significance of the following:
- George H. W. Bush
- James A. Baker III
- George W. Bush
- Bob Bullock
- Rick Perry

3. Analyzing Information Copy the graphic organizer below. Use it to identify the achievements and leadership qualities of each of the Texans listed in the outer boxes.

4. Finding the Main Idea

a. How did the Texas economy change in the 1990s and 2000s?

b. What happened on September 11, 2001, and how did the Bush presidency respond?

5. Writing and Critical Thinking myWriteSmart

Analyzing Information Write a paragraph describing the effects of major international conflicts during the George W. Bush presidency.

Consider the following:
- the terrorist attacks of September 11
- the War on Terror

Section 3

21st Century Challenges

Main Ideas

1. Migration from within the United States and immigration from other countries have led to population growth in Texas.
2. Water shortages are a problem in Texas today.

Key Terms

- **illegal immigrants**
- **deportation**
- **infrastructure**
- **desalinization**

Why It Matters Today

More than 5 million people from other parts of the country and of the world moved to Texas between 2000 and 2010. Use current events sources to learn more about migration and immigration to Texas today.

TEKS: 7F, 10B, 11A, 11B, 11C, 17A, 20D, 21B, 21C, 22D

myNotebook

Use the annotation tools in your eBook to take notes about issues that Texans face in the 21st century.

The Story Continues

Tom and Debbie Lowell lived near Detroit, Michigan. Tom was laid off from his job as a plumber, and neither he nor Debbie could find another job. They packed all their belongings into their car and headed south for Houston to look for work. When Tom went to his first job interview, the interviewer asked him, "So you've decided to come down to the land of opportunity?"

★ A Growing Population

The arrival of families like the Lowells was a common occurrence in Texas in the late twentieth and early twenty-first centuries. Between 1980 and 2010, the population of Texas swelled from about 14 million people to about 25 million. About half of this increased population came from births. The other half is the result of people moving to Texas, either from other countries or from other parts of the United States. As a result of this growth, Texas has the second-highest population of any state. Only California has more people.

As the state's population grew, so too did the size of Texas cities. By 2005 about 85 percent of Texans lived in cities. Three Texas cities—Houston, San Antonio, and Dallas—have populations of more than 1 million each, placing them among the 10 largest cities in the nation. Another three—Austin, Fort Worth, and El Paso—are home to more than half a million people and growing quickly. All three were among the fastest-growing cities in the United States in 2013.

Interpreting Visuals

Growing Cities. *Texas cities, including Dallas, have grown rapidly in recent years.* ***Based on this photo, what challenges has the growth caused?***

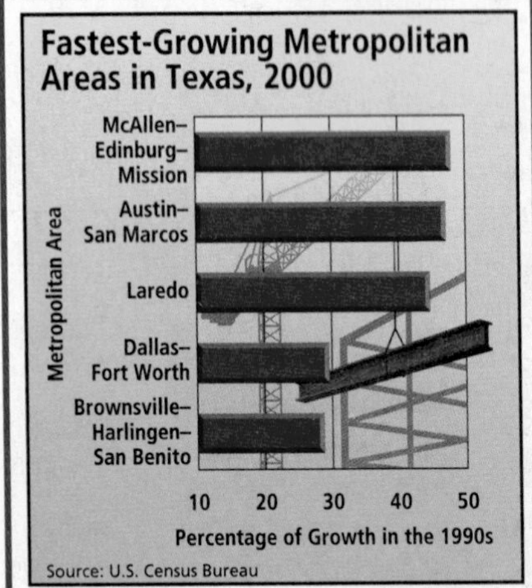

Interpreting Charts Migration and immigration contributed to urban growth in Texas. What was the fastest-growing metropolitan area?

According to 2011 estimates, more than 5 million people living in Texas—about 22 percent of the state's population—were born in other states within the United States. About half a million of them had moved to Texas within the last year. Most of those people moved to Texas for work. Since 2000, whenever the United States as a whole experienced economic difficulties, unemployment rates rose. In Texas, however, the negative effects on the economy were not as severe as in other states. Although some Texas industries felt the effects of the change in the economy, others continued to prosper. The oil and gas and high-tech industries even expanded, creating jobs and drawing people to Texas.

People also move to Texas because the cost of living is lower than in some parts of the country. Homes, for example, cost less on average in Texas than in many states. The absence of a state income tax also appeals to many people.

Texas has also seen a flood of immigrants from other countries. In 2011, about 4 million people—16 percent of the population—had been born in other countries. Like migrants from other states, most foreign-born immigrants come for work, whether as unskilled day laborers or college-educated professionals. Other immigrants come to Texas to go to school or to live with family already in the state.

Although most immigrants follow legal procedures for moving to the United States, some do not. In 2009 the U.S. Department of Homeland Security estimated that about 1.8 million **illegal immigrants** lived in Texas. The largest number was from Mexico, followed by other countries in Latin America. The issue of illegal immigration has been a source of much debate for Texas leaders. Some Texans want to return all illegal immigrants to their home countries, a process known as **deportation**. They argue that illegal immigrants use more in government services than they pay in taxes. Others disagree with deportation. They want to create programs that will help illegal immigrants become U.S. citizens.

Reading Check **Analyzing Information** What factors have drawn people to Texas in recent years?

Effects of Population Growth

As the Texas population has grown, so has the strain on government resources. More people living in the state means the need for an improved **infrastructure**—public works such as roads, bridges, electrical grids, and water systems. For example, the numbers of drivers in Texas has increased as the population has grown. Many of the state's highways were not built to handle the amount of traffic they now have. As a result, traffic congestion has become a problem in many cities.

State and local governments have tried to ease this congestion by building more roads and freeways. In 2012 the state spent more than $4.1 billion on road construction. Some Texas cities have also explored alternative means of public transportation. Dallas, for example, created the Dallas Area Rapid Transit (DART) system. DART consists of buses, light-rail, and vans that carry some 200,000 people per day. Other cities have created similar public transportation systems.

The rising number of people living in Texas has also led to an increase in the demand for services such as education and health care. Between 2000 and 2010 the number of students enrolled in public schools in Texas jumped by nearly 900,000. This has caused a need for more schools as well as more teachers and staff. Some school districts have struggled with paying for such expansions. Likewise, the number of hospitals in the state has increased. Between 2005 and 2011, 17 new hospitals began operations in Texas.

Reading Check **Evaluating** What effects has the growing population had on Texas?

Water Shortages

Another effect of the increasing state population is a strain on the state's water resources. Texas has 14 major rivers, more than 100 lakes, and 23 aquifers. These bodies of water provide most of the drinking water used by Texans, as well as water used in agriculture and other industries. In many cases, however, water is being drained from rivers, lakes, and aquifers faster than it can be replaced.

This drain is due in large part to increased water usage, which has risen tremendously in recent years. Austin, for example, used three times as much water in 2010 as it did in 1970. Part of that increase stems from population growth, but part of it is due to increasing industrial activity. Rice farms along the Gulf coast, for example, draw a huge amount of water from that region's rivers. The oil industry has also become a major user of water. In the early 2000s many oil companies turned to a process called hydraulic fracturing, or fracking, which uses water to draw oil and gas from mineral deposits.

Drought in the early 2000s killed crops across Texas.

★ Texas Cities ★

El Paso

History: In 1659, the Spanish established a mission at the site of present-day Ciudad Juárez, Mexico. In 1682 they built the Corpus Christi de la Ysleta mission—now a part of the city of El Paso.

Population in 2012: 672,538 (estimate)

Relative location: On the Rio Grande in the far western tip of Texas

Region: Mountains and Basins

County: County seat of El Paso County

Origin of name: Spanish explorer Juan de Oñate named a nearby site El Paso del Norte, "The Pass of the North."

Economy: El Paso's economy can be summarized by the "four Cs": cattle, clothing, copper, and cotton. The city is a center for cement manufacturing, cotton ginning, meatpacking, milling, mining operations, and oil refining. El Paso also has a thriving tourism industry.

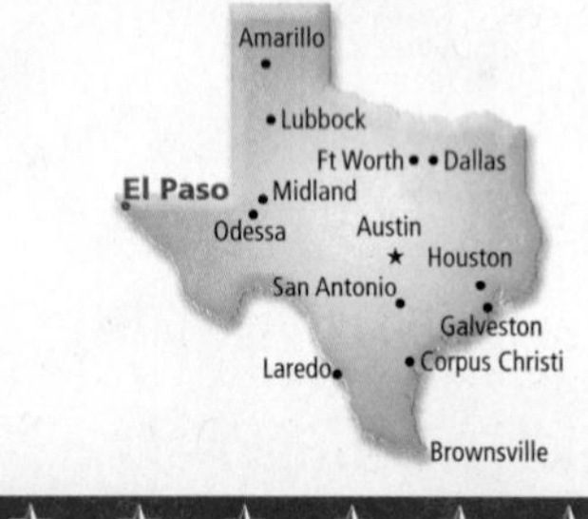

In addition to increased usage, drought has contributed to the state's water shortage. Between 2008 and 2012 much of Texas suffered from one of the worst droughts in state history. The city of El Paso, for example, went 118 days without a drop of rain in 2011. Little rain fell to replace the water drawn from rivers and lakes. As a result, the amount of water in those rivers and lakes dropped quickly. Lake Travis and Lake Buchanan, for example, dipped below 50 percent of their normal water levels. State, county, and city officials implemented measures to restrict water usage, but Texans still suffered. Many farmers and ranchers did not have enough water to keep their crops or their herds alive.

Across the state, Texans are researching ways to deal with future water shortages. Some are looking for ways to store water in case of future droughts. For example, they have proposed creating more reservoirs to store water from rivers before it runs into the Gulf of Mexico.

Others are seeking new sources of water for home or industry use. One possibility is to use water from the Gulf. Before this water could be used for drinking or irrigating crops, though, it would need to undergo **desalinization,** a process that removes salt from seawater. For now, this process is very expensive. In the meantime, cities across Texas are creating water usage plans to protect the needs of residents and businesses both now and in the future.

Reading Check Summarizing What factors have led to water shortages in Texas?

★ Section 3 Review

1. Define and explain:
- illegal immigrants
- deportation
- infrastructure
- desalinization

2. Locate on a Texas map:
- El Paso

3. Summarizing
Use the graphic organizer below to examine reasons for migration and immigration to Texas in the 21st century.

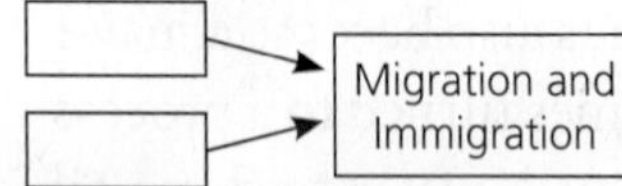

4. Finding the Main Idea
a. What are some issues regarding migration and immigration to Texas?
b. How have water shortages affected Texas?

5. Writing and Critical Thinking *my*WriteSmart
Making Generalizations and Predictions
Explain how migration and immigration have influenced Texas in the 21st century.
Consider the following:
- people's reasons for moving to Texas
- effects on transportation, education, and health care systems

Connecting To

Economics

Employment in Texas

During the 1990s the United States experienced an economic boom. Unemployment fell to its lowest level in years. By 2007, however, times had changed. Businesses were failing, and unemployment was on the rise. A major financial recession had begun. While Texas felt some effects from this recession, it fared better than most other states. Unemployment rates remained lower than the national average, and thousands of people moved to Texas in search of jobs. As a result, the number of people employed in certain industries increased.

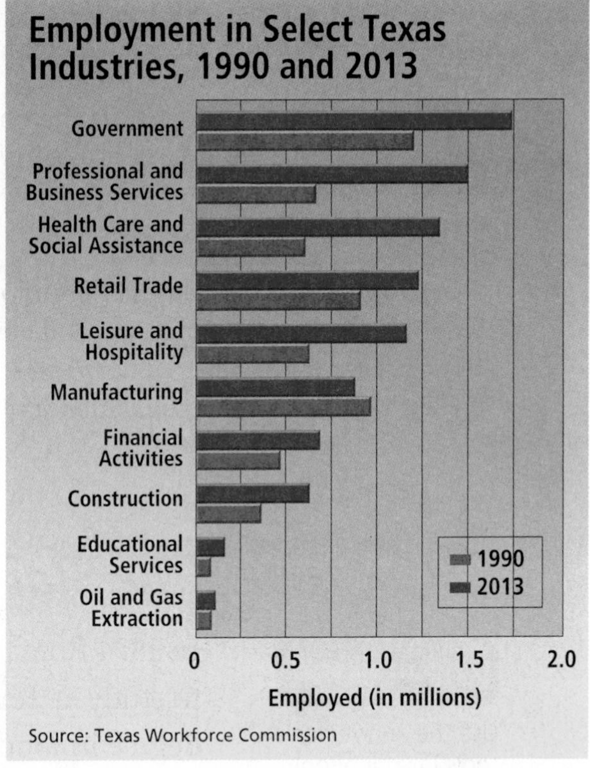

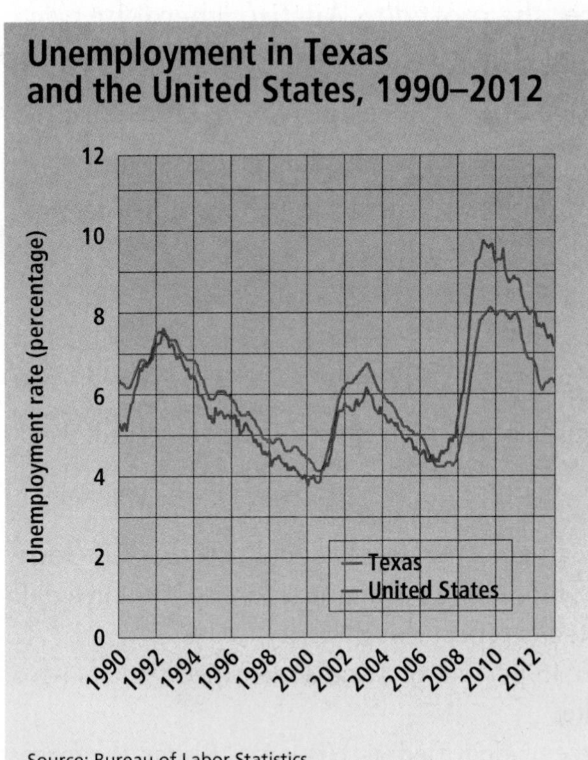

Interpreting Graphs and Charts

1. Which industry witnessed the largest growth in employment between 1990 and 2013?
2. Which industry had fewer workers in 2013 than in 1990?
3. Approximately what percentage of Texans were unemployed in 2007?
4. In what year did the national unemployment rate first exceed the Texas unemployment rate?

Section 4

Cultures of Texas

Main Ideas

1. The Texas population grew and became more diverse in the 1990s.
2. Ethnic groups in Texas celebrate their heritage.
3. Texas musicians, writers, and artists have reflected the state's diversity.

Why It Matters Today

Every 10 years the U.S. census offers information about who Texans are, where they live, and how they work. Use current events sources to learn more about the most recent census and other population statistics.

Key Terms and People

- **Cinco de Mayo**
- **Larry McMurtry**
- **John Graves**
- **Sandra Cisneros**
- **Diane Gonzales Bertrand**
- **John Biggers**
- **Amado Peña Jr.**
- **Willie Nelson**

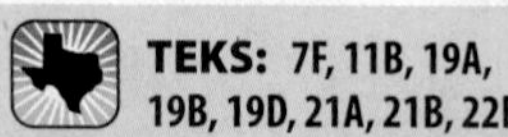

myNotebook

Use the annotation tools in your eBook to take notes on the varied cultures of Texas.

The Story Continues

In 1974 Romannee "Foo" Swasdee left Bangkok, Thailand, to study at Texas A&M University. After earning a doctoral degree in food science, she moved to Austin, where she saw no evidence of the Thai culture she had grown up in. Proud of her heritage, Swasdee opened a restaurant to showcase the foods of Thailand and other parts of Asia. Friends warned her that no one would come, because people were not familiar with Thai food. They were wrong.

★ A Land of Many Cultures

As the population of Texas has grown, its diversity has increased. People from all around the world, like Romannee Swasdee, moved into Texas, adding their own cultures to the mix already in the state. As a result, parts of the state display an amazing degree of cultural diversity today. In Houston, for example, more than 90 languages are spoken on a daily basis. The 2010 census results reflect this diversity.

- Slightly more than 45 percent of Texans identified themselves as non-Hispanic white.
- More than 37 percent identified as Hispanic. By far the largest group within the Hispanic population is of Mexican heritage.
- About 12 percent identified themselves as African American.

- Some 3.8 percent identified as Asian.
- Less than 1 percent identified as American Indian.
- Nearly 3 percent reported belonging to more than one race.

The result of so diverse a population has been the creation of a blended Texas culture. The various groups of people who live in the state have maintained elements of their traditional cultures while also absorbing elements of the cultures of other people. For example, the Tigua Indians, who live outside El Paso, have maintained their own cultural identity while adapting to the other cultures of the area, as a former leader noted.

Analyzing Primary Sources
Drawing Inferences and Conclusions How does Sierra's comment reflect the concept of diversity within unity?

TEXAS VOICES

"We have three cultures that we are trying to fit into: our own, the Spanish, and the American. . . . Some people today even claim that since we speak Spanish, we were never Indian. But, remember that we were Indians before the Spanish came and we conversed first in Tiwa, second in Spanish, and third in English."

—Joe Sierra, quoted in *Exiled: The Tigua Indians of Ysleta del Sur,* by Randy Lee Eickhoff

Today the Tigua operate tourist attractions such as a museum that showcases the group's history. They also celebrate St. Anthony's Day on June 13 every year. On this day, they carry a statue of St. Anthony from their pueblo to their mission. During the ceremony the Tigua also carry a sacred 300-year-old drum. This blending of Catholic and traditional Tigua ceremonies and performances reflects how the Tigua have combined their Spanish and American Indian heritage.

Other groups in Texas also observe special days that remind them of their ethnic heritage. Each year on May 5, Mexican Americans celebrate **Cinco de Mayo.** It was on May 5, 1862, that a Mexican army defeated an invading French force at the Battle of Puebla. Mexican Americans also celebrate Diez y Séis de Septiembre, Mexico's Independence Day.

Other festivals held throughout Texas also celebrate the state's many cultures. The Wurstfest, held every year in New Braunfels, celebrates the state's German heritage. African Americans throughout Texas celebrate Juneteenth on June 19 to mark the day in 1865 when the Emancipation Proclamation was announced in the state, freeing enslaved Texans. These and other celebrations reflect the diversity of the people of Texas.

Reading Check Summarizing What cultural activities, celebrations, and performances reflect the ethnic heritage of Texas?

Interpreting Visuals

Mexican American culture. *Mexican Americans in Texas celebrate holidays with traditional performances and costumes.* ***How are these Mexican American citizens maintaining their cultural heritage?***

 Texans in Art and Literature

Texas writers and artists have also provided the world with glimpses of the state in their work. Pulitzer Prize–winning author **Larry McMurtry** is one of the most well-known Texas writers. He has written several novels about life in Houston and on the Texas frontier. McMurtry once commented on why he writes about the frontier. "It's . . . fun to reinvent a western myth. . . . I'm renovating the cowboy."

A. C. Greene and **John Graves** are two other well-known writers who have observed the effect of the land of Texas on people's lives. Greene once called Graves's book *Goodbye to a River* "the best book ever written about Texas." The internationally known novelist James Michener wrote the novel *Texas* and spent his later years living in Austin.

Other Texas writers focus on the people of Texas. For example, Américo Paredes wrote about the folklore of Mexican Americans. **Sandra Cisneros** and **Diane Gonzales Bertrand** have also received national attention for their works, which focus on the lives of Mexican American families in America. Cisneros writes for adults, while Bertrand writes for children. Poet Carmen Tafolla uses both Spanish and English verse to examine life in San Antonio's Mexican American community.

Texans have also excelled in the visual arts. **John Biggers** of Texas Southern University has produced works of art that portray African American views and experiences. **Amado Peña Jr.** has attempted to capture the Southwest through his depictions of American Indian life. In addition, Texans can view the work of sculptor Charles Umlauf at the Umlauf Sculpture Garden in Austin. Donald C. Judd spent the last years of his life in Marfa, where he designed large sculptures made from industrial metals. These artists and others changed the way Texans have perceived their state.

Reading Check **Categorizing** How is the diversity of Texas reflected in the works of Texas authors and artists?

Connecting To Literature

Larry McMurtry

Larry McMurtry is perhaps the most noted Texas writer today. Many of his works have focused on life on the Texas frontier. In this excerpt from a collection of essays on Texas, In a Narrow Grave, *McMurtry described the importance of the history of the Texas frontier in his works.*

"Myself, I dislike frontiers, and yet the sense that my own has vanished produces in me the strongest emotion I have felt in connection with Texas, or with any place. It has **embedded**[1] itself in the titles of each of my books, and just as I think I have worn the emotion out it seizes me again, usually at some unlikely moment. I see my son, age five, riding a mechanical horse in front of the laundrymat on Sunday morning, and the sight calls up my Uncle Johnny, when he was age five, sitting on top of the McMurtry barn watching the last trail herd go by. It is indeed a complex distance from those traildrivers who made my father and my uncles determined to be cowboys to the mechanical horse that helps convince my son that he is a cowboy, as he takes a vertical ride in front of a laundrymat."

[1]**embedded:** rooted

Understanding What You Read

1. **Literature and History** How do you think the closing of the frontier and the myths and realities of cowboy life have affected McMurtry's stories?
2. **Literature and You** What aspects of Texas life have you seen change, and what stories could be written about those changes?

CONNECTING TO
The Arts

John Biggers

A native of North Carolina, John Biggers established the art department at Texas Southern University in 1949. Biggers became well known for his murals that showed aspects of African American history. Biggers taught his students to look to their African heritage and their local communities for inspiration. **How does this painting focus on Texas culture and daily life?**

★ Music, Popular Culture, and Sports

The Texas music scene also reflects the state's diversity. As author Rick Koster has noted, "Texas is a big state. But regardless of one's background or interests, it's probably possible to find the sort of music you want to hear—and find someone who's . . . good at playing it." Texans have written and performed blues, country, folk, jazz, rap, rock, Tejano, and classical music.

To many Americans, Texas is closely linked with country music. Texans such as George Jones and George Strait perform traditional country music. In the 1970s a group of Texas musicians developed what would become known as progressive country. These performers, who worked in and around Austin, included **Willie Nelson,** Waylon Jennings, and Jerry Jeff Walker. They had a number of hit songs. Nelson's popular "Blue Eyes Crying in the Rain" made him a national star. Lyle Lovett of Klein has also become an internationally known country singer.

Two of Texas's most popular music stars died tragically during the 1990s. Stevie Ray Vaughan, a gifted guitarist, studied the work of blues greats. During the 1980s he released a series of popular albums that combined blues and rock. However, he died in a helicopter crash after a concert in 1990. Selena Quintanilla was born in Lake Jackson in 1971. Her father recognized her musical talent and taught her how to perform. At age 15 Selena won the Tejano Music Award for best female vocalist. She continued to win awards, including a Grammy. Tragically, a member of Selena's business enterprises killed the young star in 1995.

CONNECTING TO
Music

Tejano Music

Tejano music has its roots in the music that Mexican Americans performed in the 1800s. They played Spanish dance music but were also influenced by other European musical styles. As a result, the polkas and waltzes that German and Czech settlers brought to Texas can still be heard in Tejano music. Freddie Fender and Flaco Jimenez are two of the best-known Tejano musicians. "Little" Joe Hernandez of Temple liked traditional Mexican music, rock 'n' roll, and country music. His music paved the way for Tejano stars such as Selena and Emilio Navaira. **How does modern Tejano music reflect a blending of traditional heritage with the larger Texas culture?**

Texas is also home to several outstanding classical musicians. Pianist Van Cliburn of Fort Worth won international acclaim for his performances after winning a prestigious international competition in 1958. In addition, Austin, Dallas, Fort Worth, Houston, and several other cities are home to professional opera companies and symphonies. The Houston Grand Opera, formed in 1955, has won numerous awards for its lavish productions. Many Texas ballet companies have also been recognized for the quality of their performances.

People around the world learned about Texas and Texans from sources other than music. During the 1980s the popular TV show *Dallas* brought worldwide attention to the state. Starring Larry Hagman of Weatherford, the show told the story of a fictional wealthy Texas oil and ranching family. Later series such as *King of the Hill* and *Friday Night Lights* also portrayed Texas life for national audiences.

Texans have also been involved in making TV shows and movies. Austin and Dallas are both home to thriving film industries, and more movies are shot in the state each year. Texas directors such as Robert Rodriguez, Richard Linklater, and Mike Judge have won national and international acclaim. People throughout the world continue to enjoy movies that are about Texas or that are made in the state.

Among the most popular forms of entertainment in Texas today is sports. The state is home to many professional sports teams in such sports as football, men's and women's basketball, baseball, soccer, and hockey. In addition, many universities have well-established sports programs for both men and women. Texas college teams compete in sports ranging from football, basketball, and baseball to volleyball, swimming, and track and field. In addition, thousands of Texans attend middle school and high school sporting events each week.

Reading Check **Drawing Inferences and Conclusions** What does Texas music and popular culture reveal about the state?

Section 4 Review

hmhsocialstudies.com
ONLINE QUIZ

1. Define:
- Cinco de Mayo

2. Identify and explain:
- Larry McMurtry
- John Graves
- Sandra Cisneros
- Diane Gonzales Bertrand
- John Biggers
- Amado Peña Jr.
- Willie Nelson

3. Analyzing Information
Copy the graphic organizer below. Use it to show how Texas musicians, writers, and artists reflect the diversity of Texas.

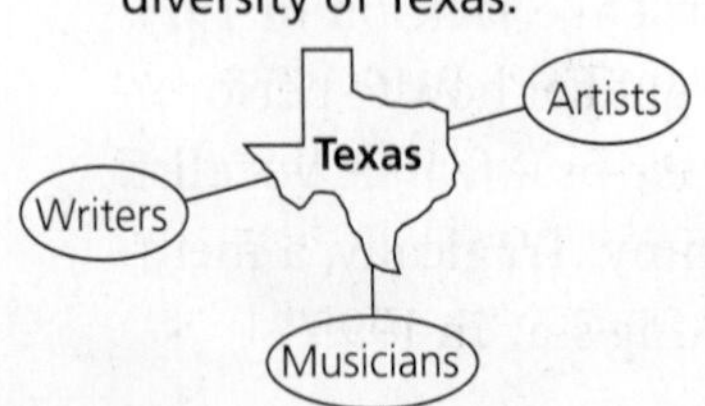

4. Finding the Main Idea
a. What has led to the created of a blended culture in Texas?
b. How do Texans celebrate their ethnic heritage?

5. Writing and Critical Thinking myWriteSmart
Summarizing Write a short story about how life in Texas has changed over time. Consider the following:
- the state's history
- the people of Texas

Texas Faces the Future

Main Ideas

1. Several challenges face Texas as it moves into the future.
2. Texans have taken steps to protect their environment.

Why It Matters Today

Companies and individuals across Texas have made great strides in harnessing the power of water, wind, and the sun as new sources of energy. Use current event sources to find information about new research into alternative sources of energy and how they will affect Texas.

Key Terms and People

- **biomass**
- **wind farms**
- **globalization**
- **Texas Commission on Environmental Quality**
- **Foreign-Trade Zones**

TEKS: 7F, 9C, 10B, 17A, 20A, 20C, 20D, 20E, 21B, 22D

myNotebook

Use the annotation tools in your eBook to take notes on the issues Texas faces as it prepares for the future.

The Story Continues

According to Cliff Etheredge, the people of Roscoe, Texas, used to hate the wind of West Texas. It blew constantly, killing much of their cotton crop and pulling moisture out of the land. In 2008, though, Etheredge and some partners developed a plan to harness the wind. They worked with an Irish company to install huge turbines that could harness the power of wind to create electricity. Roscoe became the site of what was then the largest wind farm in the world.

New Sources of Energy

Wind farms like the one in Roscoe are part of a state- and nationwide effort to develop new sources of energy. Historically, Texas has gotten most of its energy through the burning of fossil fuels, such as coal, oil, and natural gas. The state's huge oil and gas deposits have supplied most of its needs, as well as the needs of other parts of the country and the world. However, the world's oil and gas deposits are not limitless. They will run out someday. Before that happens, Texans—and the rest of the world—will need to rely on other sources of energy.

One potential source of energy is nuclear power. As of 2013, two nuclear plants operated in Texas, producing nearly 10 percent of the state's electricity. Supporters of nuclear power point out that it causes less pollution than fossil fuel burning. Opponents, however, fear that accidents or disposal of hazardous wastes could release radiation.

Many Texans are also looking to renewable energy sources, those that do not depend on limited resources like oil, gas, or nuclear material. For example, some new power plants generate energy from **biomass**—plant material and animal waste—rather than fossil fuels. Others harness the power of rivers to generate hydroelectricity. Many cities, businesses, and individuals have also installed solar panels to turn the sun's energy into electricity.

The most successful form of renewable energy in Texas today is wind power. Several companies have built **wind farms** in West Texas. These wind farms depend on the near constant winds of the Texas prairie to move turbines that generate electricity. Since 2002 the number of wind farms in Texas has grown rapidly. As a result, Texas now produces more wind power than any other state.

Reading Check **Analyzing Information** What are some new sources of energy that are being developed in Texas?

★ Protecting The Environment

As the Texas population has grown, so has demand on water and other natural resources. Texas leaders have worked hard to manage the state's resources. They do so to ensure that the people and businesses of Texas will have enough water to meet their needs.

In some parts of the state, air and water pollution have become an issue. Stopping pollution has become a goal for many Texans and other Americans. To help in this effort, the state created the **Texas Commission on Environmental Quality.** This commission tries to balance the increased costs businesses must bear to protect the environment with efforts to safeguard the state's air and water. It tracks air and water quality and enforces state and federal regulations regarding the environment. Through the combined efforts of citizens, businesses, and government, Texans are working to have a cleaner environment as well as a strong economy.

Reading Check **Analyzing Information** How has economic and population growth affected the state's natural resources?

Interpreting Visuals

Wind farms. *The Horse Hollow Wind Energy Center is a wind farm in Taylor and Nolan counties.* ***How have Texans adapted to their natural environment?***

Globalization

During the late 1900s and early 2000s the nations of the world became increasingly interdependent as goods, ideas, and people moved all across the globe. This process of **globalization** has boosted the state's economy as Texas businesses have gained greater access to global markets. This also means that Texas industries are sometimes affected by international events. For example, when Mexico experienced a financial crisis in 1995, computer exports from Texas to that country fell. Even so, the Texas economy has generally benefited from global interdependence. Many nations have offices in Texas to improve trade with the state. Texas also maintains several **Foreign-Trade Zones.** These are areas in which export regulations are reduced to promote trade. The increased trade in these areas has boosted the state's economy.

The state government has also played a role in advancing globalization. This has helped Texas become a major exporter of goods. In fact, Houston ranked first among exporting cities in the United States in 2013. Interaction between people from different parts of the world is not new, of course. Author Gordon Bennett noted that Texas had long been involved in international events.

CONNECTING TO

SCIENCE AND TECHNOLOGY

Our Future

The growth of the Internet has changed how many Texans study, work, and spend their leisure time. The Internet has become an important research tool for Texas businesses, scholars, and students. Today Texas remains a leader in producing computer and communications technologies. **How might future computer and other technological innovations affect the Texas economy and society?**

TEXAS VOICES

"Pioneer settlers represented many European nationalities: German, Norwegian, Scot, Swedish, and more. . . . Our premier oil and gas industry ebbs and flows with Middle Eastern production and international demand. Houston and Dallas are world trade centers."

—Gordon Bennett, *Global Connections*

Reading Check **Finding the Main Idea** How has globalization transformed the Texas economy?

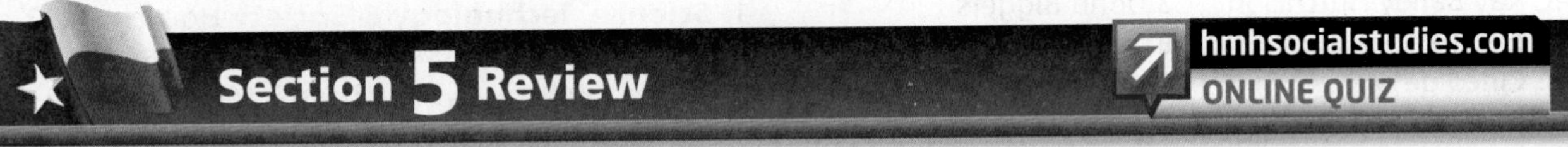

1. **Define and explain:**
   - biomass
   - wind farms
   - globalization
   - Foreign-Trade Zones
2. **Identify and explain** the significance of the following:
   - Texas Commission on Environmental Quality
3. **Summarizing** Copy the graphic organizer below. Use it to explain some of the challenges Texans face in the 2000s.

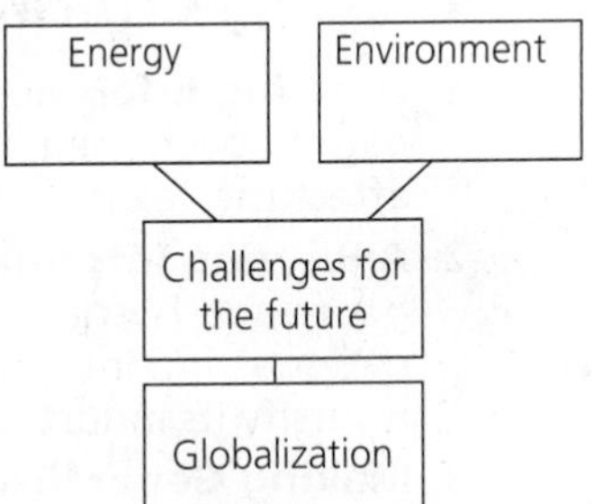

4. **Finding the Main Idea**
   - **a.** How might the search for new sources of energy affect the Texas economy?
   - **b.** What are some of the environmental consequences of the state's growth?
5. **Writing and Critical Thinking** *my* WriteSmart

   Analyzing Information Imagine you are a reporter for a Texas newspaper. Write an article describing the challenges of the future.

   Consider the following:
   - the benefits and consequences of economic and population growth
   - the economic, social, and environmental consequences that may result from future discoveries and technological innovations

The Chapter at a Glance

Examine the following visual summary of the chapter. Then, with a partner, take turns summarizing orally the information included in the chapter.

The boom in the computer and medical technology industries led to new jobs and a growing economy in the 1990s. NAFTA also affected the Texas economy as international trade expanded.

A growing population has contributed to cultural diversity in Texas and to the state's growing economy.

During the 1980s Republicans gained increasing power in Texas politics. Texas Republicans, George H.W. Bush and his son George W. Bush were elected president in 1988 and 2000, respectively.

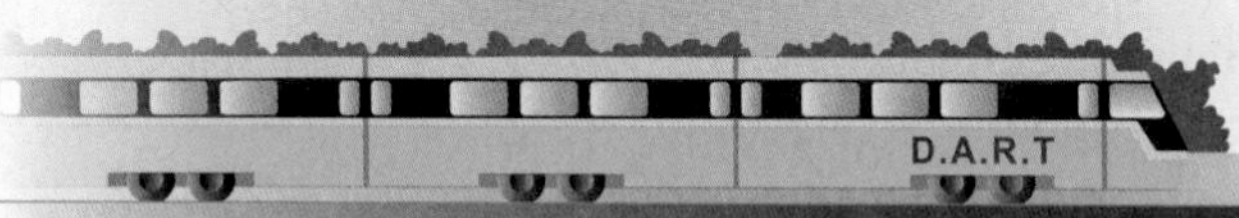

Education, transportation, globalization, and population growth will all be important issues to the next generation of Texans.

Identifying People and Ideas

Write a sentence to explain the role or significance of each of the following terms or people.

1. George W. Bush
2. Rick Perry
3. Kay Bailey Hutchison
4. two-party system
5. Cinco de Mayo
6. Amado Peña Jr.
7. Larry McMurtry
8. John Biggers
9. wind farms
10. globalization

Understanding Main Ideas

Section 1

1. What is a two-party system, and how has it affected Texas politics?
2. What happened to the oil industry in the 1980s?

Section 2

3. What leadership qualities did the two presidents Bush display while in office?
4. How did George W. Bush respond to terrorism?

Section 3

5. How have immigration and migration affected transportation systems in Texas?

Section 4

6. What contributions have Texans Diane Gonzales Bertrand and Sandra Cisneros made to the arts?

Section 5

7. How has globalization affected Texas?

You Be the Historian

Reviewing Themes

1. **Science, Technology & Society** How has technology changed the lives of Texans?
2. **Global Relations** How have international events affected the Texas economy in the late 1900s and early 2000s?
3. **Culture** How is the diversity of Texas reflected in a variety of cultural activities, celebrations, and performances?

Thinking Critically

1. **Drawing Inferences and Conclusions** How might government protection of the environment affect the Texas economy?
2. **Analyzing Information** Explain how the state's boom-and-bust economy and the demands of national and international markets led Texas to diversify its industrial base.
3. **Making Generalizations and Predictions** List characteristics of Contemporary Texas.

Texas Test Practice

Interpreting Databases

The database below lists the racial makeup of the 12 largest counties in Texas in 2012. Use it to answer the questions that follow.

Racial Makeup of Select Counties, 2012 (in percentages)

County	White	Hispanic	African American	Asian	American Indian
Harris	32.2	41.5	19.5	6.6	1.1
Dallas	32.2	38.9	22.9	5.5	1.1
Tarrant	50.7	27.4	15.6	5.0	0.9
Bexar	29.8	59.1	8.1	2.7	1.2
Travis	50.1	33.8	9.0	6.1	1.4
El Paso	13.7	81.2	3.9	1.2	1.0
Denton	63.2	18.7	9.2	7.1	0.9
Hidalgo	7.5	90.9	0.8	1.1	0.5
Collin	61.8	15.0	9.2	12.0	0.7
Fort Bend	35.7	24.0	21.4	18.1	0.6
Cameron	10.3	88.4	0.8	0.8	0.6
Nueces	31.9	61.5	4.3	1.9	0.8

1. Which county had the highest percentage of African American residents?
- **A** Tarrant
- **B** Fort Bend
- **C** Hidalgo
- **D** Dallas

2. Organize the counties by region, such as East Texas, West Texas, and so on. In which region are the highest Hispanic populations found?

Analyzing Primary Sources

Read the following quote from George H. W. Bush. Then answer the questions.

"Great nations of the world are moving toward democracy through the door to freedom. Men and women of the world move toward free markets through the door to prosperity. The people of the world agitate for free expression and free thought through the door to the . . . satisfaction that only liberty allows. We know what works: Freedom works."

3. Which of the following statements best describes Bush's point of view?
- **F** Free markets do not help the people of the world.
- **G** The people of the world are not calling for more freedom.
- **H** Freedom and free markets will help people.
- **J** Few of the world's great nations are moving toward democracy.

4. How does Bush believe free markets will affect people throughout the world?

Linking to Community

Many communities hold celebrations or performances to recognize their ethnic and cultural heritage. Contact your local chamber of commerce, tourist bureau, or a person familiar with the activities of your community. Ask them to describe a local performance or celebration related to the community's past and heritage. Find out whether the person you are speaking with has firsthand information about what you need to know. Create a poster that advertises the event, focusing on the community's cultural heritage.

Internet Activity 

Access the Internet to locate databases and media sources on the Texas economy and settlement. Analyze and interpret the data you locate to determine patterns in where people lived and how they worked. Then create a new database that contrasts economic trends and geographic patterns of the 1980s with those of today. Create a graph to represent the statistical information in your database.

Social Studies Skills

WORKSHOP

Distinguishing Fact from Opinion and Identifying Bias

Historical sources may contain both facts and opinions. Such sources as diaries, letters, and speeches express historical figures' personal views. The ability to distinguish facts from opinions is very important. It allows you to judge the accuracy of an argument or the reliability of a historical account. A document that is mostly opinions is probably not a good source for learning about what really happened.

Any piece that contains opinions, whether it is written, spoken, or visual, may also contain bias—prejudices or strong feelings about a group or issue. Modern historians try to be impartial when writing about the past. People in the past did not always feel the need to be impartial. When reading historical sources, try to identify any biases the writer may have. Many famous historical people had strong opinions that appear in their writings, speeches, and art. Remember that just because a person is famous does not mean that you must agree with his or her opinions.

How to Distinguish Fact from Opinion

1. **Identify the facts.** Ask yourself whether the statement be proven. Determine whether the idea can be checked for accuracy in a source such as an almanac or encyclopedia. If so, the statement concerns a factual matter. If not, it probably contains an opinion.
2. **Identify the opinions.** Look for clues that indicate a statement of opinion. These clues include phrases such as *I think* and *I believe,* comparative words like *greatest* and *more important,* and value-filled words like *extremely* and *ridiculous.* All of these words imply a judgment and, thus, an opinion.

How to Identify Bias

1. **Evaluate the information presented.** What are the sources of information? How reliable are they? Why might a historical figure have supported one view over another? Be sure to distinguish between provable facts and someone's opinions.
2. **Make your own judgment.** Remember that many of the historical documents you read are created by people who have their own opinions and points of view. It is up to you to read each document critically and to draw your own conclusions.

Practicing the Skill

Read the excerpt below, in which Justice Abe Fortas describes Lyndon Johnson, and then answer the questions that follow.

"He was a very emotional man and a very sensitive man, a man of enormous power, power that was communicated to others. There was a physical element in his communication of power. There was also an element of his own dedication and his own immense commitment to achieve a chosen objective. Johnson was fervently result-oriented."

1. Is this excerpt an example of a fact or an opinion? Which words let you know?
2. Compare this excerpt to other sources on Lyndon Johnson. Also find information about Abe Fortas. How can what you have learned help you evaluate the validity of the excerpt?

History in Action

UNIT 9 SIMULATION

You Make the Decision . . .

Should your family move to a city?

Complete the following activity in small cooperative groups. It is 1943. Because of the military's need for weapons and supplies, industry in Texas has boomed. Many Texans have moved from rural areas to the state's cities to take advantage of the strong job markets there. Other Texans have chosen to stay on farms and ranches. You have to decide whether your family will move to a city. You have to prepare a presentation that will convince the rest of your family that your decision is best for them. Follow these steps to reach your decision.

1. Gather information. Use your textbook and other resources to find information that might help you decide whether to move to a Texas city. Be sure to use what you've learned from this unit's Skills Workshop on Distinguishing Fact from Opinion and Identifying Bias to help you make an informed decision. You may want to divide different parts of the research among group members.

2. Identify options. Based on the information you have gathered, consider the options you might recommend for moving or not moving to a city. Your final decision may be easier to reach if you consider as many options as possible. Be sure to record your possible options for your presentation.

3. Predict consequences. Now take each option you and your group came up with and consider the possible outcomes of each course of action. Ask yourselves questions such as, "What job opportunities are available in a city that are not available where we now live?" Once you have predicted the consequences, record them as notes for your presentation.

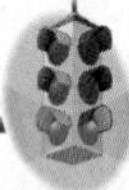

4. Take action to implement your decision. After you have considered your options, plan and create your presentation. Be sure to make your decision very clear. You will need to support your decision by including information you gathered and by explaining why you rejected other options. Your presentation needs to be visually appealing to gain the support of your family. When you are ready, decide who in your group will make each part of the presentation, and then take your decision to your family (the rest of the class). **As an audience member,** listen carefully to the words the presenter uses. Notice any connecting words used to link ideas, because these can show how ideas are related. As each group finishes, write a brief summary of what you have heard. After all groups have finished, refer to your summaries to help you decide whether each group was convincing.

UNIT 10

Handbook of Texas

(1845–PRESENT)

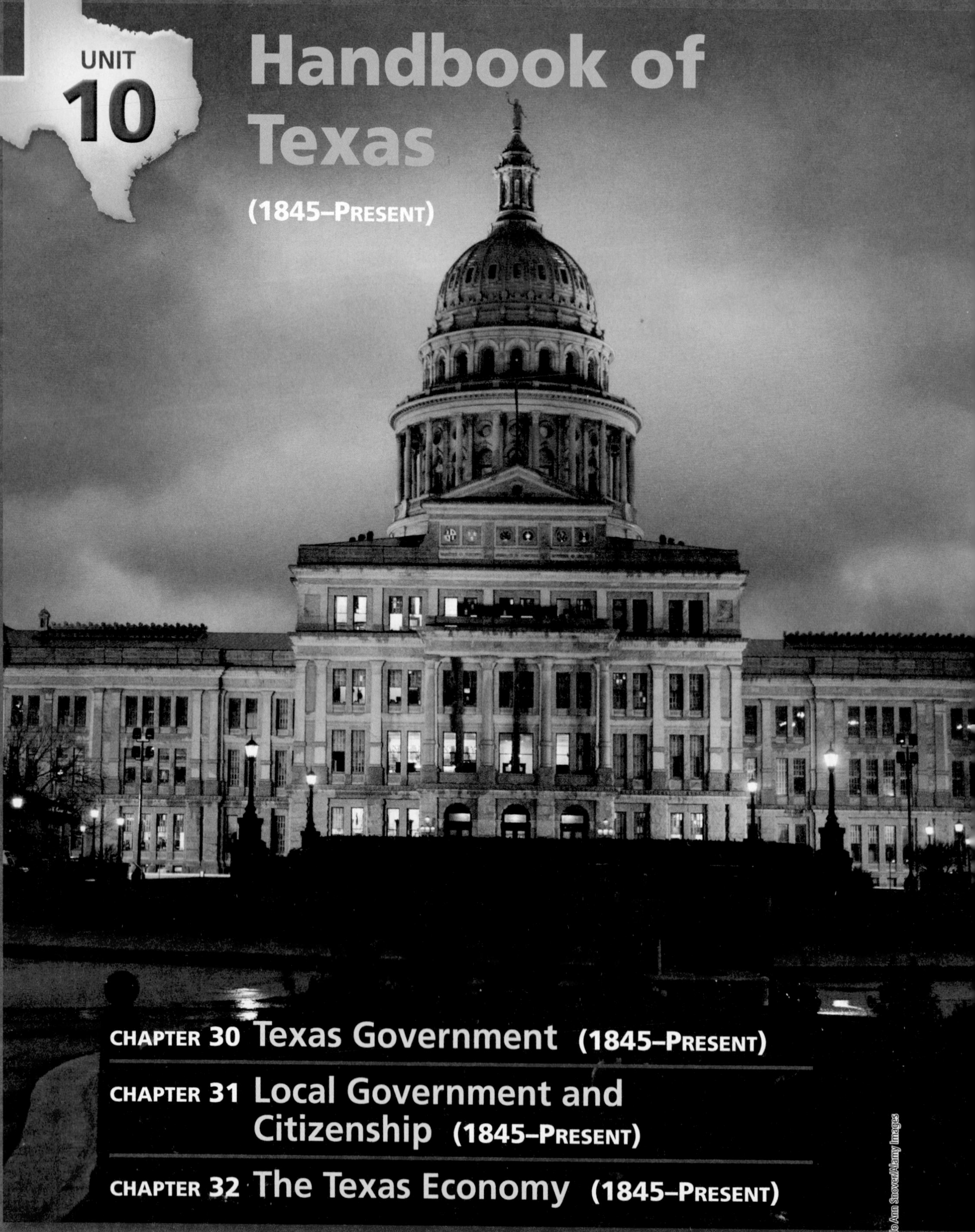

CHAPTER 30 Texas Government (1845–PRESENT)

CHAPTER 31 Local Government and Citizenship (1845–PRESENT)

CHAPTER 32 The Texas Economy (1845–PRESENT)

The Texas Capitol houses both the Texas Legislature and the governor's office and is the site of many state government meetings.

Image Credit: ©Jo Ann Snover/Alamy Images

Texas Teens

Young Politicians

In 2013 Emily Resendez from Rockdale got a rare opportunity to take part in state government. A student at the Sacred Heart School, Emily was taking part in the Texas Senate's Page for a Day program. This program allows students between the ages of 6 and 18 to get a first-hand look at the workings of the state government. Pages work with Senate messengers to run errands for members of the legislature. Participants in the program are selected by members of the state Senate.

Older students who want to learn about the workings of the state government can take part in the Boys State and Girls State programs. These programs are run by the American Legion and the American Legion Auxiliary for high school juniors who are interested in government. Participants form mock governments and take on the roles of city and state leaders. Members of the mock legislature, for example, meet to debate and vote on proposed laws, which are then sent to the student governor for approval. Participants in Boys State and Girls State must be nominated by their high schools.

College students in Texas can apply to work as legislative interns. An internship gives students an opportunity to work with elected officials and learn about the government while earning college credit. While the legislature is in session, interns work closely with state officials, including legislators, the governor, and Supreme Court justices. When the legislature is not in session, they work in the offices of state, city, and county officials. As a result, an intern can learn about all levels of Texas government. Each internship lasts one semester. **How can Texas teens use these and similar programs to learn about the government and future of the state?**

In this unit you will learn about the Texas government and economy. You will also learn about the rights and responsibilities of citizenship and other aspects of Texas politics.

The Texas Capitol

The Texas Capitol in Austin is the seat of State government—the place where Texas legislators meet to propose, debate, and pass laws. An inspiring structure, the Capitol stands as a symbol of both democracy and the rule of law.

Designed by Elijah E. Myers, the Texas Capitol was built between 1882 and 1888 in the Renaissance Revival style and was modeled after the national Capitol in Washington, D.C. A truly impressive public building, the Texas Capitol is the largest state capitol in total square footage and is slightly taller than the national Capitol. The original structure had 392 rooms, 924 windows, and 404 doors!

In February 1888, as the building was nearing completion, a statue called the Goddess of Liberty was placed atop the dome. The Goddess was made of galvanized iron and zinc coated with paint and sand to look like stone. It was nearly 16 feet tall and weighed about 2,000 pounds. The statue's exaggerated features were designed to be viewed from a distance of several hundred feet.

In 1983, nearly a century after it was built, a fire seriously damaged part of the building. The fire led to an effort to restore the Capitol. One of the first restoration projects was to replace the Goddess of Liberty, which had begun to deteriorate. In 1985 it was removed and replaced with a corrosion-resistant replica made of aluminum. The original statue was later moved to the Bullock Texas State History Museum, where it stands on permanent display.

Exploring Museum Resources

The Texas Capitol was named a National Historic Landmark in 1986 for its significant contribution to American history. Learn more about this amazing building and the story of its construction and restoration. You can find a museum resources at

hmhsocialstudies.com

Photograph Just how tall is the Texas Capitol? How did the State of Texas pay for its construction? Go online to find out.

Artifact How did workers remove the Goddess of Liberty from the Texas Capitol?

Photograph How much did the renovation and restoration of the Texas Capitol cost, and what changes were made to the building?

Reading Social Studies

Summarizing

Focus on Reading When you are reading a long section of text, such as a chapter in a textbook, it can be hard to remember everything you read. Sometimes it can be easier to remember the important information if you write a short summary of the passage.

Understanding Summarizing A **summary** is a short restatement of the most important ideas in a text. When you summarize, you can use some of the key ideas and words from the passage to write your own sentences that explain the information. Less important details can be left out.

The example below shows three steps you can use to write a summary. First underline important details. Then write a short summary of each paragraph. Finally, combine these paragraph summaries into a short summary of the whole passage.

Political participation is an important duty of citizens in a democracy. Political parties are one way for citizens to participate. Political parties organize to nominate and elect government officials and to shape government policy. Delegates are elected or appointed to attend their party's convention, where they decide the party's platform, or stated goals. Delegates also nominate candidates for office and elect party officers.

The two major political parties in Texas—and the United States—are the Democratic Party and the Republican Party. The Democratic Party dominated Texas politics for about 100 years after Reconstruction. Texas was virtually a one-party state during this time. Since the late 1970s the Republicans have held many statewide offices, and Texas has become a two-party state.

Summary of paragraph 1
By participating in political parties, citizens can help elect candidates and shape government policy.

Summary of paragraph 2
Two parties, the Democratic and Republican parties, shape Texas politics today.

Combined summary
Texans can join the Democratic or Republican parties to help elect officials and shape policy.

You Try It!

The following passage is from the unit you are about to read. As you read it, think about what you would include in a summary.

The Two Houses

The House of Representatives is one part of the legislative branch of Texas, described in Article III of the Texas Constitution. The legislative branch makes the laws that govern the state. Like the U.S. Congress, the Texas legislature is bicameral, or made up of two houses: the House of Representatives and the Senate. The House has 150 members, called representatives, who serve two-year terms. The Senate has 31 members, called senators, who serve four-year terms.

After you read the passage, read the following summaries and decide which one is the better summary statement. Explain your answer.

1. The Texas Constitution established a two-house legislature that includes a House of Representatives and a Senate.

2. The Texas legislature is described in the state Constitution. It has two houses. The House of Representatives has 150 members and the Senate has 31 members. Representatives serve for two years. Senators serve for four years.

Reading Section Assessment

1. What is the purpose of a summary?

2. What are some characteristics of a good summary?

3. How can summarizing help you make sense of what you read?

Key Terms

Unit 10

Chapter 30

limited government *(p. 641)*
checks and balances *(p. 642)*
bicameral *(p. 644)*
line-item veto *(p. 649)*
appellate courts *(p. 653)*
civil law *(p. 653)*
criminal law *(p. 653)*
judicial review *(p. 654)*

Chapter 31

precincts *(p. 662)*
home-rule charters *(p. 664)*
slander *(p. 667)*
libel *(p. 667)*
due process *(p. 667)*
eminent domain *(p. 667)*
referendum *(p. 670)*
interest groups *(p. 672)*
lobby *(p. 672)*
political action committees *(p. 673)*

Chapter 32

free enterprise *(p. 678)*
profit *(p. 678)*
supply *(p. 679)*
demand *(p. 680)*
competition *(p. 680)*
information technology *(p. 686)*
semiconductors *(p. 686)*
dot-coms *(p. 686)*
maquiladoras *(p. 692)*
embargo *(p. 692)*

As you read, use context clues to help you figure out the meaning of unfamiliar words and phrases. Context clues can help you comprehend challenging language.

CHAPTER 30

Texas Government

(1845–Present)

Texas Essential Knowledge and Skills (TEKS) 1B, 8A, 9A, 14A, 14B, 15A, 15B, 15C, 16B, 17B, 17C, 18A, 21A, 21B, 21C, 21E, 22A, 22B, 22C, 22D

Construction began on the Texas Governor's Mansion in 1854.

TEXAS

1845
On December 29 the U.S. Congress officially admits Texas to the Union and approves its first state constitution.

1876
Texans adopt the constitution that governs the state today.

1890
James Stephen Hogg—the first native-born Texan to become governor—is elected.

1915
The Texas legislature passes the first state law requiring children to attend school.

1845 — 1865 — 1885 — 1905 — 1925

U.S. and WORLD

1861
The Civil War breaks out in the United States between the North and the South.

1886
The Statue of Liberty, a gift from France to the United States, is installed on what is now Liberty Island.

1924
U.S. citizenship is granted to all American Indians born in the United States.

As a Texan . . .
How are you affected by government?

Build on What You Know

Since their state's founding, Texans have taken an active role in their government and its day-to-day processes. Many aspects of government have changed over the years. But the state's fundamental law, the Texas Constitution, has guided the state for more than 125 years.

Built in 1885, the Texas State Capitol houses the state government. Both legislative chambers and the governor's office are inside.

Texas courts apply and interpret state law to decide legal cases.

1945 | 1965 | 1985 | 2005 | Present

1954 The U.S. Supreme Court's ruling in *Brown* v. *Board of Education* leads to the racial integration of American public schools.

1955 Women are allowed to serve on Texas juries for the first time.

1974 A major attempt to adopt a new Texas constitution fails.

1981 Sandra Day O'Connor becomes the first woman appointed to the U.S. Supreme Court.

1991 The Soviet Union dissolves, and many of the republics become independent nations.

2000 The Texas state government employs more than 230,000 people in more than 200 agencies, with a two-year budget totaling more than $98 billion.

2001 The U.S. government passes the No Child Left Behind Act to regulate education.

2008 Rick Perry becomes the longest-serving governor in Texas history. He was elected governor again in 2010.

You Be the Historian

myNotebook

What's Your Opinion? Do you agree or disagree with the following statements? Support your point of view in your notebook.

- **Constitutional Heritage** State constitutions rarely reflect the influence of other constitutions.
- **Government** A weak leader results in an ineffective government.
- **Economics** All government agencies should receive equal amounts of money.

Section 1

The Texas Constitution

Main Ideas

1. Ideas from the U.S. Constitution have influenced the Texas Constitution.
2. The Texas Constitution is based on several key principles intended to protect the rights of citizens.
3. The Texas Constitution includes a bill of rights to protect people's freedoms.

Key Terms

- **federalism**
- **republicanism**
- **limited government**
- **separation of powers**
- **checks and balances**
- **veto**
- **amendments**

Why It Matters Today

The Texas Constitution shapes the state government and sets out the basic laws of the state. Use current events sources to examine the relationship between government and the law.

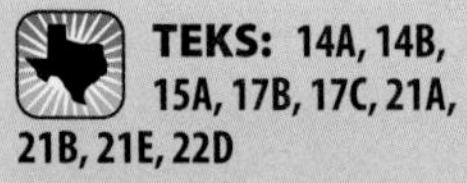

TEKS: 14A, 14B, 15A, 17B, 17C, 21A, 21B, 21E, 22D

myNotebook

Use the annotation tools in your eBook to take notes on the Texas Constitution.

The Story Continues

In 1875 delegates from around Texas met in Austin to rewrite the state's constitution. For more than 12 weeks, they met, debated, and revised the document that would define the state's government. Eventually, they created a document that was approved by the state's voters. More than 100 years later, this constitution is still in effect.

Basic Principles of Government

The Texas Constitution is the basis of the state's government and provides the fundamental, or basic, law of the state. It was approved in 1876 and is the fifth constitution Texas has had as a state. It is modeled after the Texas Constitution of 1845, which had been modeled after the U.S. Constitution. As a result, today's Texas Constitution reflects several principles found in the U.S. Constitution. Among them are popular sovereignty, republicanism, limited government, separation of powers, checks and balances, federalism, and protection of individual rights.

As a state, Texas is subject to the laws of the United States. Nothing in the state constitution can contradict federal law. At the same time, however, the U.S. Constitution grants certain authority to state governments. This division of authority between two levels of government is called **federalism**. Some powers, like coining money, belong only to the federal government. Others, like establishing school systems, are only given to state governments. Some powers are shared—for example, both the federal and state governments can collect taxes.

Popular sovereignty is the idea that political power comes from the people. The government exists because people agree to be governed. Should people become dissatisfied with the government, they have the right to change it. Popular sovereignty is the basis of both the U.S. and Texas governments. The Texas Constitution clearly states this principle.

TEXAS VOICES

"All political power is inherent in the people, and all free governments are founded on their authority, and instituted [created] for their benefit. The faith of the people of Texas stands pledged to the preservation of a republican form of government, and, subject to this limitation only, they have at all times the inalienable [undeniable] right to alter, reform or abolish their government in such manner as they may think expedient [proper]."

—Texas Constitution, art. 1, sec. 2

Analyzing Primary Sources
Finding the Main Idea What principles of government are outlined in this passage?

Because Texans give the state government its authority, the constitution is sometimes called the people's document. Its purpose is to serve Texans, protect individual rights, and promote the common good.

As the passage above notes, republicanism is central to the Texas Constitution. **Republicanism** is a system in which voters elect officials to represent them in the government. These officials are then responsible to voters. Both Texas and the United States have republican governments.

The writers of the Texas Constitution did not want the state government to be too powerful. For example, they did not want the state to be able to take away individual rights, such as the right to free speech. As a result, they created a **limited government**, or one with specific limits on its power.

Reading Check **Finding the Main Idea** How does the Texas Constitution reflect the principles of popular sovereignty?

Image Credit: ©Michael Ainsworth/Dallas Morning News/Corbis

Interpreting Visuals

Principles of democracy. *Rick Perry took an oath of office in January 2011 after being elected governor for the third time.* ***What in this photo reflects the importance of the office Perry is assuming?***

GLOBAL CONNECTIONS

English Common Law

English common law—law made primarily by judges—developed from England's early traditions and customs. The common law tradition heavily influenced U.S. and Texas law. For example, the Texas Constitution includes such common-law principles as the right to a jury trial and the right to bail. In 1840 Texas officially adopted English common law, replacing the Mexican law that had been in force before that time. The common law tradition is still the basis for the Texas legal system. **What is the legacy of English common law?**

★ Balancing Governmental Power

In order to keep balance in the government, the Constitution creates a **separation of powers.** It divides power among different government branches. This separation helps prevent any one branch from becoming too powerful. Article II of the Texas Constitution divides state government into three branches—legislative, executive, and judicial. This structure matches that of the U.S. government. Each branch has different powers and duties.

- The legislative branch makes laws. It consists of the two houses of the state legislature—the Senate and the House of Representatives.
- The executive branch carries out laws. The governor is the head of the executive branch.
- The judicial branch, or court system, interprets laws. In includes all courts in the state.

To further balance power, the Texas government employs a system of **checks and balances**. Under this system, each branch has ways to check, or restrain, the other two. These checks help prevent one branch from controlling the government. For example, the governor can check the legislature by rejecting a proposed law. This rejection is called a **veto**. In turn, the legislature can override, or reverse, a veto if enough legislators agree. The judicial branch can check the legislature if it decides that a new law violates the principles of the Texas Constitution. These checks and balances in Texas follow the pattern established at the federal level.

Reading Check **Analyzing Information** How does the principle of federalism affect the federal and state governments?

★ The Texas Bill of Rights

The protection of individual rights is another basic principle of a democracy. To protect Texans' rights, the state constitution includes a bill of rights as Article I. A bill of rights outlines the civil liberties, or individual rights, that a government promises to protect.

The Texas Bill of Rights was modeled after the U.S. Bill of Rights and lists many of the same rights and freedoms. The freedoms of speech and of the press protect Texans' right to express their ideas and opinions. The freedom of worship protects Texans' right to practice any religion they choose. The bill of rights also protects the rights of crime victims and the rights of people accused of crimes. For example, it ensures Texans' right to a trial by jury and prevents people from being tried for the same crime multiple times. The bill of rights concludes by declaring that the state can never take away these basic rights.

Reading Check **Supporting a Point of View** Explain why you think the Texas Bill of Rights is important.

★ Changing the Constitution

Like the U.S. Constitution, the Texas Constitution can be changed to address citizens' needs and views. Additions, changes, and corrections to a constitution are called **amendments**. Since 1876 the Texas Constitution has been amended more than 470 times. In comparison, the U.S. Constitution has only 27 amendments. These amendments deal with such wide-ranging topics as taxation, voting rights, and the creation of new counties.

The political climate of the 1870s strongly affected the current Texas Constitution. Its writers wanted to set limits on the power of the state government. So they created a constitution that restricts the state government's powers. Unlike the federal government, which is granted all powers "necessary and proper" to fulfill its duties, the state government does not have any powers that are not expressly stated in the Constitution. As a result, the state must ask voters to approve a constitutional amendment each time it wants to create a new power.

Article XVII of the Texas Constitution outlines the method for amending the Constitution. First, a member of the legislature proposes an amendment. Next, two thirds of the members of each chamber must approve it. Last, a majority of Texans must vote to pass the amendment.

The Texas Constitution has been the basic law of the state for more than 125 years. On three occasions, organized efforts have been made to replace the constitution entirely. These efforts—put forth in 1917, 1919, and 1972—were all defeated.

Reading Check **Drawing Inferences and Conclusions** Why might people consider the Texas Constitution to be a living document?

★ Section 1 Review

hmhsocialstudies.com
ONLINE QUIZ

1. Define and explain:
- federalism
- republicanism
- limited government
- separation of powers
- checks and balances
- veto
- amendments

2. Summarizing
Copy the chart below. Use it to explain the importance of the basic principles in the Texas Constitution.

Texas Constitution
1.
2.
3.
4.
5.
6.
7.

3. Finding the Main Idea

a. How are the principles and concepts of the Texas Constitution similar to those found in the U.S. Constitution?

b. What is the purpose of the Texas Bill of Rights? How is it similar to the U.S. Bill of Rights?

4. Writing and Critical Thinking myWriteSmart

Supporting a Point of View Imagine that you are attending a constitutional convention. Write a short speech explaining which two individual rights you think are most important and why.

Consider the following:
- who holds the power in a republic
- why a bill of rights is important

Section 2 The Texas Legislature

Main Ideas

1. The Texas legislature makes the state's laws.
2. The lawmaking process is long and complex.

Key Terms

- **bicameral**
- **sessions**
- **bill**
- **conference committee**

Why It Matters Today

Texans can influence the laws that the state legislature and Congress pass. Use current events sources to learn how the Texas legislature or U.S. Congress works today and how citizens can take part in the process.

TEKS: 1B, 14A, 15A, 21B, 21C, 22D

myNotebook

Use the annotation tools in your eBook to take notes on the duties and powers of the legislature.

The Story Continues

On January 12, 1965, Secretary of State Crawford Morgan swore in the 150 members of the newly elected Texas House of Representatives. Among those sworn in that morning was T. J. Lee, the first Chinese American ever elected to the body. After taking the oath, the representatives got to the business of creating the state's laws.

★ The Two Houses

The legislative branch of Texas is described in Article III of the Texas Constitution. The legislative branch makes the laws that govern the state. Like the U.S. Congress, the Texas legislature is **bicameral**, or made up of two houses: the House of Representatives and the Senate. The House has 150 members, called representatives, who serve two-year terms. The Senate has 31 members, called senators, who serve four-year terms.

Each representative and senator represents a district of the state. Each type of district is sized to contain roughly the same number of people. Thus, all Texans have equal representation in the legislature. Every 10 years, the legislature uses data from the new U.S. census to adjust the size of the districts. As of the 2010 census, each member of the House represented about 168,000 Texans. Each senator represented about 811,000 Texans.

To serve as legislators, Texans must meet certain requirements. All legislators must be residents of their election districts for at least one year before running for office. In addition, representatives must be at least 21 years old and have been Texas citizens for two years. Senators must be at least 26 years old and have been Texas citizens for five years. Under the Constitution, each legislator receives a salary of $7,200 per year. They also receive money to cover work-related expenses.

Reading Check **Categorizing** What are the requirements and duties of Texas representatives and Texas senators?

★ Legislative Duties and Powers

The main duty of the legislature is making laws. These laws shape the lives of the people of Texas. For example, they set taxes, create traffic regulations, and establish qualifications for teachers. Members of either house can propose new state laws. However, laws that increase taxes or otherwise raise money for the state must begin in the House.

The legislature has several other duties and powers. Only legislators can propose constitutional amendments. The Senate must approve all executive appointments. The legislature also has the power to impeach, or bring charges against, judges and executive officials. Impeachment is a two-step process. First, the House of Representatives brings impeachment charges against an official. If the House votes to impeach, the Senate then puts the official on trial. If the trial ends in a conviction, the legislature removes the official from office. The best-known case of a Texas official being removed from office is the impeachment and conviction of Governor James Ferguson in 1917.

Most of the Texas legislature's work takes place during periods called **sessions**. These sessions start on the second Tuesday of January in odd-numbered years. Regular sessions last for up to 140 days. However, the governor can call special sessions of the legislature when necessary. A special session may last up to 30 days. The governor specifies the topics, such as the state budget, that will be addressed in special sessions.

Reading Check **Summarizing** What are the legislature's main powers and duties?

BIOGRAPHY

Thomas J. Lee

(1923–1996) In 1964 Thomas J. "T. J." Lee became the first Chinese American to serve in the Texas legislature. After emigrating from China, his family eventually settled in San Antonio. Lee earned a law degree and became a successful attorney. In 1964 he ran for the Texas House of Representatives. The district in which Lee campaigned had a diverse population. During the campaign Lee spoke to voters in three languages: Chinese, English, and Spanish. **How might speaking in three languages have helped Lee get elected?**

The Texas legislature meets in the Capitol, where each house has its own chamber.

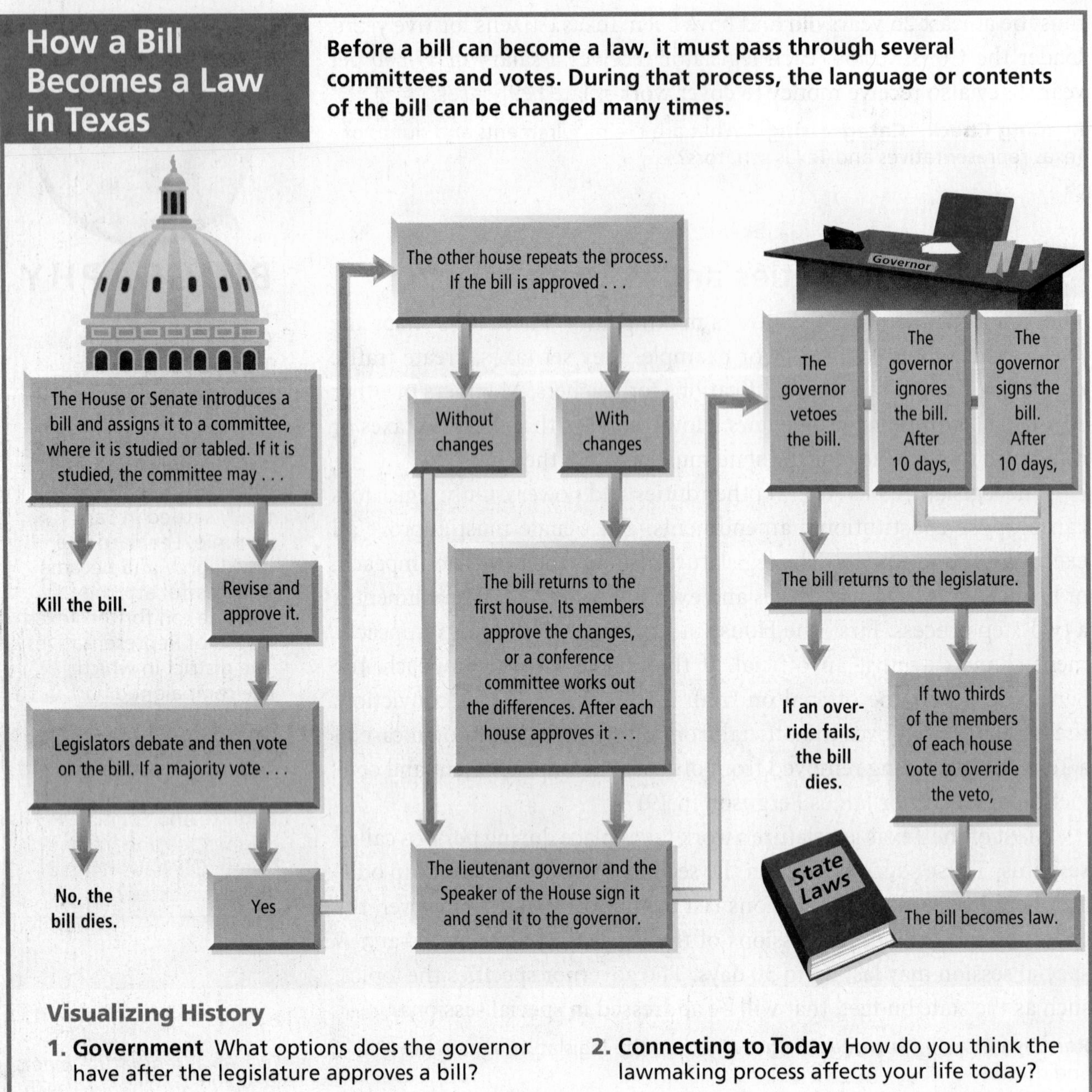

Visualizing History

1. **Government** What options does the governor have after the legislature approves a bill?
2. **Connecting to Today** How do you think the lawmaking process affects your life today?

★ How a Bill Becomes a Law

The process of creating a new law is complex. First, a legislator must propose a **bill**, or potential law. In most cases, legislators in either house can create a bill. A clerk then reads the title of the bill aloud to the members of that house.

Next, the house leader assigns the bill to a committee. The leader of the House of Representatives is the Speaker of the House. Representatives elect the Speaker. The leader, or president, of the Senate is the lieutenant governor, who is elected by the people alongside the governor. These leaders have a great deal of power. They set the agenda for debates and can influence which bills are considered.

The committees to which bills are assigned are appointed by the Speaker of the House or lieutenant governor. Each committee is led by a chairperson, also appointed by the house leader. Each committee focuses on bills that deal with a specific subject, such as education or finance. As a result, some committees are more powerful than others. Committees that meet during sessions are called standing committees. Those that meet between sessions are called interim committees.

Once a committee receives a bill for consideration, its members study the bill and decide what to do with it. Sometimes they approve the bill as it was written. Sometimes they rewrite portions of the bill. In some cases, the committee tables, or refuses to examine, the bill. Committee members may also hear citizens' opinions about the bill. After discussion, the committee approves or rejects the bill. A rejected bill dies.

If a committee approves a bill, it goes before the entire house for debate and voting. If it is approved, the bill is sent to the other house. The other house can approve or reject the bill. If rejected, the bill dies. Frequently, though, the second house approves a revised version of the bill. In such cases, the two houses form a **conference committee**. This committee revises the bill so it will satisfy both houses. After the committee is finished, both houses vote again on the bill. An approved bill then goes to the governor.

The governor can deal with a bill in three ways. He or she can sign the bill, in which case it becomes law. He or she can ignore the bill, but an ignored bill automatically becomes law after 10 days. The governor can also veto the bill. A vetoed bill returns to the legislature, which can then override the veto. If two thirds of the members of each house vote to override a veto, the bill becomes law. However, the legislature must be in session to do so. Of the thousands of bills proposed each session, fewer than half become law.

Reading Check **Finding the Main Idea** What individuals and groups are involved in passing a new law?

> **That's Interesting!**
>
> **Watching the Legislature**
>
> Each chamber of the Texas Capitol includes a gallery from which visitors can watch the proceedings of the Senate and the House of Representatives. For those who cannot make it to the Capitol, the proceedings are also broadcast online through the House and Senate Web sites. Some committee meetings can be watched online as well.

Section 2 Review

hmhsocialstudies.com ONLINE QUIZ

1. Define and explain:
- bicameral
- sessions
- bill
- conference committee

2. Analyzing Information Copy the graphic organizer below. Use it to identify two duties of the Speaker of the House and the lieutenant governor.

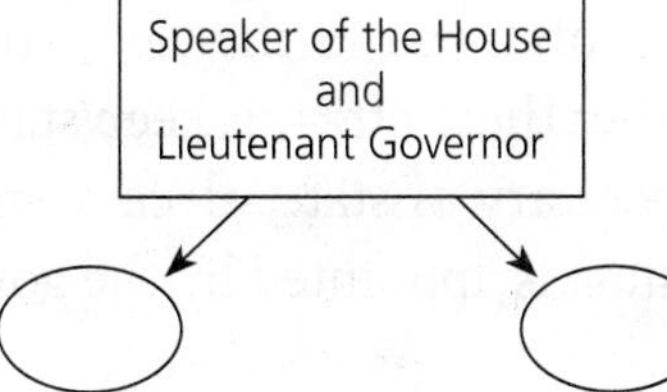

3. Finding the Main Idea

a. What is the main power of the legislature, and what other powers does it have?

b. List in order some of the steps involved in a bill becoming a law.

4. Writing and Critical Thinking myWriteSmart

Summarizing Imagine that you are writing a letter to a friend in another state. Explain how the Texas legislature serves as the voice of the state's citizens.

Consider the following:
- the principle of popular sovereignty
- the powers and duties of the legislature

Section 3

The Texas Executive Branch

Main Ideas

1. The powers and duties of the governor of Texas are outlined in the state constitution.
2. In addition to the governor, several other officials and agencies are part of the executive branch.

Key Terms

- **line-item veto**
- **pardon**

Why It Matters Today

The decisions the governor makes affect Texans in many ways. Use current events sources to find information about policies and programs supported by the state's current governor.

TEKS: 9A, 15A, 18A, 21B, 22D

myNotebook

Use the annotation tools in your eBook to take notes on the powers and duties of the governor and executive officials.

The Story Continues

During Reconstruction Texas governors had greater power than they do today. Governor Edmund J. Davis, for example, created a state police force that he used to keep order. When Davis lost his bid for reelection in 1873, he refused to give up power. However, Richard Coke—the Democrat who had defeated Davis—and his supporters took control of the Capitol. Davis summoned troops to help him, but they sided with Coke instead. Davis gave up. In 1875, delegates met to write a new state constitution. They wanted to ensure that no governor would be as powerful as Davis had been.

The Governor

The governor of Texas is the head of the state's executive branch, described in Article IV of the Texas Constitution. This branch enforces the laws passed by the legislature. It also manages and conducts the daily business of the state. In addition to the governor, the executive branch includes a lieutenant governor, a secretary of state, a comptroller of public accounts, a commissioner of the General Land Office, and an attorney general. Together these officials keep state affairs running smoothly. Other than the secretary of state, all of them are elected by the people. The secretary of state is appointed by the governor.

Texans elect a governor every four years. These elections occur in even-numbered years that do not have presidential elections, such as 2014, 2018, 2022, and 2026. The Texas Constitution does not limit the number of terms a governor can serve. You can find a list of all the men and women who have served as governor of Texas in the reference section at the back of this book.

The Texas Constitution outlines the qualifications to serve as governor. A candidate must be at least 30 years old and a citizen of the United States. He or she must also have lived in Texas for at least five years immediately prior to being elected.

The governor's salary is set by the Texas legislature. As of 2013, the governor receives $150,000 per year. He or she lives in the Governor's Mansion in Austin, built by the state in 1856. In addition, the state also provides the governor with a staff, transportation, and money for job-related expenses.

Reading Check **Finding the Main Idea** What state government official heads the executive branch in Texas?

BIOGRAPHY

Ann Richards

(1933–2006) Ann Richards was born during the Great Depression and grew up near Waco. Her parents were poor and taught her the value of hard work. "I believed I could do anything," Richards said. She started her career as a teacher before entering politics. Richards became state treasurer in 1983. Then in 1988 she captured the national spotlight when she spoke at the Democratic National Convention. She won the governor's office in 1990, becoming the second female governor in Texas history. **What political offices did Richards hold?**

★ The Powers and Duties of the Governor

As the head of the executive branch, the governor cannot make laws. He or she can, however, make recommendations for new laws to the legislature. Some of these recommendations are made in an address at the beginning of each legislative session. Called the State of the State address, this speech reports on the status of matters within Texas. It also outlines policies that the governor would like to see enacted during his or her time in office.

The legislature is not required to follow the governor's wishes. It may ignore any or all of the governor's suggestions. However, a governor with a powerful personality can have a strong impact on state affairs. For example, in 1891 Governor James Stephen Hogg urged the legislature to establish a railroad commission. Despite strong opposition, the legislature created the agency, now one of the state's most powerful.

Although the governor cannot create laws, he or she can help determine which laws go into effect. Before any new law can take effect, it must be sent to the governor for a signature. Those that he or she signs become law. Those to which he or she is opposed can be vetoed.

The veto is a powerful tool. Because it is very difficult for the legislature to override a veto, even the threat of a veto on an upcoming bill can help change policy matters. If the legislature fears that the governor will veto an upcoming bill, they may revise it before it passes. The governor also has the power of the **line-item veto**. It allows him or her to delete specific lines, or parts, of budget bills. This power increases the governor's influence on how state money is spent.

★ Texas Cities ★

Austin

History: When Anglo settlers first arrived in the Austin area about 1835, Tonkawa Indians lived in the region. In 1839 the city was chosen as the new capital of the Republic of Texas. Edwin Waller, the first mayor, designed the original plan for the city. The grid pattern of Waller's plan is still visible in the layout of downtown.

Population in 2012: 842,592 (estimate)

Relative location: On the Colorado River, 75 miles northeast of San Antonio

Region: Edge of the Blackland Prairie subregion of the Gulf Coastal Plain

County: County seat of Travis County

Special feature: The capital of Texas

Origin of name: Named for Stephen F. Austin

Economy: The state government employs a large part of Austin's workforce. The University of Texas also employs many people in the Austin area. Since the 1970s, the city has become a center for high-tech industries and for research. It has also developed active music and film industries.

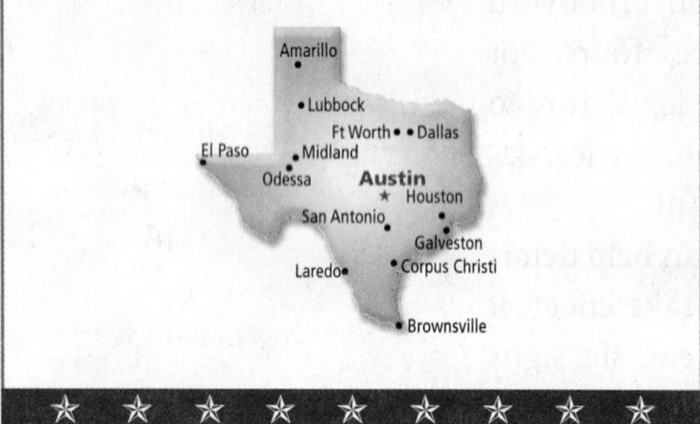

The governor can also influence the legislature by calling a special session. During a special session, the legislature may only address topics specified by the governor. The Texas Constitution does not limit the number of special sessions a governor may call.

In addition to policy making, the governor oversees many of the state's agencies, boards, and commissions and appoints officials to these agencies. During a single term, a governor appoints some 3,000 officials, including the secretary of state, who oversees elections. However, the Senate must approve most appointments. The governor can also remove appointed officials from office with the Senate's approval.

The governor also plays a role in the state judicial system. He or she appoints judges when vacancies occur. On the recommendation of the Board of Pardons and Paroles, the governor can also **pardon**, or forgive, people convicted of crimes. In addition, the governor can grant a 30-day reprieve, or delay, to a person facing the death penalty.

In addition, the governor serves as commander in chief of the state's military. In times of crisis, he or she can mobilize the Texas National Guard. The governor can also declare martial law, putting an area under military control.

An informal but important executive power is the governor's role as "first citizen" of Texas. In this role, the governor represents Texas at state functions and presents awards to outstanding Texans. He or she also issues proclamations, such as declaring a site a disaster area after a flood or a tornado.

Because the constitution limits many of his or her powers, Texas is said to have a weak governor. Despite the governor's many responsibilities, the Texas legislature has more power than the governor does. For example, the governor has little control over the state's budget. Although the governor submits a budget proposal to the state legislature, this proposal has little effect on the final budget. The legislature is responsible for officially determining the state's budget. This limited financial control represents one of the weaknesses of the governor's office.

Reading Check **Analyzing Information** List the governor's responsibilities.

Image Credit: ©SuperStock/Getty Images

★ Executive Officials and Agencies

In addition to the governor, the executive branch includes several other elected officials. The most important of these is the lieutenant governor. Elected to a four-year term at the same time as the governor, the lieutenant governor serves as the leader of the Texas Senate. He or she also chairs the powerful Legislative Budget Board. Because the legislature is the most powerful branch of the state government, the lieutenant governor has been said to have more power than the governor. Besides his or her legislative duties, the lieutenant governor serves as acting governor when the governor is out of Texas. He or she also takes over if the governor leaves office for any reason.

Other senior executive officials provide important state services. The attorney general gives legal advice and represents Texas in certain court cases. The comptroller of public accounts oversees the collection of taxes. The commissioner of agriculture enforces agricultural laws and aids farmers. The commissioner of the General Land Office manages the state's land and mineral rights.

The executive branch also includes some 200 agencies, boards, and commissions. These departments enforce state laws and provide Texans with various services. The largest of these agencies is the Department of Criminal Justice. Its goal is to protect public safety and assist the victims of crime. Another important agency is the Texas Railroad Commission. When it was formed in 1891, the agency regulated the state's railroads. Today it regulates the oil, natural gas, and mining industries in Texas—but not railroads. These and other agencies and officials help keep the state running smoothly.

Reading Check **Comparing and Contrasting** In what ways are the offices of governor and lieutenant governor similar? How do they differ?

The Texas Capitol

The Capitol Building in Austin took six years to build and was finished in 1888. The Texas Capitol is modeled after the U.S. Capitol in Washington, D.C. Just like the U.S. Capitol, it is topped by a dome. On this dome stands a statue named the Goddess of Liberty. Whereas the national Capitol is white, the Texas Capitol is made from red granite from Marble Falls. The building is the largest state capitol. It covers about 2.5 acres and is more than 300 feet tall. **How is the Texas Capitol similar to and different from the U.S. Capitol?**

Section 3 Review

hmhsocialstudies.com
ONLINE QUIZ

1. **Define and explain:**
   - line-item veto
   - pardon
2. **Locate on a Texas map:**
   - Austin
3. **Categorizing**
   Copy the graphic organizer below. Use it to describe the primary duties and powers of each part of the executive branch.

   Executive Branch — Governor; Lt. Governor; Senior Official; Senior Official; Senior Official; Senior Official; Executive Agencies

4. **Finding the Main Idea**
   a. Excluding the veto, which of the governor's powers do you believe is the most important? Why?
   b. Name two executive agencies and describe the services those agencies provide.
5. **Writing and Critical Thinking** *my*WriteSmart
   Analyzing Information Write a paragraph about the governor's importance as leader of Texas.
   Consider the following:
   - the governor's role as first citizen of Texas
   - the governor's role in directing state policy

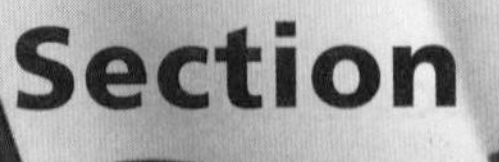

Section 4 The Texas Judiciary

Main Ideas

1. The Texas judicial system includes many levels of courts.
2. Juries play important roles in the judicial system.

Key Terms

- civil law
- criminal law
- trial courts
- appellate courts
- judicial review
- petit jury
- grand jury

Why It Matters Today

Many Texans will appear in one of the courts of the state at least once in their lives. Use current events sources to find information about a recent trial or court ruling in your area.

TEKS: 14A, 15A, 16B, 17C, 21B, 21C, 22D

myNotebook

Use the annotation tools in your eBook to take notes on the parts and functions of the Texas judicial system.

The Story Continues

In 1924 a case came before the Texas Supreme Court that involved an all-male organization to which all of the justices belonged. Under state law, none of them could rule on the case. Governor Pat Neff looked for replacement justices, but each one he considered belonged to the same organization. Eventually Neff decided to appoint three women to hear the case. In January 1925, the only all-woman Supreme Court in Texas history met. The court heard the case, ruled on it, and then disbanded. More than 50 years passed before a woman served full-time on the high court.

Judges and Courts

The Supreme Court is part of the Texas judicial system, described in Article V of the Texas Constitution. This branch includes all of the state's courts. Its main role is to decide legal cases by interpreting and applying the law. More than 3,500 judges hear cases in some 2,800 Texas courts. Most judges are elected to either four- or six-year terms. Although the qualifications for judges vary, all judges must be U.S. citizens and residents of Texas.

The Texas Supreme Court today is made up of a Chief Justice and eight justices, or judges. The members of the Supreme Court are elected to six-year terms. Their elections are staggered so that only a portion of the court is replaced in each election cycle.

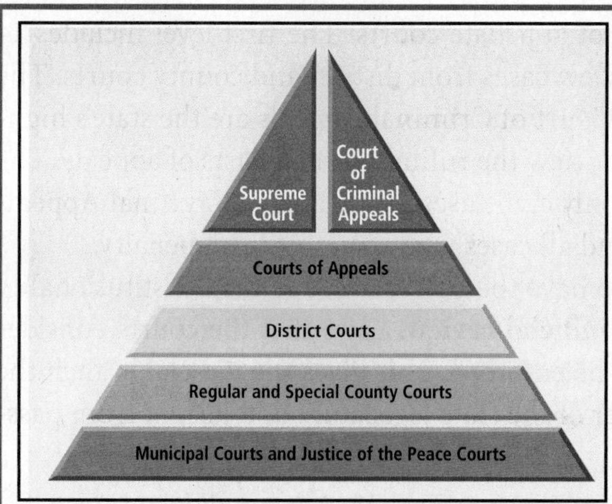

Texas Judicial System

Interpreting Charts The Texas judicial system is complex, with several thousand courts arranged in different levels. What are the highest courts in the Texas judicial system?

Texas courts hear millions of cases each year involving both civil and criminal law. **Civil law** deals with legal disputes between individuals. Examples of civil law matters include contract disputes, divorce proceedings, and property settlements. **Criminal law** deals with people accused of committing crimes. Criminal cases are brought by the government. They deal with such matters as murder, assault, and theft. Civil and criminal cases are tried in different types of courts.

Reading Check **Finding the Main Idea** What is the main role of the judicial branch?

★ The Structure of the Texas Courts

Cases that go to trial in Texas are heard in **trial courts.** These courts hear new cases and give a verdict, or ruling, in each. Texas has three levels of trial courts. Each level has a specific jurisdiction, or authority to hear certain types of cases.

- Municipal courts and justice of the peace courts hear misdemeanor, or minor crime, cases punishable by fines. Misdemeanors include such offenses as littering and speeding.
- County courts hear more serious misdemeanor cases and civil cases involving amounts between $200 and $5,000.
- District courts hear all civil cases involving sums greater than $5,000, divorce cases, and some misdemeanor cases. District courts also hear all felony, or major crime, cases. Felonies include crimes such as murder and robbery.

Several Texas cities have separate district courts for criminal, family-law, and civil cases.

After a case is heard in trial court, the losing party may appeal the case to the next level of court. These courts are called **appellate courts.** They review trials to determine whether correct procedures were followed. Based on its review of a case, an appellate court may order a new trial or overturn a trial's verdict.

Interpreting Visuals

Jury duty. *Members of a jury hand down a verdict at the end of a trial.* ***How do you think juries gather the information they need to reach a verdict?***

Texas has two levels of appellate courts. The first level includes 14 courts of appeals that review cases from district and county courts. The Supreme Court and the Court of Criminal Appeals are the state's highest courts. They mainly review the rulings of the courts of appeals. The Supreme Court reviews only civil cases. The Court of Criminal Appeals reviews criminal cases and all cases involving the death penalty.

Both high courts also have the power to judge the constitutionality of a law, a power called **judicial review.** Laws that the courts consider unconstitutional cannot be enforced. This gives the judicial branch the ability to check the power of the state legislature and keep it from passing unfair laws.

Reading Check **Analyzing Information** How does judicial review reflect the principle of checks and balances in the Texas Constitution?

★ The Jury System

Judges are not the only people involved in the judicial system. Juries are groups of six or twelve citizens who hear trial cases and make decisions. Under the Texas Bill of Rights, all Texans have the right to a trial by jury.

Serving on juries is part of every Texan's civic responsibility. Only by taking part in the legal system can we ensure that everyone receives a fair trial. However, Texans must meet several requirements to serve on a jury. For example, they must be qualified to vote and must be able to read and write English. They cannot have been convicted of a felony.

Texas courts use two very different types of juries. A **petit jury** decides the verdict in a civil or criminal trial. A **grand jury** decides whether a person accused of a felony should be indicted, or formally charged with a crime. Grand juries consist of 12 people. For a felony case to go to trial, nine of the jurors must vote to indict.

Reading Check **Drawing Inferences and Conclusions** Why is jury duty an important civic responsibility?

Section 4 Review

1. Define and explain:
- civil law
- criminal law
- trial courts
- appellate courts
- judicial review
- petit jury
- grand jury

2. Summarizing Copy the graphic organizer below. Use it to identify and describe the two main types of cases heard in Texas. Next, identify and describe the two main types of courts in Texas.

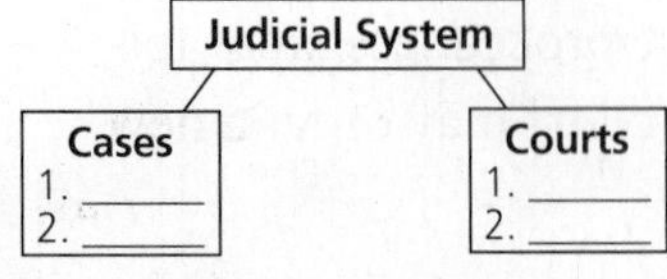

3. Finding the Main Idea
a. What are the two highest courts in Texas, and what cases do they hear?
b. What is the role of each type of jury?

4. Writing and Critical Thinking *my*WriteSmart
Evaluating Write a paragraph defending the point of view that serving on juries is an important civic duty.
Consider the following:
- the right to a trial by jury
- the importance of the jury system

Section 5 The State Budget and Public Education

Main Ideas

1. The Texas budget includes revenue from taxes, fees, and other sources.
2. Public education is funded and governed at both the state and local levels.

Key Terms

- **Legislative Budget Board**
- **appropriation bill**
- **sales tax**

Why It Matters Today

Many Texans are affected when the government raises taxes or cuts services. Use current events sources to find information related to taxes or government spending.

TEKS: 15A, 15B, 15C, 17C, 21B, 21C, 21E, 22D

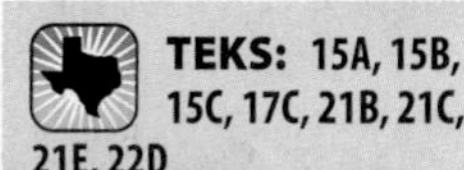

Use the annotation tools in your eBook to take notes on the state budget process and public education in Texas.

The Story Continues

In 1927 a young Texan named Lyndon B. Johnson enrolled in Southwest Texas State Teachers College. He had little money. To pay for his schooling, he worked as both a janitor and a secretary. Johnson graduated in 1930. He would go on to become the 36th U.S. president. For Texans like Johnson, state colleges make obtaining a higher education possible.

★ The State Budget

The Texas state government requires billions of dollars to function. The cost of government for 2012 and 2013 totaled $173.5 billion. The state budget specifies how much of this money will go to different parts of the government. For example, the budget gave more than $22 billion to higher education in 2012 and 2013. This state funding helps keep tuitions lower at public colleges. As a result, more Texans can afford to attend.

Texas uses a biennial, or two-year, budget. Preparing this budget is a long, complicated process that generally takes more than a year to complete. It begins with two state agencies. One is the Office of Budget, Planning, and Policy, which is part of the executive branch. The other, more powerful agency is the **Legislative Budget Board**. This board is made up of nine senior legislators and the lieutenant governor, who acts as its chair. Every two years the two boards send out instructions and goals to all state agencies. The agencies then send funding requests back to the boards.

Texas State Budget, 2012–2013

Education	$72.9 bil.
Health and Human Services	$55.4 bil.
Business and Economic Development	$23.7 bil.
Public Safety and Criminal Justice	$11.5 bil.
General Government	$4.5 bil.
Natural Resources	$3.9 bil.
Courts and the Legislature	$1.0 bil.
Regulatory	$0.7 bil.

Total State Budget: $173.5 Billion

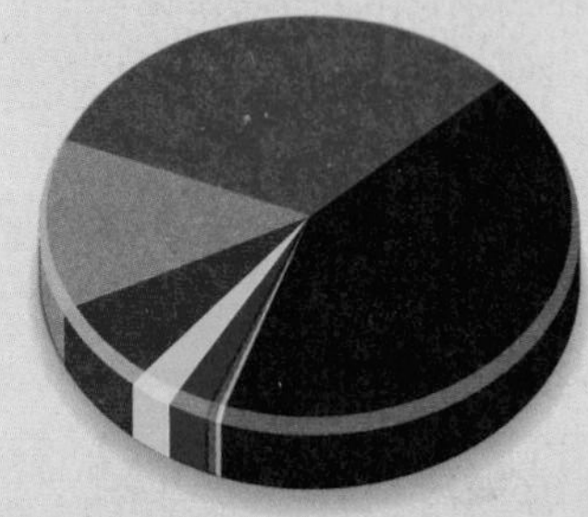

Source: Legislative Budget Board

Interpreting Charts One of the primary tasks of the Texas legislature is determining how the state government will spend its money. What area received the most funding in 2012–2013?

After receiving all requests, the Legislative Budget Board prepares an **appropriation bill**, a bill dealing with the spending of public money. The bill is sent to both houses of the Legislature for review and debate. Each house must pass the budget bill before it can move on.

If the legislature approves the budget bill, it goes to the state comptroller. This official determines whether the state will receive enough revenue, or income, to cover expenses. The Texas Constitution requires a balanced budget, one in which spending does not exceed income. Once the comptroller approves the budget bill, it goes to the governor to be signed.

Reading Check **Summarizing** Who is involved in approving the budget?

★ Revenue and Spending

The Texas state government obtains the revenue it needs from several sources. The largest source of the state's income is federal grants. In 2012 Texas received around $31 billion from the federal government. This represents more than a third of the state's revenue.

Another major source of state income is taxes. In 2013 taxes accounted for more than a fourth of all state income. More than half of this tax income came from sales taxes. A **sales tax** is added to the price paid for many goods and services at the time of purchase. Other taxes that create revenue for the state include taxes on corporations, oil production, gasoline, and motor vehicle sales.

Texas also gains revenue from fees, such as those it charges for licenses and permits. In Texas, anyone who wishes to drive a motor vehicle or hunt must first obtain a license from the state. Workers in many professions are also required to purchase licenses. Doctors, dentists, and counselors, for example, must have licenses in order to practice in Texas. Plumbers, land surveyors, cosmetologists, and many other types of workers must also have licenses. Similarly, many types of businesses must purchase permits before they can operate in the state.

In addition, the state obtains money from fines charged to people who break state laws. People who receive speeding tickets, for example, pay fines to the state. The state also charges penalties to those who do not purchase required licenses and permits.

State funds are used to build highways, pay state employees, and provide many other public services. The two areas that receive the most state money are health and human services and education. In 2012 and 2013 Texas spent about $55 billion on health and human services. These services include medical insurance and other services for Texans in need. In that same period the state spent about $73 billion on education.

Reading Check **Finding the Main Idea** What are the major sources of revenue for state government?

★ Texas Public Education

The Texas Constitution requires the legislature to maintain a free public school system. As of 2012, some 5 million students attend Texas public schools. These schools are funded through the combined efforts of state, local, and federal governments. The state provides money through the Permanent School Fund, which receives money from state taxes and investments. Local governments raise money for schools through property taxes and bond issues. Property taxes are levied on the amount of property, such as land or houses, that people own. A bond is a certificate of debt issued by a government when it borrows money, promising to repay what it has borrowed with interest. The federal government also provides funds from federal taxes, such as income tax. Much of this money funds specialized programs such as job training.

The administration of Texas public schools is divided between state and local governments. At the state level, the Texas legislature passes the laws governing public schools, including the subjects they teach. Two state agencies assist the legislature with these matters. The Texas Board of Education sets education policy and reviews textbooks for use in schools. This board has 15 elected members. The Texas Education Agency puts education policy into effect. This agency reviews standards for learning materials, schools, and teacher certification. It is directed by a commissioner of education appointed by the governor.

Locally, schools are governed by more than 1,000 independent school districts. Boards of trustees or school boards govern each district. School boards arrange for school construction, select textbooks, and set property tax rates. They also hire superintendents to run the day-to-day business of the school district. By providing a strong system of public education, Texans hope to ensure a successful future for their state.

Reading Check **Summarizing** How are Texas public schools funded?

LINKING Past to Present

Texas School Days

In the days when most children lived on farms, the school year was much shorter than it is today. Schools had long summer breaks because that was when farmers were busiest. In 1915 a Texas law required children aged 8 to 14 to attend school 100 days a year. Today school-age children in Texas are required to attend school at least 180 days a year. Some Texas schools have gone to year-round schedules. In such schools, the traditional summer break is divided into several two- to three-week vacations. **How did the state's farm-based economy affect the development of the Texas school year?**

★ Section 5 Review

hmhsocialstudies.com ONLINE QUIZ

1. **Define and explain:**
   - appropriation bill
   - sales tax
2. **Identify and explain** the significance of the following:
   - Legislative Budget Board
3. **Categorizing** Copy the graphic organizer below. Use it to identify three major sources of state revenue and two major areas of state spending.

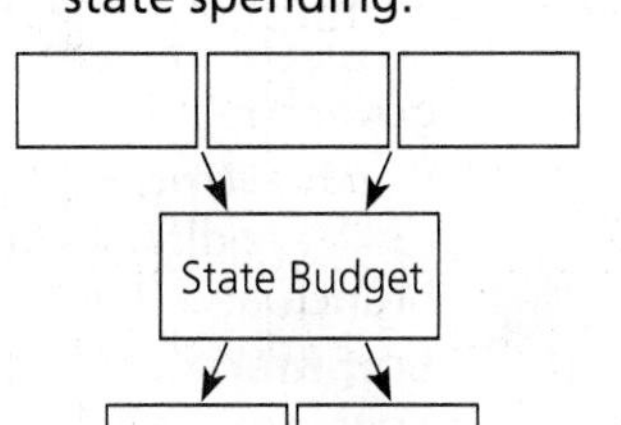

4. **Finding the Main Idea**
   - **a.** List in order the steps involved in preparing the state budget.
   - **b.** How are public schools in Texas structured and governed?
5. **Writing and Critical Thinking** myWriteSmart
   Supporting a Point of View Write a letter to the legislature and try to persuade it to increase the budget for education.
   Consider the following:
   - the overall state budget
   - the importance of education

The Chapter at a Glance

Examine the following visual summary of the chapter. Working with a partner, take turns explaining to each other the structure and functions of the Texas government. Be sure to include specific details in your explanation.

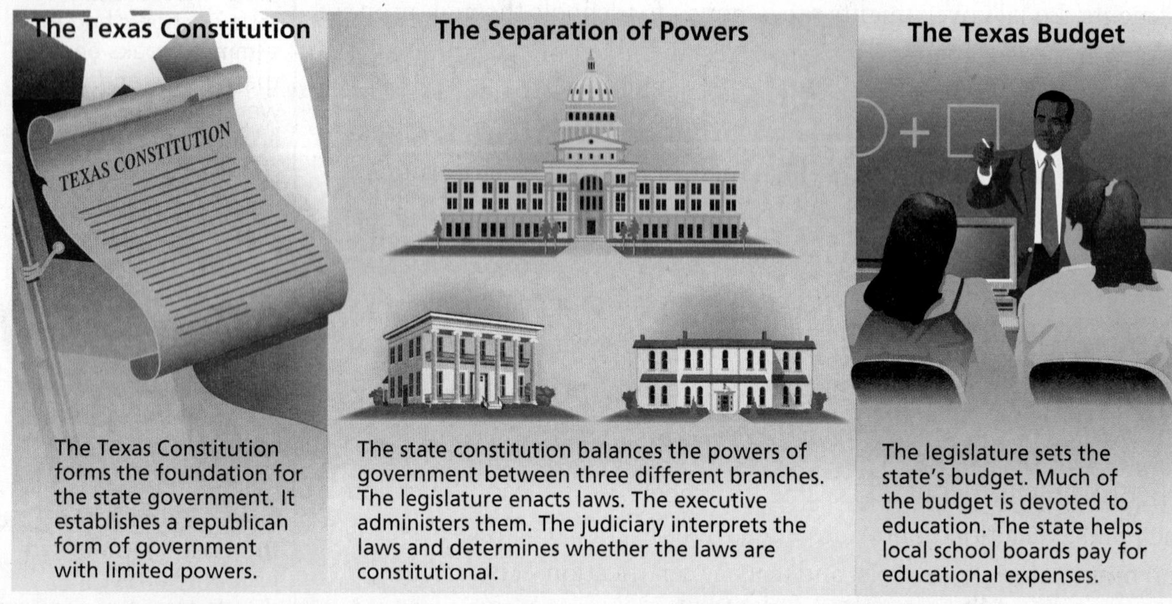

The Texas Constitution forms the foundation for the state government. It establishes a republican form of government with limited powers.

The state constitution balances the powers of government between three different branches. The legislature enacts laws. The executive administers them. The judiciary interprets the laws and determines whether the laws are constitutional.

The legislature sets the state's budget. Much of the budget is devoted to education. The state helps local school boards pay for educational expenses.

Identifying People and Ideas

Write a sentence to explain the role or significance of each of the following terms.

1. republicanism
2. limited government
3. separation of powers
4. checks and balances
5. federalism
6. veto
7. bicameral
8. line-item veto
9. appellate courts
10. appropriation bill

Understanding Main Ideas

Section 1

1. What basic principles are reflected in the Texas Constitution?
2. How does the Texas Constitution protect the individual rights of Texans?

Section 2

3. Describe the legislature's structure and its powers and duties.

Section 3

4. List some of the governor's powers.

Section 4

5. What is the basic structure of the Texas courts?

Section 5

6. What are the largest sources of state revenue?
7. Describe the funding of the state's public education system.

You Be the Historian

Reviewing Themes

1. **Constitutional Heritage** How are the principles and concepts found in the Texas Constitution and Bill of Rights similar to those in the U.S. Constitution and Bill of Rights? Why do you think the documents have similarities?
2. **Government** What are some of the advantages and disadvantages of having a weak governor system in Texas?
3. **Economics** Name the public service that you think should receive most state funds. Give three reasons why you think this service should receive funds. Be sure to use specific information to support your point of view.

Thinking Critically

1. **Evaluating** Do you think Texas judges should be elected by the public or appointed by the governor? Explain your answer.
2. **Contrasting** Explain how the powers of the judiciary differ from those of the executive branch and legislature.
3. **Summarizing** Describe the structure of the state government.

Texas Test Practice

Interpreting Outlines

Study the outline below. Then answer the questions that follow.

Texas Government

I. Legislative Branch
   A. Makes laws
   B. Includes two houses
      1. Senate
      2. House of Representatives
II. Executive Branch
   A. Enforces laws
   B. Headed by the governor
      1. Can sign or veto laws
      2. Appoints officials
   C. Other officials
      1. Lieutenant governor
      2. Heads of executive departments
III. Judicial Branch
   A. Interprets laws
   B. Includes several levels of courts

1. Which branch of the government makes laws?
   A legislative branch
   B executive branch
   C judicial branch
   D governor branch

2. Reorganize the information in this outline into a visual format, such as a graph, chart, or table.

Analyzing Primary Sources

Read the following quote from Ann Richards, taken from her inaugural address, January 15, 1991. Then answer the questions.

"Today, we have a vision of a Texas where the government treats every citizen with respect and dignity and honesty, where consumers are protected, where business is . . . valued, where good jobs are plentiful, where those in need find compassion and help, where every decision is measured against a high standard of ethics and true commitment to the public trust. . . . Nothing is more fundamentally important to me than the understanding that this administration exists to serve the taxpayers. . . . Service to the people is government's bottom line."

3. Which of the following statements best describes Ann Richards's point of view?
   F Government is too large.
   G Government should serve the people.
   H Government exists to strictly regulate business behavior.
   J Government should not help the poor.

4. What do you think Richards means when she says that the government's bottom line is to serve the people?

Linking to Community

Many people work in leadership positions in the state government. Research information about an elected or appointed leader of Texas, such as the governor, the secretary of state, a legislator, or a judge. Find out if the person was elected or appointed to office. Determine what the official's duties are and identify the leadership qualities that the person brings to the job. Then create a collage that illustrates the person's duties and leadership qualities for the class.

Internet Activity 

Access the Internet to research the state's government. Then create a visual presentation or model illustrating the structure and function of Texas government. Include information on the Texas Constitution, the branches of government, major state agencies, and the specific powers and duties of each branch or agency. Include drawings, photographs, or any other visuals you wish. Be sure to include captions for any visuals and to check your work for standard grammar, spelling, sentence structure, punctuation, and citation of sources.

CHAPTER 31

Local Government and Citizenship

(1845–Present)

Texas Essential Knowledge and Skills (TEKS) 8A, 15A, 15B, 16A, 16B, 17A, 17B, 17C, 18A, 18B, 21A, 21B, 21C, 21D, 21E, 22A, 22B, 22C, 22D

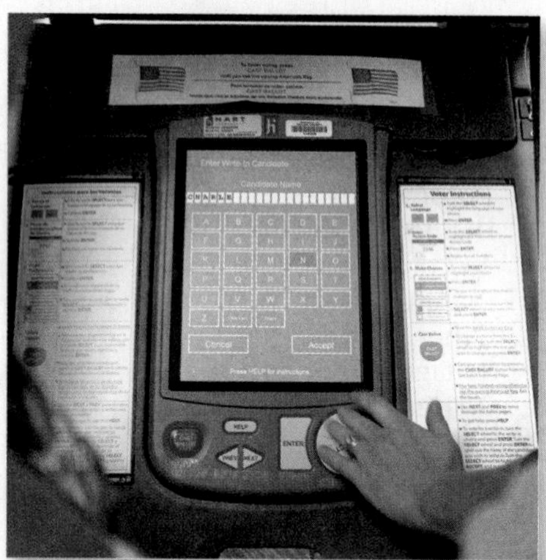

Recent technology has been used to make vote recorders that are very accurate.

TEXAS

1848 Texans cast their first votes as U.S. citizens in a presidential election.

1869 Edmund J. Davis is elected governor, the last Republican to hold the office until Bill Clements was elected in 1978.

1918 After decades of fighting for the right to vote, women are allowed to vote in Texas primary elections.

1845 — 1865 — 1885 — 1905 — 1925

U.S. and WORLD

1848 The Seneca Falls Convention calls for equal rights for women, including the right to vote.

1868 The Fourteenth Amendment, which expands and protects citizenship, is adopted.

1892 A third party, the Populist Party, holds its first national convention.

1920 The Nineteenth Amendment is adopted, giving women the right to vote..

As a Texan . . . ***How do you fulfill your civic responsibilities?***

Build on What You Know

The Texas Constitution divided state government into three branches. Below the state government are many local governments. Texans make important contributions to their state by participating in elections and by fulfilling their many other civic responsibilities.

With his election in 1978, Bill Clements became the first Republican governor in more than 100 years.

Texans have the right to assemble peacefully to protest government actions or policies.

1944
A Texas law establishing white primaries is struck down by the U.S. Supreme Court in *Smith* v. *Allwright*.

1965
Congress passes the Voting Rights Act to protect citizens' right to vote.

1972
Texan Barbara Jordan is elected to the U.S. House of Representatives. She is the first black woman from the South to serve in Congress.

1986
Raul Gonzalez is elected to the Texas Supreme Court. He is the first Mexican American elected to statewide office.

2000
Texan George W. Bush is elected president of the United States.

2010
The U.S. Supreme Court rules that corporations may support candidates in federal elections.

2012
Based on the 2010 Census, Texas gains four new seats in Congress.

1945 — 1965 — 1985 — 2005 — Present

Image Credit: (tl) ©Courtesy Jack Wilson. Houghton Mifflin Harcourt Photo/Sam Dudgeon; (tr) ©Bob Daemmrich/Alamy

You Be the Historian

myNotebook

What's Your Opinion? Do you agree or disagree with the following statements? Support your point of view in your notebook.

- **Constitutional Heritage** Free speech and press contribute little to democratic society.
- **Citizenship** Civic participation is important in a republic.
- **Government** In a democracy, citizens rarely express different political views.

Section 1

Local Government

Main Ideas

1. Local government in Texas includes county and municipal governments and special districts.
2. Local governments raise money with bonds and taxes.

Key Terms

- **commissioners' court**
- **precinct**
- **home-rule charters**
- **general-law cities**
- **special districts**

Why It Matters Today

Fire protection is just one example of a service provided by local governments. Use current events sources to find information on the public services provided by the government in your area today.

TEKS: 15A, 15B, 17C, 21B, 21C, 21E, 22D

myNotebook

Use the annotation tools in your eBook to take notes of the structure and functions of local government.

The Story Continues

As a high school student, J. D. Clark began writing for the newspaper in Chico. He was soon assigned to cover local city council meetings, and he came to realize the great impact that city government had on people's lives. While in college he was elected to the city council, and after a few years he became mayor of Chico. Mayor Clark was only 23 years old.

★ County Governments

Local governments such as the one in Chico provide police protection, roads, water, and other services to Texans. They provide leadership for the state's cities, towns, and counties. In Texas, there are two major divisions of local government: county and municipal.

Texas has 254 counties, each with its own government. The governing body for a Texas county is the **commissioners' court**, made up of five people. Four members are known as commissioners. Each represents one **precinct**, or county subdivisions. The fifth member, the county judge, is elected by voters countywide. The judge directs all court meetings.

The commissioners' court prepares the county budget and addresses local issues. It also sets county property taxes, which are the major source of revenue for most counties. The court can also propose bonds to raise money to build roads, public buildings, and other projects. These proposals need to be approved by the county's voters. Despite its name, the commissioners' court does not handle legal cases. However, in less populated counties the judge may hear certain cases.

Other officials also serve at the county level. These include the county clerk, treasurer, sheriff, and tax assessor-collector. The county clerk keeps records of the commissioners' court. He or she also keeps records of births, deaths, marriages, and land ownership. The county treasurer manages the county's money. The sheriff provides police protection and runs the county jail. He or she is responsible for keeping the people of the county safe. The tax assessor-collector makes sure that taxes are collected and issues vehicle titles. These and other officials work hard to keep counties running smoothly.

Reading Check **Contrasting** How do the duties of the commissioners' court and a regular court differ?

Texans on the Road

Maintaining the state's roads is an important function of local governments. The number of licensed drivers in Texas—about 20 million—continues to grow each year. More than 22 million cars, trucks, and other vehicles travel Texas highways, a number second in the nation to only California.

Municipal Governments and Special Districts

More than 85 percent of Texans live in cities and towns. Each of the more than 1,000 cities and towns—or municipalities—in Texas was set up by the state government. Each city or town also has its own local, or municipal, government.

There are several types of municipal governments in Texas. In a mayor-council government, voters elect a mayor and a city council to run the government. The mayor serves as the city's chief executive officer and directs council meetings.

Many cities have a council-manager government in which voters elect a mayor and a city council. These elected officials decide the city's policies. The council then chooses a city manager to carry out those policies and handle all of the city's day-to-day business. With a council-manager government, the city's administration rests in the hands of a hired professional.

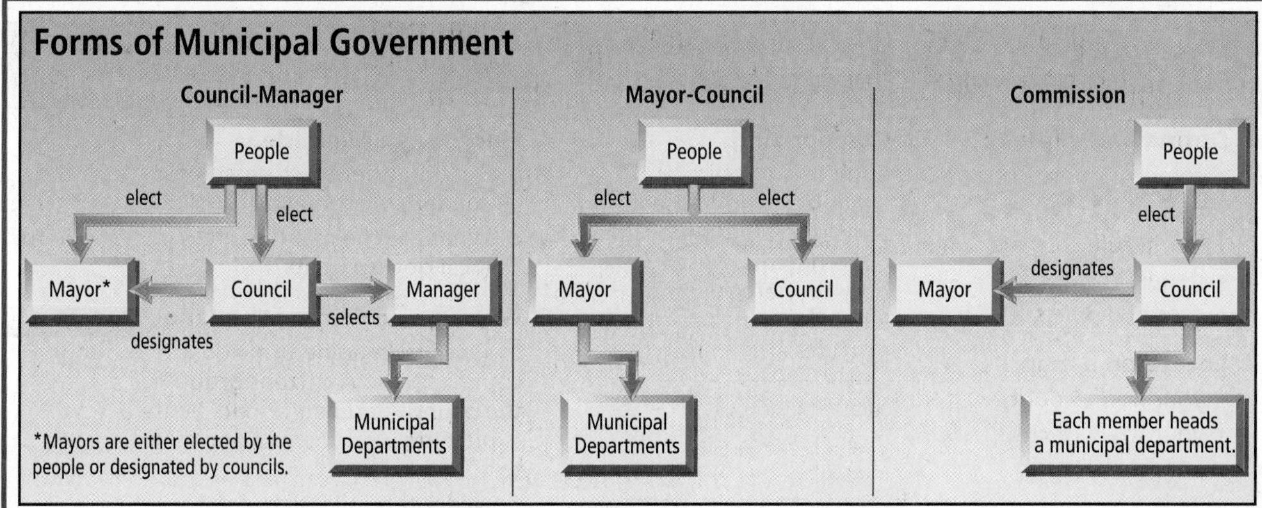

Interpreting Charts Municipal governments differ from city to city. Most include mayors, city councils, and departments such as police, fire, roads, utilities, and parks departments. In which form of government does the mayor have the most power?

Some Texas cities used to operate under a commission plan in which voters elected commissioners to serve as a city council. Each commissioner supervised a city department. However, council members had difficulty working together toward citywide goals, and cities abandoned the plan. There are no true commission governments in Texas today.

Texas cities with populations of more than 5,000 qualify for **home-rule charters**. These charters allow citizens to choose among the three forms of municipal government. Cities draft and adopt these charters within guidelines set by the state legislature. The cities then pass ordinances, or local laws. Unless an ordinance conflicts with state law, the state will not interfere with the local law.

Most small towns and villages are known as **general-law cities**. They operate under the general laws of the state. Some of these towns have charters from the state outlining the form of government they can use.

City governments raise revenue, or money, by issuing bonds and from property and sales taxes. The government uses this money to provide services such as police and fire protection, garbage collection, recycling, and utilities. Many cities build city parks, pools, and sports fields.

In addition to counties and municipalities, Texans are governed by **special districts.** Each district is formed for a particular purpose, often handling services that other local governments do not provide. A special district might be as small as a town. For example, many towns and cities operate their own independent schools districts. Other special districts are huge, serving people in several counties. The Lower Colorado River Authority, for instance, provides flood control and electricity to people throughout the Colorado River flood plain. Other examples of special districts include hospital and transportation districts. The people in charge of special districts may be either appointed or elected.

Reading Check **Summarizing** What are special districts, and why do they exist?

Section 1 Review

hmhsocialstudies.com
ONLINE QUIZ

1. Define and explain:
- commissioners' court
- precinct
- home-rule charters
- general-law cities
- special districts

2. Locate on a map:
- your home county
- your town or city

3. Categorizing
Copy the graphic organizer below. Use it to list the types of local governments. Describe how they are run and what services each provides.

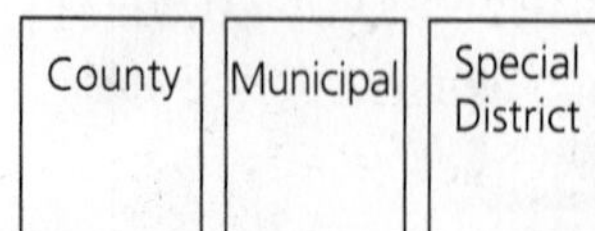

4. Finding the Main Idea
- **a.** Describe the structure and function of county government.
- **b.** What are the major sources of revenue for local governments?

5. Writing and Critical Thinking *my* WriteSmart
Evaluating Imagine that you are a county commissioner. A citizens group has asked the county to repair a road. Write a letter explaining why you will or will not agree to this.
Consider the following:
- the road's need for repair
- the county's budget

Section 2 The Rights of Texas Citizens

Main Ideas

1. The freedoms of speech, the press, and assembly are all crucial to a successful democracy.
2. The Texas Bill of Rights extends protections to Texans accused of committing crimes.
3. The Bill of Rights outlines several additional rights that cannot be taken from Texans.

Key Terms

- **slander**
- **libel**
- **due process**
- **bail**
- **eminent domain**

Why It Matters Today

The Texas Bill of Rights guarantees the right to assemble. Use current events sources to find information about a recent political meeting in your area or another part of Texas.

TEKS: 14B, 16A, 17B, 17C, 21B, 21E, 22D

The Story Continues

For days, a drama had unfolded in front of the governor's mansion where angry citizens were protesting the state's environmental policies. The police had ordered the protesters to leave so that others could use the sidewalk. After several protesters were arrested, they went to court to defend their right to protest. Their lawyer pointed to the Texas Bill of Rights and its protection of free speech and assembly.

myNotebook

Use the annotation tools in your eBook to take notes on the rights of Texas citizens.

★ Basic Rights and Freedoms

The Texas Bill of Rights protects the individual liberties of Texans. It grants many of the same rights as the U.S. Bill of Rights does. The writers of the Texas Constitution considered these rights so important that they listed the Bill of Rights as Act I of the document. This placement emphasizes its importance. Its writers wanted to ensure that no government could ever take away people's basic rights.

The Texas Bill of Rights declares that all Texans have equal rights under the law. No one can be treated differently because of his or her gender, race, religion, or national origin. Texans are free to worship however they please. The government cannot force people to practice a certain religion—or any religion at all—or support one religion over another. In addition, the government cannot name an official state religion.

Interpreting Visuals

Free speech and assembly. *Occasionally, Texans have found it necessary to conduct public protests to make their opinions heard.* ***What do you think these students are protesting?***

The Texas Bill of Rights also protects people's freedom of speech. People are free to express whatever opinions they wish. They cannot be punished for disagreeing with the government. Similarly, the press is free to publish news without interference from the government.

The freedoms of speech and the press are crucial to democracy. For democracy to work, the people must be able to stay informed and to freely discuss issues. Because media, such as newspapers and magazines, are free from government control, they can provide citizens with multiple perspectives on issues. As a result, citizens can be better informed.

These right to free speech is not unlimited, however. **Slander**—a false statement made on purpose that damages another's reputation—is not protected. **Libel**, an intentionally false written statement, is likewise not protected. Nor does freedom of speech protect statements that seriously threaten the public's safety. For example, falsely shouting "Fire!" in a crowded theater is unprotected speech.

Related to the right to free speech is the right of assembly. Texans are free to assemble to discuss political issues or to protest government policies or practices. Generally, government officials cannot break up a meeting unless the people are disruptive or breaking the law. Texans can also petition, or make a request, for particular government action.

Reading Check **Finding the Main Idea** What rights are protected in the Texas Bill of Rights?

Protection of the Accused

In addition to the basic rights described above, the Texas Constitution includes protection for people accused of wrongdoing. For example, it requires the government to take certain legal actions before it can seize a person's property or punish a person. This is known as **due process**. The Constitution prohibits "unreasonable seizures or searches" of Texans' property. This means that, in most cases, a judge must approve a search before the police can carry it out.

Even after he or she is arrested, a person is protected by law. No one can be tried for a crime without being informed of the charges, and everyone is presumed to be innocent until proven guilty in court. Those convicted of crimes are guaranteed not to receive cruel or unusual punishment. In addition, the government cannot pass a law punishing someone for conduct that was not illegal when it was committed.

Texas courts cannot set unreasonably high **bail**, or money that the defendant promises to pay to the court in exchange for release from jail. If the person does not show up for trial, he or she can be arrested. Persons facing very serious criminal charges can be denied bail.

Reading Check **Analyzing Information** What are some of the rights guaranteed to people accused of crimes?

★ Other Rights

Texans benefit from other protections as well under the Texas Bill of Rights. Some rights deal with property. For example, the Constitution gives the government the right of **eminent domain**—the ability to take land from private individuals for public use in some cases. However, the Bill of Rights ensures that the property owner must be paid for the property. In addition, Texans cannot be jailed for unpaid debts. The Bill of Rights also outlines the right of Texans to keep and bear arms.

All of the rights listed above are protected by both the federal and state bills of rights. Some protections in the Texas Bill of Rights, though, are not in the U.S. Bill of Rights. For example, the Texas document guarantees that the state will not fall under military law. In addition, it states that a citizen cannot be outlawed or banished from the state for committing a crime.

In addition, the Texas Bill of Rights includes protections that are intended to protect people from the abuse of government. Under the Texas Bill of Rights, people have the right to alter, reform, or abolish the state government if they feel it is not properly functioning. It states that the national government has authority in Texas only as long as the right of the state to govern itself is maintained. The Texas Bill of Rights also expressly forbids government favoritism toward any individual.

To ensure that people's rights would not be restricted, the Constitution clearly states that the government cannot change the Texas Bill of Rights. No branch of government has the authority to restrict the rights granted in the document, and no law that would attempt to restrict these rights can be enacted. These protections help ensure the freedom of all Texans.

Reading Check **Summarizing** What are some of the other rights guaranteed to Texans?

★ Section 2 Review

hmhsocialstudies.com
ONLINE QUIZ

1. Define and explain:
- slander
- libel
- due process
- bail
- eminent domain

2. Analyzing Information
Copy the table below. Use it to describe the freedoms of speech, press, and assembly.

Freedom of Speech	
Freedom of the Press	
Freedom of Assembly	

3. Finding the Main Idea

a. Describe the rights that a person accused of a crime has under the Texas Bill of Rights.

b. What other rights do Texans have under the Bill of Rights?

4. Writing and Critical Thinking myWriteSmart

Analyzing Information Write a paragraph explaining why freedoms of speech, the press, and assembly are important rights in a democracy.

Consider the following:
- where people get information about issues
- how people can express their political views

CELEBRATE FREEDOM WEEK

On September 17, Constitution Day, Americans celebrate the signing of the United States Constitution in 1787. In Texas, social studies classrooms also observe Celebrate Freedom Week. This important celebration focuses on the meaning and significance of the two foundational documents in United States history—the Declaration of Independence and the U.S. Constitution.

The Declaration of Independence

One of the most eloquent and influential documents ever written, the Declaration of Independence gave the reasons the American colonies were willing to fight for independence. Thomas Jefferson, the main author of the document, began by explaining the purpose of government. Part of this first section, known as the Preamble, must be recited by Texas students during Celebrate Freedom Week. It is perhaps the most famous statement from the document:

> ***"We hold these Truths to be self-evident, that all Men are created equal, that they are endowed by their Creator with certain unalienable Rights, that among these are Life, Liberty, and the Pursuit of Happiness. That to secure these Rights, Governments are instituted among Men, deriving their just Powers from the Consent of the Governed."***
>
> ***—Declaration of Independence***

IN CONGRESS, JULY 4, 1776.

The unanimous Declaration of the thirteen united States of America,

When in the Course of human events, it becomes necessary for one people to dissolve the political bands which have connected them with another, and to assume among the powers of the earth, the separate and equal station to which the Laws of Nature and of Nature's God entitle them, a decent respect to the opinions of mankind requires that they should declare the causes which impel them to the separation. —— We hold these truths to be self-evident, that all men are created equal, that they are endowed by their Creator with certain unalienable Rights, that among these are Life, Liberty and the pursuit of Happiness. — That to secure these rights, Governments are instituted among Men, deriving their just powers from the consent of the governed, — That whenever any Form of Government becomes destructive of these ends, it is the Right of the People to alter or to abolish it, and to institute new Government, laying its foundation on such principles and organizing its powers in such form, as to them shall seem most likely to effect their Safety and Happiness. Prudence, indeed, will dictate that Governments long established should not be changed for light and transient causes; and accordingly all experience hath shewn, that mankind are more disposed to suffer, while evils are sufferable, than to right themselves by abolishing the forms to which they are accustomed. But when a long train of abuses and usurpations, pursuing invariably the same Object

These powerful words established the idea that governments exist to serve their citizens, and that people have basic natural rights that government cannot take away. Throughout our history, these words have inspired Americans to fight for and expand the definitions of freedom, equality, and basic rights. For example, women's rights advocates echoed the language of the Declaration of Independence in 1848 when they demanded the right to vote by declaring that "all men and women are created equal." Abolitionists and civil rights leaders also looked to the Declaration of Independence in their struggles to end slavery and ensure that African Americans were guaranteed equal rights. Even beyond America, the Declaration of Independence has inspired independence and pro-democracy movements around the world. It continues to inspire us today.

KEY FACTS

DECLARATION OF INDEPENDENCE

Date

- Adopted July 4, 1776 by the Continental Congress

Key Author

- Thomas Jefferson

Intent

- To announce formally that the 13 American colonies considered themselves independent states no longer part of the British Empire
- To explain and justify the reasons for independence

Meaning and Importance

- Established in writing the principle that all people have certain fundamental rights that no government can take away
- Explained that the purpose of government is to serve citizens
- Influenced the U.S. Constitution and Bill of Rights
- Has inspired people throughout history in the struggle for equality, justice, and basic human rights

Independence Day

Each 4th of July, Americans celebrate the adoption of the Declaration of Independence with parades, fireworks, picnics, fairs, and ceremonies honoring our freedoms and government.

The U.S. Constitution

Building on the Declaration of Independence, the U.S. Constitution established the system of government that is still in effect today. Another truly ground-breaking document, the Constitution established the rule of law and made clear that no one, including the highest government official, is above it. The document's opening words, the Preamble, elegantly state its purpose:

> ***"We the People of the United States, in Order to form a more perfect Union, establish Justice, insure domestic Tranquility, provide for the common defense, promote the general Welfare, and secure the Blessings of Liberty to ourselves and our Posterity, do ordain and establish this Constitution for the United States of America."***
>
> ***—United States Constitution***

The three opening words, *We the People*, which were written so much larger than the others, announced dramatically that in the United States the people are the source of all government power and authority.

To protect people's rights and to balance power, the Constitution set up a system that divides power among federal and state governments. Federal power is supreme, and certain powers are shared or reserved for the states. A system of checks and balances further divides power among three equal branches of government—legislative, executive, and judicial.

The Constitution also includes a process by which it can be amended, or changed. It is sometimes referred to as "a living document" for this reason; it can be added to and improved by the people to reflect changes in society. Since it was adopted in 1787, the Constitution has been amended 27 times. These amendments have abolished slavery, guaranteed women and minorities the right to vote and to receive equal treatment under the law, changed voting and election procedures, and made other improvements to our government.

One of the most important parts of the Constitution is the Bill of Rights—the first 10 amendments. The Bill of Rights helps protect the rights described in the Declaration of Independence. For example, the Bill of Rights protects such basic rights as freedom of speech, press, and religion as well as due process rights such as the right to a fair trial. The Bill of Rights was an important early addition to the Constitution because it stated in writing some of the specific individual rights and protections guaranteed for all Americans.

KEY FACTS

THE CONSTITUTION

Date

- Adopted September 17, 1787 by the Constitutional Convention

Key Author

- James Madison

Intent

- To establish a new national government of the United States
- To replace the Articles of Confederation
- To safeguard the freedoms of all Americans, present and future

Meaning and Importance

- Established the supreme law of the land for the United States that is still in effect today
- Identifies the people as the ultimate source of government power
- Sets up a system of power sharing among the federal and state government
- Divides power into three equal branches of government
- Includes an amendment process
- Includes the Bill of Rights and other amendments that have protected and expanded individual rights and freedoms

BILL OF RIGHTS

1st Amendment	Protects freedom of religion, speech, press, assembly, petition
2nd Amendment	Protects the right to keep and bear arms
3rd Amendment	Provides restrictions on quartering soldiers in citizens' homes
4th Amendment	Bans unreasonable searches or seizures
5th Amendment	Protects citizens against self-incrimination and being tried twice for the same crime; prohibits government from depriving citizens of life, liberty, or property without due process of law
6th Amendment	Protects citizens' right to a swift and fair trial
7th Amendment	Guarantees right to trial by jury
8th Amendment	Protects citizens against cruel and unusual punishment
9th Amendment	States that citizens have rights beyond those specifically written in the Constitution
10th Amendment	States that powers not given to the government are reserved to the states, or to the people

Research Activity

As part of Celebrate Freedom Week, conduct research on the two most influential documents in U.S. history. First, read the Declaration of Independence and explore how it influenced subsequent American history and has inspired people for generations. In your own words, explain how the Declaration of Independence is still relevant in our lives today. Then, review a copy of the U.S. Constitution to explore how it has been amended throughout our nation's history. Give an example of how the Constitution or Bill of Rights protects your rights, and the rights of others.

Section 3

Citizenship and Elections

Main Ideas

1. Citizens in Texas have many responsibilities.
2. Texans take part in several types of elections.

Key Terms

- **runoff election**
- **general elections**
- **special election**
- **referendum**

Why It Matters Today

Texans go to the polls regularly to choose leaders and decide on issues. Use current events sources to find information on a recent election.

TEKS: 16A, 16B, 17C, 21B, 21E, 22D,

myNotebook

Use the annotation tools in your eBook to take notes on the responsibilities of citizens and the roles they play in government.

The Story Continues

Since 1995, people from towns along the Rio Grande—in both the United States and Mexico—have gathered once a year to celebrate the importance of the river. The annual event is called Día del Río—"Day of the River." Volunteers gather to clean up the often polluted river. Among other activities, they plant trees, build trails, and clean up litter.

★ Civic Responsibilities and Participation

Texans who participate in volunteer activities such as Día del Río are fulfilling their civic responsibilities. Civic responsibilities are duties and behaviors expected of all citizens. Fulfilling these responsibilities is necessary for keeping our democracy running properly.

One of the most fundamental civic responsibilities in our society is obeying the law. Imagine what might happen if people did not obey the law. Society would quickly fall apart. In order to obey the laws, people must know what the laws are. It is the responsibility of individual citizens to educate themselves about federal, state, and local laws. The government can punish a lawbreaker even if he or she is unaware of the law. If Texans disagree with a law, they can try to change it by speaking to their local representative or by challenging the law in court. They can also petition the government or vote for officials who oppose the law.

Paying taxes is another important civic responsibility. The government needs tax money to pay for important public services. Without taxes, the government could not provide schools, roads, and police and fire protection. Texans pay several state taxes, including sales and property taxes. They also pay federal income taxes.

Citizens are also expected to serve on juries when called to do so. For the right to trial by jury in the Texas Bill of Rights to have any meaning, citizens must serve when called.

Perhaps the most important civic responsibility for Texans is taking part in the government. Civic participation is vital for the running of any republic. As Texas Congressman Sam Rayburn explained, it can also be fun and rewarding.

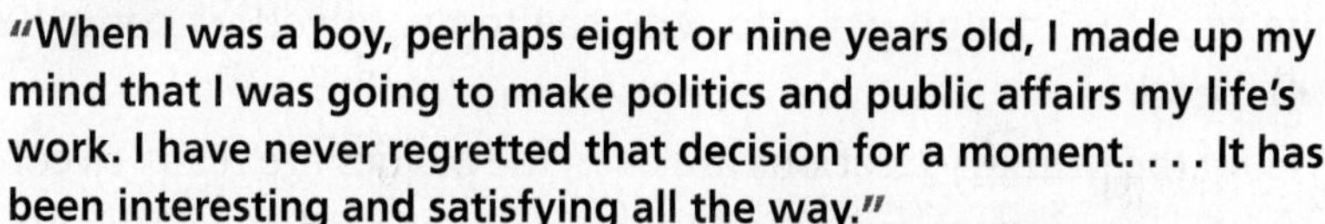

TEXAS VOICES

"When I was a boy, perhaps eight or nine years old, I made up my mind that I was going to make politics and public affairs my life's work. I have never regretted that decision for a moment. . . . It has been interesting and satisfying all the way."

—Sam Rayburn, "Mr. Sam's Legacy to Aspiring Young Politicians," Rayburn Library, Bonham, Texas

Voting is the most basic way for Texans to participate in their government. Our government is based on the consent of the governed. Therefore we must let our leaders know when we approve or disapprove of their actions. Texans do this by casting votes for or against particular candidates and issues.

Because votes affect government policy, citizens have a duty to stay informed. To cast a vote wisely, a citizen must be well informed about candidates, current events, and key issues. Staying informed involves taking an interest in government programs and activities.

Being informed is just the start of participating in the government. Democracy also needs people who are willing to join political parties and help shape their positions on issues. It also needs people who are willing to serve as elected government officials.

Reading Check **Drawing Inferences and Conclusions** Why is political participation important in a republic?

Citizenship and You

Public Service

There are many ways citizens of all ages can contribute to their communities. Many Texas teenagers have donated their time to library reading programs for young children. Others volunteer with church groups, community centers, and hospitals. **In what ways can Texans fulfill their civic responsibilities?**

★ Elections

Although most Texans will not serve in office, nearly all of them will vote in elections during their lifetimes. All citizens have the right to vote in elections. A voter must be a U.S. citizen and at least 18 years old. Texas voters must have lived in the state for at least 30 days before the election and must live in the county in which they registered to vote.

Before they can vote in an election, citizens must register. Registration ensures that a person is legally eligible to vote. To register, a potential voter fills out a simple form and sends it to the voter registrar—a county official. Within 30 days, the voter receives a registration certificate to present when it is time to vote.

Voting policies in Texas are set by law and supervised by the secretary of state. Citizens vote in the areas in which they live, either in person or by mail. Most of the hands-on work of carrying out elections is handled by county officials. Local officials print ballots and provide voting equipment. Volunteers also help the process run smoothly.

BIOGRAPHY

Kay Bailey Hutchison (1943–) Born in Galveston, Kay Bailey Hutchison attended law school at the University of Texas. In 1972 she was elected to the Texas House of Representatives but left politics for a time afterward. She became state treasurer in 1990. In 1993 she was elected to the U.S. Senate in a special election to fill the vacancy left when Senator Lloyd Bentsen resigned. In her political career, Hutchison set a trail for other women. She was the first Republican woman elected to the Texas House of Representatives and to state office, and she was the first Texas woman of either party to be a U.S. senator. What offices has Hutchison held?

There are many types of elections in Texas. Many of these elections help determine who will hold offices in the state. The election of political officials is a multi-step process.

First, political parties hold primary elections to decide who will represent the party in full elections. Voters can only participate in one party primary. For example, someone who voted in the Democratic primary cannot vote in the Republican primary that same year. Any candidate who receives more than 50 percent of the votes in a primary wins. If no one receives enough votes to win, the top vote getters compete in a **runoff election**.

When the primary elections are over, the parties are ready to compete directly. **General elections** decide who wins a particular state or local office. At the same time, citizens may be asked to vote on certain issues, such as constitutional amendments. All registered voters may participate in general elections. General elections for statewide office are held in November of even-numbered years when there is no presidential race. General elections at the local level are usually held in odd-numbered years.

If an office becomes vacant between elections, voters may return to the polls for a **special election** held to fill the vacancy. Special elections can also be held for constitutional amendments and local bond issues.

In a representative democracy such as Texas, elected officials represent the people. At times, however, Texans decide issues directly. For example, a **referendum** allows citizens to vote on such issues as constitutional amendments. A referendum can also be used to repeal, or do away with, a law. Initiatives allow voters to propose local laws and then require a vote on the measure. Citizens can propose initiatives if a given number of voters sign petitions for the measure. Another example of direct government participation in Texas is the recall. A recall is an election that gives voters the chance to remove a local official from office.

Reading Check **Analyzing Information** In what types of elections can Texas citizens vote?

Section 3 Review

1. Define and explain:
- runoff election
- general elections
- special election
- referendum

2. Sequencing
Copy the graphic organizer below. Use it to show in order the steps that a citizen must take before voting.

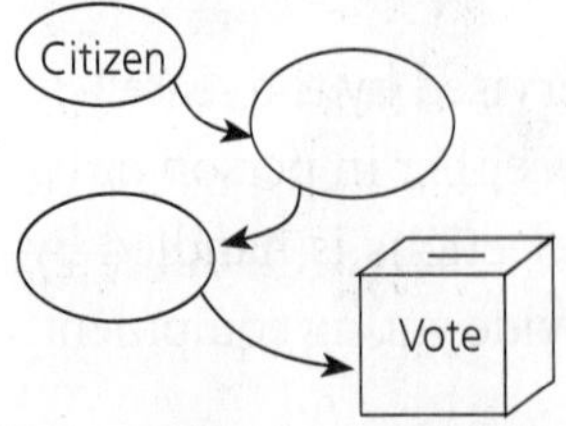

3. Finding the Main Idea
a. Why is civic participation important?
b. What types of elections are held in Texas?

4. Writing and Critical Thinking my WriteSmart
Evaluating Write a paragraph analyzing Texans' civic responsibilities. In your paragraph, identify the two responsibilities that you believe are most important.
Consider the following:
- benefits of civic responsibilities
- civic responsibility and democracy

Section 4

Political Parties and Interest Groups

Main Ideas

1. Political parties nominate candidates and help shape policy in Texas.
2. Interest groups can influence officials' points of view.

Key Terms

- **interest groups**
- **lobby**
- **political action committees**

Why It Matters Today

Political races—whether for national, state, or local office—are exciting events. Use current events sources to find information on a recent political campaign in your area.

TEKS: 16B, 17A, 17C, 21B, 21D, 21E, 22D

myNotebook

Use the annotation tools in your eBook to take notes on the roles of political parties and interest groups in the political process.

The Story Continues

Molly Beth Malcolm's parents taught her about the value of voting. Voting, she learned, was a key way to take part in the political process. She carried this belief into adulthood, serving as chairperson of the Texas Democratic Party from 1998 to 2003. She enjoys competing with Republicans. "I'm glad Texas is a two-party state. That's how democracy should be."

Political Parties

Political participation is an important duty of citizens in a democracy, and political parties are one way for citizens to participate. Parties nominate and elect government officials and thus help shape government policy. Each party has a set of stated goals called its platform. The candidates a party nominates for office generally support the goals set up in the party platform.

The two major political parties in Texas—and the United States—are the Democratic Party and the Republican Party. The Democratic Party dominated Texas politics for about 100 years after Reconstruction, making Texas virtually a one-party state during this time. In the late 1970s Republicans began winning many statewide political offices, and Texas became a two-party state. In the late 1990s and early 2000s, Republican candidates won every major election, and Republicans held every state office. This made Texas once again one-party state in practice. Although third parties sometimes have influenced Texas politics in different eras, they have not greatly affected state politics in recent years.

Interpreting Visuals

Political parties.** The Republican and Democratic parties hold national conventions every four years to choose presidential candidates. The 1992 Republican National Convention was in Houston.* ***What is the atmosphere at this convention like?

The Democratic Party is the older of the two major parties in Texas. When Texas joined the United States, the Democratic Party was the party of states' rights. Democrats believed state governments should be allowed to make decisions for their states with limited interference from the federal government. In addition, the Democrats supported slavery.

The Republican Party, in contrast, was founded to oppose slavery. Because Texas was a slave state, the Republican Party was not popular at first. After the Civil War and Reconstruction, the Republican Party became the champion of small businesses and farmers.

For much of the state's history, the Democratic Party was considered conservative, and the Republicans were seen as liberal. In the twentieth century, though, changes in party platforms brought about changes in people's perceptions. Today, the Republican Party is the more conservative party, while the Democrats tend to be more liberal. Democrats support federal programs to address such issues as protecting the environment and helping the less fortunate. Republicans, on the other hand, argue that states, individuals, and private businesses should deal with such issues.

Reading Check **Identifying Points of View** How are Democrats' and Republicans' views on some issues similar and different?

Interest Groups

Many Texans take part in the political process by forming or joining **interest groups**. Such groups try to affect decisions made by officials in the government. Interest groups **lobby**, or try to persuade, government officials to support the group's goals. Interest groups hire lobbyists to meet with public officials and argue for their goals.

Interest groups are not a new concept in Texas. For more than a century, groups of citizens have banded together to make their opinions known about key issues. For example, the Patrons of Husbandry, or Grange, pushed for legislation that would benefit farmers in the late 1800s. The Texas Women's Political Caucus in the 1970s campaigned to get women elected to offices across the state.

Many interest groups operate within Texas today. Business groups such as the Texas Mortgage Bankers Association focus on economic issues, while the League of United Latin American Citizens (LULAC) works to protect the civil rights of the state's Hispanic Americans. Mothers Against Drunk Driving (MADD) supports the passage of laws designed to prevent drunk driving.

In some cases, interest groups have different points of view on important issues and campaign against each other. In Texas today, interest groups try to sway legislators' opinions about such topics as health care, education priorities, campaign spending laws, and water usage. Some issues with which interest groups are involved, such as gun control and immigration policy, are sensitive subjects about which many Texans feel strongly. Interest groups on both sides of these issues spend hundreds of thousands of dollars lobbying the legislature to support their views.

One way that people tried to gain the support of legislators is by raising money for their campaigns. Many officials are more willing to support causes favored by those who donate to their campaigns. Contributions to political candidates can be made directly or through **political action committees** (PACs). PACs are groups that raise and spend money for a candidate. Contributions are important to political campaigns, which are expensive, particularly in races for statewide office.

Campaign money pays for advertisements on radio, television, and in the newspapers. Texas sets no limit on how much money a PAC can accept or spend. But PACs must report information about their contributors and how the money is spent. PACs provide another way for Texans to participate in the political process.

Reading Check **Summarizing** What role do political action committees play in Texas politics?

That's Interesting!

Every Vote Counts

Whether you are a voter or an elected government official, voting is crucial. In 1845 Texas became the 28th state by a very slender margin. The final vote in the U.S. Senate was 27 to 25. In 1912 Woodrow Wilson was elected president by less than one vote per precinct in one state. In the 2000 presidential election, Texan George W. Bush won the electoral college vote by receiving 537 more popular votes in Florida than candidate Vice President Al Gore did.

Section 4 Review

1. Define and explain:
- interest groups
- lobby
- political action committees

2. Evaluating
Copy the graphic organizer below. Use it to show why interest groups form and the activities in which they engage.

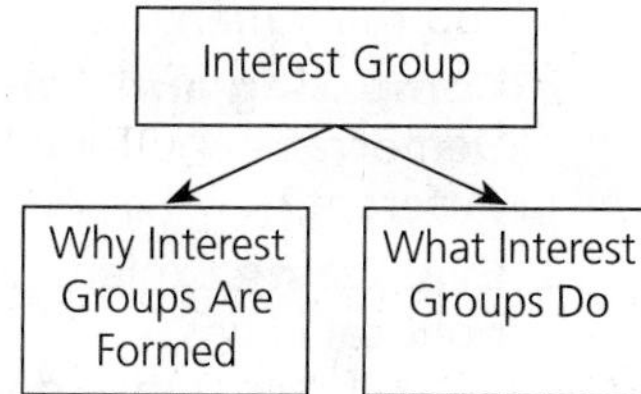

3. Finding the Main Idea

a. Describe the points of view of political parties in Texas on key issues, past and present.

b. What are some points of view supported now or in the past by interest groups in Texas?

4. Writing and Critical Thinking myWriteSmart

Supporting a Point of View Imagine that you are running for governor. Write an e-mail to an interest group explaining why it should support you.

Consider the following:
- the interest group's positions
- why you support these positions

The Chapter at a Glance

Examine the following visual summary of the chapter. Then use the visual to create an outline about local government and citizenship that you could use as a study guide.

Local Government

Local Government

County Government | Municipal Government | Special District (such as school districts)

Rights and Responsibilities

Rights

The Texas Bill of Rights ensures that each citizen has the rights to freedom of press, speech, and religion as well as a trial by jury.

Responsibilities

Texas citizens have responsibilities such as obeying the law, paying taxes, and public service. A responsible citizen is also an educated voter.

Politics

Political Parties

Texas politics is dominated by two political parties, the Democratic and Republican Parties. These parties create platforms and raise funds for their candidates.

Interest Groups

Interest groups and political action committees lobby the legislature to pass laws.

Identifying People and Ideas

Use the following terms or individuals in sentences.

1. commissioners' court
2. special districts
3. due process
4. eminent domain
5. runoff election
6. general elections
7. special election
8. referendum
9. interest group
10. lobby

Understanding Main Ideas

Section 1

1. Describe the structure and function of local governments.
2. Describe the major sources of revenue for local governments.

Section 2

3. What rights do Texans have?
4. Which rights are granted by both the Texas Bill of Rights and the U.S. Bill of Rights? Which are only granted by the Texas Bill of Rights?

Section 3

5. What are the civic responsibilities of Texans?
6. Describe the different elections in Texas, and explain why they are held.

Section 4

7. How do political parties and interest groups try to influence government policy?

You Be the Historian

Reviewing Themes

1. **Constitutional Heritage** Describe the importance of freedoms of speech and the press in a democratic society.
2. **Citizenship** What are the rights and duties of Texas citizens, and why are they important?
3. **Government** How does the Texas Bill of Rights allow Texans to debate important issues?

Thinking Critically

1. **Drawing Inferences and Conclusions** Why do you think many Texans form interest groups?
2. **Comparing and Contrasting** How are the Democratic and Republican Parties similar and different?
3. **Evaluating** Explain how being informed on political issues is an important civic responsibility in a representative democracy.

Texas Test Practice

Interpreting Graphs

Study the graph below. Use it to answer the following questions.

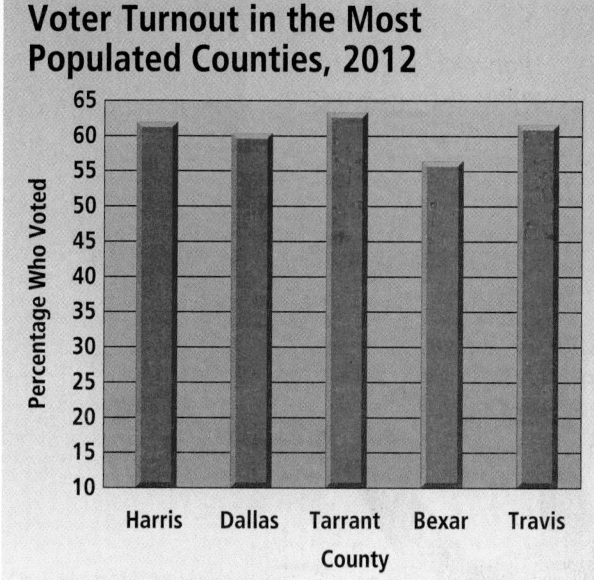

1. Which Texas county had the highest voter turnout, and what was the difference between it and the next highest county?
   - **A** Tarrant; 63 percent
   - **B** Travis; 5 percent
   - **C** Tarrant; 1.5 percent
   - **D** Bexar; 10 percent

2. What was the average voter turnout in these counties? Why might some people argue that more people should vote?

Analyzing Primary Sources

Read the following quote by former governor Bill Clements. Then answer the questions.

"You too have a responsibility to help achieve good government, and that responsibility goes beyond voting on election day. When we as individuals, and as a state are silent—when we let others make decisions for us without stating our beliefs—we forfeit [give up] our freedom. When we stand up and speak out, when we express our desires and concerns, then and only then, will we have effective government."

3. Which of the following statements best describes the author's point of view?
   - **F** Voting is the only way for people to express their points of view.
   - **G** Speaking out rarely results in better government.
   - **H** Only governmental leaders can bring about good government.
   - **J** People can best protect their freedom by speaking out.

4. What does Clements believe the people of Texas should do to create more effective government?

Interdisciplinary Connection to the Arts

Imagine that you and several of your classmates belong to a political party and are delegates to your party's convention. Create a platform for your party, describing the issues that are most important to you and considering the rights and civic responsibilities of Texans. You might want to research the platforms of the Democratic and Republican Parties for ideas and to learn their points of view on issues that are important to Texans. Work as a group to write a catchy song that expresses your party's stance on an issue.

Internet Activity 

Go online to research and identify the contributions of one of the following Texas leaders: Sul Ross, John Nance Garner, James Baker, Henry B. Gonzáles, Kay Bailey Hutchison, Barbara Jordan, Raymond Telles, Raul Gonzales, Sam Rayburn, George H.W. Bush, George W. Bush, or Lyndon B. Johnson. Then write a biography in which you examine how he or she came to participate in government. Also note his or her accomplishments and leadership skills. Be sure to check your biography for standard grammar, spelling, sentence structure, punctuation, and citation of sources.

CHAPTER 32

The Texas Economy

Texas Essential Knowledge and Skills (TEKS)

7B, 7F, 9A, 12C, 13A, 13B, 13C, 17C, 20A, 20B, 20C, 20D, 20E, 21A, 21B, 21C, 21E, 22A, 22B, 22C, 22D

High-tech products made in Texas are sold around the world.

Military advances have influenced the Texas aerospace industry.

	1900	1915	1930	1945

TEXAS

1901 The Spindletop oil strike spurs the growth of the Texas oil industry.

1939 The Southern Aircraft Corporation, the first airplane manufacturer in Texas, is formed.

U.S. and WORLD

1908 The Ford Motor Company introduces the Model T.

1938 A viable source of oil is discovered in Saudi Arabia, launching a new industry.

1946 The U.S. Army develops ENIAC, considered the world's first general-purpose computer.

As a Texan . . . *How are you tied to the world economy?*

Build on What You Know

Since people first arrived in Texas, they have sought ways to survive. From early farmers and ranchers to modern software engineers, Texans have branched into all types of economic activities. Decisions made in Texas affect life all around the world, and vice versa.

Billions of dollars worth of goods are shipped through Texas ports each year to markets around the world.

1957 The Soviet Union launches *Sputnik,* the first artificial satellite.

1960

1961 The Manned Space Center, now the Johnson Space Center, is built in Houston.

1967 Texas Instruments releases the first handheld calculator.

1975

1979 OPEC blocks the sale of oil to the United States.

1990

1994 The North American Free Trade Agreement is passed, easing trade among the United States, Mexico, and Canada.

2003 Fearing contamination, Japan bans the import of beef from the United States.

2005

2012 Texas exports more than $134 billion worth of goods.

Present

You Be the Historian

*my*Notebook

What's Your Opinion? Do you **agree** or **disagree** with the following statements? Support your point of view in your notebook.

- **Economics** Economic activities shape how people live.
- **Science, Technology & Society** Developments in technology are always beneficial to economic activities.
- **Global Relations** Countries should promote policies that make international trade easier.

Section 1

The Free Enterprise System

Main Ideas

1. The free enterprise system allows people to run businesses with little government interference.
2. Market forces like supply, demand, and competition drive business decisions.
3. The government plays several roles in the economy.

Key Terms

- **free enterprise**
- **profit**
- **supply**
- **demand**
- **competition**

Why It Matters Today

Thousands of Texans have created businesses under the free enterprise system. Use current events sources to find information about new companies in your area.

TEKS: 13B, 17C, 21B, 21C, 21E, 22D

Use the annotation tools in your eBook to take notes on the benefits of the free enterprise system.

The Story Continues

In 1978 John Mackey decided to open a health food store in Austin. He thought the people of Austin would support a business that provided them with healthier, more natural options. Mackey had to borrow $45,000 to get his business running, but it soon took off. Within a few years, he opened more locations, expanding his company into Houston, Dallas, and other cities. Today, his company—Whole Foods Market—is one of the country's biggest grocery store chains.

The Opportunity for Success

Business owners like John Mackey are able to become wealthy because Texas, like the rest of the United States, operates under the free enterprise system. **Free enterprise** is an economic system in which business can be conducted with limited direction or interference from the government. Business owners and corporations decide for themselves how to run their companies. Free enterprise is also known as the free market system or capitalism.

The free enterprise system offers Texans the opportunity to become successful and make profits. **Profit** is the money that a business has left after it pays its expenses. In a free enterprise system, profits belong to the owners of the business, whether a single owner or a huge group of corporate stockholders. The opportunity to create wealth through profits is what inspires most new business owners and investors.

Of course, a business does not have to be as big as Whole Foods to be successful. Millions of business owners make enough money to support themselves and their families without becoming wealthy. However, by starting a business, an individual also opens himself or herself to the possibility of failure. Many businesses do not perform as well as their owners hope. Others do well for a time, only to fail for reasons beyond the owner's control. The owners of such businesses can lose huge amounts of money—or even their businesses. The possibility for failure is the main risk that people face in the free enterprise system.

Texans have taken advantage of the opportunities provided by the free enterprise system. By 2012 more than half a million businesses were operating in the state. These ranged from small businesses with only a few employees to international corporations that employ thousands. The state government encourages the creation of businesses in Texas. In 2013, Governor Rick Perry emphasized freedom from government regulation that is at the heart of free enterprise.

TEXAS VOICES

"One of the reasons Texas excels both at creating jobs and creating new technology is because we free people to do their best work. And freedom breeds innovation. It's as simple as that."

—Governor Rick Perry, September 11, 2013

Reading Check **Summarizing** What role does profit play in the free enterprise system?

The Role of the Market

The American free enterprise system is one example of a market economy, a system in which people are free to buy and sell whatever goods they wish. For example, if you decide you want to buy a shirt, you can choose whichever one you want. No one will force you to buy a particular brand or style. You can choose which store to shop at, how many shirts to buy, and so on.

Because customers are free to choose which products to buy, companies must figure out how to make products that appeal to those customers. One of the main factors companies use to attract customers is pricing. You might think that a business that wants to attract customers will set its prices very low. After all, people are more likely to buy a particular product when it is priced low. However, pricing is not that simple. It is governed by two economic principles called supply and demand. **Supply** refers to how much of a given product businesses are willing to produce. In general, businesses will produce more products when they

CONNECTING TO

ECONOMICS

Small Businesses in Texas

As of 2010, more than 2 million small businesses operated in Texas. In fact, there are far more small businesses in the state than there are large ones. More than half of the companies in Texas employ fewer than five people. A huge number have no employees at all. These businesses consist of an individual—the business owner—working alone. Only about 5,000 companies, such as Whole Foods, Exxon Mobil, and AT&T, employ more than 500 employees.

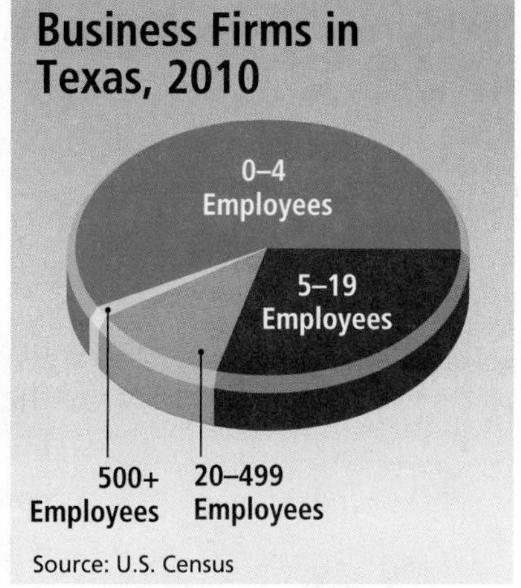

Interpreting Graphs

1. Use the graph to estimate the percentage of Texas firms with fewer than 20 employees.
2. Why do you think small firms are more common than large ones?

Interpreting Visuals

Supply and demand. *The available supply of a product often helps determine its price.* ***How might prices at this farmers' market change from season to season?***

can sell them at higher prices. They will produce fewer products when prices are low. **Demand** refers to how much of a product buyers are willing to purchase. The demand for a product is usually higher when prices are low and tends to drop as prices rise.

Supply and demand work together to determine prices. For example, suppose that a bakery in Denton makes pies. Each pie costs about $4 to make. If the bakery sells the pies for $5 each, it will make only $1 profit on each pie. As a result, the bakery owner may not be willing to make very many pies. On the other hand, if she can sell pies for $15 each, her profit on each sale will be $11. She would probably be much more eager to make pies to sell. A customer, however, would be much less likely to purchase a pie for $15 than for $5. If the bakery makes 20 pies each day but sells only one, then the owner loses money. As a result, she must carefully consider both factors—her desire for profit and her customers' willingness to buy her goods—in setting the best price for her pies.

The effects of supply and demand on prices can be seen in many industries. As droughts worsened in Texas in 2010, water supplies dwindled. In response, cities were forced to raise the rates they charged residents for water. San Antonio, for example, raised its water rates by as much as 33 percent for some residents in that year.

Supply and demand are not the only factors that affect pricing. Another is **competition**, the rivalry between companies selling similar products. If two companies produce goods of equal quality but price them differently, more customers will be drawn to the company with lower prices. As a result, the presence of competition can often force companies to lower their prices. As an example, consider the Texas cotton industry. Before the 1920s, cotton was one of the state's most valuable products. Texas cotton was sold to textile mills throughout the country, and cotton producers made huge profits. Around that time, however, other countries began shipping cotton to the United States. This imported cotton was priced lower than Texas cotton. Texas growers saw a sharp decline in their profits. Similarly, competition from oil producers in Southwest Asia in the 1950s and 1960s led to lower prices for Texas oil and—for a time—the weakening of the Texas oil industry.

Competition has effects that extend far beyond pricing, though. Competition can push a company to improve its products or develop new ones in order to lure customers. For example, an electronics company might work to make mobile devices with more data storage than its rival company makes. A car company might seek to improve the safety of its cars to encourage buyers to purchase them. In the bakery example above, the owner might look for new, better-tasting recipes. Customers are often willing to pay higher prices for products if those products are of higher quality than other options.

Reading Check **Finding the Main Idea** What are some factors that affect pricing in a free enterprise system?

Government Regulation

While government interference in a free market economy is limited, this does not mean that the government has no part. In fact, the government plays several important roles in the functioning of the Texas economy.

One of the government's roles is regulation. It passes and enforces laws that ensure businesses are run fairly and safely. For example, the government requires factories to meet basic standards for worker safety and food sellers to meet certain standards for quality. Those that do not follow government regulations can be fined or shut down. The government has also passed laws that prohibit employers from paying their workers less than a minimum amount.

The government also works to protect competition in the marketplace. As you have read, competition is central to the free enterprise system. As a result, the government works to stop practices that would limit or prevent competition. For example, the government has banned monopolies. A monopoly is a company that is the only one providing a particular good or service. Because a monopoly has no competition, it can set whatever prices it wants. Such a practice is bad for consumers, who have no choice but to pay extremely high prices.

Similarly, the government protects the ideas of the people who create products. Suppose an individual works for years to develop an exciting new product. He or she does not want rivals to copy that product and sell it for themselves. The government provides two ways to protect ideas. A patent gives an individual the exclusive right to make and sell an invention for a certain number of years. A copyright is the exclusive right to publish or sell a piece of writing, music, or art.

Reading Check **Analyzing Information** How does the government help to protect the rights of innovators?

Section 1 Review

hmhsocialstudies.com
ONLINE QUIZ

1. Define and explain:
- free enterprise
- profit
- supply
- demand
- competition

2. Summarizing
Copy the graphic organizer below. Use it to explain the effects of various elements of the free enterprise system on the Texas economy.

Profit	
Supply and demand	
Competition	
Government regulation	

3. Finding the Main Idea

a. What role does competition play in the free enterprise system?

b. How are supply and demand related to price in a free enterprise system?

4. Writing and Critical Thinking myWriteSmart

Making Generalizations Imagine that you are a business owner talking to students. Write a short speech describing the benefits of the free enterprise system.

Consider the following:
- the chance for profit
- the role of the government

Section 2

Texas Industries

Main Ideas

1. Farming and ranching have been major economic activities in Texas since the state's earliest days.
2. Oil and gas dominated the Texas economy in the twentieth century.
3. New industries have developed and expanded in Texas since World War II.

Key Terms and People

- **agribusiness**
- **feedlots**
- **information technology**
- **semiconductors**
- **Michael Dell**
- **dot-coms**

Why It Matters Today

New industries are created in Texas every year. Use current events sources to find information on developing industries in Texas today.

TEKS: 7B, 12C, 13A, 13C, 20A, 20B, 20C, 20D, 20E, 21B, 21C, 22D

***my*Notebook**

Use the annotation tools in your eBook to take notes on the industries found across Texas today.

The Story Continues

Bob Beakley owns a large farm near Ennis, Texas. He grows a variety of crops on his farm, but one of the most important is wheat. Some 1,700 acres of farmland—the same amount of land as in 1,285 football fields—is devoted to wheat. Despite planting over such a huge area, it takes only Beakley and his son to harvest all of their wheat, thanks to modern technology. However, even the latest technology cannot prevent nature from destroying crops. In 2009 a late freeze killed nearly half of Beakley's wheat crop.

Agriculture

For over two centuries, farming was the backbone of the Texas economy, and it remains important in the state today. In 2000, **agribusiness**—large-scale farming and processing of crops—and related industries employed about 14 percent of the state's workers. Agribusiness brings about $36 billion to the state each year.

Commercial farming can be a risky business. The fertile soils and mild winters in Texas make it a good place to farm, but the hot, dry summers present a challenge. Crops may wilt in the heat. Farmers turn to irrigation to bring water to their fields. Irrigation systems can be expensive, though. Plant diseases, drought, competition, and other factors can also hurt a farmer's chances for success.

Like farming, ranching has long been a major industry in Texas. Today, Texas produces more beef than any other state. The state is the country's leading producer of wool from both sheep and goats. Modern ranching bears little resemblance to the operations worked by the cowboys of the 1800s. Instead of sprawling open pastures, most cattle are raised in commercial **feedlots**. A feedlot is a large area of enclosed land on which animals are kept and fed to make ready for market. Cattle on feedlots are fed blends of grains mixed with vitamins and minerals. This feed is meant to keep cattle healthy and to guarantee that they will produce tender, flavorful beef. In addition, ranchers use modern technology such as computers and helicopters to keep track of their herds.

Interpreting Visuals

Modern ranching. *Most commercial ranching today takes place on huge feedlots.* ***Based on this photo, how is modern ranching different from ranching in the 1800s?***

Reading Check **Finding the Main Idea** What are some risks common in the agriculture industry?

 Oil and Gas Industry

Although a few companies began drilling for oil in the late 1800s, the Texas oil industry was really born in 1901. The Spindletop strike that year launched the state's first oil boom. New fields popped up all along the Gulf coast. Over time, the industry spread throughout the state, extending into North and West Texas. By the 1930s oil production had increased tremendously, and oil had become the state's major industry. By that time, oil was in high demand around the world.

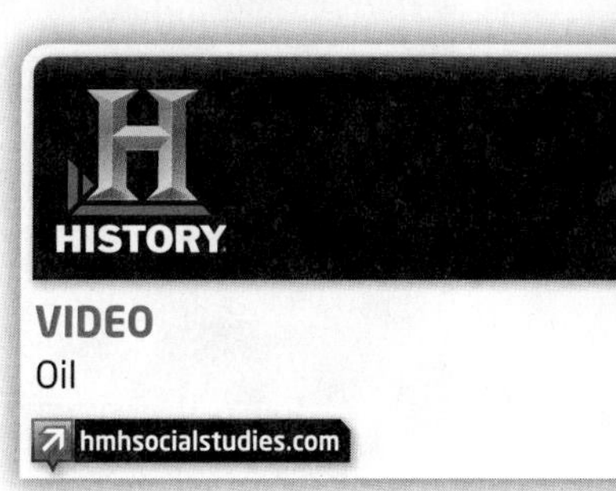

As oil production was expanding, the market for natural gas was also increasing. Gas was first discovered as a by-product of oil drilling, because the two are frequently found near each other.

CONNECTING TO

SCIENCE AND TECHNOLOGY

Drilling Technology

Much of the oil and gas in Texas is found in rock beds deep underground. Early drilling methods could not reach these deposits, so they remained untapped for decades. In the 1940s some companies began using a process called hydraulic fracturing, or "fracking," to access these deposits. Water, sand, and chemicals are shot at high pressure down wells. This mixture opens seams in the rock and allows oil and gas to be extracted. While fracking has increased oil production, some people fear that it can lead to pollution of aquifers. **How has technology changed how Texans use oil resources?**

Over the next few decades, oil prices rose and fell in response to customer demand. The biggest change came in the 1970s when the United States lost access to oil from some countries in Southwest Asia. With a major source of foreign oil cut off, the country turned to domestic sources, including Texas. When world production increased in the 1980s, Texas production dropped. Since then, prices have risen and fallen due to a number of factors. Production has increased and decreased in response. In 2013, for example, oil production in Texas was double what it had been just three years earlier.

The oil and gas industry is a major part of the Texas economy. The state has about one-fourth of all U.S. oil reserves. It produces more oil per day than any other state. The state's petroleum refineries handle about a quarter of all refining in the country. Texas is also the country's leading natural gas producer. Texas and Louisiana together account for about 40 percent of the natural gas produced in the United States.

Reading Check **Analyzing Information** How have the oil and gas industries been affected by events worldwide?

★ Aviation and Aerospace Industries

The Texas aviation industry was born shortly before the United States entered World War II. In 1939 the state's first airplane-manufacturing center opened near Houston. More centers followed, mostly in the Dallas–Fort Worth area. In addition, the U.S. military opened bases and pilot-training centers in Texas. Although production of aircraft dropped after the war ended, an industry had been born. By the 1960s aircraft manufacturing had picked up again in Texas. Fort Worth became a leading aviation and aerospace center. The choice of Houston as the base for NASA's Manned Spacecraft Center solidified the state's position in the industry.

Today, Texas remains one of the major centers for aircraft manufacturing. Companies such as Lockheed Martin Aeronautics and Bell Helicopter, both of Fort Worth, produce planes and helicopters for the U.S. military. Two major commercial airlines have headquarters in Texas. American Airlines is based in Fort Worth, and Southwest Airlines is based in Dallas. These airlines help connect passengers from Texas and the rest of the country with cities across the country and around the world.

Dallas/Fort Worth International Airport is one of the busiest airports in the world. It connects Dallas to more than 200 destinations around the world.

Reading Check **Summarizing** What elements make up the aerospace industry in Texas?

★ Medical Industry

Medical researchers in Texas have worked hard to meet the health needs of the state and the world. As a result, Texas has earned a reputation as a leader in medicine. Medical research centers around the state have drawn millions of dollars in funding for medical research. In 2012 Texas medical centers spent nearly $2.6 billion on biomedical research. Research and technological developments have led to the growth of a major medical industry in Texas. By 2012 Texas had 630 hospitals, 9 medical schools, and 100 nursing schools. The state provides medical services and devices to people and hospitals around the world. Many Texas hospitals have reputations as excellent care centers. The University of Texas M.D. Anderson Cancer Center in Houston, for instance, has been called the best cancer treatment facility in the country.

The state's leading position in the medical field is largely due to the work of prominent surgeons and researchers. For example, you read earlier about the work of surgeons Michael DeBakey, who performed the first arterial bypass surgery, and Denton Cooley, who implanted the first artificial heart. In 1998 Dr. Ferid Murad of the University of Texas was a co-winner of the Nobel Prize in Physiology or Medicine for his research on the relationship between chemicals and the heart.

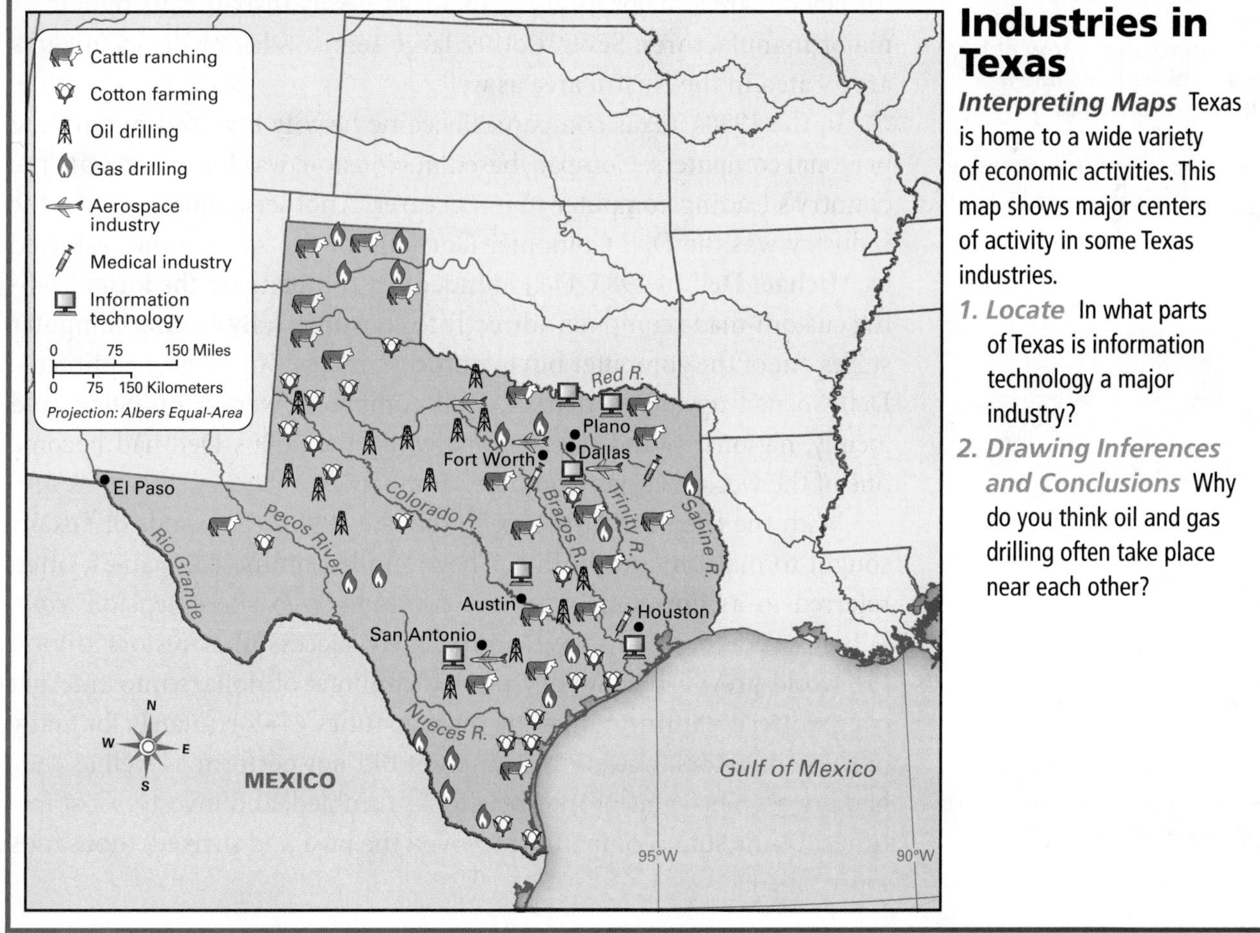

Industries in Texas

Interpreting Maps Texas is home to a wide variety of economic activities. This map shows major centers of activity in some Texas industries.

1. ***Locate*** In what parts of Texas is information technology a major industry?
2. ***Drawing Inferences and Conclusions*** Why do you think oil and gas drilling often take place near each other?

In addition to hospitals and research centers, Texas is also home to several medical equipment manufacturers and pharmaceutical companies. These companies make lifesaving devices and medicines that are used in doctors' offices and hospitals around the world.

Reading Check **Drawing Inferences and Conclusions** How does the Texas medical industry affect the lives of people around the world?

BIOGRAPHY

Michael Dell (1965–)
As the founder of Dell Inc., Michael Dell is one of the biggest names in the Texas computer industry. The company was born when Dell was a freshman at the University of Texas. At a time when computers were sold only through stores, he started a business selling built-to-order computers directly to customers. Sales took off, and Dell's company became one of the world's leading computer manufacturers. **How did Michael Dell become a leader in the high-tech industry?**

★ Computer and Information Technology Industry

One of the fastest-growing segments of the Texas economy is the computer and information technology industry. **Information technology** (IT) is the development, maintenance, and use of computer hardware and software. The computer industry in Texas began shortly after World War II, not long after the first computers were developed.

Although the computer was not invented in Texas, researchers in the state soon adapted to the new technology. In the 1950s and 1960s, for example, Texas Instruments of Dallas developed the first transistor radio and handheld calculator. Both devices used **semiconductors**, or materials that conduct some electricity, but not as much as most metals do. Semiconductors are vital to modern electronics. Today semiconductor devices are a major industry in Texas. Texas Instruments remains a major manufacturer. Several other large semiconductor device makers are located in the Austin area as well.

In the 1980s Texas companies became heavily involved in building personal computers. Compaq, based in Houston, was for many years the country's leading computer manufacturer. Another major player in the industry was the Dell Computer Corporation—now Dell Inc.—started by **Michael Dell** in 1985. Dell founded his company on the idea of selling custom-made computers directly to consumers. By cutting computer stores out of the computer buying process and selling to people directly, Dell opened up a new market. Dell computers were soon being sold locally, nationally, and internationally. By the 2000s Dell had become one of the world's largest computer companies.

With the rise of the Internet in the late 1990s, thousands of Texans sought to make money online. They founded online companies, often referred to as **dot-coms** after the common Web site extension *.com*. When several dot-coms were immediately successful, investors around the world grew excited. They poured millions of dollars into Internet companies, dreaming of making huge fortunes. Unfortunately for many of these investors, however, the market did not perform as well as they had hoped. The value of Internet stocks tumbled, and investors lost fortunes. While some companies survived the bust and thrived, thousands more failed.

Despite the bust of the early 2000s, the Texas IT industry survived and continued to grow. Concentrated in Austin, Houston, Dallas, and San Antonio, the computer industry today is one of the largest industries in the state. More than 15,000 companies are engaged in activities that range from computer manufacturing to video game programming to Internet security and more. Between 2008 and 2013, employment in computer system design rose by some 40 percent. The number of companies involved in the industry also continues to grow each year. In addition to the companies founded here, Texas is home to offices for such industry giants as Apple, Google, IBM, eBay, and National Instruments.

Reading Check **Identifying Cause and Effect** What caused the dot-com bust of the late 1990s and early 2000s?

Other Industries

In addition to those industries mentioned above, Texans participate in many more besides. Banking, insurance, and other financial corporations operate in all of the state's major cities. Mining and manufacturing take place statewide. Texas manufacturers range from the Peterbilt Motors Company, based in Denton, which makes heavy trucks, to Mary Kay Inc., based in Addison, which makes cosmetics.

One of the state's most important industries in recent years has been tourism. Texas is a huge state, and visitors are drawn to its many attractions. Some visit historic landmarks, such as the Alamo in San Antonio. Others are drawn to natural areas, such as Padre Island, Big Bend National Park, the Caverns of Sonora, or Enchanted Rock in the Hill Country. Still more choose to spend their time at the many amusement parks and water parks found in Texas. Millions attend professional

Interpreting Visuals

Texas tourism. *Each year the State Fair of Texas, held in Dallas, draws an estimated 3 million visitors.* ***What attractions might draw people to the fair?***

Production of Select Industries, 1965–2011

Interpreting Graphs The economy of Texas has changed dramatically since 1965. Which industry on this graph has seen the most booms and busts in that time?

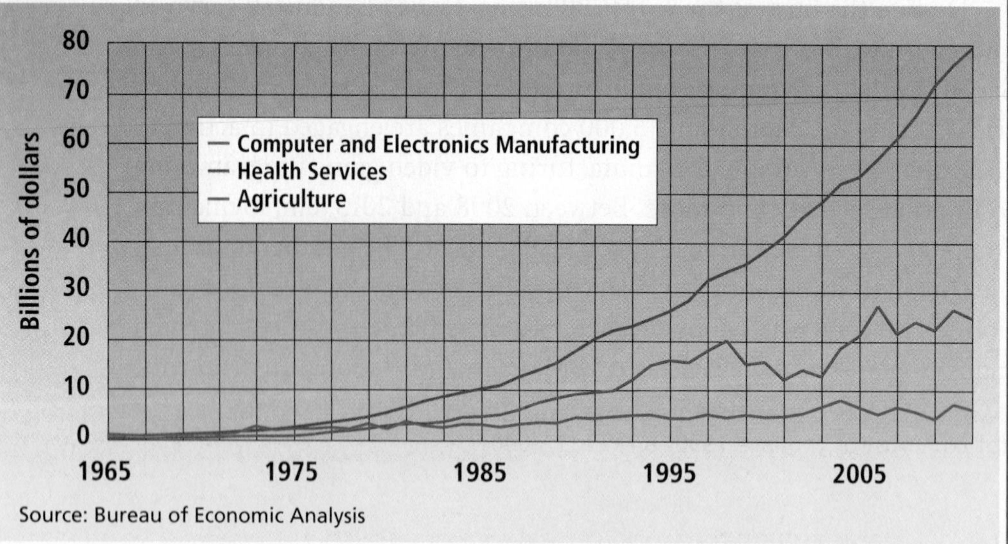

and college sporting events throughout the state. Many visitors also come to Texas for business rather than pleasure. Houston, Dallas, and San Antonio are among the most popular cities in the United States for business and trade conventions.

Texas also has a thriving entertainment industry. Film and television producers are attracted by the state's diverse scenery and skilled labor force. Austin in particular has become a center for music and film making. Austin hosts the world-famous South by Southwest (SXSW) music and film festival each year. This festival draws tens of thousands of visitors from around the world to Texas.

Reading Check **Supporting a Point of View** Do you think tourism and entertainment should be supported in Texas? Why or why not?

Section 2 Review

hmhsocialstudies.com ONLINE QUIZ

1. Define and explain:
- agribusiness
- feedlots
- information technology
- semiconductors
- dot-coms

2. Identify and explain the significance of the following in Texas history:
- Michael Dell

3. Categorizing Copy the graphic organizer below. In each circle, identify a Texas industry and describe its impact on national and international markets.

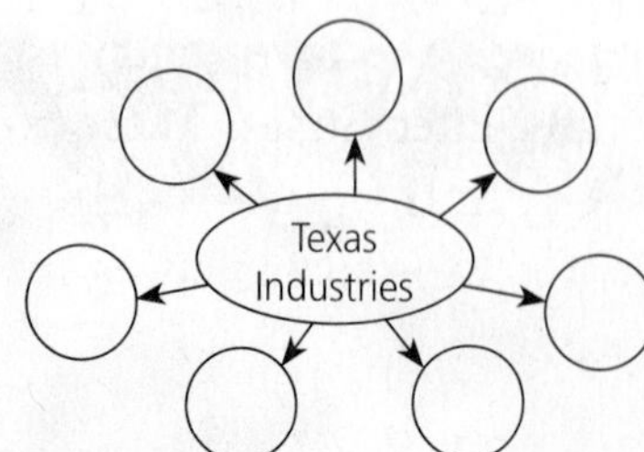

4. Finding the Main Idea

a. Look at the map in this section. What patterns can you see in Texas industries? What do you think caused those patterns?

b. Summarize the booms and busts of the computer industry since the 1990s.

5. Writing and Critical Thinking myWriteSmart

Supporting a Point of View Imagine that you work for the Texas government and are trying to attract new businesses to the state. Choose one industry and write a paragraph how Texas could benefit that industry.

Consider the following:
- the history of the industry in Texas
- possible markets for the industry

Section 3

Texas in the World Economy

Main Ideas

1. Texas trades more goods with Mexico than with any other country.
2. Products are shipped to and received from countries around the world.
3. Events in other parts of the world can affect the Texas economy.

Key Terms

- **North American Free Trade Agreement**
- **maquiladoras**
- **embargo**

Why It Matters Today

Events around the world can have lasting effects on economic issues in Texas. Use current events sources to find information about global events that are shaping the economy today.

TEKS: 7F, 9A, 13A, 13B, 13C, 20C, 20E, 21B, 21C, 22D

myNotebook

Use the annotation tools in your eBook to take notes on the role Texas plays in the global economy.

The Story Continues

Josue Cruz, a truck driver from Mexico, made history in October, 2011. As he crossed over the Rio Grande towing a huge drilling machine, he became the first Mexican truck driver allowed to deliver cargo into the United States. Before, drivers brought their goods to the border, where they would be transferred to American trucks. But under an agreement passed in 1994 drivers would now be allowed to cross the border. The new policy was part of a program intended to make trade between Mexico and the United States easier.

★ Trade with Mexico

Texas shares a long border with Mexico, more than 1,250 miles. All along the border, roads and railroads cross from one country to the other. Because they are so tied together, Texas and Mexico have been natural trading partners for many years.

Texas has long been the main entry point for Mexican products being brought to the United States. These products include machinery, vehicles, oil, and agricultural products. It is also the main transit point for goods being sent to Mexico, including machinery, oil, plastic goods, and agricultural products.

Although trade with Mexico has existed for many years, the Texas economy received a big boost in 1994 when the **North American Free Trade Agreement** (NAFTA) went into effect. This agreement eliminated many trade barriers. Many of the trade goods flowing between the United States and Mexico pass through Texas. As a result of NAFTA, trade between Texas and Mexico more than doubled. In 2012 some $94 billion worth of goods—almost half of the state's exports—went to Mexico. At the same time, $191 billion worth of goods were brought from Mexico into Texas.

Most products shipped between Texas and Mexico travel on trucks. Other products are shipped via railroads. Because all of this trade is overland, border towns have profited from it. With the passing of NAFTA, Texas cities such as Eagle Pass, Laredo, Brownsville, and El Paso boomed as trade increased. Laredo, the busiest of the border towns in terms of trade, was one of the fastest-growing cities in the country during the 1990s.

Increased border trade also created challenges. Texas cities along the border experienced rapid population growth. Most of these cities could not build infrastructure—public works such as roads and water systems—fast enough to keep pace with the growth. Hundreds of **maquiladoras**, factories near the border that build products using imported parts, have also been built in Mexico. Many of these factories are owned by American companies. Workers at the maquiladoras assemble goods that are then shipped to the United States. These factories have provided many jobs, but air and water pollution have increased in the border region. The resulting environmental and health issues continue to challenge Texas leaders.

Reading Check **Summarizing** How has NAFTA affected the Texas economy?

Interpreting Visuals

Texas–Mexico border. *More than 32 million vehicles crossed the border between Texas and Mexico in 2012, an average of more than 90,000 per day.* ***How are border crossings controlled?***

 Trade with Other Countries

Trade with Mexico accounts for just over half of Texas's international trade. However, Mexico is not the state's only trading partner. Products from Texas are shipped all around the world. In return, Texas receives imports from nearly every region of the globe. As technology and transportation have improved, international trade increases. Because shipping goods around the world is so easy today, countries have come to depend on imports from distant regions to fulfill their citizens' needs.

Besides Mexico, the countries to which Texas exports the most goods are Canada, China, and Brazil. The markets in these countries have a strong demand for Texas products. Each of them received more than $10 billion in Texan products in 2012. Among the top products exported from Texas are refined oil and other petroleum products, chemicals, machine parts, aircraft, and computers.

These exports were produced by companies all around Texas. Every year, more than 26,000 companies in the state produce goods to be sold in other countries. Not all of these producers are huge companies that sell millions of dollars worth of products each year. In fact, the majority of companies that export products have fewer than 500 employees.

Not counting Mexico, the countries from which Texas imported the most goods in 2012 were China, Saudi Arabia, Venezuela, and Canada. Each of these countries sent more than $10 billion worth of products to Texas. By far the most valuable product imported to Texas is crude oil. Other imports to the state include electronic devices such as cellular phones and televisions, computer parts, and passenger vehicles.

Most goods traded with other countries are shipped through the state's ports. The busiest port in Texas is Houston. In fact, in 2013 Houston was the busiest port in the entire United States for foreign trade. More than 200 million tons of goods move through the city's docks every year. Among the other major ports in Texas are Corpus Christi, Beaumont, Texas City, Freeport, and Port Arthur.

Texas airports are also vital to the state's international trade. Hundreds of thousands of tons of freight fly in and out of the airports each year. Dallas/Fort Worth International Airport and George Bush Intercontinental Airport in Houston are the state's busiest airports in freight carried. Airports in San Antonio, El Paso, and Laredo also handle significant amounts of cargo.

Reading Check Comparing and Contrasting How is Texas's trade with the rest of the world different from trade with Mexico?

Imports through Texas Ports, 2012

Product	Total value
Oil and oil products	$121.8 billion
Electric machinery and appliances	$67.5 billion
Vehicles	$47.2 billion
Industrial machines and computers	$44.3 billion
Iron and steel goods	$12.5 billion
Medical and technical instruments	$8.3 billion
Furniture and bedding	$7.4 billion
Other	$68.8 billion

Interpreting Tables Texas imports products from countries all around the world. Based on this table, does the state seem to import more raw materials or manufactured products?

This spacecraft was built at a facility in Houston. The Texas aerospace industry grew in part in response to events in the Soviet Union.

Image Credit: ©Yomiuri Shimbun/AP Images

Global Influence

International trade has tied Texas to countries around the world. Because of these ties, events that happen far from Texas can still affect the state's economy. These effects are particularly evident in the oil industry. Political disruption and turmoil in oil-producing regions of the world, such as Southwest Asia, have led to increased business for Texas oil companies.

In 1973, for example, a group of Arab states in Southwest Asia, including Syria and Egypt, attacked Israel. Shortly after the attack, the United States moved to assist its ally, Israel. In response, several members of OPEC, the Organization of Petroleum Exporting Countries—which included the world's leading suppliers of oil—declared an **embargo**, or ban, on shipments of crude oil to the United States. Faced with a national oil shortage, the United States turned to domestic sources, including Texas. Statewide oil production boomed.

Similar oil booms have happened several times. In 1979 the shah, or king, of Iran was overthrown. The revolution caused Iran's oil production to plummet, which in turned caused worldwide oil shortages. Once again the Texas oil industry stepped up production to meet the demand. Similarly, the Persian Gulf War in 1991 caused a spike in prices. This again led to increased Texas production, but only for a short time.

The aerospace industry in Texas also grew tremendously in response to world events. In 1957 the Soviet Union launched the world's first artificial satellite, called *Sputnik*. The United States, to keep pace with its rival, formed the National Aeronautics and Space Administration (NASA). In 1963 NASA created the Manned Spacecraft Center—now the Lyndon B. Johnson Space Center—in Houston, intended to send an astronaut into orbit. It became one of the country's major space research and training facilities and an important element of the state economy. Several related industries grew up in the Houston area.

International events can also hurt Texas industries. In the 1980s and 1990s an outbreak of the disease bovine spongiform encephalopathy (BSE), commonly called mad cow disease, led to the deaths of more than 100 people in Great Britain. When in 2003 a cow in the United States tested positive for the disease, several nations—including Japan and South Korea—banned imports of U.S. beef, which hurt the Texas cattle industry.

Prior to the ban, Japan was the largest overseas market for American beef. Even after the Japanese government lifted the ban, many people in the country were unwilling to buy beef from the United States, despite steps taken by the United States to ensure that the beef was safe for consumption. The loss of such a big market was a major blow to Texas ranchers.

Just as events around the world affect Texas industries, decisions made in Texas can have long-reaching effects. Decisions by oil and gas companies about how much to produce influence how much people in Texas, the United States, and the world pay for fuel. Similarly, choices made by ranchers and farmers affect food prices. Products developed by high-tech and aeronautics companies are shipped to markets throughout the world. Medications and medical procedures developed in Texas are used to treat patients locally, nationally, and internationally. In addition, business practices developed in Texas have influenced world commerce. For example, companies around the world have adopted the direct-to-customer online sales philosophy developed in the computer industry by Dell.

Reading Check **Finding the Main Idea** How have world events affected the Texas ranching industry?

Global Citizenship

Have you ever heard people say that the world is getting smaller? Because of improvements in communication and transportation, the world seems smaller than it did in the past. What happens in one part of the world can affect the entire planet. More than ever before, people around the world are coming together. The world is changing into a global community. As citizens of such a community, it is our responsibility to do our parts to preserve and promote it. That means treating all people equally and respectfully, regardless of where they live or whether they disagree with you about issues. It means working together to create a better future. **What does it mean to be a global citizen?**

Section 3 Review

hmhsocialstudies.com
ONLINE QUIZ

1. Define and explain:
- North American Free Trade Agreement
- maquiladoras
- embargo

2. Locate on a map:
- Houston
- Laredo
- El Paso

3. Identifying Cause and Effect
Copy the graphic organizer below. Use it to analyze the impact of international events on Texas industries.

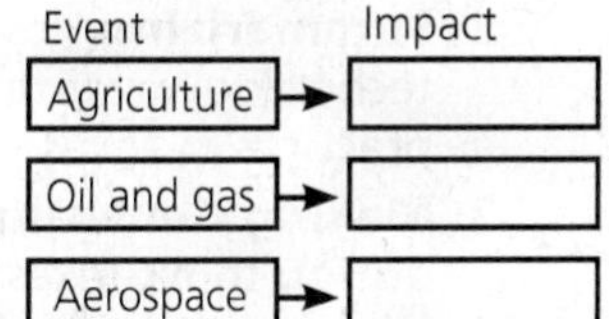

4. Finding the Main Idea
- **a.** How have international markets helped small businesses in Texas?
- **b.** How has world competition affected the Texas oil industry?

5. Writing and Critical Thinking my WriteSmart
Analyzing Information Write a short essay explaining how science and technology have led to an increasing dependence among Texas, the United States, and the world.
Consider the following:
- the products created in Texas
- changes in communication and transportation

The Chapter at a Glance

Examine the following visual summary of the chapter. Then use the visual to write an outline of the major topics covered in this chapter. Compare outlines with a classmate and organize the information in both outlines into a chapter study guide.

The Texas Economy

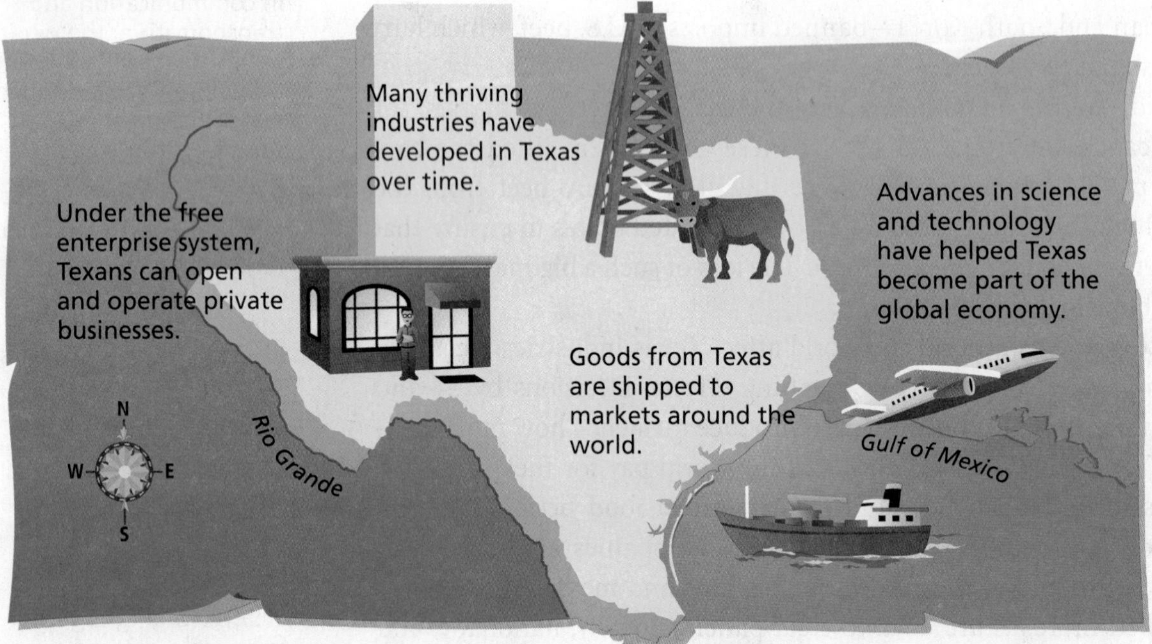

Identifying People and Ideas

Write a sentence to explain the role or significance of each of the following terms or people.

1. free enterprise
2. profit
3. competition
4. information technology
5. dot-com
6. feedlot
7. Michael Dell
8. semiconductor
9. maquiladora
10. embargo

Understanding Main Ideas

Section 1

1. What role does the government play in the free enterprise system?
2. How has international competition affected the economy of Texas?

Section 2

3. How does the Texas aerospace industry serve local, national, and international markets?
4. Which Texas industry do you think is most affected by international events? Why?

Section 3

5. How is Texas part of the global economy?

You Be the Historian

Reviewing Themes

1. **Economics** How have economic developments in Texas affected economic decisions and influenced people's lives in local, national, and international markets?
2. **Science, Technology & Society** How have changes in technology affected the oil industry and the resources of Texas?
3. **Global Relations** Do you think the North American Free Trade Agreement has been good or bad for Texas? Support your answer.

Thinking Critically

1. **Sequencing** Trace the series of booms and busts that have affected the Texas oil and gas industry.
2. **Summarizing** How have developments in technology over time influenced agricultural practices in Texas?
3. **Making Generalizations and Predictions** How do you think Texas's role in the global economy will change in the future? Why?

Texas Test Practice

Interpreting Tables

Study the table below. Then use the information in the table to answer the questions that follow.

Texas Imports by Country, 2012

Country	Value of imports
Mexico	$191.0 billion
China	$25.4 billion
Saudi Arabia	$19.3 billion
Venezuela	$19.1 billion
Germany	$8.8 billion
Russia	$8.3 billion
Iraq	$8.3 billion
Colombia	$8.1 billion
South Korea	$6.7 billion
Kuwait	$6.7 billion
Rest of the world	$82.6 billion

1. From which of the following countries did Texas import the least in 2012?

A South Korea
B Mexico
C Venezuela
D Iraq

2. Organize the countries on this table into groupings by continent. From which continent did Texas import the highest value of goods?

Summarizing

Read the following passage from this chapter. Then answer the questions that follow.

Medical researchers in Texas have worked hard to meet the health needs of the state and the world. As a result, Texas has earned a reputation as a leader in medicine. Medical research centers around the state have drawn millions of dollars in funding for medical research. In 2012 Texas medical centers spent nearly $2.6 billion on biomedical research. Research and technological developments have led to the growth of a major medical industry in Texas. By 2012 Texas had 630 hospitals, 9 medical schools, and 100 nursing schools.

3. Which of the following statements would you be most likely to find in a good summary of this passage?

F Texas had 630 hospitals in 2012.
G Medical centers spent $2.6 billion on research.
H Texas is a world leader in medical research.
J Medical researchers work hard.

4. Write a one-sentence summary of the passage above.

Cooperative Learning

Work with a small group to complete the following activity. Each person in your group should select one of the following major Texas industries: a) farming b) oil and gas production c) ranching d) real estate e) banking f) computer technology. Each member should conduct research to learn about booms and busts in that industry throughout the state's history. Then work together to create an annotated time line of the Texas economy. Include maps, pictures, and other visual elements. You may wish to create graphs or charts based on any statistical information you find in your research.

Internet Activity 

Access the Internet to research recent scientific developments or technological advances in a Texas industry. Compare the technology used in that industry today to what was used in the past. Also analyze the effects of technological advances on the use of resources such as fossil fuels, water, and land. Prepare an oral presentation in which you outline the effects of science and technology on the industry and on Texas as a whole. Before you present, check your work for proper grammar, sentence structure, and citation of sources.

Social Studies Skills

WORKSHOP

Making Presentations

In your history classes, you will be called upon to make presentations. Sharing the information you have learned with others is an important part of studying history.

Types of Presentations

There are many types of presentations that you might be called upon to make. Probably the most common is a **written presentation,** or report. Clarity is important for a written presentation. You do not want to clutter your writing with unnecessary or distracting details. State your topic clearly and provide plenty of support for it. To create a written presentation, you will probably have to conduct research. You must be careful to cite all the sources from which you gather information for your report.

You may also be called upon to create an **oral presentation.** Examples of oral presentations include speeches, lectures, and interviews. Oral presentations generally support a point of view about an event or issue. They should be more engaging and dynamic than simply reading a report out loud would be. Before you give an oral presentation, you should practice your delivery. Use a clear but lively tone of voice to keep your listeners' attention.

From time you time, you may have to create a **visual presentation**. This type of presentation could be a poster, a series of maps or charts, or a multimedia presentation. When creating a visual presentation, clarity is important. You do not want your presentation to look cluttered. Everything in the presentation should fit together. Use large, attention-getting images to get a viewer's attention, but be careful that your images do not overwhelm the message you are trying to convey.

Organizing Your Presentation

Whatever type of presentation you are making, there are some key steps you should follow:

1. **Identify your topic.**
   - Do not try to cover too broad a topic, like the entire Texas government. Instead, choose a more focused idea, such as the powers of the Supreme Court.
2. **Organize your information.**
   - Whether written, oral, or visual, your information needs to be presented in a way that makes sense to your audience.
3. **Record your sources.**
   - Keep track of where you collect the information you use in your presentation. You must give proper credit to these sources in your finished work.
4. **Express your point of view.**
   - This point is particularly important for oral presentations, but written and visual works can also indicate your perspective on your topic.
5. **Proofread.**
   - Always read through your written presentation, your notes for an oral presentation, or the captions and labels in a visual presentation. Be sure that you use proper grammar, spelling, sentence structure, and word choice.

Practicing the Skill

Select a topic from this chapter and plan a written, oral, or visual presentation about it. Remember to keep the focus of your presentation narrow. Follow the steps above to help with your final product. When you have finished, share your work with your classmates.

History in Action

UNIT 10 SIMULATION

You Solve the Problem . . .

How can I encourage Texans to vote?

Complete the following activity in small cooperative groups. U.S. citizens over the age of 18 living in Texas can register to vote. Yet many qualified Texans have not registered to vote. You have to prepare a series of presentations to convince all eligible Texans to vote. Follow these steps to solve your problem.

1. **Gather information.** Use your textbook and other resources to find information that might influence your plan of action for encouraging Texans to vote. Remember that your presentations must include information that will persuade Texans to vote. Be sure to use what you learned from this unit's Skills Workshop on Making Presentations to help you decide how to address the problem and share your information. You may want to divide different parts of the research among group members.

2. **List and consider options.** After reviewing the information you have gathered, list and consider the options you might recommend for successfully convincing Texans to vote. Think about how you can address these options in written, oral, and visual presentations.

3. **Consider advantages and disadvantages.** Now consider the advantages and disadvantages of taking each option. Ask yourselves questions such as, "What motivates a person to vote?" Once you have considered the advantages and disadvantages, record them for use in preparing your presentations.

4. **Choose, implement, and evaluate a solution.** After considering the advantages and disadvantages, plan and prepare your presentations. Have each member of your group create one type of presentation—written, oral, or visual—to help convince Texans that they should register to vote. Be sure that your group prepares all three types of presentations. Remember that your proposal for convincing Texans to vote should be very clear in each presentation. You will need to support your reasons by including information you gathered and by explaining why you rejected other options. Your presentations need to be appealing to attract potential voters' attention. When you are ready, decide which group members will deliver each presentation, and then make your presentations to the community (the rest of the class).

As you present, try to engage your audience's attention. Use different sentence types to keep listeners interested. Mix short, simple sentences with longer, more complex ones. Use connecting words to link the ideas in your sentences together.

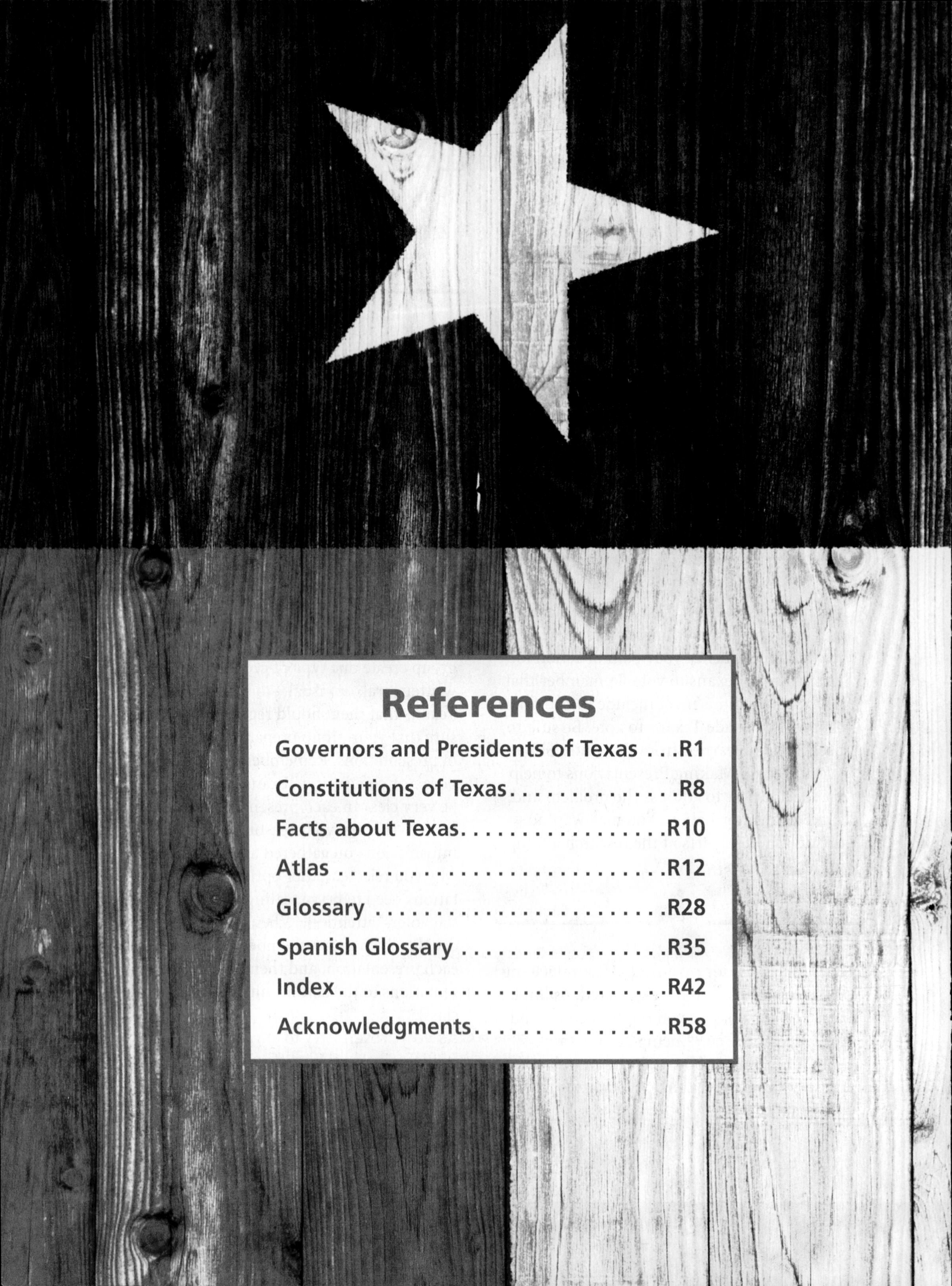

References

Governors and Presidents of Texas

Spanish Royal Governors of Texas

Domingo Terán de los Ríos
1691–1692

Gregorio de Salinas Varona
1692–1697

Francisco Cuerbo y Valdéz
1698–1702

Mathías de Aguirre
1703–1705

Martín de Alarcón
1705–1708

Simon Padilla y Córdova
1708–1712

Pedro Fermin de Echevers y Subisa
1712–1714

Juan Valdéz
1714–1716

Martín de Alarcón
1716–1719

José de Azlor, Marqués de San Miguel de Aguayo
1719–1722

Fernando Pérez de Almazán
1722–1727

Melchor de Media Villa y Azcona
1727–1730

Juan Antonio Bustillos y Ceballos
1730–1734

Manuel de Sandoval
1734–1736

Carlos Benites Franquis de Lugo
1736–1737

Prudencio de Orobio y Basterra
1737–1741

Tomás Felipe Wintuisen
1741–1743

Justo Boneo y Morales
1743–1744

Francisco García Larios
1744–1748

Pedro del Barrio Junco y Espriella
1748–1751

Jacinto de Barrios y Jáuregui
1751–1759

Ángel de Martos y Navarrete
1759–1766

Hugo Oconór
1767–1770

Barón de Ripperdá
1770–1778

Domingo Cabello
1778–1786

Bernardo Bonavía
1786 (*appointed, never served*)

Rafael Martínez Pacheco
1786–1790

The office of governor was suppressed and the province put under a provincial captain.
1788–1789

Manuel Muñoz
1790–1798

José Irigoyen
1798 (*appointed, never served*)

Juan Bautista Elguézabal
1800–1805

Antonio Cordero y Bustamante
1805–1808

Manuel María de Salcedo
1808–1813

Juan Bautista de la Casas
1811 (*revolutionary governor*)

Cristóbal Domínguez
1813–1814

Mariano Varela
1815–1816

Ignacio Pérez
1816–1817

Manuel Pardo
1817

Antonio Martínez
1817–1821

Mexican Governors of Texas

José Felix Trespalacios
1822–1823

Luciano García
1823–1824

Rafael Gonzales
1824–1826

Victor Blanco
1826–1827

José María Viesca
1827–1831

José María Letona
1831–1832

Juan Martín de Veramendi
1832–1833

Juan José de Vidaurri y Villasenor
1833–1834

Juan José Elguézabal
1834–1835

Agustín M. Viesca
1835

Provisional Colonial Governors before Independence

Henry Smith
1835–1836

James W. Robinson
1836 (*served as acting governor after Smith was impeached*)

Presidents of the Republic of Texas

David G. Burnet
March 16, 1836–October 22, 1836
(ad interim president)

Sam Houston
October 22, 1836–December 10, 1838

Mirabeau B. Lamar
December 10, 1838–December 13, 1841

Sam Houston
December 13, 1841–December 9, 1844

Anson Jones
December 9, 1844–February 19, 1846

Governors since Annexation

J. Pinckney Henderson
February 19, 1846–December 21, 1847
(Albert C. Horton served as acting governor during the U.S.–Mexican War.)

George T. Wood
December 21, 1847–December 21, 1849

Peter Hansbrough Bell
December 21, 1849–November 23, 1853

J. W. Henderson
November 23, 1853–December 21, 1853

Elisha M. Pease
December 21, 1853–December 21, 1857

Hardin R. Runnels
December 21, 1857–December 21, 1859

Sam Houston
December 21, 1859–March 16, 1861

Edward Clark
March 16, 1861–November 7, 1861

Francis R. Lubbock
November 7, 1861–November 5, 1863

Pendleton Murrah
November 5, 1863–June 17, 1865

Andrew J. Hamilton
June 17, 1865–August 9, 1866
(provisional governor)

James W. Throckmorton
August 9, 1866–August 8, 1867

Elisha M. Pease
August 8, 1867–September 30, 1869 (Between September 30, 1869, and January 8, 1870, Texas was without an acting head of government.)

Edmund J. Davis
January 8, 1870–January 15, 1874

Richard Coke
January 15, 1874–December 1, 1876

Richard B. Hubbard
December 1, 1876–January 21, 1879

Oran M. Roberts
January 21, 1879–January 16, 1883

John Ireland
January 16, 1883–January 18, 1887

Lawrence Sullivan Ross
January 18, 1887–January 20, 1891

James Stephen Hogg
January 20, 1891–January 15, 1895

Charles A. Culberson
January 15, 1895–January 17, 1899

Image Credit: (all) The State Preservation Board, Austin, Texas

Joseph D. Sayers
January 17, 1899–January 20, 1903

S. W. T. Lanham
January 20, 1903–January 15, 1907

Thomas Mitchell Campbell
January 15, 1907–January 17, 1911

Oscar Branch Colquitt
January 17, 1911–January 19, 1915

James E. Ferguson
January 19, 1915–August 25, 1917

William P. Hobby
August 25, 1917–January 18, 1921

Pat M. Neff
January 18, 1921–January 20, 1925

Miriam A. Ferguson
January 20, 1925–January 17, 1927

Dan Moody
January 17, 1927–January 20, 1931

Image Credit: (all) The State Preservation Board, Austin, Texas

Ross S. Sterling
January 20, 1931–January 17, 1933

Miriam A. Ferguson
January 17, 1933–January 15, 1935

James V Allred
January 15, 1935–January 17, 1939

W. Lee O'Daniel
January 17, 1939–August 4, 1941

Coke R. Stevenson
August 4, 1941–January 21, 1947

Beauford H. Jester
January 21, 1947–July 11, 1949

Allan Shivers
July 11, 1949–January 15, 1957

Price Daniel
January 15, 1957–January 15, 1963

John Connally
January 15, 1963–January 21, 1969

Preston Smith
January 21, 1969–January 16, 1973

Dolph Briscoe
January 16, 1973–January 16, 1979

William P. Clements
January 16, 1979–January 18, 1983

Mark White
January 18, 1983–January 20, 1987

William P. Clements
January 20, 1987–January 15, 1991

Ann Richards
January 15, 1991–January 17, 1995

George W. Bush
January 17, 1995–December 21, 2000

Rick Perry
December 21, 2000—

The Constitutions of Texas

The Constitution of 1824

The first constitution that governed the people of Texas was the Mexican Federal Constitution of 1824. Erasmo Seguín served as the representative for Texas in the assembly that created the document. Stephen F. Austin also consulted with its framers. The constitution used the U.S. Constitution and the Spanish Constitution of 1812 as models. Under this constitution a president and vice president were chosen for four-year terms by the legislative bodies of the states of Mexico. The constitution also created a national congress with a lower house of deputies and an upper house of senators. Judicial power was shared by a Supreme Court and superior courts of departments and districts. Catholicism was given a special place in the government as the state religion.

The Constitution of 1827

The Constitution of 1827 provided a government for the newly created state of Coahuila y Texas. The terms of the document were debated for more than two years. Baron de Bastrop represented Texas in the assembly at Saltillo that drafted it. The constitution divided the state into three departments and created a unicameral legislature. Executive power was delegated to a governor and vice governor who were elected to four-year terms by popular vote. The right to trial by jury was addressed by the constitution but not clearly established. Slavery was banned. As in the Constitution of 1824, Catholicism was made the state religion.

The Constitution of 1836

After Texas declared its independence from Mexico, a new constitution was created for the Republic of Texas. On March 1, 1836, 59 delegates assembled at Washington-on-the-Brazos to create the document, which was ratified by a popular vote in September 1836. The U.S. Constitution and other state constitutions were used as models for the new government. The Constitution of 1836 divided the government into three branches. The Congress was bicameral with a House of Representatives and a Senate. The executive branch was led by a popularly elected president. The judiciary included justice, county, and district courts, headed by a supreme court. The constitution barred ministers and priests from holding public office. It included a bill of rights and laws to protect homesteaders.

The Constitution of 1845

The Constitution of 1845 provided the first framework of government for Texas as a state in the United States. The framers of the state constitution used the Constitution of 1836, the Constitution of Louisiana, and the constitution created at the Convention of 1833 as models. The legislature included a Senate and a House of Representatives. The executive branch was headed by a governor who served a two-year term. The judiciary was composed of a supreme court, district courts, and inferior courts established by the legislature. Ministers were ineligible to be legislators. Banks were outlawed.

The Constitution of 1861

The Constitution of 1861 was created after Texans voted to secede from the Union. The new document was an amended version of the Constitution of 1845. Some wording was replaced. For example, the name "United States of America" was replaced by "Confederate States of America." Slavery and states' rights were more directly addressed. All state officials were required to take a loyalty oath to the Confederacy.

The Constitution of 1866

The Constitution of 1866 was created in accordance with the orders of Presidential Reconstruction. The term of the governor was increased from two to four years, and the governor was given more powers, including the ability to veto items of appropriations. The terms of office for legislators remained the same, but their salaries were increased. The number of judges on the Supreme Court was increased from three to five. The constitution also outlined improvements for public education and school funding.

The Constitution of 1869

The Constitution of 1869 was created in compliance with the Reconstruction Acts of 1867. The U.S. Constitution was declared the supreme law, and the equality and equal rights of all persons were recognized before the law. The term of office for the governor and representatives remained as they had been, but the term of senators was increased from four to six years. Legislative sessions were held annually. The number of judges on the Supreme Court was reduced from five to three. All judicial officers were appointed. African Americans were given the right to vote. A poll tax was also instituted to help fund public schools.

The Constitution of 1876

The Constitution of 1876 is the current constitution governing Texas. The document was created by a constitutional convention in 1875 and adopted after a popular vote in 1876. The convention was held after Democrats regained control of the legislature following Reconstruction. The Constitution of 1876 was influenced by provisions in the previous constitutions of Texas, including some laws that can by traced to Mexican and Spanish laws. The document contains special sections dealing with land titles and debtor relief. The constitution also prohibited the creation of banks and required a strict separation of church and state.

The powers of the governor were decreased and the term was reduced to two years. (The governor's term in office was later extended to four years by a 1972 amendment.) The term of representatives was set a two years and senators at four years. The legislature was to meet every two years. County courts were reinstated. All judges were to be elected by popular vote with the Supreme Court judges and criminal appeals court judges serving six-year terms. District court judges serve four-year terms, and all other judges serve two-year terms.

Changes to the constitution are made through amendments. Since 1876 more than 470 amendments to the constitution have been adopted. Several calls have been made over the years for a new constitution. With more than 85,000 words it is one of the longest state constitutions.

Facts about Texas

State Seal

According to the Texas Constitution, the state seal "shall be a star of five points, encircled by olive and live oak branches, and the words, 'The State of Texas.'" The reverse side of the seal, adopted in 1961, shows a shield with symbols of the Texas Revolution, including the Alamo, the cannon from Gonzales, and Vince's Bridge. Surrounding these items are the six flags that have flown over Texas.

Spain *France*

Mexico *Texas*

Confederate States of America *United States of America*

Six Flags over Texas

Through the years, six countries have claimed Texas and flown their flags over the region. Spanish explorers and colonists were the first to claim the region. The French also briefly took control of Texas. The Mexican flag flew over Texas after Mexico successfully won its independence from Spain. With the Texas Revolution, Texans established a new republic and created the lone star flag. The American flag replaced the Texas flag after annexation. When Texas seceded from the Union during the Civil War, the Confederate flag was used. When the Civil War ended in 1865, the American flag once again flew over the state.

The Pledge to the Texas Flag

On April 3, 1965, Governor John Connally signed an act of the 59th legislature, officially designating the following as the pledge to the Texas flag:

> ***Honor the Texas Flag.***
> ***I pledge allegiance to thee,***
> ***Texas, one and indivisible.***

State Bird

The mockingbird was designated the Texas state bird by the legislature on January 31, 1927. The mockingbird has the ability to imitate many things it hears. It has been characterized as fearless and aggressive in protecting itself and its offspring against enemies.

State Song

The Texas state song is "Texas, Our Texas." The music was written by William J. Marsh, and the words by Gladys Yoakum Wright and William J. Marsh. It was adopted by the legislature in 1929.

State Motto

The state motto, adopted in February, 1930, is the word *Friendship*. The motto commemorates the Caddo word *Tejas,* which means "friends" and is the origin of the name Texas.

State Flower

The bluebonnet was adopted as the state flower of Texas by the 27th legislature on March 7, 1901. The flower is said to have received its name from its resemblance to a woman's sunbonnet. It also has been called wolfflower, buffalo clover, and *el conejo* (the rabbit).

Atlas

Locating Texas

Northern Hemisphere

Western Hemisphere

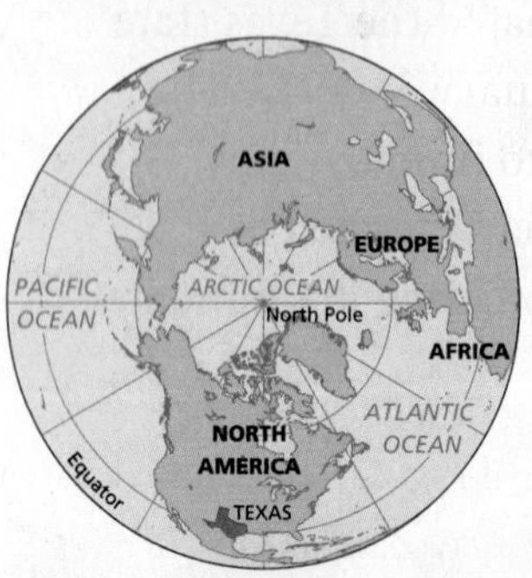

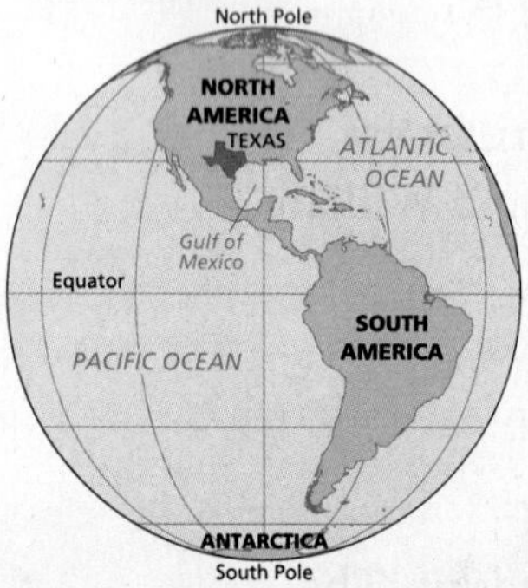

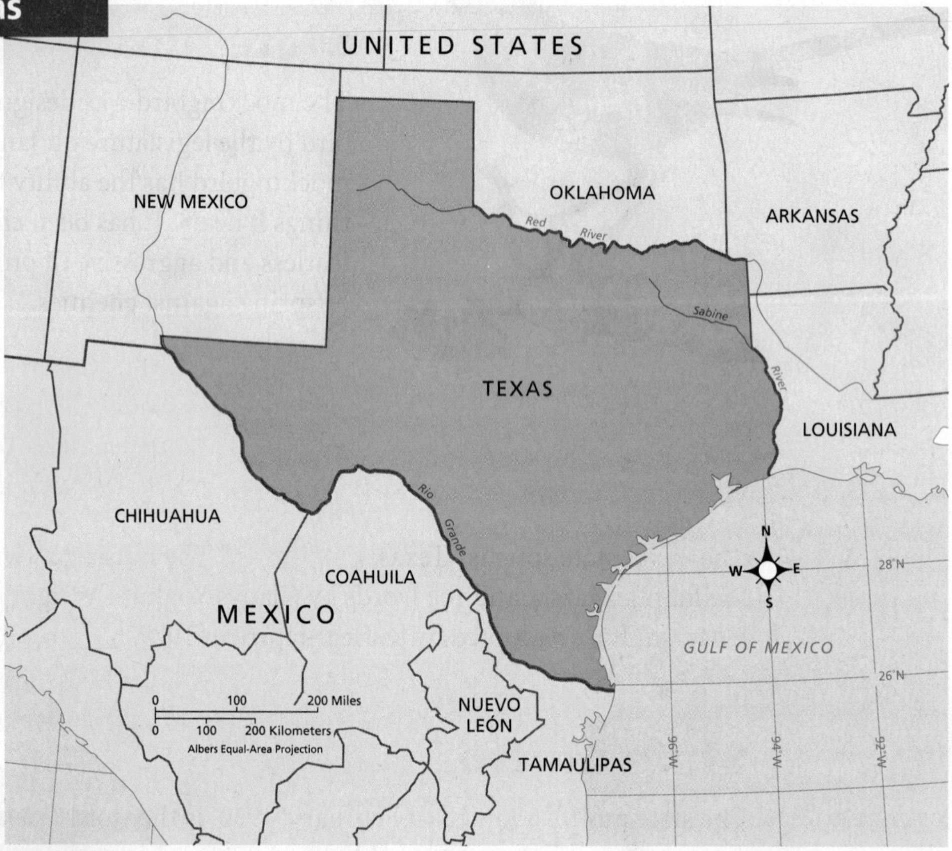

Texas: Counties

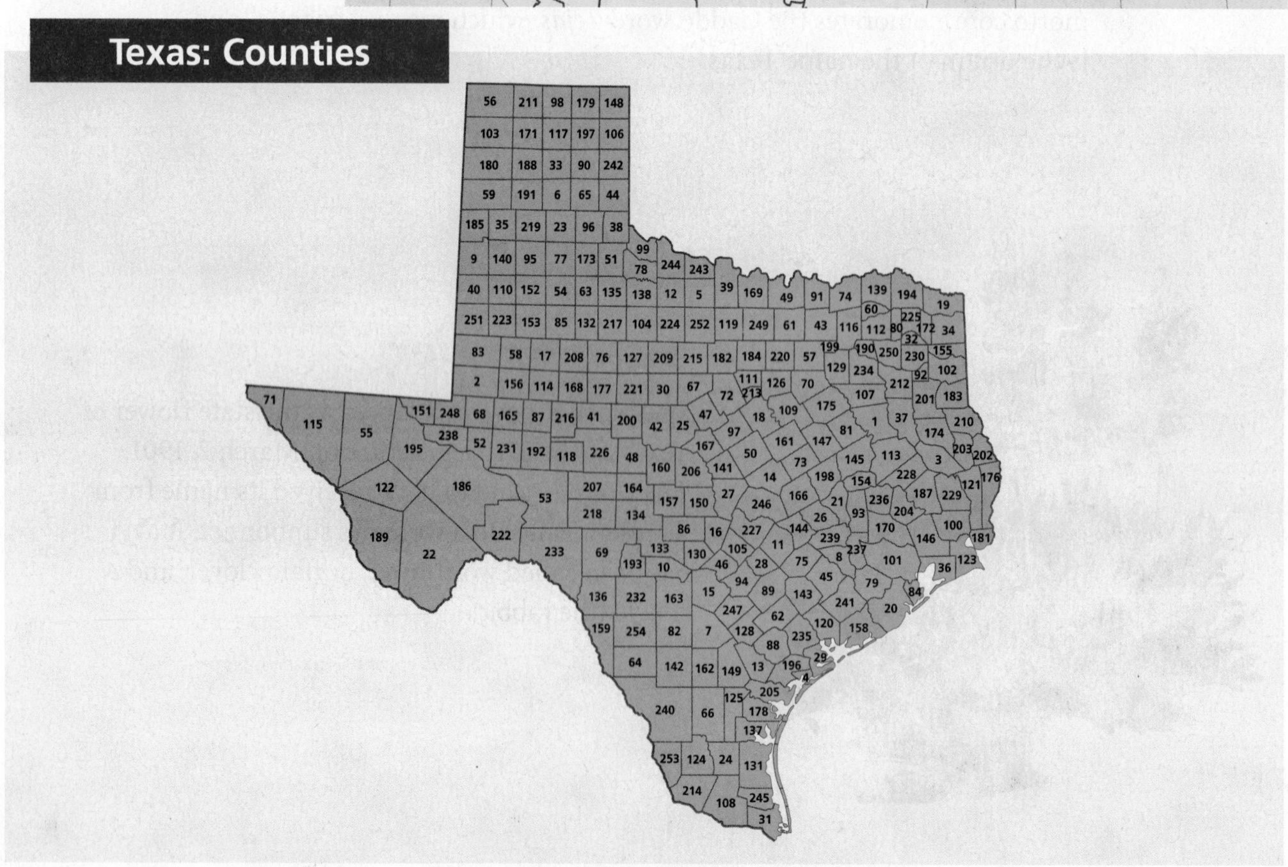

Texas Counties

County	Number on Map	2012 Population (estimate)	Area (sq. mi.)	County Seat	Date Created/ Organized	Industries/Products
Anderson	1	58,190	1,078.0	Palestine	1846	timber, cattle, manufacturing
Andrews	2	16,117	1,501.0	Andrews	1910	oil, cattle, cotton
Angelina	3	87,597	864.4	Lufkin	1846	timber, cattle, manufacturing
Aransas	4	23,818	527.9	Rockport	1871	shipping, cattle, tourism
Archer	5	8,735	925.7	Archer City	1880	cattle, oil services, dairy, agriculture
Armstrong	6	1,944	913.7	Claude	1890	agribusiness, cattle, wheat
Atascosa	7	46,446	1,232.7	Jourdanton	1856	cattle, peanuts, strawberries
Austin	8	28,618	656.3	Bellville	1837	cattle, manufacturing, tourism
Bailey	9	7,130	827.3	Muleshoe	1917	manufacturing, dairy, agriculture, cattle
Bandera	10	20,537	797.5	Bandera	1856	tourism, hunting, cattle
Bastrop	11	74,763	895.9	Bastrop	1836	cattle, hay, tourism, high-tech
Baylor	12	3,623	901.0	Seymour	1879	cattle, agribusiness, crops
Bee	13	32,527	880.3	Beeville	1858	oil, cattle, agribusiness
Bell	14	323,037	1,087.1	Belton	1850	cattle, high-tech, corn, manufacturing
Bexar	15	1,785,704	1,256.7	San Antonio	1836	tourism, cattle, crops
Blanco	16	10,655	713.3	Johnson City	1858	tourism, agribusiness, cattle
Borden	17	616	906.0	Gail	1891	cattle, oil, agribusiness, cotton
Bosque	18	18,125	1,002.6	Meridian	1854	cattle, agribusiness, hunting
Bowie	19	93,148	922.7	Boston	1840	cattle, crops, paper manufacturing
Brazoria	20	324,769	1,597.4	Angleton	1836	cattle, petrochemicals, rice
Brazos	21	200,665	590.3	Bryan	1843	education, agribusiness, cattle
Brewster	22	9,316	6,193.1	Alpine	1887	cattle, tourism
Briscoe	23	1,561	901.6	Silverton	1892	agribusiness, cotton, wheat
Brooks	24	7,161	943.6	Falfurrias	1911	oil, gas, cattle, crops
Brown	25	37,825	956.9	Brownwood	1857	manufacturing, cattle, agribusiness
Burleson	26	17,291	677.8	Caldwell	1846	oil, gas, cattle, crops
Burnet	27	43,448	1,020.0	Burnet	1854	cattle, stone, agribusiness, hunting
Caldwell	28	38,734	547.3	Lockhart	1848	oil, agribusiness, cattle
Calhoun	29	21,609	1,032.1	Port Lavaca	1846	cotton, manufacturing, oil, grain
Callahan	30	13,517	901.2	Baird	1877	cattle, wheat, feed and fertilizer
Cameron	31	415,557	1,276.3	Brownsville	1848	agribusiness, trade, tourism, cotton, vegetables, citrus
Camp	32	12,449	203.1	Pittsburg	1874	agribusiness, poultry, timber
Carson	33	6,157	924.1	Panhandle	1888	wheat, cattle, agribusiness
Cass	34	30,166	960.3	Linden	1846	poultry, cattle, timber
Castro	35	8,164	899.3	Dimmitt	1891	agribusiness, cattle, corn
Chambers	36	36,196	868.5	Anahuac	1858	oil, chemicals, rice, cattle
Cherokee	37	51,206	1,062.0	Rusk	1846	nurseries, timber, dairy, cattle
Childress	38	7,029	713.5	Childress	1887	cotton, cattle, wheat

Texas Counties						
County	**Number on Map**	**2012 Population (estimate)**	**Area (sq. mi.)**	**County Seat**	**Date Created/ Organized**	**Industries/Products**
Clay	39	10,535	1,116.1	Henrietta	1873	oil, agribusiness, cattle, crops
Cochran	40	3,046	775.2	Morton	1924	agribusiness, oil, cotton, sunflowers
Coke	41	3,231	927.9	Robert Lee	1889	oil well supplies, agribusiness
Coleman	42	8,675	1,281.5	Coleman	1864	agribusiness, oil, cattle
Collin	43	834,642	885.8	McKinney	1846	manufacturing, cattle, grain
Collingsworth	44	3,036	919.4	Wellington	1890	peanuts, cotton, agribusiness
Colorado	45	20,696	973.6	Columbus	1837	agribusiness, oil services, rice
Comal	46	114,384	574.5	New Braunfels	1846	manufacturing, cattle, crops
Comanche	47	13,765	947.6	Comanche	1856	dairy, cattle, agribusiness
Concho	48	4,010	993.7	Paint Rock	1879	agribusiness, sheep, cattle, grain
Cooke	49	38,688	898.7	Gainesville	1848	agribusiness, oil, cattle, grain
Coryell	50	77,231	1,056.7	Gatesville	1854	agribusiness, cattle, grain, military
Cottle	51	1,486	901.6	Paducah	1892	agribusiness, cotton, peanuts
Crane	52	4,562	785.6	Crane	1927	oil, oil services, cattle ranching
Crockett	53	3,743	2,807.6	Ozona	1891	sheep, cattle, oil, gas
Crosby	54	6,126	901.6	Crosbyton	1886	agribusiness, cattle, cotton
Culberson	55	2,290	3,812.8	Van Horn	1912	agribusiness, cattle, crops, tourism
Dallam	56	6,996	1,505.3	Dalhart	1891	agribusiness, cattle, hogs, grain
Dallas	57	2,453,843	908.7	Dallas	1846	telecommunications, electronics, textiles, banking
Dawson	58	13,640	902.1	Lamesa	1905	cotton, peanuts, cattle
Deaf Smith	59	19,360	1,498.3	Hereford	1890	meatpacking, farming, feedlots
Delta	60	5,329	277.8	Cooper	1870	agribusiness, tourism, cattle, crops
Denton	61	707,304	957.6	Denton	1846	horses, eggs, cattle, crops
DeWitt	62	20,465	910.4	Cuero	1846	wood, furniture, cattle
Dickens	63	2,323	905.2	Dickens	1891	agribusiness, cattle, cotton, horses
Dimmit	64	10,461	1,334.5	Carrizo Springs	1880	vegetables, cattle, agribusiness
Donley	65	3,598	933.0	Clarendon	1882	cattle, agribusiness, cotton
Duval	66	11,717	1,795.7	San Diego	1876	cattle, grain, oil, cotton
Eastland	67	18,421	931.8	Eastland	1873	agribusiness, cattle, peanuts
Ector	68	144,325	901.7	Odessa	1891	oil, cattle, horses, pecans
Edwards	69	1,968	2,120.0	Rocksprings	1883	goats, sheep, hunting, oil
Ellis	70	153,969	951.6	Waxahachie	1850	manufacturing, agribusiness, cattle
El Paso	71	827,398	1,014.6	El Paso	1850	trade, distribution, dairy, tourism
Erath	72	39,321	1,089.8	Stephenville	1856	dairy, cattle, horses
Falls	73	17,610	773.8	Marlin	1850	agribusiness, cattle, grain
Fannin	74	33,831	899.1	Bonham	1838	agribusiness, cattle, soybeans
Fayette	75	24,695	959.8	La Grange	1838	agribusiness, poultry, cattle, crops
Fisher	76	3,844	901.7	Roby	1886	agribusiness, oil, cattle, cotton

Texas Counties

County	Number on Map	2012 Population (estimate)	Area (sq. mi.)	County Seat	Date Created/ Organized	Industries/Products
Floyd	77	6,367	992.5	Floydada	1890	cotton, livestock feedlots, cattle
Foard	78	1,307	707.7	Crowell	1891	agribusiness, wheat, cotton, clothes
Fort Bend	79	627,293	886.0	Richmond	1838	agribusiness, petrochemicals, crops
Franklin	80	10,640	294.7	Mount Vernon	1875	agribusiness, dairy, hay, fruits
Freestone	81	19,515	892.1	Fairfield	1851	mining, cattle, fruits, crops
Frio	82	17,702	1,134.3	Pearsall	1871	peanuts, agribusiness, oil, crops
Gaines	83	18,413	1,502.8	Seminole	1905	cotton, oil, gas, peanuts
Galveston	84	300,484	876.3	Galveston	1839	port activities, cattle, tourism
Garza	85	6,412	896.2	Post	1907	cotton, oil, cattle
Gillespie	86	25,153	1,061.5	Fredericksburg	1848	tourism, cattle, peaches, crops
Glasscock	87	1,259	900.9	Garden City	1893	cotton, cattle, hunting, oil, gas
Goliad	88	7,351	859.3	Goliad	1837	oil, agribusiness, cattle, corn
Gonzales	89	20,045	1,069.8	Gonzales	1837	agribusiness, poultry, cattle
Gray	90	22,978	929.2	Pampa	1902	oil, cattle, wheat
Grayson	91	121,935	979.1	Sherman	1846	manufacturing, cattle, horses
Gregg	92	122,658	276.3	Longview	1873	oil, manufacturing, cattle, horses
Grimes	93	26,783	801.2	Anderson	1846	manufacturing, cattle, timber, dairy
Guadalupe	94	139,841	714.2	Seguin	1846	manufacturing, cattle, poultry
Hale	95	36,385	1,004.8	Plainview	1888	agribusiness, cattle, cotton, hogs
Hall	96	3,293	904.0	Memphis	1890	grain, cotton, peanuts, cattle
Hamilton	97	8,307	836.3	Hamilton	1858	agribusiness, dairy, cattle, hunting
Hansford	98	5,521	920.4	Spearman	1889	agribusiness, cattle, corn
Hardeman	99	4,082	697.0	Quanah	1884	agribusiness, wheat, cattle, cotton
Hardin	100	55,190	897.3	Kountze	1858	paper manufacturing, wood, cattle
Harris	101	4,253,700	1,777.8	Houston	1837	petrochemicals, port activities, aerospace, rice
Harrison	102	67,450	915.1	Marshall	1842	oil, gas, lumber, cattle, hay
Hartley	103	6,144	1,463.3	Channing	1891	cattle, corn, wheat, gas
Haskell	104	5,901	910.2	Haskell	1885	agribusiness, wheat, cotton, peanuts
Hays	105	168,990	679.8	San Marcos	1843	education, cattle, crops, tourism
Hemphill	106	4,080	912.0	Canadian	1887	oil, cattle, crops
Henderson	107	79,094	949.0	Athens	1846	agribusiness, cattle, manufacturing
Hidalgo	108	806,552	1,582.7	Edinburg	1852	food processing, sugarcane, citrus
Hill	109	35,115	985.6	Hillsboro	1853	agribusiness, cattle, manufacturing
Hockley	110	23,072	908.5	Levelland	1921	oil, gas, cotton, grain
Hood	111	52,044	436.7	Granbury	1866	tourism, cattle, hay, peanuts
Hopkins	112	35,469	792.7	Sulphur Springs	1846	dairy, cattle, horses, hay
Houston	113	23,161	1,236.8	Crockett	1837	livestock, poultry, timber
Howard	114	35,408	904.2	Big Spring	1882	agribusiness, oil, gas, cotton

Texas Counties

County	Number on Map	2012 Population (estimate)	Area (sq. mi.)	County Seat	Date Created/ Organized	Industries/Products
Hudspeth	115	3,337	4,572.2	Sierra Blanca	1917	agribusiness, mining, cotton
Hunt	116	87,079	882.0	Greenville	1846	manufacturing, cattle, education
Hutchinson	117	21,922	894.9	Stinnett	1901	oil, gas, petrochemicals, cattle, corn
Irion	118	1,573	1,051.6	Mertzon	1889	cattle, sheep, goats, wheat, oil
Jack	119	8,983	920.1	Jacksboro	1857	oil, cattle, hay, wheat
Jackson	120	14,255	857.0	Edna	1836	oil, rice, cattle, cotton
Jasper	121	35,923	969.6	Jasper	1837	timber, oil, cattle, hogs, fishing
Jeff Davis	122	2,307	2,264.6	Fort Davis	1887	tourism, greenhouse nurseries, cattle
Jefferson	123	251,813	1,111.2	Beaumont	1837	petrochemicals, rice, soybeans, cattle
Jim Hogg	124	5,249	1,136.2	Hebbronville	1913	oil, cattle, hay, dairy
Jim Wells	125	41,754	868.2	Alice	1912	oil, gas, cattle, dairy, grain
Johnson	126	153,441	734.3	Cleburne	1854	agribusiness, dairy, cattle, horses
Jones	127	19,973	937.1	Anson	1881	agribusiness, cotton, wheat, peanuts
Karnes	128	15,233	753.5	Karnes City	1854	agribusiness, cattle, poultry
Kaufman	129	106,753	806.8	Kaufman	1848	manufacturing, nursery crops, cattle
Kendall	130	35,956	662.9	Boerne	1862	agribusiness, cattle, sheep, goats
Kenedy	131	431	1,945.5	Sarita	1921	oil, hunting, cattle, horses
Kent	132	839	902.8	Jayton	1892	agribusiness, oil, cattle, sheep, goats
Kerr	133	49,786	1,107.6	Kerrville	1856	tourism, cattle, sheep, goats, crops
Kimble	134	4,560	1,250.9	Junction	1876	livestock, goats, sheep, pecans
King	135	276	913.3	Guthrie	1891	minerals, cattle, horses, cotton
Kinney	136	3,603	1,365.3	Brackettville	1874	agribusiness, cattle, goats, hay
Kleberg	137	32,025	1,090.4	Kingsville	1913	chemicals, plastics, cattle, cotton
Knox	138	3,789	855.4	Benjamin	1886	agribusiness, cattle, horses, goats
Lamar	139	49,811	932.4	Paris	1841	manufacturing, cattle, hay, soybeans
Lamb	140	14,008	1,017.7	Littlefield	1908	agribusiness, cattle, corn, wheat
Lampasas	141	20,107	713.9	Lampasas	1856	cattle, goats, military
La Salle	142	7,109	1,494.2	Cotulla	1880	agribusiness, cattle, peanuts, hunting
Lavaca	143	19,468	970.3	Hallettsville	1846	manufacturing, poultry, cattle, leather
Lee	144	16,601	634.0	Giddings	1874	manufacturing, cattle, hogs, eggs
Leon	145	16,803	1,080.4	Centerville	1846	oil, gas, cattle, hogs, poultry
Liberty	146	76,571	1,176.3	Liberty	1837	chemicals, rice, soybeans
Limestone	147	23,585	933.1	Groesbeck	1846	manufacturing, cattle, dairy, horses
Lipscomb	148	3,480	932.2	Lipscomb	1887	agribusiness, cattle, wheat, oil
Live Oak	149	11,664	1,078.8	George West	1856	oil, cattle, hogs, corn, grain
Llano	150	19,085	966.1	Llano	1856	cattle, turkeys, hunting, hogs
Loving	151	71	676.8	Mentone	1931	oil, cattle
Lubbock	152	285,760	900.6	Lubbock	1891	cotton, cattle, feedlots, manufacturing

Texas Counties

County	Number on Map	2012 Population (estimate)	Area (sq. mi.)	County Seat	Date Created/ Organized	Industries/Products
Lynn	153	5,783	893.4	Tahoka	1903	agribusiness, cotton, peanuts, grain
Madison	154	13,677	472.3	Madisonville	1854	manufacturing, nurseries, cattle
Marion	155	10,324	420.3	Jefferson	1860	timber, cattle hay, goats
Martin	156	5,017	915.6	Stanton	1884	oil, cotton, grain, cattle
Mason	157	4,003	932.2	Mason	1858	cattle, peanuts, sheep, hunting
Matagorda	158	36,547	1,612.2	Bay City	1837	oil, rice, cotton, grain
Maverick	159	55,365	1,291.7	Eagle Pass	1871	oil, cattle, pecans, vegetables
McCulloch	160	8,313	1,073.3	Brady	1876	agribusiness, manufacturing, cattle
McLennan	161	238,707	1,060.2	Waco	1850	distribution center, corn, wheat
McMullen	162	726	1,142.6	Tilden	1877	livestock, hunting, cattle, hay
Medina	163	46,765	1,334.5	Hondo	1848	agribusiness, cattle, crops, hunting
Menard	164	2,240	902.2	Menard	1871	agribusiness, oil, gas, sheep, goats
Midland	165	146,645	902.2	Midland	1885	oil, cattle, horses, sheep
Milam	166	24,157	1,021.6	Cameron	1837	aluminum, poultry, cattle, hay
Mills	167	4,828	749.8	Goldthwaite	1887	agribusiness, hunting, cattle, sheep
Mitchell	168	9,336	915.9	Colorado City	1881	agribusiness, oil, cotton, grain
Montague	169	19,565	938.4	Montague	1858	agribusiness, oil, cattle, dairy
Montgomery	170	485,047	1,076.8	Conroe	1837	lumber, oil, cattle, hay
Moore	171	22,313	909.6	Dumas	1892	oil, gas, cattle, manufacturing
Morris	172	12,787	258.6	Daingerfield	1875	steel, timber, cattle, hay
Motley	173	1,202	989.8	Matador	1891	cotton, cattle, peanuts, hunting
Nacogdoches	174	66,034	981.3	Nacogdoches	1837	agribusiness, timber, poultry, dairy
Navarro	175	47,979	1,086.2	Corsicana	1846	manufacturing, oil, cattle, cotton
Newton	176	14,200	939.5	Newton	1846	timber, cattle, crops, tourism
Nolan	177	14,924	913.9	Sweetwater	1881	manufacturing, oil, gas, cattle, sheep
Nueces	178	347,691	1,166.4	Corpus Christi	1846	oil, port activities, grain
Ochiltree	179	10,728	918.1	Perryton	1889	oil, cattle, hogs, wheat
Oldham	180	2,060	1,501.4	Vega	1880	cattle, ranching, crops
Orange	181	82,977	379.5	Orange	1852	petrochemicals, shipping, cattle, rice
Palo Pinto	182	27,856	985.4	Palo Pinto	1857	manufacturing, petroleum, cattle
Panola	183	24,020	801.0	Carthage	1846	gas, oil, cattle, forestry, dairy
Parker	184	119,712	910.0	Weatherford	1855	agribusiness, cattle, horses
Parmer	185	10,183	885.2	Farwell	1907	cattle, grain, crops, meat packing
Pecos	186	15,619	4,765.0	Fort Stockton	1872	agribusiness, oil, gas, vegetables
Polk	187	45,656	1,109.8	Livingston	1846	timber, lumber, hay, vegetables
Potter	188	122,335	922.0	Amarillo	1887	feedlots, cattle, petrochemicals, gas
Presidio	189	7,525	3,856.4	Marfa	1875	cattle, onions, hunting, bees, honey
Rains	190	10,943	258.8	Emory	1870	oil, tourism, cattle, vegetables

Texas Counties

County	Number on Map	2012 Population (estimate)	Area (sq. mi.)	County Seat	Date Created/ Organized	Industries/Products
Randall	191	125,082	922.4	Canyon	1889	agribusiness, wheat, corn, education
Reagan	192	3,475	1,176.0	Big Lake	1903	oil, gas, cotton, cattle, sheep
Real	193	3,369	700.0	Leakey	1913	tourism, cattle, sheep, goats, hunting
Red River	194	12,694	1,057.6	Clarksville	1837	agribusiness, lumber, cattle, soybeans
Reeves	195	13,798	2,642.0	Pecos	1884	agribusiness, feedlots, cattle, cotton
Refugio	196	7,259	818.6	Refugio	1837	oil, cotton, cattle, grain
Roberts	197	854	924.1	Miami	1889	agribusiness, oil services, cattle
Robertson	198	16,545	865.7	Franklin	1838	agribusiness, cattle, cotton, hay
Rockwall	199	83,021	148.6	Rockwall	1873	grain, cattle, horses, cotton
Runnels	200	10,449	1,057.2	Ballinger	1880	agribusiness, oil, manufacturing
Rusk	201	54,026	938.6	Henderson	1843	oil, lumber, cattle, dairy, poultry
Sabine	202	10,433	576.5	Hemphill	1837	timber, tourism, poultry, cattle
San Augustine	203	8,818	592.2	San Augustine	1837	lumber, shipping, manufacturing
San Jacinto	204	27,126	627.9	Coldspring	1870	timber, oil, cattle, horses
San Patricio	205	65,600	707.0	Sinton	1847	oil, petrochemicals, cotton, grain
San Saba	206	6,002	1,138.2	San Saba	1856	agribusiness, stone, cattle, poultry
Schleicher	207	3,264	1,310.7	Eldorado	1901	oil, hunting, sheep, cattle, goats
Scurry	208	17,126	907.6	Snyder	1884	oil, textiles, cotton, grain, livestock
Shackelford	209	3,356	915.5	Albany	1874	oil, manufacturing, cattle, wheat
Shelby	210	26,019	834.5	Center	1837	poultry, eggs, cattle, timber
Sherman	211	3,073	923.2	Stratford	1889	agribusiness, cattle, wheat, corn
Smith	212	214,821	949.4	Tyler	1846	agribusiness, oil, roses, cattle
Somervell	213	8,598	191.8	Glen Rose	1875	tourism, cattle, hay, grain, goats
Starr	214	61,615	1,229.3	Rio Grande City	1848	vegetable packing, shipping, cattle, trade
Stephens	215	9,464	921.5	Breckenridge	1876	oil, agribusiness, cattle, hogs, goats
Sterling	216	1,191	923.5	Sterling City	1891	cattle, sheep, hunting, oil, goats
Stonewall	217	1,475	920.2	Aspermont	1888	agribusiness, cattle, wheat, cotton
Sutton	218	3,950	1,454.4	Sonora	1890	oil, gas, agribusiness, hunting, cattle
Swisher	219	7,891	900.6	Tulia	1890	feedlots, grain, manufacturing, crops
Tarrant	220	1,880,153	897.5	Fort Worth	1850	aerospace, manufacturing, trade
Taylor	221	133,473	919.3	Abilene	1878	military, feedlots, wheat, cattle
Terrell	222	917	2,357.9	Sanderson	1905	ranching, oil, gas, tourism
Terry	223	12,613	890.8	Brownfield	1904	agribusiness, oil, cotton
Throckmorton	224	1,601	915.5	Throckmorton	1879	oil, agribusiness, hunting, cattle
Titus	225	32,663	425.6	Mount Pleasant	1846	agribusiness, manufacturing, poultry
Tom Green	226	113,281	1,540.5	San Angelo	1875	sheep, wool, mohair, cattle, cotton
Travis	227	1,095,584	1,022.1	Austin	1843	education, tourism, high-tech, government
Trinity	228	14,309	713.9	Groveton	1850	forestry, tourism, cattle, horses

Texas Counties

County	Number on Map	2012 Population (estimate)	Area (sq. mi.)	County Seat	Date Created/ Organized	Industries/Products
Tyler	229	21,458	935.7	Woodville	1846	lumber, manufacturing, cattle, hay
Upshur	230	39,995	592.6	Gilmer	1846	manufacturing, agribusiness, poultry
Upton	231	3,283	1,241.8	Rankin	1910	oil, cotton, cattle, pecans, sheep
Uvalde	232	26,752	1,558.6	Uvalde	1856	agribusiness, cattle, vegetables
Val Verde	233	48,705	3,232.6	Del Rio	1885	agribusiness, sheep, goats, military
Van Zandt	234	52,427	859.5	Canton	1848	oil, tourism, cattle, dairy
Victoria	235	89,269	888.7	Victoria	1836	petrochemicals, oil, corn, cattle
Walker	236	68,408	801.4	Huntsville	1846	education, tourism, timber, cattle
Waller	237	44,357	518.4	Hempstead	1873	agribusiness, manufacturing, cattle
Ward	238	10,879	835.7	Monahans	1892	oil, gas, cattle, cotton, alfalfa
Washington	239	34,093	621.3	Brenham	1837	agribusiness, oil, cattle, poultry
Webb	240	259,172	3,375.6	Laredo	1848	international trade, manufacturing, tourism
Wharton	241	41,285	1,094.5	Wharton	1846	oil, rice, sulfur, cotton, hunting
Wheeler	242	5,626	915.3	Wheeler	1879	oil, agribusiness, cattle, horses
Wichita	243	131,559	632.9	Wichita Falls	1882	retail trade, cattle, wheat, oil
Wilbarger	244	13,258	978.1	Vernon	1881	agribusiness, wheat, alfalfa, cattle
Willacy	245	22,058	784.2	Raymondville	1921	oil, agribusiness, cotton, corn, vegetables
Williamson	246	456,232	1,136.4	Georgetown	1848	agribusiness, cattle, high-tech
Wilson	247	44,370	808.5	Floresville	1860	agribusiness, cattle, dairy, hogs
Winkler	248	7,330	841.2	Kermit	1910	oil, gas, cattle, goats, horses
Wise	249	60,432	922.7	Decatur	1856	agribusiness, oil, cattle, dairy
Wood	250	42,022	695.7	Quitman	1850	oil, gas, dairy, cattle, poultry
Yoakum	251	8,075	799.8	Plains	1907	oil, cotton, peanuts, watermelons
Young	252	18,339	930.8	Graham	1874	oil, agribusiness, cattle, wheat
Zapata	253	14,290	1,058.1	Zapata	1858	tourism, oil, cattle, onions, fruit
Zavala	254	11,961	1,301.7	Crystal City	1884	agribusiness, cattle, vegetables, corn

Sources: *Texas Almanac; Handbook of Texas;* U.S. Census Bureau

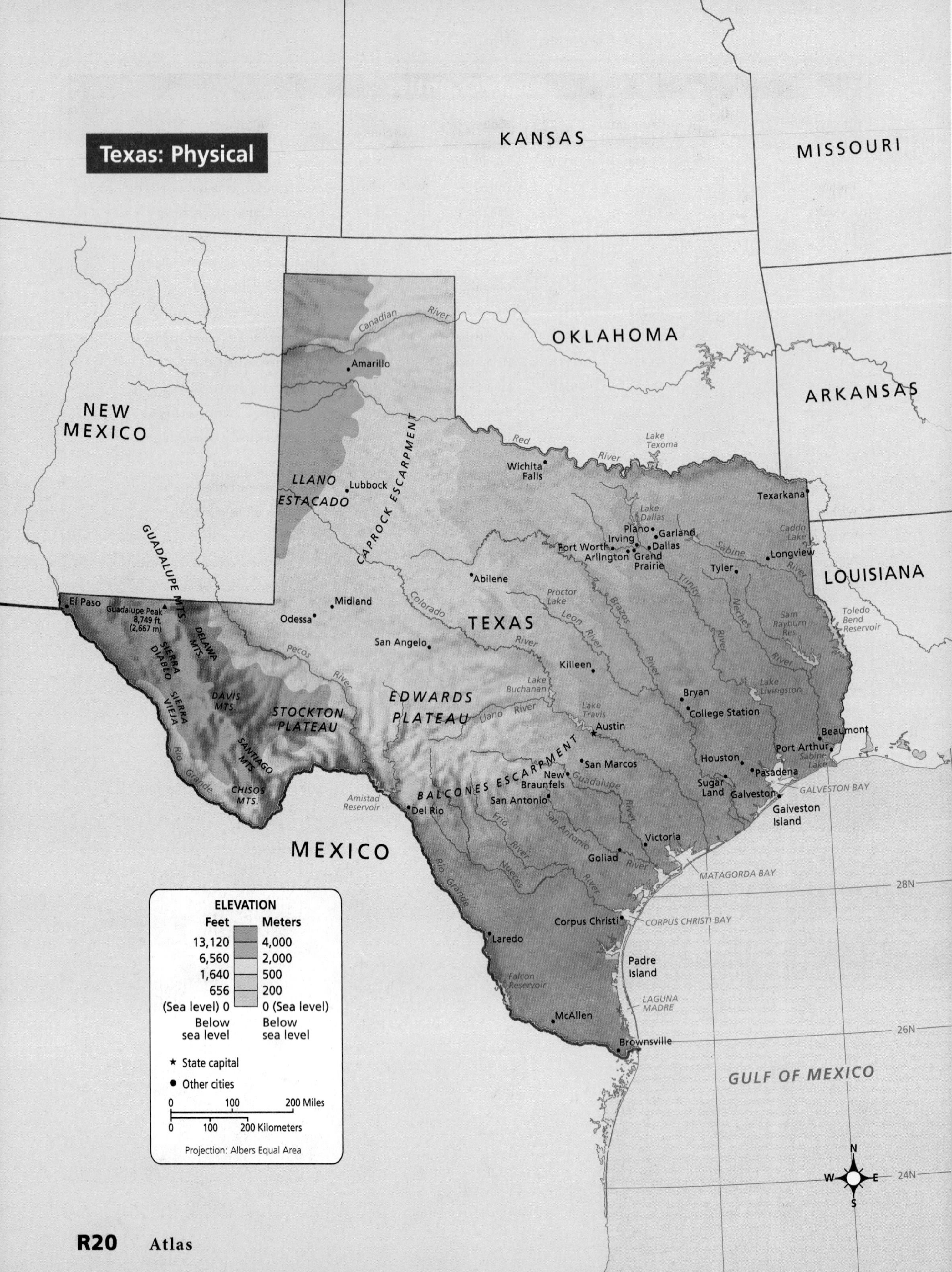

Texas: Physical
KANSAS
MISSOURI
OKLAHOMA
ARKANSAS
NEW MEXICO
LOUISIANA
TEXAS
MEXICO
GULF OF MEXICO
Canadian River
Red River
Lake Texoma
Amarillo
Lubbock
LLANO ESTACADO
CAPROCK ESCARPMENT
Wichita Falls
Texarkana
Lake Dallas
Caddo Lake
Plano
Garland
Irving
Fort Worth
Dallas
Arlington
Grand Prairie
Sabine River
Longview
Tyler
Abilene
GUADALUPE MTS.
El Paso
Guadalupe Peak 8,749 ft. (2,667 m)
Midland
Odessa
Colorado River
Proctor Lake
Leon River
Brazos River
Trinity River
Neches River
Sam Rayburn Res.
Toledo Bend Reservoir
DELAWA MTS.
SIERRA DIABLO
San Angelo
Pecos River
Killeen
Lake Buchanan
Lake Livingston
Bryan
College Station
DAVIS MTS.
SIERRA VIEJA
STOCKTON PLATEAU
EDWARDS PLATEAU
Llano River
Lake Travis
Austin
Beaumont
Port Arthur
Sabine Lake
SANTIAGO MTS.
BALCONES ESCARPMENT
San Marcos
Houston
Pasadena
New Braunfels
Guadalupe River
Sugar Land
Galveston
GALVESTON BAY
Rio Grande
CHISOS MTS.
Amistad Reservoir
Del Rio
San Antonio
Galveston Island
Frio River
San Antonio River
Victoria
Goliad
Nueces River
MATAGORDA BAY
28N
Corpus Christi
CORPUS CHRISTI BAY
Laredo
Padre Island
Falcon Reservoir
LAGUNA MADRE
McAllen
26N
Brownsville
24N
N
S
E
W
ELEVATION
Feet
Meters
13,120
4,000
6,560
2,000
1,640
500
656
200
(Sea level) 0
0 (Sea level)
Below sea level
Below sea level
State capital
Other cities
0 100 200 Miles
0 100 200 Kilometers
Projection: Albers Equal Area

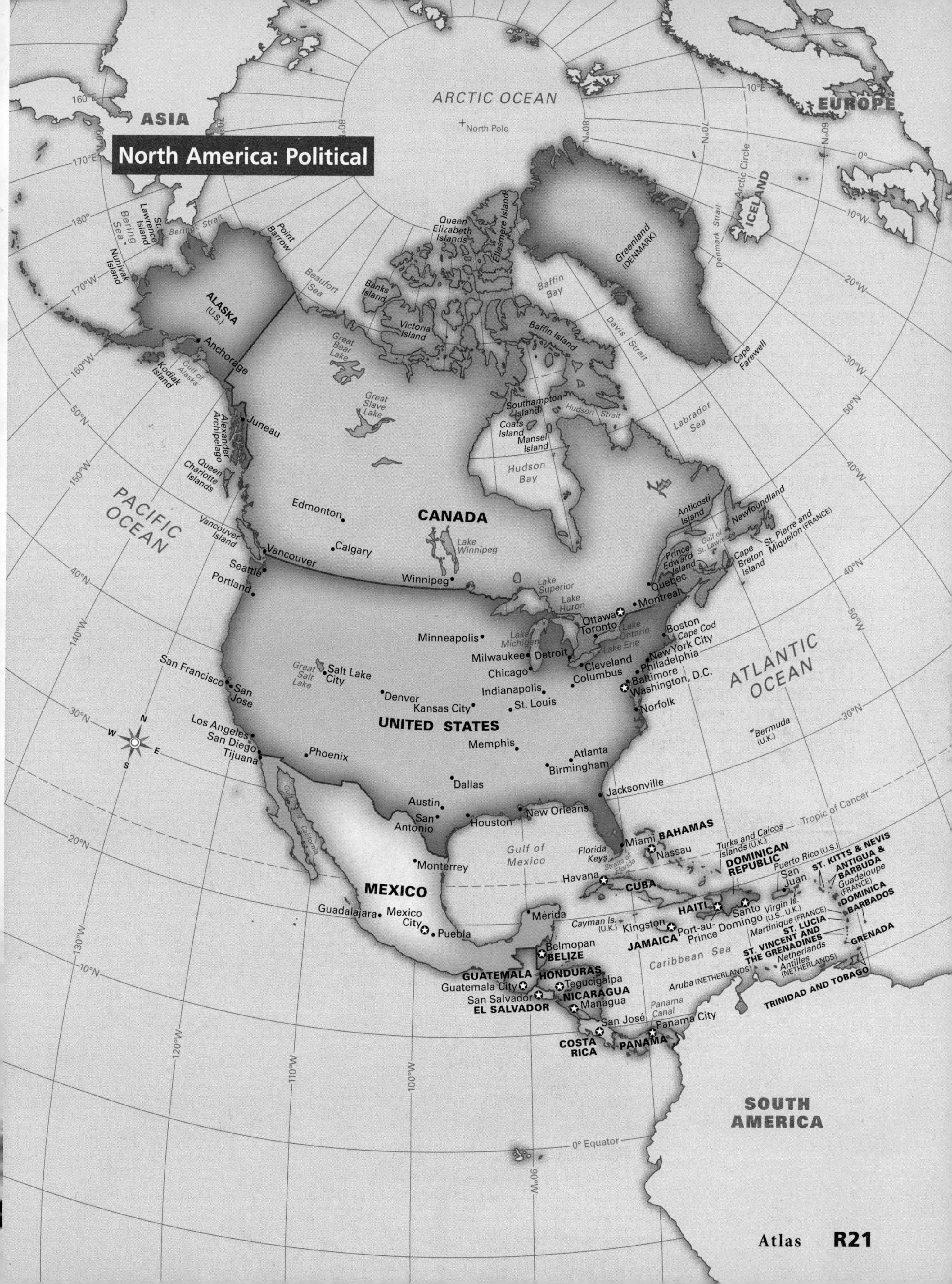
North America: Political
ARCTIC OCEAN
North Pole
ASIA
EUROPE
ICELAND
Greenland (DENMARK)
Queen Elizabeth Islands
Ellesmere Island
Baffin Bay
Baffin Island
Davis Strait
Denmark Strait
Arctic Circle
Cape Farewell
Labrador Sea
Hudson Strait
Southampton Island
Coats Island
Mansel Island
Hudson Bay
Banks Island
Victoria Island
Beaufort Sea
Great Bear Lake
Great Slave Lake
Point Barrow
Bering Strait
Bering Sea
St. Lawrence Island
Nunivak Island
ALASKA (U.S.)
Anchorage
Gulf of Alaska
Kodiak Island
Juneau
Alexander Archipelago
Queen Charlotte Islands
PACIFIC OCEAN
Vancouver Island
Vancouver
Seattle
Portland
Edmonton
Calgary
CANADA
Lake Winnipeg
Winnipeg
Lake Superior
Lake Huron
Lake Michigan
Lake Ontario
Lake Erie
Ottawa
Toronto
Montreal
Quebec
Anticosti Island
Newfoundland
Gulf of St. Lawrence
Prince Edward Island
Cape Breton Island
St. Pierre and Miquelon (FRANCE)
Boston
Cape Cod
New York City
Philadelphia
Baltimore
Washington, D.C.
Norfolk
ATLANTIC OCEAN
Bermuda (U.K.)
Minneapolis
Milwaukee
Detroit
Cleveland
Chicago
Columbus
Indianapolis
St. Louis
San Francisco
San Jose
Great Salt Lake
Salt Lake City
Denver
Kansas City
UNITED STATES
Los Angeles
San Diego
Tijuana
Phoenix
Memphis
Atlanta
Birmingham
Dallas
Jacksonville
Austin
San Antonio
Houston
New Orleans
Gulf of California
Gulf of Mexico
Florida Keys
Straits of Florida
Miami
BAHAMAS
Nassau
Tropic of Cancer
Turks and Caicos Islands (U.K.)
DOMINICAN REPUBLIC
Puerto Rico (U.S.)
San Juan
ST. KITTS & NEVIS
ANTIGUA & BARBUDA
Guadeloupe (FRANCE)
DOMINICA
BARBADOS
Monterrey
MEXICO
Havana
CUBA
HAITI
Santo Domingo
Virgin Is. (U.S., U.K.)
Martinique (FRANCE)
ST. LUCIA
ST. VINCENT AND THE GRENADINES
GRENADA
Guadalajara
Mexico City
Puebla
Mérida
Cayman Is. (U.K.)
Kingston
Port-au-Prince
JAMAICA
Caribbean Sea
Netherlands Antilles (NETHERLANDS)
Aruba (NETHERLANDS)
TRINIDAD AND TOBAGO
Belmopan
BELIZE
GUATEMALA
Guatemala City
HONDURAS
Tegucigalpa
San Salvador
EL SALVADOR
NICARAGUA
Managua
Panama Canal
San José
Panama City
COSTA RICA
PANAMA
SOUTH AMERICA
0° Equator
N
S
E
W
160°E
170°E
180°
170°W
160°W
150°W
140°W
130°W
120°W
110°W
100°W
90°W
70°W
80°W
80°N
70°N
60°N
50°N
40°N
30°N
20°N
10°N
10°E
0°
10°W
20°W
30°W
40°W
50°W
60°W

United States: Physical
Strait of Juan de Fuca
Mount Rainier 14,410 ft (4,392 m)
CASCADE RANGE
COAST RANGES
Franklin D. Roosevelt Lake
Columbia River
Pend Oreille
Clark Fork
Flathead River
Flathead Lake
Lewis Range
Milk River
Missouri River
Fort Peck Lake
Lake Sakakawea
Bitterroot Range
Salmon River
Salmon River Mts.
Sawtooth Mts.
Columbia Plateau
Snake River
Willamette River
ROCKY MOUNTAINS
CONTINENTAL DIVIDE
Yellowstone River
Yellowstone Lake
Grand Tetons
Wind River
Bighorn Mts.
Bighorn River
Powder River
GREAT PLAINS
INTERIOR PLAINS
Lake Oahe
Black Hills
Cheyenne River
White River
Niobrara River
North Platte River
Platte River
South Platte River
Republican River
Smoky Hill River
Klamath River
Goose Lake
Cape Mendocino
Shasta Lake
Pyramid Lake
Gannett Peak 13,804 ft (4,207 m)
Wind River Range
Wasatch Range
Great Salt Lake
Utah Lake
Uinta Mts.
Green River
Front Range
SIERRA NEVADA
Sacramento River
Central Valley
GREAT BASIN
Lake Tahoe
San Francisco Bay
San Joaquin River
Monterey Bay
Coast Ranges
Colorado River
Mount Elbert 14,433 ft (4,400 m)
Pikes Peak 14,110 ft (4,301 m)
COLORADO PLATEAU
Lake Powell
San Juan River
Mount Whitney 14,494 ft (4,419 m)
Death Valley
Mojave Desert
Lake Mead
Grand Canyon
Painted Desert
San Luis Valley
Sangre De Cristo Mts.
Rio Grande
Canadian River
PACIFIC OCEAN
Channel Islands
Salton Sea
Imperial Valley
Gila River
Sonoran Desert
Gulf of California
Pecos River
Amistad Reservoir
Nueces River
MEXICO
45°N
40°N
35°N
30°N
125°W
120°W
To understand the relative locations of Alaska and Hawaii, as well as the vast distances separating them from the rest of the United States, see the world map.

CANADA
Isle Royale
Lake Superior
Mesabi Range
Red River
Minnesota River
James River
Mississippi River
Wisconsin River
Lake Michigan
Lake Huron
Lake Ontario
Lake Erie
St. Lawrence River
St. Lawrence Seaway
St. John River
Longfellow Mts.
Penobscot River
Lake Champlain
Adirondack Mts.
Green Mts.
White Mts.
Connecticut River
Hudson R.
Cape Cod
Catskill Mts.
Long Island Sound
Long Island
Allegheny R.
PLATEAU
Susquehanna River
Delaware River
40°N
MOUNTAINS
Missouri River
Des Moines River
Illinois River
Wabash River
Scioto River
Monongahela R.
ALLEGHENY
Potomac River
Delaware Bay
PLAINS
Kansas R.
Ohio River
Kanawha River
APPALACHIAN
James River
Chesapeake Bay
ATLANTIC OCEAN
70°W
Lake of the Ozarks
OZARK PLATEAU
Lake Barkley
Cumberland River
Cumberland Plateau
BLUE RIDGE MOUNTAINS
Roanoke River
Pamlico Sound
Cape Hatteras
35°N
Keystone Lake
Kentucky Lake
Great Smoky Mts.
PIEDMONT
Arkansas River
White River
Eufaula Lake
Tennessee River
Ouachita Mts.
Lake Texoma
Tombigbee River
Coosa River
Oconee River
Savannah River
Trinity River
Saline River
Red River
Mississippi
Pearl River
Alabama R.
Chattahoochee River
Altamaha River
Sea Islands
Brazos River
Toledo Bend Reservoir
PLAIN
COASTAL
GULF
Okefenokee Swamp
Chandeleur Islands
Mississippi Delta
FLORIDA PENINSULA
Cape Canaveral
N
W
E
S
80°W
Gulf of Mexico
Lake Okeechobee
BAHAMAS
25°N
Padre Island
The Everglades
Cape Sable
Florida Keys
Straits of Florida
95°W
90°W
85°W
75°W

To understand the relative locations of Alaska and Hawaii, as well as the vast distances separating them from the rest of the United States, see the world map.

CANADA
MINNESOTA
WISCONSIN
MICHIGAN
IOWA
ILLINOIS
INDIANA
OHIO
PENNSYLVANIA
NEW YORK
MAINE
VT
NH
MA
CT
RI
NJ
DE
MD
WEST VIRGINIA
VIRGINIA
KENTUCKY
TENNESSEE
NORTH CAROLINA
SOUTH CAROLINA
GEORGIA
ALABAMA
MISSISSIPPI
ARKANSAS
MISSOURI
LOUISIANA
FLORIDA
BAHAMAS
ATLANTIC OCEAN
Gulf of Mexico
Grand Forks
Fargo
Duluth
Superior
Minneapolis
St. Paul
Sioux Falls
Sioux City
Omaha
Lincoln
Topeka
Wichita
Kansas City
Des Moines
Cedar Rapids
Davenport
Madison
Milwaukee
Green Bay
Marquette
Sault Ste. Marie
Grand Rapids
Lansing
Detroit
Ann Arbor
Saginaw
Rockford
Chicago
Peoria
Springfield
East St. Louis
St. Louis
Jefferson City
Gary
South Bend
Fort Wayne
Indianapolis
Evansville
Louisville
Frankfort
Lexington
Toledo
Cleveland
Youngstown
Akron
Columbus
Dayton
Cincinnati
Erie
Buffalo
Rochester
Syracuse
Albany
Pittsburgh
Harrisburg
Allentown
Philadelphia
Jersey City
Newark
New York City
Yonkers
Trenton
Camden
Atlantic City
Dover
Baltimore
Annapolis
Washington, D.C.
Charleston
Richmond
Newport News
Norfolk
Virginia Beach
Burlington
Montpelier
Augusta
Portland
Concord
Manchester
Boston
Worcester
Springfield
Providence
Hartford
New Haven
Bridgeport
Cape Cod
Long Island Sound
Long Island
Lake Superior
Lake Michigan
Lake Huron
Lake Ontario
Lake Erie
Lake Champlain
St. Lawrence River
Hudson R.
Connecticut R.
Susquehanna River
Delaware Bay
Chesapeake Bay
Red River
Minnesota River
Mississippi River
Missouri River
Illinois River
Ohio River
Lake of the Ozarks
Lake Barkley
Kentucky Lake
Keystone Lake
Tulsa
Eufaula Lake
Lake Texoma
Fayetteville
Springfield
Nashville
Knoxville
Memphis
Chattanooga
Winston-Salem
Greensboro
Durham
Raleigh
Asheville
Charlotte
Cape Hatteras
Greenville
Columbia
Charleston
Savannah River
Little Rock
Pine Bluff
Huntsville
Birmingham
Atlanta
Macon
Columbus
Savannah
Sea Islands
Vicksburg
Jackson
Meridian
Montgomery
Chattahoochee R.
Dallas
Waco
Shreveport
Toledo Bend Reservoir
Beaumont
Houston
Galveston
Baton Rouge
New Orleans
Biloxi
Mobile
Pensacola
Chandeleur Islands
Tallahassee
Jacksonville
Gainesville
Orlando
Cape Canaveral
Tampa
St. Petersburg
Lake Okeechobee
Fort Myers
Fort Lauderdale
Miami
Cape Sable
Florida Keys
Straits of Florida
N
S
E
W
40°N
35°N
30°N
25°N
70°W
75°W
80°W
85°W
90°W
95°W

World: Political

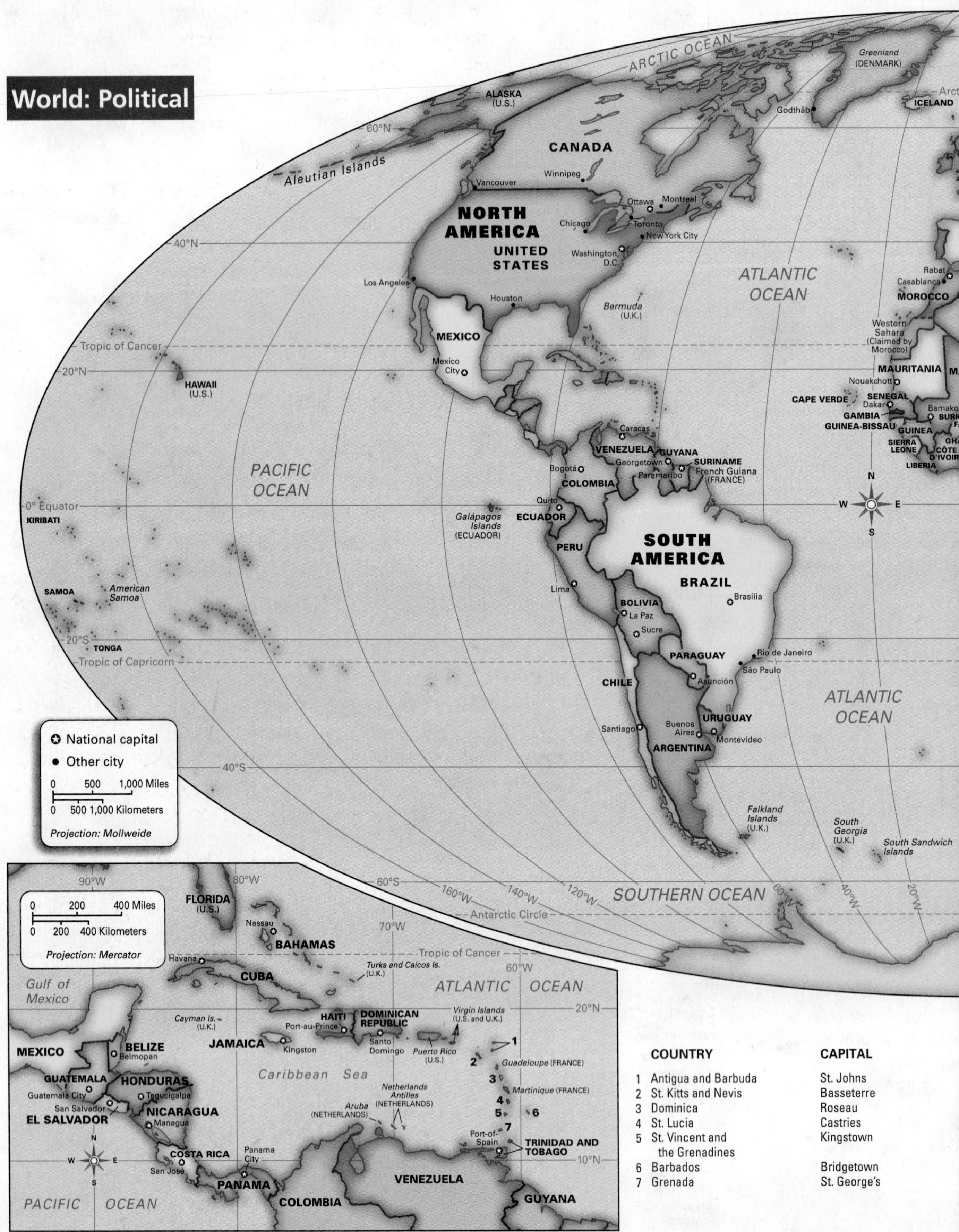

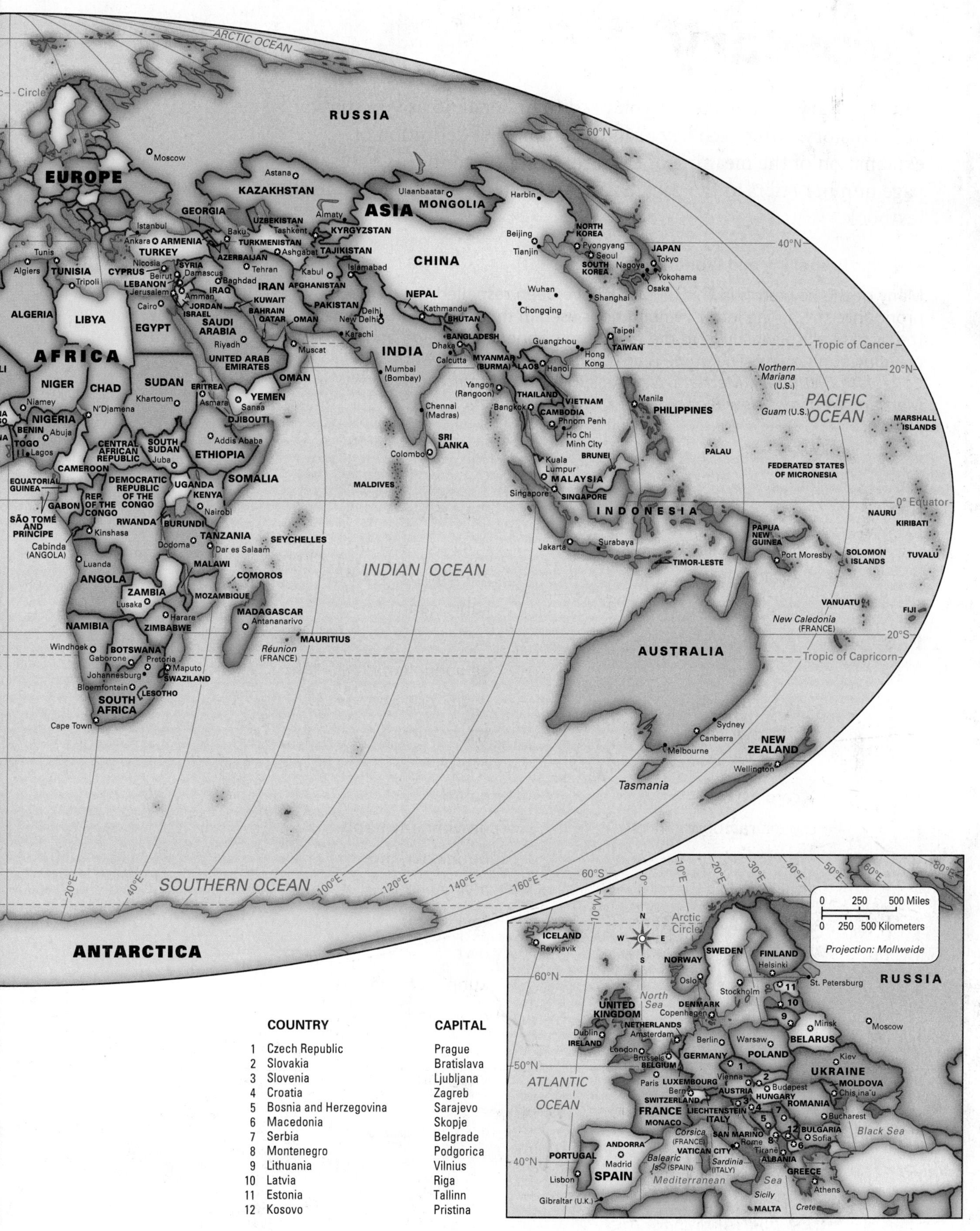

	COUNTRY	CAPITAL
1	Czech Republic	Prague
2	Slovakia	Bratislava
3	Slovenia	Ljubljana
4	Croatia	Zagreb
5	Bosnia and Herzegovina	Sarajevo
6	Macedonia	Skopje
7	Serbia	Belgrade
8	Montenegro	Podgorica
9	Lithuania	Vilnius
10	Latvia	Riga
11	Estonia	Tallinn
12	Kosovo	Pristina

Glossary

This Glossary contains terms you need to understand as you study Texas history. After each key term there is a brief definition or explanation of the meaning of the term as it is used in this book. The page number refers to the page on which the term is introduced in the textbook.

Phonetic Respelling and Pronunciation Guide

Many of the key terms in this textbook have been respelled to help you pronounce them. The letter combinations used in the respelling throughout the narrative are explained in the following phonetic respelling and pronunciation guide. The guide is adapted from *Webster's Tenth New Collegiate Dictionary, Merriam-Webster's New Geographical Dictionary,* and *Merriam-Webster's New Biographical Dictionary.*

mark	as in	respelling	example
a	alphabet	a	*al-fuh-bet
ā	Asia	ay	ay-zhuh
	alcalde, José	eh	ahl-KAHL-deh, hoh-SEH
ä	cart, top	ah	kahrt, tahp
e	let, ten	e	let, ten
ē	even, leaf	ee	ee-vuhn, leef
i	it, tip, British	i	it, tip, brit-ish
ī	site, buy, Ohio	y	syt, by, oh-hy-oh
	iris	eye	eye-ris
k	card	k	kahrd
ō	over, rainbow	oh	oh-vuhr, rayn-boh
u̇	book, wood	ooh	boohk, woohd
ȯ	all, orchid	aw	awl, awr-kid
ȯi	foil, coin	oy	foyl, koyn
au̇	out	ow	owt
ə	cup, butter	uh	kuhp, buht-uhr
ü	rule, food	oo	rool, food
yü	few	yoo	fyoo
zh	vision	zh	vizh-uhn

*A syllable printed in small capital letters receives heavier emphasis than the other syllable(s) in a word.

A

abolition The ending of slavery. **363**

absolute location The exact position of a place on Earth, often stated in latitude and longitude. **9**

academies Schools that offer classes at the high school level. **289**

ad interim Temporary. **242**

adobe Building material made of dried clay mud. **79**

aerospace Earth's atmosphere and the space beyond it. **568**

age distribution Portion of a population at each age. **33**

agribusiness The large-scale farming and processing of crops. **682**

agriculture Growing crops and raising animals. **35**

alcalde (ahl-KAHL-deh) Spanish official who had judicial and law enforcement powers in a Spanish settlement in Texas. **130**

allies Friends who support one another. **76**

amendments Additions, changes, or corrections to a constitution. **643**

Anglos Mostly white, non-Hispanic settlers who moved to Texas from the United States during the Mexican period. **161**

annexation Formal joining of one political region to another. **258**

anthropologists Scientists who study and compare peoples to learn how they live or have lived. **70**

appellate courts Courts that review trials to determine if correct procedures were followed. **653**

appropriation bill Bill that sets the amount of money to be spent by a government. **656**

aquifers Natural formations of underground gravel, rock, or sand that trap and hold rainwater. **23**

archaeologists Scientists who use remains of materials that they find to study peoples of the past. **70**

artifacts Tools, weapons, and other objects made by people. **70**

ayuntamiento (ah-yoon-tah-MYEN-toh) Governing council of a Spanish settlement in Texas. **130**

B

bail A sum of money that a defendant promises to pay to the court as a guarantee to appear at the proper time. **667**

balanced budget Budget in which spending does not exceed revenue. **271**

bands Groups of people, as in groups of American Indian families. **83**

barbed wire Fencing designed with sharp points. **454**

bar graph Chart that uses bars of differing lengths to represent numbers or percentages for comparing information about different places or time periods. **13**

barter Trade of goods or services without use of money. **193**

basins Lowlands surrounded by higher land. **57**

bayous Slow-moving, swampy sections of rivers or lakes. **47**

bicameral Having two legislative houses. **644**

biennial Every two years. **319**

bill Proposed law. **646**

bill of rights Government document that outlines the civil liberties, or individual rights, that a government promises to protect. **242**

biomass Plant and animal material used to generate energy. **630**

bipartisanship Cooperation between political parties to achieve goals. **615**

birthrate Number of births per 1,000 people. **32**

Black Codes Laws passed in southern U.S. states after Reconstruction to deny African Americans' civil rights. **399**

blues Musical form with lyrics that often reflect the difficulties people face in life. **542**

boll weevil Type of beetle that infests the cotton plant. **470**

bonds Certificates that represent money owed by a government to private citizens. **405**

boom-and-bust cycle Alternating periods of growth and depression in an industry or economy. **481**

boomtowns Towns that grow along with economic booms. **486**

brands Identification marks on livestock made by burning with a hot iron. **440**

breadlines Lines of people waiting to receive free food. **546**

buckskin Tanned deer hide. **187**

budget surplus Money remaining after all expenses have been paid, caused when income exceeds expenses. **612**

buffalo guns Powerful rifles with telescopes used by hunters to kill buffalo. **423**

buffalo soldiers Name that American Indians gave to African American troops. **428**

buffer Zone of protections between two countries or territories. **160**

C

cabinet Group of advisers to a head of state, such as a president. **259**

capitol Building in which government officials meet. **266**

carpetbaggers Northerners who moved to the South after the Civil War; so called because they often carried all they owned in bags made of carpet. **405**

casualties People who are killed, wounded, captured, or missing during a war. **239**

cattle drives The herding of large groups of cattle from the open range to market for sale. **441**

causation chart Chart that uses pictures, diagrams, boxes, or arrows to show causes and effects of events. **15**

cavalry Group of soldiers on horseback. **228**

cede To officially give, as a territory from one country to another. **136**

centennial One-hundredth anniversary. **554**

charter Document granting permission to operate. **266**

checks and balances Governmental arrangement by which each different branch has the power to check, or restrict, the power of the other branches. **642**

Chicano movement Movement by Hispanics during the 1960s for political change and the end of discrimination. **593**

Cinco de Mayo Mexican celebration of May 5, 1862, the day that a Mexican army defeated an invading French force at the Battle of Puebla. **625**

circuit riders Traveling preachers. **289**

civil law Law relating to private rights or obligations. **653**

civil rights Individual rights guaranteed by a Constitution. **399**

Cold War Term describing the tensions between the United States and the Soviet Union after World War II. **568**

Columbian Exchange Term describing the transfer of plants, animals, and diseases between the Americas and other continents since the time of Columbus. **105**

commercial farming Large-scale growing of crops for profit. **469**

commissioners Representatives of a government. **416**

commissioners' court Panel of elected commissioners that governs a county in Texas. **662**

commission plan Plan of government in which a panel of elected commissioners is in charge of city services. **508**

commute Travel back and forth, as for a job when one lives in one place and works in another. **574**

compass rose A feature on a map that points to north, south, east, and west. **11**

competition Economic rivalry between companies selling products. **680**

confederacies Alliances between different groups. **76**

conference committee A committee in a legislature that works to revise bills to satisfy both houses of the legislature. **646**

conquistadores (kahn-kees-tuh-DAWR-ez) Spanish soldiers and adventurers in search of glory, gold, and land. **91**

conservatism An approach to politics that supports gradual change and favors keeping systems and programs that have worked in the past. **570**

consumer goods Items produced for personal use. **542**

cooperative stores Businesses owned and operated for the benefit of the members of an organization. **499**

corporations Companies that sell shares of ownership to investors to raise money. **321**

cotton belt Region of the southern United States in which the majority of the nation's cotton crop was grown. **349**

cottonclads Steamboats lined with cotton bales and converted to gunboats during the Civil War. **382**

cotton diplomacy Tactic used by southern leaders to secure foreign support during the Civil War by withholding cotton shipments to other nations until they offered aid. **378**

cotton gins Devices that separate cotton fibers from seeds. **165**

criminal law Law determining what actions are illegal within a society. **653**

crop rotation System of growing different crops on the same land over a period of years to improve the soil. **75**

culture A learned system of shared beliefs, traits, and values. **4**

customs duties Import taxes. **205**

D

death rate Number of deaths per 1,000 people. **33**

delegates Representatives, as to a convention. **212**

demand In economics, the amount of a good or service that people are willing to buy. **680**

demobilization Moving from a wartime to a peacetime economy. **536**

demography Branch of geography that studies human populations. **32**

denominations Religious groups with similar beliefs. **289**

deportation The forced removal of people from a country or region. **620**

derricks Towers that support oil-drilling equipment. **479**

desalinization The process of removing salt from seawater to make it safe to drink. **622**

desegregate To free a place or institution from laws or practices separating the races. **578**

diplomatic recognition The formal acknowledgement by one government that another government exists. **294**

diplomats Individuals who represent countries in foreign affairs. **142**

dogtrot cabins Log homes with two rooms separated by an open passage. **186**

dot-coms Online companies. **686**

draft Requirement of military service. **387**

drought Long period without rain. **26**

dry farming Farming techniques, such as terracing, used in a dry climate to keep moisture in the soil. **467**

due process The legal process that governments must follow before taking away a person's property or punishing a person. **667**

Dust Bowl Parts of the southern Great Plains in which dust and drought ruined crops and killed thousands of cattle during the 1930s. **548**

E

ecosystem All of an area's plants and animals together with the nonliving parts of their environment. **7**

embargo The banning of trade with a country. **692**

eminent domain A government's power to claim privately owned land for public use. **667**

empresarios Businesspeople who promoted migration to the Texas colonies. **174**

environment Physical surroundings. **4**

epidemics Widespread outbreaks of disease. **105**

equator An imaginary line circling the globe exactly halfway between the North and South Poles. **10**

eras Periods into which historians divide the past. **68**

erosion Process by which something such as soil is worn away. **29**

escarpments Cliffs. **54**

expenditures Government expenses. **262**

exports Items made in a country and sold to other countries. **193**

extinct Died out completely. **29**

F

faction A group acting together within a larger group, usually in opposition. **217**

fault Break in Earth's crust. **55**

federalism System of government that balances powers by distributing them between one central and many regional governments. **641**

feedlot Large area of enclosed land on which animals are kept and fed to be made ready for market. **685**

filibusters Military adventurers who came to Texas from the United States in the early 1800s. **144**

flatboats Long, low boats used for river travel. **185**

flowchart Chart using boxes, arrows, or images to show a series of activities or steps. **15**

foreign relations Dealings between a country and other countries. **294**

Foreign Trade Zones Areas in which export regulations are reduced to promote trade. **631**

fossil fuel Fuel such as coal, oil, or natural gas formed underground from plant or animal remains. **478**

freedpeople Former slaves. **397**

free enterprise Economic system in which businesses operate with little interference from government. **678**

frontier Region marking the farthest edge of settlement by a country or group of people. **160**

G

general elections Elections in which voters cast their ballots for candidates for a particular state or local office or for deciding certain issues. **670**

general-law cities Small towns or cities that operate under the general laws of the state of Texas; some have a charter from the legislature outlining their form of government. **664**

geographic information systems (GIS) Computer systems that gather, store, and organize geographic information. **5**

geography The study of the special physical and human characteristics of places or regions. **4**

globalization The interdependence of the nations of the world that has been created as goods, ideas, and people move across the globe. **631**

grand jury Jury that decides if a person accused of a felony should be indicted, or formally charged. **654**

Great Depression Severe global economic slowdown in the 1930s. **545**

Great Society Program launched by President Lyndon B. Johnson that included laws improving health care, education, environmental protection, job training, and immigration. **586**

gristmills Machines for grinding grain into meal or flour. **351**

growth rate Speed of growth. **32**

H

habitat Environmental home of an animal. **29**

hides Animal skins. **79**

historians People who study the past. **68**

home-rule charters Charters that allow citizens in Texas municipalities of more than 5,000 people to choose their form of government. **664**

homestead law Law passed by the Republic Congress in 1839 that protected a family's home and up to 50 acres of land from seizure for debts. **267**

horizontal integration Owning many businesses in a particular field. **485**

humidity The amount of moisture in the air. **25**

hunter-gatherers People who hunt animals and gather wild plants for game. **72**

I

illegal immigrants People who move to a country without following the proper legal procedures. **620**

immigration Movement of people from one country to another. **31**

impeach To bring charges against a public official. **402**

imports Items that a nation buys from other countries. **193**

infantry Foot soldiers. **228**

information technology The development, maintenance, and use of computer hardware and software. **686**

infrastructure Public works such as roads and water systems. **621**

interest groups Groups united by a common interest that try to affect government policy. **672**

internal combustion engine Engine in which the combustion, or burning, that generates power takes place inside the engine. **487**

ironclads Ships used during the Civil War that were heavily armored with iron plates. **380**

irrigation Supplying water to crops by artificial methods. **23**

J, K

jacales (huh-KAW-lehs) Small, one-room huts made of sticks and mud. **151**

joint resolution Measure passed by both houses of Congress that is a formal expression of intent. **316**

judicial review Courts' power to determine if a law is constitutional. **654**

junctions Meeting places of two or more lines, as of a railroad. **465**

Juneteenth June 19; day celebrated as the day on which Union general Gordon Granger landed at Galveston and issued the Emancipation Proclamation freeing Texas slaves. **396**

L

labor unions Organizations formed to support the interests of workers. **473**

land speculators People who buy large amounts of land in hopes of selling it for great profits. **287**

latitude Imaginary lines that run east-west around the globe and measure distance north and south of the equator. **10**

legend A key that helps explain the symbols, colors, and other features on a map. **11**

libel Intentionally written false statements. **667**

lignite A type of soft coal. **49**

limited government Principle of government in which power is limited by set laws, such as those in a constitution. **641**

line graph Graph that indicates a trend or pattern over time, such as whether something is increasing, decreasing, or staying the same. **14**

line-item veto Power held by a government executive that allows for the veto of specific lines, or parts, of budget bills. **649**

lobby To try to persuade legislators about an issue. **672**

longhorn Breed of cattle that developed as Spanish breeds mixed with English cattle brought by U.S. settlers. **442**

longitude Imaginary lines that run north-south around the globe and measure distance east and west of the prime meridian. **10**

Louisiana Purchase Agreement in 1803 in which the United States purchased Louisiana from France for $15 million. **141**

M

manifest destiny The belief that the United States was meant to spread across North America. **315**

map projections Means by which mapmakers create flat representations of Earth's features. **12**

maquiladoras Mexican factories near the Mexico-Texas border that assemble products using parts imported from the United States. **622**

martial law Rule by military authority. **388**

matrilineal Traced through the mother's side of the family. **76**

migration Movement from one country, place, or location to another. **7**

militia Citizen army. **167**

missions Religious communities established by Spanish Catholics. **112**

mitotes All-night celebrations held by the Coahuiltecans and other American Indians. **74**

monopoly Sole control of a field of business. **503**

mustangs Wild offspring of the horses the Spanish brought to the Americas. **105**

N

natural gas Gas that can be used as a fuel. **485**

natural regions Distinct areas with a common physical environment. **44**

neutral Not aligned with either side during a conflict. **530**

New Deal Program initiated by President Franklin D. Roosevelt to fight the Great Depression. **550**

nomads Groups of people who move from place to place. **72**

noncombatants People who are not involved in the fighting of a war. **239**

nonrenewable resources Resources, such as coal, natural gas, and oil, that cannot be replaced by Earth's natural processes. **36**

nonviolent resistance Peaceful public demonstrations. **578**

North American Free Trade Agreement (NAFTA) Agreement between Canada, Mexico, and the United States that eliminated many trade barriers. **690**

O, P

offensive A forward troop advance. **333**

open range Unfenced land. **444**

oxcarts Large, slow two-wheeled carts with solid wheels used to haul freight before the building of railroads. **354**

pardon Power held by a government executive to free people convicted of crimes. **650**

petition Formal request made by citizens to the government. **242**

petit jury Jury that decides the verdict in a trial. **654**

petrochemicals Chemicals made from oil and natural gas. **47**

petroleum Dark, thick liquid fossil fuel commonly called oil. **478**

philanthropy The giving of money or gifts for charitable causes. **489**

pie chart Chart showing how the parts of a whole are divided. **14**

plains Areas of flat or gently rolling land without a sharp rise or fall in elevation. **21**

plantations Large farms that usually specialized in growing one kind of crop. **195**

planters Large-scale farmers. **349**

plateaus Areas of flat, elevated land that drops sharply on one or more sides. **21**

platform Statement of political goals of a political party. **502**

political action committees (PACs) Groups that raise and spend money for a candidate. **673**

political parties Groups of people who help elect government officials and influence government policies. **316**

poll tax Tax on voting. **513**

pooling Combining efforts by companies to prevent competition in an industry. **500**

popular sovereignty Principle of government that all political power comes from the people. **641**

precincts County subdivisions. **662**

prehistory Period of time before written records. **70**

presidios Military bases in Spanish colonial America. **113**

primary elections Elections in which voters select persons to run in the later general election. **539**

prime meridian An imaginary line that runs around the globe from the North Pole through Greenwich, England, to the South Pole. **10**

profit The money that a business has left after it pays expenses. **678**

progressives Reformers in the late 1800s and early 1900s who worked to improve society. **507**

prohibition The banning of the manufacture, distribution, and sale of alcoholic beverages. **511**

proration Proportionate division or distribution. **546**

provisional Temporary. **232**

Q, R

quilting bees Quilting groups. **187**

ragtime Form of music popular during the early 1900s. **525**

ranchos Ranches. **113**

ranges Groups of mountains. **21**

range wars Occasionally violent disputes caused by the fencing of the open range. **455**

ratify Approve and accept formally. **263**

Reconstruction The process of reuniting the United States after the Civil War and rebuilding the southern states. **397**

redbacks Paper money issued by the Republic of Texas during Mirabeau B. Lamar's administration to help stop an economic crisis. **267**

reference maps Maps used to find locations. **12**

referendum The practice of allowing voters to decide a legislative issue. **670**

refinery Factory where crude oil is refined, or made into usable products such as gasoline. **479**

reforms Changes in policy intended to improve a condition. **212**

refugees People forced to leave their homeland because of war or persecution. **529**

regiment A military unit made up of a number of battalions, or groups of troops. **377**

relative location Where a place is in relation to other places. **9**

remuda Spanish word for "remount"; referred to the fresh horses that cowboys kept in reserve during a cattle drive. **447**

renewable resources Resources, such as trees and wind, that are replaced by Earth's natural processes. **36**

republic Government in which authority comes from the people and power is exercised by elected officials according to set laws. **172**

republicanism System in which voters elect people to represent them in government. **641**

reservations Areas of land reserved for American Indians. **340**

reservoirs Artificial lakes that store water and are often used as a source of drinking water for towns and cities. **23**

resolutions Statements that express opinions. **209**

revenue Government income. **262**

revolt Revolution. **114**

runoff election An election to determine a winner in a contest in which no candidate received a majority of the vote. **670**

rustlers Cattle thieves. **441**

S

sales tax Tax added to the price of many goods and services at the time of purchase. **656**

savings and loan associations Banks originally established to help people buy homes. **513**

sawmills Mills in which wood is cut into usable pieces. **193**

scalawags Name given to southerners who supported Reconstruction for personal economic gain. **405**

scale A ruler indicating the relationship between distances on a map and actual distances. **11**

scandal a publicized event in which officials are disgraced for wrongdoing. **604**

scrip Paper money. **546**

secede To formally withdraw from an organized body. **374**

secularize To move from religious to civil control. **162**

segregation Forced separation of whites and African Americans in public. **409**

semiconductors Materials that conduct some electricity, but not as much as most metals do, necessary for modern electronics. **686**

separation of powers Principle of government in which powers are divided among different government branches. **642**

session Period in which the legislature meets. **644**

sharecroppers Farmers who lacked land and necessary supplies and thus promised a large part of their crop to the landowner in exchange for these items. **411**

siege Military blockade of a city or fort. **145**

sit-ins Protests that involve sitting down in a location and refusing to leave. **590**

slander A false statement made on purpose that damages another's reputation. **667**

soup kitchens Places run by charitable organizations where people can come for a free meal when in need of assistance. **546**

sovereignty Supremacy in power. **375**

special districts Type of local government that is formed for a particular purpose, often handling services that other local governments do not provide. **664**

special elections Elections in which voters cast their ballots to fill a vacant office or approve a government change such as a constitutional amendment or local bond issue. **670**

spirituals emotional Christian songs sung by enslaved people in the South that mixed African and European elements and usually expressed slaves' religious beliefs. **362**

squatters People who do not legally own the land on which they live. **184**

states' rights Rights held by states that place limits on the implied powers of the federal government over state governments. **372**

statistics Information in the form of numbers. **13**

steamboat A boat powered by steam created by the burning of wood or coal. **355**

stocks Shares of ownership in a company. **544**

stockyards Holding pens for livestock. **443**

strike Refusal by workers to do their job until a company meets their demands. **473**

subregions Smaller divisions of a region. **45**

suburbs Residential neighborhoods built outside a central city. **523**

suffrage Voting rights. **398**

Sunbelt The southern region of the United States, known for its warm climate. **42**

supply In economics, the amount of a good or service that is available for purchase. **679**

T

tanneries Businesses built for preparing animal hides. **351**

Tejanos (teh-HAW-nohs) Texas settlers of Spanish or Mexican descent. **138**

telegraphs Electronic device used to communicate over long distances by sending coded messages over wires. **358**

temperance movement Social reform effort that encouraged people to drink less alcohol. **511**

tenant farmers People who rent land to grow crops. **411**

tepees Movable homes used by some Plains Indians that were made from animal hides stretched over long poles. **82**

terrorism Use of violent attacks by individuals or small groups to advance political goals. **617**

Texas fever Disease that plagued cattle, to which longhorns were resistant. **442**

Texas Rangers Defense force that tried to keep the peace along the Texas frontier. **261**

thematic maps Maps that show a specific topic, theme, or spatial distribution of an activity. **12**

threshers Machines that separate grain or seeds from plants. **468**

tidelands Underwater lands bordering the coast. **571**

time line Chart showing a sequence of events. **15**

tourism Business of attracting visitors to a region or place. **58**

transcontinental railroad Railroad that runs across the continent. **463**

transportation center Place where goods arrive to be reshipped to many destinations. **51**

trial courts Courts that hear new cases and give a verdict, or ruling. **653**

tributaries Small streams or rivers that flow into a larger stream or river. **22**

trusts Legal arrangements in which a number of companies are grouped under a single board of trustees. **503**

two-party system Political system in which two major parties compete to gain political office. **610**

U, V

urbanization An increase in people living or working in cities. **7**

vaqueros (vah-KEHR-ohz) Cowboys. **131**

venison Deer meat. **188**

vertical integration Owning the businesses involved in each step of a manufacturing process. **485**

veto Power exercised by the executive branch of government to reject a law. **642**

viceroy Royal governor. **98**

victory gardens Small vegetable gardens planted on the home front during World War II for extra food. **566**

W, X, Y, Z

white primary Primary elections established in the 1920s in Texas in which Africans Americans were excluded from voting. **539**

wigwams Circular huts. **73**

wildcatters Oil operators who worked on their own in search of new fields. **483**

wind farm Group of wind turbines in one area used to create energy. **630**

windmills Devices using wind power to pump water from underground to the surface. **450**

wrangler One who herds or cares for livestock on the range. **447**

Glossary/Glosario

A

abolition/abolición Final de la esclavitud. **363**

absolute location/posición absoluta Posición exacta de un lugar en la Tierra, con frecuencia definido en términos de latitud y longitud. **9**

academies/academias Escuelas que imparten clases de enseñanza secundaria. **289**

ad interim/interino Temporal. **242**

adobe/adobe Material de construcción hecho de arcilla humedecida. **79**

aerospace/espacio aéreo Atmósfera de la Tierra y el espacio más allá de ésta. **568**

age distribution/distribución por edad Porción de la población que representa un grupo de determinada edad. **33**

agribusiness/agroindustria Agricultura a gran escala y procesamiento de los cultivos. **682**

agriculture/agricultura Siembra de cultivos y cría de animales. **35**

alcalde/alcalde Funcionario público que tenía poderes judiciales y legales en el asentamiento español de Texas. **130**

allies/aliados Amigos que se apoyan unos a otros. **76**

amendments/enmienda Agregados, cambios o correcciones hechas a una constitución. **643**

Anglos/anglosajones Colonos, en su mayoría blancos, que se mudaron de los Estados Unidos a Texas cuando este era parte de México. **161**

annexation/anexión Unión formal de una región política a otra. **258**

anthropologists/antropólogos Científicos que estudian y comparan diferentes culturas para aprender cómo viven o vivían. **70**

appellate courts/cortes de apelación Cortes que revisaban los casos para determinar si se habían seguido los procedimientos correctos. **653**

appropriation bill/carta de apropiación Carta que asigna una cantidad de dinero al gobierno para sus gastos. **656**

aquifers/acuíferos Formaciones naturales de grava, roca o arena debajo de la tierra en las que se almacena el agua de lluvia. **23**

archaeologists/arqueólogos Científicos que buscan restos de materiales y los usan para analizar las condiciones de vida en el pasado. **70**

artifacts/artefactos Herramientas, armas y otros objetos hechos por el hombre. **70**

***ayuntamiento*/ayuntamiento** Consejo de gobierno de las poblaciones españolas en Texas. **130**

B

bail/fianza Suma de dinero que un acusado deposita en una corte como garantía de que se presentará cuando ésta se lo pida. **667**

balanced budget/presupuesto equilibrado Presupuesto en el que los gastos de un gobierno no son superiores a sus ingresos. **271**

bands/bandas Grupos de personas, como las tribus indígenas. **83**

barbed wire/alambre de púas Material con puntas filosas usado para construir cercas. **454**

bar graph/gráfica de barras Diagrama que usa barras de diferente longitud para representar números o porcentajes y comparar información sobre distintos lugares o épocas. **13**

barter/trueque Intercambio de bienes o servicios sin usar dinero. **193**

basins/cuencas Tierras bajas rodeadas por terrenos de mayor altitud. **57**

bayous/brazos pantanosos Secciones de corrientes lentas y cenagosas de los ríos o lagos. **47**

bicameral/bicameral Que tiene dos cámaras de legisladores. **644**

biennial/bianual Que sucede cada dos años. **319**

bill/iniciativa Ley presentada para su aprobación. **646**

bill of rights/carta de derechos Documento en el que el gobierno otorga derechos civiles o individuales y se compromete a respetarlos. **242**

biomass/biomasa Materia orgánica de las plantas o animales que se usa como fuente de energía. **630**

bipartisanship/acuerdo bipartidista Acción cooperativa entre dos partidos políticos diferentes con el fin de alcanzar objetivos comunes. **615**

birthrate/tasa de natalidad Número de nacimientos por cada 1,000 habitantes. **32**

Black Codes/Códigos negros Leyes aprobadas por el Congreso estadounidense después de la Reconstrucción que niegan los derechos civiles a las personas de raza negra. **399**

blues/blues Tipo de música cuya letra refleja con frecuencia las dificultades de la vida cotidiana. **542**

boll weevil/gorgojo de algodón Tipo de escarabajo que infesta las plantas de algodón. **470**

bonds/bonos Certificados que representan el dinero que un gobierno debe a ciudadanos particulares. **405**

boom-and-bust cycle/ciclo de expansión y contracción Períodos alternos de crecimiento y depresión en la industria o la economía. **481**

boomtowns/pueblos en auge Poblados que crecieron rápidamente debido al desarrollo económico de una región. **486**

brands/marcas Señales de identificación hechas en la piel del ganado con hierros calientes. **440**

breadlines/filas del pan Hileras de personas en espera de una ración gratuita de alimentos. **546**

buckskin/cuero Piel curtida de algún animal. **187**

budget surplus/superávit Dinero que queda como excedente cuando los ingresos son mayores que los gastos. **612**

buffalo guns/rifles de búfalo Rifles poderosos con miras telescópicas usados para cazar búfalos. **423**

buffalo soldiers/soldados búfalo Nombre dado por los indígenas a las tropas estadounidense. **428**

buffer/zona de protección Área entre dos países o territorios que se encuentra protegida. **160**

C

cabinet/gabinete Grupo de consejeros de un jefe de estado como el presidente. **259**

capitol/capitolio Edificio en el que se reúnen los funcionarios del gobierno de Estados Unidos. **266**

carpetbaggers/carpetbaggers "Aventureros"; habitantes del norte que emigraron al sur después de la Guerra Civil, llamados así porque llevaban sus pertenencias en sacos. **405**

casualties/bajas Personas fallecidas, heridas o capturadas durante una guerra. **239**

cattle drives/travesías de ganado Arreo de grandes manadas de ganado de campo abierto a los puntos de venta. **441**

causation chart/diagrama de causa y efecto Diagrama que usa dibujos, recuadros y flechas para mostrar las causas y efectos de un suceso. **15**

cavalry/caballería Grupo de soldados a caballo. **228**

cede/ceder Entrega oficial de territorio de un país a otro. **136**

centennial/centenario Aniversario número cien. **554**

charter/carta Documento que otorga permiso de operación. **266**

checks and balances/revisión y balance Acuerdo entre los poderes de un gobierno para revisar o restringir la autoridad de los demás poderes. **642**

Chicano movement/Movimiento Chicano Creciente demanda de cambios políticos y el final de la discriminación iniciada por los hispanos en la década de 1960. **593**

Cinco de Mayo/Cinco de Mayo Celebración mexicana del 5 de mayo de 1862, fecha en que el ejército mexicano derrotó a las fuerzas invasoras francesas en la Batalla de Puebla. **625**

circuit riders/jinetes de circuito Predicadores viajeros. **289**

civil law/ley civil Ley que supervisa la aplicación de los derechos y obligaciones privados. **653**

civil rights/derechos civiles Derechos individuales garantizados por la Constitución. **399**

Cold War/guerra fría Término que describe las tensiones entre Estados Unidos y la Unión Soviética después de la Segunda Guerra Mundial. **568**

Columbian Exchange/intercambio colombino Término que describe el intercambio de plantas, animales e incluso enfermedades entre continentes desde llegada de Cristóbal Colón a América. **105**

commercial farming/agricultura comercial Cultivo a gran escala de productos con fines de lucro. **469**

commissioners/comisionados Representantes de un gobierno. **416**

commissioners court/corte de comisionados Panel de comisionados electos para gobernar los condados de Texas. **662**

commission plan/plan de la comisión Plan del gobierno en el que un panel de comisionados electos se encarga de la prestación de servicios públicos. **508**

commute/conmutar Viajar de ida y vuelta al lugar de trabajo cuando se vive en otro. **574**

compass rose/rosa de los vientos Figura de los mapas que indica la posición del norte, sur, este y oeste. **11**

competition/competencia Rivalidad económica entre empresas que venden productos. **680**

confederacies/confederaciones Alianzas entre grupos. **76**

conference committee/comité de conferencia Comité de legislatura que revisa las propuestas de ley para satisfacer las demandas de ambas cámaras. **646**

conquistadores/conquistadores Soldados españoles y aventureros en busca de gloria, oro y tierras. **91**

conservatism/conservadurismo Tendencia política que favorece el cambio gradual pero manteniendo los sistemas y programas que han funcionado bien en el pasado. **570**

consumer goods/bienes de consumo Productos fabricados para uso personal. **542**

cooperative stores/tiendas cooperativas Negocios de una organización operados para el beneficio de sus integrantes. **499**

corporations/corporaciones Compañías que se venden parcialmente en forma de acciones para recaudar fondos. **321**

cotton belt/región algodonera Región del sur de Estados Unidos en la que se cosechaba la mayor parte del algodón cultivado en el país. **349**

cottonclads/algodoneros Botes de vapor aislados con fardos de algodón que se usaron como botes de combate durante la Guerra Civil. **382**

cotton diplomacy/diplomacia del algodón Bloqueo de los envíos de algodón al extranjero por parte de los líderes del sur hasta obtener el apoyo de esas naciones durante la Guerra Civil. **378**

cotton gins/desmotadora de algodón Dispositivos usados para separar las fibras de algodón de las semillas. **165**

criminal law/ley criminal Ley que determina cuáles son las acciones ilegales en una sociedad. **653**

crop rotation/rotación de cultivos Sistema en el que se siembran diferentes productos en periodos alternados para evitar el desgaste de la tierra. **75**

culture/cultura Conjunto de creencias, valores y conductas aprendidas y compartidas por un grupo de personas. **4**

customs duties/derechos de aduana Impuestos de importación. **205**

D

death rate/tasa de mortalidad Número de personas fallecidas por cada 1,000 habitantes de una región. **32**

delegates/delegados Representantes; por ejemplo, en una convención. **212**

demand/demanda En términos económicos, cuantía de bienes y servicios que las personas están dispuestas a comprar. **680**

demobilization/desmovilización Transición de la economía de tiempos de guerra a tiempos de paz. **536**

demography/demografía Rama de la geografía que estudia a las poblaciones humanas. **32**

denominations/sectas Grupos religiosos con creencias similares. **289**

deportation/deportación Acción de sacar a una persona a la fuerza de un país o región. **620**

derricks/torre de perforación Bases donde se instala el equipo usado para la extracción del petróleo. **479**

desalinization/desalinización Proceso por el cual se quita la sal del agua de mar para hacerla potable. **622**

desegregate/desegregar Anulación de leyes o prácticas que separan a las razas humanas en determinado lugar o institución. **578**

diplomatic recognition/reconocimiento diplomático Aceptación formal de la existencia de un gobierno por parte de otro gobierno. **294**

diplomats/diplomáticos Individuos que representan a sus países en los asuntos internacionales. **142**

dogtrot cabins/cabañas de dos alas Cabañas de troncos que tienen dos habitaciones separadas por un pasillo. **187**

dot-coms/punto com Compañías en Internet. **686**

draft/reclutamiento militar Registro obligatorio para el servicio militar. **387**

drought/sequía Largo periodo sin lluvias. **26**

dry farming/cultivo de sequía Técnicas agrícolas usadas en climas secos para conservar la humedad del suelo. **467**

due process/proceso debido Proceso legal que las autoridades deben seguir antes de sancionar a una persona por una falta cometida. **667**

Dust Bowl/Cuenca del Polvo Parte de las Planicies del sur donde la sequía y el polvo arruinaron las cosechas y causaron la muerte del ganado en la década de 1930. **548**

E

ecosystem/ecosistema Plantas, animales y formas no vivas que comparten el entorno de una región. **7**

embargo/embargo Prohibición del comercio con un país. **692**

eminent domain/dominio eminente Autoridad del gobierno para declarar una propiedad privada como de uso público. **667**

***empresarios*/empresarios** Comerciantes que promovieron la migración a las colonias de Texas. **174**

environment/medio ambiente Entorno natural que nos rodea. **4**

epidemics/epidemia Brote de una enfermedad que afecta a un área grande. **105**

equator/ecuador Línea imaginaria que rodea a la Tierra justo a la mitad de la distancia entre ambos polos. **10**

era/eras Períodos en los que los historiadores organizan el pasado. **68**

erosion/erosión Proceso de desgaste de un material, como el suelo. **29**

escarpments/acantilados Riscos. **54**

expenditures/egresos Gastos del gobierno. **262**

exports/exportaciones Productos que un país compra a otros países. **193**

extinct/extinguida Especie que se ha agotado por completo. **29**

F

faction/facción Grupo que por lo general actúa en oposición de un grupo mayor. **217**

fault/falla Abertura importante en la corteza de la Tierra. **55**

federalism/federalismo Sistema de gobierno que reparte su poder entre un organismo federal y varios regionales para equilibrar fuerzas. **641**

feedlot/lote de engorde Espacio de terreno amplio y encerrado en el que se crían animales para enviar al mercado. **683**

filibusters/filibusteros Aventureros militares que llegaron de Estados Unidos a Texas a principios del siglo XIX. **144**

flatboats/pangas Largos botes planos usados como transporte en los ríos. **185**

flowchart/diagrama de flujo Diagrama que usa recuadros, flechas e imágenes para mostrar los pasos a seguir en un proceso. **15**

foreign relations/relaciones exteriores Asuntos que trata un país con los demás. **294**

Foreign Trade Zones/zonas de intercambio comercial Áreas donde se regulan las exportaciones con la finalidad de promover el intercambio comercial. **631**

fossil fuel/combustible fósil Combustible natural, como carbón o gas, que se forma en el subsuelo con restos de plantas y animales. **478**

freedpeople/liberados Esclavos puestos en libertad. **397**

free enterprise/libre empresa Sistema económico en que el gobierno no interfiere demasiado en la operación de los negocios. **678**

frontier/frontera Región que demarca el punto límite de un asentamiento establecido por un país o grupo de personas. **160**

G

general elections/elecciones generales Elecciones en las que los votantes usan boletas para elegir a los candidatos para un cargo particular o toman decisiones sobre ciertos asuntos. **670**

general-law cities/ciudades de ley general Pequeños pueblos y ciudades sujetos a las leyes del estado de Texas; algunos de ellos recibieron una carta de la legislatura que definía su propia forma de gobierno. **664**

geographic information systems/sistemas de información geográfica (GIS) Sistemas computarizados que recopilan, almacenan y organizan información geográfica. **5**

geography/geografía Estudio de las características físicas y humanas de cada lugar o región. **4**

globalization/globalización Interdependencia de las naciones del mundo mediante el intercambio de bienes, ideas y personas. **631**

grand jury/gran jurado Jurado que decide si una persona acusada de un delito debe someterse a cargos formales. **654**

Great Depression/Gran Depresión Severa reducción en las actividades económicas mundiales ocurrida en la década de 1930. **545**

Great Society/Gran Sociedad Programa del presidente Lyndon B. Johnson que incluía mejoras de salud, educación, protección ambiental, capacitación laboral y reformas de inmigración. **586**

gristmills/molinos Máquinas usadas para triturar granos y elaborar harina. **351**

growth rate/tasa de crecimiento Velocidad con la que crece la población. **32**

H

habitat/hábitat Ambiente en que vive un animal. **29**

hides/cuero Piel de animal. **79**

historians/historiadores Personas que estudian lo que sucedió en el pasado. **68**

home-rule charters/cartas de leyes ciudadanas Cartas que permiten a los ciudadanos de las localidades de Texas con más de 5,000 habitantes elegir su propia forma de gobierno. **664**

homestead law/Ley de Posesión de tierras Ley aprobada por el Congreso de la República en 1839 para proteger 50 acres de terreno que no puede ser embargado como propiedad de cada familia. **267**

horizontal integration/integración vertical Posesión de todos los negocios de una rama particular. **485**

humidity/humedad Cantidad de agua que flota en el aire. **25**

hunter-gatherers/cazadores-recolectores Personas que cazan animales y recolectan plantas para subsistir. **72**

I

illegal immigrants/inmigrantes ilegales Personas que se establecen en un país sin observar los procedimientos legales requeridos. **620**

immigration/inmigración Movimiento de personas que abandonan un país para irse a vivir a otro. **31**

impeach/encausar Levantar cargos contra un funcionario público. **402**

imports/importaciones Productos que una nación compra a otras naciones. **193**

infantry/infantería Soldados a pie. **228**

information technology/tecnología de la información El desarrollo, manejo y utilización de los programas y los equipos de computación. **686**

infrastructure/infraestructura Obras públicas como carreteras y sistemas de suministro de agua. **621**

interest groups/grupos de interés Grupos unidos por un interés común que tratan de afectar las políticas de un gobierno. **672**

internal combustion engine/máquina de combustión interna Máquinas que utilizan la combustión, es decir, la quema de un combustible para generar energía en su interior. **487**

ironclads/acorazados Barcos equipados con placas protectoras de acero usados durante la Guerra Civil. **380**

irrigation/riego Suministro de agua por medios artificiales para regar los cultivos. **23**

J, K

jacales/jacales Pequeñas viviendas de una sola habitación hechas con lodo y varas. **151**

joint resolution/resolución conjunta Medida aprobada por las dos cámaras del Congreso para formalizar una propuesta. **316**

judicial review/revisión judicial Autoridad de la Corte para determinar si una ley es aniticonstitucional. **654**

junctions/empalme Puntos de encuentro de dos o más conductos, como las líneas ferroviarias. **465**

Juneteenth/19 de junio Fecha en que el general de la Unión Gordon Granger emitió en Galveston la Proclama de emancipación que liberó a los esclavos de Texas. **396**

L

labor unions/sindicatos Organizaciones formadas para defender los intereses de los trabajadores. **473**

land speculators/especuladores de tierra Personas que compran vastas extensiones de tierra con la esperanza de obtener grandes ganancias. **287**

latitude/latitud Líneas imaginarias que corren de este a oeste en el globo terrestre y miden la distancia al norte y al sur del ecuador. **10**

legend/leyenda Clave que explica los símbolos, colores y características de un mapa. **11**

libel/libelo Escrito con declaraciones falsas intencionales. **667**

lignite/lignito Tipo de carbón mineral. **49**

limited government/gobierno limitado Principio de un gobierno en el que el uso de los poderes es limitado por leyes establecidas, como la Constitución. **641**

line graph/gráfica lineal Gráfica que muestra una tendencia en un periodo, es decir, algo que aumenta o disminuye con el paso del tiempo. **14**

line-item veto/veto de artículos en línea Autoridad del Poder Ejecutivo para anular ciertas leyes total o parcialmente. **649**

lobby/cabildear Tratar de convencer a los legisladores en un tema específico. **672**

longhorn/cuernos largos Raza de ganado desarrollada mediante la cruza de razas españolas e inglesas traídas por los colonizadores. **442**

longitude/longitud Líneas imaginarias que corren de norte a sur en el globo terrestre y miden la distancia al este y al oeste del primer meridiano. **10**

Louisiana Purchase/compra de Louisiana Acuerdo firmado en 1803 en el que Estados Unidos compró a Francia el territorio de Louisiana por 15 millones de dólares. **141**

M

manifest destiny/destino manifiesto Creencia de que por destino Estados Unidos debía extenderse y ocupar América del Norte. **315**

map projections/proyecciones en mapa Medios usados por los cartógrafos para crear representaciones planas de la superficie de la Tierra. **12**

maquiladoras/maquiladoras Fábricas ubicadas en la frontera entre México y Texas, que usan partes provenientes de Estados Unidos para ensamblar productos. **690**

martial law/ley marcial Ley creada por autoridades militares. **388**

matrilineal/matrilineal Descendencia originada en la parte materna de la familia. **76**

migration/migración Desplazamiento de un grupo de personas que abandona su lugar de origen. **7**

militia/milicia Ejército de civiles. **167**

missions/misiones Comunidades religiosas establecidas por católicos españoles.**112**

mitotes/mitotes Celebraciones de los coahuiltecos que duraban toda la noche. **74**

monopoly/monopolio Control absoluto de una rama comercial. **503**

mustangs/mustangs Tipo de caballos salvajes traídos a América por los colonizadores españoles. **105**

N

natural gas/gas natural Gas que puede usarse como combustible. **485**

natural regions/regiones naturales Zonas distintas con un ambiente físico común. **44**

neutral/neutral No aliado con ninguna de las partes que intervienen en un conflicto. **530**

New Deal/*New Deal* Programa iniciado por el presidente Franklin D. Roosevelt para acabar con la Gran Depresión. **550**

nomads/nómadas Grupos de personas que viajan de un lugar a otro sin establecerse. **72**

noncombatants/no combatientes Personas que no participan en los combates de una guerra. **239**

nonrenewable resources/recursos no renovables Recursos como el carbón, el gas natural y el petróleo que los procesos naturales de la Tierra no pueden regenerar. **36**

nonviolent resistance/resistencia sin violencia Demostraciones públicas pacíficas. **578**

North American Free Trade Agreement/Tratado de Libre Comercio (NAFTA, por sus siglas en inglés; TLC, en español) Acuerdo entre Estados Unidos, Canadá y México que eliminó muchas barreras comerciales. **690**

O, P

offensive/ofensiva Avance de tropas militares. **333**

open range/campo abierto Tierras no protegidas con cercas. **444**

oxcarts/carretas de bueyes Vehículos lentos con dos grandes ruedas que se usaban para el transporte de carga antes de que se construyeran los ferrocarriles. **354**

pardon/indulto Autoridad que tiene el Poder Ejecutivo para liberar a personas acusadas de algún crimen. **650**

petition/petición Solicitud formal hecha por ciudadanos al gobierno. **242**

petit jury/pequeño jurado Jurado que decide el veredicto de un juicio. **654**

petrochemicals/petroquímica Productos químicos derivados del petróleo y el gas natural. **47**

petroleum/petróleo Líquido fósil espeso y oscuro usado como combustible. **478**

philanthropy/filantropía Ofrecimiento de dinero para causas de beneficencia. **489**

pie chart/gráfica de pastel Diagrama que muestra cómo se dividen las partes de un entero. **14**

plains/planicies Áreas planas o de pendiente ligera en las que no hay grandes elevaciones ni hundimientos. **21**

plantations/plantaciones Grandes granjas que por lo general se especializan en la siembra de un solo cultivo. **195**

planters/hacendado Agricultores importantes. **349**

plateaus/mesetas Áreas de elevación plana con bordes de pendiente pronunciada en uno o más lados. **21**

platform/plataforma Declaración de objetivos por parte de un partido político. **502**

political action committees/comités de acción política (PAC, por sus siglas en inglés) Grupos que recaudan fondos para apoyar la campaña de un candidato. **673**

political parties/partidos políticos Grupos de personas que eligen a funcionarios del gobierno e influyen en las políticas del gobierno. **316**

poll tax/impuesto de voto Impuesto pagado para tener derecho a votar. **513**

pooling/consorcio Combinación de esfuerzos de varias compañías para evitar la competencia en cierta industria. **500**

popular sovereignty/soberanía popular Principio de gobierno en el que el poder político proviene de los habitantes. **241**

precincts/distritos Subdivisiones de un país. **662**

prehistory/prehistoria Periodo anterior a los registros históricos escritos. **70**

presidios/presidios Bases militares de las colonias españolas en América. **113**

primary elections/elecciones primarias Elecciones en que los votantes eligen a los candidatos que participarán en las elecciones generales. **539**

prime meridian/primer meridiano Línea imaginaria de la Tierra que va del Polo Norte al Polo Sur, y pasa por Greenwich, Inglaterra. **10**

profit/ganancia Dinero que le queda a un negocio luego de cubrir sus gastos. **678**

progressives/progresistas Reformistas de finales del siglo XIX y principios del siglo XX que lucharon por mejorar la sociedad. **507**

prohibition/prohibición Cancelación del permiso legal para la fabricación, distribución y venta de bebidas alcohólicas. **511**

proration/prorrateo División o distribución proporcional. **546**

provisional/provisional Temporal. **232**

Q, R

quilting bees/*quilting bees* "Abejas tejedoras"; grupos de mujeres tejedoras. **187**

ragtime/ragtime Tipo de música popular que surgió a principios del siglo XX. **525**

ranchos/ranchos Fincas de ganado. **113**

ranges/cordilleras Grupos de montañas. **21**

range wars/batallas a campo abierto Violentas disputas ocasionales por el control de las tierras a campo abierto. **455**

ratify/ratificar Aprobación y aceptación formal. **263**

Reconstruction/Reconstrucción Proceso de reunificación de Estados Unidos después de la Guerra Civil y la recuperación de los estados del sur. **397**

redbacks/espaldas rojas Papel moneda emitido por la República de Texas durante la administración de Mirabeau B. Lamar para detener la crisis económica. **267**

reference maps/mapas de referencia Mapas para encontrar lugares específicos. **12**

referendum/referéndum Práctica que permite a los votantes tomar decisiones sobre temas legislativos. **670**

refinery/refinería Lugar donde se refina el petróleo crudo para fabricar productos útiles como la gasolina. **479**

reforms/reformas Cambios en las políticas de un país para mejorar ciertas condiciones. **212**

refugees/refugiados Personas obligadas a abandonar su lugar natal por causas de guerra o persecución. **529**

regiment/regimiento Unidad militar de varios batallones o tropas. **377**

relative location/posición relativa Ubicación de un lugar en relación con la de otros. **9**

remuda/remuda Palabra española que significa "montura de reemplazo", se usaba para referirse a los caballos de refresco que los vaqueros reservaban en las travesías de ganado. **447**

renewable resources/recursos renovables Recursos como los árboles y el viento, que son generados de nuevo por los procesos naturales de la Tierra. **36**

republic/república Gobierno en el que el poder proviene de la población y es ejercido por funcionarios electos de acuerdo con ciertas normas legales. **172**

republicanism/republicanismo Sistema de gobierno en el que los ciudadanos eligen a sus representantes por voto popular. **641**

reservations/reservaciones Áreas exclusivas para los indígenas estadounidenses. **340**

reservoirs/embalses Lagos artificiales en los que se almacena agua que por lo general se suministra como agua potable a las ciudades. **23**

resolutions/resoluciones Declaraciones que expresan opiniones. **209**

revenue/ingresos Dinero que recibe el gobierno. **262**

revolt/revuelta Revolución. **114**

runoff election/elecciones de desempate Elecciones que designan al ganador en una competencia en la que ninguna de las partes recibe la mayoría del voto. **670**

rustlers/abigeos Ladrones de ganado. **441**

S

sales tax/impuesto a las ventas Impuesto que se cobra por bienes y servicios en el momento de la compra. **656**

savings and loan associations/sociedades de ahorro y préstamos Bancos creados inicialmente para ayudar a las personas a comprar viviendas. **612**

sawmills/aserraderos Lugares en los que los troncos de los árboles son cortados en piezas de tamaño útil. **193**

scalawags/*scalawags* "Bribones"; nombre dado a los habitantes del sur que apoyaban la Reconstrucción con fines de lucro. **405**

scale/escala Medida que muestra la relación entre las distancias usadas en un mapa y las distancias reales. **11**

scandal/escándalo Acontecimiento de carácter público que involucra a funcionarios acusados de actos ilegales. **604**

scrip/certificado Papel moneda. **546**

secede/secesión Retiro formal de un cuerpo organizado. **374**

secularize/secularizar Pasar de términos religiosos a términos civiles. **162**

segregation/segregación Separación obligada de blancos y afroestadounidenses en público. **409**

semiconductors/semiconductores Sustancias aislantes que conducen menor cantidad de electricidad que los metales, pero suficiente para el funcionamiento de ciertos aparatos eléctricos modernos. **686**

separation of powers/separación de poderes Principio de gobierno que divide los poderes en varias ramas. **642**

session/sesión Periodo de reuniones legislativas. **644**

sharecroppers/cultivo compartido Sistema en el que los campesinos carecen de tierras y herramientas, por lo que siembran en tierras ajenas a cambio de recibir una parte de la cosecha. **411**

siege/sitio Bloqueo militar de una ciudad o un fuerte. **145**

sit-ins/plantones Protestas de personas que se sientan en un lugar y se niegan a abandonarlo. **590**

slander/calumnia Declaración falsa que daña la reputación de alguien. **667**

soup kitchens/comedores de beneficencia Lugares administrados por organizaciones de beneficencia en los que se ofrecen alimentos gratuitos a personas sin hogar. **546**

sovereignty/soberanía Supremacía de poder. **375**

special districts/distritos especiales Organismo del gobierno local creado con un propósito específico, que por lo general ofrece servicios no ofrecidos por otros organismos locales. **664**

special elections/elecciones especiales Elecciones en las que los votantes pueden elegir a un funcionario para ocupar un puesto vacante o solicitar enmiendas constitucionales en temas locales. **670**

spirituals/espirituales canciones relgiosas emotivas cantadas por los esclavos del Sur que combinaban elementos de origen africano y europeo y solían expresar sus creencias religiosas. **362**

squatters/ocupantes ilegales Aquellas personas que se instalan en territorios que no les pertenecen legalmente. **184**

states' rights/derechos estatales Derechos que limitan la autoridad del gobierno federal sobre los gobiernos de los estados. **372**

statistics/estadísticas Información presentada en forma de cantidades. **13**

steamboat/barco de vapor Buque que navega a impulso del vapor creado por máquinas que queman madera o carbón. **355**

stocks/acciones Títulos parciales de propiedad de una empresa. **544**

stockyards/corrales Lugares de concentración de cabezas de ganado. **443**

strike/huelga Negativa de los trabajadores a realizar sus labores hasta que su compañía cumpla con sus demandas. **473**

subregions/subregiones Partes en que se divide una región. **45**

suburbs/suburbios Zonas residenciales construidas en las afueras de una ciudad. **523**

suffrage/sufragio Derecho al voto. **398**

Sunbelt/Cinturón del sol La región del sur de los Estados Unidos, conocida por su clima cálido. **42**

supply/oferta En términos económicos, cuantía de bienes y servicios disponibles para la compra. **679**

T

tanneries/curtiduría Lugar donde se preparan pieles de animales para su uso. **351**

Tejanos/tejanos Colonos de ascendencia española o mexicana establecidos en Texas. **138**

telegraphs/telégrafo Dispositivo eléctrico de comunicación a distancia con el que se envían mensajes codificados por medio de alambres. **358**

temperance movement/movimiento de abstinencia Reforma social que fomentaba la disminución en el consumo de bebidas alcohólicas. **511**

tenant farmers/agricultores arrendatarios Personas que rentaban tierras de cultivo. **411**

tepees/tipis Tiendas portátiles hechas con pieles de animales estiradas sobre postes, usados por los indígenas de las Grandes Planicies. **82**

terrorism/terrorismo Uso de ataques violentos por individuos o pequeños grupos con el propósito de conseguir ciertas metas políticas. **617**

Texas fever/fiebre de Texas Epidemia que atacó al ganado, con excepción de los cuernos largos, que fueron resistentes a la enfermedad. **442**

Texas Rangers/*Rangers* de Texas Cuerpo de defensa creado con la finalidad de mantener la paz en las fronteras de Texas. **261**

thematic maps/mapas temáticos Mapas que muestran un tema específico o la distribución de espacios en una actividad. **12**

threshers/trilladoras Máquinas usadas para separar los granos de las semillas de las plantas. **468**

tidelands/marismas Tierras ubicadas debajo del nivel del mar en zonas costeras. **571**

time line/línea del tiempo Diagrama que muestra una secuencia de sucesos en el tiempo. **15**

tourism/turismo Negocio que consiste en atraer visitantes a un lugar o región. **58**

transcontinental railroad/ferrocarril transcontinental Ferrocarril que cruza la parte continental de Estados Unidos. **463**

transportation center/centro de transporte Lugar de recepción de productos que son distribuidos a otros lugares. **51**

trial courts/juicios civiles Cortes que analizan casos relacionados con la sociedad y dan un veredicto o decisión. **653**

tributaries/tributarios Pequeñas corrientes o ríos que desembocan en corrientes mayores. **22**

trusts/consorcio Acuerdo legal en el que varias compañías se agrupan en un solo consejo. **503**

two-party system/sistema bipartidista Sistema político en el que los dos partidos más importantes compiten para ganar el control de un país. **610**

U, V

urbanization/urbanización Aumento del número de personas que viven o trabajan en las ciudades. **7**

vaqueros/vaqueros Arrieros. **131**

venison/*venison* Carne de venado. **188**

vertical integration/integración vertical Apropiación de los medios usados en un proceso de fabricación. **485**

veto/veto Autoridad del poder ejecutivo para rechazar una ley del congreso. **642**

viceroy/virrey Gobernador real. **98**

victory gardens/huertos del triunfo Pequeños huertos que se sembraban en los hogares como fuente adicional de alimentos durante la Segunda Guerra Mundial. **566**

W, X, Y, Z

white primary/Elecciones Primarias de Blancos Ronda de elecciones primarias establecida en Texas en la década de 1920 en las que no se permitía el voto a los afroestadounidenses. **539**

wigwams/*wigwams* Chozas indias circulares. **73**

wildcatters/buscadores de petróleo Trabajadores que buscan petróleo por su cuenta. **483**

wind farm/parque eólico Agrupación de turbinas de viento que se usan para generar electricidad en una misma área. **630**

windmills/molinos de viento Dispositivos que usan la fuerza del viento para impulsar agua de mantos subterráneos a la superficie. **450**

wrangler/arriero Persona que conduce manadas de ganado en campo abierto. **447**

Index

Key to Index
c=chart
f=feature
m=map
p=photo

A

B

C

D

E

F

G

H

I

J

K

L

M

N

O

P

Q

R

S

T

U

Acknowledgments